LAW, BUSINESS, AND SOCIETY

Tony McAdams

Professor, Management Department, University of Northern Iowa
BA (History), University of Northern Iowa
JD, University of Iowa, MBA, Columbia University

Contributing Authors

James Freeman

Associate Professor, Department of Management, University of Kentucky
BS (Economics), Wharton School, University of Pennsylvania
JD, MA (Economics), University of South Carolina
LLM, Harvard Law School
Professor Freeman contributed Chapter 9, Business Organizations and Securities Regulation

Laura Pincus

Assistant Professor, Legal Studies and Ethics, DePaul University
BS (Social Psychology), Tufts University
JD, University of Chicago
Professor Pincus contributed Chapter 6, International Ethics and Law

LAW, BUSINESS, AND SOCIETY

Fourth Edition

IRWIN

Chicago • Bogotá • Boston • Buenos Aires • Caracas
London • Madrid • Mexico City • Sydney • Toronto

Senior sponsoring editor:	Kurt L. Strand
Editorial coordinator:	Michele Dooley
Marketing manager:	Cindy Ledwith
Project editor:	Stephanie Britt
Designer:	Larry J. Cope
Cover designer:	Andrew Curtis
Compositor:	Graphic Composition, Inc.
Typeface:	10/12 Times Roman
Printer:	R. R. Donnelley & Sons Company

Library of Congress Cataloging-in-Publication Data

McAdams, Tony.
    Law, business, and society / Tony McAdams, James Freeman, Laura
Pincus. — 4th ed.
      p.   cm. — (Irwin legal studies in business series)
    Includes index.
    ISBN 0-256-14166-5
    1. Business enterprises—Law and legislation—United States.
2. Trade regulation—United States.   3. Business ethics—United
States. 4. Industry—Social aspects—United States. I. Freeman,
James, . II. Pincus, Laura B. III. Title. IV. Series.
KF1355.M28   1995
346.73'065—dc20
[347.30665]   94–21204

Printed in the United States of America
1 2 3 4 5 6 7 8 9 0 DO 1 0 9 8 7 6 5 4

To our parents

PREFACE

OVERVIEW

This text is directed to courses at both the upper-division undergraduate and masters levels in the legal environment of business and government and business, as well as business and society. To date, authors of textbooks in these areas have rather uniformly relied on a single discipline (for example, law, economics, or management) as the foundation for their efforts. In this text, we take an interdisciplinary approach, utilizing elements of law, political economy, international business, ethics, social responsibility, and management. This large task necessarily requires certain trade-offs, but we hope the product will more accurately embrace the fullness of the business environment.

We want to emphasize at the outset that our primary goal is to produce an interesting reading experience. Naturally, accuracy and reasonable comprehensiveness cannot be sacrificed. However, our feeling is that a law text can be both intellectually and emotionally engaging without sacrificing substantive ends. To meet our objective we have given extensive attention to readings, provocative quotes, and factual details (surveys, data, and anecdotes) that add flesh to the bones of legal theory.

The book is divided into five parts as follows:

Part I—Business and Society. We do not begin with the law. Rather, in Chapter 1 (Capitalism and the Role of Government). Chapter 2 (Ethics), and Chapter 3 (The Corporation and Public Policy: Expanded Responsibilities), we hope to establish the influences that determine the character of our legal system.

Part I should meet the following goals: (*a*) enhance student awareness of the many societal influences on business, (*b*) establish the business context from which government regulation arose, and (*c*) explore the roles of the free market, government intervention, and individual and corporate ethics in controlling business behavior.

The student must understand not merely the law but the law in context. What forces have provoked government intervention in business? What alternatives to our current "mixed economy" might prove healthy? These considerations help the students respond to one of the critical questions of the day: To what extent, if any, *should* we regulate business?

Part II—Introduction to Law. Chapter 4 (The American Legal System) and Chapter 5 (Constitutional Law and the Bill of Rights) survey the foundations of our legal system. Here, we set out the "nuts and bolts" of law, combining cases, readings, and narrative. Then, with Chapter 6 (International Ethics and Law), we examine business and public policy in the global context.

Part III—Trade Regulation and Antitrust. Chapter 7 (Government Regulation of Business: An Introduction) is a bit of a departure from the approach of many texts in that significant attention is directed to state and local regulations. Chapter 8 (Administrative Agencies and the Regulatory Process), Chapter 9 (Business Organizations and Securities Regulation), Chapter 10 (Antitrust Law—Monopolies and Mergers), and Chapter 11 (Antitrust Law—Restraints of Trade) survey the heart of government regulation of business (administrative law, business organizations and securities regulation, and antitrust).

Part IV—Employer–Employee Relations. Chapter 12 (Employment Law I: Protecting the Employee), Chapter 13 (Employment Law II: Discrimination), and Chapter 14 (Employment Law III: Labor–Management Relations) are intended not only to survey the law in those areas, but also to introduce some of the sensitive and provocative social issues that have led to today's extensive government intervention in the employment relationship.

Part V—Business and Selected Social Problems. The three closing chapters of this book—Chapter 15 (Consumer Protection), Chapter 16 (Product Liability), and Chapter 17 (Environmental Protection)—emphasize the dramatic expansion in the past two decades of the public's demands on the business community.

ACCREDITATION

Our text conforms to the undergraduate and MBA "Perspectives" portion of the American Assembly of Collegiate Schools of Business (AACSB) curriculum standards for accreditation:

Standard: Both undergraduate and MBA curricula should provide an understanding of perspectives that form the context for business. Coverage should include:

- Ethical and global issues,
- The influence of political, social, legal and regulatory, environmental, and technological issues, and
- The impact of demographic diversity on organizations.

Two chapters are devoted exclusively to ethics materials, while ethics themes emerge throughout the book. At the same time, law and economics clearly must remain central ingredients in meeting our goal of explaining the business and social context in which government regulation arose. The chapter on employment discrimination should be quite helpful in aiding students' understanding of the "demographic diversity" topic.

Furthermore, as required by the rapidly changing nature of commerce and as recommended by the AACSB, the text devotes extensive attention to issues arising from international business. Various topics throughout the text (for example, comparative economic systems, the Foreign Corrupt Practices Act, and global pollution) afford the student a sense of the worldwide implications of American business practice.

PHILOSOPHY

As noted, our primary goal is to provoke student thought. To that end, heavy emphasis is placed on analysis. Accordingly, retention of rules of law per se is not of paramount concern. The questions asked are considered more important than the answers. The student is acquainted with existing policy in the various areas not merely for the purposes of understanding and retention but also to provoke inquiry as to the desirability of those policies. Then, where appropriate, an effort is made to explore with the student the desired managerial role in shaping and responding to governmental policy.

Our book represents a departure from a conventional legal environment of business text. Part I of the text is, as explained, a necessary foundation on which the student can build a logical understanding of the regulatory process. But the business and society themes don't stop there. In virtually every chapter, we look beyond the law itself to other environmental forces. For example, in the antitrust chapters economic philosophy is of great importance. Antitrust is explored as a matter of national social policy. We argue that antitrust has a good deal to do with the direction of American life generally. Law is at the heart of the fair employment practices section, but materials from management, sociology, economics, and the like are used to treat fair employment as an issue of social policy rather than as a series of narrower technical legal disputes. These kinds of approaches characterize most chapters as we attempt to examine the various problems in the whole and, to some degree, from a managerial viewpoint. Having said all this, it should be understood that the law remains the bulky core of the book.

KEY FEATURES/DEPARTURES

Extensive use of readings (particularly from *The Wall Street Journal*) seeks to give the book a stimulating, real-world quality.

Ethics and social responsibility are at the heart of the text rather than an afterthought to meet accreditation standards.

International issues receive extensive attention.

Law cases are of a length sufficient to clearly express the essence of the decision while challenging the reader's intellect.

The law is studied in the economic, social, and political context from which it springs.

Attention is given to critics of business values and the American legal system.

Perhaps the key pedagogical tactic in the book is the emphasis on questions rather than on answers.

INSTRUCTOR'S MANUAL

A package of supplementary materials is included in the instructor's manual. Those materials include (*a*) chapter outlines, (*b*) general advice regarding the goals and purposes of the chapters, (*c*) summaries of the law cases, (*d*) answers for the questions raised in the text, and (*e*) a test bank.

ACKNOWLEDGMENTS

Completion of the third edition of this book depended, in significant part, on the hard work of others. The authors are pleased to acknowledge the contributions of those good people. Markedly more than was the case with the first and second editions, the third version is a product of careful guidance and hard work by the Irwin editorial staff. Likewise, this fourth edition benefited from the good work of Kurt Strand, sponsoring editor, Stephanie Britt, project editor, Michele Dooley, editorial coordinator, and Marjorie Kaplan, permissions editor, as well as Shelley Clubb, student assistant, University of Northern Iowa.

The authors also thank the following professors who reviewed portions of the manuscript and otherwise provided valuable guidance:

First edition—David Chadwick-Brown, San Diego State University; John Collins, Syracuse University; Wayne Evenson, University of Northern Iowa; Nancy Hauserman, University of Iowa; Harold Hotelling, Oakland University; Carey Kirk, University of Northern Iowa; Eric Richards, Indiana University; and Arthur D. Wolfe, Michigan State University.

Second edition—Wayne Evenson, University of Northern Iowa; Harold Hotelling, Oakland University; Michael Howard, Unviersity of Iowa; Janet Richmond, University of Northern Iowa; Linda Samuels, George Mason University; Richard Trotter, University of Baltimore; Jeff Vermeer, Eastern Oregon State College.

Third edition—Mark L. Usry, James Madison University; Anne Stich, St. Louis University; Carol Docan, California State University—Northridge; Sherry K. Schneider, University of Arizona; James T. George, Kansas State University; Janell M. Kurtz, St. Cloud State University; Andrea Giampetro-Meyer, Loyola College in Maryland; and Arnold Celnicker, The Ohio State University.

Fourth edition—Dr. Steven E. Abraham, Esq., University of Minnesota-Morris; E. Eugene Arthur, S.J., Rockhurst College; Paul Lansing, University of Illinois-Champaign; Cynthia L. Srstka, Augustana College; Keith D. Swim, Jr., Texas A&M University.

SUGGESTIONS

The authors welcome comments and criticism from all readers.

Tony McAdams

CONTENTS

PART

I

BUSINESS AND SOCIETY

———————●———————

CHAPTER

1

CAPITALISM AND THE ROLE OF GOVERNMENT

Part One—Introduction

INTERNATIONAL

[handwritten margin note: Balancing between central planning + free market / extreme example of capitalism as per Friedman]

We are lucky to have been witnesses in recent years to some of the most striking political and economic adjustments in recorded history. The Berlin Wall fell. Germany is reunited. Our primary enemy, the Soviet Union, is gone—to be replaced by Russia and the other struggling republics (the Commonwealth of Independent States—CIS). At this writing in 1994, only China, Cuba, North Korea, and a few other smaller nations remain even nominally committed to Marxist–Leninist doctrine, although the 1993 Russian election suggests that Communism appeals to those who miss the glory and security of the former Soviet Union.

In assessing the fall of Communism, former U.S. State Department policy planner Francis Fukuyama raised the provocative argument that we are approaching the end of ideological history. The fascism of the Nazis and the Marxism of the Communists have failed, and Western liberal democracy has survived as the universal expression of human government. Thus, while other approaches to government could emerge, Fukuyama says that for the foreseeable future the world will come more and more to understand that democracy, with its roots in personal freedom and capitalism, is the best method of structuring human relations.[1]

Of course, others see a more confused picture. Harvard professor and now Secretary of Labor Robert Reich:

Human civilization is at the brink of a new era. Choose which one:

(a) History is ending in bureaucratic corporatism . . . Key decisions are shifting away from elected politicians and legislative bodies toward multinational bureaucracies (such as the G-7) and global corporations unaccountable to any single population.

(b) History alternates between periods of central control and chaos, and we are again entering the latter. The 40-year interval of superpower stability is giving way to tribal fragmentation and warfare with ethnic tensions flaring over Eastern Europe and the former Soviet Union, the Asian subcontinent, and even within advanced industrial nations . . .

(c) History is ending in cultural authoritarianism. Societies like Japan and Germany, which reward group loyalty and investment, are gaining economic power over societies organized around individual liberty and personal consumption. Meanwhile, much of the Third World is succumbing to Islamic fundamentalism.

(d) History is ending in liberal democracy and individual liberty. Modern economies depend on educated work forces, which in turn are demanding rights and freedoms that only liberal democracies can provide (look at Latin America).

(e) All of the above.

The correct answer is, of course, (e). History is unfolding dramatically in every direction at once, spewing enough data to prove any grand historical design that the human imagination possibly can devise.[2]

These insights from Fukuyama and Reich capture the central political/economic question of the day and provide the starting point for our investigation of the role of law in the business life of America. Essentially, the purpose of this book is to ask (1) What is the proper role of business in American society? (2) How much, if any, government regulation of business is necessary to secure that role? Fukuyama says Western liberal thought—that is, capitalist democracy—has won. Even if Fukuyama is correct, we know that most nations and peoples feel uncomfortable in turning over their fate to a free market. Hence, a key question facing all nations is: What blend of free market principles and government intervention is in the best interests of all of the people?

Market versus Planning

In the United States, we certainly cannot understand our system of laws without a firm appreciation for the principles of capitalism from which those laws spring, in pertinent part. We chose a capitalist, democratic approach to life. Other cultures have placed less faith in the market and more in government planning. The legal systems in those countries reflect a preference for greater central authority.

In this chapter, we will explore the full range of the economic spectrum, moving from a laissez-faire, free market approach on the extreme right, to a brief reminder of command economy principles on the far left, but the bulk of our attention will rest where the world is at this moment—that is, we will examine the notion of the *mixed economy*. For now, at least, capitalism is the victor, but a vital question remains: How much government should be mixed with the market?

The free market approach assumes that we can operate our business structure and our society at large free of all but the most basic legal mechanisms such as contract and criminal law. The wisdom of the market—our individual judgments, in combination with our individual consciences—would serve to "regulate" American life. Government regulatory agencies, occupational licensure, zoning restrictions, antitrust law, and all but the most basic government services (perhaps limited to the police, the courts, and the army) would be unnecessary.

On the other hand, the collectivist alternatives (communism, socialism, and their variations) pose the notion that the business community and society at large require more expansive government intervention than that characterizing the US system. Individual judgment would be supplemented with or largely supplanted by the collective will.

Of course, today's debate is no longer about capitalism versus communism but about the mixed economy—that is, about what form of capitalism best serves the world's needs. At the moment, the center of the struggle lies in the U.S., Japanese, and

European versions of capitalism, but that will surely change as China's remarkable economic transformation so vividly reminds us. Capitalism has shown itself to be the stronger vehicle for productivity, efficiency, and personal freedom. Is it the stronger vehicle for building a sense of community, for improving the standard of living of all citizens, and for coping with the uncertainties of the future? Should we embrace the Japanese practice of close cooperation between government and business? Or the European model of capitalism with a heavy overlay of welfare programs? Or America's firmer commitment to market principles? Or some amalgam of the three? Or will a new direction emerge? Indeed, at this writing in 1994, the Japanese appear to be moving guardedly toward a less-managed market system.

Law?

Finally, this chapter should be read as a foundation for the study of law that follows. Once a society settles on some broad political and economic principles, it pours a thin veneer or many heavy coats (depending on the system chosen) of social control on that foundation to implement the goals of the larger system. The law serves as a primary method of social control. So, to understand the law, we need to understand its roots in political economy.

Part Two—Capitalism

FOUNDATIONS

We begin with a brief reminder of the ideological foundation of American capitalism. As noted, the law develops, in part, as a response to the governing economic system. That system is a product of society's values and philosophies. We need, therefore, to assess those values and philosophies to determine which economic system is most suitable to contemporary American society.

Although many intellectual forces have played a role in shaping American capitalism, this discussion will be limited to four themes of particular historical significance.

1. John Locke's Natural Right of Property.   Locke, the brilliant English philosopher, provided in his *Two Treatises of Government* (1690) much of the intellectual underpinning of the Declaration of Independence and, thus, the course of American life. Locke argued that the rights of life, liberty, and property were natural to all humans. Those rights predated any notion of an organized society. Hence, society's only control over those rights was to protect them. Locke's viewpoint was a powerful intellectual and moral argument for the establishment of industrial capitalism in which private ownership of property and freedom from government restraint were vital.

2. Adam Smith and Laissez-Faire.   Smith's *An Inquiry into the Nature and Cause of the Wealth of Nations* (1776) offered profound theoretical support to free market principles. Smith argued that the Invisible Hand of supply and demand would determine the price of goods. Competition would ensure the greatest good for the greatest number. Thus, government should not interfere in the market system. Rather, government should fulfill only those public services (defense, justice, public works, and the like) in which business cannot practically engage. He believed government interference would only disturb the natural genius of the market.

3. Herbert Spencer and Social Darwinism.   Charles Darwin's explorations of the origins of the species led him to the theory that all of life evolved through a process of natural selection, so that the strongest and the most fit survived. Spencer applied Darwin's survival of the fittest to the development of society. He argued that the more capable individuals would inevitably rise to influential positions. Government interference would only inhibit the natural selection process. Thus, Social Darwinism provided the late-19th-century leaders of industry an ideal rationale for their positions of extreme wealth and power.

4. Max Weber and the Protestant Ethic.   In his book *The Protestant Ethic and the Spirit of Capitalism,* Weber argued that Protestants, particularly Calvinists, were moved by a religious philosophy that demanded a lifetime of disciplined effort in pursuit of good work. Salvation demanded productivity. The accumulation of worldly goods was material evidence of that productivity, but one's success was not to be squandered. Rather, it was to be reinvested to enhance the value of goods placed in human hands via God's grace. Thus, hard work and thrift were moral responsibilities, and in turn, the accumulation and multiplication of worldly goods to be used for the benefit of all people served to measure one's success in meeting God's expectations. The Protestant ethic was a powerful spur to and justification for capitalist enterprise.

So, capitalism in America arose from rather noble, if debatable, intellectual premises, but capitalism also moved to the fore on the strength of promises to the people not afforded by any previous economic system. Conservative commentator Irving Kristol summarized the hope offered by capitalism:

> What did capitalism promise? First of all, it promised continued improvement in the material conditions of all its citizens, a promise without precedent in human history. Secondly, it promised an equally unprecedented measure of individual freedom for all of these same citizens. And lastly, it held out the promise that, amidst this prosperity and liberty, the individual could satisfy his instinct for self-perfection—for leading a virtuous life that satisfied the demands of his spirit (or, as one used to say, his soul)—and that the free exercise of such individual virtue would aggregate into a just society.[3]

Capitalism in Theory—Ayn Rand

Capitalism was built on a sound intellectual footing and was stimulated by the promise of unprecedented general welfare. These forces, in combination with America's natural resources and an astonishingly courageous and hardy population, led to the development of a powerful economic machine. But that machine, in the view of many Americans, ran out of control for a time. The era of the Robber Barons and abuses associated with them brought widespread popular sentiment for governmental restraints on capitalism. Thus, as is discussed in subsequent chapters, America's substantially free market economy was, in increasing increments, placed under government regulation. Today, ours is commonly labeled a *mixed economy.* And despite the striking rhetoric and significant deregulation strides of the Reagan free market era, America remains a nation of big government.

Our purpose now is to reconsider the merits of a purer form of capitalism. Did we turn too hastily from the market? Should we further shed our governmental role in economic affairs and restore our faith in the Invisible Hand? Or, even if the market in a substantially pure form cannot practically be achieved and relied on, may we not profit from a reminder of the nature of that system? Are at least some strides in that direction demanded? Can we, in large measure, do without regulation by law? Will a genuinely unfettered market better serve our needs than our current amalgam of business restrained by government? To answer these questions, we need a firm understanding of capitalism in a pure form, which has almost entirely slipped from view. The controversial philosopher and novelist Ayn Rand was an uncompromising advocate of free market principles. She believed the necessary categories of government were only three in number: the police, the armed services, and the law courts. Via her philosophy of Objectivism, Rand argued that the practice of free market principles is necessary to the pursuit of a rational, moral life. Rand's viewpoint has been the subject of vigorous criticism. Its merits are for the reader to assess, but it is fair to say that she was among America's most ardent and articulate apostles of a genuine free market.

MAN'S RIGHTS

Ayn Rand

If one wishes to advocate a free society—that is, capitalism—one must realize that its indispensable foundation is the principle of individual rights. If one wishes to uphold individual rights, one must realize that capitalism is the only system that can uphold and protect them. And if one wishes to gauge the relationship of freedom to the goals of today's intellectuals, one may gauge it by the fact that the concept of individual rights is evaded, distorted, perverted, and seldom discussed, most conspicuously seldom by the so-called "conservatives."

"Rights" are a moral concept—the concept that provides a logical transition from the principles guiding an individual's actions to the principles guiding his relationship with others—the concept that preserves and protects individual morality in a social context—the link between the moral code of a man and the legal code of a society, between ethics and politics. *Individual rights are the means of subordinating society to moral law.*

Every political system is based on some code of ethics. The dominant ethics of mankind's history were variants of the altruist-collectivist doctrine which subordinated the individual to some higher authority, either mystical or social. Consequently, most political systems were variants of the same statist tyranny, differing only in degree, not in basic principle, limited only by the accidents of tradition, of chaos, of bloody strife and periodic collapse. Under all such systems, morality was a code applicable to the individual, but not to society. Society was placed *outside* the moral law, as its embodiment or source or exclusive interpreter—and the inculcation of self-sacrificial devotion to social duty was regarded as the main purpose of ethics in man's earthly existence.

Since there is no such entity as "society," since society is only a number of individual men, this meant, in practice, that the rulers of society were exempt from moral law; subject only to traditional rituals, they held total power and exacted blind obedience—on the implicit principle of: "The good is that which is good for society (or for the tribe, the race, the nation), and the ruler's edicts are its voice on earth."

This was true of all statist systems, under all variants of the altruist-collectivist ethics, mystical or social. "The Divine Right of Kings" summarizes the political theory of the first—"*Vox populi, vox dei*" of the second. As witness: the theocracy of Egypt, with the Pharaoh as an embodied god—the unlimited majority rule or *democracy* of Athens—the welfare state run by the Emperors of Rome—the Inquisition of the late Middle Ages—the absolute monarchy of France—the welfare state of Bismarck's Prussia—the gas chambers of Nazi Germany—the slaughterhouse of the Soviet Union.

All these political systems were expressions of the altruist-collectivist ethics—and their common characteristic is the fact that society stood above the moral law, as an omnipotent, sovereign whim worshiper. Thus, politically, all these systems were variants of an *amoral* society.

The most profoundly revolutionary achievement of the United States of America was *the subordination of society to moral law.*

The principle of man's individual rights represented the extension of morality into the social system—as a limitation on the power of the state, as man's protection against the brute force of the collective, as the subordination of *might* to *right.* The United States was the first *moral* society in history.

All previous systems had regarded man as a sacrificial means to the ends of others, and society as an end in itself. The United States regarded man as an end in himself, and society as a means to the peaceful, orderly, *voluntary* coexistence of individuals. All previous systems had held that man's life belongs to society, that society can dispose of him in any way it pleases, and that any freedom he enjoys is his only by favor, by the *permission* of society, which may be revoked at any time. The United States held that man's life is his by *right* (which means: by moral principle and by his nature), that a right is the property of an individual, that society as such has no rights, and that the only moral purpose of a government is the protection of individual rights.

A "right" is a moral principle defining and sanctioning a man's freedom of action in a social context. There is only *one* fundamental right (all the others are its consequences or corollaries): a man's right to his own life. Life is a process of self-sustaining and self-generated action; the right to life means the right to engage in self-sustaining and self-generated action—which means: the freedom to take all the actions required by the nature of a rational being for the support, the furtherance, the fulfillment, and the enjoyment of his own life . . .

America's inner contradiction was the altruist-collectivist ethics. Altruism is incompatible with freedom, with capitalism, and with individual rights. One cannot combine the pursuit of happiness with the moral status of a sacrificial animal.

It was the concept of individual rights that had given birth to a free society. It was with the destruction of individual rights that the destruction of freedom had to begin.

A collectivist tyranny dare not enslave a country by an outright confiscation of its values, material or moral. It has to be done by a process of internal corruption. Just as in the material realm the plundering of a country's wealth is accomplished by inflating the currency—so today one may witness the process of inflation being applied to the realm of rights. The process entails such a growth of newly promulgated "rights" that people do not notice the fact that the meaning of the concept is being reversed. Just as bad money drives out good money, so these "printing-press rights" negate authentic rights.

Consider the curious fact that never has there been such a proliferation, all over the world, of two contradictory phenomena: of alleged new "rights" and of slave-labor camps.

The "gimmick" was the switch of the concept of rights from the political to the economic realm.

The Democratic Party platform of 1960 summarizes the switch boldly and explicitly. It declares that a democratic administration "will reaffirm the economic bill of rights which Franklin Roosevelt wrote into our national conscience 16 years ago."

Bear clearly in mind the meaning of the concept of *"rights"* when you read the list which that platform offers:

1. The right to a useful and remunerative job in the industries or shops or farms or mines of the nation.
2. The right to earn enough to provide adequate food and clothing and recreation.
3. The right of every farmer to raise and sell his products at a return which will give him and his family a decent living.
4. The right of every businessman, large and small, to trade in an atmosphere of freedom from unfair competition and domination by monopolies at home and abroad.
5. The right of every family to a decent home.
6. The right to adequate medical care and the opportunity to achieve and enjoy good health.
7. The right to adequate protection from the economic fears of old age, sickness, accidents and unemployment.
8. The right to a good education.

A single question added to each of the above eight clauses would make the issue clear: *At whose expense?*

Jobs, food, clothing, recreation (!), homes, medical care, education, etc., do not grow in nature. These are man-made values—goods and services produced by men. *Who* is to provide them?

If some men are entitled *by right* to the products of the work of others, it means that those others are deprived of rights and condemned to slave labor.

Any alleged "right" of one man, which necessitates the violation of the rights of another, is not and cannot be a right.

No man can have a right to impose an unchosen obligation, an unrewarded duty, or an involuntary servitude on another man. There can be no such thing as *"the right to enslave."*

A right does not include the material implementation of that right by other men; it includes only the freedom to earn that implementation by one's own effort.

Observe, in this context, the intellectual precision of the Founding Fathers: they spoke of the right to *the pursuit* of happiness—*not* of the right to happiness. It means that a man has the right to take the actions he deems necessary to achieve his happiness; it does *not* mean that others must make him happy . . .

Property rights and the right of free trade are man's only "economic rights" (they are, in fact, *political* rights)—and there can be no such thing as "an *economic* bill of rights." But observe that the advocates of the latter have all but destroyed the former . . .

And while people are clamoring about "economic rights," the concept of political rights is vanishing. It is forgotten that the right of free speech means the freedom to advocate one's views and to bear the possible consequences, including disagreement with others, opposition, unpopularity, and lack of support. The political function of "the right of free speech" is to protect dissenters and unpopular minorities from forcible suppression—*not* to guarantee them the support, advantages, and rewards of a popularity they have not gained . . .

Such is the state of one of today's most crucial issues: *political* rights versus *"economic"* rights. It's either-or. One destroys the other. But there are, in fact, no "economic rights," no "collective rights," no "public-interest rights." The term *individual rights* is a redundancy: there is no other kind of rights and no one else to possess them.

Those who advocate laissez-faire capitalism are the only advocates of man's rights.

Capitalism in Practice—"Privatization" in America and Abroad

Around the globe, from Russia to Eastern Europe and from the United Kingdom to Southeast Asia, expanded faith in the free market was the singular economic message of the 1980s and 1990s. The basic point to recognize is the free market argument that virtually all services now performed by the government may be more efficiently and more equitably "managed" by the impersonal forces of the market.

Most commonly, privatization follows two patterns: (1) contracting out where government, in effect, turns over a portion of its duties, such as garbage collection, to a private firm; and (2) the sale of public assets, such as an airport, to a private purchaser. Chicago, under Mayor Richard M. Daley, has been particularly aggressive in pursuing privatization, resulting, for example, in annual savings of $900,000 by turning janitorial work over to private firms. In 1989, cars were being abandoned on Chicago streets faster than the city could haul them away. The government turned to private towing firms who paid the city $25 per abandoned car and then sold them at a profit for scrap.[4] A Reason Foundation study estimates that some $227 billion in commercial airports, utilities, highways, bridges, water systems, and so on could be sold to the private sector and operated at a profit while saving money for the public.[5]

At least 14 states have privately operated prisons. Private firms are managing schools in Baltimore and Miami. New York pays a private company, America Works, to move welfare recipients to training and work. The cost? $5,300 versus the $23,000 per year that the state would otherwise pay to support the welfare client. America Works claims a 68 percent success rate.[6]

Privatization Abroad.   Capitalism has swept the globe. In five years during the late 1980s and early 1990s, Mexico sold off $22 billion of state-owned companies, including the telephone system and an airline.[7] Zambia announced in 1993 that it intended to sell 150 companies that controlled 80 percent of its economy. Ironically, the companies had been nationalized in the 1970s and 1980s, and the Zambian government intends to give the former multinational owners the first opportunity to repurchase the companies.[8] Germany is thinking of turning its highway system over to private interests,[9] and even China, virtually the last bastion of Communism, has created a semi-independent railway company to manage part of its vast system.[10]

Privatization: An Assessment.   Of course, privatization won't cure the world's economic problems. Critics argue that the savings from privatization result simply from paying substandard wages and cutting corners on quality. Professor Jonathan Goodrich lists these primary concerns regarding privatization:[11]

- Unemployment of government workers because of privatization.
- Lower quality of service.
- Government loss of control and accountability.
- The government paying too much for the services done by a private company.
- The possibility of corruption and scandal.

The article that follows offers a case study of an effective privatization effort in New Zealand.

INTERNATIONAL

IN NEW ZEALAND, FREE ENTERPRISE DELIVERS THE MAIL

John Crutcher

Just because most people think the Postal Service is a natural monopoly doesn't make it so, says the Hon. Richard Prebble, member of the New Zealand parliament . . .

Three years ago on April 1, 1987, Mr. Prebble and his colleagues in the Labor government decontrolled and corporatized the New Zealand Post. While the state retains ownership of the corporation, it has surrendered all control of its actions, any stake in its profits, and any responsibility for its losses.

While the U.S. Postal Service is announcing a 19 percent average increase in postal rates and reductions in service in order to bring its $1.6 billion deficit under control, the New Zealand Post has greatly improved service, turned a tidy profit for investors, and has handed over a substantial bundle of cash to the national treasury each year in the form of income taxes. New Zealand postal managers have slashed paper work by 90 percent, slimmed the work force by 20 percent and removed unnecessary barriers to competition—even as New Zealand Post remains obliged by law to maintain universal service and universal postal rates.

Rates went up 40 percent between 1985 and 1987—the last two years under state control—they have stuck at about 23 U.S. cents in the two years since, and will remain at that price until at least 1991—by which time a U.S. first class stamp will cost 29 cents.

The law freeing the post office also freed its competitors. New Zealand merchants may now distribute circulars in mailboxes themselves, if they prefer. In the United States, dropping a note in a neighbor's mailbox is against the law. You may think you "own" that little box, but sole access to it belongs to the postal monopoly.

Protected from competition, postal management and labor unions have made full-time career postal employees the most highly paid semiskilled workers in the world: more than $42,000 per year with benefits. Their New Zealand counterparts make about $15,000.

Postal management, protected by the monopoly, has carelessly bargained away work rules that may be the most restrictive for any large organization in this country. There is no Japanese competition to hold managers' feet to the fire. Where it has faced competition, the post office's record is dismal. For example, at the time of postal reorganization in 1970, the old Post Office Department handled nearly all of the nation's parcel business. Today its share is less than 4 percent. Its share of the express mail business has slipped to 13 percent.

There is little incentive for monopoly managers to protect the public interest at the bargaining table. There is, in fact, a material disincentive: Nearly all postal management salaries rise by roughly the same percentage given to union members at the bargaining table.

Nor do postal managers make tough business decisions. In 1988, Postmaster General Anthony Frank was handed a study done by his own Postal Inspection Service that showed that contracting local carrier delivery jobs to individuals in the community would save about 50 percent. Thousands of his own "Star Route" contract carriers prove to him each day that he could cut big chunks of money from the $10 billion cost of the delivery force by contracting the remainder of his carrier jobs, by attrition, as they become available. But even this halting form of privatization is vigorously opposed by post office management, which defends the monopoly just as vigorously as postal labor union leaders.

Change will have to come from outside, and New Zealand has indicated how it can be done. That experience should be studied. While the study is being conducted, the U.S. should proceed without delay to modify the outmoded regulations on access to the mailbox, by giving local, nonprofit community-based organizations full rights to use it for their own purposes. Meter readers for local utilities should also be granted permission to drop their bills in the mailbox.

There is little reason too for the Postal Service not to experiment with contracts to permit access to the mailbox for advertising mail.

U.S. Postal Service officials who go to New Zealand return chastened and silent. The U.S. post office is not the cheapest or most efficient in the world; it's only the biggest. And it's certainly not operating at the cutting edge of change. To the contrary it is structured to avoid change or to delay it as long as possible.

Source: *The Wall Street Journal*, March 8, 1990, p. A14. Reprinted by permission of *The Wall Street Journal*, © 1990 Dow Jones & Company, Inc. All Rights Reserved Worldwide.

Questions—Part Two

1. *a.* Should we turn the U.S. Postal Service over to the private sector? Explain.
   b. Which segments of society would be harmed most by that move? Explain.
2. Capitalism's philosophical roots lie largely in the views of Locke, Smith, Spencer, and Weber.
   a. Do those views continue to explain our reliance on capitalism? Explain.
   b. If so, does our long-term drift away from the free market suggest a flaw in that philosophical foundation? Explain.
   c. If not, can you suggest other doctrines or ethics that better explain our contemporary economic philosophy?
3. From the capitalist viewpoint, why is the private ownership of property necessary to the preservation of freedom?
4. Ayn Rand argued: "Altruism is incompatible with freedom, with capitalism, and with individual rights."
   a. Define altruism.
   b. Explain why Rand rejected altruism.
5. In describing life in aggressively commercialized Hong Kong, Alvin Rabushka praises the "single-minded pursuit of making money" and the "emphasis on the material things in life." Rabushka admits to finding "Hong Kong's economic hustle and bustle more interesting, entertaining, and liberating than its lack of high opera, music, and drama."
   a. Although it is often criticized in America, is materialism the most certain and most interesting path to personal happiness? Explain.
   b. Would "sophisticated" culture (such as opera and drama) substantially disappear in America without government support? Explain.
   c. If so, how may we justify that support? If not, how may we justify that support?
6. Assume the federal government removed itself from the purchase and maintenance of its parks.
   a. Left to the private sector, what sorts of parks would develop under the profit incentive?

    b. Would Yellowstone, for example, survive in substantially its present state? Explain.

    c. How can it be argued that the federal parks are an unethical, undemocratic expropriation of private resources?

7. Assume the abolition of the federal Food and Drug Administration. How would the free market protect the citizenry from dangerous food and drug products?

8. Should education be returned to the free market? Explain. How would poor Americans finance a private-sector education?

9. Scholar Amitai Etzioni argues that America must choose between rededication to economic growth and emphasis on a quality-of-life society (slower growth, emphasis on ecology, concern for safety, harmony with oneself and others). He argues that the monetary costs and the social-psychic strains of pursuing these two divergent courses exceed America's resources, both physical and emotional.

    a. Do you agree with Etzioni? Explain.

    b. Which path would you choose? Explain.

    c. Will the market support the quality-of-life approach? Explain.

10. Puritan leaders felt concern over the morality of merchants selling goods for "more than their worth." That concern was particularly grave when the goods were scarce or in great demand.

    a. Should our society develop an ethic wherein goods are to be sold only "for what they are worth"? Explain.

    b. Can a seller make an accurate determination of worth? Explain.

    c. Does a product's worth differ from the price that product will bring in the marketplace? Explain.

    d. Personalize the inquiry: Assume you seek to sell your Ford auto for $5,000. Assume you know of several identical Fords in a similar state of repair that can be purchased for $4,500. Assume you find a buyer at $5,000. Will you unilaterally lower your price or direct the purchaser to the other autos? Explain.

    e. If not, have you acted justly? Explain.

11. Critics of our capitalist system contend that ability and effort often are less responsible for one's success than "unearned" factors such as family background, social class, luck, and willingness to cheat. Do you agree? Explain.

12. Commentator Irving Kristol asked whether it was "just" for Ray Kroc (now deceased, formerly of McDonald's) to have made so much money by merely figuring out a new way to sell hamburgers. He concluded that capitalism says it is just because he sold a good product; people want it; it is fair.

    a. Do you agree with Kristol? Explain.

    b. Does contemporary American capitalism offer excessive rewards to those clever enough to build near-term paper profits (lawyers, accountants, financial analysts) through mergers, tax write-offs, and the like while diverting scarce resources from long-term productive ventures (such as new product development or more efficient production processes)? Explain.

    c. If so, is capitalism fatally flawed? Explain.

13. Professor Robert E. Lane argued that the person who is motivated by needs for affiliation, rather than by needs for achievement, does less well in the market. Such a person is not rewarded so well as autonomous, achievement-oriented people.

    a. Is Lane correct? Explain.

    b. Is capitalism, in the long run, destructive of societal welfare in that achievement is better rewarded than affiliation? Explain.

14. List some free market solutions for the problems of overcrowded highways and airports.

15. Explore the argument that the federal highway program, although well-intentioned, was merely one in a series of federal interventions that distorted the market, leading, in this instance, to the long-term decline of inner cities.

16. How would poor people be cared for in a free market society?

Part Three—Collectivism

The term *collectivism* embraces various economic philosophies on the left of the political–economic spectrum; principally, communism and socialism. Capitalism is characterized by economic individualism. On the other hand, communism and the various styles of socialism are characterized by economic cooperation.

COMMUNISM

INTERNATIONAL

Clearly, Soviet Communism, the *totalitarian* version of collectivism practiced by *Marxist–Leninists,* has been rejected by the bulk of the world. Nonetheless, we need to briefly remind ourselves of some fundamental Marxist principles because, as *The Wall Street Journal* reminded us a few years ago, "His Shadow Persists: Marx Can't Be Ignored. In His Critique of Capitalism The Great Analyst Helped To Shape Today's Agenda."[12] Lenin, not Marx, created the Communist dictatorship in Russia. Lenin and the other Communist totalitarians, most notably Stalin and Mao, cannot be defended. However, Marx, along with Freud and Einstein, are the thinkers that have most profoundly shaped the 20th century. For our purposes, Marx's central message concerns the severe abuses that can accompany unrestrained capitalism. Marx was particularly concerned about the growing imbalance between rich and poor. Moreover, he felt that the pursuit of wealth and self-interest would erode society's moral core. More broadly, Marx built an economic interpretation of history, arguing that "the mode of production in material life determines the general character of the social, political and spiritual processes of life."[13] The power and originality of those thoughts, along with concerns about the excesses of capitalism, mean that Marx will continue to influence our lives for the foreseeable future.

Problems.   Communism appears to have run its course philosophically. However, the problems that generated its appeal—poverty, oppression, political inequality, and so on—remain. Hence, the world continues to look to government intervention. The question is: How much? We will briefly remind ourselves of the *socialist* response to that question. Socialists reject communist totalitarianism and embrace democracy while calling for aggressive government intervention to correct economic and social ills. Socialism, as an operating philosophy for a society, is largely discredited. Around the world, from Argentina to Mexico to Zambia to Great Britain and even to the "welfare states" of Scandinavia, government is getting out of the business of managing economics. At the same time, socialist concerns and principles remain highly influential.

SOCIALISM

The distinctions between communism and socialism are not entirely clear. Historically, socialism has been associated with democratic governments and peaceful change while communism has been characterized by totalitarianism and violent revolution.

Socialists aim to retain the benefits of industrialism while abolishing the social costs often accompanying the free market. Nationalization is limited to only the most vital industries, such as steel, coal mining, power generation, and transportation. While nationalization may be relatively uncommon, the government is likely to be directly involved in regulating growth, inflation, and unemployment. In the contemporary Western world, Austria, Norway, Denmark, Sweden, South Africa, and France are among the nations where socialist principles assumed a significant presence. Now those nations have largely embraced free markets.

Socialist Goals

A critical distinction between socialists and capitalists is that the former believe a society's broad directions should be carefully planned rather than left to what some take to be the whimsy of the market. Furthermore, socialists are convinced that problems of market failure (inadequate information, monopoly, externalities, public goods, and so on—see Chapter 7) mean that the free market is simply incapable of meeting the needs of all segments of society. The socialist agenda includes:[14]

1. Liberty. To the capitalist, socialism appears to harshly restrain individual freedom. To the socialist, the freedoms of capitalism are largely an illusion, accessible only to the prosperous and powerful.

2. Social Welfare. Socialists reserve much of their concern for the condition of the lower class—poverty, exploitation, cultural deprivation, and so on. Socialists feel that the economy must be directed toward the general interest rather than left free to multiply the welfare of successful capitalists. Hence, socialists advocate income supports, free education, free health care, generous sick pay, family planning, and so on to correct the wrongs of capitalism.

3. Fulfilling Work.   Socialists object to the harshness of working life where a large segment of society is chained to degrading labor.

4. Community.   Socialists seek a communitarian approach to life where the excessive individualism of capitalism is muted by a concern for the welfare of all.

5. Equality.   Class distinctions are anathema to the collectivist. All humans are equally meritorious, and distinctions among them are inherently unjust.

6. Rationality.   Socialists fear the "irrationality" of a society based upon competition and unrestrained pursuit of industrial growth.

Coping with Capitalism

INTERNATIONAL

The collapse of communism in Eastern Europe and the former Soviet Union means that hundreds of millions of people accustomed to thorough state direction now must cope with the new and unforgiving "commands" of the free market. Economic chaos and political uncertainty—particularly in Russia—have marked this startling transition. Consider 29-year-old Olaf Viek of Thurow, a town of 160, in the former East Germany:

> Mr. Viek shudders at the price of reunification and capitalism. Although he was able to get a job at a dairy in the city up the road, many of his friends have been displaced by modern technology. "One lady milks 400 cows in one day. Can you imagine? 400 cows. We used to have 10 people to do that many," he says incredulously.
>   "We must always be profitable, day after day," he adds. "The workers own shares in the company. I must think like the cows are my own. If a cow gets sick and dies, it costs me money. We've already had to fire a number of workers who have problems thinking this way."[15]

Halfway around the world from Viek, the Chinese communists have energetically embraced what is labeled a "socialist market economy." In the People's Republic of China (PRC), communism and capitalism coexist in a delicate and exquisite dance for dominance.

ENTREPRENEURIAL ENERGY
SETS OFF A CHINESE BOOM

Nicholas D. Kristof

A few years ago, Wang Junjin was a traveling sales-man, a Chinese Willy Loman whose second home was a ponderous, creaking sardine can of a train car-rying him 38 hours each way to the factories in Hu-nan Province that bought his badges and insignias.

Mr. Wang found a better way. He and his brother started an airline.

Today Mr. Wang, a short, boy-faced tycoon who looks much younger than his 23 years, has far more need for his cellular telephone than for a razor. His Sky Dragon Charter Airline Company offers seven regularly scheduled flights a week and reported reve-nue last year of $2 million—some of which went into his $420 double-breasted suit and his $600 24-karat gold bracelet.

"If the Government lets us do it," Mr. Wang said, "we'll do it."

Profound Consequences

His boldness captures the entrepreneurial spirit in China today, and the entire Chinese economy seems to be taking off with as much energy as Mr. Wang's chartered Boeing 737's and other aircraft. Perhaps the takeoff will still be aborted, but there is a growing view that the incomes of China's nearly 1.2 billion people could soar for decades . . .

. . . [N]ever before in recorded history have so many people—or perhaps even such a large propor-tion of humanity—risen from poverty so rapidly.

Based on comparisons of purchasing power, China may now have the second largest economy in the world, ranking behind only the United States . . .

Will China Surpass U.S.?

"It may well be that when the history of the late 20th century is written 100 years from now, the most sig-nificant event will be the revolutionary changes in China, which will soon be Communist only in a rhe-torical sense," Lawrence H. Summers, the former World Bank chief economist, wrote last year.

"For more than a century, the United States has been the world's largest economy," Mr. Summers added. "The only nation with a chance of surpassing it in the next generation in absolute scale is China."

What would China look like if it sustains its course? If it reaches Taiwan's per-capita income lev-els, China will have an economy larger than all in-dustrialized countries in the world combined. It would be a bit like the rise of Japan, except that China has nuclear weapons and nearly 10 times the population.

*   *   *   *   *

Attitudes abroad about China's prospects have fluctuated sharply over the last two decades, mirror-ing the boom-bust pattern in China's economy. Skep-tics say this is simply another peak in a love-hate cycle that will lead to new disappointment in a year or two.

In the early- and mid-1980's, there was a wave of enthusiasm about China. That disappeared after troops fired on Tiananmen Square protesters in June 1989. The rise of the hard-liners coincided with a cy-clical economic slowdown, and all bets were off.

The economy suffered less damage from sanctions and ebbing investor confidence than most expected, however. Last year, China's gross national product grew by a stunning 12 percent, to an official level of about $370 per person—or perhaps to $2,000 or even $4,000, according to other estimates.

*   *   *   *   *

Even a Slowdown May Not Stop Boom

. . . Since 1980, China's economy has grown by an average of 9.5 percent a year, roughly the same level that Japan and then Taiwan and South Korea experienced at their postwar peaks.

. . . In contrast, the United States economy has expanded at an average annual rate of about 3 percent over the last 12 years.

The industrial revolution in China is most evident in cities along the eastern coast, like Wenzhou, 250 miles south of Shanghai. The atmosphere along the cluttered shop-lined streets is very much like that of Taiwan two decades ago, with frenetic activity, multitudes of small businesses and a good deal of what Marx would have called exploitation.

"We start at 7 or 8 in the morning and go on until about 11:30 at night," said Zhou Sailu, 37, a peasant who left her village three months ago to work at a shoe factory in Wenzhou.

Many of the workers maintain that routine seven days a week, month after month. They sleep in cubbyholes above the factory floor and take a break only for Chinese New Year and in the slack season around June.

Ms. Zhou left her husband in the village but brought her daughter, 19, who works beside her stitching shoes. They each earn a bit more than $100 a month. When a visitor asked if her husband objected to her leaving home to work all day in a grimy factory, Ms. Zhou smiled patronizingly at the stupidity of the question.

"How could he possibly have any objections?" she asked. "Look how much money I'm making!"

Regulation Virtually Disappears

In any case, it is clear that it is no longer very useful to describe China's economy as Communist, socialist or centrally planned. This year, for instance, the Government says the central plan will account for just 6 percent of industrial production.

Economic sectors like agriculture and industry are already slipping out of Government hands, so overall the state-owned sector accounts for less than one-third of total economic output.

*   *   *   *   *

These days, the problem occasionally seems to be not enough Government regulation rather than too much. In the last few years, for instance, dozens of factories have turned out useless contraptions that are supposed to make people taller or to expand women's breasts . . .

Similarities to Other 'Miracles'

Some economists are optimistic about China's prospects in part because of similarities they see with the "miracle economies" of Japan, South Korea, Taiwan, Singapore and Hong Kong. Though the link is unproven, some people note that all these areas were traditionally influenced by Confucianism. They say Confucianism may have left a useful legacy of respect for education and for thrift and savings.

Perhaps as a result of the emphasis on education, China's labor force—much more than Africa's, India's or Bolivia's—is literate enough to power an industrial revolution. And the 38 percent savings rate, one of the world's highest, helps finance new investment to maintain the economy's momentum.

Like Japan, Taiwan and South Korea, China went through a process of land redistribution, soon after the 1949 revolution, that evened out the worst inequities in wealth. China's peasants in effect have their own land . . .

*   *   *   *   *

A crucial economic advantage that China has over other developing countries is that it has brought its population growth under control. While China's 14-year-old family planning policies are harsh and coercive, sometimes involving forced sterilization, they give the country an economic edge over nations like Laos or Kenya, where the economy must expand by 3 percent annually just to keep up with the population.

What the statistical comparisons obscure is the powerful yearning to do business that is infecting cities and villages across China. It is often said that 70 years of Communism stunted the entrepreneurial feelings of Russians, but in China tens of millions of people are racing to start new restaurants or factories. Some say that in the current economic boom, China may be the easiest place in the world to make a fortune.

"My nephew is in California, looking after my business interests there," said Zhou Jiangning, the owner of a factory in Wenzhou that produces jade carvings. "But he says that it's easier to make money in China. Expenses are too high in America."

Mr. Zhou earned a profit of $750,000 last year on sales of about $1 million, and he says that profits and revenue are rising by about 35 percent a year. He is an apt representative of China's new gilded age: in the first 15 minutes of conversation, he mentions that his diamond-studded gold Rolex watch cost $16,000 and asks if it is true that middle-class Americans earn less than $100,000 a year.

"Oh," he said soberly, shaking his head sympathetically, "that's not very much."

To be sure, many Chinese find people like Mr. Zhou less inspiring than infuriating. The economic boom is bypassing some inland rural areas, where tens of millions live in caves or rudimentary huts, where meat is a great luxury, where parents cannot afford to send their children to school.

Life has never been fair, but to some Chinese peasants, it has rarely been so unfair. One of Communist China's great achievements was a relatively egalitarian distribution of wealth in a nation that historically had huge disparities; now those traditional disparities are returning with remarkable rapidity.

Source: *New York Times,* February 14, 1993, p. 1. Copyright ©1993, The New York Times Company. Reprinted by permission.

Questions

1. Does the rise of capitalism mean the decline of the strong sense of community, mutual support, and group solidarity that have characterized Chinese culture over the centuries? Explain.
2. Will a rise in crime inevitably accompany the movement in the People's Republic of China from collectivism to capitalism? Explain.
3. Based on your understanding of the role of government in capitalist societies, will the PRC be forced to impose more stringent regulations on Chinese business than is now the case? Explain.

MIDDLE GROUND? A MIXED ECONOMY

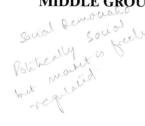

Communism has failed. Socialist principles, to the extent that they call for central planning, bloated bureaucracies, and restraints on personal freedom, are discredited. An era has passed, but the shape of the future is unclear. Some middle ground in free market and welfare state principles seems to be the next step, but the appropriate mixture is proving elusive. For years, the Scandinavian states of Sweden, Norway, and Denmark practiced their market socialism or social democracy with such success that it was labeled a "third way" between the harsher extremes of capitalism and communism. Their welfare states provided healthy economic growth with cradle to grave social care for all in a system emphasizing the collective welfare over individual preferences. Scholar Robert Livingston described Germany's similar approach:

The *social* aspects have always been as important—perhaps more important—than the profit motive. Not only is the social-welfare net essential, not only does a "social partnership" exist between employers and the employed . . . but more broadly the economic system rests upon an implicit social contract, in which employers, the employed (through their unions), the government and, less clearly, the Central Bank are all partners.[16]

Welfare

Now, in the mid-1990s, even that dream of social justice built on a capitalist foundation is foundering as the welfare states of Austria, Germany, France, Great Britain, Scandinavia, and others reluctantly acknowledge that the competitive forces of the global market are not accommodating to their generous social concerns. With deficits exploding, unemployment in the double digits, and worker absenteeism pushing toward 25 percent, even the Swedes turned away in the early 90s from the Social Democratic Labor Party that had governed for more than half a century and embraced moderates who sought to reduce government spending and reinvigorate the market. Of course, welfare state principles have not been abandoned, but in the United States and much of Europe the central question in political economy is that of the proper mixture of government and markets. The first of the two articles that follow summarizes the welfare cutbacks that are slowly and reluctantly marking the changing Western European economy. At the same time, the second article reports the admiration that many American leaders and intellectuals feel for the European model. So the search for a stable middle ground continues.

EUROPE'S SAFETY NETS BEGIN TO TEAR

Terence Roth

Hard times are eating away Europe's social-market economies.

* * * * *

. . . [A]fter decades of seemingly smooth running, Western Europe's social-market economies are beginning to indicate that regaining competitiveness could mean a wrenching overhaul.

Reversing the social-market trend means paring decades of support programs covering most facets of European life, from child allowances and generous pensions to job guarantees, industrial subsidies and cheap health care.

It won't be easy. German Economics Minister Guenther Rexrodt lowered the boom with a proposed hit list of social programs in May, declaring that Germany "increasingly exports more jobs than products."

Europe's most advanced welfare state, Sweden, has led the reverse trend since launching in 1991 the biggest assault ever on the country's social programs as part of a deficit-reduction plan. Britain is whittling down state health services, and Italy has suspended its rigid wage-indexation system and is expecting bigger changes.

Dutch riot squads clashed violently with 20,000

students in the center of The Hague in May. The students were protesting planned cuts in the availability of free transport and automatic unemployment payments beginning on graduation day.

Spain sparked a general strike last year when the government cut unemployment benefits. France is turning further from its costly tradition of state ownership with planned sell-offs of government-held companies beginning later this year.

To be sure, much isn't changing immediately. But some economists predict that reforms could gain momentum as pressure builds to tighten bloated government deficits and get industries moving again.

* * * * *

There are several reasons why the crunch is hitting now. A deepening recession has exacerbated the drag of structural deadweight piling up over decades, most visibly in the steady climb in long-term unemployment. At the same time, new competition from the Pacific Rim, a revitalized U.S. industry and cheaper producers in work-hungry Eastern Europe are cutting into European producers' profits.

The result: trimming government spending, cutting taxes and scraping the keels of industry by de-regulating labor markets and cutting social contributions that are added to employee paychecks. Policy makers are conceding now what was unutterable only a few years ago: Europeans will either have to lose benefits or lose jobs.

* * * * *

European labor is as much as 50% more expensive than its major competitors; not because hourly wages are that much higher, but because the social benefits paid by employers have exploded. The average German manufacturing worker, the highest paid in Europe, received $26.89 an hour in wages and benefits last year, of which $12.47 came in the form of social benefits such as health insurance and pension funding.

Italian workers receive more benefits than wages in their $21.09 hourly compensation. By contrast, only $4.44 of a U.S. worker's average hourly compensation of $15.89 an hour comes as benefits.

Europeans also take longer vacations and work shorter weeks. In 1992, the average German worker clocked 1,519 hours and took 40 days of paid vacation. The average French worker put in 1,646 hours. Meantime, their U.S. and Japanese competitors worked an average 1,857 and 2,007 hours last year, respectively.

* * * * *

Business leaders say it's time to begin sacrificing Europe's holy cows. "We have arrived at a point where we have to tell employees that they have to begin insuring themselves," says Peter-Ruediger Puf, chief economist of Daimler-Benz AG. "Self-responsibility is the watchword."

* * * * *

Public spending amounted to nearly 49% of the EC's gross domestic product last year, up from 37% in 1970, according to the EC Commission. That compares with 37% in the U.S. and 32% in Japan last year. In 1990, the latest figures available, social-security outlays accounted for 25% of GDP in the EC, compared with 15% in the U.S. and 11% in Japan.

* * * * *

The generous public sector helps explain why the corporate tax burden is 61% in Germany and 52% in France, but 45% in the U.S., according to calculations by the Institute of German Industry . . .

These comparisons have alerted policy makers that the structural baggage allowed to pile up over decades will frustrate classic efforts to stimulate growth, such as freer public spending or cheap credit.

"Instead of resorting to fiscal and monetary panaceas that have long been obsolete, policy makers should concentrate on removing actual impediments to growth," Bundesbank Chief Economist Otmar Issing said recently.

He was talking about Europe's albatrosses, also called "structural rigidities." These include politically inspired subsidies to nonprofitable industries. And they include regulatory hurdles and inflexible labor markets—defined as a system of unrealistic wage and benefit scales, lacking worker mobility, and elaborate rules that ban or discourage part-time or weekend work . . .

At the root of the problem is that Europeans have become richer but still demand the protection designed before widespread prosperity.

Source: Adapted from *The Wall Street Journal,* July 1, 1993, p. A10. Reprinted by permission of *The Wall Street Journal,* © 1993 Dow Jones and Company, Inc. All Rights Reserved Worldwide.

SOCIAL JUSTICE

Kay Miller

It's easier to sympathize with others when you're in pain yourself.

Battered, bruised and near economic ruin after World War II, Germans concluded individuals often are victimized by war, unemployment and illness, through no fault of their own.

Germany began devising comprehensive social policies that today insure the German people against almost every imaginable economic risk.

If Germany can do it, why can't we?

*   *   *   *   *

What we can learn from the major industrialized countries' 40-plus years of social policies was the focus of a . . . forum, "The Challenge of Social Justice in a Global Economy" held at the University of Minnesota.

*   *   *   *   *

"It's not a question of, 'Can it be done?' because it is done. The principal economic competitors of the United States today—Japan, Germany, France—are also the countries that have the highest levels of social protection, of social justice, in the contemporary world," said William Pfaff, Paris columnist for the International Herald Tribune and author of "Barbarian Sentiments: How the American Century Ends."

How do they do it?

"They spend a great deal of money," Pfaff said.

Public opinion polls have consistently shown Americans opposed to tax increases. Where the total tax bite for U.S. citizens averages 30.1 percent, it's 43.8 percent in France, 38.1 percent in Germany, 30.6 percent in Japan, and 35.3 percent in Canada.

Higher taxes are accepted in those countries because their citizens see direct benefits in their lives. In France, for example, the cities are clean, high speed trains run on time and unemployed French workers are supported and retrained. The French social contract guarantees college students a free education and French women a six-month paid maternity leave.

Covert racism also complicates our view of social policy. And it disguises the breadth of existing welfare policies that benefit the American middle class.

My home, for example, is partly subsidized by income tax deductions. I received my bachelor's degree at a state university, where other taxpayers underwrote two-thirds of the actual cost of my education. When my father was dying of cancer, Medicaid reimbursed tens of thousands of dollars worth of hospital bills. And my mother will receive many times more Social Security dollars than she put into the system.

But the U.S. system of social supports is spotty. It lacks a coherent philosophy articulating who we want to help and how we intend to pay for it, said Theodore Marmor, professor of Public Policy and Management at Yale University and author of "America's Misunderstood Welfare State."

Arriving at a consistent welfare policy is an especially difficult task, hinging as it does on values.

Americans have long prized individualism—that frontier mentality of the lone cowboy taming the frontier . . . The unspoken assumption in the myth of the rugged individualist is that people who are poor, sick or unemployed have somehow brought it on themselves.

Americans don't use the term "social justice" very much, Pfaff noted. When one conference participant suggested Americans already have purchased all the social justice they really wanted, a murmur of agreement rippled through an auditorium packed with scholars, public officials, policy wonks and concerned corporate types.

* * * * *

"We can't underestimate the ideology—and I use the word advisedly—which has dominated (U.S.) public life during the last 12 years, that the market solves all problems: That God acts through the market," Pfaff said.

By contrast, in Europe there is suspicion of capitalism and the free market. If anything is viewed as God-given, it is the call to help one's fellow citizens, said Robert Gerald Livingston, director of the American Institute for Contemporary German Studies at Johns Hopkins University.

"One of the successes of the European models is that the system has redistributed the taxes so that everyone receives benefits. There is not a stigma of benefits. And there's not this idea that the rich are being robbed to pay for people who don't deserve it," said Ezra Vogel, professor of social sciences at Harvard University and author of "Japan as Number One."

For some time, American disagreement over how much our government should do has been disguised by a rough balance between economic growth and the cost of social programs. But mounting global competition now is undermining that equation, said former Vice President Walter Mondale:

"We have something like 38 (to) 40 million Americans who work around the clock. They're not on welfare. They're not asking for anybody to help them. And when you get all done, their life is such that they could never go to a movie. They can never go out for a meal. They can never afford a baby sitter. They can never take a vacation where money's involved."

And if they get sick, they're in real trouble. Retirement looks bleak. And they've passed the aspirations of limitation on to their children.

Americans seem to have lost the feeling that we're all in this together.

Douglas Fraser, former president of the United Auto Workers, remembers coming to this country as a boy and living in a neighborhood populated by immigrants. "Maybe misery loves company, but there was a feeling of unity and solidarity in those days among those people," Fraser said.

Source: Waterloo Courier, February 28, 1993, p. E1. Reprinted with permission of the *Star Tribune,* Minneapolis-St. Paul.

Questions—Part Three

1. Taxes in the United States are much lower than those of our chief European competitors and slightly lower than those in Japan, and yet we think we are overtaxed. Why? Are we greedy? Explain.

2. According to the article "Social Justice," Americans tend to believe that "God acts through the market" while Europeans are more likely to see a God-given command to "help one's fellow citizens."

   a. Which of those characterizations corresponds most closely to your own view of life? Explain.

   b. How do you explain the pronounced difference in philosophical directions between Europeans and Americans?

3. Americans feel a great deal of faith in the free market. Explain some of the weaknesses in the market. That is, where is the free market likely to fail?

4. Writing in *Dissent,* Joanne Barkan says, "[A]lmost all Swedes view poverty, extreme inequalities of wealth, and the degradation that comes with unemployment as unacceptable."[17]

   a. Do you agree with the Swedes? Explain

   b. Why are Americans more tolerant of those conditions than Swedes?

5. In the late 1970s, correspondent R. W. Apple of the *New York Times* reported that Sweden had willfully pursued a policy of economic leveling:

   > As a result almost every family living near the sea has a boat, but almost all are small boats. A large percentage of families have summer houses, but none of them rivals the villas of the Riviera or the stately manor houses of Britain. Virtually no one has servants.
   >
   > Even among the handful of people who might be able to afford it, conspicuous consumption is frowned upon. There are fewer than 25 Rolls Royces in Sweden.[18]

   a. Is that Swedish approach preferable to the extreme conspicuous consumption permitted—and even encouraged—in this country? Explain.

   b. Is the opportunity to garner luxuries necessary to the successful operation of the American system? Explain.

   c. Does our system generate guilt among those who enjoy its fruits in quantities well beyond the norm? Explain.

6. *a.* Should an American citizen's primary duty be to her- or himself or to all other members of society? Explain.

   b. Should all humans be regarded as of equal value and thus equally worthy of our individual support? Explain.

   c. Can social harmony be achieved in a nation whose citizens fail to regard the state as a "superfamily"? Explain.

7. Distinguished professor and Pulitzer prize winner Arthur Schlesinger, Jr., commented in *The Wall Street Journal* on the emergence of "capitalistic communism" in China:

   > Mr. Deng's economic policies have brought about a considerable increase in production (especially in agriculture), in wealth, in inequality, and in corruption. White-collar crime is growing. At the end of June, the State Council promulgated a new code setting punishments for fraud, profiteering, tax evasion, unauthorized bonuses, and other "economic crimes." The State Auditing Administration has uncovered financial irregularities covering almost 2 percent of the total amount audited.

The number of lawyers is increasing; in Liaoning Province alone, 2,300 lawyers have opened 122 offices. The divorce rate is also rising. Beggars and vagrants are seen more often in the streets. The de-collectivization of agriculture has elevated short-term profit over long-term considerations of land use and conservation; weakened the traditional system of irrigation, canals, and dikes; and has exposed the countryside to new threats of soil exhaustion, erosion, pollution, and flooding.[19]

   a. Is an increase in economic crimes an inevitable by-product of the transformation from socialist–communist principles to capitalism? Explain.

   b. Schlesinger notes a general increase in social problems in China. Are social problems more pronounced in capitalist states than in those with a socialist bent? If not, why would any rational person opt for a socialist government? If so, why would any rational person opt for a capitalist government?

8. In Sweden, the spanking of children is a violation of the law.
   a. What reasoning supports that legislation?
   b. Would such legislation help reduce violence in America? Explain.

9. Collectivists believe that if the means of production reside in private hands, workers will be exploited.
   a. Does American history support that contention? Explain.
   b. Is worker exploitation necessary to the success of capitalism? Explain.

10. The Eskimos, among other cultures, regarded all natural resources as free or common goods to be used but never possessed by any individual or group. What arguments may be raised to justify our notion of private ownership of natural resources?

11. Swedish legislation and the policies of many companies, such as Volvo, provide for worker participation in management decisions. American firms have begun to take that direction. Would this "socialist" goal be desirable for America? Explain.

Part Four—America's Economic Future—Where Are We?

We have inspected the entire economic continuum. We know that communism has been discredited. Hence, the far left has little to offer. President Reagan and, to a lesser extent, President Bush gave us a 12-year view of the virtues and demerits of greater faith in the free market. Should we heed Reagan's call to place our faith in largely unrestrained capitalism, or do we need to move our present *mixed economy* a bit closer to the welfare state model, which itself is under great pressure? Or must a new model emerge? In sum, how much government do we need?

Not surprisingly, the available empirical evidence is mixed. For example, a journalist's "report card" of life in America (as compared with the balance of the globe) features grades ranging from A to D. Jonathan Peterson of the *Los Angeles Times* compiled data from dozens of studies and statistical files and concluded that the United States surpasses the other nations in some ways and ranks poorly in others:

Category	America's Grade
Things people have	A
National wealth	A
Satisfaction	B+
Climbing the ladder	B
Health, well-being	C+
Housing	C
Jobs for everyone	C
Poverty	C−
Sharing the riches	C−
Leisure time	D

Source: Jonathan Peterson, "Life in America: Report Card Helps You Keep Score," *Waterloo Courier,* April 11, 1993, p. A1.

Peterson concludes that the United States is a "hodgepodge of contradictions":

It ranks first in billionaires but first also "in children living in poverty among the 19 major industrial nations," declares author Andrew Shapiro in "We're Number One," a 1992 book of global rankings. We're No. 1 in health care spending and we're number 1 in infant mortality . . .

"The United States is wealthy and poor," Shapiro says, "medically advanced and chronically ill, highly educated and highly uninformed." [20]

Consider some of the details:

Poverty and Wealth.   According to the Census Bureau, in 1992 the percentage of Americans living below the government's official poverty line (a family of four earning $14,335 or less in 1992) rose to 14.5; up from 14.2 in 1991 for a total of 36.9 million people in serious economic distress.[21] At the same time, the income inequalities that accelerated in the early 1980s continued to expand in 1992 as the top 20 percent of American households earned 46.9 percent of the nation's income, up from 46.5 in 1991. Mean income for those people was $91,494. The bottom 20 percent of American households earned 3.8 percent of the national income, the same total as in 1991. Mean income for that group was $7,328.[22]

In the same vein, a 1992 Federal Reserve study concluded that 1 percent of America's households own 37 percent of the nation's wealth, a concentration that the study labeled the greatest of any of the industrial nations. Indeed, the 934,000 richest households in the United States have a greater total net wealth than that of the 84 million poorest households.[23]

Standard of Living by Ethnicity.   According to the Human Development Index from the United Nations, the United States ranks sixth in the world behind Japan, Canada, Norway, Switzerland, and Sweden in overall standard of living. However, white Americans rank first in the world on that Index while African-Americans come in 31st and Hispanic-Americans 35th.[24]

Health Care.   Western European babies have a much better chance of surviving their infancy and childhood than do their counterparts in the United States. The biggest factor in the difference, according to a 1991 study, is that European children have much better access to health care. Other important factors are believed to be better parental supervision in Europe and the higher incidence of drunken driving and deaths due to guns in this country.[25] Encouragingly, the United States' infant mortality rate hit an all-time low in 1990 at 9.2 babies dying before the age of one per 1,000 live births. The United States now ranks 20th among 23 developed nations, with Japan the leader at five deaths per 1,000 live births.[26]

Education.   The World Competitiveness Report, compiled by two Swiss-based economic consulting firms, concluded that the educational system in the United States ranks 21st among the industrial nations of the globe, exceeding only Greece in its ability to meet the needs of a competitive economy.[27]

Good News.   Author and commentator Ben Wattenberg reminds us that we are doing awfully well in some important respects. The Cold War is over, and, he says, we won it. He notes that American culture dominates the globe. "The mark of a great society is that it is influential," Wattenberg adds. "There has never been a nation as influential as this."[28] The facts, in many respects, are extremely encouraging: Drug use is down. Adult reading is up. We have the highest marriage rate among industrialized nations. We are unusually hard working. We handily lead the world in Nobel Prizes and significant patents. And our average tax burden of 29.8 percent of income is among the lowest in the world—with the Japanese, for example, paying 31.3 percent.[29]

No Easy Answers

These data confirm that immense problems remain in America even though the wisdom of the capitalist approach is almost universally conceded. That is, despite its remarkable productive and organizational power, the free market is not without imperfections. Nowhere are those imperfections more apparent than in Eastern Europe, where the capitalist revolutionaries who broke away from communism in 1989 have seen the free market fall tragically short of their hopes. Of course, those hopes were unrealistic; but as the following article suggests, simply unleashing the free market probably is not the route to a better life for all.

LEADERS OF REVOLUTION ACROSS
EASTERN EUROPE ARE NOW ITS VICTIMS

Roger Thurow

Calin Nemes stashed his suicide note in a friend's briefcase so the Romanian police wouldn't get to it before the newspapers did.

In a hand heavy with sarcasm, he scribbled farewell to a country "where communism has been driven away . . . where Romanians, Hungarians and even gypsies live perfectly well together . . . where prices are low and wages are high . . . where our children don't get sick." Farewell, he wrote, to the dreams of the East European revolutionaries of 1989.

Four winters ago in Transylvania, Mr. Nemes, a longhaired, provincial actor, ran into a medieval square in the gritty town of Cluj and ripped off his shirt like a madman. "Go on, kill me," he shouted to a phalanx of soldiers loyal to Communist dictator Nicolae Ceausescu. The commanding officer raised his rifle and hit the bare target with two bullets. As Mr. Nemes crumpled to the cobblestone pavement, an inspired crowd swamped the soldiers. The revolution was on.

Mr. Nemes survived. President Ceausescu was executed. But for the remaining three years, six months and 17 days of his life, Mr. Nemes believed that the tyrant got the better deal.

Instead of the envisioned democratic and free-market utopia, there is unemployment, soaring inflation and crime. Racism has spread across the land. Old Communist apparatchiks are running the new government. Despairing that this isn't the kind of Romania for which he took two bullets—the captain who wounded him is now a major—Mr. Nemes finally did in the summer of 1993 what he had challenged the soldiers to do: He killed himself at age 32 . . .

*   *   *   *   *

An Epilogue

. . . [T]he note Mr. Nemes carefully left behind and published in a Bucharest newspaper provides an unmistakable epilogue to the euphoric revolutions of 1989, when a swarm of ordinary East Germans, Czechs, Slovaks and Romanians tore down the Iron Curtain, shattered the Soviet bloc and buried the Cold War—all between Halloween and Christmas. Their heroism changed the course of the world. But what has become of them?

Today, many of the everyday heroes of 1989 have become victims. Once the shock troops of revolution, they are now the casualties of economic shock treatment.

Their revolt against Communism brought them access to the world's tourist spots, satellite television and bananas all year round. But it also introduced them to capitalism's survival-of-the-fittest competition. While a few have become fabulously successful entrepreneurs, the vast majority have discovered they were woefully unfit for the new world they established. From Bucharest to Berlin, their disillusionment and despair hang as heavy as the autumn smog, giving Europe its current instability and foreshadowing the future problems that await economic reformers in the former Soviet Union.

Social Problems

"The great losers of the revolutions are the ordinary workers," says Silviu Brucan, a Romanian *eminence grise* to East European governments past and present. "All of a sudden they have become the underdogs of the post-Communist society. That makes them an angry and unruly crowd . . . the No. 1 social problem in Europe."

Four years ago, as heroes of the revolutions, the ordinary people of Eastern Europe electrified the world's living rooms. Now, as bitter victims, they are back, agitating for change once again.

* * * * *

Oct. 9, 1989: "I had the feeling that all of Leipzig was on its feet," says Rosemarie Wunnenburger, closing her eyes and recalling how she nervously left the sanctum of a Lutheran church that night to join 70,000 fellow citizens on a protest march through the East German city. They screamed and whistled at the building housing the security police. They shook their fists at the local Communist Party headquarters. They called for free elections and the freedom to travel. Four weeks later, the Berlin Wall fell.

Last month, Mrs. Wunnenburger was out marching again, this time in Dresden at a rally protesting the German government's threatened cuts in jobless benefits and other social expenditures. Several weeks after East Germany disappeared from the world's maps, her job disappeared, too, when the meat-processing factory succumbed to competition in a unified Germany. During the Leipzig march, she carried a candle; in Dresden, she waved a huge banner damning the harshness of capitalism.

"For a long time after losing my job, I couldn't even go to concerts to hear my son play the cello," she moans. "We had a bloodless revolution, but we are nevertheless paying a high price."

Leipzig calls itself the City of Heroes for giving birth to the demonstrations that eventually brought down one of the most orthodox of the Communist states. Today, more than 40% are on the dole after losing their Communist-era jobs.

"We didn't expect things to happen this way," says Mrs. Wunnenburger, a slight, bespectacled 57-year-old. "After the revolution, we thought, 'Now comes our time. We can really do something. We can use our ideas, our energy, our work experience.' And then we find out that no one needs us."

Though Mrs. Wunnenburger finally did get a temporary job, paid for by the government's "work-creation program," it is one of supreme irony. She counsels the unemployed in an office provided by the Nikolaikirche, the Lutheran church that nurtured the revolution with its Monday night "peace prayers." Day after day, she stares sympathetically into hollow, demoralized eyes, listening to the broken promise of German reunification and staring at the roots of the nation's festering right-wing fanaticism.

"We're building new walls in Germany," she says. "Those who work and those who are unemployed don't talk to each other. They don't understand each other. Friendships, families have been destroyed by this."

Source: *The Wall Street Journal,* Oct. 22, 1993, p. A1. Reprinted by permission of *The Wall Street Journal,* © 1993 Dow Jones and Company, Inc. All Rights Reserved Worldwide.

Questions

1. Did Nemes and Wunnenburger expect too much too quickly? Explain.
2. Has capitalism failed them, or have they failed it? Explain.
3. Is a painful transition simply inevitable as communism is cast aside and the market is embraced? Explain.
4. If they stick to the free market course, will Eastern Europeans find prosperity? Happiness? Explain.

BEYOND IDEOLOGY?

We began this chapter with Francis Fukuyama's interesting suggestion that we are at the end of ideological history, by which he meant that Western liberal democracy has vanquished fascism and communism and shown itself to be the clearly superior means of ordering human affairs. As we conclude this chapter, we should consider the possibility that our hopes for a better future simply can't be found in the current debate about the proper balance of market forces and government intervention. As journalist Clarence Page says:

> We need a new definition of civil society which answers the unanswerable questions posed by both the market forces and the governmental ones, as to how we can have a society that fills us up again and makes us feel that we are part of something bigger than ourselves." [30]

Consider the following prescriptions for a life that transcends more traditional ideologies.

Universalism.   Scholar Richard Falk calls for a sense of global citizenship:

> The traditional capitalism/socialism debate is a sham, quite irrelevant to our prospects as a civilization, mere words. The real challenge is whether we can summon the courage and imagination to find ways to reorganize our society around a sustainable economic, ecological, and political ethic that brings people in diverse national societies credible hope for "life, liberty, and the pursuit of happiness." A beginning, and yet no more or less than that, is to nourish feelings, thoughts, and actions around the central idea of being a citizen of the planet, as well as a citizen of a country, a member of a family, race, and religion. Some sense of global identity is, I believe, the only basis on which to achieve enough detachment from the destructive forces of the modern world to form a judgment about what needs to be done within the political arena.
>   . . . Both capitalism and socialism are fundamentally methods for organizing production to maximize efficiency of output and, thereby, to assure social benefit. To go on as if the comparative merits of these two secular ideologies are what matters most ignores the dramatic, urgent reality that neither ideology has led to societies which offer much human promise for the future. We need an ideology that probes beneath the debate about productive efficiency and asks, "What for?" . . . Such a quest requires a commitment to a process of change that extends beyond our lifetimes. Hence it is more a religious than a political enterprise, although it partakes of both. [31]

Smaller Scale.   Journalist Lauren Soth shares Falk's view that improved productivity alone won't satisfy our hopes. Soth says that our preoccupation with goods has led us to neglect other critical goals such as distributing wealth more equitably, reducing crime, and curbing pollution. Soth suggests that in the names of *both* capitalism and socialism we have turned to ever greater aggregations of industrial firms in ever more concentrated urban masses. Soth calls for a renewed respect for smaller units of life.

> As we head into the third American century, shouldn't we look at other goals besides greater output of goods? Shouldn't we try to place a higher value on the general welfare . . . ?

* * * * *

Business executives want their firms to grow; they want to become heads of larger organizations. Prestige. Honor. How do you develop incentives for remaining small? Avoiding the bad labor relations of a huge industrial complex? Having a more pleasant life for your worker families?

Is it feasible to create the cultural advantages of large cities in smaller communities?[32]

Community.   Soth's message, in part, is one of renewed *community,* and that theme is central to a great body of thought about a new direction for America. Scholar Amitai Etzioni, a leader of the communitarian movement, argues that we have moved from the traditional 50s, to the "anything goes" 60s and 70s, to the materialistic 80s, and now we find ourselves dismayed about our moral decline and wondering what to do. Etzioni's answer is, in brief, to move from "me" to "we,"[33] a view shared by Professor William Galston:

> All in all, I believe that communitarianism represents the most promising basis so far for muting the left/right divisions that have shaped (and stalled) so much public-policy debate over the past generation. It offers the most hope for building on widely shared moral sentiments—concerning family, neighborhood, work, and citizen responsibility.[34]

Meaning.   Commentator/publisher Michael Lerner advocates an approach similar to communitarianism under the label of a "politics of meaning":

> The basic supposition is this: Human beings have psychological, ethical and spiritual needs that transcend the normal liberal agenda. Liberals have tended to focus exclusively on economic entitlements and political rights. But most people need something more: We need to be part of loving families and ethically and spiritually grounded communities that provide a meaning for our lives that transcends the individualism and me-firstism of the competitive market.[35]

Questions—Part Four

1. *a.* Do you agree that the current preoccupation with the free market–government intervention debate is too narrow to embrace the needs of genuine reform in contemporary life? Explain.
   b. Do we need reform? Explain.
   c. Do you see promise in any of the prescriptions suggested here (global "citizenship," "small is beautiful," communitarianism, and the "politics of meaning")? Explain.
2. Soth says, "Let's challenge the sacred goals of economic growth, greater output of goods and services, greater productivity."[36] How could we have a better life if we were to diminish our attention to those seemingly central requirements?
3. Scholars William Halal and Alexander Nikitin:

> [F]reedom always entails a price, and the price that Americans pay is the lack of a sense of community. The competitive stress, absence of social support, and sheer meaningless of American life seem to be a major underlying cause for a variety of

crippling social disorders that run rampant in the United States, such as crime, illiteracy, drug use, violence, and other social problems that are among the highest in the modern world.[37]

    a. Do you agree with Halal and Nikitin that America lacks a "sense of community"? Explain.

    b. Is American life "meaningless"? Explain.

CHAPTER QUESTIONS

1.   *a.* Is Francis Fukuyama correct in arguing that we are witnessing the end of ideology? Explain.

    b. Fukuyama also argues that the end of ideology will mean the replacement of politics with economics, resulting in "a very sad time," because the great political questions about how to shape a better world will be replaced by the cultural banality that is one of the products of capitalist society's preoccupation with material goods. Explain what Fukuyama means. Is he correct?

2. Commenting in *Newsweek,* economist Robert Samuelson said, "The . . . pervasive problem of capitalist economies is that almost no one fully trusts capitalists."[38] Do you agree? Why?

3. Dartmouth English professor Noel Perrin laments the explosive growth of the world population, which amounts to about 2 million additional persons per week. In 1987, the world population was 5 billion, and by 2000 the total will reach 6 billion. Perrin says, "Why not stem the population explosion by paying women not to have babies?"[39] He proposes government payments to each fertile woman each year commencing with $500 at puberty and rising by $100 for each year thereafter so long as the woman does not give birth. That total would reach nearly $100,000 by age 53, but he compares that with, for example, the nearly $200,000 cost of bringing up one abandoned child in New York City. In sum, he argues that the plan would be less expensive than our current welfare program.

    a. Would you support Professor Perrin's market-based approach to birth control? Explain.

    b. Do you consider such a program immoral? Explain.

4. "America's real problem," says former Council of Economic Advisers Chairman Herbert Stein, a conservative Republican, is that it has "serious deficiencies that one would not expect in so rich a country . . . the public is saying that even though we are very rich, we have too much crime, too much homelessness, too much illiteracy and ignorance."[40]

    a. Do you agree? Explain.

    b. How do you account for our problems?

    c. Do we need a greater measure of government intervention in order to correct those problems? Explain.

5. Currently, the top 20 percent of American families earn as much income as the remaining 80 percent combined. The upper 5 percent of the families earn as much as the next 15 percent combined. The upper 1 percent of our families earn as much as the next 4 percent combined.[41]

    a. Is this division simply "the natural order of things"; the inevitable result of inherent gradations in individual ability? Explain.

    b. Despite these enormous divisions in wealth, most middle- and upper-middle-class Americans, according to commentator Guy Molyneux, have little awareness of their relative affluence. That is, they believe that most people (excluding the truly poor) live more or less as they do. How is it possible that affluent Americans might be unaware of their good fortune?

6. Child development authority Benjamin Spock says that our total devotion to capitalism, competition, and material gain are the main forces in the destruction of the American family.

    The overriding problem is excessive competition and our glorification of it. It may contribute to our rapid technological advancement, but it has done so at a great price. We are taught to be rugged individualists, and we are obsessed with getting ahead. The family gets lost in this intense struggle. In a healthy society, family should come first, community second, and our outside jobs third. In this country, it is the other way around.[42]

a. Comment.

b. If Spock is correct, how did we reach this condition?

7. It is often argued that many intellectuals (and, in particular, many college professors) actively criticize capitalism and support welfare state principles.
   a. Has that been your experience? Explain.
   b. If that assessment is accurate, how do you account for the leftist inclinations among intellectuals?

8. As you noted in the readings, privatization is enjoying immense popularity.
   a. Make the arguments for and against turning our prisons and jails over to private enterprise.
   b. Would you favor a penal system operated for profit? Explain.

9. If we are fundamentally selfish, must we embrace capitalism as the most accurate and, therefore, most efficient expression of human nature? Explain.

10. Economist and jurist Richard Posner has suggested a free market in babies. Given that "production costs" are relatively low and the value of babies to childless people is high, Posner observed the possibilities for mutually beneficial transactions.
    a. Explain some of the advantages and disadvantages of a market in babies.
    b. Would you favor the legalization of the sale of babies? Explain.

11. Is capitalism a necessary condition for successful democracy? Or, put another way, in a democracy will increasing state control necessarily result in the destruction of that democracy? Explain.

12. Richard Falk argues for "some sense of global identity." Does capitalism enhance or impede the development of a world community? Explain.

13. Socialist Michael Harrington argued for life "freed of the curse of money":

> [A]s long as access to goods and pleasures is rationed according to the possession of money, there is a pervasive venality, an invitation to miserliness and hostility to one's neighbor.[43]

Should we strive to make more and more goods and services "free"? Raise the competing arguments.

14. The great intellect Adolph Berle once said: "A day may come when national glory and prestige, perhaps even national safety, are best established by a country's being the most beautiful, the best socially organized, or culturally the most advanced in the world."[44]
    a. Is government intervention necessary to achieving Berle's goal? Explain.
    b. If faced with a choice, would most Americans opt for Berle's model or for a nation preeminent in consumer goods, sports, and general comfort? Explain.

15. The 1970s were often referred to as the "Me Decade," a period of self-absorption. Pollster Daniel Yankelovich predicted this selfishness would be replaced in the 1980s with an ethic of commitment:

> The core idea of commitment is to make people less absorbed with self and to break through the iron age of self-centeredness. The new ethic of commitment is emerging in two chief forms of expression: a hunger for deeper personal relations and a yearning to belong to a community where people share many bonds in common. At the heart of the ethic of commitment is the moral intuition that the meaning of life lies in finding a commitment outside one's self.[45]

a. We can now look back on the 1980s. Evaluate the accuracy of Yankelovich's views.

b. If Yankelovich is correct in his contention that we seek a greater sense of community and a commitment beyond self-interest, should we opt for the free market or some significant degree of government intervention? Explain.

c. Why is selfishness often considered an evil?

16. In Scandinavia, poverty is effectively nonexistent. In America in 1992, 14.5 percent of the population had incomes below the government poverty line of $14,335 for a family of four. That is, approximately 36.9 million Americans, the equivalent of, for example, the combined populations of Ohio, Indiana, Illinois, and Michigan, led deprived economic lives.
    a. Is that condition alone sufficient justification for American adoption of the welfare state approach? Explain.
    b. It is generally assumed that giving citizens money to combat poverty reduces those

citizens' incentive to work. Do you agree? Explain.

c. As you leave college, if you were given only enough money to lift you above the poverty line, would your incentive to work be significantly reduced? Explain.

d. Regardless of your personal viewpoint, make the argument that welfare does not materially reduce the incentive to work.

17. Benjamin Barber, writing in *The Atlantic,* sees two possible political futures, which he labels, the "forces of Jihad" and the "forces of McWorld":

> The first is a retribalization of large swaths of humankind by war and bloodshed . . . culture is pitted against culture, people against people, tribe against tribe—a Jihad in the name of a hundred narrowly conceived faiths against every kind of interdependence . . . The second is being borne in on us by the onrush of economic and ecological forces that demand integration and uniformity and that mesmerize the world with fast music, fast computers, and fast food—with MTV, Macintosh, and McDonald's pressing nations into one commercially homogenous global network: One McWorld tied together by technology, ecology, communications, and commerce.[46]

a. Do either of these scenarios make sense to you? Explain.

b. Which would you prefer? Explain.

18. Critics argue that socialism requires a uniformity, a "sameness" that would destroy the individuality Americans prize.

a. Are Americans notably independent and individualistic? Explain.

b. Explore the argument that socialism would actually enhance meaningful individualism.

19. A visitor to China during the Maoist period observed that the Chinese children appeared "more cooperative than competitive, more altruistic than selfish." Maoist training taught children to "share toys, love and help each other, and, of course, venerate Mao."

a. Must we similarly curb our emphasis on competition? Explain.

b. If so, what would spur us to greater achievements?

c. Are we taught to "love and help each other"? Explain.

d. Wouldn't a tie be the optimal result in all games? Explain.

20. Hilda Scott wrote a book to which she affixed the provocative title, *Does Socialism Liberate Women?*

a. Answer her question. Explain.

b. Are minority oppression and oppression of women inevitable by-products of capitalism? Explain.

21. In Wisconsin, members of the Old Order Amish religion declined to formally educate their children beyond the eighth grade. The U.S. Supreme Court held that their First Amendment right to freedom of religion was violated by the Wisconsin compulsory education statute, which required school attendance until the age of 16. Chief Justice Burger explained:

> They object to the high school, and higher education generally, because the values they teach are in marked variance with Amish values and the Amish way of life; they view secondary school education as an impermissible exposure of their children to a "worldly" influence in conflict with their beliefs. The high school tends to emphasize intellectual and scientific accomplishments, self-distinction, competitiveness, worldly success, and social life with other students. Amish society emphasizes informal learning-through-doing; a life of "goodness," rather than a life of intellect; wisdom, rather than technical knowledge; community welfare, rather than competition; and separation from, rather than integration with, contemporary worldly society.[47]

a. Have the Amish taken the course we should all follow? Explain.

b. Could we do so? Explain.

22. Irving Kristol built the argument that American society has given rise to a "new class"—scientists, teachers, bureaucrats—who are actively opposed to business and the capitalist approach. The new class consists of:

> [S]cientists, teachers and educational administrators, journalists and others in the communications industries, psychologists, social workers, those lawyers and doctors who make their careers in the expanding public sector, city planners, the staffs of the larger foundations, the upper levels of the government bureaucracy . . . It is basically

suspicious of, and hostile to, the market precisely because the market is so vulgarly democratic—one dollar, one vote . . . The "new class"—intelligent, educated, energetic—has little respect for such a commonplace civilization. It wishes to see its "ideals" more effectual than the market is likely to permit them to be.[48]

 a. Is Kristol's argument sound? Explain.

 b. Have you had experience with people in this new class? Explain.

23. Distinguished economist Gary Becker argues for a free market approach to America's immigration difficulties:

> In a market economy, the way to deal with excess demand for a product or service is to raise the price. This reduces the demand and stimulates the supply. I suggest that the United States adopt a similar approach to help solve its immigration problems. Under my proposal, anyone willing to pay a specified price could enter the United States immediately.[49]

 Comment.

24. At Memorial Junior High in San Diego, students received 25 cents for each day of perfect attendance. The money (actually paper credits) was spent only for school-related goods dispensed in the school store. Initially, the absentee rate dropped dramatically (6 percent to 2.8 percent), but in 38 subsequent months the improvement was modest (7 percent to 6.2 percent).[50]

 a. Evaluate this approach to improved educational performance.

 b. Is the profit motive the key to improving the public sector generally? Explain.

25. Management scholars Rabindra Kanungo and Jay Conger remark that: "'Altruism' is a word rarely associated with the world of business," but they ask: "Does altruism have a place in our business lives? And does it make good economic sense?"[51] Answer their questions.

26. George C. Lodge and Ezra Vogel edited a book entitled *Ideology and National Competitiveness: An Analysis of Nine Countries,* in which they compared the industrial policies of those nine nations.[52] Lodge and Vogel argue that the success of Japan and several Southeast Asian nations in the international market is at least partially attributable to those nations' communitarian approaches to life. On the other hand, they argue that the emphasis on individualism in the United States has harmed our ability to be internationally competitive. Do you agree with Lodge and Vogel? Explain. See Professor Jeffrey A. Hart's review of the book (*Business Horizons* 30, no. 6, November–December 1987, p. 83).

NOTES

1. Francis Fukuyama, "Are We at the End of History?" *Fortune,* January 15, 1990, p. 75.

2. Robert Reich, "Is Liberal Democracy the Hallmark of Our Era?" *The Wall Street Journal,* February 6, 1992, p. A12. Reprinted by permission of *The Wall Street Journal,* © 1992 Dow Jones and Company, Inc. All Rights Reserved Worldwide.

3. Irving Kristol, "When Virtue Loses All Her Loveliness—Some Reflections on Capitalism and 'The Free Society,'" in *Capitalism Today,* ed. Daniel Bell and Irving Kristol (New York: New American Library, 1971), p. 15.

4. Richard Worsnop, "Privatization," *CQ Researcher* 2, no. 42 (November 13, 1992), p. 979.

5. Ibid., p. 980.

6. Jay Matthews, "Taking Welfare Private," *Newsweek,* June 29, 1992, p. 44.

7. Matt Moffett, "Jacques Rogozinski, Mexico's $22 Billion Man, Spreads the Gospel as an Apostle of Privatization," *The Wall Street Journal,* March 16, 1993, p. A16.

8. Richard Holman, "Zambia's Privatization Program," *The Wall Street Journal,* March 8, 1993, p. A6.

9. Richard Holman, "Germany May Privatize Roads," *The Wall Street Journal,* February 10, 1993, p. A8.

10. Richard Holman, "China Deregulates a Railway," *The Wall Street Journal,* February 10, 1993, p. A8.

11. Jonathan N. Goodrich, "Privatization in America," *Business Horizons* 31, no. 1 (January–February 1988), pp. 11, 16.

12. Henry Myers, "His Statues Topple, His Shadow Persists: Marx Can't Be Ignored," *The Wall Street Journal*, November 25, 1991, p. A1.

13. Ibid.

14. Elements of this list are drawn from Agnes Heller and Ferenc Feher, "Does Socialism Have a Future?" *Dissent*, Summer 1989, p. 371.

15. Roger Thurow, "In a Tiny Community in Eastern Germany, Change Comes Hard," *The Wall Street Journal*, January 28, 1993, p. A1.

16. Robert Livingston, "A Social-Conscience Driven Economy," *The Wall Street Journal*, February 19, 1992, p. A19.

17. Joanne Barkan, "Not Yet Paradise, But . . . ," *Dissent*, Spring 1989, pp. 147, 150.

18. R. W. Apple, Jr., "Swedes Feel They're Lumped Together in 'National Blandness,'" reprinted from The *New York Times* in *Lexington Leader*, July 26, 1978, p. A–15.

19. Arthur Schlesinger, Jr., "At Last: Capitalistic Communism," *The Wall Street Journal*, August 4, 1987, p. 32. Reprinted by permission of *The Wall Street Journal*, © 1987 Dow Jones & Company, Inc. 1987. All Rights Reserved Worldwide.

20. Jonathan Peterson, "Life in America: Report Card Helps You Keep Score," *Waterloo Courier*, April 11, 1993, p. A1.

21. Paulette Thomas, "Poverty Spread in 1992 to Total of 36.9 Million," *The Wall Street Journal*, October 5, 1993, p. A2.

22. Ibid.

23. *Parade* Intelligence Report, "Clinton's Clarion Call," *Parade*, July 12, 1992, p. 12.

24. *Los Angeles Times*, "The Standard of Living Gap," *Des Moines Register*, May 16, 1993, p. 6A.

25. Tim Friend, "Western European Kids Get Better Health Care," *USA Today*, August 14, 1991, p. D1.

26. Associated Press, "Infant Mortality at All-Time Low," *Waterloo Courier*, March 12, 1993, p. A5.

27. Associated Press, "U.S. Drops to Fifth Most Competitive, Report Says," *Des Moines Register*, June 22, 1992, p. 1A.

28. Bill Dietrich, "Hey, America: Some Good News," *Des Moines Register*, August 2, 1992, p. 1A.

29. Ibid.

30. Clarence Page, "First Couple Leaves Us Stranded," *Des Moines Register*, May 29, 1993, p. 9A.

31. Richard Falk, "A Sham Debate," in "Is Capitalism on the Way Out?" ed. Leonard Orr, *Business and Society Review* 28 (Winter 1978–79), pp. 4–6.

32. Lauren Soth, "Seek Better Care of People and Earth," *Des Moines Register*, April 24, 1993, p. 5A.

33. Jennifer Haines, "Community: A Solution for America's Decline," *Ethics Journal*, Summer 1993, p. 4.

34. William Galston, "Clinton and the Promise of Communitarianism," *The Chronicle of Higher Education*, December 2, 1992, p. A52.

35. Michael Lerner, "The Meaning of the Politics of Meaning," *The Wall Street Journal*, June 3, 1993, p. A15.

36. Soth, "Seek Better Care," p. 5A.

37. William Halal and Alexander Nikitin, "One World," *The Futurist* 24, no. 6 (November–December 1990), p. 9.

38. Robert Samuelson, "Economics Made Easy," *Newsweek*, November 27, 1989, p. 64.

39. Noel Perrin, "A Nonbearing Account," *Newsweek*, April 2, 1990, pp. 10, 11.

40. Karen Pennar, "The Free Market Has Triumphed, But What About the Losers?" *Business Week*, September 25, 1989, p. 178.

41. Guy Molyneux, "Our Economic Class System," *Des Moines Register*, May 2, 1993, p. 1C.

42. Carla McClain, "Dr. Spock: Restore the Family," *Des Moines Register*, November 7, 1993, p. 3E.

43. Michael Harrington, "Why We Need Socialism in America," *Dissent*, May–June 1970, pp. 240, 286.

44. Adolph Berle, *Power* (New York: Harcourt Brace Jovanovich, 1969), pp. 258–59.

45. Daniel Yankelovich, "Are You Taking Risks with Your Life?" *Parade*, May 24, 1981, pp. 4, 5.

46. Benjamin Barber, "Jihad Vs. McWorld," *The Atlantic* 269, no. 3 (March 1992), p. 53.

47. *Wisconsin* v. *Yoder*, 406 U.S. 205 (1972).

48. Irving Kristol, "Business and the 'New Class,'" *The Wall Street Journal,* May 19, 1975, p. 8.

49. Gary Becker, "Why Not Let Immigrants Pay for Speedy Entry?" *Business Week,* March 2, 1987, p. 20.

50. "In California: Pay-As-You-Go Pedagogy," *Time,* May 11, 1981, p. 8.

51. Rabindra Kanungo and Jay Conger, "Promoting Altruism as a Corporate Goal," *The Academy of Management Executive* 8, no. 3 (August 1993), p. 37.

52. George C. Lodge and Ezra Vogel, *Ideology and National Competitiveness: An Analysis of Nine Countries* (Boston: Harvard Business School, 1987).

ETHICS

Vice is a monster of so frightful mien,
As, to be hated, needs but to be seen;
Yet seen too oft, familiar with her face,
We first endure, then pity, then embrace.

Alexander Pope

Part One—Foundations of Ethical Theory

Chapter 1 explored the capitalism–collectivism economic continuum to remind the reader of the fundamentals of political economy and to encourage some judgment about the degree of government intervention necessary to achieve a desirable relationship between business and the balance of society. That is, might we rely on the market alone to "regulate" the course of business, or must we interpose some degree of government regulation?

Chapter 2 introduces self-regulation as a technique for achieving a more desirable role for business in society. To what extent can we rely on the ethical quality, the morality, of the businessperson and the business organization to govern the path of commerce? If we felt full faith in the free market and the ethical quality of individuals and companies, regulation by law would be reduced at least to those minimums suggested in Chapter 1 by Ayn Rand.

No effort will be made to *teach ethics*. The purpose here is not to improve the reader's "ethical quotient." Rather, the goal is to sensitize the reader to the ethical component of business life. Some sense of the ethical climate of business—some glimpse of the specific ethical problems facing the businessperson—should be useful in assessing the role of ethics in the business decision-making equation and in evaluating the utility of ethics as a "regulator" of business behavior. The three cases that follow illustrate the complexity of ethical analysis. Case 1, "'Bubba' Smith and Advertising," raises the universal theme of personal values in conflict with material gain. Case 2, "Alcohol and Advancement," presents an ethical dilemma typical of those managers must deal with in the workplace. Case 3, "Banker's Fetal Position," places the abortion controversy in the workplace and raises, in an unusually volatile setting, the perennial question of whether the manager can/should/must employ her personal ethical code in carrying out professional activities.

INTRODUCTION TO ETHICS

CASE 1. "BUBBA" SMITH AND ADVERTISING

[Charles "Bubba" Smith, a massive and very successful football lineman for Michigan State University and three professional teams, worked for several years after his football career in commercials for a brewing company. The clever commercials were successful in capitalizing on Smith's reputation for particularly vigorous play by showing Smith, for example, tearing the tops off beer cans with his bare hands. As explained in the article that follows, Smith came to have doubts about the ethics of his role in advertising alcohol.]

Filled-Up Bubba Smith Loses Taste for Lite Beer

Bubba Smith has sworn off booze. Not drinking it, but selling it.

Bubba never did drink, but he sold a ton of beer by making cute television ads. Not anymore. Bubba has kicked the habit.

Bubba Smith may be the first athlete ever, maybe the first person ever, to give up a very lucrative, stupendously easy, and really amusing job making beer commercials, just because he decided it was wrong.

Here's how it happened.

"I went back to Michigan State for the homecoming parade last year," Bubba said. "I was the grand marshall and I was riding in the back seat of this car. The people were yelling, but they weren't saying, 'Go, State, go!' One side of the street was yelling, 'Tastes great!' and the other side was yelling 'Less filling!'

"Then we go to the stadium. The older folks are yelling 'Kill, Bubba, kill!' But the students are yelling 'Tastes great! Less filling!' Everyone in the stands is drunk. It was like I was contributing to alcohol, and I don't drink. It made me realize I was doing something I didn't want to do.

"I loved doing the commercials, but I didn't like the effect it was having on a lot of little people. I'm talking about people in school. Kids would come up to me on the street and recite lines from my commercials, verbatim. They knew the lines better than I did. It was scary. Kids start to listen to things you say, you want to tell 'em something that is the truth.

"Doing those commercials, it's like me telling everyone in school, 'Hey, it's cool to have a Lite beer.' I'd go to places like Daytona Beach and Fort Lauderdale on spring breaks, and it was scary to see how drunk those kids were. It was fun talking to the fans, until you see people lying on the beach because they can't make it back to their room, or tearing up a city."

The obvious question is, why would a nondrinker like Bubba spend eight years making beer commercials?

"Making those commercials, that was a joy to me," Bubba said. "I told myself I couldn't be doing nothing wrong. It seemed so innocent. You don't see things sometimes until you step back from it. Making those commercials, we were a team. It was like football, without the pain. That was an important part of my life, especially the [annual] reunion commercials. It would be five days of sheer laughter—at the shoot, after the shoot, every night."

When Bubba quit, the brewery went out and hired L. C. Greenwood, another huge, intimidating, black former football player who wears eyeglasses and a mustache. Bubba ripped the tops off beer cans. L. C. rips trees out of the ground.

"[The ad people] don't miss a beat," Bubba said.

Source: Scott Ostler, "That Little Voice Just Kept Chanting: 'Stop, Bubba, Stop,'" Copyright 1986, *Los Angeles Times*. Reprinted by permission. Reprinted in the *Des Moines Register*, September 14, 1986, p. 12D.

Questions

1. Were you in his position, would you do as Bubba Smith did in removing himself from the lucrative alcohol-advertising business? Explain.
2. Is alcohol advertising unethical? Is such advertising unethical if directed exclusively to adults? Explain.
3. Would you decline to work in or own a bar because of the harm that your product might do to others? Explain.
4. What measure should we use to determine the degree of our personal responsibility for the conduct of others? Explain.

CASE 2. EMPLOYEE ASSISTANCE PROGRAMS AND A PROMOTION DECISION

Archer Corporation has an Employee Assistance Program (EAP) that offers counseling for alcohol and substance abuse, mental and psychiatric problems.

In 1985, Bob Spicer, a 15-year sales staff veteran and frequent winner of annual performance awards, told his boss, Joe Sampson, "I have been drinking a lot because I am depressed about my personal problems." Sampson referred him to the EAP. Before, and since that time, Spicer's job ratings have been consistently superior. The company does not have access to his medical records and does not know whether he ever obtained or is currently receiving counseling for depression. Joe Sampson, the manager whom Spicer consulted, is now CEO of Archer.

In November 1990, Spicer applied for the high-stress position of vice president, sales, a job for which his performance merits serious consideration. In reviewing his qualifications:

1. Sampson Should (pick one):

A. Ask Spicer if he is still "depressed"; his response is relevant to whether he qualifies for the job.
B. Not discuss the issue with Spicer, but his complaint of being "depressed" should be a factor in considering him for the job.

C. Ignore Spicer's 1985 "depression" complaint because his performance has been excellent and his personal problems are irrelevant in making the promotional decision.
D. Exclude the "depression" incident from consideration in the promotional decision because it occurred more than five years ago.

2. In Making His Decision Sampson (check one):

A. Is confronting ethical as well as business considerations.
B. Can resolve the issue by limiting discussion to standard personnel policies.

3. Archer's Policy with Respect to Known Employee Health Complaints Should Be to (pick one):

A. Exclude using them in making any assignments or promotions.
B. Consider them when performance related.
C. Consider if performance related, but exclude if they occurred more than three years ago.

Source: Ronald E. Berenbeim, "Corporate Ethics Practices" (New York: The Conference Board, 1992), p. 23. Reprinted with permission of the copyright holder, The Conference Board.

CASE 3. BANKER'S FETAL POSITION

Tim Williams is using his skills and connections as a businessman to fight what he regards as a sin against God: abortion. The assistant vice president and trust investment officer at First National Bank of Dayton (Ohio), belongs to Financial Professionals for Life. The group of about fifty bankers, stockbrokers, and insurance agents shares information about abortion and supports boycotts against companies that give to Planned Parenthood.

"Basically, we want to carry the life ethic into our professional lives," said Williams. "The object of corporate charity is to create good will. Why make such a controversial gift? It's not doing the company or the shareholder any good."

Financial Professionals for Life has joined a long list of groups that oppose abortion, including Life Decisions International, which has spearheaded boycotts against corporate donors to Planned Parenthood. A number of corporations, including AT&T, have cut off support to Planned Parenthood when the issue was raised or boycotts threatened.

"My wife is reminding me all the time which products we shouldn't buy or restaurants we shouldn't go to," said Williams, a father of four children with a fifth on the way.

Financial Professionals is now looking to target insurance companies that pay for abortions. "Do you want to make a premium payment to an insurance carrier that pays for—and thereby encourages—abortion?" Williams asked. He added that insurance companies may have an economic reason to cover abortions because the medical costs are less expensive than carrying a baby to term. "They lose in the long run. The baby that gets aborted doesn't get to buy insurance."

Williams said that the Dayton bank where he works does not contribute to Planned Parenthood, though some of his coworkers are pro-choice. "We agree to disagree," he says.

Source: Jeffrey Zack, "Ethics in the News," *Business and Society Review*, no. 83 (Fall 1992), p. 4. Reprinted with permission of the copyright holder, *Business and Society Review*.

Questions

1. In dealing with ethics–public policy questions such as abortion, should managers strictly divide their private and professional lives? Explain.
2. Do you have an ethics–public policy cause to which you are so committed that you will practice it as an active part of your professional life? Explain.
3. Should Williams be dismissed from his job if his antiabortion activism hurts his employer? Explain.
4. Should First National Bank of Dayton deal differently with Williams if he were, for example, a white supremacist or the leader of an antigay organization? Explain.
5. Should Williams decline to do work for his employer where that work assists a company that he knows to be a contributor to Planned Parenthood? Explain.

ETHICS THEORIES

Volumes of literature are devoted in general terms to the question of defining ethics. We cannot hope to advance that discussion here. Ethics, of course, involves judgments as to good and bad, right and wrong, and what ought to be. We seek to use reason in discovering how individuals ought to act. Business ethics refers to the measurement of business behavior based on standards of right and wrong, rather than relying entirely on principles of accounting and management. (In this discussion, morals will be treated as synonymous with ethics. Distinctions certainly are drawn between the two, but those distinctions are not vital for our purposes.)

Finding and following the moral course is not easy for any of us, but the difficulty may be particularly acute for the businessperson. The bottom line is necessarily unforgiving. Hence, the pressure to produce is intense and the temptation to cheat may be very great. Although the law provides useful guideposts for minimum comportment, no clear moral guidelines have emerged. Therefore, when the businessperson is faced with a difficult decision, a common tactic is simply to do what he or she takes to be correct at any given moment. Indeed, in one survey of ethical views in business, 50 percent of the respondents indicated that the word *ethical* meant "what my feelings tell me is right." [1]

Philosophers have provided powerful intellectual support for that approach. Existentialists, led by the famed Jean-Paul Sartre, believe standards of conduct cannot be rationally justified and no actions are inherently right or wrong. Thus, each person may reach his or her own choice about ethical principles. That view finds its roots in the notion that humans are only what we will ourselves to be. If God does not exist, there can be no human nature, because there is no one to conceive that nature.

In Sartre's famous interpretation, existence precedes essence. First humans exist, then we individually define what we are—our essence. Therefore, each of us is free, with no rules to turn to for guidance. Just as we all choose our own natures, so must we choose our own ethical precepts. Moral responsibility belongs to each of us individually.

Universal Truths?

Have we then no rules or universal standards by which to distinguish right from wrong? Have we no absolutes? Philosophers seek to provide guidance beyond the uncertainties of ethical relativism. We will survey two ethical perspectives, teleology and deontology, which form the core of ethical analysis. Before proceeding to those theories, we will note the important role of religion in ethics and take a brief look at three additional formulations—libertarianism, distributive justice, and virtue ethics—that have been increasingly influential in contemporary moral analysis.

1. Religion.   Judeo–Christian beliefs, the Moslem faith, Confucianism, Buddhism, and so on are powerful ethical voices in contemporary life. They often feature efforts such as the Golden Rule to build absolute and universal standards. Scholarly studies indicate that most American managers believe in the Golden Rule and take it to be their most meaningful moral guidepost. From a religious point of view, the deity's laws are absolutes that must shape the whole of one's life, including work. Faith, rather than reason, intuition, or secular knowledge, provides the foundation for a moral life built on religion.

2. Libertarianism.   Contemporary philosopher Robert Nozick has built an ethical theory rooted in the notion of personal liberty. For him, morality springs from the maximization of personal freedom. Justice and fairness, right and wrong are measured not by equality of results (e.g., wealth) for all, but from ensuring equal opportunity for all to engage in informed choices about their own welfare. Hence, Nozick takes essentially a free market stance toward ethics.

3. Distributive Justice.   Harvard philosopher John Rawls calls for maximizing justice, which in turn implies an "equitable" distribution of goods and services. Although his position is quite complex, in essence Rawls seeks to identify that social contract under which free, rational people would choose to order their affairs if they were situated behind a "veil of ignorance" that prevented them from knowing their status in society (intelligence, appearance, wealth). He argues that they would build a cooperative system in which benefits (e.g., income) would be distributed unequally only where doing so would be to the benefit of all—particularly the least advantaged. All those behind the veil would agree to that standard because they could not know whether they would be among the advantaged or disadvantaged. From this system of distributive economic justice, it would seem to follow that ethical justice would be measured by the capacity of the act in question to enhance cooperation among members of society.

4. Virtue Ethics.   In recent years, an increasing number of philosophers have argued that the key to good ethics lies not in rules, rights, and responsibilities but in the classic notion of character. As Plato and Aristotle argued, our attention should be given to strategies for encouraging desirable character traits such as honesty, fairness, compassion, and generosity. Aristotle believed that virtue could be taught much as any other skill. Virtue ethics applauds the person who is motivated to do the right thing and who cultivates that motivation in daily conduct. A part of the argument is that such persons are more morally reliable than those who simply follow the rules but fail to inspect, strengthen, and preserve their own personal virtues.

Teleology or Deontology—An Overview

Teleological ethical systems emphasize the end, the product, the consequences of a decision. The morality of a decision is determined by measuring the probable outcome. A morally correct decision is one that produces the greatest good. The teleological approach calls for reaching moral decisions by weighing the nonmoral consequences of an action. For the teleologist, the end is primary.

To the deontologist, principle is primary and consequence is secondary or even irrelevant. Maximizing right rather than good is the deontological standard. The deontologist might well refuse to lie even if doing so would maximize good. *Deontology,* derived from the Greek word meaning *duty,* is directed toward what ought to be, toward what is right. Relationships among people are important because they give rise to duties. A father may be morally committed to saving his son from a burning building, rather than saving another person who might well do more total good for society. Similarly, deontology considers motives. For example, why a crime was committed may be more important than the actual consequences of the crime.

The distinction here is critical. Are we to guide our behavior in terms of rational evaluations of the consequences of our acts, or are we to shape our conduct in terms of duty and principle—that which ought to be? Let's take a closer look at *utilitarianism,* the principle teleological ethical theory, and *formalism,* the principle deontological ethical theory.

Teleology

Utilitarianism.   In reaching an ethical decision, good is to be weighed against evil. A decision that maximizes the ratio of good over evil for all those concerned is the ethical course. Jeremy Bentham (1748–1832) and John Stuart Mill (1806–1873) were the chief intellectual forces in the development of utilitarianism. Their views and those of other utilitarian philosophers were not entirely consistent. As a result, at least two branches of utilitarianism have developed. According to *act-utilitarianism,* one's goal is to identify the consequences of a particular act to determine whether it is right or wrong. *Rule-utilitarianism* requires one to adhere to all the rules of conduct by which society reaps the greatest value. Thus, the rule-utilitarian may be forced to shun a particular act that would result in greater immediate good (punishing a guilty person whose constitutional rights have been violated) in favor of upholding a broader rule that results in the greater total good over time (maintaining constitutional principles by freeing the guilty person). In sum, the principle to be followed for the utilitarian is the greatest good for the greatest number.

Deontology

Formalism.   The German philosopher Immanuel Kant (1724–1804) developed perhaps the most persuasive and fully articulated vision of ethics as measured not by consequence (teleological) but by the rightness of rules. In this formalistic view of ethics, the rightness of an act depends little (or, in Kant's view, not at all) on the results of the act. Kant believed in the key moral concept of "the good will." The moral person is a person of goodwill, and that person renders ethical decisions based on what is right, regardless of the consequences of the decision. Moral worth springs from one's decision to discharge one's duty. Thus, the student who refuses to cheat on exams is morally worthy if his or her decision springs from duty, but morally unworthy if the decision is merely one born of self-interest, such as fear of being caught.

How does the person of goodwill know what is right? Here, Kant propounded the *categorical imperative,* the notion that every person should act on only those principles that he or she, as a rational person, would prescribe as universal laws to be applied to the whole of humankind. A moral rule is "categorical" rather than "hypothetical" in that its prescriptive force is independent of its consequences. The rule guides us independent of the ends we seek. Kant believed that every rational creature can act according to his or her categorical imperative, because all such persons have "autonomous, self-legislating wills" that permit them to formulate and act on their own systems of rules. To Kant, what is right for one is right for all, and each of us can discover that "right" by exercising our rational faculties.

Theory Applied to Reality

Theory must face the test of reality. The bulk of that testing will be left to the reader. However, let's apply the two dominant ethical theories to Bubba Smith's decision to remove himself from beer advertising.

1. Utilitarianism. Does the collective harm in Smith's work outweigh the collective benefit? Under this analysis, Smith must seek to maximize pleasure and reduce pain, not merely for himself, but for all. Employing a cost–benefit analysis, is the society-wide pain produced by alcohol consumption exceeded by the societywide pleasure? Does Smith bear any responsibility for either?

2. Formalism. Would we want to universally apply a rule that all those situated similarly to Smith should do as he did and desist from working in support of the consumption of beer? Remember that our concern is with intentions rather than consequences. Hence, rather than engaging in a cost–benefit analysis, we would decide whether we prefer a universal standard under which all would decline to promote activities that might be harmful to others. Or would we prefer a universal standard holding that all adults who consume beer are personally and fully responsible for the consequences of doing so?

Obviously, no ethical theory provides easy answers to life's most difficult questions. However, those theories are useful in identifying and sorting the issues that lead to better decision making.

Questions—Part One

1. Think about your approach to ethical dilemmas in your own life.
   a. Do you find yourself turning primarily to teleological or deontological reasoning to resolve those problems? Or neither? Explain.
   b. Have you developed any systematic means of addressing ethical issues? Explain.
2. Do you think that philosophers' analyses of ethics, as we have briefly explored them in this text, can be of value in your future professional life? Explain.

3. Bubba Smith withdrew from his very lucrative role advertising beer in television commercials because of his concerns regarding the ethics of encouraging young people to drink. Commentator John J. O'Connor expresses other grounds for objecting to TV ads directed to children:

> [I]n the York City area, black and Hispanic children are in the majority, but they nevertheless will have a hard time finding their reflections in the commercials surrounding the Saturday morning cartoons.
>   Black children are just about always placed in supporting roles.
>   If a basketball game is used to promote the virtues of a soft drink or cereal, the single black youth will barely get into the picture frame. The leader of the pack is invariably a white boy, preferably blond.[2]

   a. Is O'Connor correct in his assessment of the racial message of many ads directed to children? Explain.
   b. If so, are the companies that issue those ads engaging in unethical conduct? Explain.
4. Some commentators decry what they take to be a growing sense of moral uncertainty in America. *U.S. News & World Report* explains:

> Perhaps more important, heterogeneous 20th-century America has grown cautious about making value judgments. "[There is] a growing degree of cynicism and sophistication in our society," says Jody Powell, former press secretary to Jimmy Carter, "a sense that all things are relative and that nothing is absolutely right or wrong." When a New York City student last year turned in a purse she had found—complete with $1,000 in cash—not a single school official would congratulate her on her virtue. As her teacher explained, "If I come from a position of what is right and wrong, then I am not their counselor." The apparent translation: We no longer believe in black and white, only shades of gray.[3]

   a. Is moral relativism a threat to the nation's moral health? Explain.
   b. Is lying always wrong? Explain.

Part Two—Managerial Ethics: Evidence and Analysis

Suddenly, the subject of ethics is of interest to the whole of American society. The headlines fairly scream for attention to the issue of fundamental flaws in the American character: "A Nation of Liars?"[4] "The New Crisis in Business Ethics,"[5] and "What's Wrong—Hypocrisy, Betrayal, and Greed Unsettle the Nation's Soul."[6] Allegations of rampant greed and proof of surprisingly commonplace corporate crime, including well-publicized securities law violations involving Michael Milken, Ivan Boesky, and so on, left many observers wondering where we had gone wrong in the 1980s. However, a 1987 Touche Ross survey of business and political leaders, while revealing important concerns, expressed overall faith in business ethics.

> Does American business have an ethics problem? Based on the survey's findings, the answer clearly is "yes." Indeed, that viewpoint seems to be nearly unanimous. The survey found that 94 percent of respondents think the business community is troubled by ethical problems. Some 95 percent of the corporate directors and officers expressed this belief, as did 99 percent of the business school deans and 77 percent of the lawmakers . . .

Although respondents believed almost unanimously that business is troubled by ethical problems, they did not say it suffers from a wholesale breakdown in ethics. Indeed, 97 percent believed U.S. business is either highly or reasonably ethical, and only 3 percent said it is unethical.[7]

Furthermore, a 1991 survey of 200 executives found 63 percent of them holding the opinion that "adherence to ethical business behavior" had increased in America in the previous five years.[8] At the same time, we must be alarmed by mounting scholarly evidence that a very high percentage of today's businesspeople are experiencing conflict between their personal standards and organizational demands. One survey of 1,498 managers across the nation found that 46 percent of the supervisors, 29 percent of the middle managers, and 21 percent of the executives had "sometimes" compromised their personal principles to meet an organizational demand.[9] Therefore, based on the experience of those managers, the odds are approximately one in two that the entry-level manager will feel compelled to violate his or her personal moral code in order to meet company goals.

Similarly, Professors John Delaney and Donna Sockell sought to identify ethical challenges in the "real world" by surveying more than 1,000 graduates of the Columbia University Business School classes of 1953 through 1987:

> More than 82 percent of the respondents indicated that they had faced ethical dilemmas at work, with the average graduate facing four in the past year and 11 in his or her career . . .
>
> Nearly 51 percent of respondents indicated that they refused to take the action they felt was unethical, but almost 27 percent knowingly took the action and 23 percent said they did something else, such as resigning. Of those who did something else, 43 percent indicated that they simply expressed their concern.[10]

Delaney and Sockell went on to explain that employers responded by rewarding about 40 percent of those who took the unethical action and they punished about 31 percent of those who refused to engage in the wrongdoing.[11]

Women. A survey of 1,400 women by *Working Woman* magazine provides results much like those of Delaney and Sockell:

> Fully 53 percent agreed that most successful businesspeople must sometimes fudge principles to get ahead. And 78 percent of women who feel they're "highly successful" were more willing to bend and break rules than others.
>
> Just 37 percent of women who took an ethical stand say it helped their careers; 30 percent say it hurt. Over 60 percent would use a secret report stolen from a competitor. Fully 66 percent have "no problem" with a salesperson giving costly gifts to sales prospects. Flirting to make a sale was known by 43 percent, sex with a client by 10 percent, with the boss by 29 percent.
>
> *The most unethical behavior occurs in government, said 66 percent; sales, 51 percent; law, 40 percent; the media, 38 percent; finance, 33 percent; medicine, 21 percent; banking, 18 percent; manufacturing, 14 percent.*[12]

Young People. Doubtless, business ethics reflect societal ethics to some extent, and the ethics news for America generally is not encouraging. Based on a nationwide survey of high school and college students, the Josephson Institute for Ethics has concluded that American youth lack a firm moral core. For example, 33 percent of high school students and 16 percent of those in college admitted to having shoplifted within the previous year. One-third said they were willing to lie to get a job.[13] Similarly, a poll of over 6,000 students at 31 of the top American universities found 76 percent of those who were planning business careers admitted to having cheated on at least one test. Neither prospective doctors, public officials, nor lawyers reported such a high incidence of cheating. And 74 percent of female college students intending to enter MBA programs likewise admitted to cheating, a figure exceeding that of all other groups of women headed for graduate school.[14]

But young people needn't take the fall for the whole of society. Ninety-one percent of adult Americans surveyed in a recent poll admitted to "lying regularly," although only 36 percent admitted to telling "serious lies."[15] Arguably, no segment of society is immune. A survey of 245 scientists revealed that one in three suspected a colleague of falsifying scientific data.[16]

The following national poll certainly reflects great skepticism about business community ethics, but cynicism marks public attitudes toward many professions.

How would you rate the honesty and ethical standards of people in these different fields—very high, high, average, low, or very low?

July 19–21, 1993

	Very High	High	Average	Low	Very Low	No Opinion	1993 Rank*	1992 Rank*
Druggists/ pharmacists	12%	53%	31%	2%	1%	1%	1	1
Clergy	14	39	36	7	2	2	2	2
College teachers	10	42	37	5	1	5	3	4
Medical doctors	8	43	37	9	2	1	4	3
Policemen	10	40	39	7	3	1	5	7
Bankers	3	25	55	13	3	1	10	11
Business executives	2	18	57	16	3	4	13	15
Building contractors	2	18	54	18	4	4	14	13
U.S. senators	2	16	50	24	6	2	16	20
Lawyers	3	13	41	28	13	2	17	14
TV talk show hosts	2	14	41	29	11	3	18	NA
Real estate agents	1	14	57	21	4	3	19	17
Labor union leaders	3	11	39	33	10	4	20	18
Congressmen	2	12	47	30	7	2	21	22
Stockbrokers	1	12	52	20	4	11	23	19
Insurance salesmen	2	8	45	33	10	2	24	24
Advertising practitioners	1	7	46	32	8	6	25	23
Car salesmen	1	5	32	41	19	2	26	25

*Rank based on "very high" and "high" combined.

Source: Leslie McAneny, "Pharmacists Retain Wide Lead as Most Honorable Profession," *The Gallup Poll Monthly*, no. 334 (July 1993), pp. 37–38.

STEINER AND STEINER—THE ROOTS OF BUSINESS ETHICS

Scholars George and John Steiner help to clarify this muddy picture by identifying six primary sources of the business ethics construct in America.[17]

1. Genetic Inheritance.   Although the view remains theoretical, sociobiologists have in recent years amassed persuasive evidence and arguments suggesting that the evolutionary forces of natural selection influence the development of traits such as cooperation and altruism that lie at the core of our ethical systems. Those qualities of goodness often associated with ethical conduct may, in some measure, be a product of genetic traits strengthened over time by the evolutionary process.

2. Religion.   Via a rule orientation exemplified by the Golden Rule (or its variations in many religions) and the Ten Commandments, religious morality is clearly a primary force in shaping our societal ethics. The question here concerns the applicability of religious ethics to the business community. Could the Golden Rule serve as a universal, practical, helpful standard for the businessperson's conduct?

3. Philosophical Systems.   To the Epicureans, the quality of pleasure to be derived from an act was the essential measure of its goodness. The Stoics, like the Puritans and many contemporary Americans, advocated a disciplined, hardworking, thrifty lifestyle. These philosophies and others, like those cited earlier, have been instrumental in our society's moral development.

4. Cultural Experience.   Here, the Steiners refer to the rules, customs, and standards transmitted from generation to generation as guidelines for appropriate conduct. Individual values are shaped in large measure by the norms of the society.

5. The Legal System.   Laws represent a rough approximation of society's ethical standards. Thus, the law serves to educate us about the ethical course in life. The law does not and, most would agree, should not be treated as a vehicle for expressing all of society's ethical preferences. Rather, the law is an ever-changing approximation of current perceptions of right and wrong.

6. Codes of Conduct.   Steiner and Steiner identify three primary categories of such codes. Company codes, ordinarily brief and highly generalized, express broad expectations about fit conduct. Second, company operating policies often contain an ethical dimension. Express policy as to gifts, customer complaints, hiring policy, and the like serves as a guide to conduct and a shield by which the employee can avoid unethical advances from those outside the company. Third, many professional and industry associations have developed codes of ethics, such as the Affirmative Ethical Principles of the American Institute of Certified Public Accountants. In sum, codes of conduct seem to be a growing expression of the business community's sincere concern about ethics. However, the utility of such codes remains unsettled.

WHY DO SOME MANAGERS CHEAT?

Values

We may begin to answer that question by examining the value structures of those who manage. The German philosopher Edward Spranger identified six fundamental value orientations for all humans.[18] Based on Spranger's classifications, William Guth and Renato Tagiuri surveyed a group of top-level executives and arrived at the following ranking of average value scores:[19]

Value	Score
Economic	45
Theoretical	44
Political	44
Religious	39
Aesthetic	35
Social	33

Source: Reprinted by permission of the *Harvard Business Review.* Excerpt from "Personal Values and Corporate Strategy" by William D. Guth and Renato Tagiuri (September–October 1965). Copyright © 1983 by the President and Fellows of Harvard College; all rights reserved.

Thus, managers appear to value more strongly the features of the pragmatic person than the sensitivities often associated with the lower three items. By contrast, ministers, for example, ranked the values in the following order: religious, social, aesthetic, political, theoretical, and economic.[20] In the same vein, Professor George England of the University of Minnesota found that 91 percent of 1,072 managers he surveyed believed trust to be important, but only 12 percent felt trust would help them in their careers. On the other hand, 75 percent of the managers thought ambition was important, and 73 percent thought it would help them become successful.[21]

Psychological Forces

An array of personal needs and preferences clearly play an important role in why managers, and humans generally, engage in wrongdoing. *Business Week* took an interesting look at the motivations behind the Wall Street insider trading scandals of the late 1980s.[22] Young, often Ivy League–educated, highly paid traders crossed the line in order to earn yet more money. *Business Week* asked "Why Wasn't $1 Million a Year Enough?" Of course, no one has definitive answers, but *Business Week*'s interviews with traders, academics, and psychologists produced the important conclusion that the conventional response—greed—was only a partial explanation. Other influential forces included: (1) a predisposition to cut corners, (2) compulsive drives, (3) a yearning to maintain the emotional "high" that accompanied success, (4) the stimulation in danger, (5) a craving for recognition, (6) inexperience, and (7) intellectual excitement.

Moral Development

Scholars argue that some individuals are simply better prepared to make ethical judgments than are others. Psychologist Lawrence Kohlberg built and empirically tested a comprehensive theory of moral development in which he claimed that moral judgment evolves and improves primarily as a function of age and education.

Kohlberg, via interviews with children as they aged, was able to identify moral development as movement through distinct stages, with the later stages being improvements on the earlier ones.

Kohlberg identified six universal stages grouped into three levels.

1. Preconventional Level:
   Stage 1: Obey rules to avoid punishment.
   Stage 2: Follow rules only if it is in own interest, but let others do the same. Conform to secure rewards.

2. Conventional Level:
   Stage 3: Conform to meet the expectations of others. Please others. Adhere to stereotypical images.
   Stage 4: Doing right is one's duty. Obey the law. Uphold the social order.

3. Postconventional or Principled Level:
   Stage 5: Current laws and values are relative. Laws and duty are obeyed on rational calculations to serve the greatest number.
   Stage 6: Follow self-chosen universal ethical principles. In the event of conflicts, principles override laws.[23]

At Level 3, the individual is able to reach independent moral judgments that may or may not be in conformity with conventional societal wisdom. Thus, the Level 2 manager might refrain from sexual harassment because it constitutes a violation of company policy and the law. A manager at Level 3 might reach the same conclusion, but his or her decision would have been based on independently defined, universal principles of justice.

Kohlberg found that many adults never pass beyond Level 2. Consequently, if Kohlberg was correct, many managers may behave unethically simply because they have not reached the upper stages of moral maturity.

Kohlberg's model is based on very extensive longitudinal and cross-cultural studies over a period of more than three decades. For example, one set of Chicago-area boys was interviewed at three-year intervals for a period of 20 years. Thus, the stages of moral growth exhibit "definite empirical characteristics" such that Kohlberg was able to claim that his model had been scientifically validated.[24] While many critics remain, the evidence, in sum, is supportive of Kohlberg's general proposition.

Feminine Voice?   One of those lines of criticism requires a brief inspection. Carol Gilligan, a colleague of Kohlberg, contends that our conceptions of morality are, in substantial part, gender-based.[25] She claims that men typically approach morality as a function of justice, impartiality, and rights while women are more likely to build a morality based on care, support, and responsiveness. Men, she says, tend to take an impersonal, universal view of morality as contrasted with the feminine "voice" that rises more commonly from relationships and concern for the specific needs of others. Gilligan then criticizes Kohlberg because his highest stages, 5 and 6, are structured in terms of the male approach to morality while the feminine voice falls at stage 3. Further, Kohlberg's initial experimental subjects were limited to young males. The result, in Gilligan's view, is that women are underscored.

Organizational Forces

Values, psychological factors, and moral decision-making skills undoubtedly all play a role in managerial misdeeds. However, a considerable body of evidence suggests that forces external to the manager can also be quite influential. In three extensive surveys from 1961 through 1984, managers were asked to rank six factors "in order of their influence or contribution to unethical behaviors or actions by managers."

Factors Influencing Unethical Managerial Behavior

	1984 *Study*	*1977* *Study*	*1961* *Study*
Behavior of superiors	1*	1	1
Behavior of one's peers in the organization	2	4	3
Ethical practices of one's industry or profession	3	3	2
Society's moral climate	4	5	—†
Formal organizational policy (or lack thereof)	5	2	4
Personal financial need	6	6	5

*1 is most influential; 6 is least influential.
†Factor not included.

Note: Suggested by similar table in Archie B. Carroll, *Business and Society* (Cincinnati: South-Western Publishing Co., 1989), p. 120.
Sources: 1984 study—Barry Posner and Warren Schmidt, "Values and the American Manager: An Update," *California Management Review* 26, no. 3 (Spring 1984), p. 202; 1977 study—Steve Brenner and Earl Molander, "Is the Ethics of Business Changing?" *Harvard Business Review* 55, no. 1 (January–February 1977), p. 57; 1961 study—Raymond Baumhart, "How Ethical Are Businessmen?" *Harvard Business Review* 39, no. 4 (July–August 1961), p. 6.

Clearly, managers share the perception that the boss's behavior is the critical ingredient (among the six studied) in maintaining an ethical workplace. The influence of one's coworkers and one's industry or profession is likewise thought to be significant, while society's moral climate and the presence or absence of formal company policy (such as a code of conduct) are generally not perceived to be highly influential. Finally, these managers uniformly dismiss the importance of personal financial need in cheating. Of course, these studies address a limited array of issues, and it may be that these managers are merely passing the buck. In your personal experience, if any, with unethical behavior, were any of these six factors influential in your conduct? Or does the blame lie with you—your values, your personal preferences, or your moral decision-making system? Or some combination of all of those and more?

Cheating—Other Pressures

Many factors clearly are at work, and that in itself is an important lesson. We are often inclined to attribute cheating merely to the desire for personal advancement. But that force, important though it is, does not fully explain cheating. Most of us wish to advance, but some of us are not willing to cheat. Perhaps we are all genetically predisposed to cheat in order to survive. Perhaps we are actually taught to cheat. Perhaps we simply have not fully understood the fundamental moral truths. Perhaps we all too willingly submit to the unethical example and wishes of others. Perhaps, as Karl Menninger suggested, we have lost our sense of sin.[26]

THE CORPORATION AS A MORAL PERSON?

We have given a good deal of attention to the moral dilemma of the individual manager. At this point, an alternative conception should be considered. Many philosophers and commentators have now embraced the notion of the corporation as a person in the fullest sense of the word. Of course, the corporation has long been treated as a person of sorts in the eyes of the law. We can legitimately hold the corporation legally blameworthy for employee wrongs. But can we attribute moral responsibility to the corporation? Ordinarily, we consider an individual morally responsible for act or event X only (1) if the person did X or caused X to occur and (2) if the person's conduct was intentional. Does a corporation ever do or cause any event, or are all so-called corporate acts really the decisions of an individual or individuals? And even if a corporation could act, could it do so intentionally? In a sense, can a corporation think?

How might a corporation be thought of as a fully functioning moral being? Philosopher Peter French is perhaps the leading proponent of the corporate moral personhood notion.[27] For our purposes, the theory begins with what French calls the Corporate Internal Decision Structure (CID Structure), by which he means (1) an organizational system of decision making—the organizational chart—and (2) a set of procedural and policy rules. Via the CID Structure, the judgments and actions of the individual managers, officers, and directors are "processed," and those actions and judgments become the will of the corporation. Thus, the corporate action process parallels that of humans. To French, the corporation displays the characteristics necessary for intentional conduct—hence, his view of the corporation as a moral person. (French's argument goes on in a much more detailed and sophisticated fashion, but this glimpse will suffice here.) Many philosophers support French's position; many differ. The critics' arguments are multiple, but at bottom the corporation, to them, does not appear to be a person. That is, even though a corporation may be *analogous* to a person, it is not necessarily *identical* to a person. For example, do corporations possess all of the rights of a person (e.g., the right to life)?[28]

Even if a corporation can be treated as a moral person, should we want to do so? We might answer yes because, in the event of wrongdoing, we could avoid the nearly impossible task of finding the guilty party within the corporate maze. Why not simply place the blame (or at least part of it) on the organization? But if we were to do so, would we somehow depreciate perhaps the central moral precept in our society—the notion that each of us must accept responsibility for our actions?

Moral World?

Or perhaps, as Professor Jeffrey Nesteruk suggests, we need to move beyond the person/property debate and recognize that existing legal categories don't adequately express the nature of corporations.[29] Nesteruk sees the corporation as a "moral world"—not merely a legal construct or a passive framework to expedite managerial action but a persuasive moral environment actively influencing the nature of ethical decision making within it. Hence, Nesteruk calls for a third legal category reaching beyond person or property to label the corporation an *organizational actor*. Such an approach would highlight the influential role of the organization itself in the ethical choices made by individuals within that organization. The corporation, he argues, is *both* a moral person (and thus morally responsible) and a moral world in which individuals make decisions (and thus are morally responsible.)

The *Challenger* case that follows illustrates the complexity of assigning moral responsibility in contemporary organizational life.

ROGER BOISJOLY AND THE CHALLENGER DISASTER: THE ETHICAL DIMENSIONS

Russell P. Boisjoly, Ellen Foster Curtis, and Eugene Mellican

ABSTRACT. This case study focuses on Roger Boisjoly's attempt to prevent the launch of the Challenger and subsequent quest to set the record straight despite negative consequences. Boisjoly's experiences before and after the Challenger disaster raise numerous ethical issues that are integral to any explanation of the disaster and applicable to other management situations. Underlying all these issues, however, is the problematic relationship between individual and organizational responsibility. In analyzing this fundamental issue, this paper has two objectives: first, to demonstrate the extent to which the ethical ambiguity that permeates the relationship between individual and organizational responsibility contributed to the Challenger disaster; second, to reclaim the meaning and importance of individual responsibility within the diluting context of large organizations.

Introduction

On January 28, 1986, the space shuttle Challenger exploded 73 seconds into its flight, killing the seven astronauts aboard. [See Figure 1.] As the nation mourned the tragic loss of the crew members, the Rogers Commission was formed to investigate the causes of the disaster. The Commission concluded that the explosion occurred due to seal failure in one of the solid rocket booster joints. Testimony given by Roger Boisjoly, senior scientist and acknowledged rocket seal expert, indicated that top management at NASA [National Aeronautics and Space Administration] and Morton Thiokol [contractor for the space shuttle booster rocket] had been aware of problems with the O-ring seals [large rubber gaskets designed to help seal together segments of the rocket], but agreed to launch against the recommendation of Boisjoly and other engineers. Boisjoly had alerted management to problems with the O-rings as early as January, 1985, yet several shuttle launches prior to the Challenger had been approved without correcting the hazards. This suggests that the management practice of NASA and Morton Thiokol had created an environment which altered the framework for decision making, leading to a breakdown in communication between technical experts and their supervisors, and top level management, and to the acceptance of risks that both organizations had historically viewed as unacceptable. With human lives and the national interest at stake, serious ethical concerns are embedded in this dramatic change in management practice.

* * * * *

The significance of an ethical analysis of the Challenger disaster is indicated by the fact that it immediately presents one of the most urgent, but difficult, issues in the examination of corporate and individual

---

FIGURE 1   View Is Forward (Direction of Flight) or "Up" When Vehicle Is on Launch Pad

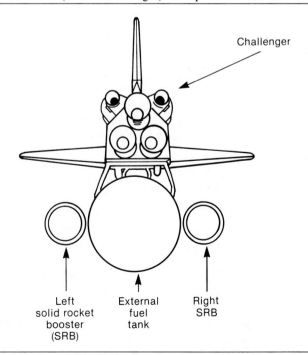

Challenger

Left
solid rocket
booster
(SRB)

External
fuel
tank

Right
SRB

Source: *Report of the Presidential Commission on the Space Shuttle Challenger Accident. June 6, 1986.*

behavior today, i.e., whether existing ethical theories adequately address the problems posed by new technologies, new forms of organization, and evolving social systems. At the heart of this issue is the concept of responsibility . . . Modern technology has . . . transformed the context and scale of human action . . . [I]t is no longer the individual that is the primary focus of power and responsibility, but public and private institutions. Thus, it would seem, it is no longer the character and virtues of individuals that determine the standards of moral conduct, it is the policies and structures of the institutional settings within which they live and work.

Many moral conflicts facing individuals within institutional settings do arise from matters pertaining to organizational structures or questions of public policy. As such, they are resolvable only at a level above the responsibilities of the individual. Therefore, some writers argue that the ethical responsibilities of the engineer or manager in a large corporation have as much to do with the organization as with the individual. Instead of expecting individual engineers or managers to be moral heroes, emphasis should be on the creation of organizational structures conducive to ethical behavior among all agents under their aegis.

* * * * *

Yet, others argue that precisely because of these organizational realities individual accountability must be reemphasized to counteract the diffusion of responsibility within large organizations and to prevent its evasion under the rubric of collective responsibility. Undoubtedly institutions do take on a kind of collective life of their own, but they do not exist, or act, independently of the individuals that constitute them, whatever the theoretical and practical complexities of delineating the precise relationships involved. Far from diminishing individuals' obligations, the reality of organizational life increases them because the consequences of decisions and acts are extended and amplified through the reach and power of that reality.

* * * * *

Preview for Disaster

On January 24, 1985, Roger Boisjoly, senior scientist at Morton Thiokol, watched the launch of Flight 51–C of the space shuttle program. He was at Cape Canaveral to inspect the solid rocket boosters from Flight 51–C following their recovery in the Atlantic Ocean and to conduct a training session at Kennedy Space Center (KSC) on the proper methods of inspecting the booster joints. While watching the launch, he noted that the temperature that day was much cooler than recorded at other launches, but was still much warmer than the 18 degree temperature encountered three days earlier when he arrived in Orlando. The unseasonably cold weather of the past several days had produced the worst citrus crop failures in Florida history.

When he inspected the solid rocket boosters several days later, Boisjoly discovered evidence that the primary O-ring seals on two field joints [The two solid rocket boosters were each composed of four large stacked tubes. The points where the tubes met were called field joints (see Figure 2).] had been compromised by hot combustion gases (i.e., hot gas blow-by had occurred), which had also eroded part of the primary O-ring. This was the first time that a primary seal on a field joint had been penetrated. When he discovered the large amount of blackened grease between the primary and secondary seals, his concern heightened . . . Post-flight calculations indicated that the ambient temperature of the field joints at launch time was 53 degrees. This evidence, coupled with his recollection of the low temperature the day of the launch and the citrus crop damage caused by the cold spell, led to his conclusion that the severe hot gas blow-by may have been caused by, and related to, low temperature. [Boisjoly surmised that the O-rings shrink and harden at lower temperatures, allowing hot gas to escape (blow-by) through the joints.] After reporting these findings to his superiors, Boisjoly presented them to engineers and management at NASA's Marshall Space Flight Center (MSFC). As a result of his presentation at MSFC, Roger Boisjoly was asked to participate in the Flight Readiness Review (FRR) on February 12, 1985, for

FIGURE 2 Cutaway View of the Solid Rocket Booster Showing Solid Rocket Motor Propellant and Aft Field Joint

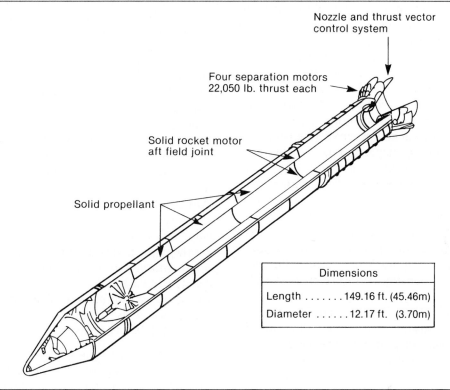

Nozzle and thrust vector control system

Four separation motors 22,050 lb. thrust each

Solid rocket motor aft field joint

Solid propellant

Dimensions	
Length . . . . 149.16 ft.	(45.46m)
Diameter . . . . . . 12.17 ft.	(3.70m)

Source: *Report of the Presidential Commission on the Space Shuttle Challenger Accident. June 6, 1986.*

Flight 51–E which was scheduled for launch in April, 1985. This FRR represents the first association of low temperature with blow-by on a field joint, a condition that was considered an "acceptable risk" by Larry Mulloy, NASA's manager for the Booster Project, and other NASA officials.

Roger Boisjoly had twenty-five years of experience as an engineer in the aerospace industry. Among his many notable assignments were the performance of stress and deflection analysis on the flight control equipment of the Advanced Minuteman Missile at Autonetics, and serving as a lead engineer on the lunar module of Apollo at Hamilton Standard. He moved to Utah in 1980 to take a position in the Ap-

plied Mechanics Department as a staff engineer at the Wasatch Division of Morton Thiokol. He was considered the leading expert in the United States on O-rings and rocket joint seals . . .

The tough questioning he received at the February 12th FRR convinced Boisjoly of the need for further evidence linking low temperature and hot gas blow-by. He worked closely with Arnie Thompson, supervisor of Rocket Motor Cases, who conducted sub-scale laboratory tests in March, 1985, to further test the effects of temperature on O-ring resiliency. The bench tests that were performed provided powerful evidence to support Boisjoly's and Thompson's theory: Low temperatures greatly and adversely affected the ability of O-rings to create a seal on solid rocket booster joints. If the temperature was too low (and they did not know what the threshold temperature would be), it was possible that neither the primary nor secondary O-rings would seal!

One month later the post-flight inspection of Flight 51–B revealed that the primary seal of a booster nozzle joint [the seal area where the flared lower portion of the rocket meets the rocket cylinder.] did not make contact during its two minute flight. If this damage had occurred in a field joint, the secondary O-ring may have failed to seal, causing the loss of the flight. As a result, Boisjoly and his colleagues became increasingly concerned about shuttle safety. This evidence from the inspection of Flight 51–B was presented at the FRR for Flight 51–F on July 1, 1985; the key engineers and managers at NASA and Morton Thiokol were now aware of the critical O-ring problems and the influence of low temperature on the performance of the joint seals.

During July, 1985, Boisjoly and his associates voiced their desire to devote more effort and resources to solving the problems of O-ring erosion. In his activity reports dated July 22 and 29, 1985, Boisjoly expressed considerable frustration with the lack of progress in this area, despite the fact that a Seal Erosion Task Force had been informally appointed on July 19th. Finally, Boisjoly wrote the following memo, labelled "Company Private," to R. K. (Bob) Lund, vice president of Engineering for Morton Thiokol, to express the extreme urgency of his concerns. Here are some excerpts from that memo:

> This letter is written to insure that management is fully aware of the seriousness of the current O-ring erosion problem . . . The mistakenly accepted position on the joint problem was to fly without fear of failure . . . is now drastically changed as a result of the SRM 16A nozzle joint erosion which eroded a secondary O-ring with the primary O-ring never sealing. If the same scenario should occur in a field joint (and it could), then it is a jump ball as to the success or failure of the joint . . . The result would be a catastrophe of the highest order— loss of human life . . .

> It is my honest and real fear that if we do not take immediate action to dedicate a team to solve the problem, with the field joint having the number one priority, then we stand in jeopardy of losing a flight along with all the launch pad facilities.

On August 20, 1985, R. K. Lund formally announced the formation of the Seal Erosion Task Team. The team consisted of only five full-time engineers from the 2,500 employed by Morton Thiokol on the Space Shuttle Program. The events of the next five months would demonstrate that management had not provided the resources necessary to carry out the enormous task of solving the seal erosion problem.

On October 3, 1985, the Seal Erosion Task Force met with Joe Kilminster [Morton Thiokol vice president of Space Booster Programs] to discuss the problems they were having in gaining organizational support necessary to solve the O-ring problems. Boisjoly later stated that Kilminster summarized the meeting as a "good bullshit session." Once again frustrated by bureaucratic inertia, Boisjoly wrote in his activity report dated October 4th:

> . . . NASA is sending an engineering representative to stay with us starting Oct. 14th. We feel that this is a direct result of their feeling that we (MTI) are not responding quickly enough to the seal problem . . . upper management apparently feels that the SRM program is ours for sure and the customer be damned.

Boisjoly was not alone in his expression of frustration. Bob Ebeling, department manager, Solid Rocket Motor Igniter and Final Assembly, and a member of the Seal Erosion Task Force, wrote in a memo to Allan McDonald, manager of the Solid Rocket Motor Project, "HELP! The seal task force is constantly being delayed by every possible means . . . We wish we could get action by verbal request, but such is not the case. This is a red flag."

At the Society of Automotive Engineers (SAE) conference on October 7, 1985, Boisjoly presented a six-page overview of the joints and the seal configuration to approximately 130 technical experts in hope of soliciting suggestions for remedying the O-ring problems. Although MSFC had requested the presentation, NASA gave strict instructions not to express the critical urgency of fixing the joints, but merely to ask for suggestions for improvement. Although no help was forthcoming, the conference was a milestone in that it was the first time that NASA allowed information on the O-ring difficulties to be expressed in a public forum. That NASA also recognized that the O-ring problems were not receiving appropriate attention and manpower considerations from Morton Thiokol management is further evidenced by Boisjoly's October 24 log entry, ". . . Jerry Peoples (NASA) has informed his people that our group needs more authority and people to do the job. Jim Smith (NASA) will corner Al McDonald today to attempt to implement this direction."

The October 30 launch of Flight 61–A of the Challenger provided the most convincing, and yet to some the most contestable, evidence to date that low temperature was directly related to hot gas blow-by. The left booster experienced hot gas blow-by in the center and aft field joints without any seal erosion. The ambient temperature of the field joints was estimated to be 75 degrees at launch time based on post-flight calculations. Inspection of the booster joints revealed that the blow-by was less severe than that found on Flight 51–C because the seal grease was a grayish black color, rather than the jet black hue of Flight 51–C. The evidence was now consistent with the bench tests for joint resiliency conducted in March. That is, at 75 degrees the O-ring lost contact with its sealing surface for 2.4 seconds, whereas at 50 degrees the O-ring lost contact for 10 minutes. The actual flight data revealed greater hot gas blow-by for the O-rings on Flight 51–C, which had an ambient temperature of 53 degrees, than for Flight 61–A, which had an ambient temperature of 75 degrees. Those who rejected this line of reasoning concluded that temperature must be irrelevant since hot gas blow-by had occurred even at room temperature (75 degrees). This difference in interpretation would receive further attention on January 27, 1986.

During the next two and one-half months, little progress was made in obtaining a solution to the O-

ring problems. Roger Boisjoly made the following entry into his log on January 13, 1986, "O-ring resiliency tests that were requested on September 24, 1985, are now scheduled for January 15, 1986."

The Day before the Disaster

At 10 AM on January 27, 1986, Arnie Thompson received a phone call from Boyd Brinton, Thiokol's manager of Project Engineering at MSFC, relaying the concerns of NASA's Larry Wear, also at MSFC, about the 18 degree temperature forecast for the launch of Flight 51–L, the Challenger, scheduled for the next day. This phone call precipitated a series of meetings within Morton Thiokol, at the Marshall Space Flight Center, and at the Kennedy Space Center that culminated in a three-way telecon involving three teams of engineers and managers that began at 8:15 PM EST.

Joe Kilminster began the telecon by turning the presentation of the engineering charts over to Roger Boisjoly and Arnie Thompson. They presented 13 charts which resulted in a recommendation against the launch of the Challenger. Boisjoly demonstrated their concerns with the performance of the O-rings in the field joints during the initial phases of Challenger's flight with charts showing the effects of primary O-ring erosion, and its timing, on the ability to maintain a reliable secondary seal. The tremendous pressure and release of power from the rocket boosters create rotation in the joint such that the metal moves away from the O-rings so that they cannot maintain contact with the metal surfaces. If, at the same time, erosion occurs in the primary O-ring for any reason, then there is a reduced probability of maintaining a secondary seal. It is highly probable that as the ambient temperature drops, the primary O-ring will not seat, that there will be hot gas blow-by and erosion of the primary O-ring, and that a catastrophe will occur when the secondary O-ring fails to seal.

Bob Lund presented the final chart that included the Morton Thiokol recommendations that the ambient temperature including wind must be such that the seal temperature would be greater than 53 degrees to proceed with the launch. Since the overnight low was predicted to be 18 degrees, Bob Lund recommended against launch on January 28, 1986, or until the seal temperature exceeded 53 degrees.

NASA's Larry Mulloy bypassed Bob Lund and directly asked Joe Kilminster for his reaction. Kilminster stated that he supported the position of his engineers and he would not recommend launch below 53 degrees.

George Hardy, deputy director of Science and Engineering at MSFC, said he was "appalled at that recommendation," according to Allan McDonald's testimony before the Rogers Commission. Nevertheless, Hardy would not recommend to launch if the contractor was against it. After Hardy's reaction, Stanley Reinartz, manager of Shuttle Project Office and MSFC, objected by pointing out that the solid rocket motors were qualified to operate between 40 and 90 degrees Fahrenheit.

Larry Mulloy, citing the data from Flight 61–A which indicated to him that temperature was not a factor, strenuously objected to Morton Thiokol's recommendation. He suggested that Thiokol was attempting to establish new Launch Commit Criteria at 53 degrees and that they couldn't do that the night before a launch. In exasperation Mulloy asked, "My God, Thiokol, when do you want me to launch? Next April?" Although other NASA officials also objected to the association of temperature with O-ring erosion and hot gas blow-by, Roger Boisjoly was able to hold his ground and demonstrate with the use of his charts and pictures that there was indeed a relationship: The lower the temperature the higher the probability of erosion and blow-by and the greater the likelihood of an accident. Finally, Joe Kilminster asked for a five minute caucus off-net.

According to Boisjoly's testimony before the Rogers Commission, Jerry Mason, senior vice president of Wasatch Operations, began the caucus by saying that "a management decision was necessary." Sensing that an attempt would be made to overturn the no-launch decision, Boisjoly and Thompson attempted to re-review the material previously presented to NASA for the executives in the room. Thompson took a pad of paper and tried to sketch out the problem with the joint, while Boisjoly laid out the photos of the compromised joints from Flights 51–C and 61–A. When they became convinced that no one was listening, they ceased their efforts. As Boisjoly would later testify, "There was not one positive pro-launch statement ever made by anybody."

According to Boisjoly, after he and Thompson made their last attempts to stop the launch, Jerry Mason asked rhetorically, "Am I the only one who wants to fly?" Mason turned to Bob Lund and asked him to "take off his engineering hat and put on his management hat." The four managers held a brief discussion and voted unanimously to recommend Challenger's launch.

* * * * *

Aside from the four senior Morton Thiokol executives present at the teleconference, all others were excluded from the final decision. The process represented a radical shift from previous NASA policy. Until that moment, the burden of proof had always been on the engineers to prove beyond a doubt that it was safe to launch. NASA, with their objections to the original Thiokol recommendation against the launch, and Mason, with his request for a "management decision," shifted the burden of proof in the opposite direction. Morton Thiokol was expected to prove that launching Challenger would not be safe.

The change in the decision so deeply upset Boisjoly that he returned to his office and made the following journal entry:

> I sincerely hope this launch does not result in a catastrophe. I personally do not agree with some of the statements made in Joe Kilminster's written summary stating that SRM–25 is okay to fly.

The Disaster and Its Aftermath

On January 28, 1986, a reluctant Roger Boisjoly watched the launch of the Challenger. As the vehicle cleared the tower, Bob Ebeling whispered, "we've just dodged a bullet." (The engineers who opposed the launch assumed that O-ring failure would result in an explosion almost immediately after engine ignition.) To continue in Boisjoly's words, "At approximately T + 60 seconds Bob told me he had just completed a prayer of thanks to the Lord for a successful launch. Just thirteen seconds later we both saw the horror of the destruction as the vehicle exploded."

Morton Thiokol formed a failure investigation team on January 31, 1986, to study the Challenger explosion. Roger Boisjoly and Arnie Thompson were part of the team that was sent to MSFC in Huntsville, Alabama. Boisjoly's first inkling of a division between himself and management came on February 13 when he was informed at the last minute that he was to testify before the Rogers Commission the next day. He had very little time to prepare for his testimony. Five days later, two Commission members held a closed session with Kilminster, Boisjoly, and Thompson. During the interview Boisjoly gave his memos and activity reports to the Commissioners. After that meeting, Kilminster chastised Thompson and Boisjoly for correcting his interpretation of the technical data. Their response was that they would continue to correct his version if it was technically incorrect.

Boisjoly's February 25th testimony before the Commission, rebutting the general manager's statement that the initial decision against the launch was not unanimous, drove a wedge further between him and Morton Thiokol management. Boisjoly was flown to MSFC before he could hear the NASA testimony about the preflight telecon. The next day, he was removed from the failure investigation team and returned to Utah.

Beginning in April, Boisjoly began to believe that for the previous month he had been used solely for public relations purposes. Although given the title of Seal Coordinator for the redesign effort, he was isolated from NASA and the seal redesign effort. His design information had been changed without his knowledge and presented without his feedback. On May 1, 1986, in a briefing preceding closed sessions before the Rogers Commission, Ed Garrison, president of Aerospace Operations for Morton Thiokol, chastised Boisjoly for "airing the company's dirty laundry" with the memos he had given the Commission. The next day, Boisjoly testified about the change in his job assignment. Commission Chairman Rogers criticized Thiokol management: ". . . if it appears that you're punishing the two people or at least two of the people who are right about the decision and objected to the launch which ultimately resulted in criticism of Thiokol and then they're demoted or feel that they are being retaliated against, that is a very serious matter. It would seem to me, just speaking for myself, they should be promoted, not demoted or pushed aside."

Boisjoly now sensed a major rift developing within the corporation. Some coworkers perceived that his testimony was damaging the company image. In an effort to clear the air, he and McDonald requested a private meeting with the company's three top executives, which was held on May 16, 1986. According to Boisjoly, management was unreceptive throughout the meeting. The CEO told McDonald and Boisjoly that the company "was doing just fine until Al and I testified about our job reassignments." McDonald and Boisjoly were nominally restored to their former assignments, but Boisjoly's position became untenable as time passed. On July 21, 1986, Roger Boisjoly requested an extended sick leave from Morton Thiokol.

Source: *Journal of Business Ethics* 8 (April 1989), pp. 217–30. © 1989. Reprinted by permission of Kluwer Academic Publishers.

Afterword

Morton Thiokol admitted no liability in the *Challenger* explosion. Both Thiokol and the government settled the claims of the estates of the six astronauts and the teacher Christa McAuliffe who were aboard the shuttle. For example, four of the families settled with the government and Thiokol for $7.7 million, 60 percent from Thiokol and 40 percent from the government. Thiokol settled with the government without "official" penalty. The company agreed to pay $10 million in profits and do $409 million in work at cost to correct the booster problems. The government decided against seeking a formal assessment of blame, thus avoiding litigation and permitting a more expeditious correction of problems in the space program.

In 1988, Morton Thiokol announced its intention not to compete for the contract to manufacture NASA's next generation of shuttle rocket motors. Thiokol indicated that it wanted to concentrate on redesigning the existing motors, which are to be used through 1997. Some observers thought that Thiokol withdrew in the belief that political opposition because of the *Challenger* tragedy would have precluded a successful bid.

Questions—*Challenger* Case

1. Does the *Challenger* case represent a problem in ethics, an accident, poor decision making, or criminal negligence? All of the above? Explain.
2. The authors see the *Challenger* case as an example of the potential conflict between individual and organizational responsibility.
   a. What do they mean?
   b. Are they correct?
   Explain.
3. The authors attribute part of the problem in the *Challenger* case to "groupthink" by the Morton Thiokol officials.
   a. What is groupthink?
   b. How did it affect the decision-making process prior to the *Challenger* loss? Explain.
4. The Rogers Commission chose, for the most part, not to focus its attention and findings on individual wrongdoing or mistakes in its *Challenger* inquiry. Was that a good decision by the Commission? Explain.
5. Would a flawless management *system* prevent disasters like *Challenger?* Explain.
6. As a matter of morality, under what circumstances should we hold an individual personally responsible for a tragedy like *Challenger?* That is, what test would you employ to assign personal responsibility?
7. Apparently, NASA's top authorities were not fully informed regarding the O-ring problem and the Thiokol engineers' concerns regarding cold weather launches.
   a. That being the case, are those top authorities in any sense morally responsible for the tragedy? Explain.
   b. Is ignorance a legitimate excuse for unethical conduct? Explain.

Questions—Part Two

1. Does a corporation have a conscience? Explain. See Kenneth Goodpaster and John B. Matthews, Jr., "Can a Corporation Have a Conscience?" *Harvard Business Review,* January–February 1982, p. 136.

2. Saul Gellerman, dean of the University of Dallas Graduate School of Management, speculated about why managers who are normally good, decent people would occasionally engage in unethical conduct. Gellerman attributes the problem in part to four rationalizations. For example, he believes managers often "rationalize" their wrongdoing by convincing themselves that they will not be caught. Identify other rationalizations that permit good managers to do bad deeds. See Saul Gellerman, "Why 'Good' Managers Make Bad Ethical Choices," *Harvard Business Review,* July–August 1986, p. 85.

3. Business schools are giving increasing attention to ethics. Will that attention make a difference in the ethical quality of actual business practice? Professor David Vogel put the issue this way in a *Wall Street Journal* commentary entitled "Could an Ethics Course Have Kept Ivan [Boesky] from Going Bad?":

   > Before we set about reforming the nation's businesses through its business schools, we might want to reflect more carefully on the relationship between these two institutions. Does anyone believe that if Mr. Levine or Mr. Siegel had been exposed to a few lectures, or even a course, on business ethics they would have been better able to resist the temptation to benefit financially from insider information?[30]

   What value, if any, is likely to be derived from the study of ethics in business schools?

4. As explained earlier, psychologist Lawrence Kohlberg developed a theory of moral development holding that humans proceed through six stages before reaching moral maturity. Kohlberg built his theory from the interviewees' responses to a series of moral dilemmas. For example (stated briefly), should you steal drugs if doing so is the only way to save your spouse's life?

   a. Is Kohlberg's theory consistent with your own view of moral development? Explain.

   b. Rank your moral development using Kohlberg's scale.

   c. Carol Gilligan has argued that men and women have differing moral languages. Gilligan suggests women make moral decisions based on responsibility and caring, whereas moral decision making for males is founded in rules and justice. Comment.

Part Three—Business Ethics in Practice

INTRODUCTION

Having established a general ethical foundation, we now turn to the pragmatics of dealing with specific ethical problems. As noted, when questioned regarding the forces that contribute to unethical decision making in working life, managers point to the behavior of their superiors and the nature of company policy regarding wrongdoing. Hence, we assume that the organization committed to ethical quality can institute some structures and procedures to encourage decency. Codes of conduct are a common corporate ethics tool. The codes vary from rather specific lists of do's and don'ts to general statements of company aspirations. The Johnson & Johnson credo (p. 65) is the most frequently cited corporate ethics statement.

Codes of Conduct

Over 80 percent of the respondents to a 1991 survey of American corporations indicated that they use an employee code of conduct, while European (71 percent) and Canadian firms (68 percent) were slightly less likely to do so.[31] The most commonly prohibited behaviors are set out in the following table. We should note that some evidence suggests that the codes may actually contribute to ethical problems. Professor William Frederick of the University of Pittsburgh argues that the "culprit is not personal values but corporate culture."[32] Professor Frederick points to studies demonstrating that corporations with codes of ethics are actually cited by federal agencies more frequently than those without such codes. And Frederick argues that the codes themselves characteristically emphasize conduct that strengthens the company's profit picture. As exhibited in the table below, company codes normally ignore the firm's role in a variety of pressing social issues.[33] In sum, Frederick's important, data-based study lends scientific support to the view that company goals often have the effect of submerging personal values.

At the same time, corporate efforts to attack ethics problems continue to grow. A 1992 survey of Fortune 1000 companies found over 40 percent of them holding ethics

---

What Company Codes of Conduct Stress

A study of 202 corporate codes of conduct found these subjects included at least 75 percent of the time and, similarly, found these subjects not mentioned at least 75 percent of the time.

Included	Frequency	Not Included	Frequency
Relations with U.S. government	86.6%	Personal character matters	93.6%
Customer/supplier relations	86.1	Product safety	91.0
Political contributions	84.7	Environmental affairs	87.1
Conflicts of interest	75.3	Product quality	78.7
Honest books or records	75.3	Civic and community affairs	75.2

Sources: William Frederick and James Weber, University of Pittsburgh; Marilynn Cash Matthews, Washington State University.

Our Credo

We believe our first responsibility is to the doctors, nurses and patients,
to mothers and fathers and all others who use our products and services.
In meeting their needs everything we do must be of high quality.
We must constantly strive to reduce our costs
in order to maintain reasonable prices.
Customers' orders must be serviced promptly and accurately.
Our suppliers and distributors must have an opportunity
to make a fair profit.

We are responsible to our employees,
the men and women who work with us throughout the world.
Everyone must be considered as an individual.
We must respect their dignity and recognize their merit.
They must have a sense of security in their jobs.
Compensation must be fair and adequate,
and working conditions clean, orderly and safe.
We must be mindful of ways to help our employees fulfill
their family responsibilities.
Employees must feel free to make suggestions and complaints.
There must be equal opportunity for employment, development
and advancement for those qualified.
We must provide competent management,
and their actions must be just and ethical.

We are responsible to the communities in which we live and work
and to the world community as well.
We must be good citizens—support good works and charities
and bear our fair share of taxes.
We must encourage civic improvements and better health and education.
We must maintain in good order
the property we are priviledged to use,
protecting the environment and natural resources.

Our final responsibility is to our stockholders.
Business must make a sound profit.
We must experiment with new ideas.
Research must be carried on, innovative programs developed
and mistakes paid for.
New equipment must be purchased, new facilities provided
and new products launched.
Reserves must be created to provide for adverse times.
When we operate according to these principles,
the stockholders should realize a fair return.

seminars while one-third have established ethics committees. And some 200 firms have recently appointed ethics officers to act as ombudspersons.[34]

The article that follows suggests some of the competing, real-life forces that cloud the manager's ethics landscape. Note that this article details *allegations* of wrongdoing.

HONDA FIRED U.S. EXECUTIVES TIED TO BRIBERY

Krystal Miller

Honda Motor Co. acknowledged it discharged some U.S. sales executives following an internal review of charges by dealers that they had to bribe company officials with money and gifts to receive adequate supplies of cars.

"The allegations relate to a few former employees," a Honda spokesman said. "The vast majority of our employees are honest people that have great integrity and dedication to the company."

* * * * *

So far, three senior executives accused of accepting bribes from dealers have left the company, the spokesman said. Six of 10 Honda regional zone managers have resigned within the last 12 months amid the charges of corruption.

The allegations of corruption in Honda's marketing operations surfaced in a lawsuit filed in 1989 by a Concord, N.H., Acura dealer. The dealer charged that Honda ignored his ailing franchise while giving special treatment to a nearby Acura dealer who bribed the district sales manager with a car and money. Acura is Honda's luxury car division.

Richard Nault, the New Hampshire dealer who filed the suit, charges that Acura dealer Paul T. Boh-

lander gave a new Acura Integra automobile to David L. Pedersen, an Acura district sales manager, according to court documents. Mr. Nault claimed that after Mr. Pedersen was promoted to assistant zone manager, Mr. Bohlander gave him four payments totaling $17,197 in cash. During testimony in U.S. District Court in Concord, Mr. Bohlander admitted he made the payments, according to court records.

Mr. Nault charged that Mr. Bohlander received preferential treatment as a direct result of the payments. For instance, Mr. Bohlander was awarded an Acura dealership in Manchester, N.H., after he gave Mr. Pedersen a new car. Mr. Nault charges in court documents that he sought an Acura dealership in Manchester but was refused.

U.S. Attorney Peter Papps of Concord said in March that he is investigating the accusations of bribery in Mr. Nault's case as well as other alleged incidents. The FBI said . . . that it is also investigating the auto maker.

Questions

1. Explain Professor Frederick's argument that corporation codes of conduct some-times actually increase ethical problems.
2. *a.* If you were a CEO of a corporation, would you institute a code of conduct? Explain.
   b. If so, how would you seek to address the problem that Professor Frederick cites?
3. Should bribes be viewed simply as a necessary cost of doing business for the one paying the bribe and as part of the recipients' "salary"? Explain.
4. Assume you are unmarried and you are opening a one-person firm.
   a. Would you pay a bribe if it were necessary to get your business underway? Explain.
   b. Would your response change if you had a family and if you employed 20 people, all of whom would lose their jobs if the bribe were not paid? Explain.
5. How would you differentiate gifts and bribes?
6. Would you accept gifts from a supplier or a customer if your company rules permitted it but you believed it to be unethical? Explain.

BUSINESS CRIME—MANAGERIAL LIABILITY

While business itself is the victim of shoplifting, employee theft, fraud, and so on, reaching tens of billions of dollars annually, our concern is with white-collar crime in which the criminals are themselves corporations and/or managers. Regrettably, we have extensive evidence of widespread business crime. Professor Amitai Etzioni summarized some of that evidence is his 1990 criminal justice testimony to Congress:

What do we know about the scope of corporate crime and who the actual perpetrators are? The Inspector General's office in the Department of Defense reports that 20 of the 100 largest defense contractors have been convicted in criminal cases since 1983. A study by the Department of Justice that looked at almost 600 of the largest U.S. publicly owned manufacturing, wholesale, retail, and service corporations with annual sales of $300 million or more, showed that during 1975 and 1976 "over 60 percent had at least one enforcement action initiated against them . . . more than 40 percent of the manufacturing corporations engaged in repeated violations." The Resolution Trust Corporation, established to manage the savings and loan bail-out, reports that criminal fraud was discovered in 60 percent of the savings institutions seized by the government in 1989. My own study of the *Fortune 500,* found that 62 percent were involved in one or more incidents of corrupt behavior, including price fixing, environmental and anti-trust violations, bribery and fraud, during the period between 1975 and 1984. VSI Corporation, the largest aircraft fastener manufacturer and a subsidiary of Fairchild Industries Inc., pleaded guilty this month to scheming to falsify test reports on parts for 15 years. A recent General Accounting Office report found that about 52% of the gasoline it sampled was labeled with a higher octane level than it actually contained. The report estimates that such misbranding costs American motorists as much as $150 million per year. Researchers at Rutgers University studied 1,000 people convicted of federal white-collar crime and found that 43 percent had previous arrest records leading to our conclusion that past penalties were not deterring continued criminal behavior. (*U.S. News & World Report,* 5/7/90, p. 24.) From oil spills to laundering drug money, from tax evasion to price fixing, corporate crime is far from rare. [35]

Punishment

Anger over corporate crime itself has been magnified for many years by the widespread sense that business criminals are not meaningfully punished even when caught. In November 1991, to supplement earlier sentencing standards for individuals, the federal government imposed new guidelines on punishments for organizations. The basic idea was to achieve similar punishments for similar offenses. The new guidelines dramatically boost the potential size of fines, corporations may be placed on probation, and management is required to report criminal conduct. Under a complicated formula, fines are assessed based on both the seriousness of the offense and the company's role in the offense. Penalties may go up depending on senior management's role in the crime, the firm's criminal history, the firm's cooperation with authorities, and the strength of the company's compliance effort.[36] At the same time, corporations doing their best to prevent and uncover crime will be treated more leniently, as explained in the accompanying table.

Federal Guidelines for Preventing Corporate Crime

Under the new Federal Guidelines for Sentencing, companies can accrue credits against potential penalties by showing they have complied with the following crime-prevention steps, among others:

- Firms must establish crime prevention standards and procedures for employees and agents. Large companies must have written programs.
- High-level employees with substantial responsibility must be assigned to enforce standards.
- Companies must take steps to prevent employees with an apparent propensity to engage in criminal activity from exercising discretionary authority.
- Companies must communicate anti-crime standards to all employees and agents either in writing or through training programs.
- The anticrime program must include strategies to prevent and detect crimes. Hotlines must be set up and whistle-blowers must be protected from reprisals.

Source: Arthur Hayes, "Businesses Are Slow to Respond to Corporate Sentencing Rules," *The Wall Street Journal*, November 1, 1991, p. B1, B7. Reprinted by permission of *The Wall Street Journal*. © 1991 Dow Jones & Company, Inc. All Rights Reserved Worldwide.

Savings and Loan

In 1993, Malaysia's law minister announced that the next session of the nation's Parliament would consider a bill to publicly whip white-collar criminals as a deterrent to others.[37] Clearly, we are not headed in that direction, but the new sentencing guidelines and much accompanying talk indicate some vigor in white-collar crime enforcement. However, as the following article suggests, serious punishment remains an elusive goal even in the most stunning case of financial mismanagement/white-collar crime of the century—the several hundred billion dollar savings and loan disaster.

TAKE THE MONEY AND RUN

Stephen P. Pizzo and Paul Muolo

Does crime pay? For the white-collar criminals who played leading roles in the savings and loan debacle, the answer appears to be a resounding yes.

A handful of high-profile figures have received stiff sentences, notably Charles H. Keating, Jr., who may spend the rest of his life behind bars for selling worthless junk bonds to depositors of Lincoln Savings and Loan Association and stealing tens of millions of dollars from Lincoln's federally insured deposits. But many have gone unpunished, and most of those who have faced prosecution were handed short sentences or probation. Even their court-imposed criminal fines and financial restitution remain largely uncollected.

Recent studies of bank fraud prosecutions by the General Accounting Office and Public Citizen's Congress Watch have come to basically the same conclusion: Crime—at least bank fraud—pays.

Among the findings: From 1987 through 1992 federal bank and thrift regulators filed a staggering 95,045 criminal referrals with the FBI. The volume was so large that more than 75 percent of these referrals have been dropped without prosecution. Those convicted of bank fraud have been sentenced to prison terms that averaged 2.4 years, compared with 7.8 years for those convicted of old-fashioned bank robbery. From October 1988 through June 1992 federal courts ordered defendants to repay more than $846.7 million in fines and restitution, of which the government has collected only 4.5 percent.

In cases where the defendant agreed to pay restitution in return for a reduction in the prison sentence, the collection rate is even worse. The courts were promised $133.8 million in return for leniency, but have collected only $577,540—or less than half a cent on the dollar.

The issues raised by these statistics go deeper than a petty need to extract satisfaction for taxpayers. They also collide with the stated values of a judicial system that seems to have boundless energy and re-sources to fight and punish so-called street crimes but comes up short when confronted with multi-million-dollar white-collar crimes.

Faced with this discrepancy, Congress imposed a set of new sentencing guidelines in 1987 that mandated minimum sentences over which judges had little discretion. But this measure did little to narrow the gap between street crime and white-collar crime. Those who committed sophisticated financial frauds continued to get off lightly. The courts simply view such crimes differently.

After a jury convicted Thomas E. Nevis, a developer in Yuba City, of defrauding an Oregon S&L out of $55 million, the federal judge, Owen Panner, ultimately reduced Nevis's sentence to six months in a halfway house and $2 million in restitution.

When the prosecutor raised objections, the judge explained his reasoning: "This man has a unique ability, and I think it can be carried out honestly as well as dishonestly . . . People who are able to accomplish what he has, if it can be done honestly, are also stimulating the economy of this country and helping those of us who are professionals to exist."

Consequently prosecutors now think twice before filing charges in such cases. Either they limit the number of charges, knowing that wealthy fraud defendants will use every means available to elude a mandatory prison term; or they bring stiff charges initially only to use them as a plea-bargaining tool, reducing them to a single, lesser charge if the defendant agrees to plead guilty.

Why aren't white-collar criminals prosecuted more zealously? Being tough on street crime is always popular because the public feels threatened by violent crime and wants violent criminals out of circulation. But prosecutors get little political mileage out of prosecuting white-collar crimes because the public simply does not feel threatened by men like Michael Milken and Charles Keating.

"Look, I can wave a pair of bloody underwear in front of a jury and have their undivided attention," one federal prosecutor said. "But I can wave $100 million in phony loan statements in front of the same jury and just watch their eyes glaze over."

*   *   *   *   *

The lack of judicial vigor has been an unexpected bonus for some of the most notorious figures in the S&L debacle.

Don Dixon owned Vernon Savings Association in Dallas, a thrift so notorious it earned the nickname "Vermin Savings" from federal regulators. Vernon Savings cost taxpayers $1.3 billion when it failed in 1987. When federal regulators autopsied Vernon Savings they found the cause of death: More than 95 percent of the thrift's loans were in default. The only explanation for such a rate was that the loans were never intended to be repaid.

Federal regulators sued Dixon for $540 million, accusing him of using his company, Dondi Financial Corporation, to loot Vernon Savings. Dixon filed for bankruptcy, claiming that he was broke in order to avoid the federal civil action. During his bankruptcy hearing the judge asked him why, if he was so broke, he was driving a Ferrari. Dixon explained that it was a "family Ferrari," and not an extravagance. Asked what made it a family Ferrari, Dixon explained that it had an automatic transmission.

When federal prosecutors tried to fashion a criminal case against Dixon, they found that the matrix of interlocking companies and subsidiaries he used to drain off Vernon's money had obscured his direct involvement behind layers of corporate subordinates.

"His signature rarely showed up on the actual documents," one prosecutor, Marvin Collins, complained.

After months of investigation the government charged Dixon with conspiring to defraud Vernon Savings of $611,200 and misusing Vernon's funds to buy a $2 million California beach house. Though the amount was low, the number of fraud counts in the indictment exposed Dixon to up to 120 years behind bars.

Dixon was convicted in late 1990, but to Collins' dismay the judge, A. Joe Fish of the federal District Court, sentenced Dixon to five years in jail, followed by five years' probation. Collins then asked that Dixon at least be ordered to pay restitution of $33.7 million. But the judge decided that Dixon should only have to repay the $611,200.

Dixon would have been eligible for parole next year had he not been indicted a second time. In February 1992, he was charged with illegally diverting additional funds from Vernon for his own uses. Dixon pleaded guilty to the second indictment; at his sentencing he pleaded with the judge for probation because of a serious heart ailment. Federal Judge Robert Maloney sentenced him to five more years, to be served consecutively with his first sentence.

Collins says Dixon has worked out a deal with prosecutors and is cooperating on other investigations in return for sentencing consideration.

And what of his $611,200 fine? "He's broke," says his lawyer, William Ravkind. "He's really broke. Dirt poor."

Questions

1. Many countries do not recognize the possibility that a corporation is capable of being a criminal.
   a. How would you argue that corporations do not have the capacity to be criminals?
   b. Who pays whatever financial penalty is imposed on criminal corporations? Explain.
   c. Why do we have difficulty in holding individual managers responsible for corporate crime?

2. The evidence suggests that corporate crime is not at all unusual. In your judgment, is the business community more tolerant of crime than is American society generally? Explain.

3. A *Fortune* study speculated that crime may be particularly common in small firms: "The bribing of purchasing agents by small manufacturers and the skimming of receipts by cash-laden small retail businesses are a commonplace of commercial life."[38] Thus, we have Etzioni's testimony demonstrating that crime is common among the larger *Fortune* 500 firms and a *Fortune* judgment that small firms (much beneath *Fortune* 500 size) are also frequent cheaters. In your judgment, does corporate size correlate in any meaningful way with the incidence of crime? Explain.

4. Dr. Donald Cressey, a leading expert on white-collar crime, said: "Restraints of trade, price fixing, and other major white-collar crimes are much more threatening to the national welfare than are burglaries, and robberies and other so-called street crimes."[39]

   a. Do you agree? Explain.

   b. Why might white-collar criminals receive more gentle treatment?

   c. What punishments would be most effective against white-collar criminals?

WHISTLE-BLOWING

Today, employees seem increasingly inclined to follow the dictates of conscience in speaking out—publicly, if necessary—against wrongdoing by their employers. Historically, complaints were taken to management and resolved there. "Going public" was considered an act of disloyalty. Americans continue to maintain a strong tradition against "squealing." Indeed, management has good reason to discourage irresponsible, precipitous whistle-blowing that might disclose legitimate trade secrets, cause unnecessary conflict among employees, unfairly tarnish the company image, and so on.

However, increased respect for whistle-blowing has provoked expanded legislative and judicial protection for whistle-blowers. Congress and President Bush agreed on the Whistleblower Protection Act of 1989, which, in brief, makes it easier for federal employees to get their jobs back if they have been demoted or fired after revealing mismanagement. More than 20 other federal laws provide some form of whistle-blower protection and most apply to both public and private employees.

Some 34 states now also have whistle-blower protection statutes for public sector employees. About half of those also offer protection to private sector employees discharged for complaining about a company action believed to violate a law or regulation. In some instances, those state whistle-blower laws apply only if the employee first gave management a chance to resolve the alleged difficulty.

Finally, some court decisions have afforded protection to whistle-blowers by denying employers the right to fire *at-will* employees (those not working under contract) because of their decision to blow the whistle. Traditionally, at-will employees could be fired for any reason (see Chapter 12), but courts have begun to restrict that right, particularly when the firing is deemed to violate public policy (as in the case of a legitimate whistle-blowing complaint).

FEDERAL JUDGE AWARDS
EX-GE STAFFER RECORD AMOUNT
IN WHISTLE-BLOWER CASE

Amal Kumar Naj

A federal judge awarded $13.4 million [subsequently set at $11.5 million] to a former General Electric Co. employee for exposing a defense-contract fraud at the company, sending a strong message of encouragement to corporate whistle-blowers.

The award is the highest ever in a whistle-blower case. In deciding in favor of the GE employee, the judge also harshly criticized GE and the U.S. Justice Department for their conduct toward employees who try to uncover wrongdoings at their companies.

The case in the Cincinnati court was closely watched because the Department of Justice, which is charged with assisting and aiding whistle-blowers, had joined GE in contending that the employee had "manipulated" the federal False Claims Act for his personal gains.

After GE pleaded guilty and paid $69 million in fines and penalties in July to settle the civil and criminal charges, the government argued that the GE employee shouldn't receive any more than $4.5 million for his role.

Responding to the award, GE said it "strongly disagrees" with the judge's decision to offer a "bounty" to Chester Walsh, the employee. Under the whistle-blower protection act, GE cannot challenge the award. But it said it will appeal the court's award of $2.5 million in attorney fees to Mr. Walsh's lawyers from GE's pocket.

Under the whistleblower protection act, Mr. Walsh was entitled to as much as $14.9 million, or 25% of the $59.5 million GE paid to settle the civil portion of the charges. The fraud involved diversion of U.S. funds by high-level company employees and an Israeli general, Rami Dotan, in connection with Israel's acquisition of GE jet engines. The scheme was orchestrated by employees at GE's Aircraft Engine unit in Cincinnati and at the company's offices in Israel.

Mr. Walsh, who was based in Tel Aviv, gathered evidence for more than four years and then sued GE in Cincinnati in November 1990 under the act. The statute allows private citizens to bring such action in behalf of the government and then collect a portion of the federal fines or assessments against the company.

GE had maintained that Mr. Walsh had violated the company's self-policing policies by not bringing the matter to the attention of the company. The Justice Department had joined GE in arguing that Mr. Walsh deliberately waited before filing his suit in order to collect a large reward. The government asked for a smaller award in order to "send a strong message" that whistleblowers shouldn't get "large windfalls" for preparing their case "in a dilatory fashion."

But in his written order, Judge Carl B. Rubin said that there's "no dispute" that without the documents Mr. Walsh had to "smuggle" out of Israel "it would have been difficult, if not impossible, to sustain a case against" GE. The Justice Department had contended that much of the information Mr. Walsh provided was already known to the media and to Israeli government investigators, all of which "ultimately would have led" U.S. investigators to the fraud.

But Judge Rubin cited a secret testimony from an agent of the Federal Bureau of Investigation to discredit the government's contention. The FBI agent was quoted as saying that GE "had taken substantial measures to cover [the fraud] up for a space of two years. I have no reason to believe that anyone within GE would have ever told us besides Mr. Walsh, [who] brought us the only information that we had."

Judge Rubin, who has presided over other whistleblower suits against GE, said the Justice Department's "pattern of behavior" in whistleblower cases "has always been a mystery."

"This is not the first case where this Court has noted antagonism of the Justice Department to a whistleblower," he said. Whistleblowing "should be encouraged by monetary rewards," he added.

* * * * *

The judge also took GE to task for maintaining that it would have put a stop to the fraud if Mr. Walsh had immediately reported to the company. He cited the example of a GE employee, Alaric Fine, who was reassigned after he reported his suspicions to the company . . .

Mr. Walsh said half of his award will go to Taxpayers Against Fraud, a Washington, D.C., group that was a co-plaintiff in his suit.

Questions

1. Why is the role of "squealer" or whistle-blower so repugnant to many Americans?
2. How would you feel about a classmate who blew the whistle on you for cheating on an examination? Would you report cheating by a classmate if it came to your attention? Explain.
3. Assume an employee of an American corporation speaks out to warn the public against a danger in one of the employer's products. The employee is fired.
   a. Can the employee successfully argue that the First Amendment guarantee of freedom of speech protects him or her from dismissal? Explain.
   b. Would it make a difference if the firm operated a nuclear reactor for generating electricity? Explain. (You can refer to Chapter 5 for discussion of the First Amendment.)
4. James Roche, former chairman of the board of General Motors Corporation, said:

   > Some critics are now busy eroding another support of free enterprise—the loyalty of a management team, with its unifying values of cooperative work. Some of the enemies of business now encourage an employee to be disloyal to the enterprise. They want to create suspicion and disharmony and pry into the proprietary interests of the business. However this is labeled—industrial espionage, whistle blowing, or professional responsibility—it is another tactic for spreading disunity and creating conflict.[40]

   Evaluate Mr. Roche's argument.
5. Other than avoiding wrongdoing, what steps might the organization take to render whistle-blowing unnecessary? (You might refer to Kenneth D. Walters, "Your Employees' Right to Blow the Whistle," *Harvard Business Review,* July–August 1975, pp. 26, 31.)
6. Carl Kaufmann, an executive assistant in public affairs at Du Pont, outlined a dilemma that arose in a giant chemicals firm:

   > For years, your corporation manufactures a dye intermediate called Betanaphthylamine without any questions of risk. Then alarming evidence begins turning up—an unusual number of tumors among workers in a plant, malignant tumors. Beta is identified by company scientists as a potent carcinogen—but hundreds of your workers were already exposed.

Would you blow the whistle on yourself or try to do a cleanup quickly to prevent future injuries?[41]

Answer Kaufmann's question.

BRIBERY ABROAD

INTERNATIONAL

Multinational business firms face a special and complex ethical dilemma. In many cultures, the payment of bribes— *baksheesh* (Middle East), *mordida* (South America), or *dash* (Africa)—is accepted as necessary and, in some cases, lawful ways of doing business. American firms and officers wishing to succeed abroad have faced great pressure to engage in practices that are, of course, illegal and unethical in the American culture. In recent years, some 370 firms, including such respected names as Gulf Oil, Lockheed, Exxon, and 3M, have confessed to questionable payments abroad totaling perhaps $745 million. For example, Lockheed expended $12.6 million in Japan alone in seeking aircraft sales. Disclosure of widespread bribery by American firms, including government officials at the highest levels, led to the 1977 enactment of the Foreign Corrupt Practices Act (FCPA). The act was amended in 1988 in an attempt to deal with complaints that it put U.S. companies at too great a competitive disadvantage with foreign companies and that the act imposed an excessive compliance burden on U.S. firms.[42]

In brief, American corporations and managers are engaging in criminal conduct under the act if they offer or provide bribes to foreign government officials to obtain or retain business. And new accounting standards were imposed to eliminate "slush funds" and other devices useful in facilitating bribes. The act does not forbid "grease" payments to foreign officials or political parties where the purpose of the payments is "to expedite or to secure the performance of a routine governmental action,"[43] such as processing papers (e.g., visas), providing police protection, and securing phone service. And those accused may offer the affirmative defense that the alleged payoff was lawful in the host country or was a normal, reasonable business expenditure directed to specific marketing and contract performance activities. Criminal penalties include fines of up to $2 million for companies, while individuals may be fined $10,000 and imprisoned for as long as five years if they either participate in a violation, know of a violation, or are "aware of the high probability of the existence" of a bribery situation "unless the person actually believes that such circumstance does not exist."[44] That is, corporations and individuals cannot use "head-in-sand" tactics to avoid knowledge of wrongdoing.

Controversy

The FCPA has been controversial from the outset. Some businesspeople see it as a blessing both because it is an honorable attempt at a firm moral stance and because it is often useful for an American businessperson abroad to say, "No, our laws forbid me from doing that." On the other hand, some see the act as damaging to our competitiveness. When the FCPA was enacted originally, we had hoped that other nations would join us. None has done so.

> "It hurts us," says an executive of a *Fortune* 500 company's subsidiary that is trying to build a presence in China. He complains that foreign competitors often entertain prospective customers far more lavishly than his company would ever judge reasonable under the act. To get around the law, he says, some American companies enlist middlemen to take care of "local business practices"—while Japanese companies take care of such matters by themselves, without paying middlemen.[45]

And one's attitude toward the act depends a great deal on one's heritage and customs. In many nations, payments to public officials are simply a staple of commerce, a routine part of doing business. Indeed, in Denmark those payments are not only legal, they are tax deductible. Danish companies trying to make deals in Eastern Europe and Africa are advised to report bribes on their tax returns as "consultant fees," which will be treated as tax deductible so long as they are necessary to make a sale.[46] Some critics have argued that the FCPA is "the highwater mark of American Paternalism."[47] What do they mean?

The article that follows details the practice of *quanxi* (influence peddling) and the legal and cultural conflicts that American businesspeople face as they try to conform to the requirements of the FCPA, company codes, and personal ethics while seeking a profit in the potentially immense Chinese market.

IF YOU DON'T PLAY THE GAME
YOU DON'T STAND TO GAIN

Karl Wilson

Whichever way you look at it, more and more businessmen are finding it impossible to clinch deals in China without offering what is euphemistically termed "financial assistance."

Safely back in Hong Kong after his first foray into China on business, the young American executive looked exhausted.

"I can't believe the amount of corruption that goes on in that place," he said. "It is impossible to get anything done unless you bribe someone . . . simply impossible."

Last week China's state-run television reported the biggest crackdown on corruption since the communists came to power in 1949: Four businessmen from Haikou, the capital of Hainan province, were arrested and charged with the misappropriation of $35 million between January and August last year.

*　*　*　*　*

Talk to anyone who has done business in China and you will be told a dozen stories about corruption. To many mainlanders, however, it is not corruption but simple business etiquette. It is not a bribe but a "gift" or a "favor."

When it comes to corruption or "favors," foreign businessmen agree it is worse in the south of China than in the north.

Veteran China traders point out living standards in China have outpaced income by so much in recent years that more people are soliciting "favors" from foreigners.

* * * * *

A national crackdown on official corruption earlier in the year netted 64,000 offenders throughout the country. But one businessman with many years of doing business in China said: "That is just a drop in the bucket."

Whether it be a senior government official or factory worker, corruption has become an ingrained part of China's business ethic.

One businessman said: "If you don't play the game you don't stand to gain. Only a fool refuses to play the game. Who would turn his back on such a market?"

Another businessman said: "Doing business anywhere in the world costs you something . . . only in China it costs you a bit more.

"I will never understand why foreign businessmen take such a sanctimonious stand towards China. You mean to tell me there isn't corruption in Australia, the UK, or the United States?

"Try dealing with the Teamsters union in America or Australia's trade unions."

* * * * *

One businessman explained the process.

"When you arrive you give the family gifts, obviously the more important the official or businessman the more expensive the gifts. But you give him nothing because that would be corruption. There is nothing wrong, however, with giving gifts to his family . . .

"But there is no guarantee a deal will be struck. That is something foreigners don't quite understand."

* * * * *

Businessmen with many years' experience in doing business in China say it does not pay to be up-front with a "favor."

One recent example of a botched "favor" was when a Hong Kong broker tried to get a licence to sell B-shares in Shenzhen.

The Canadian Chinese broker, who had little experience in doing business in China, was told to bribe an official to get the licence.

Putting $100,000 into a brown envelope, the young broker took the train to Shenzhen and his designated meeting with a senior official at the People's Bank of China.

Fifteen minutes later, the young broker handed over the envelope and grasped the banker's hand saying, "I can leave this in your capable hands." The banker threw the broker out of his office along with the $100,000.

"He should have suggested meeting him at home and taken a few expensive gifts with him for the family. I know many Chinese officials are starting to get very concerned about the level of up-front favors. The government says it is cracking down but it is the government which houses the worst offenders," one Hong Kong businessman said.

"The point is, no matter how expensive the gift, it is no guarantee that you will sign a contract."

What has become popular among Chinese businessmen and officials is the invitation by their counterparts in Hong Kong to visit the territory on "business."

"When they arrive it is important to give them 'pocket money' which can be anything from $2,000 upwards depending on how important the person is."

A Hong Kong industrialist said: "Also, you are required to cover air fares, hotel accommodation and meals. That is considered the polite thing to do.

* * * * *

"We call it corruption and it comes out of our marketing budget. In China, it is part of legitimate business practice."

Source: *South China Morning Post*, January 10, 1993, p. 4. Copyright 1993 South China Morning Post Ltd. Reprinted by permission.

Questions

1. Carl Kaufmann of Du Pont raised the following bribery issue: As the head of a multinational corporation, you learn that one of your plant managers has been arrested in a distant republic. His alleged crime is that goods found in your warehouse lack the proper customs stamp and papers. But the truth is more complicated. For years, *grease* has been a way of life in this country's bureaucracy, and your plant manager has been paying gratuities to the customs officers. But he knows it is against home office policy, and so he stops. Their inspection follows. The price for dropping all charges: $18,000.
   a. Would you pay up? Or let your man be put in jail? Explain.
   b. Which alternative is more ethical? [48] Explain.

A DISSENT

To this point, the chapter has been directed, rather conventionally, to the notion that the cause of decency in the corporate community will be enhanced if we achieve a sufficient understanding of ethical dilemmas and the decision systems necessary to deal with them. Therefore, it is fitting to look at an aggressively cynical viewpoint that rejects ideals in favor of a pragmatism often considered more in keeping with today's business reality.

NOTHING SUCCEEDS LIKE AN S.O.B.

R. H. Morrison

The real key to all success is perseverance. The willingness to hang in there, take the lumps that come, and get up off the floor more than once, is the attribute that you must have.

You will also have to become a dedicated, single-minded S.O.B. You have to change your thinking, your attitude toward reality, and develop what could be described as a Machiavellian outlook on the world.

1. First, you cannot be overconcerned with morality in the conventional sense. You must become convinced there is nothing essentially wrong with exploiting people and situations. The game of business is like the game of football. If the quarterback on the offensive team discovers that a defensive halfback simply cannot cover one of his pass receivers, he will use that weakness to his maximum advantage. The defender may wind up losing his job, but this is of no concern to the quarterback. The name of the game is winning, and exploiting situations and people is part of that game.

2. You have to learn to become cool and detached in dealing with other people. You never get emotionally involved with people or situations. Essentially you view everything in terms of objects and situations. You do not suffer with intellectual analysis of the results of your actions.

3. You actually enjoy the game. You enjoy the exploitation, you derive the satisfaction from using people, things, and situations to achieve your goal. You do not do this for amusement or self-aggrandizement, but simply to get that which you are after.

4. Above all you have a rational view of society as it exists. You are neither impressed nor bothered by philosophical viewpoints that stress that the greatest goals in life are serving your fellow man.

5. In short you are not a nice guy, you are an S.O.B., dedicated to success, and having convinced yourself you need that success, it will be achieved. As for money, that's the way you keep score.

If this attitude puts some strain on your psyche, and you feel it is overly cynical or outright debasing, I would like to engage in a brief, philosophical dissertation concerning the reality of such things as truth and morals.

In point of fact, *there is no such thing as real truth in human affairs.* Let's examine the most often quoted rule of behavior, the so-called golden rule: "Do unto others as you would have others do unto you." This sounds as though it is the perfect philosophical solution to human action. However, all humans are not the same, and there are aberrations in the human psyche. If, for example, a masochist were to apply the golden rule to everybody he came in contact with, there would be many unhappy people in the vicinity.

So even the most likely sounding philosophy has holes in it. The plain truth is, that truth is a point of view.

For example, let's take a common happening that affects everybody in the vicinity. Rain! Rain falls universally on everybody in an area. The farmer says the rain is good because it makes his crops grow, and this is the truth. The roadbuilder, the owner of the baseball team, and the people going on a picnic say the rain is bad because it stops them from doing what they need to do. And that, too, is the truth. So we have several people with exactly opposing opin-

ions about an event, and all are telling the truth. So, in fact, the truth is little more than a point of view, and it depends on whose moccasins you are standing in as to whether good or bad.

The problem with things of this nature is that people tend to take extreme viewpoints. Thus, the farmer who demands that it always rains is advocating flood. The roadbuilder who advocates that it never rains is advocating drought. The truth has to be a reasonable compromise between these points of view. And so it is with all affairs of mankind—there has to be a compromise from the extremes in order to arrive at a livable situation. But those moralists who set down rules carved in stone and hand them down as the great truth from above are little more than con men attempting to force people to live in a society that advocates a single truth or a single point of view. It very seldom works.

Morals are nothing more than social customs. They change with time, generations, and societies. For example, a cannibal is moral in a cannibalistic society. He is obviously immoral in a noncannibalistic society.

In this country we have had great changes in moral attitudes over the years, and they change every day. In the Old West, horse stealing was a hanging offense. Today it is a misdemeanor. In the early days of this country, political corruption, prostitution, slavery, and other moral outrages were common coin. Yet we had a higher percentage of people going to church in those days than we do today . . .

Such is the continuous hold of morality on a society. Therefore, the small businessman who is stepping out into the business world can be little concerned with the changing fads of human morals, or philosophical opinions about what is or is not truth.

*   *   *   *   *

When you have made it up the mountain, reached the pinnacle, you can then do what the rest of those successful entrepreneurs have done before you. You can write a code of ethics, make speeches about morality to business and civic groups, and look down with a cold smile on all the scrambling, scratching little bastards below, trying to find their path to the top. You can even do what some of the rest of them have done—roll rocks down on them just for the hell of it, and make the road a little tougher.

I like to think of the small businessman as an eagle. A high-flying loner, whose only morality is to get that which he deems is his right. He flies alone, finds what he needs himself, and lives where and as he chooses.

I think of corporations, government bureaucracies, and others as vultures. Vultures operate in groups, picking the bones of the dead and defenseless, and are simply put here to demonstrate Machiavelli's rule that only the fittest survive. Start now!

Source: *Business and Society Review* 28 (Winter 1978–79), pp. 69–70. Reprinted by permission from the *Business and Society Review.* Copyright 1978, Warren, Gorham & Lamont Inc., 210 South Street, Boston, Mass. All rights reserved.

Questions

1. What is meant by a "Machiavellian outlook on the world"?
2. Is truth merely a point of view? Evaluate the author's argument.
3. Are morals merely relative or situational, changing according to time, place, and circumstances? Explain.
4. Assume a businessperson's goal is success and that issues of morality are of insignificant concern. Is Morrison's formula the best route to success? Explain.
5. In some eras and cultures, spiritual success has been preferable to material success. Is that the case in contemporary America? Explain.

CHAPTER QUESTIONS

1. Can the realistic businessperson expect to be both ethical and successful? Explain.
2. Resolve this ethical dilemma posed by Carl Kaufmann of Du Pont:[49]

   Assume that federal health investigators are pursuing a report that one of your manufacturing plants has a higher-than-average incidence of cancer among its employees. The plant happens to keep excellent medical records on all its employees, stretching back for decades, which might help identify the source of the problem. The government demands the files. But if the company turns them over, it might be accused of violating the privacy of all those workers who had submitted to private medical exams. The company offers an abstract of the records, but the government insists on the complete files, with employee names. Then the company tries to obtain releases from all the workers, but some of them refuse. If you give

   the records to the feds, the company has broken its commitment of confidentiality. What would you do?

3. Among your classmates, would you expect to find a difference between males and females in the incidence of cheating? Explain.
4. *a.* In her book *Lying,* Sissela Bok argues that lying by professionals is commonplace. For example, she takes the position that prescribing placebos for experimental purposes is a lie and immoral. Do you agree with her position? Explain.

   b. Is the use of an unmarked police car an immoral deception? Explain.

   c. One study estimates that Americans average 200 lies per day if one includes "white lies" and inaccurate excuses. On balance, do you believe Americans approve of lying? Explain.
5. "Tonight Show" host Jay Leno performed in commercials encouraging his audience to "eat your

body weight in Doritos."[50] He says that he turned down alcohol ads at twice the money. "I don't drink . . . And I don't like to sell it. You don't see dead teenagers on the highway with bags of Doritos scattered around them."[51]

    a. Are you in agreement with the moral distinction that Leno draws between encouraging the consumption of alcohol and encouraging the consumption of Doritos? Explain.

    b. Given the influence of television and of "stars," is all television advertising by celebrities inherently unethical? Explain.

6. The following quote and questions are drawn from Leonard Lewin's "Ethical Aptitude Test."

> As with other goods and services, the medical care available to the rich is superior to that available to the poor. The difference is most conspicuous in the application of new and expensive life-saving techniques.[52]

    a. Is ability to pay an acceptable way to allocate such services? Explain.

    b. If not, how should such services be apportioned?

    c. Many life-saving drugs can be tested effectively only on human beings. But often, subjects are exposed to such dangers that only those who feel they have nothing to lose willingly participate. Are there any circumstances in which it would be right to conduct such tests without ensuring that the persons tested clearly understood the risks they were taking? Explain.

    d. How much in dollars is the average human life worth?

7. Aaron Burr said, "All things are moral to great men." Regardless of your personal point of view, defend Burr's position.

8. A pharmacist in Lexington, Kentucky, refused to stock over-the-counter weight reducers. His reasons were (1) the active ingredient is the same as that in nasal decongestants; (2) he feared their side effects, such as high blood pressure; and (3) he felt weight reduction should be achieved via self-discipline.[53] Assume the pharmacist manages the store for a group of owners who have given him complete authority about the products stocked. Was his decision ethical? Explain.

9. When *Business and Society Review* surveyed the presidents of 500 large U.S. companies, 51 responded with their reactions to hypothetical moral dilemmas. One question was:

> Assume that you are president of a firm which provides a substantial portion of the market of one of your suppliers. You find out that this supplier discriminates illegally against minorities, although no legal action has been taken. Assume further that this supplier gives you the best price for the material you require, but that the field is competitive.
>
> Do you feel that it is proper to use your economic power over this supplier to make him stop discriminating?[54]

Respond to this question.

10. The insider trading scandals of the 1980s seemed to involve an unexpectedly high percentage of younger professionals rather than Wall Street veterans. Do younger people operate with less stringent ethical guidelines than their older counterparts? Explain.

11. We are in the midst of a period of unprecedented concern regarding the ethical quality of the nation. However, to many observers our problems are no more serious now than has always been the case. Robert Bartley, editor of *The Wall Street Journal,* comments:

> No, we do not live in an age of moral collapse. We more nearly live in an age of moral zealotry. We are applying to ourselves, or at least to our public and private leaders, standards of ethics never before expected of ordinary mortals.[55]

Are we asking too much of ourselves? Explain.

12. In general, does the American value system favor "cheaters" who win in life's various competitions over virtuous individuals who "lose" with regularity? Explain.

13. Why is "virtue its own reward," while tangible productivity is ordinarily accorded material compensation?

14. In general, do smaller firms have higher ethical standards than larger firms? Explain.

15. *a.* Rank the following occupations as to your perception of their ethical quality: businesspersons, lawyers, doctors, teachers, farmers, engineers, carpenters, librarians, scientists, professional athletes, letter carriers, secretaries, journalists.

    b. In general, do you find educated professionals to be more ethical than skilled but generally less-educated laborers? Explain.

    c. Can you justify accepting an occupation that is not at or near the top of your ethical ranking?

Explain how your ranking affects your career choices.

16. Can businesspeople successfully guide their conduct by the Golden Rule?

17. Comment on the following quotes from Albert Z. Carr:

> [M]ost bluffing in business might be regarded simply as game strategy—much like bluffing in poker, which does not reflect on the morality of the bluffer.
>
> I quoted Henry Taylor, the British statesman who pointed out that "falsehood ceases to be falsehood when it is understood on all sides that the truth is not expected to be spoken"—an exact description of bluffing in poker, diplomacy, and business.

* * * * *

> [T]he ethics of business are game ethics, different from the ethics of religion.

* * * * *

> An executive's family life can easily be dislocated if he fails to make a sharp distinction between the ethical systems of the home and the office—or if his wife does not grasp that distinction.[56]

18. Anthropology professor Lionel Tiger has argued for the creation of "moral quality circles" to help improve business conduct. Tiger notes that:

> [O]ur species evolved in small groups of perhaps 25 to 200 hunters and gatherers, groups in which there was no place to hide. Over 200,000 generations or so we evolved great face-to-face sensitivity and a lively skill for "whites-of-their-eyes" assessments of others.

* * * * *

> These ancient but still-lively emotions can be tied into the nature of organizational life to help overcome the all-too-evident capacity of large groups

to yield to "if you want to get along, go along." My hunch is that moral laxity emerges when members of such groups receive little or no dignified opportunity to define their moral views on practical matters without the risk of endangering their occupational health.[57]

Our moral systems sprang from that small-group context; but today, with complex industry replacing hunter–gatherers, those moral systems no longer correspond to contemporary needs. Tiger goes on to argue that we have a kind of "gene for morality" and that most of us have a rather clear sense of right and wrong. Given these conditions, he proposes the moral quality circle, in which workers would discuss the ethical implications of their duties and of the company's conduct in much the same manner that quality circles are now used to improve productivity and reliability. Do you see any value in Tiger's proposal? Explain.

19. Assume that you are working as manager of women's clothing in a large department store. You observe that the manager of equivalent rank to you in men's clothing is performing poorly in that she arrives late for work, she keeps her records ineptly, and she is rude to customers. However, her work has no direct impact on your department.

   a. Do you have any responsibility either to help her or to report her poor performance? Explain.

   b. If the store as a whole performs poorly, but you have performed well, do you bear any degree of personal responsibility for the store's failure when you confined your efforts exclusively to your own department even though you witnessed mismanagement in other departments? Explain.

20. We are often confronted with questions about the boundaries of our personal responsibilities.

   a. How much money, if any, must you give to satisfy your moral responsibility in the event of a famine in a foreign country? Explain.

   b. Would your responsibility be greater if the famine were in America? Explain.

NOTES

1. Raymond Baumhart, *Ethics in Business* (New York: Holt, Rinehart & Winston, 1968), p. 10.

2. John J. O'Connor, "Despite Outrage, Ads for Kids Unchanged," (*New York Times,* 1989). Reprinted in *Des Moines Register,* July 16, 1989, p. 3T.

3. Merril McLoughlin, Jeffrey L., Sheler, and Gordon Witkin, "A Nation of Liars?" *U.S. News & World Report,* February 23, 1987, pp. 54–55. Copyright, 1987, *U.S. News & World Report.*

4. Ibid., p. 54.

5. Kenneth Labich, "The New Crisis in Business Ethics," *Fortune* 125, no. 8 (April 20, 1992), p. 167.

6. Walter Shapiro, "What's Wrong," *Time,* May 25, 1987, p. 14.

7. "Ethics in American Business: A National Opinion Survey," *Ethics in American Business: A Special Report* (New York: Touche Ross, 1988), p. 68.

8. "Ethics Improve, but Not on Paper," *HR Focus* 68, no. 11 (November 1991), p. 6.

9. Barry Z. Posner and Warren H. Schmidt, "Ethics in American Companies: A Managerial Perspective," *Journal of Business Ethics* 6 (July 1987), p. 383.

10. John Delaney and Donna Sockell, "Resolving Business Ethics in the Real World," *Des Moines Register,* May 8, 1990, p. 7A.

11. Ibid.

12. Albert R. Karr, *Labor Letter, The Wall Street Journal,* August 21, 1990, p. A1. Reprinted by permission of *The Wall Street Journal,* © 1990 Dow Jones & Company, Inc. All Rights Reserved Worldwide.

13. Garry Abrams, "Youths Lack an Ethical Core," *Des Moines Register,* November 13, 1992, p. A1.

14. Rick Tetzell, "Business Students Cheat Most," *Fortune* 124, no. 1 (July 1, 1991), p. 14.

15. James Patterson and Peter Kim, *The Day America Told the Truth* (New York: Prentice Hall, 1991), pp. 45–46.

16. Associated Press, "One in Three Scientists Suspects Colleagues Falsify Data," *Waterloo Courier,* August 30, 1987, p. A6.

17. George Steiner and John Steiner, *Business, Government, and Society: A Managerial Perspective,* 5th ed. (New York: Random House, 1988), pp. 329–40.

18. Edward Spranger, *Types of Men,* trans. P. Pigors (Halle, Germany: Niemeyer, 1928).

19. William D. Guth and Renato Tagiuri, "Personal Values and Corporate Strategy," *Harvard Business Review* 43, no. 5 (September–October 1965), p. 123.

20. Adapted from G. W. Allport, P. E. Vernon, and G. Lindzey, *Manual for the Study of Values* (Boston: Houghton Mifflin, 1960), p. 14, as reported in Archie B. Carroll, *Business and Society* (Boston: Little, Brown, 1981), p. 70.

21. Reported in Rick Wartzman, "Nature or Nurture? Study Blames Ethical Lapses on Corporate Goals," *The Wall Street Journal,* October 9, 1987, p. 27.

22. William Glaberson, "Why Wasn't $1 Million a Year Enough?" *Business Week,* August 25, 1986, p. 72.

23. For an elaboration of Kohlberg's stages, see, e.g., W. D. Boyce and L. C. Jensen, *Moral Reasoning* (Lincoln, NE: University of Nebraska Press, 1978), pp. 98–109.

24. L. Kohlberg, "The Cognitive-Developmental Approach to Moral Education," *Phi Delta Kappan* 56 (June 1975), p. 670.

25. C. Gilligan, "In a Different Voice: Women's Conceptions of Self and Morality," *Harvard Educational Review* 47, no. 4 (November 1977), p. 481. And see, e.g., C. Gilligan, *In a Different Voice* (Cambridge, MA: Harvard University Press, 1982); L. Blum, "Gilligan and Kohlberg: Implications for Moral Theory," *Ethics* 98, no. 3 (April 1988), p. 472; and O. Flanagan and K. Jackson, "Justice, Care and Gender: The Kohlberg-Gilligan Debate Revisited," *Ethics* 97, no. 3 (April 1987), p. 622.

26. Karl Menninger, *Whatever Became of Sin?* (New York: Hawthorn Books, 1973).

27. For an overview, see Peter French, "The Corporation as a Moral Person," *American Philosophical Quarterly* 16, no. 3 (July 1979), pp. 297–317.

28. For one critic's view, see John Ladd, "Persons and Responsibility: Ethical Concepts and Impertinent Analogies," in *Shame, Responsibility and the Corpo-*

ration, ed. Hugh Curtler (New York: Haven Publishing, 1986), p. 77.

29. Jeffrey Nesteruk, "Legal Persons and Moral Worlds: Ethical Choices within the Corporate Environment," *American Business Law Journal* 29, no. 1 (Spring 1991), p. 75.

30. David Vogel, "Could an Ethics Course Have Kept Ivan from Going Bad?" *The Wall Street Journal,* April 27, 1987, p. 18.

31. Ronald E. Berenbeim, *Corporate Ethics Practices* (New York: The Conference Board, 1992), p. 11.

32. Wartzman, "Nature or Nurture?" p. 21.

33. Ibid.

34. Labich, "The New Crisis in Business Ethics," p. 168.

35. "Oversight on the U.S. Sentencing Commission and Guidelines for Organizational Sanctions," Hearings before the Subcommittee on Criminal Justice of the Committee on the Judiciary, House of Representatives, 101st Congress, March 7 and May 24, 1990, serial no. 112, (Washington, D.C.: U.S. Government Printing Office, 1990), pp. 235–36.

36. U.S. Sentencing Commission: 1991, "Sentencing Guidelines for Organizational Defendants," *Federal Register* 56(95), p. 22786.

37. *Los Angeles Times* staff and wire reports, "Pacific Watch: Malaysia," *Los Angeles Times,* May 17, 1993, p. D3.

38. Irwin Ross, "How Lawless are Big Companies?" *Fortune,* December 1, 1980, p. 57.

39. Alluded to in congressional testimony, "White-Collar Crime," Subcommittee on Crime of the Committee on the Judiciary, U.S. House of Representatives, 95th Congress, second session on white-collar crime, no. 69 (Washington, D.C.: U.S. Government Printing Office, 1979).

40. James M. Roche, "The Competitive System, to Work, to Preserve, and to Protect," *Vital Speeches of the Day,* May 1, 1971, p. 445, as reported in Kenneth D. Walters, "Your Employees' Right to Blow the Whistle," *Harvard Business Review,* July–August 1975, p. 26.

41. Carl Kaufmann, "A Five-Part Quiz on Corporate Ethics," *Washington Post,* July 1, 1979, p. C–1.

42. Amended by certain provisions of the Omnibus Trade and Competitiveness Act of 1988.

43. 15 U.S.C. 78dd–1(b),–2(b) (1982), as amended by 1988 Trade Act 5003(a), (c).

44. Foreign Corrupt Practices Act Amendments of 1988, 15 U.S.C. 78dd–1 A (f) (2) (A) (B).

45. Ford Worthy, "When Somebody Wants a Payoff," *Fortune,* Pacific Rim, 1989, pp. 117, 118.

46. "Bribes are Tax Deductible for Danes," *The Reuter Asia—Pacific Business Report,* June 4, 1993, BC cycle.

47. Hirschhorn, "Foreign Corrupt Practices Act: Narrowed, Significantly Clarified," *The National Law Journal,* December 26, 1988–January 2, 1989, p. 16. Reported in Beverley Earle, "Foreign Corrupt Practices Act Amendments," *Selected Papers of the ABLA National Proceedings,* ed. William Elliot, vol. 18, pp. 193, 198.

48. Kaufmann, "Five-Part Quiz," p. C–4.

49. Ibid.

50. "Short Takes," *The Des Moines Register,* February 5, 1990, p. 2T.

51. Ibid.

52. Leonard C. Lewin, "Ethical Aptitude Test," *Harper's,* October 1976, p. 21.

53. Reported on WKYT TV, Channel 27, "Evening News," Lexington, Kentucky, May 12, 1980.

54. "Business Executives and Moral Dilemmas," *Business and Society Review,* no. 13 (Spring 1975), p. 51.

55. Robert Bartley, "Business Ethics and the Ethics Business," *The Wall Street Journal,* May 18, 1987, p. 18.

56. Albert A. Carr, "Is Business Bluffing Ethical?" *Harvard Business Review* 46, no. 1 (January–February 1968), pp. 143–52.

57. Lionel Tiger, "Stone Age Provides Model for Instilling Business Ethics," *The Wall Street Journal,* January 11, 1988, p. 22.

3

THE CORPORATION AND PUBLIC POLICY: EXPANDED RESPONSIBILITIES

INTRODUCTION

Before turning to the law per se, it is essential to remind the reader of the context—the environment—in which the law developed. Therefore, a major purpose of this chapter is to raise some critical issues regarding the business community's relationship to the larger society. Should we "free" business from government intervention to achieve greater productivity and profit? Should business play a larger role in politics, education, and other public-sector activities? Should business assume greater responsibilities in correcting societal ills? The reader is expected to use this chapter to make a tentative assessment of the very large question: What is the proper role of business in society? Only after acquiring some preliminary grasp of that issue can one logically and fruitfully turn to various "control devices" (such as law) as a means of enforcing that proper role.

The second major goal of this chapter is that of alerting the reader to some of the primary criticisms raised against the corporate community. The successful businessperson and the good citizen must understand and intelligently evaluate the objections of those who criticize the role of the corporation in contemporary life. Of course, government regulation is, in part, a response to those criticisms. (A detailed investigation of the forces generating government intervention is offered in Chapter 7.)

Finally, this chapter is designed to introduce what has come to be known as corporate public policy. Tomorrow's leaders must understand the interdependent relationship between business and the larger society. They must understand the public policy issues that have emerged from that relationship, and they must build the skills necessary to successfully manage that relationship. In the 1960s, the public began to demand more of business than simply producing products and services. We began to expect the business community to make a broad contribution to general societal welfare—to become a corporate citizen with all of the responsibilities that corporate wealth and power suggest. Those new demands led to the evolutionary development of public policy. We will examine that evolution in four parts: (1) criticisms of corporate America, (2) the emergence of the expectation of *corporate social responsibility*, (3) the move in recent years toward the process labeled *corporate public policy*, and (4) the examination of some specific business and society issues.

Part One—Corporate Power and Corporate Critics

Corp. has constitutional rights do person to vote except incrimination it pay taxes. it has constitutional protection

Corporate critics have long argued that the public interest has not been well served by America's big corporations. We recognize that colossal size and the economies of scale that accompany it have been critical to American competitiveness in today's unforgiving global market. At the same time, that very size, the critics say, permits continuing abuse of the American public. Of course, we recognize that big companies are a fixture of the American landscape. However, a reminder of the specifics may be useful.

GM

General Motors, crippled and struggling though it may be, remains America's most prodigious industrial machine, as measured by sales. According to *Fortune* magazine, GM's 1993 sales totaled $133.6 billion, and its assets exceeded $188 billion [third in the United States behind General Electric ($251.5 billion) and Ford ($199 billion)]. Despite highly publicized cutbacks, General Motors continues to be America's biggest corporate employer, with some 711,000 people earning their living with GM.[1] Measured by stock market value in 1993, 48 of the world's 100 largest firms are American and 30 are Japanese. On the other hand, 8 of the 10 largest banks are Japanese. The largest U.S. bank, Citicorp, ranks 27th among the 100 largest banks—a list that includes 29 Japanese banks and only 7 from the United States.[2] The extraordinary wealth of America's corporate institutions is such that they tower over most of the countries of the world in economic might. If we compare corporate sales with gross national products, General Motors annually ranks around the 20th largest *anything* in the world. For example, GM does about as much business as the nation of Finland, IBM's sales slightly exceed Poland's GNP, while General Electric and Greece are neck and neck in economic productivity.[3]

To the critics, the danger in these figures is transparent—too much power in too few hands. Consider that in recent decades about 50 percent of America's manufacturing assets have resided in just 100 companies and that more than 60 percent of those assets have been controlled by just the top 200 companies.[4]

THE CORPORATE STATE

Historically, the foundation of the critics' argument has been that giant companies hold monopoly power, permitting them to secure "excess profits" at the expense of the consumer. Considerable evidence supported that view,[5] but it has been rendered somewhat passe in this era of fierce international economic competition with the giants of Japan, Germany, and the balance of the world. Further, as we discuss below, many of America's old-line titans (GM, IBM, Sears, and so on) are struggling to retain their strength, suggesting that bigness is not a guarantor of success in the contemporary market.

A litany of societal ills—pollution, discrimination, white-collar crime, misleading advertising—has long been laid at the corporate doorstep. Now the subject of intense governmental, public, and internal corporate scrutiny, those problems, while yet very real, seem no longer attributable to mere corporate size and/or malevolence. The bulk of this book is devoted to the governmental/corporate/public attack on those serious social ills. However, the critics say, those specific ills are only symptomatic of a more encompassing malady. Basically, the concern is that America has committed its *soul* to business values in a way that is progressively undermining our national well-being. We will briefly examine that argument in order to have it in mind as we proceed through our more detailed study of corporate social responsibility and government regulation of business.

America's Soul?

became materialistic.

Generally, the critics contend the power of the business community has become so encompassing that virtually all dimensions of American life have absorbed elements of the business ethic. Values commonly associated with businesspersons (competition, profit seeking, reliance on technology, faith in growth) have overwhelmed traditional humanist values (cooperation, individual dignity, human rights, meaningful service to society). In the name of efficiency and productivity, it is argued that the warmth, decency, and value of life have been debased. We engage in meaningless work in an artificial culture. Objects dominate our existence. We operate as replaceable cogs in a vast, bureaucratic machine. Our natural environment is shredded in the pursuit of progress. Indeed, we lose ourselves, the critics argue. Charles Reich, former Yale University law professor, addressed the loss of self in his influential book of the Vietnam War era, *The Greening of America:*

> Of all of the forms of impoverishment that can be seen or felt in America, loss of self, or death in life, is surely the most devastating . . . Beginning with school, if not before, an individual is systematically stripped of his imagination, his creativity, his heritage, his dreams, and his personal uniqueness, in order to style him into a productive unit for a mass, technological society. Instinct, feeling, and spontaneity are repressed by overwhelming forces. As the individual is drawn into the meritocracy, his working life is split from his home life, and both suffer from a lack of wholeness. Eventually, people virtually become their professions, roles, or occupations, and are henceforth strangers to themselves.[6]

Reich was suggesting that the *meaning* in life, the "spiritual" tones that afford flavor and quality, are being stripped from our existence. The residue, the critics argue, is a society of hollow men and women—long on dollars, occupiers of prestigious posts, possessors of power, but bereft of the central core of goodness and purpose that affords us worth beyond worldly achievement.

Questions

1. *Washington Post* columnist David Broder reflects on his satisfaction in attending a Chicago Cubs baseball game at Wrigley Field:

   > Much—perhaps too much—has been written about Wrigley Field's fidelity to baseball's past: the real grass surface, the ivy on the outfield walls, the refusal to install lights or

play night games . . . The ballpark has no electronic scoreboards, fancy frills, or other distractions to get in the way of the spectator's experience of the game of baseball . . . Wrigley Field goes on, essentially unchanged. And that is something to celebrate in this over-gimmicked, overcomplicated world.[7] [In 1988, lights were installed and occasional night games were included in the Cubs' schedule.]

Broder laments what he takes to be an increasing impersonality and technological distance in life.

a. Is American life "over-gimmicked and overcomplicated"? Explain.
b. Do we "still have the ability to determine the course of our lives"? Are you in control of your life? Explain.

Politics

PAC
– political Action
committee

We can elaborate on the case of the corporate critics by directing our attention to some areas of special concern. We will begin with politics, where critics charge that superior resources enable the business community to unfairly slant the electoral and lawmaking processes in favor of corporate interests.

In recent years, the corporate community has taken a more direct and vigorous role in the political process. As a result, corporate critics are increasingly concerned that the financial weight of big business will prove so influential that our pluralist, democratic approach to governance may be significantly distorted. Today, money is central to the task of acquiring elective office. And following election, dollars to finance lobbying on Capitol Hill can be critical in shaping congressional opinion.

Corporate funds cannot lawfully be expended for federal campaign contributions. However, corporations can lawfully establish *political action committees* (PACs) to solicit and disburse voluntary campaign contributions. That is, corporations can solicit contributions from employees, shareholders, and others. That money is then put in a fund, carefully segregated from general corporate accounts, and is disbursed by the PAC in support of a federal election campaign.

The checkbook dominates politics at the national level. In the 1991–92 election cycle, PACs donated $205 million to legislators and political parties, with $189 million of that total (a 19 percent increase over 1989–90) going to congressional candidates—three-fourths of which went to incumbents.[8] As *Newsweek* expressed it:

> The bottom line is a grubby, demeaning and never-ending quest for campaign contributions that is the bane of a political career and a blight on the political process.[9]

Much of that money comes from business and labor PACs. The biggest contributor in the 1991–92 federal elections was the real estate PAC, totaling $3 million, while the United Auto Workers gave $2.2 million.[10] But as displayed in the accompanying table, business and labor interests are only part of the PAC story. Many special interest groups spend a great deal of money in hopes of influencing the political process. For example, the Association of Trial Lawyers of America raised their contribution by 55 percent over the previous election cycle as it sought particularly to stop tort-reform legislation.[11]

Naturally, PAC money is largely directed to those politicians who can be most useful to PAC interests:

Top Ten—Total PAC Spending 1991–92

Teamsters	$11,825,340
American Medical Association	$6,263,921
National Education Association	$5,817,975
National Rifle Association	$5,700,114
National Association of Realtors	$4,939,014
Association of Trial Lawyers of America	$4,392,462
American Federation of State, County, and Municipal Employees	$4,281,395
United Auto Workers	$4,257,165
National Congressional Club	$3,864,389
National Abortion Rights Action League	$3,831,321

Source: Gregory Cerio and Kendall Hamilton, *Newsweek*, May 24, 1993, p. 6. Drawn from Federal Election Commission data.

PACs organized by the managers of American Telegraph & Telephone Co. and RJR Nabisco Inc. were among the business PACs registering the biggest growth in 1989, with AT&T's taking in more than $1.5 million. Thomas Chilcott, the company's vice president for government affairs, says 13,700 AT&T managers contribute to the PAC. Nearly one third make their contributions through voluntary payroll deductions, an increasingly popular check-off system that has helped fatten the war chests of other business and labor PACs.

AT&T's PAC contributions "tend to be concentrated" on members of the commerce, judiciary, and tax-writing panels that have jurisdiction over many telephone and communications issues, Mr. Chilcott says.

RJR Nabisco's PAC more than doubled its receipts in 1989 from 1987, to $323,549. "The external environment has become so supercharged on tobacco issues that more of our employees want to get politically involved," said Maura Payne, a spokeswoman for the company.[12]

Reform?

At this writing in 1994, both the House and Senate have approved bills reforming election finance. The Senate bill bans PACs, while the House puts a $200,000 cap on aggregate contributions by a PAC. To offset the limitations on PAC money, the House bill calls for partial public funding of federal campaigns, while the Senate bill relies largely on a tax on campaigns that violate spending limits.[13] A House–Senate compromise is expected. Of course, many politicians and analysts are unconvinced of the need for reform. In commentator's Robert Samuelson's view, special interest efforts are merely an expression of democracy, and he argues that those efforts do not dominate the political process in any case:

PACs remain a minority of all contributions. In 1986 they were 21 percent for the Senate (up from 17 percent in 1984) and 34 percent for the House (level with 1984).

The diversity of the 4,157 PACs dilutes their power. There are business PACs, labor PACs, pro-abortion PACs, anti-abortion PACs, importer PACs, and protectionist PACs.

Contributions are fairly evenly split between Democrats ($74.6 million in 1986) and Republicans ($57.5 million).

* * * * *

Of course special interests mob Congress. That's democracy. One person's special interest is another's crusade or livelihood. To be influential, people organize.[14]

Lobbying

A lot of laws are written by lobbies.

Those who criticize corporate influence on the legislative process are not concerned with PACs alone. Sophisticated and expensive lobbying is a staple of the business community's efforts to implement its legislative agenda. Of course, lobbying is defended as an efficient method of better acquainting busy politicians with the subtleties of the diverse issues they must address, and lobbying is not confined to the "big spenders" of the business community—witness the many consumer lobbies. An estimated 20,000 lobbyists annually spend perhaps $1.5 billion (including campaign contributions) attempting to influence official Washington.[15]

Congress is considering legislation to curb lobbying influence. One bill includes stronger lobby registration requirements and limits on gifts to legislators. President Clinton urged repeal of the corporate tax deduction for lobbying expenses, and he argued for new rules preventing lobbyists from making or soliciting campaign contributions. Also at issue are methods to stop the so-called revolving door, where former lawmakers become lobbyists and return to Washington to lobby. One proposal would bar former legislators from lobbying sitting legislators for two years, bar them from lobbying their former congressional committees for five years, and permanently bar them from lobbying for foreign clients.[16]

Questions

1. The corporate community possesses vast resources. Noted economist John Kenneth Galbraith, among others, has argued that consumer "wants" can be created by skillful persuasion. Does the application of corporate resources and skills to the shaping of public and political opinion constitute a threat to democracy? Explain.
2. Anne Wexler, aide to former president Jimmy Carter, is a Washington lobbyist. She says, "There's a need here. Government officials are not comfortable making these complicated decisions by themselves.[17]
   a. Are lobbyists necessary for the effective operation of government? Explain.
   b. If we wanted to curb lobbying, how should we do so?
3. Richard Goodwin, aide to former President John F. Kennedy, speaks out on PACs:

   Morally the system is bribery. It is not criminal only because those who make the laws are themselves accomplices. Government is for sale. But the bids are sealed, and the prices are very high.

There is an easy way out: Eliminate PACs. We should place a rigorous ceiling on all congressional campaigns, allocate public funds to finance campaigns, and require television stations—the most costly component of modern political campaigns—to give a specified amount of air time to candidates.[18]

a. Should we forbid PACs? Explain.
b. Would such action be constitutionally permissible? Explain.

Business Values

The corporation is arguably the central institution in contemporary America. In every dimension of American life, business values are increasingly pervasive. To those who criticize the corporation, that near-blanket adoption of the business ethic signals a dangerous distortion of the nation's priorities. In an editorial, the *Des Moines Register* commented that commercials have become so interwoven with our total existence that they cannot effectively be "separated out":

The insinuation of commercials into American life is everywhere. On Saturday mornings, the cartoon character the kids are watching may be for sale at the toy store. On prime-time shows and in movies, the brand-name product that is used as a stage prop probably isn't there by accident.

No one seems to mind. In an ad-saturated society, people willingly pay a premium price for a shirt that is adorned with an advertising logo. By choice, people wear commercial messages.

It's the triumph of hucksterism in America.[19]

Judge for yourself as we take a quick glimpse at several areas of concern.

Schools.   In the face of nationwide alarm about elementary and secondary education, the corporate community has played an increasingly aggressive role in supporting and reforming our schools. In 1992, two-thirds of those responding to a *Fortune* poll of 1,000 of America's biggest corporations reported making contributions to elementary schools; an effort only 27 percent had made just two years previously. Twenty-eight percent of those responding gave $1 million or more to education programs and school reform.[20] Clearly, the schools welcome this much-needed attention. However, critics are concerned about the increasingly intimate ties between business and education.

From kindergarten through graduate school, the "business mentality" has become pervasive. Given the competitiveness of the job market, it is argued that students and their parents call for a "quick fix" of skills (such as accounting, management, and marketing) as a replacement for occupationally ambiguous disciplines such as history, literature, and philosophy. The bargain has been struck. The student leaves his or her formal education and hopes to proceed into the Corporate State, but did that person buy a good life or an empty existence? Charles Reich offers his opinion:

The process by which man is deprived of his self begins with his institutionalized training in public school for a place in the machinery of the State. The object of the training is not merely to teach him how to perform some specific function; it is to make him become that function, to see and judge himself and others in terms of functions, and to abandon any aspect of self, thinking, questioning, feeling, loving, that has no utility for either production or consumption in the Corporate State. The training for the role of consumer is just as important as the training for a job, and at least equally significant for loss of self.[21]

A variation on Reich's concern is the argument that universities are increasingly becoming research and development adjuncts of corporate America and, in that process, giving inadequate attention to other pressing concerns such as the environment and health care. The *Chronicle of Higher Education* raises the issue:

> Are institutions—pressured by government, business, and their own financial straits—focusing too narrowly on industrial goals? Some experts who think higher education should play a greater role in meeting national needs think so. They contend that the government and universities, in seeking new knowledge and its commercial applications, are neglecting other pressing social problems.[22]

Culture. In the late 1980s, the market for superior works of art exploded. Van Gogh's *Irises* sold for $53.9 million in 1990, Picasso's self-portrait, *Yo Picasso,* went for $47.85 million in 1989, and in 1990, another Van Gogh, *Portrait of Dr. Gachet,* set a new record at $82.5 million. Art has always been a product for sale. Indeed, Van Gogh, who sold only one painting during his lifetime, might well have lived much longer and painted many more masterpieces had the market been kinder to him. But does art lose its inherent value, its capacity to inspire, when the weight of price becomes too extreme?

Spike Lee. Consider the marketing of *Malcolm X.* Spike Lee's 1992 movie produced a spasm of commercial spinoffs including, of course, T-shirts and caps but also potato chips and auto air fresheners. Commentator Jonathan Yardley put it this way:

> Thanks to the incredible stir of avarice that has been aroused by the release of Spike Lee's film, "Malcolm X," the man who is the subject of what is represented as an act of veneration has been turned into a cornucopia of commercial gain. Even among those who most loudly profess their fealty to Malcolm as a saint of the black protest movement, he exists now primarily as a cash cow.[23]

We see the same phenomenon in rock and roll, where the beer industry alone spends tens of millions of dollars annually in subsidizing performers and concerts.

Are rock, movies, art, even the ideas and memory of a striking leader debased by their treatment as commercial products in the manner of shampoo or sneakers? Do the increasingly extensive ties between performers, promoters, and corporate sponsors threaten the integrity and quality of world culture? Are all dimensions of life merely products to be bought and sold?

Sports. To the critics, the "commercialization" of sports is simply an accomplished fact. From football to bicycling, the allure of money has become so compelling that the historical purity of amateur athletics as a venue for fun and character building has been obliterated. *Business Week* devoted a recent cover story, "Nothing Sells Like Sports," to the theme of sports marketing:

These days, everything from sled-dog racing to professional beach volleyball is likely to find corporate backing.[24]

The 1992 Barcelona Summer Olympics, featuring the U.S. men's basketball "Dream Team" (Michael Jordan, Charles Barkley et al.) may mark the end of big-time sport as anything other than very big business. Barcelona's mayor, Pasqual Maragall, called for the Olympic movement to resist the temptation to "sell out":

> We ask that sport will not be the victim of the arrogance of culture, nor culture the victim of the arrogance of money, nor cities the victims of the arrogance of commercialism."[25]

At this writing, the 1996 Atlanta Summer Games approach. Will we see the same rampant commercialism? Why? Does it matter? Some day, will athletes compete for corporations rather than nations—for example, Team Nike?

Children. Materialism—the disproportionate hunger for goods—has long been a concern in adult American life from the social critic's point of view. Now, in the 1980s and 1990s, children, too, have embraced the obsessive pursuit of consumer products. Obviously, jeans and sneakers have become important to children, but the following article demonstrates that even deodorant, if cleverly marketed, has a place in a kid's life.

BERTSHERM AIMS ITS DEODORANT AT PRE-ADOLESCENT SET

Timothy L. O'Brien

Do your kids stink at math? Do your kids stink at sports? Or do your kids just stink?

If it's body odor that plagues your youngster, a remedy is at hand: Fun 'n Fresh deodorant for seven-to-12-year-olds, the brainchild of Cleveland entrepreneur Philip B. Davis.

"A light bulb went off in my head and I thought, 'Why not a deodorant for kids?'" says the 33-year-old Mr. Davis, recalling the inspiration that led him to launch BertSherm Products Inc. four years ago. "Kids need to feel ownership in the personal hygiene process."

Some say pitching adult products to children who may not need them exploits their desire to appear grown-up. But exploitative or not, the strategy works. In recent years, purveyors of everything from designer clothing to credit cards have targeted the wet-behind-the-ears set to tap into the huge spending power of pre-adolescents.

BertSherm is no exception. It began marketing Fun 'n Fresh nationally in 1990 through such national chains as Wal-Mart Stores Inc., Revco D.S. Inc., and Kmart Corp. BertSherm says its revenue is expected to grow to $1 million this year from $500,000 last year and $400,000 the previous year.

Mr. Davis, who holds a master's degree in business administration from the University of Virginia, plans to increase his product's visibility this fall with Fun 'n Fresh advertisements printed on free textbook covers that will be distributed nationally to schoolchildren. The campaign slogan reads, "Be Cool in School."

"We feel it's important to establish a relationship with children as our core consumers so they will demand this product in the house," says Mr. Davis.

Some customers say they love the deodorant sticks, which come in brightly colored packages and sell for $1.99. "My best friend at school told me that it smelled really good," says Leah Rigall, a 12-year-old Floridian who has been using Fun 'n Fresh for two years. She says she uses it not because of a body odor problem, but because her friends use it.

* * * * *

According to the Rand Youth Poll, a New York research organization, children under 12 influenced about $169 billion in household expenditures in 1990, up from $69 billion in 1975.

Some attribute the surge to greater pressure on children to emulate adults. Others ascribe it to the increase over the past decade in the number of households with two working parents, where children are given the money and responsibility for purchases Mom and Dad used to make.

"More and more, there's specialization of marketing to kids," says Dr. James McNeal, a business professor at Texas A&M University who has written three books on marketing to children. "If you can make them a loyal customer early on, then they are a switch-resistant customer."

Cornucopia of Products

This drive to snare buyers for life has led to the cornucopia of products aimed at kids. Among them is Fun 'n Fresh, although some question whether seven year-olds really need a deodorant.

"Most [kids] don't even smell yet," says Dr. Maura Frank, a pediatrician at New York Hospital's Cornell Medical Center. "At the higher end of the seven-to-12-age range, they may need it. But definitely not at the younger end—it's almost like marketing condoms to them."

Body odor arrives with puberty, and targeting seven- to nine-year-olds "is really inappropriate," Dr. Frank says. "It's one of those things that creates a need instead of really responding to a need."

Even some mainstream makers of body-care products question the need to peddle deodorants to the pre-pubescent. "Seven-year-olds are barely out of the milk stage," says Marilyn Blood, a spokeswoman for S.C. Johnson & Son Inc. "We want to consider whether they really need it." Both Avon Products Inc. and Gillette Co. say they have no intention of marketing such a product.

* * * * *

Whether they need it or not, a sizable portion of kids apparently use deodorant regularly. In a national survey last year by the Rand Youth Poll, 29% of seven- to nine-year olds said they used it occasionally. Among those aged 10 to 12, 42% said they used it occasionally.

Source: *The Wall Street Journal,* July 16, 1992, p. B2. Reprinted by permission of *The Wall Street Journal,* © 1992 Dow Jones and Company, Inc. All Rights Reserved Worldwide.

Questions

1. *a.* Should we admire Gillette and Avon for declining to market deodorant to children? Explain.
   b. Would you decline to market deodorant to children? Explain.
2. Do you find anything objectionable about distributing free BertSherm advertising/textbook covers to school children? Explain.
3. Does a free market economy inevitably result in the exploitation of children? Explain.

4. *a.* Has your education been designed primarily to prepare you for a utilitarian role as a producer and/or consumer in the Corporate State? Explain.

   b. Have you been encouraged, as Charles Reich claims, to abandon "thinking, questioning, feeling, loving"? Explain.

5. Pop artist Andy Warhol produced a painting of 200 $1 bills. The painting sold for $385,000. Warhol once said that "Being good in business is the most fascinating kind of art."

   a. What did Warhol mean?

   b. Is business America's dominant art form? Explain.

6. Big-time sports is now a big business. Has the quality of the sports experience been depreciated? Explain.

7. *a.* Do teens need protection of some sort from excessive commercial influences, especially advertising? Explain.

   b. If such protection is needed, what form should it take?

8. According to *The Wall Street Journal*, "[S]hopping can be all things to all people. It can alleviate loneliness and dispel boredom; it can be a sport and can be imbued with the thrill of the hunt; it can provide escape, fulfill fantasies, relieve depression."[26]

   a. Is shopping an American addiction that requires treatment in the manner of alcoholism, for example? Explain.

   b. Does shopping fill a void of some sort in our lives? If so, how was that void created? Or was it always there?

   c. If you reduced shopping in your life to that which is required to meet only the necessities, how would you use the time that would then be available to you?

   d. Are shopping malls replacing the family in American life? Explain.

   e. Even if shopping has assumed excessive importance in our lives, is the business community in any way to blame for that condition? Explain.

9. *Newsweek* asked, "Has Sneaker Madness Gone Too Far?"[27] What do you think? Explain.

DINOSAURS?

Across the range of themes raised thus far—from politics to shaping children's values—the critics' concerns are essentially those of business power. Do big corporations have too much influence in American life? If so, shouldn't the government more aggressively regulate that power? Now, in the mid-1990s, in this era of unparalleled change, the irony of the situation is that the market itself may be correcting this problem—if, indeed, it is a problem. Some of America's mightiest corporations are staggering under the stress of dramatic change in the world business climate. Consider a 1993 *Fortune* article: "Dinosaurs?"[28] and a 1993 *Newsweek* article: "The Fall of the Dinosaurs."[29] The power of "dinosaurs" such as GM, IBM, and Sears remains stunning, but bigness may not, in and of itself, be the key to corporate success, and these giants may prove to be too lumbering to successfully compete. If so, the market alone may simply correct many of the critics' concerns.

Jobs

In 1992, GM announced plans to close 21 factories and cut 74,000 workers. IBM sliced employees from a 1985 high of 405,000 to a 1994 total of about 250,000. A single share of IBM stock, worth $175 at its peak in 1987, had fallen to $50 in 1993. Sears intended to slice 50,000 jobs and, perhaps most remarkably, its famous catalog, which had defined American retailing for decades, is gone. In years past, those companies were simply in command:

> With a nearly limitless supply of resources and customers, companies that could consistently develop great products enjoyed oligopolistic, if not monopolistic, power.[30]

Ironically, IBM might be a much healthier company today if it had allowed what the Justice Department sought for years—a division of the giant into seven parts. Consider AT&T, which was broken up in 1984 and is now thriving, just as are the other seven Bell units that were spun off. Those companies' combined 1992 worth was some $208 billion. If still one company, the former telephone monopoly would dwarf all other American firms.[31]

But let's not forget: Some giants, such as GE, Exxon, and AT&T are doing just fine. They and the corporate community generally—including GM, IBM, and Sears—retain enormous clout, but it is clear that size alone does not grant immunity from the discipline of the market.

Questions—Part One

1. Thinker and futurist Herman Kahn was asked to comment on the prospects for space colonization. Kahn speculated that colonies of significance would develop in the early 21st century. But he cited two obstacles. One was that the rate at which colonization could be achieved would be instrumental in determining the excitement it would generate. The other:

   > And in the United States, we can't turn people on unless it's economic. This culture, almost alone among all cultures, will not get turned on unless it makes a profit, or is scientific or military.[32]

   Creating profit is a primary and necessary corporate value.
   a. Was Kahn correct in believing that our culture is more committed to profit seeking than most other cultures? Explain.
   b. Has the supremacy of profit seeking depreciated the quality of our lives? Explain.

2. In 1980, *Fortune* magazine conducted a study of 82 25-year-olds who have "shown promise of becoming high-level managers or entrepreneurs." Thomas Griffith summarized the results of the study:

   > They are, *Fortune* says, bright, disciplined, hardworking, motivated: "They put their jobs ahead of most other diversions and commitments—including marriage, which many are in no hurry for, and children, which some claim they'll never want . . .

Single-mindedly chasing their objectives, they ignore what doesn't blend or harmonize with their purposefully limited landscape. They view work and life as a series of 'trade-offs' rather than compromises; for each opportunity surrendered, they demand an equal benefit in return." They pride themselves on the honesty with which they proclaim their ambitions.

To [former president] Ronald Reagan, these young people may embody the self-reliant American way in its purest form, but Gwen Kinkead, the writer of the *Fortune* article, can't resist a parenthetical comment: "To a stranger from another generation, they sometimes seem a grabby bunch."

The missing note in *Fortune's* young is idealism. They are not drones; they like the good life, the ski trips, the visits to Europe or Tahiti. If they tune out on causes, if they feel no obligation to help others, the explanation is not only that they have no time for these matters, but that they have no heart for them. They are a platoon of Tin Woodmen.[33]

   a. Does business demand Tin Woodmen? Explain.

   b. Are you a Tin Woodman? Explain.

3. David Gil, professor of social policy at Brandeis University, has "called for the dismantling of corporations that have destroyed 'self-directed work' and for the return of resources to the people for their own direction 'in human-sized communities where people can come together and jointly determine their economic way of life.'"[34]

   a. Does our economic way of life reflect the will of the people? Explain.

   b. Is the corporate form destructive of the quality of the work experience? Explain.

   c. Is Gil's proposal workable? Explain.

4. In *Time* magazine, commentator Walter Shapiro wonders "Why We've Failed to Ruin Thanksgiving":

Americans have grown inured to crass commercialism, with corporate sponsorship profaning everything from bowl games to the Bill of Rights. But somehow Thanksgiving has resisted the blandishments of an age of avarice. How the greeting-card sharpies and the flower-power florists must lament a national holiday in which they are doomed to play a minor role.[35]

   a. On balance, is the "commercialization" of most holidays a good or bad development? Explain.

   b. Who is to blame for the conversion of holidays to commercial feasts? Explain.

5. Should we lament the passing of the Roxbury Russet? The Russet was an American apple that, due largely to its mottled, leathery skin, did not make the commercial grade in contemporary America. Today, apple growers are further from their markets and must focus on growing those varieties of apple that are most prolific and best able to withstand shipment. The surviving apples, in general, are sweet and red in color.[36] Similarly, we've seen the passing of juicy, flavorful tomatoes in favor of the more easily harvested and transported "rubber" tomato.

   a. Are these examples of a trade-off of quality in favor of efficiency and productivity? Explain.

   b. If so, is that trade-off necessary? Explain.

   c. Who is responsible for the trade-off? Explain.

6. *a.* What does Charles Reich mean by "loss of self"? Explain.
   b. Do you sense any such loss in yourself? Explain.
7. As the editors of *Business Week* remarked in 1987, "A lot of people are bad-mouthing greed these days."[37] But the line between profit as a legitimate motivator and profit as an expression of greed is not easily drawn.
   a. How do you define the point at which one passes from legitimate pursuit of profit to greed?
   b. Is that point irrelevant? Explain.
8. In your judgment, does either of the following quotes accurately express the American attitude of the 1990s toward the accumulation of money? Explain.

   Myron Magnet of *Fortune:*

   Money, money, money is the incantation of today. Bewitched by an epidemic of money enchantment, Americans in the 80s wriggle in a St. Vitus' dance of materialism unseen since the Gilded Age or the Roaring 20s. Under the blazing sun of money, all other values shine palely. And the M&A decade acclaims but one breed of hero: He's the honcho with the condo and the limo and the Miró and lots and lots of dough.[38]

   Michael Novak of the American Enterprise Institute:

   The vast majority of Americans choose what they want to do, and they don't choose merely to seek wealth. Most of the people I know seek the work that satisfies them most completely. Of course a sliver of people want money, money, money, but I think they're only a small number.[39]

9. *a.* Do Americans *trust* the business community? Explain.
   b. Does it matter? Explain.
10. In 1980, Ted Peters, an associate professor of systematic theology at the Pacific Lutheran Seminary and the Graduate Theological Union asked:

    How will the advancing postindustrial culture influence the course of religion? It is my forecast that religion will become increasingly treated as a consumer item.

    Because our economy produces so much wealth, we are free to consume and consume beyond the point of satiation. There is a limit to what we can consume in the way of material goods—new homes, new cars, new electronic gadgets, new brands of beer, new restaurants, and so on. So we go beyond material wants to consume new personal experiences—such as broader travel, exotic vacations, continuing education, exciting conventions, psychotherapy, and sky diving.

    What will come next and is already on the horizon is the consumption of spiritual experiences—personal growth cults, drug-induced ecstasy, world-traveling gurus, training in mystical meditation to make you feel better, etc. Once aware of this trend, religious entrepreneurs and mainline denominations alike will take to pandering their wares, advertising how much spiritual realities "can do to you." It will be subtle, and it will be cloaked in the noble language of personal growth, but nevertheless the pressure will be on between now and the year 2000 to treat religious experience as a commodity for consumption.[40]

    a. Now in the mid-90s, is Peters's forecast coming true? Explain.
    b. Is marketing necessary to the survival and growth of religion? Explain.
    c. Is marketing a threat to the legitimacy and value of religion? Explain.

11. A 1989 survey of 1,100 young people, aged 15–24, found "career success" slightly eclipsing "having a close-knit family life" among the respondents' most important life goals.[41] Should we be concerned because young people appear to value career goals as much or more than family life? Explain.

12. In 1992, 1,600 faculty, staff, and students at Clifton Middle School in Houston, Texas, each received a $70 pair of K-Swiss sneakers from the manufacturer and Foot Locker. The shoes were first prize in a stay-in-school video contest.[42] The use of corporate sponsors and merchandise prizes in education contests has exploded in recent years. Critics say the students are being taught to be more materialistic and to value education, not for its intrinsic satisfactions, but for its commercial rewards. However, the adviser for the Houston students says that such prizes can attract students who otherwise would not participate, and some of them then discover the satisfactions of education. In your view, do these prizes corrupt or enhance education? Explain.

13. Whittle Communications provides classroom televised news programs by satellite in 12-minute packages, two minutes of which are commercials. In return, the elementary and secondary schools who agree to show the programming are given the necessary televisions and satellite dish. Critics argue that students become a "captive audience" for the commercial messages and that such messages simply should not be a part of an educational setting. What do you think? Explain.

14. In 1993, a scholarly book, *The Concept of Honest Poverty,* attacking Japan's money-centered society, became a huge best-seller (600,000 copies sold in eight months). The author, Koki Nakano, explained his thesis:

    > However rich Japan becomes, it will never get the respect of the world. To earn respect, we need dignity, chivalry and the philosophy of honest poverty. Our image is that of a country that's good at making things but has no culture. Foreigners say Japanese lack character and dignity, and think of us just as people with money.[43]

    a. What does he mean by "honest poverty"?
    b. Do we honor honest poverty in America? Explain.
    c. Do you admire the Japanese? Explain.
    d. Aren't rich people highly respected in America? Explain.
    e. Why is American culture so widely admired?
    f. In the end, is culture more important to the fate of a nation than wealth? Explain.

15. Do you think allegiance to the company will become more important than allegiance to the state? Is that a desirable direction? Raise the arguments on both sides of the latter question.

16. As expressed in *Business Week,* "Increasingly, the corporation will take over the role of the mother, supplying day-care facilities where children can be tended around the clock."[44] How do you feel about the corporation as mother? Explain.

Part Two—Corporate Social Responsibility

INTRODUCTION

As illustrated in Chapter 2 and in Part One of this chapter, the business community has been the subject of intense criticism even as the influence of business values in American life has grown more dominant. That increasing business influence, in conjunction with the perception of serious business misdeeds, has led in recent decades to the development of the notion of *corporate social responsibility.*

The issue is as follows: Must business decision making include consideration not merely of the welfare of the firm but of society as well? For most contemporary readers, the answer is self-evident—of course business bears a social responsibility. Business has enjoyed a central and favored role in American life. As such, it must assume a measure of the burden for the welfare of the total society. Problems such as discrimination, pollution, and poverty require the full strength of the nation, including the vast resources of business. Professors Steven Brenner and Earl Molander's survey of *Harvard Business Review* readers revealed that:

> Most respondents have overcome the traditional ideological barriers to the concept of social responsibility and have embraced its practice as a legitimate and achievable goal for business.[45]

Only 28 percent of the respondents endorsed the free market view, popularly associated with Milton Friedman, that "the social responsibility of business is to 'stick to business,'" and 69 percent agreed with the idea that "'profit' is really a somewhat ineffective measure of business's social effectiveness." Indeed, the respondents seemed to hold a rather optimistic, activist view of business's role in society. Of those responding, 77 percent disagreed with the position that "every business is in effect 'trapped' in the business system it helped create, and can do remarkably little about the social problems of our times."[46]

Corporate acceptance of social responsibility, as manifested in that 1976 survey, seems to have matured and expanded to the point that today's businesspeople feel willing to directly tackle some of our most challenging social issues. A 1990 *Business Week* Harris Poll shows that contemporary executives and graduate business students firmly endorse business's responsibility to help solve society's problems.[47]

Thy Brother's Keeper?

Should corporations become more directly involved in solving such social problems as substance abuse, homelessness, health care, and education, or not?

	Executives	*Students*
More involved in solving social problems	69%	89%
Not more involved in solving social problems	27	8
Not sure	4	3

Source: Kevin Gudridge and John Byrne, "A Kinder, Gentler Generation of Executives." *Business Week*, April 23, 1990, p. 86.

A New Ideology

The ascendance of the social responsibility concept represents one of the most striking ideological shifts in American history. From the settling of the nation until roughly 1950, business was expected to concentrate on one goal—the production and distribution of the best products at the lowest possible prices. Of course, social responsibility arguments were raised, but business was largely exempt from any affirmative duty for the resolution of social problems. Rendered practical perhaps by increasing prosperity, the public, led by business scholars and critics, began in the 1950s to consider a larger role for corporate America. In four decades, the role of business in society has been radically altered. Profit seeking remains central and essential, but for most businesspersons, the new and rather unwieldy ingredient of social responsibility must be added to the equation.

Doubts Remain

But skepticism remains. Actual performance may or may not measure up to the business community's expressions of commitment. And mighty though their resources are, how much progress can we expect businesspeople to make in solving huge social dilemmas? As economics correspondent Robert Kuttner sees it, "Despite recent ballyhoo, supporters of improved public education, worker training, and national health care won't be rescued by the white knight of Corporate America."[48]

WHAT IS SOCIAL RESPONSIBILITY?

Many definitions of social responsibility (SR) have been offered, and a broad consensus seems to have emerged, but no single expression has successfully embraced the full spectrum of views. For example, Davis and Blomstrom put it this way: "The idea of social responsibility is that decision makers are obligated to take actions which protect and improve the welfare of society as a whole along with their own interests."[49]

Kenneth Andrews suggests the same tone but offers some additional dimensions:

> By "social responsibility" we mean the intelligent and objective concern for the welfare of society that restrains individual and corporate behavior from ultimately destructive activities, no matter how immediately profitable, and leads in the direction of positive contributions to human betterment, variously as the latter may be defined.[50]

Social Responsibility Pyramid

The accompanying table, developed by Professor Archie Carroll, depicts social responsibility as much more than a form of corporate charity. Social responsibility begins with making a profit, the foundation on which all other social contributions necessarily rest. At the same time, the honorable corporation complies with those

Corporation candor or ✓

The Pyramid of Corporate Social Responsibility

Philanthropic = *charitable*
Responsibilities

Be a good corporate citizen.
Contribute resources
to the community;
improve quality of life.

Ethical
Responsibilities

Be ethical.
Obligation to do what is right, just,
and fair. Avoid harm.

Legal
Responsibilities

Obey the law.
Law is society's codification of right and wrong.
Play by the rules of the game.

Economic
Responsibilities

Be profitable.
The foundation upon which all others rest.

Source: Archie B. Carroll, "The Pyramid of Corporate Social Responsibility: Toward the Moral Management of Organizational Stakeholders." Reprinted from *Business Horizons* 34, no. 4 (July–August 1991), pp. 39, 42. Copyright 1991 by the Foundation for the School of Business at Indiana University. Used with permission.

legal and ethical obligations that all citizens must meet. Having fulfilled those duties, the firm that seeks to be a good citizen and contribute to its own long-term best interests may also choose to engage in voluntary philanthropic efforts (in the form of money, facilities, management time, etc.) to build a better community.

Profit Maximization

While social responsibility, framed in terms of business's duty to society, appears broadly accepted in business and among the general public, recall that a significant body of sentiment adheres to the free market view alluded to previously and perhaps best expressed by Milton Friedman:

> [In a free economy] there is one and only one social responsibility of business—to use its resources and engage in activities designed to increase its profits, so long as it stays within the rules of the game, which is to say, engages in open and free competition, without deception or fraud.[51]

Friedman believes the firm, maximizing its profits, is necessarily maximizing its contribution to society. He believes social responsibility is both unworkable and unjust. He asks how selected private individuals can know what the public interest is. He also argues that any dilution of the profit-maximizing mode—such as charitable contributions—is a misuse of the stockholders' resources. The individual stockholder, he contends, should dispose of assets according to her or his own wishes.

SOCIAL RESPONSIBILITY IN PRACTICE

> Faced with increased public scrutiny, businesses are scrambling to become socially responsible.[52]

That observation by *Newsweek* suggests what has so clearly come to pass. The debate is over. The corporate community, perhaps reluctantly, now acknowledges its increased responsibility to the larger society. Today, the question is one of what to do and how to do it. The accompanying "Corporate Report Card" suggests some of the activities that companies are doing (or failing to do) to make a contribution to society beyond providing quality products and services.

A Corporate Report Card

Socially responsible companies got stars from the Council on Economic Priorities. Other corporations with less than stellar records received dishonorable mentions.

GOOD GRADES

Pitney Bowes: For its affirmative-action, profit-sharing and child-care-leave practices.

Xerox: For allowing employees with three years of service to take a leave with full pay to do community work.

Cummins Engine: Gets high marks for giving 5 percent of its domestic pretax profits to charity.

BAD GRADES

Perdue Farms: For its unsafe facilities and for allegedly firing workers with job-related injuries.

USX: Recently settled federal charges for workplace health and safety violations, paying $3.3 million in fines.

Exxon: For its poor handling of the 1989 Alaskan oil spill and for the explosion of an oil pipe near Staten Island.

Source: Council on Economic Priorities. In Karen Springen and Annetta Miller, "Doing the Right Thing." *Newsweek*, January 7, 1991, p. 42.

Ben & Jerry's

The unorthodox but highly successful East Coast ice-cream company has integrated social responsibility into the heart of the company's approach to business. Each year, 7.5 percent of pretax profits goes to worthy causes. Ben & Jerry's supports an entrepreneurial fund to encourage new businesses. Employees are urged to volunteer for community service, for which they are paid their normal salaries by the company. Founder Ben Cohen says, "Business has a responsibility to give back to the community."[53]

But Is Corporate Social Responsibility Good Business?

The empirical evidence is mixed. Many studies show highly responsible firms with very favorable economic returns.[54] Others show little or no relationship between social responsibility and performance.[55] In some sense, the question is moot because the public has spoken so clearly:

> Studies have shown that the public is paying ever-closer attention to corporate behavior. A recent Roper poll of 1,496 U.S. consumers found that 52 percent said they would pay 10 percent more for a so-called socially responsible product and 67 percent said they are concerned about a company's social performance when they shop.
>
> Loblaws, a Canadian grocery chain, reports it sees a 10 to 60 percent increase in sales of products after they are labeled with the company's environmental seal. Ethical mutual funds are also paying off. In a test that compared the return of [Domini Social Index] listed companies and the S&P 500 from 1986 to 1990, the DSI's total return was 80 percent, almost identical to the S&P's.[56]

Part Three—Corporate Public Policy

SOCIAL RESPONSIVENESS

As the principle of social responsibility became increasingly acceptable to the corporate community, the nature of the debate shifted a bit to whether corporate *performance* conformed to those principles. The idea of *corporate social responsiveness* then emerged. The movement was away from the moral theme of responsibility, obligation, and duty to the more practical notion of how best to manage the firm's response to social issues. However, social responsiveness, being reactive in character, proved inadequate to the demands of an increasingly complicated corporate–societal compact. Mere responsiveness to social problems in this era cannot meet the needs of the business community nor the demands of the larger society.

PUBLIC POLICY

Hence, in recent years, we have witnessed the evolution of *corporate public policy,* wherein business takes a more activist stance in addressing contemporary social issues. Public policy refers to the process by which the total society identifies and manages its problems and goals. The corporate public policy approach calls for the business community to recognize that it should play a part in setting the larger public policy agenda and dealing with it. Hence, business, rather than taking a responsive role, must be an active player in social themes. Business now must be closely attuned not merely to market signals but to government signals and to the larger society's preferences. All of this, of course, requires the contemporary manager to learn about a much broader range of issues than was the case historically. Profit now rests not merely in providing the best product or service at the lowest price but in understanding and dealing with the very complex interplay between the corporation, government, and society. Thus, today's socially responsible firm is likely to be ever more involved in identifying and attempting to manage social issues. To do so, many corporations have now built the public policy process into their management structure and systems.

Planning and Implementing Corporate Public Policy

For the firm that accepts the notion of social responsibilities beyond meeting fundamental economic and legal requirements, it becomes immediately apparent that a mechanism must be established to identify and deal with those responsibilities. That is, social responsibility may be internalized and "managed" in a planned, coordinated manner that weaves social concerns into the total operation of the firm. Social issues become a critical part of the firm's larger strategic planning process. Essentially, the process falls into five states:

1. Scanning the environment.
2. Assessing organizational assets.
3. Setting policy.
4. Implementing policy.
5. Measuring results.

1. Scanning the Environment. Many corporations have established mechanisms to keep abreast of, and even anticipate, social trends that may affect corporate policy. Some firms establish entire departments to deal with the external social and political environment. Others vest an individual with specific scanning duties. Others hire consultants. However implemented, the process is that of reading, talking, and exploring so that management can be alerted to and involved in preparing for new social trends. By taking a more active role in the political process and in the total complex of forces *play active role in identifying societal preferences.*

by which public policy is formulated, business can make a positive contribution to societal preferences. Clearly, business has the legal and moral right to have its voice heard, and thus, presumably, to enhance the quality of the ultimate decision. But to some critics, the proactive approach raises the possibility of business using its enormous resources to unfairly shape policy according to narrow commercial interests.

2. Assessing Organizational Assets. Having identified pressing social issues and trends, the firm must determine whether and to what extent it is capable of dealing with those challenges. For example, as our population ages, environmental scanners have identified the need for increasing attention to the interests of elderly Americans. The firm will then determine whether it possesses the resources in terms of management, finance, commitment, and so forth, to make a contribution and presumably benefit the company in the long run.

Directors should be set to towards working to work towards realizing the policy.

3. Setting Policy. Having completed steps 1 and 2, the critical policy decision must be made. Here, it is a matter of capturing the time and attention of top-level executives, not only so that directions will be set but also so that the project will be imbued with the full will of the organization.

4. Implementing Policy. Obviously, it is at this stage where glorious ideas often get lost in the vast bureaucratic bog. A detailed, standardized operating procedure must be established. Many approaches are employed—a social responsibility officer, a task force, a management committee—but the point is that social issues must be treated in the same responsible, systematic fashion as, for example, product development. And social responsibility advocates would argue that, in the long term, their concerns will be at least as important to the firm as traditional icons such as financial planning and marketing strategies.

5. Measuring Results. All successful planning/management processes require some sort of evaluation or control mechanism both to determine the success of the effort and to shape continuing strategic planning. A direction is taken (e.g., the corporation decides to establish an on-site day care center for employee use), the success of that direction is evaluated, and adjustments are made, as necessary, to bring that direction ever closer to the goals of the larger strategic plan.

Of course, measuring the costs and benefits of social projects is very difficult. Although various approaches might be employed, the primary effort has been some form of a social audit that, like an accounting audit, seeks to measure results—in this case, the company's involvement in social issues and the success of that involvement. Broadly, a firm catalogs its social issues activities and tries to evaluate their effectiveness through a cost-benefit analysis. The task is daunting. To quantify not just costs (many of which do not come in the form of direct, out-of-pocket dollars) but benefits as well (Is the benefit to society in sponsoring a Little League baseball team merely equal to the costs of uniforms and equipment?) taxes our ingenuity.

Part Four—Business and Society Issues

Managing the volatile business and society interface is immensely demanding. The materials that follow raise three contemporary social responsibility issues—inner-city jobs, alcohol marketing, and human rights violations abroad—that are presently causing headaches for corporate leaders who must produce a profit but who also must conform to society's expectations for responsible conduct. Note that issues like these often generate calls for new laws and/or regulations. Thus, these three themes raise the question of where a company's social responsibility lies, but they also call into play the larger theme of this book—can the business community successfully regulate itself, or must government intervene?

SOCIAL RESPONSIBILITY

1. Inner-City Jobs?

SOCIAL RESPONSIBILITY AND NEED FOR LOW COST CLASH AT STRIDE RITE

Joseph Pereira

At the gleaming headquarters building of Stride Rite Corp. in bustling Kendall Square here, plaques on the walls honor the shoe company for its good deeds.

In the past three years alone, Stride Rite has received 14 public-service awards . . .

While doing good, Stride Rite also has done well. It has posted a profit, usually a record, for the past 32 quarters. This year, its sales are expected to top $625 million, more than double the 1986 level. Its stock has increased sixfold since then, making it a favorite on the New York Stock Exchange and among socially conscious investors.

But just a few miles away, in Boston's rough inner-city Roxbury neighborhood, stands another Stride Rite building: a weather-beaten, red-brick structure surrounded by empty lots, crumbling roads and chain-link fences. It once housed corporate headquarters and employed 2,500 people making the company's Keds sneakers and Sperry Top-Sider shoes.

Today, the building is just a distribution center employing only 175 workers. Next year, even they will be gone. Stride Rite plans to close the warehouse—and another one in New Bedford, Mass.—and move the operations to Kentucky.

In Roxbury, so close to corporate headquarters but yet so far, Stride Rite's citations for corporate citizenship ring hollow. With the local unemployment rate estimated at nearly 30%, the soon-to-be-jobless workers see a bleak future.

"Where are you supposed to go?" wonders Miguel Brandao, a 46-year-old Cape Verdean immigrant who has worked at the plant 11 years. "There is no place to go."

* * * * *

And last June, Stride Rite closed another plant, in Tipton, Mo., and laid off 280 workers. The unemployment rate is grim there, too. Three other shoe companies also closed nearby factories at about the same time, idling 1,400 workers. Angie and Stanley Shewmaker, who both worked for Stride Rite in Tipton, are still unemployed. They have been in job training—and in counseling for a marriage strained by money worries. "I'm all nerves," Mrs. Shewmaker says. "I'm on tranquilizers. I can't sleep at night. It's been hard. I'm fighting depression all the time."

In the past decade, Stride Rite has prospered partly by closing 15 factories, mostly in the Northeast and several in depressed areas, and moving most of its production to various low-cost Asian countries. The company still employs 2,500 workers in the U.S., but that is down from a peak of about 6,000.

Difficult Questions

So yet-another departure from yet-another inner-city neighborhood such as Roxbury is hardly surprising. Neither is the transfer of work to the Far East. But when the company behind the moves is a Stride Rite, one that has received so many accolades, it raises difficult questions: What makes a company socially responsible? And how far can social responsibility be expected to go?

Is it sufficient to do good deeds, as everyone agrees Stride Rite has done? It has contributed 5% of its pretax profit to a foundation, sent 100,000 pairs of sneakers to strife-torn Mozambique, paid Harvard graduate students to work in a Cambodian refugee camp, given scholarships to inner-city youths, permitted employees to tutor disadvantaged children on company time and been a pioneer in setting up on-site day-care and elder-care facilities.

Or is something more basic needed, such as providing jobs in depressed areas even at the expense of profits? To many who have watched much of corporate America leave inner cities, the answer is clear. "The most socially responsible thing a company can do is to give a person a job," argues Donald Gillis, executive director of Boston's Economic Development and Industrial Corp., which tried to persuade Stride Rite to stay.

Adds Gilda Haas, an economic and urban-planning lecturer at the University of California at Los Angeles: "It strikes me as strange that we're having this conversation about inner-city jobs only a year after the civil unrest in South Central Los Angeles. What exactly did the corporate sector mean when they spoke of the need for inner-city jobs last year as Los Angeles burned?"

Stride Rite contends that it has been socially responsible but nevertheless has to balance the demands of two masters—shareholders and society. If a company doesn't stay competitive, its executives contend, it can't grow, it would provide even fewer jobs, it would earn too little to afford its community programs, and, at worst, it might jeopardize its survival. "Putting jobs into places where it doesn't make economic sense," Chairman Ervin Shames says, "is a dilution of corporate and community wealth."

So, even while Stride Rite was nurturing social programs, it slowly and reluctantly began closing plants in Maine and New Hampshire in the late 1960s and shifting production overseas. And as the quality and efficiency of foreign workers improved, Stride Rite, and its competitors, started to export jobs more rapidly. Higher-priced American workers simply weren't competitive; even Stride Rite's efforts to run small, cost-efficient factories in rural New England failed.

Nike Inc., too, briefly tried running a factory in Maine in the late 1970s, but gave up after losing more than $5 million a year. "Athletic shoes are best made in parts of the world other than the U.S.," a Nike spokesman says. "If the Air Jordan shoe were to be made in the U.S. today, it could retail for $280 to $310 a pair." The Taiwan-made shoe costs about $100.

By the early 1980s, only half of Stride Rite's shoes were U.S.-made. "You could stay in the U.S. if you were doing high-end shoes," a niche Stride Rite wasn't in, says Myles Slosberg, a director and former executive vice president. "Otherwise, it was going to be pretty darn difficult."

One of the company's biggest layoffs, of 2,500 people, came in 1984. Stride Rite closed three plants, including its children's shoe factory in Roxbury, and moved the jobs overseas. It had to, it says, to survive.

That year, its net income plummeted 68% to $5.4 million from $16.8 million in 1983—the first drop in 13 years. In 1986, the company closed two more Massachusetts plants, in Brockton and Lawrence. It still operates two factories in Missouri, but it now makes only 10% of its shoes in the U.S. It doesn't own the overseas factories or directly employ the workers; instead, it contracts with local companies.

The labor savings are huge. Andy Li, a Taiwan contractor who has found subcontractors to work for Stride Rite, says skilled workers in China earn $100 to $150 a month, working 50 to 65 hours a week. Unskilled workers—packers and sorters—get $50 to $70 a month. By comparison, Stride Rite's U.S. workers average $1,200 to $1,400 per month in wages alone, plus modest fringe benefits.

"It has become virtually impossible to manufacture sneakers in the U.S. and still be in the competition," says Carl Steidtmann, chief economist at Price Waterhouse's merchandise-consulting division. The obvious consequence in Missouri: Shoe-making jobs dwindled to 8,250 last year from a peak of 25,000 in 1968.

Even overseas, Stride Rite continues its quest for labor bargains. In recent years, it has switched from factories in South Korea as pay rose there to lower-wage Indonesia and China. . .

Stride Rite also contends it has little choice but to pull its distribution centers out of Roxbury and New Bedford. "It was a difficult decision," Mr. Shames says. "Our hearts said, 'Stay,' but our heads said, 'Move.'" Stride Rite will save millions of dollars, he adds, by going to the Midwest. When the company profiled its retailers, he says, "the average customer tended to be in the Midwestern or Southern part of the nation."

Moreover, the central location will make shipping generally more efficient. Now, most Stride Rite shoes are shipped from the Far East to Los Angeles and Seattle and then trucked to Boston and New Bedford, where they are sorted and labeled and then dispatched to retailers nationwide. The new distribution center in Louisville will eliminate 800 to 1,200 miles on some truck routes, speeding delivery by 2 1/2 to four days . . .

Within Stride Rite's top management, however, the decision has caused soul-searching. Arnold Hiatt, a former chairman who retired last year but remains a director, says, "I objected to that decision as much as I could. I was overruled." He passionately espoused a "Jeffersonian vision" linking corporate and social responsibility. When Stride Rite joined 54 other companies to form Businesses for Social Responsibility last year, he said, "If you're pro-business, you also have to be concerned about things like jobs in the inner city and the 38 million Americans living below the poverty line."

But Mr. Hiatt concedes that the issue is complicated. For three months, officials reviewed offers in connection with the warehouse from Indiana, Ohio, Massachusetts and Kentucky. Kentucky won mainly because of a $24 million tax break over 10 years, vs. a $3 million offer from Massachusetts. Lower wage rates also played a role.

Mr. Hiatt acknowledges that he himself moved many jobs out of Roxbury in his 24 years as a top officer. "To the extent that you can stay in the city, I think you have to," he says. But "if it's at the expense of your business, I think you can't forget that your primary responsibility is to your stockholders."

It was under Mr. Hiatt, a staunch liberal who served as treasurer for Sen. Eugene McCarthy's 1968 presidential campaign, that Stride Rite became known for progressive policies. In 1971, he opened a day-care center at the Roxbury plant, a move that cost some money but more than paid off in goodwill. In 1988, another day-care center, at the Cambridge headquarters, was expanded to become a widely praised "intergenerational center," caring for the aged as well.

Stride Rite also contributes heavily to charity. In 1991, its board decided to allot 5% of pretax profits—or about $5 million last year—to the Stride Rite Charitable Foundation. Part of that money helps 40 inner-city students attend Harvard. . .

*   *   *   *   *

For a long time, the Roxbury site, then the company headquarters, was relatively unscathed despite the sharply deteriorating neighborhood. Then, in

1981, came a stunning blow: Stride Rite moved its offices to Cambridge. "We held out as long as we could," Mr. Hiatt says, "but it became clear that people that had the more skilled jobs at Stride Rite were coming from other parts of the city and were increasingly reluctant to go into Roxbury." One day, a bullet smashed through his window, he says, "and I knew it was time to go."

To soften the impact on Roxbury, Stride Rite moved in distribution centers from Atlanta and Salem, N.H. But the respite was brief. In 1984, it closed the factory.

Now, the departure of the warehouse compounds Roxbury's problems. Ames Department Stores Inc. closed its Roxbury store in March and Digital Equipment Corp. shut its factory in the neighborhood this month.

"It is very devastating," says Roderick Dowdell, a worker at the nearby Common Bostonian restaurant. "It is like back-to-back grand slams by the opposing team." A few doors from Stride Rite in Roxbury, Edward Williams says his Hair Salon is struggling. "We did 150 clients a week; now, I'm lucky to do 25," he says.

In the wake of the closings, community leaders called a huddle, seeking ways to stimulate new businesses and hold onto existing ones. But one ray of hope, a proposed biotechnology center that will create 150 jobs, is little consolation to Stride Rite employees; many speak little or no English and lack the skills that even entry-level jobs at the center will require. Stride Rite employees need "$3,000 worth of education" to have hope of getting in the door, says Sue Swartz, director of the Boston Workers Assistance Center. But her project allows for only half that.

* * * * *

The talk of schooling draws looks of amusement from a few workers. With eight children, Mr. Brandao, a sorter at the warehouse, says he must work an average of 14 hours overtime a week to make ends meet. "Who will feed my children?" he asks in thickly accented English.

The approximately 500 employees at the Roxbury and New Bedford facilities could request transfers to Kentucky but would compete with local applicants for the 275 positions. Many probably won't even try. "Why would we want to go there?" says Carol Pitta, an inventory controller at New Bedford. "There won't be a union, the pay will be less and what happens if in two months they don't want you? Who'll pay my way home?"

* * * * *

The federal government offered retraining because the [shoe factory] jobs lost in Missouri went abroad. Not all the unemployed could take advantage of the programs.

"It costs $80 a week for a baby sitter, and I'm getting $175 a week in unemployment assistance," explains Anita Bracht, a former Stride Rite employee in Tipton who has four children. Her husband, Donny, worked at Stride Rite, too, and also is unemployed. "He's tried everything," Mrs. Bracht says. "The union tells him there are 500 people on the waiting list" for jobs contracted by the union. With their unemployment benefits nearing an end, she adds, "I'm about ready to panic."

Among the many lessons learned from the closings, one has struck especially close to home for Mr. Brandao in Roxbury. A 70-year-old Irish immigrant, who rented a room from him, died recently, leaving behind a 32-year-old mentally disabled son. "I don't have the heart to ask him to leave," he says with the help of a translator. "If I did, I would be doing to him what my company is doing to me."

Afterword

Stride Rite sales rose only 2 percent in 1992 after annual increases in the high teens during the mid- and late-1980s. Low-priced "knockoffs" and a modest decline in sneaker interest contributed to Stride Rite's problems. Stride Rite reduced its retail outlets from approximately 250 in 1989 to about 170 in 1993. Following CEO Ervin Shames's surprise resignation in 1993 after less than one year on the job, Stride Rite was faced with its third CEO search in four years.

Questions

1. Answer these questions drawn from the "Stride Rite" article.
    a. "What makes a company socially responsible?"
    b. "And how far can social responsibility be expected to go?"
    c. "Is it sufficient to do good deeds, as everyone agrees Stride Rite has done?" Explain.
2. If you were a Stride Rite shareholder, what would you expect the company to do with its inner-city operations? Explain.
3. Is corporate-funded training for inner-city, disadvantaged workers a good investment? Explain.
4. Is the business community partially responsible for the 1992 Los Angeles riots? Explain.
5. How can government help industry in rebuilding the inner cities?

2. Targeted Alcohol Marketing?

CRITICS SHOOT AT
NEW COLT 45 CAMPAIGN

Laura Bird

In a new TV commercial that began airing nationally this week, a message of hope and reformation is delivered in hip, stream-of-consciousness narration over bleak, grainy shots of an inner-city neighborhood.

"I was the first one in my family to go to college," says the earnest young black man in shirt and tie. "It was a night-school thing, which is cool, because now I can do some good things. Give back what I learned." He sits on a front porch and beckons to an even younger friend to join him. "And the brothers, they see me and maybe they'll want to do something better for themselves, y'know," the role model says.

It may look like an ad for Big Brothers or the United Negro College Fund. But the college grad and his front-porch pal sip from bottles of Colt 45 malt liquor in the new spot from G. Heileman Brewing Co. It marks a sharp departure from the campaign Colt 45 has used since the mid-1980s, featuring the older-appeal, middle-aged leading man, Billy

Dee Williams, beautiful women and the tag line "Colt 45. It works every time."

The new spot is part of a controversial effort to hone a hipper image for Colt 45 and appeal more directly to the malt-liquor market's most important customers: young inner-city blacks. It is already re-opening the pitched debate over the ethics of aiming high-octane malt liquor at young drinkers in the inner city.

Deutsch/Dworin, the New York ad agency that created the new Colt 45 commercials, says they are meant to portray the values and concerns of inner-city consumers. But critics call them cynical, just a more subtle version of Mr. Williams's glitzy spots linking the drink with romantic and financial prowess.

* * * * *

"It's the same old success tie-in, portraying drinkers as those who are successful," says George Hacker, director of the alcohol-policies project at the Center for Science in the Public Interest, of the commercial's text. "But here it's so cynical because drinking those high-alcohol products frequently leads to the exact opposite result."

The issue is all the more heated because of the Heileman name. Two summers ago, the company was planning to introduce PowerMaster, an especially potent malt aimed directly at urban blacks, but backed off after widespread outcry. Later, Heileman took heat for its part in producing and distributing St. Ides, a malt brand that features rappers like Ice Cube in its ads. After that came still more criticism for Heileman for brewing the high-power Crazy Horse malt liquor.

Now comes the commercial blitz for Colt 45, using an all-black cast of youthful actors. The complaints may grow when Heileman harnesses the new campaign to Cool Colt, a lighter, flavored malt liquor that the company says is designed to "broaden the Colt 45 franchise." Cool Colt's slogan is "Taste the Cool," and such lighter, flavored versions often appeal to younger consumers. (Cool Colt is the only aspect of this article on which Heileman would comment.)

Many brewing-industry executives see nothing wrong with such efforts. Targeting low-income African-Americans for malt liquor is no different from selling the Mercedes-Benz line to white, affluent suburbanites, their argument goes. It reeks of paternalism and racism to suggest it is inappropriate, says Donny Deutsch, executive vice president and creative director at Deutsch/Dworin. Why should Colt 45 shy away from portraying its core consumers just because more than 90% of them are male and black?

"I don't understand why beer can't be segmented with intelligence, respect, honesty and relevance" to black consumers, Mr. Deutsch says. "Just like you can target to affluent businessmen, you should be able to target urban downscale white women, or urban black men, or children. That's marketing. Who are these people who are sitting as judge and jury on who should be targeted?"

But critics of the targeting technique say malt makers have drawn a bead on the very market—urban blacks and other minorities—that suffers disproportionately from alcohol-related disease and inadequate access to health care. For instance, African-American men are nearly twice as likely as white men to die from liver-related ailments and almost three times as likely to die due to other alcohol-related circumstances, according to a 1989 report by the Centers for Disease Control and Prevention. That renders targeting such people fundamentally wrong, critics contend.

Makani Themba, a public-policy analyst at the Marin Institute in San Rafael, Calif., and others say the malt business pursues the black urban market because it is one of the few growth segments left. Inner-city blacks have historically lower levels of alcohol consumption than whites, and they are more likely to purchase malt as a cheaper and higher-kick alternative to beer, critics of the malt-liquor ads say.

Malt liquor was a rare bright spot in the beer industry last year, according to M. Shanken Communications' Impact Databank, which tracks industry sales. Malt-liquor sales were up 15% last year to $1.1 billion at retail, compared with flat sales in the overall $35 billion beer category.

But Colt, with its dated image, hasn't kept up with the category. Colt sales were up 12.5% last year, according to Impact, to about $280 million. That compares with 18% growth for Pabst Brewing's Olde

English 800, now the No. 1 selling malt, thanks in part to a blizzard of outdoor ads featuring blatant use of macho imagery.

*   *   *   *   *

Among the criticism [sic], some health activists charge the Colt 45 ads portray underage drinking as acceptable. And they contend that Heileman is breaching the beer industry's self-imposed restrictions against advertising alcohol to customers under the legal drinking age of 21.

The Marin Institute's Ms. Themba says the spots have been calculated to send two dangerous messages: "That the way to appropriately bond is through malt liquor, and that malt liquor is a better alternative to the other dangerous things that are out there."

Source: *The Wall Street Journal,* February 17, 1993, p. B1. Reprinted by permission of *The Wall Street Journal,* © 1993 Dow Jones and Company, Inc. All Rights Reserved Worldwide.

Questions

1. Do you agree with the following statement: "Targeting low-income African-Americans for malt liquor is not different from selling the Mercedes-Benz line to white, affluent suburbanites?" Explain.
2. For adults, is the decision to drink simply a matter of personal responsibility regardless of the direction or effectiveness of advertising campaigns? Explain.
3. Several scholarly studies have shown that cigarette ads featuring cartoonlike characters are particularly effective in reaching children. One study found that nearly three-fourths of the seventh- and eighth-grade students surveyed liked R. J. Reynolds's Joe Camel ads, while 43 percent liked those with human characters.[57] Another study showed that smokers aged 12–18 prefer the most heavily advertised cigarettes (Marlboro, Newport, and Camel), while adult smoking was much less concentrated by brand.[58] The tobacco companies say that friends and family are most influential in smoking habits and that no evidence supports a link between enjoying ads and subsequently using a product.
   a. In your opinion, do tobacco ad campaigns "target" young people? Explain.
   b. Would you personally participate in such an ad campaign if you worked for a tobacco company? Explain.
   c. Should we simply banish tobacco advertising? Explain.
4. Peter Hoult, an RJR Nabisco executive vice president, responded to the campaign against Reynolds's plans for an Uptown brand targeted at blacks:

   We regret that a small coalition of antismoking zealots apparently believes that black smokers are somehow different from others who choose to smoke.[59]

   Reynolds's Dakota brand was to have been directed to high school educated, 18- to 20-year-old "virile females" who, according to a marketing study,

   tend to wear jeans, watch nighttime soap operas, go to parties, bars and shopping centers, and hang out with their boyfriends at drag races, tractor pulls, professional wrestling matches and the like.[60]

   a. What did Mr. Hoult mean? Do you agree with his view? Explain.
   b. Were Reynolds's plans for Uptown and Dakota ethically improper? Explain.

INTERNATIONAL

5. In 1990, Harvard University decided to divest itself of its stock in tobacco companies because, according to Harvard President Derek Bok, tobacco products "create a substantial and unjustifiable risk of harm to other human beings."[61] Harvard held $3.5 million in tobacco stocks.

   a. Should all those who disapprove of smoking express that displeasure by divesting themselves of any holdings they may have in tobacco companies? Explain.

   b. Should Harvard divest itself of its holdings in companies producing alcohol for drinking? Explain.

   c. Would you decline to work for alcohol and tobacco companies? Explain.

6. Do you believe yourself to be influenced either by ads promoting alcohol consumption or by ads encouraging moderation in drinking? Explain.

3. Human Rights Abroad?

THE SUPPLY POLICE

John McCormick and Marc Levinson

Companies that make tools and building materials usually love to take orders from Home Depot. But last month the Atlanta retailer demanded more from its 300 foreign suppliers than the customary shipments of wrenches and lumber. A new questionnaire asked whether any factory in Home Depot's worldwide supply chain employs children or prison convicts. Lest suppliers think the company isn't dead serious about disreputable business practices, Home Depot added an ultimatum: you have 72 hours to respond.

Home Depot desperately wants to avoid a new strain of public-relations disaster. The Christmas-week NBC show asserting that Wal-Mart's "Buy American" program misleads consumers also leveled a more sinister charge: that children as young as 9 churn out clothes for the nation's largest retailer in Bangladeshi sweatshops. Other big-name U.S. importers aren't waiting to see whether the public buys Wal-Mart's denials. Instead they're making sure their own suppliers are free of environmental, human-rights or other potential embarrassments. The supplier police had better hurry. Jeff Fiedler, the AFL-CIO official who helped NBC mug Wal-Mart,

says that he's drawing beads on a dozen new targets, including apparel and dress-shoe companies.

. . . Activists pushing a variety of causes have discovered that exposing corporate exploitation will accomplish what tamer strategies, such as leafleting annual meetings, have not. Scrutiny by labor unions, activists and socially conscious investors is forcing importers to monitor not just their foreign subsidiaries but their far-flung networks of independent suppliers—and their suppliers' suppliers as well. Says Donna Katzin of the Interfaith Center on Corporate Responsibility, "Just because companies don't make a product themselves doesn't relieve them of all obligations."

Take the case of H. J. Heinz. The Pittsburgh-based food processor doesn't catch its own tuna, but that made little difference when environmental groups enlisted schoolchildren in a campaign to end fishing techniques that kill large numbers of dolphins. After a barrage of mail from young consumers, Heinz announced in 1990 that its Star-Kist brand would buy tuna only from fishing boats that used approved methods. "Consumer response has been extremely positive," says Star-Kist spokeswoman Susan Halberstadt. The victory emboldened environmentalists to broaden their knowledge of who buys what from whom overseas. Unions have followed suit, seeking to discourage imports and win new trade barriers by exposing poor working conditions and suppliers' avoidance of U.S. import quotas.

Is it fair to hold Third World suppliers to U.S. standards of conduct? Even many of those who say it is admit to ambivalence about imposing their values on countries and companies halfway around the world. "It's easy to take cynical views of American corporations," says Northwestern University business ethicist David Messick. "But what gives us the right to decide at what age people in Bangladesh should work?"

Avoiding Risks

To which image-conscious executives might answer: why take risks? As the Wal-Mart case demonstrates, even perceived transgressions can lead to big embarrassment. Wal-Mart's heavy reliance on imports has long rankled the AFL-CIO. Fiedler says NBC called him first, but didn't have to twist his arm. In the television footage, it was the union guy who looked authoritative and Wal-Mart CEO David Glass who appeared not to know how his company buys its merchandise. Wal-Mart maintains that the NBC report was blatantly false. But the fact that an executive of Glass's stature could be tripped up by one obscure link in his company's vast chain of thousands of suppliers shows how vulnerable a major corporation can be.

Several companies have made pre-emptive strikes to avoid similar pratfalls. Last March, Sears said it wouldn't import forced-labor products from China. Phillips-Van Heusen explicitly threatens to terminate orders to apparel suppliers that violate its broad ethical, environmental and human-rights code. And Dow Chemical asks suppliers to conform not just to local pollution and safety laws, but to the often tougher U.S. standards. At least one major U.S. company acted merely to stamp out falsehoods: persistent rumors that McDonald's suppliers grazed their cattle on cleared rain-forest land finally led it to ban the practice in writing.

Executives may well take the increased scrutiny as a sign of an antibusiness conspiracy. But three distinct types of tactics are now evident. Socially conscious investors and mainstream religious groups promote the positive message that companies should extend their own high standards to all their business partners. Environmentalists and other activists tend toward the more direct pressure that comes from naming names. Union officials are taking a more investigative approach to locate human-rights and other violations, including schemes in which foreign manufacturers, especially in China, circumvent U.S. textile quotas by misidentifying the country in which their goods were made . . .

Exasperated importers say they can't possibly patrol the world. For openers, there is no central repository of information about exporters. "How can you know what's happening in Bangladesh when everyone between here and there has reason to lie?" says John Schultz, president of Ethical Investments, which helps bleeding-heart investors pick stocks. Some charges of misbehavior reach the United States through regional groups like Hong Kong's Committee for Asian Women, which exposes beatings and other factory abuses. But in a global market of component parts, generic goods and layers of middlemen, it's hard to keep score. "I can't control the factory that supplies my supplier," says Russell Berrie, whose New Jersey company is a big buyer of trinkets from China.

Exacting Reforms

How can importers behave honorably—or at least watch their backs? The model of aggressive enforcement is Levi Strauss & Co., which last March laid down tough standards of conduct to its 600 suppliers worldwide. After inspecting each one, the company ditched about 30 suppliers and exacted reforms from an additional 120. Levi Strauss also pulled out of Myanmar, citing that government's pervasive human-rights violations. And in Bangladesh, where factories routinely employ youngsters under the legal age of 14, the company struck a bargain to protect 40 children who would have been fired under its new rules. That could have impoverished entire families.

Instead Levi Strauss will help to educate the kids while local suppliers pay them regular wages until they turn 14.

Separating right from wrong overseas doesn't guarantee a company high praise at home. Just ask Nike, which ran afoul of cultural relativism late in 1992. Harper's magazine printed a U.S. labor activist's dissection of a pay stub for an Indonesian woman; she netted the equivalent of $37.46 a month for making sneakers. Later, an article in the Far Eastern Economic Review reported that Indonesians who make Nikes earn far more than most workers lucky enough to get factory jobs in the impoverished country. "Americans focus on wages paid, not what standard of living those wages relate to," says Nike's Dusty Kidd. But such reasoned argument misses the point. When it comes to social responsibility, it's not enough for a company to be right. It also has to convince its increasingly touchy customers.

Source: *Newsweek,* February 15, 1993. © 1993 Newsweek, Inc. All rights reserved. Reprinted by permission.

Questions

1. "Just because companies don't make a product themselves doesn't relieve them of all obligations." Do you agree? Explain.
2. *a.* Are the corporate critics trying to impose American values on the balance of the world? Explain.
   b. Is it morally acceptable to argue for human rights around the world, but morally unacceptable to endeavor to secure those rights via commercial (i.e., financial) pressure? Explain.
   c. Is this campaign to police international suppliers unfair to the average American consumer? Explain.
3. Should American companies refuse to do business in countries:
   a. Which do not practice democracy?
   b. Which routinely practice discrimination?
   c. Which tolerate or even encourage the abuse of children? Explain.
4. The Worldwatch Institute says that the richest one-fifth of the planet, the "consumer class," is ruining the planet because of excessive consumption that leads to environmental harm such as acid rain and greenhouse gases. Worldwatch recommends longer vacations in place of higher wages and curbs on advertising.[62]
   a. Do American consumer practices amount to abuse of the lesser developed world?
   b. Would lesser wages and longer vacations be a good prescription for what ails America and the world? Explain.
5. American culture clearly dominates the globe. Three hundred million Chinese watch the Super Bowl. In 1990, *Pretty Woman* was the leading movie in Germany, Sweden, Italy, Spain, Australia, and Denmark. CNN is watched in 122 countries.[63] Madonna and Michael Jackson are citizens of the world.
   a. Is America's cultural dominance in the best interest of all the citizens of the globe? Explain.
   b. Are American ads ("Drink Coca Cola") the key to a cohesive, peaceful global village? Explain.

ADDITIONAL CASES FOR DISCUSSION

CASE 1. THE FORD PINTO

Background

The Ford Pinto two-door sedan was introduced on September 11, 1970, as a 1971 model year vehicle. A three-door runabout version was introduced in February 1971, and the Pinto station wagon model was brought out on March 17, 1972. The design and location of the fuel tank in the Ford Pinto, and identically designed Mercury Bobcat, were unchanged until the 1977 model year, when revision was required to meet new federal safety standards for rear-impact collisions. By that time over 1.5 million two- and three-door Pinto sedans and nearly 35,000 Bobcat sedans had been sold. Because of the different configuration of the station wagon model, the fuel tank was mounted differently and, consequently, was less susceptible to damage from rear-end collisions.

The 1971–1976 Pinto fuel tank is constructed of sheet metal and is attached to the undercarriage of the vehicle by two metal straps with mounting brackets. The tank is located behind the rear axle. Crash tests at moderate speeds have shown that, on rear-impact collisions, the fuel tank is displaced forward until it impacts the differential housing on the rear axle and/or its mounting bolts or some other underbody structure.

The Cause for Concern

Public awareness and concern over the Pinto gas tank design grew rapidly following the 1977 publication of an article by Mark Dowie in *Mother Jones,* a West Coast magazine. This article was widely publicized in the press and reprinted in full in *Business and Society Review.* The article, based on interviews with a former Ford engineer, alleged that Ford Motor Company had rushed the Pinto into production in much less than the usual time in order to gain a competitive edge. According to the article, this meant that tooling began while the car was still in the product design stage. When early Ford crash tests allegedly revealed a serious design problem in the gas tank, the tooling was well underway. Rather than disrupt this process, at a loss of time and money, to incorporate more crashworthy designs which Ford allegedly had tested, the article stated that the decision was made to market the car as it was then designed.

The Dowie article further included calculations reportedly contained within an internal company memorandum showing that the costs of making the fuel tank safety improvement ($11 per car) were not equal to the savings in lives and injuries from the estimated proportion of crashes that would otherwise be expected to result in fires. These "benefits" were converted into dollar figures based on a value or cost of $200,000 per death and $67,000 per injury, figures which were obtained from [the National Highway Traffic Safety Administration] (NHTSA). In addition the article stated that Ford had lobbied for eight years to delay the federal standard for fuel tank safety that came into force with the 1977 model year. The article alleged that Ford's opposition to Federal Motor Vehicle Safety Standard 301 was stimulated by the costly retooling that would have been required when the Pinto was first scheduled for production. In response, a Ford official characterized the allegations made in the Dowie article as distorted and containing half-truths.

The NHTSA Investigation

Based on allegations that the design and location of the fuel tank in the Ford Pinto made it highly susceptible to damage on rear impact at low to moderate closing speeds, . . . NHTSA initiated a formal defect investigation on September 13, 1977. In response to the NHTSA's requests, Ford provided information concerning the number and nature of known incidents in which rear impact of a Pinto reportedly caused fuel tank damage, fuel system leakage, or fire. Based on this information and its own data sources, in May 1978 NHTSA reported that, in total, it was aware of 38 cases in which rear-end collisions of Pinto vehicles had resulted in fuel tank damage, fuel system leakage, and/or ensuing fire. These cases had resulted in a total of 27 fatalities sustained by Pinto occupants, of which one is reported to have resulted from impact injuries. In addition, 24 occupants of these Pinto vehicles had sustained nonfatal burn injuries.

In addition, the NHTSA Investigation Report stated that prior to initial introduction of the Pinto for sale Ford had performed four rear-impact barrier crash tests. However, as Ford reported, "none of the tested vehicles employed structure or fuel system designs representative of structures and fuel systems incorporated in the Pinto as introduced in September 1970." These tests were conducted from May through November 1969.

Following initial introduction of the Pinto for sale, Ford continued with a program of rear-impact tests on Pintos which included assessment of post-impact conditions of the fuel tank and/or filler pipe. Reports of 55 such tests were provided to NHTSA, including tests of Mercury Bobcats. Three items developed a history of consistent results of concern at impact speeds as low as 21.5 miles per hour with a fixed barrier: (1) the fuel tank was punctured by contact with the differential housing or some other underbody structure; (2) the fuel filler neck was pulled out of the tank; and (3) structural and/or sheet metal damage was sufficient to jam one, or both, of the passenger doors closed. Review of the test reports in question suggested to the NHTSA investigators that Ford had studied several alternative solutions to the numerous instances in which fuel tank deformation, damage, or leakage occurred during or after impact.

The NHTSA investigation concluded that the fuel tank and filler pipe assembly installed in the 1971–1976 Ford Pinto is subject to damage which results in fuel spillage and fire potential in rear-impact collisions by other vehicles at moderate closing speeds. Further, examination by NHTSA of the product liability actions filed against Ford and other codefendants involving rear impact of Pintos with fuel tank damage/fuel leakage/fire occurrences, showed that at that time nine cases had been completed. Of these, the plaintiffs had been compensated in eight cases, either by jury awards or out-of-court settlements.

Following this initial determination that a defect existed and less than a week before a scheduled NHTSA public hearing on the Pinto fuel tank problem, Ford agreed to a voluntary recall.

The Cost of Dying in a Pinto

Printed below are figures from a Ford Motor Company internal memorandum on the benefits and costs of an $11 safety improvement which would have made the Pinto less likely to burn. The memorandum purports to "prove" that the improvement is not cost effective:

Benefits
   Savings: 180 burn deaths, 180 serious burn injuries, 2,100 burned vehicles.
   Unit cost: $200,000 per death; $67,000 per injury; $700 per vehicle.
   Total benefit: 180 × ($200,000) + 180 × ($67,000) + 2,100 × ($700) = **$49.5 million.**

Costs
   Sales: 11 million cars, 1.5 million light trucks.
   Unit cost: $11 per car, $11 per truck.
   Total cost: 11,000,000 × ($11) + 1,500,000 × ($11) = **$137 million.**

Source: Mark Dowie, "How Ford Put Two Million Firetraps on Wheels," *Business and Society Review* 23 (Fall 1977), pp. 46, 51. © Mark Dowie. Originally published in *Mother Jones* magazine. Reprinted with permission.

Criminal Charges

On September 12, 1978, following an accident involving the burning and death of three young women in a Pinto, a county grand jury in Indiana indicted Ford Motor Company on three counts of reckless homicide and one count of criminal recklessness. The charge of reckless homicide was brought under a 1977 revision of the Indiana Penal Code that allows a corporation to be treated as a person for the purposes of bringing criminal charges. On March 13, 1980, more than two months after the trial began, the jury found Ford not guilty.

Source: Library of Congress Congressional Research Service. Background material for hearings on H. R. 7040, Subcommittee on Crime of the Committee on the Judiciary, House of Representatives, 96th Congress, 2nd session, May 1980.

Was Ford Liable under Civil Law?   Note that Ford has argued throughout the Pinto episode that, based on government data, the Pinto was less susceptible to fires from rear-end collisions than the average car on the road. The Pinto conformed to all federal safety standards at the time. Fuel tank standards for rear-end collisions were not established until 1977.

The many civil suits arising from Pinto fires have resulted in a number of large judgments and settlements against Ford. For example, the families of two Pennsylvania children killed in a Pinto fire received, according to the families' attorney, more than $2 million in an out-of-court settlement. But the most striking such trial was that of Richard Grimshaw, who received a jury verdict of $127.8 million. Grimshaw was subjected to more than 60 operations. Among other injuries he sustained the loss of his nose, left ear, and four fingers. The California Fourth Circuit Court of Appeals upheld the Grimshaw decisions against Ford with a reduced damages total of $6.3 million.

Was Ford Liable under Criminal Law?   Of course, the most publicized and, in terms of legal and social policy, far-reaching Pinto trial was the Indiana criminal prosecution mentioned in the Library of Congress study. A loss in the Indiana case presumably would have opened Ford to tens of millions of dollars in punitive damage claims in the many undecided Pinto civil suits. Despite Ford's victory, some observers think the case is demonstrative of an appropriate new zeal for holding corporations and their executives criminally accountable for their behaviors. An excerpt from an editorial appearing in *The Nation* reflects that sentiment.

> Ford got off this time—perhaps as a result of the judge's controversial decision to exclude on technical grounds evidence in the form of Ford internal documents.
>
> Despite a sympathetic judge and a defense war chest of a reported $3 million (the budget of the small-town prosecutor in Winamac, Indiana, was $20,000), Ford very nearly lost the case. The jury deliberated for four days before reaching a decision.[64]

The Pinto—20 Years Later.   A 1991 law review article challenges the conventional reading of Ford as a villain in the Pinto case. Walter Olson summarized that article in a *Wall Street Journal* commentary:

Remarkably, even the affair of the "exploding" Ford Pinto—universally hailed as the acme of product liability success—is starting to look like hype . . . UCLA law professor Gary Schwartz demolishes "the myth of the Pinto case." Actual deaths in Pinto fires have come in at a known 27, not the expected thousand or more. More startling, Mr. Schwartz shows that everyone's perceived ideas about the fabled "smoking gun" memo are false. The actual memo did not pertain to Pintos, or even Ford products, but to American cars in general; it dealt with rollovers, not rear-end collisions; it did not contemplate the matter of tort liability at all, let alone accept it as cheaper than a design change; it assigned a value to human life because federal regulators, for whose eyes it was meant, themselves employed that concept in their deliberations; and the value it used was one that they, the regulators, had set forth in documents.

In retrospect, Mr. Schwartz writes, the Pinto's safety record appears to have been very typical of its time and class.[65]

Questions

1. Defend the use by automakers and the government of seemingly callous cost/benefit analyses that sometimes balance the cost of safety improvements versus the cost of deaths and injuries.
2. What organizational characteristics contribute to the occurrence of arguably regrettable decisions like those associated with the Pinto?
3. Would an episode like that of the Pinto be less likely to transpire in a socialist state? Explain.
4. If the various allegations against Ford proved to be true, would you decline to work for the organization? Put another way, what dollar sum would be required for you to accept employment with Ford in a job commensurate with your interests and skills? Explain.
5. Is criminal prosecution a sensible, desirable approach to the Pinto case? Explain.
6. If the choice were yours, would you award Richard Grimshaw the original $127.8 million, the appeals court decision of $6.3 million, or some lesser amount? Explain.
7. Are large civil penalties effective in discouraging future wrongdoing? Explain.
8. Professor Terrence Kiely argues for personal, criminal liability for executives involved in cases like the Pinto: "The only way we're going to get quality products as consumers is to make corporate executives feel personally responsible for their decisions. The aim is to get them to worry and think about more than just the bottom line."[66] Comment.
9. Ford had argued that attempting to apply the criminal law in cases like the Pinto "would wipe out the basic distinction between civil wrongs and criminal offenses."[67] What did Ford mean?

CASE 2. FIRMS TRY HARDER, BUT OFTEN FAIL, TO HELP WORKERS COPE WITH ELDER-CARE PROBLEMS

Sue Shellenbarger

Just over the horizon looms a demographic time bomb for the nation's employers, and nobody has figured out yet how to defuse it.

If you were to draw a picture of this bomb, stenciled on its side would be two words: Elder Care.

As the workforce ages and more employees begin caring for elderly parents and in-laws, research shows these caretakers experience stress and productivity losses on the job. But only 43% of 1,026 employers surveyed in 1992 by Hewitt Associates, Lincolnshire, Ill., benefits consultants, offered elder-care benefits, compared with 74% offering some kind of child-care aid. A 1992 survey of 1,004 employers by the Society for Human Resource Management, Alexandria, Va., showed that two-thirds were not at all involved in elder-care services.

"One of the most significant reasons companies are not moving faster on elder care is that they just

don't know what to do," says Dana Friedman, co-president of the Families and Work Institute, a non-profit New York research and consulting concern . . .

Many experts believe the worries and distractions caused by elder care can be more damaging in the workplace than child-care problems. Roughly one-third of employed caregivers live more than 100 miles from their elders. Worse yet, elders' needs often erupt as crises, and they can be complex and emotionally harrowing.

When Robert Plummer's phone rang at 1 A.M. last month in his home near Chicago, he awoke to learn that his 80-year-old father-in-law had had a stroke in his home 250 miles away in Columbus, Ind. Unable to use his right side, the father-in-law had been trying for five hours to get to the phone. After persuading his reluctant relative to call an ambulance and ask a

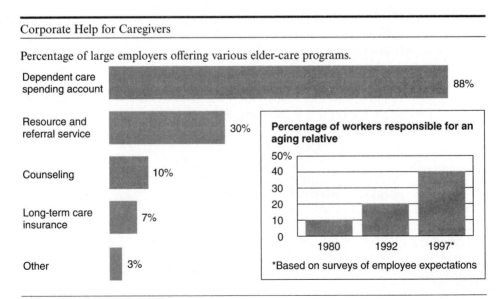

Corporate Help for Caregivers

Percentage of large employers offering various elder-care programs.

Dependent care spending account — 88%
Resource and referral service — 30%
Counseling — 10%
Long-term care insurance — 7%
Other — 3%

Percentage of workers responsible for an aging relative

1980 — 10
1992 — 20
1997* — 40

*Based on surveys of employee expectations

Source: Hewitt Associates, Lincolnshire, Ill.

neighbor to care for his bedridden mother-in-law, Mr. Plummer and his wife drove to Columbus.

Though his father-in-law recovered, his health problems have meant missed time from work for Mr. Plummer, who administers American Telephone & Telegraph Co.'s Midwestern employee-volunteerism efforts, and his wife, a teacher. Over the years, Mr. Plummer's role has ranged from helping his father-in-law cope with chest pain to helping with estate planning, signing up for home health aides and persuading him to enroll in Meals on Wheels. The role of a caregiver for the elderly, he says, is costly and "awfully stressful."

In caring for his father-in-law, Mr. Plummer says he was greatly helped by AT&T's resource and referral service, a telephone network offering information about available elder-care services. And despite his problems, he has been more fortunate than many of his generation. In a 1992 study of 305 employed caregivers of the elderly by the Families and Work Institute and the Older Women's League, Washington, D.C., almost one-fourth of those interviewed changed their employment drastically as a result of their eldercare responsibilities, including changing jobs, quitting or taking several part-time jobs.

Caregivers typically are absent $1\frac{1}{2}$ times more often for family reasons than average, and productivity losses from elder care cost employers about $2,500 per year per caregiving employee, estimates Andrew Scharlach, a professor of aging at the University of California at Berkeley.

Yet many of employers' best-intentioned efforts to ease elder-care burdens have fallen flat. An offer by Remington Products Co. to pay half the cost of re-

spite care for elderly relatives to give employees a break was cited as "a model initiative" in a 1991 Families and Work Institute publication. But only a few employees signed up and the Bridgeport, Conn., electric-shaver maker discontinued the program after about a year. Many employees apparently chose to use their own families as a backup, rather than pay half of the $10 to $15 an hour charged by visiting nurses.

"It's a failed example" people can learn from, Ms. Friedman says . . .

Intergenerational Center

Though nearly 80% of companies start elder-care programs partly as an outgrowth of child-care assistance, according to a 1992 study by the Conference Board, a New York business-research group, most child-care ideas don't transplant well as elder-care solutions. For example, Stride Rite Corp., Cambridge, Mass., and Lancaster Laboratories Inc., Lancaster, Pa., began offering intergenerational on-site day care in recent years but have seen little employee demand for the elder-care slots. "Adult day care is still a fairly new concept," says Carol Miller, executive vice president, human resources, for Lancaster. Both companies predict greater use of elder-care facilities in the future.

Others are more skeptical. "My mom doesn't want to go to work with me, and I don't suppose very many others do either," says the University of California's Mr. Scharlach.

Questions

1. *a.* What benefits might businesses derive from being involved in elder care?
   b. Should they do so? Explain.
2. *a.* Have you given thought to caring for your elders as they and you age? Explain.
   b. In your opinion, are younger people responsible for the welfare and comfort of aging people? Explain.
3. Assume you are the CEO of a major corporation and you determine that your company can only afford to offer either a child-care program or an elder-care program, but not both. Which would you choose? Explain.

CHAPTER QUESTIONS

1. *a.* In general, do you think employers are more concerned with profits or with delivering quality goods and services? Explain.
   b. Which *should* they be more concerned about? Explain.
   c. Are you most concerned about receiving a quality education or earning a degree? Explain.

2. Scholar Denis Goulet argued that we will find no facile resolution to the conflict between the values of a just society and the sharply opposing values of successful corporations.
   a. Do you agree that the values of a just society oppose those of successful corporations? Explain.
   b. Can a solution be found? Explain.

3. In November 1980, a fire in the Las Vegas MGM Grand Hotel resulted in 84 deaths and 500 injuries. Prior to the fire, Las Vegas fire chief Roy Parrish said fire officials and building inspectors had met with hotel officials to urge the expansion of the sprinkler system, even though the change was not required under existing law. The hotel did not undertake the expansion. (At the time of the fire, sprinklers were installed in the basement and the 1st and 26th floors.)
   a. In this case, is the legal standard also the proper ethical standard? Explain.
   b. Safety is purchased. Is the failure to make that purchase unethical? Explain.
   c. How can you decide when the cost of doing right is too high?

4. In criticizing General Motors, Ralph Nader is reported to have said:

   > Someday we'll have a legal system that will criminally indict the president of General Motors for these outrageous crimes. But not as long as this country is populated by people who fritter away their citizenship by watching TV, playing bridge and Mah-Jongg, and just generally being slobs.[68]

   a. Is the citizenry generally unconcerned about unethical corporate conduct? Explain.
   b. To the extent that corporations engage in misdeeds, does the fault really lie with the corporate community or with society at large? Explain.

5. Michael Kinsley, a senior editor of *New Republic,* expresses some serious reservations about corporate social responsibility:

   > In particular, I am not impressed by corporate charity and cultural benefaction, which amount to executives playing Medici with other people's money. You wouldn't know, from the lavish parties corporate officers throw for themselves whenever they fund an art exhibit or a PBS series, that it's not costing them a penny. The shareholders, who aren't invited, pick up the tab.[69]

   Comment on Kinsley's statement.

6. Should corporate chief executive officers submit to press conferences on a regular basis? Explain.

7. Must the corporation adjust to changing societal sentiments (social responsibility), or is the future health of the nation dependent on the corporate community manifesting the strength to adhere to traditional free market principles? Explain.

8. Is the ethical climate of business improving or declining? Explain.

9. In 1992, the rapper Ice-T released a song entitled "Cop Killer" as part of his album, "Body Count." President Bush labeled the rap "sick" as a glorification of killing law enforcement officers. Some music retail chains removed "Body Count" from their shelves. However, Time Warner continued to distribute the album. Ice-T eventually decided to remove "Cop Killer" from the album.
   a. Was Time Warner socially irresponsible in its decision to market the album while it included the "Cop Killer" tune?
   b. Defend Time Warner.
   c. Assume the rap had said "fag killer," or "black killer," or "Jew killer," or "woman killer." Explain what you would have done had you been in charge of Time Warner and Ice-T included one of those raps on his album.
   d. Rap and heavy metal music often degrade women and glorify sexual violence. Do you decline to purchase music of that character? Explain.

10. The Institute for Transportation and Policy Development (a nonprofit organization addressing Third World needs) argues for the use of bicycles rather than autos in the Third World:

    > The oil and automobile companies, having already made Americans auto-dependent, are targeting Asia, Latin America, and Africa for future growth, aided by large loans from the World

Bank and other international funding sources. Many developing countries, by repeating our mistakes, are deep in debt and often spend half of their foreign exchange earnings to pay for oil and cars that fail to meet the basic mobility needs of the majority.[70]

a. Have the oil and auto companies *made* Americans auto-dependent? Explain.

b. Should the socially responsible auto or oil company discourage the purchase of autos in Third World nations? Explain.

c. On balance, if we could somehow turn back the technology clock, would the United States be a better place to live had we not so thoroughly embraced the automobile to meet our transportation needs? Explain.

11. a. Are you a "socially conscious" consumer in the sense that your buying habits are influenced by your perception of a firm's stance on social issues?

b. Should you be? Explain.

c. If we were able to successfully rate firms according to a social responsibility index, and if most or all Americans were guided in their buying, investing, and employment decisions by that index, would ours be a better society? Explain.

12. You are the sole owner of a neighborhood drugstore that stocks various brands of toothpaste. Assume that scientific testing has established that one brand is clearly superior to all others in preventing tooth decay.

a. Would you remove from the shelves all brands except the one judged best in decay prevention? Explain.

b. What alternative measures could you take?

c. Should the toothpaste manufacturers be required to reveal all available data regarding the effectiveness of their products? Explain.

13. IBP, the world's largest fresh beef and pork processor, brought 1,300 jobs and a $23 million payroll to the town of Columbus Junction, Iowa (population 1,400), when it reopened and expanded a Rath Packing Co. plant. The plant "saved" the local economy. Because the company cannot meet its labor needs locally, IBP recruits in "the nation's most desperate pockets of unemployment."[71] Many of those people come to Columbus Junction with little in the way of resources. (IBP's blue-collar wages begin at $6 per hour.) The result was social upheaval for the com-

munity. The police chief estimates that crime has risen 400 percent since IBP arrived. In the fall of 1989 alone, junior high and high school pupil turnover was 25 percent. Many of the new recruits and their children cannot speak English.[72]

a. What responsibility, if any, does IBP have to help Columbus Junction deal with its new circumstances? Explain.

b. Higher wages would attract additional local employees. Should IBP be expected to increase its wage scale in order to reduce its reliance on recruiting the urban unemployed? Explain.

c. Defend IBP.

14. In 1987, 79 percent of all worldwide film and television exports originated in the United States; in 1991, European TV productions accounted for just 20,000 hours of the total 125,000 hours of airtime of all European TV stations. About three-quarters of all computer programs in the world operate by English commands.[73]

a. Is it good for the world that America dominates the globe's popular culture?

b. Is it good for America?

c. Are we guilty of "cultural imperialism?" Explain.

15. Approximately $10 million is expended annually for alcohol ads in college newspapers. Many millions more are expended in other youth-oriented publications such as *National Lampoon* and *Rolling Stone.* The beer industry sponsors many campus athletic contests. And brewers have established promotional relationships with rock bands. Is beer and liquor advertising directed to the youth market unethical? Explain.

16. Many jurisdictions curb alcoholic beverage advertising. Quebec forbids endorsements by famous personalities. Ecuador has banned such ads prior to 9 P.M. Finland forbids all alcohol ads. Even news pictures displaying bottle labels are not allowed. Advertising of hard liquor is forbidden on American TV. Should the United States banish all advertising of alcoholic beverages?[74] Explain.

17. Professor Albert Huebner decries American exports of tobacco to the Third World:

As efforts to expose and to stop the irresponsible promotion of bottle feeding [of babies] have grown, a new invasion of many of the same countries has begun. Transnational tobacco companies are vigorously stepping up sales efforts in the Third World, which is now seen as the major growth area for their products. These efforts are likely to be more intensive, more successful in achieving their goal, and more disastrous for the health of people in the countries involved than the breast-to-bottle campaign.[75]

a. Is the promotion and sale of tobacco products in the Third World nations socially irresponsible behavior? Explain.

b. Should the U.S. government attempt to curb such promotion and sales? Explain.

18. In 1992, Congress passed a bill that prevented Hornell Brewing Co. from using the brand name Crazy Horse (a Sioux Indian chief) for one of its malt liquors. Native Americans and others objected to the brand name as offensive to Indian dignity and history and argued that the liquor was targeted to Native Americans. How would you have voted on the bill? Explain.

19. Former General Motors vice president John Z. DeLorean wrote in his book, *On a Clear Day You Can See General Motorstore:*

> It seemed to me then, and still does now, that the system of American business often produces wrong, immoral, and irresponsible decisions, even though the personal morality of the people running the business is often above reproach. The system has a different morality as a group than the people do as individuals, which permits it willfully to produce ineffective or dangerous products, deal dictatorially and often unfairly with suppliers, pay bribes for business, abrogate the rights of employment, or tamper with the democratic process of government through illegal political contributions.[76]

a. How can the corporate "group" possess values at odds with those of the individual managers?

b. Is DeLorean merely offering a convenient rationalization for corporate misdeeds? Explain.

c. Realistically, can one expect to preserve individual values when employed in a corporate group? Explain.

20. Do you agree or disagree with the following statements? Explain.

a. "Social responsibility is good business only if it is also good public relations and/or preempts government interference."

b. "The social responsibility debate is the result of the attempt of liberal intellectuals to make a moral issue of business behavior."

c. "'Profit' is really a somewhat ineffective measure of business's social effectiveness."

d. "The social responsibility of business is to 'stick to business.'"[77]

21. U.S. consumers are in the midst of a "circle of poison." Pesticides that are banned in this country are shipped abroad where they are used in fruit and vegetable production. That "poisoned" food is then exported to the United States. Key members of Congress indicated in 1990 that they intend to stop that practice by barring the export of those pesticides. Critics labeled that proposed legislation "environmental imperialism" and argued that it would not work, in any case.[78]

a. What do the critics mean by "environmental imperialism"?

b. Why would a U.S. ban on such exports not solve the problem?

c. Should the pesticide makers voluntarily decline to export those products? Explain.

22. Increasingly, we are treating education as a product and students as consumers. Do you see any problems in that trend? Explain.

23. Boycotts usually do not work, but they can pose a major strategic dilemma for corporate America. In 1992, an estimated 100 boycotts were underway nationwide, including those against General Electric (for making nuclear weapons), Anheuser Busch (for keeping whales in captivity in its theme parks), and Coca-Cola (for investing in South Africa).[79]

In 1990, antiabortion activists protested Dayton-Hudson's annual grant ($18,000) to Planned Parenthood, and the department store chain decided to discontinue the grant.

a. Can you deduce what happened next?

b. How would you have handled the situation?

NOTES

1. "The *Fortune* 500," *Fortune* 129, no. 8 (April 8, 1994), pp. 220 and 254.

2. "The Global Giants," *The Wall Street Journal,* September 24, 1993, p. R25.

3. Rick Tetzeli, "How Countries Stack Up with Companies," *Fortune* 125, no. 8 (April 20, 1992), p. 14.

4. Bureau of Census. Unpublished data, 1989.

5. Peter Asch, *Industrial Organization and Antitrust Policy* (New York: John Wiley & Sons, 1983), p. 162.

6. Charles Reich, *The Greening of America* (New York: Bantam Books, 1970), pp. 7–8.

7. David Broder, "Wrigley Field, an Anchor in an Insecure World," *Des Moines Register,* June 10, 1987, p. 7A.

8. "Top Ten PAC Spenders," *Newsweek,* May 24, 1993, p. 6.

9. Tom Morganthau, "Checkbook Politics," *Newsweek,* April 2, 1990, p. 32.

10. Associated Press, "Incumbents Got 70% of PAC Money," *Waterloo Courier,* April 30, 1992, p. C2.

11. Glenn Simpson, "Study: PAC Spending Jumps 18% in 1992," *Roll Call,* June 3, 1993, p. 1.

12. Jill Abramson and Brooks Jackson, "Debate over PAC Money Hits Close to Home as Lawmakers Tackle Campaign-Finance Bill," *The Wall Street Journal,* March 7, 1990, p. A20.

13. "Inside Congress," *Congressional Quarterly,* December 11, 1993, p. 3,357.

14. Robert Samuelson, "The Campaign Reform Fraud," *Newsweek,* July 13, 1987, p. 43.

15. Evan Thomas, "Peddling Influence," *Time,* March 3, 1986, pp. 26–27.

16. Jeffrey Birnbaum and John Harwood, "Campaign-Finance, Lobbying Overhaul Picks Up Steam after Years of Hot Air," *The Wall Street Journal,* May 7, 1993, p. A4.

17. Thomas, "Peddling Influence," pp. 26, 33.

18. Richard N. Goodwin, "PACs Gobbling Up Congress," *Waterloo Courier,* December 17, 1985, p. A4.

19. Editorial, "Triumph of Hucksterism," *Des Moines Register,* May 29, 1989, p. 8A.

20. Nancy Ramsey, "How Business Can Help the Schools," *Fortune* 126, no. 8 (November 16, 1992), p. 14.

21. Reich, *Greening of America,* pp. 141–42.

22. Colleen Cordes, "Debate Flares over Growing Pressures on Academia for Ties with Industry," *The Chronicle of Higher Education,* September 16, 1992, p. A26.

23. Jonathan Yardley, "Making Money on Malcom X," *Des Moines Register,* November 22, 1992, p. 1C.

24. *Business Week,* August 31, 1987, p. 48.

25. Associated Press, "Barcelona Will Be Remembered as Games the Professionals Took Over," *Waterloo Courier,* August 10, 1992, p. B3.

26. Betsy Morris, "As a Favored Pastime, Shopping Ranks High with Most Americans," *The Wall Street Journal,* July 30, 1987, pp. 1, 13.

27. Todd Barrett, "Has Sneaker Madness Gone Too Far?" *Newsweek,* December 18, 1989, p. 51.

28. Carol Loomis, "Dinosaurs?" *Fortune,* May 3, 1993, p. 36.

29. Jolie Solomon, "The Fall of the Dinosaurs," *Newsweek,* February 8, 1993, p. 42.

30. Ibid., p. 43.

31. Loomis, "Dinosaurs?" p. 36.

32. Herman Kahn, "Self-Indulgence, Survival, and Space," *The Futurist,* October 1980, pp. 10–11.

33. Thomas Griffith, "Me First," *The Atlantic,* July 1980, p. 20.

34. *University of Iowa Spectator,* March 1980, p. 4.

35. Walter Shapiro, "Why We've Failed to Ruin Thanksgiving," *Time,* November 27, 1989, p. 94.

36. Peter Wynn, *Apples, History, Folklore, Horticulture, and Gastronomy,* as reported by Joanee Will for the *Chicago Tribune* and reprinted in the *Lexington Leader,* October 1, 1980, p. D-1.

37. "For What Shall It Profit a Man . . . ?" *Business Week,* July 6, 1987, p. 104.

38. Myron Magnet, "The Money Society," *Fortune,* July 6, 1987, p. 26.

39. Forum, "Is There Virtue in Profit?" *Harper's Magazine,* December 1986, pp. 37, 42.

40. Ted Peters, "The Future of Religion in a Post-Industrial Society," *The Futurist,* October 1980, pp. 20, 22.

41. Associated Press, "Poll: Youths Are Tuning Out the Community," *Des Moines Register,* November 21, 1989, p. 4A.

42. Ann de Rouffignac, "School Contests Help Concerns Promote Brands," *The Wall Street Journal,* July 3, 1992, p. B1.

43. Richard Holman, "Book Captures Japan's New Mood," *The Wall Street Journal,* May 6, 1993, p. A11.

44. "More Leisure in an Increasingly Electronic Society," *Business Week,* September 3, 1979, pp. 208, 212.

45. Steven N. Brenner and Earl A. Molander, "Is the Ethics of Business Changing?" *Harvard Business Review* 55, no. 1 (January–February 1977), pp. 57, 59.

46. Ibid., p. 68.

47. Kevin Gudridge and John Byrne, "A Kinder, Gentler Generation of Executives?" *Business Week,* April 23, 1990, p. 86.

48. Robert Kuttner, "U.S. Business Isn't About to Be Society's Savior," *Business Week,* November 6, 1989, p. 29.

49. Keith Davis and Robert L. Blomstrom, *Business and Society: Environment and Responsibility,* 3rd ed. (New York: McGraw-Hill, 1975), p. 6.

50. Kenneth R. Andrews, *The Concept of Corporate Strategy* (Homewood, IL: Dow Jones-Irwin, 1971), p. 120.

51. Milton Friedman, *Capitalism and Freedom* (Chicago: University of Chicago Press, 1962), p. 133.

52. Karen Springen and Annetta Miller, "Doing the Right Thing," *Newsweek,* January 7, 1991, p. 42.

53. Jennifer Laabs, "Ben & Jerry's Caring Capitalism," *Personnel Journal* 71, no. 11 (November 1992), pp. 50, 55.

54. See Phillip I. Cochran and Robert Wood, "Corporate Responsibility and Financial Performance," *Academy of Management Journal* 27, no. 1 (March 1984), p. 42, for an excellent study of the issue and a survey of previous research.

55. For a summary of some of these studies, see Alfred A. Marcus, Philip Bromiley, and Robert Goodman, "Preventing Corporate Crises: Stock Market Losses as a Deterrent to the Production of Hazardous Products," *Columbia Journal of World Business* 22, no. 1 (Spring 1987), p. 33.

56. Springen and Miller, "Doing the Right Thing," pp. 42, 43.

57. Kevin Goldman, "Kids and Camels," *The Wall Street Journal,* February 5, 1993, p. B6.

58. Glenn Ruffenach, "Study Says Teen-Agers' Smoking Habits Seem to be Linked to Heavy Advertising," *The Wall Street Journal,* March 13, 1992, p. B3.

59. *The Washington Post,* "Reynolds Snuffs Ad Campaign," *Des Moines Register,* January 20, 1990, p. 5S.

60. Editorial, "Targeting 'Virile Females,'" *Des Moines Register,* March 5, 1990, p. 4A.

61. "Kicking Butts Off Campus," *Time,* June 4, 1990, p. 71.

62. Associated Press, "Study: Consumerism, Malls Ruining Planet," *Des Moines Register,* July 26, 1992, p. 2A.

63. Associated Press, "Americanizing the World: Good? Bad? Inevitable?" *Waterloo Courier,* March 10, 1992, p. A1.

64. *The Nation,* March 29, 1980, pp. 356–57.

65. Walter Olson, "The Most Dangerous Vehicle on the Road," *The Wall Street Journal,* February 9, 1993, p. A14.

66. Andy Pasztor, "Pinto Criminal Trial of Ford Motor Company Opens Up Broad Issues," *The Wall Street Journal,* January 4, 1980, pp. 1, 23.

67. Ibid.

68. Charles McCarry, *Citizen Nader* (New York: Saturday Review Press, 1972), p. 301.

69. Michael Kinsley, "Companies as Citizens: Should They Have a Conscience?" *The Wall Street Journal,* February 19, 1987, p. 29.

70. Michael Replogle, Fund-Raising Letter for Institute for Transportation and Policy Development, 1990.

71. Dennis Farney, "A Town in Iowa Finds Big New Packing Plant Destroys Its Old Calm," *The Wall Street Journal,* April 3, 1990, A1.

72. Ibid.

73. Reinhold Wagnleitner, quoted in "The Controversy about Popular Culture," *The American Enterprise* 3, no. 3 (May–June 1992), pp. 72, 76.

74. Michael Jacobson, Robert Atkins, and George Hochers, "Booze Merchants Cheer On Teenage Drinking," *Business and Society Review,* no. 46 (Summer 1983), p. 46.

75. Albert Huebner, "Tobacco's Lucrative Third World Invasion," *Business and Society Review,* no. 35 (Fall 1980), p. 49.

76. John Z. DeLorean with J. Patrick Wright, "Bottom-Line Fever at General Motors" (excerpted from *On a Clear Day You Can See General Motors*), *The Washington Monthly,* January 1980, pp. 26–27.

77. Brenner and Molander, "Ethics of Business," p. 68.

78. David Hess, "Ban Sought on Pesticides Sold to Foreign Growers," *Des Moines Register,* April 29, 1990, p. 4A.

79. Marcus Mabry, "Do Boycotts Work?" *Newsweek,* July 6, 1992, p. 58.

PART

II

INTRODUCTION TO LAW

—————•—————

4

THE AMERICAN LEGAL SYSTEM

●

INTRODUCTION/JUSTICE

Presumably, we can agree that some business practices have unfavorable consequences for society. Thus, the issue becomes: What should be done, if anything, to change those consequences? The fundamental options in the United States have been three-fold: let the market "regulate" the behavior; leave the problem to the individual decision maker's own ethical dictates; or pass a law. Market regulation was discussed in Chapter 1. Self-regulation through ethics was explored in Chapters 2 and 3. This chapter, then, begins the discussion of the legal regulation of business with a brief outline of the American legal system and how it functions.

This chapter will also introduce a fourth alternative for addressing business/society conflicts. This alternative looks at conflict resolution processes other than those resorting to the legal system, such as negotiation, mediation, and arbitration. Although these alternatives are not new, they have been receiving much more attention in recent years.

Before turning to our detailed examination of the technical dimensions of the law, we should remind ourselves of the central purpose of our legal system—the pursuit of justice. As you read this chapter, ask yourself repeatedly: "Does this rule (this procedure, this case) contribute to the search for justice? While not our primary concern, criminal law is a vivid vehicle for introducing the notion of justice. In a 1993 national survey of 2,512 adult Americans, 87 percent said that our criminal justice system does not treat people equally. Among those who doubt the fairness of the system, 93 percent believe that rich people receive special treatment, while 61 percent say minorities aren't treated fairly and 77 percent say the same of poor people. Eighty-five percent of whites and 64 percent of black and Hispanic-Americans have a "positive attitude" toward the police. Overall, 57 percent expressed faith in the criminal justice system.[1]

Of course, the issue of justice was at the forefront of our thoughts in 1992–93 with the Rodney King beating, the resulting police officers' trials, and the devastating riot in South Central Los Angeles. King, a black man, was struck more than 50 times by police officers' batons during his arrest after a high-speed chase in Los Angeles. The beating happened to be recorded on videotape by a civilian onlooker. The officers' acquittal in their initial trial led to the April 1992 riot where 52 people were killed, perhaps 2,300 were injured, and property damage was estimated at $1 billion.

The confusion mounted when two black men accused of attacking truck driver Reginald Denny (a white man) during the LA riots were acquitted of the most serious charges against them. Prosecutors used television videotape of the Denny beating to link the suspects to the crimes. The jury found the suspects guilty of some mayhem and assault charges but did not find sufficient evidence of attempted murder or aggravated mayhem, both of which required evidence of "specific intent."

The following reading recounts the second of the King trials and raises some of the cultural issues (e.g., racism and poverty) and procedural problems (such as double jeopardy and where a trial should be heard and by whom) that influence the course of justice.

VERDICT IN KING CASE OWES MUCH TO LESSONS OF STATE-COURT TRIAL

Amy Stevens

The convictions of two of four Los Angeles police officers for violating the civil rights of a black motorist confirm what had seemed obvious in America's living rooms: Rodney King didn't deserve to be beaten senseless.

The government's victory—greeted with relief around the country—vindicated federal prosecutors' strategy of putting the defendants on trial again . . .

But the federal prosecution, while widely praised, also raises questions about the role of the federal government in holding people accountable a second time, essentially for the same offense.

The highly charged King case, involving white defendants, a black victim and broad issues of racial justice, was largely a repeat of the Simi Valley trial of the officers last year on state assault-related charges. In that case, a suburban jury that included no blacks acquitted three of the policemen and failed to reach a verdict on the fourth, setting off the worst urban riots of the century.

In the federal case, a Los Angeles jury, which included two blacks and a Hispanic, announced . . .

that Officer Laurence Powell, who had struck most of the blows during the March 1991 incident, was guilty of violating Mr. King's constitutional right to be free from an arrest made with "unreasonable force." Sgt. Stacey Koon, the officer in charge at the scene, was convicted of permitting the civil-rights violation to occur.

Appeal Expected

But the jury determined that the government hadn't adequately proved its charges against Timothy Wind, a rookie at the time of the incident who had been under the supervision of both the convicted defendants. Also acquitted was Theodore Briseno, who had stomped on Mr. King but had also moved to block one of Mr. Powell's blows.

* * * * *

From the start, federal prosecutors were faced with a more difficult legal case than were their state-court predecessors. They were required to prove both that the policemen used too much force in arresting Mr. King, and that it was their conscious objective to do so. Prosecutors in the state trial couldn't prove the first element, and didn't have to prove the second.

But if their case was made tougher by that added "intent" requirement, U.S. prosecutors had the significant strategic edge of having seen a run-through. In particular, they benefited from knowing that the notorious 81-second video-

tape of Mr. King's beating had been perceived as ambiguous in places by the first jury, and that more evidence would be needed to translate into legal terms what the tape said in visceral terms. Indeed, two jurors speaking anonymously on television over the weekend said the videotape within its new context was a crucial piece of evidence.

While typically lauding the result of the retrial, some legal commentators question the fairness of giving prosecutors that second chance. "A retrial like this provides a tremendous opportunity to learn from your mistakes," says Alan Dershowitz, a Harvard law professor and criminal-defense lawyer. "There's always going to be a lingering suspicion that the prosecutors' case this time was improved by the rehearsal in the state case . . . and there's something about that that's inconsistent with the spirit of the constitutional protection against double jeopardy."

Indeed, the federal government's decision to come into the King case after the furor over the results in the state trial was hotly debated among legal scholars because of the double-jeopardy implications. Although the Constitution says that no person shall "be subject for the same offense to be twice put in jeopardy of life or limb," the Supreme Court ruled in 1959 that the federal government can try a person for conduct that didn't result in a conviction in state court. The theory was that the state and federal governments are "separate sovereigns," entitled to prosecute their own crimes in their own courts.

Source: *The Wall Street Journal,* April 19, 1993, p. A1. Adapted with permission of *The Wall Street Journal,* © 1993 Dow Jones & Company, Inc. All Rights Reserved Worldwide.

Afterword

In a May 1994 civil injury trial, Mr. King was awarded more than $3.8 million in damages from the City of Los Angeles for his actual financial losses including medical expenses, suffering, and potential lifetime earnings. Then in June 1994 the jury rejected King's plea for punitive (penalty) damages from the police officers themselves. At the same time, Officers Koon and Powell, serving 30-month terms for their role in the beatings, are appealing their convictions.

Questions

1. *a.* Was justice achieved in the second Rodney King/police officers' trial? Explain.
   b. Should Mr. King receive compensatory and punitive damages? Explain.
2. In an editorial subsequent to the second King verdict, *The Wall Street Journal* commented that the trials had become "national melodramas of justice" but that what the populace really yearns for is "to be safe in their homes and neighbor-

hoods."[2] Did the second King verdict contribute to the goal of greater safety? Explain.

3. Sociologist Franz Schurmann says:

> No issue so suggests the existence of a dual justice system in America as the composition of its prison population. Those being fed into the prison system are overwhelmingly young, poor or darkskinned. They are the people without rights, who are, in effect, its modern, legal slaves.[3]

   a. In your opinion, is ours a dual justice system? Explain.
   b. Are the young, poor, and darkskinned of our prisons the equivalent of slaves? Explain.

4. Bernard McCummings was shot in the back and paralyzed from the waist down while he was robbing and beating a 72-year-old man in a subway station. McCummings was shot by a plainclothes police officer. McCummings pleaded guilty to robbery and served 32 months in prison. McCummings brought a civil action for his injuries. At trial, the officer testified that he shot when McCummings lunged at him. McCummings testified that he was running away when he was shot. Some corroborating evidence supported McCummings' testimony, and McCummings won a $4.3 million negligence judgment. New York's highest court upheld the jury's judgment for McCummings, saying the officer "did not exercise that degree of care which would reasonably be required of a police officer under similar circumstances."

   On the other hand, dissenting high court justice Bellacosa said the decision was an "inversion of justice." He went on to say, "the instant case approaches the surreal zone. It involves split-second decisions by public safety employees made in the most dangerous and volatile circumstances."

   In your judgment, was justice achieved in this case? Explain. See *McCummings* v. *New York City Transit Authority,* 619 N.E. 2d 664 (NY 1993); cert. den., *New York City Transit Authority* v. *McCummings,* 62 *Law Week* 3375 (1993).

Part One—Legal Foundations

LAW DEFINED

Just as this text investigates how business fits into society, we should begin our look at the legal system by considering how law fits into our society—from the perspectives of both those intimately associated with the law and outsiders looking at law as a social phenomenon. We begin by asking, what exactly is law?

Judges' Interpretations.   The great jurists Oliver Wendell Holmes and Benjamin Cardozo held similarly pragmatic visions of the meaning of law. "The prophecies of what the courts will do in fact, and nothing more pretentious, are what I mean by the law," said Holmes.[4] To Cardozo, the law was "a principle or rule of conduct so established as to justify a prediction with reasonable certainty that it will be enforced by the courts if its authority is challenged."[5]

The notion of law as rules of conduct enforced by courts will form our working definition for much of the remainder of the text. These rules, however, are not static; they are changing and changeable by both court and legislative action.

Sociologist's Interpretation.   The influential thinker Max Weber emphasized the role of external force in explaining the meaning of law.

> An order will be called law if it is externally guaranteed by the probability that coercion (physical or psychological), to bring about conformity or avenge volition, will be applied by a staff of people holding themselves specially ready for that purpose.[6]

Anthropologist's Interpretation.   The respected scholar of primitive law Bronislaw Malinowski seemed to regard the law as the natural product of cooperative, reciprocal human relationships.

> The rules of law stand out from the rest in that they are felt and regarded as the obligations of one person and the rightful claims of another. They are sanctioned not by mere psychological motive, but by a definite social machinery of binding force, based . . . upon mutual dependence, and realized in the equivalent arrangement of reciprocal services.[7]

Thus, under this approach, binding social custom is appropriately referred to as law.

Philosophers' Interpretations.   To Plato, law was one method of social control, while Cicero found the heart of the law in the distinction between the just and the unjust. Perhaps the most influential legal philosopher, Roscoe Pound, built on the social control theme to argue that the law is a mechanism for ordering private interests for the good of the whole society:

> Looked at functionally, the law is an attempt to satisfy, to reconcile, to harmonize, to adjust these overlapped and often conflicting claims and demands . . . so as to give effect to the greatest total of interests or to the interests that weigh most in our civilization, with the least sacrifice of the scheme of interests as a whole.[8]

A Dissenting Opinion.   To the critics of the American legal system, including those in the Critical Legal Studies movement, the foregoing explanations fail to capture the reality of the law as an instrument of repression. For example, "radical" sociologist Richard Quinney argues that we should be freed from "the dead hand of the legalistic mentality." Quinney asks us to imagine a life without law because, to him, law as practiced in America is the unjust product of the power of special interests.

> While law is to protect all citizens, it starts as a tool of the dominant class and ends by maintaining the dominance of that class. Law serves the powerful over the weak . . . Moreover, law is used by the state (and its elitist government) to promote and protect itself . . . We are indoctrinated with the ideology that it is our law, to be obeyed because we are all citizens of a single nation. Until law is the law of the people, law can be nothing other than official oppression.[9]

Questions

1. *a.* Under which definitions of law would provisions in a corporate code of employee conduct be considered law?
   b. Under which definitions would the Clean Air Act, for example, be considered law?
2. Terence Cannon, a Marxist "radical activist" and a member of the "Oakland Seven":

   > If you didn't know anything about how the law works in America, if all you did was read the papers, you would know that American courts and American laws are the enemies of the people. If you're too poor to pay the rent, who puts you out on the street? The law. If workers go out on a wildcat strike, who lays the injunction down on them? The law . . . Law is the tool that politicians and businessmen use to keep down the people they oppress.
   >
   > Did you ever hear of a cop busting in the head of a supermarket owner because he charged too much for food? . . . No. Law is the billyclub of the oppressor. He isn't about to use it on himself.[10]

   a. What definition(s) of law is Cannon using?
   b. Comment on the substance of the statement.

OBJECTIVES OF THE LAW

Law is shaped by social forces. The values, history, ideas, and goals of society are among the forces that determine the nature of a society's legal system. The diverse character of American society leads inevitably to differences of opinion regarding the proper direction for our legal system. However, certain broad goals can be identified.

1. Maintain Order. The law is instrumental in imposing necessary structure on America's diverse and rapidly changing society. Whether with stop signs, zoning ordinances, marriage licenses, or homicide statutes, the legal system seeks to prevent harm by imposing certain established codes of conduct on the mass of persons. Immediate self-interest is muted in favor of long-term general welfare. The problem then becomes one of how far to go in seeking to preserve a valuable but potentially oppressive commodity. Should the law require all motorcyclists to wear helmets? Or all businesses to close on Sunday? Or all motorists to limit their speed to 55 miles per hour?

2. Resolve Conflict. Because society cannot and would not wish to successfully regulate all dimensions of human conduct, a system for solving differences is required. An effort is made to substitute enlightened dispute resolution for the barbarism that might otherwise attend inevitable differences of opinion. With the law of contracts, for example, we have developed a sophisticated, generally accepted, and largely successful system for both imposing order and resolving conflict. Nevertheless, enormous problems remain, and new ones always arise.

One test of the vitality and merit of a legal system is its ability to adapt to change. Consider the 1992 case of 12-year-old Gregory Kingsley, who was granted a divorce from his parents.[11] Gregory's parents were separated. He lived rather unhappily with each of them for a time, but after his mother said that she wanted to put him up for adoption, he was placed with a foster family. He initiated his divorce action in a Florida trial court in order to permit himself to be adopted by his foster family. His mother then resisted the divorce. Gregory won at the lower court, and he won on appeal on abandonment grounds, although the appeals court overturned the lower court's judgment that he had the right (the *standing,* as it is labeled in the law) to sue on his own. The decision is a good example of our legal system struggling to maintain order and resolve new varieties of conflicts born of stunning societal change. Should children be able to bring lawsuits on their own? Will this decision lead to frivolous claims by other children?

3. Preserve Dominant Values. Americans have reached general accord regarding many values and beliefs, and the law has been put to work in preserving those standards. For example, in the Bill of Rights we have set out those fundamental freedoms that must be protected to preserve the character of the nation. Of course, in many instances societal opinion is divided. What happens when no clear consensus emerges about an issue? What if the issue involves a conflict between two values long clutched firmly to the American breast? Freedom of speech is central to a meaningful life, but what if that speech consists of anti-Semitic parades and demonstrations organized by the Ku Klux Klan?

4. Guarantee Freedom. That Americans are free and wish to remain so is the nation's most revered social value. It is, in a sense, a subset of the third goal in this list, but because of its preeminence, it properly stands alone. The problem, of course, is that freedom must be limited. Drawing the line often gives rise to severe societal conflict.

In general, you are free to do as you like so long as you do not violate the rights of others. But what are those rights? Do I have a right to smoke-free air, or do you have a right to smoke wherever you wish? Even if the rights of others are not directly violated, personal freedom is limited. The so-called victimless crimes—vagrancy, gambling, pornography, prostitution—are examples of instances where the law retards freedom in the absence of immediate injury to the rights of others. Should each citizen be free to do as he or she likes so long as harm does not befall others? Or does pornography, for example, inevitably give rise to societal harm? Should homosexuals and lesbians be permitted to serve in America's armed services?

5. Preserve Justice. In sum, justice, as we noted in the Rodney King materials, is the goal of the American legal system. Professor Franz Schurmann traces a bit of the evolution of the notion of justice.

> Since ancient times, great sprawling empires with many diverse peoples were held together not only by armies but by common systems of justice. The first such system was that of the Babylonian ruler Hammurabi at the end of the third millennium B.C. While most Americans

would view his rigid "eye for an eye and tooth for a tooth" with horror, in his time it represented a great step forward for humankind. It announced that Babylon would treat all its subjects according to the same system of justice.

* * * * *

Rome, as a republic and then an empire, inspired America's founding fathers. Rome's grandeur lasted a millennium. If the "great American experiment" is to last well into the next century, history indicates that, besides strength, it will need justice—the guarantee that every member of the polity will be treated fairly and equitably.

* * * * *

Roman law took a long time evolving but reached its fullest development when Rome became a great empire ruling over a vast human diversity. After it started freeing its slaves, its core practical principle became encapsulated in the phrase *suum cuique,* "to each his own," meaning that everyone has a legitimate place in the realm and a right to expect fair and equal treatment from the state.[12]

More than any other, the issue of justice should be at the forefront of all legal studies. In the Rodney King materials, you read about a number of the cultural and procedural problems that sometimes stand in the way of justice in the *criminal* system. Those problems and others also trouble our system of *civil* justice. The *Graff* case that follows illustrates the frustrations in the search for fairness given persuasive competing claims. More broadly, *Graff* depicts the legal system struggling simply to determine where justice lies. That is, even if the system is fair, some questions are so difficult that justice, at least in the sense of finding the truth, may remain elusive.

The Case Law: Locating and Analyzing

To prepare for *Graff,* the first law case in this text, a bit of practical guidance may be useful. The study of law is founded primarily on the analysis of judicial opinion. Except for the federal level and a few states, trial court decisions are filed locally for public inspection rather than being published. Appellate opinions, on the other hand, are generally published in volumes called *reports.* State court opinions are found in the reports of that state, as well as a regional reporter published by West Publishing Company that divides the United States into units, such as South Eastern (S.E.) and Pacific (P.).

Within the appropriate reporter, the cases are arranged in a workable fashion and are *cited* by case name, volume, reporter name, and page number. For example, *Royce Graff, Debra Graff, Bobby Hausmon and Betty Hausmon* v. *Brett Beard and Dorothy Beard,* 858 S.W.2d 918 (Texas S.Ct. 1993) means that the opinion will be found in volume 858 of the Southwestern Reporter, 2d series, at page 918 and that the decision was reached in 1993 by the Texas Supreme Court. Federal court decisions are found in several reporters, including the *Federal Reporter* and the *United States Supreme Court Reports.*

Briefing the Case

Most law students find the preparation of *case briefs* (outlines or digests) to be helpful in mastering the complexities of the law. A brief should evolve into the form that best suits the individual student's needs. The following approach should be a useful starting point.

1. Parties.   Identify the plaintiff and the defendant.
2. Facts.   Summarize only those facts critical to the outcome of the case.
3. Procedure.   Who brought the appeal? What was the outcome in the lower court(s)?
4. Issue.   Note the central question or questions on which the case turns.
5. Holding.   How did the Court resolve the issues? Who won?
6. Reasoning.   Explain the logic that supported the Court's decision.

ROYCE GRAFF, DEBRA GRAFF, BOBBY HAUSMON AND BETTY HAUSMON v. BRETT BEARD AND DOROTHY BEARD
858 S.W.2d 918 (Texas S.Ct. 1993)

Justice John Cornyn

We are asked in this case to impose a common-law duty on a social host who makes alcohol available to an intoxicated adult guest who the host knows will be driving . . .

Houston Moos consumed alcohol at a party hosted by the Graffs and Hausmons, and allegedly left in his vehicle in an intoxicated condition. En route from the party, Moos collided with a motorcycle, injuring Brett Beard. Beard sued both Moos and his hosts for his injuries. The trial court ultimately dismissed Beard's claims against the hosts for failure to state a cause of action. An en banc divided court of appeals reversed the trial court's judgment and remanded the case, holding for the first time in Texas jurisprudence that social hosts may be liable to third parties for the acts of their intoxicated adult guests.

Under the court of appeals' standard, a social host violates a legal duty to third parties when the host makes an alcoholic beverage available to an adult guest who the host knows is intoxicated and will be driving. In practical effect, this duty is twofold. The first aspect of the host's duty is to prevent guests who will be driving from becoming intoxicated. If the host fails to do so, however, a second aspect of the duty comes into play—the host must prevent the intoxicated guest from driving.

The legislatures in most states, including Texas, have enacted dram shop laws that impose a statutory duty to third parties on commercial providers under specified circumstances. We have recently held that when the legislature enacted the Texas dram shop statute it also imposed a duty on the provider that extends to the patron himself. Because the dram shop statute applies only to commercial providers, however, it does not govern the duty asserted in this case.

We think it significant in appraising Beard's request to recognize common-law social host liability that the legislature has considered and declined to create such a duty. A version of the bill that eventually became our dram shop statute provided for social host liability. Although that version passed the Senate, the House rejected it. The Senate-House conference committee deleted social host liability from the bill the legislature eventually enacted.

The highest courts in only four states have done what we are asked to do today: judicially impose a duty to third parties on social hosts who make alcohol available to adult guests. In two of these states, California and Iowa, the legislatures subsequently abrogated the judicially-created duty. Neither of the two remaining jurisdictions, Massachusetts and New Jersey, had dram shop statutes when their courts acted. Rather, their courts first imposed a common-law duty to third parties on commercial establishments and then extended the duty to social hosts.

* * * * *

Deciding whether to impose a new common-law duty involves complex considerations of public policy. We have said that these considerations include "'social, economic, and political questions,' and their application to the particular facts at hand." Among other factors, we consider the extent of the risk involved, "the foreseeability and likelihood of injury weighed against the social utility of the actor's conduct, the magnitude of the burden of guarding against the injury, and the consequences of placing the burden on the defendant." We have also emphasized other factors. For example, questions of duty have turned on whether one party has superior knowledge of the risk, and whether a right to control the actor whose conduct precipitated the harm exists.

Following our decisions in Seagrams and Otis Engineering Corp., we deem it appropriate to focus on two tacit assumptions underlying the holding of the court of appeals: that the social host can reasonably know of the guest's alcohol consumption and possible intoxication, and possesses the right to control the conduct of the guest. Under Texas law, in the absence of a relationship between the parties giving rise to the right of control, one person is under no legal duty to control the conduct of another, even if there exists the practical ability to do so.

* * * * *

Instead of focusing on the host's right of control over the guest, the court of appeals conditioned a social host's duty on the host's "exclusive control" of the alcohol supply. The court defined "exclusive control," however, as nothing more than a degree of control "greater than that of the guest user." Under the court's definition, at a barbecue, a wedding reception, a back-yard picnic, a pachanga, a Bar Mitzvah—or a variety of other common social settings—the host would always have exclusive control over the alcohol supply because the host chooses whether alcohol will be provided and the manner in which it will be provided. The duty imposed by the court of appeals would apparently attach in any social setting in which alcohol is available regardless of the host's right to control the guest. Thus, as a practical matter, the host has but one choice—whether to make alcohol available to guests at all.

But should the host venture to make alcohol available to adult guests, the court of appeals' standard would allow the host to avoid liability by cutting off the guest's access to alcohol at some point before the guest becomes intoxicated. Implicit in that standard is the assumption that the reasonably careful host can accurately determine how much alcohol guests have consumed and when they have approached their limit. We believe, though, that it is far from clear that a social host can reliably recognize a guest's level of intoxication. First, it is unlikely that a host can be expected to know how much alcohol, if any, a guest has consumed before the guest arrives on the host's premises. Second, in many social settings, the total number of guests present may practically inhibit the host from discovering a guest's approaching intoxication. Third, the condition may be apparent in some people but certainly not in all . . .

* * * * *

This brings us to the second aspect of the duty implicit in the court of appeals' standard: that should the guest become intoxicated, the host must prevent the guest from driving. Unlike the court of appeals, however, we cannot assume that guests will respond to a host's attempts, verbal or physical, to prevent the guests from driving. Nor is it clear to us precisely what affirmative actions would discharge the host's duty under the court of appeals' standard. Would a simple request not to drive suffice? Or is more required? Is the host required to physically restrain the guests, take their car keys, or disable their vehicles? The problems inherent in this aspect of the court of appeals' holding are obvious.

* * * * *

Ideally, guests will drink responsibly, and hosts will monitor their social functions to reduce the likelihood of intoxication. Once a guest becomes impaired by alcohol to the point at which he becomes a threat to himself and others, we would hope that the host can persuade the guest to take public transportation, stay on the premises, or be transported home by an unimpaired driver. But we know that too often reality conflicts with ideal behavior. And, given the ultimate power of guests to control their own alcohol consumption and the absence of any legal right of the host to control the guest, we find the arguments for shifting legal responsibility from the guest to the host, who merely makes alcohol available at social gatherings, unconvincing. As the common law has long recognized, the imbiber maintains the ultimate power and thus the obligation to control his own behavior: to decide to drink or not to drink, to drive or not to drive. We therefore conclude that the common law's focus should remain on the drinker as the person primarily responsible for his own behavior and best able to avoid the foreseeable risks of that behavior.

We accordingly reverse the judgment of the court of appeals and render judgment that Beard take nothing.

Dissenting Opinion—Justice Gammage joined by Justice Doggett

I respectfully dissent. The majority errs in holding that the legislature must "create" the duty for social hosts not to send intoxicated guests driving in our streets to maim and kill. Logic, legal experience and this court's own earlier decisions dictate a contrary result. The legislature may enact a statute that creates a duty. But the legislature's failure to act does not "un-create" an existing duty. A duty created by the common law continues to exist unless and until the legislature changes it, and such an existing common law duty applies to the defendants here.

The majority confuses issues of proof with issues of whether to recognize the tort duty. The majority is concerned that the social host might not be able to persuade or control his intoxicated guest to keep him or her from driving. The host, however, clearly does control whether alcohol is being served, and in what quantities and form. The answer to the "duty" question is that the host should not let the driving guest have the alcohol in intoxicating quantities. If the guest becomes inebriated, however, just as with any other dangerous situation one helps create, the host has the duty to make every reasonable effort to keep the dangerously intoxicated guest from driving. If the guest resists those efforts, then there is a question for the factfinder to resolve whether the host's efforts were all that reasonably could be done under the circumstances.

The majority expresses concern that "the reasonably careful host" may not be able to detect when some guests are intoxicated. If that is so, then the factfinder should have no difficulty determining that the host did not serve them while they were "obviously intoxicated." The majority further asserts, without citation to authority, that the "guest . . . is in a far better position to know the amount of alcohol he has consumed" than the host.

This assertion defies common sense, because from personal observation we know that most persons, as they become intoxicated, along with losing their dexterity and responsive mental faculties, gradually become less and less cognizant of how much they've had and how badly intoxicated they are. Even if the host is also intoxicated, as a third party viewing the guest, the host is probably in a better position to evaluate the guest's intoxication. Intoxicated guests need someone to tell them not to drive . . .

If circumstances do not permit the social host to adequately monitor and control the quantity of alcoholic beverages a guest consumes, the host still retains absolute control over whether alcoholic beverages should be served at all . . .

* * * * *

. . . All culpable parties should be liable—the social host who knowingly intoxicated the guest and the guest who drunkenly caused the accident. I am persuaded that both should be liable to the extent of their responsibility for the accident. The television commercial says, "Friends don't let friends drive drunk." That is sound public policy. But today the majority says, "Intoxicate your friends and send them out upon the public streets and highways to drive drunk. Don't worry, you won't be liable." That is, in the kindest term I can muster, unsound policy.

Questions

1. Who won this case and why?
2. What do the dissenting justices mean by saying "the majority confuses issues of proof with issues of whether to recognize the tort duty"?
3. In your judgment, does the Texas Supreme Court decision represent a just result? Explain.

CLASSIFICATIONS OF LAW

Some elementary distinctions will make the role of law clearer.

Substantive and Procedural Law.   *Substantive laws* create, define, and regulate legal rights and obligations. Thus, in terms of the topics of this course, the Sherman Act forbids restraints of trade. By judicial interpretation, price-fixing between competitors is a restraint of trade.

Procedural law embraces the systems and methods available to enforce the rights specified in the substantive law. So, procedural law includes the judicial system and the rules by which it operates. Questions of where to hear a case, what evidence to admit, and which decisions can be appealed fall within the procedural domain.

Law by Judicial Decision and Law by Enactment.   In general, American rules of law are promulgated by court decisions (*case law*) or via enactments by constitutional assemblies, legislatures, administrative agencies, chief executives, and local government authorities. Enactments include constitutions, statutes, treaties, administrative rules, executive orders, and local ordinances.

Case Law (Judicial Decisions).   Our case law has its roots in the early English king's courts, where rules of law gradually developed out of a series of individual dispute resolutions. That body of law was imported to America and is known as the *common law.* (This term may be confusing because it is frequently used to designate not just the law imported from England of old but also all judge-made or case law.)

The development of English common law rules and American judicial decisions into a just, ordered package is attributable in large measure to reliance on the doctrine of *stare decisis* (let the decision stand). That is, judges endeavor to follow the precedents established by previous decisions. However, following precedent is not mandatory. The previous decision can be overruled.

As societal beliefs change, so does the law. For example, a Supreme Court decision approving racially separate but equal education was eventually overruled by a Supreme Court decision mandating integrated schools. However, the principle of stare decisis is generally adhered to because of its beneficial effect. It offers the wisdom of the past and enhances efficiency by eliminating the need for resolving every case as though it were the first of its kind. Stare decisis affords stability and predictability to the law. It promotes justice by, for example, reducing "judge-shopping" and neutralizing judges' personal prejudices.

Statutes (Enactments).   In this section, our primary concern is with the laws that have been adopted by the many legislative bodies—Congress, the state legislatures, city councils, and the like. These enactments are labeled *statutory law.* Some areas of law, such as torts, continue to be governed primarily by common law rules, but the direction of American law lies largely in the hands of legislators. Of course, legislators are not free of constraints. Federal legislation cannot conflict with the U.S. Constitution, and state legislation cannot violate either federal law or the constitutions of that state and the nation.

Law and Equity.   Following the Norman conquest of England in 1066, a system of king's courts was established in which the king's representatives settled disputes. Those representatives were empowered to provide remedies of land, money, or personal property. The king's courts became known as *courts of law,* and the remedies were labeled *remedies of law.* However, some litigants sought compensation other than the three provided. They took their pleas to the king.

Typically, the chancellor, an aide to the king, would hear these petitions and, guided by the standard of fairness, could grant a remedy (such as an injunction or specific performance) specifically appropriate to the case. The chancellors' decisions accumulated over time such that a new body of remedies—and with it a new court system, known as *courts of equity*—evolved. Both court systems were adopted in the United States following the American Revolution, but today actions at law and equity are typically heard in the same court.

Public Law and Private Law.   *Public law* deals with the relationship between government and the citizens. Constitutional, criminal, and administrative law (relating to such bodies as the Federal Trade Commission) fall in the public law category. *Private law* regulates the legal relationship between individuals. Contracts, agency, and commercial paper are traditional business law topics in the private law category.

Civil Law and Criminal Law.   The legislature or other lawmaking body normally specifies that new legislation is either *civil* or *criminal* or both. Broadly, all legislation not specifically labeled criminal law falls in the civil law category. *Civil law* addresses the legal rights and duties arising among individuals, organizations such as corporations, and governments. Thus, for example, a person might sue a company raising a civil law claim of breach of contract. The *criminal law,* on the other hand, involves wrongs against the general welfare as formulated in specific criminal statutes. Murder and theft are, of course, criminal wrongs because society has forbidden those acts in specific legislative enactments. Hence, wearing one's hat backwards would be a crime if such a statute were enacted and if that statute met constitutional requirements.

Crimes.   Crimes are of three kinds. In general, *felonies* are more serious crimes, such as murder, rape, and robbery. They are typically punishable by death or by imprisonment in a federal or state penitentiary for more than one year. In general, *misdemeanors* are less serious crimes, such as petty theft, disorderly conduct, and traffic offenses. They are typically punishable by fine or by imprisonment for no more than one year. *Treason* is the special situation in which one levies war against the United States or gives aid and comfort to its enemies.

Elements of a Crime.   In a broad sense, crimes consist of two elements: (1) a wrongful act or omission (*actus reus*) and (2) evil intent (*mens rea*). Thus, an individual who pockets a ball-point pen and leaves the store without paying for it may be charged with petty theft. However, the accused may defend by arguing that he or she merely absentmindedly and unintentionally slipped the pen in a pocket after picking it off the shelf to consider its merits. Intent is a state of mind, so the jury or judge must reach a determination from the objective facts as to what the accused's state of mind must have been.

Criminal Defenses. The law recognizes certain defenses to criminal prosecution. Infancy, intoxication, insanity, and self-defense are some of the arguments available to the defendant. Precise standards for each of these and other defenses differ from state to state, depending on the relevant statutory and case law. The federal Constitution and the various state constitutions also afford protections to the accused.

The Fourth Amendment to the federal Constitution prevents unreasonable searches and seizures; the Fifth Amendment requires a grand jury indictment for capital crimes, forbids double jeopardy and self-incrimination, and mandates due process of law; the Sixth Amendment guarantees a speedy and public trial by jury, the right to confront and obtain witnesses, and the right to a competent lawyer; and the Eighth Amendment prohibits excessive bail or fines and cruel and unusual punishment.

Criminal Procedure. In general, criminal law procedure is structured as follows: For more complex, arguably more serious, crimes the process begins with the prosecuting officials bringing their charges before a grand jury or magistrate to determine whether the charges have sufficient merit to justify a trial. If so, an *indictment* or *information* is issued, charging the accused with specific crimes. (Grand juries issue indictments; magistrates issue informations.) In those instances where action by a grand jury or magistrate is not required, cases are initiated by the issuance of a warrant by a judge, based on a showing of probable cause that the individual has committed or will commit a crime. Where necessity demands, arrests may be made without a warrant, but the legality of the arrest will be tested by probable cause standards.

After indictment or arrest, the individual is brought before the court for arraignment, where the charges are read and a plea is entered. If the individual pleads not guilty, he or she will go to trial, where guilt must be established *beyond a reasonable doubt.* (In a civil trial, the plaintiff must meet the lesser standard of *a preponderance of the evidence.*) In a criminal trial, the burden of proof is on the state. The defendant is, of course, assumed innocent. He or she is entitled to a jury trial but may choose to have the case decided by the judge alone. If found guilty, the defendant can, among other possibilities, seek a new trial or appeal errors in the prosecution. If found innocent, the defendant may, if necessary, invoke the doctrine of *double jeopardy* under which a person cannot be prosecuted twice in the same tribunal for the same criminal offense.

The column that follows outlines some elements of the criminal justice process as it applies to white-collar crime.

BEFORE YOU ARE INDICTED . . .

Daniel J. Broderick

Although most executives are aware of the increased emphasis being placed on white-collar fraud by federal and state investigative law agencies, few executives know much about the actual criminal process. Here's a look at some key points, along with some advice:

The Initial Complaint

Most criminal investigations begin with a complaint by a private citizen. It may be several months before a grand jury is convened or any contact is made directly with anyone in your company. It may take even longer in the defense industry, where whistle-blowers can sue civilly and develop a case before the government decides whether to get involved. Northrop, for example, is currently battling an employee group that alleges the firm overcharged the government in its Stealth bomber project. Clearly, any disclosures Northrop is forced to make in this civil case could hurt its posture in any criminal investigation.

* * * * *

The Start of Parallel Proceedings

It is increasingly common for criminal, civil, and administrative proceedings to operate at the same time. Do not assume that a criminal investigation will await the completion of other matters or vice versa. You *should* assume that virtually anything revealed in one proceeding will ultimately end up in the files of attorneys involved in the other.

* * * * *

The Investigation

The most fruitful investigative techniques in white-collar cases remain grand jury subpoenas. Nonetheless, law-enforcement agents have become increasingly bold and creative. In one recent Los Angeles

investigation, agents hired two prostitutes to get close to the targets of the probe, in order to discover any bedroom admissions. In another, the FBI created and operated an entire lobbying group to examine corruption in the California Legislature.

Even standard investigative techniques have become more sophisticated. It is the rule now for agencies to mount a joint investigation involving the FBI, U.S. Postal authorities, the Internal Revenue Service, and local police. These agencies employ electronic-surveillance and undercover techniques once confined to organized-crime or narcotics investigations.

In a criminal investigation that is still continuing, involving an alleged network of attorneys in Southern California that may have cost insurance companies more than $200 million in fictitious or unnecessary legal bills, one attorney member of the "alliance" wore a wire for almost two years. Like Ivan Boesky, he also recorded his telephone conversations with the others . . .

Once a criminal probe has begun, exercise extreme caution in communicating with anyone even remotely connected with the allegedly improper conduct. Even innocent actions could be perceived as efforts to obstruct justice, tamper with witnesses or influence testimony.

Interviews with Law Enforcement

Law-enforcement agents are required to advise you of your Miranda rights only when you are in custody. This same principle applies to undercover agents or informants sent in to talk to you. Any conversations with law-enforcement officials or their agents are at your own risk.

Grand Jury Investigations

At some point in any serious federal white-collar criminal investigation, a grand jury will be used to obtain witness testimony or business records, or both. Most grand jury investigations into major fraud cases take well over one year to complete . . .

Prosecutors are required to remain silent about secret grand jury investigations but witnesses are not. You or your counsel should do what reporters do: Ask witnesses to tell you the questions the grand jury asked, so that you can divine the potential subjects or targets. If you are a target, and you merely appear before a grand jury to produce records but not answer questions, your appearance with such records can be used against you in a subsequent prosecution . . .

In one investigation, the prosecutor subpoenaed two recalcitrant witnesses at the same time. The first was escorted into the grand jury room in plain view of the other and asked to sit quietly inside the room for 30 minutes. He was escorted out before he could talk to the second witness, who was then brought in. After being told that the whole story was out now, the second witness, assuming that the first had

talked, agreed to cooperate and tell all against the first witness.

Plea-Bargaining and Immunity Agreements

The best time to approach a prosecutor is early on in an investigation, when information is scarce. If you or your company is not a major target, the prosecutor may agree to grant immunity in return for cooperation.

* * * * *

It's best to obtain competent legal advice early. Although corporate liability is rather straightforward, individual liability is not. Under certain statutes, responsible corporate officers are potentially liable for certain criminal acts committed without their direct involvement.

Source: *The Wall Street Journal,* February 5, 1990, p. A14. Reprinted by permission of *The Wall Street Journal,* © 1990 Dow Jones & Company, Inc. All Rights Reserved Worldwide.

Questions—Part One

1. Daniel Broderick notes the government's increased emphasis on white-collar fraud. Is the government misallocating its resources when that money and effort might be directed to street crime, the drug trade, and so forth? Explain.
2. The federal government and the states have passed laws to restrict the sale of drug paraphernalia (pipes, spoons, bongs, and the like). Through the decade of the 1970s, paraphernalia was sold lawfully and openly in so-called head shops. Increased concern regarding drug use has prompted legislation to retard sales.
   a. Raise the competing arguments regarding criminal penalties for paraphernalia trade.
   b. Should we rely on the free market to "regulate" commercial enterprise of this nature? That is, should we permit the government to destroy the operations of businesses designed to meet a need expressed by the market and heretofore considered free of any illegality? Explain.
3. In two recent Milwaukee, Wisconsin, criminal trials, defense lawyers have raised a new line of argument for their inner-city clients, claiming they are the victims of "urban psychosis." Both clients were accused of murder. Both claimed to have been traumatized by extraordinary violence (assaults, rapes, murders) that had been inflicted on them or that they had witnessed. The result, according to their lawyers, was a psychological condition akin to post-traumatic stress disorder, which some courts have already recognized in cases involving Vietnam veterans, rape victims, and battered spouses and children.

    a. In effect, who are these defendants blaming for their alleged crimes?

    b. How would you respond to the urban psychosis defense if you were serving on a jury? See Junda Woo, "Urban Trauma Mitigates Guilt, Defenders Say," *The Wall Street Journal,* April 27, 1993, p. B1.

4. Should we remove criminal penalties from the so-called victimless crimes of vagrancy, prostitution, pornography, and gambling? Should we regulate those practices in any way? Explain.

5. What steps would you advocate to reduce crime in America?

6. A Rhode Island man pleaded guilty to child molestation. As an alternative to imprisonment and as a condition of his probation, the judge ordered him to purchase a newspaper ad displaying his picture, identifying himself as a sex offender, and encouraging others to seek assistance. A number of courts across the country have required apologies or other forms of humiliation in criminal cases.

    a. What objections would a defendant's lawyer raise to that method of punishment?

    b. Would you impose a "humiliation sentence" were you the judge in a case like that in Rhode Island? Explain.

Part Two—The Judicial Process

One of the functions of the law, as mentioned above, is the resolution of conflicts. Most disputes are, in fact, settled without resort to litigation; but when agreement cannot be reached, the citizenry can turn to the courts—a highly technical and sophisticated dispute resolution mechanism.

STATE COURT SYSTEMS

While state court systems vary substantially, a general pattern can be summarized. At the heart of the court pyramid in most states is a *trial court of general jurisdiction,* commonly labeled a *district court* or a *superior court.* It is here that most trials—both civil and criminal—arising out of state law would be heard, but certain classes of cases are reserved to courts of limited subject matter jurisdiction or to various state administrative agencies (such as the state public utilities commission and the workers' compensation board). Family, small claims, juvenile, and traffic courts are examples of trial courts with limited jurisdiction. At the top of the judicial pyramid in all states is a court of appeals, ordinarily labeled the *supreme court.* A number of states also provide for an intermediate court of appeals located in the hierarchy between the trial courts and the highest appeals court.

State and Federal Court Systems

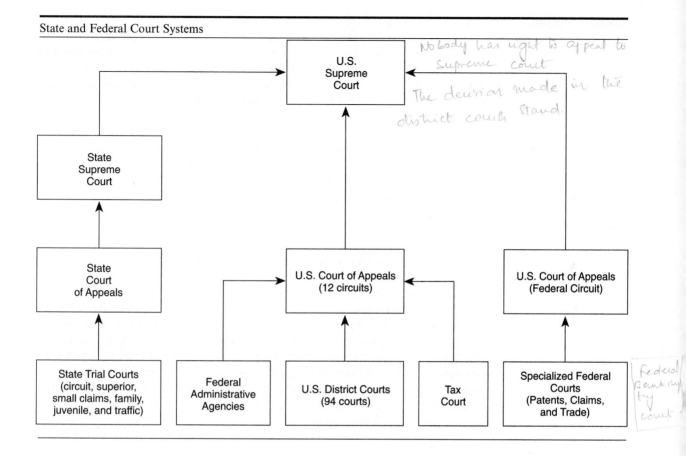

[handwritten: Nobody has right to appeal to Supreme court]

[handwritten: The decision made in the district courts stand]

[handwritten: Federal Bankruptcy court]

FEDERAL COURT SYSTEM   *[handwritten: No common law]*

District Courts

The district courts provide the foundation of the federal judicial system. The Constitution provides for a Supreme Court and such inferior courts as Congress shall authorize. Pursuant to that authority, Congress has established at least one district court for each state and territory. These are trial courts where witnesses are heard and questions of law and fact are resolved. More populous areas with heavier case loads have additional district courts. As circumstances demand, Congress adds courts at the district level. Most federal cases begin in the district courts or in a federal administrative agency (such as the Interstate Commerce Commission or the Federal Communications Commission). Congress has also provided for several courts of limited jurisdiction, including a Tax Court and a U.S. Claims Court.

[handwritten: Trial court → 94 federal District Court.]

Court of Appeals

Congress has divided the United States geographically into 11 judicial circuits and the District of Columbia and has established a court of appeals for each. Those courts hear appeals from the district courts within their circuit and review decisions and enforce orders of the various federal administrative agencies.

In 1982, Congress created the U.S. Court of Appeals for the Federal Circuit. That court hears, among others, all patent appeals and all appeals from the U.S. Claims Court (monetary claims against the United States).

Supreme Court

Hear cases that have high national imp

The Supreme Court consists of nine justices appointed for life by the president and confirmed by the Senate. In limited instances, the Supreme Court serves as an original or trial court. However, almost all of the Supreme Court's work consists of reviewing lower court decisions, principally from the courts of appeal and from state high courts. Recent congressional legislation has dramatically limited the number of mandatory appeals that come to the Court "as a matter of right." Now, virtually all parties seeking Supreme Court review must petition the Court for a *writ of certiorari,* which commands the lower court to forward the trial records to the Court. Decisions regarding those petitions are entirely discretionary with the Court. Typically it will hear those cases that will assist in resolving conflicting courts of appeal decisions, as well as those that raise questions of special significance about the Constitution or the national welfare. The Court annually receives more than 5,000 cases but agrees to a full hearing for 110 to 140 of those.

JURISDICTION

A plaintiff may not simply proceed to trial at the court of his or her preference. The plaintiff must go to a court with *jurisdiction*—that is, a court with the necessary power and authority to hear the dispute. The court must have jurisdiction over both the subject matter and the persons (or, in some instances, the property) involved in the case.

Subject-Matter Jurisdiction

Subject-matter jurisdiction imposes bounds on the classes of cases a court may hear. The legislation or constitution creating the court will normally specify that court's jurisdictional authority. For example, state courts of general jurisdiction may hear most types of cases, but a criminal court or probate court is limited in the subject matter it may hear.

The outer bounds of federal jurisdiction are specified in the Constitution, while Congress has further particularized that issue by statute. Essentially, the federal district courts may hear two types of cases: (1) those involving a federal question and (2) those involving diversity of citizenship and more than $50,000.

Federal question jurisdiction exists in any suit where the plaintiff's claim is based on the U.S. Constitution, a U.S. treaty, or a federal statute. Thus, litigants can bring to the federal courts cases involving, for example, the federal antitrust statutes, federal criminal laws, constitutional issues such as freedom of the press, and federal tax questions. Federal question jurisdiction does not require an amount in controversy exceeding $50,000. Further, federal and state courts have *concurrent jurisdiction* for some federal questions. Thus, some federal question cases are decided in state courts applying federal law. Congress has accorded the federal courts exclusive jurisdiction over certain subjects, including federal criminal laws, bankruptcy, and copyrights. Under *diversity jurisdiction,* federal district courts may hear cases involving more than $50,000 where the plaintiff(s) and the defendant(s) are citizens of different states. (Corporations are treated as citizens both of their state of incorporation and the state in which their principal place of business is located.) Diversity cases may also be heard in state courts, but plaintiffs frequently prefer to bring their actions in federal courts. The quality of the federal judiciary is generally believed to be superior to that of the states, and the federal courts are considered less likely to be influenced by local bias. Federal court action may also have procedural advantages, such as greater capacity to secure witnesses' testimony.

Personal Jurisdiction

Judicial authority over the person is known as *in personam jurisdiction.* In general, a state court's powers are limited to the bounds of the state. While the matter is fraught with complexities, it is fair to say that state court jurisdiction can be established in three ways: (1) When the defendant is a resident of the state, a summons may be served at that residence. (2) When the defendant is not a resident, a summons may be personally served should he or she be physically present in the state. (3) All states have legislated "long-arm" statutes that allow a court to secure jurisdiction against an out-of-state party where the defendant has committed a tort in the state or where the defendant is conducting business in the state. Hence, in an auto accident in Iowa involving both an Iowa resident and an Illinois resident, the Iowan may sue in Iowa and achieve service of process over the Illinois defendant as a consequence of the jurisdictional authority afforded by the long-arm statute.

A state court may also acquire jurisdiction via an *in rem action.* In that instance the defendant may be a nonresident, but his or her property, which must be the subject of the suit, must be located within the state.

The following case illustrates some of these jurisdictional issues.

ASAHI METAL INDUSTRY CO. v. SUPERIOR COURT
480 U.S. 102 (1987)

Justice O'Connor

INTERNATIONAL

This case presents the question whether the mere awareness on the part of a foreign defendant that the components it manufactured, sold, and delivered outside the United States would reach the forum State in the stream of commerce constitutes "minimum contacts" between the defendant and the forum State such that the exercise of jurisdiction "does not offend 'traditional notions of fair play and substantial justice.'"

I

On September 23, 1978, on Interstate Highway 80 in Solano County, California, Gary Zurcher lost control of his Honda motorcycle and collided with a tractor. Zurcher was severely injured, and his passenger and wife, Ruth Ann Moreno, was killed. In September 1979, Zurcher filed a product liability action in the Superior Court of the State of California in and for the County of Solano. Zurcher alleged that the 1978 accident was caused by a sudden loss of air and an explosion in the rear tire of the motorcycle, and alleged that the motorcycle tire, tube, and sealant were defective. Zurcher's complaint named, *inter alia,* Cheng Shin Rubber Industrial Co., Ltd. (Cheng Shin), the Taiwanese manufacturer of the tube. Cheng Shin in turn filed a cross-complaint seeking indemnification from its codefendants and from petitioner, Asahi Metal Industry Co., Ltd. (Asahi), the manufacturer of the tube's valve assembly. Zurcher's claims against Cheng Shin and the other defendants were eventually settled and dismissed, leaving only Cheng Shin's indemnity action against Asahi.

California's long-arm statute authorizes the exercise of jurisdiction "on any basis not inconsistent with the Constitution of this state or of the United States." Asahi moved to quash Cheng Shin's service of summons, arguing the State could not exert jurisdiction over it consistent with the Due Process Clause of the Fourteenth Amendment.

In relation to the motion, the following information was submitted by Asahi and Cheng Shin. Asahi is a Japanese corporation. It manufactures tire valve assemblies in Japan and sells the assemblies to Cheng Shin, and to several other tire manufacturers, for use as components in finished tire tubes. Asahi's sales to Cheng Shin took place in Taiwan. The shipments from Asahi to Cheng Shin were sent from Japan to Taiwan. Cheng Shin bought and incorporated into its tire tubes 150,000 Asahi valve assemblies in 1978; 500,000 in 1979; 500,000 in 1980; 100,000 in 1981; and 100,000 in 1982. Sales to Cheng Shin accounted for 1.24 percent of Asahi's income in 1981 and 0.44 percent in 1982. Cheng Shin alleged that approximately 20 percent of its sales in the United States are in California. Cheng Shin purchases valve assemblies from other suppliers as well, and sells finished tubes throughout the world.

In 1983 an attorney for Cheng Shin conducted an informal examination of the valve stems of the tire tubes sold in one cycle store in Solano County. The attorney declared that of the approximately 115 tire tubes in the store, 97 were purportedly manufactured in Japan or Taiwan, and of those 97, 21 valve stems were marked with the circled letter "A," apparently Asahi's trademark. Of the 21 Asahi valve stems, 12 were incorporated into Cheng Shin tire tubes. The store contained 41 other Cheng Shin tubes that incorporated the valve assemblies of other manufacturers. An affidavit of a manager of Cheng Shin whose duties included the purchasing of component parts stated: "'In discussions with Asahi regarding the purchase of valve stem assemblies the fact that my Company sells tubes throughout the world and specifically the United States has been discussed. I am informed and believe that Asahi was fully aware that valve stem assemblies sold to my Company and to others would end up throughout the United States and in California.'" An affidavit of the president of Asahi, on the other hand, declared that Asahi "'has never contemplated that its limited sales of tire valves to Cheng Shin in Taiwan would subject it to lawsuits in California.'"

Primarily on the basis of the above information, the Superior Court denied the motion to quash summons, stating: "Asahi obviously does business on an international scale. It is not unreasonable that they defend claims of defect in their product on an international scale."

The Court of Appeal of the State of California issued a peremptory writ of mandate commanding the Superior Court to quash service of summons. The court concluded that "it would be unreasonable to require Asahi to respond in California solely on the basis of ultimately realized foreseeability that the product into which its component was embodied would be sold all over the world including California."

The Supreme Court of the State of California reversed and discharged the writ issued by the Court of Appeal. The court observed: "Asahi has no offices, property or agents in California. It solicits no business in California and has made no direct sales [in California]." Moreover, "Asahi did not design or control the system of distribution that carried its valve assemblies into California." Nevertheless, the court found the exercise of jurisdiction over Asahi to be consistent with the Due Process Clause. It concluded that Asahi knew that some of the valve assemblies sold to Cheng Shin would be incorporated into tire tubes sold in California, and that Asahi benefited indirectly from the sale in California of products incorporating its components. The court considered Asahi's intentional act of placing its components into the stream of commerce—that is, by delivering the components to Cheng Shin in Taiwan—coupled with Asahi's awareness that some of the components would eventually find their way into California, sufficient to form the basis for state court jurisdiction under the Due Process Clause.

II

A

The Due Process Clause of the Fourteenth Amendment limits the power of a state court to exert personal jurisdiction over a nonresident defendant. "[T]he constitutional touchstone" of the determination whether an exercise of personal jurisdiction comports with due process "remains whether the defendant purposefully established 'minimum contacts' in the forum State." Most recently we have reaffirmed that minimum contacts must have a basis in "some act by which the defendant purposefully avails itself of the privilege of conducting activities within the forum State, thus invoking the benefits and protections of its laws."

* * * * *

Some courts have understood the Due Process Clause to allow an exercise of personal jurisdiction to be based on no more than the defendant's act of placing the product in the stream of commerce. Other courts have understood the Due Process Clause . . . to require the action of the defendant to be more purposefully directed at the forum State than the mere act of placing a product in the stream of commerce.

* * * * *

We now find this latter position to be consonant with the requirements of due process. The "substantial connection," between the defendant and the forum State necessary for a finding of minimum contacts must come about by *an action of the defendant purposefully directed toward the forum State.* The placement of a product into the stream of commerce, without more, is not an act of the defendant purposefully directed toward the forum State. Additional conduct of the defendant may indicate an intent or purpose to serve the market in the forum State, for example, designing the product for the market in the forum State, advertising in the forum State, establishing channels for providing regular advice to customers in the forum State, or marketing the product through a distributor who has agreed to serve as the sales agent in the forum State. But a defendant's awareness that the stream of commerce may or will sweep the product into the forum State does not convert the mere act of placing the product into the stream into an act purposefully directed toward the forum State.

Assuming, *arguendo,* that respondents have established Asahi's awareness that some of the valves sold to Cheng Shin would be incorporated into tire tubes sold in California, respondents have not demonstrated any action by Asahi to purposefully avail itself of the California market. Asahi does not do business in California. It has no office, agents, employees, or property in California. It does not advertise or otherwise solicit business in California. It did not create, control, or employ the distribution system that brought its valves to California. On the basis of these facts, the exertion of personal jurisdiction over Asahi by the Superior Court of California exceeds the limits of due process.

B

The strictures of the Due Process Clause forbid a state court to exercise personal jurisdiction over Asahi under circumstances that would offend "'traditional notions of fair play and substantial justice.'"

* * * * *

Certainly the burden on the defendant in this case is severe. Asahi has been commanded by the Supreme Court of California not only to traverse the distance between Asahi's headquarters in Japan and the Superior Court of California in and for the County of Solano, but also to submit its dispute with Cheng Shin to a foreign nation's judicial system. The unique burdens placed upon one who must defend oneself in a foreign legal system should have significant weight in assessing the reasonableness of stretching the long arm of personal jurisdiction over national borders.

When minimum contacts have been established, often the interests of the plaintiff and the forum in the exercise of jurisdiction will justify even the serious burdens placed on the alien defendant. In the present case, however, the interests of the plaintiff and the forum in California's assertion of jurisdiction over Asahi are slight. All that remains is a claim for indemnification asserted by Cheng Shin, a Taiwanese corporation, against Asahi. The transaction on which the indemnification claim is based took place in Taiwan; Asahi's components were shipped from Japan to Taiwan. Cheng Shin has not demonstrated that it is more convenient for it to litigate its indemnification claim against Asahi in California rather than in Taiwan or Japan.

Because the plaintiff is not a California resident, California's legitimate interests in the dispute have considerably diminished. The Supreme Court of California argued that the State had an interest in "protecting its consumers by ensuring that foreign manufacturers comply with the state's safety standards." The State Supreme Court's definition of California's interest, however, was overly broad. The dispute between Cheng Shin and Asahi is primarily about indemnification rather than safety standards. Moreover, it is not at all clear at this point that California law should govern the question whether a Japanese corporation should indemnify a Taiwanese corporation on the basis of a sale made in Taiwan and a shipment of goods from Japan to Taiwan . . .

* * * * *

Considering the international context, the heavy burden on the alien defendant, and the slight interests of the plaintiff and the forum State, the exercise of personal jurisdiction by a California court over Asahi in this instance would be unreasonable and unfair.

III

Because the facts of this case do not establish minimum contacts such that the exercise of personal jurisdiction is consistent with fair play and substantial justice, the judgment of the Supreme Court of California is reversed, and the case is remanded.

Questions

1. Trace the path of the *Asahi* case through the judicial system.
2. The Supreme Court ruled that the state court did not have jurisdiction over Asahi.
   a. What *kind* of jurisdiction is the court lacking?
   b. Why did the Supreme Court rule that jurisdiction was wanting in this case?
3. The Robinsons filed a product liability suit in an Oklahoma state court to recover for injuries sustained in an automobile accident in Oklahoma. The auto had been purchased in New York from the defendant, World-Wide Volkswagen Corp. Oklahoma's long-arm statute was used in an attempt to secure jurisdiction over the defendant. World-Wide conducted no business in Oklahoma. Nor did it solicit business there.
   a. Build an argument to support the claim of jurisdiction for the Oklahoma court.
   b. Decide. See *World-Wide Volkswagen Corp.* v. *Woodson,* 100 S.Ct. 559 (1980).
4. Burger King conducts a franchise, fast-food operation from its Miami, Florida, headquarters. John Rudzewicz and a partner, both residents of Michigan, secured a Burger King franchise in Michigan. Subsequently, the franchisees allegedly fell behind in payments, and after negotiations failed, Burger King ordered the franchisees to vacate the premises. They declined to do so, and continued to operate the franchise. Burger King brought suit in a federal district court in Florida. The defendant franchisees argued that the Florida court did not have personal jurisdiction over them because they were Michigan residents and because the claim did not arise in Florida. However, the district court found the defendants to be subject to the Florida long-arm statute, which extends jurisdiction to "[a]ny person, whether or not a citizen or resident of this state" who, "[b]reach[es] a contract in this state by failing to perform acts required by the contract

---

to be performed in this state." The franchise contract provided for governance of the relationship by Florida law. Policy was set in Miami, although day-to-day supervision was managed through various district offices. The case ultimately reached the U.S. Supreme Court.

a. What constitutional argument would you raise on behalf of the defendant franchisees?

b. Decide. See *Burger King Corp.* v. *Rudzewicz,* 471 U.S. 462 (1985).

STANDING TO SUE

Resorting to the courts is frequently an undesirable method of problem solving. Therefore, all who wish to bring a claim before a court may not be permitted to do so. To receive the court's attention, the litigant must demonstrate that she or he has *standing to sue.* That is, the person must show that her or his interest in the outcome of the controversy is sufficiently direct and substantial to justify the court's consideration. The litigant must show that she or he personally is suffering, or will be suffering, injury. Mere interest in the problem at hand is insufficient to grant standing to sue.

THE CIVIL TRIAL PROCESS

Civil procedure varies by jurisdiction. The following generalizations merely typify the process.

Pleadings

Pleadings are the documents by which each party sets his or her initial case before the court. A civil action begins when the plaintiff files his or her first pleading, which is labeled a *complaint.* The complaint specifies (1) the parties to the suit, (2) evidence as to the court's jurisdiction in the case, (3) a statement of the facts, and (4) a prayer for relief (a remedy).

The complaint is filed with the clerk of court and a *summons* is issued, directing the defendant to appear in court to answer the claims alleged against him or her. A sheriff or some other official attempts to personally deliver the summons to the defendant. If personal delivery cannot be achieved, the summons may be left with a responsible party at the defendant's residence. Failing that, other modes of delivery are permissible, including a mailing. Publication of a notice in a newspaper will, in some instances, constitute good service of process. Ordinarily, a copy of the complaint accompanies the summons, so the defendant is apprised of the nature of the claim.

The defendant has several options. He or she may do nothing, but failure to respond may result in a default judgment in favor of the plaintiff. The defendant may choose to respond by filing a *demurrer* or a *motion to dismiss,* the essence of which is to argue that even if the plaintiff's recitation of the facts is accurate, a claim on which relief can be granted has not been stated. For example, a student may be offended by a teacher's "bizarre" manner of dress; but, barring unusual circumstances, the student could not, as a matter of law, successfully challenge the teacher's costume.

Alternatively, the defendant may file with the court an initial pleading, called an *answer,* wherein the defendant enters a denial by setting out his or her version of the facts and law, or in which the defendant simply concedes the validity of the plaintiff's position. The answer may also contain an *affirmative defense* that would bar the plaintiff's claim. For example, the defendant might assert the statute of limitations or the statute of frauds. The defendant's answer might include a counterclaim or cross-claim. A *counterclaim* is the defendant's assertion of a claim of action against the plaintiff. A *cross-claim* is the defendant's assertion of a claim of action against a codefendant. In some states, these would be labeled *cross-complaints.* In the event of a counterclaim or the assertion of new facts in the answer, the plaintiff will respond with a *reply.* The complaint, answer, reply, and their components are the pleadings that serve to give notice, to clarify the issues, and to limit the dimensions of the litigation.

Motions

As necessary during and after the filing of the pleadings, either party may file motions with the court. For example, a party may move to clarify a pleading or to strike a portion deemed unnecessary. Of special importance is a motion for a judgment on the pleadings or a motion for summary judgment. In a *motion for a judgment on the pleadings,* either party simply asks the judge to reach a decision based on the information in the pleadings. However, the judge will do so only if the defendant's answer constitutes an admission of the accuracy of the plaintiff's claim, or if the plaintiff's claim clearly has no foundation in law.

In a *motion for a summary judgment,* the party filing the motion is claiming that no facts are in dispute. Therefore, the judge may make a ruling about the law without taking the case to trial. In a summary judgment hearing, the court can look beyond the pleadings to hear evidence from affidavits, depositions, and so on. These motions serve to avoid the time and expense of trial. The following case is an example of the use of a summary judgment motion.

WOODRUFF v. GEORGIA STATE UNIVERSITY ET AL.
304 S.E.2d 697 (Ga 1983)

Justice Weltner

Woodruff brought this action against the Board of Regents, Georgia State University and certain Georgia State University professors alleging state and federal constitutional violations, tort, and breach of contract claims. The trial court granted summary judgment and Woodruff appeals.

Woodruff was admitted to a master's degree program in the music department of Georgia State University in 1972. In the fall of 1973, she received an "F" on the basis of plagiarism, and appealed that grade to an appeals committee within the university. The committee changed the grade to an "incomplete." She alleges that thereafter her professors were "hostile and sarcastic" to her, refusing to help her with course work and thesis preparation, changing course requirements prior to graduation, placing damaging information about her in an open file, and giving her undeservedly low grades in an attempt to block her graduation.

In 1979, after seven years in a program which normally takes two or three years to complete, Woodruff was awarded the degree of Master of Arts in Music. She then applied for admittance into a doctoral program at the University of Georgia in Athens, which required recommendations from former professors. Woodruff's former professors either refused or ignored her request for recommendations. In their depositions, several professors testified that Woodruff was an "argumentative and troublesome" student who was erratic in her studies and not academically qualified to proceed to a doctoral program. They offered academic reasons for withholding their recommendations.

Woodruff filed suit in January, 1982, alleging libel and slander, intentional infliction of mental distress, conspiracy in withholding recommendations, negligent supervision of her graduate studies, breach of contract, and constitutional violations . . .

* * * * *

. . . [T]he central issue is whether or not a dispute concerning academic decisions of a public education institution is a justiciable controversy.

In the general realm of educational institutions, we have reviewed standards of dismissals and student discipline. We have examined the denial of student eligibility to participate in sports, and we have refused to permit the judiciary to referee high school football games. The Court of Appeals has upheld the authority of a local board of education to impose proficiency requirements as a prerequisite to graduation from high school.

We have not thus far, however, entertained an individual student's complaint seeking money damages for alleged impropriety in academic assessment of her work.

* * * * *

We now decline to review a teacher's academic assessment of a student's work.

This is clearly consistent with the authorities we have mentioned. It is restraint which stems from confidence that school authorities are able to discharge their academic duties in fairness and with competence. It is born alike of the necessity for shielding the courts from an incalculable new potential for lawsuits, testing every Latin grade and every selection for the Safety Patrol.

It protects every teacher from the cost and agony of litigation initiated by pupils and their parents who would rely upon the legal process rather than the learning process.

It protects every school system—all of them laboring under pressures of financing, personnel problems and student discipline, academic performance, taxpayer revolt and patron unrest, and a rising tide of recalls—from an added and unbearable burden of continuous legal turmoil.

Judgment affirmed.

Questions

1. *Woodruff* is the decision of what court?
2. Who were the defendants in *Woodruff* and why did they move for a summary judgment?
3. What was the legal issue facing the appellate court in *Woodruff?* Do you agree with its decision? Explain.

Discovery

Justice is the goal of the legal system. Information is central to reaching a just result. *Discovery* is the primary information-gathering stage in the trial process. Discovery (1) preserves the testimony of witnesses who may not be available for trial, (2) reduces the likelihood of perjury, (3) aids in defining and narrowing the facts and issues, (4) promotes pretrial settlements, (5) increases the likelihood of concluding the case with a summary judgment, and (6) helps prevent surprises at the trial.

In general, five discovery techniques are provided.

1. *Depositions.* A party or a witness may be required to appear before a court officer to give recorded, sworn testimony in response to questions raised by the attorneys for both sides of the controversy. Testimony is much like that at trial. *Depositions* are particularly helpful in trial preparation.
2. *Interrogatories.* Written questions calling for written answers signed under oath may be required. Unlike depositions, *interrogatories* may only be directed to parties, and they can call for information outside the party's personal knowledge, requiring the party to peruse her or his records.
3. *Discovery of documents and property.* Either party may request access to documents, as well as real and personal property, for the purpose of inspection relevant to the trial.
4. *Physical and mental examinations.* When the physical and/or mental state of a party is at issue, the court may be asked to enter an order calling for an examination. Good cause must be shown, and the court must be satisfied that the need for information outweighs the party's constitutional right to privacy.
5. *Admissions.* Either party may make written request of the other, seeking an *admission* as to the truth of a specified issue of fact or law. If the receiving party agrees

to or fails to deny the truth of the admission, that issue of fact or law is conclusively established for trial purposes. For example, in a suit alleging a defective transmission in a recently purchased automobile, the auto dealer might be asked to agree that the auto was sold under a warranty and that the warranty included the transmission.

Changes?   Because of widespread concerns about delays and expenses associated with litigation, the federal rules governing trials were changed in 1993. Basically, the new rules require the parties to voluntarily disclose all "reasonably available," relevant documents, data, names, and phone numbers of anyone likely to have discoverable information, insurance coverage, and so on. The new rules also limit interrogatories and depositions and require the parties to confer and develop a discovery plan and discuss settlement possibilities. At this writing in 1994, Congress is under pressure to amend the new rules, which many lawyers believe to be too sweeping in their requirements.

Pretrial Conference

Either party may request, and many courts require, a pretrial meeting involving the attorneys, the judge, and occasionally the parties. Usually following discovery, the conference is designed to plan the course of the trial in the interests of efficiency and justice. The participants seek to define and narrow the issues through informal discussion. The parties also attempt to settle the dispute in advance of trial. If no settlement is reached, a trial date is set.

The Judge and Jury

The federal Constitution and most state constitutions provide for the right to a jury trial in a civil case (excepting equity actions). Some states place dollar minimums on that guaranty. At the federal level and in most states, unless one of the parties requests a jury, the judge alone will hear the case and decide all questions of law and fact. If the case is tried before a jury, that body will resolve questions of fact.

Jurors are selected from a jury pool composed of a cross section of the community. A panel is drawn from that pool. The individuals in that panel are questioned by the judge, by the attorneys, or by all to determine if any individual is prejudiced about the case such that he or she could not reach an objective decision on the merits. The questioning process is called *voir dire.*

From an attorney's point of view, jury selection is often not so much a matter of finding jurors without bias as it is a matter of identifying those jurors who are most likely to reach a decision favorable to one's client. To that end, elaborate mechanisms and strategies have been employed—particularly in criminal trials—to identify desirable jurors. For example, sophisticated, computer-assisted surveys of the trial community have been conducted to develop objective evidence by which to identify jurors who would not admit to racial prejudice but whose "profile" suggests the likelihood of such prejudice. A few attorneys have taken the rather exotic tactic of employing body language experts to watch potential jurors during *voir dire* for those mannerisms said to reveal their inner views.

After questioning, the attorneys may *challenge for cause,* arguing to the judge that the individual cannot exercise the necessary objectivity of judgment. Attorneys are also afforded a limited number of *peremptory challenges,* by which the attorney can have a potential juror dismissed without the judge's concurrence and without offering a reason. However, peremptory challenges may not be used to reject jurors on the basis of race or gender.

Jury selection and the jury system are the subject of considerable debate in the legal community. Are juries necessary to a just system? How small can a jury be and still fulfill its duty? Is the jury process too slow and expensive? Should very long and complex cases, such as those in the antitrust area, be heard only by judges?

The article that follows looks at the use of science in winning jury trials.

NEW TRIAL WEAPON: PROF OFFERS GLIMPSE INTO MIND OF JURIES

Bruce Vielmetti

Call him a guru of group-think, a visionary of verdicts, a maverick professor or a slick entrepreneur.

But if you're in a high-stakes jury trial, just call him—before the other side does.

Harvey Moore—Chicago gang member-turned-Ph.D.—has become a not-so-secret weapon for lawyers. He combines social research and high technology to predict how supposedly unpredictable juries will vote.

In the past two years, Moore has gone from moonlighting sociology professor to star trial consultant . . .

Moore and his associates at Trial Practices Inc. have been on the winning side in about 72 of 78 trials they have worked on . . .

Until recently, the lawyers who hired Moore didn't like to talk about it.

"Attorneys fear that they'll be portrayed as manipulating this American institution," Moore said. "But I've thought about it, and hell, I'm proud of the work we do."

Earlier this year, he stood in front of 24 pretend jurors at Trial Practices Inc. in the First Florida Tower in downtown Tampa. The jurors came from a list of 3,500 names of people who responded to his newspaper ads. They will get $10 an hour to hear about the plaintiff in a mock personal injury case, an elderly man whose leg was amputated at a nursing home.

* * * * *

Before a case ever gets to Moore's high-tech lab, his staff has gone to the malls to question shoppers' attitudes toward the people and institutions involved in a particular case, such as nursing homes, chiropractors, lawyers or newspapers. Based on their reactions, Moore's staff creates a "framing strategy," their acknowledged euphemism for a "good story." Given a jury's likely prejudices, how can the client's story best be told?

Moore frames one or two versions of the story, then hits the malls again. Shoppers' reactions help refine the story. He may follow up with a telephone survey. The demographic data help establish profiles of what kind of jurors tend to accept or reject the story.

In the nursing home case, lawyer Jim Wilkes outlined the story of his client, a 92-year-old man whose leg was amputated. Wilkes contends the nursing home violated his client's rights by allowing the leg to deteriorate.

As a favor, another lawyer presents the nursing home's anticipated defense.

Back in a master control room, Moore watches the faces of jurors, brought to him by a pair of turning, zooming video cameras.

"That one woman is lost," he says, and notes her name. Then he sees that all the jurors perk up and lean forward for a videotaped interview with Wilkes' client; the elderly man talks about how it hurts, physically and emotionally, to have only one real leg.

Audience members record their individual verdicts before splitting into four groups to deliberate in separate, fully wired rooms.

Back in the control room, Wilkes and his partners are watching. They react like kids on Christmas morning. They frantically swap headphones in front of four TV monitors, trying to watch and hear all four juries at once. For a few moments, they gain the ultimate, intimate access into the jury's collective conscience.

"This one's already decided liability!" Wilkes shouts eagerly.

His brother, Tim Wilkes, also a lawyer, is watching another screen. "They're discussing whether you were appointed by the court!" he says. "I had no idea they talked about stuff like that."

"The things they're not supposed to be talking about—insurance, attorneys fees—they're all talking about," Jim Wilkes says. In a real case, a judge would instruct the jurors to decide only the facts pertinent to the injury, not whether a defendant has insurance or how much of the award would go to the plaintiff's lawyer.

Wilkes said he learned valuable lessons. One was that he needed to suggest a figure for damages because jurors wanted a starting point. Without one, the awards ranged from $50,000 to $1 million.

Using videotapes of those deliberations, Wilkes eventually won a favorable settlement from the nursing home.

This kind of help is not cheap. Moore's services start around $4,500 for some initial surveys, to $100,000 for a full package of extensive polling, a mock trial, in-court help and post-trial jury interviews.

* * * * *

"What his real genius is for is picking a theme out of the possible themes that are true, that will resonate with the jury," said Patrick Doherty, a lawyer. "He quotes the mall people, so in opening statement, you're using potential jurors' own words. If I want to say (an opponent's argument is) 'disingenuous,' he'll (tell me to) say, 'It's a damn lie.'"

Source: *Waterloo Courier*, October 2, 1992. Reprinted with permission of the copyright holder, *The St. Petersburg Times*.

Questions

1. Do Professor Moore's techniques amount to manipulation of the jury process? Explain.
2. In your judgment, does litigation consulting strengthen or weaken the "odds" of securing justice in a jury trial? Explain.

The Trial

The trial begins with the opening statement by the attorney having the burden of proof. Then the opposing attorney offers his or her statement. Each is expected to outline what he or she intends to prove. The plaintiff then presents evidence, which may include both testimony and physical evidence, such as documents and photos, called *exhibits.*

The attorney secures testimony from his or her own witness via questioning labeled *direct examination.* After the plaintiff's attorney completes direct examination of the plaintiff's own witness, the defense attorney may question that witness in a process labeled *cross-examination.* *Redirect* and *re-cross* may then follow. The plaintiff's attorney then summarizes the testimony and the exhibits and "rests" his or her case.

At this stage, the defense may make a motion for a *judgment as a matter of law,* arguing, in essence, that the plaintiff has offered insufficient evidence to justify relief, so time and expense may be saved by terminating the trial. Understandably, the judge considers the motion in the light most favorable to the plaintiff. Such motions ordinarily fail, and the trial goes forward with the defendant's presentation of evidence.

At the completion of the defendant's case, both parties may be permitted to offer *rebuttal* evidence, and either party may move for a directed verdict. Barring a directed verdict, the case goes forward, with each party making a *closing argument.* When the trial is by jury, the judge must instruct the jurors as to the law to be applied to the case. The attorneys often submit to the judge their views of the proper instructions. Because the law lacks the clarity that lay persons often attribute to it, framing the instructions is a difficult task, frequently resulting in an appeal to a higher court. Finally, the verdict of the jury is rendered and a judgment is entered by the court.

Post-Trial Motions

The losing party may seek a *judgment notwithstanding the verdict (judgment n.o.v.)* on the grounds that in light of the controlling law, insufficient evidence was offered to permit the jury to decide as it did. Such motions are rarely granted. The judge is also empowered to enter a judgment n.o.v. on his or her own initiative.

Either party may also move for a new trial. The winning party might do so on the grounds that the remedy provided was inferior to that warranted by the evidence. The losing party commonly claims an error of law to support a motion for a new trial. Other possible grounds for a new trial include jury misconduct or new evidence.

Appeals

After the judgment is rendered, either party may appeal the decision to a higher court. The winner may do so if he or she feels the remedy is inadequate. Ordinarily, of course, the losing party brings the appeal. The appealing party is the *appellant* or the *petitioner,* while the other party is the *appellee* or *respondent.* The appeals court does not try the case again. In theory, at least, its consideration is limited to mistakes of law at the trial level. For example, the appellant will argue that a jury instruction was erroneous or that the judge erred in failing to grant a motion to strike testimony alleged to have been prejudicial. The appeals court does not hear new evidence. It bases its decision on the trial record, materials filed by the opposing attorneys, and oral arguments.

The appellate court announces its judgment and ordinarily explains that decision in an accompanying document labeled an *opinion.* (Most of the cases in this text are appellate court opinions.) If no error is found, the lower court decision is *affirmed.* In finding prejudicial error, the appellate court may simply *reverse* (overrule) the lower court. Or, the judgment may be to *reverse and remand,* wherein the lower court is overruled and the trial court must try the case again in accordance with the law as articulated in the appeals court opinion. After the decision of the intermediate appellate court, a further appeal may be directed to the highest court of the jurisdiction. Most of those petitions are denied.

Class Actions

A *class action* allows a group of individuals to sue or be sued in one judicial proceeding, provided they are "similarly situated"—that is, their claim or the claim against them arises out of similar or closely related grievances. For example, if hundreds of people were injured in a hotel fire, a subset of that group might file an action against the hotel on behalf of all the injured parties. The class action thus permits lawsuits that might otherwise be impractical due to the number of people involved or the small amount of each claim. The class action is also expedient; many potential causes of action can be disposed of in one suit. Recently, a federal district court approved the use of a class action in a sexual harassment case, an area of the law where claims had previously been restricted to individual plaintiffs. In this case, the court ruled that the Eveleth Taconite Company's mines are a hostile environment for all hourly female workers.[13]

Questions—Part Two

1. What are the purposes and uses of the concept of jurisdiction? Why do we limit the courts to which a claim can be taken?
2. Law cases often read like soap operas while they reveal important truths. A woman and man, each married to others, had engaged in a long-term love affair. The

woman's husband died, and she pleaded with her paramour to leave his New York home to visit her in Florida. She affirmed her love for the man. They made arrangements to meet in Miami, but on his arrival at the airport he was served a summons informing him that he was being sued. His Florida "lover" sought $500,000 for money allegedly loaned to him and for seduction inspired by a promise of marriage.

    a. Does the Florida court have proper jurisdiction over him?

    b. What if he had voluntarily come to Florida on vacation? See *Wyman* v. *Newhouse,* 93 F.2d 313 (2d Cir. 1937).

3. The Incompatibility Clause of the Constitution provides that "no person holding any office under the United States shall be a member of either House during his continuance in the office." An association of Armed Forces reservists, including several U.S. citizens and taxpayers, was opposed to the Vietnam War. The association brought a class action on behalf of all U.S. citizens and taxpayers against the secretary of defense and others. The association argued that several members of Congress violated the Incompatibility Clause by virtue of their Armed Forces Reserve membership. Do the plaintiffs have standing to sue? Explain. See *Schlesinger* v. *Reservists Committee to Stop the War,* 418 U.S. 208 (1974).

4. The Fifth and Fourteenth Amendments to the U.S. Constitution guarantee that the citizenry will not be deprived of life, liberty, and property without due process of law, while the Seventh Amendment guarantees the right to trial by jury. In an unusually complex antitrust case, it was argued that the due process clause prohibits trial by jury in instances where the complexity of the case exceeds a jury's ability to reach a reasoned judgment.

    a. Should unusually complex cases be heard by a judge alone? Explain. See *In Re U.S. Financial Securities Litigation,* 609 F.2d 411 (9th Cir. 1979) cert. denied 446 U.S. 929 (1979). But see *In Re Japanese Electronic Products Antitrust Litigation* (U.S. Court of Appeals for the 3rd Circuit, No. 79–2540) *Antitrust and Trade Regulation Report,* No. 973, July 17, 1980, p. F–1.

    b. Are juries usually successful in reaching fair, impartial verdicts, or do the personal deficiencies and prejudices of the ordinary citizen result in unfair, irrational decisions? Explain.

5.   Only two people interviewed by *The Washington Post* in a nationwide poll of 1,005 persons could name all nine members of the U.S. Supreme Court.

    While only 9 percent of those polled could name the chief justice of the United States (William Rehnquist), 54 percent could name the judge on TV's "The People's Court" (Joseph Wapner).[14]

    a. The Supreme Court intentionally operates in relative obscurity. Should we be concerned that Judge Wapner is much better known than are members of the Supreme Court? Explain.

    b. Why are we more interested in judges as entertainers than judges as shapers of American life?

    c. Should the Supreme Court televise its proceedings? Explain.

Part Three—Criticisms and Alternatives

CRITICISM

To many Americans, our system of justice is neither systematic nor just, and in recent years our court system has come under increasing criticism. Broadly, the concerns are twofold: (1) our society too readily turns to litigation to solve disputes, and (2) the justice system is unfair.

Too Many Lawyers and Lawsuits?

In 1991, then Vice President Dan Quayle generated enormous, generally favorable, publicity in a speech to the American Bar Association when he said, among other things:

> Let's ask ourselves: Does America really need 70 percent of the world's lawyers? Is it healthy for our economy to have 18 million new lawsuits coursing through the system annually? Is it right that people with disputes come up against staggering expense and delay?

In fact, most countries do not collect reliable data regarding lawyer numbers, and definitions about what actually constitutes a lawyer vary widely. However, based on United Nations' data regarding individuals receiving law degrees (most of whom become law providers, in some fashion), a recent study concluded that the United States ranks 35th in the world in lawyers per 10,000 population.[15] On the other hand, another recent scholarly study claims that the United States is so overpopulated with lawyers that our total economic productivity has been reduced by more than 10 percent. On an individual basis, the study finds that the average worker's pay is reduced about $2,500 annually because we have an estimated 40 percent more lawyers than would be best for maximum economic productivity.[16] That study, in turn, is challenged by another suggesting that a higher ratio of lawyers to white-collar workers, generally, was associated with *faster* economic growth in the 1980s.[17] Clearly, we do not have definitive evidence about the impact of lawyers on the American economy. However, we can be sure that litigation has become a favorite American pastime. For example, in 1992, state courts received over *100 million* new cases.[18] And we know the system is expensive. The cost of dealing with civil injuries (torts) alone is estimated at $132 billion annually.[19] The bill is split as follows: insurance industry administrative costs (24 percent), payments for economic loss (22 percent), payments for pain and suffering (21 percent), defense lawyers (18 percent), and plaintiffs' lawyers (15 percent).[20] Note that victims, in the end, receive less than 50 percent of the total payout. On a comparative basis, the bill for justice in the United States also appears high. Tort litigation in this country consumes 2.3 percent of the GNP, compared to "fairly crude" estimates of 0.6 percent in Britain, 1.2 percent in West Germany, and 0.7 percent in Japan.[21]

At the same time, the widely embraced notion that the tort system has run wild does not seem fully supported by the more careful evidence. A recent, very extensive inquiry found, for example, that (1) plaintiffs, on the average, are undercompensated in tort cases, (2) only 5 percent of total civil grievances ever become lawsuits, and (3) only one in six of those seriously injured by medical malpractice actually file suits.[22]

Is the System Unfair?

We can confidently say that former Vice President Quayle's charges were overstated, but we can also say that our justice system is flawed. The following article describes some of the fundamental complaints made by lawyers and judges themselves.

LAWYERS AND JUDGES
TERM SYSTEM OF CIVIL SUITS
UNFAIR, COSTLY, SLOW

Stephen Wermiel

An unusual, in-depth poll of lawyers and judges reveals dissatisfaction with rising costs and delays of civil lawsuits and shows surprising agreement that the system is unfair to individuals or small businesses with limited resources.

The survey, covering a broad spectrum of lawyers from public interest firms to in-house corporate counsels to federal judges, reported that the majority believes the current civil-court system gives an unfair advantage to large institutions or wealthy individuals and "unreasonably impedes" use of the courts by "ordinary citizens."

* * * * *

The poll [was] conducted by Louis Harris & Associates.

* * * * *

Patrick Head, general counsel of FMC Corp., says the survey reflects the view that "the courts are extremely clogged up and are generally unresponsive to the needs of the public, including the corporate public."

* * * * *

The survey explored the problems of so-called transaction costs, the total cost of a lawsuit from its preparation to its conclusion, and of delays. Among the survey's findings were:

—Most lawyers said transaction costs were "a major problem," although defense lawyers were less troubled.

* * * * *

—A majority of lawyers and a sizable minority of judges thought delays have increased "somewhat" or "greatly."

—A majority in all categories said that "large interests" have an "unfair advantage" in the civil courts, and that use of the system by the average individual is impeded "unreasonably."

—More than 60 percent in all groups thought discovery abuse was a major cause of problems, and a majority of all but public interest lawyers called it the most important. Lawyers, except those in the public interest category, said about 60 percent of the costs were in discovery.

—At least 40 percent of all lawyers, and even one-third of the judges, thought inadequate case management by judges created problems.

—Significant majorities in all groups favored setting 18-month limits on discovery and allowing judges to sometimes impose the costs on the party asking for the documents.

—A majority of most groups, and 49 percent of public interest lawyers, favored making the loser pay the discovery costs in disputes between solvent corporations.

—Substantial majorities in all segments said judges should hold early-pretrial conferences, monitor and limit discovery, and set early and firm trial dates.

*   *   *   *   *

Source: *The Wall Street Journal,* April 7, 1989, p. B7. Reprinted by permission of *The Wall Street Journal,* © 1989, Dow Jones & Company, Inc. All Rights Reserved Worldwide.

On the Other Hand

Even as we reflect on its weaknesses, we should not forget why our legal system has been so important in building America. We are the envy of the oppressed people of the world in our efforts to maximize freedom, fairness, and democracy for all. Furthermore, laws and lawyers are central to economic efficiency. Lawyers devise the rules, processes, and structures that permit capitalism to operate effectively. Former communist states in Eastern Europe are clamoring for American legal expertise to help them put together governments founded in constitutional principles along with the legal infrastructures necessary for smoothly functioning free markets. Even the People's Republic of China, where law practice was actually forbidden prior to 1979, has now recognized the importance of lawyers in building a strong economy:

INTERNATIONAL

Beijing expects the number of lawyers in China to double to 100,000 by the year 2000, which the government hopes will strengthen the legal system and expedite judicial reforms. The increase is an integral part of China's economic modernization program, which has prompted a rapid rise in litigation, arbitration and contract negotiations, straining the country's young legal system.[23]

Questions

1. List some of the services performed by lawyers and the legal system that are necessary to an efficient free market.
2. Do you see it as a sign of progress that China is encouraging the growth of its legal infrastructure? Explain.
3. *a.* In your opinion, why do lawyers in America have such an unfavorable image?
   b. Is that image deserved? Explain.

ALTERNATIVE DISPUTE RESOLUTION (ADR)

In response to problems like those cited in the previous section (particularly expense and delay), we are witnessing the advance stages of what may prove to be a revolution in dispute resolution. More and more businesses and individuals are seeking alternatives to the mainstream judicial process. Some examples follow.

- Small claims courts (e.g., Judge Wapner's "People's Court") have proven so successful and efficient that smaller businesses, in particular, are encouraging legislatures to increase the maximum recovery limits (currently $1,000 to $4,000 in most states) in order to permit more cases to avoid the full-blown judicial process. Small claims courts typically have relaxed procedural requirements, lawyers are actually forbidden in some states, and cases can be resolved in a few weeks rather than the years sometimes required in conventional courts.[24]
- In 1993, New York state established a new all-business court designed eventually to handle the bulk of all commercial disputes (contracts, sales, securities) arising in New York City. In order to increase efficiency, judges for the new court will specialize in commercial matters and will be permitted to develop some special procedures for expediting cases and for reaching settlements.[25]
- About 500 larger companies now employ ombudsmen (or ombudswomen) as informal problem solvers who can receive workplace complaints and endeavor to resolve them before bigger problems emerge. Ombudsmen take a neutral perspective rather than acting as management representatives, and conversations with ombudsmen are confidential unless the employee says otherwise.[26]
- Of course, the heart of the alternate dispute resolution movement lies in mediation and arbitration. A 1993 Deloitte and Touche survey of 246 attorneys found nearly three-quarters of them had had some experience with ADR and most of that three-quarters expected to make greater use of it in the future. Sixty-five percent of those with ADR experience said they had saved money, ranging typically from 11 to 50 percent of the expected litigation costs.[27]

Mediation

Mediation introduces a neutral third party into the resolution process. Ideally, the parties devise their own solution, with the mediator as a facilitator, not a decision maker. Even if the mediator does propose a solution, its character will be in the nature of a compromise, not a determination of right and wrong. The bottom line is that only the disputing parties can adopt any particular outcome. The mediator may aid the parties in a number of ways, such as opening up communication between them.

Arbitration

Arbitration is a process in which a neutral third party is given the power to determine a binding resolution of the dispute. Depending on the situation, the resolution may be either a compromise solution or a determination of the rights of the parties and a win/lose solution. Even in the latter case, however, it may be quicker and less costly than a trial, and the arbitrator may be an expert in the subject area of the dispute instead of a generalist, as a judge would be. It is procedurally more formal than mediation, with the presentation of proofs and arguments by the parties, but less formal than court adjudication.

The following article depicts the extraordinary expansion of interest in ADR.

MEDIATION FIRMS ALTER
THE LEGAL LANDSCAPE

Ellen Joan Pollock

Imagine a legal system in which companies could put their disputes before judges of their choice, get speedy decisions, avoid the uncertainty of jury verdicts and keep legal bills to a minimum.

This is the system that hundreds of corporations are, in fact, choosing . . . Instead of going to court, such companies are letting a burgeoning industry of private mediation and arbitration firms resolve their legal disputes, ranging from auto-accident cases to the biggest antitrust suits.

Last year alone, more than 40,000 civil cases that once would have been handled in the nation's courts were resolved by four major firms that sell quicker, less costly, less procedurally complex dispute resolution. And every week, it seems, key players in another industry—from banking to food to insurance—announce that they will submit a major area of litigation to some form of mediation or arbitration.

Tremendous Savings

The savings for companies so far have been tremendous. Since 1990, 406 companies tracked by the Center for Public Resources, a nonprofit group that provides mediators and arbitrators, saved more than $150 million in legal fees and expert-witness costs by using litigation alternatives. The cases involved disputes with more than $5 billion at stake.

"I think that we're witnessing the emergence of a [free] market in dispute resolution which is challenging the traditional state-owned monopoly in dispute resolution—which, of course, is the courts," says Howard V. Golub, general counsel of Pacific Gas & Electric Co.

With the help of a mediator, Pacific Gas & Electric recently settled six disputes stemming from the crash of a helicopter that hit one of the utility's electrical lines. Such a case typically would have taken two years to wind its way through court. PG&E estimates that it would have cost $300,000 to $500,000 to litigate if the case settled just before trial, double that if it was tried to a verdict. Instead, the case was brought to a close within 10 months of the accident, and litigation costs were about $20,000. Terms of the settlement were confidential—another reason companies like mediation.

* * * * *

It was the reluctance of law firms that made mediation a fringe movement of the legal profession for so long. Quite simply, there was no financial incentive for lawyers to give up endless court battles for which they billed at hourly rates . . .

* * * * *

But now companies are taking the lead in pushing for litigation alternatives . . . At the same time, litigation alternatives have become easier to use . . .

Customized Proceedings

The new mediation firms were the answer. They customize mediation or arbitration proceedings to fit the needs of the disputing parties. Mediators can engage in shuttle diplomacy or express their opinion on the value of a case. Lawyers can be banned from the conference room. And most significantly, the pretrial fact-finding stage known as discovery, which can last years, can be streamlined to the simple exchange of a few documents.

* * * * *

Going private also allows businesses to circumvent the lottery systems by which courts assign judges. Michael J. Dontzin, a former New York state judge now with Endispute, sums up the attractions of mediation this way: "Here you write your own rules and pick your own judge."

* * * * *

Critics warn that the growth of private mediation firms is draining the public court system of some of its best judges and removing some important civil cases from the courts' domain—and thus from the public's view. If the trend continues, they say, the nation could end up with a dual system in which the rich buy high-quality justice on the private market and the poor get what's left over.

Many lawyers and judges worry in particular that the move to private dispute resolution will rob the public of the legal precedents that are the foundation of the justice system. Even Matthew Crosson, chief administrator of New York's overburdened courts and a supporter of litigation alternatives, believes that secret arbitration and mediation decisions may be bad for the public in some cases. The secret resolution of a product-liability case, he notes, means "the product defect may go uncorrected because the dispute was resolved in a private setting."

Looking for Alternatives

But the corporate world finds the advantages of mediation hard to resist . . .

* * * * *

General Motors Corp. launched an arbitration and mediation program for its dealers about two years ago with the help of Endispute. So far 78 cases have gone through, or are going through, the program. The cases generally settle, according to H. Richard Elmquist, a GM in-house lawyer. Disputes, he says, typically are resolved in a day.

William Coulter, whose Phoenix Cadillac dealership generates $55 million in revenues a year, settled a dispute with GM over charges for repair work he did on cars under warranty. GM claimed it had over-reimbursed him by $100,000. After a mediation that lasted less than a day, Mr. Coulter agreed to pay GM $25,000. Mr. Coulter felt that he could have pushed GM harder but decided not to "quibble." "It was more important for me to resolve the problem and have a good working relationship with the factory," he says.

Source: *The Wall Street Journal,* March 22, 1993, p. B1. Reprinted by permission of *The Wall Street Journal,* © 1993 Dow Jones & Company, Inc. All Rights Reserved Worldwide.

Questions

1. The article cites some problems associated with mediation.
   a. List them and any other problems you find with ADR.
   b. In your opinion, is justice as likely to be achieved via ADR as through the judicial system? Explain.

2. In an effort to reduce legal expenses, some major American banks have announced that all complaints by depositors and credit-card customers will be subject to arbitration. Some of those banks limit arbitration to claims involving large sums of money, and some permit judicial appeal of the arbitration decision. Is mandatory arbitration fair to consumers? Explain. See, e.g., Ralph King, "Banks Force Griping Customers to Forgo Courts for Arbitration," *The Wall Street Journal,* January 20, 1993, p. B1.

Questions—Part Three

1. Yale law professor George Priest recommends a constitutional amendment to limit those civil cases that may be heard by a jury.[28] A five-year wait to go to trial has become common. However, plaintiffs hold the hope that a jury will grant a large award. Therefore, they are reluctant to settle prior to trial. The result, according to Priest, is big delays. Therefore, he argues for restricting routine cases such as auto accidents to judges. Priest believes that judges' decisions would be more predictable than those of jurors. Knowing the likely outcome, the parties would then be more likely to settle in advance.

   Would justice be served if we were to follow Priest's suggestion and reserve civil juries to cases (about 5 percent of the total) where people are suing the government for violation of their rights, those claiming to have been defamed, and those injured in an "uncommon and devastating way"? Explain.

2. Total tort costs (legal and administrative expenses, jury awards, and settlements) in the United States total about 2.3 percent of the gross domestic product. For other industrialized nations, those costs average perhaps 0.5 percent of gross domestic product.[29] Some argue that our tort costs are so high relative to other nations because we have inadequate government social programs.
   a. Explain that argument. Do you agree?
   b. How do you explain the high cost of tort actions in the United States?

3. Economist Stephen Magee argues that one way to strengthen the American economy would be to close the law schools:

   "Every time you turn out one law school graduate you've got a 40-year problem on your hands," he says. "These guys run around and generate a lot of spurious conflict. They're like heat-seeking missiles."[30]

   Comment.

Part Four—Law in China

INTERNATIONAL

Having surveyed the American legal system, we should conclude by reminding ourselves that our approaches to life, including our methods of finding justice, are increasingly intertwined with the cultures of the other nations of the world. In a shrinking and increasingly competitive economic environment, we cannot afford to be ignorant about the balance of the globe. Therefore, let's take a look at one example of a justice system abroad—in this case, the law of China.

From the founding of the People's Republic of China (PRC) in 1949 to the death of Mao and the fall of the "Gang of Four" in 1976, the official Chinese position was one of hostility to law. Statutes were few and almost no one studied law. Indeed, law had played a limited role in the entire history of China. But today the Chinese are rapidly adding statutes dealing with all dimensions of their lives. Officials enroll in short courses in the law, and press coverage of legal issues is prominent.[31]

In 1986, China approved its *General Principles of Civil Law,* a code modeled not on Oriental traditions but on Roman and German law. Fundamentally, the Chinese leaders came to understand that a strong, rational legal system would be instrumental for commercial growth. Foreign investment in China, export business, and a stronger domestic market would all require a dependable, workable legal system. So to the Chinese, the law became, in part, an economic development vehicle. Of course, ultimate authority remains in the central government, and bureaucrats perform many functions left to civil law in this country.[32] Also, economic change has been accompanied by some problems. Crime is increasing at an annual rate of nearly 8 percent despite a system where defendants seldom go free. Similarly, the filing of civil lawsuits has grown about 10 percent annually since 1988, reflecting, in part, the move toward capitalism.[33]

So Chinese law is beginning to take on some of the dimensions of Western systems, but fundamental differences in attitudes remain:

> Most Chinese persons engage in a large variety of economic and social activities and resolve disputes involved in those activities without coming in contact with the formal legal system. As in Japan, litigation in a court of law is not considered a normal way to resolve a dispute. Custom and extrajudicial dispute settling mechanisms are utilized not only by private parties but by public entities. Decisions declaring someone right and someone wrong are not a desirable goal. Settlements and compromises are preferable. Even in court, Chinese litigants generally do not obtain a clear defeat or victory.[34]

The following case may be helpful in demonstrating that while China has begun to build a legal system in the individualistic, Western mode, that system operates within the parameters of ancient Chinese communal values. This case involved a subject of intense concern in China, the protection of reputation. The resolution of the case demonstrates the quite substantial difference in Chinese and American approaches to dispute resolution in that the Chinese court deemphasized compensation for loss while giving great attention to restoration of reputation and the making of an apology. Loss of face, not loss of money, was the critical issue.[35]

> *The Case of* Shanghai Xinya Medical Rubber Factory v. Wujin Medical Facilities Factory. In 1983, the plaintiff began to manufacture and sell feminine hygiene devices. The market was good, and by 1985 the plaintiff was selling more than 600,000 units a year. That year, the defendant began to manufacture and sell the same product. In order to sell its overproduction, the defendant printed hundreds of advertisements and sent them to medical supply stores in Shanghai. In these flyers, the defendant claimed that women could injure themselves by using the plaintiff's product, and that the plaintiff had inventoried 1.05 million devices that were either partially effective or completely ineffective. In the wake of these notices, the plaintiff experienced a marked drop in sales and [an] increase in returns.

The court decided that the defendant should place an announcement in a municipal daily newspaper apologizing to the plaintiff, thereby eliminating the effect of the infringement and restoring the plaintiff's reputation, and should also compensate the plaintiff for damages in the amount of 30,000 RMB (approximately US $7,500).[36] [The plaintiff's actual losses totaled about 560,000 RMB.]

Questions—Part Four

1. Explain how China's new legal system may actually operate as an economic development device.
2. Would our society be improved were we to adopt the ancient Chinese preference for compromise settlements over clear victories and defeats? Explain.
3. The difficult role of our legal system in blending the U.S. culture with those of other countries in our increasingly intertwined world was made dramatically apparent by a 1993 criminal trial in Baton Rouge, Louisiana, where Rodney Peairs was acquitted of manslaughter charges in the death of a 16-year-old Japanese exchange student. Peairs shot Yoshihiro Hattori when the student mistakenly went to Peairs's door in search of a Halloween party. Peairs felt his home was threatened, and Louisiana's "shoot the burglar" law allows the use of deadly force to protect against an intruder. The Japanese people were outraged by the decision and mystified that it could have happened since, for the most part, owning a gun in that country is forbidden.
   a. Why have we not adopted the Japanese position on the private ownership of guns?
   b. Why are some rules appropriate in one nation but not in another?
4. Should we punish immigrants to the United States for committing acts that are crimes here but that are lawful in their native states? For example, an African woman moved to England and thereafter scarred her daughter's face as part of a tribal initiation. In the interests of genuine diversity and multiculturalism, must the U.S. justice system recognize a "cultural defense" in such criminal situations? Explain.

CHAPTER QUESTIONS

1. Are the flaws in our legal system of such magnitude that respect for the law is threatened? Explain.
2. According to Warren Avis, founder of Avis Rent-a-Car:

   We've reached a point in this country where, in many instances, power has become more important than justice—not a matter of who is right, but of who has the most money, time, and the largest battery of lawyers to drag a case through the courts.[37]

   a. Should the rich be entitled to better legal representation, just as they have access to better food, better medical care, better education, and so on? Explain.
   b. Should we employ a nationwide legal services program sufficient to guarantee competent legal aid to all? Explain.
3. As discussed in the readings, peremptory challenges may not constitutionally be used to exclude a potential juror from a trial on racial or gender grounds.

a. Must a criminal jury reflect the ethnic or racial diversity of the community? Explain. See *Powers* v. *Ohio*, 111 S.Ct. 1364 (1991)

b. Could potential jurors lawfully be rejected on the basis of their place of residence? Explain. See *U.S.* v. *Bishop*, 959 F.2d 820 (1992).

4. French correspondent Alain Clement, commenting on the role of lawyers in America:

> Truly, American lawyers come as close to being a "ruling class" as is possible in a country too vast and varied to produce one. Since Franklin D. Roosevelt, each president has had around him lawyer-confidants, so that Congress and state legislatures are dominated—even if less so than before—by a majority who come from the bar.[38]

a. Do you agree with Clement? Explain.

b. If so, have lawyers earned their influence? Explain.

5. Clement also offered a partial explanation for Americans' increasing reliance on lawsuits to resolve their conflicts:

> Diverse causes explain the growth of the contentious mood in America. One could be called the devaluing of the future. In 1911, the Russian political scientist Moise Ostrgorski wrote: "Confident of the future, Americans manifest a remarkable endurance to an unhappy present, a submissive patience that is willing to bargain about not only civic rights, but even the rights of man."[39]

a. What does Clement mean?

b. How do you explain our increased reliance on litigation?

6. Maintenance of our adversary system of justice sometimes compels lawyers to engage in practices that some consider unethical. Anne Strick relates one such situation.

> Once upon a time, Williston, called by a colleague "one of the most distinguished and conscientious lawyers I or any man have ever known," was defending a client in a civil suit. In the course of the trial, Williston discovered in his client's letter file material potentially damaging to the man's case. The opposition failed to demand the file; nor did Williston offer it. His client won. But, recounts Williston in his autobiography, the judge in announcing his decision made clear that his ruling was based in part on his belief in one critical fact: a

fact Williston, through a letter from the file in his possession, knew to be unfounded.

> Did Williston, that "most conscientious lawyer," speak up? Did he correct the Court's unfounded belief, the better to serve both truth and justice? He did not.

> "Though," he wrote, "I had in front of me a letter which showed his [Honor's] error," Williston kept silent. Nor did he question the propriety of his behavior. For, said he, the lawyer "is not only not obliged to disclose unfavorable evidence, but it is a violation of his duty to his client if he does so."[40]

a. Did Williston act properly? Explain.

b. Should we turn to more cooperative, less combative, approaches to dispute resolution? Explain.

7. On July 5, 1884, four sailors were cast away from their ship in a storm 1,600 miles from the Cape of Good Hope. Their lifeboat contained neither water nor much food. On the 20th day of their ordeal, Dudley and Stevens, without the assistance or agreement of Brooks, cut the throat of the fourth sailor, a 17- or 18-year-old boy. They had not eaten since day 12. Water had been available only occasionally. At the time of the death, the men were probably about 1,000 miles from land. Prior to his death, the boy was lying helplessly in the bottom of the boat. The three surviving sailors ate the boy's remains for four days, at which point they were rescued by a passing boat. They were in a seriously weakened condition.

a. Were Dudley and Stevens guilty of murder? Explain.

b. Should Brooks have been charged with a crime for eating the boy's flesh? Explain. See *The Queen* v. *Dudley and Stephens,* 14 Queen's Bench Division 273 (1884).

8. Tompkins was a citizen of Pennsylvania. While walking on a railroad footpath in that state, he was struck by an object protruding from a passing freight train owned by the Erie Railroad Company, a New York corporation. Tompkins, by virtue of diversity of citizenship, filed a negligence suit against Erie in a New York federal court. Erie argued for the application of Pennsylvania common law, in which case Tompkins would have been treated as a trespasser. Tompkins argued that the absence of a Pennsylvania statute addressing the topic meant that federal common law had to be applied to the case. Should the court apply

the relevant Pennsylvania state law, or should the federal court be free to exercise its independent judgment about what the common law of the state is or should be? See *Erie Railroad* v. *Tompkins* 304 U.S. 64 (1938).

9. Can minorities secure justice in America? Explain. See Ellen Pollock and Stephen Adler, "Legal System Struggles to Reflect Diversity," *The Wall Street Journal,* May 8, 1992, p. A1.

10. Robert Malott, CEO of FMC, argued that Americans, more than Europeans and the Japanese, are willing to turn to the courts to resolve disputes. Assuming Malott is correct, what would explain that condition?

11. As explained in the readings, alternate dispute resolution offers many advantages in resolving business conflicts. However, some cases do not lend themselves well to ADR. Can you list some of the considerations a company should evaluate in deciding between ADR and litigation? See Campbell Killefer, "Some Disputes Still Deserve Their Day in Court," *The Wall Street Journal,* October 12, 1992, p. A10.

12. Lawyers have recently begun pursuing two new damage claims. One is labeled "fear of death," which typically arises in air crashes where the severe stress of the accident, including the fear of dying, gives rise to flashbacks and continuing anguish after the accident. The second is a suit for loss of joy or loss of pleasure, as in the case of an accident victim who is in a coma and cannot receive the pleasures of a normal life. Historically, damages in these situations have been limited to economic loss and perhaps some narrowly defined emotional losses (e.g., pain and suffering).

  a. What problems for the court do you see in these causes of action?

  b. Would you permit those claims were you the judge? Explain.

13. Judicial reform advocates often argue that the United States should adopt the English rule providing that the winner in a lawsuit is entitled to recover its reasonable litigation expenses from the loser.

  a. In brief, what are the strengths and weaknesses of the English rule?

  b. Would you favor it? Explain. See Herbert Kritzer, "Searching for Winners in the Loser Pays Rule," *ABA Journal,* November 1992, p. 55.

14. In deciding whether to confirm a president's nominee for the Supreme Court, policy analyst Terry Eastland suggests that senators ask, among others, the following question: "[I]f there is an injustice in society, and Congress or the states have failed to act, should the Supreme Court fill the void?" Answer Eastland's question. See Terry Eastland, "What Republicans Should Ask the Supreme Court Nominee," *The Wall Street Journal,* April 14, 1993, p. A15.

NOTES

1. Mark Clements, "Findings from *Parade*'s National Survey on Law and Order," *Parade Magazine,* April 18, 1993, p. 4.

2. Editorial, "L.A.: Catharsis and Reality," *The Wall Street Journal,* April 19, 1993, p. A12.

3. Franz Schurmann, "Justice for All Is a Fragile Ideal," *Des Moines Register,* April 25, 1993, p. 1C.

4. Oliver Wendell Holmes, *Collected Legal Papers* (New York: Harcourt Brace Jovanovich, 1920), p. 173.

5. Benjamin Cardozo, *The Growth of Law* (New Haven, Conn.: Yale University Press, 1924), p. 52.

6. Max Weber, *Law in Economy and Society,* ed. Max Rheinstein (Cambridge, Mass.: Harvard University Press, 1954), p. 5.

7. Bronislaw Malinowski, *Crime and Custom in Savage Society* (Patterson, N.J.: Littlefield, 1959), p. 55. Originally published in 1926.

8. Roscoe Pound, "A Survey of Social Interest," *Harvard Law Review* 57 (1943), pp. 1, 39.

9. Richard Quinney, "The Ideology of Law: Notes for a Radical Alternative to Legal Oppression," *Issues in Criminology* 7 (1972), p. 1, as reported in *The Sociology of Law: A Conflict Perspective,* ed. Charles E. Reasons and Robert M. Rich (Toronto: Butterworth, 1978), p. 42.

10. Terence M. Cannon, "Law and Order in America," in *Up Against the American Myth,* ed. Tom Christoffel, David Finkelhor, and Dan Gilbarg (New York: Holt, Rinehart & Winston, 1970), pp.

348–49, as quoted in Frederick Sturdivant, *Business and Society—A Managerial Approach,* rev. ed. (Burr Ridge, IL: Richard D. Irwin, 1981), p. 52.

11. Helene Cooper, "Child-Divorce Case Marks Legal Evolution," *The Wall Street Journal,* September 28, 1992, p. B6.

12. Schurmann, "Justice for All," p. 1C.

13. *Lois E. Jenson, et al.* v. *Eveleth Taconite Co.,* U.S. District Court, Minnesota, Third Division, Civil No. 5–88–163 (1993) reported in Milo Geyelin, "Sex-Harassment Ruling," *The Wall Street Journal,* May 17, 1993, p. B2.

14. Editorial, "The Anonymous Justices," *Des Moines Register,* July 18, 1989, p. 6A.

15. Ray August, "The Mythical Kingdom of Lawyers," *ABA Journal* 78 (September 1992), p. 72.

16. Stephen Magee, "How Many Lawyers Ruin an Economy?" *The Wall Street Journal,* September 24, 1992, p. A17.

17. Charles Epp, "Let's Not Kill All the Lawyers," *The Wall Street Journal,* July 9, 1992, p. A13.

18. "Today," National Broadcasting Company, June 22, 1993.

19. Junda Woo and Milo Geyelin, "Cost of Civil Justice System Is Estimated at $132 Billion," *The Wall Street Journal,* October 15, 1992, p. B10.

20. Ibid.

21. Ibid.

22. Michael Saks, "Do We Really Know Anything about the Behavior of the Tort Litigation System—and Why Not," University of Pennsylvania Law Review 140, no. 4 (April 1992), p. 1,147.

23. Richard Holman, "China Sees Doubling of Lawyers," *The Wall Street Journal,* January 12, 1993, p. A10.

24. Edward Felsenthal, "Expansion of Small-Claims Arena Debated," *The Wall Street Journal,* December 4, 1992, p. B14.

25. Edward Felsenthal, "It's All Business for Novel Court Now in Session," *The Wall Street Journal,* January 5, 1993, p. B1.

26. Junda Woo, "Ombudsmen Proliferate in the Workplace," *The Wall Street Journal,* February 19, 1993, p. B6.

27. Arthur Hays, "Litigation Alternatives," *The Wall Street Journal,* May 6, 1993, p. B10.

28. Ted Rohrlich, "Professor's Solution: Limit Use of Juries," *Los Angeles Times,* May 19, 1990, p. A26.

29. Woo and Geyelin, "Cost of Civil Justice," p. B10.

30. "An Economist Out to Be Sued," *Los Angeles Times,* October 8, 1990, p. D1.

31. William Jones, "Sources of Chinese Obligation Law," *Law and Contemporary Problems* 52, no. 3 (Spring 1989), p. 69.

32. Percy Luney, "Traditions & Foreign Influences: Systems of Law in China and Japan," *Law and Contemporary Problems* 52, no. 3 (Spring 1989), p. 129.

33. Richard Holman, "Crime in China Rises Steadily," *The Wall Street Journal,* March 23, 1993, p. A11.

34. Luney, "Traditions & Foreign Influences," p. 136.

35. Ye Lin, "The Tort System in China," *Law and Contemporary Problems* 52, no. 3 (Spring 1989), p. 143.

36. Ibid., p. 161.

37. Warren Avis, "Court before Justice," *New York Times,* July 21, 1978, p. 25.

38. Alain Clement, "Judges, Lawyers Are the Ruling Class in U.S. Society," *The Washington Post,* August 22, 1980, p. A–25.

39. Ibid.

40. Anne Strick, *Injustice for All* (New York: Penguin Books, 1978), p. 123.

CHAPTER 5

CONSTITUTIONAL LAW AND THE BILL OF RIGHTS

•

We the people of the United States, in order to form a more perfect union, establish justice, insure domestic tranquility, provide for the common defense, promote the general welfare, and secure the blessings of liberty to ourselves and our posterity, do ordain and establish this Constitution for the United States of America.

The Preamble to our Constitution, the words that opened this chapter, summarizes the "Founding Fathers'" lofty goals for America. The idealism embodied in the Preamble is both inspiring and touching. In reading it, we should reflect on the dream of America and the Constitution's role in molding and protecting that entirely new image of a nation. That we continue to be guided, more than 200 years later, by those rather few words is testimony to the brilliance and wisdom of its creators and to our determination to build a free, democratic, just society. Our Constitution is a remarkable document; so powerful in its ideas and images that it has reshaped the world.

CREATING A CONSTITUTION

You may recall that the Constitution grew out of the Articles of Confederation as enacted by Congress in 1778. The Articles contemplated a "firm league of friendship," but each state was to maintain its "sovereignty, freedom and independence." The Articles soon proved faulty.

Seven years of war had nearly bankrupted the colonies, and both credit and currency were almost worthless. The supposedly united states quarreled fiercely over economic resources, such as oyster-harvesting rights in Chesapeake Bay, and Congress had no real power to keep the peace.[1]

Thus, as described in the following article, the Constitutional Convention began in Philadelphia on May 25, 1787.

HOW THE DEED WAS DONE

Otto Friedrich

Actually the 55 delegates who concocted that re-markable Constitution over the course of a long, hot summer had no real mandate to do what they did. They had gathered only to consider some possible improvements in the Articles of Confederation . . . Neither Congress nor anyone else had authorized the delegates to invent a whole new political system.

* * * * *

[T]he basic issue was the comparative voting strengths of large states and small. Most of the big states demanded a powerful national government; the small ones feared coercion and insisted on states' rights. And neither side put much trust in the other.

* * * * *

As with many battles that have long since been won, it is hard now to realize how near the delegates came to failure, an event that might have led to the breakdown of the fledgling confederation, even to the reappearance of European forces eager to recapture their lost lands.

* * * * *

It took 60 ballots before the convention could agree on how to pick a president. It voted five times to have the president appointed by Congress and voted once against that. It voted repeatedly on whether a president could be impeached and how long his term should be and whether he must be native born.

The delegates also avoided settling some things, like the future of slavery.

* * * * *

With the coming of September, the framers could finally see the beginning of the end. The Pennsylvania state legislature had reconvened, and it needed the chamber where the Constitutional Convention was meeting. The dwindling collection of delegates, a dozen of whom had already gone home for one reason or another, picked a five-man Committee of Style and Arrangement to undertake the actual writing of the Constitution.

Although they were not supposed to change the substance of what the convention had so far decided, it was hardly accidental that all five were strong-government advocates, and that one of them was [James] Madison [of Virginia].

When the committee presented its constitution on September 12, the delegates eagerly began trying to change things all over again, in ways large and small. [George] Mason of Virginia declared for the first time that summer that there should be a bill of rights. He was voted down by 10 states to none.

The changing continued right up to the scheduled closing day, September 17, but then it was finally time to sign. Three of the delegates present still had objections and refused, among them Virginia's Governor [Edmund] Randolph. The rest, however, generally subscribed to [Benjamin] Franklin's [of Pennsylvania] declaration that although he too still had doubts and reservations, "I consent, sir, to this Constitution because I expect not better."

Still ahead lay nine months of bitter debate before the necessary nine states ratified what had been written that summer in Philadelphia. Ahead lay the creation of the Bill of Rights.

✳ STRUCTURE AND PURPOSE

[handwritten margin notes:]
State Court had more powers about 80/ more federal Courts like Interstate Commerce.

Federal Govt tries to expand its Powers

federal law has more power than state law in case where the former had made a treaty or bill regarding the issue

Powers given to federal Govt but national were minor in scope

The Constitution is reprinted for you in Appendix A. We now take some time to review its structure.

The Preamble identifies certain goals for our society, such as unity (among the various states), justice, domestic tranquility (peace), defense from outsiders, an increasing general welfare, and liberty. Article I sets up Congress and enumerates its powers. Article I, Section 8, Clause 3 is particularly important because it gives Congress the power to regulate commerce (the Commerce Clause). Article II sets up the executive branch, headed by the president, while Article III establishes the court system. Articles IV and VI, as well as the Fourteenth Amendment, address the relationship between the federal government and the states. Article VI provides in Clause 2 (the Supremacy Clause) for the supremacy of federal law over state law. Article V provides for amendments to the Constitution. The first 10 amendments, known as the Bill of Rights, were ratified by the states and put into effect in 1791. The remaining 16 amendments (Eleven through Twenty-six) were adopted at various times from 1798 through 1971.

From this review we can see that the Constitution serves a number of broad roles:

1. It establishes a national government.
2. It controls the relationship between the national government and the government of the states.
3. It defines and preserves personal liberty.
4. It contains provisions to enable the government to perpetuate itself.[2]

In establishing a national government, the Constitution sets up three branches and provides mechanisms for them to check and balance each other, as illustrated in the next section, "The Flag."

Another role of the Constitution is to balance the central federal authority with dispersed state power. As established by the Constitution, the federal government holds only those powers granted to it by the states. The people via the states hold all of those powers not expressly denied them by the Constitution.

Recall that the Constitution was enacted to protect the citizenry from the government. The Constitution does not protect the citizenry from purely private concentrations of power, such as large corporations. In fact, corporations themselves are often entitled to the protections of the Constitution.

Furthermore, the Constitution originally only protected the personal rights in the Bill of Rights from encroachment by the federal government. However, under a process known as the *incorporation doctrine* or *absorption doctrine,* the Supreme Court has interpreted the Due Process Clause of the Fourteenth Amendment, which is directed at the states, to incorporate or absorb those fundamental liberties against intrusion by state government as well.

The Flag

Americans, in recent years, have received a priceless lesson in constitutional law. State and federal courts and Congress have been forced to address the legally complex, highly emotional, and uniquely visible question of whether one may burn the American flag as an act of political expression and get away with it.

During the 1984 Republican National Convention, Gregory Lee Johnson burned an American flag in Dallas as a protest against the Reagan administration. He was arrested for violating a Texas law forbidding "desecration of a venerated object." He was convicted and sentenced to a year in jail, but the Texas Court of Criminal Appeals reversed that conviction on First Amendment grounds. In 1989, the U.S. Supreme Court, by a 5–4 margin, upheld that Texas decision ruling that Johnson's act was a form of political expression—of speech—and as such was protected by the First Amendment.[3] That decision excited intense political passion around the country, including strong sentiment for a constitutional amendment to protect the flag. Congress addressed the matter quickly by enacting the Flag Protection Act of 1989, which provided for a fine and a maximum of one year in jail for anyone who "knowingly mutilates, defaces, physically defiles, burns, maintains on the floor or ground or tramples upon any flag of the United States" (excepting disposing of a worn or soiled flag). While preferring a constitutional amendment, President Bush signed the legislation.

Then shortly after midnight on October 28, 1989, when the new federal law went into effect, protesters in Seattle and Washington, D.C., were charged with violating the law by burning American flags. In both instances, federal judges found the act unconstitutional, and the Justice Department appealed directly to the Supreme Court. In June 1990, the Supreme Court, by the same 5–4 vote that decided the Texas case, struck down the Flag Protection Act as an unconstitutional infringement on First Amendment rights.[4] The sum of the majority position was that the government may not forbid the expression of an idea merely because that idea is offensive to the majority. Those objecting to the majority position argued for the "societal interest in preserving the symbolic value of the flag."

Of course, the story was not over at that point. As so wisely provided for by the Founding Fathers, the balance of powers inherent in our government of three branches came once more to the fore. Predictably, the Supreme Court decision stirred outrage across the country. Many politicians, including President Bush, called once again for a constitutional amendment to protect the flag. The proposed language: "The Congress and the States shall have power to prohibit the physical desecration of the Flag of the United States." The House of Representatives took up the issue almost immediately and despite the political danger of casting a vote "against the flag," the proposed amendment failed to capture the two-thirds majority required for approval. The 254–177 vote in favor represented a 59 percent approval. The Senate then followed with a 58–42 vote supporting the amendment, which fell nine votes short of the necessary two-thirds. Opposition to the amendment was founded in perhaps three principal arguments: (1) we simply should not adjust our remarkable Bill of Rights in the absence of the most compelling circumstances; (2) "tampering" with the First Amendment would cast a shadow on our ideal of free expression; and (3) physical desecration might be interpreted by law enforcement authorities to embrace, for example, the work of artists or those who sell shirts that bear a likeness to the flag.

Had the amendment been affirmed by Congress and the president, it would then have required approval by three-quarters of the states before becoming effective as the Twenty-Seventh Amendment to the Constitution. Doubtless the issue will return since it provokes so much emotion—both sincere and politically inspired. But if history is a guide, we will not have a flag desecration amendment:

> In the 200 years since the Constitution was adopted, political leaders have tried to reverse high court decisions on everything from income taxes—in which they succeeded—to school busing—in which repeated attempts failed. Only four such amendments ever have been adopted.
>
> Efforts by politicians to overturn high-court decisions usually fail because the writers of the Constitution planned it that way, setting up a long, difficult path that amendments must traverse . . . Usually, no matter how much a high court decision upsets people, passions cool by the time the amendment process is half over, and efforts to change the Constitution run out of steam.[5]

THE BILL OF RIGHTS AND BUSINESS

The Constitution profoundly shapes the practice of American business. The Constitution embodies and supports America's belief in capitalism. Indeed, it has been argued that the economic self-interest of the framers had a persuasive impact on the principles embodied in the Constitution. Article 1, Section 8, Clause 3 of the Constitution (the Commerce Clause) affords Congress enormous authority in regulating business. Further discussion of the Commerce Clause will be deferred to Chapter 7. The bulk of this chapter will be directed to some of the key intersections between the business community and the Bill of Rights. When we think of the Bill of Rights, corporations ordinarily do not come to mind. However, extensive litigation in recent years serves notice that the relationship between the corporate "person" and the fundamental freedoms is both important and murky. We hope the reader will acquire an appreciation for the complex tensions that arise as the government attempts to identify and ensure individual rights while seeking to defend and promote both U.S. commerce and the rights of American business.

THE FIRST AMENDMENT

Congress shall make no law respecting an establishment of religion, or prohibiting the free exercise thereof; or abridging the freedom of speech, or the press; or the right of the people peaceably to assemble, and to petition the Government for a redress of grievances.

These few words constitute one of the most powerful and noble utterances in history. The freedoms guaranteed in the First Amendment reflect the basic beliefs of

American life. Much of the magnificence that we often associate with America is embodied in the protections of the First Amendment. After 200 years, it remains a source of wonder that our vast bureaucratic system and our approximately 250 million independent citizens continue to rely on that sentence as a cornerstone of our way of life.

1. Freedom of Religion

The First Amendment forbids (1) the establishment of an official state religion (the Establishment Clause), and (2) undue state interference with religious practice (the Free Exercise Clause). Government may neither encourage nor discourage the practice of religion generally, nor may it give preference to one religion over another. Broadly, the idea of the First Amendment is to maintain a separation between church and state. However, the precise boundary of that separation has become one of the more contentious social issues in contemporary life.

Schools

The issue of church/state separation appears in a variety of contexts such as the annual question of whether biblical displays in a public park at Christmas are constitutional (yes, according to a recent Ninth Circuit Court of Appeals decision),[6] but the dispute is most vivid in the schools where prayer is often at issue. The question appeared to be settled by a 1992 Supreme Court decision in *Lee* v. *Weisman* barring school-sponsored prayers from school ceremonies (graduation, etc.), even where those prayers are inclusive and nonsectarian. The 5–4 decision was based on the danger of religious coercion where school officials are involved in the religious remarks.[7] However, the power, volatility, and confusion of the school prayer theme is well illustrated by a series of lower court decisions following *Lee,* most of which have held that some school prayer is permissible if student-initiated and student-led. In 1993, the Supreme Court declined to review *Jones* v. *Clear Creek,* a court of appeals decision supporting student-led prayer.[8] Thus, the law is simply unclear on the question of school prayer controlled by students themselves.

How Much Separation?   In June 1994, the Supreme Court returned to the separation of church and state controversy. By a 6–3 vote, in the *Kiryas Joel* case[9], the Supreme Court ruled unconstitutional New York state's creation of a separate public school district to accommodate disabled Hasidic Jewish children who had been attending a general public school but were withdrawn by their parents. The parents' position was that the children were traumatized by being forced to attend school outside the religious enclave that is their home. Hence, they demanded and were granted a separate school district for their disabled children. The Supreme Court explained that "the government should not prefer one religion to another or prefer religion to irreligion." In reaching the decision the Court appears to have left largely intact its controversial three-part test for interpreting questions of church–state separation. The 1971 *Lemon* v. *Kurtzman* decision, in essence, held that the constitutionally permissible government action (1) would have a secular purpose, (2) would neither advance nor promote religion, and (3) would not excessively entangle government and religion.[10]

Blue Laws

Perhaps surprisingly, religious beliefs often become a source of dispute in business practice. Consider the so-called blue laws, those statutes and ordinances limiting or prohibiting the conduct of business on Sundays. For more than 200 years, until the 1950s, U.S. stores were rather uniformly closed for business on Sundays. Then exceptions emerged; food and newspapers, in particular. Jewish merchants began to object on discrimination grounds because they closed on Saturdays to observe their Sabbath and then were also forced to close on Sundays. Lawsuits followed. In the leading case of *McGowan* v. *Maryland,* the Supreme Court upheld the constitutionality of a blue law on the grounds that the primary purpose of the law was the furtherance of a legitimate social goal (in this case, provision of a uniform day of rest), rather than a furtherance of religious goals.[11] The Court felt that the practice of treating Sunday as a religious holiday had fallen into disuse. Now, Sunday closings are left to the states and localities to decide for themselves. Conflict remains surprisingly common. For example, in 1994 the Connecticut Supreme Court ruled that a Connecticut blue law forbidding auto sales on Sunday was an unconstitutional violation of due process because, among other reasons, it arbitrarily singled out car dealers for Sunday closing while almost all other businesses were free to operate on that day.[12] A group of auto dealers had challenged the statute claiming that it gave an unconstitutional advantage to next-door New York dealers who were free to sell seven days per week. Many Connecticut dealers opposed the Sunday openings, feeling that the extra hours would not produce additional business. Now, liquor stores are the only businesses in Connecticut that must close on Sundays.

Blue laws remain common around the world. Great Britain's pervasive but often ignored blue law was recently tested and upheld in the European Community's Supreme Court:

INTERNATIONAL

> The European Community's highest court upheld Britain's right to outlaw Sunday shopping, but stores hungry for . . . profits vowed to continue defying the much-flouted law.
>
> The EC Court of Justice ruled that the restrictions in England and Wales don't violate EC rules on free movement of goods, because the curbs equally affect sales of domestic and imported goods.
>
> . . . Many retailers have ignored the law, much mocked for its patchwork provisions. For example, stores may sell fresh produce but not canned vegetables, gin but not milk powder . . .
>
> . . . The issue pits unions and consumer groups, which want Sunday shopping deregulated, against the Keep Sunday Special Campaign, which insists Sunday should be a day of rest.[13]

Texaco and Sunday Closing.   In the reading that follows, we see the blue law issue turned on its head. Here, a gas station owner wants to close on Sunday, but Texaco says he must operate as usual.

CAN TEXACO WIN A BATTLE
IF THE LORD IS ON THE OTHER SIDE?

Bill Richards

Texaco Corp. has a divinely inspired mess on its hands here [Salem, Oregon] these days.

Texaco's troubles began when Barry Davis, a devout Christian fundamentalist who runs three Texaco service stations in Oregon, says he had a talk with the Almighty. Mr. Davis, 50 years old, credits God for making him Texaco's all-time top gasoline pumper—not to mention helping him earn nearly $470,000 last year. Texaco's star says God told him to shut his stations each week for the 24-hour biblical Sabbath—sunset Friday to sunset Saturday. The closings began on Jan. 1.

That also happens to be prime gas-pumping time, but Mr. Davis says he was sure Texaco would understand. "Texaco is the most religious oil company in the nation," he declares.

'Sabbath' in Texaco Red

That may be debatable. The company says Mr. Davis's uplifting gesture caused a 26% slide in his stations' January sales. Texaco sued Mr. Davis in federal court in Portland, Ore., . . . demanding he pay less attention to the Almighty and more to his contract, which calls for a seven-day-a-week, 24-hour-a-day operation. The company obtained a court order directing Mr. Davis to stay open on the Sabbath.

Mr. Davis, insisting that he can easily make up lost sales during the other six days, ignored the order. Friday night, precisely at 8:17 as the sun slipped below the horizon here, he slapped four-foot-high signs in his gas station windows saying, in Texaco red, "Closed for the Sabbath."

*   *   *   *   *

. . . [L]egal experts say Mr. Davis isn't covered by the 1964 federal civil rights act, which protects employees against religious discrimination by employers. The problem: Mr. Davis is not an employee. He is a contractor, who leases the land from Texaco. "In the eyes of the law, he might as well be General Motors," says Lewis Maltby, director of the American Civil Liberties Union's workplace-rights office in New York City. "I don't think he has a legal leg to stand on."

Mr. Davis has countered that while the civil rights act may not cover Texaco, his religious freedom was violated when federal Judge Helen Frye ordered him to reopen last week. A federal court can't enforce a private agreement in a way that violates a contractor's constitutional right, says David Shannon, Mr. Davis's attorney. "We feel the federal action occurred when the judge ordered Mr. Davis to be open on the Sabbath," Mr. Shannon says.

Judge Frye rejected that argument Monday, while granting Texaco a preliminary injunction against Mr. Davis's Sabbath closing. The judge said the fight is simply a dispute between the oil company and Mr. Davis. Mr. Shannon says he will appeal.

*   *   *   *   *

Texaco says that while Mr. Davis has a right to his religious beliefs, the company also has a contractual right to terminate his contracts. "This is a contract dispute and has nothing to do with religious beliefs," says the company's public relations official, who adds quickly, "I'd certainly like to be talking about other things."

*   *   *   *   *

Texaco's uneasiness may be justified. Company officials acknowledge they have already started getting letters from customers supporting Mr. Davis's stand . . .

Mr. Davis's dealer colleagues are also lining up. Michael Sherlock, executive director of the Oregon Gasoline Dealers Association, which represents operators of 1,800 gasoline outlets in the state, says Mr. Davis's agreement with God may be a bit unusual, "but we have plenty of dealers who would like to close on Sundays because of their own religious beliefs." Mr. Davis's case could also set a precedent for other dealers who don't want to stay open all night when traffic is light, Mr. Sherlock says.

Mr. Davis seems content to stay above the fray. In his hilltop house here, with a discreet wooden cross on the door and photos of his eight children scattered through the living room, he says Texaco knows full well that God is on his side.

Source: *The Wall Street Journal,* May 6, 1993, p. A1. Reprinted by permission of *The Wall Street Journal,* © 1993 Dow Jones & Company, Inc. All Rights Reserved Worldwide.

Afterword

In late May 1993, Texaco announced that it had terminated Mr. Davis' leases after Mr. Davis declined to follow the court order to remain open on Sundays. Mr. Davis indicated that he would be appealing the termination under the U.S. Petroleum Marketing Practices Act, which provides for 90 days notice and reasonable grounds prior to termination.

In 1993, Congress and the president approved the Religious Freedom Restoration Act, which clearly affirms America's high regard for religious freedom. The bill says that the government can infringe on religious freedom only for the most "compelling" reasons. That had been the accepted legal standard until a 1990 Supreme Court decision had made it easier for the government to interfere with religious practice. The bill is expected to have the greatest impact for "minority" religions whose practices sometimes conflict with state regulations. For example, the Amish have objected to state laws requiring bright safety reflectors on their horse-drawn buggies.

Questions

1. In your view, what is the ethically proper course of action for Texaco? Explain.
2. A Seventh Day Adventist was discharged by her employer when she refused to work on Saturday. Those of her faith celebrate the Sabbath on Saturday. She sought unemployment compensation, but the South Carolina Employment Security Commission denied her petition. The commission ruled that she had failed, without good cause, "to accept available work when offered." She carried an appeal to the

Supreme Court. How would you rule? Explain. See *Sherbert* v. *Verner,* 374 U.S. 398 (1963).
3. For purposes of applying the First Amendment, how should "religion" be defined? That is, how do we tell the difference between a cult and a religion . . . or do we?

2. Freedom of Speech

As illustrated by the flag-burning case, none of the remarkable freedoms guaranteed by the Constitution receives greater respect from the judiciary than the right to free expression. And so it should be. Freedom of speech is the primary guarantor of the American approach to life. In particular, Americans believe the free expression of ideas is the most likely path to finding the best of ideas. We believe in a marketplace of ideas just as we believe in a marketplace of goods. So freedom of speech is central to self-respect, to political freedom, and to the maximization of wisdom.

Freedom of speech is not an absolute. Clearly, we cannot make slanderous statements about another or publicly utter obscenities at will or yell "fire" in a crowded theater. Nonetheless, in general, the state cannot tell us what we can lawfully say; that is, the state cannot, for the most part, regulate the *content* of our speech. On the other hand, the state does have greater authority to regulate the *context* of that speech; that is, the state may be able to restrict where and when we say certain things if that regulation is necessary to preserve compelling state interests. Therefore, the Ku Klux Klan clearly can express hatred for black people, but the state may restrict where and when those expressions are made if necessary for the public safety. Of course, we have no right to freedom of speech expressed on the private property of another such as our place of employment or even, most courts have ruled, the common areas of an enclosed shopping mall. Remember, the Constitution protects us from the government, not from private parties. In general, however, we can say what we wish on public property such as a park or a state-supported college campus or a community sidewalk. Even in those places, however, the state may need to impose reasonable time and place regulations.

Sometimes, the question becomes one of what constitutes speech. As we saw in the flag-burning case, the First Amendment clearly extends to expression in forms other than actual verbiage or writing. In the leading case in this area, the Supreme Court extended First Amendment protection to the wearing of black armbands to high school as a protest against the Vietnam War where no evidence of disruption was presented.[14] Does panhandling (begging) on a public street constitute speech? (See *Loper* v. *New York City Police Dept.,* 802 F.Supp. 1029 (S.D.N.Y., 1992).)

Hate Speech

In recent years, First Amendment controversies have become a routine ingredient in daily life. The most highly publicized episodes have involved "hate crimes" and university speech codes.

Hate Crimes.   How can we stop cross burnings and other expressions of bigotry without violating free speech rights? In 1992, the Supreme Court unanimously struck down a St. Paul, Minnesota, ordinance that forbade cross burnings and bias-motivated "disorderly conduct." While governments may constitutionally regulate so-called fighting words, those regulations may not be based on the *message* conveyed by those words.[15]

Many states and localities have passed laws increasing penalties for crimes committed where discrimination motivated the behavior. For example, a Wisconsin statute imposed additional penalties against those who "intentionally" selected their criminal victim "because of the race, religion, color, disability, sexual orientation, national origin or ancestry of that person." Todd Mitchell, a black man, was sentenced to two years in prison for aggravated assault; but because he said, "There goes a white boy; go get him," his sentence was increased by two years. The Wisconsin Supreme Court struck down the statute, but the U.S. Supreme Court reversed.[16] The Court said that a judge may properly consider a defendant's motivation so long as the crime in question involved conduct rather than expression. The Court concluded that the Wisconsin statute was directed to conduct while the St. Paul ordinance was directed to expression. Do you agree with the Court's treatment of cross burning as *expression* rather than *conduct?*

Speech Codes.   In an effort to stop on-campus expressions of bigotry, a number of colleges and universities have established codes that forbid certain specified classes of speech. For example, a code might prohibit language that *intentionally demeans or disparages the race, religion, color, sex, national origin, creed, sexual preference, disability, height, weight, or age of the person to whom the remarks are directed.* Such codes, particularly where broadly drawn, appear to be constitutionally suspect, but the controversy continues at this writing in 1994. In the most highly publicized of these cases, the University of Pennsylvania accused a first-year student, Eden Jacobowitz, of racial harassment because he shouted the phrase "water buffalo" at a group of black women who were making noise sometime after midnight outside the dormitory where he was studying. Mr. Jacobowitz admitted making the remark but denied that it was racially motivated. A campus judicial officer concluded that the remark was a racial slur, although experts on the subject were prepared to testify that the phrase has no racial connotations whatsoever. Eventually, the women decided to drop their action, believing it was compromised by unfair publicity, but they continued to believe the remark was racially motivated and they claimed that the student's complete expression was "black water buffalo."[17]

The implementation of speech codes and subsequent cases like that at the University of Pennsylvania have been criticized for mandating so-called politically correct speech. The charge is that only language acceptable to "liberals" is tolerated on college campuses. Columnist Stephen Chapman put the claim this way:

> If you call someone a black SOB, you're in trouble; if you call someone a rich SOB, you're blessed. Racial minorities, women, homosexuals and other favored blocs are allowed to use terms of abuse against other groups that other groups are not allowed to use against them.[18]

Of course, those speech codes are simply designed to stop hurtful, purposeless insults that have their roots in bigotry. Achieving that laudable goal in a constitutional manner is, however, a very difficult task in a nation that properly venerates free speech.

A Campus Dispute.   The decision that follows illustrates the role of the First Amendment in campus life. In this case, a fraternity's "ugly woman contest" raised claims of racism, sexism, and general insensitivity.

IOTA XI CHAPTER v. GEORGE MASON UNIVERSITY
993 F.2d 386 (4th Cir. 1993)

Senior Circuit Judge Sprouse

George Mason University appeals from a summary judgment granted by the district court to the IOTA XI Chapter of Sigma Chi Fraternity in its action for declaratory judgment and an injunction seeking to nullify sanctions imposed on it by the University because it conducted an "ugly woman contest" with racist and sexist overtones. We affirm.

I

Sigma Chi has for two years held an annual "Derby Days" event, planned and conducted both as entertainment and as a source of funds for donations to charity. The "ugly woman contest," held on April 4, 1991, was one of the "Derby Days" events. The Fraternity staged the contest in the cafeteria of the student union. As part of the contest, eighteen Fraternity members were assigned to one of six sorority teams cooperating in the events. The involved Fraternity members appeared in the contest dressed as caricatures of different types of women, including one member dressed as an offensive caricature of a black woman. He was painted black and wore stringy, black hair decorated with curlers, and his outfit was stuffed with pillows to exaggerate a woman's breasts and buttocks. He spoke in slang to parody African-Americans.

There is no direct evidence in the record concerning the subjective intent of the Fraternity members who conducted the contest. The Fraternity, which later apologized to the University officials for the presentation, conceded during the litigation that the contest was sophomoric and offensive.

Following the contest, a number of students protested to the University that the skit had been objectionably sexist and racist. Two hundred forty-seven students, many of them members of the foreign or minority student body, executed a petition, which stated: "[W]e are condemning the racist and sexist implications of this event in which male members dressed as women. One man in particular wore a black face, portraying a negative stereotype of black women."

On April 10, 1991, the Dean for Student Services, Kenneth Bumgarner, discussed the situation with representatives of the objecting students. That same day, Dean Bumgarner met with student representatives of Sigma Chi, including the planners of and participants in the "ugly woman contest." He then held a meeting with members of the student government and other student leaders. In this meeting, it was agreed that Sigma Chi's behavior had created a hostile learning environment for women and blacks, incompatible with the University's mission.

The Dean met again with Fraternity representatives on April 18, and the following day advised its officers of the sanctions imposed. They included suspension from all activities for the rest of the 1991 spring semester and a two-year prohibition on all social activities except pre-approved pledging events and pre-approved philanthropic events with an educational purpose directly related to gender discrimination and cultural diversity. The University's sanctions also required Sigma Chi to plan and implement an educational program addressing cultural differences, diversity, and the concerns of women. A few weeks later, the University made minor modifications to the sanctions, allowing Sigma Chi to engage in selected social activities with the University's advance approval.

On June 5, 1991, Sigma Chi brought this action under 42 U.S.C. § 1983* against the University and Dean Bumgarner. It requested declaratory judgment and injunctive relief to nullify the sanctions as violative of the First and Fourteenth Amendments. Sigma Chi moved for summary judgment on its First Amendment claims on June 28, 1991, filing with its motions numerous affidavits explaining the nature of the "ugly woman contest." . . .

In addition to the affidavit of Dean Bumgarner explaining his meetings with student leaders, the University submitted the affidavits of other officials, including that of University President George W. Johnson and Vice-President Earl G. Ingram. President Johnson, by his affidavit, presented the "mission statement" of the University:

> (3) George Mason University is committed to promoting a culturally and racially diverse student body . . . Education here is not limited to the classroom.
>
> (4) We are committed to teaching the values of equal opportunity and equal treatment, respect for diversity, and individual dignity.
>
> (5) Our mission also includes achieving the goals set forth in our affirmative action plan, a plan incorporating affirmative steps designed to attract and retain minorities to this campus.

* * * * *

> (7) George Mason University is a state institution of higher education and a recipient of federal funds.

Vice President Earl G. Ingram's affidavit represented:

> (6) The University's affirmative action plan is a part of an overall state plan designed, in part, to desegregate the predominately "white" and "black" public institutions of higher education in Virginia . . . The behavior of the members of Sigma Chi that led to this lawsuit was completely antithetical to the University's mission, as expressed through its affirmative action statement and other pertinent University policies, to create a non-threatening, culturally diverse learning environment for students of all races and backgrounds, and of both sexes.

---

*Every person who, under color of any statute, ordinance, regulation, custom, or usage, of any State or Territory or the District of Columbia, subjects, or causes to be subjected, any citizen of the United States or other person within the jurisdiction thereof to the deprivation of any rights, privileges, or immunities secured by the Constitution and laws, shall be liable to the party injured in an action at law, suit in equity, or other proper proceeding for redress. 42 U.S.C. § 1983.

(7) While the University has progressed in attracting and retaining minority students, it cannot expect to maintain the position it has achieved, and make further progress on affirmative action and minority issues that it wishes to make, if behavior like that of Sigma Chi is perpetuated on this campus.

The district court granted summary judgment to Sigma Chi on its First Amendment claim, 773 F.Supp. 792 (E.D.Va.1991).

II

The University urges that the district court's grant of summary judgment was premature. It stresses that there remain factual issues which the district court should have weighed in its conclusion. According to the University, the Fraternity's intent in staging the contest is crucial to the issue of whether its conduct was expressive. The University also stresses that if given time it could demonstrate more completely the harm the contest caused to its educational mission. It is, of course, beyond cavil that summary judgment should not be granted while a viable issue of material fact remains. Summary judgment principles require the court to find that the evidence is such that a jury could not reasonably find for the party opposing summary judgment . . .

In our view, for the reasons that follow, the district court was correct in concluding that there was no outstanding issue of material fact.

III

We initially face the task of deciding whether Sigma Chi's "ugly woman contest" is sufficiently expressive to entitle it to First Amendment protection. From the mature advantage of looking back, it is obvious that the performance, apart from its charitable fund-raising features, was an exercise of teenage campus excess. With a longer and sobering perspective brought on by both peer and official disapproval, even the governing members of the Fraternity recognized as much. The answer to the question of whether the First Amendment protects the Fraternity's crude attempt at entertainment, however, is all the more difficult because of its obvious sophomoric nature.

A

First Amendment principles governing live entertainment are relatively clear: short of obscenity, it is generally protected. As the Supreme Court announced in *Schad v. Borough of Mount Ephraim,* 452 U.S. 61, 101 S.Ct. 2176, 68 L.Ed.2d 671 (1981), "[e]ntertainment, as well as political and ideological speech, is protected; motion pictures, programs broadcast by radio and television, and live entertainment . . . fall within the First Amendment guarantee." Expression devoid of "ideas" but with entertainment value may also be protected because "[t]he line between the informing and the entertaining is too elusive." *Winters v. New York,* 333 U.S. 507, 510, 68 S.Ct. 665, 667, 92 L.Ed. 840 (1948).

Thus, we must determine if the skit performed by Sigma Chi comes within the constitutionally protected rubric of entertainment. Unquestionably, some forms of entertainment are so inherently expressive as to fall within the First Amendment's ambit regardless of their quality. For example, in *Ward v. Rock Against Racism,* 491 U.S. 781, 109 S.Ct. 2746, 105

L.Ed.2d 661 (1989), the Supreme Court flatly ruled that "[m]usic, as a form of expression and communication, is protected under the First Amendment."

* * * * *

Even crude street skits come within the First Amendment's reach. In . . . *Schacht v. United States,* 398 U.S. 58, 61–62, 90 S.Ct. 1555, 1558–59, 26 L.Ed.2d 44 (1970), . . . Justice Black [declared] that an actor participating in even a crude performance enjoys the constitutional right to freedom of speech.

Bearing on this dichotomy between low and high-grade entertainment are the Supreme Court's holdings relating to nude dancing. *See Barnes v. Glen Theatre, Inc.,* 111 S.Ct. 2456, 2460, 115 L.Ed.2d 504 (1991).

[I]n *Barnes,* the Supreme Court conceded that nude dancing is expressive conduct entitled to First Amendment protection.

* * * * *

. . . [I]t appears that the low quality of entertainment does not necessarily weigh in the First Amendment inquiry. It would seem, therefore, that the Fraternity's skit, even as low-grade entertainment, was inherently expressive and thus entitled to First Amendment protection.

B

The University nevertheless contends that discovery will demonstrate that the contest does not merit characterization as a skit but only as mindless fraternity fun, devoid of any artistic expression. It argues further that entitlement to First Amendment protection exists only if the production was intended to convey a message likely to be understood by a particular audience. From the summary judgment record, the University insists, it is impossible to discern the communicative intent necessary to imbue the Fraternity's conduct with a free speech component.

As indicated, we feel that the First Amendment protects the Fraternity's skit because it is inherently expressive entertainment. Even if this were not true, however, the skit, in our view, qualifies as expressive conduct under the test articulated in *Texas v. Johnson* [491 U.S. 397 (1989)]. It is true that the *Johnson* test for determining the expressiveness of conduct requires " '[a]n intent to convey a particularized message' " and a great likelihood " 'that the message would be understood by those who viewed it.' " [T]he intent to convey a message can be inferred from the conduct and the circumstances surrounding it. Thus viewed, the University's argument is self-defeating. The affidavit from the University's Vice-President, Earl Ingram, stated that the message conveyed by the Fraternity's conduct—that racial and sexual themes should be treated lightly—was completely antithetical to the University's mission of promoting diversity and providing an educational environment free from racism and sexism . . .

* * * * *

[T]he affidavits establish that the punishment was meted out to the Fraternity because its boorish *message* had interfered with the described University mission. It is manifest from these circumstances that the University officials thought the Fraternity intended to convey a message. The Fraternity members' apology and post-conduct contriteness suggest that they held the same view. To be sure, no evidence suggests that the Fraternity advocated segregation or inferior social status for women. What is evident is that the Fraternity's purposefully nonsensical treatment of sexual and racial themes was intended to impart a message that the University's concerns, in the Fraternity's view, should be treated humorously. From the Fraternity's conduct and the circumstances surrounding it, we have no difficulty in concluding that it intended to convey a message.

As to the second prong of the *Johnson* test, there was a great likelihood that at least some of the audience viewing the skit would understand the Fraternity's message of satire and humor. Some students paid to attend the performance and were entertained . . .

* * * * *

. . . [W]e are persuaded that the Fraternity's "ugly woman contest" satisfies the *Johnson* test for expressive conduct.

IV

If this were not a sufficient response to the University's argument, the principles relating to content and viewpoint discrimination recently emphasized in *R.A.V. v. City of St. Paul,* 112 S.Ct. 2538, 120 L.Ed.2d 305 (1992), provide a definitive answer. Although the Court in *St. Paul* reviewed the constitutional effect of a city "hate speech" ordinance, and we review the constitutionality of sanctions imposed for violating University policy, *St. Paul*'s rationale applies here with equal force. Noting that St. Paul's city ordinance prohibited displays of symbols that "arouse[d] anger, alarm or resentment in others on the basis of race, color, creed, religion or gender," but did not prohibit displays of symbols which would advance ideas of racial or religious equality, Justice Scalia stated: "The First Amendment does not permit St. Paul to impose special prohibitions on those speakers who express views on disfavored subjects."

As evidenced by their affidavits, University officials sanctioned Sigma Chi for the message conveyed by the "ugly woman contest" because it ran counter to the views the University sought to communicate to its students and the community. The mischief was the University's punishment of those who scoffed at its goals of racial integration and gender neutrality, while permitting, even encouraging, conduct that would further the viewpoint expressed in the University's goals and probably embraced by a majority of society as well. "The First Amendment generally prevents government from proscribing . . . expressive conduct because of disapproval of the ideas expressed."

The University, however, urges us to weigh Sigma Chi's conduct against the substantial interests inherent in educational endeavors. The University certainly has a substantial interest in maintaining an educational environment free of discrimination and racism, and in providing gender-neutral education. Yet it seems equally apparent that it has available numerous alternatives to imposing punishment on students based on the viewpoints they express. We agree wholeheartedly that it is the University officials' responsibility, even their obligation, to achieve the goals they have set. On the other hand, a public university has many constitutionally permissible means to protect female and minority students. We must emphasize, as have other courts, that "the manner of [its action] cannot consist of selective limitations upon speech." The University should have accomplished its goals in some fashion other than silencing speech on the basis of its viewpoint.

Affirmed.

Questions

1. Is speech that consists merely of entertainment without benefit of meaningful ideas protected by the First Amendment? Explain.

2. Explain the Court's conclusion that the fraternity skit met the *Texas* v. *Johnson* test of "an intent to convey a particularized message" and a great likelihood "that the message would be understood by those who viewed it."

3. *a.* Should racist/sexist remarks be forbidden in college classrooms?

   b. Are speech codes a good methodology for dealing with campus bigotry?

   c. Do we give too much attention to freedom of speech at the expense of community civility? Explain.

4. Could a college lawfully banish a T-shirt depicting a sombrero-wearing man holding a beer bottle where the picture was designed to serve as the logo for a fraternity's "South of the Border party" and where some Hispanic students found the logo offensive? Explain.

5. Does the First Amendment prohibit public schools from teaching moral values? Explain.[19]

6. The Port Authority of New York enforced a regulation prohibiting the distribution of literature or solicitation of money within New York City airport terminals. The International Society for Krishna Consciousness (Hare Krishnas) challenged the regulation on First Amendment grounds. How would you rule? Explain. See *International Soc'y for Krishna Consciousness, Inc.* v. *Lee,* 112 S.Ct. 2701 (1992), and *Lee* v. *International Soc'y for Krishna Consciousness, Inc.,* 112 S.Ct. 2709 (1992).

7. The album "As Nasty as They Wanta Be" by rappers 2 Live Crew was described as brutal and sexually explicit.

   a. How would you defend the album from a charge of obscenity?

   b. If you have heard the album, do you consider it obscene? Explain. See *Luke Records, Inc.* v. *Nick Navarro,* 960 F.2d 134 (1992), and *Nicholas Navarro* v. *Luke Records,* 113 S.Ct. 659 (1992).

8. A homeless man, Richard Kreimer, frequented the Morristown, New Jersey, public library. Testimony indicated that he spent much of his time staring at other patrons or following them around the library. Testimony also indicated that he was unkempt and his extreme body odor made the reading room unusable to some in his presence. The library barred the man for his violation of library rules requiring civil behavior, reasonable personal hygiene, and actual use of the library (rather than simply loitering there). Mr. Kreimer, with the assistance of the American Civil Liberties Union and others, filed suit claiming a violation of, among others, his First Amendment rights.

   a. How can Mr. Kreimer claim that his freedom of expression rights were violated by the library rules?

   b. Decide the case. See *Kreimer* v. *Bureau of Police for Town of Morristown,* 958 F.2d 1242 (3d Cir., 1992).

Corporate Speech

Corporations, of course, are not natural persons. Instead, as expressed so eloquently by Chief Justice Marshall in the *Dartmouth College* case of 1819, the corporation is an "artificial being, invisible, intangible, and existing only in contemplation of law." Are the expressions of artificial beings accorded constitutional protection equivalent to that of a person? The question has become increasingly important in recent years as corporations have taken a much more active role in public affairs.

Advocacy Advertising.   Historically, corporate America had maintained a low profile in political life and public affairs. Quiet, behind-the-scenes negotiation was the preferred method of achieving the business community's public affairs agenda. Then, in the late 1960s and early 1970s, some corporations began *advocacy advertising* programs where they bought advertising space to express a point of view on public issues such as taxes, free trade, energy policy, and environmental concerns. That new, high-profile approach was spurred, in part, by the public's outrage over high oil company profits (during and following the oil shortages of 1972–73) and a rather widespread public unease with corporate America in the Vietnam War era. Now corporations, labor unions, foreign governments, and all manner of public interest organizations regularly engage in advocacy advertising in an attempt to educate and persuade the citizenry on issues of public policy. The Johnson & Higgins ad, page 196, illustrates one corporation's use of its First Amendment rights.

Corporate Political Speech.   As explained in Chapter 3, corporate funds cannot lawfully be expended for federal campaign contributions. Some states likewise forbid such contributions. However, corporations can lawfully establish *political action committees* (PACs) to solicit and disburse voluntary campaign contributions. Consequently, corporations have firmly established themselves in the political process. To some, that development is as it should be. Corporations should be able to defend their stake in American life, and the marketplace of ideas profits from a more complete dialogue. To others, corporations, with their enormous resources, are a threat to the democratic process. The fear is that the corporate view, supported by extraordinary wealth and power, may "drown out" other opinions.

Commercial Speech

On occasion, governments seek to regulate communications of a profit-seeking nature (e.g., ads for abortion services). In 1942, the Supreme Court held that commercial speech was not entitled to the protection of the First Amendment.[20] However, a series of decisions beginning in 1975 have accorded constitutional protection to commercial speech. Governments may yet impose reasonable restrictions on commercial speech where those restrictions are necessary for the public welfare.

A 1993 Supreme Court decision affirmed First Amendment protection for commercial speech where the city of Cincinnati revoked permits to place 62 freestanding newsracks on public property. The newsracks contained free magazines designed primarily to advertise the services of a pair of businesses—one selling real estate, the other providing adult educational programs. The city labeled the magazines "commercial handbills," the distribution of which was prohibited by a city ordinance, and said that the newsracks raised aesthetic and safety concerns. Distribution of newspapers on public property, however, was explicitly authorized under the city code. The businesses filed suit, claiming a First Amendment violation, and ultimately the U.S. Supreme Court, by a 6–3 vote, affirmed their claim. The city had failed to make clear the distinction between commercial circulars and conventional newspapers, and it

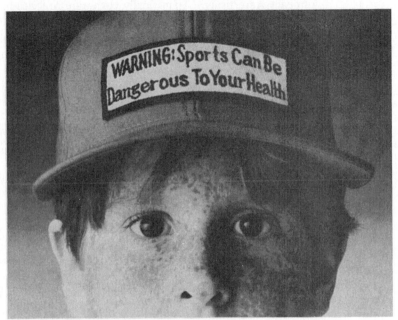

Is It Coming To This?

Once when you took the field you took your chances. Not anymore.

The courts have slipped a third strike past the venerable doctrine of "assumption of risk."

Judgments traditionally reserved for serious injury cases are hemorrhaging into claims from which organized athletics once were virtually immune.

Observes one leading specialist in sports-related law: "Participants have the attitude that someone should be forced to pay. They're suing for the slightest injury, regardless of fault."

One alarming result: at every level of sport, coaches, trainers, athletic directors—even volunteers—are at risk for failure to warn participants in detail of a sport's inherent dangers.

For municipalities and schools, this is an especially tough situation to handle. Court-cultivated expansion of the joint and several liability doctrine makes recreation departments and schools easy targets as "deep pockets" in injury suits.

Regardless of degree of fault, they may (and often do) wind up paying everything.

A return to the concept of genuine fault is clearly necessary. Many states recently have made substantial progress toward this goal by reforming their tort laws. Legislatures that have yet to act should be urged to do so.

The playing field must be level for everyone.

Consulting on a lot more than insurance.

RISK AND INSURANCE MANAGEMENT SERVICES: HUMAN RESOURCE AND ACTUARIAL CONSULTING THROUGHOUT THE WORLD

Source: Used with permission from Johnson & Higgins.

had failed to show a clear connection between its safety/aesthetic goals and the removal of 62 racks out of some 1,500 to 2,000 on public property. In general, the case has the effect of affirming the court's shield for commercial speech, although the majority was careful to say that the case applied to the particular Cincinnati facts and that commercial speech generally deserves a lesser degree of protection than not-for-profit expression.[21]

The case that follows illustrates the application of the commercial speech doctrine to professionals. This instance concerns a certified public accountant's personal solicitation of new clients.

EDENFIELD v. FANE
113 S.Ct. 1792 (1993)

Justice Kennedy

In previous cases we have considered the constitutionality of state laws prohibiting lawyers from engaging in direct, personal solicitation of prospective clients. In the case now before us, we consider a solicitation ban applicable to Certified Public Accountants (CPAs) enacted by the State of Florida. We hold that, as applied to CPA solicitation in the business context, Florida's prohibition is inconsistent with the free speech guarantees of the First and Fourteenth Amendments.

I

Respondent Scott Fane is a CPA licensed to practice in the State of Florida by the Florida Board of Accountancy. Before moving to Florida in 1985, Fane had his own accounting CPA practice in New Jersey, specializing in providing tax advice to small and medium-sized businesses. He often obtained business clients by making unsolicited telephone calls to their executives and arranging meetings to explain his services and expertise. This direct, personal, uninvited solicitation was permitted under New Jersey law.

When he moved to Florida, Fane wished to build a practice similar to his solo practice in New Jersey but was unable to do so because the Board of Accountancy had a comprehensive rule prohibiting CPAs from engaging in the direct, personal solicitation he had found most effective in the past. The Board's rules provide that a CPA "shall not by any direct, in-person, uninvited solicitation solicit an engagement to perform public accounting services . . . where the engagement would be for a person or entity not already a client of [the CPA], unless such person or entity has invited such a communication." "[D]irect, in-person, uninvited solicitation" means "any communication which directly or implicitly requests an immediate oral response from the recipient," which, under the Board's rules, includes all "[u]ninvited in-person visits or conversations or telephone calls to a specific potential client."

The rule, according to Fane's uncontradicted submissions, presented a serious obstacle, because most businesses are willing to rely for advice on the accountants or CPAs already serving them. In Fane's experience, persuading a business to sever its existing accounting relations or alter them to include a new CPA on particular assignments requires the new CPA to contact the business and explain the advantages of a change. This entails a detailed discussion of the client's needs and the CPA's expertise, services and fees.

Fane sued the Board in the United States District Court for the Northern District of Florida, seeking declaratory and injunctive relief on the ground that the Board's antisolicitation rule violated the First and Fourteenth Amendments. Fane alleged that but for the prohibition he would seek clients through personal solicitation and would offer fees below prevailing rates.

In response to Fane's submissions, the Board relied on the affidavit of Louis Dooner, one of its former Chairmen. Dooner concluded that the solicitation ban was necessary to preserve the independence of CPAs performing the attest function, which involves the rendering of opinions on a firm's financial statements. His premise was that a CPA who solicits clients "is obviously in need of business and may be willing to bend the rules." In Dooner's view, "[i]f [a CPA] has solicited the client he will be beholden to him." Dooner also suggested that the ban was needed to prevent "overreaching and vexatious conduct by the CPA."

The District Court gave summary judgment to Fane . . . [T]he Court of Appeals for the Eleventh Circuit affirmed.

We granted certiorari.

II

In soliciting potential clients, Fane seeks to communicate no more than truthful, non-deceptive information proposing a lawful commercial transaction . . .

. . . [I]t is clear that this type of personal solicitation is commercial expression to which the protections of the First Amendment apply. While we did uphold a ban on in-person solicitation by lawyers in *Ohralik* v. *Ohio State Bar Assn.,* 436 U. S. 447 (1978), that opinion does not hold that all personal solicitation is without First Amendment protection. There are, no doubt, detrimental aspects to personal commercial solicitation in certain circumstances, but these detriments are not so inherent or ubiquitous that solicitation of this sort is removed from the ambit of First Amendment protection.

In the commercial context, solicitation may have considerable value. Unlike many other forms of commercial expression, solicitation allows direct and spontaneous communication between buyer and seller. A seller has a strong financial incentive to educate the market and stimulate demand for his product or service, so solicitation produces more personal interchange between buyer and seller than would occur if only buyers were permitted to initiate contact. Personal interchange enables a potential buyer to meet and evaluate the person offering the product or service, and allows both parties to discuss and negotiate the desired form for the transaction or professional relation. Solicitation also enables the seller to direct his proposals toward those consumers whom he has a reason to believe would be most interested in what he has to sell. For the buyer, it provides an opportunity to explore in detail the way in which a particular product or service compares to its alternatives in the market. In particular, with respect to nonstandard products like the professional services offered by CPAs, these benefits are significant.

In denying CPAs and their clients these advantages, Florida's law threatens societal interests in broad access to complete and accurate commercial information that First Amendment coverage of commercial speech is designed to safeguard. The commercial marketplace, like other spheres of our social and cultural life, provides a forum where ideas and information flourish. Some of the ideas and information are vital, some of slight worth. But the general rule is that the speaker and the audience, not the government, assess the value of the information presented. Thus, even a communication that does no more than propose a commercial transaction is entitled to the coverage of the First Amendment.

* * * * *

III

To determine whether personal solicitation by CPAs may be proscribed under the test set forth in *Central Hudson* [447 U.S. 557 (1980)] we must ask whether the State's interests in proscribing it are substantial; whether the challenged regulation advances these interests in a direct and material way; and whether the extent of the restriction on protected speech is in reasonable proportion to the interests served. Though we conclude that the Board's asserted interests are substantial, the Board has failed to demonstrate that its solicitation ban advances those interests.

A

To justify its ban on personal solicitation by CPAs, the Board proffers two interests. First, the Board asserts an interest in protecting consumers from fraud or overreaching by CPAs. Second, the Board claims that its ban is necessary to maintain both the fact and appearance of CPA independence in auditing a business and attesting to its financial statements.

The State's first interest encompasses two distinct purposes: to prevent fraud and other forms of deception, and to protect privacy . . . [T]here is no question that Florida's interest in ensuring the accuracy of commercial information in the marketplace is substantial.

Likewise, the protection of potential clients' privacy is a substantial state interest. Even solicitation that is neither fraudulent nor deceptive may be pressed with such frequency or vehemence as to intimidate, vex, or harass the recipient . . .

The Board's second justification for its ban—the need to maintain the fact and appearance of CPA independence and to guard against conflicts of interest—is related to the audit and attest functions of a CPA. In the course of rendering these professional services, a CPA reviews financial statements and attests that they have been prepared in accordance with generally accepted accounting principles and present a fair and accurate picture of the firm's financial condition. In the Board's view, solicitation compromises the independence necessary to perform the audit and attest functions, because a CPA who needs business enough to solicit clients will be prone to ethical lapses. The Board claims that even if actual misconduct does not occur, the public perception of CPA independence will be undermined if CPAs behave like ordinary commercial actors.

* * * * *

B

That the Board's asserted interests are substantial in the abstract does not mean, however, that its blanket prohibition on solicitation serves them . . . [T]he *Central Hudson* test requires that a regulation impinging upon commercial expression "directly advance the state interest involved." . . . We agree with the Court of Appeals that the Board's ban on CPA solicitation as applied to the solicitation of business clients fails to satisfy this requirement.

* * * * *

The Board has not demonstrated that, as applied in the business context, the ban on CPA solicitation advances its asserted interests in any direct and material way. It presents no studies that suggest personal solicitation of prospective business clients by CPAs creates the dangers of fraud, overreaching, or compromised independence that the Board claims to fear. The record does not disclose any anecdotal evidence, either from Florida or another State, that validates the Board's suppositions . . .

. . . In contrast to the Board's anxiety over uninvited solicitation, the literature on the accounting profession suggests that the main dangers of compromised independence occur when a CPA firm is too dependent upon or involved with a long-standing client . . .

* * * * *

C

Relying on *Ohralik,* the Board seeks to justify its solicitation ban . . .

We reject the Board's argument and hold that, as applied in this context, the solicitation ban cannot be justified . . . *Ohralik* does not stand for the proposition that blanket bans on personal solicitation by all types of professionals are constitutional in all circumstances. Because "the distinctions, historical and functional, between professions, may require consideration of quite different factors," the constitutionality of a ban on personal solicitation will depend upon the identity of the parties and the precise circumstances of the solicitation . . .

Ohralik was a challenge to the application of Ohio's ban on attorney solicitation and held only that a State Bar "constitutionally may discipline a lawyer for soliciting clients in person, for pecuniary gain, under circumstances likely to pose dangers that the State has a right to prevent." . . . [T]he opinion made clear that a preventative rule was justified only in situations "inherently conducive to overreaching and other forms of misconduct." . . .

* * * * *

The solicitation here poses none of the same dangers. Unlike a lawyer, a CPA is not "a professional trained in the art of persuasion." A CPA's training emphasizes independence and objectivity, not advocacy. The typical client of a CPA is far less susceptible to manipulation than the young accident victim in *Ohralik.* Fane's prospective clients are sophisticated and experienced business executives who understand well the services that a CPA offers . . .

The manner in which a CPA like Fane solicits business is conducive to rational and considered decisionmaking by the prospective client, in sharp contrast to the "uninformed acquiescence" to which the accident victims in *Ohralik* were prone. While the clients in *Ohralik* were approached at a moment of high stress and vulnerability, the clients Fane wishes to solicit meet him in their own offices at a time of their choosing. If they are unreceptive to his initial telephone solicitation, they need only terminate the call. Invasion of privacy is not a significant concern.

If a prospective client does decide to meet with Fane, there is no expectation or pressure to retain Fane on the spot; instead, he or she most often exercises caution, checking references and deliberating before deciding to hire a new CPA . . .

* * * * *

Even under the First Amendment's somewhat more forgiving standards for restrictions on commercial speech, a State may not curb protected expression without advancing a substantial governmental interest. Here, the ends sought by the State are not advanced by the speech restriction, and legitimate commercial speech is suppressed. For this reason, the Board's rule infringes upon Fane's right to speak, as guaranteed by the Constitution.

Affirmed.

Justice O'Connor, dissenting

I continue to believe that this Court took a wrong turn with *Bates* v. *State Bar of Arizona,* 433 U. S. 350 (1977), and that it has compounded this error by finding increasingly unprofessional forms of attorney advertising to be protected speech. These cases consistently focus on whether the challenged advertisement directly harms the listener: whether it is false or misleading, or amounts to "overreaching, invasion of privacy, [or] the exercise of undue influence." This focus is too narrow. In my view, the States have the broader authority to prohibit commercial speech that, albeit not directly harmful to the listener, is inconsistent with the speaker's membership in a learned profession and therefore damaging to the profession and society at large.

* * * * *

Questions

1. *a.* What interests did the Florida Board of Accountancy claim to protect with its personal solicitation rule?
   b. From Fane's point of view, what interest was the rule designed to protect? Explain.
2. Why did the Court find for Fane?
3. How did the Court distinguish the CPA situation from that of lawyers?
4. Do you believe, as Justice O'Connor argues in dissent, that commercial speech of this kind is damaging to the accounting profession and to society at large? Explain.
5. Hornell Brewing Co. marketed a malt liquor labeled Crazy Horse. The name brought protests on the grounds that it amounted to targeting Native Americans and because it was considered disrespectful to the memory of the highly respected Sioux leader. Responding to that criticism, Congress attached a rider to an appropriations bill that forbade the use of the name Crazy Horse on an alcoholic beverage label. Hornell then challenged the constitutionality of the federal law.
   a. What is the nature of that challenge?
   b. How would you rule on it? Explain. See *Hornell Brewing Co.* v. *Nicholas Brady,* 819 F. Supp. 1227 (E.D.N.Y., 1993), and Laura Bird, "Makers of a Brew Called 'Crazy Horse' . . . ," *The Wall Street Journal,* April 14, 1993, p. B8.
6. A U.S. statute forbade the mailing of unsolicited advertisements for contraceptives. Youngs, which sold contraceptives, mailed contraceptive ads to the public at large. The ads included information regarding the public health benefits of contraceptives (e.g., family planning and prevention of venereal disease).
   a. Do the ads constitute commercial speech? Explain.
   b. Does the government have a "substantial interest" in preventing the mailings where the statute shields citizens from material that they are likely to find offensive and where the statute helps parents control their children's access to birth control information? Explain. See *Bolger* v. *Youngs Drug Products Corp.,* 463 U.S. 60 (1983).
7. Why is commercial speech accorded less protection than other categories of expression?
8. The Township of Willingboro prohibited the posting of real estate "For Sale" or "Sold" signs. The town's purposes were to promote racial integration and to retard the flight of white homeowners. Is the Willingboro action constitutionally permissible? See *Linmark Associates, Inc.* v. *Willingboro,* 431 U.S. 85 (1977).

THE FOURTH AMENDMENT

In an increasingly complex and interdependent society, the right of the individual to be free of unjustified governmental intrusions has taken on new significance. The Fourth Amendment provides that:

> [T]he right of the people to be secure in their persons, houses, papers, and effects, against unreasonable searches and seizures, shall not be violated, and no Warrants shall issue, but upon probable cause.

Some constitutional limitations on the police powers of government officials are a necessity. However, the boundaries of freedom from unreasonable search and seizure are the subject of continuing dispute. The police are under great pressure to cope with America's horrific crime problems, but they must do so within the confines of the Constitution, which is designed to protect us all—including criminals—from the power of an unfair, overreaching government.

Certainly, the most controversial dimension of Fourth Amendment interpretation is the *exclusionary rule,* which provides that, as a matter of due process, no evidence secured in violation of the Fourth Amendment may be admitted as evidence in a court of law. As ultimately applied to all courts by the 1961 U.S. Supreme Court decision in *Mapp* v. *Ohio,*[22] we can see that the exclusionary rule, while a very effective device for discouraging illegal searches, seizures, and arrests, also, from time to time, has the effect of freeing guilty criminals.

Drugs

Of course, search and seizure rules are often at issue in the government's efforts to stop illegal drug distribution. In general, a search warrant issued by a judge is necessary to comply with the Constitution in making a narcotics search. However, a warrantless search is permissible where reasonable, as in association with an arrest or where probable cause exists to believe a drug-related crime has been committed but circumstances make securing a warrant impracticable. Incident to an arrest, a search may lawfully include the person, a car, and the immediate vicinity of the arrest. Further, a police officer may lawfully secure drugs that have been abandoned or that are in plain view even though a warrant has not been obtained. For example, a juvenile, Hodari, fled after spotting some police officers in an unmarked car. Just as he was about to be apprehended by one of the pursuing officers, Hodari tossed aside what looked like a rock but turned out to be crack cocaine. In the subsequent prosecution, the State conceded that the officer did not have the "reasonable suspicion" necessary to justify pursuing Hodari. Therefore, the question became whether the officer had, in fact, "seized" Hodari at the moment the youth saw the officer on the verge of apprehending him. To constitute either the arrest or seizure of a person, physical force must be applied or the subject must have submitted to the officer's "show of authority." Neither had happened in this case at the time Hodari threw away the cocaine.

Therefore, the Supreme Court ruled, Hodari had not been seized, and the cocaine did not need to be suppressed as the "fruit of an illegal seizure."[23]

Questions

1. Had Hodari simply kept the cocaine on his person, could it have been used as evidence against him? Explain.
2. *a.* Can the police lawfully search an individual's garbage once it has been placed at the curb for disposal? In a recent case, a Connecticut resident, Paul DeFusco, was convicted of drug trafficking based on evidence found in his home. The police conducted the home search with a warrant secured on the basis of an informant's information as well as evidence (some short cut straws, glassine baggies, and prescription bottles) turned up in sifting through DeFusco's garbage.
   b. Explain the central issue in this case. See *State of Connecticut* v. *Paul DeFusco,* 620 A.2d 746 (Conn. S.Ct., 1993).
3. An informant told the police that a man, whom the informant described, was selling narcotics from the trunk of his car at a particular location. Police drove there, saw the car, and later stopped the car and arrested the driver who matched the informant's description. An officer opened the car's trunk, saw a brown bag, opened it, and found glassine bags of heroin. The car was then driven to police quarters where another warrantless search of the trunk produced a leather pouch containing money. At trial, may the heroin and cash lawfully be introduced as evidence? Explain. See *United States* v. *Ross,* 456 U.S. 798 (1982).

Business Searches

So we know that the Fourth Amendment has been the subject of dispute in criminal cases, but it may come as a surprise to learn that the contentious issues surrounding search and seizure have also been of importance in civil actions involving the government's efforts to regulate the conduct of business. As stated by the Supreme Court:

> The Warrant Clause of the Fourth Amendment protects commercial buildings as well as private homes. To hold otherwise would belie the origin of that Amendment, and the American colonial experience . . . "[T]he Fourth Amendment's commands grew in large measure out of the colonists' experience with the writs of assistance . . . [that] granted sweeping power to customs officials and other agents of the king to search at large for smuggled goods." . . . Against this background, it is untenable that the ban on warrantless searches was not intended to shield places of business as well as of residence.[24]

The case that follows illustrates one application of the Fourth Amendment to commercial property.

DOW CHEMICAL COMPANY v. UNITED STATES
106 S. Ct. 1819 (1986)

Chief Justice Burger

We granted certiorari to review the holding of the Court of Appeals . . . that EPA's aerial photography of petitioner's 2,000-acre plant complex without a warrant was not a search under the Fourth Amendment.

I

Petitioner Dow Chemical Co. operates a 2,000-acre facility manufacturing chemicals at Midland, Michigan. The facility consists of numerous covered buildings, with manufacturing equipment and piping conduits located between the various buildings exposed to visual observation from the air. At all times, Dow has maintained elaborate security around the perimeter of the complex barring ground-level public views of these areas. It also investigates any low-level flights by aircraft over the facility. Dow has not undertaken, however, to conceal all manufacturing equipment within the complex from aerial views. Dow maintains that the cost of covering its exposed equipment would be prohibitive.

In early 1978, enforcement officials of EPA, with Dow's consent, made an on-site inspection of two powerplants in this complex. A subsequent EPA request for a second inspection, however, was denied, and EPA did not thereafter seek an administrative search warrant. Instead, EPA employed a commercial aerial photographer, using a standard floor-mounted, precision aerial mapping camera, to take photographs of the facility from altitudes of 12,000, 3,000, and 1,200 feet . . .

EPA did not inform Dow of this aerial photography, but when Dow became aware of it, Dow brought suit in the district court alleging that EPA's action violated the Fourth Amendment . . . The district court granted Dow's motion for summary judgment on the ground that EPA had no authority to take aerial photographs and that doing so was a search violating the Fourth Amendment. EPA was permanently enjoined from taking aerial photographs of Dow's premises and from disseminating, releasing or copying the photographs already taken . . .

* * * * *

The Court of Appeals reversed . . .

* * * * *

II

The photographs at issue in this case are essentially like those commonly used in mapmaking. Any person with an airplane and an aerial camera could readily duplicate them. In common with much else, the technology of photography has changed in this century. These developments have enhanced industrial processes, and indeed all areas of life; they have also enhanced law enforcement techniques . . .

Dow . . . relies heavily on its claim that trade secret laws protect it from any aerial photography of this industrial complex by its competitors, and that this protection is relevant to our analysis of such photography under the Fourth Amendment. That such photography might be barred by state law with regard to competitors, however, is irrelevant to the questions presented here . . . [E]ven trade secret laws would not bar all forms of photography of this industrial complex; rather, only photography with an intent to use any trade secrets revealed by the photographs may be proscribed. Hence, there is no prohibition of photographs taken by a casual passenger on an airliner, or those taken by a company producing maps for its mapmaking purposes.

* * * * *

IV

We turn now to Dow's contention that taking aerial photographs constituted a search without a warrant, thereby violating Dow's rights under the Fourth Amendment. In making this contention, however, Dow concedes that a simple flyover with naked-eye observation, or the taking of a photograph from a nearby hillside overlooking such a facility, would give rise to no Fourth Amendment problem.

* * * * *

In the instant case, two additional Fourth Amendment claims are presented: whether the common-law "curtilage" doctrine encompasses a large industrial complex such as Dow's, and whether photography employing an aerial mapping camera is permissible in this context. Dow argues that an industrial plant, even one occupying 2,000 acres, does not fall within the "open fields" doctrine of *Oliver* v. *United States* but rather is an "industrial curtilage" having constitutional protection equivalent to that of the curtilage of a private home. Dow further contends that any aerial photography of this "industrial curtilage" intrudes upon its reasonable expectations of privacy. Plainly a business establishment or an industrial or commercial facility enjoys certain protections under the Fourth Amendment . . .

* * * * *

As the curtilage doctrine evolved to protect much the same kind of privacy as that covering the interior of a structure, the contrasting "open fields" doctrine evolved as well . . . In *Oliver,* we held that "an individual may not legitimately demand privacy for activities out of doors in fields, except in the area immediately surrounding the home." . . . To fall within the open fields doctrine the area "need be neither 'open' nor a 'field' as those terms are used in common speech." . . .

Dow plainly has a reasonable, legitimate, and objective expectation of privacy within the interior of its covered buildings, and it is equally clear that expectation is one society is prepared to observe . . . Moreover, it could hardly be expected that Dow would erect a huge cover over a 2,000-acre tract . . .

The Court of Appeals held that whatever the limits of an "industrial curtilage" barring *ground*-level intrusions into Dow's private areas, the open areas exposed here were more analogous to "open fields" than to a curtilage for purposes of aerial observation . . . In *Oliver,* the Court described the curtilage of a dwelling as "the areas to which extends the intimate activity associated with the 'sanctity of a man's home and the privacies of life.'" . . . The intimate activities associated with family privacy and the home and its curtilage simply do not reach the outdoor areas or spaces between structures and buildings of a manufacturing plant.

Admittedly, Dow's enclosed plant complex, like the area in *Oliver,* does not fall precisely within the "open fields" doctrine. The area at issue here can perhaps be seen as falling somewhere between "open fields" and curtilage, but lacking some of the critical characteristics of both . . .

* * * * *

Oliver recognized that in the open field context, "the public and police lawfully may survey lands from the air." . . . Here, EPA was not employing some unique sensory device that, for example, could penetrate the walls of buildings and record conversations in Dow's plants, offices or laboratories, but rather a conventional, albeit precise, commercial camera commonly used in mapmaking. The government asserts it has not yet enlarged the photographs to any significant degree, but Dow points out that simple magnification permits identification of objects such as wires as small as one-half inch in diameter.

It may well be, as the government concedes, that surveillance of private property by using highly sophisticated surveillance equipment not generally available to the public, such as satellite technology, might be constitutionally proscribed absent a warrant. But the photographs here are not so revealing of intimate details as to raise constitutional concerns. Although they undoubtedly give EPA more detailed information than naked-eye views, they remain limited to an outline of the facility's buildings and equipment. The mere fact that human vision is enhanced somewhat, at least to the degree here, does not give rise to constitutional problems . . .

We conclude that the open areas of an industrial plant complex with numerous plant structures spread over an area of 2,000 acres are not analogous to the "curtilage" of a dwelling for purposes of aerial surveillance; . . . such an industrial complex is more comparable to an open field and as such it is open to the view and observation of persons in aircraft lawfully in the public airspace immediately above or sufficiently near the area for the reach of cameras.

We hold that the taking of aerial photographs of an industrial plant complex from navigable airspace is not a search prohibited by the Fourth Amendment.

Affirmed.

Questions

1. Why is the Dow industrial complex "more comparable" to an open field than to the "curtilage" of a home for purposes of aerial surveillance?
2. Should businesses be accorded the same constitutional search protections given to homes? Explain.
3. Joseph Burger owned and operated an automobile junkyard where, among other things, he dismantled autos and sold the parts. A New York statute permitted police to conduct warrantless inspections of auto junkyards. Without objection by Burger, police conducted a warrantless inspection of his business. The inspection revealed stolen vehicles and stolen parts. Burger was charged with possession of stolen property. In court, Burger moved to suppress the evidence arising from the search on the grounds that the New York statute under which the search was conducted was unconstitutional.
    a. Does the statute violate the Fourth Amendment's prohibition of unreasonable searches and seizures? Explain.

b. Why do many states, including New York, explicitly permit the warrantless inspection of automobile junkyards? See *New York* v. *Joseph Burger* 482 U.S. 691 (1987).

4. Occupation Safety and Health Administration (OSHA) inspectors received permission from the Army Corps of engineers to inspect a federal construction site where an accident had occurred. The contractor declined consent, but OSHA secured a federal district court order allowing inspection. OSHA found some obvious violations, but others were apparent only after initial observations led to follow-up interviews with employees and closer looks at equipment. The contractor objected to the search on Fourth Amendment grounds.

a. Explain the nature of that objection.

b. Decide the case. See *National Engineering & Contracting Co.* v. *Occupational Safety and Health Administration,* 928 F.2d 762 (1991).

Recently, Fourth Amendment issues have been prominent in cases involving drug testing and searching of employees. For a discussion of those issues, turn to Chapter 12.

THE FIFTH AND FOURTEENTH AMENDMENTS

Takings

The Fifth Amendment prohibits the taking of private property for a public purpose without just compensation to the owner. Thus, the Fifth Amendment imposes bounds on the eminent domain processes commonly used by governments to condemn property for such projects as new highways.

One important issue under the Takings Clause is exactly what amounts to a taking. Obviously, if property is transferred to a new owner, a taking has occurred. The harder question is when regulation, such as requiring a developer to set aside land for a park area, amounts to a taking. In spite of recent Supreme Court cases, considerable uncertainty remains.[25] (See Chapter 7.)

Due Process

The Due Process Clauses of both the Fifth Amendment (applying to the federal government) and the Fourteenth Amendment (applying to the states) forbid the government to deprive citizens of life, liberty, or property without due process of law.

• *Substantive due process.* Laws that arbitrarily and unfairly infringe on fundamental personal rights and liberties such as privacy, voting, and the various freedoms specified in the Bill of Rights may be challenged on due process grounds. Basically, the purpose of the law must be so compelling as to outweigh the intrusion on personal liberty or the law will be struck down. For example, the U.S. Supreme Court ruled that a Connecticut statute forbidding the use of contraceptives violated the constitutional right to privacy (although the word *privacy* itself does not appear in the U.S. Constitution).[26] By judicial interpretation, the Fourteenth Amendment Due Process Clause "absorbs" the fundamental liberties of the *federal* Constitution and prohibits *state* laws (in this case, the Connecticut contraceptive ban) that abridge those fundamental liberties such as privacy.

• *Procedural due process.* Basically, procedural due process means that the government must provide a fair hearing before taking an action affecting a citizen's life, liberty, or property. A fair hearing might require, among others, notice of the hearing, the right to present evidence, the right to a decision maker free of bias, and the right to appeal. However, the precise nature of procedural due process depends on the situation. A murder trial requires meticulous attention to procedural fairness; an administrative hearing to appeal a housing officer's decision to banish a student from a dormitory, while required to meet minimal constitutional standards, can be more forgiving in its procedural niceties.

Equal Protection

The Fourteenth Amendment provides that no state shall "deny to any person within its jurisdiction the equal protection of the laws." The Due Process Clause of the Fifth Amendment has been interpreted to provide that same protection from the federal government. Fundamentally, these provisions forbid a government from treating one person differently than another where there is no rational basis for doing so. In short, the equal protection provisions forbid discrimination by the government. Chapter 13 gives extensive attention to discrimination, and the "Lesbian Roommate" reading that follows shortly raises the equal protection and due process themes of the Fifth and Fourteenth Amendments, as well as the fundamental liberty of privacy.

COMPETING CONSTITUTIONAL ISSUES

Guaranteed freedoms and protections sometimes appear to be in direct conflict, and the courts must sort through the resulting intellectual rubble. The article that follows examines some of the competing considerations involved in a conflict between a lessor's right to privacy and a lessee's right to be free of discrimination in housing.

PRIVACY AND THE 'LESBIAN ROOMMATE' CASE

Katherine Dalton

The very public presence of male and female homosexuals at the Democratic National Convention this past week raises an important issue. How far, exactly, do the rights of homosexuals in our society extend? What about instances where protection from discrimination comes into conflict with other, older, American rights, such as the right to privacy? Privacy prevailed in a recent decision by the Equal Opportunities Commission of Madison, Wis., in what has become known as "the lesbian roommate case." But the costs leading up to that decision by the municipal agency were high. And, in our current environment of "gay rights," cases like Madison's are likely to become more frequent.

The facts in the "roommate case" are worth looking at, because they show the astounding point to which this issue has moved in the U.S. More than three years ago, two young women, Anne Hacklander Ready and Maureen Rowe, ran an ad in the local newspaper in search of a new roommate for the house they were renting. Caryl Sprague, a lesbian, replied to the ad. Ms. Ready and Rowe accepted her deposit check, but then chose to turn her down after Ms. Sprague told them explicitly she was a lesbian. Ms. Sprague filed a complaint with the Madison Equal Opportunity Commission, a body appointed by the mayor and confirmed by the city council.

Homosexual Discrimination

Ms. Sprague's May 1989 complaint was filed under a then-new city ordinance that prevented discrimination in housing against homosexuals. According to Bruce Davey, the attorney who defended Ms. Ready and Rowe *pro bono,* the resulting legal work came to the equivalent of between $7,500 and $10,000 in billable time.

Ms. Sprague's complaint against the two women was brought under a city ordinance that reads, in part: "It shall be an unfair discrimination practice and unlawful and hereby prohibited: (a) For any person having the right of . . . transfer, sale, rental, or lease of any housing . . . to refuse to transfer, sell, rent or lease . . . [to] any person such housing because of . . . sexual orientation."

As the sole leaseholder of a house whose owner was living abroad, Anne Ready had the authority to sublease. According to an EOC hearing examiner who later reviewed the case, Sheilah O. Jakobson, this made Ms. Ready in effect the lessor. Under the ordinance, lessors are barred from discriminating against protected classes of people.

The EOC staff apparently felt Ms. Ready was guilty. That is to say, they felt Ms. Ready and Ms. Rowe had had no choice but to accept a lesbian roommate. In 1989, at a meeting set up to investigate Caryl Sprague's complaint, EOC investigator Mary M. Pierce drew up an "Agreement in Principle" that ordered Ms. Ready and Ms. Rowe to pay Ms. Sprague $1,000 in damages. Ms. Pierce then went beyond fines, and ordered Ms. Ready and Ms. Rowe to write Ms. Sprague "an acceptable letter of apology" (in the words of the agreement). They were also to have their rental practices monitored for two years, and to attend a two-hour sensitivity training class conducted by the United, a homosexual organization.

After a discussion Anne Ready characterized to me in a phone interview as emotional, and at which she and Maureen Rowe were not represented by a lawyer, the women signed the agreement. Then they contacted the attorney, Bruce Davey, who questioned the propriety of the meeting and who asked for a formal hearing before an EOC examiner. That hearing was finally held more than two years later, on Oct. 14, 1991, before Sheilah Jakobson.

When I tried to reach Caryl Sprague, she declined through her lawyer to be interviewed. But according to Ms. Jakobson's decision, Ms. Sprague testified at the October hearing that she had felt humiliated at losing the apartment and suffered from crying spells and an inability to concentrate. For her emotional distress, Ms. Jakobson decided she should get an award of $3,000 in damages from Ms. Ready and Ms. Rowe, plus $300 to make up for a security deposit she lost later in the summer on another apartment. In her decision, dated Dec. 27, 1991, Ms. Jakobson also ordered Ms. Ready and Ms. Rowe to pay Ms. Sprague's lawyer's fees as well. Christopher Kelly, Ms. Sprague's lawyer, wouldn't tell me what those fees were, but he did concede that they would run in the thousands of dollars.

Narrowly interpreting the original ordinance, Ms. Jakobson stated that Ms. Ready and Ms. Rowe lost their constitutional right to privacy "when they entered the public marketplace by advertising for unknown women to live with them."

She cited a 1987 Supreme Court decision, *Rotary Club of Duarte v. International Rotary Club,* and a 1984 decision, *Hishon v. King and Spaulding,* to buttress her judgment. Ms. Jakobson did not draw any distinction between the privacy rights of a social club in selecting a member (the first instance) or a law firm in selecting partners (the second instance), and the privacy rights of individuals in their own home. The fact that each woman would have had her own bedroom, she maintained, gave them privacy enough.

Ms. Ready and Ms. Rowe, Ms. Jakobson wrote, "sought strangers as roommates by entering the marketplace, admittedly to gain an economic benefit by reducing their share of the $740.00 per month rent for the house. Consequently, I find that there was no intimate relationship subject to constitutional protection for the right of free association."

Ms. Ready and Rowe then appealed to the full 11-member board of the Madison EOC to review the case. On June 26, the board decided that Madison's Common Council (the town's city council) had never intended to hold roommates to the same antidiscrimination laws standards applied to landlords. "If you're living in the same place as someone else, we really think you should be able to decide whether you want to live with that person or not, for whatever reason," said Joseph Szwaja, a city alderman and member of the EOC board. This reversal means that Ms. Ready and Ms. Rowe will not have to pay the $3,300 in damages, or Ms. Sprague's legal fees.

The town of Madison, for its part, had already decided it sided with Ms. Ready and Ms. Rowe on this issue. After the case got a wide public airing in 1989, the Common Council voted 19–2 in September 1989 to amend the ordinance to allow people to choose their roommates freely.

*   *   *   *   *

The question is: Where do we draw the line? The lesbian roommate case was a painful one, both for Ms. Ready and Ms. Rowe and for Ms. Sprague. As the definition of discrimination continues to expand, the definition of privacy continues to shrink. Today the fight is apparently over in Madison. But tomorrow in some other city [someone] may find himself in court, defending the very basic issue of whether he has the right to choose with whom he will live.

Source: *The Wall Street Journal,* July 20, 1992, p. A10. Reprinted by permission of *The Wall Street Journal,* © 1992 Dow Jones & Company, Inc. All Rights Reserved Worldwide.

Question

1. Answer Katherine Dalton's question: "Where do we draw the line?" Explain.

AN INSPIRATION FOR ALL

INTERNATIONAL

The remarkable insights and idealism of our Constitution have not been lost on the balance of the world. Ever since its writing, other nations have read and copied it. Today, the Czech Republic, Slovakia, Bulgaria, Poland, and other newly liberated Eastern European nations are in the process of building new governmental structures. Many American legal experts have been asked to aid in that process. They report that the Eastern Europeans look to our Constitution for its inspirational vigor, but the actual documents turn out to be more in the Western European tradition. Our Constitution is one of soaring, idealized generalities, while the Europeans tend toward detailed specifications—for example, a provision in a draft of the Bulgarian Constitution that forbade anyone to injure the reputation of another. This is quite a contrast to the United States, where we have a largely unrestrained right to criticize government officials.[27] So our constitutional principles have certainly not been embraced in whole around the globe. However, as the following article attests, one of America's most powerful export products, shaping the nature of government and life for billions, is our 200-year-old expression of the role of government in a free, democratic society. Note that this article, while dated, remains an effective summation of the enduring influence of our conception of government.

A GIFT TO ALL NATIONS

John Greenwald

INTERNATIONAL

In overwhelmingly Catholic Ireland, the constitution outlaws abortion and divorce and proclaims the Holy Trinity the source of all political power. Japan's national charter renounces war. Portugal's forbids private ownership of television stations. Peru reprints its charter in the Lima telephone directory, filling 10 pages of fine print. Yet beneath such diversity, each document can trace its rights and freedoms to U.S. soil. Says Joseph Magnet, a law professor at Canada's University of Ottawa: "America has been and remains the great constitutional laboratory for the entire world."

Of the 170 countries that exist today, more than 160 have written charters modeled directly or indirectly on the U.S. version. Those states range from the giant Soviet Union to the tiny Caribbean island country of Grenada. While Poland and France became the first to follow America's lead when they drafted modern constitutions in 1791, the largest impact has been recent. More than three quarters of today's charters were adopted after World War II. Jawaharlal Nehru, India's first prime minister, could have been speaking for the rest of the Third World when he told the U.S. Congress in 1949, "We have been greatly influenced by your own Constitution."

Some charters are roundly ignored. China's declaration of human rights was powerless to stop the abuses of the 1960s' Cultural Revolution. In Latin America dictators often simply disregard national charters during times of unrest. Many African leaders have stymied democracy by outlawing opposing political parties and turning their countries into one-party states, often without bothering to amend their charters. Yet so strongly have constitutional ideals taken hold worldwide that few countries dare to abandon them completely.

Indeed, constitutions are living documents that are constantly being created and reshaped. Voters in the Philippines went to the polls in January to approve a new charter, the country's fifth, that prohibits human rights violations and retains Corazon Aquino as president until 1992. In Nicaragua this year, the Marxist-influenced Sandinista leadership unveiled that country's 12th constitution in 149 years. Haitians in March approved their 23rd charter since 1804 in the country's first free election in three decades.

As such figures show, many constitutions have managed to survive only until the next upheaval or military coup. Three quarters of the world's constitutions have been completely rewritten since they were first adopted, making America's fidelity to a single charter highly unusual. Some experts contend that frequent constitutional changes can be healthy. Says Albert Blaustein, a Rutgers University law professor who has helped draft six foreign charters: "Jefferson concluded that every 20 years the new generation should have its own constitution to meet current needs. That might not be a good idea for the United States, but it's really not a bad idea for other countries."

Some constitutions are born of disaster. After World War II, Americans played a key role in drafting charters for the defeated nations of Japan and West Germany. The Japanese charter declares that the country will never again make war or maintain an army, navy, or air force. As a result, Japan spends only about 1 percent of its gross national product on defense, freeing the economy for more productive purposes. Ironically, the United States is pressing the Japanese to boost defense outlays.

The West German constitution, written under the watchful eye of U.S. occupation leaders, sought to prevent the rise of another Hitler by limiting the executive branch. Recalls Joachim von Elbe, a Bonn legal expert: "We did not want to make the Germans just imitate the American constitutional model but

rely on themselves to reform, rebuild, and overcome the Nazi period." The framers decreed that the Bundestag, or parliament, could not oust a chancellor without first choosing a successor. That has helped prevent a return of the political chaos that brought the Nazis to power in the 1930s.

Italians, with memories of Mussolini still fresh in their minds, went even further than the Germans in reining in the executive branch. While this has guarded against a new outbreak of tyranny, the inability of any one of Italy's parties to win a majority in parliament has led to frequent political turnover: Italy has had 46 governments since 1945.

*   *   *   *   *

[A] gulf between rhetoric and reality exists in China. The country's current charter, its fifth since 1949, grants "freedom of speech, of the press, of assembly, of association, of procession, and of demonstration." Peking nonetheless responded to widespread student protests last winter by detaining the leaders, firing university officials, and halting demonstrations. Authorities then shut down half a dozen liberal periodicals and banned scores of books, magazines, and films throughout the country.

Among Third World nations, India has often seemed the most faithful to its U.S.-inspired constitutional ideals. The world's largest democracy included a declaration of "fundamental rights" in its 1949 charter and backed them up by borrowing the U.S. system of judicial review. "Thank God they put in the fundamental rights," says Nani Palkhivala, a constitutional expert who was India's ambassador to Washington in the late 1970s. He observes, "Since 1947 we have had more harsh and repressive laws than were ever imposed under British rule." Indian courts, however, overturned most of them.

Leaders in Africa, confronted by tribal rivalries and the constant threat of coups, have taken far greater pains to stay in power than to preserve democratic rights. Troublesome constitutions are usually ignored or tailored to suit. "If any one speaks to you about a multi-party political system, catch him and hit him hard," declared Gabon President Albert-

Bernard (Omar) Bongo in a widely quoted 1983 speech. At least 28 of the continent's 53 states have only one political party, and 27 African nations are under military rule. Countries ranging from Guinea in West Africa to Somalia in the east have gone so far as to declare dissent a treasonable crime that can be punished by death. Notes British historian Lord Blake: "The political tradition in many parts of Africa is authoritarian, and that's what has taken over."

In Latin America, coups and military dictatorships have often been the rule. Chile's 1981 constitution grants dictatorial authority to President Augusto Pinochet, the general who seized power in 1973. In Argentina, the three-year effort at civilian rule under constitutionally mandated human rights principles still sways precariously if the military glowers too hard. Mexico is politically stable and boasts a constitution that provides for separation of powers between branches of government, but the Institutional Revolutionary Party and its forerunner have controlled the presidency—and much of the other branches—since 1929.

Though many U.S.-inspired constitutions have gone their own ways over the years, the seed planted in Philadelphia in 1789 should continue to flower. "The idea that individuals have rights against government is probably the most profound influence of the U.S. Constitution," says Oscar Schachter, professor emeritus of international law and diplomacy at Columbia University. "The whole notion of human rights as a worldwide movement was grounded in part in the Constitution." Those rights may not always be honored, but they have fired the imaginations of individuals, free and otherwise, around the world. After two centuries, the U.S. Constitution remains the standard against which people of all sorts measure their governments, and some governments even measure themselves.

Source: *Time,* July 6, 1987, pp. 92–95. Copyright 1987 Time Warner. All rights reserved. Reprinted by permission from Time Warner.

CHAPTER QUESTIONS

1. The Labor Department conducts regular investigations of business records to ensure compliance with the wages and hours provisions (e.g., higher pay for overtime) of the Fair Labor Standards Act. When a compliance officer sought to inspect certain financial records at the Lone Steer restaurant/motel in Steele, North Dakota, the restaurant declined his admittance until the government detailed the scope of the investigation. Not receiving a satisfactory response, the Lone Steer demanded a search warrant prior to inspection. As provided for under the FLSA, the government secured an administrative subpoena, which, unlike a search warrant, does not require judicial approval. Once again, Lone Steer denied admission. The government then filed suit. Decide. Explain. See *Donovan* v. *Lone Steer,* 464 U.S. 408 (1984).

2. A Texas statute forbade the practice of optometry under a trade name. The Texas legislature feared possible deception in optometric practice, such as changes in the staff of optometrists while the trade name remained unchanged or the use of different trade names at shops under common ownership, which practices might create a false impression of competition between the shops. Was the Texas statute a violation of the freedom of speech safeguards of the First Amendment? Explain. See *Friedman* v. *Rogers,* 440 U.S. 1 (1979).

3. This chapter noted a number of decisions affording protection to commercial speech. Why are corporations unlikely to begin using their vast resources to speak out on the wide range of public issues from abortion to organized prayer in schools to the death penalty? Explain.

4. The California Public Utilities Commission ordered a regulated private utility, Pacific Gas and Electric Company, to include in its billing envelopes the comments of a rate reform group with whose views the company disagreed. The company appealed, claiming its First Amendment rights were violated.

Decide. Explain. See *Pacific Gas and Electric Company* v. *Public Utilities Commission of California,* 106 S. Ct. 903 (1986).

5. Restaurant owner Smith reads of studies suggesting that women typically work more diligently than men. He decides therefore to hire only women for his new restaurant. He runs an employment ad in the local newspaper and includes the language, "Only women need apply." Smith is challenged in court on the grounds that the ad violates Title VII of the Civil Rights Act of 1964, which forbids discrimination in employment on the basis of race, religion, color, sex, or national origin. Smith loses the lawsuit, but he appeals the decision on constitutional grounds.
   a. What constitutional law argument might be raised in Smith's behalf?
   b. Decide. Explain. See *Pittsburgh Press* v. *Human Relations Commission,* 413 U.S. 376 (1973) for a relevant decision.

6. Members of Local 590 were picketing a grocery store located in Logan Valley's shopping center. The grocery store had hired only nonunion personnel. An injunction was served barring the picketing on the grounds of trespass. The decision was appealed to the U.S. Supreme Court.
   a. What constitutional law argument would you raise on behalf of Local 590?
   b. What argument would you raise on behalf of Logan Valley?
   c. Decide. Explain. See *Amalgamated Food Employees Union Local 590 et al.* v. *Logan Valley Plaza, Inc. et al.,* 391 U.S. 308 (1968).

7. Tanner and others sought to distribute handbills in the interior mall of the Lloyd Corporation shopping center. The literature concerned an anti-Vietnam War meeting. Lloyd Corporation had a strict rule forbidding handbilling. When security guards terminated distributions within the center, Tanner et al. claimed a violation of their First Amendment rights. Both the district court and the Court of Appeals relied on *Amalgamated Food* (see question 6) in finding a violation of constitutional rights. The decision was appealed to the U.S. Supreme Court. Decide. Explain. See *Lloyd Corporation* v. *Tanner,* 407 U.S. 551 (1972).

8. Philip Zauderer, an Ohio attorney, ran a newspaper ad promising a full refund of legal fees if clients accused of drunk driving were convicted. He later ran an ad soliciting clients who believed themselves to have been harmed by the Dalkon Shield intrauterine contraceptive. That ad included a line drawing of the device as well as a promise that "[i]f there is no recovery, no legal fees are owed by our clients." The Office of Disciplinary Counsel of the Supreme Court of Ohio charged that Zauderer violated several provisions of the Disciplinary Rules of the Ohio Code of Professional Responsibility, including:
   i. The drunk-driving ad was deceptive because it purported to allow a contingent fee arrangement in a criminal case when that payment method was explicitly forbidden by Ohio rules.
   ii. The Dalkon Shield ad failed to disclose the fact that clients might be liable for *litigation costs* (rather than *legal fees*) and, therefore, was deceptive.
   iii. The Dalkon Shield ad violated rules forbidding the use of illustrations in ads.
   iv. The Dalkon Shield ad violated rules forbidding "soliciting or accepting legal employment through advertisements containing information or advice regarding a specific legal problem."

   Zauderer was found to have violated the Ohio Disciplinary Rules, and a public reprimand was issued. He took his case to the U.S. Supreme Court.
   a. What constitutional claim should be raised on behalf of Zauderer?
   b. Decide. Explain. See *Zauderer* v. *Office of Disciplinary Counsel of the Supreme Court of Ohio,* 471 U.S. 626 (1985).

9. American Bar Association rules seek to discourage lawyers from aggressive pursuit of clients in an "ambulance-chasing" fashion. In-person solicitation of clients is entirely forbidden. General mass mailings not directed to individuals known to be in need of legal assistance are permissible under the bar's guidelines. Some attorneys have used targeted mailings to potential clients known to be facing legal difficulties. For example, attorneys have offered their legal assistance via express mail messages to families whose relatives have been killed or injured in crashes or other disasters. ABA rules discourage targeted advertising, and many states have followed

the ABA's advice by adopting guidelines restraining that type of advertising by lawyers.

A Kentucky lawyer sought to mail letters to individuals against whom home foreclosure proceedings had been instituted. He offered "free information on how you can keep your home." Kentucky rules forbade targeted mailings. The attorney claimed a First Amendment violation. How would you rule? Explain. See *Shapero* v. *Kentucky Bar Association,* 486 U.S. 466 (1988).

10. A California sales and use tax of 6 percent on all personal property sales was applied to the distribution of religious materials by religious organizations. The Jimmy Swaggart Ministries challenged the tax on constitutional grounds.

 a. What constitutional issue was raised by the plaintiff?

 b. Decide. Explain. See *Jimmy Swaggart Ministries* v. *Board of Equalization of California,* 493 U.S. 378 (1990).

11. Southwest Texas State University adopted a rule that restricted the distribution of commercial newspapers on its campus to specified locations, newspaper boxes, or subscriptions. The *Hays County Guardian* sued, claiming interference with its First Amendment rights.

 a. How does the University defend its position?

 b. Decide.

 c. Would the result be different if Southwest Texas were a private college? Explain. See *Hays County Guardian* v. *Supple,* 969 F.2d 111 (5th Cir. 1992); cert. den. 113 S.Ct. 1067 (1993).

12. J. R.'s Kitty Kat Lounge in South Bend, Indiana, featured young women dancers who progressively removed their clothing until they were performing in the nude. Public nudity is banned by statute in Indiana. On the strength of that statute, the city tried to close the Kitty Kat Lounge. The dancing was not obscene as a matter of law. As the judge saw it, the issue was "whether nonobscene nude dancing of the barroom variety, performed as entertainment, is expression and thus entitled to protection under the First Amendment." How would you rule? Ex-

plain. See *Barnes* v. *Glen Theatre,* 111 S.Ct. 2456 (1991).

13. In recent years, Congress and various state legislatures and municipalities have considered legislation designed to make pornographers pay damages to sexual abuse victims. For example, the Pornography Victims' Compensation Act of 1991, a federal proposal that was not approved, would have permitted those who believe their attackers were spurred on by obscene material to sue producers, distributors, and sellers of that material.

 a. How would you vote on such legislation? Explain.

 b. Would you favor extending such legislation to sexually explicit movies or to television violence? Explain.

 c. Could we lawfully ban all material that "subordinates or degrades" women in that such material would constitute a form of sex discrimination? Explain. For a related decision, see *American Booksellers Ass'n* v. *Hudnut,* 771 F.2d 323 (1985); Aff'd on Appeal, 475 U.S. 1001 (1986). Also see *Regina* v. *Butler,* 89 D.L.R. 4th 449 (S.Ct. of Canada, 1992).

14. *a.* Could the federal government lawfully ban all tobacco advertising? Explain.

 b. Should it do so? Explain.

15. The sons of a murder victim brought a wrongful death/negligence action against a magazine, *Soldier of Fortune,* alleging that it had published an ad creating an unreasonable risk of violent crime. A former police officer had placed the ad offering his services as a bodyguard under the heading, "Gun for Hire." The ad resulted in the officer being hired to kill the plaintiffs' father. The ad included the phrases "professional mercenary," "very private," and a statement indicating that "all jobs" would be considered, but it also included a list of legitimate jobs that involved the use of a gun. The plaintiffs won the negligence action and were awarded a $4.3 million judgment. *Soldier of Fortune* appealed on First Amendment grounds. Decide. See *Braun* v. *Soldier of Fortune Magazine, Inc.,* 968 F.2d 1110 (11th Cir. 1992); cert. den., 113 S.Ct. 1028 (1993).

NOTES

1. Otto Friedrich, "How the Deed Was Done," *Time,* July 6, 1987, p. 59.

2. Jerre Williams, *Constitutional Analysis in a Nutshell* (St. Paul, Minn.: West Publishing, 1979), p. 33.

3. *Texas* v. *Johnson,* 105 L.Ed. 342 (1989).

4. *United States* v. *Eichman,* 496 U.S. 310 (1990).

5. Davis Lauter, "Overruling High Court Usually a Futile Effort," *Los Angeles Times,* June 12, 1990, p. A5.

6. *Kreisner* v. *City of San Diego,* 988 F.2d 883 (9th Cir. 1993).

7. *Lee* v. *Weisman,* 112 S.Ct. 2649 (1992).

8. *Jones* v. *Clear Creek Independent School District,* 977 F.2d 963 (5th Cir. 1992); cert. den. 113 S.Ct. 2950 (1993).

9. *Board of Education of Kiryas Joel Village School District* v. *Grumet,* U.S. Supreme Court, mos. 93–517, 93–527, and 93–539 (6127194). For a journalistic account of the case, see Paul Barrett, "High Court Rules Hasidic School Unit Unconstitutional," *The Wall Street Journal,* June 28, 1994, p. A4.

10. *Lemon* v. *Kurtzman,* 403 U.S. 602, 612 (1971).

11. 366 U.S. 420 (1961).

12. *Fair Cadillac* v. *Bailey,* 229 Conn. 312 (Conn. S. Ct. 1994).

13. Richard Holman, "Britain's Sunday Shopping Ban," *The Wall Street Journal,* December 17, 1992, p. A11.

14. *Tinker* v. *Des Moines School District,* 393 U.S. 503 (1969).

15. *R.A.V.* v. *St. Paul,* 112 S.Ct. 2538 (1992).

16. *Wisconsin* v. *Todd Mitchell,* 113 S.Ct. 2194 (1993).

17. Editorial, "Buffaloed at Penn," *The Wall Street Journal,* April 26, 1993, p. A14; and Associated Press, "Case Dropped in University 'Race' Incident," *Des Moines Register,* May 25, 1993, p. 4A.

18. Stephen Chapman, "Speech Codes on the Way Out," *Waterloo Courier,* July 9, 1992, p. B7.

19. This question was suggested by a reviewer, Professor Cynthia Srstka, Augustana College (South Dakota).

20. *Valentine* v. *Chrestensen,* 316 U.S. 52 (1942).

21. *City of Cincinnati* v. *Discovery Network,* 113 S.Ct. 1505 (1993).

22. 367 U.S. 643.

23. *California* v. *Hodari,* 111 S.Ct. 1547 (1991).

24. *Marshall* v. *Barlow's, Inc.,* 436 U.S. 307 (1978).

25. See, for example, *Keystone Bituminous Coal Association* v. *DeBendictis,* 107 S. Ct. 1232 (1987); *Nollan* v. *California Coastal Commission,* 107 S. Ct. 3141 (1987); and *Lucas* v. *South Carolina Coastal Council,* 112 S.Ct. 2886 (1992).

26. *Griswold* v. *Connecticut,* 381 U.S. 479 (1965).

27. Henry Reske, "U.S. Constitution Unpopular," *ABA Journal* 77 (December 1991), p. 28.

CHAPTER

6

INTERNATIONAL ETHICS AND LAW

●

INTRODUCTION

The preceding chapters have addressed general concepts of ethics and American law. As companies today expand, not only within their domestic borders but many times across continents and seas, an understanding of ethics and law across borders is critical. Unless a firm continues to meet the demands of worldwide constituents (clients, customers, consumers), it may be left behind without the means to effectively challenge its competitors. By globalizing, firms have more efficient access to resources, reduce tariffs paid, and take advantage of the geographical area that provides the best return for the firm's investment. And companies are not alone in this effort to globalize; they are supported by their governments, which have entered into agreements with other countries in order to facilitate the process. For instance, in the fall of 1993, Canada, the United States, and Mexico joined in the North American Free Trade Agreement (NAFTA), which opened the trade borders of North America, allowing easier access and growth opportunities for affected firms.

But what are the implications of this expansion around the globe? To what laws are companies subject if they cannot even determine what is their "home" country? As firms become companies of the world, rather than of one nation, conflicts that might otherwise have been easily settled are now legal quagmires.

THE INTERNATIONAL ENVIRONMENT

Since Adam Smith, many have argued that it is axiomatic that a decrease in trade barriers between any number of countries will stimulate the world economy, not simply those of the countries involved in the specific trade agreement. Accordingly, the NAFTA was successful in the U.S. Congress because the legislators believed that a stimulation of the Mexican and Canadian economies would lead to a boost in the American economy. At the same time, during the national debate on the NAFTA, labor leaders contended that, with a lowering of trade barriers, U.S. firms would immediately take advantage of lower cost labor locations in Mexico and thus sacrifice American jobs. This, however, is seen by some as a short-term setback to the

American economy in trade for long-term gains by the creation of more robust markets for American goods.

The desire to reach some common legal ground in international business is not a recent development. As is explained later in the *Sumitomo* case, United States commercial treaties, negotiated as early as 1778, regulated shipping and trading rights and rules between individuals of different countries. However, with the advent of the multinational enterprise, these early international treaties have become outmoded. With new agreements come new concerns.

As is evidenced by the NAFTA debate, countervailing forces are at work in the global economy. On the one hand, consider the practically unprecedented expansion of world trade through agreements such as the NAFTA, the General Agreement on Tariffs and Trade (GATT), the MERCOSUR Common Market (created by Argentina, Brazil, Paraguay, and Uruguay), and the East African Community (created by Kenya, Tanzania, and Uganda), among others. These alliances represent not only legislative victories but also resistance to a growing isolationist tendency in the United States and elsewhere.

For example, despite the support of every living president in the United States, as well as Nobel Prize–winning economists, almost half of the American public opposed the NAFTA. The alliance, which will expand trade across the North American continent, was passed in Congress by only a slight margin. In addition, after years of negotiation, the current round of the GATT was finally successfully concluded in December 1993, eliminating many tariff barriers between and among most countries worldwide. Economists believe that "within the mindnumbing text of GATT lies an enormous stimulus to the world economy as tariffs are reduced and new markets are opened." [1]

Countervailing Forces.   On the other hand, there are forces that are, in effect, limiting the globalization of world business. First, the European Community (EC) is painfully mired in several issues that do not seem to be easily resolved. The EC's aims have been retarded since the failure of the Maastricht Conference, which sought to establish a common currency for member countries. Financial and immigration concerns, as well as power struggles, have characterized the debate on this topic, slowing efforts at trade expansion. Second, the former Soviet Union is experiencing growing pains that have frustrated Russian leader Boris Yeltsin's original time line for reform and a free market economy. In December 1993, Yeltsin had to deal with the election of a number of right-wing legislators who opposed the swiftness and direction of his reforms. Consequently, he was forced to decelerate the privatization process, which in turn accelerates inflation and, for the time being, slows international trade. Finally, China too is experiencing rampant inflation as it endures growth at a pace of 13 percent per year and the resulting "demand pull" inflation. There are too many yuan chasing too few goods, and the consequence could be reduced exports and imports. Again, a potentially enormous market player may be delayed in playing the game.

The following article illustrates the dramatic recent changes in the European trading market.

EUROPE'S BORDERS FADE AND PEOPLE AND GOODS CAN MOVE MORE FREELY

Tony Horwitz

Barry Cotter is the unlikely face of the new Europe. A florid, beer-bellied Englishman, he speaks no foreign languages and jokes about "cloggies" (the Dutch) and "Kermits" (as in "frogs," or Frenchmen). But as he steers his 18-wheel tanker through the Pyrenees between Spain and France, he assumes a less provincial role: a European Community passport holder, driving for a German transport firm and hauling Spanish-made chemicals to Italy.

Not that anyone at the border cares. On January 1, 1993, officials here—as at many borders in Europe—stopped making passport, customs, and other checks that used to delay Mr. Cotter for hours, even days. "On most trips, I made worse time than Hannibal," he says, referring to the Carthaginian general who crossed this same mountain pass with elephants in 218 BC. Now, Mr. Cotter speeds across a border without so much as a glance from a lone, idle guard. With the traditional delays vanishing across Europe, he can span the Continent in three days, against four or more just six months ago. "In this business, time is money," he says, "and these days I've got a lot more of both."

His glee contrasts sharply with the gloom in European capitals. There, the conventional wisdom holds that the dream of a United States of Europe is evaporating amid recession, political bickering, and paralysis over Bosnia. But viewed from the ground, reports of the new Europe's demise appear greatly exaggerated. A visit to the borders of seven nations finds a quiet revolution under way as people vote with their feet and wallets against high taxes and heavy revolution.

Frontier regions have become laboratories of new Europe, a place where shoppers, smugglers, entrepreneurs and savers hunting for the best bank are testing the bounds of a much heralded but still novel entity: a border-free market of 12 nations and 345 million consumers.

* * * * *

The Danish border shows how the new Europe spells doom for uncompetitive tax rates and prices. Already, a traditional and rather surreal tax dodge—driving to Germany to buy Danish beer at supermarkets with Danish-speaking staff and Tuborg-lined aisles—has forced Copenhagen to lower its beer tax. Now, a bizarre scheme devised by Fleggaard, a household goods company, may force down Denmark's hefty value-added tax as well.

At Fleggaard outlets across Denmark, shoppers simply ask to pay the German VAT of 15% rather than the 25% Danish rate. Fleggaard prints out an invoice at a small office just across the border in Germany, loads an appliance at a warehouse on the Danish side and drives across the frontier. Then the truck turns around and delivers the machine to the Danish buyer. The invoice and short trip make Germany the point of sale, and of taxation. Fleggaard says its sales so far this year have more than doubled, with over five million kroners ($800,000) going into German tax coffers.

* * * * *

Such tactics wouldn't be possible without the freeing-up of cross-border transport, once a clotted and corrupt sector that exemplified Europe's economic stagnation, its "Eurosclerosis." Until recently, differing fees and inspections at each border stalled truckers and inflated their costs. Some nations limited how much diesel fuel truckers could carry, forcing them to buy it at that country's pumps. Others required obscure checks to boost employment and tax revenue. Bribes were routine, particularly in Italy.

*   *   *   *   *

But it is the Spanish border town of La Jonquera that drivers regard as a shrine to the *ancien regime.* Here, paperwork that took 10 minutes in Denmark and Germany typically required a day. The procedures were so tangled that truckers hired middlemen to fill out forms and get them stamped while they themselves waited in the town's shops, bars and brothels. Once a desolate, windblown town of 2,500, known only for its arsenic mines, La Jonquera became a bustling place where even clerks could earn 300,000 pesetas (about $2,500) a month—not counting rake-offs.

Now 35% of La Jonquera's work force is unemployed, and shops that had enjoyed a captive market of bored truckers are silent. "Paperwork is finished as a career," Pere Brugat, the town's mayor says wistfully as the 4,000 or so trucks that once stopped here daily now whiz past on the highway outside his window.

He and other officials concede that the red tape was largely unnecessary. But they fear that without it, EC states such as Spain and Portugal can't compete with the countries like Germany.

"Bureaucracy helped equalize things," says Jose Guanter, a reference librarian for the few remaining customs agents. His computer is turned off, his shelves filled with dusty tomes of defunct regulations. "Without all this," he adds, "we are in Darwin's world, where only the strong ones survive."

La Jonquera, at least, is evolving. Having once thrived as a gatekeeper, it now hopes to become a gateway instead. The town is turning a vast parking lot where trucks waited out the delays into an industrial park, and it is offering free land to companies that relocate there. Its offer—advertised with glossy brochures titled "A Doorway to Europe"—has already lured a few Spanish and French concerns, which plan to open distribution warehouses.

"From here, you can move quickly to anywhere in France or Spain, without bureaucracy," says Mr. Brugat, smiling at the irony of his boast.

Source: Tony Horwitz, "Europe's Borders Fade and People and Goods Can Move More Freely," *The Wall Street Journal,* May 18, 1993, p. A1. Reprinted by permission of *The Wall Street Journal,* © 1993 Dow Jones & Company, Inc. All Rights Reserved Worldwide.

Questions

1. What is your reaction to La Jonquera Mayor Pere Brugat's concern that Spain and Portugal will not be able to compete with countries like Germany?
2. What other ideas could you offer Brugat in connection with the revitalization of his town?
3. Why do you believe that it has taken until now to open borders? What incentives did countries have to maintain tighter border controls?

THE INTERCULTURAL ENVIRONMENT: ETHICS ACROSS INTERNATIONAL BORDERS

Consistency in Behavior

Do ethical concepts and standards cross borders? If it is ethical to act in a certain way in one country, is it similarly ethical to do so in another? Many ethical dilemmas have arisen due to variations among cultures. It might be a firm's general practice to conform to the legal standards in any country in which it does business, but this does not mean that the firm is consistent in its ethical stance.

For example, the United States requires that cigarette companies place a label on all products and product advertisements warning of the hazardous effects of smoking. This warning label is not required worldwide. Consequently, cigarette manufacturers place the label on their products sold in the United States but generally do not place the label on products marketed in countries that do not require the labeling. If putting the label on the product has been deemed ethical behavior by American society, are the companies acting unethically by not doing so in other countries?

A second approach adopted by some firms is to maintain consistent standards without regard to the country in which the firm is doing business, rather than conforming behavior only to what is required by the country. The problem with this approach is that maintaining standards that are higher than those required in the host country may impose higher costs on the firm, and, consequently, raise prices to consumers. The firm would be hurt competitively because other firms would not have this additional cost.

American firms also claim that their opportunity to compete has been hampered by the U.S. government. For example, our government has attempted to encourage Vietnam to recognize a code of human rights and to turn over information regarding MIAs. Because Vietnam is extremely interested in economic ties with the United States, we have been able to use trade as a bargaining chip for our interests in human rights. However, American industry does not want to be foreclosed from the very promising Vietnamese market. Thus, early in 1994, President Clinton announced that he was lifting the 19-year embargo on trade with Vietnam.

The Foreign Corrupt Practices Act (FCPA)

As we saw in Chapter 2, the Foreign Corrupt Practices Act prohibits U.S. companies and some joint ventures from making certain payments or gifts to government officials for the purpose of influencing business decisions. While the FCPA appears to be well motivated, some critics argue that it is inappropriate for the United States to "unilaterally attempt to legislate morality in foreign trade."[2] In addition, others argue that the FCPA unduly restricts American companies operating in other countries and prevents them from effectively competing with other firms.

In Chapter 2, we examined bribery in the emerging Chinese market. The following article shows that even a powerful, highly respected industrialist in the relatively prosperous, mature Italian economy may feel compelled to buy influence to be successful.

DE BENEDETTI SAYS POLITICAL
BRIBES WERE COMMONPLACE
IN THE 1980s

Lisa Bannon

If he had to do it all over again, Italian industrialist Carlo De Benedetti says he would do the same thing: he would pay bribes to politicians to get public works contracts, because those were the rules of the game in Italy in the 1980s.

"And I'd do it with the same disgust I did then," said the 58-year-old chairman and controlling shareholder of C. Olivetti & Co. In an interview, a relatively tranquil Mr. De Benedetti reflected on his many battles, financial and political, with the Italian political establishment over the years and discussed why he is optimistic about the outcome of the latest one. Mr. De Benedetti's description of the political pressures brought to bear in Italy in the 1980s sheds light on the general Italian business climate for both Italian and foreign companies operating in Italy in the past decade.

Historical Context.   Emphasizing that people and acts must be judged in their historical context, Mr. De Benedetti doesn't apologize for making kickbacks to Italian political parties to obtain contracts. "When Olivetti arrived at a state of desperation [with a state agency], when our sales representatives weren't even received by the ministry, when [then postal minister Giuseppe] Parella said everybody else paid so we had to pay, then I authorized the agreement," he said. "And when we stopped paying in 1991, we didn't get one order."

As reported, Mr. De Benedetti voluntarily told Milan magistrates . . . that Olivetti paid 10 billion lire ($6.8 million) in kickbacks to the Ministry of Post and Telecommunications to obtain contracts in the 1980s. He also told magistrates of four or five other instances but declined to elaborate on details of those cases . . . Mr. De Benedetti said he hasn't

received formal notice that he is under investigation in the corruption scandal, but Italian news reports indicate that his name appears on an undisclosed list of those under investigation.

Long considered a maverick industrialist who operated outside the traditional Italian political system, Mr. De Benedetti reflected on being caught up in the same system he had denounced repeatedly over the years.

Blocked Sale.   "I was prepared to pay not a small price to maintain my independence," he said. He recalled when in 1985, then Socialist Prime Minister Bettino Craxi blocked the sale of state food group SME to Mr. De Benedetti after the deal had been signed. Mr. De Benedetti implied that Mr. Craxi blocked the sale because Olivetti didn't offer bribe money.

In another incident, Mr. De Benedetti said, he failed to gain control of then financially troubled publishing group Rizzoli in 1981 because of political pressure. Then Socialist Finance Minister Salvatore Formica said that "he would send the police to Olivetti if we got near Rizzoli," Mr. De Benedetti recalled. It was a "vendetta Mafiosa," he said. The deal was ultimately blocked by the government. "There were businessmen friends and businessmen enemies," he said, "I was part of the enemies."

He said it would have been impossible for him to report the kickback system at the time. "Why didn't I denounce [systematic extortion] in 1988? Because today is a very different place than back then—even six months ago nobody thought Italy would change as much as it has." He said he didn't step forward to confess the bribes over the past year because he was acting first as the chairman of Olivetti, with responsibilities to the company and its shareholders. "You can't go damage your company on purpose," he said. "I can't go denounce my company if it wasn't yet involved."

However, Mr. De Benedetti said other businessmen shouldn't wait until their companies are investigated before reporting extortion to magistrates. "We're at the point where it's no longer dangerous for companies to come forward [and confess]," he said.

Ultimately, the effects of Italy's "tangentopoli"— or "kickback city"—scandals will have a positive effect on business in general and Olivetti in particular, Mr. De Benedetti said. But only if the process is completed rapidly and if the investigators get to the very bottom of their probe.

Source: Lisa Bannon, "De Benedetti Says Political Bribes Were Commonplace in the 1980s," *The Wall Street Journal,* May 20, 1993, p. A15. Reprinted by permission of *The Wall Street Journal,* © 1993 Dow Jones & Company, Inc. All Rights Reserved Worldwide.

Questions

1. If the only way to run a business in a country is to pay bribes to public officials, what is the ethical response for a foreign company? Explain.
2. In the 1980s and early 1990s, powerful interests lobbied against corporate investment in South Africa. Those opposed to investment there argued that foreign money would only serve to support apartheid (the former policy of racial oppression in South Africa). They contended that by divesting or refusing further investment, U.S. firms could exert a greater influence on the white minority then in power in South Africa. Others argue that divestment only took U.S. companies out of positions of power. If foreign firms continued to invest in South Africa, they would then be able to use their influence to effect changes. Of course, South Africa has now abolished apartheid and embraced democracy. With the benefit of hindsight, was divestment the correct policy for American firms in white-ruled South Africa? Explain.

Social Responsibility to Host Country

Where a firm is involved in business abroad, does that firm have social duties to the host country beyond those required by the market and the law? This issue has arisen most recently in connection with the environment. For instance, are firms that engage in business that may result in a depletion of the rain forests responsible for protecting the forests, even where there are no laws that require them to do so? Power companies AES Corporation and New England Electric System evidently believed that they were responsible. When they learned that the carbon dioxide emissions from fossil-fueled power plants in the United States were dangerous to trees in the rain forests, they engaged in a voluntary program to replant the forest with new trees in order to offset the effects of their industry.[3] On the other hand, Chiquita, Dole, and Del Monte have all been cited as companies that have engaged in harmful practices. These companies have expanded their banana plantations in Central and South America, increasing the amount of pesticides used in those areas, which has then led to extreme deforestation.

Social Responsibility to Home Country

Notwithstanding a potential responsibility to the countries in which a firm does business, does that firm have any special obligation to its home country? In 1993, the federal government had prohibited American firms from participating in an embargo of Israel imposed by Arab countries, including Iraq, Kuwait, Libya, Yemen, Saudi Arabia, and Syria. The Arab countries refused to do business not only with Israel but also with any firm that did business with Israel.

Baxter Pharmaceuticals allegedly cooperated with the Arab embargo by refusing to do business with Israel because it wanted to maintain certain lucrative Arab contracts. Vernon Loucks, Baxter's CEO, was called on the carpet by Baxter's institutional stockholders and was at risk of losing his position because of this decision. In fact, when Loucks introduced himself as the CEO at Baxter's annual meeting, he was met with a response of "Not for long!" from one of the shareholders. While he kept his job (he did step down from his position on the board of Yale University as a result of student protests regarding his involvement in the Arab boycott), Baxter suffered gravely in the U.S. press and paid $6.5 million in fines. In addition, one month after the fines were imposed, the Defense Department banned Baxter from new business contracts with the department.

Baxter, in this situation, argued that it should be able to contract with whomever it chooses, that it owes no obligation to the foreign policy matters of the U.S. government. In this case, the firm was in violation of U.S. law; in other cases, the line may not be so clearly drawn. For instance, McDonnell Douglas was faced with similar allegiance questions when it proposed a sale of a portion of its manufacturing interests to Taiwan Aerospace. After years of defense contracts with the U.S. government, opponents of the plan were concerned that privileged information regarding America's defense would fall into the wrong hands. Opponents contended that McDonnell Douglas had a duty to the United States to maintain the confidentiality of this information within America's borders. McDonnell Douglas, on the other hand, argued that it was a private company and could sell its assets to the highest bidder, which was Taiwan by a wide margin. U.S. law did not prohibit the sale in this instance, and McDonnell Douglas was faced with the prospect of violating the wishes of its home government in order to stay afloat, or complying with the government's request to stop the sale and perhaps sacrificing the survival of the company. Ultimately, McDonnell Douglas did not sell to Taiwan Aerospace.

Having briefly examined some international ethics themes, we now turn our attention to problems of global law.

FOUNDATIONS OF INTERNATIONAL LAW

A firm with manufacturing plants in Argentina and Thailand, and corporate headquarters in Bangkok, enters into a contract with a French firm to distribute its products produced in the Argentinean plant. The French firm is not satisfied with the quality of the products being sent. What law would apply to this situation? Argentinean? Thai? French? The answer to this question is not simple, even for seasoned lawyers; yet the firms involved will be greatly affected by the decision, since contract law varies from country to country.

The source of law applicable to an international issue depends on the issue involved. In general, private parties are free to form agreements in whatever manner they wish. The parties to the agreement can determine, for instance, which nation's law shall govern the contract, where disagreements in connection with the contract shall be settled, and even in which language the transactions shall be made. This is considered *private law.* Whenever the parties to a transaction are from different jurisdictions and are involved in a lawsuit, the court will look to the agreement of the parties to resolve these issues. Otherwise, where the contract is silent as to the choice of law, jurisdiction, and other questions, the court must decide. Generally, the choice of law rule of the jurisdiction in which the transaction occurred is applied. If the transaction is done by mail, as are many international trade negotiations, most often the law of the jurisdiction of the seller's place of business applies. Recall, however, that the parties to the contract may always reach an agreement on the law to be applied.

Public law, on the other hand, includes those rules of each nation that regulate the contractual agreement between the parties—for instance, import and export taxes, packaging requirements, and safety standards. In addition, public law regulates the relationships between nations.

Public law derives from a number of sources. The most familiar source of public law is a *treaty* or *convention* (a contract between nations). For example, the United States, Canada, and Mexico have the NAFTA, a convention regarding free trade between those countries. Public law is also found in *international custom* or *generally accepted principles of law.* These terms refer to those practices that are commonly accepted as appropriate business or commercial practices between nations. For instance, sovereign immunity is an accepted principle of international law. A custom is derived from consistent behavior over time that is accepted as binding by the countries who engage in that behavior.

The Development of Customs.   One might better understand the concept of custom if it is analogized to the law of sales in the United States. For years, merchants would follow certain accepted customs or principles in connection with the sale of goods. These customs or manners of dealing between merchants were later codified in the Uniform Commercial Code (UCC) that regulates the sale of goods and has certain provisions specifically related to the sale of goods between merchants. In this way, customs or practices traditionally followed by merchants have become accepted principles of law.

On the other hand, in the international legal arena, customary practices are not stagnant; the development of custom as a guide for behavior or decision making is in a constant state of evolution. For instance, in connection with personal privacy or information flow between countries, it has always been the custom that personal information flow freely between countries in order to encourage the free flow of information in the business world. However, recently, the European Community began to examine the potential for invasions of privacy and has now proposed minimum standards which must be maintained by a country receiving information from an EC country.

To determine whether a custom exists, one must look to two factors: consistency and repetition of the action or decision; and recognition by nations that this custom is binding. The first requirement merely holds that the action or decision must be accepted by a number of nations for a time long enough to establish uniformity of application. The second requirement dictates that the custom be accepted as binding by nations observing the custom. Where the custom is accepted as merely persuasive, the custom does not rise to the level of a generally accepted principle of law. Through persistent objections of one or several nations, those nations may ensure that certain customs are not applied in cases which involve them.

Courts.   Public international law is also found in *judicial decisions.* The only court that is devoted entirely to hearing cases of public law is the International Court of Justice (ICJ) in the United Nations. The ICJ is made up of 15 judges from 15 different member countries. The ICJ may issue two types of decisions depending on its jurisdiction. The court has *advisory jurisdiction* where the United Nations asks the court for an opinion on a matter of international law. These opinions are merely advisory and do not bind any party. The ICJ may also have *contentious jurisdiction.* This exists only where two or more nations (not individual parties) have consented to the jurisdiction of the court and have requested an opinion. In this case, the opinion would be considered binding on the parties involved. The court, however, is not bound by its own earlier decisions as precedent.

Comity

The unique aspect of public international law is that countries are generally not subject to law in the international arena unless they consent to such jurisdiction. For instance, a country is not bound by a treaty unless that country has signed the treaty. A country is not bound by international custom unless it has traditionally participated in that custom. And prior judicial decisions are only persuasive where a country is persuaded by and accepts these decisions as precedent. In fact, perhaps the most critical element in understanding international law is understanding that it is not actually "law" in the way that we generally consider law. Countries are not bound to abide by it except through "comity." *Comity* is the concept that countries *should* abide by international custom, treaties, and other sources of international direction because that is the civil way to engage in relationships. Nations must respect each other and respect some basic principles of dealing in order to have effective relationships.

It may be helpful to analogize the concept of comity to deontological ethical theory; the view of ethical reasoning which suggests that there are certain universal principles of a civilized society to which all involved should adhere. This type of reasoning assumes that there are certain acts which are right and certain acts which are wrong, no matter where you are or where you are from. The belief that countries *should* abide by international agreements would be a universal principle which is arguably right according to comity, no matter what situation is proposed.

While some believe that the origins of law are in religion and its commandments, others have argued that, instead, law derives from a natural tendency to prevent chaos. International law is that attempt to prevent chaos in the international marketplace through the application of universal principles, and comity is the means by which it is encouraged.

DOING BUSINESS IN A FOREIGN COUNTRY

UN Convention on Contracts for the International Sale of Goods

In 1988, 10 nations signed and became bound by the UN Convention on Contracts for the International Sale of Goods (CISG). Twenty-six nations, including the United States, have now become parties to the Convention. The CISG applies to contracts between parties of countries that have signed the convention and provides uniform rules for the sale of goods.

The CISG contains rules regarding the interpretation of contracts and negotiations and the form of contracts. Many obligations of the parties are enunciated by the CISG. For instance, the seller is required to deliver the goods and any documents relating to the goods, as well as to make sure that the goods are in conformance with the contract terms. The buyer, on the other hand, is required to pay the contract price and to accept delivery of the goods. The CISG, however, does not answer all questions that may arise in the course of a transaction. For instance, questions of a contract's validity are left to national law. Under American law, an enforceable contract requires four elements:

- *Capacity* to enter the contract.
- *Offer and acceptance* of the terms of the contract.
- *Consideration* for the promises in the contract.
- *Legality* of purpose of the contract.

Capacity refers to the parties' ability to understand the nature and consequences of the contract. For example, an individual who is under the influence of alcohol might not have capacity to enter into a contract. The offer and acceptance must evidence a "meeting of the minds" between the parties; that is, there must be a mutual understanding regarding the terms of the contract. Consideration means that something of value (whether monetary or otherwise) has passed between the parties. For example, one party agrees to pay money, and the other party agrees to deliver the goods requested. Countries that are not based in the common law, but instead in civil law systems, do not require consideration for a contract. The final element requires that the contract's purpose be legal. For instance, under American law, if a company agreed to pay money to import certain goods to a country where those goods are not allowed, that agreement would not be enforceable.

Generally, once a contract has been created, it is enforceable according to its terms by all parties to the contract. The following case highlights the "commercial impracticability" defense to a contract, where one party may rescind or modify a contract on the basis that performance of the contract's terms are not impossible, but commercially impracticable.

TRANSATLANTIC FINANCING CORPORATION v. UNITED STATES
363 F.2d 312 (D.C. Cir. 1966)

[In 1956, Transatlantic Financing, a steamship operator, contracted with the United States to ship wheat from Texas to Iran. Six days after the ship left port for Iran, the Egyptian government was at war with Israel and blocked the Suez Canal to shipping. The steamer therefore was forced to sail around the Cape of Good Hope. Transatlantic accordingly sued the United States for its added expenses as a result of this change of circumstances. Transatlantic contended that it had contracted only to travel the "usual and customary" route to Iran and that the United States had received a greater benefit than that for which it contracted. The district court held for the United States; Transatlantic appealed.]

Judge Skelly Wright

Transatlantic's claim is based on the following train of argument. The charter was a contract for a voyage from a Gulf port to Iran. Admiralty principles and practices, especially stemming from the doctrine of deviation, require us to [infer] into the contract the term that the voyage was to be performed by the 'usual and customary' route. The usual and customary route from Texas to Iran was, at the time of contract, via Suez, so the contract was for a voyage from Texas to Iran via Suez. When Suez was closed this contract became impossible to perform. Consequently, appellant's argument continues, when Transatlantic delivered the cargo by going around the Cape of Good Hope, in compliance with the Government's demand under claim of right, it conferred a benefit upon the United States for which it should be paid on quantum meruit.

The contract in this case does not expressly condition performance upon availability of the Suez route. Nor does it specify 'via Suez' or, on the other hand, 'via Suez or Cape of Good Hope.' Nor are there provisions in the contract from which we may properly [infer] that the continued availability of Suez was a condition of performance. Nor is there anything in custom or trade usage, or in the surrounding circumstances generally, which would support our constructing a condition of performance. The numerous cases requiring performance around the Cape when Suez was closed indicate that the Cape route is generally regarded as an alternative means of performance. So the implied expectation that the route would be via Suez is hardly adequate proof of an allocation to the promisee of the risk of closure. In some cases, even an express expectation may not amount to a condition of performance. The doctrine of deviation supports our assumption that parties normally expect performance by the usual and customary route, but it adds nothing beyond this that is probative of an allocation of the risk.

If anything, the circumstances surrounding this contract indicate that the risk of the Canal's closure may be deemed to have been allocated to Transatlantic. We know or may safely assume that the parties were aware, as were most commercial men with interest affected by the Suez situation, that the Canal might become a dangerous area. No doubt the tension affected freight rates, and it is arguable that the risk of closure became part of the dickered terms. We do not deem the risk of closure so allocated, however. Foreseeability or even recognition of a risk does not necessarily prove its allocation. Parties to a contract are not always able to provide for all the possibilities of which they are aware, sometimes because they cannot agree, often simply because they are too busy. Moreover, that some abnormal risk was contemplated is probative but does not necessarily establish an allocation of the risk of the contingency which actually occurs. In this case, for example, nationalization by Egypt of the Canal Corporation and formation of the Suez Users Group did not necessarily indicate that the Canal would be blocked even if a confrontation resulted. The surrounding circumstances do indicate, however, a willingness by Transatlantic to assume abnormal risks, and this fact should legitimately cause us to judge the impracticability of performance by an alternative route in stricter terms than we would were the contingency unforeseen.

We turn then to the question whether occurrence of the contingency rendered performance commercially impracticable under the circumstances of this case. The goods shipped were not subject to harm from the longer, less temperate Southern route. The vessel and crew were fit to proceed around the Cape. Transatlantic was no less able than the United States to purchase insurance to cover the contingency's occurrence. If anything, it is more reasonable to expect owner-operators of vessels to insure against the hazards of war. They are in the best position to calculate the cost of performance by alternative routes (and therefore to estimate the amount of insurance required), and are undoubtedly sensitive to international troubles which uniquely affect the demand for and cost of their services. The only factor operating here in appellant's favor is the added expense, allegedly $43,972.00 above and beyond the contract price of $305,842.92, of extending a 10,000 mile voyage by approximately 3,000 miles. While it may be an overstatement to say that increased cost and difficulty of performance never constitute impracticability, to justify relief there must be more of a variation between expected cost and the cost of performing by an available alternative than is present in this case, where the promisor can legitimately be presumed to have accepted some degree of abnormal risk, and where impracticability is urged on the basis of added expense alone.

We conclude, therefore, as have most other courts considering related issues arising out of the Suez closure, that performance of this contract was not rendered legally impossible.

Affirmed.

Questions

1. Would there be a different result in this case if the shipment had been tomatoes as opposed to wheat? Explain.
2. Would there be a different result in this case if the United States and Transatlantic agreed by contract that shipment was to arrive in Iran within a period of time that was only possible if the shipper used the canal route? Explain.
3. What do you think it would take for a court to render a contract commercially impracticable? In this case, the shipper was forced to spend almost $44,000 more than it had expected to spend in performing the $305,000 contract. What if the added cost had amounted to $100,000? Would you be persuaded that the contract was then commercially impracticable? What if the closing of the canal doubled the price of the contract? Explain.

Afterword

As stated above, questions of a contract's validity are left to national law. Contract law does vary from country to country. For instance, in a number of countries, contract law developed not through precedent and judicial interpretation, but instead through the institution of a civil code. Note that, while the United States has adopted the Uniform Commercial Code (UCC) in connection with the interpretation and enforcement of contracts, even that Code was based in large part on prior legal decisions.

Germany is a country which relies on its civil code for the interpretation of contracts. The civil code in Germany provides for several differences from those rules applied in the United States. For instance, an offer must be held open for a reasonable period of time if no time is specified. In the United States, an offer may be withdrawn at any time prior to acceptance, unless someone has paid to keep it open.

Second, consideration is not required for a contract. In other words, a mere promise by one party which is accepted by the other is enforceable. The same holds true for Japan. In America, this would not be the case in most circumstances.

Third, while an acceptance is valid in the United States once it is dispatched, and therefore the offer can no longer be withdrawn, an acceptance under German civil law is valid only when it is received. Consequently, since the rules vary significantly from country to country, a businessperson would be wise to investigate the national rules of each country in addition to becoming familiar with the common rules of the CISG.

Different Forms of Global Business Expansion

Multinational Enterprise (MNE)   The term *multinational enterprise* traditionally refers to a company that conducts business in more than one country. Any of the following operations, except for a direct contract with a foreign purchaser, may qualify a company as a MNE.

Direct Contract.   A firm may expand its business across territorial borders using a variety of methods. The most simplified, from a contractual perspective, occurs where a firm in one country enters into an agreement with a firm or individual in another country. Using the example of sales, a firm might decide to sell its product to a purchaser in another country through a basic contractual agreement. This is called a *direct sale* to a foreign purchaser. In this situation, the parties agree on the terms of the sale and record them in the contract.

Where the contract is silent as to a term of the sale, the law that will apply in connection with the missing term will be the law specified in the contract or, where none is specified, the applicable law will depend on the country in which the court is located. Some courts will apply the *vesting of rights doctrine,* where the applicable law is the law of the jurisdiction in which the rights in the contract vested. Other courts may apply the *most significant relationship doctrine,* where the applicable law is that of the jurisdiction that has the most significant relationship to the contract and the parties. Finally, some courts will apply the *governmental interest doctrine,* where the court will apply the law either of its own jurisdiction or of the jurisdiction that has the greatest interest in the outcome of the issue.

One of the most complicated issues pertaining to direct sales is that of *payment.* The seller should and usually does require an *irrevocable letter of credit,* which the buyer obtains from a bank after paying that amount to the bank (or securing that amount of credit). The bank then promises to pay the seller the amount of the contract after conforming goods have been shipped. The "irrevocable" component is that the bank may not revoke the letter of credit without the consent of both the buyer and the seller. In this way, the seller is protected because the buyer already has come up with adequate funds for the purchase, confirmed by a bank. The buyer is protected because the funds are not turned over to the seller until it has been determined that the goods conform to the contract. It is important to the buyer, however, that the letter of credit be specific as to the conformance of the goods, as the bank will only ensure that the goods conform to the letter of credit and not to the contract itself.

Foreign Representation.   A second type of foreign expansion is a sale through a representative in the foreign country, whether it is through a distributor, agent, or other type of representative. In this way, the firm has some representation in the foreign country and, depending on the type of representation, someone with experience dealing with that country's customs and regulations. A firm may decide to sell through an *agent*—that is, it hires an individual who will remain permanently in the foreign country, negotiate contracts, and assist in the performance of the contracts. The agent would be compensated on a commission basis. On the other hand, the firm may act through a *representative,* who may solicit and take orders but, unlike an agent, may not enter into contracts on behalf of the firm. *Distributors* purchase the goods from the seller, then negotiate sales to foreign purchasers on their own behalf. In doing so, a distributor may be more likely to invest resources to develop the foreign market for the good.

It is important to note that *exclusive dealing agreements* with a distributor, where the distributor agrees to sell only the goods of one manufacturer and the manufacturer agrees to sell only to that distributor in that area, generally are not allowed in many countries. While the antitrust laws of the United States are more lax in this area, foreign antitrust laws such as those in the European Community consider this practice a restrictive trade practice that unreasonably restrains trade.

Export trading companies are firms that specialize in acting as the intermediary between businesses and purchasers in foreign countries. The firm will take title to the good being sold and then proceed to complete the sale in the foreign country. *Export management companies,* on the other hand, merely manage the sale but do not take title to the goods; consequently they do not share in any of the risk associated with the sale.

Joint Venture.   Foreign expansion may also occur through an agreement of a joint venture between two or more parties. This type of agreement is usually for one or several specific projects and is in effect for a specified period of time. For instance, several Japanese automobile manufacturers have entered into joint ventures with American firms in order to manufacture some or all of certain models in America. For instance, Mitsubishi entered into a joint venture with Chrysler Corporation in connection with the Eclipse and Eagle Talon models. In this way, companies such as

Mitsubishi can market certain models by claiming that they were made in America, using American parts and labor.

Branch Office or Subsidiary.   A branch office is a wholly owned extension of a corporate entity in a foreign country. A subsidiary is a separate corporation formed in a foreign country and owned in whole or in part by the parent company. For example, an Indian paper company may open a branch office in London in order to market and sell its products. That office would be a mere extension of the offices established already in India. On the other hand, the Indian firm may create a separate subsidiary to handle its British orders, which might then have an office in London. A subsidiary or branch office relationship may also come about through an acquisition of an existing firm in the foreign country.

The primary difference between branch offices and subsidiaries comes into play with the question of liability. In most situations, where a subsidiary is sued, the parent company is not liable. To the contrary, however, the liabilities of a branch office immediately become the liabilities of the main office. In addition, the income of a branch office is considered income to the parent firm and must be reported on that firm's income tax return. Income to a subsidiary remains on the balance sheet of the subsidiary. On the other hand, there is a benefit to opening a branch office. The branch office is considered by all dealing with it as merely an arm of the parent firm. In this respect, loans and insurance may be easier to obtain for a branch, as opposed to a subsidiary.

The following case addresses the complicated issue of which country's laws apply to a subsidiary, those of the country in which it is located or those of the country in which the parent is located.

SUMITOMO SHOJI AMERICA, INC. v. AVAGLIANO
102 S.Ct. 2374 (1982)

[Sumitomo is a New York corporation which is a wholly owned subsidiary of Sumitomo Shoji Kabushiki Kaisha, a Japanese trading company. Female secretarial employees of Sumitomo brought an action against their employer based on its policy that it would only hire male Japanese citizens to fill executive, managerial, and sales positions. The corporation moved to dismiss the complaint, claiming that the issue was subject to the Friendship, Commerce, and Navigation Treaty between the United States and Japan. The lower court held that, because the subsidiary was a New York corporation, it was not subject to the Treaty. The Court of Appeals reversed the decision and the Supreme Court held that the Treaty provided no defense to a Title VII employment discrimination action since an American subsidiary is not a Japanese company and thus not covered by the Treaty.]

Chief Justice Burger

Interpretation of the Friendship, Commerce and Navigation Treaty between Japan and the United States must, of course, begin with the language of the Treaty itself. The clear import of treaty language controls unless "application of the words of the treaty according to their obvious meaning effects a result inconsistent with the intent or expectations of its signatories."

Article VIII(1) of the Treaty provides in pertinent part:

"[C]ompanies of either Party shall be permitted to engage, within the territories of the other Party, accountants and other technical experts, executive personnel, attorneys, agents and other specialists of their choice."

* * * * *

Clearly Article VIII(1) only applies to companies of one of the Treaty countries operating in the other country. Sumitomo contends that it is a company of Japan, and that Article VIII(1) of the Treaty grants it very broad discretion to fill its executive, managerial, and sales positions exclusively with male Japanese citizens.

Article VIII(1) does not define any of its terms; the definitional section of the Treaty is contained in Article XXII. Article XXII(3) provides:

"As used in the present Treaty, the term 'companies' means corporations, partnerships, companies and other associations, whether or not with limited liability and whether or not for pecuniary profit. Companies constituted under the applicable laws and regulations within the territories of either Party shall be deemed companies thereof and shall have their juridical status recognized within the territories of the other Party."

Sumitomo is "constituted under the applicable laws and regulations" of New York; based on Article XXII(3), it is a company of the United States, not a company of Japan. As a company of the United States operating in the United States, under the literal language of Article XXII(3) of the Treaty, Sumitomo cannot invoke the rights provided in Article VIII(1), which are available only to companies of Japan operating in the United States and to companies of the United States operating in Japan.

The Governments of Japan and the United States support this interpretation of the Treaty. Both the Ministry of Foreign Affairs of Japan and the United States Department of State agree that a United States corporation, even when wholly owned by a Japanese company, is not a company of Japan under the Treaty and is therefore not covered by Article VIII(1).

* * * * *

Our role is limited to giving effect to the intent of the Treaty parties. When the parties to a treaty both agree as to the meaning of a treaty provision, and that interpretation follows from the clear treaty language, we must, absent extraordinarily strong contrary evidence, defer to that interpretation.

Sumitomo maintains that although the literal language of the Treaty supports the contrary interpretation, the intent of Japan and the United States was to cover subsidiaries regardless of their place of incorporation. We disagree.

Contrary to the view of the Court of Appeals and the claims of Sumitomo, adherence to the language of the Treaty would not "overlook the purpose of the Treaty." The Friendship, Commerce, and Navigation Treaty between Japan and the United States is but one of a series of similar commercial agreements negotiated after World War II. The primary purpose of the corporation provisions of the Treaties was to give corporations of each signatory legal status in the territory of the other party, and to allow them to conduct business in the other country on a comparable basis with domestic firms. Although the United States negotiated commercial treaties as early as 1778, and thereafter throughout the 19th century and early 20th century, these early commercial treaties were primarily concerned with the trade and shipping rights of individuals. Until the 20th century, international commerce was much more an individual than a corporate affair.

As corporate involvement in international trade expanded in this century, old commercial treaties became outmoded. Because "corporation[s] can have no legal existence out of the boundaries of the sovereignty by which [they are] created," it became necessary to negotiate new treaties granting corporations legal status and the right to function abroad. A series of Treaties negotiated before World War II gave corporations legal status and access to foreign courts, but it was not until the postwar Friendship, Commerce and Navigation Treaties that United States corporations gained the right to conduct business in other countries. The purpose of the Treaties was not to give foreign corporations greater rights than domestic companies, but instead to assure them the right to conduct business on an equal basis without suffering discrimination based on their alienage.

The Treaties accomplished their purpose by granting foreign corporations "national treatment" in most respects and by allowing foreign individuals and companies to form locally incorporated subsidiaries. These local subsidiaries are considered for purposes of the Treaty to be companies of the country in which they are incorporated; they are entitled to the rights, and subject to the responsibilities of other domestic corporations. By treating these subsidiaries as domestic companies, the purpose of the Treaty provisions—to assure that corporations of one Treaty party have the right to conduct business within the territory of the other party without suffering discrimination as an alien entity—is fully met.

We are persuaded, as both signatories agree, that under the literal language of Article XXII(3) of the Treaty, Sumitomo is a company of the United States; we discern no reason to depart from the plain meaning of the Treaty language. Accordingly, we hold that Sumitomo is not a company of Japan and is thus not covered by Article VIII(1) of the Treaty. The judgment of the Court of Appeals is vacated, and the case is remanded for further proceedings consistent with this opinion.

Questions

1. In your opinion, is it fair to hold an American subsidiary of a Japanese company to the laws of the United States? Can you think of a reason why it would not be fair?
2. Under what method of doing business in the United States could Sumitomo have avoided problems such as those presented in the above case?
3. Do you believe that foreign companies *should* have rights equal to those of domestic firms to conduct business in the United States?

Licensing. Where a company has no interest in commencing operations in a foreign country but instead merely wants to have its product or name on the market there, the company may decide to license the rights to the name or to manufacturing the product to another company. For instance, assume an American firm owns the rights to the name "Wash 'n Dry" car-wash service. This firm manufactures and operates car-washing machines for instant washes. A firm in Italy may license the right to use the name, product, and process in Italy in exchange for a royalty fee and would then be responsible for all aspects of the business operation.

The benefit to this type of relationship is that the licensor (holder of the right) has the opportunity to enter the foreign market, while the licensee assumes all of the obligations of running the business. In addition, the foreign government may be more hospitable to a domestic company's operations than a foreign firm's. On the other hand, it is critical in a licensing situation that the license contract be particular as to the quality of the good produced or service provided. Imagine the problems that could arise where a firm licenses the right to use its name on something that is of a much lower quality than the original good.

Franchising. In a franchise agreement, the franchisee pays the franchisor for a license to use trademarks, formulas, and other trade secrets. The difference between a franchising agreement and a licensing contract is that a franchise agreement may be made up of a number of licensing arrangements, as well as other obligations. For instance, in a typical franchise agreement for a fast-food franchise, the franchisor will license to the fanchisee the right to use its trademark, name, logo, recipes, menus, and other recognized resources. The agreement may also include a commitment from the franchisor to lease a space for the franchisee, or to provide advertising or training; or it may include a commitment from the franchisee to comply not only with quality standards but also with hours of operation, marketing, and sales programs.

For many U.S. cable operators expanding in foreign countries, it's not the rules holding them back—it's the rule-breakers. In India and several other countries with scant cable development, some scofflaw entrepreneurs have become mini-cable operators, erecting a satellite dish and wiring up entire neighborhoods with a roll of coaxial cable.

That's great for the consumers. But there is a drawback: "The only problem," says one cable-industry watcher, "is that everybody's channel changes at the same time."

Source: Mark Robichaux, "Hey! I Was Watching the Game," *The Wall Street Journal,* March 26, 1993, p. R4. Reprinted by permission of *The Wall Street Journal,* © 1993 Dow Jones & Company, Inc. All Rights Reserved Worldwide.

REGULATION OF INTERNATIONAL TRADE

As explained above, there is no such thing as one body of international law per se that regulates international contracts and trade. Instead, contracts between firms in different countries may be subject to the laws of one country or the other, depending on (1) whether it is a sales contract subject to the CISG, (2) whether the contract itself stipulates the applicable law and forum in which a dispute will be heard, and (3) the rules regarding conflict of laws in each jurisdiction.

On the other hand, many countries have domestic laws that regulate business conducted within their borders or by their domestic firms outside of its borders. These laws govern the areas of employment-related activities and discrimination, product liability, intellectual property, antitrust and trade practices, and import taxes, to name a few.

The concept of extraterritorial application of national laws, that is, application of those laws beyond the borders of the country imposing them, may pose ethical dilemmas. For instance, if the culture of one country holds that it is unethical for a woman to work, the extraterritorial application of America's antidiscrimination laws may pose an ethical dilemma to an American manager in that foreign country. Does the manager abide by American law or abide by the business ethics of that foreign country? The same may be true in connection with the abhorrence of bribes in American business. If an American firm is operating in another country where a bribe is required, does the manager break American law and pay the bribe or follow American business ethics but risk financial failure?

Employment–Related Regulations

When the U.S. Congress passed the Civil Rights Act of 1991, it expressly provided for *extraterritorial* application of Title VII's antidiscrimination provisions. In doing so, Congress extended American firms' liability for discrimination against their employees to situations that occur outside of the United States. For instance, if a firm conducts operations in Saudi Arabia, where women are not expected to hold certain management positions, that firm is still held to Title VII's prohibition against gender discrimination. Similarly, if an American firm does business in Taiwan but prefers to have American workers serve in management positions, unsuccessful applicants might have a claim for national origin discrimination under Title VII, even though that office of the firm is not located in the United States.

Other U.S. employment-related statues also survive the trip across borders and oceans. For instance, the Occupational Safety and Health Act and the Employee Retirement Income Security Act do not distinguish between workers for American firms who work in the United States and those who work in other parts of the world. Moreover, labor regulations of other countries may differ to a large extent from those in the United States, and an American firm doing business in that country may be responsible for complying with those regulations. For instance, Italy requires that employees receive the benefit of the government pension plan, a staff medical scheme, a relocation allowance, insurance coverage to reimburse medical expenses, and scholarships to the staff's children. In Spain, companies with more than 100 workers must have a committee in charge of all matters relating to health and safety at work; and all employees are statutorily entitled to an appropriate health and safety policy at work.

Product Liability Statutes

Product liability (see Chapter 16) refers to the legal responsibility of a manufacturer for any harm that results from the ordinary use of its products. For instance, in the United States, if one drinks from a pop can, swallows a shard of glass, and suffers physical harm, the manufacturer of that beverage will likely be held responsible for the harm, no matter how careful the manufacturer was in preventing the harm (i.e., even if the firm's quality inspection program is the best in the country).

Liability laws differ from country to country, as do damage awards and requirements of proof. The following article addresses some of the problems that might arise from a system that differs from our own.

IN JAPAN, LAX LIABILITY
LAWS SHROUD BLAME

Merrill Goozner

Last Fall, a major drug company here introduced a new drug to combat skin disease. Within a month, 14 patients died, victims of the drug's fatal reaction with an anti-cancer medication they also were taking. The government hastily withdrew the drug from the market.

Had that happened in the United States, attorneys for the victims' families would be tripping over each other in their race to the courthouse. That's not what happened here.

According to Nippon Shoji Kaisha, Ltd., the Osaka-based pharmaceutical company that co-developed, manufactured and sold the anti-shingles drug Sorivudine, not a single suit has been filed against the company.

Shocking press accounts of Japan's "most deadly drug debut ever" have shrouded blame for the incident in a mystery. The company, which refused to discuss details of the case, put the drug on the market even though it knew a cancer patient died during clinical trials.

In its application for government approval of the new drug, Nippon Shoji told the Ministry of Health and Welfare that it was "unknown" if a reaction between Sorivudine and that patient's anti-cancer medication led to the death.

Last September, its approval in hand, the company began shipping the drug to doctors and hospitals. It included a warning that it shouldn't be taken in combination with cancer-treatment drugs. But the warning never said it could result in serious injury or death.

*   *   *   *   *

For consumer activists and Japan's tiny legal community, the Sorivudine disaster has dramatized the need for stronger product liability laws. Over the years, Japan has endured its share of major and minor product mishaps, a natural byproduct of its national obsession with promoting export industries and a lax regulatory structure overseeing domestic business activities.

But consumers here have had little recourse when something goes horribly wrong, as it did in the Sorivudine case. Since World War II, there have been only 160 successful lawsuits against manufacturers because of unsafe products.

*   *   *   *   *

Business concerns here echo the complaints frequently heard from industry in the U.S.—that an overly liberal product liability system will sap Japan of its competitiveness and inhibit product innovation. They also fear a rash of expensive lawsuits.

"Many industrial groups feel if we change the product liability system too much, we will become like the U.S.—a litigious society," said Yashiro Kawaguchi, deputy director of the consumer affairs division of the Economic Planning Agency.

*   *   *   *   *

The Japanese court system doesn't allow for trials by juries, which might be sympathetic to an injured consumer. All product liability cases are heard by judges who narrowly interpret laws that define who is to blame for manufacturing defective products. . . . Once the case is filed, Japanese lawyers do not have the right to discovery, which is considered indispensable by U.S. attorneys trying to determine if a company knew that its product might cause harm. Consumers in Japan seeking to prove that a product is unsafe usually have to pay for their own laboratory tests.

* * * * *

On top of all the structural barriers to court access, Japanese society frowns on open displays of disharmony like a court suit. Ritual apologies and discreet payments to those who have suffered grievous harm are the norm.

Source: Merrill Goozner, "In Japan, Lax Liability Laws Shroud Blame," *Chicago Tribune,* January 9, 1994, section 7, p. 1. Reprinted by permission.

Questions

1. In the United States, a consumer must prove that the manufacturer's product was responsible for the harm suffered. What would be the potential problems for a plaintiff under the American system in the above case?
2. *a.* Are you persuaded by business's argument that product liability laws may sap industry of its competitiveness and inhibit product innovation? Explain.
   b. What are the ethical ramifications of your argument? Explain.
3. What are the benefits to businesses and/or consumers of Japan's tendency to downplay conflict and resolve it in ways distinct from the traditional American way of handling a conflict?

Intellectual Property Regulation

Intellectual property generally refers to copyrights, patents, and trademarks—as opposed to real property, which encompasses land or real estate, and personal property, which refers to all other tangible items.

Trademarks.   A *trademark* is what identifies a product, whether it is the trade name, the packaging, the logo, or other distinguishing mark. When the law protects a trademark, it grants to the holder of the mark a limited monopoly: No one else may use that mark without the holder's permission. Under section 526 of the Tariff Act of 1930, it is unlawful to import goods bearing a trademark that has been registered with the Patent Office that is "owned by a citizen of, or by a corporation or association . . . organized within the United States" without the permission of the mark holder.

This provision regulates the importation of goods that would infringe on a trademark holder's rights in the United States. But what about an American company that wants to obtain trademark protection in other countries? Each country has distinct trademark regulations and different levels of protection offered marks registered in other countries. The following article addresses problems involved in the protection of American trademarks worldwide.

ASIAN NATIONS FACE U.S. LISTING OF INTELLECTUAL PROPERTY OFFENDERS

The U.S. releases Friday its annual list of the world's intellectual property pirates, and the usual suspects are taking last minute stabs at damage control. Taiwan, South Korea and China—all regulars on the list—are pledging to clamp down on those who ply trades such as plagiarizing computer software, bootlegging Hollywood's new releases and counterfeiting pharmaceuticals.

But others—most notably Thailand—risk millions of dollars in trade sanctions in what has become an annual ritual for some governments: feign a crackdown as the list deadline looms, only to slack off later.

"In the Endgame"

"We're in the endgame," says Eric H. Smith, executive director of the International Intellectual Property Alliance, a Washington-based lobby representing members of the U.S. publishing, recording, computer software and motion picture industries. At least 10 Asian governments will be cited Friday, industry officials predict. For the most part, the list simply puts countries on notice that Washington is alarmed at their poor safeguards against counterfeiting. But any nation that receives the most serious designation, "priority foreign country," is subject to an investigation of six to nine months that can lead to U.S. trade sanctions.

Mr. Smith's organization says that piracy, along with patent and trademark infringement, results in billions of dollars in trade losses annually, hurting U.S. profits and job growth. His cause has found sympathy in the Clinton administration, which is keen to use its powers to enhance U.S. competitiveness and reduce America's gaping trade deficit. "We have met with Ambassador (Mickey) Kantor and I think he is going to be very tough," Mr. Smith says. Mr. Kantor is the U.S. trade representative.

Stolen Property

Estimated 1992 U.S. trade losses due to copyright infringement,* in millions of U.S. dollars

Pakistan	40
Malaysia	41
Indonesia	96
Philippines	116
Thailand	123
India	169
China	415
South Korea	416
Taiwan	669

*Figures do not include additional substantial losses as a result of patent and trademark infringement.

Promises, Promises

That point hasn't been lost on governments in Asia. This month, after years of U.S. pressure, the Philippines signed a landmark agreement promising protections of copyrights, trademarks and patents. Likewise, China [agreed to] become a member of an international convention that combats illegal duplication of foreign recordings. . . . China has long been a producer of bootleg recordings and other products. However, over the past two years it has taken steps to protect intellectual property rights and has joined in several major international agreements.

But the biggest convert is Taiwan, considered the worst violator of U.S. rights in dollar terms. The International Intellectual Property Alliance, Mr. Smith's organization, estimates piracy there cost U.S. companies $669 million last year. Taiwan was named a priority country last April. Subsequently, under heavy pressure from the Bush administration, it signed a broad agreement that included commitments to pass several pieces of legislation and a bilateral copyright treaty originally signed in 1989.

But in January, Taiwan lawmakers reviewing the treaty decided to remove eight passages they found objectionable. That brought an angry reaction from Washington, which insisted that Taiwan approve the accord without alteration or risk retaliation. Last week, however, lawmakers approved the treaty, with the eight passages reinstated, citing the pressure from the United States. The legislators also revised Taiwan's copyright law to reflect an agreement reached recently with the U.S. on specific copyright issues.

"The parliament's approval should help us avert possible U.S. trade sanctions," said Economics Minister Chiang Pin-kung. Mr. Chiang and three other cabinet ministers say that they will resign if the U.S. still imposes sanctions. Authorities in Thailand and South Korea also have stepped up their campaigns against piracy, recently conducting high profile raids on shops and factories.

* * * * *

Other countries likely to be cited by the Clinton administration, but that don't face imminent sanctions, are Australia, India, Indonesia, Malaysia, Pakistan and Singapore.

Source: "Asian Nations Face U.S. Listing of Intellectual Property Offenders," *The Asian Wall Street Journal Weekly,* April 26, 1993, p. 4. Reprinted by permission of *The Wall Street Journal* © 1993 Dow Jones & Company, Inc. All Rights Reserved Worldwide.

Questions

1. Do you believe that governments should be held responsible for the pirating acts of firms based in their countries? Explain.
2. What type of sanctions by the U.S. government against the perpetrator will prevent this type of unfair trade practice? Explain.
3. How should the U.S. respond where countries merely step up campaigns against these types of problems just before the list comes out? Should those efforts be ignored, or should the countries who put forth those efforts be rewarded? Explain.

Paris Convention.   In 1883, several countries entered into an agreement called the International Convention for the Protection of Intellectual Property, which was revised in 1971. As of 1988, 98 countries, including the United States, were parties to the agreement, now called the Paris Convention. In short, according to the Paris Convention, member countries ensure trademark protection to marks registered in other member countries. The Convention also provides for *national treatment* requiring that any individual claiming infringement will have the same protections as would a national of that country. A member country may not favor its own nationals as against foreigners. The Madrid Agreement, established after the Paris Convention, attempts to create an international trademark system. If a holder registers a trademark with the World Intellectual Property Organization in Switzerland, that mark is protected in all member countries requested by the holder. The United States has yet to adopt the Madrid Agreement.

Inventions. A *patent* is a monopoly on a product, process, or device where the item or process claimed is an innovation, unique and inventive, and useful. The Paris Convention refers to patents as well as trademarks; however, it does not establish a worldwide network of protection. Instead, it requires that member countries follow simplified procedures for registration. The most important provision provides the *right of priority,* which grants the first person to obtain a patent in any member country priority over other individuals seeking to register the same patent. In addition, since a patent must be original to be registered in any country, many countries hold that patents previously awarded in other countries automatically preclude additional patent registration. The European Patent Convention was established in 1978 in order to create an international registration procedure for patents. Individuals who obtain patents through the European Patent Office have valid patents in each member country.

Authors/Artists. A *copyright* is a government grant giving the copyright holder exclusive control over the reproduction of a literary, musical, or artistic work. Most developed nations provide copyright protection within their borders, but many also belong to international copyright protection pacts. The Berne Convention of 1886 and the Universal Copyright Convention (UCC) of 1952 both provide a measure of international protection against the unauthorized reproduction of one's original books, photos, drawings, movies, and the like. Copyright protection extends for a period provided by national law. For example, in the United States, the copyright spans the author's life plus 50 years. The United States is a party to the UCC but not to the Berne Convention.

Broadly, we should recognize that we have not succeeded in establishing a solid international system of protection for intellectual property. As the following case illustrates, those who believe their rights are infringed must rely on national legal systems for protection, and proof of intellectual property infringements is very difficult, indeed.

COMITE INTERPROFESSIONEL DU VIN DE CHAMPAGNE v. WINEWORTHS GROUP, LTD.
2 N.Z.L.R. 432 (1991) High Court of Wellington, New Zealand

[An Australian company sought to sell Australian sparkling wine, made from Australian grapes, in the New Zealand market. The Australian company wanted to use the word *champagne* on the bottle labels. A group of French champagne producers (the Comite Interprofessionel du Vin de Champagne) sought an injunction against the Australian company's use of the word *champagne.* The French producers argued that the Australians were, in effect, "passing off" Australian wine as though it had been produced in the famous Champagne region of France.]

Judge Jeffries

These proceedings are brought by the plaintiffs to protect their claimed property right in the word "Champagne." As an editorial policy in this judgment I am using the word champagne with a capital when it refers to the district and the wine from the district. The plaintiffs seek in effect to prevent the defendant from importing into New Zealand sparkling wine from Australia labelled champagne.

The *Comite Interprofessionel du Vin de Champagne* (hereafter referred to by the acronym CIVC) is . . . a semi-official body . . . whose purposes include the protection of the name Champagne for the sparkling wine produced in Champagne, a district of France, from grapes grown in that district.

In essence French wine interests are disputing with Australian wine interests the New Zealand market for sparkling wines which Australian manufacturers and exporters to this country seek to label and sell as champagne. The plaintiffs say according to the law of New Zealand they cannot do that for it constitutes deceptive conduct because the wine labelled champagne was made in Australia from grapes grown there.

Champagne as we know it is relatively new, having its origin in time at the end of the seventeenth century but its final development was a nineteenth century phenomenon. Dom Perignon of the Benedictine Abbey of Hautvillers near Epernay in the Champagne district is credited with its beginning. There are four generally acknowledged ingredients of Champagne being its wine type, the grapes used, most importantly the location of a sparkling wine, usually but not always, white in colour. The two features of Champagne of prime importance for its uniqueness are the soil and climate in which the grapes are grown, and the method of manufacture by skilled personnel. The first of those elements cannot be exactly duplicated anywhere in the world, but the second can.

For the production of grapes for Champagne there are strict geographical limitations imposed by law. On 22 July 1927 a law strictly delimited the boundaries of the vine growing Champagne area. Within those boundaries, and in each village, the soil suitable for planting vines has been meticulously indexed. By law the wine allowed to carry the appellation Champagne must be produced exclusively within precise zones . . .

* * * * *

New Zealand has . . . no history of material consumption, or manufacture, of sparkling wine prior to 1980. Today several wine producers here market a wine using the methode champenoise process. One demands special mention. In about 1981 Montana Wines, Ltd., which is New Zealand's largest maker, launched a sparkling wine produced by methode champenoise and labelled it "Lindauer New Zealand Champagne." There were two other New Zealand makers who followed suit . . . [T]here had been a tiny importation of Australian wines calling themselves champagne through the 1960s and 1970s which did not provoke a response from the CIVC.

Proceedings were issued in 1982 against Montana and after four years were settled by a consent order of the Court issuing an injunction generally restraining the use of the word champagne on that defendant's products. Over about the last four years all New Zealand makers have observed that order and all leading wine importers have declined to import

Australian sparkling wine labelled champagne. Absenting the events now to be described New Zealand, judged by the attitude of markers and importers, conceded to the plaintiffs their legal proprietary right in the appellation champagne.

Indigenous wine making and consumption were much more a part of Australian life than they were in New Zealand until about thirty years ago. Australia has a record of well over a century of making acceptable wines of great variety and styles which have been consumed by its people. Sparkling wine calling itself champagne made from grapes grown in Australia by the methode champenoise, and by other methods, has been entirely accepted and without direct challenge from the CIVC. The plaintiffs recognize, and although reluctantly accept, for Australia, like Canada and the United States of America, there is no legal protection available to them over the use of the appellation champagne.

The sparkling wine market in New Zealand changed dramatically with the introduction here from Australia in 1986 of Yalumba Angas Brut Champagne. The wine was of good quality and reasonably priced. It was a stunning success and other wine importers began a serious search in Australia for competitors.

It is appropriate now to focus directly on the acts of Australia's wine maker, Penfolds Wine Pty., Ltd. (hereafter referred to as Penfolds) which brought about these proceedings. In August 1987 Penfolds reached agreement with the defendant Wineworths Group, Ltd., to export into New Zealand a sparkling wine made by its wholly owned subsidiary Seaview Winery Pty., Ltd., bearing the label "Australian Champagne." Before this arrangement Penfolds through another agent in 1986 had sold a Seaview wine labelled "Brut Champagne."

It is appropriate here to emphasize the plaintiffs' view of what makes the product and therefore the name of Champagne so special. First, Champagne as a product is a unique wine which must be elaborated from particular grape varieties, grown in conducive soil and climate, and made into wine by an exceptional technique performed by highly skilled persons. The product is a quality one and by virtue of the cost of manufacture it is necessarily expensive, which is part of its exclusivity. From the quality product the reputation has developed, which reflects the specialness of the wine itself arising from factors outlined above . . .

The particular attraction of Seaview was that its champagne was made by methode champenoise. . . .

The Court thinks a deliberate choice was made by Penfolds to test the New Zealand law with a middle- to upper-bracket sparkling wine made by methode champenoise rather than a wine made by the [inferior] transfer method, and specifically labelled it "Australian Champagne." That action by Penfolds set up these proceedings.

[The court discusses the dilution of the word *champagne* in the Australian and United States markets.] . . . Apparently there is some evidence of the change in the United States as well. That trend clearly suggests that the word champagne has been so devalued in the market in Australia that the public now needs a word, or words, that will convey the excitement and quality surrounding the word champagne say in New Zealand or the United Kingdom. It was a point consistently made by the plaintiffs' wine writers and experts that it is for the public's good in New Zealand to maintain the legitimate pretensions of the word champagne.

The defendant, of course, does not deny the origin of the name champagne, or that the wine made in the Champagne district is a fine and special wine having the attributes claimed for it. What the defendant does say is that the word champagne has in New Zealand lost its distinctive significance so as to be properly defined now as a generic term having generic use within the wine market. It is in the same category as many other words whose origins are almost identical such as sherry, port, burgundy, graves, and chablis.

No case was cited to the Court how it should go about making a decision on a fact of that nature. To decide whether a word has become (for there is no doubt it once was not) a generic word is not a how, when, where fact. The task of the Court is to decide how the adult population of New Zealand as a group perceives the word. One has only to frame the task in that way to demonstrate its immense difficulty.

Market research is a powerful source of information but its value is not always consistent. There were two studies performed in New Zealand, one in 1987 for the defendant and one in 1989 for the plaintiffs.

The Court holds both studies supported the contention that there is significant evidence that champagne is not a generic word by usage in New Zealand. The evidence of the plaintiffs' survey in 1989 shows about 43 percent link champagne with France as the country of origin. The defendant's survey of 1987 less directly confirmed the link between the word and France . . .

* * * * *

Notwithstanding some interesting and persuasive evidence to the contrary, the Court's decision is that the word champagne in New Zealand is not generically used to describe any white sparkling wine.

The word champagne does in my view, have a special impact or impression on ordinary, average New Zealanders for whom wine drinking generally plays no significant part in their lives. This non-expert, phlegmatic, even uninterested representative New Zealander does have a definite response to the word champagne over and above noting it to be a white sparkling wine, or one with bubbles in it . . . Finally, I think the whole case of the defendant is that it well understands that the word champagne is one invested with considerable commercial charm and does not rank with sherry, port or chablis as was argued to the Court.

* * * * *

The plaintiffs in this case must establish sufficient reputation or goodwill in the name of Champagne.

In this Court's view that has been established by the evidence. The plaintiffs have had a presence in this country now for 150 years approximately. There has already been a finding that the word champagne retains a distinctive reputation and goodwill and it has not become a generic word.

The question for the Court is whether importation into New Zealand as aforesaid by the defendant advertising and selling Seaview Champagne, is deceptive in the way complained of by the plaintiffs. The Court's decision is that it is deceptive . . .

In short the Court says the word champagne is distinctive in New Zealand for the French product and it would be deceptive for other traders, foreign or domestic, to seek to attach themselves to that reputation by using the word champagne to describe sparkling wine made out of Champagne, France.

[For the plaintiffs.]

Questions

1. Is there anything that Penfolds could have done in order to use the word *champagne* in such a way as to emphasize a more generic meaning, rather than its geographical usage?
2. How does CIVC protect its mark, "champagne"?
3. Would the result in this case have been different if it were brought in Australia? The United States? Explain.

Antitrust and Trade Regulation

Trade is regulated in the United States, in part, by the Sherman Antitrust Act, which prohibits (1) any contract that unreasonably restrains trade, as well as (2) any action that tends to lessen competition or to create a monopoly. (See Chapter 10.) The purpose of the act is to preserve competition for the benefit of American consumers. So, how does this relate to multinational businesses? The act applies to all conduct that has a direct and substantial effect on U.S. commerce, domestic consumers, or export opportunities of domestic firms.

For example, Sherman prohibits two retailers from agreeing on the price they will both charge for a certain item. The act also prohibits those two retailers from agreeing on territories that they each would serve, where no competition would be allowed between them. Predatory pricing is prohibited; this occurs where a seller prices items at below cost in order to oust others from the market, only to raise prices after it has the market all to itself.

Where actions such as these are conducted outside U.S. borders but have a substantial and direct effect on U.S. commerce, the Sherman Act would apply. On the other hand, where few or no U.S. interests are at stake, courts are less likely to intervene. Take, for instance, the case of *Montreal Trading* v. *Amax, Inc.*[4] In that case, Canadian subsidiaries of American firms refused to sell Canadian potash to a Canadian company because that company was going to resell it to North Korean buyers. The court determined that there was an insignificant and remote effect on U.S. commerce and, as a result, held that it lacked jurisdiction to hear the case.

Certain corporate activities are considered *per se* illegal by the courts, no matter the motivation. Where the purpose of an agreement, for instance, is to fix prices, courts do not look to the effect on the market but instead presume that this activity will have a negative effect and will hold the parties in violation of the act. In connection with international business operations, courts allow a certain amount of latitude and instead will generally apply the "rule of reason"; in other words, the courts will look to whether the procompetitive effect of the activity outweighs the anticompetitive effect.

Trade is also regulated by the Clayton Act, which prohibits mergers of firms that may substantially lessen competition. (See Chapter 10.) If Coca-Cola proposed a merger with PepsiCo, this merger presumably would be prohibited by the Clayton Act because of its potential to lessen competition in the soda pop industry. (In order to determine whether a merger is in violation of the Clayton Act, the court will look not only to the size and competitive position of the merging firms but also to the barriers to entry in that market, the market's definition, and the degree of concentration in that market.) The European Community Commission performs a similar analysis, as is evidenced in the following article.

EC COMMISSION GIVES THE GREEN LIGHT TO TWO VENTURES AND TWO ACQUISITIONS

The European Community Commission cleared two joint ventures and allowed two acquisitions. The Commission said it cleared a joint venture between Phillips Electronics NV, Thomson-CSF, and Societe D'Applications Generales D'Electricite et de Mechanique SA, or Sagem, that will manufacture liquid crystal display screens.

The agency gave the venture exemption from its broad ban on anti-competitive linkups because of its "strategic importance" to the Community. The cooperation in the specific area of active matrix liquid crystal displays doesn't endanger current competition between the companies in other flat screen, cathode ray tube, and liquid crystal display fields, the Commission added.

Under the linkup, the three companies will create Flat Panel Displays BV, the first European company capable of producing AMLCD screens. These will be used in televisions and display projectors. Phillips will have an 80% stake in the venture. Thomson and Sagem will each hold 10%.

The EC Commission cleared a joint venture between British Harrison Chemicals, Ltd. and Dutch Akzo Chemical International BV for the production and sale of polyvinylchloride processing additives, radiation cure additives, paint dryers, and other specialty chemical products. In a statement, the Commission said the linkup would increase the degree of concentration for PVC additives in the EC. However, the large number of rival suppliers and increased imports from outside the EC meant competition would be maintained, it said.

* * * * *

The Commission also cleared Swedish Procordia AB's acquisition of Italy's Montedison's pharmaceutical divisions. The companies' activities don't overlap and the presence of strong rivals should ensure competition, the Commission said. It also said the companies have been losing market share in some areas to rivals.

And the Commission cleared the proposed takeover by Credit Suisse of Swiss Volksbank under EC merger rules. The main activities of the two banks don't overlap since Credit Suisse mainly focuses on international investment banking and Swiss Volksbank centers on domestic banking for small and medium sized businesses and private customers, the Commission said.

* * * * *

Source: Special to *The Wall Street Journal,* "EC Commission Gives the Green Light to Two Ventures and Two Acquisitions," *The Wall Street Journal,* May 3, 1993, p. A7A. Reprinted by permission of *The Wall Street Journal,* © 1993 Dow Jones & Company, Inc. All Rights Reserved Worldwide.

Questions

1. Given the above, to what do you believe the Commission looks in reaching a conclusion regarding clearance of joint ventures and acquisitions? Explain.
2. If you managed a firm that was about to enter into a joint venture with a competing firm, what type of information would support your petition to the EC Commission?

Imports

free trade - no import duties and tariff

The General Agreement on Tariffs and Trade (GATT) regulates import duties among signatory countries in order to reduce barriers to trade and to ensure fair treatment. There are several important components of the GATT that affect decisions about where a company may conduct operations and to which country that company may export its products.

In order to promote fair trading practices, the GATT identifies two practices that are prohibited in its member countries. The first is called *dumping.* Dumping occurs where a manufacturer sells its goods in a foreign country for less than their normal value. If this practice causes or threatens material injury to a domestic or established foreign manufacturer in the foreign country, the act is prohibited. The price is considered less than normal value if it is less than the price charged in the producer's home country. A firm may want to dump its goods in a foreign market for two reasons. First, its home market may be saturated and cannot support any further supply. Second, in an effort to establish itself and perhaps drive other firms out of the market, the firm may sell its goods in a foreign market at a price below other competitors and support that price with higher prices in its home country. In this way, its competitors may be forced from the market, and the producer may then raise prices to the normal level or above.

The GATT also prohibits the payment of *unfair subsidies* by governments. This occurs where a government, in an effort to encourage growth in a certain industry, offers subsidies to producers in that industry. The producers are therefore able to sell their goods at a price lower than those of its worldwide competitors. Subsidies are considered unfair where they are used by the governments to promote export trade that harms another country. Where unfair subsidization or dumping has been found to occur in the United States, the U.S. Department of Commerce may impose *countervailing duties* on those products in an amount sufficient to counteract the effect of the subsidy or the decreased price.

International trade barriers are discussed during trade "rounds" in which a number of countries negotiate duties and other agreements. One negotiation principle is called *"most favored nation" (MFN) status.* If the United States has MFN status with France, the United States has the right to the lowest applicable tariff on its goods imported by France. If France negotiates a lower tariff with Korea, the United States is entitled to a reduction in its tariff rates as well. In fact, all nations having MFN status with France would be entitled to that lower tariff rate. A second negotiating principle is called *national treatment.* This concept dictates that, once goods have been imported into a country, they must be treated as if they were domestic goods. Consequently, the only place where a tariff may be felt is at the border. The excerpt that follows details some of the procedural burdens involved in responding to a dumping complaint.

LEGAL HARASSMENT OF FOREIGN FIRMS: THE CASE OF THE U.S. STEEL INDUSTRY

Hiroshi Matsumoto*

Political Manipulation of "Dumping" Rulings

On June 30, 1992, the American Steel industry filed anti-dumping complaints against foreign companies from 21 countries with the Department of Commerce and the International Trade Commission. Two million pages of documents, which had taken U.S. steel companies six months to prepare, were filed with the two agencies for their investigation into the alleged dumping cases against the foreign companies.

Once sued in an anti-dumping case, the accused (respondent) company must answer thousands of pages of questionnaires from the Commerce Department, including the confidential data on export prices and domestic salaries, in a very short period of time. All the foreign documents must be translated into English at the respondent company's expense. Although it is physically impossible for the respondent to answer all of the questions in such a short period of time, each respondent is forced to prepare the requested data. As a result, about 30 full-time employees of our company had to work exclusively on collecting and compiling necessary information demanded by the U.S. Department of Commerce. They worked even on weekends for months on end. The petitioners can request as much volume of information as they wish from the respondents. This rule

has been easily abused by the petitioners to harass the respondents. If the respondents fail to satisfy the requests, [they are] deemed to have admitted guilt of dumping actions.

Once the requested data is submitted by the respondent, the U.S. Department of Commerce manipulates the so-called "Fair Market Value (FMV)" yardstick of the products in question and calculates dumping margins of steel imports for each accused respondent company. Following the Commerce Department's decisions on dumping margins, the ITC has to decide whether the imports in question have caused any injury to the petitioners.

In the case of the steel dumping allegation, the Commerce Department used two types of make-believe "prices." The first price was based on the Commerce Department analysts' recalculation of foreign respondent companies' cost of production, often by arbitrarily increasing component costs and other cost factors. On top of this guestimated cost are added 8% for profit margins and 10% for administrative overhead. All of these number manipulations are designed to raise the FMV of foreign products in the U.S. market. In reality, no steel

*Matsumoto is the senior representative in the Washington, D.C., office of NKK America, Inc., a respondent in the suit discussed in this reading.

company—American or foreign—has profit margins as large as 8% of their production costs. In the case of American steel firms, their administrative overhead is about 5–6% of their production costs. The larger the FMV is, the larger are the "dumping margins" that are assessed as the difference between the FMV and the actual prices of foreign products in the U.S. market.

The second pricing method consisted of invoking the "Best Information Available (BIA)" standard. The BIA is often nothing but the self-serving estimates of foreign competitors' prices submitted by the American steel petitioner companies to prove their anti-dumping allegations. If the U.S. Com-

merce Department finds even small or trivial mistakes in the bulk of the data submitted by the foreign respondent, it reaches a decision based on the BIA. Furthermore, even when the foreign respondent properly submitted all of the requested data, the Commerce Department often substituted data concocted by the American steel companies in place of the respondent's actual cost and price data. This is why the Commerce Department decided on incredibly large dumping margins—up to 109% in one steel case.

Source: Hiroshi Matsumoto, "Legal Harassment of Foreign Firms: The Case of the U.S. Steel Industry," *Pacific Basin Quarterly,* Fall 1993, p. 3. Reprinted by permission.

Questions

1. Do you believe the author's implications that a complainant in an antidumping case could use the law to harass foreign firms? Is this an efficient use of resources for the alleged harassing firm? Explain.
2. How would you amend the antidumping regulations and procedure in order to avoid problems such as those addressed above? Explain.
3. If you represented the American steel industry, how would you respond to each of the author's contentions regarding the unfairness of the procedures?
4. Why would the Commerce Department try to increase the FMV of foreign steel for purposes of the steel industry's complaint?

Import Duties. The tariff treatment that the United States imposes on an imported product often depends on such considerations as whether the product was made with American raw materials and whether the product was actually fabricated abroad or whether it was simply assembled abroad using American-made components. The case that follows examines the question of the appropriate duty for Samsonite luggage imported from Mexico.

SAMSONITE CORPORATION v. UNITED STATES
889 F. 2d 1074 (Fed. Cir. 1989)

[Samsonite assembles luggage in Mexico and imports the completed bag into the United States. Samsonite shipped steel strips from the United States to Mexico in order to use them in the assembly of the bags. The steel pieces were shipped as 5-inch, oil-coated strips with a value of between 95 cents and $1.26. Once in Mexico, the strips were cleaned, bent into a baggage-handle form, covered with vinyl, riveted to a plastic frame, then attached to vinyl bags to form soft-sided luggage. When the luggage was later imported to the United States, the Customs Service assessed a duty on the entire bag, including the value of the steel strips, at a rate of 20 percent ad valorem. The Court of International Trade upheld the Customs Service's decision that the steel strips were not "exported in a condition ready for assembly." Samsonite appealed.]

Senior Circuit Judge Friedman

To obtain a deduction for American-fabricated articles assembled abroad, the components (a) must have been exported from the United States "in condition ready for assembly without further fabrication," (b) not have lost their physical identity in the articles by change in form, shape, or otherwise, and (c) not have been advanced in value or improved in condition "except by being assembled" and except "by operations incidental to the assembly process such as cleaning, lubricating, and painting." As the Court of International Trade correctly pointed out, since the "foregoing three conditions for a deduction are set forth in the conjunctive, . . . each must be satisfied before a component can qualify for duty-free treatment." We agree with that court that the steel strips involved in this case did not meet those conditions.

The critical inquiry is whether the bending and shaping that the strips underwent constituted "fabrication" or mere assembly and operations incidental to the assembly process. We hold that what was done to the strips in Mexico was fabrication and not mere assembly.

When the steel strips were exported from the United States, they were just that: five-inch strips that could not serve as the frame of the luggage without undergoing a complete change in shape. Prior to assembling the luggage, the strips were bent by machine into a carefully and specially configured rectangular shape that was necessary before the original strip would serve its ultimate function as part of the frame of the luggage.

In short, what emerged after the bending operation was a different object from that which left the United States. The latter was a steel strip, the former was a metal frame for a piece of luggage. The transformation of the strip in this manner into a luggage frame was a fabrication. The strips therefore had not been exported from the United States "in condition ready for assembly without further fabrication."

Samsonite contends, however, that prior decisions of the Court of Customs and Patent Appeals require a contrary conclusion. It relies particularly on *General Instrument Corp. v. United States,* 499 F.2d 1318 (CCPA 1974). That case involved wire wound on spools that had been exported from the United States to Taiwan. There the wire was removed from the spools, formed into a horizontal coil by a winding machine, taped to prevent unraveling, dipped in cement, dried, precision shaped, removed from the spools, and wound around a core. The end product made from the wire was a component of a television set that was imported into the United States.

The Court of Customs and Patent Appeals held that: "The steps performed upon the wire after its exportation to Taiwan are not 'further fabrication' steps, but rather assembly steps within the meaning of [the statute]."

Samsonite argues that far more was done to the wire in *General Instrument* than was done to the steel strips in this case. It argues that if the processing the wire underwent in *General Instrument* was not "fabrication," a fortiori "the one simple-minded act of bending a straight frame into a 'C' was neither 'a further fabrication' nor 'a nonincidental operation.'"

The critical inquiry in determining whether fabrication rather than mere assembly took place here, is not the amount of processing that occurred in the two cases, but its nature. In *General Instrument,* the wire, when it left the United States and when it returned as part of a finished product, was a coil. The wire was taken directly from the supply spool on which it was wound and, after processing, was used in assembling the TV set components. The wire underwent no basic change in connection with its incorporation into the television set component.

In contrast, in the present case the steel strips had to undergo a significant change in shape before the actual assembly of luggage could begin. Until the steel strips had been made into "C" shapes they could not be used as a part of the luggage. Unlike the "assembly" that the court in *General Instrument* held the processing of the wire involved, here "further fabrication" of the steel strips was required in order to change them into frames for luggage, before the assembly of the luggage could take place.

[Affirmed.]

Questions

1. *a.* Do you agree with the factual distinction that the court draws between Samsonite and the *General Instrument* case?
   b. Aren't the steps performed on the steel strips in this case merely "assembly steps within the meaning of the statute"? Explain.
2. If Samsonite wanted to continue its practice of importing steel strips to be used in the assembly process in Mexico, is there a way in which it could alter its process in order to avoid the higher duty? Explain.

Exports

While imports are regulated in order to protect American businesses, exports by these businesses may also be regulated. Export regulation serves several purposes, articulated in the Export Administration Act of 1979, which states that:

> It is the policy of the United States to use export controls only after full consideration of the import on the economy of the United States and only to the extent necessary
> (a) to restrict the export of goods and technology that would make a significant contribution to the military potential of any other country . . . which could prove detrimental to the national security of the United States;
> (b) to restrict the export of goods and technology where necessary to further significantly the foreign policy of the United States or to fulfill its declared international obligations; and
> (c) to restrict the export of goods where necessary to protect the domestic economy from the excessive drain of scarce materials and to reduce the serious inflationary impact of foreign demand.

Under the act, anyone wishing to export any type of goods or technology from the United States to a foreign country must obtain a license. Violations of the licensing requirement may bring imprisonment and/or fines.

Two types of licenses are available, General or Validated licenses. The shipper must determine which type of license is required. In order to obtain a General license, the shipper must merely fill out a declaration form at the time of shipping. A Validated license is required when a firm exports certain goods or technology to specified "controlled" countries. Firms must apply for the license from the Office of Export Administration in the Department of Commerce prior to shipping.

In determining whether to award a license, the Department of Commerce will look to several factors, including the type and amount of the exported good, the importing country, the good's use or purpose, the unrestricted availability of the same or comparable item in the importing country(ies), and the intended market in the importing country.

FOREIGN BUSINESSES IN THE UNITED STATES

Foreign firms may wish to establish operations in the United States because Americans are more inclined to buy goods made in this country. As we have seen, foreign car companies have built manufacturing plants in the United States and consequently have used as a marketing theme the fact that many of their cars sold in the United States are now also made in the United States. On the other hand, doing business in the United States brings with it the requirement that these foreign businesses comply with U.S. laws and regulations. As a result of a growing foreign trade deficit in the United States, the U.S. government has been more diligent in enforcing regulations against unfair trade practices of foreign businesses. The Department of Justice has been actively enforcing antidumping and countervailing duty laws, as well as requiring that certain countries (e.g., Japan) open their markets to U.S. exports where that country engages in voluminous exports to the United States.

RESTRICTIONS ON INTERNATIONAL DISPUTE RESOLUTION

As we have seen to this point, international ethical/legal relationships are highly complex. Disputes are inevitable. Resolution of these international disputes often faces several road blocks. First, as mentioned above, the interpretation of contract terms, the language of the contract, the law applicable to the resolution of the conflict, and the appropriate jurisdiction in which to resolve the dispute all raise dilemmas that are not easily dismissed. Moreover, two doctrines, accepted as general principles of international law, also pose quandaries to the courts and barriers to judicial enforcement of rights: the *act of state doctrine* and the *doctrine of sovereign immunity*.

Act of State Doctrine

It is generally accepted that a country has absolute rule over what occurs within its borders. Consequently, the act of state doctrine holds that a judge in one country does not have the authority to examine or challenge the acts of another country within that

Nationalisation: Assets of firm or company appropriated by the court in power.

Expropriation: Taking of property from a company.

country's borders. For instance, an American court may not declare the acts of the British government invalid, because it is presumed that the foreign country acted legally within its own territory.

One area that has caused a great deal of dispute in connection with the act of state doctrine is *expropriation*. Expropriation is the taking by a national government of property and/or rights of a foreign firm within its borders. The United States contends that international law dictates that an individual or firm be compensated for the taking by the government. Not all governments agree with this statement of law. On the other hand, where a government expropriates property or rights without offering just compensation, the foreign government of the firm affected may retaliate economically or otherwise.

Doctrine of Sovereign Immunity

The doctrine of sovereign immunity is based on the concept that "the king can do no wrong." In other words, if the king makes the rules, how could the king ever be wrong? As Chief Justice Marshall explained in *The Schooner Exchange* v. *McFaddon*,[5] "The jurisdiction of the nation within its own territory is necessarily exclusive and absolute. It is susceptible of no limitation not imposed by itself, deriving validity from an external source would imply a diminution of its sovereignty to the extent of the restriction, and an investment of that sovereignty to the same extent in that power which could impose such restriction."

The doctrine has been codified in the United States by the Foreign Sovereign Immunities Act of 1976 (FSIA), which provides that foreign countries may not be sued in American courts, subject to several exceptions. Accordingly, it would not be possible for a U.S. citizen to sue Britain in the U.S. courts. A foreign country may be sued in American courts if the claim falls into one of the following FSIA exceptions:

1. The foreign countries have waived their immunity (i.e., they have consented to be sued in another country's courts). Or
2. The legal action is based on a *commercial activity* by the foreign country in the United States or outside the United States but having a direct effect in the United States.

Therefore, a country that conducts a commercial activity in a foreign country may not hide behind sovereign immunity if sued, while a country acting on its own behalf and not for a commercial purpose would be able to avail itself of the protection. This "restrictive theory of immunity" is to be contrasted with the policies of some countries, which contend that immunity is absolute—no exceptions exist.

The following case illustrates the requirement that there must be a direct effect in the United States in order for exception (2) to apply.

MARTIN v. REPUBLIC OF SOUTH AFRICA
836 F.2d 91 (2d Cir. 1987)

[Barry Martin, a black professional dancer, was injured in an automobile accident during a visit to South Africa. Two state-controlled hospitals refused to provide him with emergency medical service because of his race. As a result of the failure to provide him with responsive care, Martin became permanently disabled and filed suit against South Africa. The District Court held in favor of South Africa, finding that it was subject to sovereign immunity under the FSIA, as its acts did not cause a direct effect in the United States. As the omissions of South Africa caused him to return to the United States permanently disabled, Martin argued that there was a direct effect in the United States.]

Judge Timbers

The Fifth Circuit in *Zernicek v. Brown & Root, Inc.* recently has supported the "direct effect" clause of [the FSIA]. There, an agency of the government of Mexico (Pemex) was conducting mineral exploration in the Bay of Campeche. It contracted with an American company for its support services. Zernicek, a U.S. citizen and an employee of the American company, was exposed to excessive doses of radiation as a result of the negligence of Pemex. After returning to the United States, Zernicek suffered continued sickness from the effects of his exposure. The issue before the court was whether physical suffering and substantial medical expenses incurred by Zernicek after his return to the United States constituted a "direct effect in the United States." In holding that it did not, the court stated:

> Congress' use of the term "direct" in the Act was obviously intended to invoke the court's judgment. The distinction between an effect that is "direct" and one that is indirect is not quantitative and cannot be programmed into a computer. The district court properly followed the cases holding that the eventual effect in the United States of the personal injury or death of an American citizen while abroad is not direct within the meaning of the Act.

Here, [Martin] makes substantially the same claim as the appellant did in *Zernicek*. Appellant here asserts that, where South Africa's activities have caused a citizen to return to the United States permanently disabled, the foreign state has caused a "direct effect in the United States." We disagree. We find the analysis in the *Zernicek* case to be persuasive.

Our holding on the issue raised on this appeal conforms with the holdings of all courts that have considered a claim for *personal injuries* sustained in a foreign state when the plaintiff asserted that the "direct effect in the United States" was the continued suffering and consequential damages that persisted once the plaintiff returned. For example, in *Tucker v. Whitaker Travel, Ltd.*, the plaintiff sued the Commonwealth of the Bahamas and the Ministry of Tourism for injuries he sustained while riding horseback in the Bahamas. The district court dismissed the action for lack of subject matter jurisdiction. The court held that

> The direct effects of the various defendants' tortious conduct are plaintiffs' injuries, which occurred outside the United States. Whatever pain and pecuniary loss plaintiffs suffer in the United States are indirect consequences of the accident in the Bahamas.

Likewise, in *Upton v. Empire of Iran,* the court held that subject matter jurisdiction was absent. There an action was brought against the Empire of Iran and Iran's Department of Civil Aviation, as owner and operator of an airport, for personal injuries sustained as the result of the collapse of the roof at Mehrabad International Airport in Tehran. The district court, holding that no direct effects were caused in the United States by the defendants' negligent operation and maintenance of the Mehrabad Airport, stated,

> The common sense interpretation of a "direct effect" is one which has no intervening element, but, rather, flows in a straight line without deviation or interruption.

The court also stated that, although the effects of the plaintiff's injuries may be endured in the United States, the injury itself was caused in Tehran.

At oral argument, appellant's counsel recognized the number of opinions contrary to the position he advocated. He argued that these opinions incorrectly applied the statute and created an anomaly between the treatment of corporations and the treatment of individuals under the "direct effect" provision. We disagree.

We do not believe that such a distinction exists nor do we create one here. Appellant was not in the United States at the time of the accident. He was in South Africa. Indeed, he did not return to the United States until more than one year after the date of the accident. Application of the plain language of [the FSIA] leads us to conclude that South Africa's conduct did not cause a direct effect in the United States. Appellant nevertheless invites us to interpret [the FSIA] so as to conclude that there is subject matter jurisdiction in this case. We decline the invitation.

* * * * *

To summarize: we hold that South Africa's acts did not have a "direct effect in the United States" within the meaning of §1605(a)(2) of the FSIA, and that the district court therefore correctly dismissed the complaint for lack of subject matter jurisdiction.

Affirmed.

Questions

1. Do you agree with the court's opinion that there is no distinction between the *Zernicek* case and the *Martin* case? Explain.
2. Does the holding of the *Zernicek* case create an anomaly between the treatment of corporations and the treatment of individuals under the "direct effect" provision? If so, how could you justify this distinction?

Arbitration

In light of the difficulty of obtaining jurisdiction and the choice of laws, language, and forum issues, parties to an international contract may prefer to insert a clause that calls for international arbitration in case of a dispute. Arbitration is a nonjudicial means to settle a conflict where the parties agree to a hearing in front of a third party who will issue a binding award decision. (See Chapter 4.) The arbitration clause will specify the identity of the third party (or the association from which the parties will seek a third party), the place of arbitration and, in many cases, the laws that will apply.

While arbitration is considered binding on the parties who consent to it, there are times where a losing party may opt not to satisfy the award to the other party. In that case, the successful party must petition a court of law to enforce the award. In that regard, the United Nations Convention on the Recognition and Enforcement of Foreign Arbitral Awards provides that the successful party obtain possession of the property of the losing party located in any signatory country for the purpose of satisfying the debt.

The following case illustrates the problems that may arise, even where an arbitration clause is apparently clear.

MITSUBISHI MOTORS v. SOLER CHRYSLER-PLYMOUTH
473 U.S. 614 (1985)

[Soler Chrysler-Plymouth distributed Plymouth automobiles in Puerto Rico for CISA, a Swiss subsidiary of Chrysler. CISA and Mitsubishi Heavy Industries, Inc., entered into a joint venture called Mitsubishi Motors. CISA, Soler, and Mistubishi Motors entered into an agreement stating that all disputes that arose in connection with the agreement would be settled by arbitration in Japan in accordance with the rules of the Japan Commercial Arbitration Association. After several years, Mitsubishi requested arbitration in Tokyo and filed a federal district court action to compel arbitration under the agreement. Soler argued that antitrust and other violations were involved in the dispute and that these issues were not appropriate for arbitration. The District Court ordered arbitration; the Court of Appeals reversed the decision regarding the arbitration of the antitrust matters. Mitsubishi appealed to the Supreme Court.]

Justice Blackmun

---

* * * * *

We also reject the proposition that an arbitration panel will pose too great a danger of innate hostility to the constraints on business conduct that antitrust law imposes. International arbitrators frequently are drawn from the legal as well as the business community; where the dispute has an important legal component, the parties and the arbitral body with whose assistance they have agreed to settle their dispute can be expected to select arbitrators accordingly. We decline to indulge the presumption that the parties and arbitral body conducting a proceeding will be unable or unwilling to retain competent, conscientious, and impartial arbitrators . . .

There is no reason to assume at the outset of the dispute that international arbitration will not provide an adequate mechanism. To be sure, the international arbitral tribunal owes no prior allegiance to the legal norms of particular states; hence, it has no direct obligation to vindicate their statutory dictates. The tribunal, however, is bound to effectuate the intentions of the parties. Where the parties have agreed that the arbitral body is to decide a defined set of claims which includes, as in these cases, those arising from the application of American antitrust law, the tribunal therefore should be bound to decide that dispute in accord with the national law giving rise to the claim . . .

Having permitted the arbitration to go forward, the national courts of the United States will have the opportunity at the award-enforcement stage to ensure that the legitimate interest in the enforcement of the antitrust laws has been addressed. The Convention reserves to each signatory country the right to refuse enforcement of an award where the 'recognition or enforcement of the award would be contrary to the public policy of that country.' While the efficacy of the arbitral process requires that substantive review at the award-enforcement stage remain minimal, it would not require intrusive inquiry to ascertain that the tribunal took cognizance of the antitrust claims and actually decided them.

As international trade has expanded in recent decades, so too has the use of international arbitration to resolve disputes arising in the course of that trade. The controversies that international arbitral institutions are called upon to resolve have increased in diversity as well as in complexity. Yet the potential of these tribunals for efficient disposition of legal disagreements arising from commercial relations has not yet been tested. If they are to take a central place in the international legal order, national courts will need to 'shake off the old judicial hostility to arbitration,' and also their customary and understandable unwillingness to cede jurisdiction of a claim arising under domestic law to a foreign or transnational tribunal. To this extent, at least, it will be necessary for national courts to subordinate domestic notions of arbitrability to the international policy favoring commercial arbitration.

[Affirmed in part, reversed in part.]

Questions

1. What were the bases for Soler's contention that matters such as antitrust should not be submitted to arbitration?
2. How does the court propose that Soler's concerns will be addressed?

CHAPTER QUESTIONS

1. Nigeria contracted to purchase large quantities of cement from Portland Cement in order to support its rapidly expanding infrastructure. Nigeria overpurchased the cement and the country's harbors became clogged with ships waiting to unload. Imports of other goods ground to a halt as well. Nigeria consequently repudiated its contracts with those shippers, who then filed suits to enforce the contracts. Nigeria responded that it is immune from prosecution in connection with these contracts under the Foreign Sovereign Immunities Act, claiming that its contracts were governmental and not of a commercial nature. What should be the result? See *Texas Trading and Milling Corp.* v. *Federal Republic of Nigeria,* 647 F.2d 300 (2d Cir. 1981).

2. Original Appalachian Artworks (OAA) is the manufacturer and license holder of Cabbage Patch Kids Dolls. Granada Electronics imported and distributed Cabbage Patch Kids dolls to the United States that were made in Spain by Jesmar under a license from OAA. Jesmar's license permitted manufacture and distribution of the dolls in Spain, the Canary Islands, Andorra, and Ceuta Melilla. Under the license, Jesmar agreed not to make, sell, or authorize any sale of the dolls outside its licensed territory and to sell only to those purchasers who would agree not to use or resell the licensed products outside the territory as well. Jesmar's argument that Granada's sales do not constitute "gray market" sales is that OAA's dolls sold in the United States have English-language

adoption papers, birth certificates, and instructions while Granada's dolls come equipped with Spanish-language adoption papers, birth certificates, and instructions. In addition, Granada argues that the role of trademark law is to prevent an infringer from passing off its goods as being those of another. Such is not the case here. Are these sales prohibited? Explain. See *Orig. Appalachian Artworks* v. *Granada Electronics,* 816 F.2d 68 (2d Cir. 1987).

3. What are the relative advantages and disadvantages of each form of doing business in a foreign country? Why would a firm choose one form over another?

4. Assume that you are interested in importing silk blouses from Bangkok to France. What facts might persuade you to enter into an agency agreement with the Thai blouse manufacturer rather than a distributorship, and vice versa?

5. Prior to 1941, Kalmich owned a business in Yugoslavia. In 1941, the Nazis confiscated his property as a result of Kalmich's Jewish heritage and faith. Bruno purchased the business from the Nazis in 1942 without knowledge of the potential unlawful conversion. Kalmich contends that, as the confiscation was in violation of well-defined principals of international law prior to the German occupation, the transfer to Bruno was ineffective. Kalmich seeks to apply a 1946 Yugoslavian law called "Law Concerning the Treatment of Property Taken Away from the Owner." That law provides that where property is taken from its owners, the owner may bring an action against "responsible persons" for recovery. Does the act of state doctrine apply here? If not, what should be the result in an American court? Explain. See *Kalmich* v. *Bruno,* 450 F. Supp. 227 (N.D.Il 1978).

6. Bandes owned and managed 73 percent of the shares of Industria Nacional de Clavos y Alambres (INCA), a Nicaraguan corporation. In 1978, INCA paid $460,000 to Harlow & Jones, Inc. (H & J), a U.S. company, for steel billets. However, the events of the Nicaraguan civil war prevented INCA from taking delivery of the goods after they had been paid for and caused Bandes to flee the country. Decree no. 10, enacted by the new Nicaraguan government, gave the state the right to intervene in any business that had been abandoned. In 1979, the Nicaraguan government confiscated the shares held by others in the company and stripped Bandes of all power to represent INCA. In February 1980, the government issued another decree stating that all individuals who lost rights under the prior decree no. 10 must appear in Nicaragua within 10 days to contest the taking; otherwise, the property would belong to the state with no further right to contest. Bandes did not appear because his act of abandonment would have been considered a crime under the decree, but he later filed suit in the U.S. district courts seeking to get back from H & J the money INCA had paid to it, which Bandes believed he was rightly due.

   Does the act of state doctrine apply here? Are the acts of the Nicaraguan government in line with U.S. law and policies? Does it make a difference that the funds sought by Bandes are located in the United States? Explain. See *Bandes* v. *Harlow & Jones, Inc.,* 852 F.2d 661 (1988).

7. Lee Bun entered Hong Kong illegally by boat from China. He sought to claim refugee status on the basis that he had been involved in political protests in China and feared persecution if he returned. After judicial review of deportation orders was dismissed, Lee Bun claimed that he had been denied the right to a fair hearing, guaranteed by the Geneva Convention. The Department of Immigration responded that, while Britain had ratified the Convention, it had not been extended to Hong Kong and was not, therefore, part of the law of Hong Kong. What arguments could Lee Bun make in his favor supporting the application of the Geneva Convention or his right to a fair hearing? See *Lee Bun* v. *Dir. of Immigration,* 2 HKLR 466 (1990).

8. Zedan received a telephone call from a Saudi Arabian organization offering him an engineering position at a construction project in Saudi Arabia. The Ministry of Communications, an agency of the government, guaranteed payment to Zedan for any work he performed there, whether for the government or for a nonsovereign third party. After three years, Zedan left the country without being fully paid. After he returned to the United States, he filed an action in federal court seeking to enforce the Ministry's guarantee. The Ministry argued that it was protected under the Foreign Sovereign Immunities Act. Was Zedan's recruitment in the United States a commercial activity as required by the act? Did this action have a direct effect in the United States as required by the act? Explain. See *Zedan* v. *Kingdom of Saudi Arabia,* 849 F.2d 1511 (1988).

9. Dubai and Sharjah were Arab territories under the protection of Great Britain since 1892 but without clearly defined boundaries. The extent of territory the ruler of each controlled in each of these areas depended on which tribes offered him allegiance. Since the tribes were nomadic and moved around a great deal, the areas controlled by each ruler were indefinite. At the territories' request, Britain intervened in the 1950s, awarding certain lands to one or the other territory. However, uncertainty and dissatisfaction continued, notwithstanding the fact that the parties had requested that Britain arbitrate the boundaries. A compromise between the parties was signed in 1976 that provided for continued arbitration regarding the boundary dispute. One of the recurring issues was the choice of law to be applied as, unfortunately, no applicable law had been specified. Dubai argued that international law governed, which would dictate that equity reign, whereas Sharjah argued that the federal law of the United Arab Emirates applied, which would have given greater weight to allegiance of the tribes. What should be the result here? How would you arrive at a decision regarding the delineation of territory? What factors are important to your decision? See *Dubai-Sharjah Border Arbitration, International Court of Justice, Court of Arbitration,* October 19, 1981.

10. In 1954, Italy filed a petition with the International Court of Justice based on a 1951 war reparations declaration made by America, Britain, and France. The declaration concerned the removal of certain Albanian gold from Italy in 1943 by German authorities (who then turned over the gold to Albania). The issue that concerned Italy at this hearing was whether the gold was in fact property of Italy or Albania at the end of World War II. In fact, Italy was not asking the court to order Albania to return the gold but to order the United States, Britain, and France to make reparations to Italy under the declaration. Just to complicate matters, the court was also asked to decide whether, if the gold was found to be Italy's, it should still be given to Britain in settlement of a prior judgment by Britain against Albania. Britain argued that its claim for the gold from Albania had priority over Italy's claim to the gold. Notwithstanding these truly complex matters, however, the first concern of the court was whether it had jurisdiction over all of the parties. Which parties to this action must have consented to the action in order for the court to finally decide the issues presented to it and enforce a judgment? See *Monetary Gold Removed From Rome, I.C.J. Reports 1954,* p. 19.

11. Must a rule be universal in order to be considered customary international law? For instance, if a majority of states consider the limit of one country's territorial waters to be 10 miles out from each point along the coast, but a number of states do not follow this basic rule, can it be said that the rule is still a custom of international law? Explain.

12. Camel Manufacturing imported nylon tents to the United States. The tents held nine people and weighed over 30 pounds. The tents' floors ranged from 8 feet by 10 feet to 10 feet by 14 feet. The tents were to be used as shelter during camping. The importer categorized the goods as "sports equipment," which carried a 10 percent import duty, while the U.S. Customs Service considered the tents "textile articles not specifically provided for," with a duty of $.25 per pound plus 15 percent import duty. The importer appealed the decision. What should be the result? Explain. See *Camel Manufacturing Co.* v. *United States,* 686 F.Supp. 912 (C.I.T. 1988).

NOTES

1. Michael Elliot, "Dining on Goose, Talking Turkey," *Newsweek,* December 20, 1993, p. 40.

2. Bader and Shaw, "Amendment of the Foreign Corrupt Practices Act," 15 N.Y.U. J. Int. L. & Pol. 627, 628 (1983).

3. Desda Moss, "Report: Companies Help Rain Forests Breathe a Little Easier," *USA Today,* September 15, 1993, p. 5A.

4. 661 F.2d 864 (10th Cir. 1981).

5. 11 U.S. (7 Cranch) 116 (1812).

P A R T

III

TRADE REGULATION AND ANTITRUST

7

GOVERNMENT REGULATION OF BUSINESS: AN INTRODUCTION

———————————————————————●———————————————————————

INTRODUCTION

Chapter 1 introduced the issue of the proper balance between the free market and government as systems by which the role of business in society may be "controlled." Chapter 2 addressed the utility of individual and corporate ethics as self-regulatory mechanisms for governing the behavior of the corporate community. Chapter 3 continued our exploration of the proper role of business in society. Chapters 4, 5, and 6 offered a brief overview of the justice system.

The balance of the text is largely devoted to the legal system, both here and abroad. Throughout that investigation, the reader is urged to keep in mind the issues of the introductory chapters. What is the proper role of business in society? Has business abused the public trust? If so, is government the answer to the problem? Or might we rely on self-regulation (ethics and social responsibility) and market "regulation"? What is the proper blend of these "control" devices as well as others left unexplored (e.g., custom)?

The phrase *mixed economy* is commonly applied to the contemporary American system. In an honorable pursuit of the greatest good for the greatest number, America has turned to the government to ameliorate the injustices and discomforts of contemporary life. Market "regulation" and self-regulation have been supplemented by government intervention.

Government regulation pervades our existence. The government directly controls certain dimensions of the economy, such as the public utilities. The government indirectly intervenes across the spectrum of the economy in matters as diverse as child labor and zoning restrictions; and, in the larger sense of national economic policy, the government engages in antitrust activity designed to preserve our conception of a free, efficient marketplace. To the proponents of government intervention, the successes are evident: cleaner air, safer cars, fewer useless drugs, more jobs for minorities, safer workplaces, and so on. To the critics, many government regulatory efforts either did not achieve their purpose or did so at a cost exceeding the benefits. The late 1970s and the 1980s were marked by increasingly insistent calls from virtually all segments of society to retard the reach of government. Indeed, significant deregulation has been effected (see Chapter 8). More specifically, freeing business from a portion of its regulatory burden was a key ingredient in former President Reagan's plans to reorder the nation. His intentions for deregulation were broadly applauded, but it stretches credulity to think that the American government will ever play less than a prepossessing role in American business.

WHY REGULATION?

Market Failure

In theory, government intervention in a free enterprise economy would be justified only when the market is unable to maximize the public interest—that is, in instances of market failure.

Market failure is attributed to certain inherent imperfections in the market itself.

Inadequate Information. Can the consumer choose the best pain reliever in the absence of complete information about the virtues of the competing products? An efficient free market presumes reasoned decisions about production and consumption. Reasoned decisions require adequate information. Because we cannot have perfect information and often will not have adequate information, the government, it is argued, may impose regulations either to improve the available information or to diminish the unfavorable effect of inadequate information. Hence we have, for example, labeling mandates for consumer goods, licensure requirements for many occupations, and health standards for the processing and sale of goods.

Monopoly. Of course, the government intervenes to thwart anticompetitive monopolies and oligopolies throughout the marketplace. (That process is addressed in Chapter 10.) Of immediate interest here is the so-called natural monopoly. Telephone and electrical services are classic examples of a decline in per unit production costs as the firm becomes larger. Thus, a single large firm is more efficient than several small ones, and a natural monopoly results. In such situations, the government has commonly intervened (in the form of public service commissions) to preserve the efficiencies of the large firm while preventing that firm from taking unfair advantage of the consumer.

Externalities. When all the costs and/or benefits of a good or service are not fully internalized or absorbed, those costs or benefits fall elsewhere as what economists have labeled *externalities, neighborhood effects,* or *spillovers.* Pollution is a characteristic example of a negative externality. The environment is used without charge as an ingredient in the production process (commonly as a receptacle for waste). Consequently, the product is underpriced. The consumer does not pay the full social cost of the product, so those remaining costs are thrust on parties external to the transaction. Government regulation is sometimes considered necessary to place the full cost burden on those who generated it, which in turn is expected to result in less wasteful use of resources. Positive externalities are those in which a producer confers benefits not required by the market. An example of such a positive externality is a business firm that, through no direct market compulsion, landscapes its grounds and develops a sculpture garden to contribute to the aesthetic quality of its neighborhood. Positive externalities ordinarily are not the subject of regulation.

Public Goods.   Some goods and services cannot be provided through the pricing system because we have no method for excluding those who choose not to pay. In such situations, the added cost of benefiting one person is zero or nearly so, and, in any case, no one can effectively be denied the benefits of the activity. National defense, insect eradication, and pollution control are examples of this phenomenon. Presumably most individuals would refuse to voluntarily pay for what others would receive free. Thus, in the absence of government regulations, public goods would not be produced in adequate quantities.

Philosophy and Politics

The correction of market failure could explain the full range of government regulation of business, but an alternative or perhaps supplemental explanation lies in the political process. Three general arguments have emerged.

1. One view is that regulation is considered necessary for the protection and general welfare of the public. We find the government engaging in regulatory efforts designed to achieve a more equitable distribution of income and wealth. Many believe government intervention in the market is necessary to stabilize the economy, thus curbing the problems of recession, inflation, and unemployment. Affirmative action programs seek to compensate for the racism and sexism of the past. We even find the government protecting us from ourselves, both for our benefit and for the well-being of the larger society. For example, cigarette advertising is banned on television, and in most states motorcyclists must wear helmets.

2. Another view is that regulation is developed at the behest of industry and is operated primarily for the benefit of industry. Here, the various subsidies and tax advantages afforded to business might be cited. In numerous instances, government regulation has been effective in reducing or entirely eliminating the entry of competitors. Antitrust law has been instrumental in sheltering small businesses. Government regulation has also permitted legalized price-fixing in some industries. Of course, it may be that although regulation is often initiated primarily for the public welfare, industry eventually "captures" the regulatory process and ensures its continuation for the benefit of the industry. As we see in the historical overview that follows, both the public interest and business interests have been very influential in generating government intervention in the marketplace.

3. Finally, bureaucrats who perform government regulation are themselves a powerful force in maintaining and expanding that regulation.

THE HISTORY OF GOVERNMENT REGULATION OF BUSINESS

Government has always played some role in American commerce. In the early years of the republic, tariffs were imposed to protect manufacturers, subsidies were provided to stimulate commerce, and a few agencies were established (e.g., the Army Corps of Engineers in 1824 and the Patent and Trademark Office in 1836).

Prior to the Civil War the major, if weak, link between government and business was the national bank, which possessed very limited authority. Banking remained a fundamentally private enterprise restrained only by weak state statutes. A meaningful federal banking system simply did not exist. Indeed, it is estimated that by 1860 "some 1,500 banks were issuing about 10,000 different types of bank notes."[1] Then the need for a centralized approach to the Civil War forced Congress to pass the National Banking Act of 1864, which laid the foundation for the dual system of extensive federal and state banking regulation that we know today. However, Americans continued to stoutly resist government intrusion in business affairs. The years following the Civil War were perhaps the zenith of the capitalist era. The "Robber Barons" (Carnegie, Rockefeller, and their colleagues) came to the fore. Philosopher Herbert Spencer adapted Darwin's "survival of the fittest" theory to the world of commerce, thereby giving the business community an intellectual foundation for asserting its leadership. Extraordinary industrial growth followed.

But the public began to feel the impact of big business in the late 1880s, and the feeling often was not pleasant. Anger over the conduct of the rail and industrial trusts manifested itself in the Populist movement, which embodied the struggle of the "common people" against the predatory acts of the moneyed interests. The railroads, then the nation's most powerful private economic force, were bent on growth and seemed unconcerned with the general welfare.

> By discriminating in freight charges between localities, articles, and individuals, the railroads were terrorizing farmers, merchants, and even whole communities until, as a government agency said in 1887, matters "had reached such a pass, that no man dared engage in any business in which transportation largely entered without first obtaining permission of a railway manager."[2]

Rural discontent led to the Grange movement, which became an important lobbying force for agrarian interests. Several states enacted railroad regulatory legislation. By then the confusion and abuse in the rail industry prompted Congress to pass the Interstate Commerce Commission Act of 1887 and ban, among other practices, rate discrimination against short hauls and the practice of keeping rates secret until the day of shipment. In addition to the farmers, small merchants and shippers and the railroads themselves ultimately supported federal intervention. Apparently the railroad owners felt regulation would be meaningless or even advantageous to them. Subsequently, the Hepburn Act of 1906 greatly strengthened Interstate Commerce Commission (ICC) effectiveness. The Mann-Elkins Act of 1910 extended ICC jurisdiction to interstate telegraph, telephone, cable, and wireless enterprises.

As explained in greater detail in Chapter 10, the development of giant trusts and holding companies (e.g., Standard Oil) led to extraordinary commercial advances but also to widespread abuse in the form of price-fixing, price-slashing to drive out

The four ways assumed by federal Govt to increase its power.

① Power of the Purse.
Eg: In the field of Education.

② The evolutionary change in Inter-State Comm are.

70% was Intrastate. Now 90% is interstate being regulated by federal Govt.

competitors, market sharing, and the like. Blacklists and other antilabor tactics were common. At the same time, small merchants and wholesalers were being squeezed by the weight of big manufacturing interests. Around the turn of the century, commercial giants (such as American Tobacco, Quaker Oats, Heinz, Swift, and Anheuser Busch) made purchases directly from farmers and other suppliers and sold directly to retailers. The result was that wholesalers, who had previously occupied a key economic role in most communities, were increasingly unnecessary. Similarly, retail giants (such as Sears and Woolworth) were applying extreme competitive pressure on smaller businesses. The passage of the Sherman Antitrust Act in 1890 had relatively little immediate impact; however, Presidents Roosevelt, Taft, and Wilson all took up the regulatory cause, and with the passage in 1914 of the Clayton and Federal Trade Commission acts, antitrust law became an important ingredient in American business life. The fever for regulation subsided somewhat during the prosperous 1920s, but the Depression prompted detailed government regulation.

The Depression compelled many archconservatives to surrender to the need for government intervention. President Roosevelt took office in 1933, and the first 100 days of his term saw the passage of 15 major pieces of legislation. In all, Roosevelt secured approval of 93 major bills during his first two terms in office. The federal government became the biggest voice in America as the administration sought to correct the tragedy of the Depression. The legislation literally changed the character of American life. Congress established the Civilian Conservation Corps to place the unemployed in public works projects. The Federal Emergency Relief Act funded state-operated welfare programs. The Tennessee Valley Authority established the government as a major participant in producing electrical energy. The Glass-Steagall Act divided investment and commercial banking and provided for insurance on bank deposits. The list went on and on, and the result was a new view of the business-government relationship. Effectively, the government and the citizenry conceded that the old view of an automatically self-correcting economy was invalid. The Depression revealed a fundamental instability in the unregulated market.[3]

Distrust of the market provoked further government regulation in the decades subsequent to the Depression, and that regulation has followed a much broader path. Rather than regulating single industries (transportation, banking, communication), the government interventions of recent years have swept across the entire economy to address such issues as discrimination, pollution, and worker safety. In the 1960s and the bulk of the 1970s, no social problem seemed too daunting for the government's regulatory efforts.[4] But as we explore in Chapter 8, the late 1970s and the entire decade of the 1980s were years of resistance to government intervention resulting in significant *deregulation* of some dimensions of the economy.

THE CONSTITUTIONAL FOUNDATION OF BUSINESS REGULATION

The Commerce Clause of the U.S. Constitution broadly specifies the power accorded to the federal government to regulate business activity. Article I, Section 8 of the Constitution provides that: "The Congress shall have the power . . . To regulate Commerce with foreign Nations, and among the several States, and with the Indian

Tribes . . ." State authority to regulate commerce resides in the police power reserved to the states by the Constitution. *Police power* refers to the right of the state governments to promote the public health, safety, morals, and general welfare by regulating persons and property within each state's jurisdiction. The states have, in turn, delegated portions of the police power to local government units.

Supremacy Clause

Sometimes state or local law conflicts with federal law. Such situations are resolved by the *Supremacy Clause* of the Constitution, which provides that, "This Constitution and the Laws of the United States . . . shall be the Supreme Law of the Land."

Ours is a federalist form of government wherein we divide authority between federal, state, and local units of government. Conflicts between the preferences of each level are inevitable. However, the Supremacy Clause, as interpreted by the Supreme Court, establishes that, in the event of an irreconcilable conflict, federal law will prevail and the state/local law will be ruled unconstitutional. Were it not so, we would have great difficulty in achieving a unified national policy on any issue.

At the same time, the Supreme Court recently affirmed the states' strong role in our dual system of government by announcing that "it will read federal law to preempt state governmental functions only if Congress plainly states its intent to do so."[5] In a 1991 decision, *Gregory* v. *Ashcroft,*[6] the Court stressed the constitutionally mandated balance of power between the federal and state governments. In that case, some Missouri state court judges challenged a provision in the Missouri constitution that required them to retire at age 70. Essentially, they argued that the retirement provision violated the federal Age Discrimination in Employment Act. The lower court dismissed the claim. Both the federal court of appeals and the U.S. Supreme Court affirmed. The Supreme Court argued that this was an area traditionally left to the states, and that Congress, if it wishes to exercise its constitutional authority under the Supremacy Clause to preempt a state law, must make that intention unmistakably clear in the statute. That was not the case with the ADEA. Thus, while the Supremacy Clause gives the federal government the authority to preempt state laws, *Gregory* reminds us of the states' important powers in this delicate balancing act.

Commerce Clause

The Commerce Clause, as interpreted by the judiciary, affords Congress exclusive jurisdiction over foreign commerce. States and localities, nevertheless, sometimes seek in various ways to regulate foreign commerce. For example, a state may seek, directly or indirectly, to impose a tax on foreign goods that compete with those locally grown or manufactured. Such efforts violate the Commerce Clause.

Federal control over interstate commerce was designed to create a free market throughout the United States, wherein goods would move among the states, unencumbered by state and local tariffs and duties. Not surprisingly, that profoundly sensible policy has been the source of extensive conflict and litigation. As with foreign commerce, the states and localities have endeavored in ways subtle and sometimes not so subtle to influence the course of interstate commerce. The judiciary has not been sympathetic with those efforts. Indeed, to the great chagrin of states' rights advocates, judicial decisions have very dramatically expanded the reach of the federal government. Even intrastate activities having an effect on interstate commerce are now subject to federal regulation. In *Wickard* v. *Filburn,* the Supreme Court, in interpreting a federal statute regulating the production and sale of wheat, found that 23 acres of homegrown and largely home-consumed wheat affected interstate commerce and that it was subject to federal regulation.[7] (As a small test of the mind, the student may wish to deduce the economic reasoning that supported the Court's position.) Clearly, the federal lawmakers with the approval of the judiciary have expanded the power of the central government at the expense of states and localities. The argument goes that expansion has been necessary to maximize the general good, which might otherwise be thwarted by narrowing self-interest or prejudice in specific states and localities. The following case illustrates both the technical difficulties in determining the constitutional bounds of federal regulation and the conflict between individual rights and the government's view of the general welfare.

HEART OF ATLANTA MOTEL v. UNITED STATES
379 U.S. 241 (1964)

Justice Clark

This is a declaratory judgment action, attacking the constitutionality of Title II of the Civil Rights Act of 1964 . . . [The lower court found for the United States.]

1. The Factual Background and Contentions of the Parties

 . . . Appellant owns and operates the Heart of Atlanta Motel, which has 216 rooms available to transient guests. The motel is located on Courtland Street, two blocks from downtown Peachtree Street. It is readily accessible to interstate highways 75 and 85 and state highways 23 and 41. Appellant solicits patronage from outside the State of Georgia through various national advertising media, including magazines of national circulation; it maintains over 50 billboards and highway signs within the state, soliciting patronage for the motel; it accepts convention trade from outside Georgia and approximately 75 percent of its registered guests are from out of state. Prior to passage of the act the motel had followed a practice of refusing to rent rooms to Negroes, and it alleged that it intended to continue to do so. In an effort to perpetuate that policy this suit was filed.

The appellant contends that Congress in passing this act exceeded its power to regulate commerce under [Article I] of the Constitution of the United States; that the act violates the Fifth Amendment because appellant is deprived of the right to choose its customers and operate its business as it wishes, resulting in a taking of its liberty and property without due process of law and a taking of its property without just compensation; and, finally, that by requiring appellant to rent available rooms to Negroes against its will, Congress is subjecting it to involuntary servitude in contravention of the Thirteenth Amendment.

The appellees counter that the unavailability to Negroes of adequate accommodations interferes significantly with interstate travel, and that Congress, under the Commerce Clause, has power to remove such obstructions and restraints; that the Fifth Amendment does not forbid reasonable regulation and that consequential damage does not constitute a "taking" within the meaning of that amendment; that the Thirteenth Amendment claim fails because it is entirely frivolous to say that an amendment directed to the abolition of human bondage and the removal of widespread disabilities associated with slavery places discrimination in public accommodations beyond the reach of both federal and state law . . .

[A]ppellees proved the refusal of the motel to accept Negro transients after the passage of the act. The district court sustained the constitutionality of the sections of the act under attack and issued a permanent injunction . . . It restrained the appellant from "[r]efusing to accept Negroes as guests in the motel by reason of their race or color" and from "[m]aking any distinction whatever upon the basis of race or color in the availability of the goods, services, facilities, privileges, advantages, or accommodations offered or made available to the guests of the motel, or to the general public, within or upon any of the premises of the Heart of Atlanta Motel, Inc."

2. The History of the Act

. . . The act as finally adopted was most comprehensive, undertaking to prevent through peaceful and voluntary settlement discrimination in voting, as well as in places of accommodation and public facilities, federally secured programs and in employment. Since Title II is the only portion under attack here, we confine our consideration to those public accommodation provisions.

3. Title II of the Act

This Title is divided into seven sections beginning with § 201(a) which provides that:

"All persons shall be entitled to the full and equal enjoyment of the goods, services, facilities, privileges, advantages, and accommodations of any place of public accommodation, as defined in this section, without discrimination or segregation on the ground of race, color, religion, or national origin."

4. Application of Title II to Heart of Atlanta Motel

It is admitted that the operation of the motel brings it within the provisions of § 201(a) of the act and that appellant refused to provide lodging for transient Negroes because of their race or color and that it intends to continue that policy unless restrained.

The sole question posed is, therefore, the constitutionality of the Civil Rights Act of 1964 as applied to these facts. The legislative history of the act indicates that Congress based the act on § 5 and the Equal Protection Clause of the Fourteenth Amendment as well as its power to regulate interstate commerce . . .

[Part 5 omitted.]

6. The Basis of Congressional Action

While the act as adopted carried no congressional findings the record of its passage through each house is replete with evidence of the burdens that discrimination by race or color places upon interstate commerce . . . This testimony included the fact that our people have become increasingly mobile with millions of people of all races traveling from state to state; that Negroes in particular have been the subject of discrimination in transient accommodations, having to travel great distances to secure the same; that often they have been unable to obtain accommodations and have had to call upon friends to put them up overnight, and that these conditions have become so acute as to require the listing of available lodging for Negroes in a special guidebook which was itself "dramatic testimony to the difficulties" Negroes encounter in travel. These exclusionary practices were found to be nationwide, the Under Secretary of Commerce testifying that there is "no question that this discrimination in the North still exists to a large degree" and in the West and Midwest as well. This testimony indicated a qualitative as well as quantitative effect on interstate travel by Negroes. The former was the obvious impairment of the Negro traveler's pleasure and convenience that resulted when he continually was uncertain of finding lodging. As for the latter, there was evidence that this uncertainty stemming from racial discrimination had the effect of discouraging travel on the part of a substantial portion of the Negro community. This was the conclusion not only of the Under Secretary of Commerce but also of the Administrator of the Federal Aviation Agency, who wrote the Chairman of the Senate Commerce Committee that it was his "belief that air commerce is adversely affected by the denial to a substantial segment of the traveling public of adequate and desegregated public accommodations." We shall not burden this opinion with further details since the voluminous testimony presents overwhelming evidence that discrimination by hotels and motels impedes interstate travel.

7. The Power of Congress over Interstate Travel

The power of Congress to deal with these obstructions depends on the meaning of the Commerce Clause.

* * * * *

In short, the determinative test of the exercise of power by the Congress under the Commerce Clause is simply whether the activity sought to be regulated is "commerce which concerns more States than one" and has a real and substantial relation to the national interest. Let us now turn to this facet of the problem.

* * * * *

The same interest in protecting interstate commerce which led Congress to deal with segregation in interstate carriers and the white-slave traffic has prompted it to extend the exercise of its power to gambling, to criminal enterprises, to deceptive practices in the sale of products, to fraudulent security transactions, and to racial discrimination by owners and managers of terminal restaurants . . .

That Congress was legislating against moral wrongs in many of these areas rendered its enactments no less valid. In framing Title II of this act Congress was also dealing with what it considered a moral problem. But that fact does not detract from the overwhelming evidence of the disruptive effect that racial discrimination has had on commercial intercourse. It was this burden which empowered Congress to enact appropriate legislation, and, given this basis for the exercise of its power, Congress was not restricted by the fact that the particular obstruction to interstate commerce with which it was dealing was also deemed a moral and social wrong.

It is said that the operation of the motel here is of a purely local character. But, assuming this to be true, "[i]f it is interstate commerce that feels the pinch, it does not matter how local the operation which applies the squeeze."

* * * * *

Thus the power of Congress to promote interstate commerce also includes the power to regulate the local incidents thereof, including local activities in both the states of origin and destination, which might have a substantial and harmful effect upon that commerce. One need only examine the evidence which we have discussed above to see that Congress may—as it has—prohibit racial discrimination by motels serving travelers, however "local" their operations may appear.

Nor does the act deprive appellant of liberty or property under the Fifth Amendment. The commerce power invoked here by the Congress is a specific and plenary one authorized by the Constitution itself. The only questions are: (1) whether Congress had a rational basis for finding that racial discrimination by motels affected commerce, and (2) if it had such a basis, whether the means it selected to eliminate that evil are reasonable and appropriate. If they are, appellant has no "right" to select its guests as it sees fit, free from governmental regulation.

There is nothing novel about such legislation. Thirty-two states now have it on their books either by statute or executive order and many cities provide such regulation. Some of these acts go back four-score years. It has been repeatedly held by this Court that such laws do not violate the Due Process Clause of the Fourteenth Amendment.

* * * * *

It is doubtful if in the long run appellant will suffer economic loss as a result of the act. Experience is to the contrary where discrimination is completely obliterated as to all public accommodations. But whether this be true or not is of no consequence since this Court has specifically held that the fact that a "member of the class which is regulated may suffer economic losses not shared by others . . . has never been a barrier" to such legislation . . . Likewise in a long line of cases this Court has rejected the claim that the prohibition of racial discrimination in public accommodations interferes with personal liberty . . . Neither do we find any merit in the claim that the act is a taking of property without just compensation. The cases are to the contrary . . .

We find no merit in the remainder of the appellant's contentions including that of "involuntary servitude." . . . We could not say that the requirements of the act in this regard are in any way "akin to African slavery." . . .

We, therefore, conclude that the action of the Congress in the adoption of the act as applied here to a motel which concededly serves interstate travelers is within the power granted it by the Commerce Clause of the Constitution, as interpreted by this Court for 140 years . . .

Affirmed.

Questions

1. In your judgment, does the Commerce Clause afford the federal government the authority to regulate a local business like the Heart of Atlanta motel? Explain.
2. Should the federal government regulate local business to further the cause of racial equity? Explain.
3. What arguments were offered by the government to establish that the Heart of Atlanta racial policy affected interstate commerce? Are you persuaded by those arguments? Explain.
4. Explain the Fifth and Thirteenth Amendment arguments raised in *Heart of Atlanta.*
5. What test did the Court articulate to determine when Congress has the power to pass legislation based on the Commerce Clause?
6. Ollie's Barbecue, a neighborhood restaurant in Birmingham, Alabama, discriminated against black customers. McClung brought suit to test the application of the public accommodations section of the Civil Rights Act of 1964 to his restaurant. In the suit, the government offered no evidence to show that the restaurant ever had served interstate customers or that it was likely to do so. Decide the case. See *Katzenbach* v. *McClung,* 379 U.S. 294 (1964).
7. May a private club lawfully decline to serve liquor to a black person who is accompanying a white person to the club bar? Build the argument that the club is not "private" as a matter of law. See *Moose Lodge No. 107* v. *Irvis,* 407 U.S. 163 (1972).
8. What economic consequences would you project from a judicial decision permitting Congress to regulate public accommodations clearly interstate in character, while leaving more preponderantly local public accommodations to the regulation of state and local governments?

STATE AND LOCAL REGULATION OF INTERSTATE COMMERCE

As noted, the states via their constitutional police power have the authority to regulate commerce within their jurisdictions for the purpose of maintaining the general welfare. That is, in order to assist in maintaining the public health, safety, and morals, states must be able to control persons and property within their jurisdictional authority. However, we have seen that the Commerce Clause, as interpreted, accords the federal government broad authority over commerce. As explained, the federal government has exclusive authority over foreign commerce. Purely intrastate commerce, having no significant effect on interstate commerce, is within the exclusive regulatory jurisdiction of the states. Of course, commerce purely intrastate in nature is quite rare. The confusion arises in the middle ground of interstate commerce where regulation by the federal government or state governments or both may be permissible. While federal government regulation of interstate commerce is pervasive, it is not exclusive. In broad terms, states may regulate interstate commerce where all of these conditions obtain:

1. The commerce being regulated does not require uniform, consistent treatment throughout the nation.

2. Congress has not preempted the area by its own complete regulation.
3. The state regulation does not discriminate against interstate commerce in favor of state interests.
4. The state regulation is not an undue burden on commerce.
5. The state regulation is not in conflict with federal law.

In the *Chemical Waste Management* case that follows, we see how the Supreme Court dealt with a conflict between state waste disposal laws and the general interest in the smooth flow of interstate commerce.

CHEMICAL WASTE MANAGEMENT v. GUY HUNT [Governor of Alabama]
112 S.Ct. 2009 (1992)

Justice White

Alabama imposes a hazardous waste disposal fee on hazardous wastes generated outside the State and disposed of at a commercial facility in Alabama. The fee does not apply to such waste having a source in Alabama. The Alabama Supreme Court held that this differential treatment does not violate the Commerce Clause. We reverse.

I

Petitioner, Chemical Waste Management, Inc., a Delaware corporation with its principal place of business in Oak Brook, Illinois, owns and operates one of the Nation's oldest commercial hazardous waste land disposal facilities, located in Emelle, Alabama. Opened in 1977 and acquired by petitioner in 1978, the Emelle facility is a hazardous waste treatment, storage, and disposal facility operating pursuant to permits issued by the Environmental Protection Agency (EPA). Alabama is 1 of only 16 States that have commercial hazardous waste landfills, and the Emelle facility is the largest of the 21 landfills of this kind located in these 16 States.

The parties do not dispute that the wastes and substances being landfilled at the Emelle facility "include substances that are inherently dangerous to human health and safety and to the environment. Such waste consists of ignitable, corrosive, toxic and reactive wastes which contain poisonous and cancer causing chemicals and which can cause birth defects, genetic damage, blindness, crippling and death." Increasing amounts of out-of-state hazardous wastes are shipped to the Emelle facility for permanent storage each year. From 1985 through 1989, the tonnage of hazardous waste received per year has more than doubled, increasing from 341,000 tons in 1985 to 788,000 tons by 1989. Of this, up to 90% of the tonnage permanently buried each year is shipped in from other States.

Against this backdrop Alabama enacted Act No. 90-326 (the Act). Among other provisions, the Act includes a "cap" that generally limits the amount of hazardous wastes or substances that may be disposed of in any 1-year period, and the amount of hazardous waste disposed of during the first year under the Act's new fees becomes the permanent ceiling in subsequent years. The cap applies to commercial facilities that dispose of over 100,000 tons of hazardous wastes or substances per year, but only the Emelle facility, as the only commercial facility operating within Alabama, meets this description. The Act also imposes a "base fee" of $25.60 per ton on all hazardous wastes and substances disposed of at commercial facilities, to be paid by the operator of the facility. Finally, the Act imposes the "additional fee" at issue here, which states in full:

> For waste and substances which are generated outside of Alabama and disposed of at a commercial site for the disposal of hazardous waste or hazardous substances in Alabama, an additional fee shall be levied at the rate of $72.00 per ton.

. . . In addition to state law claims, petitioner contended that the Act violated the Commerce, Due Process, and Equal Protection Clauses of the United States Constitution, and was preempted by various federal statutes. The Trial Court declared the base fee and the cap provisions of the Act to be valid and constitutional; but, finding the only basis for the additional fee to be the origin of the waste, the Trial Court declared it to be in violation of the Commerce Clause. Both sides appealed. The Alabama Supreme Court affirmed the rulings concerning the base fee and cap provisions but reversed the decision regarding the additional fee. The court held that the fee at issue advanced legitimate local purposes that could not be adequately served by reasonable nondiscriminatory alternatives and was therefore valid under the Commerce Clause.

. . . [W]e granted certiorari limited to petitioner's Commerce Clause challenge to the additional fee. We now reverse.

II

No State may attempt to isolate itself from a problem common to the several States by raising barriers to the free flow of interstate trade . . . [I]n *Philadelphia* v *New Jersey,* 37 U.S. 617 (1978), we found New Jersey's prohibition of solid waste from outside that State to amount to economic protectionism barred by the Commerce Clause:

> [T]he evil of protectionism can reside in legislative means as well as legislative ends. Thus, it does not matter whether the ultimate aim is to reduce the waste disposal costs of New Jersey residents or to save remaining open lands from pollution, for we assume New Jersey has every right to protect its residents' pocketbooks as well as their environment. And it may be assumed as well that New Jersey may pursue those ends by slowing the flow of *all* waste into the State's remaining landfills, even though interstate commerce may incidentally be affected. But whatever New Jersey's ultimate purpose, it may not be accompanied by discriminating against articles of commerce coming from outside the State unless there is some reason, apart from their origin, to treat them differently.
>
> The Court has consistently found parochial legislation of this kind to be constitutionally invalid, whether the ultimate aim of the legislation was to assure a steady supply of milk by erecting barriers to allegedly ruinous outside competition, or to create jobs by keeping industry within the State, or to preserve the State's financial resources from depletion by fencing out indigent immigrants.

To this list may be added cases striking down a tax discriminating against interstate commerce, even where such tax was designed to encourage the use of ethanol and thereby reduce harmful exhaust emissions, or to support inspection of foreign cement to ensure structural integrity. For in all of these cases, "a presumably legitimate goal was sought to be achieved by the illegitimate means of isolating the State from the national economy."

The Act's additional fee facially discriminates against hazardous waste generated in States other than Alabama, and the Act overall has plainly discouraged the full operation of petitioner's Emelle facility. Such burdensome taxes imposed on interstate commerce alone are generally forbidden: "[A] State may not tax a transaction or incident more heavily when it crosses state lines than when it occurs entirely within the State." Once a state tax is found to discriminate against out-of-state commerce, it is typically struck down without further inquiry.

The State, however, argues that the additional fee imposed on out-of-state hazardous waste serves legitimate local purposes related to its citizens' health and safety. Because the additional fee discriminates both on its face and in practical effect, the burden falls on the State "to justify it both in terms of the local benefits flowing from the statute and the unavailability of nondiscriminatory alternatives adequate to preserve the local interests at stake." . . .

The State's argument here does not significantly differ from the Alabama Supreme Court's conclusions on the legitimate local purposes of the additional fee imposed, which were:

> The Additional Fee serves these legitimate local purposes that cannot be adequately served by reasonable nondiscriminatory alternatives: (1) protection of the health and safety of the citizens of Alabama from toxic substances; (2) conservation of the environment and the state's natural resources; (3) provision for compensatory revenue for the costs and burdens that out-of-state waste generators impose by dumping their hazardous waste in Alabama; (4) reduction of the overall flow of wastes traveling on the state's highways, which flow creates a great risk to the health and safety of the state's citizens.

These may all be legitimate local interests, and petitioner has not attacked them. But only rhetoric, and not explanation, emerges as to why Alabama targets *only* interstate hazardous waste to meet these goals. As found by the Trial Court, "[a]lthough the Legislature imposed an additional fee of $72.00 per ton on waste generated outside Alabama, there is absolutely no evidence before this Court that waste generated outside Alabama is more dangerous than waste generated in Alabama. The Court finds under the facts of this case that the only basis for the additional fee is the origin of the waste." In the face of such findings, invalidity under the Commerce Clause necessarily follows, for "whatever [Alabama's] ultimate purpose, it may not be accomplished by discriminating against articles of commerce coming from outside the State unless there is some reason, apart from their origin, to treat them differently."

Ultimately, the State's concern focuses on the volume of the waste entering the Emelle facility. Less discriminatory alternatives, however, are available to alleviate this concern, not the least of which are a generally applicable per-ton additional fee on *all* hazardous waste disposed of within Alabama, or a per-mile tax on *all* vehicles transporting hazardous waste across Alabama roads, or an evenhanded cap on the total tonnage landfilled at Emelle, which would curtail volume from all sources. To the extent Alabama's concern touches environmental conservation and the health and safety of its citizens, such concern does not vary with the point of origin of the waste, and it remains within the State's power to monitor and regulate more closely the transportation and disposal of *all* hazardous waste within its borders. Even with the possible future financial and environmental risks to be borne by

Alabama, such risks likewise do not vary with the waste's State of origin in a way allowing foreign, but not local, waste to be burdened. In sum, we find the additional fee to be "an obvious effort to saddle those outside the State" with most of the burden of slowing the flow of waste into the Emelle facility. "That legislative effort is clearly impermissible under the Commerce Clause of the Constitution."

[Reversed.]

Questions

1. Why did the Supreme Court strike down the Alabama statute?
2. Oregon imposed an $.85 per ton surcharge on the disposal of solid waste generated within the state and a $2.50 per ton charge for solid waste generated in other states. The Oregon plan was challenged as a violation of the Commerce Clause.
   a. Explain the plaintiff's argument.
   b. Defend the Oregon approach. (Reference to the *Chemical Waste* decision will be helpful here.)
   c. Decide. Explain. See *Oregon Waste Systems* v. *Department of Environmental Quality of the State of Oregon,* 62 *Law Week* 4209 (1994).
3. *a.* What were Alabama's stated reasons for enacting this statute?
   b. Why were those reasons insufficient to meet constitutional standards?
   c. What other reason(s) might have motivated the Alabama statute?
4. An Indiana statute prohibited the practice of backhauling municipal waste. Indiana was trying to prevent truckers from hauling trash on the homeward bound leg of a trip after having delivered other goods on the outbound leg. On its face, the statute applied evenly to intrastate and interstate carriers. Most in-state waste is hauled in "dedicated" garbage trucks (those used exclusively for garbage). The Indiana statute was challenged by two companies engaged in brokering waste disposal.
   a. What constitutional challenge was raised by the plaintiffs?
   b. What defense is raised by Indiana?
   c. Decide. See *Government Suppliers Consolidating Services and Jack Castenova* v. *Evan Bayh and Kathy Prosser,* 975 F.2d 1267 (1992); cert. den., 113 S.Ct. 977 (1993).
5. North Dakota rules require those bringing liquor into the state to file a monthly report, and out-of-state distillers selling to federal enclaves (military bases, in this instance) must label each item indicating that it is for consumption only within the enclave. The United States challenged those rules after sellers said they would discontinue dealing with the military bases or they would raise their prices in order to meet the cost of dealing with the two rules.
   a. What are the constitutional foundations of the federal government's challenge?
   b. What were the state's reasons for adopting the rules?
   c. Decide. Explain. See *North Dakota* v. *United States,* 495 U.S. 423 (1990).
6. During the 1973 gasoline shortage, Maryland gasoline stations operated by producers or refiners had received, according to a state government survey, preferential treatment over "independent" dealers in obtaining supplies of gasoline. Thereafter, a statute was enacted providing "a producer or refiner of petroleum products (1) may not operate any retail service station within the state, and (2) must extend all 'voluntary allowances' uniformly to all service stations it supplies." Exxon challenged the statute.
   a. What is the essence of Exxon's claim?
   b. Decide the case. See *Exxon Corp.* v. *Governor of Maryland,* 98 S. Ct. 2207 (1978).

7. In the interest of safety, an Illinois statute required rear fender mudguards of a special contoured design on trucks using Illinois roadways. The required design was not typical of that in use in the industry and possessed no clearly established safety advantage. Was the statute constitutional? See *Bibb* v. *Navajo Freight Lines, Inc.,* 359 U.S. 520 (1959).

8. A New York state statute prohibited the export of milk produced in the state to other states. New York argued that the statute was necessary to avoid milk shortages. Is the statute constitutional? See *H. P. Hood & Sons* v. *DuMond,* 336 U.S. 525 (1949).

The States in "Combat"

As we have seen, our careful constitutional balancing act between the federal, state, and local governments is not free of problems. Each governmental unit is in constant competition for scarce economic resources even as each tries to look out for the human needs of its citizens. As a consequence, states and localities routinely erect trade barriers to protect their own interests while burdening commerce from other states and localities. For example, "one study found more than 1,500 agricultural restrictions on interstate trade in 11 western states alone."[8] Since 1967, the sale of Florida grapefruit has been banned in Texas. Licensing and certification procedures for professionals (e.g., lawyers, doctors, and teachers) restricts the mobility of their labor from state to state such that, in the case of dentists, one study found their incomes 12 percent higher than would have been the case in a genuine free market.[9] Some of that protectionism has been swept away by the courts, but much remains. And arguably much needs to remain because, under their constitutionally granted police power, the state governments have the authority and the responsibility to protect the welfare of their citizens.

EUROPEAN COMMUNITY—ONE MARKET?

INTERNATIONAL

We are seeing played out around the world an important economic and political parallel to the continuing effort of the United States to balance federal and states' rights. With the former Soviet Union ripped apart and further fissures threatening, with the former Yugoslavia in warring pieces, with even California contemplating dividing itself into three states, the difficulties in maintaining a unified nation that nonetheless allows freedom for its parts (as we have done so successfully) is apparent. The material that follows demonstrates the efforts of the European Community [The European Community consists of 12 nations—Belgium, Britain, Denmark, France, Germany, Greece, Ireland, Italy, Luxembourg, the Netherlands, Portugal, and Spain. At this writing in 1994, Sweden, Finland, Norway, and Austria have been approved for membership and will join the EC if supported by forthcoming referenda in those four countries.] to achieve its economic goal of one market as a step toward its political goal of one nation. The tractor illustration is suggestive of the regulations that inhibited trade between the European nations. The "Barriers Slowly Fall" article summarizes the progress the Europeans have made toward an open market more like what we have known in the United States over the years.

Tractor Regulations in Europe

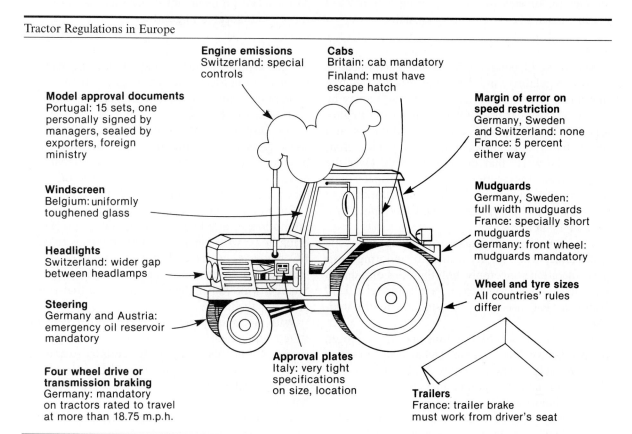

Engine emissions
Switzerland: special controls

Cabs
Britain: cab mandatory
Finland: must have escape hatch

Model approval documents
Portugal: 15 sets, one personally signed by managers, sealed by exporters, foreign ministry

Margin of error on speed restriction
Germany, Sweden and Switzerland: none
France: 5 percent either way

Windscreen
Belgium: uniformly toughened glass

Mudguards
Germany, Sweden: full width mudguards
France: specially short mudguards
Germany: front wheel: mudguards mandatory

Headlights
Switzerland: wider gap between headlamps

Wheel and tyre sizes
All countries' rules differ

Steering
Germany and Austria: emergency oil reservoir mandatory

Approval plates
Italy: very tight specifications on size, location

Four wheel drive or transmission braking
Germany: mandatory on tractors rated to travel at more than 18.75 m.p.h.

Trailers
France: trailer brake must work from driver's seat

Source: *The Financial Times*, June 1988.

INTERNATIONAL

ACROSS THE EC, THE BARRIERS SLOWLY FALL; NATIONAL INTERESTS CLASH WITH SINGLE-MARKET GOAL

Patrick Oster

For the last several years, Bernard DuBois has wasted half an hour each time he crossed the Belgian-French border here with his truckloads of bottled gas. He had to present his passport, then stop at the steel-and-glass French customs building to process a multipage document and hand over a sample of his hazardous cargo.

He isn't stopping now.

The customs office in this French village and the booths of suspicious passport checkers have all been closed as the 12-nation European Community takes another major step toward becoming a borderless market, much like the 50 American states.

* * * * *

Across the Community, the seven-year project to remove regulatory and legal barriers to the free movement of goods, services, people and money by Jan. 1 of this year was supposed to give a mighty forward shove to the continent's economies and boost the profits of countless companies from around the world that do business here. Over the next six years, the creation of a single European market with 345 million consumers was supposed to boost economic growth inside the Community by a total of 4.5 percent.

The improved efficiencies of selling into one Community-wide market instead of tailoring business operations to comply with the rules of a dozen separate nations promised to save companies $270 billion a year, according to estimates in the mid-1980s.

There are winners like DuBois and his employer, the Belgian trucking firm De Dijcker, which now can pick up loads in France or any EC country, a right now controlled by quotas that protect national trucking industries.

But many other businesses are still waiting for the payoff. And some, due to compromises made in constructing the single market, may never get their prize.

The EC has managed to make a dent in nearly all of 282 categories of trade restrictions—like the time-consuming red tape for cross-border trucking. Some of the barriers have been dismantled completely, but others have merely been nudged. As a result, the concept of a single market still remains a goal and not a reality.

* * * * *

The most obvious shortfall was a delay in achieving the goal of unrestricted travel. Residents and visiting foreigners traveling within the Community will still have to present passports at airports until Dec. 1 next year.

In the United Kingdom, Ireland and Denmark, passport and baggage checks may continue even longer at all border posts as those countries deal with special problems involving rabid animals, terrorists and illegal immigrants.

* * * * *

The EC has had more success in removing barriers to the cross-border movement of goods than in lowering barriers for tourists, though there are some embarrassing exceptions.

For example, a 1992 ruling by the EC's highest court gives its countries the right to block cross-border shipments of wastes. And cheap bananas—generally those not coming from former EC colonies—are restricted by quotas and stiff tariffs.

But in a dramatic departure from the past, there are no longer any limits or duties on goods people bring home with them from shopping trips to other EC countries. Cars and trailers are likely to be stuffed with dozens of bottles of French, Italian or Spanish wine rather than the five or so that is now generally the limit.

With prices for electronic goods, clothes, cameras, stereo equipment and other products varying as much as 50 percent from one EC country to another, other cross-border shopping should blossom as Europeans shake off centuries of parochial buying habits.

There is now a new minimum sales tax of 15 percent and similar minimums for levies on alcohol and gasoline. But because of opposition from revenue-pinched EC members, there are no maximum rates. With sales tax rates as high as 25 percent in some places in Europe such as Denmark, the low-tax countries, such as Luxembourg, should remain discount-shopping havens.

* * * * *

Corporate taxes didn't get reformed at all. Rates will continue to vary from 33 percent in the United Kingdom to 57.5 percent in Germany . . .

The EC did establish broad, harmonized safety, health and environmental standards for many products to replace as many as 12 differing national standards. Goods inspected in one EC country now have an EC "passport" authorizing their sale in any other EC nation without further testing. Philips Electronics NV, which used to have to make 12 different television models to satisfy national standards, will now be able to make just one.

Nonetheless, the EC, faced with a demand for 10,000 product standards, did not nearly get them all done. Out of 1,500 "priority" standards, EC officials have finished only 310.

*   *   *   *   *

The list of exceptions, qualifying footnotes and exemptions goes on: While other EC countries ended controls on cross-border transfers of money in 1990, Greece doesn't have to lift them until mid-1994.

Liberalization of the stock brokerage business won't begin until 1996 as a sop to weak stock firms in Italy and France. Because of objections by protected German truckers, trucking firms, such as DuBois' employer, aren't able to operate like domestic firms in other EC countries at all.

Postal, electric and energy services didn't get opened to cross-border competition. Basic and long-distance telephone service didn't either, although sales of some phone equipment and nonbasic services, such as fax mail, did. Common rules on establishing an EC corporation or attempting a hostile takeover don't exist. And there will be no EC trademark because of bickering about which country would get the trademark office.

In addition, a fifth of the approved single-market reforms that need national legislation to become effective still haven't been passed by EC parliaments. Italy, Belgium and Luxembourg are the leading scofflaws. And several laws that have been approved and implemented contain vaguely worded safety-valve clauses that allow EC countries to enact new trade barriers in "the common good."

*   *   *   *   *

Despite the lengthy list of shortcomings and exceptions, just enough has been done to justify calling the EC a "single market" in fact as well as in name . . .

EC airlines established in one country will be able to operate in any other, a prospect that has caused Belgium's ailing Sabena World Airlines to merge with Air France to stay alive in the face of the stiffer competition it now expects.

Banks, stock brokerages and insurance companies have EC "passports" to operate anywhere in the EC once they are chartered by one EC country. Professionals and technicians may work in any EC country once certified anywhere in the EC.

Lucrative government contracts have to be advertised and awarded to the lowest or best bidder rather than to local champions. And common rules for reviewing large mergers and joint ventures for antitrust violations have been in effect for two years.

Source: Patrick Oster, *The Washington Post,* January 3, 1993, p. H1. © 1993 *The Washington Post.* Reprinted with Permission.

Questions

1. On balance, is the EC single market good or bad for American business? Explain.
2. *a.* Can you envision a time when all of the nations of the world are able to agree on the elimination of regulatory barriers to trade such as those illustrated by the example of the tractor in Europe? Explain.
   b. Would you favor that development? Explain.
3. The U.S. Congress has passed laws effectively imposing rather uniform federal standards on a number of areas of business practice, including securities trading, civil rights, and copyrights. Now, businesses are lobbying Congress requesting uniformity in other areas in order to avoid the costs and frustrations of dealing with a patchwork of state laws.

    a. What areas of law might benefit from greater uniformity across the states? Explain.

    b. Make the arguments for and against greater uniformity in those areas. See Edward Felsenthal, "Firms Ask Congress to Pass Uniform Rules," *The Wall Street Journal,* May 10, 1993, p. B5.

SUMMARY OF STATE AND LOCAL REGULATION

The magnitude and visibility of federal regulation of business has obscured our bountiful web of state and local rules. Indeed, as measured by jobs, local government is growing more rapidly than state government and state government is growing more rapidly than the federal government. In May 1992, state and local government employment had reached 4,368,000,[10] a new record, and one that substantially exceeds the federal total of about three million.[11] Of course, part of that growth is attributable to population increase, particularly in Sun Belt states. However:

> By 1988, there were 147 "fulltime equivalent" (FTE) positions in state government for every 10,000 Americans, against only 61 in 1952. At the local level, the comparable figures were 358 versus 195.[12]

We need to remember that this upward spiral, however lamentable in some ways, often springs from our demands for a better life, including improvements in education, health care, infrastructure, and so on. Furthermore, the states and localities serve the important civic purpose of bringing government close to the people. Those governments, as former President Bush reminded us, are "laboratories" of democracy and incubators for new approaches to public problems.

Just as state and local employee rolls have grown, so have the rules that some of those employees enforce. Many of those rules are designed to regulate business behavior. Those regulations fall into three broad categories: (1) controlling entry into business, (2) regulating competition, and (3) preventing consumer fraud.

The states are primarily responsible for regulating the insurance industry and are heavily involved in regulating banking, securities, and liquor sales. Many businesses and professions—from funeral preparations to barbering to the practice of medicine—require a license from the state. Public utilities (e.g., gas, electricity, and sewage disposal) are the subject of extensive regulation governing entry, rates, customer service, and virtually the fullness of the companies' activities. All states have some form of public service commission charged with regulating utilities in the public interest. Many states seek to directly enhance competition via antitrust legislation. Many states have passed laws forbidding usury, false advertising, stock fraud, and other practices harmful to the consumer.

Local regulation is much less economically significant than state regulation. Local government intervention in business typically involves various licensure requirements. For example, businesses like bars and theaters are often required to obtain a local permit to operate. Certain tradespeople (such as plumbers, electricians, and builders) may be required to gain local (and/or state) occupational licensure to legally engage in their craft. Licensure, it is argued, serves to protect the public from unsafe, unhealthy, and substandard goods and services, but critics contend that the presumed benefits of licensure are exceeded by its costs in increased prices, decreased services, and administrative overhead.

The following article summarizes some likely areas of state and local regulatory growth in the mid-1990s. Note that some of these proposals are initiated by legislators, but some come from the business community itself.

SMALL FIRMS LOOK TO STATES FOR NEW APPROACHES TO ISSUES

Barbara Marsh

[S]mall-business groups . . . are pressing state legislatures to take fresh approaches on crucial issues: insurance costs, mandated benefits, regulation, labor and help for minority firms.

State lawmakers, meanwhile, are pushing ahead with their own agendas . . . Here is a summary of their efforts.

Family Leave

States won't let the federal government have the last word on this mandated benefit, causing small businesses to worry about state efforts to extend benefits beyond those stipulated in the recent federal law. That law gives employees of most firms as much as 12 weeks of unpaid leave to care for a child, spouse or parent.

"Now we have a federal law, it's energized the issue," especially in states with existing laws, says Bill Smith, state director of the National Federation of Independent Business in Wisconsin. Small businesses hope to block a Wisconsin measure allowing parents to miss four hours of work a year to attend school events, such as a teacher conference or a sports event.

Meanwhile, small businesses in Massachusetts aim to stop a bill pushed by Democratic state Sen.

Lois Pines, chairman of the Commerce and Labor Committee, to expand mandated leave to companies not covered by federal law. The federal law covers companies with at least 50 employees; the Massachusetts measure would include those with at least 15.

*   *   *   *   *

Workers Compensation

Small businesses are looking for new ways to rein in soaring costs of insurance for workers injured on the job. Such coverage includes medical care, sick pay and legal expenses for victims. In Florida, for instance, where premiums have jumped 72% in five years, small businesses are backing a bill that would provide government lawyers to represent injured victims.

Proponents say the program would eliminate the high fees businesses pay to private personal-injury lawyers, estimated at $120 million statewide last year. It would only cost $8 million annually, they say. If passed, "we won't have attorneys taking questionable cases to court," says William Herrle, NFIB state director.

*   *   *   *   *

Health Insurance

Despite the Clinton administration's pledge to resolve the nation's health-care crisis, states are going ahead with their own proposed solutions.

Small businesses in Georgia back a state proposal there that would make coverage available to everyone able to buy it, proponents say. The plan would guarantee that coverage be renewable, "portable" for workers switching employers and priced the same for everybody in a locale, regardless of sex, age and health status.

* * * * *

Child Labor

Small businesses are trying to reduce the hassles involved in hiring teenagers. In Washington state, which cut the allowable workweek for 16-year-olds and 17-year-olds during the school year to 20 hours from 40 hours, effective July 1, small businesses back legislation to reduce paperwork involving parent and school approvals for hiring teens.

* * * * *

Minority Contractors

More states are weighing programs to help minority-owned and women-owned contractors obtain surety bonds, a requirement of general contractors on public construction work. Surety bonds, typically issued by insurance firms, guarantee that a contractor will complete a project on time and pay subcontractors. Minority-owned and women-owned firms have had difficulty in persuading insurance firms to issue them bonds, say minority-business advocates.

* * * * *

Regulations

The small-business battle against red tape is heating up. In California, small businesses are pushing a plan to create a one-stop state source for all business permits required by state and local agencies.

Source: *The Wall Street Journal,* March 15, 1993, p. B2. Reprinted by permission of *The Wall Street Journal,* © 1993 Dow Jones & Company, Inc. All Rights Reserved Worldwide.

Questions

1. Would you vote for any of the proposals outlined in the preceding article? Explain.
2. As you see it, why are many state and local governments growing so rapidly?
3. In general, do we rely too much on government in the United States? Explain.
4. Two Dallas, Texas, ordinances were challenged in court. One gave the police very broad authority to deny licenses to "adult" businesses such as bookstores. The other, which was directed at prostitution, barred motel owners from renting rooms for fewer than 10 hours.
   a. What challenges would you raise against these ordinances?
   b. How would you rule? Explain. See *FW/PBS Inc.* v. *City of Dallas,* 493 U.S. 215 (1990).
5. The city of Pomona, California, passed an ordinance requiring, among other things, that businesses having on-premises signs in foreign alphabetical characters must devote one-half of the space in those signs to English alphabetical characters. The city took the position that the ordinance was necessary in case of emergencies. The ordinance was challenged in court.
   a. What constitutional challenges would you raise against the ordinance?

      b. How would you rule? Explain. See *Asian American Business Group* v. *Pomona,* 716 F. Supp. 1328 (CD Cal) 1989.

6. The city of Los Angeles, California, recently enacted an ordinance that created a dress code for cab drivers and imposes fines for violations. For example, tank tops and cutoff pants are forbidden. In addition, being rude to passengers can also lead to fines.

      a. By what constitutional authority does Los Angeles instruct cab drivers regarding dress and behavior?

      b. Do you favor the ordinance? Explain.

TAKINGS

At local, state, and federal levels, government bodies have been increasingly willing in recent decades to take private property for public use—a procedure called *eminent domain.* If the state wants to build a road, or a dam, or an airport, for example, a property owner ordinarily cannot stop the *taking* of the required land, assuming a necessary and proper public purpose. However, the Fifth Amendment provides that private property shall not be "taken for public use, without just compensation." Therefore, the government can take the land, but the owner must be paid.

Now, what happens when the government does not *take* the property but rather, under its police power, simply *regulates* it in a manner that deprives that property of some or all of its economic usefulness? For example, without providing *just compensation,* can the state lawfully limit the amount a landlord can charge for rent in an effort to preserve housing for low-income citizens? Or can a state forbid roadside billboards? Or can the government forbid logging in a timber area inhabited by an endangered species—for example, spotted owls? The case that follows demonstrates the recent inclination of the Supreme Court to be more protective of private property interests in such situations than has been the case for several decades.

LUCAS v. SO. CAROLINA COASTAL
112 S. Ct. 2886 (1992)

Justice Scalia

In 1986, petitioner David H. Lucas paid $975,000 for two residential lots on the Isle of Palms in Charleston County, South Carolina, on which he intended to build single-family homes. In 1988, however, the South Carolina Legislature enacted the Beachfront Management Act, which had the direct effect of barring petitioner from erecting any permanent habitable structures on his two parcels. A state trial court found that this prohibition rendered Lucas's parcels "valueless." This case requires us to decide whether the Act's dramatic effect on the economic value of Lucas's lots accomplished a taking of private property under the Fifth and Fourteenth Amendments requiring the payment of "just compensation."

I
A

... In its original form, the South Carolina Act required owners of coastal zone land that qualified as a "critical area" (defined in the legislation to include beaches and immediately adjacent sand dunes) to obtain a permit from the newly created South Carolina Coastal Council (respondent here) prior to committing the land to a "use other than the use the critical area was devoted to on [September 28, 1977]."

In the late 1970's, Lucas and others began extensive residential development of the Isle of Palms, a barrier island situated eastward of the City of Charleston. Toward the close of the development cycle for one residential subdivision known as "Beachwood East," Lucas in 1986 purchased the two lots at issue in this litigation for his own account. No portion of the lots, which were located approximately 300 feet from the beach, qualified as a "critical area" under the 1977 Act; accordingly, at the time Lucas acquired these parcels, he was not legally obliged to obtain a permit from the Council in advance of any development activity. His intention with respect to the lots was to do what the owners of the immediately adjacent parcels had already done: erect single-family residences. He commissioned architectural drawings for this purpose.

The Beachfront Management Act brought Lucas's plans to an abrupt end. Under that 1988 legislation, the Council was directed to establish a "baseline" [from the beach.] [Land between the baseline and the beach could not be developed. Lucas's lots lay between the line and the beach.]

B

Lucas promptly filed suit in the South Carolina Court of Common Pleas, contending that the Beachfront Management Act's construction bar effected a taking of his property without just compensation. Lucas did not take issue with the validity of the Act as a lawful exercise of South Carolina's police power, but contended that the Act's complete extinguishment of his property's value entitled him to compensation regardless of whether the legislature had acted in furtherance of legitimate police power objectives. Following a bench trial, the court agreed. Among its factual determinations was the finding that "at the time Lucas purchased the two lots, both were zoned for singlefamily residential construction and ... there were no restrictions imposed upon such use of the property by either the State of South Carolina, the County of Charleston, or the Town of the Isle of Palms." The trial court further found that the Beachfront Management Act decreed a permanent ban on construction insofar as Lucas's lots were concerned, and that this prohibition "deprive[d] Lucas of any reasonable economic use of the lots, ... eliminated the unrestricted right of use, and render[ed] them valueless." The court thus concluded that Lucas's properties had been "taken" by operation of the Act, and it ordered respondent to pay "just compensation" in the amount of $1,232,387.50.

The Supreme Court of South Carolina reversed. It found dispositive what it described as Lucas's concession "that the Beachfront Management Act [was] properly and validly designed to preserve ... South Carolina's beaches." Failing an attack on the validity of the statute as such, the court believed itself bound to accept the "uncontested . . . findings" of the South Carolina legislature that new construction in the coastal zone—such as petitioner intended—threatened this public resource. The Court ruled that when a regulation respecting the use of property is designed "to prevent serious public harm," no compensation is owing under the Takings Clause regardless of the regulation's effect on the property's value.

* * * * *

We granted certiorari.

[Part II omitted.]

III

A

Prior to Justice Holmes' exposition in *Pennsylvania Coal Co.* v *Mahon,* [it was] generally thought that the Takings Clause reached only a "direct appropriation" of property, or the functional equivalent of a "practical ouster of [the owner's] possession." Justice Holmes recognized in Mahon, however, that if the protection against physical appropriations of private property was to be meaningfully enforced, the government's power to redefine the range of interests included in the ownership of property was necessarily constrained by constitutional limits [and] . . . while property may be regulated to a certain extent, if regulation goes too far it will be recognized as a taking."

. . . In 70-odd years of succeeding "regulatory takings" jurisprudence, we have generally eschewed any "'set formula'" for determining how far is too far. . . . We have, however, described at least two discrete categories of regulatory action as compensable without case-specific inquiry into the public interest advanced in support of the restraint. The first encompasses regulations that compel the property owner to suffer a physical "invasion" of his property. In general (at least with regard to permanent invasions), no matter how minute the intrusion, and no matter how weighty the public purpose behind it, we have required compensation . . .

The second situation in which we have found categorical treatment appropriate is where regulation denies all economically beneficial or productive use of land.

* * * * *

We have never set forth the justification for this rule. Perhaps it is simply, as Justice Brennan suggested, that total deprivation of beneficial use is, from the landowner's point of view, the equivalent of a physical appropriation . . .

* * * * *

We think, in short, that there are good reasons for our frequently expressed belief that when the owner of real property has been called upon to sacrifice *all* economically beneficial uses in the name of the common good, that is, to leave his property economically idle, he has suffered a taking.

B

The trial court found Lucas's two beachfront lots to have been rendered valueless by respondent's enforcement of the coastal-zone construction ban.

* * * * *

It is correct that many of our prior opinions have suggested that "harmful or noxious uses" of property may be proscribed by government regulation without the requirement of compensation. For a number of reasons, however, we think the South Carolina Supreme Court was too quick to conclude that that principle decides the present case.

* * * * *

Where the State seeks to sustain regulation that deprives land of all economically beneficial use, we think it may resist compensation only if . . . the nature of the owner's [legal title] shows that the [forbidden use was] not part of his title to begin with.

* * * * *

Where "permanent physical occupation" of land is concerned, we have refused to allow the government to decree it anew (without compensation), no matter how weighty the asserted "public interests" involved—though we assuredly would permit the government to assert a permanent easement that was a pre-existing limitation upon the landowner's title. We believe similar treatment must be accorded confiscatory regulations, i.e., regulations that prohibit all economically beneficial use of land: Any limitation so severe cannot be newly legislated or decreed (without compensation), but must inhere in the title itself, in the restrictions that background principles of the State's law of property and nuisance already place upon land ownership . . .

On this analysis, the owner of a lake bed, for example, would not be entitled to compensation when he is denied the requisite permit to engage in a landfilling operation that would have the effect of flooding others' land. Nor the corporate owner of a nuclear generating plant, when it is directed to remove all improvements from its land upon discovery that the plant sits astride an earthquake fault. Such regulatory action may well have the effect of eliminating the land's only economically productive use, but it does not proscribe a productive use that was previously permissible under relevant property and nuisance principles . . .

The "total taking" inquiry we require today will ordinarily entail analysis of, among other things, the degree of harm to public lands and resources, or adjacent private property, posed by the claimant's proposed activities, the social value of the claimant's activities and their suitability to the locality in question, and the relative ease with which the alleged harm can be avoided through measures taken by the claimant and the government (or adjacent private landowners) alike. The fact that a particular use has long been engaged in by similarly situated owners ordinarily imports a lack of any common-law prohibition (though changed circumstances or new knowledge may make what was previously permissible no longer so). So also does the fact that other landowners, similarly situated, are permitted to continue the use denied to the claimant.

It seems unlikely that common-law principles would have prevented the erection of any habitable or productive improvements on petitioner's land . . . The question, however, is one of state law to be dealt with on remand. We emphasize that to win its case South Carolina must do more than proffer the legislature's declaration that the uses Lucas desires are inconsistent with the public interest . . . Instead, as it would be required to do if it sought to restrain Lucas in a common-law action for public nuisance, South Carolina must identify background principles of nuisance and property law that prohibit the uses he now intends in the circumstances in which the property is presently found. Only on this showing can the State fairly claim that, in proscribing all such beneficial uses, the Beachfront Management Act is taking nothing.

* * * * *

[Reversed and remanded.]

Afterword

Following the Supreme Court decision, South Carolina paid Lucas $425,000 for each lot, as well as $725,000 for interest, attorney's fees, and costs, and then took over the property, which was placed on the market for sale.

Questions

1. Summarize the Court's holding.
2. Does this decision settle cases where the property in question can still be put to economic use but at a lower rate of return than in the absence of the regulation? Explain.
3. The Court specified a pair of exceptions to its general rule. Explain them.
4. Marilyn and James Nollan applied for a permit to replace their beachfront home with a larger structure. The California Coastal Commission agreed on the condition that the Nollans grant an easement on their beach that would allow the public to cross that property and thus facilitate movement between the public beaches that lay on both sides of the Nollan beach. The Nollans sued, claiming a violation of the Takings Clause. Decide. Explain. See *Nollan* v. *California Coastal Commission,* 483 U.S. 825 (1987).
5. Alarmed by a decline in low-rent housing, New York City passed a law placing a moratorium on the conversion or demolition of hotels and "single-room occupancy" buildings while requiring owners to rehabilitate those properties so that each unit was habitable. The idea was to involve developers in the effort to increase housing for the aged, ill, and poor. Property owners sued, contending the law constituted an unlawful taking in violation of the Fifth Amendment. Decide. Explain. See *Seawall Associates* v. *City of New York,* 542 N.E.2d 1059 (1989), 492 U.S. 935 (1989).

TOO MUCH REGULATION?

The dominant public policy debate of the 1980s and 1990s has been the question of how much government we need in America. We have seen that state and local governments, in particular, have expanded rapidly and are imposing or seeking to impose a wide array of new rules on the business community. Our natural and perhaps correct reaction is to call for a reduction in government intervention. However, we need a balanced view of that critical issue. The article that follows serves as a reminder that, in general at least, government rules seek to address real problems with effective remedies.

A GOVERNMENT SUCCESS STORY:
LIVES SAVED ON NATION'S HIGHWAYS

Joan Claybrook

One of the most rewarding aspects of the effort expended on legislative battles is seeing the payoff from bills successfully enacted. In highway safety, both federal and state legislators can take credit for a number of smashing success stories. And they are important to Americans all over the country whose loved ones are surviving highway crashes rather than suffering fatal or crippling injuries by the tens of thousands each year.

* * * * *

When Congress created NHTSA [the National Highway Traffic Safety Administration] it recognized both the traditional functions of the states in regulating drivers and highway design and the newer precepts that the design and performance of the vehicle are critical in saving lives.

As required by the 1966 law, NHTSA set standards to measure state achievements under newly authorized grant-in-aid programs.

Proven Life-Savers

Over the past 20 years, the efficacy, the cost effectiveness, and the rigor of NHTSA standards and guidelines have been challenged, researched, reviewed, and amended. In some cases, new legislation has been enacted. This process has resulted in a series of programs that are saving thousands of lives and mitigating tens of thousands of injuries per year.

Those with the highest payoff are:

• **55-Mile-per-Hour (MPH) Speed Limit.** Enacted in 1973 to conserve energy, this law saved an estimated 25,000 to 50,000 lives in its first decade. The National Academy of Sciences has estimated that the lower speed limit prevents 2,500 to 4,500 serious, severe, and critical injuries and 34,000 to 61,000 minor and moderate injuries annually. The Academy's

Transportation Research Board declared, "Few safety policies can rival the impact of the 55-MPH speed limit in reducing accidental deaths of Americans as they travel about the country. In addition, this law results in the saving of approximately 60 million barrels of petroleum each year, or about 1 percent of the total U.S. consumption." Despite these incredible savings over the past 14 years, these laws continue to be challenged by individuals who argue that saving a few minutes of travel time is more important than saving lives and reducing crippling injuries on the highway. [Speed limits may now be raised to 65 MPH on rural interstates.]

* * * * *

• **Child Restraints.** Nearly 50 percent of all children age four or younger are now protected by special car seats or other safety restraints, compared to less than 5 percent in 1974. The payoff has been significant. Nearly 200 children up to four years old were saved by child restraints (158 lives) or lap belts (34 lives) in 1984. This dramatic change occurred because every state requires use of child restraints by law. Tennessee enacted the first child restraint law in 1977 under pressure from pediatricians . . . [P]romotion of the concept throughout the country by NHTSA culminated in adoption of similar laws in most states by 1983.

• **Age 21 for Drinking.** In 1970, many states dropped their drinking age from 21 to 18, rationalizing that those old enough to be drafted and vote should be able to drink legally. However, extensive research showed that age 21 for drinking would prevent hundreds of teenage highway deaths each year. Driving while alcohol impaired is the leading cause of death for young adults aged 16–24. In 14 states that raised their legal drinking age to 21, nighttime highway fatalities among youths under 21 declined by a total of 380 per year. If the higher drinking age were adopted in all states, an estimated additional 600 young people per year might be saved nationwide. [All states have now adopted the 21 standard rather than face the threat of losing federal highway aid.]

Crash Safety—Lap Belts to Air Bags

The more than 50 standards for motor vehicle safety performance issued since the federal government began doing so in 1967 have significantly reduced highway deaths and injury. Vehicle manufacturers routinely oppose new standards as too onerous or costly. When the first safety standards were proposed in 1966, Henry Ford II furiously objected to this government intrusion into the decision-making prerogatives of the manufacturers. He protested, "Many of the temporary standards are unreasonable, arbitrary, and technically unfeasible . . . If we can't meet them when they are published, we'll have to close down."

Many motor vehicle standards have been delayed, indefinitely postponed, or cut back by industry lobbying. Despite these setbacks to safety protection in cars, very significant improvements have been adopted.

The standards require improved padding and the removal of sharp edges and knobs, installation of lap and shoulder restraints, improved door locks, side-impact protection devices, crashworthy fuel tanks, head restraints, collapsible steering assemblies, and, most recently, automatic restraint systems (air bags or automatic seat belts).

NHTSA estimates that the crash safety standards have saved over 100,000 Americans from being killed on the highway since 1968, a proud record indeed. The number of injuries mitigated are in the many hundreds of thousands.

Under the Department of Transportation standard, automatic restraints are now being installed in 10 percent of all new cars . . . NHTSA estimates that this standard will save between 6,000 and 9,000 lives and reduce 150,000 injuries per year when the automatic systems are installed in all cars. Other standards are under consideration for pedestrian protection, for side-impact protection, and extension of the car standards to vans and light trucks, which will save hundreds of additional lives per year.

In short, the highway and auto safety programs are something to boast about in an era when the effectiveness of government programs is questioned and ridiculed.

Source: Joan Claybrook, "A Government Success Story: Lives Saved on Nation's Highways," State Government News, April 1987, pp. 8–9. © 1987 The Council of State Governments. Reprinted with permission from State Government News.

CASES FOR DISCUSSION

Having taken an introductory look at government regulation of business, we turn now to a pair of "real-life" situations where new rules have been imposed. Your task is to evaluate these situations and make a judgment: Was the government wise to intervene?

1. Motorcycle Helmets

Most states require the use of motorcycle helmets, and federal highway laws impose a financial penalty on states that don't have helmet rules. Consider the competing arguments.

MOTORCYCLE HELMET LAWS
HELP PROTECT EVERYBODY

Our View: Laws Requiring Motorcyclists to Wear Helmets Make Sense—for Riders and Taxpayers

The motorcycle helmet controversy is on the road again in California.

It revved up . . . when a new law ordered all motorcyclists—youths and adults—to wear helmets.

Outraged cyclists scrambled to revive the national debate on this travel-weary topic. But they haven't realized—or won't acknowledge—that the dialogue shifted long ago from personal freedom to public responsibility.

Wayne Thomas of the California Motorcyclist Association argues against helmet laws by citing lower accident and death rates in the three states without such laws—Colorado, Illinois and Iowa. He says those rates indicate that helmets reduce cyclists' caution and actually restrict their driving ability.

More persuasive arguments appear on the other side of the debate.

Of 474 motorcycle-accident victims treated during almost four years in Orange County, Calif., only six of the 20 who died wore helmets—just one from a head injury. The 238 wearing helmets had no serious neck injuries, had fewer and less-serious head injur-

ies, spent less time on respirators and suffered less permanent physical and mental damage.

And their hospital bills averaged $16,000, compared to $30,000 for those who crashed without helmets.

When cyclists who don't wear helmets run up hospital bills almost twice as costly as those of riders with helmets, everyone's insurance costs go up.

That—not death rates—may have been the most telling consideration for the 22 states that make minors wear helmets and the 24, plus the District of Columbia, that mandate them for all riders.

Add other factors—disability and unemployment payments, rehabilitation costs—and states with helmet laws have 43% lower societal costs from motorcycle accidents, says California Assemblyman Richard Floyd's office.

That takes the issue far beyond whether motorcyclists should be protected from themselves.

With soaring costs driving even basic health care beyond many families' reach, it's time for cyclists to give this road show rerun a rest.

Source: Editorial, *USA Today,* January 3, 1992, p. 10A. Copyright 1992, *USA Today.* Reprinted with permission.

THESE LAWS MOCK FREEDOM

Paul Lax

Opposing View: Mandatory Helmet Laws Don't Work and Are a Precedent for Taking Away Other Freedoms

Last March, I was in Sacramento lobbying against the proposed California helmet law. A large yellow bow was tied around the Capitol dome and Gov.

Pete Wilson made a speech about the debt we all owed to those fighting against Iraq for the cause of freedom. Freedom. The word trips effortlessly from the lips of politicians, but lip service is all it got in California.

What's wrong with helmet laws? One, they don't work. Two, they destroy individual freedom.

In California, we put evidence of the ineffectiveness of helmet laws before the legislature. Fatality rates in states that require everyone to wear helmets are higher, per 100 accidents, than in free states. Helmet laws are a placebo.

The second reason should worry everyone, even if you never go near a motorcycle. The helmet law was passed on the claim that freedom was costing the state money. Proponents blamed unhelmeted riders for avoidable medical costs. The numbers used to pass the law were false, it's now been acknowledged.

But even if they had been correct, what sort of precedent does this establish?

Whether I wear a helmet or not, who is affected?

Obviously, only me. To the best of my knowledge, no one is yet claiming that a head injury can result from being near a person who isn't wearing a helmet.

If cost is the prime factor, then there is no activity the state cannot regulate. The reasoning used to pass this law could be used to outlaw smoking or require us all to eat a good breakfast.

Is liberty still an inalienable right, or can you yell "costs" at our legislators and have them trample freedom like so many frightened sheep? If so, one of your most cherished freedoms may be next.

Source: *USA Today,* January 3, 1992, p. 10A. Copyright 1992, *USA Today.* Reprinted with Permission.

Questions

1. Has the market failed such that regulation is required to compel riders to wear motorcycle helmets? Explain.
2. List the competing considerations in this debate.
3. Should bicycle riders be required to wear helmets? Explain.
4. How would you vote on laws requiring the use of motorcycle helmets? Explain.

2. Tanning Salons

The following article and accompanying table describe the 1991 decision in the state of Iowa to impose new rules on the tanning industry.

RULES CUT DOWN ON NUMBER OF TANNING BEDS

Jennifer Dukes

Some local businesses have pulled the plug on the "electric beach."

State tanning bed regulations that clamped down on "fake bake" operations have given some area hair salon owners headaches. And while bed operators-owners agree that industrywide regulation is neces-sary, they say the extra work required for just a few beds isn't worth the added effort.

The Iowa Department of Public Health, acting on recently passed legislation, established stricter rules for commercial tanning operations in March 1991. The requirements came about in response to escalating concern among doctors that skin cancer was increasing in young women . . .

Tanning bed operators are now required to take a short course ranging from three to eight hours. An open book exam tests the operators' knowledge on safety procedures, lighting specifications and equipment information.

In addition, there is a $35 registration fee to be paid annually for each tanning bed, under the rule change.

Inspectors are also now expected to make annual visits to commercial tanning beds to make sure business owners are in compliance with the state regulations.

Larger businesses who specialize only in tanning typically aren't burdened by the added safety measures and ensuring paperwork. But some hair salon owners who have tanning beds as a sideline to their regular business feel that the extra work is a hassle.

Large and small tanning businesses alike agree that operators of hair salons have a more difficult time running the beds because they are essentially juggling two businesses.

"It just wasn't feasible to keep one bed," said Jean Boss, owner of Shear Artists . . . "The regulations are a good thing, but you just get tired (of operating beds) after a while."

It's not that tanning business was bad at Shear Artists, Boss said. In fact, the bed, open from 9 A.M. until 8 P.M. was often in use.

Boss said the extra $500 in insurance costs for one bed was a secondary factor in her decision to stop her tanning business. She said insurance expense for the booths is more feasible if the operator has more than one bed.

Wayne Sadler, owner of Wayne's Style Salon . . . agrees with the state's decision to take control of the industry, but with only two beds, "it's just not worth the effort."

Sadler said tanning business at Wayne's salon in Cedar Falls, with only one bed, was halted last year.

Rogers said the stiffer regulations have probably weeded out a few smaller businesses in the tanning industry, but on the whole, most people have been receptive.

For the larger companies, the rules actually improve business.

"People will go somewhere and get burned, and that will only hurt business," [said Charlene Rogers of the Iowa Department of Public Health]. And more regulation should mean less burning.

She said one woman called in and complained that her contacts had melted to her eyes. Others were burned, had tanned in unclean beds or had received no tan at all . . .

*   *   *   *   *

Another concern among smaller tanning businesses is that an angry customer will sue, and that has scared some operators to get out before the fear becomes a reality.

*   *   *   *   *

Customers who run the highest health risks are the ones who abuse the beds, tanning salon owners contend. People who tan in more than one bed in a day, or tan both inside and outside each day are hurting their bodies, tanning bed proprietors said.

But Betty Dotson, co-owner of Custom Pools and Spas. . . . said her customers are becoming more aware of potential dangers. They understand that 20 minutes in a tanning bed is equivalent to an afternoon in the sun.

Source: *Waterloo Courier*, June 10, 1992, p. C1. Reprinted by permission of the copyright holder, *Waterloo Courier*.

Tanning Rules; Possible Hazards

Some of the tanning salon rules issued by the Iowa Department of Public Health:

- All persons operating a tanning facility must pay a fee of $35 per tanning device per year, up to a maximum of $350 per year.
- Warning signs of red on white saying "Danger, Ultraviolet Radiation" with the hazards listed shall be visible to persons entering the establishment and within one meter of the tanning device.
- Facilities must provide each customer with a written statement about hazards of tanning and the substances that might make them more sensitive to ultraviolet light.
- Facility temperature should not be more than 100 degrees.

* * * * *

- Each consumer shall provide his own protective eyewear or purchase it from the facility.
- A trained operator shall be present when a tanning device is operated and must have received instruction through a course of training.
- A record shall be kept of each customer's total number of visits and tanning times.

* * * * *

- Contact surfaces should be cleansed between each use.
- A tanning facility cannot claim or distribute materials stating that a tanning device is safe or risk-free.
- Any violation of the tanning regulations is a simple misdemeanor, punishable by a maximum of not more than 30 days in jail and fine of not more than $100.

Source: The Iowa Department of Public Health. In Ann Langel, "'Fake Bake' Worshippers," *Waterloo Courier,* April 14, 1991, pp. C1, C3. Reprinted by permission of the copyright holder, *Waterloo Courier.*

Questions

1. Has the market failed such that regulation is required to protect consumers? Explain.
2. List the competing considerations in deciding whether state rules should be imposed on tanning salons.
3. Should the federal government regulate tanning salons? Explain.
4. Why do businesses sometimes welcome or even encourage government regulations?
5. List the array of regulatory strategies (e.g., education requirements) that might be imposed on salon operators in order to achieve the state's goals.
6. How would you vote on the question of regulating tanning salons? Explain.

CHAPTER QUESTIONS

1. Notwithstanding the deregulation efforts of recent years, the clear trend in the United States over the past 50 years has been that of increased government regulation of business. How do you explain that trend?

2. Define: Positive and negative externalities. Public goods.

3. If we had not experienced the Depression, would government regulation of business be substantially less pervasive than it is now? Explain.

4. As a safety measure, Arizona enacted a statute that limited the length of passenger trains to 14 cars and freight trains to 70 cars. Trains of those lengths and greater were common throughout the United States. The Southern Pacific Railroad challenged the Arizona statute.
   a. What was the legal foundation of the Southern Pacific claim?
   b. Decide the case. Explain. See *Southern Pacific Railroad* v. *Arizona,* 325 U.S. 761 (1945).

5. Many large American cities, including Philadelphia, Denver, Pittsburgh, and New York City, closely regulate cab service and severely restrict the number of cabs that may lawfully serve the community.
   a. Why would cities choose to limit a useful service for its citizens that also provides much-needed jobs?
   b. Who is harmed by these regulations? Explain. See Allen Randolph, "New York Taxi Policy Is a Lemon," *The Wall Street Journal,* March 17, 1992, p. A14.

6. Taalib-Dan Abdul Uqdah owns and operates Cornrows & Co., a hair-braiding salon in Washington, D.C. The D.C. Board of Cosmetology pursued Uqdah for years because he and his 10 employees had not secured cosmetology licenses. At one point, Uqdah was fined $1,000 and ordered to close unless he and his employees went to school for nine months. The schooling would have cost about $5,000 per person and did not teach the natural African techniques that are Uqdah's practice. Uqdah's business does not employ the use of chemicals.
   a. Why was the Washington, D.C., Board imposing the license requirement on Uqdah?
   b. Should it have done so? Explain. See Editorial, "Forgotten Civil Rights," *The Wall Street Journal,* August 14, 1992, p. A12, and Editorial, "Barring Entry," *The Wall Street Journal,* December 23, 1992, p. A8.

7. A *Journal of the American Medical Association* study indicates that a state-mandated drinking age of 21 has been quite successful in reducing auto deaths among drivers aged 19 and 20. The study of Tennessee drivers found that single-vehicle nighttime crash deaths in that age group fell by 38 percent after Tennessee changed its drinking age from 19 to 21.[13]
   a. What constitutional authority allows the states to regulate the age at which one may lawfully consume alcoholic beverages?
   b. Were the power yours, at what age would you allow drinking? Explain.

8. The following excerpt is from an article criticizing local and state regulations designed to stem growth.

   The growth control and environmental movements have had a very favorable press, stressing the widespread benefits they can achieve by protecting the quality of our common environment against the onslaught of the bulldozer.

   A closer look at how the growth control and environmental coalition operates in local controversies shows that its effects are far less benign. It has made a clear and substantial contribution to the escalation of new home prices, yet its success in discouraging home building has failed to produce important environmental benefits for the public at large. Instead, it has protected the environmental, social, and economic advantages of *established* suburban residents who live near land that could be used for new housing.[14]

   a. What are the opposing factors in weighing a no-growth policy?
   b. Should a state or locality be permitted to enact such a policy? Explain.

9. The preponderant government regulatory thrust is currently at the federal level. Should we shift that emphasis to the state and local levels? Explain.

10. In recent years, hundreds of local communities have banished or limited billboards on the grounds that they constitute traffic hazards and are unsightly. Many of the communities permit phase-out periods

of five years or so for existing billboards, and they allow the billboards to be relocated.

a. What constitutional questions are raised by these policies?

b. Are these policies lawful? Explain. See Arthur Hayes, "Signs of Battles over Billboards are Easy to See," *The Wall Street Journal,* March 23, 1993, p. B1.

11. Many states and localities ban smoking in public places and require employers to establish smoking and nonsmoking areas satisfactory to employees.

a. Do you favor those laws? Explain.

b. Should the federal government enact similar legislation? Explain.

c. Why might such laws be to the advantage of much of the business community?

12. A provision of the Airline Deregulation Act of 1978 prohibits states from enforcing any law "relating to rates, routes, or services" of any air carrier. In 1987, the National Association of Attorneys General (representing all 50 states) passed guidelines designed to regulate fare advertisements in order to prevent deception. A specific concern was ads that displayed reduced fares in large print, with taxes and add-ons in small print. Several airlines filed suit to block the guidelines.

a. What constitutional argument did they raise?

b. Decide. Explain. See *Morales* v. *Trans World Airlines,* 112 S.Ct. 2031 (1992).

13. Alabama's legislature imposed a higher tax on out-of-state insurance companies than on in-state firms. Out-of-state companies could reduce, but not eliminate, the differential by investing in Alabama.

a. What constitutional objection was raised by the out-of-state firms?

b. What defense was raised by the state?

c. Decide. Explain. See *Metropolitan Life Ins. Co.* v. *Ward,* 470 U.S. 869 (1985).

14. The Pennsylvania legislature passed legislation requiring all trucks over a specified weight to display an identification marker and pay a $25 annual fee for that marker. Trucks registered in Pennsylvania were exempted from the marker fee on the grounds that the $25 would be treated as a part of the general state vehicle registration fee. Later, the Pennsylvania legislature reduced the $25 fee to $5 and imposed a $36-per-axle fee on all trucks over a specified weight. At the same time, the legislature reduced the fee for registering trucks (of the specified weight class) in Pennsylvania by the amount of the axle tax. The American Trucking Associations challenged the Pennsylvania laws.

a. Identify the central constitutional issue in this case.

b. Decide the case. Explain. See *American Trucking Associations, Inc.* v. *Scheiner,* 483 U.S. 266 (1987).

15. Monroe County, which embraces the Florida Keys, is concerned (like so many coastal communities) with the problem of population growth exceeding the county's capacity to produce adequate public services (roads, utilities, schools, and so on). Therefore, in 1987, the country designated 16,000 lots as unsuitable for building. The result, in some instances, was that property owners who held two adjacent lots were told they could build only one structure on the two lots combined.

a. What constitutional argument would you make on behalf of those lot owners?

b. Should the government be permitted to restrain growth in this manner, or should we allow the free market to work its will? Explain.

16. Overall, which level of government (local, state, or federal) do you consider the more trustworthy? Explain.

17. In the interest of safety, an Iowa statute prohibited the use of 65-foot double-trailer trucks within its borders. Scientific studies revealed that 65-foot doubles were as safe as 55-foot singles (permissible under Iowa law). The State of Iowa argued that the statute promoted safety and reduced road wear by diverting much truck traffic to other states. Consolidated Freightways challenged the statute. Decide. See *Raymond Kassel et al.* v. *Consolidated Freightways Corporation of Delaware,* 101 S.Ct. 1309 (1981).

NOTES

1. Karl Schriftgiesser, *Business and the American Government* (Washington, D.C.: Robert B. Luce, 1964), p. 14.

2. Ibid., p. 27.

3. The remarks in this paragraph are drawn, in part, from "Interventionist Government Came to Stay," *Business Week,* September 3, 1979, p. 39.

4. Ibid.

5. "Federalism—Clear Congressional Mandate Required to Preempt State Law," *Harvard Law Review* 105, no. 1 (November 1991), p. 196.

6. 111 S.Ct. 2395 (1991).

7. 317 U.S. 111 (1942).

8. David R. Francis, "A War between the States: Home-grown U.S. Trade Barriers Costly," *The Christian Science Monitor,* September 20, 1984, p. 23.

9. Ibid.

10. Christopher Conte, "What Shakeout?" *The Wall Street Journal,* July 21, 1992, p. A1.

11. Timothy Noah, "Fiscal Crisis or No, States' Bureaucracies Just Keep Swelling," *The Wall Street Journal,* July 1, 1991, p. A1.

12. Editorial, "Punched In," *The Wall Street Journal,* March 25, 1991, p. A10.

13. Associated Press, "Raising Drinking Age Does Cut Traffic Fatalities, Study Finds," *Des Moines Register,* December 23, 1988, p. 4T.

14. Bernard Frieden, "Regulating the American Dream," *Across the Board,* August 1979, p. 67.

8

ADMINISTRATIVE AGENCIES
AND THE REGULATORY PROCESS

●

This chapter is divided into four parts. Parts One through Three discuss the nature and duties of the many federal regulatory agencies. Part Four evaluates the strengths and weaknesses of the federal regulatory process.

Part One–Introduction to Administrative Agencies[1]

The articles that follow raise the central themes in this chapter: (1) our lives suffer from excessive government regulation, but (2) some regulation is necessary in an increasingly complex society; therefore, (3) where do we draw the line? As you proceed through this chapter, these issues should guide your reading.

SO YOU WANT TO GET
YOUR ROOF FIXED . . .

Richard Rosenow

Suppose you own a roofing business, and one morning you get a call from your neighbor, whose garage roof is leaking. He tells you that the roof is asphalt-based, and you agree to send a repair crew to try to fix it. In order to fully comply with federal regulations that are in effect today, you would have to:

First examine the roof to determine whether asbestos is present. There is a good chance that an asphalt roof will at least include asbestos-containing base flashings and cements; if they do, Environmen-

tal Protection Agency regulations will apply, and Occupational Safety and Health Agency regulations may apply.

It is very likely that you won't know from a visual examination whether asbestos is present. In that case, you will have to cut a sample from the roof, and patch it to avoid leaks at the point of the sample cut. You will then send the sample, after you have bagged it properly, to an accredited laboratory, and delay your repair work until the sample is analyzed.

(In some states, only a certified abatement contractor is allowed to make this test cut.)

If you discover that asbestos is contained in the roof, you must:

Notify the owner (your neighbor) in writing;

notify the EPA Regional Office (10 days prior to beginning work, which will mean your neighbor's roof will continue to leak);

be sure that at least one person on your repair crew is trained to satisfy EPA requirements;

conduct air monitoring on the job, once you are able to start work, to determine whether emissions of asbestos will exceed OSHA's action level. You can't do this, of course, until the 10-day EPA notification period has passed.

Once you begin any repair work, you will have to "adequately wet" the materials. EPA defines this as "thoroughly penetrating" the asbestos-containing material, which is an interesting concept for a waterproof material like asphalt. EPA also stipulates that there be no "visible emissions" on the job, even if you can demonstrate that the emissions contain no asbestos fibers.

You will then have to vacuum the dust generated by any "cutting" that you do, put it in double bags, and take it to an approved landfill.

You will also be responsible for prohibiting smoking on the job site, and are subject to fine if one of your employees lights up.

You will probably wonder why your neighbor will be asked to absorb all of the costs associated with these steps, since hundreds of test samples have shown no asbestos exposures above acceptable limits in roofing operations.

You must ensure that your crew is trained about any hazardous materials that they may encounter. (These will include the gasoline you use to power the pump on your roofing kettle.) You will also have to be sure that copies of the appropriate Material Safety Data Sheets are present at the work site, and that all containers are properly labeled.

Your crew must also be thoroughly trained in handling these materials. This will be determined not by what steps you have taken to train them, but by what your employees tell the OSHA inspector who asks them what they have been taught.

Because you are transporting asphalt at a temperature above 212 degrees, so that your crew won't have to wait two or three hours at your neighbor's home for the asphalt to heat, you must:

Mark the side of your roofing kettle with a sticker that says "HOT" in capital letters;

complete shipping papers before the truck leaves your yard;

have emergency response procedures developed in the event the kettle should turn over en route to your neighbor's home;

be sure that your driver has been drug-tested, and has a commercial driver's license;

be sure that the driver completes his log sheets for the day, and stops 25 miles after he leaves your yard to see if the load has shifted;

be sure that your kettle has a hazardous material placard, in addition to the "HOT" sticker mentioned above.

Because your vehicle is being driven for work-related matters, you must be sure that the driver wears his seat belt, and has received driver training. If he does not wear his seat belt, you, of course, will be fined.

Assuming you have met other OSHA safety standards, and are satisfied you will be in compliance with local and state regulations, it is now safe for you to begin. Your most dangerous act, however, is yet to come: presenting your neighbor with his bill, and explaining why your costs have increased so dramatically in the three years since these regulations have been promulgated.

Source: *The Wall Street Journal,* February 4, 1992, p. A14. Reprinted by permission of *The Wall Street Journal,* © 1992 Dow Jones & Company, Inc. All Rights Reserved Worldwide.

"REGULATION" ISN'T A DIRTY WORD

Vermont Royster

Every time I leave my house I seem to fall into a web of regulation. If I drive, the township tells me how fast I'm allowed to go, ranging from 25 to 35 miles per hour. If I leave town, the state steps in . . .

*   *   *   *   *

If I go afoot I don't escape. At the intersections there are those signs reading "walk" or "don't walk." Car drivers at the same corner are regulated by red, yellow, and green lights, sometimes with little arrows pointing left or right . . .

I suppose I should object to all this since the cry of our time is for "deregulation."

*   *   *   *   *

If I hesitate to join the hue for deregulation, even when much of the regulation is misguided, it's because I shudder at the thought of a wholly deregulated society. I prefer knowing my pharmacist has to be licensed and that somebody checks on him; so also with the butcher so that I have some assurance his scale registers a true measure.

As a matter of fact, regulation to protect consumers is almost as old as civilization itself. Tourists to the ruins of Pompeii see an early version of the bureau of weights and measures, a place where the townsfolk could go to be sure they weren't cheated by the local tradesmen. Unfortunately a little larceny is too common in the human species.

So regulation in some form or other is one of the prices we pay for our complex civilization. And the more complicated society becomes, the more need for some watching over its many parts. We shouldn't forget that a great deal of the regulation we encounter today in business or in our personal lives arose from a recognized need in the past.

Take the drug companies. It wasn't so very long ago that the countryside was flooded with snake-oil salesmen hawking cures for every ailment and bamboozling credulous folk with worthless nostrums. The Food and Drug Administration Act in 1906 was the outgrowth of a real need.

Source: *The Wall Street Journal,* September 9, 1987, p. 30. Reprinted by permission of *The Wall Street Journal,* © 1987 Dow Jones & Company, Inc. All Rights Reserved Worldwide.

Question

1. Does the government intrude excessively in your present life? Explain.

THE AGENCIES

That branch of the law governing the administrative operations of government is *administrative law.* The Federal Administrative Procedure Act defines an *agency* as any government unit other than the legislature and the courts. Thus, administrative law technically addresses the entire executive branch of government. However, our attention will be directed to the prominent regulatory agencies (Interstate Commerce Commission, Federal Communications Commission, Securities and Exchange Commission, etc.) rather than the various executive departments (Agriculture, Defense, etc.) and nonregulatory, welfare agencies (Social Security Administration, Veterans Administration, and the Public Health Service). Although our fundamental concern lies at the federal level, administrative law principles are fully applicable to the conduct of state and local governments. At the local level, planning and zoning boards and property tax assessments appeals boards are examples of administrative agencies. At the state level, one might cite public utility commissions and the various state licensure boards for law, medicine, architecture, and the like.

History

Congress established the Interstate Commerce Commission (ICC), the first federal regulatory agency, in 1887 for the purpose of regulating railroad routes and rates. The Food and Drug Administration (FDA—1907) and the Federal Trade Commission (FTC—1914) followed, but federal regulation became pervasive only in response to the Great Depression of the 1930s. Congress created the Securities and Exchange Commission (SEC), the Federal Communications Commission (FCC), the Civil Aeronautics Board (CAB), and the National Labor Relations Board (NLRB), among others, as a response to the widely shared belief that the stock market crash and the Depression were evidence of the failure of the free market.

The next major burst of regulatory activity arrived in the 1960s and 1970s when Congress created such agencies as the Equal Employment Opportunity Commission (EEOC—1965), the Environmental Protection Agency (EPA—1970), the Occupational Safety and Health Administration (OSHA—1970), and the Consumer Product Safety Commission (CPSC—1972).

Note that the work of most of the early agencies was directed to controlling entire industries such as transportation or communications and that the primary purpose of most of those agencies was to address economic concerns. Then with the arrival of the prosperity and social turbulence of the 1960s and 1970s, Congress built a rather massive array of new agencies directed not to economic issues but to social reform in such areas as discrimination, the environment, job safety, and product safety.

As we explore later in the chapter, the free market enthusiasm of the 1980s resulted in strenuous efforts to deregulate the economy and reduce the influence of the federal agencies and the government generally. Now, in the 1990s, we appear to be in a period of respect for the free market tempered by concern that government oversight remains vital to the general welfare. In any case, the federal regulatory agencies remain dominant institutions, issuing tens of thousands of pages of rules annually and directly affecting virtually every corner of American life.

Creating the Agencies

The so-called independent agencies (e.g., Federal Trade Commission, Interstate Commerce Commission, National Labor Relations Board, and Securities and Exchange Commission) are created by Congress via statutes labeled *enabling legislation*. For example, the Federal Trade Commission is empowered to pursue unfair trade practices by the authority of its enabling legislation, a portion of which follows:

Federal Trade Commission Act (excerpts)

Section 1: A commission is created and established, to be known as the Federal Trade Commission, which shall be composed of five commissioners, who shall be appointed by the President, by and with the advice and consent of the Senate . . .

　　Section 5: Unfair methods of competition in or affecting commerce, and unfair or deceptive acts or practices in or affecting commerce, are hereby declared unlawful.[2]

In creating an agency, Congress delegates a portion of its authority to that body. Congress acknowledges the existence of a problem and recognizes that it is not the appropriate body to address the specific elements of that problem—hence, the agency. The president, ordinarily with the advice and consent of the senate, appoints the administrator or the several commissioners who direct each agency's affairs. Commissioners are appointed in staggered terms, typically of seven years' duration. The appointment of commissioners for most of the independent agencies must reflect an approximate political balance between the two major parties.

In effect, Congress has created a fourth branch of government. Recognizing that it possesses neither the time nor the expertise to handle problems arising from nuclear power, product safety, racial discrimination, labor unions, and much more, Congress wisely established "minigovernments" with the necessary technical resources and day-to-day authority to address those problems.

The president likewise delegates authority by creating so-called executive agencies. Those agencies (e.g., Department of Commerce, Department of Labor, Department of Justice, and Department of State) are, in most instances, headed by cabinet officers who serve at the behest of the president and may be removed at will.

Agency Duties

The authority of the federal regulatory agencies falls broadly into three categories.

1. Control of Supply. Some agencies control entry into certain economic activities. The Federal Communications Commission grants radio and television licenses. The Food and Drug Administration decides which drugs may enter the American market. The Securities and Exchange Commission (See Chapter 9) acts as a gatekeeper, preventing the entry of new securities into the marketplace until certain standards are met. The general feeling in these areas and others like them is that the market alone cannot adequately protect the public interest.

2. Control of Rates.   Historically, those federal agencies charged with regulating utilities and carriers (Federal Energy Regulatory Commission, ICC, and CAB) set the prices to be charged for the services offered within their jurisdictions. For example, the consumer facing an interstate change of address found little value in comparison shopping for the least expensive furniture mover because the rates, regulated by the Interstate Commerce Commission, were virtually identical. Government rate setting remains important at the state level. However, at the federal level, the deregulation movement resulted in the elimination of the CAB and the general withdrawal of the other administrative agencies from the rate-setting process. That is, the federal government decided to turn such decisions as the price of airline tickets back to the free market.

3. Control of Conduct

   (a) Information.   A major element of government regulation is simply requiring information. Agencies commonly compel companies to disclose consumer information that would otherwise remain private. For example, warning labels may be mandated.

   (b) Standards.   Where simply requiring information is deemed inadequate to the public need, the government may establish minimum standards that the private sector must meet. For example, a ladder might be required to safely hold at least a specified weight, or workers might lawfully be exposed to only a specified maximum level of radiation.

   (c) Product Banishments.   In those unusual instances where information alone is deemed inadequate to protect the public, products can be banned from the market. The Consumer Product Safety Commission banned the flame retardant Tris (used in children's sleepwear) because of evidence of the product's cancer-causing properties.

   The article below illustrates FCC practice in regulating conduct in the communications industry.

FCC TAKES NEW LOOK
AT TV PROGRAMMING
AIMED AT CHILDREN

The Federal Communications Commission is taking a new look at television programming aimed at children.

   The agency said it was taking the step because it found little change in children's programming in recent years, despite passage of the Children's Television Act of 1990. The FCC said it compared lists of children's shows contained in recent applications for broadcast license renewals with congressional findings when lawmakers were considering the 1990 law. Broadcasters, the agency concluded, "may remain uncertain as to the scope of their programming obligations, and this uncertainty may largely explain the apparent lack of growth in children's programming."

   The agency asked for public comment on whether it should define more precisely the levels and types of programming that broadcasters must carry to meet the informational needs of children. The commission suggested that both the agency and broadcasters might benefit from clear examples and better definitions of programming requirements.

The FCC also tentatively concluded it should specify that the primary objective of a broadcaster's core programming for children is educating or informing children; entertaining them should be a secondary goal.

Questions—Part One

1. The phrase *government regulation* embraces many functions. Define it.
2. Is the federal regulatory process limited in its goals to the correction of market failures? Should it be so limited? Explain.
3. In 1975, Scholar James Q. Wilson said, "All democratic regimes tend to shift resources from the private to the public sector and to enlarge the size of the administrative component of government."[3]
   a. Is Wilson correct? Explain.
   b. Given the striking economic and political changes around the world, would he say the same today? Explain.
4. Scholar George Stigler asked, "What benefits can a state provide to an industry?"[4] Answer Stigler's inquiry.
5. Does the real origin of government regulation of business lie in the citizen's fear? That is, do the people consider the market too risky and, therefore, opt for a system that affords them some protection from economic loss? Explain.
6. Have we reason for concern because the federal agencies have become a fourth branch of government not directly accountable to the public via the electoral process? Explain.

Part Two—Summary of the Administrative Process

As we have noted, the administrative agencies act as minigovernments, performing quasi-executive, quasi-legislative (rule-making), and quasi-judicial (adjudicatory) roles broadly involving control of supply, rates, and conduct in large segments of American life. Let's look now at how those agencies undertake their business.

OPERATING THE AGENCIES

Executive Functions

The basic executive duty of the various agencies is to implement the policy provided for in the enabling legislation and in the agencies' own rules and regulations. A large part of agency activity consists of performing mundane, repetitive tasks that are necessary for a smoothly operating society but that do not merit the day-to-day attention of Congress or the courts. Thus, agencies enter into contracts, lease federal lands, register security offerings, award grants, resolve tax disputes, settle workers' compensation claims, administer government benefits to the citizenry, and so on. Some agencies, such as the Food and Drug Administration, are charged with protecting the public by engaging in inspections and testing. Most agencies offer informal advice, both in response to requests and on their own initiative, to explain agency policy and positions. For example, each year, the Federal Trade Commission receives many inquiries regarding the legal sufficiency of warning labels on various potentially dangerous products. Supervisory duties, including most notably the active and close attention given to the banking industry, are a further illustration of agency executive duties.

Of course, a big part of the agencies' executive duties is the protection of the public in one way or another by ensuring compliance with laws and regulations. Therefore, most agencies spend a great deal of time conducting inspections and investigations and collecting information. For example, the Occupational Safety and Health Administration regularly checks businesses for safety hazards. The agencies' efforts may result in formal adjudicatory proceedings, but the agencies seek to informally resolve all disputes. OSHA, for example, might specify that warning signs are needed near a piece of equipment, and the business often will simply comply. If informal resolution cannot be achieved, a citation may be issued calling for, as appropriate, a fine, suspension of an operating license, rehiring an employee, paying a claim, or the like.

Legislative Functions

The agencies create *rules* that, in effect, are laws. These rules provide the details necessary to carry out the intentions of the enabling legislation. In day-to-day business practice, the rules are likely to be much more important than the original congressional legislation. The Occupational Safety and Health Act calls for a safe and healthy workplace, but the rules necessary for interpreting and enforcing that general mandate come, not from Congress, but from OSHA.

Rules.   Agencies enact three types of rules: (1) procedural rules, (2) interpretive rules, and (3) legislative rules. *Procedural rules* delineate the agency's internal operating structure and methods. *Interpretive rules* offer the agency's view of the meaning of those statutes for which the agency has administrative responsibility. The agency seeks to clarify for interested parties the meaning of congressional statutory language that is often very broadly drawn. Interpretive rules do not have the force of law, but they are important expressions of opinion as to what the governing legislation requires. Internal Revenue Service regulations are an example of interpretive rules. *Legislative rules* are policy expressions having the effect of law. The agency is exercising the lawmaking function delegated to it by the legislature. Federal Trade Commission rules providing for a cooling-off period of three business days within which the buyer may cancel door-to-door sales contracts are an example of agency lawmaking that significantly affects business behavior.

The Rule-Making Process.   The Administrative Procedure Act provides for both *informal* and *formal* rule-making processes for legislative rules. Under both approaches, the process begins with the publication of a Notice of Proposed Rule Making in the *Federal Register* (a daily publication of all federal rules, regulations, and orders). Thereafter, in the case of informal rule making, the agency must permit written comments on the proposal and may hold open hearings. Having received public comments, the agency either discontinues the process or prepares the final rule.

In the case of formal rule making, after providing notice, the agency must hold a public hearing that must be conducted with most of the procedural safeguards of a trial, where all interested parties may call witnesses, challenge the agency evidence, and so on. The agency decision must be based on the formal record only.

Final agency rules are published in the *Federal Register* and later compiled in the *Code of Federal Regulations.*

Agency Rule-Making Process	
Informal Agency Rule Making (*legislative in character*)	*Formal Agency Rule Making* (*legislative/judicial* *in character*)
Public notice in *Federal Register* Public comment (informal) Final rule in *Federal Register*	Public notice in *Federal Register* Public comment (formal) Final rule in *Federal Register*

Informal rule making is the standard approach. It provides an efficient mechanism for agency action; however, it does so at some cost in procedural safeguards and opportunities for public input. In recent years, concerns over too much discretion in the hands of the agencies has led Congress to specify formal rule making for most of the new health, safety, and environmental agencies, including the Occupational Safety and Health Administration, the Consumer Products Safety Commission, and the Environmental Protection Agency. In 1990, Congress passed the Negotiated Rule Making Act,[5] which is designed to encourage all interested parties to engage in face-to-face negotiations and cooperation while developing agency rules, the better to avoid subsequent litigation.

The article that follows illustrates the rule-making process.

FCC ADOPTS RULES
TO CURB TELEMARKETING

Mary Lu Carnevale

The Federal Communications Commission adopted rules to help consumers avoid calls from pesky telemarketers and to regulate the use of automatic dialers, prerecorded messages and facsimile machines.

Under the rules, telemarketing companies will be required to maintain an in-house list of residential telephone subscribers who don't want to be called. And it banned telemarketing calls to homes before 8 A.M. and after 9 P.M.

Critics charged that the agency didn't go far enough in establishing rules to carry out the Telephone Consumer Protection Act of 1991. They argue that the lawmakers intended for the FCC to develop a nationwide database of consumers who don't want to be bothered by so-called cold calls from stock brokers, long-distance carriers and other salespeople who work the phones to drum up business.

"The FCC chose the path of least resistance, a do-not-call list run by the companies making the calls," said Rep. Edward J. Markey (D., Mass.), chairman of the House telecommunications subcommittee . . ." Rep. Markey, who sponsored the legislation in the House, also faulted the FCC for not setting up a procedure for notifying customers of their new rights to curb the number of unwanted calls.

Instead of a directive for marketers or others to notify citizens directly, the agency said it would issue a "consumer alert" to consumer groups and state consumer protection agencies as well as industry associations and local telephone companies.

The Direct Marketing Association, the nation's leading trade association for telemarketers, had worried that the law would result in stricter rules, but expressed enthusiasm over the agency's action . . .

* * * * *

The FCC suggested that when consumers get unsolicited calls and don't want to be bothered again, they state clearly that they don't want further calls. The marketer is then required to record the request on in-house, regional or industry-based calling lists. If a consumer continues to receive unwanted calls, he can take the telemarketer to state court for damages of up to $500.

* * * * *

[The FCC] also barred telemarketers from placing calls to homes using artificial or recorded voice messages, unless the call is for an emergency or the resident had earlier consented to receiving such calls. Under the new rules, prerecorded calls made with an automatic dialer must identify the caller, give the caller's phone number or address and free up the called party's line within five seconds if the called party hangs up the line.

* * * * *

The commission said it didn't adopt a nationwide database because it would cost too much—perhaps as much as $20 million in the first year and about $10 million a year thereafter. Moreover, the commission said, it would require complicated safeguards to protect consumers' privacy.

Questions

1. In your experience, do we need greater protection from telemarketers? Explain.
2. Do we need a nationwide database of those who don't want to be bothered by telemarketers even if it would cost $10 to $20 million annually? Explain.
3. *a.* In theory, how do the forces of the free market act to "regulate" the number of telemarketing pleas we receive?
   b. In fact, does the market offer that protection? Explain.

Judicial Functions

Although informal procedures such as settlements are preferred, agencies commonly must turn to judicial proceedings to enforce agency rules. The National Labor Relations Board may hold a hearing to determine if an employee was wrongfully dismissed for engaging in protected union activities. The Federal Communications Commission may decide whether to remove a radio license because of a failure to serve the public interest. The Federal Trade Commission may judge whether a particular ad is misleading. Adjudicatory administrative hearings are equal in significance and much superior in numbers to all federal court trials each year.

Rule Making or Adjudication?   Many issues facing agencies could properly be resolved in either the rule-making or the adjudicatory format. The distinction between the two cannot be drawn vividly. Characteristically, however, an adjudication addresses specific parties involved in a specific present or past dispute. Rule making ordinarily involves standards to be applied to the future conduct of a class of unspecified parties. The rule-making/adjudication decision is discretionary with the agency (subject to judicial review) and is based on the nature of the issue and fairness to the parties. Regardless, the agencies are, in effect, "making law" either by setting a judicial-like precedent in the case of an adjudication or by passing a rule that has authority much like a law.

Administrative Hearing.   Typically, after an investigation, a violation of a statute and/or rule may be alleged. Affected parties are notified. An effort is made to reach a settlement via a *consent order,* in which the party being investigated agrees to steps suitable to the agency but under which the respondent makes no admission of guilt (thus retarding the likelihood of subsequent civil liability). Federal law also encourages the use of alternate dispute resolution methods such as arbitration.

ALJ.   Failing a settlement, the parties proceed much as in a civil trial. Ordinarily, the case is heard by an *administrative law judge (ALJ).* The respondent may be represented by counsel. Parties have the right to present their cases, cross-examine, file motions, raise objections, and so on. However, they do not have the right to a jury trial. The ALJ decides all questions of law and fact and then issues a decision (*order*).

In general, that decision is final unless appealed to the agency/commission. After exhausting opportunities for review within the agency, appeal may be taken to the federal court system.

CONTROLLING THE AGENCIES

As noted, agency influence in business practice and in American life generally is enormous. However, none of these agencies and their thousands of employees are directly accountable to the people and all of them operate under necessarily broad grants of power. What is to keep them from abusing their discretion? Just as with our constitutional system generally, certain checks and balances are in place to constrain agency conduct while allowing the latitude necessary to achieve effectiveness.

Executive Constraints

As noted, the president appoints the top administrators for the various agencies, thus significantly influencing the conservative/liberal slant of the agency. Further, the president obviously has great influence in the budget process. Recent presidents, particularly Ronald Reagan, have sought to extend executive influence over the regulatory process via the Office of Management and Budget (OMB). Two *executive* (presidential) *orders* designed to restrain regulatory growth have imposed significant constraints on agency action. One order requires the executive (but not the independent) agencies to submit their regulatory plans to OMB and, in effect, secure OMB approval (subject to appeal—ultimately, to the president). The second order requires a cost-benefit analysis of all significant regulatory proposals, with the expectation that agencies will take the most economically sound regulatory approach—which has often meant the rejection of proposed regulations. In effect, the OMB has become a funnel through which all new regulation must pass.

Reform? At this writing in 1994, President Clinton is taking steps to reduce executive branch constraints on agency action. The White House seeks to depreciate OMB power to stall new regulations, and the administration is working on ways to expand the measure of benefits in cost-benefit analyses. Rather than limiting benefits to readily quantifiable ingredients such as lives saved, the president proposes a more expansive picture that would include such things as improved environmental quality and reduced racial discrimination. The problem lies, of course, in the measuring.

Congressional Constraints

Congress creates and can dissolve the agencies. Congress controls agency budgets and thus can encourage or discourage particular agency action. Broadly, Congress oversees agency action, and agencies often check with Congress before major initiatives are undertaken. Congress can directly intervene by amending the enabling legislation or by passing laws that require agencies to take specific directions.

Judicial Review

Agency rules and orders may be challenged in court, and the threat of judicial review is probably the chief constraint on agency power. However, the sheer bulk of agency activities means only a very small portion of those activities will receive judicial scrutiny. Indeed, many appeals of agency actions may be denied on technical grounds (as when the appealing party does not have standing to sue). However, assuming those procedural hurdles are scaled and review is granted, the question becomes that of the scope of judicial review. Into which issues will the court inquire? Historically, the courts have taken a rather narrow approach to judicial review. Two common-sense considerations support that restrained judicial stance. The first is deference to the presumed expertise of the administrative agencies. The jurists, being generalists in the field of law, have been reluctant to overrule the judgment of specialists specifically chosen to regulate within their area of expertise. Second, very crowded judicial calendars act as a natural brake on activist judicial review. For those reasons, judges have traditionally disposed of administrative law cases in an expeditious manner, by readily sustaining the judgment of the agency. Of course, the courts have overruled the agencies when appropriate. Indeed, of late we can see evidence of a firmer judicial role.

Not surprisingly, judicial review of agency decisions raises a variety of technical, esoteric issues of law. The nature of those issues depends, in part, on whether the court is reviewing an agency's rule-making function or its adjudicatory function. Cases turn on questions like these:

1. Does the legislature's delegation of authority meet constitutional requirements?
2. Has the agency exceeded the authority granted by the enabling legislation?
3. Has the appealing party exhausted all the available administrative remedies?
4. Are the agency's findings of fact supported by substantial evidence in the record as a whole?

These issues are close to the heart of the administrative law practitioner, but their exploration is not necessary to the layperson's understanding of the larger regulatory process. The case that follows will be our only consideration of the formalities of judicial review. This appeal from a Federal Communications Commission adjudication sheds some light on the agency regulatory process and judicial review; but, much more importantly, the case raises fundamental questions regarding freedom of speech in a technologically advanced society.

F.C.C. v. PACIFICA FOUNDATION
98 S.Ct. 3026 (1978)

Justice Stevens

This case requires that we decide whether the Federal Communications Commission has any power to regulate a radio broadcast that is indecent but not obscene.

A satiric humorist named George Carlin recorded a 12-minute monologue entitled "Filthy Words" before a live audience in a California theater. He began by referring to his thoughts about "the words you can't say on the public, ah, airwaves, um, the ones you definitely wouldn't say, ever." He proceeded to list those words and repeat them over and over again in a variety of colloquialisms. The transcript of the recording . . . indicates frequent laughter from the audience.

At about 2 o'clock in the afternoon on Tuesday, October 30, 1973, a New York radio station, owned by respondent Pacifica Foundation, broadcast the "Filthy Words" monologue. A few weeks later a man, who stated that he had heard the broadcast while driving with his young son, wrote a letter complaining to the commission. He stated that, although he could perhaps understand the "record's being sold for private use, I certainly cannot understand the broadcast of same over the air that, supposedly, you control."

The complaint was forwarded to the station for comment. In its response, Pacifica explained that the monologue had been played during a program about contemporary society's attitude toward language and that, immediately before its broadcast, listeners had been advised that it included "sensitive language which might be regarded as offensive to some." Pacifica characterized George Carlin as a "significant social satirist" who "like Twain and Sahl before him, examines the language of ordinary people . . . Carlin is not mouthing obscenities, he is merely using words to satirize as harmless and essentially silly our attitudes toward those words." Pacifica stated that it was not aware of any other complaints about the broadcast.

On February 21, 1975, the commission issued a declaratory order granting the complaint and holding that Pacifica "could have been the subject of administrative sanctions." . . . The commission did not impose formal sanctions, but it did state that the order would be "associated with the station's license file, and in the event that subsequent complaints are received, the commission will then decide whether it should utilize any of the available sanctions it has been granted by Congress."

* * * * *

[T]he commission concluded that certain words depicted sexual and excretory activities in a patently offensive manner, noted that they "were broadcast at a time when children were undoubtedly in the audiences (i.e., in the early afternoon)" and that the prerecorded language, with these offensive words "repeated over and over," was "deliberately broadcast." . . .

In summary, the commission stated: "We therefore hold that the language as broadcast was indecent and prohibited." . . .

The United States Court of Appeals for the District of Columbia Circuit reversed, with each of the three judges on the panel writing separately . . .

Judge Tamm concluded that the order represented censorship and was expressly prohibited by ¶ 326 of the Communications Act. Alternatively, Judge Tamm read the commission opinion as the functional equivalent of a rule and concluded that it was "overbroad." . . .

Chief Judge Bazelon's concurrence rested on the Constitution. He was persuaded that ¶ 326's prohibition against censorship is inapplicable to broadcasts forbidden by ¶ 1464 (prohibiting "obscene, indecent, or profane language by means of radio communications"). However, he concluded that ¶ 1464 must be narrowly construed to cover only language that is obscene or otherwise unprotected by the First Amendment . . .

Judge Leventhal, in dissent, stated that the only issue was whether the commission could regulate the language "as broadcast." . . .

Emphasizing the interest in protecting children, not only from exposure to indecent language, but also from exposure to the idea that such language has official approval, . . . he concluded that the commission had correctly condemned the daytime broadcast as indecent.

Having granted the commission's petition for certiorari, . . . we must decide: (1) whether the scope of judicial review encompasses more than the commission's determination that the monologue was indecent "as broadcast"; (2) whether the commission's order was a form of censorship forbidden by ¶ 326; (3) whether the broadcast was indecent within the meaning of ¶ 1464; and (4) whether the order violates the First Amendment of the United States Constitution.

(I)

The general statements in the commission's memorandum opinion do not change the character of its order. Its action was an adjudication . . . It did not purport to engage in formal rule making or in the promulgation of any regulations. The order "was issued in a specific factual context"; questions concerning possible action in other contexts were expressly reserved for the future. The specific holding was carefully confined to the monologue "as broadcast." . . .

(II)

The relevant statutory questions are whether the commission's action is forbidden "censorship" within the meaning of ¶ 326 and whether speech that concededly is not obscene may be restricted as "indecent" under the authority of ¶ 1464 . . .

* * * * *

The prohibition against censorship unequivocally denies the commission any power to edit proposed broadcasts in advance and to excise material considered inappropriate for the airwaves. The prohibition, however, has never been construed to deny the commission the power to review the content of completed broadcasts in the performance of its regulatory duties.

* * * * *

Entirely apart from the fact that the subsequent review of program content is not the sort of censorship at which the statute was directed, its history makes it perfectly clear that it was not intended to limit the commission's power to regulate the broadcast of obscene, indecent, or profane language. A single section of the [Radio Act of 1927] is the source of both the anticensorship provision and the commission's authority to impose sanctions for the broadcast of indecent or obscene language. Quite plainly, Congress intended to give meaning to both provisions. Respect for that intent requires that the censorship language be read as inapplicable to the prohibition on broadcasting obscene, indecent, or profane language.

We conclude, therefore, that ¶ 326 does not limit the commission's authority to impose sanctions on licensees who engage in obscene, indecent, or profane broadcasting.

(III)

The only other statutory question presented by this case is whether the afternoon broadcast of the "Filthy Words" monologue was indecent within the meaning of ¶ 1464 . . .

The commission identified several words that referred to excretory or sexual activities or organs, stated that the repetitive, deliberate use of those words in an afternoon broadcast when children are in the audience was patently offensive and held that the broadcast was indecent. Pacifica takes issue with the commission's definition of indecency, but does not dispute the commission's preliminary determination that each of the components of its definition was present. Specifically, Pacifica does not quarrel with the conclusion that this afternoon broadcast was patently offensive. Pacifica's claim that the broadcast was not indecent within the meaning of the statute rests entirely on the absence of prurient appeal.

The plain language of the statute does not support Pacifica's argument. The words "obscene, indecent, or profane" are written in the disjunctive, implying that each has a separate meaning. Prurient appeal is an element of the obscene, but the normal definition of "indecent" merely refers to nonconformance with accepted standards of morality.

* * * * *

Because neither our prior decisions nor the language of history of ¶ 1464 supports the conclusion that prurient appeal is an essential component of indecent language, we reject Pacifica's construction of the statute. When that construction is put to one side, there is no basis for disagreeing with the commission's conclusion that indecent language was used in this broadcast.

(IV)

Pacifica makes two constitutional attacks on the commission's order. First, it argues that the commission's construction of the statutory language broadly encompasses so much constitutionally protected speech that reversal is required even if Pacifica's broadcast of the "Filthy Words" monologue is not itself protected by the First Amendment. Second, Pacifica argues that inasmuch as the recording is not obscene, the Constitution forbids any abridgement of the right to broadcast it on the radio.

A

The first argument fails because our review is limited to the question of whether the commission has the authority to proscribe this particular broadcast. As the commission itself emphasized, its order was "issued in a specific factual context." . . .

That approach is appropriate for courts as well as the commission when regulation of indecency is at stake, for indecency is largely a function of context—it cannot be adequately judged in the abstract.

* * * * *

It is true that the commission's order may lead some broadcasters to censor themselves. At most, however, the commission's definition of indecency will deter only the broadcasting of patently offensive references to excretory and sexual organs and activities. While some of these references may be protected, they surely lie at the periphery of First Amendment concern . . .

B

When the issue is narrowed to the facts of this case, the question is whether the First Amendment denies government any power to restrict the public broadcast of indecent language in any circumstances. For if the government has any such power, this was an appropriate occasion for its exercise.

The words of the Carlin monologue are unquestionably "speech" within the meaning of the First Amendment. It is equally clear that the commission's objections to the broadcast were based in part on its content. The order must therefore fall if, as Pacifica argues, the First Amendment prohibits all governmental regulation that depends on the content of speech. Our past cases demonstrate, however, that no such absolute rule is mandated by the Constitution.

The classic exposition of the proposition that both the content and the context of speech are critical elements of First Amendment analysis is Mr. Justice Holmes's statement . . .

We admit that in many places and in ordinary times the defendants in saying all that was said in the circular would have been within their constitutional rights. But the character of every act depends upon the circumstances in which it was done . . . The most stringent protection of free speech would not protect a man in falsely shouting fire in a theatre and causing a panic. It does not even protect a man from an injunction against uttering words that may have all the effect of force . . . The question in every case is whether the words used are used in such circumstances and are of such a nature as to create a clear and present danger that they will bring about the substantive evils that congress has a right to prevent.

Other distinctions based on content have been approved . . . The government may forbid speech calculated to provoke a fight . . . It may pay heed to the "commonsense differences between commercial speech and other varieties." . . . It may treat libels against private citizens more severely than libels against public officials . . . Obscenity may be wholly prohibited . . .

The question in this case is whether a broadcast of patently offensive words dealing with sex and excretion may be regulated because of its content. Obscene materials have been denied the protection of the First Amendment because their content is so offensive to contemporary moral standards . . . But the fact that society may find speech offensive is not a sufficient reason for suppressing it. Indeed, if it is the speaker's opinion that gives offense, that consequence is a reason for according it constitutional protection. For it is a central tenet of the First Amendment that the government must remain neutral in the marketplace of ideas. If there were any reason to believe that the commission's characterization of the Carlin monologue as offensive could be traced to its political content—or even to the fact that it satirized contemporary attitudes about four-letter words—First Amendment protection might be required. But that is simply not this case. These words offend for the same reasons that obscenity offends . . .

* * * * *

In this case it is undisputed that the content of Pacifica's broadcast was "vulgar," "offensive," and "shocking." Because content of that character is not entitled to absolute constitutional protection under all circumstances, we must consider its context in order to determine whether the commission's action was constitutionally permissible.

C

We have long recognized that each medium of expression presents special First Amendment problems . . . And of all forms of communication, it is broadcasting that has received the most limited First Amendment protection . . . The reasons for [that distinction] are complex, but two have relevance to the present case. First, the broadcast media have established a uniquely pervasive presence in the lives of all Americans. Patently offensive, indecent material presented over the airwaves confronts the citizen, not only in public, but also in the privacy of the home, where the individual's right to be left alone plainly outweighs the First Amendment rights of an intruder . . . Because the broadcast audience is constantly tuning in and out, prior warnings cannot completely protect the listener or viewer from unexpected program content . . .

Second, broadcasting is uniquely accessible to children, even those too young to read . . .

It is appropriate, in conclusion, to emphasize the narrowness of our holding. This case does not involve a two-way radio conversation between a cab driver and a dispatcher, or a telecast of an Elizabethan comedy. We have not decided that an occasional expletive in either setting would justify any sanction or, indeed, that this broadcast would justify a criminal prosecution. The commission's decision rested entirely on a nuisance rationale under which context is all-important. The concept requires consideration of a host of variables. The time of day was emphasized by the commission. The content of the program in which the language is used will also affect the composition of the audience, and differences between radio, television, and perhaps closed-circuit transmissions, may also be relevant . . .

The judgment of the court of appeals is reversed.

[Omitted are the appendix containing a transcript of the "Filthy Words" monologue, as well as the concurring opinions of Justices Powell and Blackmun and the dissenting opinions of Justices Brennan, Marshall, Stewart, and White.]

Afterword

Congress and the FCC tried to impose a 24-hour ban on indecent broadcasting, but it was struck down in a 1991 federal appeals court decision. Thereafter, the FCC, at the direction of Congress, officially forbade indecent radio and television broadcasts between 6 AM and midnight. However, that too was challenged, and in 1993, a federal appeals court threw it out as a First Amendment violation.[6] At this writing in 1994, the FCC, in response to the appeals court decision, has returned to its "old" policy of banning indecency from 6 AM to 8 PM

Howard Stern.   This continuing First Amendment struggle is well illustrated by the FCC's pursuit of radio "shock jock" Howard Stern. From 1988 through early 1994, the FCC proposed more than $1.7 million in fines on Stern's employer, Infinity Broadcasting. Stern's 6 to 11 morning program held the no. 1 rating in both New York City and Los Angeles. For an extended period of time, much of Stern's programming was devoted to sexual matters. He and celebrities discussed sexual fantasies, he invited women to disrobe in his studio, and he described the process over the radio. He talked at length about masturbation and "spewing evil gunk all over everybody," he discussed anal intercourse and rectal bleeding, and remarked that two of his critics might be stranded at sea and "be forced to drink their own urine."

Responding to the FCC decision, columnist James Kilpatrick said:

> By any standard known to the law, the broadcasts were in fact indecent, and the fine was appropriate to the offense.[7]

Do you agree? Do you see any risk to society in curbing Stern's speech? At this writing in 1994, Infinity lawyers are arguing that the fines can no longer be lawfully imposed, since the 6 AM to midnight ban has been ruled unconstitutional.

Questions

1. Why was the question of whether the Federal Communications Commission's decision constituted adjudication or rule making significant to the subsequent judicial appeals? Explain the Supreme Court's resolution of that issue.
2. What is "prurient appeal"?
3. Are you persuaded by the Court's distinction between "obscene" language and "indecent" language? Explain.
4. Why was the commission's action not considered censorship?
5. Do children of all ages require the same degree of FCC protection? Explain.
6. The *Pacifica* decision is explicitly limited to the facts of the case. But the Court conceded that the decision might lead to some self-censorship. "At most, however, the commission's definition of indecency will deter only the broadcasting of patently offensive references to excretory and sexual organs and activities." Do you agree that the commission's position is casting only a very limited chill over broadcasting? Explain.
7. What is the significance of the distinction the Court draws between the content and the context of the speech in question?
8. Should the Court adopt Pacifica's view that the First Amendment prohibits all government regulation that depends on the content of the speech? Explain.

9. Is any group, however well qualified, capable of specifying national standards of broadcasting decency? Explain.
10. Develop the argument that rule making is preferable to litigation as a means of settling public policy issues.

Part Three—An Example: The Food and Drug Administration

Having achieved an overview of the agency *procedures,* we turn now to the *substance,* the actual business, of one of the more prominent agencies.

The Food and Drug Administration, a division of the Department of Health and Human Services, is responsible for protecting the public from dangerous food, drugs, and cosmetics and for ensuring the effectiveness of drugs. Our inquiry will be limited largely to those situations in which the FDA governs the entry of new products into the market and in which the agency recalls products from the market that fail to meet government standards (on grounds of mislabeling, subpotency, etc.)

HISTORY OF THE FDA

Today's FDA had its roots in the Bureau of Chemistry in the Department of Agriculture beginning in the 1880s. Consumer abuse of a magnitude that would today generate outrage was commonplace around the turn of the century. For example, adulterated, dangerous, worthless, sometimes habit-forming patent medicines, sold as miracle cures, constituted a significant health hazard. The muckraking literature of the day (e.g., Upton Sinclair's *The Jungle,* an exposé of unsanitary conditions in the meat-packing industry) and the increasing support of the American Medical Association and various industry trade associations led Congress in 1906 to approve the Food and Drug Act. In essence, the act prohibited the adulteration and misbranding of foods and drugs under federal jurisdiction. The legislation had been encouraged by the colorful tactics of Dr. Harvey Wiley, head of the Bureau of Chemistry, who formed what he called a "poison squad"—a group of 12 volunteers who ate meals laced with common preservatives of the era (borax, boric acid, formaldehyde, sulfurous acids, and others)—and then submitted the results to Congress.[8]

Weaknesses in the 1906 law generated appeals for further legislation. In 1937, a drug manufacturer released a new sulfa drug without benefit of toxicity tests. The first 40 gallons of "Elixir Sulfanilamide-Massengill" caused more than 100 deaths before its removal from the market.[9] Soon thereafter, Congress approved the Food, Drug, and Cosmetics Act of 1938, which, among other requirements, prevented the marketing of new drugs until their safety was established and authorized the new FDA to remove from the market drugs found to be hazardous.

The final major piece of legislation investing the FDA with its current authority was the 1962 Kefauver Drug Amendments Act, which, among other provisions, required the effectiveness of a drug to be established by "substantial evidence" before it could lawfully be marketed. Interestingly, passage of the Kefauver Act was likewise secured by a major scandal. Many pregnant women in Europe and Canada who had used the sedative thalidomide gave birth to children with deformed or missing limbs. The drug had been limited to experimental use in the United States. Although the Kefauver Amendment would have had no impact on the thalidomide product, the publicity surrounding that horror was instrumental in passage of the act.

FDA DUTIES

Under the aggressive leadership of Commissioner David Kessler, the FDA has been busy (critics say too busy) on many fronts. Let's look at some of those initiatives.

FDA Initiatives: Cigarettes as Drugs?

At this writing in 1994, Commissioner Kessler, in congressional testimony, has cited some evidence that tobacco companies may sell cigarettes with nicotine levels intentionally manipulated to cause addiction. If true, cigarettes would then be considered a drug and would fall under FDA jurisdiction. Kessler said that the FDA does not yet have sufficient evidence to assert regulatory authority over tobacco, but he called upon Congress to provide guidance in how to address the problem if the evidence leads the FDA to conclude that cigarettes are, in effect, a drug. Congressional support would be necessary to further regulate or ban cigarettes. That support has been considered unlikely, but recent allegations that some tobacco executives may have suppressed evidence about the addictiveness and other health risks of smoking may put great pressure on congress (see Chapter 16, Product Liability.) The tobacco industry denies any effort to manipulate nicotine levels, and the Philip Morris Tobacco Company, in March 1994, filed a $10 billion lawsuit against ABC News because of a February 28, 1994, "Day One" program allegedly suggesting that the tobacco industry was adding nicotine to cigarettes.

How would you advise approaching the issue of cigarettes as a drug? Would you call for a ban on the sale of cigarettes?

FDA Initiatives: Drug Approval

From a free market viewpoint, one of the most frustrating elements of FDA activity has been the slow pace at which new drugs are introduced to the market. In 1991, an average of 23 months were required for new drug clearance except for breakthrough formulations urgently needed for illnesses such as AIDS and cancer, which were approved in an average of 11 months. Those clearance times are a significant improvement over the historical record and now, further progress has arrived. In 1992, Congress approved new legislation that is expected to cut those review times to 12 months and 6 months, respectively, by 1997, thus aiding those suffering, saving drug companies millions, and presumably leading to increased drug development. The expedited approval is financed by new fees on drug companies, which will permit the FDA to hire 600 new employees.[10] That the FDA has made good progress in recent years is suggested by the recent approval of the cancer drug taxol in a period of 5 months and 2 days.[11]

FDA Initiatives: Silicone Implants

Some 150,000 women annually chose to receive silicone implants. Then, many women began to claim that the implants were leaking silicone and producing serious health problems, particularly autoimmune disease. In 1992, although the evidence was not conclusive, the FDA restricted the use of silicone gel implants to those with pressing medical needs (e.g., breast reconstruction) and those involved in clinical studies designed to test the risks. That decision was prompted, in part, by Dow Corning (the leading manufacturer) internal memos questioning implant safety:

> Memos and other corporate documents from 1975 to 1985 depict the nation's largest breast-implant manufacturer as rushing a new silicone-gel implant to market in 1975 and failing to do certain safety tests for years. The documents portray the company as misleading plastic surgeons about the risk that silicone could ooze out and spread to other parts of the body. In one memo, a salesman expressed his opinion that a decision to market a "questionable lot" of "greasy" implants "has to rank right up there with the Pinto gas tank." [12]

Then, in late 1992, Dow's outside counsel and former U.S. attorney general Griffin Bell concluded that Dow employees had falsified certain important records associated with the manufacture of the implants.[13] Manufacturers continued to insist that no proof of a link between the implants and health problems had been established, but increasing evidence supported those claims[14] and plaintiffs began to win some of the thousands of civil suits springing from the implants. A tentative $4.25 billion global settlement was announced in 1993. Women suffering from the implants were to receive from $200,000 to $2 million each. Under the terms of the proposed settlement, women with silicon implants were to give notice by June 17, 1994, if they did not want to participate in the settlement. Then federal judge Sam Pointer was to conduct an August 1994 hearing to determine if the settlement was fair and reasonable. At this writing in 1994, several new studies have called into question the link between the implants and a number of illnesses. The table on page 321 summarizes the early history of the implant controversy.

FDA Initiatives: Food Labeling

FDA rules, effective in 1994, create food label standards designed to improve consumer nutrition and discourage misleading claims. Terms such as *light, cholesterol free,* and *source of* can be used only if the food actually conforms to specific FDA definitions. Nutritional information and a list of all sweeteners must be provided, and health claims (such as "helps prevent heart disease") cannot be used without meeting

---

The Breast Implant Controversy

- **July 9, 1991.** The Food and Drug Administration, acting in 1988, sets this deadline for manufacturers of silicone-gel breast implants to provide detailed safety data.
- **Sept. 23, 1991.** Bristol-Myers Squibb Co. says it will close its breast implant business because it can't meet the FDA deadline to prove safety.
- **Dec. 13, 1991.** A San Francisco federal court jury issues a $7.3 million verdict against Dow Corning Corp., concluding the company concealed evidence linking ruptures to immune disorders.
- **Jan 6, 1992.** FDA Commissioner David Kessler, after reviewing company documents, announces a 45-day moratorium on the sale of silicone implants.
- **Feb. 10, 1992.** Dow Corning shakes up top management in the wake of an FDA inquiry into silicone implant safety.
- **Feb. 18–20, 1992.** An FDA panel hears testimony about the safety of silicone implants and decides to recommend limited sale of the devices.

- **March 19, 1992.** Dow Corning says it will stop making silicone implants.
- **April 16, 1992.** The FDA limits implants to clinical trials and to women needing reconstructive surgery because of effects of breast cancer, for example.
- **Nov. 2, 1992.** Dow Corning says its outside counsel, Griffin Bell, found evidence that company employees for several years faked records about the preparation of some silicone gel used in implants.
- **Nov. 28, 1992.** A Scripps Research Institute study, published in the *Lancet,* strengthens the link between silicone implants and autoimmune disorders. Women whose implants leaked experienced symptoms years sooner than women whose implants were intact.
- **Dec. 23, 1992.** A Houston woman wins a $25 million verdict against Bristol-Myers Squibb over silicone implants.
- **Jan. 5, 1993.** The FDA begins evaluating the safety of breast implants containing saline solution.

Source: *The Wall Street Journal,* February 4, 1993. p. B1. Reprinted by permisison of *The Wall Street Journal,* © 1993 Dow Jones & Company, Inc. All Rights Reserved Worldwide.

specific FDA requirements. The 882 pages of new rules will affect 250,000 products at a cost of perhaps $2 billion, but with an anticipated savings of many billions in reduced medical costs.[15] In 1994, the FDA and Agriculture Department announced new rules for food makers' use of the label "healthy." Food described as healthy must have low levels of fat, sodium, and cholesterol and must contain certain minimum levels of six basic nutrients, such as vitamin A. Critics say these rules represent regulatory overkill.

FDA Initiatives: Abortion Pill

The FDA is facing a potential storm with the May 1994 announcement that the French producer of the abortion drug, RU-486, has agreed to give a nonprofit group, the Population Council, the American licensing rights to the drug. The Population Council will choose an American manufacturer. Clinical trials, commencing in late 1994 and involving some 2000 women, will require about 14 months. Thereafter, FDA review is expected to require about six months. More than 120,000 Swedish, French, and British women have used the drug, which successfully terminates pregnancies in about 96 percent of the cases.[16]

Questions—Part Three

1. One critic's description of the new FDA food labeling rules included: "costly," "confusing," "condescending," and "controversial." Explain. See Elizabeth Whelan, "Food Label Folly," *The Wall Street Journal,* December 9, 1992, p. A20.
2. In 1993, the FDA banned all over-the-counter aids (gums, pills, etc.) for those who seek to quit smoking. Eleven years of studies and debate failed to provide proof of the products' effectiveness.
   a. Should the FDA ban these products or simply provide the public with the available evidence and let us decide for ourselves? Explain.
   b. Why doesn't the FDA banish tobacco products?
3. Jane King sued Collagen Corporation, claiming that she developed autoimmune disease after using Zyderm, a medical device inserted under the skin to smooth wrinkles. She raised various claims, including negligence in manufacturing. The device had been approved for distribution by the FDA and, according to a federal appeals court, was the subject of "extensive regulation." The court ruled that the FDA approval preempted the plaintiff's claims.
   a. Legal issues aside, was the decision in the best interests of the American public? Explain the competing public policy considerations.
   b. Why didn't the plaintiff sue the FDA for approving a product that subsequently proved to be dangerous?
   c. In a concurring opinion, two of the judges said, "Perfection is impossible and a few individuals may be denied full protection at the cost of benefitting the rest." What do they mean? As a matter of public policy and morality, how do you feel about their position? Explain. See *King* v. *Collagen,* 983 F.2d 1130, 1138 (1993).
4. On May 25, 1979, an American Airlines DC-19 crashed in Chicago, Illinois, with 273 persons aboard.

   The Federal Aviation Administration [FAA] certified the DC-10 wide-bodied jet without having its own employees check all preproduction tests and design plans, an FAA official says.

   Douglas Sharman, an FAA aerospace engineer, told a National Transportation Safety Board hearing that only a fraction of the work approved by aircraft manufacturing engineers designated as agents of the FAA actually is checked by the government agency. Thus McDonnell Douglas Corporation, which made the DC-10, "approved" its own work for the government.[17]

   a. Can American corporations be trusted to do their own testing prior to product approval? Explain.
   b. Does the presence of the various regulatory agencies afford the public a false sense of security? Explain.

5. A past director of the FDA's Bureau of Drugs, in speaking of his agency's regulation of prescription medicines, stated that "We do not pay any attention to the economic consequences of our decisions."[18]
   a. Defend that seemingly arrogant and wasteful attitude.
   b. Should economic considerations be irrelevant to regulations regarding human health and safety? Explain.
6. Oraflex, an arthritis drug manufactured by Eli Lilly & Co., was rejected for the American market in 1980. It was subsequently admitted to the British market. Later, the FDA reversed its position and permitted the sale of Oraflex in the United States. After reports of many illnesses and a number of deaths apparently linked to the drug, it was removed from the market by Lilly. In a subsequent congressional investigation, the acting director of the FDA testified that Lilly had submitted data revealing various side effects from Oraflex, but the FDA did not look at the data, and Lilly failed to bring the data directly to the attention of the FDA.[19]
   a. Should all new drug applicants be required to explicitly identify all hazards known to be associated with their products? Explain.
   b. Should cigarette manufacturers be required to reveal all the evidence in their possession regarding the health hazards associated with their products? Explain.
   c. In either of the cases explored in (*a*) and (*b*), should producers be required not merely to reveal known hazards but to advertise that information broadly? Explain.

Part Four—*The Federal Regulatory Process Evaluated*

Free market advocates seek to reduce government, while others favor a restrained market where the government plays an important role in preventing and correcting market failure. The economic signature of the late 1980s and early 1990s was the stunning ascendance of market economics in Eastern Europe, the former Soviet Union, Great Britain, and now China. (See Chapter 1.) At the same time, the Reagan administration worked to sharply reduce the regulatory role of the federal government in American life. The Bush and Clinton administrations have moved back toward the center on the question of government intervention. Against that historical backdrop, the argument continues—should the government be more or less involved in American business? The principal criticisms of the regulatory process follow.

CRITICISMS

Excessive Regulation

In brief, the argument of excessive regulation is that government regulations reduce business efficiency, curb freedom, and unjustly redistribute resources. Consider some of the more specific costs:

- *Total bill.* The most recent comprehensive study puts the total cost of federal government regulation in 1990 at about $400 billion—or $4,000 per household.[20] (Note that those figures do not reflect the benefits derived from those regulations.)
- *Personnel and paper.* The 1992 federal budget provided for 122,400 "regulators," the largest number ever and 16,400 more than in 1989.[21] As of October 1991, federal agencies were working on nearly 5,000 regulations.[22]
- *Jobs.* Economist Robert Hahn reminds us that those direct costs are only the most visible regulatory tax:

> The measurable costs of regulation pale against the distortions that sap the economy's dynamism. The public never sees the factories that weren't built, the new products that didn't appear, or the entrepreneurial idea that drowned in a cumbersome regulatory process.[23]

Note that the regulatory impact is particularly great for small businesses, which do not have the resources and the mechanisms in place (as giant firms do) to cope with the weight of regulation.

Summary. In addition to the expense of the regulations, the business community's primary complaints can be summarized as follows:

1. Overlap and conflict among agencies.
2. Overextension of agency authority, not merely in setting goals but in dictating how those goals are to be met.
3. Adversarial attitudes toward business.
4. Agency delay in issuing required permits, rules, and standards.
5. Escalating reporting requirements.

The following article presents a clear picture of the burdens of government regulation, but it also reminds us of the benefits—in this case, allegedly safer food.

FDA REGULATORY TIDE SWALLOWS UP MCCURDY FISH CO.

Brent Bowers

This is the story of how government regulation killed the U.S. smoked-herring industry.

Unfortunately for John McCurdy, *he* was the industry. He says he was forced to shut down his herring smokehouse in Lubec, Maine—by all accounts, the last one in America—because he refused to gut freshly caught fish before dumping them into brine tanks.

With only $250,000 in annual revenue, McCurdy Fish Co. was no match for the U.S. Food and Drug Administration. Undaunted, Mr. McCurdy is still pressing the FDA to modify the policy that did in his family business in 1991 ... His battle underscores the vulnerability of small companies to sudden shifts in the regulatory environment.

The FDA says that it intervened to protect the public from the threat of botulism. The 62-year-old Mr. McCurdy says that the agency overreacted. He says his company produced three million pounds of herring—roughly 54 million fillets—in his 20 years at the helm without a single report of food poisoning.

Mr. McCurdy's run-in with the FDA began in 1990, when the agency informed him that it could no longer tolerate his methods. The company had used these methods since Mr. McCurdy's grandfather founded the concern at the turn of the century. The notification grew out of the agency's 1988 "policy guide" that fish must be eviscerated before being salted and smoked. Failing to do so posed "a potentially life-threatening, acute health hazard," the FDA told Mr. McCurdy. The company eviscerated the fish after the salting and smoking process.

Nonsense, Mr. McCurdy retorted. Not only had he never had any complaints, he says, but FDA inspectors found nothing amiss in their almost yearly tests of his fish . . .

*   *   *   *   *

The confrontation raged for a year. The crux of the problem, Mr. McCurdy says, was that he couldn't afford to pay $75,000 for the equipment needed to meet the FDA's demands. With little lobbying clout and no money to wage an uphill legal battle, he finally closed in May 1991.

The demise of McCurdy Fish wiped out 22 jobs in Lubec, a coastal village of 1,900 people. Today, a "for sale" sign is affixed to Mr. McCurdy's salting shed, a red building covered with cedar shingles that sits on pilings in Johnson Bay. So far, Mr. McCurdy has been unable to find a buyer. No wonder: half of the 20-plus stores in downtown Lubec are boarded up, victims of a long economic decline . . .

Mr. McCurdy still chokes with anger at the way things turned out. He says "tons and tons" of smoked herring continue to pour into the U.S. from Canada, some processed by the same methods that he used. "It's a double standard that has destroyed my livelihood and cost this town more than 20 jobs and an industry that was part of the community since the early 1800s," he says bitterly.

The FDA counters that a U.S. agreement with Canada blocks exports of smoked fish that aren't eviscerated before processing. At least one Canadian fish processor, however, privately acknowledges that it ignores this official requirement.

*   *   *   *   *

Considering Americans' phobia about contaminated food, the FDA probably had no choice, says Roy Martin, vice president for science and technology at the National Fisheries Institute, a trade group in Washington, D.C. But he wonders whether the crackdown is justified by the three deaths in the 1980s.

"There's a risk-benefit question here the country hasn't addressed yet," Mr. Martin says. "The only villain is 'the possibility of a public-health problem.' When you have the word 'may' in there, you can drive a truck through it."

Would he have eaten Mr. McCurdy's smoked fish? "Sure," Mr. Martin says. "I'm sure it was perfectly safe."

Thomas Billy, director of the FDA's office of seafood, bristles at any suggestion that the agency engaged in overkill. "What we're talking about is not some bureaucratic, arbitrary whimsy," but people's lives, he says. After all, he notes, Mr. McCurdy had the option of buying widely available evisceration equipment. The FDA official says there also was a lack of "quality control" at the Lubec plant.

Insufficient Regulation

Our society is rapidly changing, complex, and, in many ways, troubled. Consequently, calls for new government regulations and more money for existing regulatory efforts are routine. For example, aren't most Americans pleased that the Federal Communications Commission in 1990 issued new rules that make it more difficult for minors to listen to so-called dial-a-porn messages? Advocates of increased regulation point to the many successes of government intervention: legal equality for minorities and women; prevention of the sale of dangerous food and drugs; the Auto Safety Act, which, by some estimates, saves 12,000 lives per year; child labor laws; increasingly safe workplaces; cleaner air; and on and on. Indeed, one recent study's "best guess" is that social regulation (environment, health, and safety), unlike economic regulation, generated *net benefits* to society of about $2 billion in 1988.[24]

As we see in the following article, the industry being regulated may itself call for further regulation. Perhaps paradoxically, the government in this instance subsequently resisted that appeal (see p. 329).

AIRLINES URGE FAA: ORDER TOT SAFETY SEATS

Jane Norman

The airline industry . . . asked the Federal Aviation Administration to require that infants traveling on aircraft be strapped into safety seats.

The proposal, which comes in the wake of a crash in Sioux City, Ia., last year in which an unrestrained 23-month-old boy was killed, could require parents to buy tickets for children who now fly free.

Children under two years old are not required to use safety seats under . . . FAA rules, and passengers usually are advised to hold infants tightly or place them on the floor in case of turbulence or a crash. Airlines recently have encouraged use of the seats, which are mandated for babies traveling in motor vehicles.

Why Not?

"If we buckle up our children at 50 miles per hour, why not at 550 miles per hour?" asked Robert Aaranson, president of the Air Transport Association . . . He said 5,000 to 10,000 infants travel with their parents on commercial aircraft every day . . .

*   *   *   *   *

Safety seats most likely would be provided by parents, not the airlines. The seats would be the same ones parents use in their cars or trucks, as long as the seats bear stickers indicating they meet federal Department of Transportation regulations.

*   *   *   *   *

In the case of the Sioux City crash, passenger Sylvia Tsao told federal investigators that she wrapped her son, Evan, in blankets and placed him on the floor of the aircraft, following flight attendants' orders. But when the crippled DC-10 flipped over, "I saw for an instant my son's body floating and flying at a very high speed down the right aisle toward the back of the plane, his head first, his face away from me. He must have been traveling at an incredible speed."

Source: Reprinted by permission of the *Des Moines Register,* February 23, 1990, pp. 1A, 10A.

Excessive Industry Influence

As we have noted, the industries to be regulated were often instrumental in spawning the various federal agencies. Noted economist George Stigler summarizes the argument: "[R]egulation is acquired by the industry and is designed and operated primarily for its benefit."[25] Stigler further contends that, where possible, firms will encourage government regulations restricting entry (licensing), thus limiting competition: "Every industry or occupation that has enough political power to utilize the state will seek to control entry."[26]

As evidence of industry influence in agency affairs, critics argue that agency employees who leave federal service frequently turn to jobs in the industry they were formerly charged with regulating. Similarly, agency recruits are often drawn from the industry being regulated. Industry influence over the regulatory process is considerable. Industry expertise is invaluable, and the industry voice should be heard. The question is one of the "volume" of the voice.

The Ethics Reform Act of 1989 seeks to reduce some of these problems. Among other provisions, the act bars high government officials from lobbying the executive branch of government for one year after leaving their government posts.[27]

In 1993, President Clinton issued an executive order designed to open the regulatory process and reduce the quiet, "back-door" influence of special interests. The order also requires the use of cost-benefit analyses in considering new regulations. Additional concerns, such as the burden of new rules on business, must also be taken into consideration.

Underrepresentation of Public Opinion

Agency critics also charge that the diffuse voice of public opinion does not receive the attention accorded the pleas of special interests. It is generally acknowledged that public sentiment, being largely unorganized, is greatly underrepresented in regulatory matters, while well-financed, skillfully organized special interests carry political weight far beyond the numbers they represent.

Mechanics.   These complaints are not meant to represent the full range of criticisms of the federal regulatory process. In particular, the mechanics of agency conduct are frequently assailed. Allegations of inefficiency, incompetence, and arbitrariness are commonplace. The pace of work is said to be slow, and enforcement of policy often appears weak and ineffectual.

DEREGULATION

In response to those criticisms, both Democrats and Republicans, beginning in the late 1970s, began to reduce the quantity of federal regulatory intervention. Primarily, the deregulation movement consisted of shrinking the federal bureaucracy, eliminating as many government rules as possible, and expediting the process of complying with those rules that could not be removed.

In those cases where a government role continued to be considered necessary, the deregulation advocates argued for applying free market incentives and reasoning to the achievement of regulatory goals. Thus, rather than forbidding undesirable conduct (such as pollution and industrial accidents), the government might impose a tax on those behaviors society wants to discourage. In effect, a business would purchase the right to engage in conduct society considers injurious or inefficient. Similarly, rather than rationing portions of the radio spectrum or the right to land at airports at peak times, the government might auction those rights to the highest bidder. Market incentives would (1) encourage companies to use cost-effective compliance means and (2) raise the price of dangerous products, thus discouraging their use. However, monitoring difficulties, particularly in the case of pollution, render the taxing or auction methods inexact at best. Some object to the idea of allowing businesses to engage in undesirable conduct or highly prized conduct merely because they have the resources to pay for those privileges.

Similarly, cost-benefit analysis would be applied to all regulations. Regulations would be imposed only if added benefits equaled or exceeded added costs. The accompanying table, based on data by Professor Kip Viscusi, illustrates that some regulations are, in a cost-benefit sense, much more sensible than others.

How the Costs Vary

Regulation	Agency	Annual Number of Deaths (per 100,000 of exposed population)	Cost Per Life Saved
Mandatory seat belts for cars	National Highway Traffic Safety Administration	9.1	$390,000
Prohibitions on alcohol and drug use by railroad employees	Federal Railroad Administration	0.2	$650,000
Control and disposal standards for benzene	Environmental Protection Agency	2.1	$4,000,000
Disposal standards for uranium mine wastes	Environmental Protection Agency	43.0	$69,000,000
Restrictions on worker exposure to asbestos	Occupational Safety and Health Administration	6.7	$117,000,000
Restrictions on worker exposure to formaldehyde	Occupational Safety and Health Administration	0.1	$94,000,000,000

Source: Louis Richman, "Bringing Reason to Regulation," *Fortune*, October 19, 1992, pp. 94, 96. Reprinted by permission.

In 1992, the FAA announced that it had decided against the proposal to require child safety seats on American flights (see p. 326). That decision was based on a cost-benefit analysis, which is described in the following article.

FAA ARGUES AGAINST REQUIRING CHILD SAFETY SEATS ON AIRPLANES

Requiring child-safety seats for infants on airliners would cost more lives than it would save, the Federal Aviation Administration said . . .

"While the chance of survival aboard an airplane may be slightly improved, the costs . . . will divert a significant number of families from . . . air travel to far less safe travel by automobile," Associate FAA Administrator Anthony Broderick told a House subcommittee.

* * * * *

The long-awaited FAA study concluded that requiring safety seats would increase the average airfare for a family by 31 percent, or $185.

Those higher costs, the study said, would cause about 20 percent of the families now using airlines for long-distance trips to opt to drive or stay home, which also would expose them to higher risks associated with increased local travel.

While estimating that mandated safety seats would save one infant's life in an airline crash over the next decade, the resulting increased auto traffic would produce at least nine additional highway deaths, 52 serious injuries and more than 2,300 minor injuries, the study said.

Source: Associated Press, *Des Moines Register,* July 13, 1990, p. 3A. Reprinted by permission of the Associated Press.

FURTHER DEREGULATION OR REREGULATION?

The United States remains the least regulated of all the industrialized nations. Central planning, direct government investment, and social welfare regulation greatly exceeding our own are represented in varying proportions among all other advanced economies. Indeed, some of those nations, such as Japan and Germany, currently enjoy economic health in many respects exceeding our own. Highly regarded economist and MIT dean Lester Thurow reminds us that America's economic performance has improved since the onset of the intensive government intervention of the New Deal.[28] Government regulation in America normally arises not from ideology but from actual problems.[29] America is not committed to government regulation as a matter of political policy. Rather, regulation in this country has, in many instances, resulted from an honorable effort to correct evident wrongs. Much-maligned agencies such as the EPA, OSHA, and the FDA were not born of a desire for big government and central planning. Pollution, industrial accidents, and dangerous food and drugs were clearly the impetus for the creation of those agencies.

Less Government?

We turn now to the encompassing inquiry: Should we further deregulate the American economy? Some argue for more regulations. Others would favor exclusive reliance on the free market. Most fall somewhere between. In recent years, we have engaged in a national debate about the proper measure of government regulation of business.

Is deregulation desirable? In the 1990s, neither the American public nor politicians are displaying much zeal for further deregulation. Virtually everyone favors reducing paperwork, eliminating red tape, and getting bureaucrats off our backs. But when addressing specific issues such as auto safety, banking, job health and safety, the environment, and the stock market, very few Americans want less regulation. Most either favor the current balance or prefer greater government intervention.[30] Furthermore, as discussed later in this chapter, the federal government has recently "reregulated" the cable television industry. Now that the dust has settled a bit, we are reminded by economist Roger Noll that "the regulatory structure that was in place 20 years ago is almost intact."[31] Nonetheless, in specific industries (most notably, transportation, banking, and communications), the impact has been quite pronounced. Meanwhile, the central issue remains: What is the proper business–government mix in America?

The Evidence

Arguably, the biggest legacy of the deregulation effort is its effectiveness in reminding us of the virtues of the free market and of the immense power of the pricing mechanism in addressing virtually all issues. More specifically, both consumers and producers have enjoyed some obvious tangible benefits.

The Good News.   In the key deregulated industries of transportation and communications, productivity is up and prices are down. According to a 1992 Interstate Commerce Commission study, productivity in those industries, except for telephones, improved (or declined at a slower rate) after deregulation than before. Furthermore, the data show that productivity gains were greatest where deregulation was most thorough (railroads, trucking, and airlines). Similarly, prices fell in all deregulated industries, although in the telephone business the price decline was greater before deregulation than after.[32]

In a similar vein:

- *New businesses.* "The number of new businesses increased by 12.3 percent in the deregulated industries of transportation and financial services, compared to 8.2 percent for the whole economy."[33]
- *Airlines.* According to one study airfares fell about 29 percent following deregulation.[34] Many more people are now able to fly.
- *Shipping.* Consumers are estimated to have saved some $72 billion between 1980 and 1987 in lower prices for goods as freight rates fell.[35]

- *Telephones.* Long-distance telephone rates have fallen by perhaps 20 percent,[36] and striking technological advances are emerging.

Perhaps the strongest support for deregulation is that others around the world have looked at the American experience and are beginning to do the same. The following article notes that even the Japanese, so long and successfully committed to government/private-sector cooperation, are considering deregulation initiatives.

INTERNATIONAL

JAPAN INCHES TOWARD DEREGULATION, BUT ECONOMISTS DON'T SEE QUICK FIXES

David P. Hamilton

Japan's new government, after weeks of talking about deregulating the economy to benefit consumers, took a few steps in that direction, albeit baby ones.

Private economists in Japan say the cautious deregulation proposals, which government ministers described as the core of their efforts to pull the nation out of its economic slump, might help in the long term but aren't likely to have much effect in the short run.

Officials said the proposals . . . are intended to increase business opportunities in Japan, expand market access and pass on the benefits of the high yen to consumers.

For instance, various ministries have suggested allowing the transmission and reception of international television broadcasts, easing license restrictions on new liquor stores, allowing importers to set their own testing standards for some goods and raw materials, and liberalizing taxi fares and trucking rates.

Lower Prices

* * * * *

Officials also said they intend to lower prices of some consumer goods and of utility charges such as

gas and electricity by capitalizing on the yen's 20% appreciation this year . . .

* * * * *

Deregulation will have "a very slow, invisible impact, and in that sense it's going to be disappointing," said Donald Kimball, senior economist at Mitsubishi Bank. "You simply can't depend on any sort of deregulation to snap this economy out of recession. It takes time to rewrite regulations—you don't just suddenly sweep them off the books," he said.

* * * * *

Bank of Tokyo economist Soichi Enkyo said that, within two to three years, deregulation—if it actually occurs—could have several effects. It likely would spread the benefits of the yen's appreciation and bring down consumer prices; it could boost productivity at many inefficient industrial sectors, such as distribution and services, and it could improve the U.S.-Japan trade imbalance, to boot.

The Bad News.   Deregulation has not been a panacea for what ails America or even for the problems of the deregulated industries. The accompanying material summarizes deregulation concerns.

Deregulation Means Never Having to Say You're Sorry

The orthodoxy of deregulation that characterized the 1980s was supposed to bring with it intense competition. Instead, consumers have seen less competition, higher prices, and deteriorating service in industry after industry. Paul Stephen Dempsey, professor of law at the University of Denver, offers his assessment of the failures of deregulation:

Airlines

- Deteriorating service (unrealistic scheduling, deliberate overbooking, false and misleading advertising, etc.).
- Large number of failures (150 bankruptcies).
- Unprecedented industry concentration (eight firms control 90 percent of the passenger market; only three to five airlines are viable).
- Erosion of the margin of safety.
- Pricing discrimination.
- Prices (in real dollars and adjusted for changing fuel costs) higher than preregulation trend.
- Deterioration in labor-management relations.

Banks and S&Ls

- More fraudulent transactions.
- More failed institutions.
- Federal deposit insurance funds near bankruptcy.
- Taxpayers will pay $500 billion—more than $2,000 for every man, woman, and child in the United States—to bail out failed thrifts.

Bus Industry

- Unprecedented concentration (industry duopoly becomes an anemic monopoly that faces bankruptcy).
- Deterioration of service (4,500 small communities abandoned).
- Deterioration in labor-management relations.

Cable Television

- Sharply increased prices.
- Deterioration of service.
- Unprecedented concentration.

Railroads

- Unprecedented concentration (seven major railroads control 85 percent of the freight).
- Pricing discrimination (bulk shippers prejudiced).
- Higher coal rates result in significant increase in electricity prices for consumers.
- Deterioration in labor-management relations.

Telecommunications

- Deterioration in service.
- Industry concentration (long-distance service dominated by AT&T).
- Local and rural rate increases outpace declining toll rates.

Trucking

- Large number of failures (60 percent of general freight companies disappear with no significant new entries).
- Unprecedented concentration.
- Deterioration in safety.
- Highly discriminatory pricing (prejudicing small and rural shippers).
- Deterioration in labor-management relations.

Source: Paul Stephen Dempsey, "Has Deregulation Derailed American Industry?" *Business and Society Review* 77 (Spring 1991), 53, 55. Reprinted with permission of the copyright holder, *Business & Society Review.*

Reregulate?

Predictably, we are now experiencing something of a backlash against deregulation. Cable television was deregulated in 1986. Then, in 1992, Congress approved, over President Bush's veto, a new regulatory scheme for the industry.[37] The bill was designed to curb rapidly rising rates while encouraging competition for monopoly cable systems. In those markets where the cable company does not have competition, the bill requires *basic* service rates set according to a Federal Communications Commission formula based on market rates in communities where cable companies face competition (such as satellite systems). Basic service must include local over-the-air channels as well as public access, educational, and government channels. Local authorities can no longer grant *exclusive* cable franchises, and over-the-air television stations can now negotiate to require payment to carry their programming on cable systems.

Rates.   From 1986 when cable was deregulated to 1992, average monthly cable rates for basic service rose from just over $10 to nearly $19.[38] The 1992 law was expected to significantly reduce rates, but by 1994 it became apparent that loopholes in the legislation compromised that goal and actually resulted in rising rates for about one-third of cable subscribers. Hence, the FCC announced a further rate cut, effective in May 1994, which, in combination with the original rollback, was targeted to achieve as much as a 17 percent rate decrease for some consumers and an estimated three billion dollars in annual savings. Ninety percent of cable users were projected to realize a rate reduction.[39]

However, changes in the number or nature of channels in the basic package, increases in rates for the unregulated premium channels (HBO, etc.) and other programming changes may mean that actual consumer savings will be modest.

Is reregulation a good idea? Prior to passage of the bill, a *Des Moines Register* editorial urged Congress to resist voter pressure and stay with the free market.

DON'T RE–REGULATE CABLE TV

Consumers may not have liked it when the chain that operates all but one movie theater in the Des Moines area raised its rates last year. But despite increases in movie-ticket prices, from $4 to $5.50 since 1988, nobody has given an instant thought to calling for federal regulation of movie-theater prices. Why? Because going to the movies isn't an essential activity. There's simply no need for government involvement.

That's the way it is with cable television, or at least the way it ought to be. It's a nonessential activity, an add-on entertainment service that expands on what most consumers can get, at no charge, over the airwaves. But Congress nonetheless is on a tear to reregulate cable rates. Lawmakers, for the second time in two years, are trying to make their constituents happy by fighting the cable industry.

*   *   *   *   *

There's no question that since cable operations were deregulated in 1984, increases in rates have been outrageous, three times the rate of inflation.

Proponents of re-regulation argue that the industry gets by with hefty price hikes because 97 percent of cable systems operate where there is no effective competition.

But tinkering by Congress may not help. One way or the other, cable operators will get their profit . . .

*   *   *   *   *

Still, cable is increasingly popular—more than 60 percent of all homes now are wired. Those paying the bills in those households have an effective option if they don't like the price: They can discontinue the service. That's a much better option than what's now being considered in Washington.

Source: *Des Moines Register,* August 3, 1992. Copyright 1992, *Des Moines Register.* Reprinted with permission.

Questions

1. *a.* Has deregulation affected your life? *Explain.*
   b. Do you *trust* the free market? The government? Both? Neither? Explain.
   c. On balance, has business deregulation been a good direction for America? Explain.
2. The *Des Moines Register* advocated a free market approach to cable television, labeling it a "nonessential activity." Should the government be involved in regulating only those products and services that we cannot do without? Explain.

CASE FOR DISCUSSION

General Motors Pickup Trucks

Shannon Moseley, a teenager, died in a fiery crash while driving a General Motors pickup truck. In February 1993, his family was awarded $105.2 million, $101 of which was for punitive damages. The decision was overturned on appeal, and at this writing in 1994, the family has indicated that they will seek a retrial. The Moseley case was one of many contending GM's Chevrolet and GMC 1973–1987 model heavy pickup trucks are unreasonably dangerous because their side-mounted gas tanks are especially vulnerable to puncture or rupture. The point of contention is that the GM gas tanks, unlike those of the competition, are located outside the frame rails of the pickups. GM had previously lost three multimillion dollar cases involving those pickups, and it had settled several others out of court. GM contends the pickups are safe, but in the Moseley trial a GM engineer, who had defended GM in 15 previous cases, "defected" and testified that the truck design was "indefensible." He did so after learning of GM crash tests showing the tanks splitting open. Another GM engineer testified that GM had shredded critical files while facing litigation in the early 1980s.[40] GM is appealing the Moseley decision.

GM maintains the trucks are safe, and with 4.7 million of them still on the road, a recall might cost $2 billion at a time when GM is floundering financially. Auto safety advocates say the likely cost is about $65 per vehicle, for a total of $300 million.[41]

Settlement?   In 1993, GM, facing several dozen class action suits seeking money (a likely total of about $2 billion) lost due to the reduced resale value of the trucks, reached a tentative settlement providing pickup owners with $1,000 coupons to be used toward the purchase of a new GM truck. (In early 1994, the settlement is being challenged in court.)

According to National Highway Traffic Safety Administration data, the GM pickups are actually safer than most vehicles on the road (see table).

Crash tests: Each year you drive a heavy pickup truck, these are your odds of dying in an accident:

Dodge	1 in 8,606
Ford	1 in 6,916
GM	1 in 6,605
Nissan (light model)	1 in 4,521
All passenger cars	1 in 6,053

Source: NHTSA, in Rich Thomas, "Just as Safe at Any Speed," *Newsweek,* May 10, 1993, p. 52.

So what is the problem? Government data show that the chances of dying in a fire after a side collision in a GM pickup are nearly two and one-half times greater than in a comparable Ford or Dodge pickup.[42] Understand that a driver is not more likely to die in a GM pickup in a side collision than in a Ford; rather, if one were to die in such a collision, the odds are greater that the death would be caused by fire. In total, then, the GM pickups are safe by government standards but below average with respect to fire safety in side collisions. Specifically, NHTSA estimates that the challenged design will result in five to six additional deaths per year.[43]

Fatalities have declined significantly since 1988, when GM moved the tanks inside the frame.[44] Further, the government is concerned that while the GM tanks did meet government standards at the time of production, they may be subject to wear and rust that will make them especially vulnerable to leakage or rupture.

Recall?   Because of the horrid image of fire deaths, because of a wave of adverse publicity (including an NBC documentary later conceded to have been rigged), and because of a public that demands maximum safety, GM is under attack. The government has sought a recall, and GM has declined. Our concern in this instance is not so much with GM's social responsibility in this case, although that is obviously a pressing issue, but with a federal agency's handling of the case. The following article explains the National Highway Traffic Safety Administration's approach to the pickup controversy. As you read this article, think about (1) whether GM has been fairly treated by the government, (2) how we decide when the government should seek a product recall, and (3) what GM's duties are.

IS U.S. RECALL REQUEST ON GM TRUCKS DRIVEN BY SAFETY OR POLITICS?

Douglas Lavin and Bruce Ingersoll

For more than a year, record red ink and a board-room revolt have put General Motors Corp. under increasing scrutiny. Now the company must deal with its latest crisis: the federal government's request that it recall 4.7 million pickup trucks equipped with "side-saddle" gasoline tanks. GM's official response to the National Highway Traffic Safety Administration is due tomorrow.

But as GM prepares a legal battle over the trucks, many experts believe that a harsh light ought to be shone on the government as well. For more than two decades, they say, the traffic-safety agency's evaluation of the GM trucks has smacked of consistent bureaucratic bumbling. And now, by seeking what could become a multibillion-dollar recall, regulators are responding to pressure from an advocacy group by trying to make up for what some view as earlier ineptitude. Consider:

• For almost two years, the agency investigated whether 1.6 million of the GM pickups, built between 1984 and 1986, were leaking fuel through rusting gas tanks. Investigators found few owner complaints, no reports of leaks causing fires and no evidence of an "unreasonable risk" of fires in side-impact collisions. In February 1992, they pronounced the trucks safe.

• Nearly two decades earlier, when the side-saddle pickups were being introduced, the agency had the perfect opportunity to correct any design flaw. In 1973, regulators were drafting a new standard governing fuel-tank integrity in crashes. But they set the side-impact standard at just 20 miles per hour, which the GM trucks easily met. Only in 1990 did the agency concede that its own standard was inadequate. And not for another two years did the agency begin the process of making the rule more stringent.

• The NHTSA is seeking a recall only after being pushed by trial lawyers and by the Washington-based Center for Auto Safety, a group founded by GM foe Ralph Nader. The trucks were also pilloried by the media and, unfairly it turned out, by NBC News last fall. The regulators are basing their recall request on the same historical accident data that they have had, and disregarded, for years.

Laxness Denied

* * * * *

Agency officials bristle at the suggestion that they have been lax. "You can always look in hindsight, 20–20, and say, 'Gee, you should have picked that up,'" says William A. Boehly, who is heading up NHTSA's investigation into the pickups. But, he says, the safety administration generally launches inquiries only after it receives complaints from consumers. Mr. Boehly says there have been very few complaints.

That fact raises the question: Are the trucks then safe? The answer is yes, overall, as Mr. Boehly acknowledges. Their fatal-accident record is substantially better than most cars' and only slightly worse than that of Ford and Dodge trucks, according to both NHTSA and GM.

Stricter Testing

What is more, GM's internal tests for side-impact safety have long been more stringent than the government's. In the early 1970s, the company was testing its vehicles in side-impact crashes at 30 miles an hour, which was above the federal standard. By 1984 GM had increased its internal standard to 50 mph. That prompted the company to improve the design of the gas tanks, protecting them with a plastic shield.

However, ever since the side-saddle trucks were introduced in 1973, their gas tanks have sometimes ripped open and exploded in side-impact collisions. The GM trucks are 2.4 times as likely as pickups made by Ford Motor Co. to be involved in deadly side crashes with fires, NHTSA says. That translates into about five deaths a year out of more than 40,000 on the nation's highways.

Such crashes, then, are quite rare. In the U.S., for every 10,000 vehicle crashes, there are only 30 fires; only three or four of them involve side-impact collisions. At most, one of those accidents would involve a pickup truck of any make.

So, then, what is the proper statistical standard for determining whether a vehicle is unsafe and in need of recall? That is a judgment call, and Washington's judgment clearly has changed. The Clinton administration has a more activist regulatory bent than its Republican predecessors. Federico Pena, the secretary of transportation, could have overruled the NHTSA staff's recommendation that the GM trucks be recalled, but he didn't.

During the 12 years of Republican deregulatory policies, the decision almost certainly would have been different. Had the staff recommended a GM-pickup recall during the Bush era, then-administrator Jerry Curry says he would have booted them out of his office . . .

Down a New Road

NHTSA itself says it is plowing new regulatory ground with this case. Never before has the agency asked for a recall of a vehicle that met a precisely applicable government safety standard at the time it was built.

To General Motors, which in 1988 changed the design of its pickup trucks to put the gas tank inside the steel underframe, this amounts to changing the rules after the game is over . . . [T]he NHTSA could hold hearings on the matter before ordering a recall. GM then could appeal the agency's decision in court.

* * * * *

In the midst of this, it is clear that federal regulators had opportunity to act on GM's design much earlier—and with relatively little cost.

Early Doubts

Shortly after the 1973 GM pickups were first marketed, questions were being raised about the safety of side-saddle gas tanks. Ford printed diagrams of the positioning of Ford and Chevrolet gas tanks in a 1973 sales brochure and pointed out that "Ford has mounted the tank between the steel frame siderails for protection." Chrysler Corp.'s pickups are similar to Ford's, leaving GM alone among the Big Three with tanks near the exterior of the vehicle.

Also at this time, NHTSA was developing a new rule, Federal Motor Vehicle Safety Standard 301, which limits the amount of fuel that can leak from vehicles in test crashes to an ounce a minute. The government's test crashes for side-impact collisions were conducted at 20 miles an hour—a standard that still stands.

"The standard is ludicrously low," says L. L. "Mick" McBee Jr., a plaintiff's attorney in Dallas who has won millions of dollars from GM in three pickup-case settlements.

Mr. McBee has a point of view, of course. But in November 1990 the NHTSA published a statistical examination of Rule 301's effectiveness over the years. It found the standard had helped to reduce car fires by 14%, but didn't cut fire-related deaths. The rule had no effect at all on pickups. "No significant reduction in crash fires was found for post-standard light trucks," the report says.

The safety agency didn't follow up on that report for two years. Then, last December, NHTSA opened its standard for review. It questioned whether any of the crash tests simulate what happens in the real world. In the tests, a dummy vehicle is thrust into the side of the pickup truck at a precise 90-degree angle. The broad impact of the test crash may blunt the penetration of the side of the pickup, the agency said, and thus fail to replicate the spearing that sometimes happens on the road.

Auto Maker's Defense

The validity of the federal side-impact standard is crucial, because it is at the heart of GM's defense. The company says its trucks shouldn't be recalled because they are safe and because they meet federal Rule 301.

Meanwhile, even though NHTSA tested 1979, 1981 and 1984 model pickups, none of the tests the agency conducted involved side hits. "All the vehicles were doing very well in compliance with that standard," says NHTSA's Mr. Boehly. "It was a matter of enforcement resources. Other things were more important to test."

As it turns out, the agency didn't conduct any side-impact crash tests until earlier this year. In one series of tests at East Liberty, Ohio, investigators found a 1987 Chevy pickup leaked 10 times more fuel than either a 1987 Dodge or 1987 Ford pickup when broadsided by the same kind of car at 60 mph. In another series at 50 mph, they found that three 1986 GM pickups had sprung leaks of more than 10 gallons within the first minute, far in excess of the Rule 301 limit of one ounce a minute.

What concerned Mr. Boehly is that test results on dummies in the GM pickups indicate that the drivers would have survived the 50-mph crash—but if trapped in the wreckage, they could have been burned to death.

Also among the signals missed by NHTSA in the 1980s: two multimillion-dollar verdicts awarded accident victims or their survivors in GM pickup cases.

But perhaps the most glaring example of an omission came in 1990, when the agency launched a two-year investigation into whether the gas tanks on some of the later model pickups were rusting.

Safety investigators examined whether the tanks on 1.6 million 1984–86 model pickups were corroding and leaking fuel—without stumbling upon the risk of side-impact fires.

The concern was that the plastic shield GM installed in 1984 was trapping dirt and moisture against the tank and causing corrosion.

The agency focused on wear, not accidents. But it did examine some state accident data that showed the trucks weren't more prone to fires than their competitors. The agency closed the investigation after finding very few owner complaints and no reports of tank leaks causing fires. "We didn't see anything to suggest a recall was warranted," says Mr. Boehly. "These were old vehicles with lots of miles on them."

Conflicting Data

Then this year, in a more comprehensive review of federal fatal-accident reports, NHTSA found the opposite. The different finding stemmed from a separate set of data—federal instead of state. The agency also has recently reopened its corrosion inquiry as part of a broader fire-risk investigation.

NHTSA officials, defending their handling of the GM case, say they primarily respond to complaints from the public. The agency doesn't have the resources, regulators say, to regularly analyze federal fatal-accident data to search for numerical spikes that might be linked to a defect.

Source: *The Wall Street Journal,* April 29, 1993, p. A1. Reprinted by of *The Wall Street Journal,* © 1993 Dow Jones & Company, Inc. All Rights Reserved Worldwide.

Afterword

In March 1994 two victims of crash fires and the families of eight others who died in GM pickup fires filed a $100 million suit claiming that General Motors destroyed accident evidence and faked crash tests involving 1973–87, full-sized Chevrolet and GMC pickups. GM says that the claims are false and that the trucks are safe.[45]

At this writing in 1994, the National Highway Traffic Safety Institute is studying the safety of the trucks.

Questions

1. "In crass terms, the question is, should GM spend hundreds of millions of dollars modifying its trucks to save a few lives a year?" What do you think? Explain. See Andrew Serwer, "GM Gets Tough with Its Critics," *Fortune,* May 31, 1993, pp. 90, 94.
2. Should the government retroactively impose new safety standards on the GM trucks? Explain.
3. In federal testing (mentioned in the article), three GM pickups were struck in the side at 45 miles per hour and did not leak.[46] The pickups did leak substantially more than comparable Ford and Dodge models when struck at 50 and 60 miles per hour.
   a. In your judgment, should a truck be considered "safe" if it leaks substantial gasoline in a 50 MPH crash, but little at 45 MPH? Explain.
   b. How would you decide what standard of safety is adequate?
   c. Why was the 20 MPH standard acceptable in the past but under question today?
4. The article explains NHTSA manager William Boehly's concern that while the trucks are safe enough to preserve life in a 50 MPH crash, those survivors might then burn to death if trapped in the vehicle. Should fuel system safety standards be at least equal to the vehicle's overall crash safety standards? Explain.
5. a. Should GM simply acknowledge that the trucks are not as safe as they could be and recall them? Explain.
   b. Should the government simply apprise the public of the test data and withdraw from the GM inquiry? Explain.

CHAPTER QUESTIONS

1. A major complaint about the federal regulatory process is that the regulators share an excessively "cozy" relationship with those being regulated. In Japan, cooperation between government, business, workers, and the public seems to have been instrumental in that nation's remarkable economic success. Indeed, it is commonplace for retiring high-level bureaucrats to be hired as top executives of the companies they once regulated. The practice is labeled *amakudari* (descent from heaven).

   Should the United States emulate the Japanese *amakudari* policy as a step toward a more unified, cooperative industrial policy? Explain.

2. Transportation deregulation has resulted in an immediate loss of service to some smaller communities. Some of that loss has been compensated for with the entry of smaller, independent firms.
   a. Has deregulation endangered small-town America? Explain.
   b. Should we apply free market principles to the postal service, thus, among other consequences, compelling those in small and remote communities to pay the full cost of service

rather than the "subsidized" cost now paid?
Explain.

3. The expense of government regulation is not limited
to the direct cost of administering the various agencies. Explain and offer examples of the other expenses produced by regulation.

4. To the extent the federal government achieves deregulation, what substitutes will citizens find for
protection?

5. Motor carriers have argued that by allowing open
entry to new carriers, the government has confiscated their property. Explain that argument.

6. Make the argument that increasing government
rules and jobs lead to decreasing private sector businesses and jobs.

7. *a.* How might a student such as yourself usefully
employ cost-benefit reasoning to improve your
academic performance?

    b. Do you do so? Explain.

8. A study by Professor Andrew Chalk of Southern
Methodist University concludes, in effect, that the
free market is more effective than the rules of the
Federal Aviation Administration in ensuring air
safety.[47] Assume the role of Professor Chalk. Explain the market mechanisms that have been influential in building our present impressive safety record in air travel.

9. As you know, deregulation of the American airline
industry has resulted in a rapid series of consolida-
tions, with fewer, bigger companies emerging from
the scramble. In Europe, some 21 national airlines
(British Airways, Lufthansa, Air France, etc.) were
operational in 1988. The nations of the European
Community are gradually reducing regulation of
their air system. Assume you are an advisor to the
EC. What advice would you offer about European
airline deregulation in light of deregulation in
America?

10. Charles Koch of Koch Industries: "The majority of
businessmen today are not supporters of free enterprise capitalism."[48] Does the bulk of the business
community favor government intervention? Explain.

11. A major issue facing the Federal Aviation Administration is that of congestion in the airways caused
by too many planes seeking to take off or land at
peak times at high-demand airports. How might we
solve that problem while maintaining reasonable
service?

12. In 1987, 20 men, frustrated with the quality of radio
programming, put together $100,000 to convert a
rusty, 200-foot freighter into a radio station. Taking
the craft five miles off the Long Island shore, the
group began transmission even though they were
not licensed by the FCC. Radio Newyork [sic] International, as they called themselves, used a playlist
of rock songs from the 1960s to today, many with a
strong emphasis on antiwar messages. RNI felt that
FCC guidelines interfered unfairly with the ability
of the disc jockeys to impose their personality and
views on the music and other programming. After a
few days of broadcasting, agents of the FCC and
other federal units boarded the ship, handcuffed the
deejays, neutralized the broadcasting equipment,
and charged RNI with operating a radio station
without a license. Felony charges against the group
were subsequently dropped.[49]

    a. Assuming the station's signal was not interfer-
ing with the broadcasts of licensed stations,
should the FCC intervene? Explain.

    b. RNI argued that they were in international wa-
ters and thus not subject to FCC jurisdiction.
How would you handle a situation where an
unlicensed television station operating well offshore aired sexually explicit material 24 hours
per day?

    c. In your view, does American radio program-
ming suffer from blandness provoked by excessive government oversight? Explain.

13. In calculating the costs and benefits of a new rule,
make the argument that added regulation normally
slows the economy and leads to increased deaths.

14. According to a study by economist John Morrall of
the federal Office of Management and Budget,[50] the
total cost (based on government estimates) of government regulations regarding vehicle collapsible
steering column protections is about $100,000 per
life saved. Based on government studies, the steering column rules save about 1,300 lives per year.
Rules mandating airbags or automatic seat belts
cost us about $300,000 for each of the estimated
1,850 lives saved annually. Rules on children's
sleepwear flammability cost us about $1.3 million
for each of the estimated 106 lives saved annually.
At the other end of the scale, an OSHA standard
protecting us from arsenic costs about $92.5 million
for each of the estimated 11.7 lives saved per
year.

    If the power were yours, which of these rules
would you banish? Explain, including your standard
for assessing the value of a human life.

NOTES

1. The organizational structure of Parts One and Two of this chapter owe a great deal to the suggestions of Professor Cynthia Srstka.

2. 15 U.S.C. 41, 45 (a)(1), 1914.

3. James Q. Wilson, "The Rise of the Bureaucratic State," *The Public Interest* 41 (Fall 1975), as quoted in *Perspectives on the Administrative Process,* ed. Robert L. Rabin (Boston: Little, Brown, 1979), pp. 16, 33.

4. George Stigler, "The Theory of Economic Regulation," *Bell Journal of Economics and Management Science* 2 (Spring 1971), p. 3.

5. 5 U.S.C. 594, et seq.

6. *Action for Children's Television* v. *FCC,* No. 93–1092, No. 93–1100, United States Court of Appeals for the District of Columbia Circuit (1993).

7. James Kilpatrick, "Indecent Radio Broadcasts Deserve Fine," *Des Moines Register,* December 27, 1992, p. 3C.

8. Jerry Mashaw, "Regulation, Logic, and Ideology," *Regulation,* November–December 1979, p. 48.

9. Ibid.

10. Bruce Ingersoll, "Plan to Speed Drug Approvals Clears Congress," *The Wall Street Journal,* October 8, 1992, p. B1.

11. Web Bryant, "Speeding Up Approval," *USA Today,* December 30, 1992, p. 1A.

12. Bruce Ingersoll, "FDA Review of Dow Corning Documents Led to Call for Moratorium on Implants," *The Wall Street Journal,* January 13, 1992, p. A3.

13. Thomas Burton, "Dow Corning Employees Falsified Data on Breast Implants, Counsel Concludes," *The Wall Street Journal,* November 3, 1992, p. A3.

14. Thomas Burton, "Breast Implants Raise More Safety Issues," *The Wall Street Journal,* February 4, 1993, p. B1.

15. Richard Gibson, "Label Law Stirs Up Food Companies," *The Wall Street Journal,* June 2, 1993, p. B1.

16. Associated Press, "Firm to License Abortion Pill to U.S. Group," *Waterloo Courier,* April 21, 1993, p. A3.

17. "DC-10 Jet Was 'Certified' but Never Seen by FAA," *Lexington Leader,* August 7, 1979, p. A-4.

18. J. Richard Crout, in *Drug Development and Marketing,* ed. Robert Helms (Washington, D.C.: American Enterprise Institute, 1975), p. 197, as quoted in Murray Weidenbaum, *The Future of Business Regulation* (New York: AMACOM, 1979), p. 116.

19. "Congress Wondering How Oraflex Was Approved," *Waterloo Courier,* August 4, 1982, p. B-1.

20. William Niskanen, "The Costs of Regulation (continued)," *Regulation* 15, no. 2 (Spring 1992), p. 25.

21. Jeanne Saddler, "Small Businesses Complain that Jungle of Regulations Threatens Their Futures," *The Wall Street Journal,* June 11, 1992, p. B1.

22. Doug Bandow, "Is Business Drowning in a New Regulatory Tide?" *Business & Society Review* 82 (Summer 1992), p. 45.

23. Louis Richman, "Bringing Reason to Regulation," *Fortune,* October 19, 1992, p. 94.

24. Reported in William Niskanen, "The Total Cost of Regulation?" *Regulation* 14, no. 3 (Summer 1991), p. 23.

25. Stigler, "Theory of Economic Regulation," p. 3, as cited in *The Politics of Regulation,* ed. James Q. Wilson (New York: Basic Books, 1980), p. 358.

26. Ibid., p. 5.

27. For a journalistic interpretation of the act, see Associated Press, "New Ethics Law Targets Federal Workers," *Waterloo Courier,* December 27, 1990, p. B6.

28. Lester Thurow, *The Zero-Sum Society* (New York: Penguin Books, 1980), p. 140.

29. Ibid., p. 136.

30. See, e.g., Laurie McGinley, "Federal Regulation Rises Anew in Matters that Worry the Public," *The Wall Street Journal,* April 21, 1981, p. 1.

31. Associated Press, "Deregulation of American Business Had a Price," *Des Moines Register,* December 20, 1989, p. 5S.

32. Niskanen, "The Costs of Regulation," p. 26.

33. Louis Rukeyser, ed., *Louis Rukeyser's Business Almanac* (New York: Simon & Schuster, 1988), p. 165.

34. Associated Press, "Deregulation of American Business Had a Price," p. 55.

35. Stephen Koepp, "Rolling Back Regulation: A De-

bate Rages over How Much Freedom Should Be Given to Industry," *Time,* July 6, 1987, p. 50.

36. Ibid.

37. Cable Television Consumer Protection and Competition Act of 1992, PL 102–385.

38. Jeanne Saddler and Mark Robichaux, "Billion-Dollar Rollback Is Set for Cable Rates," *The Wall Street Journal,* April 2, 1993, p. B1.

39. Joanne Kelly, "FCC Wants Larger Cuts in Rates for Cable TV," *The Des Moines Register,* February 23, 1994, p. A1.

40. Kenneth Jost, "GM Cover-Up Charged in Truck Case," *ABA Journal* 79 (May 1993), p. 22.

41. Andrew Serwer, "GM Gets Tough with Its Critics," *Fortune,* May 31, 1993, p. 90.

42. Serwer, "GM Gets Tough," p. 90.

43. Ibid.

44. Ibid.

45. Michael Clements, "Suit Claims GM Falsified Truck Data," USA TODAY, March 17, 1994, p. 1A.

46. Douglas Lavin, "GM to Reject Recall of Pickup Trucks and Focus Instead on Regulators' Tests," *The Wall Street Journal,* April 30, 1993, p. B4.

47. Andrew Chalk, "Market Outperforms FAA as Air-Safety Enforcer," *The Wall Street Journal,* September 1, 1987, p. 26.

48. Charles Koch, "Business Can Have Free Enterprise—If It Dares," *Business & Society Review,* no. 28 (Winter 1978–79), p. 54.

49. See, for example, Joseph Berger, "Seafaring Protesters Challenge FCC Rules," *New York Times,* July 27, 1987, p. 1.

50. John F. Morrall III, "A Review of the Record," *Regulation* 10, no. 2 (November–December 1986), p. 25.

9

BUSINESS ORGANIZATIONS AND SECURITIES REGULATION

Part One—Business Organizations

When starting a business, one of the first decisions that must be made by its promoters is which legal format is best for the firm. This decision can be crucial, for it will determine many of the rules and requirements governing the operations of the fledgling business. Most large-scale concerns opt for the corporate form, while many smaller ones choose to begin as partnerships or sole proprietorships. Size alone, however, does not determine which form the promoters of a business should prefer. All of the available options—sole proprietorships, partnerships, corporations, Sub S corporations, and so on—offer various advantages and disadvantages, each of which must be considered, given the circumstances of the particular investment opportunity.

After deciding how the business will be set up, its promoters must determine how and from whom to raise the money needed to establish the business and commence operations. Many small businesses rely solely on their owners for capital, perhaps supplementing their available money with loans from friends or relatives, loans guaranteed by a federal agency (such as the Small Business Administration), or loans collateralized by the owner's house or other assets. Other promoters choose to raise money from banks, insurance companies, or other financial institutions by using the assets of the business or the attractiveness of the investment opportunity to convince the lender that the loan can be repaid. Others rely on risk-taking venture capitalists who are willing to back new companies with impressive expertise, product lines, or ideas in return for a share of ownership in the business, while still other firms opt for issuing stock or securities to small segments of the public, such as friends or acquaintances, or even to the public at large.

The decision of how to raise capital is dictated by market forces. If no bank is willing to extend credit, or no broker is willing to attempt to sell shares or bonds in the company, those avenues of money-raising activity must be eliminated from consideration. From those economically viable possibilities, however, the promoters must choose wisely if they are to raise the needed capital at the lowest possible cost to the business and their ownership of it. As will be seen in the second section of this chapter, major expenses can be avoided if the firm can raise capital without subjecting itself to the requirements of federal securities laws. Many deals are structured in a particular manner solely for the purpose of ensuring that the capital raised will not cause the business to fall under the scrutiny of the Securities and Exchange Commission and its mandates.

FORM OF THE ORGANIZATION

When determining which legal form a business will adopt, most thoughtful promoters focus on five factors: cost, continuity, control, liability, and taxes. The order of importance of these considerations will vary from business to business, but all five certainly merit serious analysis before a final decision is made. Cost reflects the initial and subsequent expenses (direct and indirect) associated with a particular form of organization. Continuity refers to the consequences of an owner dying or otherwise withdrawing from participation in the firm, or a new owner joining the business. Control focuses on who will set firm policy and run the business. Liability concerns what assets of the owners may be used to pay firm debts, while tax considerations are based on maximizing the share of corporate resources available to the owner and minimizing those due the government.

Partnerships

Many small businesses start out as sole proprietorships or partnerships. A partnership can be defined as two or more persons carrying on as co-owners of a business for profit. A sole proprietorship exists when there is but a single owner of the business. Under either of these arrangements, costs are minimal. There are no legal requirements, other than obtaining local business licenses and permission to operate under the proposed partnership name. A group of persons who agree to form a partnership or who act like partners have done just that—created a partnership. No written agreement, filings at the courthouse, or other legal notice must be given in advance for a legal partnership to exist. While a written partnership agreement is advisable to set forth rights and responsibilities and to limit confusion, it is not usually required. Furthermore, the partners' agreement, whether written or oral, can be changed at any time with their consent.

In those situations in which a partnership is formed without the partners agreeing to the terms under which it will operate, state laws supply the operating conditions for the partnership. Most jurisdictions have, in essence, adopted the Uniform Partnership Act (UPA), which sets forth a traditional allocation of powers and responsibilities for partnerships. Among some of its provisions are:

1. All partners share equally in partnership profits and losses.
2. All partners are expected to devote their full time and energies to partnership business, without compensation, and to act in the best interests of the partnership at all times.

Sharing of profit is the primary facts of partnership.

3. An agreement made by any partner may bind the entire partnership to the terms of the agreement.
4. Unanimous consent is necessary to admit a new partner.
5. The partnership can be terminated at any time for any reason by any partner.

A partnership is free to tailor the provisions of its agreement to the particular needs of the partners. Many times, profits and losses are not shared equally, or one partner receives a salary in addition to his or her share of profits, but such variances from the UPA must be spelled out and agreed to. Failure to do so automatically triggers the UPA's provisions and may have costly and perhaps fatal consequences when disputes arise.

Continuity. Continuity is a problem for many partnerships that were not set up to last solely for a fixed period of time. Every time a partner leaves for any reason (e.g., death, insanity, voluntary or involuntary withdrawal, or personal bankruptcy) or a new partner joins, the partnership must be legally dissolved and a new one created. While under most circumstances, the partnership continues to operate during the process, dissolution requires all firm creditors to be notified and appropriate arrangements made. The value of the partnership must be determined, and the withdrawing partner must be given his or her appropriate share or its monetary equivalent of the partnership assets. This process can provoke many disputes and is often time-consuming and expensive. If the partners cannot reach an agreement, the dissatisfied partner may be able to force the partnership to sell all of its assets and give each partner his or her appropriate share. From a business point of view, it can be disastrous if partnership assets must be sold quickly to pay off a withdrawing partner. While a good partnership agreement can limit the potential problems caused by a partner's withdrawal, it can never totally eliminate them.

Control. Control in a partnership is relatively simple. Either each partner has an equal say-so in partnership policy, or the partnership agreement sets forth an alternative scheme under which some partners have a greater voice than others. On most issues, unless otherwise agreed to by the partners, a majority vote is necessary to approve a course of action. Thus, if the initial partners are willing, it is easy to set up a system in which one or more partners own less than half the interest of the partnership but have more than half—or effective control—for voting purposes. Other than to benefit or protect individual partners, the most critical issue that must be addressed concerning control is making certain that tie votes among the partners do not occur continually. Many small partnerships fail because the partners are not able to muster a majority to approve a policy (typically 1–1 or 2–2 votes on a crucial issue) and have not established procedures to prevent the deadlock from becoming a permanent pitfall capable of stifling any partnership action.

Liability. Liability is often the issue that forces promoters to choose the corporate form over a partnership. All members of a partnership are personally liable to the full extent of their assets for all partnership debts. If, for instance, the partnership were to lose money and be unable to pay a bank loan on time, or if a partnership truck were to cause environmental damage, the partners might be forced to sell their houses, stocks, bonds, and other personal possessions to meet the demands of various creditors. Because of this uncertainty, many people with substantial assets refuse to invest or participate in partnerships. Clearly, if the business is likely to be sued regularly or face catastrophic losses from accidents or other tort liability, a partnership probably would not be appropriate. On the other hand, if the partners are judgment proof (i.e., have no unencumbered assets) or the risks they face are insurable, the penalty associated with the unlimited personal liability for partnership debts is largely illusory.

Taxation. Taxation is the reason many small businesses choose to be partnerships. Partnerships merely serve as conduits for profits flowing from the business directly to the partners. The partners then report partnership profits or losses on their tax returns and pay the appropriate taxes at the ordinary personal income tax rate. The partnership itself merely reports the amount of income to appropriate taxing agencies and does not actually pay any income tax. Many states also levy a yearly tax against the authorized shares of corporations chartered in their states. Partnerships typically escape such taxes.

Corporations

Partnerships and sole proprietorships make economic sense for people who are essentially selling their own and their partners' labor, expertise, or experience (three doctors, eight attorneys, or five radio repairers). Businesses that utilize many different factors in production, need large amounts of capital, and expect to continue unabated after the founding owners have departed often find partnerships unwieldy and economically unfeasible. For these businesses, a corporate entity is more appropriate. Corporations do business under a charter provided by a state and are an economic entity totally separate and distinct from their owners. Typically, but not always, corporations are chartered in the state where their headquarters are located. Many corporations, however, choose to incorporate in states like Delaware or Texas regardless of where they plan on doing business because the corporate laws and low-taxation policies of these jurisdictions give management more leeway in how it runs the corporation, controls its policies, and benefits itself and the shareholders. Quite often, such state regulations and laws are decisive tools in corporate mergers or takeover attempts.

Cost. The cost of setting up a corporation is often higher than that associated with a partnership. Obtaining a charter typically requires an attorney and the completion of numerous forms and procedures dictated by the state. Taxes and license fees often have to be paid. The corporation must also undertake similar obligations in other states in which it plans to do business. After the corporation is chartered, it must file regular reports with the state, pay appropriate taxes and fees, maintain an agent for service of process, and generally comply with the state's corporate laws. This might require election of a board of directors, regular audits, shareholder meetings, and any number of items thought necessary by the state to ensure the corporation is run fairly for the benefit of all shareholders.

As long as all state requirements are met, a corporation may enjoy a perpetual existence, thus eliminating continuity problems (such as those occurring in a partnership when an important partner decides to withdraw at an inopportune time). Ownership of stock in a corporation does not connote a personal, fiduciary duty like that existing between partners, who must always act in the best interests of the partnership, even if it is not personally advantageous. Shares typically may be transferred freely to anyone without corporate approval, and the corporation is usually under no obligation to buy back the shares of a disgruntled or departing shareholder. Likewise, on the death of a shareholder, the shares simply transfer to his or her heirs, and the corporate structure remains unchanged.

Control. Control is usually much easier to maintain in a corporation than in a partnership. Shares of stock are often sold to widely diverse groups of people who have no connection with each other, little in common, and no interest in being involved in corporate dealings. For publicly traded companies, large blocks of shares are controlled by banks, mutual funds, or insurance companies, which tend to vote for the continuation of current management except in the most unusual situations. The groups that control major corporations often own or control very small percentages of the company's stock but are able to maintain their positions as board members or top corporate officers. Corporations sometimes issue nonvoting as well as voting stock. This nonvoting stock participates in firm profits and dividends but does not vote at shareholder meetings. Through this technique, existing owners can raise additional capital for the firm without risking loss of control.

Liability. Shareholder liability is much more limited than partner liability. Because a corporation is a separate entity, it can sue and be sued. Corporate debts are the sole obligations of the corporation and must be paid from corporate assets. In other words, a party aggrieved by an action of a corporation (an unpaid debt or an automobile accident), but unable to recoup adequate damages from the corporation cannot expect to recover its losses from the personal assets of the individual shareholders. Except in the most egregious or unusual circumstances, shareholders' losses are limited to their original investment in the corporation.

This inability of creditors to use personal shareholder assets to satisfy corporate debts or obligations is referred to as the "corporate veil" and is often a powerful incentive to incorporate. By incorporating, a person starting a small business can rest at night with the assurance that a business reverse will not cause the owner's house, automobiles, jewelry, and so on to be sold to pay corporate debts.

Taxation. The issue of taxation presents the major drawback for choosing a corporate existence. Because a corporation is a separate economic entity, it is also a separate taxable entity. As such, corporations must pay a corporate income tax to the federal government as well as to most states in which they conduct business. Joint state and federal income taxes can approach 40 percent of profits. Furthermore, an individual receiving dividends from a corporation must pay income tax on the dividend to state and federal authorities. Thus, corporate profits are said to be subject to "double taxation"—first when the corporation reports a profit, and later when those profits are distributed to owners in the form of dividends. For each dollar of corporate profits, it would not be inconceivable to suggest that less than 40 cents would eventually find its way into the shareholders' pockets. Dividends paid to other corporations are partially exempt from taxation, thus minimizing "triple taxation."

Hybrid Organizations

Because corporations and partnerships have various shortcomings, businesses have sought other alternatives. State legislatures and Congress have responded by authorizing three other forms of organization—limited partnerships, Sub S corporations, and limited liability companies.

1. Limited Partnerships. A limited partnership is like a partnership in many respects: It is not a taxable entity, and all losses or gains are passed through to the partners. The principal difference is that there are two classes of partners. One class, typically investors, is referred to as limited partners. They are not allowed to participate in management decision making, but they are also granted limited liability so that their maximum liability in case of failure is their original investment in the project. The other class, typically the promoters, is referred to as general partners. They manage the business and are personally liable for all losses. A corporation can be the general partner in many instances, thus offering the actual general partners (the owners of the corporation) the equivalent of limited liability. Limited partnerships are particularly suitable for raising capital for single-project alliances among diverse groups of investors (e.g., developing an office building or shopping mall) and when one of the primary motivations for investing in the project is to shelter other income from taxation. In a limited partnership, the shares or interests of the limited partners may be sold or transferred freely. Death, bankruptcy, insanity, and so on have no effect on the partnership. The general partners, on the other hand, are subject to roughly the same restrictions as in a regular partnership. However, provision is usually made in the limited partnership agreement for an alternate general partner so that the project can continue unabated should a general partner be forced to withdraw. Limited partnerships are often more complicated than corporations to form. Failure to comply with all the requirements may subject the limited partners to unlimited liability just as if they were general partners.

2. Sub S Corporations. Some business projects call for the formation of a Sub S corporation. This creation of federal tax law allows, in certain situations, an incorporated business to escape most corporate income tax. The owners of the business then have the best of both worlds—limited liability without double taxation. In order to qualify, a corporation must have fewer than 35 shareholders, over 80 percent of its income must be "earned" income (i.e., not derived from dividends, interest, royalties, and other passive sources), and almost all of its income or losses must be distributed to the owners each year. The shareholders then pay the appropriate personal income tax on their earnings just as partners would. Because of these restrictions, Sub S corporations are suitable only for smaller projects that do not need to retain capital for growth purposes. A typical situation might be eight individuals who decide to develop 100 acres of land into 200 lots, which will then be sold over a period of years. The early losses generated from building roads, sewers, parks, and so on will be passed through to the individual shareholders to reduce their current income tax, while the taxable gains will be deferred to later years. Furthermore, no additional capital will be needed by the business. When all the lots have been sold, the deal will end and the corporation will simply cease operations.

3. LLC. Limited liability companies (LLC) are creations of state law and have been accepted by over 35 states. Due to an IRS ruling, LLCs retain the limited liability of corporations but are not taxable like partnerships. LLCs tend to be easier to create than limited partnerships and have no restrictions on the maximum number of investors, as do Sub S corporations. Furthermore, unlike a limited partnership, in which the general partners have unlimited liability, no one in a LLC retains unlimited personal liability. Many attorneys believe that LLCs will gradually become more and more prevalent, with Sub S corporations, general partnerships, joint ventures, and even limited partnerships being used less. Currently, tax consequences make it difficult for existing, profitable businesses to become LLCs, but new businesses do not face this issue. It must be remembered that while LLCs are a creation of the laws in many states, their popularity is due to a 1988 IRS ruling that the IRS could modify or Congress would void if abuses of LLC status become significant.

OPERATING THE ORGANIZATION

While the rules for operating or managing the business organization vary depending on which form is used, one common element is present—the fiduciary duty. Officers, directors, managers, or partners have a particularly strong responsibility to act in the best interest of the business and its shareholders, even if that means putting the needs of the business ahead of personal needs or financial gain. The fiduciary standard is often expressed by such terms as acting in "good faith" or in a "reasonably prudent manner." Obviously, these definitions are not situation specific and leave considerable discretion to the individual involved to decide what is best for the business in a particular circumstance. This lack of specificity, however, does not open up all business decisions to second-guessing by courts or irate shareholders. Protection is offered to managers whose decisions turn out to be in error. The "business judgment" rule says that if a manager acts in a reasonable manner (often defined as "could another manager have rationally made the same decision?"), then the courts will not hold the manager liable for the fact that his or her judgment ultimately turned out to be wrong. Courts are often more concerned, however, when partners or employees use business assets for their own benefit, or take for their own an idea or process they developed while working for an enterprise. Judges often invoke the "corporate opportunity doctrine," which states that an employee who develops something of value may not use it for personal gain until it has first been offered to the employer for its benefit and rejected.

Likewise, courts are often very concerned when it appears that entrenched management is using its power in a manner that is detrimental to minority shareholders. The paying of extremely large salaries or bonuses, failure to treat shareholders fairly, or refusal to bargain in good faith with prospective purchasers may be examples of breaches of fiduciary duties by board members. One method that has been developed for protecting shareholders' interests is the "derivative suit," in which shareholders may sue the board or management on behalf of the corporation if the shareholders believe that the board has breached its fiduciary duties. If the lawsuit is successful, the actions may be stopped and the board members may have to personally pay compensation for their breaches. If damages are awarded, the money goes directly back to the corporation, with the shareholders who brought the suit being compensated only for their expenses. This rule tends to limit the derivative suit process to egregious situations, since the shareholders can only benefit indirectly—through their holdings of the stock.

Another remedy available to minority shareholders who believe that their board has not acted fairly in buying or selling their shares is to request an accounting. In this procedure, shareholders who are required to sell or transfer their stock on terms approved by the board may ask an independent expert to calculate the value of their shares. If the expert determines that the shares are worth more than the value being received, the minority shareholders are entitled to additional compensation. The requirements for receiving an accounting are a matter of state corporate law. The process can be time-consuming and very expensive, especially for minority interests in small businesses.

Other types of friction between majority and minority interests often arise. Recent trends appear to be giving minority shareholders more rights in a variety of situations than historically has been the case. The following article discusses these conflicts in the context of *closely held corporations* (where the stock is owned by a small number of persons; often family members or friends).

MINORITY SHAREHOLDERS STAND UP, DEMAND TO BE HEARD

Barbara Marsh

Karen Goettsche is fed up with being shut out of her family's Chicago manufacturing company.

As a minority shareholder she feels stuck with a poor investment. "I'd like to be able to inherit what my dad left me," including a job, says 50-year-old Ms. Goettsche, whose father founded the company. But she says that her efforts to land a job there created antagonism with the six family members who already work at the company. Directors blocked her attempt to join the board, she adds.

Like many minority shareholders in closely held companies, Ms. Goettsche considers her stock dividends "a pittance." She has rejected company offers to buy her shares as too low. Unlike public company shareholders, she can't easily escape her fix by selling her shares. "I'm at their mercy," she complains.

*   *   *   *   *

Requests for help from minority shareholders in closely held corporations have risen to several a month from one a year in the last two years, reports the United Shareholders Association, a Washington advocacy group for shareholders of public companies. Some requests involve "pitiful cases" of minority shareholders being "squeezed out" of private concerns, says Ralph Whitworth, the group's president.

These troubles typically arise over conflicting priorities of minority and majority shareholders in private firms, legal experts say. Majority stockholders usually control management and often hold highly paid jobs. This encourages them to promote the company's growth and capital reinvestment. They keep dividends low—and salaries high—because dividends are taxed at both the corporate and individual level. Salaries are taxed only at the individual level.

But minority shareholders often rely solely on dividends to make money from their holdings. In the past, legal specialists note, minority investors' complaints about their low dividends or other ill treatment prompted majority shareholders essentially to say: "Tough luck." When the majority offered to buy the minority's shares, the price was generally discounted against a company's value because the shares lack marketability.

Increasingly, however, "courts and legislatures have recognized [that] the position of minority shareholders needs enhancement," says Robert Thompson, a Washington University law professor who has written extensively about minority shareholder rights. He says that more judges now let minority shareholders bring cases charging the majority with breaching their fiduciary duty. And more courts are ordering remedies such as buyouts of minority shares.

In addition, Mr. Thompson continues, judges have reduced or eliminated the traditional buyout discount on minority shares when a minority shareholder gets forced out. Consider the three Pedro brothers. They worked together for most of their adult lives, with each man holding one-third of their family's Minnesota luggage and leather goods firm, according to an August 1992 opinion by that state's appeals court.

The opinion said that a falling out arose after Alfred Pedro, the brother who was manufacturing manager, questioned an apparent discrepancy in the company's financial records. When internal investigations didn't resolve the issue, Mr. Pedro testified that his managerial authority was undermined. In 1987, his brothers—then the firm's chairman and president—fired him. The appeals court noted that as a minority shareholder in such a closely held corporation, Mr. Pedro could reasonably expect "a job, salary, a significant place in management, and economic security for his family."

The court said Mr. Pedro should be awarded fair market value for his stock, despite a company agreement that pegged the buyout of shares at a 25% discount from their book value. The court agreed with a lower court that Mr. Pedro deserved fair-market value to compensate him for being forced to sell his shares. It upheld the lower court finding that his brothers had breached their fiduciary duty to him and wrongfully terminated his contract for lifetime employment. It also upheld a $2 million award.

To avoid such nasty legal tangles, prospective minority shareholders are bargaining harder upfront. Some investors now insist on a board seat, a salary based on company performance or a buyout arrangement if they lose their jobs, says J. C. Bruno, a Detroit lawyer and small-business specialist. To prevent a low-ball buyout bid for minority shares, he adds, some investors are winning the right to turn around and buy out majority shareholders at the same per-share level that the majority offers.

Meanwhile, more private companies are trying to avert costly litigation by treating minority shareholders better. Firms are creating separate classes of stock, such as a high-dividend class with no voting rights for passive shareholders, and a low-dividend class with voting rights for paid managers, says Mr. de Visscher, the consultant.

In addition, the consultant notes, some firms create occasional markets for their stock. A concern sets aside certain amounts—say, 1% to 10% of its yearly earnings or cash flow—for a special liquidity fund. Then, for a fixed period every year, generally a month to six weeks, the business uses the fund to buy stock from shareholders. The sale price is based on an independent evaluation or a multiple of earnings.

Source: *The Wall Street Journal,* February 23, 1993, p. B2. Reprinted by the permission of *The Wall Street Journal,* © 1993 Dow Jones & Company, Inc. All Rights Reserved Worldwide.

SPECIAL SITUATIONS

Piercing the Corporate Veil

Although shareholders in corporations are said to have limited liability for the debts of the corporation, in certain instances they can be held personally liable when the corporation is unable to pay its obligations. For instance, the corporate veil of limited liability can be pierced if a business is started with so little capital that it is obvious to the courts that the sole purpose of incorporating was for the shareholders to escape liability for their actions.

Suppose a corporation with little or no capital was established to supply propane gas to civic arenas, theaters, and so on. This business kept no insurance, had no assets, and would have nothing to lose should a tank explode, killing or injuring numerous people. Although its owners might think themselves to be insulated from liability and the corporation to be judgment proof, a court might pierce the corporate veil and hold the owners personally liable on the theory that the gross undercapitalization of their business so abused the corporate privileges granted them in their charter that they should be denied limited liability. In other situations, limited liability may be denied the owners of a corporation that received a corporate charter but does not comply with all the state requirements that directors be elected, board meetings be held, and so on. Typically, this occurs when one corporation sets up another corporation to perform some activity but the original corporation does not allow the new one to be run as an independent entity, treating it instead like it was simply another division of the original corporation. If the new corporation suffers large losses, the courts might hold the founding corporation liable for its debts on the grounds that the two were run like a single corporation even though they were issued two charters. One is said to be the *alter ego* of the other and thus liable.

Reality of Limited Liability

Many businesspeople automatically assume they want to form a corporation because of their concern about personal liability for business debts. These debts could come from two main sources: tort liability resulting from an incident involving business activities (such as an accident caused by a firm truck) or contract liability occurring because the firm is unable to pay its obligation to a supplier of goods or a lender of money. Concerning tort liability, very few businesses, partnerships, or corporations would fail to have insurance adequate to pay foreseeable losses resulting from accident or death due to negligence. Thus, in most situations short of catastrophic loss, personal tort liability can be as easily avoided in a partnership as in a corporation. Insurance is not normally obtainable to pay contract liabilities resulting from a firm's inability to meet its debts and other obligations, so the corporate form might appear advantageous, as many more businesses fail due to contractual indebtedness than to tort actions. Banks and other lenders, however, recognize this economic fact of life and want to protect themselves from the limited liability afforded corporate shareholders. The principal way they do this is by refusing to lend money to small or new corporations unless the owners personally guarantee the loans. This usually means the owners must pledge their houses, stocks, bonds, and other assets to the bank. If the business fails, their personal fortunes are just as likely to be lost in a corporation as in a partnership. For a small corporation, limited liability is not always the advantage it seems.

Avoidance of Double Taxation

One of the principal problems for small businesses that choose the corporate form is double taxation. Many smaller corporations that are owned and managed by the same people can take various steps to minimize the bite of corporate taxation. In all instances, the strategy revolves around the same simple principle: maximize the benefits received by the owners and minimize the profitability of the corporation. Corporate assets are used in a way that is advantageous to the owners and deductible to the corporation. For instance, the owners can pay themselves large salaries and substantial fringe benefits for running the business. They receive those salaries and benefits directly, much as they would receive dividends if they were passive shareholders, and if they can arrange it so that the corporation earns no profit each year, no corporate income tax will be paid and thus double taxation will be avoided. The IRS recognizes this game, however, and will allow only the deduction of reasonable salaries and benefits. Still, salaries and benefits can be stretched to minimize corporate profitability.

The owners could also choose to lend the firm money and receive interest, rather than purchase stock in the corporation and receive dividends in return. As interest is deductible to the corporation while dividends are not, and both are taxable to the recipients at ordinary income tax rates, this strategy also eliminates double taxation. Again, the IRS is not blind to the possibilities of abuse and has the power to disallow interest payments it believes are excessive. Clearly, a business funded 100 percent with debt provided by its owner would not pass IRS muster, but a 50 percent debt/50 percent equity ratio would probably appear reasonable in most circumstances.

Some businesses choose to minimize double taxation by not paying dividends and accumulating earnings. In effect, taxes are deferred until the business is sold or dividends are paid. In the meantime, the money can be used to help the business grow or to invest in other stocks or bonds. The IRS can minimize this ploy by taxing excess accumulated earnings, which it defines as earnings accumulated not for business-related reasons but for tax avoidance purposes. Before the IRS can consider levying the tax, several million dollars of earnings must be accumulated and there must be no valid reason, such as future plans for expansion, for retaining the earnings.

As was discussed earlier, these techniques for avoiding double taxation may cause disputes between shareholders employed by the corporation and those that are not employees.

Changing the Form of a Business

Within certain IRS-imposed limitations, businesses are free to change their legal form as they deem advantageous. One simple strategy is to start out as a partnership, because it is cheaper and easier and because any business losses can be deducted immediately from the partners' personal income. (If the corporate form were initially chosen, business losses would not reduce taxes until such time as the corporation itself earned money, which might not occur for years.) Later, after profitability is attained and as the needs for continuity and increased capital become more pressing, a transfer to corporate status might be appropriate.

Tax Shelters

The theory of tax shelters is based on taking advantage of provisions in the tax code that allow certain bookkeeping entries (such as depreciation and depletion) to be deducted from the profits of specific investments. If economically viable and properly set up, these projects can have a negative taxable income plus a positive cash flow for a period of years, thus offering shelter from taxation to some part of a wealthy person's income. Suppose, for instance, that a real estate salesperson wants to buy a building but has no money. Doctors have money and tax problems but do not have real estate management skills. This marriage made in heaven results in a limited partnership. Typically, the doctors (limited partners) would invest money to make the down payment on the building, and the real estate salesperson (general partner) would borrow the remaining money, using the building as collateral. The general partner would receive a small percentage of ownership in the building and a fee for managing it, while the limited partner would receive the remaining economic and tax benefits.

The rules on tax shelters are continually being tightened. For instance, in the past much of the desirability of tax shelters was based on the fact that no limited partner was personally obligated to pay back the borrowed money if the project failed (nonrecourse financing). Currently, nonrecourse financing can yield tax-sheltered income only on real estate. Bulls, movie scripts, and myriad other shelter offerings can no longer use borrowed, nonrecourse money to leverage their expected returns to extremely high levels. Lower personal tax rates have also made tax shelters much less attractive to many investors.

Buy/Sell Agreements

Many small businesses fail because one of the principal owner/managers dies. The death causes numerous hardships for the firm. First of all, the deceased's expertise is unexpectedly lost. Second, he or she will have to be replaced, often with more than one person, and the new people must be trained and paid. The time and expense can be substantial. Also, from the deceased's point of view, any spouse and children need to be provided for. Most small-business investments are totally illiquid in that no ready purchaser is available to buy the deceased's shares. The remaining owners will probably be unable to purchase the shares because of the increased costs to the business associated with the death and the precarious financial position that the firm is likely to find itself in at this time.

One attractive solution to this dilemma is a buy/sell agreement. This consists of an agreement *negotiated at the formation of the business* concerning the terms under which the business will be valued and ownership transferred should an owner die. Once the valuation formula is agreed to, the firm purchases a joint life insurance policy, which pays a specified amount on the first death of an owner. When a death occurs, the firm uses the proceeds of the policy to purchase the shares at the agreed-on price. All remaining parties benefit, as well, because their pro rata ownership interests in the business rise. The spouse and children receive cash to pay estate taxes and living expenses, and the firm receives a cash infusion just when it is needed most. Although the premiums on the policy typically are not deductible, the proceeds normally escape taxation. The only caveat is that these agreements must be negotiated before an owner's health fails. When all parties are healthy, buy/sell agreements are easy to negotiate because all sides want the purchase price to be relatively low. They all expect to be purchasing the stock (i.e., alive), not selling it for the benefit of their heirs. Once it becomes apparent who is likely to survive, the issue of valuation becomes much more difficult.

Questions—Part One

1. According to *The Wall Street Journal,* courts have pierced the corporate veil fewer than 150 times in the past 10 years. What are the ramifications for business if piercing the corporate veil becomes more common?
2. *a.* Why are partnerships not taxable entities for income tax purposes, yet corporations are taxable? Does this distinction make sense? Explain.
   b. What would be the ramifications of taxing corporations at much lower rates or not taxing them at all?
3. *a.* Why does federal law allow Sub S corporations? Do they serve any useful purpose? What?
   b. Do limited partnerships serve any useful purpose? Explain.
4. *a.* In an episode of "LA Law," Arnie Becker decided to leave his firm (a partnership). Before he announced he was leaving, he contacted all of his clients and asked them to transfer their legal business to his new law firm. Is this type of conduct permissible? Should it be? Explain.

b. Would it matter if Arnie Becker were a computer salesman who was switching from IBM to Apple? Explain.

5. *a.* Before tax rates were lowered, the total tax on unearned income in Great Britain exceeded 90 percent. In other words, the government's share of an individual's income derived from rent, interest, and so on exceeded 90 percent, while the investor kept less than 10 percent. Likewise, the government's share of any losses suffered by an investor exceeded 90 percent, if the investor had other income to offset the losses. What are the ramifications of such a policy?

b. A developer in England built a large office building during this period. Because inflation was so high, the developer decided he could make more money by leaving the building empty, depreciating it, deducting his losses from his other income, and then leasing the building at a higher rate the following year. The following year, inflation was still high, and he made the same decision. This practice continued for several years, until the developer had almost totally depreciated the still-empty building. At that point, the developer demolished the building—and built another. Discuss.

Part Two—Securities Regulation

PUBLIC OFFERING OF NEW SECURITIES

Once the form of organization has been established and the business has started operation and begun to progress, the need for additional funds beyond the financial capacity of the founders and promoters becomes acute. At this time, many firms choose to "go public" or to attempt to raise capital from the general public in a variety of ways to finance their business or personal plans for expansion and growth. To attract this new money, a business not only must offer an attractive investment opportunity but also must comply with numerous state and federal requirements concerning the sale and resale of securities. This section discusses some of the applicable statutes and regulations.

Condominiums	Stocks
Gold	Annuities
Bonds	Warehouse receipts
Orange groves	Limited partnerships
Bourbon	

Any of the above can be securities and thus subject to many state and federal laws. As these examples suggest, the definition of a security is broad, and care has to be taken so that inadvertent violations of securities laws do not occur. State laws, referred to as "blue sky" laws, must be complied with in each state in which the securities are to be sold. Furthermore, one or more federal statutes may be applicable. For instance, the Securities Act of 1933 regulates the public offering of new, nonexempt securities and prohibits their sale until they have been properly registered with the Securities and Exchange Commission (SEC). Fraudulent and deceptive practices are barred by this act. The Securities Exchange Act of 1934 controls the resale of securities and sets up the SEC for the purpose of exercising that responsibility. This act prohibits manipulative or deceptive practices, requires the registration of brokers and dealers, and limits their activities in many respects. Stock exchanges, clearinghouses, and other participants involved in transferring securities also come under its broad umbrella of coverage. The Investment Advisors Act of 1940 is roughly analogous to the 1934 act in the requirements it places on investment counselors.

The Investment Company Act of 1940 regulates any publicly owned entities that primarily invest in or buy and sell securities. Insider dealings, capital requirements, sales charges, and so on are covered by this statute. The Securities Investor Protection Act of 1970 set up the Securities Investor Protection Corporation, which aids customers of bankrupt or illiquid securities companies. Finally, the Insider Trading and Securities Fraud Enforcement Act of 1988 increases criminal penalties and fines for investors engaging in insider trading or failing to file proper notice of certain trading activities.

While the SEC is the primary federal agency established to regulate the securities industry, it cannot do the entire job itself. Thus, all regulatory schemes involve a good deal of "self-regulation," in which the regulated entities become participants in their own regulation. The New York Stock Exchange, with SEC approval and oversight, continues to establish many regulations for its members and is active in investigating insider abuses and manipulations by its members. The National Association of Securities Dealers plays a similar role for dealers in over-the-counter securities.

DEFINITION OF A SECURITY

The Securities Act of 1933 defines a security as:

> any note, stock, treasury stock, bond, debenture, evidence of indebtedness, certificate of interest or participation in any profit-sharing agreement, collateral-trust certificate, preorganizational certificate or subscription, transferable share, investment contract, voting-trust certificate, certificate of deposit for a security, fractional undivided interest in oil, gas, or other mineral rights, or, in general, any interest or instrument commonly known as a "security," or any certificate of interest or participation in, temporary or interim certificate for, receipt for, guarantee of, or warrant or right to subscribe to or purchase, any of the foregoing.

Any instrument called a *bond, stock, debenture, share,* and so on will almost certainly be considered a security. Most of the disputes involving the applicability of securities laws involve investment contracts or certificates of participation in a profit-sharing agreement. Typically, these involve attempts by promoters to raise money for various schemes in which investors pool their money with the expectation of future returns, but no pieces of paper that look like securities are involved. In *SEC v. W. J. Howey Co.,* set out below, orange groves were held to be securities and the following test was put forward: "the person invests his money in a common enterprise and is led to expect profits solely from the efforts of the promoter or a third party."

SECURITIES & EXCHANGE COMMISSION v. W. J. HOWEY CO.
328 U.S. 293 (1946)

Justice Murphy

This case involves the application of § 2(1) of the Securities Act of 1933 to an offering of units of a citrus grove development coupled with a contract for cultivating, marketing and remitting the net proceeds to the investor.

* * * * *

Most of the facts are stipulated. The respondents, W. J. Howey Company and Howey-in-the-Hills Service, Inc., are Florida corporations under direct common control and management. The Howey Company owns large tracts of citrus acreage in Lake County, Florida. During the past several years it has planted about 500 acres annually, keeping half of the groves itself and offering the other half to the public "to help us finance additional development." Howey-in-the-Hills Service, Inc., is a service company engaged in cultivating and developing many of these groves, including the harvesting and marketing of the crops.

Each prospective customer is offered both a land sales contract and a service contract, after having been told that it is not feasible to invest in a grove unless service arrangements are made. While the purchaser is free to make arrangements with other service companies, the superiority of Howey-in-the-Hills Service, Inc., is stressed. Indeed, 85 percent of the acreage sold during the three-year period ending May 31, 1943, was covered by service contracts with Howey-in-the-Hills Service, Inc.

The land sales contract with the Howey Company provides for a uniform purchase price per acre or fraction thereof, varying in amount only in accordance with the number of years the particular plot has been planted with citrus trees. Upon full payment of the purchase price the land is conveyed to the purchaser by warranty deed. Purchases are usually made in narrow strips of land arranged so that an acre consists of a row of 48 trees. During the period between February 1, 1941, and May 31, 1943, 31 of the 42 persons making purchases bought less than five acres each. The average holding of these 31 persons was 1.33 acres and sales of as little as 0.65, 0.7, and 0.73 of an acre were made. These tracts are not separately fenced and the sole indication of several ownership is found in small land marks intelligible only through a plat book record.

The service contract, generally of a 10-year duration without option of cancellation, gives Howey-in-the-Hills Service, Inc., a leasehold interest and "full and complete" possession of the acreage. For a specified fee plus the cost of labor and materials, the company is given full discretion and authority over the cultivation of the groves and the harvest and marketing of the crops. The company is well established in the citrus business and maintains a large force of skilled personnel and a great deal of equipment, including 75 tractors, sprayer wagons, fertilizer trucks and the like. Without the consent of the company, the land owner or purchaser has no right of entry to market the crop; thus there is ordinarily no right to specific fruit. The company is accountable only for an allocation of the net profits based upon a check made at the time of picking. All the produce is pooled by the respondent companies, which do business under their own names.

The purchasers for the most part are nonresidents of Florida. They are predominantly business and professional people who lack the knowledge, skill, and equipment necessary for the care and cultivation of citrus trees. They are attracted by the expectation of substantial profits. It was represented, for example, that profits during the 1943–1944 season amounted to 20 percent and that even greater profits might be expected during the 1944–1945 season, although only a 10 percent annual return was to be expected over a 10-year period. Many of these purchasers are patrons of a resort hotel owned and operated by the Howey Company in a scenic section adjacent to the groves. The hotel's advertising mentions the fine groves in the vicinity and the attention of the patrons is drawn to the groves as they are being escorted about the surrounding countryside. They are told that the groves are for sale; if they indicate an interest in the matter they are then given a sales talk.

It is admitted that the mails and instrumentalities of interstate commerce are used in the sale of the land and service contracts and that no registration statement or letter of notification has ever been filed with the commission in accordance with the Securities Act of 1933 and the rules and regulations thereunder.

Section 2(1) of the act defines the term "security" to include the commonly known documents traded for speculation or investment. This definition also includes "securities" of a more variable character, designated by such descriptive terms as "certificate of interest or participation in any profit-sharing agreement," "investment contract" and "in general, any interest or instrument commonly known as a 'security.'" The legal issue in this case turns upon a determination of whether, under the circumstances, the land sales contract, the warranty deed and the service contract together constitute an "investment contract" within the meaning of § 2(1). An affirmative answer brings into operation the registration requirements of § 5(a), unless the security is granted an exemption under § 3(b). The lower courts, in reaching a negative answer to this problem, treated the contracts and deeds as separate transactions involving no more than an ordinary real estate sale and an agreement by the seller to manage the property for the buyer.

. . . [A]n investment contract for purposes of the Securities Act means a contract, transaction or scheme whereby a person invests his money in a common enterprise and is led to expect profits solely from the efforts of the promoter or a third party, it being immaterial whether the shares in the enterprise are evidenced by formal certificates or by nominal interests in the physical assets employed in the enterprise. Such a definition necessarily underlies this Court's decision in *S.E.C.* v. *Joiner Corp.* and has been enunciated and applied many times by lower federal courts. It permits the fulfillment of the statutory purpose of compelling full and fair disclosure relative to the issuance of "the many types of instruments that in our commercial world fall within the ordinary concept of a security." H. Rep: No. 85, 73d Cong., 1st Sess., p. 11. It embodies a flexible rather than a static principle, one that is capable of adaptation to meet the countless and variable schemes devised by those who seek the use of the money of others on the promise of profits.

The transactions in this case clearly involve investment contracts as so defined. The respondent companies are offering something more than fee simple interests in land, something different from a farm or orchard coupled with management services. They are offering an opportunity to contribute money and to share in the profits of a large citrus fruit enterprise managed and partly owned by respondents. They are offering this opportunity to persons who reside in distant localities and who lack the equipment and experience requisite to the cultivation, harvesting, and marketing of the citrus products. Such persons have no desire to occupy the land or to develop it themselves; they are attracted solely by the prospects of a return on their investment. Indeed, individual development of the plots of land that are offered and sold would seldom be economically feasible due to their small size. Such tracts gain utility as citrus groves only when cultivated and developed as component parts of a larger area. A common enterprise managed by respondents or third parties with adequate personnel and equipment is therefore essential if the investors are to achieve their paramount aim of a return on their investments. Their respective shares in this enterprise are evidenced by land sales contracts and warranty deeds, which serve as a convenient method of determining the investors' allocable shares of the profits. The resulting transfer of rights in land is purely incidental.

Thus all the elements of a profit-seeking business venture are present here. The investors provide the capital and share in the earnings and profits; the promoters manage, control and operate the enterprise. It follows that the arrangements whereby the investors' interests are made manifest involve investment contracts, regardless of the legal terminology in which such contracts are clothed. The investment contracts in this instance take the form of land sales contracts, warranty deeds and service contracts which respondents offer to prospective investors. And respondents' failure to abide by the statutory and administrative rules in making such offerings, even though the failure results from a bona fide mistake as to the law, cannot be sanctioned under the act.

This conclusion is unaffected by the fact that some purchasers choose not to accept the full offer of an investment contract by declining to enter into a service contract with the respondents. The Securities Act prohibits the offer as well as the sale of unregistered, nonexempt securities. Hence it is enough that the respondents merely offer the essential ingredients of an investment contract.

We reject the suggestion of the Circuit Court of Appeals, that an investment contract is necessarily missing where the enterprise is not speculative or promotional in character and where the tangible asset which is sold has intrinsic value independent of the success of the enterprise as a whole. The test is whether the scheme involves an investment of money in a common enterprise with profits to come solely from the efforts of others. If that test be satisfied, it is immaterial whether the enterprise is speculative or nonspeculative or whether there is a sale of property with or without intrinsic value. The statutory policy of affording broad protection to investors is not to be thwarted by unrealistic and irrelevant formulae.

Reversed.

DEFINITION OF A SECURITY—CONTINUED

In subsequent cases, various courts have expanded on the *Howey* doctrine of whether the scheme involves an investment of money in a common enterprise with profits to come solely from the efforts of others. For instance, it would be quite easy to avoid this definition and ensuing SEC regulation by structuring the investment so that some effort on the part of investors was required. As the circuit court in *SEC* v. *Koscot Interplanetary, Inc.,* and other cases pointed out, however, the critical question is "whether the efforts by those other than the investor are the undeniably significant ones, those essential managerial efforts which affect the failure or success of the enterprise."[1] In *Koscot Interplanetary,* the court discussed a pyramid scheme in which people gave the company money in return for the right to wholesale cosmetics to "beauty advisers" who then sold the cosmetics to the public. For a larger sum, the person could obtain the rights to distribute cosmetics to wholesalers and the beauty advisers and to recruit new participants. These "supervisors" and "distributors" were also allowed to keep a substantial portion of the money that any new prospect they recruited paid to Koscot for the right to participate in the cosmetics scheme. The court held that the involvement of the "supervisors," "distributors," and "beauty advisers" in selling cosmetics was merely incidental to the pyramid scheme of attracting more money from new prospects, and that such payments to Koscot for the right to introduce other prospects to the company, thus receiving a share of *their* initiation payments, was properly an investment subject to SEC jurisdiction.

Given that the courts appear to take an expansive view of what constitutes a security, several other cases yield somewhat surprising results. For instance, in *United Housing Foundation* v. *Forman,* subsidized cooperative nonprofit housing communities were held not to be securities.[2] In a co-op, one buys shares in a corporation that owns or builds an apartment building. Ownership of the shares gives these purchasers the right to occupy certain rooms (an apartment) in the building as long as all fees, rents, expenses, and so on are paid. Typically, there are restrictions on the occupancy of the apartment and the transferability of shares. In this instance, prospective dwellers bought the shares with the expectation that the rent would be around $23 per room. Ten years later, the estimate had escalated to almost $40 per room. Claims by purchasers that this was a securities offering that should have been registered with the SEC were rejected by the Supreme Court on the grounds that the primary motive of the participants was to obtain decent housing. In other words, this "investment" was for personal consumption, not an attempt to receive profits from the efforts of others. The mere inclusion of the word *stock* or *shares* in the deal did not automatically make it a "security" pursuant to federal securities laws.

In *International Brotherhood of Teamsters* v. *Daniel,* nonparticipatory retirement plans were held excluded from securities law. Daniel worked as a driver from 1950 to 1973, with the exception of a six-month layoff in 1961.[3] During this period, his employer contributed money on a weekly basis to the Teamsters Union, which invested it for the purpose of paying Daniel and others a pension on retirement. Daniel himself directly contributed no money to the fund. When Daniel retired, he expected a pension of about $500 monthly but was totally denied it because the pension fund rules required 20 years continuous service to qualify for any pension. Despite the compelling facts of this case and the obvious unfairness to Daniel, the court held that a compulsory, noncontributory pension fund was not the type of investment Congress had in mind when it passed the securities acts and that no relief for this unfairness could be had. While the securities laws have a broad scope, they do not encompass all investments.

EXEMPTIONS

Any securities issued or guaranteed by federal, state, or local governments are exempt from all securities laws, as are those of banks and savings and loans, charitable and religious institutions, and common carriers such as motor carriers and railroads (for certain types of offerings). The issuance of most insurance and annuity contracts and commercial paper are also exempt from federal securities laws. Reselling these securities may be subject to one or more provisions of the various laws; however, constitutional concerns play a key role in the exemptions of government, religious, and charitable securities. Most of the others are removed from SEC jurisdiction because their issuance is regulated by other state or federal agencies, such as the Federal Reserve System or the Interstate Commerce Commission.

In recent years, major cities like New York and Cleveland have defaulted on some bond issues, and numerous industrial development bonds issued under the auspices of local governments have gone bad. Furthermore, speculation in these securities has proliferated because of their unregulated status. From a stodgy, low-pressure backwater of the securities industry, trading in municipal securities has now become, for many, a very speculative and aggressive arena. By 1985, trades of government securities exceeded by many times (in dollar volume) trades on the New York Stock Exchange and were in excess of $60 billion daily.

S&Ls

Recently, many savings and loan associations have likewise gone bankrupt or become insolvent. Some have failed because of fraud or mismanagement; others because of poor real estate markets; but quite a few have failed because they speculated in leveraged, unregulated assets such as government securities, the value of which is highly dependent on changes in interest rates. Often, an investment of as little as $3 can be used to buy (or control) $100 worth of government bonds. A small upward change in interest rates can totally wipe out the value of the investment and thus bankrupt the investor. Likewise, a reduction in interest rates can lead to enormous profits for the skilled (or lucky) investor. As many commentators have pointed out, what is now called "the savings and loan crisis" can be traced to a regulatory system that allowed these institutions to issue unregulated securities (most of which we guaranteed by federal or state government insurance schemes). Many of the funds thus raised were then invested in highly speculative, also unregulated, financial instruments. As these investments soured, savings and loan losses soared, with the end result being massive demands on the federal insurance system.

"NEW GAMES"

Crafty marketers are constantly inventing new financial instruments to help investors and institutions meet their objectives more effectively. Some of these "new games," such as those involving interest rate swaps, may reduce the cost of capital to large firms, although risks may be associated with the savings. These instruments may also avoid SEC regulation or fall into regulatory gaps. Other financial vehicles appear to be bald-faced attempts to structure highly speculative, and occasionally fraudulent, deals to take advantage of regulatory loopholes. Even bonds issued by state and local governments can cause problems for unwary investors.

TAX–FREE BOND PROBES BY FEDERAL AGENCIES STIR TALK OF REGULATION

Steve Swartz and John Connor

A federal investigation of Matthews & Wright, Inc., a once-obscure New York municipal bond house, is turning a spotlight on a longstanding problem: The tax-exempt market can be hazardous to some investors' financial health.

The Matthews & Wright Group subsidiary had prospered by specializing in transactions that were too small or too risky for other securities firms and that were arranged on behalf of some unlikely places. These included a $399 million bond offering for the U.S. territory of Palau and a $9 million offering for Lenexa, Kansas. "I've never heard of a Lenexa, Kansas, bond," says Barnet Sherman, a municipal bond analyst at Smith Barney, Harris Upham & Co. Lenexa "isn't even in our atlas."

Now, Matthews & Wright is at the center of one of the largest federal investigations of the municipal bond business in history. Investigators from several agencies, including the Federal Bureau of Investigation and the Securities and Exchange Commission, are looking into possible fraud, bribery, and tax law violations involving more than $1 billion of tax-exempt bonds underwritten by Matthews & Wright in 1985 and 1986, people familiar with the investigation say.

Largely Unregulated

The investigation raises questions about the nation's largely unregulated $730 billion municipal bond market. Unlike the market for corporate bonds, municipal bond offerings aren't scrutinized by either the SEC or any other federal agency before the issues are sold. And federal laws give virtually no clues to what must be disclosed to investors beforehand.

* * * * *

Congress Interested

The investigation of Matthews & Wright could ignite a regulatory fire in Congress.

* * * * *

Any move toward tougher federal regulation of the municipal bond market would rile states' rights proponents. And many municipals professionals argue that the market is already well policed by state regulators and municipal officials. Michael D. Hernandez, the head of the municipal securities division at First Boston Corp., contends, for example, that municipalities often disclose more information about their offerings than corporate issuers do because cities and towns aren't sure what they have to disclose.

And Robert D. Pope, the president-elect of the National Association of Bond Lawyers, says "the first line of enforcement" is the industry professionals who structure bond sales for local governments. But the investigation of Matthews & Wright and other firms suggests that the self-regulatory mechanisms failed to catch bond-underwriting activities that should have had the professionals raising red flags.

A bond attorney's primary role is to ensure that a bond offering has been validly issued under state law and is tax exempt under state and federal laws. The trustee's job, which varies with the issue, generally is to ensure that the bond proceeds are invested and eventually spent under the terms set out in bond documents. Both professionals normally are hired by the municipality, but the underwriter typically has a strong say over who is selected.

Thus, like accountants doing corporate audits, bond lawyers and trustees can be subject to pressure from underwriters to approve their activities. Industry professionals complain privately of "shopping" by some underwriters, particularly for favorable bond law opinions.

* * * * *

The question of who should "keep up" with the vast municipal market has long been a contentious issue. The last major regulatory push came in 1975 when Congress, reacting to a series of scandals, created the Municipal Securities Rulemaking Board, a self-regulatory organization that sets standards for municipal underwriters.

The board is barred by law from requesting information from local-government issuers or in any other way regulating them. "The board has been asked to regulate with less than all the tools available to regulate the corporate world," says Christopher Taylor, the board's executive director.

Corporate Requirements

Mr. Taylor notes that corporate bond issuers must, by law, register offerings with the SEC and follow specific guidelines on what information is to be disclosed. Corporations must file quarterly and annual financial statements with the SEC and disclose any material events affecting their financial status.

Although the antifraud provisions of federal securities laws apply to municipal offerings, regulation of the market is largely left to state and local officials. "Some states, like New Jersey, require the filing of financial reports [by municipal issuers] with the secretary of state," Mr. Taylor notes. "Others have little or no supervision of the local units."

The Government Finance Officers Association has published guidelines on disclosure, but they are voluntary and don't apply to private projects, such as apartment complexes built with tax-free funds.

Richard Ciccarone, a vice president of municipal research at Van Kampen Merritt, Inc., in Chicago, scoffs at the notion that any regulators are watching the municipals market effectively. "It's most definitely unregulated," he says.

Questions

1. Investors in certain western states are being offered the opportunity to buy unprocessed gold ore from a company that will extract pure metal from the ore and deliver it to the investor at a future date. The investor is asked to pay the stated price for the unprocessed ore immediately, and the company agrees to provide any pure gold extracted from the ore at a below-market rate. By some estimates, investors are paying over $150 million per year for unprocessed ore. In effect, if substantial quantities of gold are in the ore, the investor stands to reap a windfall profit after the ore is processed. If no gold is found, the initial investment becomes worthless. Recent court decisions have held that such investments are not securities because investors may profit from future increases in the market price of gold, and thus they are not relying "solely" on the efforts of the promoters to obtain their profits.

    Do you agree with this interpretation? What are its drawbacks from the standpoint of a securities regulator? What types of abuses may occur?

2. The SEC is generally considered one of the most effective regulatory bodies, yet problems and potential new abuses keep arising. Can the SEC ever effectively regu-

late all the new schemes thought up by promoters? Why do investors, often rich, sophisticated individuals or even institutions, continue purchasing these highly speculative, unregulated instruments? Are other methods available for regulators to stamp out abuses? What are the drawbacks to other approaches?

3. If federal regulations are needed to protect investors who purchase securities newly issued by most private businesses, why should government securities and securities issued by a few types of private businesses such as insurance companies, banks, and so on be exempt from these laws?

EXEMPTIONS—CONTINUED

While some securities are totally exempt from federal securities laws, others are only exempt from certain provisions of the laws. Primarily, Congress has chosen to exempt certain types of securities from registration and disclosure under the 1933 act, although they may still be subject to the antifraud provisions of the law. The issuer of a security attempting to qualify for an exemption has an affirmative duty to demonstrate that it fits under the explicit terms of the particular exemption. In other words, if challenged, the company issuing the security must prove the exemption requirements were satisfied—the SEC does not have to prove they were not complied with. Recordkeeping, then, becomes paramount for a company attempting to qualify for an exemption.

Despite the problems of claiming an exemption, the alternatives can be much worse from the point of view of the company promoting the investment. The legal, accounting, and professional fees involved in registering a nonexempt security can be substantial, as are the printing and underwriting costs. Delays in getting approval from regulatory bodies or other costly mistakes can also make prohibitive the expense of obtaining regulatory approval. The costs of floating a $10 million initial public offering could easily exceed $1 million. Thus, for financial reasons, there is quite an incentive to structure a proposed offering so that it is exempt from federal registration requirements.

Types of Exemptions

The three main types of exemptions from compliance with SEC registration requirements are private placements, intrastate offerings, and simplified registrations. *Private placements* are securities sold to a limited number of investors, to "institutional" investors—banks, insurance companies, and pension plans—and to financially sophisticated, wealthy individuals and businesses. The 1933 Act exempts these people on the theory that they do not need the government to protect them. To qualify for the exemption, all investors must be provided with information similar to that required by the SEC for the sale of new securities, and stringent limitations are placed on the resale of these securities for a period of time. No advertising of these securities is allowed. These prohibitions keep private placements from becoming a tool to avoid

SEC registration requirements, and they prevent immediate marketing of the securities to the general public.

In recent years, approximately 35 percent of all corporate financings have been accomplished via private placements. Typically insurance companies, pension funds, or other entities would buy the securities and hold them for the lengthy period of time required by law. In 1990, however, the SEC loosened the rules so that institutions owning more than $100 million in securities can trade them without SEC registration (Rule 144a).

Intrastate offerings are those sold only in a single state to residents of that state. Even if this requirement is met, the issuer must demonstrate that 80 percent of its business (sales, assets, and so on) and 80 percent of the proceeds from the issue are to be used in that state. This exemption is designed to aid purely local businesspeople in obtaining funds without meeting costly SEC registration requirements. To qualify for this exemption, no resale to nonresidents may be made for nine months after the offering is complete.

A company desiring to issue less than about $1.5 million within 12 months to persons other than those involved with the company may file a much-simplified offering circular with the SEC. While not a complete exemption, this *simplified registration* procedure for small placements can lower offering costs substantially and encourage small businesses needing to raise capital to seek it from the public. This partial exemption also helps insulate the company and other people involved in the issuance of the security from liability arising from mistakes in the offering circular. Companies may issue securities worth $500,000 or less to anyone, without providing them with any information. Thus, the SEC has attempted to ensure that small businesses do not face insurmountable transactions costs.

Although an issue may qualify for a total or partial exemption from SEC rules, state blue sky laws in those jurisdictions in which the security is to be sold may not offer the same exemptions. In that case, issuers would still have to comply with state laws.

REGISTRATION REQUIREMENTS

If no total or partial exemption is available to the issuers, both state and federal laws will have to be considered. State blue sky laws are based on the theory that the state has the duty to protect its citizens from unwise, fraudulent, or excessively speculative investments. Before a security can be sold, most states require the state securities regulator to be convinced that the issue has some investment merit and is not a fraudulent scheme. Normally, securities that qualify under federal laws have no difficulty (just expense) in meeting state blue sky requirements. However, as recently as the 1970s, Massachusetts initially denied its residents the opportunity to buy Apple Computer stock when it was offered because the state felt the risk was too great and the price too high. The clamor was so great and so many residents simply decided to have brokers in other states purchase the stock for them that Massachusetts was finally forced to relent.

The Securities Act of 1933, on the other hand, is not concerned with the value or speculative nature of an issue; rather, it focuses on full disclosure of all the material facts. Before an offering can be sold, a detailed registration statement must be submitted to the SEC, which can then scrutinize it to make sure it contains all the data investors need to evaluate the desirability of a security for their investment purposes. A major part of the registration statement is the *prospectus,* which must be given to all potential investors before they are allowed to purchase the security. The prospectus contains all relevant data, such as the nature of the business and the background of the principals, the uses of the funds, the risks inherent in the enterprise, possible benefits, and various financial statements.

The SEC reviews the prospectus and other data it requires before the security can be sold. It can require additional data or information to be added and risks or other unusual factors to be highlighted. While the SEC cannot reject an offering based on its perception of the likelihood of success, the SEC can lengthen the approval process (and increase the expense) so that offerings it deems undesirable or misleading become practically impossible to market.

The prospectus and any other data on file with the SEC have to be updated if necessary due to changed conditions since the prospectus was originally created. The company issuing the security cannot take any unusual actions, such as advertising on television or exceptional press conferences, that gain favorable publicity for the company. The only advertising it may undertake relating to the sale of new securities is a tombstone ad, which simply sets forth what is being offered, when it is available, and from whom a prospectus may be obtained. The purpose of these restrictions is so that the purchaser can make decisions based on the data in the prospectus, not on some flattering facts put together by the company and contained in a glossy brochure that has not met SEC scrutiny. This is not to imply that all investors read the prospectus and develop informed opinions based on it. Many rely on brokers and other professionals, independent newspaper columns, their own experiences with the product, and so on; but before they buy the stock, they must have received a prospectus. The SEC does not protect foolish investors from folly; rather, it ensures that all investors have access to information adequate to reach a reasonable conclusion about the merits of the offering. Whether the potential investor properly evaluates the available data or chooses to ignore the proffered prospectus entirely is totally the investor's business.

While the SEC has normally been vigorous in demanding that investors have access to a prospectus, it has recognized that prior perusal of a prospectus is not always necessary to protect investors, especially in areas where competition exists. The following article discusses one possible instance.

SEC WILL PROPOSE LOOSER RULES
ON MARKETING MUTUAL FUNDS

Christi Harlan and Jonathan Clements

Buying a mutual fund could soon get as easy as leafing through the newspaper ads or responding to a piece of junk mail.

That at least is the plan of the Securities and Exchange Commission, which tomorrow will unveil for public comment a proposed overhaul of its rules governing mutual-fund advertising.

The big surprise in the SEC's proposal: Fund companies would be able to sell funds by mail without first furnishing the formal offering document known as the prospectus. Most fund executives hadn't expected the sale by direct-mail plan to be allowed. What they did expect, correctly, is that newspaper and magazine ads would be allowed to offer funds for sale to investors who hadn't first seen a prospectus. Under this provision of the new rules, investors also would be able to send a check without first seeing the prospectus.

* * * * *

The only funds eligible for sale under the expanded advertising rules would be those that have been registered with the SEC for two years or longer. "These won't be new funds," Mr. Breeden said. "These are funds with a track record."

The expanded advertising horizon will give a boost to no-load and low-load funds, which sell shares to the public with little or no sales charge. Under current regulations, such funds do advertise in newspapers but a would-be investor has to request a prospectus before a sale can take place. The no-loads have complained that this is unfair because rival funds are marketed through commissioned brokers, who can sell a mutual fund over the phone and mail a prospectus to the investor along with the confirmation of the sale.

The new regulations will shorten the turnaround time by allowing investors to read an ad for a direct-marketed fund and mail in a check. But the ads will be heavy on verbiage: The funds will have to disclose any fees or expenses involved, historic performance data, investment risks, policies on dividends and distributions, tax consequences, and redemption procedures.

By expanding the permitted advertising to include direct mail, the SEC would alleviate concerns of some smaller mutual funds that say they can't afford newspaper ads. "The problem with limiting it [to newspapers and magazines] is that it makes it only available to the largest funds," SEC Commissioner Richard Roberts said yesterday.

The SEC will require that advertisements and direct-mail literature be filed and cleared before publication with the National Association of Securities Dealers or, for non-NASD members, the SEC itself. If funds live up to the ad regulations for a full year, the filing rule will be relaxed to allow them to file ads within three days before or after publication, Mr. Breeden said.

* * * * *

Mr. Breeden called the plan "an attempt to reduce the barriers to competition between mutual funds that are offered through a commissioned sales force and those that are direct-marketed to investors . . . the result should be more choices for investors, and more vigorous competition."

Among the six largest fund companies that sell funds directly to investors, five say they would probably take advantage of the new advertising rules, if they are introduced.

"We think it's a fine idea, because it lifts out of the prospectus all the key information," says Diane

Coffey, a spokeswoman for New York's Dreyfus Corp. Roger Servison, a managing director with Boston's Fidelity Investments, the country's largest mutual fund group, reckons the fund industry could save $50 million a year since "a good 80% of the prospectuses we now send out end up going to people who never open an account."

The exception is Vanguard Group, the Valley Forge, Pa., company that ranks as the fund industry's third largest fund group. "It's a terrible idea," says John Bogle, Vanguard's chairman. "The advertisements would have to have some mighty big warnings in them before they would satisfy me."

Mr. Bogle notes that the push for new advertising rules is partly driven by complaints by no-load fund companies that they are at a disadvantage compared with broker-sold fund groups.

If this disadvantage needs to be erased, it should be done by forcing brokers to deliver a prospectus before making a sale, argues Mr. Bogle. "I don't see what the hurry is," he says. "If you're investing for 20 years, surely the additional 48 hours that lapses won't make much difference."

Source: *The Wall Street Journal,* March 17, 1993, p. C1. Reprinted by permission of *The Wall Street Journal,* © 1993 Dow Jones & Company, Inc. All Rights Reserved Worldwide.

REMEDIES FOR VIOLATIONS

Common Law Fraud.   In the absence of securities laws, if one has been sold a share of the Brooklyn Bridge, a Ponzi scheme, or a nonexistent South African gold mine, common law fraud theory may be used to recover money from the promoter or the company, assuming that either can be found and is solvent. To recover for fraud, the investor must show all of the following:

1. A material fact was misstated or omitted from the data given the purchaser.
2. The promoter/seller had knowledge of the error—scienter.
3. Reliance on the misstatement by the purchaser.
4. Intent to defraud the purchaser by the seller.
5. Privity of contract between seller and purchaser.
6. The misstatement was the cause of the investor's losses—proximate cause.
7. Damages.

At common law, failure to properly prove any one of these elements of fraud prohibits recovery by the seller. Thus, only in the most egregious cases could an investor recover any money. Typically, the person committing the fraud—the promoter—was unavailable, bankrupt, or in jail and therefore judgment proof, while the other persons the investor had dealt with (such as a broker and financial adviser, the firm's accountants, and attorneys for the firm) had not actively participated in the fraud and could not be liable for the fraud of the promoter.

Statutory Liability.   The 1933 Act, however, gave investors much greater potential for recovery when they felt they were defrauded. First of all, criminal liability may be imposed for willful violations of the act. The 1933 Act also imposes civil liability for all material misstatements, misleading data, or omissions in the prospectus and other registration material filed with the SEC. Quite simply, anyone who purchases a new security that is subject to registration requirements and contains errors, omissions, or misleading statements or for which no registration material is filed may be able to recover damages in an amount up to the original purchase price for all money lost as a result of the investment. No proof of reliance and causation is necessary. The mere fact that the error was made and that the investor lost money (the price of the security fell) is enough to entitle the investor to a recovery if the error or omission is deemed to be material. This means an investor can be perfectly satisfied with a purchase for a long period of time, but if the investment goes bad at a later date, the purchaser can then scan the prospectus for the error, misstatement, or omission. Finding such a problem with the prospectus can lead to the recovery of the total damages resulting from the decline in price of the original purchase.

Furthermore, another section of the act has been used to hold promoters and others liable for material misstatements or omissions regarding the offer or sale of securities not subject to the filing of a registration statement. Under either of these provisions, the company; any officer or director of the company; its accountants, attorneys, real estate appraisers, and other experts who helped develop the offering and registration; the underwriters; and anyone who signed the registration statement are personally liable for damages suffered by purchasers of the security. Thus, an aggrieved purchaser can have a veritable field day in finding the "deepest pockets" from the available, solvent parties and forcing a recovery from them. Once the error or omission has been found, the only significant defense these persons have to a suit by an investor is that they exercised due diligence and the mistake was made by someone else. In other words, the CPA firm cannot be held liable for a mistake by the law firm. However, the issuer of the security is absolutely liable for the mistake regardless of who was at fault.

It should now be readily apparent why the underwriting and registration process is so expensive. Each time an underwriter, accountant, attorney, appraiser, or financial printer becomes involved in a new offer, that person is potentially liable for the total amount of the offering—not only for intentional omissions and misstatements, but also for the most mundane typographical error, skipped line, or misplaced modifier. It is not surprising that Wall Street lawyers often become the world's most expensive proofreaders for many hours before a prospectus is released. An error could translate into hundreds of millions of dollars of liability for their firm and the other involved parties.

Questions

1. Rule 144a allows approximately 4,000 large institutions to trade privately placed securities that may not be offered to or traded by small (or many) individual investors.
   a. As these securities make up approximately 35 percent of all recent offerings, what problems will the ruling cause small investors?
   b. Is the volume of private placements likely to rise or fall? Explain.

      c. What are the implications for a regulatory system in which investors are willing to commit billions of dollars to investments that may not have complied with all the requirements of SEC regulation?

      d. Is it possible that SEC rules are counterproductive in some situations? List some examples of this problem.

2. The following excerpt does not depict a typical public offering, but it does clearly show the types of negative information that must be inserted in a prospectus because it is deemed to be material:

> The fact that the Mustang Ranch is a legal brothel isn't the only thing that makes the current attempt to turn it into a publicly traded company an eye-opener for investors.
>
> Not only has the Reno, Nev., operation been under protection of Chapter 11 of the Bankruptcy Code since 1982, but the Internal Revenue Service stands to be one of the big winners if the initial public offering succeeds.
>
> Indeed, leaving aside the purient details, the offering might be an object lesson about what investors can learn from a prospectus. "This isn't your typical IPO," says Alan Hadhazy, senior research analyst at the Institute for Econometric Research in Fort Lauderdale, Fla.
>
> The offering seeks to raise $17 million by selling 1.7 million shares at $10 each.
>
> * * * * *
>
> According to the prospectus, the brothel and the rest of the [owners'—Joseph and Sally Conforte] property is subject to an IRS lien. In fact, the IRS was scheduled to seize the property last month, but an extension was worked out, says Peter Perry, chief executive officer and director. "They're willing to extend it as many times as necessary to complete the offering." Adds Donald Clough, the company's president and treasurer, "They want the money, too."
>
> * * * * *
>
> Another notable feature of the prospectus is a discussion of a dispute about one aspect of the brothel's accounting methods. The Confortes have treated the prostitutes as self-employed independent contractors for tax purposes. But the IRS contends that they should be treated as employees and that the brothel is liable for employment taxes. The matter is the subject of an administrative appeal pending before the IRS.
>
> If the IRS prevails, it would "likely have a materially adverse effect upon the Company's prospects for profitability," the prospectus warns. Taking into account the disputed taxes, it says, earnings reported for four of five recent years would have been losses. For 1988, the last complete year for which figures are shown, the prospectus says the brothel earned $58,881 (after deducting disputed tax liabilities) on total revenue of $5.3 million.
>
> The prospectus also says investors in Mustang Ranch "will experience immediate and substantial dilution" in their stock. While the shares are being offered at $10 each, the prospectus puts the company's net tangible book value (essentially, assets minus liabilities) at between $1.09 and $2.13. Additional dilution could occur through exercise of warrants or sales of additional stock, the prospectus says.
>
> Typically, IPO principals keep a low profile during the offering stage. But Mr. Conforte allowed television personality Geraldo Rivera to tape two programs at the brothel last spring. In November and December, Mr. Conforte made a number of widely reported

comments, claiming increases in brothel earnings and plans to open a facility catering to women.

But according to a supplement to the prospectus filed Jan. 19, the company "cannot confirm the accuracy of the statements" regarding earnings. There is no plan to open a facility staffed by male prostitutes, it says.

An ad for the offering appeared in the January issue of Penthouse, where "you don't see too many Wall Street firms advertising," says Mr. Hadhazy. "It's being sold on the strength of the novelty . . . The sole hope is for publicity to get mom-and-pop investors to call." [4]

[Three efforts to take the Ranch public failed, and in 1990 it was sold at auction to pay taxes. However, the novel idea of a bordello as investment vehicle was not a complete failure. An eight-million dollar Broadway musical, "The Best Little Whorehouse Goes Public," which opened in May 1994 and closed shortly thereafter, was inspired by the Mustang Ranch story.]

    a. What problems would have faced investors who bought this security?
    b. Why did the ranch go to the expense of amending its prospectus to point out that it has no plans to open a facility staffed by male prostitutes?

3. Because of liability concerns, many underwriters put so much information into prospectuses that they can easily become almost book length. To combat eye fatigue and short attention spans, many underwriters also send potential investors a 4- to 12-page glossy, full-color summary of the highlights of the investment as part of the prospectus.
    a. Does this defeat the purpose of the prospectus?
    b. Should the SEC require that less data be contained in the prospectus in order to make it more readable for the average investor?

4. The issuance of securities is one of the many areas of regulation in which state and federal agencies substantially overlap in their oversight.
    a. Should the federal government "preempt" the regulation of securities from state jurisdiction?
    b. Would a partial preemption be appropriate?
    c. What types of offerings should be preempted?

REGULATION OF PUBLICLY HELD COMPANIES

The Securities Exchange Act of 1934 regulates many aspects of the financial dealings of publicly held companies. Any company with more than $1 million in assets and 500 shareholders may be subject to some provisions of the act, as are any businesses that have issued a class of securities traded on a national securities exchange. All companies required to register with the SEC must file annual and quarterly reports with the SEC, as well as monthly reports if certain specified occurrences take place. Investment companies, banks, insurance companies, and various other industries are exempt from these disclosure requirements, but over 10,000 firms are required to disclose the specified data to the SEC and the public on a regular basis.

In addition, the 1934 Act sets up the SEC and gives markets like the New York Stock Exchange some power of self-regulation, to be exercised with SEC oversight.

Furthermore, the SEC is authorized to regulate the extension of credit to buy securities, trading by members of the exchanges, and manipulative practices by members. It may also suspend trading of securities if it becomes necessary. The SEC also requires the regulation of brokers and dealers, municipal securities dealers, clearing and transfer agencies, and entities dealing in securities information.

The SEC also has the power to establish accounting rules for listed securities. While the commission typically defers to the expertise of the Financial Accounting Standards Board (FASB), it need not do so. Because of the role that accounting rules may have played in exacerbating the savings and loan bankruptcies and because of concerns that FASB standards do not accurately reflect financial realities, the SEC is taking a harder look at the independence it has given the FASB. The following article looks at one area of concern.

WHAT'S IT WORTH? TACKLING ACCOUNTING, SEC PUSHES CHANGES WITH BROAD IMPACT

Kevin G. Salwen and Robin Goldwyn Blumenthal

The Securities and Exchange Commission is shaking up the world of accounting.

The overhaul, so far, is a sedate one in a notoriously sedate field. But it could radically change companies' financial reports, and so the way companies are evaluated by investors. Even small variations in accounting can translate into big changes in stock prices, and some of the contemplated rule changes aren't small.

* * * * *

Right now, the SEC is focusing solely on debt securities and certain types of loans held by banks and other financial institutions. Next to be affected will probably be other companies with significant financial assets. Finally, much of corporate America, ranging from General Motors to a Silicon Valley startup, may feel pressure to revise the way it accounts for assets.

No Complete Overhaul

Although no one is suggesting that the SEC will revamp financial statements altogether, it wants to force companies to go a long way toward putting up-to-date values on assets currently on their books at historical cost—the original purchase price. It has launched an aggressive campaign in Congress and with the accounting profession to get fast action.

"If accounting standards aren't adequate to give an accurate picture of a firm's condition, they're not doing the job they need to do," says SEC Chairman Richard C. Breeden.

The agency's focus on accounting is another indication of its renewed scrutiny of corporate America, and its shift away from targeting Wall Street stock-trading abuses. The SEC recently adopted rules making it easier for companies to sell debt directly to large institutions and is awaiting congressional approval to toughen enforcement against wrongdoing by corporate officials.

* * * * *

Should the SEC decide to change the rules, it has a lot of weapons at its disposal besides just pressuring accounting bodies. For example, it has the power simply to change accounting rules by voting a rule proposal at an open meeting. After a period for public comment, the commission could pass a final rule. Alternatively, the agency can issue interpretative releases, telling public companies and the accounting industry how it reads a specific rule and that they should abide by that reading.

'A Statement of History'

Under today's standards, financial companies—banks, thrifts, and insurance concerns—holding stacks of investment securities can make their own judgments on whether to use historical accounting or current, "market" standards. "Financial-institution balance sheets should have the words 'once upon a time' on top of them," Mr. Breeden says scornfully. "They are a statement of history." Under the SEC plan, recently rejected by an industry accounting panel, only current values of a financial company's securities would be listed on the balance sheet and reflected in quarterly profit-and-loss statements.

Some financial concerns already are sharpening their pencils to current accounting and stepping away from historical levels. Rouse Co., a real-estate developer based in Columbia, Md., which began the switch in 1976, shows the differences on the balance sheet in its annual report. At year-end 1989, for example, the company's assets, largely land and buildings, totaled $4.13 billion, nearly $2 billion more than the assets would reflect on a cost basis. (The company does the same on the liabilities side of the ledger.)

"Initially, it came about as a result of the SEC requesting that companies do replacement cost accounting," says David Tripp, Rouse's director of investor relations. Rather than trying to estimate what it would cost to build a new project, Rouse values its assets on what it would cost to replace the income stream from them.

Not surprisingly, Mr. Tripp notes, the company's stock has tended to trade much closer to the value achieved by the current-cost model. At the end of 1989, based on historical cost, Rouse had shareholder equity of $52.9 million, or roughly $1.11 a share, Mr. Tripp says. But under the current-value model, shareholder equity was $1.73 billion, or about $34.80 a share. Only recently, with the real-estate slump, has the stock been trading at a deep discount to current value, Mr. Tripp says.

But James W. Otto, chief financial officer of Ameritrust Corp., a Cleveland-based banking company, says marking assets to current value "would be a very significant and costly effort that wouldn't be useful . . . It's an estimation of the liquidation value of a company that is totally irrelevant to a going concern."

Moreover, Mr. Otto adds, "A majority of the assets and liabilities don't have a ready market." Therefore, he argues, "some very subjective assumptions" would be needed to arrive at current values for those assets and liabilities.

At the root of SEC's new zeal are lessons drawn from the thrift crisis. Mr. Breeden cites 1978 numbers that show the thrift industry with a positive net worth. But a harder look—using current instead of historical accounting—shows that the industry was already ailing, with a negative net worth of as much as $118 billion.

* * * * *

According to Pat McConnell, a Bear, Stearns & Co. managing director, a major advantage of historical-cost accounting, he argues, is that value is determined by competing interests—a buyer and a seller agreeing on a price. Relying on a company's current valuation requires appraisals. "There's only one danger with doing an appraisal: Believing it," he says. The wild real-estate appraisals emerging from the devastated thrift industry have increased that anxiety.

But that hasn't stopped some companies from relying more heavily on internal systems of current accounting. "We may not be accurate in our current cost estimates," says David G. Harmer, FMC Corp.'s comptroller, "but we're a hell of a lot closer than erroneous historical-cost basis. We know [those] are understated."

* * * * *

Mr. Harmer acknowledges that the current-cost accounting is no panacea. Intangibles such as good will and training pose insurmountable problems; the company uses standard historical accounting for them.

[SEC Commissioner Philip] Lochner sees that as just one stumbling block. "What is the current value of Coca-Cola's trademarks? Your guess is as good as theirs," he says. "But we all know it's worth more than the $1 or so it's carried for on Coke's books." (Actually, it's on the books at zero.)

Source: *The Wall Street Journal,* September 27, 1990, p. A1. Reprinted by permission of *The Wall Street Journal,* © 1990 Dow Jones & Company, Inc. All Rights Reserved Worldwide.

REGULATION OF PUBLICLY HELD COMPANIES—CONTINUED

Besides registration and submission of various reports, publicly held companies are regulated concerning their recordkeeping, repurchases of securities, proxy solicitations, director changes, corrupt foreign practices, and many other areas of day-to-day activities. Stockholders who are officers or directors of a company or who own large blocks of the stock are required to report their transactions involving the company's securities to the SEC and are prohibited from engaging in certain stock transactions in which their position could give them an unfair advantage over the uninformed public. It is also a violation for anyone to trade shares on the basis of inside information—information not available to the investing public at the time. An officer of the company might have the ability to do this frequently, but on occasion so could a low-level employee (such as a field engineer who learns of an oil strike before it is announced to the public). Restrictions also are placed on tender offers (explained below), purchases of substantial blocks of stock, and institutional investment managers. Misleading statements in proxy solicitations or about the purchase or sale of a security, along with other unfair or deceptive practices, can result in criminal or civil liability under the 1934 Act.

Information

Just as the 1933 Act mandates issuance of a prospectus to notify potential investors of all relevant information about the security, the 1934 Act is also very concerned about keeping the investing public informed about all relevant facts concerning publicly traded companies. Thus, all significant information about the company must be made public in a timely manner. Not only does the prompt dissemination of information limit the possibilities for insider trading, but it also allows the financial markets to operate more efficiently.

Information on Wall Street equals power and success. To the extent that information is public, the financial markets can process that information and trade the underlying securities so that their market values reflect that new data. Obviously, a person with access to accurate information prior to the time it is made public can reap substantial rewards. Most financial institutions spend huge sums of money on analysts, whose jobs revolve around performing in-depth studies of particular industries. In the rough-and-tumble world of Wall Street, analysts who can predict industry trends, or more accurately predict a company's earnings or future conduct, will have a profitable career. As the following article indicates, even a few minutes can make the difference between profit and loss in a volatile situation. While many individuals go to extreme (but legal) lengths to ferret out information about companies, others use illegal means to gain an economic advantage. Insider trading, which will be discussed later in this chapter, is a prime example of such abuses, and takeover attempts such as this one present fertile grounds for inside trading.

The Paramount-Viacom Merger Hearings (Paramount's Stock Price at Five-Minute Intervals Yesterday)

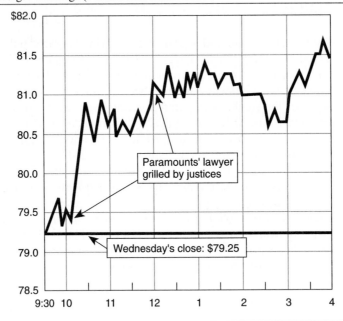

Source: *Knight-Ridder TradeCenter*

PARAMOUNT-TAKEOVER HEARING
GLUES TRADERS TO TV SCREENS

William Power

It was Wall Street's answer to "The People's Court."

A key hearing in the Paramount Communications Inc. takeover battle was put on national cable television yesterday morning, and instantly became the hottest show on Wall Street.

The two hours of live coverage from Delaware Supreme Court was studied, blow-by-blow, by traders and brokers with access to Courtroom Television Network (Court TV) and other channels that carried the network's feed. Remarkably, Paramount's stock price appeared to react instantaneously with developments from the courtroom, eventually closing $2.75 higher at $82 a share in heavy New York Stock Exchange composite trading.

Judging by all the traders and securities lawyers who watched it yesterday morning—and by the rapid price reaction of Paramount shares to courtroom developments—the business of takeover-stock speculation may never be the same.

Tough Questions

Paramount stock started stirring just after 10 a.m. Eastern time, when Paramount lawyer Barry Ostrager began his presentation. The Delaware justices put Mr. Ostrager on the defensive with tough questions.

The red-haired Mr. Ostrager looked scared, many traders concluded. They began bidding up Paramount's stock, convinced that the court was leaning toward killing Viacom Inc.'s takeover agreement with Paramount and allowing a more-lucrative one from QVC Network Inc. to go forward. (And after the market closed, that's exactly what happened.)

"We and all of our arbitrage clients were riveted to it," said Frank Baxter, chairman of Jefferies Group Inc., which pulled in the feed on its four televisions in its Los Angeles trading room. The show was watched everywhere from the trading desk of giant Merrill Lynch & Co. in New York to the smallest independent takeover trader, or risk arbitrager. "It was sensational. It was high drama," said one of these arbitragers. "It speeded up [trading in Paramount] to real time."

It was the first time that a major takeover battle got such a spot on Court TV.

During many mid-1980s takeover fights, traders relied on rumors or frantic phone calls from colleagues outside courtrooms. But yesterday's telecast could be a preview of the 21st-century stock market—when most traders will probably have TVs built right into their trading screens, and market-moving court hearings will be telecast routinely.

High Stakes, Top Lawyers

If so, not all trials will be as interesting as the Paramount hearing in Wilmington. Many Wall Street cases are as boring as they come, filled with lawyers posturing about obscure rules of law and procedure. The Paramount hearing, in contrast, had big stakes and top-notch lawyers (including, to be fair, Mr. Ostrager).

TV-watching traders thought that QVC's lawyer who appeared after Mr. Ostrager, Herbert Wachtell, was more impressive though he also faced tough questions; after all, two of the justices seemed to nod their heads in agreement with one of Mr. Wachtell's points.

Paramount's stock held its ground during Mr. Wachtell's testimony, and again jumped upward when Mr. Ostrager made a second appearance around noon. During that appearance, Justice Andrew Moore was particularly aggressive about why Paramount turned down a good offer from QVC. It "doesn't sound like you're dealing openly with both sides," he said.

The stock continued to rise at 12:15 P.M. as Viacom's attorney, Stuart Baskin, also got a tough reception from the justices. The stock eased in the afternoon, once the court adjourned and the television sets were shut off . . .

Paramount stock rallied again in the last hour of trading, before the post-trading court decision was announced.

* * * * *

Before TV got in the act, traders had to be more enterprising. Traders, lawyers and aides representing outside investors swarmed over court hearings, jamming into the best seats near exit routes to nearby telephones.

A few years ago, the Delaware Supreme Court cited one New York lawyer for contempt after he lied about smuggling a cellular telephone into the courtroom during a hearing on the Polaroid-Shamrock takeover battle. At that time, the court also scolded Mr. Wachtell, the lawyer who did so well in yesterday's television testimony, after one of his partners was accused of improperly leaking a document during the Time Inc. takeover battle.

Traders insist that the popularity of yesterday's televised hearing doesn't mean that takeover-stock investors can get all they need to know from TV, without using their highly paid brokers.

"There's still a tremendous amount of subjectivity to trading," says Mr. Baxter. "There are many ways of looking at the same piece of information."

Source: *The Wall Street Journal,* December 10, 1993, p. C1. Reprinted by permission of *The Wall Street Journal,* © 1993 Dow Jones & Company, Inc. All Rights Reserved Worldwide.

Tender Offers

When one company attempts to take over another, SEC rules can often be crucial. All such *tender offers* must be registered with the SEC. Furthermore, certain disclosure rules are triggered when groups purchase more than 5 percent and more than 10 percent of a company's outstanding stock. In recent years, as hostile takeover attempts have become more frequent, many strategies have been developed to limit their success. The raiders, however, are sometimes able to use the rules to their advantage. In many such takeovers, both state laws and SEC requirements play a part. Typically, management uses state requirements to slow down or eliminate the possibility of a hostile takeover, while the raiders usually enlist the aid of SEC rules. This is not a hard-and-fast rule, and in this fast-paced, tricky area, the positions can flip-flop regularly.

Bidders for a company can rely on recent amendments to the 1934 Act to get more information about a target company and to shorten the period of time during which shareholders can decide whether to accept the offer. These amendments also have placed additional restrictions on a company's ability to use state law to fend off a takeover. For instance, in the Mobil–Marathon takeover battle, the "lockout" defense was rejected by the courts. In this maneuver, the target's board opposed a "totally inadequate" offer by giving another friendly corporation ("white knight") the right to purchase 10 million authorized but unissued shares and a contingent option to purchase a major oil field in the event of a hostile takeover. The purpose of this transaction was to make the takeover candidate more expensive and financially unattractive to the raider. The court held this practice to be "manipulative" in that it set an artificial ceiling on what the shareholders could expect to receive should the company or its assets be sold. In effect, the shareholders were being harmed in order to keep the company from being sold and to keep existing management in power.

Other Strategies

On the other hand, such other defenses as questioning whether a takeover violates antitrust law and claiming access to insider information by the bidder or violations of SEC disclosure rules remain important in stopping hostile bids. Another effective technique is to buy a business, such as a radio or television station, railroad, bank, insurance company, or airline, for which state or federal regulatory approval is necessary prior to a change in ownership. Getting necessary regulatory approval may add to the time and expense involved in a takeover and may force a bidder to reconsider. For instance, several attractive takeover candidates have bought Florida-based insurance companies because of that state's rules concerning sales of insurance companies. Other options involve selling large blocks of stock to employees, issuing much new debt, attempting to take over the hostile bidder, requiring that the same sale or exchange terms be offered to all shareholders, mandating that the board or a supermajority of all shareholders must approve takeover bids, selling off the most attractive corporate assets, finding another purchaser, or buying out the bidder at a profit ("greenmail"). Clearly, some of these techniques are more desirable than others from the standpoint of the corporation, and many, such as taking on substantial new debt or selling off attractive corporate assets ("scorched earth" defense), can seriously damage the long-run prospects of the business. One last defense, which has been used frequently but is likely to be curtailed, is "golden parachutes," in which officers are paid large bonuses in the event of a hostile takeover. The shareholder ill will engendered by these bonuses is often substantial, and their legality may be subject to question.

The best way to avoid a takeover remains unchanged, however—run a well-managed company with attractive share prices. Only companies whose assets are thought to be undervalued or whose parts can be spun off at prices greater than current share prices become takeover targets.

THE STATES RESPOND

To stem hostile takeovers, management has been turning to state legislatures. Takeover candidates are using their political clout to convince legislators of the harmful effects a takeover could have for the state where the business is incorporated or has a major presence. Such economic issues as plant closings, wholesale transfers, or moving the headquarters appear to strike a responsive chord. From the standpoint of investors, regulators, and raiders, such tactics are troublesome.

HOW INDIANA SHIELDED A FIRM AND CHANGED THE TAKEOVER BUSINESS

Michael W. Miller

One day in December 1985, James K. Baker, the chairman of Arvin Industries, Inc., summoned his friend Robert Garton to lunch and let him in on a startling secret. Arvin Industries, an auto-parts gi-ant, had received a letter from Canada's Belzberg family threatening a takeover.

Jim Baker and Bob Garton, the president of the Indiana Senate, went back a long way together in

Columbus, a town of tree-lined streets and ginger-bread storefronts. They were fellow Rotarians, members of the same gourmet cooking club, and parents of former classmates at Southside Junior High School. Now, Mr. Baker asked his old friend to help stop the takeover and save Arvin Industries and Columbus from wrenching change.

Mr. Garton didn't let him down. Within four weeks, he had steered a tough anti-takeover bill, drafted by Arvin's own lawyers, through the Indiana legislature and onto the governor's desk, where it was promptly signed. The bill, in effect, outlawed most hostile takeovers in the Hoosier state.

Preserving Small Towns

Twenty-one states restrict takeovers, and most of the laws sprang from the same impulse that moved Mr. Baker and Mr. Garton: to preserve small company towns and their ways. For many years, judges across the country deemed those laws touching but unconstitutional. The courts said the states were meddling illegally in the nationwide securities market.

That changed last spring. In a ruling on a second Indiana law—also backed by Arvin—the Supreme Court upheld the right of states to regulate takeovers.

The decision promises to have a sweeping impact on the takeover game, hobbling corporate raiders and giving management a powerful new defense weapon. It will give state takeover laws unprecedented power and spur states that don't yet have them on their books to consider them.

* * * * *

Fossilizing Industry

At the heart of the saga lies some far-reaching economic issues: How much power should a community have to prevent economic upheavals within its borders? And will towns use this power to preserve harmony and stability or to fossilize aging industrial and social structures?

The assault on Arvin began December 3, 1985, when the Belzberg family wrote the company that it

had amassed a 4.9 percent shareholding and was considering buying the remaining shares. The Belzbergs are a powerful Canadian family, immensely wealthy and well-scarred after a decade of tumultuous takeover attempts.

* * * * *

About eight years ago, the Belzberg sons started showing up on the doorsteps of large U.S. companies, brandishing minority shareholdings in the companies and threatening to take over. They gained a reputation as raiders who could be bought off, and one company after another paid the Belzbergs greenmail—buying back the shares at a juicy premium over the market price.

Grave Misgivings

The Belzbergs confronted a dozen companies, extracting large payments from Ashland Oil, Inc.; USG Corp.; Potlatch Corp.; and others. In 1985, they surprised Wall Street by actually following through on a raid, buying Scovill, Inc. The family likes to work in secret and, through a spokesman, refused to be interviewed for this article.

The Belzbergs are exactly the sort of takeover artists chief executives have in mind when they bemoan the excesses of merger mania. But people in Columbus (population 30,200) weren't only worried about the Belzbergs' brand of corporate raiding. They had grave misgivings about how their town would fare if Arvin was ever taken over.

The fortunes of Columbus have been closely bound to Arvin since 1931, when Q. G. Noblitt moved the company's forerunner, Indianapolis Air Pump Co., into town. Last year, Arvin had sales of nearly $1 billion and a profit of $41 million. It makes mufflers, exhaust pipes, catalytic converters, and scores of other industrial and electronic products; it employs about 2,000 people in Columbus, making it the town's second-largest employer, after Cummins Engine Co.

Arvin is the kind of company that chambers of commerce adore. Hundreds of Columbus children go to a pair of schools that Mr. Noblitt donated to the town in the 1950s. In the summers, they play in a 70-acre wooded youth camp, another Noblitt donation.

When Columbus needed a new superintendent of schools two years ago, Arvin executives helped in the nationwide search. Then the company donated money to help the town lure its top prospect to south-central Indiana. A few years ago, Shirley Lyster, an English teacher at Columbus North High School, called Chairman Baker and told him she wished her class could read Homer in the out-of-print George Herbert Palmer translation. Arvin printed a special edition for her.

Columbus is a town with a social fabric so tight-knit that people joke, "You have to pull the blinds to change your mind in Columbus." When the Belzbergs loomed, the town fathers believed a takeover would shatter the town's long, cozy relationship with Arvin. And it raised the specter of a fate local residents dreaded: Columbus as a mere branch-plant town.

"Had [the Belzbergs] bought Arvin, you'd see that company's personality change overnight," says Brooke Tuttle, an official at the Columbus Chamber of Commerce. "There's a kind of attitude you get from an out-of-town owner—the focus is on the bottom line and the return to shareholders."

Mistrust of Outsiders

"Communities don't become great just being branch-plant towns," declares Robert Stewart, the mayor of Columbus.

But the town's staunch support of Arvin also springs from some emotional biases, including a deep mistrust of outsiders. "The farther away from Columbus you get," says Mr. Baker, "the more we look at them with the suspicion that they're not coming from the same place as us."

It also glosses over a fact that has been painfully clear in Columbus in the 1980s: No matter how hard the town and the state work to keep Arvin, economic necessities are forcing the company to stray far from its beloved hometown. Arvin, the company that doesn't want to become a branch plant, has its own

branches in dozens of U.S. cities. In 1970, it opened an electronics factory in Taiwan, which now employs 1,500 people. Meanwhile, unemployment in Bartholomew County, which Columbus dominates, has been nearly 9 percent in the 1980s, up from about 5 percent in the 70s. Today one out of six Columbus households lives on an income at or below the poverty level.

In short, Indiana and Columbus were fighting to stay wedded to an industry of the past.

* * * * *

Too Vulnerable

[In an attempt to repel the Belzbergs, Arvin turned to the legislature for help.] "We decided we'd better bring Brother Garton [the Senate president] into the fold," says Mr. Baker.

As Mr. Baker saw it, the stock market values companies inefficiently, making them vulnerable to raiders. It was, he thought, an inequity so deep that only new laws could remedy it.

A lawyer working for Arvin, James Strain, quickly drafted just such a law and sent it to Senator Garton. Modeled on laws in New York and other states, it banned hostile business combinations for five years after an investor buys 10 percent of a company.

Senator Garton made the anti-takeover bill the state Senate's first bill of the session, a slot reserved for matters of pressing importance. The bill was officially declared "emergency legislation," and it went into effect as soon as the governor signed it. The legislature's haste drew a scolding from the Indianapolis *Star:* "This is not a topic to be whipped through the legislature with a smile and a prayer and no debate."

Two months later, the Indiana legislature passed a second anti-takeover statute as part of a major revision of the state's corporate code. Arvin's lawyer, Mr. Strain, was one of three Indianapolis attorneys who drafted it.

With that law, the trio came up with a novel way to thwart a hostile bidder. The law springs a booby trap on an investor who acquires 20 percent of an Indiana company: He loses his shares' voting rights unless the other shareholders move to reinstate them.

Arvin says the new laws helped repel the Belzbergs' takeover attempt. Shortly after the second law passed, the two sides settled. Arvin agreed to buy for $39 million a Belzberg-owned tire-valve company it had declined to purchase just one year earlier. (Arvin says the Belzbergs lowered the price to a reasonable level.) It also bought for $20.4 million the Belzbergs' Arvin shares, paying $25.25 each, which was below the market price at the time but still gave the raiders a handsome profit, according to Arvin officials.

* * * * *

Economy "Balkanized"

A slew of lower courts had struck down similar state laws, mostly on the grounds that they blocked interstate commerce.

* * * * *

But on April 21, one year after the Belzbergs backed off from Arvin, the Supreme Court rejected the challenge by a 6–3 vote.

* * * * *

Their opinion dismissed the Indiana law's effect on interstate commerce as "limited." And it declared that the law fell well within states' rights to regulate their corporations and define the kinds of stock they can issue.

The decision came on the heels of Wall Street's insider-trading scandals and amid a national uproar against takeovers. While the justices didn't directly acknowledge that background, their tone indicated that they, too, believed the merger game had gone too far.

The law, according to the court, would allow "shareholders collectively to determine whether the takeover is advantageous to their interests [which] may be especially beneficial where a hostile tender offer may coerce shareholders into tendering their shares."

Justice Antonin Scalia also upheld the law, but he would not sign his name to Justice Powell's broad endorsement of state takeover laws. A law "can be both economic folly and constitutional," he wrote. "The Indiana Control Shares Acquisition Chapter is at least the latter."

Source: *The Wall Street Journal,* July 1, 1987, p. 1. Reprinted by permission of *The Wall Street Journal,* © 1987 Dow Jones & Company, Inc. All Rights Reserved Worldwide.

STATE TAKEOVER LAWS: CONSTITUTIONAL BUT DUMB

Roberta Romano

The Supreme Court recently upheld Indiana's state takeover statute. Such legislation may be constitutional, but is it wise? State takeover statutes are controversial because there are serious questions whether these laws benefit shareholders. These new provisions might increase the premium shareholders receive in a takeover bid, but that effect could be swamped by a decrease in the likelihood of an offer being made. The statutes could thus be a lever for preserving management's jobs while reducing shareholder wealth.

In promoting state regulation of takeovers, managers often claim to be furthering shareholders' interests. They also suggest that the interest of workers and local communities are served by these statutes. One way to gauge better who benefits from takeover laws is to examine the politics of the legislation—to investigate, for instance, who initiates the bills and who lobbies for their adoption. If the broad-based constituency to which proponents of the legislation refer were truly benefited, we would expect to see the supposed beneficiaries, who have their own powerful lobbying organizations, at the forefront in the making of takeover statutes. The politics of takeover statutes does not, however, fit such a scenario.

* * * * *

The supposed beneficiaries of takeover bills either oppose the legislation or are neutral. The shareholder groups that do lobby oppose most legislation regulating takeovers. Nor do unions and community-based groups actively initiate or lobby for takeover laws. Unions, for instance, are far more concerned with regulating plant closings, and other

matters that directly affect their members, than with takeover statutes that give managers tools with which to impede hostile acquisitions.

* * * * *

Justice Antonin Scalia, in his concurring opinion on state takeover statutes, noted that a law can be both constitutional and foolish. Takeover statutes, while constitutional, are troublesome because they can undermine the shareholder sovereignty on which all of corporate law is premised. For it is most plausible that the principal beneficiaries of this regulation are its prime promoters—managers seeking to circumvent a shareholder vote because they fear the loss of their jobs.

Source: *The Wall Street Journal,* May 14, 1987, p. 22. Reprinted by permission of *The Wall Street Journal,* © 1987 Dow Jones & Company, Inc. All Rights Reserved Worldwide.

SEC CHIEF URGES CONGRESS TO GIVE AGENCY POWER TO PREEMPT STATE SECURITIES LAWS

Bruce Ingersoll

Securities and Exchange Commission Chairman David Ruder urged lawmakers to give the SEC sufficient rule-making power to preempt state laws that interfere with the "national market" for securities.

The commission, Mr. Ruder said, needs more statutory authority over tender offers, largely because of the recent Supreme Court ruling on Indiana's takeover law. The ruling upheld for the first time state regulation of corporate takeovers.

The rush by the states to adopt similar or more restrictive legislation "threatens to create a maze of overlapping and conflicting regulation," the former Northwestern University law professor testified yes-

terday before the House Energy and Commerce Committee's securities panel.

State attempts to shield their corporations from hostile bids have "presented serious impediments to the free and efficient operation" of the stock markets, Mr. Ruder said. "Drawing the line between appropriate state regulation of internal corporate affairs and improper state regulation of national tender offers is not easy," he added, "but the task is unavoidable."

Source: *The Wall Street Journal,* September 18, 1987, p. 17. Reprinted by permission of *The Wall Street Journal,* © 1987 Dow Jones & Company, Inc. All Rights Reserved Worldwide.

DISGRUNTLED INVESTORS

Although the Supreme Court affirmed the right of states to adopt antitakeover legislation, large shareholders are attempting to use their economic leverage to minimize the potential impact of those laws on their investments. As the following article reinforces, ultimately the only certain defense to takeovers is the support of a majority of the firm's owners.

HOLDERS PUSHING PENNSYLVANIA CONCERNS TO FORSAKE THE STATE'S TAKEOVER SHIELD

Dana Milbank

Pennsylvania companies that accepted protection under the state's controversial anti-takeover law are getting hit by a barrage of challenges from disgruntled shareholders.

Members of the United Shareholders of America, a Washington, D.C.-based group backed by T. Boone Pickens, have filed holder initiatives against Aluminum Co. of America, PPG Industries Inc., and AMP Inc., and also will file a proposal at Zurn Industries Inc. The initiatives direct the companies to reincorporate elsewhere, or take other measures, to escape the state takeover protection. In addition, the influential California Public Employee Retirement System filed resolutions directing Armstrong World Industries Inc. and Scott Paper Co. to reincorporate in Delaware.

These six companies are the largest Pennsylvania concerns that accepted protection under the state law. Alcoa, AMP, and Scott confirmed they had received proposals. Armstrong and PPG declined to comment. Zurn said it hadn't yet received a proposal.

Proponents believe they have widespread support for the initiatives, which will appear on the ballot at the companies' annual meetings this spring unless they are withdrawn or are found to violate Security and Exchange Commission guidelines.

The companies are expected to oppose the resolutions, and—as with all such resolutions—won't be formally bound by them if passed. Still, the initiatives underscore the hostility that many investors feel toward both the antitakeover act and the companies that accepted its protection.

"This law is the worst ever," asserts Ralph Whitworth, United Shareholders president. "Pennsylvania's winning the race to the bottom."

The Pennsylvania law is considered by many investors to be among the nation's toughest against takeovers. Shareholders claim it violates their rights and hurts stock value. Of the 117 companies with capitalization of over $10 million in Pennsylvania, 80 opted out of protection under the new law.

* * * * *

Investors have been particularly irked by one provision in the law that amends the "fiduciary duty" standards so that company directors needn't consider shareholder interests dominant over employee, community and creditor interests. The law also provides a "disgorgement" provision, which directs takeover bidders to return profits to the company that they made by putting the company into play.

Delaware

> While the Pennsylvania law appears to lower fiduciary duty standards concerning directors' obligations to act in the best interests of shareholders, other influential states such as Delaware seem to be putting more emphasis on the rights of shareholders by allowing directors less discretion in exercising their "business judgment." As the following article notes, this is especially true when the directors have opted to consider selling the company.

PARAMOUNT IS TOLD BY COURT
TO CONSIDER OFFER BY QVC

Johnnie L. Roberts and Randall Smith

The Delaware Supreme Court upheld a resounding lower court defeat for Paramount Communications Inc., forcing Paramount to consider QVC Network Inc.'s $10.1 billion offer on an equal basis with Viacom Inc.'s friendly bid.

The three-judge panel yesterday strongly rebuked Paramount's directors for failing shareholders by ignoring unwelcome suitor QVC in favor of an inferior deal with Viacom.

* * * * *

The ruling also appears to scale back the freedom given to corporate boards to pursue the long-term strategies of their choice. That freedom came in a 1989 Delaware Supreme Court decision allowing Time Inc. to proceed with an acquisition of Warner Communications Inc., despite the fact that Paramount had made a $200 per share offer for Time. In its ruling, the court said the Time Warner precedent didn't apply because Paramount was selling control to Viacom's chairman, Sumner Redstone.

In a brief oral order from the bench, Chief Justice E. Norman Veasey said that because Paramount directors agreed to sell control to Viacom on Sept. 12, they erred by failing to consider other offers. The directors "had a duty to continue their search for the best value available to shareholders," Justice Veasey said.

Having decided to sell the company, Paramount directors were "required to evaluate critically whether or not all material aspects of the Paramount-Viacom transaction were reasonable and in the best interests of the Paramount stockholders," the ruling said. The directors failed to do so, the court added.

The ruling sent the takeover battle back to the lower Delaware Chancery court, where Vice Chancellor Jack Jacobs must now instruct the Paramount board how to comply. It wasn't clear how much discretion he would give the board to set up fair bidding procedures.

* * * * *

Though Paramount had argued that its merger agreement with Viacom prevented it from negotiating with QVC, Justice Veasey rejected that defense in reading the court's decision. He said the so-called "no-shop" clauses in the Paramount agreement with Viacom prevented the directors from fulfilling their fiduciary duty to search for the best value for Paramount shareholders, and thus the provisions were "invalid and unenforceable."

* * * * *

At one point near the end of the hearing, Justice Andrew G. T. Moore II asked Barry Ostrager, the

Paramount lawyer, why Paramount directors weren't told that Paramount's investment banker believed that QVC could get financing for its offer at a meeting Nov. 15.

Exchange with Attorney

When Mr. Ostrager responded that the directors had been told, Justice Moore asked, "Where is that in the record?" And he repeated the same questions three more times when Mr. Ostrager couldn't cite specifics in the voluminous court documents.

At that meeting, Paramount's board concluded that a $90-a-share cash bid by QVC for 51% of Paramount was too conditional to consider because Paramount's contract with Viacom barred Paramount from talking to a bidder whose bid was subject to financing.

* * * * *

The court noted that Paramount's directors had based their decision to approve a deal with Viacom on "their best business judgment." But the court said the "traditional business judgment rule," which allows directors to pursue a merger they deem to be in the best interests of shareholders, didn't apply because the transaction was a sale of control.

Viacom's Mr. Redstone is the controlling shareholder of that company and would end up with 69.8% of the voting stock and 38.5% of the equity in a merged Paramount Viacom. That is clearly a change of control and would give Mr. Redstone the voting power "to cause a breakup of the company, to cash out the minority stockholders, or to alter materially the equity interest of the minority public shareholders," the ruling said.

Strategic Alliance Vision

Regardless of the Paramount directors' vision of a long-term strategic alliance with Viacom, the court said, "once control passes to Redstone, he has the power to alter that vision."

The court was especially critical of provisions in the Paramount-Viacom sale agreements which it said were designed to discourage competing offers. In the event Paramount was sold to a higher bidder, Viacom was owed a $100 million fee, plus the right to buy 23.7 million new Paramount shares at $69.14 each, the price when the bidding began.

It ruled that those so-called "lockup" agreements were "improperly designed to deter other potential bidders," and thus deprive shareholders of a possible opportunity for a higher offer.

The Delaware court indicated that a critical turning point in the takeover battle involved a Paramount board decision on Oct. 24 to substitute a Viacom tender offer at a higher price of $80 a share for the original merger agreement between the two companies.

The tender offer was Viacom's response to a similar tender offer that QVC had announced about a week earlier, after Paramount ignored a takeover proposal by QVC. The court ruled that directors had a duty at the board meeting and afterward to critically evaluate both offers.

The court said the directors should have tried to determine whether the two offers could be improved, and whether each would likely be completed, among other things. [For the outcome of the QVC/Viacom battle for Paramount, see p. 431.]

Source: *The Wall Street Journal,* December 10, 1993, p. A3. Reprinted by permission of *The Wall Street Journal,* © 1993 Dow Jones & Company, Inc. All Rights Reserved Worldwide.

Questions

1. Who benefits from the antitakeover provisions in corporate charters or state laws? Who is harmed? How? Do these provisions violate management's fiduciary duty to its shareholders? Explain.

2. What effect, if any, will these provisions have concerning the efficiency of the U.S. economy?

3. Do managers and workers need greater protection from corporate raiders? Should state governments intervene in takeover battles? Can you think of any unintended consequences of intervention? Explain.

SECURITIES FRAUD

The 1934 Act and SEC Rule 10b–5 prohibit securities fraud with respect to the sale of registered or unregistered securities. While SEC requirements are greater than those under state common law fraud rules, they are not as burdensome as those of the 1933 Act. Clearly, those who are direct participants in securities fraud are in violation of the 1934 law and Rule 10b–5. However, the more troublesome question in recent years has been the liability of third parties—often accountants, lawyers, and other professionals who "aided or abetted" a fraudulent scheme. Since the 1940s many federal court decisions have upheld private lawsuits against those third parties. Large, solvent accounting firms have made particularly attractive targets for suits by investors who have lost money as a result of corporate fraud or financial failure. While the law has long held that the 1934 act holds accountants responsible for investor losses if the accountants were active participants in the fraud (e.g., intentionally overlooked improprieties or accepted money or other payoffs in return for changing their opinion), the more difficult question is one of liability for accountants, lawyers, and others when they are "third parties" to a fraud. Since a crooked or incompetent investment promoter is often penniless and/or hard to reach, investors often have turned to the deep pockets of those professionals who worked for the promoter. Now in a surprising decision that overturns decades of precedent the Supreme Court has ruled that those who aid and abet a stock fraud may *not* be sued under the 1934 Securities Act. The article that follows explains that decision.

JUSTICES DEAL INVESTORS
A BLOW IN CERTAIN SUITS

Paul M. Barrett

The Supreme Court took away a major legal weapon that investors have used in lawsuits alleging securities-fraud schemes.

In a 5–4 ruling, the court said the main federal securities-fraud law, Section 10(b) of the 1934 Securities Exchange Act, doesn't allow investors to file suits charging that someone "aided or abetted" deceptive acts involving stock or bond transactions.

The main beneficiaries of the ruling will be lawyers, accountants and other financial advisers who are commonly swept into securities-fraud suits even if their roles were tangential to the purported wrongdoing.

While the decision directly involved private suits, the rationale also seems to bar the Securities and Exchange Commission from taking civil enforcement actions against defendants who play secondary roles in alleged fraud schemes. Writing for the majority, Justice Anthony Kennedy said Section 10(b), as written, simply doesn't prohibit aiding securities fraud. He said lower courts have been wrong to read the provision as doing so.

Justice Kennedy failed to clarify the ruling's effect on the SEC, which had filed a friend-of-the-court brief urging the justices to preserve aiding-and-abetting liability under Section 10(b). In a dissenting opinion, Justice John Paul Stevens asserted that the majority's strict reading of Section 10(b) "leaves little doubt" that the SEC would be affected.

But the commission's general counsel, Simon Lorne, argued that the Kennedy opinion "left open the commission's ability to bring" aiding-and-abetting cases under Section 10(b). The SEC lawyer said a reference by Justice Kennedy to "vexatious" investor lawsuits suggests that the court was more concerned with private cases than government actions.

The ruling won't stop the SEC from enforcing other, narrower provisions of the securities laws that explicitly prohibit aiding and abetting such wrongdoing as trading stock based on "inside" information. The decision likewise won't interfere with criminal prosecutions of secondary players in

securities-fraud cases. Nor will it affect the right of investors to bring suits against those they believe were directly involved in wrongdoing.

The case before the justices arose after investors sued participants in a 1988 sale of municipal bonds intended to finance a planned community in Colorado Springs, Colo. The suit, brought after the issuing authority defaulted on the bonds, named, among others, Central Bank of Denver, which had served as trustee for the offering and allegedly helped defraud the investors. The federal appeals court in Denver ruled that bondholders could sue Central Bank.

Reversing the Denver court, the Supreme Court majority rejected an array of arguments by investor advocates and the SEC, including the notion that a broad reading of Section 10(b) is consistent with the general purpose of the New Deal-era securities laws.

In Congress, the SEC's backers were wary of attacking the high court's action for fear they would open the door to attempts to further limit investors' rights to sue. "We are going to consider whether to draft legislation to reverse this decision," said a senior aide to Rep. Edward Markey (D., Mass.), chairman of the House Telecommunications and Finance Subcommittee. But, the aide added, "The prospect of it getting tangled up with efforts to limit private rights of action isn't appealing." [*Central Bank of Denver N.A.* vs. *First Interstate Bank of Denver, N.A.,* 62 *Law Week* 4230 (1994)]

Source: *The Wall Street Journal*, April 20, 1994, p. A2. Reprinted by permission of *The Wall Street Journal*, © 1994 Dow Jones & Company, Inc. All Rights Reserved Worldwide.

RICO

A concern that is often raised in complaints about government prosecutions of securities fraud is the use of the Racketeer Influenced and Corrupt Organizations Act to obtain guilty pleas. Under the 1970 law, which was originally designed to stop organized crime activities, a company that, within a 10-year period, commits two or more offenses such as securities fraud, mail or wire fraud, or illegal drug dealing can be found guilty of a pattern of "racketeering." In addition to normal criminal penalties, the government may be able to seize a significant portion of the business's assets.

Furthermore, the business will be subject to often crippling civil litigation once it is deemed a "racketeer." In order to avoid that stigma, which may well force a financial institution into bankruptcy before its guilt is determined, several companies have chosen to plead guilty to lesser offenses rather than risk a RICO verdict at trial.

The striking reach of RICO was illustrated in a 1994 Supreme Court decision where the justices unanimously ruled that abortion-rights activists may use the law against protesters who endeavor to close abortion clinics.[5] Because RICO permits recoveries that triple the actual damages sustained, the decision could open protestors to crippling claims. However, the Court made it clear that its ruling did not address the substantive question of whether protesters have actually violated RICO in pursuing antiabortion activities.

Professionals such as accountants and attorneys have been sued under RICO when they have rendered services to companies that eventually failed or lost money. A recent Supreme Court decision, however, may restrict such suits in the future.

HIGH COURT GIVES ACCOUNTANTS A SHIELD AGAINST CIVIL RACKETEERING LAWSUITS

Paul M. Barrett

The Supreme Court gave the embattled accounting profession a new shield against civil racketeering lawsuits.

Accountants for financial institutions that go out of business have come under heavy legal fire from investors searching for villains with money left in their pockets. But the high court said outside professionals who don't help run corrupt businesses can't be sued under the Racketeer Influenced and Corrupt Organizations Act, known as RICO.

Accountants were relieved, if not ecstatic. The 7–2 ruling "is a step in the right direction," said Kathryn Oberly, who won the case for the accounting firm Ernst & Young. But, she added, "it doesn't mean that suits against auditors are gone." The decision didn't provide protection against suits alleging that professionals were negligent. Nor did it disallow racketeering lawsuits alleging that professionals were directly involved in fraud.

Although they lost, investor advocates and proponents of aggressive racketeering suits said the high court's ruling could have been much worse. "The big danger," explained Robert Blakey, a Notre Dame Law School professor, "was that [the justices] would say that RICO is a 'kingpin' statute, applying to top management only. They didn't do that."

In fact, Justice Harry Blackmun, who wrote the majority opinion, went out of his way to explain that yesterday's ruling shouldn't be read too broadly . . .

Impact on Settlement Talks

The ruling's most immediate and significant impact probably will come in pretrial settlement talks, where most civil litigation is resolved. The threat of RICO claims has prompted some white-collar defendants to agree to generous settlements because the law allows plaintiffs to collect triple their actual damages. With that threat removed, accountants, lawyers and other professionals will gain important leverage outside the courtroom.

RICO has been the focus of intense attacks from

business interests. They contend that the law, which was designed primarily to go after organized crime, has been misused by plaintiffs' lawyers in civil cases. On the other side, advocates for investors blame outside auditors and lawyers for helping turn savings and loan associations and other financial institutions into precisely the type of crooked enterprises that RICO should punish.

The law has both criminal and civil components, but yesterday's ruling won't affect the prosecution of criminal activities.

The part of RICO at issue in the Ernst & Young case makes it unlawful for anyone "employed by or associated with" an interstate business "to conduct or participate, directly or indirectly, in the conduct" of the business "through a pattern of racketeering activity." Racketeering activity is defined as commission of two or more infractions such as securities and wire fraud.

Trouble with a Farmers' Co-Op

The accounting firm Arthur Young & Co., which has been absorbed by Ernst & Young, got into trouble for its auditing in the early 1980s of a farmers' cooperative in Van Buren, Ark. By selling uninsured notes, the co-op had expanded from a small operation that bought farmers' crops and sold supplies into a multimillion-dollar business. The co-op's manager, Jack White, used some of the proceeds for his personal business ventures. He poured $4 million of the co-op's money into a company that made gasohol, a gasoline-and-alcohol fuel mixture. But when it still lost money, he transferred ownership of the operation to the co-op.

In early 1981, Mr. White was convicted of federal tax fraud based on allegations of self-dealing unrelated to the gasohol project. Before he went to prison later that year, he arranged to have Arthur Young hired as the co-op's auditor. According to the note holders, Arthur Young overvalued the gasohol proj-

ect as part of a scheme to protect Mr. White and keep the co-op as a client.

Arthur Young prepared allegedly misleading audit reports and financial statements. Representatives from the firm also made presentations at co-op meetings, but failed to tell directors or investors how they came up with the valuation of the gasohol plant.

After the co-op filed for bankruptcy-law protection in 1984, farmers and other investors sued Arthur Young, among others, accusing the accountants of helping to conceal the looting of the co-op by Mr. White. A jury in federal court in Fort Smith, Ark., found that Arthur Young had committed securities fraud, but the trial judge excluded a claim for triple damages under RICO.

Middle Course Prevails

The U.S. Court of Appeals for the Eighth Circuit in St. Louis affirmed the verdict and the RICO exclusion. "It is clear that Arthur Young committed a number of reprehensible acts," the appeals court said. But the Eighth Circuit has interpreted RICO to mean that outside professionals aren't covered unless they "participate in the management or operation" of the corrupt business at issue. Ernst & Young's activities didn't meet the test, the appeals court said.

*   *   *   *   *

After picking apart dictionary definitions of individual words in the disputed portion of RICO, Justice Blackmun concluded that to be liable, defendants must participate in the "direction" of the business. He didn't define "direction," but said "the 'operation or management' test expresses this requirement in a formulation that is easy to apply."

[See Reves v. Ernst & Young, 113 S.Ct. 1163 (1993)]

Source: *The Wall Street Journal,* March 4, 1993, p. A3. Reprinted by permission of *The Wall Street Journal,* © 1993 Dow Jones & Company, Inc. All Rights Reserved Worldwide.

INSIDER TRADING

For the stock market to be free market, insider trading should not be there

While criminal behavior is not the norm in the corporate community, neither is it rare. In recent years, stock market manipulators, defense contractors, savings and loan executives, and pharmaceutical firms have been accused (and often convicted) of white-collar crime. The Wall Street insider trading scandals involving Michael Milken (who, technically, did not plead guilty to insider trading), Ivan Boesky, and others have been front page news for several years.

In 1990, Milken, the junk-bond genius and almost certainly the most highly paid executive of all time, entered a guilty plea to six felony counts in the government's 98-count securities fraud indictment. He was sentenced to 10 years in jail, and he agreed to pay $600 million in fines and restitution. Even after those payments, Milken will not be a poor man. He earned $550 million in 1987 alone, and his personal worth might still approach $1 billion.

Milken's employer, Drexel Burnham Lambert, Inc., was seriously harmed by the scandal. In 1989, it paid $650 million in fines to settle the government's securities violations charges, and finally declared bankruptcy in 1990.

While no one has condoned the practices of Boesky, which consisted of paying suitcases full of money for obviously inside information, some people on Wall Street have attacked the government's prosecution of Milken and others on the grounds that the violations to which they admitted guilt were highly technical and did not involve the types of blatant actions that caused Boesky's downfall. Those commentators point to the difficulty in determining who was actually harmed by Milken's actions and the fact that the law contains no explicit definition of insider trading; that is, the government determines after the fact whether someone's actions crossed an unknown line of illegality.

The Law

In subsequent pages, the debate over what types of actions constitute insider trading and what types of people are subject to insider trading statutes will be discussed. Once a person is determined to have inside information, however, the rules on insider trading appear to be very simple—anyone who has access to nonpublic information of a material nature (such as a recent oil strike, results of a major lawsuit, huge earnings increases, an impending takeover bid) must (1) refrain from trading in the stock and telling friends, relatives, and so on to trade in the stock or (2) release the information to the public, wait a reasonable period of time, and then trade as desired. The SEC and the courts have interpreted Rule 10b–5 (forbidding securities fraud) to prohibit insider trading. In recent years, the question of who is an *insider* under Rule 10b–5 and the conditions under which someone can be held liable for dealing in insider information have been in a state of flux. Clearly, corporate officers, directors, and attorneys may have access to inside information; in particular instances, engineers in an oil field also could—but so could brokers, analysts, printers, and journalists.

Short-Swing Profits

One of the earliest SEC concerns was that insiders would use access to financial reports and other data to buy (or sell) shares just prior to releasing positive (negative) information about the company and then almost immediately sell (or buy) back the shares at a profit when the market price of the stock had responded to this new information. In an attempt to limit the ability of major participants in corporate affairs to gain a short-term economic advantage due to their early access to earnings reports and other inside, nonpublic information that might cause a change in stock prices when made public, the 1934 Act prohibits officers, directors, and 10 percent beneficial owners of a corporation from receiving *short-swing profits.* These are any profits made on company stock held for less than six months. Any such profits must be returned to the company, and applicable attorneys' fees may also have to be paid by the person violating the rule. As mentioned previously, the SEC interprets short-swing profits as occurring if any sale price is greater than any purchase price during any six-month period. This interpretation can have some surprising results for someone unaware of how it works, as the following example indicates. A director:

Buys 500 shares at $35 on June 4.
Sells 300 shares at $30 on September 15.
Buys 1,000 shares at $25 on November 20.
Sells 800 shares at $20 on December 19.

Pursuant to this provision, the director has short-swing profits of $1,500 (300 shares × $5) because he sold on September 15 at $30 and bought on November 20 at $25. From the example given, either he was not trading on nonpublic information or the information was erroneous, because the stock fell continually during the period. Adding insult to his trading losses is this extra SEC penalty for violating the short-swing profit rule.

Rule 10b–5

The prohibition against short-swing profits leaves open the possibility that an insider could still profit by buying (selling) shares just prior to the release of positive (negative) information, but not engaging in another transaction for at least six months. While the trade would not trigger the short-swing profits provision, it would still be insider trading under Rule 10b–5, and the insider could be prosecuted. While the short-swing profits restriction spells out exactly who is an insider and what transactions are forbidden, the persons and behavior covered by Rule 10b–5 can be much less clear.

HIGH COURT UPHOLDS
CONVICTION OF WINANS,
TWO CO–CONSPIRATORS

James B. Stewart and Stephen Wermiel

In a decision that is likely to give new impetus to the government's crackdown on insider trading on Wall Street, the Supreme Court upheld the convictions of former *Wall Street Journal* reporter R. Foster Winans and two co-conspirators.

Government lawyers immediately hailed the ruling as vindication of a campaign that has already produced guilty pleas from such leading Wall Street figures as former arbitrager Ivan F. Boesky and former takeover specialist Martin A. Siegel.

* * * * *

Surprising Decision

The Supreme Court's opinion, which surprised many court observers, is as important for what it doesn't do as much as for what it does. In upholding Mr. Winans' conviction for securities, mail, and wire fraud, the Supreme Court didn't reject the so-called misappropriation theory, a doctrine that has been the legal backbone of insider-trading prosecution. And in reinterpreting the law of mail and wire fraud, the Supreme Court handed prosecutors a powerful new weapon, one that could easily eclipse misappropriation as the dominant theory of insider-trading prosecution.

* * * * *

Facts Not in Dispute

From the time criminal charges were first lodged against Mr. Winans in 1984, the facts have never been in serious dispute: Mr. Winans, a former writer of the *Journal's* "Heard on the Street" stock market column, leaked advance information, usually from pay phones, about the timing and the content of those columns to Peter Brant, a former stockbroker at Kidder Peabody & Co.

Mr. Brant used the information to trade in the stocks mentioned in the columns, later enlisting a Kidder Peabody colleague, Kenneth Felis. Both agreed to give Mr. Winans a stake in the profits. All told, the scheme netted $690,000 in profits, of which $31,000 went to Mr. Winans.

Mr. Brant pleaded guilty to two counts of securities fraud and became the government's star witness against Mr. Winans and the two co-conspirators—Mr. Felis and Mr. Winans' former roommate, David Carpenter, a former *Journal* news clerk, who also shared in the profits from the scheme.

* * * * *

Legal Implications

It was the legal theory supporting the criminal charges against Mr. Winans and his co-conspirators that immediately attracted attention. The government alleged that Mr. Winans had misappropriated, or stolen, confidential information entrusted to him about the contents and the timing of columns that potentially could have affected securities prices. This misappropriation constituted fraud, both under the securities laws and under the mail- and wire-fraud statutes, the government argued.

Others have been convicted of insider trading on similar theories, most notably Adrian Antoniu, a former Morgan Stanley & Co. investment banker, whose 1982 case gave rise to the doctrine. But the theory is judge-made law never legislated by Congress, and it has never been explicitly approved by the Supreme Court. In the past, the high court had simply refused to hear the petitions of those convicted. Nor had the doctrine ever been used to indict a newspaper reporter, someone who wasn't directly involved in the securities industry.

*   *   *   *   *

Academic experts were quickly parsing the opinion for future hypothetical cases, but there was widespread agreement that the government's hand has been greatly strengthened for the kinds of cases that have recently dominated the headlines. Noting that the Court didn't overturn the misappropriation theory even when stretched to include a reporter, they say that it is highly unlikely the Court would do so in a case involving stockbrokers, arbitragers, or other Wall Streeters.

OUTSIDER TRADING, THAT NEW CRIME

John C. Coffee, Jr.

Legal principles have a tendency to expand to the limits of their logic—and often beyond. This process may now be at work with respect to the law of insider trading, where a critical case has just been reargued in Manhattan before all the judges of the U.S. Court of Appeals for the Second Circuit.

Earlier this year, a three-judge panel of that court overturned the criminal conviction for insider trading of Robert Chestman. The government asked for, and the Second Circuit granted, a full court reargument, which was heard Friday. A decision is expected next year. At issue is whether "insiders" and "outsiders" should be equally subject to criminal liability and if there is a difference between stealing information and stumbling across it. Eventually, *U.S. v. Chestman* may compel the courts to choose between two competing rationales for the prohibition on insider trading: one, narrow; the other, broad.

The first and narrower theory holds that the corporation has a property right in confidential business information that it develops; thus, when its employees or agents trade on such information, they are essentially stealing (or "misappropriating," in securities-law parlance) this corporate asset. The second theory is based on broader notions of fairness and equity and postulates that all who trade in the securities markets are entitled to a level playing field; from this perspective, it is wrongful for anyone to trade on material, nonpublic information, however acquired.

The critical difference between these theories is that the first reaches only corporate insiders and those in conspiracy with them, while the second theory can cover outsiders as well—i.e., market professionals, securities analysts and others whose profession it is to search for new, undiscovered information about corporate securities. For such outsiders, if the *Chestman* conviction is reinstated, the business of searching for new information will become dangerously entangled with the criminal law.

Chain of Gossip

Factually, the *Chestman* case involves an attenuated chain of family gossip. When Ira Waldbaum, the president of Waldbaum Inc., decided to sell his supermarket chain to A&P, he called his elderly sister, Shirley, and told her to go to her bank and collect her stock certificates. Shirley asked her daughter Joan to drive her to the bank; Joan asked her sister

Susan to substitute for her in carpooling the children that day and vaguely alluded to taking their mother somewhere. Fearing illness, Susan called her mother and learned the reason for her trip. Susan passed this information on to her husband, Keith Loeb, who allegedly called his stockbroker, Robert Chestman, who traded on the information for his discretionary accounts.

Mr. Chestman is thus what the law calls a "remote tippee." But unlike Ivan Boesky he did not bribe or trick anyone. Confidential information was not embezzled from Waldbaum Inc.; rather, the information leaked out the way it often does—by inadvertence, not fraud.

Still, if the level-playing-field rationale governs, Mr. Chestman arguably traded on material, nonpublic information and could be convicted. Which theory does govern? The modern Supreme Court cases have essentially articulated a property-rights rationale and have said that mere possession of material, nonpublic information is insufficient. Rather, a second element must be shown: namely, a fiduciary breach by which the tipper gave the tippee the information in an attempt by the former to realize a direct or indirect pecuniary gain. In layman's terms, the Supreme Court's decisions have viewed insider trading as essentially a theft of information. To prove theft, there must be a wrongful taking of the information. Even the prosecution concedes Mr. Chestman did not steal information from Waldbaum Inc.

But, if so, how was Mr. Chestman indicted and convicted? There are two answers: first, in response to the Supreme Court, the Securities and Exchange Commission adopted a special rule (Rule 14e–3) that applies only to tender offers and that does not require any fiduciary breach or wrongful taking of the information for conviction. It was this level-playing-field rule that the Second Circuit panel essentially invalidated in the *Chestman* case.

Second, Mr. Chestman was also convicted under the standard SEC rule used to prosecute insider trading (Rule 10b–5) on the theory that he breached a duty not to the corporation but to the Waldbaum family. Here, the prosecution's theory was that Mr. Chestman aided Keith Loeb in breaching Mr. Loeb's

duty to maintain the confidences entrusted to Mr. Loeb by his wife's family.

This theory never quite explains why the protection of spousal communications is deemed a purpose of the federal securities laws, but it does illustrate how overcriminalization occurs. Through a semantic twist, the sensible idea that "temporary" insiders—such as investment bankers, lawyers and financial printers—who receive confidential business information for a special corporate purpose cannot misuse that information for their own personal benefit is extended to prohibit anyone from using information received from a friend or other person under circumstances suggesting that the information was given in confidence. Such an extension treats family gossip on a par with business property.

Chestman is only one of several recent decisions that have extended the reach of misappropriation theory so that it applies not only when business information is stolen, but whenever any breach of a "confidential relationship" occurs. Thus, a psychiatrist has been criminally convicted of trading on information disclosed to him during treatment by a patient. Undoubtedly, the psychiatrist's behavior was sleazy and merits professional discipline, but it is less clear that the federal securities laws should serve as the vehicle by which to deter professional misconduct of this sort.

In *Chestman,* the three-judge panel rejected the prosecution's theory that Mr. Chestman had violated a confidential relationship, because no evidence showed that Mr. Chestman knew Mr. Loeb had violated his family's confidence and because it was unclear that Mr. Loeb even owed such a duty to his wife's family when there had been no prior pattern of information-sharing within the family. Valid as this response was, however, the real problem goes deeper. The concept of "confidential relationship" is hopelessly overbroad.

Looking back after the events in question, prosecutors can often claim that some confidential relationship was abused—whether between lovers, family members, longtime friends, or simply that well-known confidential relationship between bartender and drunk. Such a test inherently creates legal uncertainty and invites selective prosecutions. Ultimately, the subjectivity inherent in this test quietly but effectively moves the law of insider trading from a property-rights rationale to a level-playing-field rationale.

Professionals as Criminals

In the wake of recent scandals, some may favor such a broader rationale. What's wrong with it? Essentially, the problem is that such a test fails to distinguish insiders from outsiders. While insiders should be restricted, the securities markets depend for their efficiency on a vigorous competition among securities analysts and other outsiders to ferret out nonpublic information.

Securities professionals constantly receive a flow of market rumors and other soft information and regularly seek to confirm this data with their sources in corporate management. While such outsiders should not be permitted to bribe insiders or steal information, all investors, large and small, benefit from the outsiders' search for new information. A perfectly level playing field thus means a slower, less accurate market.

The role of a securities analyst can be fairly compared to that of an investigative journalist. Society would not tolerate the prosecution of journalists who coaxed, begged, or wheedled information from their political contacts on the vague theory that they thereby violated a confidential relationship. Similarly, securities analysts deserve a comparable freedom to seek information, which freedom an uncertain legal standard denies them. Thus a "bright line" standard is needed so that outsider trading not be lumped together with insider trading. Outsider trading is not yet criminal, but scandals make bad law, and, unfortunately, in the near future it could become so.

Source: *The Wall Street Journal,* November 14, 1990, p. A14. Reprinted by permission of *The Wall Street Journal,* © 1990 Dow Jones & Company, Inc. All Rights Reserved Worldwide.

Afterword

On rehearing, the Court of Appeals affirmed *Chestman*'s Rule 14e–3 (tender offer) convictions and reversed the Rule 10b–5 and mail fraud convictions.[6]

REGULATION CLUB WON'T CURB WALL STREET EXCESSES

Michael Kinsley

I was curled up with a drink and *The Wall Street Journal*'s latest tirade against insider-trading laws last Friday, and was just starting, per instructions, to "ponder whether the securities laws may do more harm than good," when word came that the feds had nailed Ivan Boesky—an event that probably has brought more innocent pleasure to more people than anything the government has done since the Apollo moon landing.

*   *   *   *   *

Some conservative economists maintain that no one is really hurt by insider trading. It's true that you can get dizzy trying to pinpoint the loss. Those who sold shares to Mr. Boesky would have sold to someone else at about the same price (or a lower one!) if he'd stayed out of the market. Are the losers these sellers? Or the unknown people whom Mr. Boesky edged out of buying? And who are the losers when someone refrains from acting on inside information?

Nevertheless, it's absurd to say there's no loss just because the loss is hard to find. Insider trading doesn't change the price of a stock in the long run. (The value of inside information is knowing where the stock is headed anyway.) Nor does it increase the total value of stocks in the market. Therefore, it's a zero-sum game. If Ivan Boesky is $50 million richer as a result of inside information, others are a total of $50 million poorer, even if exactly who lost exactly how much is unknowable. The conventional wisdom about insider trading—that the loss is to the market in general—isn't just a metaphor. It's a mathematical certainty.

For this reason, the *Journal*'s position that restrictions on the use of inside information should be a matter of private contract between employer and employee, or banker and client, makes no sense.

* * * * *

On the other hand, the *Journal* is right that any effort to make the stock market an "honest crap game" by putting outsiders and insiders on exactly the same footing would destroy the market's function as an efficient capitalizer of business information. It's an impossible puzzle. The Securities and Exchange Commission's search for a middle ground has led it down several theoretical blind alleys. My own conclusion is that the "loss of public confidence" feared by financial graybeards is perfectly justified. The market is indeed stacked against the typical *Wall Street Journal* reader. Sorry.

Source: *The Wall Street Journal,* November 20, 1986, p. 27. Reprinted by permission of *The Wall Street Journal,* © 1986 Dow Jones & Company, Inc. All Rights Reserved Worldwide.

Insiders Abroad

While the United States has a long history of vigorously ferreting out insider trading, other countries tend to take a more relaxed view.

EUROPE MOVES TO CURB
INSIDER TRADING

Glenn Whitney

For most shares, April 23 was a lackluster day on the London Stock Exchange. Not for Savage Group PLC. The hardware maker's stock leapt 34% to 67 pence from 50 pence during the morning—without any news being disclosed.

Then, toward the end of the day, Savage announced it had received an inquiry about a possible takeover. Within days, McKechnie PLC said it would pay £47.2 million ($69.5 million), or about 75 pence a share, for Savage.

"It's easy to assume that it was insider trading," says Michael Ost, chief executive officer for McKechnie, which is cooperating with authorities examining the trading case.

But after months of investigation, the source of the presumed leak hasn't yet been determined. Judging by experience, the culprits may never be found.

Spotty Enforcement

And so it goes in Europe. While most European countries in recent years have adopted laws making insider trading illegal, enforcement is spotty at best and nonexistent in some cases.

But investment funds are tired of everyone shrugging at the problem. A common belief that certain investors have access to confidential information and profit from it is a major reason why comparatively few Europeans own stocks, some professionals contend. In contrast to the U.S., where some 35% of adults own shares directly, only 7% in Germany, 14% in France, and 20% in Britain own stock.

"We need to fight insider dealing with teeth and vigor," argues Paul Myners, chairman of Gartmore Investment Management Ltd. in London. "As fund managers, we're placed in a position of great trust, and it reflects very poorly on the industry when there are these blatant violations."

John Hickling, a European fund manager for the giant Boston-based group Fidelity Investments, treads carefully on the Continent, keeping *caveat emptor* in mind at all times. "It's clear outsiders like ourselves don't have access to equal information," Mr. Hickling says. "If there were credible regulatory institutions" institutional investors' confidence in the markets would increase significantly, he adds.

Getting Serious

Some countries hear the complaints, and are acting. There are hopes that Germany, for instance, is finally getting serious on the topic. Chancellor Helmut Kohl's government yesterday approved draft legislation that would make insider dealing a crime. If accepted by Parliament, the new proposals would also create a German equivalent of the Securities and Exchange Commission and broaden the disclosure requirements for major shareholders . . . [F]inal passage isn't expected until mid-1994, nearly two years after the European Community deadline for enacting anti-insider dealing legislation.

Meanwhile, London's International Stock Exchange plans to publish draft guidelines today on how companies should disseminate information.

But while it's relatively easy to create laws and institutions, it's another thing to actually prosecute offenders.

Indeed, ridding Europe of insider dealing will require a radical shift in the mindset of market participants, some contend. "The puritanical morality in the Anglo-Saxon culture says insider trading is wrong. Here, that particular kind of morality doesn't exist," concedes Alberto Rolla, an analyst with Milla & Co. Sim SpA in Milan. "People who make money because they're sly are admired in Italy."

"We've gone from 15 or 20 years ago when you only traded on the basis of insider information to perceiving it as a crime," says Peter Seabrook, a director at Fleming Investment Management Ltd. in London. "Some countries are still about a decade behind."

British and French Convictions

Of the 14 major Western European countries, just Britain and France can claim an insider-trading conviction at all. In the 13 years that insider trading has been an offense, U.K. authorities have brought only 30 cases to trial and won just 17 convictions—a period in which the U.S. SEC has filed well over 350 cases, most of which resulted in punitive action.

In some countries, enforcement responsibility is spread among a number of bodies, so none has enough power to be effective. Generally, it is a criminal and not a civil offense, meaning that the burden of proof is higher.

Mike Feltham, head of the London Stock Exchange's surveillance group, doubts insider trading will be effectively combated until Britain has a centralized enforcement agency. "You need to be able to hit people with a big stick and we don't have that right now," he says.

Moreover, there is nothing remotely close to a unified EC financial markets regulatory body to coordinate cross-border investigations. "The law may be good, but it's a bit of a paper tiger," notes Robert de Haze Winkelman, a spokesman at the Vereniging van Effectenbezitters, a Dutch shareholder rights association. He says insider traders often hide behind partners across borders, particularly in Luxembourg, which has tight banking secrecy.

Source: *The Wall Street Journal,* November 4, 1993, p. A13. Reprinted by permission of *The Wall Street Journal,* © 1993 Dow Jones & Company, Inc. All Rights Reserved Worldwide.

Questions

1. *a.* Do you support rules against insider trading? Explain.
   b. Should they be general or specific prohibitions? Explain.
   c. Why do you think the SEC would want a general rule against insider trading?
   d. What are the consequences if insiders do not have specific examples or guidance about what they can and cannot do?
2. *a.* Are there degrees of insider trading? Explain.
   b. Is some "good" and some "bad"? Explain.
   c. Can the two be distinguished? Explain.
3. Financial printers are paid large sums of money to prepare documents for tender offers, registration statements, and so on. Advance knowledge of the data contained in these documents could be very valuable, and thus great steps are taken to stop any premature leaks. The printing may be divided up among many printers, or the printers may even be kept incommunicado for a period of time. If a printer were to use information in a document for his or her own benefit, would this constitute insider trading? Explain. See *Chiarella* v. *United States,* 445 U.S. 222 (1980).

CHAPTER QUESTIONS

1. Recent crises in the government securities market have provoked calls for increased government regulation. Do you favor that direction? Explain.
2. Define: *(a)* security, *(b)* private placements, *(c)* blue sky laws, *(d)* fraud, *(e)* short-swing profits, *(f)* tender offers, *(g)* buy/sell agreements, *(h)* partnerships, *(i)* Sub S corporation, *(j)* registration, and *(k)* prospectus.
3. Should accountants be expected to discover and reveal fraud perpetrated by their clients? Explain.
4. Why is insider trading unlawful?
5. X, Y, and Z desire to start a business. X is concerned about liability because he is rich. Y wants to have the right to control all decisions made in running the firm. X and Z do not plan to participate in managing the firm but will contribute money to start it. They expect to lose money for at least three years. How should they structure their organization?
6. Explain the ramifications of abolishing the "business judgment" rule.
7. Should tax shelters be eliminated? How?
8. Discuss the advantages and disadvantages of partnerships and corporations.
9. Discuss the exemptions available for certain types of securities.
10. Explain how federal securities laws attempt to make provisions for small businesses.

11. Ivan Landreth and his sons owned all of the stock in a lumber business they operated in Tonasket, Washington. The owners offered the stock for sale. During that time a fire severely damaged the business, but the owners made assurances of rebuilding and modernization. The stock was sold to Dennis and Bolten, and a new organization, Landreth Timber Company, was formed with the senior Landreth remaining as a consultant on the side. The new firm was unsuccessful and was sold at a loss. The Landreth Timber Company then filed suit against Ivan Landreth and his son seeking rescission of the first sale, alleging, among other arguments, that Landreth and sons had widely offered and then sold their stock without registering it as required by the Securities Act of 1933. The district court acknowledged that *stocks* fit within the definition of a *security,* and that the stock in question "possessed all of the characteristics of conventional stock." However, it held that the federal securities laws do not apply to the sale of 100 percent of the stock of a closely held corporation. Here, the district court found that the purchasers had not entered into the sale with the expectation of earnings secured via the labor of others. Managerial control resided with the purchasers. Thus, the sale was a commercial venture rather than a typical investment. The Court of Appeals affirmed, and the case reached the Supreme Court. Decide. See *Landreth Timber Co.* v. *Landreth,* 471 U.S. 681 (1985).

12. For two years, representatives of Basic Incorporated and Combustion Engineering, Inc., had engaged in various meetings and conversations regarding the possibility of a merger. During that time, Basic issued three public statements indicating that no merger talks were in progress. Then, in 1978, the two firms merged. Some Basic shareholders had sold their stock between the first public denial of merger talks and the time when the merger was announced. Those stockholders filed a class action claiming Basic had made false and misleading statements in violation of Section 10(b) of the 1934 Securities Act and SEC Rule 10b–5. The plaintiff stockholders claimed they had suffered injury by selling their stocks at prices artificially depressed by the allegedly false statements. They argued that they would not have sold their stocks had they been truthfully informed of the merger talks. The trial court, in finding for Basic, took the position that preliminary merger discussions are immaterial. But the lower court certified (approved) the stockholders' class action, saying that reliance by the plaintiffs on Basic's statements could be presumed (and thus reliance need not be proved by each plaintiff in turn). In certifying the class action, the lower court embraced the efficient-market theory or the fraud-on-the-market theory. The court of appeals agreed with the lower court's class action certification based on efficient-market reasoning, but the appeals court reversed the immateriality finding regarding preliminary discussions. The case went to the Supreme Court.

    a. Explain the efficient-market theory and its role in this case.

    b. Decide the materiality issue. Explain. See *Basic, Inc.* v. *Max L. Levinson,* 485 U.S. 224 (1988).

13. Christopher Farrell commented in *Business Week* regarding the 1987 stock market crash, which resulted in an immediate 23 percent "devaluation of corporate America":

    > Economists will argue for years over what caused the crash of 1987. But it's already clear that the October 19 cataclysm marks the failure of the most pervasive belief in economics today: an unquestioning faith in the wisdom of free markets.

    Do you agree? Explain. See "Where Was the Invisible Hand?" *Business Week,* April 18, 1988, p. 65.

14. This chapter addresses insider trading and other suspect practices in the securities markets. Commentator George Will thinks those (and similar) problems, as popularized in the movie *Wall Street,* are "draining capitalism of its legitimacy":

    > A moral vulnerability of capitalism today is the belief that too much wealth is allocated capriciously, not only by the randomness of luck but by morally tainted shortcuts around a level playing field for all competitors. The legitimacy of the economic order depends on a consensus that, on balance, rewards are rationally related to the social value of the effort involved.

    Do you agree? Explain. See "Capitalist Flaws Should Worry GOP," *Des Moines Register,* December 30, 1987, p. 6A.

15. What would be the consequences of legalizing insider trading?
16. During a therapy session, assume that a patient tells her psychiatrist information that relates to the future value of a publicly traded company, and that the psychiatrist financially benefits by buying the company's shares.

　　a. Is this insider trading? Explain.
　　b. Is it unethical? Explain.
　　c. What other information would you need to make an informed decision?

NOTES

1. 497 F.2d 473 (5th Cir. 1974).
2. 421 U.S. 837 (1975).
3. 439 U.S. 551 (1979).
4. Ellen E. Schultz, "IRS May Emerge as the Big Winner if Brothel's Public Offering Succeeds," *The Wall Street Journal,* March 5, 1990, p. C6. Reprinted by permission of *The Wall Street Journal,* © 1990 Dow Jones & Company, Inc. All Rights Reserved Worldwide.
5. For a journalistic account, see Paul M. Barrett, "New Legal Weapon in Abortion Fight Is Hard to Use and Hard to Enforce," *The Wall Street Journal,* January 28, 1994, p. B1.
6. *U.S.* v. *Chestman,* 947 F.2d 551 (1991); cert. den., 112 S.Ct. 1759 (1992).

CHAPTER 10

ANTITRUST LAW—MONOPOLIES AND MERGERS

INTRODUCTION

Perhaps more than any other branch of the law, antitrust is a product of political and economic tides. During President Reagan's tenure, a free market mentality prevailed, and reliance on antitrust law declined. While the federal government continued to avidly pursue collusion between competitors and certain other antitrust violations, the prevailing temperament was that the market would function most effectively in the absence of government intervention. That view, so successfully fostered by the so-called Chicago School of free market economics, was dominant through the Reagan years.

Historically, antitrust law sought, broadly expressed, to maintain an approach to life based on free market principles where every American, at least in theory, had the opportunity to reach the top. More specifically, antitrust advocates were concerned about:

1. *The preservation of competition.* Antitrust law was designed to provide free, open markets permitting the virtues of capitalism to be fully expressed. The belief was (and continues to be) that competition would bring the best products and services at the lowest possible prices.

2. *The preservation of democracy.* Many businesses in competition meant that none of them could corner economic, political, or social power.

3. *The preservation of small businesses, or more generally, the preservation of the American Dream.* Antitrust was designed to preserve the opportunity for the "little people" to compete with the giants.

4. At least for a segment of society, antitrust laws were *an expression of political radicalism.* Those laws were meant to be tools for reshaping America to meet the needs of all of the people, rather than those of big business.

Antitrust Resurgent?

Today in the federal courts, conservative Reagan/Bush judges are dominant and antitrust, while important in ensuring a competitive economy, is certainly not being used aggressively as a lever for social change. Nonetheless, recent developments indicate that antitrust may be a more visible force in the mid- and late-1990s:

1. Of course, the election of President Clinton suggests a shift away from the appointment of doctrinaire conservatives to the bench.

2. In December 1992, soon after President Clinton's election, the Justice Department filed a far-reaching price-fixing charge against the major airlines.

3. Soon after the Clinton administration assumed its duties in 1993, the Transportation Department forced Northwest Airlines to abandon plans to start three new routes in order to compete with Reno-Air, a Nevada line that had entered the market only months before. Reno-Air claimed that Northwest pursued the Nevada to California routes simply to crush the new competition. The federal government does not have the authority to prevent a domestic airline from opening a new domestic route, but Transportation Secretary Federico Pena told Northwest that he would urge the Justice Department to file antitrust charges if Northwest went ahead with its plans. Patrick Murphy of the Transportation Department summed up the significance of the Northwest–Reno action:

> It was an important change in policy . . . The academics have complained that we deregulated without enforcing the antitrust laws. They say we allowed the law of the jungle. From now on, we're not going to allow certain kinds of behavior to go unexamined."[1]

4. In 1992, the Supreme Court itself emphatically demonstrated that antitrust was not "dead," as some had thought. In a case involving Eastman Kodak and Image Technical Services (see Chapter 11), a 6–3 majority, as *The Wall Street Journal* noted, engaged in an "apparent downgrading of economic analysis" and, in effect, told the lower courts to be more sparing in allowing antitrust defendants "off the hook" via summary judgments.[2]

A Centrist Role

Do not misunderstand. We will not see the government routinely intervening in the market. Nor do these signals suggest any rejection of the general idea of deregulation. What seems likely is simply a more centrist role for antitrust where, in appropriate cases, the legal system will be employed to deal with market imperfections.

Part One—The Roots of Antitrust Law

The essence of America is personal freedom. The constitutions of the United States and the 50 states are designed to preserve our individual freedom against encroachment by government. As we saw in Chapter 3, Americans likewise fear excessive concentrations of power in private hands. Because the federal constitution and state constitutions afford us little protection from abuse of private power, it has been thought necessary to turn to legislation to curb private concentrations of authority. The primary components of that legislation are the various federal antitrust statutes to which this chapter is addressed.

Anger directed at corporate power came to the fore following the Civil War. Farmers and small-business persons were particularly incensed by high railroad freight charges and high prices for commodities. Interest groups such as "The National Anti-Monopoly Cheap Freight Railway League" called for action to abate the power of the railroads and the so-called trusts in sugar, whiskey, fuel oil, and others.[3] Indeed, by 1914, the upper 2.2 percent of all manufacturing firms employed 35.3 percent of the manufacturing workers and produced 48.7 percent of the manufactured products.[4]

The Standard Oil trust of John D. Rockefeller was the most conspicuous example of big business abuse. At one point, Rockefeller's oil cartel controlled nearly 90 percent of U.S. refining capacity. Secret rebates were negotiated with railroads in order to strengthen Standard Oil's competitive advantage. Then the cartel moved from horizontal cooperation to a vertically integrated system controlling the entire product stream from initial crude oil production, through refining, distribution, and retail sales.[5] Smaller firms were simply crushed, as C. B. Matthews, former president of the Buffalo Lubricating Oil Company, testified:

> [Standard controlled] more than half of the territory of the United States, so that independents could not ship there, they have been able to reap such large profits in those districts that they could sell where there was competition at a point below the cost of manufacturing for the purpose of destroying the competitor.[6]

Farmers, wholesalers, small businesses, and the mass of ordinary workers all felt that a handful of companies and owners at the top of America enjoyed astonishing wealth and power while all the rest were poor, helpless, and increasingly desperate.

Monopoly power was more than an economic issue; it became, in the late 1800s, the dominant domestic political issue of the day.[7] Bigness was perceived as a threat to democracy, as lawyer Louis Brandeis said in congressional testimony:

> You cannot have true American citizenship, you cannot preserve political liberty, you cannot secure American standards of living unless some degree of industrial liberty accompanies it.[8]

The federal government responded in 1887 by passing the Interstate Commerce Commission Act to stop discriminatory rail rates. The Sherman Antitrust Act was approved in 1890. Then both state and federal governments pursued Standard Oil (and other cartels) in the courts until in 1911 the United States won the Supreme Court victory that broke the Standard Oil monopoly and resulted in the oligopoly pattern that we see in the oil business today.[9] That new view that market forces must be tempered by government intervention has, of course, profoundly altered American life.

ANTITRUST STATUTES

A brief look at the various antitrust statutes will serve to place them in historical context. A further examination will accompany the case materials.

Sherman Antitrust Act, 1890

Section 1 of the Sherman Antitrust Act forbids restraints of trade, and Section 2 forbids monopolization, attempts to monopolize, and conspiracies to monopolize. Several enforcement options are available to the federal government:

1. Violation of the Sherman Act opens participants to criminal penalties. The maximum corporate fine is $10 million per violation, while individuals may be fined $350,000 and imprisoned for three years. Sherman Act violations are classified as felonies.
2. Injunctive relief is provided under the civil law. The government or a private party may secure a court order preventing continuing violations of the act and affording appropriate relief (such as dissolution or divestiture).

Perhaps the most important remedy is that available to private parties. An individual or organization harmed by a violation of the act may bring a civil action seeking three times the damages (treble damages) actually sustained. Thus, the victim is compensated, and the wrongdoer is punished.

Clayton Act, 1914

Sherman forbade the continued practice of specified anticompetitive conduct, but it did not forbid conduct that was *likely to lead to* anticompetitive behavior. Furthermore, many felt that judicial interpretations of Sherman had seriously weakened that legislation. Hence, the 1914 approval of the Clayton Act. The Clayton Act forbids price discrimination, exclusive dealing, tying arrangements, requirements contracts, mergers restraining commerce or tending to create a monopoly, and interlocking directorates.

Civil enforcement of the Clayton Act is similar to the Sherman Act in that the government may sue for injunctive relief, and private parties may seek treble damages. Injunctive relief was also extended to private parties under both the Clayton and Sherman Acts. In general, criminal law remedies are not available under the Clayton Act.

Federal Trade Commission Act (FTC)

The Federal Trade Commission Act created a powerful, independent agency designed to devote its full attention to the elimination of anticompetitive practices in American commerce. The FTC proceeds under the Sherman Act, the Clayton Act, and Section

5 of the FTC Act itself, which declares unlawful "unfair methods of competition" and "unfair or deceptive acts or practices in or affecting commerce." The commission's primary enforcement device is the cease and desist order, but fines may be imposed. The agency's action is subject to judicial review under the principles articulated in Chapter 8.

1915 to the Present

The antitrust zeal that produced the Clayton and FTC Acts was muted by World War I and largely extinguished by a strong free enterprise spirit following the war. The Harding, Coolidge, and Hoover administrations of 1920 to 1932 constituted perhaps the zenith of faith in capitalist principles in America. In time, the suffering of the Depression era brought a search for solutions in the form of renewed government intervention. Among President Roosevelt's many legislative programs to achieve economic recovery, the Robinson-Patman Act of 1936 and the Miller-Tydings Act of 1937 were the only antitrust measures. Robinson-Patman amended the Clayton Act in an effort to achieve firmer controls over price discrimination. Miller-Tydings legalized "fair-trade" pricing where state law allowed such pricing. *Fair-trade pricing* is a policy of *resale price maintenance* wherein the seller specifies the price at which its product may be resold. In 1975, the Consumer Goods Pricing Act repealed Miller-Tydings. However, many states still retain fair-trade pricing, and, as will be discussed, resale price maintenance arrangements remain a common merchandising strategy.

Since World War II, antitrust legislative activity has been relatively sparse. Of particular note, however, was the 1950 passage of the Celler-Kefauver Act, which strengthened the Clayton Act, and the 1976 Hart-Scott-Rodino Antitrust Improvement Act, which requires notice to the FTC and the Justice Department in advance of major mergers.

EXEMPTIONS FROM FEDERAL ANTITRUST LAWS

For reasons both practical and political, selected industries have been excused by Congress from the antitrust laws. In some instances, such as the so-called natural monopolies, open competition is economically undesirable. In others, government regulation seems the most sensible method of oversight. And yet others have been exempted for public policy reasons, which occasionally meant that certain industries simply had sufficient political influence to gain exemption.

Labor Unions

Congress has accorded labor unions partial exemption from antitrust law. One result of the exemption is that unions are able to restrict the supply of labor, thus "artificially" raising prices. The labor exemption has provoked complaints. Robert Tollison observes:

For a variety of reasons, the most serious cases of monopoly have traditionally been those monopolies sanctioned by the government . . . It seems clear that without legal sanction, the monopoly power of unions would be quickly eroded by competition in labor markets.[10]

Why have unions been partially shielded from federal antitrust laws? Should unions be fully subject to free market forces? If so, how would all our lives be altered?

State Action

Regulated industries (e.g., insurance, utilities, shipping, banking, and securities) have been, in the main, free of the impact of the antitrust laws. Congress and the courts have recognized the government's direct supervisory authority in such critical areas as entry, exit, and pricing and thus have generally declined to apply the antitrust laws. However, at this writing in 1994, Congress is considering legislation to reduce the antitrust exemptions provided to the insurance industry by the 1945 McCarran-Ferguson Act, which generally entrusted insurance regulation to the states.

State laws and regulations often result in anticompetitive effects. For example, a state monopoly over the sale of liquor is state action that inhibits competition; however it is exempt from the Sherman Act because that state action is believed to further public welfare while providing sufficient oversight to meet antitrust goals.

In 1992, the Supreme Court put some antitrust teeth in the state action area by holding that *active supervision* is necessary before an industry may claim exemption from antitrust laws.[11] In *Ticor,* the Federal Trade Commission charged five leading title insurers with price-fixing. The federal court of appeals held that the states involved, Wisconsin and Montana, had clearly articulated their plans to displace competition with regulation, thus qualifying the insurers for antitrust immunity. However, the Supreme Court ruled that those states had failed to actively supervise the regulatory systems they had put in place, thus precluding a claim of antitrust immunity for the alleged price-fixing scheme.

Professional Sports

Curt Flood, the distinguished outfielder, sued baseball when he resisted a trade and sought to sell his services openly on the market. In that 1972 case, the U.S. Supreme Court affirmed 50 years of precedent by ruling that professional baseball is exempt from the antitrust laws.[12] Of course, the other professional sports are subject to antitrust, and football, in particular, has been the subject of extensive litigation.

Professional Services

Historically, the professional services (e.g., law, medicine, engineering, and accounting) were not threatened by antitrust action, but that immunity has been altered dramatically in recent years. In 1975, the Supreme Court in the *Goldfarb* case held that the Sherman Act applies to at least some anticompetitive conduct by lawyers.[13] Mr. and Mrs. Goldfarb successfully argued that the minimum fee schedule published by the Virginia State Bar constituted a price-fixing scheme in violation of Sherman 1. The Goldfarbs' victory has led to a continuing series of challenges to the professions, making it evident that professional services do constitute commerce and that anticompetitive practices may be challenged. However, as explained in *Goldfarb,* the judiciary clearly believes regulation of the professions is a matter not best administered at the federal level:

> In holding that certain anticompetitive conduct by lawyers is within the reach of the Sherman Act we intend no diminution of the authority of the State to regulate its professions.[14]

FEDERAL ANTITRUST LAW AND OTHER REGULATORY SYSTEMS

State Law

Most states, through legislation and judicial decisions, have developed their own antitrust laws. Sparked perhaps by the Reagan administration's restrained approach to antitrust enforcement, many states have lately asserted their own antitrust authority. And a recent Supreme Court decision involving a California challenge to the proposed merger of two large supermarket chains affirms the capacity of the states to become very important forces in antitrust action.[15] The 9–0 decision upheld the right of states and others to use the federal Clayton Act to require divestiture of assets as a remedy in harmful mergers. The Court's conclusion was particularly striking in that it permits states and private citizens to raise the divestiture threat in challenging mergers even though those mergers have already received approval from the Federal Trade Commission or the U.S. Justice Department. Presumably, the decision will result in greatly increased premerger negotiations with affected states in order to resolve disputes in advance.

Patents, Copyrights, and Trademarks

Each of these devices constitutes a limited, government-granted monopoly. As such, they are in direct conflict with the general thrust of antitrust law. However, each device serves to protect—and thus encourage—commercial creativity and development. The resulting antitrust problem is essentially that of limiting the patent, copyright, or trademark holder to the narrow terms of its privilege.

Law of Other Nations

Part Four of this chapter addresses international antitrust issues. Refer also to the antitrust and trade regulation materials in Chapter 6, International Ethics and Law.

Part Two—Monopoly

Principal legislation: Sherman Act, Section 2.

> Every person who shall monopolize, or attempt to monopolize, or combine or conspire with any other person or persons, to monopolize any part of the trade or commerce among the several States, or with foreign nations, shall be deemed guilty of a felony punishable by a fine.

Throughout chapters 10 and 11, the two antitrust chapters, the principal legislation is identified. But it should be understood that most, if not all, antitrust violations are subject to more than one piece of legislation. In particular, Section 5 of the Federal Trade Commission Act is arguably applicable to all antitrust violations.

From an economic viewpoint, a *monopoly* is a situation in which one firm holds the power to control prices and/or exclude competition in a particular market. By contrast, an *oligopoly* is the situation in which a few firms share monopoly power.

The general test for monopolization is

1. The possession of monopoly power in the relevant market.
2. The willful acquisition or maintenance of that power, as distinguished from growth or development as a consequence of a superior product, business acumen, or historic accident.[16]

Thus, the critical inquiries are the percentage of the market held by the alleged monopolist and the behavior that produced/maintained that market share. The Sherman Act does not, as interpreted, punish efficient companies who legitimately earn and maintain large market shares.

It is important to note that a considerable debate rages in the legal community about whether *conduct* or *structure* (or, indeed, several other possibilities) constitutes the best test of anticompetitive conditions. Should we concern ourselves with a firm's behavior, or should we focus on those industries in which a few firms control a large percentage of the market? Is a concentrated market undesirable in and of itself, or should we challenge market concentration only when it has been acquired and/or maintained via abusive conduct? In this free market era, the conduct view predominates, but the student is advised to consider the implications of each policy.

Purists. Finally, "pure" free market advocates hold a markedly different view of monopoly than that just articulated. Alan Greenspan, noted economist and chairman of the Federal Reserve Board, explains:

> The necessary precondition of a coercive monopoly is closed entry—the barring of all competing producers from a given field. This can be accomplished only by an act of government intervention, in the form of special regulations, subsidies, or franchises. Without government assistance, it is impossible for a would-be monopolist to set and maintain his prices and production policies independent of the rest of the economy. For if he attempted to set his prices and production at a level that would yield profits to new entrants significantly above those available in other fields, competitors would be sure to invade his industry.[17]

To some laissez-faire advocates, the alleged monopolies that, in part, provoked the creation of the Interstate Commerce Commission and the Sherman Act were really the product of government intervention. For example, the railroads, which engendered the farmers' rage over their rate policies in the latter half of the 1800s, were able to secure market dominance in the West only after unusually favorable government treatment, including grants of tens of millions of acres.

MONOPOLIZATION ANALYSIS

While the case law is not a model of clarity, a rather straightforward framework for monopoly analysis has emerged:

1. Define the relevant *product market.*
2. Define the relevant *geographic market.*
3. Compute the defendant's *market power.*
4. Assess the defendant's *intent.*
5. Raise any available *defenses.*

1. Product Market

Here, the court seeks, effectively, to draw a circle that encompasses categories of goods in which the defendant's products or services compete and excludes those not in the same competitive arena. The fundamental test is that of interchangeability, as determined primarily by the price, use, and quality of the product in question.

An analysis of cross elasticity of demand is a key ingredient in defining the product market. Assume that two products, X and Y, appear to be competitors. Assume that the price of X doubled and Y's sales volume was unchanged. What does that tell us about whether X and Y are, in fact, in the same product market?

Defining the product market is really the process we all go through in routine purchasing decisions. Let us assume that you feel a rather undefined hunger for salty snack food. You proceed to the nearby convenience store. Many options confront you, but for simplicity, let's confine them to chips, nuts, and popcorn. Of course, each of those food types is composed of variations. As you sort through the choices—corn chips, cheese curls, Spanish peanuts, rippled potato chips, and so on—you employ the criteria of price, use, and quality in focusing your decision. In so doing, you are defining the product market for "salty junk food." Products closely matched in price, use, and quality are interchangeable, and thus competitors, and thus in the same product market. But, for example, an imported salty cheese at $10 per quarter pound presumably is not in the same product market as salted sunflower seeds.

Expressed as a matter of elasticity, the critical question becomes something like the following: If the price of potato chips, for example, falls by 10 percent, does the sales volume of salted nuts likewise fall? If so, we have a strong indication that potato chips and salted nuts lie in the same product market and thus are competitors.

2. Geographic Market

Once the product market has been defined, we still must determine where the product can be purchased. The judicial decisions to date offer no definitive explanation of the geographic market concept. A working definition might be "any section of the country where the product is sold in commercially significant quantities." From an economic perspective, the geographic market is defined by elasticity. If prices rise or supplies are reduced within the geographic area in question (e.g., New England) and demand remains steady, will products from other areas enter the market in quantity sufficient to affect price and/or supply? If so, the geographic market must be broadened to embrace those new sources of supply. If not, the geographic market is not larger than the area in question (New England). Perhaps a better approach is to read the cases and recognize that each geographic market must simply be identified in terms of its unique economic properties.

3. Market Power

Market Share.   We have no firm guidelines as to what percentage of the market must be controlled to give rise to a monopoly. In the *Alcoa* case, Judge Hand found a monopoly where Alcoa had 90 percent of the virgin ingot aluminum market.[18] In *U.S. v. United Shoe Machinery Corporation*[19] a 75 percent share of the shoe machinery market was a monopoly share, but a 50 percent share in some supply markets was not large enough to constitute a monopoly. The Fifth Circuit Court of Appeals once indicated that "something more than 50 percent of the market is a prerequisite to a finding of monopoly."[20]

Additional Factors.   Market share alone cannot be determinative of monopoly power. The courts are interested in other features of the market, including *barriers to entry,* the strength of the competition, *economies of scale,* trends in the market, and pricing patterns. The point of these inquiries is to determine whether the market in question remains competitive even though one firm has a large market share. Why are the courts interested in barriers to entry?

4. Intent

Assuming the market share is of threatening proportions, the next test element is proof of an intent to monopolize. A monopoly finding requires both a showing of monopoly power and evidence of the willful acquisition or maintenance of that power. A showing of intent does not demand, for example, an internal memo, setting out a plan to acquire monopoly power. Rather, a showing of purposeful or deliberate acts that are predatory or unfair (such as price-fixing) will normally suffice to establish the requisite intent.

5. Defenses

The defendant may yet prevail if the evidence demonstrates that the monopoly was *"thrust upon"* the firm, rather than that the firm affirmatively sought its monopoly posture. The thrust-upon defense had its genesis in Judge Learned Hand's opinion in the aforementioned *Alcoa* case, where that most aptly named jurist suggested the Sherman Act would not be violated if monopoly power were innocently acquired via superior skill, foresight, or industry or by failure of the competition as a consequence of changes in costs or consumer preference. Depending on the circumstances, other defenses (such as possession of a patent, for example) may be persuasive.

ATTEMPTED MONOPOLIZATION

The Sherman Act forbids attempts to monopolize as well as monopoly itself. In the 1993 *Spectrum Sports* decision,[21] the Supreme Court set out its three-part test for attempted monopolization: (1) that the defendant has engaged in predatory or anti-competitive conduct with (2) a specific intent to monopolize and (3) a dangerous probability of achieving monopoly power.[22] The Court made it clear that part 3 of the test requires proof of the relevant market and evidence that the defendant had a "realistic probability" of achieving monopoly power in that market. A showing of unfair or predatory conduct alone will not suffice to establish the dangerous probability.

MONOPOLY CASES

The two cases that follow illustrate the interesting balance in current monopoly law. *Syufy,* the first case, probably reflects the dominant "ideological" view among federal court judges. The decision embodies the free market philosophy of the Reagan/Bush administrations and their judicial appointees, and it suggests an increasing judicial acceptance of the position that what might be considered monopoly market shares may be earned and maintained legitimately—particularly where competition may easily enter the market.

The case is also notable for the fact that Judge Kozinski, in the spirit of the facts, managed to insert the names of nearly 200 movies in his 25-page opinion (only a small portion of which is reprinted here.)

The *Aspen Skiing* case, on the other hand, shows that ample vitality remains in antimonopoly law. Furthermore, with President Clinton and the Democrats in control of judicial appointments at least through the mid-90s, we can expect to see some backing away from the free market zeal of recent years. As noted above, what seems likely to emerge is a centrist view, where monopoly law is enforced but not used as an instrument for social change, and where the virtues of the free market are respected but where market failure is acknowledged and addressed in the courts.

U.S. v. SYUFY ENTERPRISES
903 F.2d 659 (9th Cir. 1990)

Circuit Judge Kozinski

Suspect that giant film distributors like Columbia, Paramount and Twentieth Century–Fox had fallen prey to Raymond Syufy, the canny operator of a chain of Las Vegas, Nevada, movie theaters, the United States Department of Justice brought this civil antitrust action to force Syufy to disgorge the theaters he had purchased in 1982–84 from his former competitors. The case is unusual in a number of respects: The Department of Justice concedes that moviegoers in Las Vegas suffered no direct injury as a result of the allegedly illegal transactions; nor does the record reflect complaints from Syufy's bought-out competitors, as the sales were made at fair prices and not precipitated by any monkey business; and the supposedly oppressed movie companies have weighed in on Syufy's side. The Justice Department nevertheless remains intent on rescuing this platoon of Goliaths from a single David.

After extensive discovery and an eight-and-a-half day trial, the learned district judge entered comprehensive findings of fact and conclusions of law, holding for Syufy. He found, *inter alia,* that Syufy's actions did not injure competition because there are no barriers to entry—others could and did enter the market—and that Syufy therefore did not have the power to control prices or exclude the competition . . .

Facts

Gone are the days when a movie ticket cost a dime, popcorn a nickel, and theaters had a single screen: This is the age of the multiplex. With more than 300 new films released every year—each potentially the next *Batman* or *E.T.*—many successful theaters today run a different film on each of their 6, 12, or 18 screens . . .

Raymond Syufy understood the formula well. In 1981, he entered the Las Vegas market with a splash by opening a six-screen theater. Newly constructed and luxuriously furnished, it put existing facilities to shame. Syufy's entry into the Las Vegas market caused a stir, precipitating a titanic bidding war. Soon, theaters in Las Vegas were paying some of the highest license fees in the nation, while distributors sat back and watched the easy money roll in.

It is the nature of free enterprise that fierce, no-holds-barred competition will drive out the least effective participants in the market, providing the most efficient allocation of productive resources. And so it was in the Las Vegas movie market in 1982. After a hard-fought battle among several contenders, Syufy gained the upper hand. Two of his rivals, Mann Theatres and Plitt Theatres, saw their future as rocky and decided to sell out to Syufy. While Mann and Plitt are major exhibitors nationwide, neither had a large presence in Las Vegas. Mann operated two indoor theaters with a total of three screens; Plitt operated a single theater with three screens. Things were relatively quiet until September 1984; in September, Syufy entered into earnest negotiations with Cragin Industries, his largest remaining competitor. Cragin sold out to Syufy midway through October, leaving Roberts Company, a small exhibitor of mostly second-run films, as Syufy's only competitor for first-run films in Las Vegas.

It is these three transactions—Syufy's purchases of the Mann, Plitt, and Cragin theaters—that the Justice Department claims amount to antitrust violations. As government counsel explained at oral argument, the thrust of its case is that "you may not get monopoly power by buying out your competitors." . . .

Discussion

* * * * *

[O]f significance is the government's concession that Syufy was only a monopsonist, not a monopolist. Thus, the government argues that Syufy had market power, but that it exercised this power only against suppliers (film distributors), not against its consumers (moviegoers). This is consistent with the record, which demonstrates that Syufy always treated moviegoers fairly: The movie tickets, popcorn, nuts, and the Seven-Ups cost about the same in Las Vegas as in other, comparable markets. While it is theoretically possible to have a middleman who is a monopolist upstream but not downstream, this is a somewhat counterintuitive scenario. Why, if he truly had significant market power, would Raymond Syufy have chosen to take advantage of the big movie distributors while giving a fair shake to ordinary people? And why do the distributors, the alleged victims of the monopolization scheme, think that Raymond Syufy is the best thing that ever happened to the Las Vegas movie market?

The answers to these questions are significant because, like all antitrust cases, this one must make economic sense . . . Keeping in mind that competition, not government intervention, is the touchstone of a healthy, vigorous economy, we proceed to examine whether the district court erred in concluding that Syufy does not, in fact, hold monopoly power. There is universal agreement that monopoly power is the power to exclude competition or control prices . . . The district court determined that Syufy possessed neither power. As the government's case stands or falls with these propositions, the parties have devoted much of their analysis to these findings. So do we.

1. Power to Exclude Competition

It is true, of course, that when Syufy acquired Mann's, Plitt's, and Cragin's theaters he temporarily diminished the number of competitors in the Las Vegas first-run film market. But this does not necessarily indicate foul play; many legitimate market arrangements diminish the number of competitors . . . If there are no significant barriers to entry, however, eliminating competitors will not enable the survivors to reap a monopoly profit; any attempt to raise prices above the competitive level will lure into the market new competitors able and willing to offer their commercial goods or personal services for less . . .

* * * * *

The district court . . . found that there were no barriers to entry in the Las Vegas movie market . . . Our review of the record discloses that the district court's finding is amply supported by the record.

* * * * *

Immediately after Syufy bought out the last of his three competitors in October 1984, he was riding high, having captured 100 percent of the first-run film market in Las Vegas. But this utopia proved to be only a mirage. That same month, a major movie distributor, Orion, stopped doing business with Syufy, sending all of its first-run films to Roberts Company, a dark-horse competitor previously relegated to the second-run market. Roberts Company took this as an invitation to step into the major league and, against all odds, began giving Syufy serious competition in the first-run market. Fighting fire with fire, Roberts opened three multiplexes within a 13-month period, each having six or more screens. By December 1986, Roberts was operating 28 screens, trading places with Syufy, who had only 23. At the same time, Roberts was displaying a healthy portion of all first-run films. In fact, Roberts got exclusive exhibition rights to many of its films, meaning that Syufy could not show them at all.

By the end of 1987, Roberts was showing a larger percentage of first-run films than was the Redrock multiplex at the time Syufy bought it. Roberts then sold its theaters to United Artists, the largest theater chain in the country, and Syufy continued losing ground. It all boils down to this: Syufy's acquisitions did not short-circuit the operation of the natural market forces; Las Vegas' first-run film market was more competitive when this case came to trial than before Syufy bought out Mann, Plitt, and Cragin.

The Justice Department correctly points out that Syufy still has a large market share, but attributes far too much importance to this fact. In evaluating monopoly power, it is not market share that counts, but the ability to *maintain* market share . . . Syufy seems unable to do this. In 1985, Syufy managed to lock up exclusive exhibition rights to 91 percent of all the first-run films in Las Vegas. By the first quarter of 1988, that percentage had fallen to 39 percent; United Artists had exclusive rights to another 25 percent, with the remaining 36 percent being played on both Syufy and UA screens.

Syufy's share of box office receipts also dropped off, albeit less precipitously. In 1985, Syufy raked in 93 percent of the gross box office from first-run films in Las Vegas. By the first quarter of 1988, that figure had fallen to 75 percent. The government insists that 75 percent is still a large number, and we are hardpressed to disagree; but that's not the point. The antitrust laws do not require that rivals compete in a dead heat, only that neither is unfairly kept from doing his personal best. Accordingly, the government would do better to plot these points on a graph and observe the pattern they form than to focus narrowly on Syufy's market share at a particular time. The numbers reveal that Roberts/UA has steadily been eating away at Syufy's market share: In two and a half years, Syufy's percentage of exclusive exhibition rights dropped 52 percent and its percentage of box office receipts dropped 18 percent. During the same period, Roberts/UA's newly opened theaters evolved from absolute beginners, barely staying alive, into a big business.

* * * * *

Confronted with this record and the district court's clear findings, the government trots out a shopworn argument we had thought long abandoned: that efficient, aggressive competition is itself a structural barrier to entry. According to the government, competitors will be deterred from entering the market because they could not hope to turn a profit competing against Syufy . . .

The notion that the supplier of a good or service can monopolize the market simply by being efficient reached high tide in the law 44 years ago in Judge Learned Hand's opinion in *United States* v. *Aluminum Co. of Am.,* 148 F.2d 416 (2d Cir. 1945). In the intervening decades the wisdom of this notion has been questioned by just about everyone who has taken a close look at it . . .

* * * * *

The Supreme Court has distanced itself from the *Alcoa* legacy, taking care to distinguish unlawful monopoly power from "growth or development as a consequence of a superior product, business acumen, or historic accident."

* * * * *

2. Power to Control Prices

The crux of the Justice Department's case is that Syufy, top gun in the Las Vegas movie market, had the power to push around Hollywood's biggest players, dictating to them what prices they could charge for their movies. The district court found otherwise. This finding too has substantial support in the record.

Perhaps the most telling evidence of Syufy's inability to set prices came from movie distributors, Syufy's supposed victims. At the trial, distributors uniformly proclaimed their satisfaction with the way the Las Vegas first-run film market operates; none complained about the license fees paid by Syufy . . . Particularly damaging to the government's case was the testimony of the former head of distribution for MGM/UA that his company "never had any difficulty . . . in acquiring the terms that we thought were reasonable," . . . explaining that the license fees Syufy paid "were comparable or better than any place in the United States. And in most cases better." . . .

The documentary evidence bears out this testimony. Syufy has at all times paid license fees far in excess of the national average, even higher than those paid by exhibitors in Los Angeles, the Mecca of Moviedom. In fact, Syufy paid a higher percentage of his gross receipts to distributors in 1987 and 1988 than he did during the intensely competitive period just before he acquired Cragin's Redrock.

While successful, Syufy is in no position to put the squeeze on distributors . . .

* * * * *

It is a tribute to the state of competition in America that the Antitrust Division of the Department of Justice has found no worthier target than this paper tiger on which to expend limited taxpayer resources. Yet we cannot help but wonder whether bringing a lawsuit like this, and pursuing it doggedly through 27 months of pretrial proceedings, about two weeks of trial and now the full distance on appeal, really serves the interests of free competition.

* * * * *

Affirmed.

District Judge Quackenbush concurring

I concur in the result reached in Parts 1 and 2 of the opinion . . .

I do not agree with those portions of Parts 1 and 2 which state that if there are no significant barriers to entry, there can be no monopoly as a matter of law . . .

* * * * *

If the opinion stands for the proposition that a finding of lack of barriers to entry *mandates* a finding of lack of monopoly power, then I disagree with the opinion. While I agree that the issue of monopoly power often depends heavily upon market share and barriers to entry, the analysis should also include consideration of the extent of the alleged monopolist's market share, the ability to maintain that share, the power to control prices, and capability of excluding competitors, and the intent of the alleged monopolist, along with the existence of barriers to entry.

Questions

1. At one point, Syufy held 100 percent of the first-run market. Why was Syufy not a monopolist?
2. Is this decision rooted more in structural (market share) or conduct (e.g., predatory pricing) considerations? Explain.
3. What role did the issue of Syufy's intent to monopolize play in this case? Explain.
4. Assume we have historical data showing that when the price of rolled steel has increased, the sales volume of rolled aluminum has remained constant. What, if anything, does that fact tell us about the product market for rolled steel?
5. Define the product market for championship boxing matches. See *United States v. International Boxing Club of New York, Inc.,* 358 U.S. 242 (1959).

ASPEN SKIING COMPANY v. ASPEN HIGHLANDS SKIING CORPORATION
105 S.Ct. 2847 (1985)

Justice Stevens

In a private treble damages action, the jury found that petitioner Aspen Skiing Company (Ski Co.) had monopolized the market for downhill skiing services in Aspen, Colorado. The question presented is whether that finding is erroneous as a matter of law because it rests on an assumption that a firm with monopoly power has a duty to cooperate with its smaller rivals in a marketing arrangement in order to avoid violating § 2 of the Sherman Act.

I

Aspen is a destination ski resort with a reputation for "super powder," "a wide range of runs," and an "active night life," including "some of the best restaurants in North America." Between 1945 and 1960, private investors independently developed three major facilities for downhill skiing: Aspen Mountain (Ajax) [owned by Ski Co.], Aspen Highlands (Highlands), and Buttermilk. A fourth mountain, Snowmass [owned by Ski Co.], opened in 1967.

The development of any major additional facilities is hindered by practical considerations and regulatory obstacles. The identification of appropriate topographical conditions for a new site and substantial financing are both essential. Most of the terrain in the vicinity of Aspen that is suitable for downhill skiing cannot be used for that purpose without the approval of the United States Forest Service. That approval is contingent, in part, on environmental concerns. Moreover, the county government must also approve the project, and in recent years it has followed a policy of limiting growth.

Between 1958 and 1964, three independent companies operated Ajax, Highlands, and Buttermilk. In the early years, each company offered its own day or half-day tickets for use of its mountain. In 1962, however, the three competitors also introduced an interchangeable ticket. The six-day, all-Aspen ticket provided convenience to the vast majority of skiers who visited the resort for weekly periods, but preferred to remain flexible about what mountain they might ski each day during the visit. It also emphasized the unusual variety in ski mountains available in Aspen.

As initially designed, the all-Aspen ticket program consisted of booklets containing six coupons, each redeemable for a daily lift ticket at Ajax, Highlands, or Buttermilk. The price of the booklet was often discounted from the price of six daily tickets, but all six coupons had to be used within a limited period of time—seven days, for example. The revenues from the sale of the three-area coupon books were distributed in accordance with the number of coupons collected at each mountain.

In 1964, Buttermilk was purchased by Ski Co., but the interchangeable ticket program continued . . . [Thus, by 1967 when Snowmass opened, Ski Co. owned three areas: Ajax, Buttermilk and Snowmass with Aspen Highlands remaining a separate company.]

In the 1971–1972 season, the coupon booklets were discontinued and an "around the neck" all-Aspen ticket was developed. This refinement on the interchangeable ticket was advantageous to the skier, who no longer found it necessary to visit the ticket window every morning before gaining access to the slopes. Lift operators at Highlands monitored usage of the ticket in the 1971–1972 season by recording the ticket numbers of persons going onto the slopes of that mountain. Highlands officials periodically met with Ski Co. officials to review the figures recorded at Highlands, and to distribute revenues based on that count.

There was some concern that usage of the all-Aspen ticket should be monitored by a more scientific method than the one used in the 1971–1972 season. After a one-season absence, the four-area ticket returned in the 1973–1974 season with a new method of allocating revenues based on usage. Like the 1971–1972 ticket, the 1973–1974 four-area ticket consisted of a badge worn around the skier's neck. Lift operators punched the ticket when the skier first sought access to the mountain each day. A random-sample survey was commissioned to determine how many skiers with the four-area ticket used each mountain, and the parties allocated revenues from the ticket sales in accordance with the survey's results.

* * * * *

In the 1970s the management of Ski Co. increasingly expressed their dislike for the all-Aspen ticket. They complained that a coupon method of monitoring usage was administratively cumbersome. They doubted the accuracy of the survey and decried the "appearance, deportment, [and] attitude" of the college students who were conducting it. In addition, Ski Co.'s president had expressed the view that the four-area ticket was siphoning off revenues that could be recaptured by Ski Co. if the ticket was discontinued. In fact, Ski Co. had reinstated its three-area, six-day ticket during the 1977–1978 season, but that ticket had been outsold by the four-area, six-day ticket nearly two to one.

In March 1978, the Ski Co. management recommended to the board of directors that the four-area ticket be discontinued for the 1978–1979 season. The board decided to offer Highlands a four-area ticket provided that Highlands would agree to receive a 12.5% fixed percentage of the revenue—considerably below Highland's historical average based on usage. Later in the 1978–1979 season, a member of Ski Co.'s board of directors candidly informed a Highland's official that he had advocated making Highlands "an offer that [it] could not accept."

Finding the proposal unacceptable, Highlands suggested a distribution of the revenues based on usage to be monitored by coupons, electronic counting, or random sample surveys. If Ski Co. was concerned about who was to conduct the survey, Highlands proposed to hire disinterested ticket counters at its own expense—"somebody like Price Waterhouse"—to count or survey usage of the four-area ticket at Highlands. Ski Co. refused to consider any counterproposals, and Highlands finally rejected the offer of the fixed percentage.

As far as Ski Co. was concerned, the all-Aspen ticket was dead. In its place Ski Co. offered the three-area, six-day ticket featuring only its mountains. In an effort to promote this ticket, Ski Co. embarked on a national advertising campaign that strongly implied to people who were unfamiliar with Aspen that Ajax, Buttermilk, and Snowmass were the only ski mountains in the area. For example, Ski Co. had a sign changed in the Aspen Airways waiting room at Stapleton Airport in Denver. The old sign had a picture of the four mountains in Aspen touting "Four Big Mountains" whereas the new sign retained the picture but referred only to three.

Ski Co. took additional actions that made it extremely difficult for Highlands to market its own multi-area package to replace the joint offering. Ski Co. discontinued the three-day, three-area pass for the 1978–1979 season, and also refused to sell Highlands any lift tickets, either at the tour operator's discount or at retail. Highlands finally developed an alternative product, the "Adventure Pack," which consisted of a three-day pass at Highlands and three vouchers, each equal to the price of a daily lift ticket at a Ski Co. mountain. The vouchers were guaranteed by funds on deposit in an Aspen bank, and were redeemed by Aspen merchants at full value. Ski Co., however, refused to accept them.

Later, Highlands redesigned the Adventure Pack to contain American Express Traveler's Checks or money orders instead of vouchers. Ski Co. eventually accepted these negotiable instruments in exchange for daily lift tickets. Despite some strengths of the product, the Adventure Pack met considerable resistance from tour operators and consumers who had grown accustomed to the convenience and flexibility provided by the all-Aspen ticket.

Without a convenient all-Aspen ticket, Highlands basically "becomes a day ski area in a destination resort." Highlands' share of the market for downhill skiing services in Aspen declined steadily after the four-area ticket based on usage was abolished in 1977: from 20.5 percent in 1976–1977, to 15.7 percent in 1977–1978, to 13.1 percent in 1978–1979, to 12.5 percent in 1979–1980, to 11 percent in 1980–1981. Highlands' revenues from associated skiing services like the ski school, ski rentals, amateur racing events, and restaurant facilities declined sharply as well.

II

In 1979, Highlands filed a complaint in the United States District Court for the District of Colorado naming Ski Co. as a defendant. Among various claims, the complaint alleged that

Ski Co. had monopolized the market for downhill skiing services at Aspen in violation of §2 of the Sherman act, and prayed for treble damages. The case was tried to a jury which rendered a verdict finding Ski Co. guilty of the §2 violation and calculating Highlands' actual damages at $2.5 million.

In her instructions to the jury, the District Judge explained that the offense of monopolization under §2 of the Sherman Act has two elements: (1) the possession of monopoly power in a relevant market, and (2) the willful acquisition, maintenance, or use of that power by anticompetitive or exclusionary means or for anticompetitive or exclusionary purposes. Although the first element was vigorously disputed at the trial and in the Court of Appeals in this Court Ski Co. does not challenge the jury's special verdict finding that it possessed monopoly power. Nor does Ski Co. criticize the trial court's instructions to the jury concerning the second element of the §2 offense.

On this element, the jury was instructed that it had to consider whether "Aspen Skiing Corporation willfully acquired, maintained, or used that power by anticompetitive or exclusionary means or for anticompetitive or exclusionary purposes."

* * * * *

III

* * * * *

Ski Co. is surely correct in submitting that even a firm with monopoly power has no general duty to engage in a joint marketing program with a competitor. Ski Co. is quite wrong, however, in suggesting that the judgment in this case rests on any such proposition of law. For the trial court unambiguously instructed the jury that a firm possessing monopoly power has no duty to cooperate with its business rivals.

The absence of an unqualified duty to cooperate does not mean that every time a firm declines to participate in a particular cooperative venture, that decision may not have evidentiary significance, or that it may not give rise to liability in certain circumstances . . . The high value that we have placed on the right to refuse to deal with other firms does not mean that the right is unqualified.

* * * * *

IV

The question whether Ski Co.'s conduct may properly be characterized as exclusionary cannot be answered by simply considering its effect on Highlands. In addition, it is relevant to consider its impact on consumers and whether it has impaired competition in an unnecessarily restrictive way. If a firm has been "attempting to exclude rivals on some basis other than efficiency," it is fair to characterize its behavior as predatory. It is, accordingly, appropriate to examine the effect of the challenged pattern of conduct on consumers, on Ski Co.'s smaller rival, and on Ski Co. itself.

Superior Quality of the All-Aspen Ticket

The average Aspen visitor "is a well-educated, relatively affluent, experienced skier who has skied a number of times in the past . . ." Over 80 percent of the skiers visiting the resort each year have been there before—40 percent of these repeat visitors have skied Aspen at least five times. Over the years, they developed a strong demand for the six-day, all-Aspen ticket in its various refinements. Most experienced skiers quite logically prefer to purchase their tickets at once for the whole period that they will spend at the resort; they can then spend more time on the slopes and enjoying apres-ski amenities and less time standing in ticket lines. The four-area attribute of the ticket allowed the skier to purchase his six-day ticket in advance while reserving the right to decide in his own time and for his own reasons which mountain he would ski on each day. It provided convenience and flexibility, and expanded the vistas and the number of challenging runs available to him during the week's vacation.

While the three-area, six-day ticket offered by Ski Co. possessed some of these attributes, the evidence supports a conclusion that consumers were adversely affected by the elimination of the four-area ticket. In the first place, the actual record of competition between a three-area ticket and the all-Aspen ticket in the years after 1967 indicated that skiers demonstrably preferred four mountains to three . . .

Highlands' Ability to Compete

The adverse impact of Ski Co.'s pattern of conduct on Highlands is not disputed in this Court. Expert testimony described the extent of its pecuniary injury. The evidence concerning its attempt to develop a substitute product either by buying Ski Co.'s daily tickets in bulk, or by marketing its own Adventure Pack, demonstrates that it tried to protect itself from the loss of its share of the patrons of the all-Aspen ticket . . .

Ski Co.'s Business Justification

Perhaps most significant, however, is the evidence relating to Ski Co. itself, for Ski Co. did not persuade the jury that its conduct was justified by any normal business purpose. Ski Co. was apparently willing to forgo daily ticket sales both to skiers who sought to exchange the coupons contained in Highlands' Adventure Pack, and to those who would have purchased Ski Co. daily lift tickets from Highlands if Highlands had been permitted to purchase them in bulk. The jury may well have concluded that Ski Co. elected to forgo these short-run benefits because it was more interested in reducing competition in the Aspen market over the long run by harming its smaller competitor.

That conclusion is strongly supported by Ski Co.'s failure to offer any efficiency justification whatever for its pattern of conduct. In defending the decision to terminate the jointly offered ticket, Ski Co. claimed that usage could not be properly monitored. The evidence, however, established that Ski Co. itself monitored the use of the three-area passes based on a count taken by lift operators, and distributed the revenues among its mountains on that basis. Ski Co. contended that coupons were administratively cumbersome, and that the survey takers had been disruptive and their work inaccurate. Coupons, however, were no more burdensome than the credit cards accepted at Ski Co. ticket windows. Moreover, in other markets Ski Co. itself participated in interchangeable lift tickets using coupons. As for the survey, its own manager testified that the problems were much overemphasized by Ski Co. officials, and were mostly resolved as they arose. Ski Co.'s explanation for the rejection of Highlands' offer to hire—at its own expense—a reputable national accounting firm to audit usage of the four-area tickets at Highlands' mountain, was that there was no way to "control" the audit.

In the end, Ski Co. was pressed to justify its pattern of conduct on a desire to disassociate itself from—what it considered—the inferior skiing services offered at Highlands. The all-Aspen ticket based on usage, however, allowed consumers to make their own choice on these matters of quality. Ski Co.'s purported concern for the relative quality of Highlands' product was supported in the record by little more than vague insinuations, and was sharply contested by numerous witnesses. Moreover, Ski Co. admitted that it was willing to associate with what it considered to be inferior products in other markets.

. . . [T]he record in this case comfortably supports an inference that the monopolist made a deliberate effort to discourage its customers from doing business with its smaller rival. The sale of its three-area, six-day ticket, particularly when it was discounted below the daily ticket price, deterred the ticket holders from skiing at Highlands. The refusal to accept the Adventure Pack coupons in exchange for daily tickets was apparently motivated entirely by a decision to avoid providing any benefit to Highlands even though accepting the coupons would have entailed no cost to Ski Co. itself, would have provided it with immediate benefits, and would have satisfied its potential customers. Thus the evidence supports an inference that Ski Co. was not motivated by efficiency concerns and that it was willing to sacrifice short-run benefits and consumer goodwill in exchange for a perceived long-run impact on its smaller rival . . .

Affirmed.

Questions

1. Summarize the fundamental lessons of *Aspen*.
2. Write a brief dissenting opinion for the *Aspen* case.
3. As the *Aspen* Court says, "Aspen Skiing Company (Ski Co.) had monopolized the market for downhill skiing services in Aspen, Colorado." That being the case, why doesn't the government challenge Aspen Skiing Company's market dominance?
4. Kodak dominated the American market for provision of amateur photographic films, cameras, and film-processing services. Berkey was a much smaller, but still significant, competitor in that market. In some markets Kodak served as Berkey's supplier. In the "amateur conventional still camera" market (consisting primarily of 110 and 126 instant-loading cameras), Kodak's share of the sales volume between 1954 and 1973 ranged from 64 to 90 percent. Kodak invented both the "126" and "110" cameras. The introduction of the 110 "Pocket Instamatic" and the companion Kodacolor II film in 1972 resulted in a dramatic Kodak camera sales increase of from 6.2 million units in 1971 to 8.2 million in 1972. Rivals were unable to bring competitive units into the market until nearly one year later. Even then, Kodak retained a strong lead. Thereafter, Berkey filed suit claiming that the introduction of the 110 system was an illegal monopolization of the camera market. The essence of the Berkey argument was as follows:

> Kodak, a film and camera monopolist, was in a position to set industry standards. Rivals could not compete effectively without offering products similar to Kodak's. Moreover, Kodak persistently refused to make film available for most formats other than those in which it made cameras. Since cameras are worthless without film, the policy effectively prevented other manufacturers from introducing cameras in new formats. Because of its dominant position astride two markets, and by use of its film

monopoly to distort the camera market, Kodak forfeited its own right to reap profits from such innovations without providing its rivals with sufficient advance information to enable them to enter the market with copies of the new product on the day of Kodak's introduction.

On appeal, the Court noted "little doubt that . . . Kodak had monopoly power in cameras," and the Court observed that Kodak had sometimes "predisclosed" its innovations to its rivals, and sometimes it had not done so.

a. Was Kodak under a legal duty to predisclose innovations to rivals?

b. What defense would you offer to counter Berkey's monopolization claim?

c. Decide the case, and explain the reasons for your decision. See *Berkey Photo, Inc.* v. *Eastman Kodak Company,* 603 F. 2d 263 (2 Cir. 1979). Cert. denied, 444 U.S. 1093 (1980).

Questions—Parts One and Two

1. A federal district court found IBM guilty of unlawful monopolization in a portion of the computer industry. IBM manufactured and distributed both central processing units (CPUs) and various peripheral devices (PDs), including magnetic tape drives and printers. Telex manufactured PDs compatible with IBM's CPUs, but not with the CPUs of other manufacturers. It was established at trial that relatively inexpensive interfaces could be used to make Telex PDs compatible with the CPUs of manufacturers other than IBM, and at a relatively modest cost Telex could produce PDs compatible with CPUs other than those of IBM. The district court concluded that the relevant product market was PDs compatible with IBM CPUs and that IBM controlled at least 80 percent of that market. Given IBM's monopoly power, the district court also found IBM guilty of predatory behavior. For example, in response to competition from Telex and others, IBM lowered its leasing fees for PDs and offered more desirable leasing terms. Similarly, IBM reduced the sales prices of its PDs. In setting those prices, IBM considered the ability or inability of its competitors to respond to those prices. At the reduced prices, IBM achieved a 20 percent profit margin and increased its market share.

   Was the district court correct? Explain. See *Telex Corporation* v. *IBM Corporation* (10th Cir. 1975) 510 F.2d 894, cert. denied, 423 U.S. 802 (1975).

2. *a.* A traditional concern about monopolies is that a lack of competition discourages efficiency and innovation. Argue that monopolies may actually *encourage* innovation.

   b. Even if monopolies do not discourage invention, we have firm economic grounds for opposing monopolies. Explain.

4. Historically, perhaps the most important interpretation of the Sherman Act's proscription of monopolization was Judge Learned Hand's opinion in the *Alcoa* case. After finding that Alcoa controlled 90 percent of the aluminum ingot market,

Hand had to determine whether Alcoa possessed a general intent to monopolize. Hand concluded that Alcoa's market dominance could have resulted only from a "persistent determination" to maintain control [148 F.2d 416, 431 (1945)].

> It was not inevitable that it should always anticipate increases in the demand for ingots and be prepared to supply them. Nothing compelled it to keep doubling and redoubling its capacity before others entered the field. It insists that it never excluded competitors; but we can think of no more effective exclusion than progressively to embrace each new opportunity as it opened, and to face every newcomer with new capacity already geared into a great organization.

Comment on Judge Hand's remarks.

5. Is a monopolist who makes only a "fair" profit in violation of the law? Explain.

6. May a monopolist lawfully increase its market share, assuming it does so without recourse to predatory or exclusionary tactics? Explain. Should it be able to do so? Explain.

7. The U.S. government sued Du Pont, claiming a monopolization of the cellophane market. Du Pont produced almost 75 percent of the cellophane sold in the United States. Cellophane constituted less than 20 percent of the "flexible packaging materials" market. The lower court found "[g]reat sensitivity of customers in the flexible packaging markets to price or quality changes."

   a. What is the relevant product market?

   b. Who wins the case? Explain. See *United States* v. *E.I. du Pont de Nemours & Co.,* 351 U.S. 377 (1956).

8. The National Football League was organized in 1920. During the 1960 season, it had 14 teams located in 13 cities—Chicago (two teams), Cleveland, New York, Philadelphia, Pittsburgh, Washington, Baltimore, Detroit, Los Angeles, San Francisco, Green Bay, Dallas, and Minneapolis. The rival American Football League commenced play in 1960 with eight teams in eight cities—Boston, Buffalo, Houston, New York, Dallas, Denver, Los Angeles, and Oakland.

   In its first season, the AFL was successful in competing for outstanding players and in acquiring a desirable television contract. "[R]epresentatives of the American League declared that the League's success was unprecedented." Nevertheless, the AFL sued the NFL, claiming monopolization. A central issue in the case was that of the geographic market. The AFL characterized the market as those 17 cities either having an NFL franchise or seriously considered for a franchise. The NFL saw the market as nationwide.

   Define the geographic market in this case. Explain. See *American Football League* v. *National Football League,* 323 F.2d 124 (4th Cir. 1963).

9. Consider the accompanying table, which depicts airline market shares at the Pittsburgh Airport. Do these figures suggest that USAir is a monopolist in that market? Explain.

Taking Control (Passenger Market Share at Greater Pittsburgh International Airport)

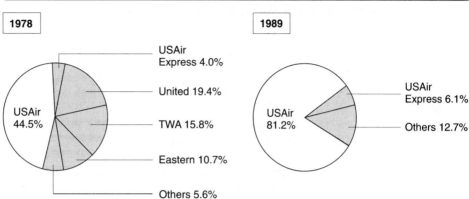

Source: Allegheny, PA, County Department of Aviation. Published in Asra Q. Nomani and Paul M. Barrett, "Control of Major Airports by Carriers Is Focus of Justice Department Inquiry," *The Wall Street Journal,* June 18, 1990, p. A3. Reprinted by permission of *The Wall Street Journal.* © 1990 Dow Jones & Company, Inc. All Rights Reserved Worldwide.

10. Several smaller airlines sued the two giants, United and American, claiming that the two violated the Sherman Act through their computerized reservation systems (CRSs). The heart of the plaintiffs' position was that United and American were monopolists who violated the law by denying other airlines reasonable access to their CRSs. American and United had the largest CRSs, but other airlines also maintained CRSs. Neither had blocked any other airline's access to its CRS, but they had charged fees (in American's case, $1.75 per booking to the airline who secured a passenger through American's CRS). United and American each controlled about 12 to 14 percent of the total air transportation market. According to the court, the plaintiffs were "unhappy" about United and American's ability to extract booking fees from them for the use of the CRSs. The U.S. Ninth Circuit Court of Appeals ruled for the defendants and the Supreme Court declined to review this case.

    a. Explain why the plaintiffs felt wronged by American and United.

    b. Explain the defendants' argument that they could not successfully charge "excessive" prices for the use of the CRSs. See *Alaska Airlines* v. *United Airlines,* 948 F.2d 536 (1991), cert. den., 112 S.Ct. 1603 (1992).

11. A principal fear about monopoly is that of *predatory pricing,* where large firms price their goods below cost in order to drive their competition out of the market, then raise those prices to monopoly levels.

    a. As a matter of economics, explain why predatory pricing of that nature is quite unlikely.

    b. On the other hand, as a matter of economics, explain how predatory pricing might be successful where a monopolist operates in several markets and sells below cost in one or two of them.

Part Three—Mergers

GILLETTE AND PARKER PEN MERGER

Preface

INTERNATIONAL

This preface details the regulatory and judicial story of the 1993 purchase of Parker Pen, a British corporation, by Gillette Co., headquartered in Boston. Characteristic of today's global mergers, the Gillette–Parker Pen deal required government regulatory approval in four foreign countries as well as two federal court decisions in the United States. Of course, the impact of these immense mergers ripples throughout the global economy. Often, thousands of jobs and billions of dollars are at stake. Vital economic efficiencies may be achieved, or delicate competitive balances may be destroyed. As you read this account, take note of the arguments for and against this merger, and reflect on the extraordinary complexity of global corporate management. Note, too, that the center of this case, as with many mergers, is that of market definition. Did the market consist of $50 to $400 refillable fountain pens, as the U.S. government contended, or was it a much larger slice of writing instruments generally, as Gillette argued?

Chronology

September 10, 1992: The Deal Is Announced.   Gillette, with a stationery division but best known for its razors, announced that it was paying $561 million to acquire the British firm Parker Pen. Gillette's Paper Mate line is very strong in the inexpensive market, while its Waterman brand is a leader among premium pens. Parker Pen is particularly strong in the mid-priced market. The purchase would make Gillette the global leader in the $5 billion writing instrument market.

Parker, a 98-year-old company, is headquartered in Newhaven, England, while its U.S. headquarters and manufacturing unit are in Jamesville, Wisconsin. Parker, with 2,500 employees, holds about 7 percent of the worldwide pen market. For the 1991–92 fiscal year, Parker earned operating profits of $70.7 million on revenues of $356 million.

Gillette's stationery division produces Liquid Paper correction fluids in addition to Paper Mate and Waterman. The stationery division's 1991 operating profits were $49 million on revenues of $460 million, a figure representing just under one-tenth of the total Gillette revenues of $4.7 billion.[23]

October 22, 1992: Britain to Review Merger.   British law allows an investigation of a merger that "creates or intensifies" a monopoly. Basically, a monopoly is defined as 25 percent of the U.K. market or a takeover exceeding £30 million ($51 million).[24] The British procedure:

Michael Heseltine, Secretary for Trade and Industry, announced that [the merger was to be investigated.] He followed the advice of the Director General of Fair Trading, Sir Bryan Carsberg, to refer the proposed acquisition, by the Gillette Company, to the Monopolies and Mergers Commission. The investigation has been ordered under the Fair Trading Act of 1973.[25]

January 6, 1993: France Approves Merger.   Although the merger would give the new company a dominant position, 42.5 percent of the French market for refillable pens, the government gave its approval. Gillette had acquired the French brand Waterman pens in 1987. The French government approved the Gillette–Parker merger in the belief that Waterman's international competitiveness would be improved through "Parker's technological achievements and marketing network."[26] The approval was conditioned on the understanding that Gillette would maintain the Waterman pens in the French market and would report to the government in three years to detail its steps to fulfill that commitment.[27]

February 10, 1993: UK Approval.   The British Monopolies and Mergers Commission cleared the merger on the general grounds that Gillette would be prevented from exploiting its market power by the strength of the larger retailers who would be Gillette's primary market and by those retailers' ability to turn to other existing or potential suppliers:

> Although more expensive pens have better quality nibs, finishes and mechanisms, there is no great technical difference between pens and production processes are comparatively simple. There have been a number of recent entrants and some multiple retailers who have successfully introduced own-brand pens.[28]

Gillette, of course, welcomed the approval, saying it would allow the sharing of technology and other resources that would ensure global competitiveness for its pens.

March 19, 1993: U.S. Justice Department Issues Challenge.   The Justice Department announced its intention to challenge the merger in court on the grounds that it would significantly increase concentration in an already concentrated market and lead to higher prices in the U.S. market for premium fountain pens, thus violating the Clayton Act. The total premium fountain pen market in the United States in 1991 was about $46 million. Gillette (through its Waterman brand) had 21 percent of that market, while Parker held about 19 percent. Richemont, maker of Montblanc pens, was the leader with just under 40 percent. The Justice Department argued that fountain pens of lesser quality or brand image were not likely to be able to apply the market pressure that would prevent Gillette and Parker from raising prices after the merger.[29]

March 24, 1993: Judge Approves Merger.   Federal District Court Judge Stanley Sporkin rejected the Justice Department's request for an order barring the purchase. Gillette had argued that competition in the United States would not be harmed, since 80 percent of Parker's sales and 90 percent of Waterman's were outside the United States.

Judge Sporkin was not moved by the government's claim that the merger would permit price increases in the premium pen market:

> "You're dealing in an area where rich people are concerned," Sporkin said. "I don't think poor people buy these pens. You think these lawyers on Wall Street are going to complain if they have to pay so much for these pens? It's a status thing for them. I buy an 87-cent pen and it does the same thing," Sporkin said, pulling one from the shirt pocket inside his robe and, with a smile on his face, waving it in the courtroom.[30]

May 5, 1993: Gillette Can Acquire Parker Pen.   Following Judge Sporkin's decision, the case proceeded to the federal District Court for the District of Columbia. District Court Judge Royce Lamberth denied the government's request for a preliminary injunction to block the merger. Judge Lamberth rejected the government's market definition—refillable fountain pens with a suggested retail price of between $50 and $400—as too narrow. The judge saw those pens as a submarket within a much larger market of all premium writing instruments, including mechanical pencils and refillable ballpoint, rollerball, and fountain pens priced from $40 to $400. The government failed to show harm in that larger market, and failed even to show that the larger market was highly concentrated. Indeed, the judge referred to the larger market as "awash" with manufacturers. As to the narrower submarket defined by the government, the judge did find it highly concentrated, but his judgment was that no competitive harm would result. Gillette and the other defendants were able to satisfy the judge that unilateral price increases by Gillette–Parker would be blocked due to competition from other writing instruments and the lack of technological barriers to entry in the fountain pen market. Further, innovation would not be stifled by the merger, and the court found no evidence of the likelihood of collusion between Gillette and Richemont (Montblanc).[31]

Questions

1. Explain the reasoning by which France, Great Britain, and the United States permitted the Gillette–Parker merger.
2. Do you agree with Judge Lamberth's definition of the product market? Explain.
3. What did the British Monopolies and Mergers Commission mean by its judgment that the strength of the larger retailers would prevent Gillette from exploiting its market power?
4. What was the point of Judge Sporkin saying, in effect, that only rich people seeking another status symbol would be hurt by the merger?

INTRODUCTION TO MERGERS

Principal legislation: Sherman Act, Section 1, and Clayton Act, Section 7:

That no person engaged in commerce or in any activity affecting commerce, shall acquire, directly or indirectly, the whole or any part of the stock or other share capital and no person subject to the jurisdiction of the Federal Trade Commission shall acquire the whole or any part of the assets of another person engaged also in commerce or in any activity affecting commerce, where in any line of commerce or in any activity affecting commerce in any section of the country, the effect of such acquisition may be substantially to lessen competition, or to tend to create a monopoly.

No person shall acquire, directly or indirectly, the whole or any part of the stock or other share capital and no person subject to the jurisdiction of the Federal Trade Commission shall acquire the whole or any part of the assets of one or more persons engaged in commerce or in any activity affecting commerce, where in any line of commerce or in any activity affecting commerce in any section of the country, the effect of such acquisition, of such stocks or assets, or of the use of such stock by the voting or granting of proxies or otherwise, may be substantially to lessen competition, or to tend to create a monopoly.

Technically, a merger involves the union of two or more enterprises wherein the property of all is transferred to the one remaining firm. However, antitrust law embraces all those situations wherein previously independent business entities are united—whether by acquisition of stock, purchase of physical assets, creation of holding companies, consolidation, or merger.

Mergers fall, somewhat awkwardly, into three categories:

1. *Horizontal mergers* are those where the firms are in direct competition and occupy the same product and geographic markets. A merger of two vodka producers in the same geographic market would clearly fall in the horizontal category. Would the merger of a vodka producer and a gin producer constitute a horizontal merger?
2. *Vertical mergers* are those involving two or more firms at different levels of the same channel of distribution, such as a furniture manufacturer and a fabric supplier.
3. *Conglomerate mergers* involve firms dealing in unrelated products. Thus, the conglomerate category embraces all mergers that are neither horizontal nor vertical. An example of such a merger would be the acquisition of a pet food manufacturer by a book publisher.

Identification of the type of merger being dealt with is essential because, as will be seen, the analysis differs for each.

ENFORCEMENT

Because a challenged merger would allegedly involve either an unlawful monopoly or another restraint of trade, the Sherman Act can be used as the necessary legislative vehicle. However, remember that Sherman requires a showing of the *existence* of anticompetitive conditions, while Clayton requires only a showing of a *reasonable probability* of lessening competition or a *tendency* toward monopoly. However, because Clayton has no criminal provision, the government must rely on Sherman in those cases where a criminal suit is warranted.

Clayton 7 is enforced by the government via the Justice Department and the FTC, as well as by companies and individuals. Those challenging mergers often seek injunctions either to stop the merger or to secure relief after the consummation of a merger.

PREMERGER/MERGER GUIDELINES

Mergers involving firms of significant size (as defined by government rules) must be reported to the FTC and the Justice Department. That premerger notification gives the government time to decide whether to challenge the merger before it takes place and before the companies have undertaken the expense of combining their enterprises. To provide warnings about likely challenges, the FTC and the Justice Department jointly issued 1992 horizontal merger guidelines. Justice Department policy in recent years has not regarded most vertical and conglomerate mergers as threatening to competition—hence the focus on horizontal mergers.

Market Power

The guidelines are designed to identify mergers that may result in "market power," which is defined as the ability of a seller "profitably to maintain prices above competitive levels for a significant period of time." The guidelines set out a five-step methodology for analyzing horizontal mergers:

1. Market definition.
2. Measurement of market concentration.
3. Identification of potential adverse effects.
4. Appraisal of ease of entry into the market.
5. Appraisal of possible defenses.[32]

1. Market.   The market will be defined as the smallest product and geographic market in which a hypothetical monopolist could raise prices a "small but significant and nontransitory" amount (usually set at 5 percent) above current prices.[33]

2. Market Concentration.   The formidable-sounding Herfindahl–Hirschman Index (HHI) is employed to measure market concentration. Notwithstanding the forbidding title, the index is computed quite easily. The market share of each firm in a market is squared and the results are summed. Thus, if five companies each had 20 percent of a market, the index for that market would be 2,000. The HHI is useful because it measures both concentration and dispersion of market share between big and small firms. If 10 firms each have 10 percent of the market, the resulting HHI is 1,000. The larger the HHI, the more concentrated the market. The new guidelines establish "safe harbors" for mergers which are considered unlikely to produce anti-competitive effects. Hence, a post-merger HHI of 1,000 or less ordinarily would not be challenged.

On the other hand, a post-merger concentration of more than 1,800 accompanied by a change in the HHI above 50 (from the pre-merger HHI) is *presumed* to be threatening. The presumption can be overcome by a showing that market harm is unlikely. That showing would be established by reference to the other factors in the Guidelines; that is, adverse effects, ease of entry, efficiencies, and so on. In the middle ground involving post-merger HHI figures of 1000 to 1800 accompanied by changes in the HHI above 100, the Guidelines find the *potential* for competitive concerns depending on the analysis of the other factors in the Guidelines. To illustrate, consider again a market composed of five companies, each with 20 percent of the market. If two of them merge, the HHI would rise from 2,000 to 2,800, and the merger would be presumed threatening pending consideration of the other factors in the Guidelines. Thus the government's new guidelines reject the older notion of market size *alone* as a threat to the welfare of the economy.

3. Adverse Effects. While the guidelines provide highly complex instructions about conditions likely to raise adverse competitive effects, the basic point is that the government is worried that the merger may permit cartel-like behavior in the merged firm's market.

4. Ease of Entry. The idea here is that the newly merged firm cannot arbitrarily raise prices or otherwise abuse the market if entry by competitors is "timely, likely and sufficient," since those new competitors will force the existing firms to charge competitive prices and otherwise conform to the discipline of the market.

5. Defenses. An otherwise unacceptable merger may be saved by certain defenses. Most prominent among these are *efficiencies* and the *failing company doctrine.* Efficiencies would include such desirable economic results as economies of scale or reduced transportation costs as a result of the merger. The failing company doctrine permits a merger in order to preserve the assets of a firm that would otherwise be lost to the market.

Merger Data

Merger activity develops in waves. The early 1990s were a quiet period. In 1992, total U.S. mergers were valued at just $94.9 billion, but in 1993 that total leaped to $176.4 billion, although the total number of transactions (2,664) represented only a 4 percent increase from 1992.[34]

At this writing in 1994, we have just now witnessed one of the most highly publicized and bitter merger struggles in history. Viacom, which owns MTV, Showtime, and other media resources, won Paramount with its movie studio, sports teams, and so on, in a $10 billion bidding war with QVC, the home-shopping network. This titanic, five-month struggle achieved even greater media pizazz when Viacom merged with Blockbuster Entertainment Corporation (video rentals and other entertainment ventures) in part as a means of strengthening its resources in bidding for Paramount. However, that deal now appears to be unraveling due to the falling value of Viacom shares in the wake of the very expensive battle for Paramount.

MERGER PROBLEMS

Naturally, some acquisitions prove to have been sensible; some do not. Scholar Michael Porter's examination of the merger record of 33 major American firms from 1950 to 1986 showed that more than half of their acquisitions failed and were sold off.[35] The result, the critics say, is poor economic performance, wasted stockholder funds, and lumbering corporate giants often unsuited to the competitive demands of the day. More broadly, merger excesses are accused of exacerbating the problems of bigness that were outlined in Chapter 3. Political and economic power will reside in fewer hands. Barriers to entry may increase. Absentee owners, ignorant of local needs, will alter community lifestyles. Lives will be disrupted by plant closings, changes in management, and relocations.

As we noted in Chapter 3, the recent performance of the corporate dinosaurs such as General Motors, Sears, and IBM suggest that simply being bigger is no longer (if it ever was) a guarantee of success.

MERGER VIRTUES

Nevertheless, many mergers are clearly beneficial. Some of the potential virtues of mergers include the following:

1. Mergers permit the replacement of inefficient management. Similarly, the threat of replacement disciplines managers to achieve greater efficiency.
2. Mergers may permit stronger competition with formerly larger rivals.
3. Mergers may improve credit access.
4. Mergers may produce efficiencies and economies of scale.
5. Mergers frequently offer a pool of liquid assets for use in expansion.
6. Very often, mergers offer tax advantages to at least one of the participants.
7. Growth by merger is often less expensive than internal growth.
8. Mergers help to satisfy the personal ambitions and needs of management.

A recent *Business Week* study of the mergers, acquisitions, and takeovers of the 1980s found "evidence of many more failures than successes." But the *Business Week* study reported a division of opinion among academics:

> [S]cholars such as Northwestern University's Alfred Rappaport argue that the U.S. companies are leaner than they were at the start of the decade. The threat of a takeover has forced many managers to work their companies into fighting trim. Moreover, shareholders saw enormous gains through acquisitions, leveraged buyouts, and recapitalizations. Leverage, says Rappaport, "was a fantastically good tool to make management become more shareholder-value oriented."
>
> But even Rappaport admits that merger mania was "a two-edged sword." As companies took on more leverage to feed increasing shareholder expectations, the U.S. economy was put at risk . . . In the end, it seems, neither side can make a convincing case.[36]

A 1992 study by Professor Frank Lichtenberg offers strong support for the value of acquisitions in toughening the economy. He concluded that the 1980s corporate restructuring led to increased productivity and firmer international competitiveness for U.S. firms. (His study covered all acquisitions including mergers.) He also concluded that white-collar workers suffered job loss and reduced wages (except for research and development personnel), but that blue-collar workers were not similarly harmed.[37]

MERGERS AND ACQUISITIONS IN PRACTICE

Mergers and acquisitions have become a central tool in American corporate strategy. Mammoth deals have reshaped the business landscape. Between 1981 and 1984, five of America's largest oil firms (Gulf, Getty, Conoco, Marathon, and Cities Service) were gobbled up by mergers. In 1989, the Bristol Meyers–Squibb merger totaled $12.5 billion. The 1992 alliance of BankAmerica and Security Pacific, with assets totaling $192 billion, was the largest bank merger in history.

For America's managers, these deals have profound professional and personal consequences. They are part of a thorough restructuring of the American economy (a corporate housecleaning of sorts) that hit high gear in the 1980s and continues today. How are we to compete in a fierce world market if we fail to become "lean and mean?" Probably, we cannot. At the same time, the human consequences are staggering. Job losses are a particularly poignant product of America's industrial consolidation:

> Between 1980 and 1990, more than 10 million Americans were laid off due to buyouts, mergers and company restructuring.[38]

Not all of those job losses are the product of mergers, but many are. For example, Chemical Bank shed 5,700 white-collar jobs in the two years following its 1991 merger with Manufacturers Hanover.[39] For the first time in history, the total number of unemployed white-collar workers (more than three million in 1993) exceeded jobless blue-collar workers.[40] Furthermore, new white-collar jobs often do not carry the fulsome benefits of the past. One study found that the portion of new jobs offering pensions and health benefits has declined as much as 35 percent since the 1970s.[41]

Mergers and acquisitions have become a strategic tool in this overall restructuring process, and the consequences, while personally very painful, may be necessary to the reinvigoration of a somewhat flabby American economy.

Before examining the merger case law, a cautionary note from conservative antitrust scholar and former Supreme Court nominee Robert Bork is appropriate:

> The Supreme Court has not decided a major merger case in the past 15 years. Antitrust concern with conglomerate mergers seems to have disappeared without a trace. Although the government has a few guidelines about the circumstances in which it will move against vertical mergers, the guidelines are quite mild, and there seem to be few, if any, challenges to such mergers. Horizontal mergers remain a subject of the law, as they should, but the enforcement agencies challenge mergers only in much larger size ranges than they once did. Though the agencies have not relaxed their policies to the degree I believe is desirable, the law is no longer doing major damage.[42]

Of course, Bork has a strong free market preference, but the facts are as he expresses them. During the Reagan and Bush years, merger challenges were uncommon. As suggested by the Gillette–Parker Pen case, the federal government remains quite concerned about horizontal mergers, in particular, and active oversight in that area, at least, should be expected. Furthermore, many states have become aggressive in pursuing antitrust claims in light of the federal government's relatively passive approach. However, the preponderantly conservative federal judiciary is unlikely to be sympathetic to antitrust activism in the absence of compelling evidence of economic harm arising from a proposed merger.

HORIZONTAL AND VERTICAL MERGERS—ANALYSIS

Horizontal

The government's concern with *horizontal mergers* rests on the presumed decline in competition and increase in market concentration that accompanies the acquisition by one firm of another firm in the same market. The resulting firm raises concerns similar to those in a monopoly situation, and, indeed, the market analysis to be applied to horizontal mergers is very similar to that previously discussed in the monopoly section. Essentially, we must define the product and geographic markets and then apply the Clayton Act, Section 7 test—that is, some unspecified probability of substantially lessening competition or tending to create a monopoly.

Vertical

A *vertical merger* involves an alliance between a supplier and a purchaser. The primary threat thus arising is that of market foreclosure. As illustrated in the accompanying diagram, a vertical merger may deny a source of supply to a purchaser or an outlet for sale to a seller, which might then threaten competition so as to violate the Clayton Act.

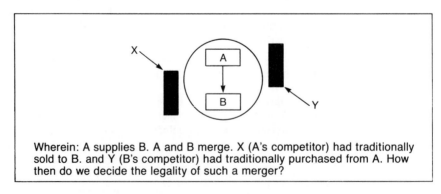

Wherein: A supplies B. A and B merge. X (A's competitor) had traditionally sold to B. and Y (B's competitor) had traditionally purchased from A. How then do we decide the legality of such a merger?

Some other economic considerations may influence the legality of a vertical merger.

1. *Deep pockets.* The merger may provide the merged firm with financial advantages that smaller rivals could not match.
2. *Price squeeze.* In the diagram, the newly merged AB may be able to arbitrarily raise prices of raw materials to Y while temporarily depressing the price of its finished goods. The result may, of course, severely pinch Y.
3. *Barriers to entry.* A market composed of integrated—and thus often larger—firms would pose a more formidable hurdle in terms of capital requirements and courage than one of many small suppliers and purchasers.

The following *Brown Shoe* case illustrates the Court's early efforts to interpret Congress's intent in passing the amended Clayton Act. Note that *Brown* embraces both horizontal and vertical dimensions. Note also that the federal government, in recent years, has shown little concern regarding vertical mergers.

BROWN SHOE CO. v. UNITED STATES
370 U.S. 294 (1961)

Chief Justice Warren

This suit was initiated in November 1955 when the Government filed a civil action alleging that a contemplated merger between the G. R. Kinney Company, Inc. (Kinney), and the Brown Shoe Company, Inc. (Brown), through an exchange of Kinney for Brown stock, would violate Sec. 7 of the Clayton Act . . .

* * * * *

In the district court, the Government contended that the effect of the merger of Brown— the third largest seller of shoes by dollar volume in the United States, a leading manufacturer of men's, women's, and children's shoes, and a retailer with over 1,230 owned, operated or controlled retail outlets—and Kinney—the eighth largest company, by dollar volume, among those primarily engaged in selling shoes, itself a large manufacturer of shoes, and a retailer with over 350 retail outlets—"may be substantially to lessen competition or to tend to create a monopoly."

* * * * *

The Industry

The district court found that although domestic shoe production was scattered among a large number of manufacturers, a small number of large companies occupied a commanding position. Thus, while the 24 largest manufacturers produced about 35 percent of the Nation's shoes, the top 4—International, Endicott-Johnson, Brown (including Kinney), and General Shoe—alone produced approximately 23 percent of the Nation's shoes or 65 percent of the production of the top 24.

In 1955, domestic production of nonrubber shoes was 509.2 million pairs, of which about 103.6 million pairs were men's shoes, about 271 million pairs were women's shoes, and about 134.6 million pairs were children's shoes. The district court found that men's, women's, and children's shoes are normally produced in separate factories.

The public buys these shoes through about 70,000 retail outlets, only 22,000 of which, however, derive 50 percent or more of their gross receipts from the sale of shoes and are classified as "shoe stores" by the Census Bureau. These 22,000 shoe stores were found generally to sell (1) men's shoes only, (2) women's shoes only, (3) women's and children's shoes, or (4) men's, women's, and children's shoes.

The district court found a "definite trend" among shoe manufacturers to acquire retail outlets. For example, International Shoe Company had no retail outlets in 1945, but by 1956 had acquired 130; General Shoe Company had only 80 retail outlets in 1945 but had 526 by 1956 . . . Brown, itself, with no retail outlets of its own prior to 1951, had acquired 845 such outlets by 1956. Moreover, between 1950 and 1956 nine independent shoe store chains, operating 1,114 retail shoe stores, were found to have become subsidiaries of these large firms and to have ceased their independent operations.

And once the manufacturers acquired retail outlets, the district court found there was a "definite trend" for the parent-manufacturers to supply an ever-increasing percentage of the retail outlets' needs, thereby foreclosing other manufacturers from effectively competing for the retail accounts. Manufacturer-dominated stores were found to be "drying up" the available outlets for independent producers.

Another "definite trend" found to exist in the shoe industry was a decrease in the number of plants manufacturing shoes. And there appears to have been a concomitant decrease in the number of firms manufacturing shoes. In 1947, there were 1,077 independent manufacturers of shoes, but by 1954 their number had decreased about 10 percent to 970.

Brown Shoe

Brown Shoe was found not only to have been a participant, but also a moving factor, in these industry trends. Although Brown had experimented several times with operating its own retail outlets, by 1945 it had disposed of them all. However, in 1951, Brown again began to seek retail outlets by acquiring the Nation's largest operator of leased shoe departments, Wohl Shoe Company (Wohl), which operated 250 shoe departments in department stores throughout the United States. Between 1952 and 1955 Brown made a number of smaller acquisitions . . .

The acquisition of these corporations was found to lead to increased sales by Brown to the acquired companies . . .

During the same period of time, Brown also acquired the stock or assets of seven companies engaged solely in shoe manufacturing. As a result, in 1955, Brown was the fourth largest shoe manufacturer in the country, producing about 25.6 million pairs of shoes or about 4 percent of the Nation's total footwear production.

Kinney

Kinney is principally engaged in operating the largest family-style shoe store chain in the United States. At the time of trial, Kinney was found to be operating over 400 such stores in more than 270 cities. These stores were found to make about 1.2 percent of all national retail shoe sales by dollar volume . . .

In addition to this extensive retail activity, Kinney owned and operated four plants which manufactured men's, women's, and children's shoes and whose combined output was 0.5 percent of the national shoe production in 1955, making Kinney the 12th largest shoe manufacturer in the United States.

Kinney stores were found to obtain about 20 percent of their shoes from Kinney's own manufacturing plants. At the time of the merger, Kinney bought no shoes from Brown; however, in line with Brown's conceded reasons for acquiring Kinney, Brown had, by 1957, become the largest outside supplier of Kinney's shoes, supplying 7.9 percent of all Kinney's needs.

It is in this setting that the merger was considered and held to violate § 7 of the Clayton Act. The district court ordered Brown to divest itself completely of all stock, share capital, assets or other interests it held in Kinney . . .

Legislative History

The dominant theme pervading congressional consideration of the 1950 amendments [to the Clayton Act, Section 7] was a fear of what was considered to be a rising tide of economic concentration in the American economy . . .

Other considerations cited in support of the bill were the desirability of retaining "local control" over industry and the protection of small businesses. Throughout the recorded discussion may be found examples of Congress' fear not only of accelerated concentration of economic power on economic grounds, but also of the threat to other values a trend toward concentration was thought to pose.

The Vertical Aspects of the Merger

. . . The primary vice of a vertical merger or other arrangement tying a customer to a supplier is that, by foreclosing the competitors of either party from a segment of the market otherwise open to them, the arrangement may act as a "clog on competition." . . .

The Product Market

The outer boundaries of a product market are determined by the reasonable interchangeability of use or the cross-elasticity of demand between the product itself and substitutes for it. However, within this broad market, well-defined submarkets may exist which, in themselves, constitute product markets for antitrust purposes . . . The boundaries of such a submarket may be determined by examining such practical indicia as industry or public recognition of the submarket as a separate economic entity, the product's peculiar characteristics and uses, unique production facilities, distinct customers, distinct prices, sensitivity to price changes, and specialized vendors . . .

Applying these considerations to the present case, we conclude that the record supports the district court's finding that the relevant lines of commerce are men's, women's, and children's shoes. These product lines are recognized by the public; each line is manufactured in separate plants; each has characteristics peculiar to itself rendering it generally noncompetitive with the others; and each is, of course, directed toward a distinct class of customers. . . .

The Geographic Market

We agree with the parties and the district court that insofar as the vertical aspect of this merger is concerned, the relevant geographic market is the entire nation. The relationships of product value, bulk, weight and consumer demand enable manufacturers to distribute their shoes on a nationwide basis, as Brown and Kinney, in fact, do . . .

The Probable Effect of the Merger

Once the area of effective competition affected by a vertical arrangement has been defined, an analysis must be made to determine if the effect of the arrangement "may be substantially to lessen competition, or to tend to create a monopoly" in this market.

Since the diminution of the vigor of competition which may stem from a vertical arrangement results primarily from a foreclosure of a share of the market otherwise open to competitors, an important consideration in determining whether the effect of a vertical arrangement "may be substantially to lessen competition, or to tend to create a monopoly" is the size of the share of the market foreclosed. However, this factor will seldom be determinative.

* * * * *

[I]t is apparent both from past behavior of Brown and from the testimony of Brown's President, that Brown would use its ownership of Kinney to force Brown shoes into Kinney stores . . .

Another important factor to consider is the trend toward concentration in the industry . . .

The existence of a trend toward vertical integration, which the district court found, is well substantiated by the record. Moreover, the court found a tendency of the acquiring manufacturers to become increasingly important sources of supply for their acquired outlets. The necessary corollary of these trends is the foreclosure of independent manufacturers from markets otherwise open to them . . .

Brown argues, however, that the shoe industry is at present composed of a large number of manufacturers and retailers, and that the industry is dynamically competitive. But remaining vigor cannot immunize a merger if the trend in that industry is toward oligopoly. It is the probable effect of the merger upon the future as well as the present which the Clayton Act commands the courts and the commission to examine.

Moreover, as we have remarked above, not only must we consider the probable effects of the merger upon the economics of the particular markets affected but also we must consider its probable effects upon the economic way of life sought to be preserved by Congress. Congress was desirous of preventing the formation of further oligopolies with their attendant adverse effects upon local control of industry and upon small business. Where an industry was composed of numerous independent units, Congress appeared anxious to preserve this structure . . .

The Horizontal Aspects of the Merger

. . . The acquisition of Kinney by Brown resulted in a horizontal combination at both the manufacturing and retailing levels of their businesses. Although the district court found that the merger of Brown's and Kinney's *manufacturing* facilities was economically too insignificant to come within the prohibitions of the Clayton Act, the government has not appealed from this portion of the lower court's decision. Therefore, we have no occasion to express our views with respect to that finding. On the other hand, appellant does contest the district court's finding that the merger of the companies' *retail* outlets may tend substantially to lessen competition.

The Product Market

. . . In . . . this opinion we hold that the district court correctly defined men's, women's, and children's shoes as the relevant lines of commerce in which to analyze the vertical aspects of the merger. For the reasons there stated we also hold that the same lines of commerce are appropriate for considering the horizontal aspects of the merger.

The Geographic Market

The criteria to be used in determining the appropriate geographic market are essentially similar to those used to determine the relevant product market. Moreover, just as a product submarket may have § 7 significance as the proper "line of commerce," so may a geographic submarket be considered the appropriate "section of the country." Congress prescribed a pragmatic, factual approach to the definition of the relevant market and not a formal, legalistic one. The geographic market selected must, therefore, both "correspond to the commercial realities" of the industry and be economically significant. Thus, although the geographic market in some instances may encompass the entire nation, under other circumstances it may be as small as a single metropolitan area.

* * * * *

We agree that the district court properly defined the relevant geographic markets in which to analyze this merger as those cities with a population exceeding 10,000 and their environs in which both Brown and Kinney retailed shoes through their own outlets. Such markets are large enough to include the downtown shops and suburban shopping centers in areas contiguous to the city, which are the important competitive factors, and yet are small enough to exclude stores beyond the immediate environs of the city, which are of little competitive significance.

The Probable Effect of the Merger

. . . The market share which companies may control by merging is one of the most important factors to be considered when determining the probable effects of the combination on effective competition in the relevant market. In an industry as fragmented as shoe retailing, the control of substantial shares of the trade in a city may have important effects on competition. If a merger achieving 5 percent control were now approved, we might be required to approve future merger efforts by Brown's competitors seeking similar market shares.

* * * * *

At the same time appellant has presented no mitigating factors, such as the business failure or the inadequate resources of one of the parties that may have prevented it from maintaining its competitive position, nor a demonstrated need for combination to enable small companies to enter into a more meaningful competition with those dominating the relevant markets . . .

The judgment is affirmed.

Questions

1. As to the vertical element of *Brown Shoe,* what potential harm did the Court identify?
2. In *Brown Shoe,* why did the Supreme Court settle on different geographic markets for the horizontal and vertical elements of the merger?
3. In *Brown Shoe,* the Court followed the mandate of Congress that tendencies toward concentration are to be curbed in their incipiency. Why must the Court bow to the will of Congress in this matter?
4. How did the Supreme Court justify its prohibition of the merger in light of the rather small market shares involved (e.g., Brown produced 4 percent of the nation's shoes, while Kinney sold about 1.2 percent of the nation's total)?
5. In 1958, Pabst Brewing Company acquired Blatz Brewing Company. Pabst was America's 10th-largest brewer, while Blatz was the 18th largest. After the merger, Pabst had 4.49 percent of the nationwide beer market and was the fifth-largest brewer. In the regional market of Wisconsin, Michigan, and Illinois, the merger gave Pabst 11.32 percent of the sales. After the merger, Pabst led beer sales in Wisconsin with 23.95 percent of that state-wide market. The beer market was becoming increasingly concentrated, with the total number of brewers declining from 206 to 162 during the years 1957 to 1961. In *United States* v. *Pabst Brewing Co.,* 384 U.S. 546 (1966), the Supreme Court found the merger violated the Clayton Act, Section 7. The Court did not choose among the three geographic market configurations, saying that the crucial inquiry is whether a merger may substantially lessen competition *anywhere* in the United States. Thus, the Court held that, under these facts, a 4.49 percent share of the market was too large.

   Respected scholar and jurist Richard Posner labeled the *Pabst* decision an "atrocity" and the product of a "fit of nonsense" on the part of the Supreme Court.[43] What economic arguments would support Posner's colorful complaint?
6. In the period 1917–19, Du Pont acquired 23 percent of the stock in the then-fledgling General Motors Corporation. By 1947, Du Pont supplied 68 percent of GM's automotive finish needs and 38 percent of its fabric needs. In 1955, General Motors ranked first in sales and second in assets among all U.S. industrial corporations, while accounting for approximately two-fifths of the nation's annual automobile sales. In 1949, the Justice Department challenged Du Pont's 1917–19 acquisitions of GM stock.

   a. Why did the government challenge Du Pont's acquisition?
   b. May an acquisition be properly challenged 30 years after the fact, as in *Du Pont?*
   c. Given your general understanding of finishes and fabrics, how would you defend Du Pont?
   d. Decide. Explain. See *United States* v. *E. I. du Pont de Nemours & Co.,* 353 U.S. 586 (1957).

7. In 1961, Ford Motor Company acquired the trade name and other assets of the Electric Autolite Company, a producer and distributor of spark plugs and other automotive parts. At the time of the acquisition, three firms controlled 95 percent of the spark plug market: Champion (50 percent), General Motors-AC (30 percent), and Autolite (15 percent). Spark plug producers traditionally sold them to automakers at a price below cost. The profit came in the replacement market, where mechanics ordinarily replaced the original plug with the same brand of aftermarket plug. Ford, in seeking entry to the profitable aftermarket, concluded that it would require five to eight years to successfully create its own spark plug division, and the cost involved would be greater than that of buying Autolite. Ford accounted for approximately 9.6 percent of all the spark plugs sold in America. After the acquisition, Autolite began a new spark plug business that garnered 1.6 percent of the market by 1964. The government challenged the acquisition.

   a. What category—or categories—of merger are we dealing with here?

   b. What harm did the government fear with the acquisition of Electric Autolite?

   c. Argue that the Ford–Electric Autolite merger strengthened competition.

   d. Decide. Explain. See *Ford Motor Company* v. *United States,* 405 U.S. 562 (1972).

CONGLOMERATE MERGERS—ANALYSIS

Although the federal government, at present, is unlikely to challenge a conglomerate merger, we believe the reader will find intellectual value in understanding the government's historical concerns regarding those mergers.

In essence, conglomerate mergers fall into four categories of analysis:

1. Potential Entrant.   When a firm might have entered a market on its own but chose instead to acquire an existing firm, the government may raise a challenge under Clayton § 7. Potential entrant mergers are of two types: product extension and market extension.

Product extension involves two products that are not competitors but are closely related in their production or distribution. The merger of Procter & Gamble, a soap manufacturer, and Clorox, a bleach manufacturer, exemplifies the product extension conglomerate merger.

Market extension involves two companies that produce the same product but sell it in different geographic markets. The merger of Narragansett Brewing, marketing its products in New England, and Falstaff Brewing, marketing in 32 states but not in New England, is an example of the market extension conglomerate.[44]

2. Market Power Entrenchment.   The government may challenge those conglomerate mergers involving a large firm acquiring a leading firm in a concentrated market in cases when the acquisition may solidify or entrench the acquired firm's already strong market posture. For example, where the acquiring and acquired firms deal in related products, the size of the acquiring firm may convince distributors to accord the acquired firm favored treatment. The government is concerned that some conglomerate mergers will enhance the ability of the merged firm to increase product differentiation. That is, the acquiring firm can use its superior resources in the acquired firm's market, via advertising and the like, with the result that competition is reduced and barriers to entry are increased. The general area of market entrenchment is sometimes referred to by the terms *deep pockets* or *rich parent*. Consideration of the merger guidelines and the *Procter & Gamble* case that follows will clarify this line of analysis.

3. Reciprocity. Essentially, reciprocity involves a "you scratch my back, and I'll scratch yours" sales arrangement in which two parties agree to both buy from and sell to each other. For example, A buys chemicals from B on the condition that B agrees to buy soap from A. Reciprocity takes two forms:

1. *Coercive reciprocity* is the situation in which one of the parties uses its purchasing power to force the other to enter a reciprocal buying arrangement. A says to B, in effect, I buy plenty of chemicals from you. You need my business. To keep my business, you must agree to purchase soap from me. Coercive reciprocity exhibits the characteristics of tying arrangements (see Chapter 11) where a seller with market power forces a buyer to take unwanted product X in order to be supplied with desired product Y.

2. *Mutual patronage reciprocity* involves the same mutual purchase, but no force is involved. Both parties merely believe themselves to be advantaged by buying from each other. The argument is frequently made that mutual patronage reciprocity is harmless in that it involves no abuse and presumably results in maximum consumer welfare and efficiency. However, the historically dominant view in this modestly litigated area is as expressed in a 1966 *General Dynamics* case: "Reciprocity, whether mutual or coercive, serves to exclude competitors by the exercise of large-scale purchasing power."[45]

Conglomerate mergers sometimes exacerbate reciprocity. The accompanying diagram illustrates the problem.

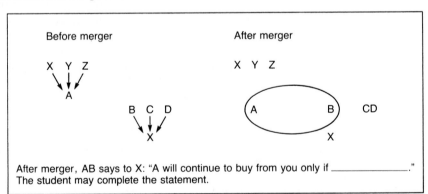

After merger, AB says to X: "A will continue to buy from you only if _____."
The student may complete the statement.

4. Aggregate Concentration. In several cases, the Justice Department has secured consent decrees on the grounds that the mergers in question would have resulted in unacceptable increases in overall commercial concentration. The argument is that commerce is already substantially concentrated—therefore, further significant concentration should be challenged on that ground alone. Despite the Justice Department's occasional success with this line of analysis, no recorded judicial opinion has explicitly supported it.

A careful reading of the *Procter & Gamble* case should provide a reasonably clear picture of the main lines of conglomerate analysis.

FTC v. PROCTER & GAMBLE CO.
386 U.S. 568 (1967)

Justice Douglas

This is a proceeding initiated by the Federal Trade Commission charging that respondent, Procter & Gamble Co., had acquired the assets of Clorox Chemical Co. in violation of § 7 of the Clayton Act . . . The charge was that Procter's acquisition of Clorox might substantially lessen competition or tend to create a monopoly in the production and sale of household liquid bleaches.

[The FTC found the merger unlawful and ordered divestiture.] The Court of Appeals for the Sixth Circuit reversed and directed that the Commission's complaint be dismissed . . . We find that the Commission's findings were amply supported by the evidence, and that the Court of Appeals erred.

. . . This merger may most appropriately be described as a "product-extension merger," as the Commission stated . . .

At the time of the merger, in 1957, Clorox was the leading manufacturer in the heavily concentrated household liquid bleach industry. It is agreed that household liquid bleach is the relevant line of commerce . . . It is a distinctive product with no close substitutes . . . The relevant geographical market is the nation and a series of regional markets. Because of high shipping costs and low sales price, it is not feasible to ship the product more than 300 miles from its point of manufacture. Most manufacturers are limited to competition within a single region since they have but one plant. Clorox is the only firm selling nationally; it has 13 plants distributed throughout the nation. Purex, Clorox's closest competitor in size, does not distribute its bleach in the northeast or mid-Atlantic states; in 1957, Purex's bleach was available in less than 50 percent of the national market.

At the time of the acquisition, Clorox was the leading manufacturer of household liquid bleach, with 48.8 percent of the national sales—annual sales of slightly less than $40 million. Its market share had been steadily increasing for the five years prior to the merger. Its nearest rival was Purex, which accounted for 15.7 percent of the household liquid bleach market. The industry is highly concentrated; in 1957, Clorox and Purex accounted for almost 65 percent of the nation's household liquid bleach sales, and, together with four other firms, for almost 80 percent. The remaining 20 percent was divided among over 200 small producers. Clorox had total assets of $12 million; only eight producers had assets in excess of $1 million, and very few had assets of more than $75,000.

* * * * *

Since all liquid bleach is chemically identical, advertising and sales promotion are vital. In 1957 Clorox spent almost $3.7 million on advertising, imprinting the value of its bleach in the mind of the consumer. In addition, it spent $1.7 million for other promotional activities. The Commission found that these heavy expenditures went far to explain why Clorox maintained so high a market share despite the fact that its brand, though chemically indistinguishable from rival brands, retailed for a price equal to or, in many instances, higher than its competitors.

Procter is a large, diversified manufacturer of low-price, high-turnover household products sold through grocery, drug, and department stores. Prior to its acquisition of Clorox, it did not produce household liquid bleach. Its 1957 sales were in excess of $1.1 billion, from which it realized profits of more than $67 million; its assets were over $500 million. Procter has been marked by rapid growth and diversification . . .

In the marketing of soaps, detergents, and cleansers, as in the marketing of household liquid bleach, advertising and sales promotion are vital. In 1957, Procter was the nation's largest advertiser, spending more than $80 million on advertising and an additional $47 million on sales promotion. Due to its tremendous volume, Procter receives substantial discounts from the media. As a multiproduct producer Procter enjoys substantial advantages in advertising and sales promotion. Thus, it can and does feature several products in its promotions, reducing the printing, mailing, and other costs for each product. It also purchases network programs on behalf of several products, enabling it to give each product network exposure at a fraction of the cost per product that a firm with only one product to advertise would incur.

Prior to the acquisition, Procter was in the course of diversifying into product lines related to its basic detergent-soap-cleanser business. Liquid bleach was a distinct possibility since packaged detergents—Procter's primary product line—and liquid bleach are used complementarily in washing clothes and fabrics, and in general household cleaning.

* * * * *

The anticompetitive effects with which this product-extension merger is fraught can easily be seen: (1) the substitution of the powerful acquiring firm for the smaller, but already dominant, firm may substantially reduce the competitive structure of the industry by raising entry barriers and by dissuading the smaller firms from aggressively competing; (2) the acquisition eliminates the potential competition of the acquiring firm.

The liquid bleach industry was already oligopolistic before the acquisition, and price competition was certainly not as vigorous as it would have been if the industry were competitive. Clorox enjoyed a dominant position nationally, and its position approached monopoly proportions in certain areas. The existence of some 200 fringe firms certainly does not belie that fact. Nor does the fact, relied upon by the court below, that, after the merger, producers other than Clorox "were selling more bleach for more money than ever before."

. . . In the same period, Clorox increased its share from 48.8 percent to 52 percent. The interjection of Procter into the market considerably changed the situation. There is every reason to assume that the smaller firms would become more cautious in competing due to their fear of retaliation by Procter. It is probable that Procter would become the price leader and that oligopoly would become more rigid.

The acquisition may also have the tendency of raising the barriers to new entry. The major competitive weapon in the successful marketing of bleach is advertising. Clorox was limited in this area by its relatively small budget and its inability to obtain substantial discounts. By contrast, Procter's budget was much larger; and, although it would not devote its entire budget to advertising Clorox, it could divert a large portion to meet the short-term threat of a new entrant. Procter would be able to use its volume discounts to advantage in advertising Clorox. Thus, a new entrant would be much more reluctant to face the giant Procter than it would have been to face the smaller Clorox.

Possible economies cannot be used as a defense to illegality. Congress was aware that some mergers which lessen competition may also result in economies but it struck the balance in favor of protecting competition . . .

The Commission also found that the acquisition of Clorox by Procter eliminated Procter as a potential competitor . . . The evidence . . . clearly shows that Procter was the most likely entrant . . . Procter was engaged in a vigorous program of diversifying into product lines closely related to its basic products. Liquid bleach was a natural avenue of diversification since it is complementary to Procter's products, is sold to the same customers through the same channels, and is advertised and merchandised in the same manner . . . It is clear that the existence of Procter at the edge of the industry exerted considerable influence on the market. First, the market behavior of the liquid bleach industry was influenced by each firm's predictions of the market behavior of its competitors, actual and potential. Second, the barriers to entry by a firm of Procter's size and with its advantages were not significant. There is no indication that the barriers were so high that the price Procter would have to charge would be above the price that would maximize the profits of the existing firms. Third, the number of potential entrants was not so large that the elimination of one would be insignificant. Few firms would have the temerity to challenge a firm as solidly entrenched as Clorox. Fourth, Procter was found by the Commission to be the most likely entrant . . .

The judgment of the Court of Appeals is reversed and remanded with instructions to affirm and enforce the Commission's order.

Questions

1. Make the argument that Procter & Gamble beneficially influenced and disciplined the bleach market, even though it had not actually entered that market.
2. Argue that Procter & Gamble was not a likely potential entrant into the bleach market.
3. Could General Motors lawfully acquire Clorox? Explain.
4. Could Procter & Gamble lawfully acquire Purex, at that time the number two liquid bleach producer with 15.7 percent of the market? Explain.
5. Would the outcome of the *Procter & Gamble* case be altered if bleaches were of differing chemical composition and quality? Explain.

Part Four—American Antitrust Laws and the International Market

INTERNATIONAL

America's commercial market now very clearly embraces the entire globe. Multinational corporations dominate international business. Antitrust questions can become extremely complex in transactions involving multiple companies, in multiple nations, where those transactions are potentially governed by U.S. and foreign antitrust laws. U.S. antitrust laws are, of course, applicable to foreign firms doing business here. The Sherman, Clayton, and FTC acts, among others, are all potentially applicable to American business abroad.

Sherman Act

The Sherman Act applies to the conduct of American business abroad when that business has a direct effect on domestic commerce. That the business was conducted entirely abroad or that the agreement was entered in another nation does not excuse an American firm from the reach of the Sherman Act (assuming American courts can achieve the necessary jurisdiction).

Clayton Act

Section 7 of the Clayton Act is clearly applicable to acquisitions combining domestic and foreign firms and is potentially applicable to acquisitions not involving American firms if the effect would be harmful to competition in the American market.

Federal Trade Commission Act

As noted earlier, the FTC shares antitrust enforcement authority with the Justice Department, and Section 5 of the act strengthens Clayton 7.

Enforcement

The complexity and uncertainty of the antitrust laws can be particularly daunting in the international arena. However, the Justice Department has provided a mechanism for achieving greater clarity. Under its Business Review Procedure, the Justice Department will prepare a statement of its likely response to a proposed transaction so that the parties will have advance notice of the government's antitrust stance.

FOREIGN ANTITRUST LAWS

INTERNATIONAL

The United States historically has taken a much more aggressive attitude toward antitrust policy and enforcement than have the nations of Western Europe and Japan. Indeed, those nations generally regard cooperative economic arrangements and concentrations of industrial power as necessary and desirable components of economic success. Of course, Japan and the European Community historically have practiced economic policies involving government quite directly in regulating and "managing" commercial practice for the general good.

Radical changes in both Eastern and Western Europe and the advent of the European common market have forced companies to prepare strategies for dealing with the new realities. To some, the choice was one of merge or be overrun.[46] Hence, the merger climate in Europe in the early 1990s looks a bit like the acquisitions wave of the 1980s in the United States:

> In comparison with those in the U.S.A., the number of mergers and acquisitions in the EC may still be small but . . . more enterprises are placing their trust in the concept of merging, ignoring often unfortunate past experience. According to research conducted by a German institute in the 1980s, nine out of ten mergers failed to provide the success envisaged by their initiators.[47]

EC Antitrust Rules

The European Community has now put in place a set of competition rules that roughly parallel our treatment of antitrust problems. Like Sherman Section 1, the EC rules forbid concerted practices that harm competition. Abuse of market dominance (monopoly) is also forbidden, and in that instance, the EC law appears to be more aggressive than ours because, to be considered threatening, a market share in the EC need not be so large as what we would require for a challenge here in the United States.[48] Further, the EC rules are more aggressive than ours in the sense that charging "excessive" prices is considered abusive and may be attacked under the antitrust laws.

Mergers in the EC are regulated like those in the United States, with premerger notification requirements and the European Communities Commission to review those proposed mergers. Broadly, Commission review is limited to cases with EC implications (rather than those limited to one nation). Judicial review is available via the European Court of Justice. In its first 12 months, the Commission reviewed 50 mergers and disapproved one while negotiating adjustments in several others.[49] The chief concern is that one firm will secure market dominance as a consequence of a merger.

In addition to the EC antitrust rules, each nation can continue to enforce its own national laws in those cases not exhibiting EC implications. The following brief article describes a monopoly claim in the EC.

AIRPORT MONOPOLIES CHALLENGED

Krishnan Anantharaman

In a complaint filed with the European Community Commission, seven European airlines challenged the monopolies that some airport authorities in the EC allow in services such as refueling and unloading baggage. Dutch carrier KLM claimed that in Spanish airports, as well as in Milan and Frankfurt, foreign carriers must use the services of one airport handling company, which determines the cost and quality of the services. In some cases, KLM said, monopolies' rates are 30% to 50% higher than at airports with several handlers. Joining KLM's complaint were Air France, Alitalia, British Airways, Lufthansa, Scandinavian Airlines System and Sabena.

ANTITRUST AND GLOBAL COMPETITIVENESS

INTERNATIONAL

Antitrust law figures prominently in American trade policy. The approach has two dimensions: (1) relaxed enforcement and (2) extraterritoriality.

1. Relaxed Enforcement.   In the 1980s and early 1990s, federal policy was to relax antitrust oversight. Congress passed legislation giving U.S. companies greater latitude to enter joint research agreements abroad and to create export cartels. The Justice Department adopted a more permissive attitude toward foreign companies doing business here, which also allowed U.S.-foreign joint ventures greater flexibility. That general policy continues today, with Congress expected to approve new joint venture legislation that would actually encourage competitors to cooperate during the production stage, a direction quite at odds with our historical fear of collusion between competitors.

A four-year, 10-nation study by highly regarded Harvard Business School professor Michael Porter questions the wisdom of that general direction. Porter says that we need intense domestic competition in order to build stronger firms that are then better prepared to compete globally. Porter's study indicates that Japan has ample domestic competition while the United States has too little. In his view, the more fierce the competition, the more successful the nation. Thus, he is critical of the relaxed joint venture stance as well as the Reagan/Bush indifference to large horizontal mergers.[50]

2. Extraterritoriality.   The much more controversial role of antitrust in trade policy is the Justice Department decision, announced in 1992, to apply American antitrust law abroad. The general idea is to prosecute foreign firms that violate U.S. antitrust laws even when the anticompetitive actions take place overseas (extraterritorial application). In practice, the Justice Department would bring suit in U.S. courts against American subsidiaries of foreign companies where those foreign parents are believed to be violating American antitrust law. Very few such actions are expected.

Keiretsu

The particular concern of the plan is to signal our frustration with the Japanese keiretsu system, which involves closely linked financial and industrial firms that operate, we claim, to unfairly exclude American business from the Japanese market. Keiretsu are often built around banks such as Fuji and Sanwa, but others are headed by large companies such as Toyota or Sony. Particularly in the industrial area, the keiretsu operate as large amalgams of affiliates, subsidiaries, and subcontractors that are dominated by the major firm at the top. These huge enterprise groups compete vigorously with each other but are resistant, we claim, to doing business with foreign firms. Consider one prominent keiretsu arrangement:

> For example, Matsushita Electric, which is known for its Panasonic products, has almost 600 subsidiaries and affiliates in which it holds at least 10 percent of the shares. It has some 200 subsidiaries and affiliates of which Matsushita holds over 50 percent of the shares. Around each of these important affiliates and subsidiaries in the Matsushita group are doz-

ens to 100 smaller suppliers and sales companies in which one or another of the Matsushita companies may have a shareholding interest. Nearly every member company will be engaged in a narrow range of activities so that each will be dependent on the rest.[51]

The article that follows examines the wisdom of applying American antitrust law abroad as part of an overall strategy to strengthen our economic competitiveness.

INTERNATIONAL

ANTITRUST LAW "BAD WEAPON" TO COMBAT TRADE IMBALANCE, ATTORNEY SAYS

U.S. antitrust law is a "bad weapon" to use in export–import grievances, Washington attorney Joel Davidow of Dickstein, Shapiro, and Morin said . . . at a symposium on the overseas application of the laws.

Davidow, formerly chief of the foreign commerce section of the Justice Department's antitrust division, acknowledged that "there is some truth to the point" that Japan's system of keiretsu can be blamed for the U.S. trade imbalance with Japan . . .

Whether the United States can or should limit Japanese imports because Japan may not be enforcing its own competition law against keiretsu adequately is a "thin theory."

Davidow . . . said that antitrust law is neutral in relationship to the U.S.–Japanese trade balance.

The Japanese government has "moved" in the direction of tougher enforcement, although the "results are hard to see," Davidow said, citing the low number of complaints received by the Japan Fair Trade Commission. [JFTC].

He predicted the keiretsu system will weaken because of social changes, political pressures, and some Japanese law changes. "But the U.S. antitrust role will likely be very limited."

* * * * *

. . . [D]espite the highly publicized April 1992 change in U.S. policy that the antitrust division of Justice will challenge anti-competitive behavior by foreigners that hurts U.S. exporters, there have been no cases in the area, Davidow observed.

He explained there have been no cases because of changes over the last 15 years in U.S. antitrust theory, in which "economists have found that partial exclusive dealings, partial vertical mergers" domestically are "simply too minor and too flexible" to be attacked. Thus, he reasoned, for the U.S. to challenge such a situation in a delicate international context would be particularly infeasible.

In comments on Davidow's paper, former Assistant Attorney General James Rill, of Collier, Shannon, Rill & Scott, took issue with the theory that antitrust is "neutral" in relation to trade. It promotes trade instead by opening markets, he said.

Davidow's paper, Rill noted, underscores how little is known about keiretsu—a subject he said cries out to be examined. Furthermore, he continued, Davidow is too optimistic about the prospects of enforcement by the JFTC.

Alex Seita of Albany Law School agreed with Rill that Davidow is overly optimistic about the JFTC's ability to solve keiretsu problems.

"Simply letting the JFTC do its job without significant American interaction is politically unwise" because merely solving the antitrust problems will not affect the larger trade picture, Seita said. Further, if the keiretsu are weakened, it may not be the United States that benefits, but other Japanese companies and other foreigners.

Source: Reprinted with permission from *Daily Report for Executives,* No. 19, p. A-13 (Feb. 1, 1993). Copyright 1993 by The Bureau of National Affairs, Inc., (800) 372-1033.

Questions

1. *a.* In your judgment, must we nudge Japan more vigorously than we have to date by bringing antitrust litigation in American courts to challenge business practices in Japan? Explain.

   b. If we do so, could Japan then legitimately raise challenges in Japanese courts using Japanese law against American business practices such as "Buy American" programs or a community that declined to buy Toyota autos for its municipal police force? See Editorial, "Barr vs. Consumers," *The Wall Street Journal,* March 3, 1992, p. A12.

2. William G. Shepherd, University of Michigan economist and economic advisor to the Justice Department's Antitrust Division during the administration of President Lyndon Johnson:

   > It may not be too late to turn back from this road to serfdom by reviving the case for antitrust, but the odds aren't favorable. More probably, antitrust will continue to sink.[52]

   a. As you see it, what is the future of antitrust law in the United States?

   b. Is bigness bad, or is it necessary in today's global economy? Explain.

Questions—Parts Three and Four

1. Antitrust attorney Joel Davidow says that four policy measures have been critical to the success of formerly socialist nations that are moving to a market economy: privatization, restructuring, deregulation, and adoption of competition legislation (antitrust). Now, in the late 1980s and early 1990s, almost all of the industrial nations of the world, including Russia, Poland, Hungary, and Bulgaria, are taking all of these measures.

   a. Why is antitrust law important to the success of the new market economies in these formerly collectivist nations?

   b. Is antitrust of importance to developing nations such as India, Argentina, and Brazil? Explain. See Joel Davidow, "The Relevance of Antimonopoly Policy for Developing Countries," *The Antitrust Bulletin* 37, no. 1 (Spring 1992), p. 277.

2. In 1993, French competition policy expert Jean-Marie Descarpentries said that "social factors" must play a role in competition (antitrust) law. Descarpentries pointed to a forecast of 30 million unemployed in the EC as an example of such a social factor. He went on to say that social factors were considered in France's decision to approve the Gillette–Parker Pen merger (discussed earlier in this chapter) on the condition that the French brand, Waterman, was maintained.

   Should social factors play a role in antitrust policy or should it be purely a matter of law and economics? Explain. See "EEC Is Urged to Clarify Merger Control Regulations," *Antitrust and Trade Regulation Report* 64, no. 1599 (January 28, 1993), p. 91.

3. In 1992, Coca Cola controlled about 41 percent of the U.S. soft drink market, while Pepsi Cola controlled just over 31 percent. Should their 72 percent combined market share be challenged by the government? Explain.

4. Today, our grocery shelves offer about 150 brands of cereal. Some of them cost $5 per pound or more and prices have risen at about double the rate of all foods. The number one cereal company, Kellogg, holds about 37 percent of the market; General Mills, number two, has about 25 percent; and numbers three through six (Kraft, General Foods/Post, Quaker, and Ralston Purina) share about 28 percent.

   a. Why don't other companies try to tap into this very lucrative market?

   b. *Common Cause Magazine* says that the big cereal companies establish so-called flanker brands, "oddball varieties that occupy the territory [grocery shelf space] adjacent to name products." "When these short-lived varieties sputter out of sight, new ones step in." (Deborah Baldwin, "The Cornflake Cartel," *Common Cause Magazine,* April/May/June, 1993.) What is the economic point of establishing these unlikely-to-succeed flanker brands?

5. Nintendo of America is a Redmond, Washington, subsidiary of Nintendo of Kyoto, Japan, the world's largest manufacturer of video games. Both were sued by a rival game maker, Atari, on the grounds, among others, that Nintendo monopolized the home video game business in the United States. At times, Nintendo controlled 90 percent of the relevant market. Evidence introduced at trial showed that Nintendo was able to maintain its prices for more than four years while other consumer electronics prices were falling. According to Atari's translation of the minutes, a Nintendo board meeting included an open discussion of its "monopoly" position. Atari claimed that Nintendo maintained its market dominance by requiring game makers to give Nintendo an exclusive two-year license for their games. Atari had suffered severe financial reverses, but Nintendo's evidence suggested that those problems were caused by Atari's own missteps.

   Is Nintendo a monopolist? Explain. See *Atari Corp.* v. *Nintendo Co. Ltd. and Nintendo of Am., Inc.,* no. C-89–0824-FMS (N.D. Cal. May 1, 1992).

6. Is the influence of big business so persuasive that it nullifies the effective enforcement of the antitrust laws? Explain.

7. On the average, would firms pursuing expansion via an active merger policy be more or less profitable than those firms not involved in frequent acquisitions? See Linda Hayes, "Twenty-Five Years of Change in the Fortune 500," *Fortune,* May 5, 1980, p. 88.

8. Consolidated, a large food processor and distributor, acquired Gentry, a producer of dehydrated onion and garlic. Consolidated made substantial purchases from various food processors who, in turn, used dehydrated onion and garlic in preparing and packaging their foods. Prior to the merger, Gentry had 32 percent of its market, its chief competitor, Basic, held about 58 percent, with two other firms splitting the balance. Eight years after the merger, Gentry's share rose to 35 percent, while Basic's fell to 55 percent. Basic's products were considered, even by Gentry's president, to be superior to Gentry's products. The Federal Trade Commission challenged the merger as a violation of Section 7 of the Clayton Act. See *Federal Trade Commission* v. *Consolidated Foods Corp.,* 380 U.S. 592 (1965).

   a. What anticompetitive practice did the FTC allege?

   b. Decide the case. Explain.

9. The Justice Department has traditionally been reluctant to accept economies of scale as a defense to an otherwise unlawful merger. Why?

10. How can a merger benefit society?

11. Which economic considerations support the view that unilateral growth is preferable to growth by merger?
12. Excel, a division of Cargill, was the second-largest firm in the beef-packing market. It sought to acquire Spencer Pack, a division of Land-O-Lakes, and the third-largest beef packer. After the acquisition, Excel would have remained second ranked in the business, but its market share would have been only slightly smaller than that of the leader, IBP. Monfort, the nation's fifth-largest beef packer, sought an injunction to block the acquisition, claiming a violation of Clayton Section 7. In effect, Monfort claimed the merger would result in a dangerous concentration of economic power in the beef-packing market, with the result that Excel would pay more for cattle and charge less for its processed beef, thus placing its competitors in a destructive and illegal price–cost squeeze. Monfort claimed Excel's initial losses in this arrangement would be covered by its wealthy parent, Cargill. Then, when the competition was driven from the market, Monfort claimed, Excel would raise its processed beef prices to supracompetitive levels. Among other defenses, Excel averred that the heavy losses Monfort claimed were merely the product of intense competition, a condition that would not constitute a violation of the antitrust laws. The district court found for Monfort and the appeals court, considering the cost–price squeeze a form of predatory pricing, affirmed. Excel appealed to the Supreme Court. Decide. Explain. See *Cargill, Inc.* v. *Monfort of Colorado, Inc.,* 479 U.S. 104 (1986).

NOTES

1. Martin Tolchin, "Antitrust Signal Sent to Airlines," *New York Times,* April 5, 1993, p. D1.
2. Charles F. Rule, "Back to the Dark Ages of Antitrust," *The Wall Street Journal,* June 17, 1992, p. A17.
3. See A. D. Neale, *The Antitrust Laws of the U.S.A.,* 2nd ed. (Cambridge: Cambridge University Press, 1970), p. 190.
4. Solomon Fabricant, *The Output of Manufacturing Industries, 1899–1937* (New York: National Bureau of Economic Research, 1940), pp. 84–85, as reported in Martin C. Schnitzer, *Contemporary Government and Business Relations* (Skokie, IL: Rand McNally, 1978), p. 114.
5. Tony Freyer, *Regulating Big Business Antitrust in Great Britain and America, 1880–1990* (Cambridge: Cambridge University Press, 1992), p. 31.
6. Ibid., p. 52.
7. Ibid., p. 64.
8. Ibid., p. 66.
9. *Standard Oil Co. of New Jersey* v. *United States,* 221 U.S. 1 (1911).
10. Robert Tollison, "Labor Monopoly and Antitrust Policy," *Policy Report,* April 1979.
11. *Federal Trade Commission* v. *Ticor Title Insurance Co.,* 112 S.Ct. 2169 (1992).
12. *Flood* v. *Kuhn,* 407 U.S. 258 (1972).
13. *Goldfarb* v. *Virginia State Bar et al.,* 95 S.Ct. 2004 (1975).
14. Ibid., p. 2016.
15. *California* v. *American Stores Co.,* 495 U.S. 271 (1990).
16. *United States* v. *Grinnell,* 384 U.S. 563, 570–1 (1966).
17. Alan Greenspan, "Antitrust," in *Capitalism: The Unknown Ideal,* ed. Ayn Rand (New York: Signet, 1967), p. 68.

18. *U.S.* v. *Aluminum Company of America,* 148 F.2d 416 (2d Cir. 1945).

19. 110 F. Supp. 295 (Mass. 1953), aff'd per curium, 347 U.S. 521 (1954).

20. *Cliff Food Stores, Inc.* v. *Kroger Co.,* 417 F.2d 203, 207 n.2 (5th Cir. 1969).

21. *Spectrum Sports, Inc.* v. *Shirley McQuillan,* 113 S.Ct. 884 (1993).

22. Ibid., p. 4126.

23. Ronald Rosenberg, "Gillette to Buy Parker," *Boston Globe,* September 11, 1992, p. 73.

24. The Bureau of National Affairs, "Gillette's Proposed Acquisition of Parker Pen Is Referred to MMC," *Antitrust and Trade Regulation Report* 63, no. 1587 (October 22, 1992), p. 516.

25. Ibid.

26. The Bureau of National Affairs, "French Ministers Clear Acquisition in Pen Sector," *Antitrust and Trade Regulation Report* 64, no. 1598 (January 21, 1993), p. 63.

27. Ibid.

28. The Bureau of National Affairs, "UK Commission Clears Bid by Gillette to Buy Parker Pen," *Antitrust and Trade Regulation Report* 64, no. 1602 (February 18, 1993), p. 179.

29. "Justice Department Challenges Proposed Acquisition by Gillette of Parker Pens," *U.S. Newswire,* March 19, 1993.

30. "Gillette's Takeover Plan OK'D," *Boston Globe,* March 24, 1993, p. 41.

31. *United States of America* v. *The Gillette Company,* 828 F. Supp. 78 (1993).

32. L. C. Griffiths, "Regulation of Monopolistic Methods," *Journal of Marketing* 57 (January 1993), p. 102.

33. Wayne D. Collins and Steven C. Sunshine, "Rigor and Sophistry in the New Merger Guidelines," *The American Enterprise* 4, no. 2 (March–April 1993), p. 61.

34. *The Wall Street Journal,* "Mergers, Acquisitions Value Increased 86% Last Year," *The Wall Street Journal,* January 25, 1994, p. C-15.

35. Reported in Walter Adams and James W. Brock, "The Big Business Establishment," in *Ethics, Leadership, and the Bottom Line,* ed. Charles Nelson and Robert Cavey (Croton-On-Hudson, NY: North River Press, 1991), pp. 202, 208.

36. Michael Oneal et al., "The Best and Worst Deals of the '80s," *Business Week,* January 15, 1990, pp. 52, 53–54.

37. Frank Lichtenberg, *Corporate Takeovers and Productivity* (Cambridge, MA: MIT Press, 1992).

38. Jay Bookman, "Voices of Anger: Atlantans Discuss How the Country Lost Its Way," *Atlanta Journal and Constitution,* July 12, 1992, p. C3.

39. David Hage, Linda Grant, and Jim Impoco, "White Collar Wasteland," *U.S. News & World Report,* June 28, 1993, p. 42.

40. Ibid.

41. Ibid.

42. Robert Bork, "The New Vision of Antitrust," *The American Enterprise* 4, no. 1 (January–February 1993), pp. 60, 67.

43. Richard Posner, *Antitrust Law* (Chicago: The University of Chicago Press, 1976), p. 130.

44. *U.S.* v. *Falstaff Brewing Corp.,* 410 U.S. 526 (1973).

45. *United States* v. *General Dynamics Corp.,* 258 F. Supp. 36, 66 (S.D.N.Y. 1966).

46. Michael Schmittmann and Wolfgang Vonnemann, "Mergers and Acquisitions in Europe 1993: The New EC Merger Control Regulation and Its Effects on National Merger Control in Germany," *Antitrust Bulletin* 37, no. 4 (Winter 1992), p. 1025.

47. Ibid., p. 1026.

48. Margot Horspool and Valentine Korah, "Competition," *Antitrust Bulletin* 37, no. 2 (Summer 1992), p. 337.

49. Ibid., p. 343.

50. Michael Porter, "Why Nations Triumph," *Fortune,* March 12, 1990, p. 94.

51. Tomoko Hamada, *American Enterprise in Japan* (Albany, NY: SUNY Press, 1991), p. 53.

52. William G. Shepherd, "Bust the Reagan Trustbusters," *Fortune,* August 4, 1986, pp. 225, 227.

CHAPTER

11

ANTITRUST LAW—RESTRAINTS OF TRADE

INTRODUCTION

The past 20 years or so have produced a revolution of sorts in our view of antitrust law. The "Chicago School," with its advocacy of free market economics, has been successful in reshaping antitrust analysis. Efficiency has become the goal and cornerstone of the new view of antitrust. And businesses, the Chicago School argues, should be free to pursue whatever arrangements best serve their needs so long as those arrangements are not designed to exclude a competitor on some basis other than efficiency (e.g., horizontal price-fixing). Long-standing governmental and public fear of bigness has been muted. But even so, dramatic Supreme Court reversals of "old" antitrust law have been the exception. Mistrust of big business and doubts about the free market as a complete cure for our problems will continue to compete with the undeniable intellectual power of efficient markets thinking.

Democrats

As noted in Chapter 10, with the advent of the Clinton administration, we are seeing some balancing of free market/government intervention approaches to antitrust. In any case, the declining antitrust activism of recent years should not be interpreted as an open door to business abuse. As illustrated by the following article, restraint of trade remains a problem in American commerce, and antitrust law is our primary tool for addressing that problem. The balance of the chapter will describe the antitrust law that has evolved to deal with allegations like these in the baby food business.

METHODS OF MARKETING INFANT FORMULA LAND ABBOTT IN HOT WATER

Thomas M. Burton

Like clockwork, Abbott Laboratories for two decades has posted 15% profit increases annually. For much of that achievement, credit baby formula, the concoction of milk and vitamins that Abbott sells at princely pharmaceutical-level prices.

On 18 occasions from 1980 through this year, Abbott raised the price of its Similac formula by a total of 207%—six times the increase in the consumer price of milk, its basic ingredient. By last year, the nation's top maker of formula was selling $1.1 billion of it annually, or 14% of its total sales and about 16% of profits.

But Abbott's lucrative baby-formula prosperity resulted from a multiyear offensive that included talks with other formula makers and cash grants to the American Academy of Pediatrics. Meanwhile, Abbott's Ross Laboratories formula-making unit also engaged in the systematic destruction of internal documents. Company and industry records show that Abbott played a central role in persuading rivals to agree to an industry sales code that erected a barrier to new competitors by discouraging consumer advertising of formula.

Medical Assistance

U.S. formula companies also have lavished millions of dollars on pediatricians and the American Academy of Pediatrics, which in turn helped the companies sell their formula. The academy issued proclamations opposing formula advertising, though it denies any link to Abbott's contributions. Abbott and some other formula makers also paid for doctors' trips to medical meetings, according to people familiar with these practices.

This formula for Abbott's success, however, could pose a financial threat to the company. Facing federal antitrust allegations from 27 drugstore and food chains, along with charges from the Florida attorney general of bid-rigging, Abbott yesterday settled for more than $140 million. The settlement, whose precise terms weren't disclosed, wraps up consolidated antitrust litigation in federal court in Tallahassee, Fla., and highlights a series of recent cases alleging antitrust violations in the infant-formula industry.

While Abbott declined to comment for this article, it said yesterday that it was "pleased to conclude this matter." It denied any wrongdoing and said that it competes "responsibly, aggressively and completely within the law" and that the settlement "will not have an impact on reported net earnings." The company declined to elaborate.

*   *   *   *   *

The stakes are high for American families . . . At current prices, many babies consume $75 or more of formula a month . . . Florida's attorney general calculates that of any dollar Abbott charged wholesale for formula in 1991, only 16 cents represents its cost of production and delivery.

For the most part, baby formula is pretty much the same. Pediatric-nutrition experts agree that healthy babies whose mothers don't breast-feed thrive equally well on all commercial baby formula . . .

Rivalry from Abroad

Abbott entered the baby nutrition business in 1964, purchasing for $42 million in stock the company now called Ross Laboratories of Columbus, Ohio. Abbott built it to U.S. industry leadership. By 1980, though, a dark cloud loomed. Word emerged that Nestle S.A., the world's largest food company and the leading formula seller overseas, planned to jump into the U.S. market.

But the Swiss concern had an Achilles heel. Nestle had been hit with a consumer boycott over the way it marketed infant formula to Third World mothers; health professionals claimed it urged women to give up breast feeding, which medical experts say generally has health advantages over formula.

William Smart, Ross Labs' president in the early 1980s, devised the idea of a formula-industry code of behavior that would, among other things, condemn consumer advertising, according to depositions in the Florida litigation. This provision, not incidentally, would hamper Nestle's ability to compete in the U.S. market because the company relied heavily on consumer marketing.

Abbott didn't need to advertise because of its network of sales representatives with contacts at hospitals and with doctors. Abbott had cultivated such relationships over decades—links Nestle couldn't easily duplicate. These medical sales methods are known as "ethical marketing."

The ethics have been dubious. Formula makers, including Abbott, have extended benefits to medical students and pediatricians that included school loans, grants, payments for medical articles and trips to conferences, according to people familiar with these tactics. In testimony before joint Senate panels in 1991, Jerome W. Hoffman, antitrust chief in the Florida attorney general's office, told of outright cash grants of "thousands of dollars" from formula companies apparently to induce physicians to recommend specific products.

*   *   *   *   *

. . . Lael F. Johnson, Abbott's general counsel and senior vice president, began in the early 1980s to contact counterparts at Bristol-Myers and American Home Products to push for an antiadvertising code, according to a deposition he gave in the Florida litigation. Extensive negotiations—invariably including the three formula makers who once shared about 98% of the U.S. market—ensued as the industry prepared a code to attack consumer advertising.

At a Sept. 2, 1983, meeting at the O'Hare Hilton in Chicago, Mr. Johnson urged the no-advertising clause on other members of an industry group called the Infant Formula Council. A memo from one IFC

lawyer shows Mr. Johnson was concerned even then about whether these activities might violate antitrust law.

Avoiding Problems

The memo, by attorney Steven M. Kowal, which was entered as evidence in Florida, says Mr. Johnson was looking for code language that would "not present intolerable antitrust problems." The memo describes Mr. Johnson as saying that if federal antitrust enforcers objected to portions of the code, companies "would then unilaterally address these areas in unilaterally adopting their own code." Abbott declines to comment on the memo.

While these talks continued, Abbott and the other manufacturers regularly raised formula prices in what critics describe as lock-step fashion. Companies would raise prices within weeks, or often days, of one another. The difference among the three companies in wholesale price per can often ranged from zero to three cents . . .

In a January 1985 meeting at New York's Park Hyatt/United Nations Plaza Hotel, executives from Abbott and the other companies hammered out points of agreement over language of an antiadvertising code, according to those familiar with the meeting. The following month, at the Sonesta Beach Resort on Key Biscayne, Fla., the formula makers' industry council approved the code. A memo by Mr. Kowal, the attorney, says it was Mr. Johnson who devised the industry's rationale for the provision: that breast-feeding was so important as to outweigh any restrictions on competition.

However, in congressional testimony in 1991, the FTC's deputy director of competition, Mary Lou Steptoe, said about the formula industry: "The antitrust laws do prohibit agreements among competitors to refrain from advertising, even where the competitors profess laudatory motives such as the public health or safety." . . .

Academy Steps In

It was at this point that the American Academy of Pediatrics entered the picture, restating its opposition to advertising. It worried that advertising could diminish breast-feeding. But the academy may not have been a disinterested third party, given the contributions received from the formula industry . . .

* * * * *

In 1988, Nestle finally entered the U.S. market following its acquisition of Carnation. It began selling Good Start and Good Nature (now called Follow-Up) brands. The following year, Bristol-Myers teamed with Gerber Products Co., based in Michigan, to sell a Gerber formula brand. The new products were to be largely advertised directly to parents. (An ad campaign ultimately was launched.)

Abbott renewed its attacks on advertising. Richard Gast, then president of Ross Labs, began to write pediatricians about what he called "a development that undermines your control over the infant's diet and health." . . .

Slow Road to Success

Since then, Nestle and Gerber brands have been slow to find success in the U.S.; they currently hold about 5% and 3% of the market, respectively. Abbott, despite a two-point drop in the past year, holds about a 51% share of the U.S. market, followed by Bristol-Myers's 27% and American Home's 11%.

* * * * *

Nestle's Carnation formulas, though, have begun making inroads into the lucrative federal low-income program for Women, Infants and Children (WIC), which makes up one-third of U.S. industry sales, by volume . . .

Undercutting the Competition

Carnation recently won its first WIC bid, to supply the Western states, by substantially undercutting its competition in price. This may portend a growing WIC price war among manufacturers.

Even so, in at least four other WIC bids in 1990—in Montana, Nevada, West Virginia and Iowa—Abbott and Bristol-Myers bid exactly the same amount, a rebate to the state of 75 cents off its regular commercial price for 13-ounce cans of concentrated milk-based formula. (There were a number of states where the companies' WIC bids didn't match.)

Abbott actually had begun bidding 75-cent rebates in Connecticut in 1989. At the time, John Kane, then president of Abbott's Ross Labs unit, wrote in an internal memo about bid rebates that competitors "may respond to our strong consistent signal," apparently referring to the repeated 75-cent bids. Abbott declined comment.

Shortly thereafter, a Bristol-Myers letter publicly announced it would bid a 75-cent rebate in several other states—a move the Center for Budget and Policy Priorities described as "undermining the sealed bidding procedures."

But destruction of documents at Abbott's Ross unit could pose as many problems as these underlying events. Many of the document-purge orders took place after Florida Assistant Attorney General Patricia A. Conners had filed civil subpoenas . . . for Ross documents. Denying talk of a coverup, Abbott maintains it had a routine policy of discarding records for efficiency's sake. But surviving documents suggest a fixation not with efficiency, but secrecy.

"Be sensitive to what you put in writing," wrote Charles F. Himes, Ross Labs' vice president of marketing and sales, in a July 1988 memo to Ross executives. Ross meeting minutes that month show that Mr. Himes "emphasized the need to protect confidential information."

Questions

1. *a.* Why would an industry agreement that discouraged consumer advertising of infant formula constitute a barrier to entry by new competitors?
   b. How would such an agreement affect prices for infant formula?
2. *a.* What objection might the government raise to the alleged use by John Kane (President of Abbott's Ross Labs in 1989) of repeated $.75 bid rebates in the WIC program as price "signals"?
   b. What objection might the government raise to Bristol-Myers's public announcement that it would offer a $.75 bid rebate in several states?
3. Make a list of the practices cited in this article that you take to be anticompetitive.
4. Could infant formula companies "unilaterally" adopt their own antiadvertising codes without thereby violating the law? Explain.
5. Why would the government object to price cuts, which are, by definition, beneficial to consumers, even if those cuts appear to be signals to others?

Part One—Horizontal Restraints

RULE OF REASON

Not surprisingly, our legal system casts a particularly unyielding eye on horizontal restraints of trade. After all, cooperation among putative competitors nullifies much of the virtue of the market system. The various horizontal restraints are governed by Section 1 of the Sherman Act, which forbids contracts, combinations, or conspiracies in restraint of trade. The statute was, of course, broadly drawn to embrace the many possibilities that arise in American commerce. Therefore, the courts were left to determine what Congress meant by the phrase *restraint of trade.* In the *Standard Oil*[1] decision of 1911 (see Chapter 10), the U.S. Supreme Court articulated what has come to be known as the Rule of Reason. In essence, the Court said that the Sherman Act forbids only *unreasonable* restraints of trade. The Rule of Reason has remained a source of considerable controversy because it recognized the possibility of lawful restraints of trade and "good" as well as "bad" trusts. However, that 1911 interpretation, as applied to both Sections 1 and 2, remains the law today.

PER SE VIOLATIONS

Some antitrust violations such as horizontal price-fixing are perceived to be so injurious to competition that their mere existence constitutes unlawful conduct. Plaintiffs must prove that the violation in question occurred, but they need not prove that the violation caused, or is likely to cause, harm. Such violations are simply unreasonable on their face.

However, in recent years, the use of the per se doctrine has declined. The economics-based notions of efficiency and consumer welfare are increasingly causing jurists to insist on a showing of the defendant's economic abuse before finding an antitrust violation.[2]

HORIZONTAL PRICE-FIXING

Principal legislation: Sherman Act, Section 1.

> Every contract, combination in the form of trust or otherwise, or conspiracy, in restraint of trade or commerce, among the several States, or with foreign nations, is hereby declared to be illegal.

Historically, a contract, combination, or conspiracy among competitors that reduced price competition was an unreasonable restraint of trade and per se unlawful. An inquiry into the reasonableness of the price or proof of a harmful effect was unnecessary. However, recent decisions demonstrate that the judiciary is questioning the per se rule in some instances of horizontal price-fixing. Some courts are taking a Rule of Reason approach under some limited conditions. The per se/Rule of Reason debate continues to evolve.

Proof

The major dilemma in price-fixing and all other Sherman Act section 1 violations is what measure of proof satisfies the requirement of a contract, combination, or conspiracy? As suggested in the infant formula article, evidence of alleged collusion arises in a variety of ways. Broadly, a showing of cooperative action amounting to an agreement must be established. In general, that showing may be developed by any of the following four methods of proof:

1. *Agreement with direct evidence.* In the easiest case, the government can produce direct evidence such as writings or testimony from participants proving the existence of collusion.
2. *Agreement without direct evidence.* Here, the defendants directly but covertly agree, and circumstantial evidence such as firm behavior must be employed to draw an inference of collusion.
3. *Agreement based on a tacit understanding.* In this situation, no direct exchange of assurances occurs, but the parties employ tactics that act as surrogates for direct assurances and thus "tell" each other that they are, in fact, in agreement.
4. *Agreement based on mutual observation.* These defendants have simply observed each others' pricing behavior over time, and they are able therefore to anticipate each others' future conduct and act accordingly without any direct collusion but with results akin to those that would have resulted from a direct agreement.[3]

Parallel Conduct.   An unlawful conspiracy is to be distinguished from independent but parallel business behavior by competitors. So-called *conscious parallelism* is fully lawful because the competitors have not agreed either explicitly or by implication to follow the same course of action. Rather, their business judgment has led each to independently follow parallel paths. In a variation on the general conspiracy theme, the Supreme Court in 1984 firmly rejected the "intra-enterprise conspiracy" doctrine in holding that a parent corporation and its wholly owned subsidiary are incapable, as a matter of law, of conspiracy in violation of Sherman 1.[4]

Contemporary Cases.   Price-fixing is a regrettably common commercial tactic:

- *Abbott.* We began this chapter with Abbott's settlement of price-fixing and other charges.
- *Borden.* In 1993, Borden agreed to pay an $8 million fine to settle federal charges of bid rigging in selling milk to schools. Other milk suppliers are also being pursued by the government in a widespread investigation into unlawful bidding practices, which are estimated to cost consumers hundreds of millions of dollars.[5]
- *Airlines.* In 1993, the nation's biggest airlines agreed to a $458 million settlement of a class action suit by consumers claiming price-fixing by the airlines. The claim was that the airlines used their jointly owned computerized fare database to unlawfully signal each other about prices. Most of the settlement ($408 million) was to be paid in the form of discount coupons to be applied to future flights.[6]
- *Universities.* An unusual price-fixing claim was litigated in 1992, when the Massachusetts Institute of Technology was found guilty of price-fixing with other schools in the so-called Ivy Overlap Group. The schools shared financial information about applicants who applied to more than one of the schools. The schools limited price competition by agreeing on aid to each students in amounts that would equalize the net tuition cost of going to each of the schools. The purpose of the arrangement was to avoid "bidding wars" over students, thus enabling the schools to spread aid more broadly and fairly.

  The price-fixing decision was subsequently overturned on appeal, whereupon the government and MIT reached a settlement permitting sharing of student financial aid information with other schools but forbidding discussions of individual grants to specific students. The agreement permits other nonprofit schools to similarly share information and seems to call into question the Supreme Court's long-standing position that improving social welfare is not a justification for horizontal price-fixing.[7]

ATTEMPTED PRICE-FIXING

Historically, the Federal Trade Commission has not been aggressive in pursuing attempted price-fixing schemes, but in 1993, the Commission displayed a new activism over these *invitations to collude*. YKK, Inc., the largest U.S. zipper maker, and its chief rival, Talon, controlled 82 percent of the market. The FTC accused YKK of attempting to fix prices with Talon:

> [T]he FTC said that in a 1988 letter and follow-up meeting, YKK's lawyer asked Talon to stop offering free equipment to customers who buy zipper components at the same time. YKK said it would stop providing free installation equipment to its customers if Talon did the same, according to the FTC complaint.[8]

With neither admitting nor denying wrongdoing, YKK agreed not to engage in such practices in the future. The day previous to the YKK settlement, the FTC announced that it had settled charges against A. E. Clevite, a manufacturer of locomotive bearings, and that it had invited a foreign competitor to fix prices.[9]

Crandall. The most famous alleged invitation to collude was a February 1982 conversation between Robert L. Crandall, chief executive officer of American Airlines, and Howard Putnam, then president of Braniff. The conversation became a matter of public record after it was submitted to a federal court.

Mr. Crandall

I think it's dumb as hell for Christ's sake, all right, to sit here and pound the [expletive] out of each other and neither one of us making a [expletive] dime.

Mr. Putnam

Well . . .

Mr. Crandall

I mean, you know, goddamn, what the [expletive] is the point of it?

Mr. Putnam

Do you have a suggestion for me?

Mr. Crandall

Yes I have a suggestion for you. Raise your goddamn fares 20 percent. I'll raise mine the next morning.

Mr. Putnam

Robert, we . . .

Mr. Crandall

You'll make more money and I will too.

Mr. Putnam

We can't talk about pricing.

Mr. Crandall

O [expletive], Howard. We can talk about any goddamn thing we want to talk about.[10]

Business Week later commented editorially on the Crandall affair:

Most businessmen would interpret Crandall's remarks as an illegal invitation to fix prices. So did the Justice Department . . . In February, 1983, Justice filed a complaint in federal court charging American and Crandall with trying to fix prices and asking the court to bar Crandall for two years from any airline job with authority over prices. Then followed two years' negotiations with American and Crandall. On July 14, 1985, Justice allowed American and Crandall to sign a consent decree without admitting any guilt in the Braniff affair. Deterrence, anyone?[11]

Questions

1. In the YKK–Talon case, why would an agreement to stop providing free equipment and installation constitute price-fixing?
2. *a.* Why does the government settle so many of its antitrust cases rather than taking them to court for a full review of the issues?
   b. What does the government lose when it settles rather than litigating?

NCAA

The *NCAA* case that follows illustrates the Supreme Court's approach to price-fixing and what is known as *output restriction.* The Court analyzed horizontal price-fixing under the Rule of Reason rather than the per se standard.

NATIONAL COLLEGIATE ATHLETIC ASSOCIATION v. BOARD OF REGENTS OF THE UNIVERSITY OF OKLAHOMA AND UNIVERSITY OF GEORGIA ATHLETIC ASSOCIATION
468 U.S. 85 (1984)

Justice Stevens

The University of Oklahoma and the University of Georgia contend that the National Collegiate Athletic Association has unreasonably restrained trade in the televising of college football games. After an extended trial, the District Court found that the NCAA had violated § 1 of the Sherman Act . . . The Court of Appeals agreed that the statute had been violated but modified the remedy in some respects . . . We granted certiorari . . . and now affirm.

I. The NCAA

Since its inception in 1905, the NCAA has played an important role in the regulation of amateur collegiate sports. It has adopted and promulgated playing rules, standards of amateurism, standards for academic eligibility, regulations concerning recruitment of athletes, and rules governing the size of athletic squads and coaching staffs. In some sports, such as baseball, swimming, basketball, wrestling and track, it has sponsored and conducted national tournaments. It has not done so in the sport of football, however. With the exception of football, the NCAA has not undertaken any regulation of the televising of athletic events.

The NCAA has approximately 850 voting members. The regular members are classified into separate divisions to reflect differences in size and scope of their athletic programs. Division I includes 276 colleges with major athletic programs; in this group only 187 play intercollegiate football. Divisions II and III include approximately 500 colleges with less extensive athletic programs. Division I has been subdivided into Divisions I–A and I–AA for football.

Some years ago, five major conferences together with major football-playing independent institutions organized the College Football Association (CFA). The original purpose of the CFA was to promote the interests of major football-playing schools within the NCAA structure. The Universities of Oklahoma and Georgia, respondents in this Court, are members of the CFA . . .

The Current [Television] Plan

The plan adopted in 1981 for the 1982–1985 seasons is at issue in this case. This plan, like each of its predecessors, recites that it is intended to reduce, insofar as possible, the adverse effects of live television upon football game attendance. It provides that "all forms of television of the football games of NCAA member institutions during the Plan control periods shall be in accordance with this Plan." . . .

The plan recites that the television committee has awarded rights to negotiate and contract for the telecasting of college football games of members of the NCAA to two "carrying networks."

* * * * *

The plan also contains "appearance requirements" and "appearance limitations" which pertain to each of the two-year periods that the plan is in effect. The basic requirement imposed on each of the two networks is that it must schedule appearances for at least 82 different member institutions during each two-year period. Under the appearance limitations no member institution is eligible to appear on television more than a total of six times and more than four times nationally, with the appearances to be divided equally between the two carrying networks . . .

Thus, although the current plan is more elaborate than any of its predecessors, it retains the essential features of each of them. It limits the total amount of televised intercollegiate football and the number of games that any one team may televise. No member is permitted to make any sale of television rights except in accordance with the basic plan.

Background of this Controversy

Beginning in 1979 CFA members began to advocate that colleges with major football programs should have a greater voice in the formulation of football television policy than they had in the NCAA. CFA therefore investigated the possibility of negotiating a television agreement of its own, developed an independent plan, and obtained a contract offer from the National Broadcasting Co. (NBC). This contract, which it signed in August 1981, would have allowed a more liberal number of appearances for each institution, and would have increased the overall revenues realized by CFA members . . .

In response the NCAA publicly announced that it would take disciplinary action against any CFA member that complied with the CFA-NBC contract . . . On September 8, 1981, respondents commenced this action in the United States District Court . . . and obtained a preliminary injunction preventing the NCAA from initiating disciplinary proceedings or otherwise interfering with CFA's efforts to perform its agreement with NBC . . .

Decision of the District Court

After a full trial, the district court held that the controls exercised by the NCAA over the televising of college football games violated the Sherman Act. The district court defined the relevant market as "live college football television" because it found that alternative programming has a significantly different and lesser audience appeal . . . The district court then concluded that the NCAA controls over college football are those of a "classic cartel" with an

> almost absolute control over the supply of college football which is made available to the networks, to television advertisers, and ultimately to the viewing public. Like all other cartels, NCAA members have sought and achieved a price for their product which is, in most instances, artificially high. The NCAA cartel imposes production limits on its

members and maintains mechanisms for punishing cartel members who seek to stray from these production quotas. The cartel has established a uniform price for the products of each of the member producers, with no regard for the differing quality of these products or the consumer demand for these various products.

The district court found that competition in the relevant market has been restrained in three ways: (1) NCAA fixed the price for particular telecasts; (2) its exclusive network contracts were tantamount to a group boycott of all other potential broadcasters and its threat of sanctions against its own members constituted a threatened boycott of potential competitors; and (3) its plan placed an artificial limit on the production of televised college football . . .

In the district court the NCAA offered two principal justifications for its television policies: that they protected the gate attendance of its members and that they tended to preserve a competitive balance among the football programs of the various schools. The district court rejected the first justification because the evidence did not support the claim that college football television adversely affected gate attendance. With respect to the "competitive balance" argument, the district court found that the evidence failed to show that the NCAA regulations on matters such as recruitment and the standards for preserving amateurism were not sufficient to maintain an appropriate balance . . .

Decision of the Court of Appeals

The Court of Appeals held that the NCAA television plan constituted illegal per se price-fixing.

* * * * *

II

There can be no doubt that the challenged practices of the NCAA constitute a "restraint of trade" in the sense that they limit members' freedom to negotiate and enter into their own television contracts. In that sense, however, every contract is a restraint of trade, and as we have repeatedly recognized, the Sherman Act was intended to prohibit only unreasonable restraints of trade.

It is also undeniable that these practices share characteristics of restraints we have previously held unreasonable. The NCAA is an association of schools which compete against each other to attract television revenues, not to mention fans and athletes. As the district court found, the policies of the NCAA with respect to television rights are ultimately controlled by the vote of member institutions. By participating in an association which prevents member institutions from competing against each other on the basis of price or kind of television rights that can be offered to broadcasters, the NCAA member institutions have created a horizontal restraint—an agreement among competitors on the way in which they will compete with one another. A restraint of this type has often been held to be unreasonable as a matter of law. Because it places a ceiling on the number of games member institutions may televise, the horizontal agreement places an artificial limit on the quantity of televised football that is available to broadcasters and consumers. By restraining the quantity of television rights available for sale, the challenged practices create a limitation on output; our cases have held that such limitations are unreasonable restraints of trade. Moreover, the district court found that the minimum aggregate price in fact operates to preclude any price negotiation between broadcasters and institutions, thereby constituting horizontal price-fixing, perhaps the paradigm of an unreasonable restraint of trade.

Horizontal price-fixing and output limitation are ordinarily condemned as a matter of law under an "illegal per se" approach because the probability that these practices are anti-competitive is so high; a per se rule is applied when "the practice facially appears to be one that would always or almost always tend to restrict competition and decrease output." *Broadcast Music, Inc.* v. *CBS,* 441 U.S. 1, 19–20 (1979). In such circumstances a restraint is presumed unreasonable without inquiry into the particular market context in which it is found. Nevertheless, we have decided that it would be inappropriate to apply a per se rule to this case. This decision is not based on a lack of judicial experience with this type of arrangement, on the fact that the NCAA is organized as a nonprofit entity, or on our respect for the NCAA's historic role in the preservation and encouragement of intercollegiate amateur athletics. Rather, what is critical is that this case involves an industry in which horizontal restraints on competition are essential if the product is to be available at all.

As Judge Bork has noted: "[S]ome activities can only be carried out jointly. Perhaps the leading example is league sports. When a league of professional lacrosse teams is formed, it would be pointless to declare their cooperation illegal on the ground that there are no other professional lacrosse teams." . . . What the NCAA and its member institutions market in this case is competition itself—contests between competing institutions. Of course, this would be completely ineffective if there were no rules on which the competitors agreed to create and define the competition to be marketed. A myriad of rules affecting such matters as the size of the field, the number of players on a team, and the extent to which physical violence is to be encouraged or proscribed, all must be agreed upon, and all restrain the manner in which institutions compete.

. . . Thus, the NCAA plays a vital role in enabling college football to preserve its character, and as a result enables a product to be marketed which might otherwise be unavailable. In performing this role, its actions widen consumer choice—not only the choices available to sports fans but also those available to athletes—and hence can be viewed as procompetitive.

III

Because it restrains price and output, the NCAA's television plan has a significant potential for anticompetitive effects. The findings of the district court indicate that this potential has been realized. The district court found that if member institutions were free to sell television rights, many more games would be shown on television, and that the NCAA's output restriction has the effect of raising the price the networks pay for television rights. Moreover, the court found that by fixing a price for television rights to all games, the NCAA creates a price structure that is unresponsive to viewer demand and unrelated to the prices that would prevail in a competitive market. And, of course, since as a practical matter all member institutions need NCAA approval, members have no real choice but to adhere to the NCAA's television controls.

* * * * *

Petitioner argues, however, that its television plan can have no significant anticompetitive effect since the record indicates that it has no market power—no ability to alter the interaction of supply and demand in the market. We must reject this argument for two reasons, one legal, one factual.

As a matter of law, the absence of proof of market power does not justify a naked restriction on price or output. To the contrary, when there is an argument not to compete in terms of price or output, "no elaborate industry analysis is required to demonstrate the anticompetitive character of such an agreement." . . .

As a factual matter, it is evident that petitioner does possess market power. The district court employed the correct test for determining whether college football broadcasts constitute a separate market—whether there are other products that are reasonably substitutable for televised NCAA football games . . . It found that intercollegiate football telecasts generate an audience uniquely attractive to advertisers and that competitors are unable to offer programming that can attract a similar audience. These findings amply support its conclusion that the NCAA possesses market power . . .

IV

Relying on *Broadcast Music,* petitioner argues that its television plan constitutes a cooperative "joint venture" which assists in the marketing of broadcast rights and hence is procompetitive . . .

The district court did not find that the NCAA's television plan produced any procompetitive efficiencies which enhanced the competitiveness of college football television rights; to the contrary it concluded that NCAA football could be marketed just as effectively without the television plan. There is therefore no predicate in the findings for petitioner's efficiency justification. Indeed, petitioner's argument is refuted by the district court's finding concerning price and output. If the NCAA's television plan produced procompetitive efficiencies, the plan would increase output and reduce the price of televised games. The district court's contrary findings accordingly undermine petitioner's position . . .

V

Throughout the history of its regulation of intercollegiate football telecasts, the NCAA has indicated its concern with protecting live attendance.

* * * * *

There is, however, a . . . fundamental reason for rejecting this defense. The NCAA's argument that its television plan is necessary to protect live attendance is not based on a desire to maintain the integrity of college football as a distinct and attractive product, but rather on a fear that the product will not prove sufficiently attractive to draw live attendance when faced with competition from televised games. At bottom the NCAA's position is that ticket sales for most college games are unable to compete in a free market. The television plan protects ticket sales by limiting output—just as any monopolist increases revenues by reducing output.

VI

Petitioner argues that the interest in maintaining a competitive balance among amateur athletic teams is legitimate and important and that it justifies the regulations challenged in this case. We agree with the first part of the argument but not the second.

* * * * *

The NCAA does not claim that its television plan has equalized or is intended to equalize competition within any one league. The plan is nationwide in scope and there is no single league or tournament in which all college football teams compete . . .

The television plan is not even arguably tailored to serve such an interest. It does not regulate the amount of money that any college may spend on its football program, nor the way in which the colleges may use the revenues that are generated by their football programs, whether derived from the sale of television rights, the sale of tickets, or the sale of concessions or program advertising. The plan simply imposes a restriction on one source of revenue that is more important to some colleges than to others. There is no evidence that this restriction produces any greater measure of equality throughout the NCAA than would a restriction on alumni donations, tuition rates, or any other revenue-producing activity. At the same time, as the district court found, the NCAA imposes a variety of other restrictions designed to preserve amateurism which are much better tailored to the goal of competitive balance than is the television plan, and which are "clearly sufficient" to preserve competitive balance to the extent it is within the NCAA's power to do so.

Affirmed.

Questions

1. Why was the NCAA's challenged television arrangement analyzed under the Rule of Reason rather than the per se rule?
2. What defenses were offered by the NCAA?
3. Does the *NCAA* ruling mean colleges and universities may not lawfully join together in groups to arrange mutually agreeable television football packages? Explain.
4. Assume two drugstores, located across the street from each other and each involved in interstate commerce, agree to exchange, on a monthly basis, a list of prices charged for all nonprescription medications. Is that arrangement lawful in the absence of any further cooperation? Explain.
5. As common sense and the cases reveal, sharing of price information among competitors can facilitate anticompetitive collusion, but how might that sharing facilitate competition?
6. Justify the use of per se rulings.
7. The gasoline dealers association in a community reaches an agreement providing: (1) both major brands and independents will not give trading stamps or other premiums and (2) majors agree not to advertise their prices except on the pumps.
   a. What is the purpose of the arrangement?
   b. What violation of law might be alleged? Decide the case. Explain. See *U.S.* v. *Gasoline Retailers Association,* 285 F.2d 688 (1961).
8. Assume that 10 real estate firms operate in the city of Gotham. Further assume that each charges a 7 percent commission on all residential sales.
   a. Does that uniformity of prices in and of itself constitute price-fixing? Explain.
   b. Assume we have evidence that the firms agreed to set the 7 percent level. What defense would be raised against a price-fixing charge?
   c. Would that defense succeed? Explain. See *McLain* v. *Real Estate Board of New Orleans, Inc.,* 444 U.S. 232 (1980).

HORIZONTAL DIVISION OF MARKETS

Principal legislation: Sherman Act, Section 1.

The issue here is whether competitors can lawfully agree (1) to divide their market geographically and/or (2) to allocate customers among themselves. In simplest terms, could Company X lawfully agree to sell only on the east side of the Mississippi River if Company Y (X's competitor) agrees to sell only on the west side? Why would they wish to do so? Under what conditions might such an arrangement enhance competition? Similarly, could Manufacturers X and Y lawfully agree to sell only to retailers rather than to wholesalers? The *Topco* case answers these questions.

UNITED STATES v. TOPCO ASSOCIATES, INC.
405 U.S. 596 (1972)

Justice Marshall

I

Topco is a cooperative association of approximately 25 small and medium-sized regional supermarket chains that operate stores in some 33 states. Each of the member chains operates independently; there is no pooling of earnings, profits, capital, management, or advertising resources. No grocery business is conducted under the Topco name. Its basic function is to serve as a purchasing agent for its members. In this capacity, it procures and distributes to the members more than 1,000 different food and related nonfood items, most of which are distributed under brand names owned by Topco. The association does not itself own any manufacturing, processing, or warehousing facilities, and the items that it procures for members are usually shipped directly from the packer or manufacturer to the members. Payment is made either to Topco or directly to the manufacturer at a cost that is virtually the same for the members as for Topco itself . . .

Topco was founded in the 1940s by a group of small, local grocery chains, independently owned and operated, that desired to cooperate to obtain high-quality merchandise under private labels in order to compete more effectively with larger national and regional chains . . . By 1964, Topco's members had combined retail sales of more than $2 billion; by 1967, their sales totaled more than $2.3 billion, a figure exceeded by only three national grocery chains.

Members of the association vary in the degree of market share that they possess in their respective areas. The range is from 1.5 percent to 16 percent, with the average being approximately 6 percent. While it is difficult to compare these figures with the market shares of larger regional and national chains because of the absence in the record of accurate statistics for these chains, there is much evidence in the record that Topco members are frequently in as strong a competitive position in their respective areas as any other chain. The strength of this competitive position is due, in some measure, to the success of Topco-brand products. Although only 10 percent of the total goods sold by Topco members bear the association's brand names, the profit on these goods is substantial and their very existence has improved the competitive potential of Topco members with respect to other large and powerful chains.

II

. . . The United States charged that, beginning at least as early as 1960 and continuing up to the time that the complaint was filed, Topco had combined and conspired with its members to violate § 1 . . . [T]he government alleged that there existed:

> a continuing agreement, understanding and concert of action among the co-conspirator member firms acting through Topco, the substantial terms of which have been and are that each co-conspirator member firm will sell Topco-controlled brands only within the marketing territory allocated to it, and will refrain from selling Topco-controlled brands outside such marketing territory.

Following approval, each new member signs an agreement with Topco designating the territory in which that member may sell Topco-brand products. No member may sell these products outside the territory in which it is licensed. Most licenses are exclusive, and even those denominated "coextensive" or "non-exclusive" prove to be *de facto* exclusive . . . When combined with each member's veto power over new members, provisions for exclusivity work effectively to insulate members from competition in Topco-brand goods. Should a member violate its license agreement and sell in areas other than those in which it is licensed, its membership can be terminated . . .

From the inception of this lawsuit, Topco accepted as true most of the government's allegations regarding territorial divisions and restrictions on wholesaling, although it differed greatly with the government on the conclusions, both factual and legal, to be drawn from these facts . . .

Topco essentially maintains that it needs territorial divisions to compete with larger chains; that the association could not exist if the territorial divisions were anything but exclusive; and that by restricting competition in the sale of Topco-brand goods, the association actually increases competition by enabling its members to compete successfully with larger regional and national chains.

* * * * *

While the Court has utilized the "rule of reason" in evaluating the legality of most restraints alleged to be violative of the Sherman Act, it has also developed the doctrine that certain business relationships are per se violations of the act without regard to a consideration of their reasonableness . . .

. . . One of the classic examples of a per se violation of § 1 is an agreement between competitors at the same level of the market structure to allocate territories in order to minimize competition. Such concerted action is usually termed a "horizontal" restraint, in contradistinction to combinations of persons at different levels of the market structure, e.g., manufacturers and distributors, which are termed "vertical" restraints. This Court has reiterated time and time again that "[h]orizontal territorial limitations . . . are naked restraints of trade with no purpose except stifling of competition." . . .

Such limitations are per se violations of the Sherman Act . . .

* * * * *

In applying these rigid rules, the Court has consistently rejected the notion that naked restraints of trade are to be tolerated because they are well intended or because they are allegedly developed to increase competition.

* * * * *

The district court determined that by limiting the freedom of its individual members to compete with each other, Topco was doing a greater good by fostering competition between members and other large supermarket chains. But, the fallacy in this is that Topco has no authority under the Sherman Act to determine the respective values of competition in various sectors of the economy. On the contrary, the Sherman Act gives to each Topco member and to each prospective member the right to ascertain for itself whether or not competition with other supermarket chains is more desirable than competition in the sale of Topco-brand products . . .

There have been tremendous departures from the notion of a free-enterprise system as it was originally conceived in this country. These departures have been the product of congressional action and the will of the people. If a decision is to be made to sacrifice competition in one portion of the economy for greater competition in another portion, this too is a decision that must be made by Congress and not by private forces or by the courts. Private forces are too keenly aware of their own interests in making such decisions and courts are ill-equipped and ill-situated for such decision making. To analyze, interpret, and evaluate the myriad of competing interests and the endless data that would surely be brought to bear on such decisions, and to make the delicate judgment on the relative values to society of competitive areas of the economy, the judgment of the elected representatives of the people is required.

* * * * *

We reverse the judgment of the District Court and remand the case . . .

Chief Justice Burger, dissenting

This case does not involve restraints on interbrand competition or an allocation of markets by an association with monopoly or near-monopoly control of the sources of supply of one or more varieties of staple goods. Rather, we have here an agreement among several small grocery chains to join in a cooperative endeavor that, in my view, has an unquestionably lawful principal purpose; in pursuit of that purpose they have mutually agreed to certain minimal ancillary restraints that are fully reasonable in view of the principal purpose and that have never before today been held by this Court to be per se violations of the Sherman Act.

In joining in this cooperative endeavor, these small chains did not agree to the restraints here at issue in order to make it possible for them to exploit an already established line of products through noncompetitive pricing. There was no such thing as a Topco line of products until this cooperative was formed. The restraints to which the cooperative's members have agreed deal only with the marketing of the products in the Topco line, and the only function of those restraints is to permit each member chain to establish, within its own geographical area and through its own local advertising and marketing efforts, a local consumer awareness of the trademarked family of products as that member's "private-label" line. The goal sought was the enhancement of the individual members' abilities to compete, albeit to a modest degree, with the large national chains which had been successfully marketing private-label lines for several years. The sole reason for a cooperative endeavor was to make economically feasible such things as quality control, large-quantity purchases at bulk prices, the development of attractively printed labels, and the ability to offer a number of different lines of trademarked products. All these things, of course, are feasible for the large national chains operating individually, but they are beyond the reach of the small operators proceeding alone.

After a careful review of the economic considerations bearing upon this case, the district court determined that "the relief which the government here seeks would not increase competition in Topco private label brands"; on the contrary, such relief "would substantially diminish competition in the supermarket field." . . . This Court has not today determined, on the basis of an examination of the underlying economic realities, that the district court's conclusions are incorrect . . .

Questions

1. In *Topco,* how does the defendant association seek to justify its division of the market? How do you evaluate that defense?
2. In exchange for royalties, Sealy allocated mutually exclusive sales territories among the various firms it licensed to construct and sell mattresses bearing the Sealy label. Sealy's agreement with each licensee provided that Sealy would not license others to manufacture or sell in the designated area, and the licensee agreed not to manufacture or sell Sealy products outside its designated area. Sealy's licensees numbered approximately 30. Those licensees owned substantially all of Sealy's stock. Sealy's business was managed by its board of directors. Each director had to be a stockholder or stockholder's nominee. Sealy contended that its primary purpose in its licensing arrangement was to exploit the Sealy name and trademark. The government filed suit against Sealy, alleging price-fixing and horizontal territorial limitations. At the trial level, Sealy was found guilty of price-fixing but innocent as to territorial restraint. The government appealed the latter, while Sealy chose not to contest the former.
   a. Defend Sealy.
   b. Decide the case. See *United States* v. *Sealy, Incorporated,* 388 U.S. 350 (1967).
   c. Would your decision in *Sealy* be changed if the U.S. Supreme Court were to embrace Judge Bork's reasoning in *Rothery* (see next section)? Explain.
3. In analyzing horizontal territorial restraints, Professor Wesley Liebeler argues:

   But it does not appear that collusion between dealers who handle the product of only one manufacturer—White truck dealers, Chevrolet dealers, or Sylvania television dealers, for example—will result in higher prices and restricted output.

   What economic logic supports his position? See Wesley J. Liebeler, 1980 Cumulative Supplement to *Antitrust Advisor,* 2nd ed. (Colorado Springs: Shepard's/McGraw-Hill, 1978).

Afterword

One of the most interesting and provocative antitrust decisions in recent years casts some doubt on the *Topco* reasoning. In *Rothery Storage & Van Co.* v. *Atlas Van Lines, Inc.,* the District of Columbia Federal Circuit Court of Appeals reasoned that recent U.S. Supreme Court decisions, including the *NCAA* price-fixing case had, in effect, overruled *Topco* "as to the per se illegality of all horizontal restraints."[12]

The *Rothery* facts were not in dispute. Rothery and other independent moving companies operated under contracts with Atlas Van Lines in which the independents would act as agents of Atlas, moving furniture and other goods as instructed. The advent of deregulation permitted the independents to move furniture on their own in interstate commerce, a power that prior to deregulation had largely been beyond their grasp. The result was that Atlas was then in competition with its own agents. Therefore, Atlas announced it would terminate the contract of any agent that persisted in handling interstate business on its own as well as for Atlas. Rothery and other Atlas agents sued, claiming (among other possibilities) that Atlas was guilty of a per se illegality (in this case, horizontal price maintenance because the agents were required to adhere to the shipping rates established by Atlas). The district court upheld the Atlas policy based on a balancing of the benefits and harms from the arrangement (a Rule of Reason analysis). The circuit court affirmed, but in so doing the panel reasoned that a balancing of good and bad was unnecessary in the case because Atlas' less-than-6-percent share of the market could not create any harm. To the circuit court, the Atlas arrangement was an efficient method of providing nationwide moving services that also prevented the Atlas agents from free riding on the Atlas name when those agents moved goods on their own. Judge Robert Bork, writing for the majority, seemed to treat market share as perhaps the only measure of anticompetitive impact in Rule of Reason cases. Whether Bork's reasoning will ultimately carry the day remains to be seen. In her concurring opinion in *Rothery,* Judge Patricia Wald declined to adopt market power as an exclusive measure in all such cases:

> Until the Supreme Court indicates that the *only* goal of antitrust law is to promote efficiency, as the panel uses that term, I think it is more prudent to proceed with a . . . Rule of Reason analysis, than to adopt a market power test as the exclusive filtering-out device for all potential violators who do not command a significant market share. Under any analysis, market power is an important consideration; I am not yet willing to say it is the only one.[13]

REFUSALS TO DEAL

Principal legislation: Sherman Act, Section 1.

A *group boycott* is yet another instance of concerted action in which a collectivity of traders jointly refuses to deal with another trader or traders. Typically, the purpose of such an arrangement is to remove or "police" a competitor. Depending on the facts, group boycotts may be analyzed under the Rule of Reason or they may be treated as per se violations. What boycott might arise from the facts diagrammed here?

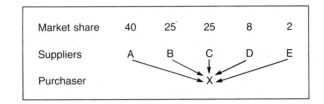

In a 1959 case, *Klor's* v. *Broadway-Hales Stores, Inc.* 359 U.S. 207 (1959), the Supreme Court applied the per se rule to boycotts. Klor's, Inc., operated a retail store on Mission Street, San Francisco, California. Broadway-Hale Stores, Inc., a chain of department stores, operated one of its stores next door. The two stores competed in the sale of radios, television sets, refrigerators, and other household appliances.

Klor's filed suit against Broadway-Hale and 10 appliance manufacturers and made the following allegations: George Klor started an appliance store some years before 1952. Klor's was as well equipped as Broadway-Hale to handle all brands of appliances. Nevertheless, manufacturers and distributors of such well-known brands as General Electric, RCA, Admiral, Zenith, Emerson, and others conspired among themselves and with Broadway-Hale either not to sell to Klor's or to sell to it only at discriminatory prices and highly unfavorable terms. Broadway-Hale used its "monopolistic" buying power to bring about this situation.

Broadway-Hale submitted unchallenged affidavits showing there were hundreds of other household appliance retailers, some within a few blocks of Klor's, who sold many competing brands of appliances, including those the defendants refused to sell to Klor's.

The Court found a group boycott in violation of the Sherman Act in that the combination deprived Klor's of the opportunity to buy appliances in the open market, thus driving Klor's out of business in the retail market for those appliances.

Question

1. Sears, issuer of the Discover credit card, acquired a savings and loan, MountainWest. Sears then sought to issue a low-interest, "Prime Option" Visa card through MountainWest. However, a Visa bylaw barred membership by "any applicant which is issuing, directly or indirectly, Discover cards or American Express cards, or any other cards deemed competitive by the board of directors. Hence, Visa, a joint venture, refused MountainWest's application for membership. MountainWest then filed suit claiming a violation of the Sherman Act by Visa. Visa responded by saying that the Sherman Act should not apply to a joint venture that, in effect, simply refuses to share its property. And Visa noted that Sears, with it Discover card, is a direct competitor and one of the largest issuers of credit cards in the United States.

   a. What charge(s) would you raise on behalf of Sears?

   b. Defend Visa.

   c. Decide. Explain. See *SCFL ILC Inc. d/b/a Mountainwest Financial* v. *Visa U.S.A. Inc.,* 819 F. Supp. 956 (DC Utah, 1993).

Part Two—Vertical Restraints

RESALE PRICE MAINTENANCE/VERTICAL TERRITORIAL AND CUSTOMER RESTRAINTS

Principal legislation: Sherman Act, Section 1; Federal Trade Commission Act, Section 5.

Manufacturers and distributors often seek to specify the price at which their customers may resell their products. Having sold its product, why should a manufacturer or distributor seek to influence the price at which the product is resold? The primary reasons are twofold: (1) by establishing a minimum price, the product's reputation for quality may be enhanced and (2) resale price maintenance policy seeks to prevent discount stores from undercutting regular retail outlets. (Why does the manufacturer or distributor prefer its products to be sold in traditional retail stores rather than in discount enterprises?)

Colgate Doctrine

An *agreement* between a seller and its buyer, fixing the price at which the buyer may resell the product, is a per se violation. However, sellers may lawfully engage in resale price maintenance if they do nothing more than specify prices at which their products are to be sold and unilaterally refuse to deal with anyone who does not adhere to those prices. This is the so-called *Colgate* doctrine, announced in *United States* v. *Colgate & Co.,* 250 U.S. 300 (1919).

Nonprice Restraints

In addition to price restraints, manufacturers commonly wish to impose restrictions on where and to whom their product may be resold. Those restrictions typically afford an exclusive sales territory to a distributor. Similarly, manufacturers may prevent distributors from selling to some classes of customers (e.g., a distributor might be forbidden to sell to an unfranchised retailer). Of course, such arrangements necessarily retard or eliminate intrabrand competition. Because price and service competition among dealers in the same brand ordinarily is of benefit to the consumer, the courts have frequently struck down such arrangements. Still, it is generally agreed that territorial and customer allocations also have merits. The *GTE Sylvania case*[14] enunciated those virtues and established the position that vertical restrictions are to be judged on a case-by-case basis, balancing interbrand and intrabrand competitive effects. Thus, the Rule of Reason is to be applied to vertical territorial and customer restraints.

At this point, the student will want to understand the critical distinction between horizontal and vertical territorial and customer allocations. The former is per se unlawful. The latter is to be resolved under the Rule of Reason unless it involves an agreement on prices. *Horizontal* restrictions are those arising from an agreement among the *competitors* themselves, while *vertical* restrictions are those imposed on *buyers* by their *suppliers.* The *Business Electronics Corporation* (B.E.C.) case that follows offers a summary of the Supreme Court's analysis of both vertical price and nonprice restraints.

BUSINESS ELECTRONICS CORPORATION v. SHARP ELECTRONICS CORPORATION
485 U.S. 717 (1988)

Justice Scalia

Petitioner Business Electronics Corporation seeks review of a decision of the United States Court of Appeals for the Fifth Circuit holding that a vertical restraint is per se illegal under § 1 of the Sherman Act, only if there is an express or implied agreement to set resale prices at some level. We granted certiorari to resolve a conflict in the Courts of Appeals regarding the proper dividing line between the rule that vertical price restraints are illegal per se and the rule that vertical nonprice restraints are to be judged under the rule of reason.

I

In 1968, petitioner became the exclusive retailer in the Houston, Texas, area of electronic calculators manufactured by respondent Sharp Electronics Corporation. In 1972, respondent appointed Gilbert Hartwell as a second retailer in the Houston area. During the relevant period, electronic calculators were primarily sold to business customers for prices up to $1,000. While much of the evidence in this case was conflicting—in particular, concerning whether petitioner was "free riding" on Hartwell's provision of presale educational and promotional services by providing inadequate services itself—a few facts are undisputed. Respondent published a list of suggested minimum retail prices, but its written dealership agreements with petitioner and Hartwell did not obligate either to observe them, or to charge any other specific price. Petitioner's retail prices were often below respondent's suggested retail prices and generally below Hartwell's retail prices, even though Hartwell too sometimes priced below respondent's suggested retail prices. Hartwell complained to respondent on a number of occasions about petitioner's prices. In June 1973, Hartwell gave respondent the ultimatum that Hartwell would terminate his dealership unless respondent ended its relationship with petitioner within 30 days. Respondent terminated petitioner's dealership in July 1973.

Petitioner brought suit in the United States District Court for the Southern District of Texas, alleging that respondent and Hartwell had conspired to terminate petitioner and that such conspiracy was illegal per se under § 1 of the Sherman Act. The case was tried to a jury. The district court submitted a liability interrogatory to the jury that asked whether "there was an agreement or understanding between Sharp Electronics Corporation and Hartwell to terminate Business Electronics as a Sharp dealer because of Business Electronics' price cutting." The district court instructed the jury at length about this question:

The Sherman Act is violated when a seller enters into an agreement or understanding with one of its dealers to terminate another dealer because of the other dealer's price cutting. Plaintiff contends that Sharp terminated Business Electronics in furtherance of Hartwell's desire to eliminate Business Electronics as a price-cutting rival.

If you find that there was an agreement between Sharp and Hartwell to terminate Business Electronics because of Business Electronics' price cutting, you should answer yes to Question Number 1.

* * * * *

A combination, agreement or understanding to terminate a dealer because of his price cutting unreasonably restrains trade and cannot be justified for any reason. Therefore, even though the combination, agreement or understanding may have been formed or engaged in . . . to eliminate any alleged evils of price cutting, it is still unlawful.

If a dealer demands that a manufacturer terminate a price-cutting dealer, and the manufacturer agrees to do so, the agreement is illegal if the manufacturer's purpose is to eliminate the price cutting.

The jury answered Question 1 affirmatively and awarded $600,000 in damages . . .

* * * * *

The Fifth Circuit reversed . . .

II
A

Section 1 of the Sherman Act provides that "[e]very contract, combination in the form of trust or otherwise, or conspiracy, in restraint of trade or commerce among the several States, or with foreign nations, is declared to be illegal." Since the earliest decisions of this Court interpreting this provision, we have recognized that it was intended to prohibit only unreasonable restraints of trade. Ordinarily, whether particular concerted action violates § 1 of the Sherman Act is determined through case-by-case application of the so-called rule of reason . . . Certain categories of agreements, however, have been held to be per se illegal, dispensing with the need for case-by-case evaluation . . .

* * * * *

Although vertical agreements on resale prices have been illegal per se since *Dr. Miles Medical Co.* v. *John D. Park & Sons Co.,* we have recognized that the scope of per se illegality should be narrow in the context of vertical restraints. In *Continental T.V. Inc.* v. *GTE Sylvania Inc.* we refused to extend per se illegality to vertical nonprice restraints, specifically to a manufacturer's termination of one dealer pursuant to an exclusive territory agreement with another. We noted that especially in the vertical restraint context "departure from the rule-of-reason standard must be based on demonstrable economic effect rather than . . . upon formalistic line drawing." We concluded that vertical nonprice restraints had not been shown to have such a "'pernicious effect on competition'" and to be so "'lack[ing] [in] . . . redeeming value'" as to justify per se illegality. Rather, we found, they had real potential to stimulate interbrand competition, "the primary concern of antitrust law":

[N]ew manufacturers and manufacturers entering new markets can use the restrictions in order to induce competent and aggressive retailers to make the kind of investment of capital and labor that is often required in the distribution of products unknown to the consumer. Established manufacturers can use them to induce retailers to engage in promotional activities or to provide service and repair facilities necessary to the efficient marketing of their products. Service and repair are vital for many products . . . The availability and quality of such services affect a manufacturer's goodwill and the competitiveness of his product. Because of market imperfections such as the so-called free-rider effect, these services might not be provided by retailers in a purely competitive situation, despite the fact that each retailer's benefit would be greater if all provided the services than if none did.

Moreover we observed that a rule of per se illegality for vertical nonprice restraints was not needed or effective to protect *intra*brand competition. First, so long as interbrand competition existed, that would provide a "significant check" on any attempt to exploit intrabrand market power. In fact, in order to meet that interbrand competition, a manufacturer's dominant incentive is to lower resale prices. Second, the per se illegality of vertical restraints would create a perverse incentive for manufacturers to integrate vertically into distribution, an outcome hardly conducive to fostering the creation and maintenance of small businesses.

* * * * *

Our approach to the question presented in the present case is guided by the premises of *GTE Sylvania:* that there is a presumption in favor of a rule-of-reason standard; that departure from that standard must be justified by demonstrable economic effect, such as the facilitation of cartelizing, rather than formalistic distinctions; that interbrand competition is the primary concern of the antitrust laws; and that rules in this area should be formulated with a view towards protecting the doctrine of *GTE Sylvania.* These premises lead us to conclude that the line drawn by the Fifth Circuit is the most appropriate one.

There has been no showing here that an agreement between a manufacturer and a dealer to terminate a "price cutter," without a further agreement on the price or price levels to be charged by the remaining dealer, almost always tends to restrict competition and reduce output. Any assistance to cartelizing that such an agreement might provide cannot be distinguished from the sort of minimal assistance that might be provided by vertical nonprice agreements like the exclusive territory agreement in *GTE Sylvania,* and is insufficient to justify a per se rule. Cartels are neither easy to form nor easy to maintain . . .

The District Court's rule on the scope of per se illegality for vertical restraints would threaten to dismantle the doctrine of *GTE Sylvania.* Any agreement between a manufacturer and a dealer to terminate another dealer who happens to have charged lower prices can be alleged to have been directed against the terminated dealer's "price cutting." In the vast majority of cases, it will be extremely difficult for the manufacturer to convince a jury that its motivation was to ensure adequate services, since price cutting and some measure of service cutting usually go hand in hand. Accordingly, a manufacturer that agrees to give one dealer an exclusive territory and terminates another dealer pursuant to that agreement, or even a manufacturer that agrees with one dealer to terminate another for failure to provide contractually obligated services, exposes itself to the highly plausible claim that its real motivation was to terminate a price cutter. Moreover, even vertical restraints that do not result in dealer termination, such as the initial granting of an exclusive territory or the requirement that certain services be provided, can be attacked as designed to allow existing dealers to charge higher prices. Manufacturers would be likely to forgo legitimate and competitively useful conduct rather than risk treble damages and perhaps even criminal penalties.

We cannot avoid this difficulty by invalidating as illegal per se only those agreements imposing vertical restraints that contain the word "price," or that affect the "prices" charged by dealers. Such formalism was explicitly rejected in *GTE Sylvania.* As the above discussion indicates, all vertical restraints, including the exclusive territory agreement held not to be per se illegal in *GTE Sylvania,* have the potential to allow dealers to increase "prices" and can be characterized as intended to achieve just that. In fact, vertical nonprice restraints only accomplish the benefits identified in *GTE Sylvania* because they reduce intrabrand price competition to the point where the dealer's profit margin permits provision of the desired services. As we described it in *Monsanto:* "The manufacturer often will want to ensure that its distributors earn sufficient profit to pay for programs such as hiring and training additional salesmen or demonstrating the technical features of the product, and will want to see that 'free-riders' do not interfere."

* * * * *

. . . Petitioner has provided no support for the proposition that vertical price agreements generally underlie agreements to terminate a price cutter. That proposition is simply incompatible with the conclusion of *GTE Sylvania* and *Monsanto* that manufacturers are often motivated by a legitimate desire to have dealers provide services, combined with the reality that price cutting is frequently made possible by "free riding" on the services provided by other dealers. The district court's per se rule would therefore discourage conduct recognized by *GTE Sylvania* and *Monsanto* as beneficial to consumers.

* * * * *

Affirmed.

Justice Stevens, with whom Justice White joins, dissenting

In its opinion the majority assumes, without analysis, that the question presented by this case concerns the legality of a "vertical nonprice restraint." As I shall demonstrate, the restraint that results when one or more dealers threatens to boycott a manufacturer unless it terminates its relationship with a price-cutting retailer is more properly viewed as a "horizontal restraint." Moreover, an agreement to terminate a dealer because of its price cutting is most certainly not a "nonprice restraint." The distinction between "vertical nonprice restraints" and "vertical price restraints," on which the majority focuses its attention, is therefore quite irrelevant to the outcome of this case.

* * * * *

Questions

1. Summarize the essence of the *B.E.C.* holding.
2. What practical effects would you expect the *B.E.C.* decision to have on the behavior of (*a*) manufacturers and (*b*) discounters?

3. *a.* What is the *Colgate* doctrine?

   b. Is the *Colgate* doctrine a practical, workable standard of conduct? Explain.

4. Assume a manufacturer communicates to its distributors a "suggested retail price" for its product. Further assume the distributors individually decide to follow that suggestion.

   a. Does that conduct violate the law? Explain.

   b. Would it matter whether the product is heavily advertised? Explain.

   c. What is fair-trade pricing?

   d. What is its current status?

5. In *Albrecht* v. *Herald Co.,* 390 U.S. 145 (1968), a newspaper distributor, Albrecht, lost his distributorship because he charged a retail price in excess of that specified by the *Herald.*

   a. Is the setting of a maximum resale price illegal? Explain.

   b. Argue the case both for and against Albrecht.

6. In *Continental T.V., Inc.,* v. *GTE Sylvania Inc.,* 433 U.S. 36 (1977), the Supreme Court took the position that interbrand, rather than intrabrand, agreements must be the primary concern of antitrust law.

   a. Why does the Court take that view?

   b. Is the Court correct? Explain.

7. The *GTE* decision distinguished vertical "nonprice" restrictions (such as location clauses) from vertical price restrictions (resale price maintenance). Make the argument that the Court's distinction was not meaningful.

8. What is the "free-rider" problem that frequently concerns the courts in cases involving vertical territorial restraints?

9. Assume a manufacturer assigns an "area of primary responsibility" to a distributor. The distributor's sales are not confined to that area, but he or she must devote his or her best efforts to that area, and failure to do so may result in termination of the distributorship. Is that arrangement lawful? Explain.

10. In 1977, Michelin failed to renew its dealership agreement with the Donald B. Rice Tire Company of Frederick, Maryland. After seven years with Michelin, approximately 80 percent of Rice's business was derived from wholesaling the tires to smaller authorized and unauthorized dealers. Other authorized dealers complained to Michelin of Rice's wholesale business. In an effort to assume primary wholesaling responsibility, Michelin chose not to renew its relationship with Rice. Rice contended that the nonrenewal was a consequence of its refusal to comply with Michelin's customer and territorial restraints, and Rice filed an antitrust action on that basis. Michelin argued that it was a new entrant into a concentrated market, and as such, restraints on intrabrand competition were necessary to induce retailers to carry Michelin tires. However, the court found frequent shortages of Michelin tires. Michelin also argued that nonrenewal was "necessary to prevent free riding by retailers on the services provided by other dealers."

   Rice had not advertised in a quantity commensurate with his sales volume. He sold to unauthorized dealers who were not bound to do any advertising and could thus reap the benefits of advertising by authorized dealers. Michelin wanted to encourage point-of-sales services and the offering of specialized services but feared authorized dealers would not invest the necessary expenditures because of their fear of being underpriced by unauthorized dealers. Decide the case. See *Donald B. Rice Tire Company Inc.* v. *Michelin Corporation,* 483 F. Supp. 750 (D.Md., 1980), 638 F.2d 15 (1981), cert. den., 454 U.S. 864 (1981).

Afterword

B.E.C. has been sharply criticized as an "anti-consumer" decision, one that allows manufacturers to prevent discounting of their products. In August 1993, the Clinton Justice Department announced that it will take a more aggressive stance toward vertical pricing arrangements than did the Reagan administration, which had issued guidelines largely removing the federal government from the business of questioning vertical pricing deals.

The practical effect of the change in policy is unclear. Written price agreements are seldom imposed on distributors, since that practice would clearly be unlawful. Many manufacturers do employ suggested retail prices, and they sometimes put pressure on distributors to adhere to those guidelines. The government may now pursue antitrust claims in some carefully chosen cases of that kind. Whether the government will be successful is debatable in light of the Supreme Court's interpretation of the law in *B.E.C.*

In announcing the new aggressiveness on resale price maintenance, the Justice Department antitrust chief, Anne Bingaman, indicated that the Justice Department would continue to be supportive of some *nonprice* vertical arrangements where consumer benefit is clear (as where a distributor is given exclusive territorial rights to a product in exchange for improved customer service.)[15]

TYING ARRANGEMENTS

Principal legislation: Clayton Act, Section 3; Sherman Act, Sections 1 and 2; Federal Trade Commission Act, Section 5.

> Clayton Act, Section 3. That it shall be unlawful for any person engaged in commerce, in the course of such commerce, to lease or make a sale or contract for sale of goods . . . or other commodities . . . or fix a price charged therefore, or discount from or rebate upon, such price, on the condition, agreement or understanding that the lessee or purchaser thereof shall not use or deal in the goods . . . or other commodities of a competitor or competitors of the lessor or seller, where the effect of such lease, sale, or contract for sale or such condition, agreement, or understanding may be to substantially lessen competition or tend to create a monopoly in any line of commerce.

The typical tying arrangement permits a customer to lease or buy a desired product (the tying product) only if she or he also leases or buys another product (the tied product). Of course, such an arrangement may harm consumers, but the primary antitrust concerns are twofold: (1) a party who already enjoys market power over the tying product is able to extend that power into the tied product market; and (2) competitors in the tied product market are foreclosed from equal access to that market.

In brief, proof of the following conditions constitutes a per se violation:

1. Proof of a tying arrangement (that is, two products bound together, not merely one product consisting of two or more components bound together, or two entirely separate products that happen to be a part of a single transaction).

2. Market power in the tying product.
3. That a substantial amount of commerce in the tied product is adversely affected.

While the courts have clearly looked with disfavor on tying agreements, certain conditions do justify such arrangements. For example, a tying agreement is more likely to be acceptable when employed by a new competitor seeking entry against established sellers. What argument would the reader offer in defense of a computer lessor who required its lessee to use only the tabulating cards supplied by the lessor? See *IBM* v. *U.S.*, 298 U.S. 131 (1936).

The 1992 *Kodak* case that follows illustrates tying arrangement analysis and affirms the Supreme Court's continuing interest in antitrust action under appropriate economic and legal circumstances.

KODAK v. IMAGE TECHNICAL SERVICES
112 S.Ct. 2072 (1992)

Justice Blackmun

This is yet another case that concerns the standard for summary judgment in an antitrust controversy. The principal issue here is whether a defendant's lack of market power in the primary equipment market precludes—as a matter of law—the possibility of market power in derivative aftermarkets.

Petitioner Eastman Kodak Company manufactures and sells photocopiers and micrographic equipment. Kodak also sells service and replacement parts for its equipment. Respondents are 18 independent service organizations (ISOs) that in the early 1980s began servicing Kodak copying and micrographic equipment. Kodak subsequently adopted policies to limit the availability of parts to ISOs and to make it more difficult for ISOs to compete with Kodak in servicing Kodak equipment.

* * * * *

I
A

Kodak equipment is unique. . . . Kodak parts are not compatible with other manufacturers' equipment, and vice versa. . . .

* * * * *

Kodak provides service and parts for its machines to its customers. It produces some of the parts itself; the rest are made to order for Kodak by independent original-equipment manufacturers (OEMs). Kodak does not sell a complete system of original equipment, lifetime service, and lifetime parts for a single price. Instead, Kodak provides service after the initial warranty period either through annual service contracts, which include all necessary parts, or on a per-call basis. It charges, through negotiations and bidding, different prices for equipment, service, and parts for different customers. Kodak provides 80% to 95% of the service for Kodak machines.

Beginning in the early 1980s, ISOs began repairing and servicing Kodak equipment. They also sold parts and reconditioned and sold used Kodak equipment. Their customers were federal, state, and local government agencies, banks, insurance companies, industrial enterprises, and providers of specialized copy and microfilming services. ISOs provide service at a price substantially lower than Kodak does. Some customers found that the ISO service was of higher quality.

Some of the ISOs' customers purchase their own parts and hire ISOs only for service. Others choose ISOs to supply both service and parts. ISOs keep an inventory of parts, purchased from Kodak or other sources, primarily the OEMs.

In 1985 and 1986, Kodak implemented a policy of selling replacement parts for micrographic and copying machines only to buyers of Kodak equipment who use Kodak service or repair their own machines.

As part of the same policy, Kodak sought to limit ISO access to other sources of Kodak parts. Kodak and the OEMs agreed that the OEMs would not sell parts that fit Kodak equipment to anyone other than Kodak. Kodak also pressured Kodak equipment owners and independent parts distributors not to sell Kodak parts to ISOs. In addition, Kodak took steps to restrict the availability of used machines.

Kodak intended, through these policies, to make it more difficult for ISOs to sell service for Kodak machines. It succeeded. ISOs were unable to obtain parts from reliable sources, and many were forced out of business, while others lost substantial revenue. Customers were forced to switch to Kodak service even though they preferred ISO service.

B

In 1987, the ISOs filed the present action in the District Court, alleging that Kodak had unlawfully tied the sale of service for Kodak machines to the sale of parts, in violation of § 1 of the Sherman Act. [Sherman 2 claims omitted.]

* * * * *

. . . Without a hearing, the District Court granted summary judgment in favor of Kodak.

The court found that respondents had provided no evidence of a tying arrangement between Kodak equipment and service or parts. The court, however, did not address respondents' claim that is at issue here. Respondents allege a tying arrangement not between Kodak *equipment* and service, but between Kodak *parts* and service . . .

The Court of Appeals for the Ninth Circuit, by a divided vote, reversed. 903 F2d 612 (1990) . . . The court first found that whether service and parts were distinct markets and whether a tying arrangement existed between them were disputed issues of fact. Having found that a tying arrangement might exist, the Court of Appeals considered a question not decided by the District Court: was there "an issue of material fact as to whether Kodak has sufficient economic power in the tying product market [parts] to restrain competition appreciably in the tied product market [service]."

* * * * *

The court then considered the three business justifications Kodak proffered for its restrictive parts policy: (1) to guard against inadequate service, (2) to lower inventory costs, and (3) to prevent ISOs from free-riding on Kodak's investment in the copier and micrographic industry. The court concluded that the trier of fact might find the product quality and inventory reasons to be pretextual and that there was a less restrictive alternative for achieving Kodak's quality-related goals. The court also found Kodak's third justification, preventing ISOs from profiting on Kodak's investments in the equipment markets, legally insufficient.

* * * * *

II

* * * * *

A

For the respondents to defeat a motion for summary judgment on their claim of a tying arrangement, a reasonable trier of fact must be able to find, first, that service and parts are two distinct products, and, second, that Kodak has tied the sale of the two products.

* * * * *

Kodak insists that because there is no demand for parts separate from service, there cannot be separate markets for service and parts. By that logic, we would be forced to conclude that there can never be separate markets, for example, for cameras and film, computers and software, or automobiles and tires. That is an assumption we are unwilling to make.

* * * * *

Kodak's assertion also appears to be incorrect as a factual matter. At least some consumers would purchase service without parts, because some service does not require parts, and some consumers, those who self-service for example, would purchase parts without service. . . .

Finally, respondents have presented sufficient evidence of a tie between service and parts. The record indicates that Kodak would sell parts to third parties only if they agreed not to buy service from ISOs.

B

Having found sufficient evidence of a tying arrangement, we consider the other necessary feature of an illegal tying arrangement: appreciable economic power in the tying market. Market power is the power "to force a purchaser to do something that he would not do in a competitive market." *Jefferson Parish,* 466 US, at 14 . . .

1

Respondents contend that Kodak has more than sufficient power in the parts market to force unwanted purchases of the tied market, service. Respondents provide evidence that certain parts are available exclusively through Kodak. Respondents also assert that Kodak has control over the availability of parts it does not manufacture. According to respondents' evidence, Kodak has prohibited independent manufacturers from selling Kodak parts to ISOs, pressured Kodak equipment owners and independent parts distributors to deny ISOs the purchase of Kodak parts, and taken steps to restrict the availability of used machines.

Respondents also allege that Kodak's control over the parts market has excluded service competition, boosted service prices, and forced unwilling consumption of Kodak service. Respondents offer evidence that consumers have switched to Kodak service even though they preferred ISO service, that Kodak service was of higher price and lower quality than the preferred ISO service, and that ISOs were driven out of business by Kodak's policies. Under our prior precedents, this evidence would be sufficient to entitle respondents to a trial on their claim of market power.

2

Kodak counters that even if it concedes monopoly *share* of the relevant parts market, it cannot actually exercise the necessary market *power* for a Sherman Act violation. This is so, according to Kodak, because competition exists in the equipment market. Kodak argues that it could not have the ability to raise prices of service and parts above the level that would be charged in a competitive market because any increase in profits from a higher price in the aftermarkets at least would be offset by a corresponding loss in profits from lower equipment sales as consumers began purchasing equipment with more attractive service costs.

Kodak does not present any actual data on the equipment, service, or parts markets . . .

* * * * *

Kodak contends that there is no need to examine the facts when the issue is market power in the aftermarkets. A legal presumption against a finding of market power is warranted in this situation, according to Kodak, because the existence of market power in the service and parts markets absent power in the equipment market "simply makes no economic sense," and the absence of a legal presumption would deter procompetitive behavior. *Matsushita,* 475 US, at 587.

* * * * *

Kodak . . . bears a substantial burden in showing that it is entitled to summary judgment. It must show that despite evidence of increased prices and excluded competition, an inference of market power is unreasonable. To determine whether Kodak has met that burden, we must unravel the factual assumptions underlying its proposed rule that lack of power in the equipment market necessarily precludes power in the aftermarkets.

* * * * *

To review Kodak's theory, it contends that higher service prices will lead to a disastrous drop in equipment sales. Presumably, the theory's corollary is to the effect that low service prices lead to a dramatic increase in equipment sales. According to the theory, one would have expected Kodak to take advantage of lower-priced ISO service as an opportunity to expand equipment sales. Instead, Kodak adopted a restrictive sales policy consciously designed to eliminate the lower-priced ISO service, an act that would be expected to devastate either Kodak's equipment sales or Kodak's faith in its theory. Yet, according to the record, it has done neither. Service prices have risen for Kodak customers, but there is no evidence or assertion that Kodak equipment sales have dropped.

Kodak and the United States attempt to reconcile Kodak's theory with the contrary actual results by describing a "marketing strategy of spreading over time the total cost to the buyer of Kodak equipment." In other words, Kodak could charge subcompetitive prices for equipment and make up the difference with supracompetitive prices for service, resulting in an overall competitive price. This pricing strategy would provide an explanation for the theory's descriptive failings—if Kodak in fact had adopted it. But Kodak never has asserted that it prices its equipment or parts subcompetitively and recoups its profits through service. Instead, it claims that it prices its equipment comparably to its competitors, and intends that both its equipment sales and service divisions be profitable . . .

Respondents offer a forceful reason why Kodak's theory, although perhaps intuitively appealing, may not accurately explain the behavior of the primary and derivative markets for complex durable goods: the existence of significant information and switching costs . . .

For the service-market price to affect equipment demand, consumers must inform themselves of the total cost of the "package"—equipment, service and parts—at the time of purchase; that is, consumers must engage in accurate lifecycle pricing . . .

Much of this information is difficult—some of it impossible—to acquire at the time of purchase . . .

Kodak acknowledges the cost of information, but suggests, again without evidentiary support, that customer information needs will be satisfied by competitors in the equipment markets . . .

Moreover, even if consumers were capable of acquiring and processing the complex body of information, they may choose not to do so. Acquiring the information is expensive. If the costs of service are small relative to the equipment price, or if consumers are more concerned about equipment capabilities than service costs, they may not find it cost-efficient to compile the information . . .

* * * * *

Given the potentially high cost of information and the possibility a seller may be able to price-discriminate between knowledgeable and unsophisticated consumers, it makes little sense to assume, in the absence of any evidentiary support, that equipment-purchasing decisions are based on an accurate assessment of the total cost of equipment, service, and parts over the lifetime of the machine.

Indeed, respondents have presented evidence that Kodak practices price-discrimination by selling parts to customers who service their own equipment, but refusing to sell parts to customers who hire third-party service companies . . .

A second factor undermining Kodak's claim that supracompetitive prices in the service market lead to ruinous losses in equipment sales is the cost to current owners of switching to a different product. If the cost of switching is high, consumers who already have purchased the equipment, and are thus "locked-in," will tolerate some level of service-price increases before changing equipment brands. Under this scenario, a seller profitably could maintain supracompetitive prices in the aftermarket if the switching costs were high relative to the increase in service prices, and the number of locked-in customers were high relative to the number of new purchasers.

* * * * *

We conclude, then, that Kodak has failed to demonstrate that respondents' inference of market power in the service and parts markets is unreasonable, and that, consequently, Kodak is entitled to summary judgment. It is clearly reasonable to infer that Kodak has market power to raise prices and drive out competition in the aftermarkets, since respondents offer direct evidence that Kodak did so. It is also plausible, as discussed above, to infer that Kodak chose to gain immediate profits by exerting that market power where locked-in customers, high information costs, and discriminatory pricing limited and perhaps eliminated any long-term loss. Viewing the evidence in the light most favorable to respondents, their allegations of market power "mak[e] . . . economic sense." . . .

* * * * *

We therefore affirm the denial of summary judgment.

Questions

1. *a.* What is the tying product in this case?
   b. The tied product?
2. What is the central issue in this case?
3. Kodak claims that "lack of power in the equipment market necessarily precludes power in the aftermarkets." Explain.
4. *a.* Explain the meaning of "cost of information."
   b. What is its significance in this case?
5. Explain Kodak's "free rider" concern.
6. The plaintiff ISOs prevailed in this case. What did they win?
7. Explain the legal result if Kodak had tied its parts and services to its original equipment.
8. Antitrust expert Gordon Spivak says the *Kodak* decision contains three messages: "(1) facts are more important than theory; (2) theory is still important; and (3) antitrust protects things other than allocative efficiencies—namely, it protects against unfairness."[16] Spivak went on to say that after *Kodak,* there will be "more litigation, more development of facts, and litigation will consider factors other than allocative efficiencies."[17]
   Explain what Spivak means in each instance.
9. When "Late Night with David Letterman" was an NBC show, the network, for some time, required those wanting to advertise on "Late Night" to also buy spots on the "Tonight Show."
   a. Does that packaging constitute a tying arrangement?
   b. Was it lawful? Explain.
10. Chrysler included the price of a sound system in the base price of its cars. Chrysler's share of the auto market was 10 to 12 percent. Chrysler did not reveal the "subprice" for the sound systems. Independent audio dealers objected on antitrust grounds. Explain their claim. Decide. See *Town Sound and Custom Tops, Inc.* v. *Chrysler Motor Corp.,* 959 F.2d 468 (1992); cert. den., 113 S.Ct. 196 (1992).

EXCLUSIVE DEALING AND REQUIREMENTS CONTRACTS

Principal legislation: Clayton Act, Section 3; Sherman Act, Section 1.

An *exclusive dealing* contract is an agreement in which a buyer commits itself to deal only with a specific seller, thus cutting competing sellers out of that share of the market. A *requirements* contract is one in which a seller agrees to supply all of a buyer's needs, or a buyer agrees to purchase all of a seller's output, or both. These arrangements have the disadvantage of closing markets to potential competitors. After defining the relevant product and geographic markets, the test is essentially that applied to vertical mergers—what percentage of the relevant market is foreclosed by the agreement? Does the agreement foreclose a source of supply of sufficient magnitude as to substantially lessen competition? Does the agreement foreclose a market for sales of sufficient magnitude to substantially lessen competition?

Exclusive dealing and requirements contracts do not constitute per se violations of the law. Indeed, it is important to recognize some of the merits of such arrangements, as once articulated by Justice Frankfurter of the U.S. Supreme Court.[18] For the buyer, these merits include:

1. Ensuring supply.
2. Protecting against price rises.
3. Enabling long-term planning on the basis of known costs.
4. Reducing the risk and expense of storing products with fluctuating demand.

For the seller, the merits include:

1. Reducing selling expenses.
2. Protecting against price fluctuation.
3. Offering a predictable market.

PRICE DISCRIMINATION

Principal legislation: Clayton Act, Section 2, as amended by the Robinson-Patman Act:

That it shall be unlawful for any person engaged in commerce . . . to discriminate in price between different purchasers of commodities of like grade and quality, where either or any of the purchases involved in such discrimination are in commerce . . . and where the effect of such discrimination may be substantially to lessen competition or tend to create a monopoly in any line of commerce, or to injure, destroy, or prevent competition with any person who either grants or knowingly receives the benefit of such discrimination, or with customers of either of them . . . Provided that nothing herein contained shall prevent differentials which make only due allowance for differences in the cost of manufacture, sale, or delivery resulting from the differing methods or quantities in which such commodities are to such purchasers sold or delivered . . . And, provided further, that nothing herein contained shall prevent price changes from time to time where in response to changing conditions affecting the market for or the marketability of the goods concerned, such as but not limited to actual or imminent deterioration of perishable goods, obsolescence of seasonal goods, distress sales under court process, or sales in good faith in discontinuance of business in the goods concerned . . .

Provided, however, that nothing herein contained shall prevent a seller rebutting the prima facie case thus made by showing that his lower price or the furnishing of services or facilities to any purchaser or purchasers was made in good faith to meet an equally low price of a competitor, or the services or facilities furnished by a competitor.

In brief, *price discrimination* involves selling substantially identical goods (not services) at reasonably contemporaneous times to different purchasers at different prices, where the effect may be to substantially lessen competition or to tend to create a monopoly. A seller may prevail against such a charge by establishing one of the following defenses: (1) The price differential is attributable to cost savings associated with the least expensive sale. However, in practice, the difficulties in proving cost savings have made successful defenses on that ground quite uncommon. (2) The price differential is attributable to a good faith effort to meet the equally low price of a competitor. (3) Certain transactions are exempt from the act. Of special note is a price change made in response to a changing market. Thus, prices might lawfully be altered for seasonal goods or perishables. Price discrimination is perhaps best understood by reference to diagrams.[19]

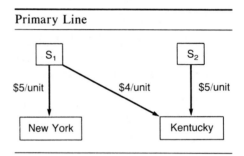

The harm here falls at the seller's level, the primary line, in that S_1's pricing policy may harm S_2. The specific fear is that S_1 will use its income from sales in New York to subsidize its lower price in Kentucky. S_1 may then be able to drive S_2 from the market. This is precisely the harm that Congress feared would be generated by the advance of chain stores across the nation. Of course, S_1 may be able to offer a defense to explain the pricing differential. For example, the price differential might be permissible if designed to allow S_1 to get a foothold in a new market. Remember that a price discrimination violation requires a showing of competitive injury.

Now turn to the "Secondary Line" table on the next page. B_1 and B_2 are direct competitors. Absent a defense, S_1 is clearly engaging in price discrimination. Here, the harm falls at the buyers' level (secondary line).

Harm may also fall on customers of customers, that is, tertiary price discrimination.

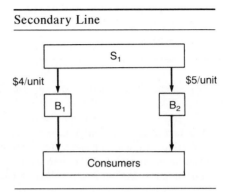

Secondary Line

Predatory Pricing

In 1993, an Arkansas state trial court found the giant retailer Wal-Mart guilty of violating an Arkansas law that forbids selling goods below cost for the purpose of injuring competitors and destroying competition. Three local pharmacies accused Wal-Mart of selling drugs and other items below cost at their Conway, Arkansas, superstore. The judge awarded $298,407 in damages to the three pharmacies, triple their actual damages. Wal-Mart conceded that it had sold some items below cost, but it denied any intent to harm competition. A loss for Wal-Mart on appeal would be quite important, because 22 other states have statutes similar to the Arkansas law.

The *Brooke* case that follows is the definitive federal judicial interpretation of predatory pricing. As you will see, had the Wal-Mart case been tried at the federal level, it likely would have been rejected because Wal-Mart could not have driven out all of the competition. And had it had some success in driving out competition via predatory prices, it would then have needed to raise prices to recoup its losses, which, in turn, would have invited new competitors to enter the market.

In the *Brooke* case, Liggett (now Brooke) tries to show that Brown & Williamson engaged in primary line price discrimination by selling generic cigarettes at prices below its average variable cost. Liggett claimed that Brown & Williamson's volume rebates constituted price discrimination, which facilitated predatory pricing. A showing of predatory pricing satisfies the Robinson-Patman requirement that the effect of the pricing "may be substantially to lessen competition."

BROOKE GROUP v. BROWN & WILLIAMSON
113 S. Ct. 2578 (1993)

Justice Kennedy

This case stems from a market struggle that erupted in the domestic cigarette industry in the mid-1980's. Petitioner Brooke Group, Inc., whom we, like the parties to the case, refer to as Liggett because of its former corporate name, charges that to counter its innovative development of generic cigarettes, respondent Brown & Williamson Tobacco Corporation introduced its own line of generic cigarettes in an unlawful effort to stifle price competition in the economy segment of the national cigarette market. Liggett contends that Brown & Williamson cut prices on generic cigarettes below cost and offered discriminatory volume rebates to wholesalers to force Liggett to raise its own generic cigarette prices and introduce oligopoly pricing in the economy segment.

I

In 1980, Liggett pioneered the development of the economy segment of the national cigarette market by introducing a line of "black and white" generic cigarettes. The economy segment of the market, sometimes called the generic segment, is characterized by its bargain prices and comprises a variety of different products: black and whites, which are true generics sold in plain white packages with simple black lettering describing their contents; private label generics, which carry the trade dress of a specific purchaser, usually a retail chain; branded generics, which carry a brand name but which, like black and whites and private label generics, are sold at a deep discount and with little or no advertising; and "Value-25s," packages of 25 cigarettes that are sold to the consumer some 12.5% below the cost of a normal 20-cigarette pack. By 1984, when Brown & Williamson entered the generic segment and set in motion the series of events giving rise to this suit, Liggett's black and whites represented 97% of the generic segment, which in turn accounted for a little more than 4% of domestic cigarette sales. Prior to Liggett's introduction of black and whites in 1980, sales of generic cigarettes amounted to less than 1% of the domestic cigarette market.

. . . Cigarette manufacturing has long been one of America's most concentrated industries . . . and for decades, production has been dominated by six firms: R. J. Reynolds, Philip Morris, American Brands, Lorillard, and the two litigants involved here . . . R. J. Reynolds and Philip Morris, the two industry leaders, enjoyed respective market shares of about 28% and 40% at the time of trial. Brown & Williamson ran a distant third, its market share never exceeding 12% at any time relevant to this dispute. Liggett's share of the market was even less, from a low of just over 2% in 1980 to a high of just over 5% in 1984.

The cigarette industry also has long been one of America's most profitable, in part because for many years there was no significant price competition among the rival firms. List prices for cigarettes increased in lock-step, twice a year, for a number of years, irrespective of the rate of inflation, changes in the costs of production, or shifts in consumer demand . . .

By 1980, however, broad market trends were working against the industry. Overall demand for cigarettes in the United States was declining . . . Once a major force in the industry, with market shares in excess of 20%, Liggett's market share had declined by 1980 to a little over 2%. With this meager share of the market, Liggett was on the verge of going out of business.

. . . Liggett took an unusual step to revive its prospects: It developed a line of black and white generic cigarettes. When introduced in 1980, black and whites were offered to consumers at a list price roughly 30% lower than the list price of full-priced, branded cigarettes . . . Liggett's black and whites were an immediate and considerable success, growing from a fraction of a percent of the market at their introduction to over 4% of the total cigarette market by early 1984.

. . . In general, the growth of generics came at the expense of the other firms' profitable sales of branded cigarettes. Brown & Williamson was hardest hit, because many of Brown & Williamson's brands were favored by consumers who were sensitive to changes in cigarette prices. Although Brown & Williamson sold only 11.4% of the market's branded cigarettes, 20% of the converts to Liggett's black and whites had switched from a Brown & Williamson brand. Losing volume and profits in its branded products, Brown & Williamson determined to enter the generic segment of the cigarette market. In July 1983, Brown & Williamson had begun selling Value-25s, and in the spring of 1984, it introduced its own black and white cigarette.

* * * * *

. . . At the retail level, the suggested list price of Brown & Williamson's black and whites was the same as Liggett's, but Brown & Williamson's volume discounts to wholesalers were larger . . .

Liggett responded to Brown & Williamson's introduction of black and whites in two ways. First, Liggett increased its own wholesale rebates. This precipitated a price war at the wholesale level, in which Liggett five times attempted to beat the rebates offered by Brown & Williamson. At the end of each round, Brown & Williamson maintained a real advantage over Liggett's prices. Although it is undisputed that Brown & Williamson's original net price for its black and whites was above its costs, Liggett contends that by the end of the rebate war, Brown & Williamson was selling its black and whites at a loss . . .

Liggett's second response was to file a lawsuit.

* * * * *

[Liggett alleged that Brown & Williamson's volume rebates to wholesalers amounted to price discrimination. Liggett claimed] that Brown & Williamson's discriminatory volume rebates were integral to a scheme of predatory pricing, in which Brown & Williamson reduced its net prices for generic cigarettes below average variable costs. According to Liggett, these below-cost prices were not promotional but were intended to pressure it to raise its list prices on generic cigarettes, so that the percentage price difference between generic and branded cigarettes would narrow . . .

* * * * *

After a 115-day trial . . . the jury [found] . . . that Brown & Williamson had engaged in price discrimination . . . The jury awarded Liggett $49.6 million in damages, which the District Court trebled to $148.8 million. After reviewing the record, however, the District Court held that Brown & Williamson was entitled to judgment as a matter of law on three separate grounds: lack of injury to competition, lack of antitrust injury to Liggett, and lack of a causal link between the discriminatory rebates and Liggett's alleged injury. *Liggett Group, Inc.* v. *Brown & Williamson Tobacco Corp.,* 748 F. Supp. 344 (MDNC 1990) . . .

The United States Court of Appeals for the Fourth Circuit affirmed. *Liggett Group, Inc.* v. *Brown & Williamson Tobacco Corp.,* 964 F. 2d 335 (1992) . . .

II
A

* * * * *

Liggett contends that Brown & Williamson's discriminatory volume rebates to wholesalers threatened substantial competitive injury by furthering a predatory pricing scheme designed to purge competition from the economy segment of the cigarette market. This type of injury, which harms direct competitors of the discriminating seller, is known as primary-line injury . . .

* * * * *

. . . [P]rimary-line competitive injury under the Robinson-Patman Act is of the same general character as the injury inflicted by predatory pricing schemes actionable under § 2 of the Sherman Act . . . [T]he essence of the claim under either statute is the same: A business rival has priced its products in an unfair manner with an object to eliminate or retard competition and thereby gain and exercise control over prices in the relevant market.

Accordingly, whether the claim alleges predatory pricing under § 2 of the Sherman Act or primary-line price discrimination under the Robinson-Patman Act, two prerequisites to recovery remain the same. First, a plaintiff seeking to establish competitive injury resulting from a rival's low prices must prove that the prices complained of are below an appropriate measure of its rival's costs* . . .

* * * * *

The second prerequisite to holding a competitor liable under the antitrust laws for charging low prices is a demonstration that the competitor had a reasonable prospect, or, under § 2 of the Sherman Act, a dangerous probability, of recouping its investment in below-cost prices . . .

That below-cost pricing may impose painful losses on its target is of no moment to the antitrust laws if competition is not injured: It is axiomatic that the antitrust laws were passed for "the protection of *competition,* not *competitors."* . . .

For recoupment to occur, below-cost pricing must be capable, as a threshold matter, of producing the intended effects on the firm's rivals, whether driving them from the market, or, as was alleged to be the goal here, causing them to raise their prices to supracompetitive levels within a disciplined oligopoly . . .

* * * * *

---

*Because the parties in this case agree that the relevant measure of cost is average variable cost, we again decline to resolve the conflict among the lower courts over the appropriate measure of cost.

B

Liggett does not allege that Brown & Williamson sought to drive it from the market but that Brown & Williamson sought to preserve supracompetitive profits on branded cigarettes by pressuring Liggett to raise its generic cigarette prices through a process of tacit collusion with the other cigarette companies. Tacit collusion, sometimes called oligopolistic price co-ordination or conscious parallelism, describes the process, not in itself unlawful, by which firms in a concentrated market might in effect share monopoly power, setting their prices at a profit-maximizing, supracompetitive level by recognizing their shared economic interests . . .

* * * * *

III
A

* * * * *

Although Brown & Williamson's entry into the generic segment could be regarded as procompetitive in intent as well as effect, the record contains sufficient evidence from which a reasonable jury could conclude that Brown & Williamson envisioned or intended this anticompetitive course of events. There is also sufficient evidence in the record from which a reasonable jury could conclude that for a period of approximately 18 months, Brown & Williamson's prices on its generic cigarettes were below its costs and that this below-cost pricing imposed losses on Liggett . . . Liggett has failed to demonstrate competitive injury as a matter of law, however, because its proof is flawed in a critical respect: The evidence is inadequate to show that in pursuing this scheme, Brown & Williamson had a reasonable prospect of recovering its losses from below-cost pricing through slowing the growth of generics . . .

* * * * *

B

Based on Liggett's theory of the case and the record it created, there are two means by which one might infer that Brown & Williamson had a reasonable prospect of producing sustained supracompetitive pricing in the generic segment adequate to recoup its predatory losses: first, if generic output or price information indicates that oligopolistic price coordination in fact produced supracompetitive prices in the generic segment; or second, if evidence about the market and Brown & Williamson's conduct indicate that the alleged scheme was likely to have brought about tacit coordination and oligopoly pricing in the generic segment, even if it did not actually do so.

1

In this case, the price and output data do not support a reasonable inference that Brown & Williamson and the other cigarette companies elevated prices above a competitive level for generic cigarettes. Supracompetitive pricing entails a restriction in output . . .

Following Brown & Williamson's entry, the rate at which generic cigarettes were capturing market share did not slow; indeed, the average rate of growth doubled . . .

* * * * *

In arguing that Brown & Williamson was able to exert market power and raise generic prices above a competitive level in the generic category through tacit price coordination with the other cigarette manufacturers, Liggett places its principal reliance on direct evidence of price behavior. This evidence demonstrates that the list prices on all cigarettes, generic and branded alike, rose to a significant degree during the late 1980's . . .

A reasonable jury, however, could not have drawn the inferences Liggett proposes. All of Liggett's data is based upon the list prices of various categories of cigarettes. Yet the jury had before it undisputed evidence that during the period in question, list prices were not the actual prices paid by consumers. As the market became unsettled in the mid-1980s, the cigarette companies invested substantial sums in promotional schemes, including coupons, stickers, and giveaways, that reduced the actual cost of cigarettes to consumers below list prices . . .

* * * * *

2

Not only does the evidence fail to show actual supracompetitive pricing in the generic segment, it also does not demonstrate its likelihood. At the time Brown & Williamson entered the generic segment, the cigarette industry as a whole faced declining demand and possessed substantial excess capacity. These circumstances tend to break down patterns of oligopoly pricing and produce price competition . . .

* * * * *

Even if all the cigarette companies were willing to participate in a scheme to restrain the growth of the generic segment, they would not have been able to coordinate their actions and raise prices above a competitive level unless they understood that Brown & Williamson's entry into the segment was not a genuine effort to compete with Liggett. If even one other firm misinterpreted Brown & Williamson's entry as an effort to expand share, a chain reaction of competitive responses would almost certainly have resulted, and oligopoly discipline would have broken down . . .

* * * * *

Finally, although some of Brown & Williamson's corporate planning documents speak of a desire to slow the growth of the segment, no objective evidence of its conduct permits a reasonable inference that it had any real prospect of doing so through anticompetitive means. It is undisputed that when Brown & Williamson introduced its generic cigarettes, it offered them to a thousand wholesalers who had never before purchased generic cigarettes. The inevitable effect of this marketing effort was to expand the segment, as the new wholesalers recruited retail outlets to carry generic cigarettes. Even with respect to wholesalers already carrying generics, Brown & Williamson's unprecedented volume rebates had a similar expansionary effect . . . By providing substantial incentives for wholesalers to place large orders, Brown & Williamson created strong pressure for them to sell more generic cigarettes . . . [M]any wholesalers passed portions of the rebates about which Liggett complains on to consumers, thus dropping the retail price of generics and further stimulating demand. Brown & Williamson provided a further, direct stimulus, through some $10 million it spent during the period of alleged predation placing discount stickers on its generic cartons to reduce prices to the ultimate consumer. In light of these uncontested facts about Brown & Williamson's conduct, it is not reasonable to conclude that Brown & Williamson threatened in a serious way to restrict output, raise prices above a competitive level, and artificially slow the growth of the economy segment of the national cigarette market.

* * * * *

IV

. . . We hold that the evidence cannot support a finding that Brown & Williamson's alleged scheme was likely to result in oligopolistic price coordination and sustained supracompetitive pricing in the generic segment of the national cigarette market. Without this, Brown & Williamson had no reasonable prospect of recouping its predatory losses and could not inflict the injury to competition the antitrust laws prohibit . . .

Affirmed.

Justice Stevens, with whom Justice White and Justice Blackmun join, dissenting.

---

* * * * *

. . . The evidence presented supports the conclusion that B&W's price war was intended to discipline Liggett for its unprecedented use of price competition in an industry that had enjoyed handsome supracompetitive profits for about half a century . . . [T]his . . . must be viewed against a background of supracompetitive, parallel pricing, in which "prices for cigarettes increased in lockstep, twice a year . . . irrespective of the rate of inflation, changes in the cost of production, or shifts in consumer demand." . . .

* * * * *

As a matter of economics, the Court reminds us that price-cutting is generally pro-competitive, and hence a "boon to consumers." This is true, however, only so long as reduced prices do not fall below cost . . . When a predator deliberately engages in below-cost pricing targeted at a particular competitor over a sustained period of time, then price-cutting raises a credible inference that harm to competition is likely to ensue.

Questions

1. Why did Liggett's claim fail in this case?
2. *a.* Why was Liggett required to show that Brown & Williamson could recoup its losses from price discrimination in order to prove a Robinson-Patman violation?
   b. How might Brown & Williamson harm its competitor, Liggett, and yet not harm competition?

3. Price-cutting is desirable. Why does the dissent object to Brown & Williamson's price-cutting scheme?
4. Define average variable cost.
5. Texaco sold gasoline at its retail tank wagon prices to Hasbrouck, an independent Texaco retailer, but granted discounts to distributors Gull and Dompier. Dompier also sold at the retail level. Gull and Dompier both delivered their gas directly to retailers and did not maintain substantial storage facilities. During the period in question, sales at the stations supplied by the two distributors grew dramatically, while Hasbrouck's sales declined. Hasbrouck filed suit against Texaco, claiming that the distributor discount constituted a Robinson-Patman violation. Texaco defended, saying the discount reflected the services the distributors performed for Texaco, and that the arrangement did not harm competition.

   Decide. Explain. See *Texaco* v. *Ricky Hasbrouck,* 496 U.S. 543 (1990).
6. Utah Pie produced frozen pies in its Salt Lake City plant. Utah's competitors, Carnation, Pet, and Continental, sometimes sold pies in Salt Lake City at prices beneath those charged in other markets. Indeed, Continental's prices in Salt Lake City were beneath its direct costs plus overhead. Pet sold to Safeway using Safeway's private label at a price lower than that at which the same pies were sold under the Pet label. Pet employed an industrial spy to infiltrate Utah Pie and gather information. Utah Pie claimed that Carnation, Pet, and Continental were in violation of Robinson-Patman. Decide. Explain. See *Utah Pie Co.* v. *Continental Baking Co.,* 386 U.S. 685 (1967).

BUYER DISCRIMINATION

Robinson-Patman also forbids price discrimination on the part of buyers—a buyer may not knowingly induce or receive a discriminatory price. This prohibition resulted from the legislators' concern that large purchasers (e.g., supermarket chains and discount stores) would take advantage of their buying power to compel suppliers to sell to them at much lower prices than would be accorded to smaller purchasers (e.g., the corner grocery store). The result would be to give a competitive advantage to the larger purchasers. In such situations, buyers may assert the Robinson-Patman defenses in the manner we have described for sellers.

Afterword

Managers must take antitrust law seriously. For example, Du Pont distributed a small plastic card (like a credit card) to its employees on which were printed the following "Ten Don'ts of Antitrust." As you can see, those "don'ts" are a brief summary of most of the primary issues in this chapter.

---

1. Don't discuss prices with competitors.
2. Don't divide customers, markets, or territories with competitors.
3. Don't agree upon or attempt to control a customer's resale price.
4. Don't attempt to restrict a customer's resale activity.
5. Don't offer a customer prices or terms more favorable than those offered competing customers.
6. Don't require a customer to buy a product only from you.
7. Don't use one product as bait to sell another.
8. Don't disparage a competitor's product unless the statements are true.
9. Don't make sales or purchases conditional on reciprocal purchases or sales.
10. Don't hesitate to consult with your legal counsel.

CHAPTER QUESTIONS

1. After reading this entire chapter, what is your judgment about the antitrust system?
   a. Does it work? Explain.
   b. How might it be altered?
   c. Could we place more reliance on the market? Explain.
   d. Do the statutes and case law, as a body, seem to form a rational package? Explain.

2. Scholar and jurist Richard Posner argues:

   > [T]he protection of small business whatever its intrinsic merit cannot be attained within the framework of antitrust principles and procedures. The small businessman is, in general, helped rather than hurt by monopoly, so unless the antitrust laws are stood completely on their head they are an inapt vehicle (compared, say, to tax preferences) for assisting small business.[20]

   a. Is antitrust law an inappropriate vehicle for protecting small business? Explain.
   b. Should we protect small business? Explain.
   c. How does the presence of monopolies benefit small business?
   d. If it is not the proper vehicle for protecting small business, what role should antitrust law properly serve? For example, should social considerations (such as the maintenance of full employment and the dispersal of political power) assume greater importance? Or should antitrust policy hew as closely as possible to economic goals? Explain.

3. Falls City, formerly a brewer in Evansville, Indiana, raised prices to its wholesale distributor in Kentucky, just across the state line from Evansville. At the same time, Falls City raised its prices to its distributor in Indiana, Vanco Beverages, by a greater margin than that to the Kentucky distributor. The resulting price differential caused higher retail beer prices in the Indiana market than in Kentucky. (Indiana law prohibited wholesalers from selling out of state and prohibited retailers from going out of state to make purchases. Further, brewers were required to maintain a uniform price throughout Indiana.) The higher Indiana price was, at least in part, a product of Falls City's policy of following the pricing patterns of other Indiana brewers. Vanco sued, claiming a violation of the Robinson-Patman Act.
   a. Are the facts sufficient to support a prima facie case of price discrimination? Explain.
   b. What defense would you raise on behalf of Falls City?
   c. Decide the case. Explain. See *Falls City Industries, Inc.* v. *Vanco Beverage, Inc.,* 103 S. Ct. 1282 (1983).

4. A group of lawyers in private practice in the District of Columbia agreed to decline further appointments to represent indigent criminal defendants until the

local government increased their compensation to a level believed satisfactory by the lawyers. That agreement was challenged by the Federal Trade Commission.

   a. What violation(s) was asserted by the FTC?
   b. What defenses were offered by the group of lawyers?
   c. Decide. Explain. See *Federal Trade Commission* v. *Superior Court Trial Lawyers Association,* 493 U.S. 411 (1990).

5. A utility charged home building contractors up to $200 as the fee for completing underground connections, but no charge for connection was assessed where the builder agreed to make the home "all electric." The plaintiff alleged a violation of the antitrust laws.

   a. What was the alleged violation?
   b. Decide the case. Explain. See *Washington Gas Light Co.* v. *Virginia Elec. and Power Co.,* 438 F.2d 248 (4th Cir. 1971).

6. Could Amana, the appliance manufacturer, lawfully refuse to deal with any purchaser who sells the products of a competitor such as Maytag? Explain.

7. Assume you seek to build and operate a clothing store. You hire a contractor, who purchases cement blocks from a manufacturer. After the building is complete, you discover evidence suggesting that your contractor was overcharged for the blocks because of a price-fixing scheme to which the block manufacturer was a party. Does the law permit you as an indirect purchaser to file an antitrust suit to recover the damages you sustained as a consequence of the conspiracy? Explain. See *Illinois Brick Co.* v. *Illinois,* 431 U.S. 720 (1977), for a similar situation.

8. SIDA, the State Independent Drivers Association, Inc., was the largest taxi company on Oahu, Hawaii. SIDA's membership was limited to independent taxis. Fleet operators were not admitted. Hawaii's Department of Transportation awarded SIDA the exclusive right to provide taxi service from Honolulu Airport. No restrictions were placed on taxi service to the airport. Charley's Taxi Radio Dispatch Corporation, the largest fleet service on the island, filed suit, challenging, among other things, SIDA's refusal to grant membership to Charley's. At trial, the facts demonstrated that taxi competition was strong on the island of Oahu.

   a. What violation was alleged by Charley's?
   b. Decide. Explain. See *Charley's Taxi Radio Dispatch* v. *SIDA of Hawaii,* 810 F.2 869 (9th Cir. 1987).

9. Assume two fertilizer dealerships, Grow Quick and Fertile Fields, hold 70 percent and 30 percent, respectively, of the fertilizer business in the farm community of What Cheer, Iowa. Assume the owner of Fertile Fields learns via inquiry, hearsay, and the like of Grow Quick's price quotes. Then, each growing season the Fertile Fields owner sets her prices exactly equal to those of her competitor. Is that practice unlawful? Explain.

10. Given identical competing products, why is identical pricing virtually inevitable—at least over the long run?

11. The FTC found the Boise Cascade Corporation in violation of Section 5 of the Federal Trade Commission Act (forbidding unfair methods of competition) for using a delivered pricing system for southern plywood, the price for which was based in part on a rail freight charge computed as though the shipping point of origin was the Pacific Northwest. Historically, plywood had originated largely in the Northwest, but technological developments spurred southeastern production. However, southeastern producers continued to quote plywood prices as though the material had been shipped from the West Coast. The commission contended that the practice inhibited price competition. Boise Cascade argued that the freight factor eased price comparisons between southeastern and northwestern plywood. No agreement among southern plywood producers as to West Coast–delivered pricing was proved. In the absence of an agreement, is this practice unlawful? Explain. *Boise Cascade Corp.* v. *FTC,* 637 F.2d 573 (9th Cir. 1980).

12. Assume firms A, B, C, D, E are charged with price-fixing under Sherman 1 because they have a program of exchanging pricing information among themselves.

   a. What element of Robinson-Patman might be used as a defense in that Sherman 1 action?
   b. Would the court find that defense persuasive? Explain.

13. The A. E. Staley Manufacturing Company, located in Decatur, Illinois, sold its glucose products at a delivered price computed as though Chicago was the shipping point, when in fact shipments originated

EMPLOYER–EMPLOYEE RELATIONS

EMPLOYMENT LAW I:
PROTECTING THE EMPLOYEE

INTRODUCTION

Employee suits against employers are turning the workplace into a legal combat zone.[1]

In 1960, about one-third of the American workforce belonged to unions. Today, that figure is about 11 percent. Collective bargaining (see Chapter 14), established to protect the interests of workers, has proven inadequate to the task.[2] Not surprisingly, federal and state regulations governing work practices have exploded. The variety of protections is prodigious: wage and hour laws, worker safety laws, unemployment compensation, workers' compensation, and social security, to name a few. All managers should have at least an introductory sense of this web of rules that now profoundly influences business conduct.

Part One—Hiring/Retention/Training/Supervision: Employer Liability

Employers increasingly bear civil liability both for their employees' job-related mistakes and misconduct and for rather new forms of negligence claims against the employers for their decisions in hiring, retaining, training, and supervising employees.

SCOPE OF EMPLOYMENT

Under the doctrine of *respondeat superior* (Let the master answer), employers have long been held vicariously (indirectly) liable for harm to third parties caused by the intentional or negligent acts of their employees. Of course, those acts must have occurred in the scope of employment.

In a 1991 case, *Mary M.* v. *City of Los Angeles,*[3] the City was held liable under the doctrine of *respondeat superior* for a sexual assault committed by a police officer. At 2:30 AM on October 3, 1981, Sergeant Leigh Schroyer was on duty, in uniform, carrying a gun, and patrolling in his marked police car. He stopped Mary M. for erratic driving. She pleaded not to be arrested. He ordered her to enter his patrol car and took her to her home. He entered her home and said that he expected "payment" for not arresting her. He raped her and was subsequently sentenced to a term in state prison.

Mary M. sued the City of Los Angeles. The general inquiry was whether Schroyer was acting within the scope of his employment during the rape episode. The jury found for Mary M. and awarded $150,000 in damages. The Court of Appeals reversed, saying the Schroyer was not acting within the scope of his employment. The case went to the California Supreme Court. The City argued that Schroyer was acting on behalf of his own interests rather than those of the City, and that the City had not authorized his conduct. Therefore, Schroyer could not have been acting within the scope of employment. However, the Court said that the correct question was not whether the rape was authorized but whether it happened in the course of a series of acts that were authorized. The Court reversed, saying that a jury could find the City vicariously liable (imputed to the principal from the agent) given the unique authority of police officers in our society.

The Test

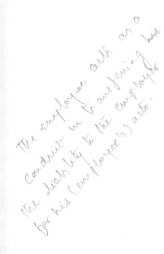

Of course, finding the employer liable does not excuse the employee from her liability. But the *respondeat superior* doctrine does have the potential effect of opening the employer's deeper pockets to the plaintiff. The general trend in these cases has been to expand the definition of the scope of employment. Presently, the standard requires all of the following ingredients:

1. The employee was subject to the employer's supervision.
2. The employee was motivated, at least in part, by desire to serve the employer's business interests.
3. The problem arose substantially within normal working hours and in a work location.
4. The act in question was of the general kind the employee had been hired to perform.

The case that follows, like *Mary M.,* springs from a sexual assault and involves a *respondeat superior* situation, but here the facts are set in the private sector, a crucial difference, as it turns out.

CAPITOL CITY FOODS, INC. v. THE SUPERIOR COURT OF SACRAMENTO COUNTY COURT OF APPEAL OF CALIFORNIA, THIRD APPELLATE DISTRICT 7 Cal. Rptr. 2d 418; 58 Fair Empl. Prac. Cas. (BNA) 1150; 59 Empl. Prac. Dec. (CCH) P41,593; (1992)

Judge Marler

This case raises the issue of an employer's liability for sexual harassment due to the conduct of a supervisory employee while off duty and not at the workplace. The superior court granted defendant Capitol City Foods, Inc.'s motion for summary judgment on all remaining causes of action in plaintiff Mary T.'s lawsuit except the first cause of action for sexual harassment. Defendant petitioned this court for a writ of mandate directing the trial court to grant the motion for summary judgment in its entirety. Defendant contends the undisputed facts reveal an insufficient nexus between the supervisor's conduct and his employment to hold the employer liable.

Factual and Procedural Background

Mary T. began working at defendant's Burger King franchise in January of 1989. Vernon Johnson was the night shift supervisor. On January 29, Mary and a coworker asked Johnson to go with them for a drink. Johnson could not go then, but suggested another time. Mary and Johnson made arrangements to go out on the 31st. They both believed the coworker would accompany them. Neither Johnson nor Mary was scheduled to work that day, but unbeknownst to Johnson, Dan Singh had changed the schedule and scheduled Mary to work that day at 5 P.M. At that time Mary was still in training and had a flexible schedule as she learned the job alongside more experienced workers. On January 31, as arranged, Johnson picked up Mary, who was in her Burger King uniform, at a grocery store at 4 P.M.; the coworker did not show up. They drove around for 45 minutes, during which time Johnson made two phone calls. He called the Burger King and told Dan Singh that he should not have changed the schedule without Johnson's approval and that if Mary wanted to work she would come in late. He also called his parents' house. Johnson took Mary to his parents' house, where they had sexual intercourse. Johnson then dropped Mary off at an auto repair store, and he went to the Burger King. The next day Mary told the manager what had happened, and quit shortly thereafter.

* * * * *

A lawsuit was filed by Mary, her three brothers and their mother as guardian. Named as defendants were Capitol City Foods, Inc., Burger King, Inc., and Vernon Johnson and his parents.* Seven causes of action were stated against Capitol City Foods, Inc. (hereafter defendant): (1) sexual harassment; (2) intentional infliction of emotional distress; (3) misrepresentation; (4) promissory fraud; (5) negligent employment; (6) assault and battery; and

---

*The trial court granted Burger King, Inc.'s motion for summary judgment. Only Capitol City Foods, Inc., is a party to this appeal.

(7) negligent infliction of emotional distress. The complaint also sought punitive damages. [We consider only the first cause of action.]

The first cause of action alleged there was unlawful discrimination on the basis of sex (sexual harassment) against Mary, which included requiring her "to work in an intimidating, hostile and offensive environment." The primary factual allegation to support this cause of action read: "On January 31, 1989, defendant Johnson, abusing his position of authority as shift manager and supervisor of plaintiff Mary [T.], instructed plaintiff Mary [T.], who was dressed in her Burger King uniform and about to enter the premises at 2335 Florin Road, Sacramento, California, to report to her regularly assigned shift, to get into his car and accompany her [sic] to his residence. Defendant Johnson advised her he had made arrangements so that she would not have to punch in on the time clock at work at that time. Defendant Johnson thereupon transported plaintiff Mary [T.] to his residence and raped her." The complaint further alleged Mary was required to then work in the presence of Johnson although he was a known sexual harasser.

* * * * *

Defendant moved for summary judgment . . . the ground as to the first cause of action was that Johnson was not acting as Capitol City's agent when the alleged rape occurred.

* * * * *

Defendant set forth 20 undisputed facts relating to the first cause of action. In addition to the facts of the incident related above, defendant indicated that prior to January 30, Johnson had not made any sexual advances towards Mary, asked her for a date, or indicated her job was conditioned upon sexual favors; she thought he was a good manager. Further, while driving around on the 31st, Johnson did not mention having sex; and, at least until they were in his bedroom, Mary did not object to being with him, nor did Johnson do or say anything that indicated coercion. Defendant had policies against sexual harassment and prohibiting dating among employees. Johnson was aware of the policy against dating, but he did not think it was his employer's business whom he dated on his own time. These facts were supported by excerpts of depositions of Mary and Johnson.

Plaintiff opposed the motion for summary judgment on the grounds that Johnson's conduct was within the scope of his employment . . .

* * * * *

Discussion

The [Fair Employment and Housing] Act makes it an unlawful employment practice for an employer to harass an employee because of sex. For purposes of this subdivision an employer includes anyone acting as an agent of the employer, directly or indirectly . . .

Regulations promulgated under the Act indicate that under the theory of respondeat superior, an employer is liable for harassment by supervisors, managers or agents committed within the scope of employment or the relationship with the employer.

Defendant contends the court abused its discretion by failing to grant its motion for summary judgment on the first cause of action. Defendant argues before an employer can be held strictly liable for the harassing conduct of an employee, even one in a supervisory position, agency principles must first be applied . . .

* * * * *

. . . [D]efendant argues the undisputed evidence reveals an insufficient nexus between Johnson's conduct and his employment to permit the inference that his conduct arose in the course of his employment. Therefore, defendant asserts the issue must be determined in the negative as a matter of law. Defendant points to the undisputed facts that Johnson was off-duty during the incident, the parties agreed to the date, and there was no evidence Johnson used his authority as a supervisor to compel Mary's presence. She did not object to going with him and there was no evidence of coercion. The single fact that he made a phone call regarding her work schedule was insufficient to bring his conduct within the scope of employment.

Precedential decisions of the Fair Employment and Housing Commission have recognized that while the harassing conduct need not occur in the workplace, it must occur in a work-related context . . .

* * * * *

Plaintiff alleged Johnson was acting under his authority as shift manager and supervisor at the time of the harassment. The undisputed evidence, however, negated plaintiff's allegations that Johnson abused his authority by instructing Mary to accompany him. It was undisputed that Mary agreed to meet and accompany Johnson. Nor did she dispute that until she and Johnson entered his bedroom she did not object to being with him and he did or said nothing to indicate coercion.†

Plaintiff contends the nexus between Johnson's conduct and employment is "overwhelming." She argues "but for" his position as her supervisor, the rape would not have occurred. Even assuming this speculative assertion were true, plaintiff must establish Johnson was acting within the scope of his employment or as defendant's agent. To show a sufficient nexus plaintiff points to the following: the "date" was arranged in Johnson's office; when he picked her up she was in her Burger King uniform; and he exercised his authority to excuse her from work so she could be with him, facilitating the rape. This argument overlooks the fact that defendant conclusively refuted the allegation Johnson forced plaintiff to accompany him or coerced her in any way prior to entering his bedroom. In light of this refutation Johnson's phone call to Burger King to excuse Mary from work is insufficient to support an inference that Johnson was acting within the scope of his employment or as the agent of defendant.

* * * * *

Disposition

Let a writ of mandate issue directing the respondent superior court to vacate its order denying defendant's motion for summary judgment on the first cause of action, and to enter a new order granting such motion . . .

Questions

1. Why did Mary M. win in the police case while Mary T. lost in the *Capitol City* case?
2. Why was Vernon Johnson not seen by the court to be operating in the scope of his employment?

† In her deposition Mary said Johnson never told her she had to go out with him. When asked if he ever told her her job depended on her going out with him, she responded: "While he was raping me, yes." . . .

3. What policy justifications support the imposition of liability on an employer for the wrongs of an employee operating within the scope of employment?
4. A plaintiff lost one leg and the use of an arm in an accident involving a defendant's employee. The employee had asked his nephew, the plaintiff, to ride on a tractor with him while he disked the defendant's orchard. The plaintiff sat on the toolbox since the tractor had only one seat. The plaintiff was struck by a tree and knocked into the path of the disk. Company rules forbade tractor passengers.
   a. What is the central issue in this lawsuit?
   b. Who wins? Explain. See *Perez* v. *Van Groningen & Sons, Inc.*, 227 Cal. Rptr. 106 (1986).

HIRING/RETENTION

Negligence

In recent years, employers' potential liability for employee wrong has been significantly expanded by a line of cases finding employers liable for negligence in hiring an employee or retaining an employee who subsequently causes harm to a third party. Typically, the employer is liable on negligence grounds for hiring or retaining an employee whom the employer knew or should have known to be dangerous, incompetent, dishonest, or the like where that information was directly related to the injury suffered by the plaintiff.

For example, an International House of Pancakes restaurant in Georgia was sued when DeLima, a waitress, became upset with two patrons, Jackson and Odom, whom DeLima believed to be intoxicated and excessively boisterous. DeLima "manhandled" Jackson. Then she grabbed Odom by the hair, punched her face several times, and poured coffee down her back (after Odom had thrown a cup of coffee at DeLima). The patrons sued IHOP for negligent hiring, among other claims, but the court dismissed that claim because the restaurant had no knowledge of prior violent behavior by the waitress, and she had denied having had any such problems when completing her employment application.[4]

Question

1. A truck driver sexually assaulted a hotel clerk during the driver's course of employment. On his employment application, the driver had stated that he did not have a criminal record. The employer did not conduct a background check of the driver's criminal record. Had the employer done so, it would have discovered the driver's previous convictions for lewd conduct, assault, theft, and other crimes. Was the employer liable for its failure to undertake a more thorough investigation? Explain. See *Connes* v. *Molalla Transp. Sys. Inc.*, 831 P.2d 1316 (Col. S.Ct. 1992).

Discrimination/Privacy

Employers' interests in avoiding negligent hiring problems sometimes conflict with the state's duty to erase employment discrimination. Equal employment opportunity laws and privacy considerations limit employers' permissible lines of inquiry in employment interviews. For some time, employers have been cautioned against inquiring into applicants' arrest/conviction records in the absence of clear job relatedness. Similarly, questions about sexual preference and marital status raise discrimination concerns. Now, with the passage of the Americans with Disabilities Act (see Chapter 13), questions regarding medical history and impairments must be carefully constructed. Further, such seemingly reasonable questions as how the applicant would meet child care duties or whether the applicant could be available on weekends might raise concerns about discrimination based on gender and religion.[5]

Recently, the Target chain of discount stores, without admitting fault, agreed to pay $1.3 million to settle the claims of an estimated 2,500 applicants for security positions who took the Rodgers Condensed CPI-MMPI "psychscreen" test in California. The true-false questions that follow illustrate those that raised discrimination and privacy concerns:

- I have never been in trouble because of my sex behavior.
- I have not had difficulty starting or holding my bowel movement.
- I am fascinated by fire.
- I believe there is a God.
- I would like to be a florist.[6]

Understand that lawsuits based on wrongful interview questions are uncommon and difficult to prove. Further, if the interview is restricted to job-related questions, no legal problems are likely.

References

Similarly, a sharp growth in defamation claims against employers has limited the usefulness of checking references when undertaking a hiring decision. Approximately 40 percent of larger American corporations have written policies declining to comment on employees without their permission.[7] Of course, the truth is a complete defense in these cases, and firms that avoid secondhand information, personal issues, and potential discrimination themes such as age are very likely not to have problems. However, a mistake can be expensive.

As an example of how costly it can be to violate somebody's rights when giving a job reference, a salesman was awarded $1.9 million when his former employer told a prospective employer that the salesman was a "classical sociopath," a "zero" and was disliked by office personnel.

In another case, four dental-claim adjusters for an insurance company were fired for gross insubordination following a dispute over filling out an expense report. Although the company did not inform any prospective employer of the reasons for the firing, the former employees had to list the reason for their termination on new job applications.

The court awarded the workers $570,000 on grounds that when they were forced to tell a new employer the reason for their firings, it was the same as the insurance company's offering the damaging reason.[8]

Broadly, a successful defamation suit requires:

1. A false and defamatory statement.
2. The statement must be "published" to a third party.
3. The employer must be responsible for the publication.
4. Damages must occur.

Truth in Hiring

Some courts have recently begun to look favorably on employee causes of action alleging employer misrepresentations during the hiring process.[9] Typically, the employee claims that promises made during the hiring process were not fulfilled or that the employee was fraudulently induced to take the job because of falsehoods during the hiring process. In the leading case, a lawyer, Victoria Stewart, convinced a federal court of appeals that she should be able to take to trial her claim that her New York City law firm, Jackson & Nash, had enticed her to work with them with representations that they had secured a major environmental law client and needed her to head their new environmental law department. That work never materialized, and eventually she was dismissed from the firm.[10]

Part Two—Fair Labor Standards Act

The Depression of the 1930s shattered many Americans' faith in an unfettered free market and led, among other things, to extensive government regulation of employment relations. The Fair Labor Standards Act (FLSA), passed in 1938 and later amended, is directed to these major objectives:

1. The establishment of a minimum wage that provides at least a modest standard of living for employees.
2. A flexible ceiling on hours worked weekly, the purpose of which is to increase the number of employed Americans.
3. Child labor protection.
4. Equal pay for equal work regardless of gender. (See Chapter 13).

WAGES AND HOURS

The FLSA requires covered employees to be paid a specified minimum wage and to be paid "time and a half" for any work in excess of 40 hours per week.

Generally speaking, employees and enterprises are covered by the FLSA if they are engaged in producing goods for interstate commerce. A number of occupations are exempted from some or all of the act. Professional, administrative, and executive employees as well as outside salespersons are exempt from the minimum wage and overtime provisions. The FLSA applies to state and local government workers as well as those in the private sector. And every state has its own wage and hour laws, which often reach workers not covered by the federal act.

Problems

A variety of problems arise under the FLSA wage and hour provisions. For example, must an employer pay employees for required activities (such as putting on protective gear) before proceeding to workstations and after leaving them? (Yes, according to one recent decision.[11]) If the federal minimum wage were raised from its current $4.25 per hour, would unemployment increase in low-wage jobs? (Yes, according to most studies.[12]) Should on-call workers be paid overtime wages for the hours spent waiting to be paged? (Federal appeals court decisions are split, but the weight of opinion at this writing in 1994 suggests that some on-call workers may be able to collect overtime pay if the employer's rules effectively prevent the employee from using the on-call time for personal purposes.[13]

In 1993, Food Lion, the supermarket chain, reached a $16.2 million settlement with the Labor Department to resolve allegations of overtime violations. The settlement was the largest of its kind in history, but will provide workers with only about $330 each in back pay. Food Lion had set time limits for its employees to complete various tasks. The Labor Department contended that the time limits were inadequate, thus effectively forcing the employees to work overtime without pay in order to complete their work.

Japan

INTERNATIONAL

Other countries struggle as the United States does with these wage and hour questions that are so important in shaping the character and quality of daily life. Japanese public policy in recent years has directed employment conditions more toward the Western model of increased leisure time. Japan seeks to reduce annual work-hours per person from an average of 1,958 in 1992 to 1,800 by 1997. Toward that goal, the Japanese Parliament in 1993 approved new rules reducing the national workweek from 44 to 40 hours and requiring holiday overtime pay up to 50 percent over the regular hourly wage, rather than 25 percent, as required previously.[14]

CHILD LABOR

Under federal law, with certain exceptions (principally agriculture), children under 14 years of age may not be employed. Those aged 14 and 15 may engage in sales and certain other jobs outside school hours for a limited time. At age 16, children may engage in any nonhazardous work. Then at 18, young adults may enter certain jobs (such as mining) that the government deems to be hazardous.

A shrinking labor pool, shifting immigration patterns, and difficult economic conditions for many have led to a concern that young workers may be threatened in the workplace. In the late 19th century, we were worried about eight-year-old children who were employed for 12-hour days in sweatshops or who lost fingers in textile milling machines. Now, new concerns about safety are being raised, both in underdeveloped nations that export goods to us and in the United States itself.

Exploitation?

INTERNATIONAL

The National Consumer League reports that 20 percent of all garment workers in Bangladesh are under 12 years of age, with some as young as 7 or 8.[15] Bangladesh is the fourth largest supplier of cotton clothing to the United States. Young girls and boys work 12- to 14-hour days, six to seven days per week, in firetrap factories in less developed nations for perhaps $9 to $10 per month.[16] As one "influential industry source" said, "Does any American consumer care that there are 9-year-olds making their sweaters in mainland China?"[17] Indeed, now some do care, and recent efforts by American firms (see Chapter 3) such as Levi Strauss to audit the child labor practices of their suppliers will improve this situation.

In America?

Ironically, as American companies are taking steps to improve child labor conditions abroad, we find those problems emerging more seriously and poignantly in the United States than has been the case in many years. As *Fortune* reported in 1993:

> Like tuberculosis and measles, child labor is making a comeback in the U.S. From New York to California, employers are breaking the law by hiring children of 7 to 17 who put in long, hard hours and often work in dangerous conditions.[18]

Migrant child labor up to 12 hours per day is common in south Florida and along parts of the Mexican border. In December 1993, the Labor Department fined Burger King $500,000 for allowing 14- and 15-year-old employees to work late at night on school evenings. And in New York City and Los Angeles, sweatshops akin to those we deplore in other countries have reemerged in the garment industry.[19] In 1990, 139 children died from job-related causes (one-third of those on farms) and 71,660 were injured.[20] Labor Department data indicate that child labor violations approximately doubled from 1980 to 1992.[21] Beyond physical injury and personal privation, a great concern about the reemergence of child labor problems in America is that educational opportunities are being depreciated by time spent working:

> The number of students working part-time has grown nearly 18 percent in the last 15 years, government statistics show. Now, more than 60 percent work some time during high school. Meanwhile, the number working 20 hours or more per week has jumped 40 percent, to 27 percent of students.[22]

Enforcement

A big part of the problem lies in our inability or unwillingness to enforce the child labor laws:

> Child labor laws . . . rarely are enforced. In 1980 the U.S. Labor Department had 1,059 investigators. Today, after several budget cuts, it deploys only 833 agents to enforce not only the child labor laws but a dozen other major regulations, among them the minimum wage laws. According to the National Safe Workplace Institute, . . . a business can expect a visit by a federal labor inspector once every 50 years.[23]

Values?

Of course, for some families, child labor may be an important income supplement. Further, a safe job at a fair wage for a youngster can be a valuable tool in personal maturation. However, the reemergence of child labor problems suggests the possibility that we are not significantly concerned about child labor abuses. Do Americans most value education or income? Do we most value cheap clothing for ourselves or safe working conditions for Third World children? On the other hand, is child labor simply a necessity for economic subsistence and subsequent progress in portions of America as well as the Third World?

Questions

1. How do you explain the reemergence of widespread child labor problems in the United States?
2. Is this a problem that should be left to families? Explain.
3. Is racism at the root of our attitudes toward child labor abuses? Explain.
4. Senator Tom Harkin of Iowa introduced legislation to bar imports from offshore industries that employ children under 15.
   a. What are the competing considerations?
   b. How would you vote? Explain.

Part Three—Health and Safety at Work

DEATHS

Recent government studies of workplace deaths provide a mixed picture of occupational safety in the United States:

- Workplace deaths decreased from 7,405 in 1980 to 5,714 in 1989.
- The fatality rate also fell from 8.9 deaths per 100,000 workers in 1980 to 5.6 in 1989.

- From 1980 through 1989, a total of 62,289 civilians died on the job, or an average of about 17 per day.
- The riskiest occupation was mining, followed by construction.
- Workplace homicides had declined 24 percent, from 914 murders in 1980 to 694 in 1989, but by 1992, workplace murders had risen to 1,004.
- In 1992, for all workers, homicide was the second leading cause of job-related deaths (trailing vehicle crashes). For women, in 1992, homicide was the number one cause of on-the-job death.[24]

INJURIES

In 1992, 6.4 million injuries were sustained in private-sector jobs. Reported occupational illness cases totaled 450,000 in 1992.[25] *Rates* of injury and illness per worker have been stable in recent years while workdays lost per full-time worker have increased.

OSHA

In 1970, Congress approved the Occupational Safety and Health Act (OSHA) in response to increasing concerns that workplaces were unnecessarily hazardous. Broadly, OSHA imposes a *general duty* on employers to provide a workplace free of "recognized hazards causing or likely to cause death or serious physical harm to employees." Employers have an absolute duty to remove any serious and preventable workplace hazards that are generally recognized in the industry and are known to the employer or should be known to the employer. That general duty is then supplemented with numerous, detailed, and demanding specific *standards*. A federal agency, the Occupational Safety and Health Administration (also labeled OSHA), is responsible for ensuring safe workplaces.

Standards

OSHA, through the secretary of labor, promulgates and enforces health and safety standards that identify and seek to correct specific workplace hazards and problems. These can range from exposure to cancer-causing agents (e.g., the chemical benzyne), to the surprisingly commonplace problem of one worker restarting a machine while another is servicing it, to mundane requirements for sanitary toilet facilities in agricultural jobs. These rules are readily available in OSHA publications, and employers must become familiar with them and comply with them.

After proposed OSHA rules are published in the *Federal Register* (see Chapter 8), industry representatives and other interested parties have the opportunity to comment. Most rules are imposed only after some form of cost-effectiveness inquiry.

New Standards

In 1991, OSHA issued detailed new rules designed to protect health care workers from AIDS and other blood-borne diseases. The rules set standards for protective clothing and workplace cleanliness. They require engineering controls such as puncture-resistant containers for used needles. They mandate specific cleanliness procedures, including written cleaning schedules and rules for disposing of needles and waste. The government estimates the cost of the rules at $821 million annually, while the American Dental Association (ADA) and others claim the cost is much higher. The rules are expected to prevent more than 200 deaths and 9,200 infections annually.[26]

In a court challenge, the new rules were upheld, but the Seventh U.S. Circuit Court of Appeals agreed with the ADA that the rules would be costly and perhaps unnecessary in some circumstances. However, the Court said the plaintiffs had failed to show that the rules were unreasonable.[27]

OSHA Loses

By contrast with the blood-borne disease rules, a federal appeals court, in 1992, nullified toxic substance standards that governed over 400 hazardous substances (e.g., chloroform, wood dust, and carbon monoxide) because OSHA did not provide separate scientific evidence for each chemical but rather bundled them in a manner that the court found "so flawed" that the standards could not be allowed to stand.[28] About half of the substances continue to be covered by earlier standards, and at this writing in 1994, Congress is considering new legislation that would put all of the standards back in place.

Variances

Employers may seek both permanent and temporary variances (exceptions) from OSHA standards. A permanent variance may be granted only if the workplace will be as safe as if the variance were enforced. A temporary variance permits additional time to put in place the necessary compliance measures. Employees have a right to a hearing to contest variances.

OSHA INFORMATION REQUIREMENTS

Right to Know

OSHA has adopted an employee *hazard communication standard* to protect employees from the dangers associated with chemicals and other toxins in the workplace. Chemical manufacturers and importers must develop *material safety data sheets* for all chemicals. Employers must then label all chemical containers so that employees will know about the chemical and its dangers, and employers must educate employees about chemical hazards and how to deal with them.

Records

Businesses (with exceptions) must maintain records listing and summarizing injuries, illnesses, and deaths on the job. A summary of those records must be posted at the job. Notice of any OSHA citations or of any imminent dangers on the job must also be posted at the job site. Fatalities as well as injuries requiring the hospitalization of five or more workers (a pending rule change would reduce that to three or more) must be reported to the area OSHA office within 48 hours (which would be reduced to eight hours under the pending rule).

Enforcement

OSHA's most publicized enforcement mechanism is the unannounced on-site inspection. Inspections arise at the initiative of the agency itself or at the request of employees or their representatives. The inspections must be conducted in a reasonable manner during working hours or other reasonable times, and ordinarily they must not be announced in advance. As discussed in Chapter 5, an employer can insist that the inspector produce a warrant prior to undertaking an inspection. Employer and employee representatives may accompany the inspector. Citations may be issued if violations are discovered. Immediate, serious threats can be restrained with a court order.

Citation.   A citation explains the rules that have been violated and the date by which corrective action must be in place. That citation must be posted near the location of the wrong. Following a citation, the employer may request to meet with an area OSHA official to discuss the problem. Often, a settlement emerges from these meetings. Failing a settlement, the employer can appeal to OSHA's Review Commission and thereafter to the federal court of appeals. Violations may lead to significant fines and/or imprisonment.

For example, in 1988, the meat packer John Morrell & Co. was fined $4.3 million for "exposing 40 percent of 2,000 workers at its Sioux Falls, South Dakota, plant to crippling hand, wrist, and arm injuries."[29] These included repetitive motion injuries such as carpal tunnel syndrome. Then, in 1990, the parties negotiated a settlement, including a $990,000 fine that, among other things, requires Morrell to:

- Hire a neurologist to oversee its program.
- Allow workers to see a doctor within four days of reporting an injury.
- Conduct education and training in those injuries.
- Reduce injury risks in at least 171 jobs.[30]

Criminals? In recent years, prosecutors have been increasingly aggressive in bringing criminal charges for labor safety and health violations. However, such prosecutions are very difficult to win. Reportedly, only seven state cases of this kind, all in California, have resulted in incarcerations.[31] California's Corporate Criminal Liability Act is the most sweeping law of its kind in America. Labeled the "be a manager, go to jail" act by critics, it requires severe criminal penalties for companies and managers that *fail to report* workplace dangers or potential hazards in products. In the first prosecution under the act, Cargill Inc. entered a no-contest plea in a case prompted by the death of an employee who was pulled between two conveyor belts when his hand was caught on a machine.[32]

Industrial Fire. As a result of the most tragic industrial accident in recent U.S. history, a North Carolina poultry plant owner pleaded guilty in 1992 to involuntary manslaughter for the deaths of 25 workers in a fire at his processing plant. The plant had no sprinkler system or fire alarms, and inspectors said that many exits were locked or blocked. Some doors allegedly had been locked in order to keep insects out, to keep employees in during breaks, and to prevent theft.[33] The owner was sentenced to nearly 20 years in prison, but he will probably be eligible for release after two to three years. The plant had never been inspected by North Carolina OSHA officials during its 11 years of operation.[34] Indeed, records indicated that only 40 of North Carolina's 83 chicken-processing plants had been inspected in the past 20 years.[35]

REGULATORY ZEAL

In the 1970s and early 1980s, OSHA was criticized for giving undue attention to comparatively trivial issues and for intruding excessively and unproductively into business life by creating too many rules with too much complexity and detail. The Reagan administration reacted by redirecting OSHA's efforts. The agency focused on health and safety *performance* standards (e.g., maximum levels of exposure to cotton dust) and moved away from specifying particular measures for achieving those standards. Further, the business community was relied on to better regulate its own health and safety.

However, critics contend that employers then relaxed worker safety efforts. Indeed, America's work injury rate rose 14 percent from 1975 to 1988.[36] By contrast, Japan's work injury rate has declined steadily since 1968 such that our occupational injury and illness rate in the mid-80s was seven times that of the Japanese.[37]

In recent years, the Bush administration and now that of President Clinton have taken a more balanced approach toward OSHA, with government oversight and free market reasoning both playing influential roles. Currently, inspections are targeted to industries where injuries are more likely, and inspections may be limited to perusal of company safety records. Where those records reveal problems in excess of national industry norms, full inspections may follow. Less dangerous locations such as retailers are unlikely to be inspected at all without an employee complaint.

Cooperation?

Some scholarly opinion holds that the comparative Japanese advantage in worker safety is at least partially attributable to the tradition of labor/management/government cooperation in Japan—as opposed to the more punitive role of government here and our tendency toward confrontation between labor and management.[38] The article that follows demonstrates one American plant's great success with the more cooperative route.

HOW A PLANT HANDLES OCCUPATIONAL HAZARD WITH COMMON SENSE

Joan E. Rigdon

The problem began with some special orders at the bakery. Customers wanted croissants whose tips curled forward and touched.

When Sara Lee Corp.'s bakery in this rural town started making them, and also filling orders for hand-decorated cakes, its workers had to twist their wrists more than before. At first no one noticed. Employees, standing on concrete floors with their arms extended over conveyor belts, even raced one another at times, with winners handling almost 100 pieces a minute. "They wanted so many and we went so fast, faster and faster," recalls one worker, Carol Panoch.

Their prize: carpal tunnel syndrome, a debilitating wrist disorder caused by repeated hand motions. It and other so-called cumulative trauma disorders caused by repetitive motion today make up the fastest growing, most widespread U.S. occupational hazard, according to the Bureau of Labor Statistics. Cumulative trauma disorders, or CTDs, afflicted 185,400 American workers in 1990, almost nine times the number reported for 1982.

Symptoms suffered by the bakery workers here were typical: shooting pains in the arms, numb and tingling fingers and aching wrists. Some workers wore splints to work or bed. Some had surgery. The town's small hospital leased a deluxe physical therapy machine to help handle the case load.

Big Improvement

But today, five years after that machine was purchased, it is more or less foreign to Sara Lee workers. While hundreds of U.S. businesses, from manufacturing plants to data-processing centers, continue to grapple with complaints of CTDs, the bakery here has nearly eliminated them. It did so—after an initial balky start—by using a homespun approach that stresses prevention and relies on close observation of work procedures and small modifications in them.

The bakery hired a hand surgeon to come in and evaluate its procedures. It brought its labor union into the game. Instead of buying new equipment off the shelf—ergonomically designed chairs and keyboards for offices can cost $100 to $1,000 a pop—it used its own maintenance department whenever possible to make dozens of small changes. In some cases, workers themselves invented devices they thought would alleviate problematic physical motions. For instance, one engineer devised a new icing gun that weighed less and took less strength to squeeze.

The result is that employees missed only eight days of work because of carpal tunnel syndrome in the first seven months of this year, after being out 181 days during all of last year . . .

Slow Start

This is not to say the Sara Lee bakery has been a paragon of enlightenment. Like many businesses, it was initially quite skeptical of workers' seemingly vague complaints . . . Bakery workers' early suggestion to slow down the production line was dismissed out of hand.

Nor is the Sara Lee bakery here the only business at the forefront in combating the problem. Facing lawsuits and huge government fines, many other plants have also changed procedures. In the past decade, unions have prodded meatpackers and auto makers to finance studies and redesign work stations.

What distinguishes this Sara Lee bakery is that it tackled the problem before it became epidemic. The majority of companies either do nothing about complaints of repetitive motion injuries or offer limited treatment, such as mandatory stretching exercises. This is so even though carpal tunnel and other CTDs are a costly and growing problem. They made up nearly 56% of work-related illnesses in 1990, according to the Bureau of Labor Statistics, compared with 21% in 1982. And the CTD cases cost an average of $29,000 in lost wages and medical treatment, says the National Council on Compensation Insurance. That doesn't include legal damages, which have been averaging $50,000 per plaintiff, or fines levied by OSHA, which have been as high as $3 million.

Source: *The Wall Street Journal,* September 28, 1992, p. A1. Reprinted by permission of *The Wall Street Journal,* © 1992 Dow Jones & Company, Inc. All Rights Reserved Worldwide.

Questions

1. *a.* How would free market forces work to provide job safety?
   b. Should we abolish OSHA? Explain.
2. Answer job safety critic Joseph Kinney's questions: "Why does the federal government spend 20 times more on the Environmental Protection Agency than on OSHA?" "Why do we have at least six fish and game inspectors in the U.S. for every job safety inspector?" See Bob Baker, "Death on the Job—A Lifework," *Los Angeles Times,* April 28, 1990, p. A1.

State Action?

Dissatisfied with federal efforts, pushed by exploding workers' compensation costs, and encouraged by successes abroad and at plants like Sara Lee, a number of states are now mandating worker–management cooperative efforts in attacking job safety problems.

AS U.S. MULLS WORKER–SAFETY MANDATE, SOME STATES REQUIRE COMPANY ACTION

Jyoti Thottam and Kevin G. Salwen

A string of states has begun forcing companies to set up worker-safety committees to reduce injury rates, while the federal government wrestles with whether to create a similar national mandate.

Next week, Connecticut companies must begin establishing worker-management teams to investigate accidents, evaluate prevention programs and determine possible safety fixes. The law applies to companies with at least 25 employees or higher-than-average injury rates. Similar or tougher laws are already on the books or going into effect in such states as Minnesota, Oregon and North Carolina.

The laws are being enacted as state legislatures are being asked by business and state governments to slash workers' compensation costs. At the same time, worker groups, led by unions, are showing that the programs are successful at cutting corporate injury and death rates.

* * * * *

The problems are painfully obvious. Nearly 10,000 workers are killed on the job each year, though many of those are in motor vehicle accidents. At the same time, the Occupational Safety and Health Administration, the government's watchdog on worker safety, has only 1,000 inspectors, a number matched by the states. They are responsible for keeping the safety standards high at six million U.S. businesses.

On Capitol Hill, efforts to reform the 20-year-old Occupational Safety and Health Act to mandate worker-safety committees have struggled . . .

So, states are moving ahead . . .

* * * * *

. . . In Oregon, where safety teams were first required in 1990 after the Legislature tried to cut workers' compensation costs, the state has slashed average base premiums for such costs by double-digit percentages each year. The state's national rank for the most costly workers' compensation has fallen to 22 from eight in 1990.

* * * * *

In a half-dozen or so other states, legislatures have refused to mandate committees, requiring instead that companies set up safety and health programs to educate employees and managers. In California, for example, all employers must set up an injury and illness prevention program, including identification of a responsible person, worker training, and communication of hazards to workers . . .

* * * * *

But Republicans worry about added burdens on companies. "One thing is certain," Rep. William Goodling (R., Pa.), the ranking Republican on the House Labor Committee, said at a recent hearing. "The bill contains a host of new mandates and costs for employers . . . We certainly had better understand what we're doing before imposing those kinds of costs on the American economy."

Questions

1. Will worker–management cooperation eventually replace the current need for OSHA oversight of job safety and health? Explain.
2. In what sense does job safety and health affect the international economic competitiveness of the United States?
3. Make the argument that new OSHA safety rules that raise employer costs and thus produce employee layoffs might actually increase worker deaths and injuries.
4. A 23-year-old college student was working part-time for a construction crew. At work, he grabbed a chain to help guide a sewer pipe into a trench. A backhoe was being used to lift the pipe. The operator of the backhoe was the president of the company. By accident, the backhoe came into contact with an overhead high-voltage power line. The student died immediately from the resulting electrical shock.

   OSHA regulations require that construction equipment must not be operated within 10 feet of electrical wires. Further, police reports cited in a *Boston Globe* article indicate that the backhoe operator had several times on that day been warned by workers to keep the machine away from the wires. Under OSHA requirements, a criminal conviction requires proof of *willful* violation of safety standards.

   Assume you are the judge in the criminal negligence case that arose from these facts. How would you rule? Explain. See Wade Lambert and Stephen Wermiel, "Employer . . . Negligence in Worker Safety Case," *The Wall Street Journal,* October 4, 1990, p. B4.

Afterword

The Comprehensive Occupational Safety and Health Reform Act, being considered by Congress at this writing in 1994, would require:

1. Written workplace health and safety plans for all employers.
2. Mandatory labor–management health and safety committees for all employers having 11 or more employees.
3. Strengthened criminal penalties.

WORKERS' COMPENSATION

Historically, when a worker was injured on the job, her recourse was to sue the employer. Typically, the employee would bring a negligence claim, and commonly the employer would assert one of three defenses: (1) *contributory negligence,* meaning the employee was at least partially responsible for her own harm; (2) *assumption of the risk,* meaning the employee recognized or should have recognized a potentially harmful workplace situation but proceeded voluntarily to engage in her duties; and (3) *fellow servant rule,* meaning the harm to the employee was the result of a coworker's conduct. Proof of any of these defenses acted as a complete bar to recovery for the injured employee. The burden of overcoming these defenses and combating the superior resources of the employer meant that employees often could not secure compensation for workplace injuries.

Then, early in this century, the states began enacting workers' compensation laws to provide an administrative remedy for those injured or killed on the job. Now all states provide some form of protection. Rather than filing a lawsuit, workers or their families simply apply for compensation based on illness, injury, or death. Typically, the system is governed by a state board or commission. Most decisions are routine and are accomplished by completing the necessary forms. Often, a claims examiner will check to verify the nature and severity of the injury. Commission decisions can be appealed to the courts.

In all but three states (Texas, New Jersey, and South Carolina)[39] employers are compelled to participate in workers' compensation, depending on state law, either by purchasing insurance privately, contributing to a state-managed fund, or by being self-insured (paying claims directly from their own funds). Of course, firms with good safety records are rewarded with lower premium payments.

Benefits

The amount of recovery for injury or death is determined by a benefits schedule, which specifies the sum to be awarded for the injury in question. The amount of the award is normally a percentage of the worker's salary either for a specified period of time or indefinitely, depending on the severity of the injury. Injury benefits normally amount to one-half to two-thirds of regular wages. Death benefits ordinarily are tied to the wages of the deceased and range from enough to pay funeral arrangements to approximately $100,000 (depending on the number of dependents) in California. Weekly maximum benefits for workers with total but temporary disabilities range from just over $200 in some states to over $700 in others.

Coverage

Certain employment classifications such as agriculture may be excluded from workers' compensation, but about 90 percent of the labor force is covered, and some of those not covered are shielded by other statutes such as the Federal Employer's Liability Act.

In general, injuries (as well as illnesses and deaths) are compensable where (1) the injury was accidental, and (2) it arose in the course of employment. Thus, workers' compensation provides a form of no-fault protection in the workplace. In brief, workers give up the right to sue and the burdens that accompany that course, and employers participate in an insurance system that recognizes the inevitability of injury and death on the job.

All states provide that the workers' compensation recovery is the *exclusive* remedy available for workplace injury, illness, or death. However, recent court decisions have begun to find limited exceptions that, in certain jurisdictions, permit employees to sue for damages beyond the (often inadequate) recoveries permitted under workers' compensation.

Litigation

Notwithstanding its no-fault character, workers' compensation has generated extensive litigation. For example, one court found an employee's "chronic anxiety" to be work-related and not the result of normal "bodily wear and tear."[40] And a 16-year-old employed as a "gas jockey" was covered by workers' compensation for injuries sustained when, during a slow time at work, he showed a friend a "trick" in which a match might be tossed into oil, gasoline, and grease without causing an explosion. On this occasion, an explosion did result, but the Workers' Compensation Board ruled and the court agreed that this "horseplay" was covered by the New York statute since it was "related to his employment."[41] On the other hand, a United Parcel Service driver who sustained a back injury while bending over to tie his shoe while on the job was excluded from compensation because, among other reasons, the injury did not arise from activity that was peculiar to the work setting.[42]

Jandrucko.   The following *Washington Post* account describes perhaps the most controversial workers' compensation award in the history of the system.

PHOBIA ABOUT BLACKS BRINGS WORKERS' COMPENSATION AWARD; FLORIDA WOMAN FILED CLAIM AFTER PARKING-LOT MUGGING

William Booth

Ruth Jandrucko has a problem. She cannot work with black people. They make her nervous.

Because of this, Jandrucko, 65, has been awarded full disability and workers' compensation benefits by Florida authorities, who found that she suffers from "a post-traumatic stress disorder" after being mugged by a black man.

The attack occurred in 1986 while Jandrucko, who is white, was working as a troubleshooter for Colorcraft Corp., a photo-processing company.

In 1990 and again last year, a Florida compensation-claims judge ruled that Jandrucko is incapable of working because of her phobia about blacks, particularly "large, black males." She has been paid about $50,000 in workers' compensation by Colorcraft, now Qualex Inc.

A federal judge here denied Colorcraft's request for permanent injunctive relief, which would have freed the company from paying compensation.

* * * * *

Lawyers who deal with civil rights and workers' compensation cases have called this one of the most unusual clashes before the appeals court because it pits a worker's right to receive benefits after a work-related injury against a company's need to preserve an integrated work force.

Renee Pelzman, Jandrucko's attorney, said her client is not a racist. "She is a sweet little old lady," Pelzman said. "To know Ruthie is to love her."

Before the mugging and phobia, Jandrucko was friendly with blacks, said Pelzman, who described her as a woman who grew up in a Mennonite community in Pennsylvania and was the kind of co-worker "who brought chicken soup to people who were sick." Jandrucko's two sons are police officers.

According to court records, a man Jandrucko described as "a large black male" attacked her from behind in a Miami parking lot, threw her to the ground and took her purse. She suffered a fractured vertebra and saw her attacker fleeing.

Pelzman said Jandrucko "never saw his face, and the man was never apprehended . . . There was no way to know parentage, what shade of black. Jandrucko knew he was black."

Jandrucko also experienced what her psychologist described as a post-traumatic stress disorder. Pelzman said this caused her "to be hyper-vigilant and extremely nervous in any situation where she might encounter black persons, especially young black males such as the person who had attacked her."

In testimony in 1991, Jonathan Alpert, Colorcraft's lawyer, asked Jandrucko why she could not work around blacks.

"It's the anxiety," Jandrucko said.

Alpert: "From coming in contact with black people?"

Jandrucko: "Yes."

Alpert: "And it's the anxiety of coming into contact with black people in the work place, correct?"

Jandrucko: "I would say yes."

Questioned about her phobia, Jandrucko testified that seeing black men in grocery and department stores frightens her. She said that when a black man once came up behind her in a department store, she had a panic attack and had to sit down and do breathing exercises prescribed by her psychologist.

Jandrucko testified that she did not fear her manicurist, a black woman, nor was she afraid of seeing CNN's Bernard Shaw on television. But seeing big black males on television "sometimes" upset her, she said.

Pelzman has argued that her client displayed no anxiety about blacks before the mugging, that she has lived and worked around blacks and that she simply suffers from a psychiatric condition. "It's medical," Pelzman said. "The rest is a red herring."

Alpert and others disagree, saying the state is sanctioning racial discrimination by awarding compensation for race-based prejudices.

"They can give her benefits for any reason they want, but not for disliking blacks," said Mark Brown, a law professor at Stetson University in St. Petersburg representing the American Civil Liberties Union, which filed a brief in the case. "If everybody starts doing it, where do you end up?"

John G. Tomlison Jr., the workers' compensation judge who awarded Jandrucko disability payments, said, "It is not relevant what the subject of her phobia is." Tomlison has said Jandrucko was not exercising a "private racial prejudice" but has a work-related phobia.

Source: *The Washington Post,* August 13, 1992, p. A3. © 1992 *The Washington Post.* Reprinted with permission.

Afterword

The parties settled the *Jandrucko* case in December 1992 by agreeing on a $50,000 award for Jandrucko and on $450,000 for her attorneys. The attorneys indicated that the $450,000 did not fully reflect the 2,500 hours they had put into the case, and they said that they believed full compensation should have amounted to $800,000 to $900,000.[43]

Despite the settlement, the employer, Fuqua Industries, carried an appeal of the administrative law judge's original decision to the federal court of appeals, where Fuqua claimed that the award was "race-based" and put the company in the position of violating civil rights laws. However, that appeal was dismissed without comment.[44]

At this writing in 1994, the Florida legislature is expected to pass legislation to exclude phobias based on discrimination from the state's workers' compensation coverage.

Questions

1. Does the *Jandrucko* case appear to meet the legal test for securing workers' compensation? Explain.
2. As you see it, does the *Jandrucko* decision constitute an ethical wrong? Explain.
3. Journalist Lynne Duke, commenting in *The Washington Post* about the *Jandrucko* decision:

   > If color-based stress is to be a legitimate basis for compensation, then what of the "post-traumatic stress disorder" that could be claimed by the untold number of dark people who've been catching hell from the lighter hues for years?[45]

   Comment.
4. Joseph Smyth, a college mathematics instructor, was killed while driving his personal auto home from work. At the time, Smyth had student papers with him, which he intended to grade that evening. He often worked at home. Many faculty members took work home in the evenings. However, the college did not require that practice. Indeed, the college neither encouraged nor discouraged working at home.

   The widely adopted "going and coming rule" provides that employees injured while commuting to and from work, in general, are not covered by workers' compensation.

   a. Should Smyth (and other teachers) be exempted from the going and coming rule, thus permitting recovery by Smyth's family? Explain. See *Santa Rosa Junior College* v. *Workers' Compensation Appeals Board and Joann Smyth,* 708 P.2d 673 (Cal.1985).

   b. Would you reach a different conclusion had a student been accompanying Smyth? Explain.
5. Casimer Gacioch worked at a Stroh Brewery. The company provided free beer at work. When he began work in 1947 he drank only three to four beers on the weekend. He was fired in 1974, by which time he was drinking 12 bottles of beer daily. After Mr. Gacioch's death, his wife sought workers' compensation benefits. The evidence indicated that Mr. Gacioch had a predisposition to alcoholism but was not an alcoholic at the time he was hired. How would you rule on the widow's workers' compensation claim? Explain. See Associated Press, "Alcoholic Brewery Worker's Widow . . ." *Waterloo Courier,* October 30, 1990, p. A2.

Reform?

Indisputably, the biggest issue in the workers' compensation field today is cost containment. From 1980 to the early 1990s, the nation's workers' compensation costs nearly tripled, to a total of $70 billion.[46] While overall health care costs rose an astonishing 102 percent between 1980 and 1987, workers' compensation care costs zoomed up at a rate of 151 percent.[47] The situation has become something of a crisis for the business community, and many states are initiating reforms.

In 1993, California passed new legislation that is expected to reduce employers' annual $11 billion workers' compensation bill by $1.5 billion. The chief reforms:

1. For claimants with stress claims, the new rules require that at least 51 percent of the stress must be job provoked. The old rules had set that standard at 10 percent.
2. The number of doctors a worker may visit to secure estimates was reduced from 8 to 3.
3. Retraining costs for disabled workers are limited to $16,000. Previously, those had averaged $20,000.[48]

Economic Growth

In assessing the value of government programs such as workers' compensation, we must balance the evident value to society of our relatively efficient, fair system of caring for workers and their families against the market's insistence on economic efficiency. During its recession from the late 1980s through the early 1990s, California lost more than a million jobs, many of which moved to other states.[49] Management often cited uncompetitive workers' compensation costs as a reason for leaving California. Reportedly, Intel, a large California computer microchip firm, chose New Mexico for a new plant, in part because its workers' compensation costs would have been $80 million higher in California.[50]

Part Four—Employee Privacy

Perhaps the most explosive employment issue of the 1990s is privacy on the job. Increasingly, employers are engaging in an array of testing and monitoring procedures both before and after hiring. Drug testing, integrity tests, personality tests, AIDS tests, spying, television and computer monitoring of work performance, and so forth are routine personnel practices in many firms. Employers have a legitimate interest in these strategies not only to hire better employees and improve productivity but to protect coworkers, reduce insurance claims, and protect consumers from poor products and service. On the other hand, job applicants and employees often feel the intrusive presence of "Big Brother" in their lives.

DRUGS AND DRUG TESTING: INTRODUCTION

American Management Association (AMA) annual survey results suggest that drug use among American workers has declined dramatically. As demonstrated in the following table, positive results on drug tests have fallen significantly for both applicants and employees.

	Job Applicants Testing Positive (%)	*Employees Testing Positive (%)*
1989	11.4%	8.1%
1990	5.8	4.2
1991	4.6	2.7
1992	4.3	2.5

Source: "Fewer People Fail as Workplace Drug Testing Increases," *HR Focus* 70, no. 6 (June 1993), p. 24.

In 1993, 84 percent of the firms in the AMA survey engaged in drug testing.[51] When an applicant tests positive, only 3 out of 503 companies responding to the survey indicated that they would hire that individual on a probationary basis.[52] When employees test positive, 57 percent of the companies reported that the employees are referred for counseling and treatment, 15 percent immediately dismiss those people, 20 percent apply a suspension or some other discipline, and 3 percent assign them to other duties.[53] Eighty-seven percent of the firms use urinalysis for drug testing, while 14.4 percent took blood samples and 1.3 percent used hair samples.[54]

DRUG-FREE WORKPLACE

Congress encouraged the effort against drug abuse by passing the Drug-Free Workplace Act of 1988. The act applies to employers who do business ($25,000 or more) with the federal government or who receive aid from the government. They are required to develop an antidrug policy for employees. They must provide drug-free awareness programs for employees, and they must acquaint employees with available assistance for those with drug problems while also warning them of the penalties that accompany violation of the policy. The act requires employees to adhere to the company policy and to inform the company within five days if they are convicted of or plead no contest to a drug-related offense in the workplace. Of course, in the event of a violation, company policy might include a mandatory rehabilitation program or termination.

The High Cost of Substance Abusers

Did you know that drug abusers are:

- Late for work three times more often than nonabusers
- Absent 2.5 times more often
- One-third less productive
- 3.6 times more likely to be involved in an accident
- 10 times more likely to be involved in employee theft
- Four times more likely to be involved in job-related death?

Source: Stephanie Lawrence, "For Your Information," *Personnel Journal* 69, no. 4 (April 1990), p. 10.

LEGAL CHALLENGES TO ALCOHOL AND DRUG TESTING

Notwithstanding the seriousness of the drug problem in America, critics are concerned that personal rights may be trampled in our zeal to attack substance abuse. Some of the concerns are that the tests (1) are often unreliable, (2) invade employee privacy, and (3) do not measure actual job impairment.

Challenges to drug testing are rooted primarily in the following legal claims/defenses.

1. Federal Constitution.   As explained in Chapter 5, the Fourth Amendment to the U.S. Constitution forbids unreasonable searches and seizures. Drug tests, depending on the circumstances, arguably violate those constitutional rights. But remember that the Constitution, in general, protects us from the government, not from private sector employers.

2. State Constitutions.   Many state constitutions offer protection similar to that at the federal level, and some strengthen that protection. For example, California's constitutional right to privacy extends to both private and public sector employees.

3. Common Law Claims.   Judge-made (common law) claims that might provide a challenge to drug testing, depending on the circumstances, include privacy, defamation (dissemination of erroneous information about an employee), negligence (in testing or selecting a test provider), and wrongful discharge (discussed later in this chapter).

4. State and Local Laws.   A number of states and communities have enacted drug testing laws. In general, those laws place limits on testing. For example, Connecticut forbids private employers from requiring drug tests of job applicants unless written notice of the test is provided, the applicant receives a copy of any positive test report, and other procedural requirements are met.[55] On the other hand, Utah specifically permits testing both for prospective and current employees.[56]

LEGALITY OF ALCOHOL AND DRUG TESTING: SUMMARY

Broadly, employment-based alcohol and drug testing occurs in four circumstances: preemployment screening, routine physical examinations, "reasonable suspicion" testing, and random testing.[57]

1. Preemployment testing is commonplace. Ordinarily it is lawful, but some state and local laws impose restrictions.
2. Assuming proper standards are met, drug testing as a part of periodic physical examinations is lawful in most states.
3. Reasonable suspicion is something less than probable cause and means that the employer has evidence, such as lapses in performance, that would justify a drug test. Such tests, given a sound factual foundation, probably are permissible.
4. Random drug testing raises particularly difficult legal issues. The Supreme Court has upheld such testing for public sector employees where public safety was involved (police and transportation workers) and for those having access to particularly sensitive information.[58] In the limited number of private sector cases addressing random testing, the courts are split.[59]

Privacy and Testing[60]

A recent Court of Appeals decision imposed some privacy limits on workplace drug screening. Sarah Borse, a 15-year employee of Piece Goods Shop of Bethlehem, Pennsylvania, was fired because she refused to take a drug test that was required under a new company policy. She raised various claims, including right to privacy, freedom from unreasonable searches, and violation of Pennsylvania public policy. Using state law rather than the federal constitution, and thus somewhat limiting the decision's impact, the court found that drug testing could constitute an invasion of privacy under at least two circumstances: if the methods used "fail to give due regard to the employee's privacy" or if the test results reveal "private facts about an employee."

The federal court of appeals, in remanding the *Borse* case to the federal district court, specified that a balancing test is to be employed in which the employee's privacy rights are weighed against the employer's need for a drug-free workplace to determine if the "alleged invasion of privacy is substantial and highly offensive to the reasonable person."[61] Though limited to Pennsylvania law, the case seems to open the door a bit for challenging some workplace drug testing.

OTHER TESTS AND SURVEILLANCE

In 1988, President Reagan approved legislation banning most uses of polygraph tests by private employers. The law forbids the use of lie detector tests in screening job applicants and in random testing of employees, but it does permit the test in special security situations involving, for example, pharmaceutical companies or where the employer has sound evidence tying an employee to theft or other wrongdoing.[62]

Integrity Tests

Now that lie detectors are normally not permissible, employers have turned to "paper and pencil" integrity tests to accomplish similar goals. In general, such tests are lawful and, according to recent research, surprisingly useful. The tests have been shown to be rather effective in identifying those who are more likely to cheat in some way at work. Furthermore, some intriguing evidence suggests that those tests are also helpful in measuring "general conscientiousness." One study that statistically evaluated the results of 40 other studies and data involving more than 500,000 test subjects found that the tests are useful in identifying those who are likely to be tardy, absent, and generally disruptive on the job.[63] Of course, such tests often raise privacy concerns.

Spying

Testing is only one of a broad array of employer strategies that raise invasion of privacy concerns in applicants and employees but are viewed as necessary efficiency measures by management. An estimated 20 million Americans are subject to electronic monitoring on the job.[64] Snooping is practiced by tabulating keystrokes, searching computer files, reviewing E-mail, and so on. Some companies keep tabs on how many times an employee goes to the bathroom or talks on the telephone, and some use video cameras to watch over work areas. One southern California medical company even requires that workers with visible "hickeys" be sent home without pay.[65] That policy was instituted in response to complaints from both patients and other workers. Monitoring is chiefly an effort to increase productivity or to investigate thefts and espionage.[66]

Some companies notify their employees about surveillance policies, but many believe their goals cannot be accomplished without secrecy. In any case, the law at this point is decidedly supportive of employer spying. In particular, if a company announces a reasonable policy of searches and surveillance where reasonably justified by work circumstances, such measures are lawful even if they include such tactics as searching desks, lockers, and offices.

Smoking

Facing surging health insurance costs, many companies now require employees to take measures to improve their health. Workers are rewarded for losing weight, reducing cholesterol counts, curbing high blood pressure, and so forth; others are penalized when they fail to do so or even when they choose to engage in dangerous activities such as skiing or sky diving. In recent years, many firms have moved to bar smoking, but as the following article explains, those antismoking policies have produced a dazzling legislative response around the country fueled by very effective tobacco industry lobbying.

EMPLOYERS FUME OVER NEW LEGISLATION BARRING DISCRIMINATION AGAINST SMOKERS

Junda Woo

Laws forbidding discrimination against smokers are on the rise—and some companies that prefer nonsmoking employees are doing a slow burn.

Faced with an antismoking fervor that stretches from the corporate office to the Oval Office, the tobacco industry has turned to state legislatures to protect the right to smoke. Largely in the past two years, 28 states and the District of Columbia have made job discrimination against smokers illegal. And at least two states have made it a civil right for workers to smoke outside the workplace.

. . . The laws don't affect office smoking bans or smoke-free zones in the workplace. But they bar companies from refusing to hire smokers and from firing employees who fail to kick the habit.

The legislation comes in response to policies many companies have adopted in recent years against hiring smokers because of health and safety concerns. In Washington state, for instance, about 10% of all employers refuse to hire smokers, according to Smokenders International, a Phoenix-based consulting concern that helps people stop smoking . . .

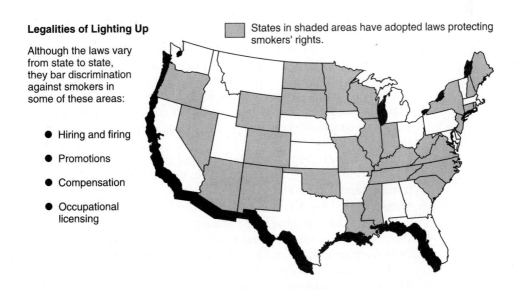

Legalities of Lighting Up

Although the laws vary from state to state, they bar discrimination against smokers in some of these areas:

● Hiring and firing

● Promotions

● Compensation

● Occupational licensing

States in shaded areas have adopted laws protecting smokers' rights.

Fines and Compensatory Damages

Some of the laws also prohibit discrimination in compensation and benefits, although higher insurance rates for smokers generally are allowed. In most of the states, companies that violate the laws face fines and can be sued for compensatory damages. Apparently none of the laws has been tested in court by smokers seeking protection.

A 1991 "smokers' rights" law in New Jersey forced Fortunoff, a retail chain based in Westbury, N.Y., to dump a policy prohibiting all employees from smoking on or off the job. The 10-year-old policy was adopted after a worker caused a fire by smoking in a storeroom. Fortunoff stopped hiring smokers, and anyone caught sneaking a cigarette was sent to smoking-cessation programs at company expense.

"There were no real victims of the nonsmoking policy," says Vice President Louis W. Fortunoff. "People who couldn't get a job with us, they got a job at Macy's. They didn't care. The real purpose of this legislation is to legitimize tobacco use—it was purely a ploy by the tobacco industry."

The company now prohibits smoking indoors . . .

* * * * *

Help from the ACLU

In some states, the tobacco lobby is getting a boost from the American Civil Liberties Union, which says off-the-job antismoking policies are a corporate intrusion into private lives. The civil-liberties group helped win laws in eight states, including New York, that broadly bar discrimination against employees who use any lawful product or who engage in lawful activities in their off hours.

Such laws protect not only smokers but alcohol drinkers and devotees of risky recreational sports, such as motorcycle riding. "As long as the behavior doesn't affect job performance, people should be allowed to do it on their own time," says Lewis Maltby, director of the ACLU's workplace-rights office in New York.

Even in states without antidiscrimination laws that address smoking, smokers have gained some workplace protection under the Americans with Disabilities Act of 1990.

Questions

1. In addition to rising health care costs, what other fears are pushing businesses to try to curb smoking on the job?
2. In what sense does the Americans with Disabilities Act provide protection to smokers against employers' nonsmoking policies?
3. If you owned a company, would you forbid vital, highly paid employees from engaging in dangerous practices such as bungee jumping, sky diving, skiing, and motorcycle riding? Explain.
4. Since the use of drugs outside of medical care is unlawful in the United States, shouldn't employers be free to engage in drug testing as they see fit as long as the testing meets appropriate scientific standards? Explain.
5. Should federal constitutional protections accorded to public sector workers likewise be extended to those in the private sector? Explain.
6. In 1990, U-Haul International announced a plan to deduct up to $130 per year from the paychecks of those employees who smoke or who have difficulty maintaining a healthful weight. Those correcting the problem would receive a refund. The policy is designed to address U-Haul's $17 million annual bill for insurance and medical expenses.

a. Build an argument against the U-Haul policy.

b. Would you impose such a policy if you were in charge? Explain.

7. Is employer spying ethically permissible if employees are informed of the practice? Explain.

Part Five—Employee Benefits and Income Maintenance

What were once "fringe benefits"—health insurance, life insurance, pensions, and so forth—are now central ingredients in employee compensation. Employers pay 37 cents to the average employee in benefit payments for every dollar paid in wages.[67] And those costs are escalating. A recent nationwide survey showed per employee expenses for health and dental coverage rising from an average of $2,354 per year in 1988 to an estimated $3,200 per year in 1990.[68] And demands for expanded benefits—particularly child care—are growing. Consequently, many employers are reducing benefits, increasing deductibles, instituting copayment requirements, or offering "cafeteria" benefit plans.

FAMILY LEAVE

The 1993 Family and Medical Leave Act provides up to 12 weeks of unpaid leave in any 12-month period for family needs such as birth or adoption of a child, caring for a child or parent, or the employee's own serious illness. Employees taking leave are entitled to reinstatement to the same (or equivalent) job. The bill applies to all companies employing 50 or more workers and is expected to cover about 40 percent of the workforce. In practice, the impact of the bill may prove to be modest. Many workers simply cannot afford to take unpaid leave. Further, many large companies already had such rules in place and at least 12 states had previously imposed rules as strong as the new federal standard. In any case, as the accompanying table illustrates, the new U.S. standard is quite modest in comparison with those of our competitors abroad. But have those countries been too generous?

INTERNATIONAL

Family Leave Policies around the World		
Country	Duration of Leave (weeks)	Number of Paid Weeks and Percent of Normal Pay (paid by government and/or employer)
Canada	17–41	15 weeks/60%
France	18	16 weeks/90%
Germany	14–26	14–19 weeks/100%
Japan	12	12 weeks/60%
Sweden	12–52	38 weeks/90%

Source: Women at Work, International Labour Office, Global Survey. Reprinted in Karen Mathes, "Is Family Leave Legislation Necessary?" *HR Focus,* 69, no. 3 (March 1992), p. 3.

AIDS

Expenses for chronic, serious illnesses have skyrocketed. The average treatment for an AIDS patient is estimated to cost something over $100,000.[69] As a consequence, many employees who most desperately need health care are threatened with the loss of their employer-provided coverage. John McGann, a Texas employee of H & H Music Company, was diagnosed with AIDS. H & H's insurance plan had a $1 million lifetime cap, and at least in that sense, McGann felt secure. Then, when his bills began to mount, the company changed to a new plan that had an AIDS cap of $5,000. McGann died in 1991, and that same year a federal court ruled that H & H had been within its rights in *retroactively* changing its insurance plan.[70] McGann's executor took the case to the U.S. Supreme Court, which declined to hear it.[71] H & H had switched to a self-insured plan where the company pays its own insurance claims. Such plans are governed by the federal benefits law, ERISA (discussed later in this chapter), under the terms of which H & H's change was lawful. About 40 percent of American workers are covered by self-insured plans. Many company insurance plans, self-insured and otherwise, limit or exclude coverage for such things as psychiatric care and infertility treatments.

At this writing in 1994, Congress is considering legislation to prohibit retroactive changes in coverage, and the Americans with Disabilities Act (ADA) (see Chapter 13) forbids discrimination in insurance plans, although the language of the statute is unclear.[72] McGann may have been able to use the ADA to block the H & H action under recently released Equal Employment Opportunity Commission guidelines interpreting the act. However, disease-specific insurance caps are permissible where they are not simply a "subterfuge" to avoid the ADA—that is, where the distinction in treatment is the result not of discrimination but of legitimate actuarial/financial/risk classification considerations. Several years of litigation will likely be necessary to resolve this issue.

COBRA

Also of note in the area of health insurance is the Consolidated Budget Reconciliation Act of 1985 (COBRA), which, among other provisions, requires most employers to permit employees to retain group health coverage at their own expense when they leave the company unless they were fired for gross misconduct. That option also extends to the spouse and children of an employee, even if the employee dies or is divorced. Coverage must be available to the employee and family for a period of 18 to 36 months, depending on the circumstances.

UNEMPLOYMENT COMPENSATION/WARN

The tragedy of the Depression, when up to 25 percent of the workforce was unemployed, led in 1935 to the passage of the Social Security Act, one portion of which provided for an unemployment insurance program. Today, all 50 states and the federal government are engaged in a cooperative system that helps to protect the temporarily jobless. The system is financed through a payroll tax paid by employers.

The actual state tax rate for each employer varies, depending on the employer's *experience* ratings—the number of layoffs in its workforce. Thus, employers have an incentive to retain employees. In 1992, combined federal and state unemployment taxes per employee ranged from a high of about $630 in Rhode Island to a low of just over $90 in South Dakota.

Rules vary by state, but, in general, employees qualify for unemployment benefits by reaching a specified total of annual wages. Those losing their jobs must apply to a state agency for unemployment compensation, which varies by state and ranges from approximately $150 per week to over $400. Benefits may be collected up to a specified maximum period, usually 26 weeks. During that time, those collecting compensation must be ready to work and must make an effort to find suitable work. Workers may be disqualified from unemployment coverage for a variety of reasons, including quitting work or being fired for misconduct. Because of disqualifications, failure to reach the necessary wage total for eligibility, and a variety of other reasons, only about one-third of those losing their jobs subsequently collect unemployment compensation.

WARN

In 1988, Congress sought to ease some job loss situations by enacting the Worker Adjustment and Retraining Notification Act (WARN), which requires firms to provide 60 days notice if they lay off one-third or more of their workers at any site employing at least 150 workers, drop 500 employees at any site, or close a plant employing at least 50 workers. However, a 1993 General Accounting Office study concluded that the law had been ineffectual, with half of plant closings not covered by the law and many firms simply remaining ignorant of the law's requirements. Congress is considering stiffer requirements, although critics fear that any change will simply encourage increased use of contract and part-time employees.

SOCIAL SECURITY

The 1935 Social Security Act, as amended, protects those retired workers who qualified for the program by paying taxes to the social security fund for a specified number of quarters. The act also provides payments for disability, hospital insurance (Medicare for the aged), and survivors of deceased workers. About 90 percent of the workforce is covered by social security. With some exceptions, workers are required to pay a tax, which is deducted from payroll checks by employers. That sum is then matched by the employers and forwarded to the federal government.

Crisis?

Serious problems are on the horizon. Happily, average life expectancies continue to climb, but that means the ratio of employed workers to those retired is falling. In 1935, 10 adults were working to support each retiree; today, there are 5 or so; and by the year 2035, only 2 adults will be working for every adult who is retired.[73]

PENSIONS

As early as the late 1800s, some employers began to adopt pension plans for their employees. In 1974, Congress approved the Employee Retirement Income Security Act (ERISA), under which the government regulates pension funds to help ensure their long-term financial security by reducing fraud and mismanagement. ERISA requires that fund managers keep detailed records, engage in prudent investments, and provide an annual report that has been certified by qualified, impartial third parties.

ERISA also establishes strict *vesting* rights (the point at which the employee has a nonforfeitable right to the funds) to ensure that employees actually receive the pensions to which they are entitled. ERISA requires that employee contributions must vest fully and immediately. Employer contributions typically vest after 10 years of work, but other options are available. Furthermore, those vested funds are not lost should the employee change jobs.

ERISA also included provisions for establishing the Pension Benefit Guaranty Corporation to protect retirees in the event of the failure of a pension fund. The PBGC guarantees that vested persons will be paid up to a specified maximum, even if the pension fund does not have sufficient resources to meet its obligations. PBGC funding is provided by company contributions.

Problems?

Despite the PBGC, ERISA, union efforts, and many well-meaning companies, millions of employees in retirement and more to come cannot be assured of the security that we have come to expect in old age. The basic problem, of course, is money. The rocky course of our economy in recent years is now being felt by retirees:

1. A recent survey found that two-thirds of the major American corporations have reduced retiree health plans or intend to do so.[74] Under ERISA, those benefits can be reduced or eliminated, as established in the *McGann* case, discussed earlier in this chapter.
2. About 15 percent of the PBGC-backed pension funds (representing 41 million Americans) are not fully funded. For example, General Motors agreed in 1990 to add $3 billion to its employees' pension benefits, even though its existing plan was underfunded by many billions of dollars. In 1992, GM remained about $12 billion short of full funding in its pension fund, but it hopes to be fully funded by the end of the century.[75]

Questions

1. *a.* Why should corporations be required to provide unpaid leave for employees as specified in the 1993 Family Leave bill?
   b. How would you have voted on that bill? Explain.
2. Clearly, cutting the health benefits of workers like McGann (an AIDS victim) or retirees seems unfair, but would you make such cuts if necessary to maintain your company's competitiveness in the market? Explain.

Part Six—Termination: Protection from Wrongful Discharge

Most Americans work without benefit of an employment contract for a specified period of time. They are labeled *at-will employees* in that they may be fired at any time, but they may also quit at any time. One study estimates that 150,000 U.S. workers are *unjustly* discharged annually.[76] During the 1970s, wrongful discharge suits totaled fewer than 200, while in 1989 alone more than 20,000 such suits were litigated in some fashion.[77]

Historically, the at-will worker in the United States could be discharged at any time for good reasons, bad reasons, or no reason at all. Harsh though it may seem, the employment-at-will doctrine is merely an extension of well-settled contract principles: Employer and employee both freely entered the bargain understanding its terms, and thus the court should, in general, enforce those terms, including the right of dismissal and the right of the employee to quit at any time. Critics argue that the doctrine ignores the obvious inequality of bargaining power between employers and employees. Nonetheless, the general rule remains that employees without a contract for a specified term are presumed to be working at will and thus may be dismissed for any reason. However, in recent decades the at-will rule has been softened by certain legislative and judicially imposed limitations. While the law varies greatly from state to state, those limitations are increasingly common. Statutory exceptions to the at-will rule include our labor laws protecting union workers and the equal employment opportunity laws that forbid the dismissal of an employee for discriminatory reasons.

Judicial Limitations on At-Will Principles

Recent court decisions have provided new grounds for dismissed at-will employees to claim that they have been wronged. Those judicial decisions were often provoked by transparently unjust dismissals including, for example, whistleblowers who exposed their employers' misdeeds and employees who declined to commit perjury on behalf of their employers. Those judicial limitations to the at-will doctrine fall into four categories: (1) express or implied contracts, (2) implied covenant of good faith and fair dealing, (3) public policy, and (4) tort claims.

Express or Implied Employment Contracts. A number of states have recognized a contract protection for at-will employees that arises, typically, either from the employee handbook or from employer conduct and oral representations. The notion here is that the courts will imply a contract based either on language in the handbook or on such assurances of continued employment as routine promotions, no notice of poor performance, longevity, and oral communications.

Implied Covenant of Good Faith and Fair Dealing.   A few state courts, including those in California most emphatically, have held that neither party to a contract may *act in bad faith* to deprive the other of the benefits of the contract. For example, a California court held that a newly hired, at-will employee who quit his former job, moved across country, and set up an office and was then dismissed before actually beginning work was damaged by his employer's breach of the implied covenant.[78]

Public Policy.   The majority of the states have now adopted some form of public policy (the general preference of the citizenry) exception providing that a dismissal is wrongful if it results from employee conduct that is consistent with the will of the people as expressed in statutes, constitutions, and so on. Those exceptions are established on a case-by-case basis, and they differ from state to state. In addition to those noted above, the exception often protects, for example, those fired for pursuing a lawful claim (e.g., workers' compensation) and those fired for fulfilling a civic responsibility (e.g., jury duty).

Tort Claims.   An influential California decision in the *Foley* case[79] and other similar cases around the country have limited dismissed at-will employees' rights to recover damages in actions for breach of contract and breach of the implied warranty of good faith and fair dealing to *economic losses* (out-of-pocket costs and lost wages). One of the consequences of that line of reasoning is that dismissed employees are increasingly turning to various kinds of tort actions (often labeled *tag-along torts*) where the potential financial recovery, including punitive damages, is much greater than for contract claims alone. Those tort possibilities include, among others, defamation, intentional infliction of emotional distress, interference with contract, and invasion of privacy.[80]

The following case addresses the public policy limitation on the at-will rule.

WAGENSELLER v. SCOTTSDALE MEMORIAL HOSPITAL
710 P.2d 1025 (Arizona S.Ct. 1985)

Justice Feldman

Catherine Sue Wagenseller petitioned this court to review a decision of the Court of Appeals affirming in part the trial court's judgment in favor of Scottsdale Memorial Hospital and certain Hospital employees (defendants). The trial court had dismissed all causes of action on defendants' motion for summary judgment . . .

Catherine Wagenseller began her employment at Scottsdale Memorial Hospital as a staff nurse in March 1975, having been personally recruited by the manager of the emergency department, Kay Smith. Wagenseller was an "at-will" employee—one hired without specific contractual term. Smith was her supervisor. In August 1978, Wagenseller was assigned to the position of ambulance charge nurse, and approximately one year later was promoted to the position of paramedic coordinator . . . Three months later, on November 1, 1979, Wagenseller was terminated.

Most of the events surrounding Wagenseller's work at the Hospital and her subsequent termination are not disputed, although the parties differ in their interpretation of the inferences to be drawn from and the significance of these events. For more than four years, Smith and Wagenseller maintained a friendly, professional, working relationship. In May 1979, they joined a group consisting largely of personnel from other hospitals for an eight-day camping and rafting trip down the Colorado River. According to Wagenseller, "an uncomfortable feeling" developed between her and Smith as the trip progressed—a feeling that Wagenseller ascribed to "the behavior that Kay Smith was displaying." Wagenseller states that this included public urination, defecation and bathing, heavy drinking, and "grouping up" with other rafters. Wagenseller did not participate in any of these activities. She also refused to join in the group's staging of a parody of the song "Moon River," which allegedly concluded with members of the group "mooning" the audience. Smith and others allegedly performed the "Moon River" skit twice at the Hospital following the group's return from the river, but Wagenseller declined to participate there as well.

Wagenseller contends that her refusal to engage in these activities caused her relationship with Smith to deteriorate and was the proximate cause of her termination. She claims that following the river trip Smith began harassing her, using abusive language and embarrassing her in the company of other staff. Other emergency department staff reported a similar marked change in Smith's behavior toward Wagenseller after the trip, although Smith denied it.

Up to the time of the river trip, Wagenseller had received consistently favorable job performance evaluations. Two months before the trip, Smith completed an annual evaluation report in which she rated Wagenseller's performance as "exceed(ing) results expected," the second highest of five possible ratings. In August and October 1979, Wagenseller met first with Smith and then with Smith's successor, Jeannie Steindorff, to discuss some problems regarding her duties as paramedic coordinator and her attitude toward the job. On November 1, 1979, following an exit interview at which Wagenseller was asked to resign and refused, she was terminated.

She appealed her dismissal . . . When this appeal was denied, Wagenseller brought suit against the Hospital, its personnel administrators, and her supervisor, Kay Smith.

Wagenseller, an "at-will" employee, contends that she was fired for reasons which contravene public policy and without legitimate cause related to job performance. She claims that her termination was wrongful, and that damages are recoverable under both tort and contract theories. The Hospital argues that an "at-will" employee may be fired for cause, without cause, or for "bad" cause . . .

* * * * *

In recent years there has been apparent dissatisfaction with the absolutist formulation of the common law at-will rule . . .

The trend has been to modify the at-will rule by creating exceptions to its operation. Three general exceptions have developed. The most widely accepted approach is the "public policy" exception, which permits recovery upon a finding that the employer's conduct undermined some important public policy . . .

The public policy exception to the at-will doctrine began with a narrow rule permitting employees to sue their employers when a statute expressly prohibited their discharge. This formulation was then expanded to include any discharge in violation of a statutory expression of public policy . . . Courts later allowed a cause of action for violation of public policy, even in the absence of a specific statutory prohibition. The New Hampshire Supreme Court announced perhaps the most expansive rule when it held an employer liable for discharging an employee who refused to go out with her foreman. The court concluded that termination "motivated by bad faith or malice or based on retaliation is not [in] the best interest of the economic system or the public good and constitutes a breach of the employment contract." . . .

. . . The leading case recognizing a public policy exception to the at-will doctrine is *Palmateer v. International Harvester Co.,* which holds that an employee stated a cause of action for wrongful discharge when he claimed he was fired for supplying information to police investigating alleged criminal violations by a co-employee. Addressing the issue of what constitutes "clearly mandated public policy," the court stated:

> There is no precise definition of the term. In general, it can be said that public policy concerns what is right and just and what affects the citizens of the State collectively. It is to be found in the State's constitution and statutes and when they are silent, in its judicial decisions . . .

Other courts have allowed a cause of action where an employee was fired for refusing to violate a specific statute . . . Similarly, courts have found terminations improper where to do otherwise would have impinged on the employee's exercise of statutory rights or duties . . . A division of our Court of Appeals recently adopted the public policy exception, ruling that the discharge of an at-will employee who refused to conceal a violation of Arizona's theft statute was contrary to public policy . . .

It is difficult to justify this court's further adherence to a rule which permits an employer to fire someone for "cause morally wrong." So far as we can tell, no court faced with a termination that violated a "clear mandate of public policy" has refused to adopt the public policy exception. Certainly, a court would be hard pressed to find a rationale to hold that an employer could with impunity fire an employee who refused to commit perjury . . . It may be argued, of course, that our economic system functions best if employers are given wide latitude in dealing with employees. We assume that it is in the public interest that employers continue to have that freedom.

We, therefore, adopt the public policy exception to the at-will termination rule. We hold that an employer may fire for good cause or for no cause. He may not fire for bad cause—that which violates public policy . . .

We turn then to the question of where "public policy" may be found and how it may be recognized and articulated. As the expressions of our founders and those we have elected to our legislature, our state's constitution and statutes embody the public conscience of the people of this state. It is thus in furtherance of their interests to hold that an employer may not with impunity violate the dictates of public policy found in the provisions of our statutory and constitutional law.

We do not believe, however, that expressions of public policy are contained only in the statutory and constitutional law, nor do we believe that all statements made in either a statute or the constitution are expressions of public policy. Turning first to the identification of other sources, we note our agreement with the following:

> Public policy is usually defined by the political branches of government . . . Thus, we will look to the pronouncements of our founders, our legislature, and our courts to discern the public policy of this state.

All such pronouncements, however, will not provide the basis for a claim of wrongful discharge. Only those which have a singularly public purpose will have such force . . .

* * * * *

In the case before us, Wagenseller refused to participate in activities which arguably would have violated our indecent exposure statute, A.R.S. Section 13–1402. She claims that she was fired because of this refusal . . .

While this statute may not embody a policy which "strikes at the heart of a citizen's social rights, duties and responsibilities" as clearly and forcefully as a statute prohibiting perjury, we believe that it was enacted to preserve and protect the commonly recognized sense of public privacy and decency. The statute does, therefore, recognize bodily privacy as a "citizen's social right." We disagree with the Court of Appeals' conclusion that a minor violation of the statute would not violate public policy. The nature of the act, and not its magnitude, is the issue. The legislature has already concluded that acts fitting the statutory description contravene the public policy of this state. We thus uphold this state's public policy by holding that termination for refusal to commit an act which might violate A.R.S. Section 13–1402 may provide the basis of a claim for wrongful discharge . . .

From a theoretical standpoint, we emphasize that the "public policy exception" which we adopt does not require the court to make a new contract for the parties . . .

* * * * *

. . . [We] adopt the "public policy" exception to the at-will termination rule and hold that the trial court erred in granting judgment against plaintiff on this theory. On remand plaintiff will be entitled to a jury trial if she can make a prima facie showing that her termination was caused by her refusal to perform some act contrary to public policy, or her performance of some act which, as a matter of public policy, she had a right to do . . .

The decision of the Court of Appeals is vacated and the case remanded to the trial court.

Questions

1. Express the central issue(s) in *Wagenseller.*
2. In reading *Wagenseller,* did you have the sense that the Arizona Supreme Court was "stretching" the law in some sense in order to achieve justice? Explain.
3. An employer provided medical insurance, a pension, and a profit-sharing plan for its at-will employees. After successfully completing the company's probationary period, an employee at will was dismissed. The employee sued.
   a. Based on these facts, build an argument for the plaintiff's wrongful discharge claim.
   b. Decide. Explain. See *Luedtke* v. *Nabors Alaska Drilling, Inc.,* 768 P.2d 1123 (1989).
4. Freeman, a television anchorperson employed by KSN, gave birth to her second child. On the day she returned from the hospital, she was notified that she had been dismissed. Six weeks later, she became unable to lactate. She sued KSN for wrongful discharge, tortious interference with contract, and negligent infliction of emotional distress. Decide. Explain. See *Freeman* v. *Medevac Midamerica of Kansas, Inc.,* 719 F. Supp. 1014 (D Kan. 1989).
5. An applicant received a job offer, which was confirmed in a letter stating that his annual salary would be $80,000. He was terminated seven months into his first year of work. Was the dismissal a breach of contract? Explain. See *Bernard* v. *IMI Sys., Inc.,* 618 A.2d 338 (N.J. S.Ct. 1993).

TERMINATION: HANDLE WITH CARE

Remember that employment at will remains overwhelmingly the law of the land. We have been looking at *limitations* on that doctrine. Those limitations have become increasingly prevalent. Nonetheless, in most instances, the at-will employee can be dismissed without fear of the courts. How, then, do we actually go about the practice of termination in a manner designed to maximize fairness to all parties and to minimize legal fallout? Consider three potential pitfalls: (1) employee handbooks, (2) employer conduct, and (3) defamation.

Employee Handbooks. Employee handbooks are important to establish a code of conduct for a business and to outline the employer's responsibilities along with the employee's rights and benefits. Unfortunately, sloppy handbooks often lead to legal problems. The handbook should include unambiguous language, uncontradicted by provisions elsewhere in the handbook, indicating that the employee is serving at will.

Employer Conduct. At the actual moment of termination, the language and procedures employed are important both for the dignity of the employee and to prevent subsequent legal problems.

Advice on Termination

Interviews with consulting firms indicate various methods to be followed when employees must be let go. Some of this advice is as follows:

Do's	*Don'ts*
• Give as much warning as possible for mass layoffs.	• Don't leave room for confusion when firing. Tell the individual in the first sentence he is terminated.
• Sit down one-on-one with the individual, in a private office.	• Don't allow time for debate during a firing session.
• Complete a firing session within 15 minutes.	• Don't make personal comments when firing someone; keep the conversation professional.
• Provide written explanations of severance benefits.	• Don't rush a fired employee off-site unless security is really an issue.
• Provide outplacement services away from company headquarters.	• Don't fire people on significant dates, like the 25th anniversary of their employment or the day their mother died.
• Be sure the employee hears about his termination from a manager, not a colleague.	• Don't fire employees when they are on vacation or have just returned.
• Express appreciation for what the employee has contributed, if appropriate.	

Source: Suzanne Alexander, "Firms Get Plenty of Practice at Layoffs, but They Often Bungle the Firing Process," *The Wall Street Journal,* October 14, 1991, p. B1. Reprinted by permission of *The Wall Street Journal,* © 1991 Dow Jones & Company, Inc. All Rights Reserved Worldwide.

Defamation. Errors in the firing process can become very expensive, as Procter & Gamble learned in 1993 when a Texas jury awarded a dismissed P&G employee $15.6

million. Don Hagler had worked for Procter for 41 years when he was publicly accused of stealing a $35 phone and was fired. Hagler said the phone was his, and he accused P&G of libel because notices accusing him of theft were posted on company bulletin boards and included in the company E-mail system. Procter & Gamble may appeal the decision.[81] Consider the following advice for avoiding defamation in the firing process.

Some Do's and Don'ts of Firing

- **Be certain of the facts** when firing someone. Conduct a thorough investigation and bring in experts in employment law and labor relations either from corporate headquarters or from the outside.
- **Be factual and avoid innuendo** when discussing a firing with other people or when recording what happened. Such caution should extend to personnel files as well.
- **Tell only those who need to know** the details of a worker's firing. Limiting the number of people who know gives the fired employee less ammunition for suing for defamation of character. It shows professionalism and good faith on the part of the company.
- **Avoid making examples** of fired employees. Let the fired employee's behavior and the facts speak for themselves. The details of a firing often seep out in the workplace and indirectly serve as a deterrent.
- **If an example must be made** of someone to prevent similar actions, be extremely careful in the wording of any announcement. Accuse someone of something as serious as theft or sexual harassment only if you're sure of the facts.

Source: Gabriella Stern, "Companies Discover that some Firings Backfire into Costly Defamation Suits," *The Wall Street Journal,* May 5, 1993, p. B1. Reprinted by permission of *The Wall Street Journal,* © 1993 Dow Jones & Company, Inc. All Rights Reserved Worldwide.

Reform?

Wrongful discharge suits can be very expensive for employers and often not particularly remunerative for fired employees. A study by the Rand Institute for Civil Justice found a median verdict of $177,000. After appeals, settlements, and lawyer fees, the median net recovery was $74,500.[82] From both sides of the fence, the system seems not to make a lot of sense. Furthermore, the greater cost from wrongful discharge litigation may lie in workers not hired. Another Rand study estimates that employment may drop as much as 5 percent in some states because of fear of wrongful discharge suits. Companies simply turn to temporaries, retain poor performers, and engage in elaborate screening measures as strategies for avoiding lawsuits.[83]

Avoid Litigation.   Because of the problems terminations can cause, employers and lawyers alike are looking to methods of avoiding wrongful discharge suits. In some instances, workers waive the right to sue in exchange for mandatory arbitration of disputes.[84] Other companies have given up the right to dismissal at will. For example, Federal Express lets employees appeal discharges to appeals panels composed of five members, three of whom are chosen from a pool by the employee.[85] Finally, the

National Conference of Commissioners on Uniform State Laws has drafted a "Model Employment Termination Act" for possible adoption by the states. The model act has three key ingredients:

1. Termination for good cause only.
2. Arbitration as the preferred method of settling termination cases.
3. Strict limits on employer liability for wrongful discharge.[86]

Part Seven—Social Issues

IMMIGRATION

INTERNATIONAL

Given that America is a nation founded on immigration and proudly open to the "huddled masses" of the globe for more than 200 years, it now comes as something of a jolt that immigration policy has become one of the most hotly disputed issues in American life.

Part of the unease lies simply in the numbers. From 1980 to 1990, approximately 9.5 million legal and illegal immigrants entered the United States, the most in any decade since we became a nation.[87] Those immense numbers in a time of economic distress, of course, cause alarm. Further, many Americans, but particularly those in southern California and Texas, are troubled that we are unable to stop the influx of illegal aliens. Others worry that we won't be able to assimilate the new immigrants in a manner that respects multiculturalism but maintains a nation basically of one language, political tradition, and will. Finally, some say the current distress is really just another manifestation of racism, in that most of the newer immigrants are not European Caucasians.

In any case, a 1993 *USA Today* poll found nearly two-thirds of Americans wanting a reduction in immigration.[88] Likewise, nearly two-thirds think that immigrants hurt the economy (by holding down wages) more than they help it.[89] Seventy-five percent believe that Irish immigrants benefit America and 65 percent think the same of Poles, but only 19 percent share that sentiment about Haitians and 20 percent about Iranians.[90]

We have responded to this situation with legislation:

1. The 1986 Immigration Reform and Control Act (IRCA) sought to slow the entry of illegal aliens by subjecting employers to criminal and civil penalties for knowingly hiring unauthorized aliens. IRCA also contained an amnesty provision that permitted illegal aliens already in the United States to come forward and secure permanent resident status. Nearly 3 million formerly illegal aliens have secured permanent resident status under the act, but illegal entry continues to flourish.[91]

2. In an effort to boost our economy, legislation was approved in 1990 to triple the number of visas annually allotted to highly skilled workers such as scientists, engineers, artists, athletes, and managers to about 140,000. Additional visas were set aside for investor-immigrants who can create jobs in America. However, as the following article suggests, the new investor program is off to a slow start.

GIVE US YOUR TIRED,
YOUR POOR . . .
YOUR MILLIONAIRES

Jeffrey A. Tannenbaum and Brent Bowers

After attracting millions of the huddled masses yearning to breathe free, the U.S. is having trouble wooing a new group: fat cats.

So far, a new program that would offer permanent residence-permits to foreigners willing to invest in U.S. businesses has landed exactly six people.

Foreign capitalists, it turns out, aren't rushing to buy their way into the citadel of capitalism. Among their reasons: They don't like to pay taxes or take unnecessary risks. The land of the free may offer Disney World, but some foreigners think other countries offer sweeter deals.

Turning Investors into Americans

The 1990 U.S. immigration law laid out the welcome mat for the wealthy, partly to compete with Canada, Australia and other nations that had taken similar steps. The U.S. set aside a quota of 10,000 "green cards," or permanent residence-permits, for foreigners who invest a minimum of $1 million (or $500,000 in a depressed area) in a business that creates at least 10 jobs . . .

. . . [O]nly 225 potential investors, largely from Taiwan and China, had filed visa petitions by the end of last month. The government has approved only six. (Canada's program, which requires less money, has attracted more than 30,000 investors in five years.)

"Everybody thought the 10,000 [green cards] would be gobbled up," says Miami attorney Jeffry Brauwerman . . . But foreigners able to afford the $1 million investment can usually find other routes to long-term residence or other places to go, he says. "I call the program a bust."

While some are more hopeful, other specialists agree that the initiative failed to take practical realities into account. For example, says Austin Frago-

Competing for Millionaires (conditions for taking part in programs designed to attract immigrant-investors)

	United States	Canada
Investment required in U.S. currency	$500,000– $1,000,000	$210,000– $420,000
Number of new jobs that must be created	5 to 10	No requirement
Pre-approved investment opportunities available	No	Yes

Sources: American Immigration Lawyers Association; Canadian government.

men, an attorney with Fragomen Del Rey & Bernsen of New York, the law requires investors to document that their funds were acquired lawfully and were duly reported to their home governments.

"Get real," says Mr. Fragomen . . .

The biggest drawback for potential investors is Washington's imposition of its taxing authority on the world-wide income of permanent residents, says Mr. Leiden of the American Immigration Lawyers Association. Other foreigners with U.S. operations are taxed only on U.S. earnings.

Uncertainties about Rules

The law's vagueness is another problem. The government still hasn't posted exact criteria for converting conditional investor visas into permanent ones . . .

Some specialists also complain that the investment and job-creation requirements are impractical. "If the government would reduce the amounts to $500,000 and five employees, they'd have a lot more applicants," says Martin J. Lawler, an immigration lawyer in San Francisco . . .

*   *   *   *   *

What to do? New York lawyer Michael Phulwani thinks the only hope is to give foreign entrepreneurs "a freer hand." He says he has gotten close to 40 inquiries about the program, but all but one of the potential investors backed away upon learning of all the conditions.

Source: The Wall Street Journal, March 19, 1992, p. B2. Reprinted by the permission of *The Wall Street Journal,* © 1992 Dow Jones & Company, Inc. All Rights Reserved Worldwide.

Questions

1. An excerpt from a *Wall Street Journal* commentary:

   > Just as countries compete in a worldwide market where goods and services are exchanged, they also compete in the market for people . . .
   >
   > In both Canada and Australia, visas are now allocated through a point system, which grades visa applicants in terms of educational attainment, age, and occupational background. The presence of relatives in the country is only one factor among many. Canada and Australia also "sell" visas to persons who have sufficient financial resources to open businesses and create employment opportunities for natives . . .
   >
   > **Discrimination?**
   >
   > Of course, a visa allocation system based on the applicant's ability to pay discriminates against people who lack these financial resources. Similarly, a point system discriminates against people who lack the favored skill characteristics. Any visa allocation system, however, is bound to lead to inequities, and the inequities that would be created by a merit-oriented immigration policy would be no more egregious than those associated with present or previous immigration policies.[92]

   The 1990 U.S. immigration law puts our policy more in line with those in Australia and Canada. Have we taken the proper course? Explain the competing considerations.

2. *a.* Should we simply sell immigration slots to the highest bidders, as suggested by free market economist Gary Becker?

   b. What are some of the competing policy considerations? See Gary Becker, "An Open Door for Immigrants—the Auction," *The Wall Street Journal,* October 14, 1992, p. A16.

BENEFITS FOR HOMOSEXUAL PARTNERS

Should the partners and dependents of unmarried homosexual employees receive employment benefits such as those accorded to the spouses and dependents of married employees? The article that follows explains that a small but growing number of American companies are taking that direction.

GAYS MAKE GAINS IN HEALTH CARE

Julia Lawlor

Software giant Microsoft is the latest and the largest company to extend health benefits to partners and dependents of its gay employees.

Could GM, GE, and IBM be next? Not likely, say benefits experts. At least in the foreseeable future.

While Digital Equipment and Du Pont are studying it, most large companies have been slow to add these benefits. AT&T has angered gay employees for refusing to pay death benefits to the partner of a gay employee who died.

Most of the 27 firms and groups that now offer unmarried-partner health benefits are either small, progressive companies like Ben & Jerry's; cities like Berkeley, Calif.; or high-tech firms that have younger management and enlightened policies. Apple Computer, Silicon Graphics and Borland International added gay-partner benefits to recruit and keep good employees, says Mark Wagoner of Foster Higgins consultants.

The companies are "definitely younger, definitely hipper," says Alan Emery, a corporate consultant from San Francisco.

Only about 75 companies offer any kind of benefit to employees' unmarried partners—gay or heterosexual. Those benefits can range from access to the company gym to full health benefits. Lotus Development lets gay partners withdraw funds from employees' 401(k) retirement plans.

Despite the high cost of AIDS treatment, companies that give gay-partner health benefits say added costs have been low. That's because only 1% to 4% of eligible employees sign up. Microsoft estimates its health-care costs will rise only 1% as a result of the change.

Why do so few employees sign up for these benefits?

For one, they have to pay taxes on them. The IRS doesn't recognize unmarried partners as dependents.

And to get the benefits, you have to admit that you're gay. That's a big problem. Says Paula Ettelbrick, a former official of a gay-rights group: "The fear of discrimination at work is so widespread that most people remain closeted."

Source: *USA Today*, April 23, 1993, p. 1B. Copyright 1993, *USA Today*. Reprinted with permission.

Questions

1. List the nonfinancial issues that a company should consider in deciding whether to follow the direction taken by Microsoft and others.
2. In your mind, is this issue akin to race and gender discrimination? Explain.
3. Would you offer these benefits, as Microsoft decided to do? Explain.

CHAPTER QUESTIONS

1. In general, employers are forced to bear (or at least share) the legal burden for their employees' negligent conduct on the job.

   a. Why do we force employers to bear that responsibility?

   b. Should we do so? Explain.

2. The government's recent aggressiveness in pursuing child labor violations has been called into question by some scholars and commentators. Some are arguing that jobs and school in combination are the best track for some young people. And Jeff Riggenbach, a freelance writer, argues that the real motivation for aggressive child labor enforcement is to prevent young people from competing with their elders in the job market:

> This is the real purpose of child labor laws—not the protection of children but the protection of privilege. You aren't "protecting" a 15-year-old by telling him he can't take a part-time job at a burger emporium because the hours are 5–8 P.M. and it's against the law for kids under 16 to work later than 7 on school nights.
>
> That's not protection—it's unfair discrimination.[93]

Should we vigorously enforce the child labor laws? Explain.

3. Many companies refer to credit reports when investigating job applicants. The Fair Credit Reporting Act (see Chapter 15) requires employers to notify applicants if they are rejected because of information in a credit report.
   a. In your judgment, does evidence of failure to pay debts constitute useful information in the job selection process? Explain.
   b. Is the use of that information an "invasion of privacy" as you understand it? Explain.

4. In some instances, a worker may voluntarily quit a job and still recover unemployment compensation.
   a. How might that happen?
   b. Is that policy fair to the employer? Explain.

5. Dismissing an employee whom the employer believes to have committed a theft at work might lead to a civil suit by the former employee claiming tort violations of the kind discussed in the materials on wrongful discharge.
   a. What tort claims might arise from such a dismissal?
   b. What tort claims might arise if the employer declined to allow the employee to go to the bathroom or to leave the building during questioning about the theft? See, for example, "Warning: Be Cautious in Worker-Theft Cases," *The Wall Street Journal,* May 14, 1990, p. B1.

6. In Iowa, a waitress was dismissed from a Maid-Rite Cafe for misconduct after she told others that the cafe was going to be closed. She had received that information from another employee. She learned that the original source of the story was an individual who was not associated with the cafe. Later, four people asked the waitress if the business was closing and she said that she had heard that to be the case. She lost her job, and she sought unemployment compensation. About 20 people in the community signed a petition saying that she was a good waitress and not the kind to start a rumor. How would you rule on her unemployment compensation claim? Explain. See Gene Raffensperger, "Woman Fired for Passing Rumor," *Des Moines Register,* April 29, 1989, p. 2A.

7. Stephen Bokat, vice president and general counsel of the U.S. Chamber of Commerce: "You fully expect that every time you discharge an employee, or don't promote an employee, or demote an employee, you're going to get a lawsuit. That was not true even 10 years ago."[94]
   a. Why are we experiencing an expansion in employee lawsuits?
   b. In general, is that trend toward litigation a necessary response to a historical abuse of power by employers? Explain.
   c. Can you suggest means other than litigation for settling workplace disputes?

8. As discussed in this chapter, many recent judicial decisions have afforded at-will employees much-improved protection against unfair dismissals. A special area of concern is whether at-will employees can be dismissed for off-duty conduct. The decisions are split, but the trend seems to be toward greater respect and protection for employee privacy. Nonetheless, companies still retain broad latitude to dismiss. For example, an employee convicted of selling drugs would most likely not be protected by the courts from a company dismissal.

   Virginia Rulon-Miller, an IBM salesperson, had been dating another IBM employee, Matt Blum, for several years. Her superiors were aware of the relationship. Blum left IBM to join a competitor, QYX, and he moved from San Francisco to Philadelphia. QYX transferred him back to San Francisco, and he and Rulon-Miller resumed dating. Again, her superiors were aware of the relationship, and one mentioned that he didn't "have any problem" with her romance. Rulon-Miller did well in her sales role and was promoted to a management position, where she continued to do well, as evidenced by a $4,000 raise. Nonetheless, one week after receiving notice of the raise, Rulon-Miller was either dismissed (her version) or "transferred" (the company's version). IBM felt her romance and her concern for the success of Blum created a conflict of interest. Despite being an at-will employee, Rulon-Miller argued that she was protected by IBM's written policies that detail those circumstances under which an employee's private life can become a company issue. She filed suit, claiming wrongful discharge. Decide. Explain. See *Rulon-Miller* v. *IBM,* 1 BNA IER Cases 405, 162 Cal App 3d 241 (1984).

9. Illinois state law forbids the retaliatory discharge of employees who file workers' compensation claims. The law provides that the employee must show that he or she was discharged and that the employer's motive for doing so was to deter the employee's exercise of workers' compensation rights.

   Assembly-line worker Jonna Lingle, a union member, filed a workers' compensation claim for a wrist injury suffered on her job making washing machine parts for the Norge Division of Magic Chef, Inc. She was fired. The company said her claim was fraudulent. The union filed a grievance on her behalf, claiming a violation of their collective bargaining agreement protecting employees from discharge in the absence of "just cause." While that action was proceeding, Lingle sued Norge, claiming an unlawful retaliatory discharge. The lower court dismissed her case, saying it was preempted by the Labor-Management Relations Act of 1947 because her claim was "inextricably intertwined" with the union-management agreement prohibiting discharge without just cause. And the court found that allowing the state law case to proceed would undermine the arbitration proceedings provided for under the collective bargaining agreement. The federal court of appeals affirmed, finding that the disposition of the retaliatory discharge claim would require an interpretation of the collective bargaining agreement and that any such interpretation was to employ federal labor law principles, thus assuring uniformity across the country and effectively preempting the application of state laws.

   Lingle appealed to the U.S. Supreme Court. A victory for her would significantly expand potential protections for those filing workers' compensation claims, whistle-blowers, victims of discrimination, and others who are parties to contracts but seek the shelter of state statutes providing protection greater than the contracts. The key to the case is whether the resolution of her state-law retaliatory discharge claim requires an interpretation of the meaning of the collective bargaining agreement to which she was a party. Decide. Explain. See *Jonna R. Lingle* v. *Norge Division of Magic Chef, Inc.,* 486 U.S. 399 (1988).

10. On the average, European workers enjoy very much better job benefits than their American counterparts. For example, if we include Social Security, the typical American worker will receive a pension providing about one-third of her preretirement income, while that average ranges from 50 to 90 percent in other industrialized nations.[95]

    a. Do we need to provide more generous pension provisions in the United States? Explain.

    b. If so, should the money come from employees, employers, the government, or some combination of all? Explain.

11. *Sweatshop* refers to a business that violates health and safety codes and, in general, provides dirty, unhealthy, unsafe, and poorly paid jobs. Recently, *Newsweek* observed:

    > After progressive labor laws and the growing muscle of unions almost vanquished old-style sweatshops in the 1950s and 1960s, they have returned. Once again, pieceworkers attach beads to belts in decrepit manufacturing lofts in Manhattan where piles of fabric block fire exits; seamstresses stitching together denim togs in El Paso are denied wages when owners make ends meet by stiffing their workers. But sweatshops have expanded beyond the rag trade into everything from plastics to flowers, thanks to the largest influx of immigrants ever to reach America since the great waves of Europeans lapped these shores late in the last century.[96]

    a. If we were to slow immigration, thus shrinking the labor pool, would wages and working conditions improve? Explain. Should we do so?

    b. What forces have led to a rebirth of sweatshop conditions?

    c. Can the free market protect workers from sweatshop conditions? Explain.

12. In the *Newsweek* article cited in question 11, economist Ruben Quiroz referred to the sweatshops as "modern slavery." Comment.

13. Kent Waldrep played football for Texas Christian University and received a scholarship for doing so. While playing in 1974, he was paralyzed. Waldrep had signed a letter of intent prior to coming to TCU indicating his commitment to play football for the University. In return for his scholarship, he was required to perform certain functions for the University—play football, practice, and travel.

    Waldrep sought workers' compensation for his injury. Decide. Explain. See Douglas Lederman, "Texas Panel . . . Workers' Compensation to Injured Athlete," *The Chronicle of Higher Education,* April 7, 1993, p. A33.

14. Employers often require employees to sign agreements not to compete with the employer if the employee should be dismissed from a job or leave it voluntarily.
    a. Why do employers seek such agreements?
    b. Are those agreements enforceable? Explain.

15. *Newsweek* argues that one of our most serious economic problems is the growing gap in wages and benefits between college graduates and high school graduates.

    > Back in 1979, a 30-year-old man with a college degree earned, on average, 27 percent more than a 30-year-old high school graduate. By 1991, the differential had widened to 65 percent.

    Newsweek suggests several government mandates to address this problem.
    a. What new legislation might the government impose on business in order to help protect blue-collar workers?
    b. Would you vote for those initiatives? Explain. See Marc Levinson, "Uphill Battle," *Newsweek,* December 7, 1992, p. 36.

16. Wisconsin and Iowa have approved legislation limiting an employer's right to do genetic testing of employees and applicants.
    a. Why do some employers give such tests?
    b. Should such tests be forbidden? Explain.

NOTES

1. Donald C. Bacon, "See You in Court," *Nation's Business* 77, no. 7 (July 1989), p. 17.

2. Clyde Summers, "Effective Remedies for Employment Rights: Preliminary Guidelines and Proposals," *University of Pennsylvania Law Review* 141, no. 2 (December 1992), p. 457.

3. *Mary M.* v. *City of Los Angeles,* 814 P.2d 1341 (1991).

4. *Odom* v. *Hubeny, Inc.,* 345 S.E.2d 886 (Ga. Ct. App. 1986).

5. Junda Woo, "Job Interviews Pose Rising Risk to Employers," *The Wall Street Journal,* March 11, 1992, p. B5.

6. Associated Press, "Strange Questions Cost Target $1.3 Million," *Waterloo Courier,* July 11, 1993, p. A3.

7. Ted Shelsby, "Lawsuits Curtail Checking References of Job Applicants," *Waterloo Courier,* January 29, 1990, p. B5.

8. Ted Shelsby, "Rules Change for Personnel Managers," *Waterloo Courier,* January 29, 1990, p. B5.

9. Jonathan Moses, "Employers Face New Liability: Truth in Hiring," *The Wall Street Journal,* July 9, 1993, p. B1.

10. *Stewart* v. *Jackson & Nash,* 976 F.2d 86 (2d Cir. 1992).

11. *Reich* v. *IBP, Inc.,* 820 F. Supp. 1315 (D. Kan. 1993).

12. See Daniel Seligman, "A Minimal Debate," *Fortune,* March 22, 1993, p. 180.

13. Junda Woo, "More 'On-Call' Workers Sue for Overtime," *The Wall Street Journal,* July 13, 1992, p. B6.

14. Albert Karr, "Japan's Diet Slims the National Work Week by Four Hours," *The Wall Street Journal,* July 13, 1993, p. A1.

15. Patricia McLaughlin, "Child Labor Issue Causing a Rift in Garment Industry," *Waterloo Courier,* May 9, 1993, p. D1.

16. Ibid.

17. Ibid.

18. Brian Dumaine, "Illegal Child Labor Comes Back," *Fortune,* April 5, 1993, p. 86.

19. Ibid.

20. Cathy Trost, "Don't Forget the Children," *The Wall Street Journal,* September 8, 1992, p. A1.

21. Dumaine, "Illegal Child Labor Comes Back," p. 86.

22. Jim Stanton, "More Teen-agers Mixing School, Job Responsibilities," *Waterloo Courier,* May 9, 1993, p. C1.

23. Dumaine, "Illegal Child Labor Comes Back," pp. 86, 87.

24. Associated Press, "Murder is Top Workplace Killer in Five States," *Des Moines Register,* November 29, 1993, p. 1A; and Stuart Silverstein, "Safety in the Workplace is Becoming a Growing Concern," *Waterloo Courier,* March 18, 1994, p. C1.

25. U.S. Department of Labor data.

26. Jeanne Saddler, "OSHA Sets Broader Rules to Protect Health-Care Workers from Infections," *The Wall Street Journal,* December 3, 1991, p. B4.

27. *American Dental Association* v. *Lynne Martin,* 984 F.2d 823 (1993). Petition for certiorari filed June 28, 1993.

28. *American Federation of Labor* v. *OSHA,* 965 F.2d 962 (11th Cir. 1992).

29. Anne Willette, "Morrell Settlement Calls for Health and Safety Plan," *Des Moines Register,* March 22, 1990, p. 10S.

30. Ibid.

31. Laurie Grossman, "Owner Sentenced to Nearly 20 Years over Plant Fire," *The Wall Street Journal,* September 15, 1992, p. C12.

32. Jonathan Moses and Junda Woo, "First Prosecution," *The Wall Street Journal,* February 10, 1992, p. B2.

33. Grossman, "Owner Sentenced," p. C12.

34. Associated Press, "More than Half of Poultry Plants Never Checked in North Carolina," *Waterloo Courier,* November 12, 1991, p. B4.

35. Ibid.

36. Christopher Conte, "Falling Behind: The U.S. Is Losing the Job-Safety War to Japan, Too," *The Wall Street Journal,* May 26, 1992, p. A1.

37. Ibid.

38. Ibid.

39. Roger Thompson, "Reforming Workers' Compensation," *Editorial Research Reports* 1, no. 14 (April 13, 1990), pp. 206, 209.

40. *Joseph Albanese's Case,* 389 N.E. 2d 83 (Mass. 1979).

41. *Lubrano* v. *Malinet,* 480 N.E. 2d 737 (N.Y. 1985).

42. *United Parcel Service* v. *Fetterman,* 336 S.E. 2d 892 (Va. 1985).

43. Edward Felsenthal and Arthur Hayes, "Race-Phobia Case Settled," *The Wall Street Journal,* December 23, 1992, p. B6.

44. *Fuqua Industries* v. *John G. Tomlinson, Jr.,* 983 F.2d 236 (11th Cir. 1992).

45. Lynne Duke, "Color Me Stressed; What If We All Sought Compensation for Our Race-Based Problems?" *The Washington Post,* August 16, 1992, p. C5.

46. Eric Schine, "Workers' Comp Goes under the Knife," *Business Week,* October 19, 1992, p. 90.

47. Larry Reynolds, "States Are Trying to Avoid Disaster with Workers' Comp," *HR Focus* 69, no. 12 (December 1992), p. 1.

48. Jim Carlton, "California Law Alters Workers' Compensation," *The Wall Street Journal,* July 19, 1993, p. A2.

49. Ibid.

50. Ibid.

51. "Fewer People Fail as Workplace Drug Testing Increases," *HR Focus* 70, no. 6 (June 1993), p. 24.

52. Ibid.

53. Ibid.

54. Ibid.

55. Littler, Mendelson, Fastiff, and Tichy, *The 1990 Employer,* vol. I, p. Q-11.

56. Ibid.

57. Ibid., p. Q-13.

58. See, e.g., *National Treasury Employees Union* v. *Von Raab,* 109 S.Ct. 1385 (1989).

59. See *Luck* v. *Southern Pacific Transportation Company,* 218 Cal. App. 3d 1 (1990). But see *Luedtke* v. *Nabors Alaska Drilling Co.,* 768 P. 2d 1123 (Alaska 1989).

60. The "Privacy and Testing" section draws heavily on Wade Lambert and Milo Geyelin, "Drug Testing by Companies May Be Grounds for Invasion-of-Privacy Claim," *The Wall Street Journal,* May 22, 1992, p. B2.

61. *Sarah Borse* v. *Piece Goods Shop, Inc.,* 963 F.2d 611 (3d Cir. 1992). Rehearing denied, 963 F.2d 626 (1992).

62. "Ban on Most Uses of Polygraph Tests Clears Congress," *The Wall Street Journal,* June 10, 1988, p. 40.

63. Daniel Seligman, "Searching for Integrity," *Fortune* 127, no. 5 (March 8, 1993), p. 140.

64. Wire Reports, "Bosses Peek at E-Mail," *USA Today,* May 24, 1993, p. B1.

65. Associated Press, "Company Cracking Down on Workers with Hickeys," *Waterloo Courier,* January 21, 1993, p. A6.

66. "Bosses Peek at E-Mail," p. B1.

67. Littler et al., *The 1990 Employer,* vol. I, p. K-1.

68. Dan Dundon, "Explosive Costs Could Rewrite Company-Employee 'Contract'", *Waterloo Courier,* February 4, 1990, p. A1.

69. Bruce Shenitz, "Patients Left Out in the Cold," *Newsweek,* November 23, 1992, p. 48.

70. *McGann* v. *H & H Music Co.,* 946 F.2d 401 (5th Cir. 1991).

71. *Greenburg* v. *H & H Music Co.,* 113 S.Ct. 482 (1992).

72. Shenitz, "Patients Left Out in the Cold," p. 48.

73. Editorial, "Avoiding a Social Security Crisis," *Des Moines Register,* December 26, 1992, p. 8A.

74. Melinda Beck, "Big Costs, Broken Promises," *Newsweek,* January 11, 1993, p. 59.

75. Albert Karr, "Risk to Retirees Rises as Firms Fail to Fund Pensions They Offer," *The Wall Street Journal,* February 4, 1993, p. A1.

76. Jack Stieber, "Recent Developments in Employment-at-Will," *Labor Law Journal* 36, no. 8 (August 1985), p. 557.

77. John Skipper, "Employer's Right to Make Choices Erodes," *Des Moines Register,* July 5, 1990, p. 8A.

78. *Sheppard* v. *Morgan Keegan & Co.,* 218 Cal. App. 3d 61 (1990).

79. *Foley* v. *Interactive Data Corp.,* 47 Cal. 3d 654 (1988).

80. This discussion of judicial limitations on the at-will doctrine relies heavily on Littler et al., *The 1990 Employer,* vol. I, Section E.

81. Gabriella Stern, "Companies Discover that Some Firings Backfire into Costly Defamation Suits," *The Wall Street Journal,* May 5, 1993, p. B1.

82. Summers, "Effective Remedies for Employment Rights," p. 457.

83. Milo Geyelin and Jonathan Moses, "Rulings on Wrongful Firing Curb Hiring," *The Wall Street Journal,* April 7, 1992, p. B3.

84. Wade Lambert, "Employee Pacts to Avoid Suits Sought by Firms," *The Wall Street Journal,* October 22, 1992, p. B1.

85. Christopher Conte, "Who Fires? Some Companies Give Up the Right to Dismiss Employees at Will," *The Wall Street Journal,* May 12, 1992, p. A1.

86. Jeremy Fox and Hugh Hindman, "The Model Employment Termination Act: Provisions and Discussion," *Employee Responsibilities and Rights Journal* 6, no. 1 (March 1993), p. 33.

87. Maria Puente, "Sentiment Sours as Rate of Arrival Rises," *USA Today,* July 14, 1993, p. 1A.

88. Ibid.

89. Ibid.

90. Ibid.

91. Harry Bernstein, "How Immigration Reform Law Helps U.S. Workers," *Los Angeles Times,* January 30, 1990, p. D3.

92. George Borjas, "The U.S. Takes the Wrong Immigrants," *The Wall Street Journal,* April 5, 1990, p. A22.

93. Jeff Riggenbach, "End Labor Laws' Bias against Teen Workers," *USA Today,* March 19, 1990, p. 10A.

94. Bacon, "See You in Court," p. 17.

95. Associated Press, "Specialists Sound Warnings about 'Strong' Pension System," *Waterloo Courier,* August 5, 1992, p. B6.

96. Sharon Begley, "The New Sweatshops," *Newsweek,* September 10, 1990, p. 50.

CHAPTER

13

EMPLOYMENT LAW II: DISCRIMINATION

PREFACE

In 1993 and 1994, Denny's restaurants and its parent, Flagstar, were caught squarely in the midst of the racial conflict that has become one of the defining themes in American life. In March 1993, 32 black customers in California filed suit, alleging that some Denny's restaurants treat black customers differently than whites by requiring blacks to pay in advance and to pay cover charges. Likewise, in March 1993, the Justice Department announced that it had substantiated charges of racial bias against the chain. Therefore, in April 1993, Flagstar (then called TW Holdings) signed a consent decree providing for antidiscrimination training for its employees and a nondiscrimination statement in its advertising. Then, soon after reaching the understanding with the Justice Department, six black federal Secret Service agents accused a Denny's restaurant in Maryland of ignoring them while promptly serving nearby white customers.

Agreement I. In July 1993, Flagstar negotiated an agreement with the National Association for the Advancement of Colored People (NAACP) requiring Denny's and the other Flagstar restaurants to do just over $1 billion in minority hiring, franchising, and purchasing over an eight-year period. Fifty-four of Denny's 1,487 restaurants were minority-owned in 1993 (only 1 of which was owned by an African-American), but the agreement provides that 107 are to be minority-owned by 1997. Over an eight-year period, 325 black managers are to be hired and, among other terms, 12 percent of Flagstar's annual $800 million purchasing budget is to go to minority firms through 1997.[1]

Agreement II. In May, 1994, Denny's settled class action suits in Maryland and California that will resolve the bulk of the 4,300 complaints against the company. The Maryland settlement, which embraces the nation except California, totaled $19.6 million, including attorneys' fees of $1.9 million, and will provide $35,000 to each federal

Secret Service agent mentioned above and similar or lesser sums to others who can show that they were victims of discrimination by Denny's. The California settlement involved claims in that state only and totaled $34.8 million, including attorneys' fees of $6.8 million. In addition, Denny's has agreed to take certain steps, such as closer monitoring of civil rights compliance and greater use of black people in ads, in order to prevent future discrimination.[2]

Question

1. As a matter of ethics, did Denny's/Flagstar do the right thing in agreeing to numerical quotas for minority franchisees, managers, and so on? Explain.

Part One—Introduction

Denny's problems are representative of a tidal wave of discrimination claims, lawsuits, settlements, and affirmative action plans that have taken up an increasingly large space in American management practice. Discrimination in its many forms has been perhaps the most damaging social problem in American history. Of course, we all know that, but do we know what discrimination is?

EMPLOYMENT DISCRIMINATION: THE FOUNDATION IN LAW

History

In 1941, A. Philip Randolph, president of the predominantly black Brotherhood of Sleeping Car Porters, organized black leaders who threatened a massive protest march in Washington, D.C. In response, President Franklin Roosevelt issued Executive Order 8802 (such orders have the force and effect of law), which created a Fair Employment Practice Committee. Congress was hostile to the order and limited the committee's budget, but Roosevelt's action was a striking first step for the federal government in addressing racial discrimination. Likewise, during the 1940s, several states enacted their own fair employment laws.

The next striking step toward racial equality was the landmark *Brown* v. *Board of Education*[3] decision in 1954 in which the Supreme Court forbade "separate but equal" schools. *Brown* repudiated the doctrine enunciated in an 1896 Supreme Court case, *Plessy* v. *Ferguson,*[4] in which the Court held that a Louisiana statute requiring equal but separate accommodations for whites and blacks on trains was not unconstitutional. (The history of *Plessy* and *Brown* is a particularly apt illustration of the living, changing character of the law. While stability and hence predictability in the law are important, they must not stand in the way of achieving justice in a changing society.) A period of intense activism followed *Brown,* as citizens engaged in sit-ins, freedom rides, boycotts, and the like to press claims for racial equality in housing, public transportation, employment, and so on. It was a turbulent, sometimes violent era, but those activities were critical ingredients in subsequent advances for the black population. Then, in 1964, the National Labor Relations Board asserted its jurisdiction over racial discrimination where it constitutes an unfair labor practice. With the passage of the 1964 Civil Rights Act, the campaign against discrimination solidified as one of the most energetic and successful social movements in American history.[5]

Constitutional Provisions

The Fourteenth Amendment to the federal Constitution provides that no state shall deny to any person life, liberty, or property without *due process of law* or deny him or her the *equal protection of the laws.* Thus, citizens are protected from discrimination at the instigation of a state government. Then, by Supreme Court decision in 1954, the due process clause of the Fifth Amendment ("nor shall any person . . . be deprived of life, liberty, or property, without due process of law") was interpreted to forbid invidious discrimination by the federal government. Thus, the Fifth and Fourteenth Amendments have been useful tools against government discrimination.

Civil Rights Act of 1866

Of course, the constitutional provisions are broadly drawn and thus open to variation in interpretation. The Constitution protects the citizenry from the government but not from private-sector abuse. Therefore, statutes and executive orders were necessary to attack discrimination more explicitly and to reach private-sector problems. The Civil Rights Act of 1866, as amended in 1991, forbids all forms of racial bias arising out of contract. Employment relationships are, of course, founded in contract. Thus, when a black person is discriminated against by a private employer or by a labor union, the act has been violated.

Executive Orders

Although a number of executive orders (EO) address discrimination issues, one is of special importance here. EO 11246 requires each government agency to include an "equal opportunity" clause in its agreements with federal contractors. Thus, firms doing business with the federal government must agree, in a broad sense, not to discriminate because of race, color, religion, sex, or national origin and to take affirmative action to avoid and correct underutilization of minorities and women. The Office of Federal Contract Compliance (OFCCP) uses the government's enormous leverage as a purchaser to enforce EO 11246. Noncompliance may result in contract termination or in rendering firms ineligible for future federal business.

Civil Rights Act of 1964

Relying on its authority to regulate interstate commerce, Congress forbade (in Title VII of the Civil Rights Act of 1964) discrimination in employment because of race, color, religion, sex, or national origin. The act applies to private-sector employers with 15 or more employees, employment agencies, and labor unions operating a hiring hall. The Equal Employment Opportunity Act of 1972 amended the 1964 Act to extend coverage to all state and local governments. The Civil Rights Act forbids employment discrimination in most units of the federal government, but Congress itself and those judicial and legislative positions not subject to competitive civil service standards are exempt. Private clubs are exempt from the act, and religious organizations may discriminate in employment on the basis of religion.

The act, as interpreted, prohibits discrimination in hiring, discharge, and general conditions of employment. While the act forbids employment discrimination against the specified protected classes (race, color, religion, sex, national origin), a number of exceptions are recognized. The more important exceptions are those regarding seniority, employee testing, bona fide occupational qualifications, and veterans' preferences.

Civil Rights Act of 1991

After two years of bickering and political posturing and sometimes sincere debate about racial quotas, Congress and President Bush agreed on new legislation designed primarily to reverse parts of seven recent Supreme Court decisions. The practical effect of those decisions had been to add difficulty to plaintiffs' efforts to redress perceived civil rights violations. The bill was a rebuff to the conservative direction that the Supreme Court had taken in those cases, and it serves as a useful reminder of the importance of the balance of powers notion in our approach to federal governance. The Civil Rights Act of 1991, while creating some new law, primarily serves to return the law more nearly to where it had been prior to those Supreme Court decisions. The substance of that law is discussed throughout this chapter.

Other Federal Statutes

Several more federal statutes, including the Equal Pay Act, the Age Discrimination in Employment Act, and the Americans with Disabilities Act, offer protection against discrimination. The impact of those statutes is discussed later in this chapter.

ENFORCEMENT

The Equal Employment Opportunity Commission (EEOC), a federal agency created under the terms of the Civil Rights Act of 1964, is primarily responsible for enforcing the provisions of the act. The commission imposes recordkeeping requirements on businesses, unions, and employment agencies in order to build a record should a discrimination issue emerge. The EEOC also investigates discrimination claims, attempts to resolve disputes via *conciliation,* and, if necessary, engages in litigation. Most complaints are settled through the conciliation process.

In essence, Title VII of the 1964 Act established two methods of enforcement: individual actions and "pattern or practice" suits.

Individual Actions

Normally, a private party seeking redress under Title VII must satisfy a series of administrative requirements before litigation is permitted. A job applicant or employee with a discrimination grievance must begin by filing a complaint with the appropriate local or state fair employment practices agency, where provided for by state law. After 60 days, the grievant may turn to the EEOC for aid. Charges must be filed with the EEOC within 180 days of the discriminatory act (or 300 days if preceded by a local or state filing).

Going forward with an EEOC action is often frustrating because the agency is always burdened with a backlog of cases. When a charge is filed, the commission must investigate. The commission may decide that the complaint does not appear to raise a violation, in which case the charges will be dismissed and a "right-to-sue" letter will be issued releasing the grievant to file his or her own lawsuit. If reasonable cause is found to believe that a violation has occurred, the EEOC will attempt to conciliate the dispute. That failing, the commission may file a civil suit or a right-to-sue letter may be issued to the grievant. Thus, several years may pass before the administrative process and any subsequent lawsuits have run their course.

Pattern or Practice Suits

In brief, the commission has the authority to investigate and take action on charges of a pattern or practice of discrimination. Pattern or practice claims seek to prove a general policy of discrimination rather than a specific instance of bias. Pattern or practice suits are based primarily on a statistically significant "deficiency" in the percentage of minority employees in the employer's workforce, as compared with the percentage of minority employees in the relevant labor pool. The employer may be able to rebut the discriminatory inference in a variety of ways. For example, it might be demonstrated that the relevant labor market was improperly drawn or that the statistical disparity is the result of nondiscriminatory conditions.

REMEDIES

Remedies under Title VII of the Civil Rights Act of 1964 include granting back pay, affording seniority relief, imposing reporting requirements, and so on. One of the more contentious portions of the Civil Rights Act of 1991 greatly expands employers' potential financial liability for civil rights violations. Victims of *intentional* discrimination based on sex, religion, or disability may seek compensatory and punitive damages that had previously been available only in discrimination cases based on race or ethnicity. Such damages are capped at $50,000 to $300,000, depending on the size of the employer's workforce. The Civil Rights Act of 1866 provides for the possibility of unlimited damages in race discrimination cases arising out of all aspects of the employment contract relationship. The 1991 Act also provides that plaintiffs suing under Title VII or the Americans with Disabilities Act may now seek jury trials. Since juries often award large recoveries, employment discrimination claims now raise very worrisome financial risks for the employer.

Arbitration

Given the potential damages, attorneys' fees, and so on, employers quite naturally try to avoid litigation. Recent court decisions suggest that a sound, fair arbitration system can be a legally permissible route for reducing reliance on litigation of discrimination claims.

Settlements

Of course, many cases are simply resolved among the parties. For example, in 1991, the Marriott hotel chain, while not admitting wrongdoing, settled a sex discrimination suit regarding promotion policies.[6] The class action involved about 3,000 women and claimed that Marriott engaged in discrimination by systematically excluding women from managerial roles in the chain's food and beverage division. In the settlement, Marriott adopted specific promotion goals, placed $3 million in a settlement fund, and agreed to revise its promotion system.

Part Two—Discrimination on the Basis of Race, Color, or National Origin

Title VII of the 1964 Act places race, color, and national origin among those "protected classes" against which discrimination is forbidden. The act was directed primarily to improving the employment opportunities of blacks, but it applies to all races and colors (including whites and Native Americans). The national origin proviso forbids discrimination based on one's nation of birth, ancestry, or heritage. Therefore, an employment office sign reading "Mexicans need not apply" would clearly be unlawful. To put the law in perspective, we will examine the socioeconomic conditions of minority Americans, beginning with the black community.

Progress?

Responding to a 1992 Gallup Poll, 51 percent of black Americans said that the quality of life for blacks had declined over the previous 10 years.[7] The data suggest that

African-Americans have made great strides in some ways, but that pronounced inequalities remain. All Americans should take pride in the striking successes of the civil rights movement, the Voting Rights Act, the integration of the schools, and the end of "Jim Crow" in the South. In a more tangible sense, black people have made significant economic and educational advances:

- In 1940, the average black man's weekly wage was about 44 percent of that of the average white man; by 1980, that figure was about 72. For black women, that figure rose from 40 to over 90 percent of white women's pay.[8]
- In 1972, we had only 19,000 black accountants in America; by 1991, that figure rose to 110,000. Black managers rose from 243,000 to 858,000. Black lawyers rose from 5,000 to 19,000.[9]
- Educated black women appear to have turned an economic corner. "For every $1,000 a white person with four years of college earns, a black woman with four years of college earns $1,002."[10]

However, immense problems remain.

- The unemployment rate for blacks in June 1993 was 13.3 percent, as compared with 6.1 for whites.[11]
- Nearly one in three African-Americans (31.9 percent) were living beneath the government's official poverty line ($14,350 annually for a family of four) in 1991, while 10.7 percent of whites fell into that category.[12]
- As of 1991, the average black person could expect to live to age 70, while the average white person could expect about 76.4 years.[13] Indeed, the life expectancy of black males is actually in decline, due especially to homicides among young black men.[14]
- A 1993 United Nations study places the United States sixth in the world in human development (life expectancy, education, and purchasing power); but if black Americans were a separate nation, they would rank 30th out of 173 countries and would fall behind such nations as Barbados, Hong Kong, and Cyprus.[15]
- Black family income as compared with that of white families has fallen significantly since 1970:

Median Income of U.S. Families (1991 dollars)

	Black	*White*	*Ratio*
1970	19,144	31,209	61.3
1978	19,739	33,327	59.2
1988	19,329	33,915	57.0
1991	21,548	37,783	57.0

Source: Census Bureau and Urban League, *The State of Black America (1993)*.

Education?   In 1968, black men earned 45 percent less than white men, but by 1977, that gap had narrowed to 29 percent.[16] Then, in the 1980s, that closure stopped. Why?

Clearly, racism remains a wearing burden in America, but the more specific cause here appears to be a want of education. Due to declining financial aid and other forces, the gap in education between black and white males, which closed dramatically in the 1970s, did not change in the 1980s.[17]

In Summary.   The socioeconomic landscape for African-Americans really consists of two pictures: (1) middle-class Americans whose economic condition substantially overlaps that of whites (a success that is much more likely to require both parents working than is the case with white families), and (2) a black underclass consisting of families headed by unmarried females. Nearly half of all black families and 73 percent of all poor black families fit the latter picture.[18]

CHANGING DEMOGRAPHICS

Of course, the disadvantages of minority life in America are not limited to blacks. A recent study, the first of its kind, shows that Hispanic-Americans are three times more likely to live in poverty than are "non-Hispanic whites." While 9 percent of non-Hispanic whites live in poverty, 29 percent of America's Hispanics fall below the poverty line.[19] These figures, in concert with America's rapidly changing demographic makeup, suggest that our view of race-based problems, including discrimination, will need to be broadened in the coming years. A 1993 Census Bureau study projects a rather dramatic new picture of America's racial balance (percentages are rounded to nearest whole number):

- Hispanics in 2010 will replace blacks as the nation's largest minority group.
- Non-Hispanic whites' share of the population will drop from 76 percent now to 68 percent in 2010 and 53 percent in 2050.
- Blacks, with 12 percent of the population today, will rise to 13 percent in 2010 and to 16 percent in 2050.
- Asian-Americans, the fastest growing portion of the population, will rise from today's 3 percent share to 10 percent by 2050.
- Hispanics, now at 9 percent of the population, will rise to 14 percent in 2010 and 23 percent in 2050.
- Our Native American population will nearly double to 4.3 million by mid-century, but the percentage share will rise only slightly to about 1 percent.[20]

Question

1. Does the evolving demographic "face" of America portend changes in the nature of American life? Explain.

Afterword

INTERNATIONAL

In fairness, we should note that U.S. discrimination problems are by no means unique. Throughout the 1990s, Germany has been dealing with right-wing extremist attacks against the more than 6 million Turks, Slavs, Romanians, and other foreigners who came to Germany seeking work and asylum. Those attacks, which resulted in 17 deaths in 1992, are the product of both racism and a difficult job market following German reunification. France, in recent years, has absorbed some 5 million (mostly North African) immigrants. The result has been greatly increased tension:

> A survey on race relations, ordered by their Socialist government in Paris, discloses that 76 percent of the French people believe there are too many Arabs in their country, 46 percent declare there are too many blacks, 40 percent say there are too many Asians, and 24 percent complain that there are too many Jews.[21]

Of course, the truth abroad, as here, is an ambiguous package of conflicting feelings, as the following article suggests.

INTERNATIONAL

BLACKS SEE MUCH POSITIVE IN RACE RELATIONS IN JAPAN

Leon Wynter

Conflicting visions of race relations in Japan are illuminated by a new documentary.

"Struggle & Success: The African-American Experience in Japan" shows the Japan where children cherish grotesque Sambo dolls, blackface buffoonery is a television staple and politicians make overtly racist comments. But it also shows another side, through the eyes of black professionals and entrepreneurs, some with Japanese spouses. They speak of Japan's appreciation of black popular culture and respect for people of any color who prove themselves in business. And they say their adopted home has no race-tinged crime or open class conflicts.

As a result, "Japan offers you a form of psychic freedom. You don't have to talk about race on a daily basis," says CBS television reporter Bill Whittaker, interviewed for the film during a Tokyo posting.

In the film, Mr. Whittaker recalls an instance of housing discrimination. But, notes P. Bai Arkridge, a black IBM executive who worked in Japan for three years, most African-Americans grow up expecting housing discrimination in the U.S. What Mr. Arkridge didn't expect was the way Japanese people accepted his authority the instant he displayed his business card; he says that doesn't always happen in the U.S.

Regge Life, a Los Angeles-based documentary filmmaker who directed and produced the film, credits Japanese respect for *majime,* or seriousness of purpose, for blacks' reports of personal validation in one of the most competitive societies on Earth.

Questions

1. Joe DiMaggio, Hall of Fame centerfielder for the New York Yankees, once husband of Marilyn Monroe, and immensely admired American, was the subject in 1939 of a photo-article in *Life* magazine. Contemporary sports columnist Bill Conlin recounted segments of that 1939 article:

   > Italians, bad at war, are well suited for milder competitions . . . Although he learned Italian first, Joe, now 24, speaks English without an accent, and is otherwise well adopted [sic] to most U.S. mores. Instead of olive oil or smelly bear grease he keeps his hair slick with water. He never reeks of garlic and prefers chicken chow mein to spaghetti . . . Joe DiMaggio's rise in baseball is a testimonial to the value of general shiftlessness . . . His inertia caused him to give up school after one year in high school . . . He is lazy, rebellious and endowed with a bad stomach.[22]

   As Mr. Conlin demonstrates, 50 years ago Italians were the subject of offensive stereotypes. Today, we find those views foolish.

   a. Are blacks in contemporary America the subjects of stereotypes? Explain.

   b. If so, will those stereotypes become absurd historical artifacts 50 years hence? Explain.

2. Hong Kong–based Hawley and Hazel Chemical Company produced one of the most popular tooth cleansers in Asia, Darkie Toothpaste. The package was adorned with the face of a black man displaying a "toothy smile." The logo was based on popular singer Al Jolson, a white American man who performed as a minstrel in black face in the early 1900s. The product has been popular in Asia for more than 60 years.[23]

   a. Would you label the name or the logo "racist"? Explain.

   b. Should Americans or the American government apply pressure to change international brand names and logos that are considered offensive in this country? Explain.

   c. In 1985, Colgate-Palmolive bought a 50 percent interest in Hawley and Hazel. Is Colgate-Palmolive obliged to apply American values to the marketing of Darkie Toothpaste? Explain.

3. Joseph Boyce, a senior editor at *The Wall Street Journal,* explaining what he labels "the black tax":

   > The black tax is the hidden charge in rents and mortgages blacks pay because of housing and lending discrimination. It is the higher expense of owning an automobile because, as studies have shown, car dealers give larger discounts to whites than blacks. It's the greater cost of doing business in the black community because of higher insurance and security rates.[24]

   a. In your judgment is Boyce correct in alleging that black people in America pay an extra "tax"? Explain.

   b. If so, who is to blame? Explain.

4. In your judgment, do blacks and whites have equal opportunities for success in America? Explain.

5. Would you expect companies that are aggressive in hiring minorities and women to be more or less financially successful than companies that are not aggressive about equal opportunity? Explain.

EMPLOYMENT DISCRIMINATION ANALYSIS

The Civil Rights Act of 1964 as amended by the Civil Rights Act of 1991 is the primary vehicle for pursuing employment discrimination claims. However, the reader is reminded of the other constitutional, statutory, and executive order protections mentioned above. Title VII of the 1964 Act provides two primary theories of liability—disparate treatment and disparate impact. (A third theory of liability, perpetuation of past intentional discrimination, will not be discussed here.)

Disparate Treatment

The basic elements of disparate treatment exist where an employer *intentionally* treats some people less favorably than others because of their race, color, religion, sex, or national origin. Intent ordinarily is established by circumstantial evidence. In a simplified form, a claim under disparate treatment analysis would proceed as follows:

1. Plaintiff's (Employee's) Prima Facie Case (sufficient to be presumed true unless proved otherwise).   Optimally the plaintiff would present direct, explicit evidence of intentional disparate treatment. For example, that evidence might take the form of a letter from an employer to an employment agency indicating that "women would not be welcome as applicants for this physically taxing job." Because direct evidence of that nature is ordinarily unavailable, the plaintiff must then build the following prima facie case from which intent and, hence, disparate treatment may be inferred:

a. Plaintiff belongs to a protected class.
b. Plaintiff applied for a job for which the defendant was seeking applicants.
c. Plaintiff was qualified for the job.
d. Plaintiff was denied the job.
e. The position remained open, and the employer continued to seek applications.

2. Defendant's (Employer's) Case.   If the plaintiff builds a successful prima facie case, the burden shifts to the defendant to "articulate some legitimate, nondiscriminatory reason for the employee's rejection" (for example, greater work experience). However, the defendant need not prove its decision not to hire the plaintiff was, in fact, based on that legitimate, nondiscriminatory reason. The defendant simply must raise a legitimate issue of fact disputing the plaintiff's discrimination claim. Further, and perhaps most important, the defendant is not required to prove that it is *not* guilty of discrimination.

3. Plaintiff's Response.   Assuming the defendant was successful in presenting a legitimate, nondiscriminatory reason for its action, the burden of proof shifts back to the plaintiff to show that:

a. The reason offered by the defendant was not the true reason but was, in fact, merely a *pretext* to hide discrimination.
b. Discrimination was the real reason for the defendant employer's action.[25]

Disparate Impact

Disparate impact analysis arose out of situations in which employers used legitimate employment standards that, despite their apparent neutrality, worked a heavier burden on a protected class than on other employees. For example, a preemployment test, offered with the best of intentions and constructed to be a fair measurement device, may disproportionately exclude members of a protected class and thus be unacceptable (barring an effective defense). Alternatively, an employer surreptitiously seeking to discriminate may establish an apparently neutral, superficially valid employment test that has the effect of achieving the employer's discrimination goal. For example, a tavern might require its "bouncer" to be at least 6 feet 2 inches tall and weigh at least 180 pounds. Such a standard disproportionately excludes women, Orientals, and Hispanics from consideration and probably is impermissible (barring an effective defense). Disparate impact analysis is similar to that of disparate treatment, but critical distinctions mark the two approaches. In particular, note that disparate treatment requires proof of intent, while disparate impact does not.

1991 Act.   A 1989 Supreme Court decision in the *Wards Cove* case had greatly increased the plaintiff's (employee's) burden in winning a disparate impact case. The Civil Rights Act of 1991 directly addressed that case by significantly increasing the demands of proof on the defendant (employer). Because the act is new and little tested in court, we cannot yet be sure of its ultimate meaning. However, the best evidence at this writing in 1994 is that the law returns at least generally to the direction that the Court elaborated in the *Griggs* case that follows shortly.

The Test.   Disparate impact following the 1991 Act appears to require the following:

1. The plaintiff must prove (often with statistical evidence) that a protected class is suffering an *adverse impact* in the workplace in question. The statistical analysis to establish disparate impact (against black job applicants, for example) must be based on a comparison of the racial composition of the group of persons actually holding the jobs in question versus the racial composition of the *job-qualified* population in the relevant labor market.

2. The plaintiff must identify the *specific employment practice or policy* (e.g., test score, skill, or height) that caused the disparate impact on the protected class. However, if the employer's decision-making process cannot be divided into pieces for analysis, the plaintiff may allege that a combination of practices and policies was responsible for the disparate impact.

3. Assuming the plaintiff/employee establishes a prima facie case in steps 1 and 2, the burden of proof then shifts to the employer to demonstrate that the employment practice/policy is (*a*) *job related* and (*b*) *consistent with business necessity.*

4. If the employer succeeds in demonstrating job relatedness and consistency with business necessity, the plaintiff/employee may yet prevail by demonstrating that *an alternative, less discriminatory business practice is available and that the employer refuses to adopt it.*

GRIGGS v. DUKE POWER CO.
401 U.S. 424 (1971)

Chief Justice Burger

We granted the writ in this case to resolve the question whether an employer is prohibited by the Civil Rights Act of 1964, Title VII, from requiring a high school education or passing of a standardized general intelligence test as a condition of employment in or transfer to jobs when (a) neither standard is shown to be significantly related to successful job performance, (b) both requirements operate to disqualify Negroes at a substantially higher rate than white applicants, and (c) the jobs in question formerly had been filled only by white employees as part of a longstanding practice of giving preference to whites.

Congress provided, in Title VII of the Civil Rights Act of 1964, for class actions for enforcement of provisions of the Act and this proceeding was brought by a group of incumbent Negro employees against Duke Power Company . . .

The district court found that prior to July 2, 1965, the effective date of the Civil Rights Act of 1964, the company openly discriminated on the basis of race in the hiring and assigning of employees at its Dan River plant. The plant was organized into five operating departments: (1) Labor, (2) Coal Handling, (3) Operations, (4) Maintenance, and (5) Laboratory and Test. Negroes were employed only in the Labor Department where the highest-paying jobs paid less than the lowest-paying jobs in the other four "operating" departments in which only whites were employed. Promotions were normally made within each department on the basis of job seniority. Transferees into a department usually began in the lowest position.

In 1955 the company instituted a policy of requiring a high school education for initial assignment to any department except Labor, and for transfer from the Coal Handling to any "inside" department (Operations, Maintenance, or Laboratory). When the company abandoned its policy of restricting Negroes to the Labor Department in 1965, completion of high school also was made a prerequisite to transfer from Labor to any other department. From the time the high school requirement was instituted to the time of trial, however, white employees hired before the time of the high school education requirement continued to perform satisfactorily and achieve promotions in the "operating" departments. Findings on this score are not challenged.

The company added a further requirement for new employees on July 2, 1965, the date on which Title VII became effective. To qualify for placement in any but the Labor Department it became necessary to register satisfactory scores on two professionally prepared aptitude tests, as well as to have a high school education. Completion of high school alone continued to render employees eligible for transfer to the four desirable departments from which Negroes had been excluded if the incumbent had been employed prior to the time of the new requirement. In September 1965 the company began to permit incumbent employees who lacked a high school education to qualify for transfer from Labor or Coal Handling to an "inside" job by passing two tests—the Wonderlic Personnel Test, which purports to measure general intelligence, and the Bennett Mechanical Comprehension Test. Neither was directed or intended to measure the ability to learn to perform a particular job or category of jobs. The requisite scores used for both initial hiring and transfer approximated the national median for high school graduates.

The District Court had found that while the company previously followed a policy of overt racial discrimination in a period prior to the Act, such conduct had ceased. The District Court also concluded that Title VII was intended to be prospective only and, consequently, the impact of prior inequities was beyond the reach of corrective action authorized by the Act.

. . . The Court of Appeals concluded there was no violation of the Act.

* * * * *

The objective of Congress in the enactment of Title VII is plain from the language of the statute. It was to achieve equality of employment opportunities and remove barriers that have operated in the past to favor an identifiable group of white employees over other employees. Under the Act, practices, procedures, or tests neutral on their face, and even neutral in terms of intent, cannot be maintained if they operate to "freeze" the status quo of prior discriminatory employment practices.

The Court of Appeals' opinion, and the partial dissent, agreed that, on the record in the present case, "whites register far better on the company's alternative requirements" than Negroes. This consequence would appear to be directly traceable to race. Basic intelligence must have the means of articulation to manifest itself fairly in a testing process. Because they are Negroes, petitioners have long received inferior education in segregated schools.

. . . Congress did not intend by Title VII, however, to guarantee a job to every person regardless of qualifications. In short, the Act does not command that any person be hired simply because he was formerly the subject of discrimination, or because he is a member of a minority group. Discriminatory preference for any group, minority or majority, is precisely and only what Congress has proscribed . . .

. . . The Act proscribes not only overt discrimination but also practices that are fair in form, but discriminatory in operation. The touchstone is business necessity. If an employment practice which operates to exclude Negroes cannot be shown to be related to job performance, the practice is prohibited.

On the record before us, neither the high school completion requirement nor the general intelligence test is shown to bear a demonstrable relationship to successful performance of the jobs for which it was used. Both were adopted, as the Court of Appeals noted, without meaningful study of their relationship to job-performance ability. Rather, a vice president of the company testified, the requirements were instituted on the company's judgment that they generally would improve the overall quality of the work force.

The evidence, however, shows that employees who have not completed high school or taken the tests have continued to perform satisfactorily and make progress in departments for which the high school and test criteria are not used . . .

The Court of Appeals held that the company had adopted the diploma and test requirements without any "intention to discriminate against Negro employees." We do not suggest that either the District Court or the Court of Appeals erred in examining the employer's intent; but good intent or absence of discriminatory intent does not redeem employment procedures or testing mechanisms that operate as "built-in headwinds" for minority groups and are unrelated to measuring job capability.

* * * * *

The facts of this case demonstrate the inadequacy of broad and general testing devices as well as the infirmity of using diplomas or degrees as fixed measures of capability . . .

The company contends that its general intelligence tests are specifically permitted by § 703(h) of the Act. That section authorizes the use of "any professionally developed ability test" that is not "designed, intended *or used* to discriminate because of race . . ." (Emphasis added.)

The Equal Employment Opportunity Commission, having enforcement responsibility, has issued guidelines interpreting § 703(h) to permit only the use of job-related tests. The administrative interpretation of the Act by the enforcing agency is entitled to great deference. Since the Act and its legislative history support the commission's construction, this affords good reason to treat the guidelines as expressing the will of Congress.

. . . From the sum of the legislative history relevant in this case, the conclusion is inescapable that the EEOC's construction of § 703(h) to require that employment tests be job related comports with congressional intent.

Nothing in the Act precludes the use of testing or measuring procedures; obviously they are useful. What Congress has forbidden is giving these devices and mechanisms controlling force unless they are demonstrably a reasonable measure of job performance. Congress has not commanded that the less qualified be preferred over the better qualified simply because of minority origins. Far from disparaging job qualifications as such, Congress has made such qualifications the controlling factor, so that race, religion, nationality, and sex become irrelevant. What Congress has commanded is that any tests used must measure the person for the job and not the person in the abstract.

The judgment of the Court of Appeals is . . . reversed.

Questions

1. According to the Supreme Court, what was Congress's objective in enacting Title VII?
2. Had Duke Power been able to establish that its reasons for adopting the diploma and test standards were entirely without discriminatory intent, would the Supreme Court have ruled differently? Explain.
3. What is the central issue in this case?
4. Why was North Carolina's social and educational history relevant to the outcome of the case?
5. Statistical evidence showed that 35 percent of new hires in grocery and produce at Lucky Stores, a retail grocery chain, were women, while 84 percent of new hires in deli, bakery, and general merchandise were women. Statistical evidence also showed that 31 percent of those promoted into apprentice jobs in grocery and produce were women, while women comprised 75 percent of those promoted into apprentice jobs in deli, bakery, and general merchandise. Grocery and produce jobs generally were higher paying jobs than those in deli, bakery, and general merchandise. Women received significantly fewer overtime hours.

   Do these facts regarding Lucky Stores suggest discrimination? Explain. See *Stender* v. *Lucky Stores, Inc.* 803 F. Supp. 259 (DC Cal. 1992).

6. Gregory, a black male, was offered employment by Litton Systems as a sheet metal worker. As part of a standard procedure he completed a form listing a total of 14 non-traffic arrests but no convictions. Thereupon the employment offer was withdrawn. Gregory then brought suit, claiming he was a victim of racial discrimination.

   a. Explain the foundation of his argument.

   b. Decide the case. See *Gregory* v. *Litton,* 412 F.2d 631 (9th Cir. 1972).

7. Eighty-one percent of the hires at Consolidated Service Systems, a small Chicago janitorial company, were of Korean origin. The EEOC brought a disparate treatment claim, saying the firm discriminated in favor of Koreans by relying primarily on word-of-mouth recruiting. Mr. Hwang, the owner, is Korean. Seventy-three percent of the job applicants were Korean. One percent of the Chicago-area workforce is Korean, and not more than 3 percent of the janitorial workforce for the area is Korean. The court found no persuasive evidence of intentional discrimination, although the government claimed that 99 applicants were denied jobs because they were not Koreans.

   a. Does restricting hiring to members of one ethnic group constitute discrimination where hiring is accomplished by word of mouth? Explain.

   b. What if a firm, using the word-of-mouth approach, hired only white applicants? Explain.

   c. In this case, the EEOC brought but dropped a disparate impact claim. Analyze the case using the disparate impact test. See *Equal Employment Opportunity Commission* v. *Consolidated Service Systems,* 989 F.2d 233 (7th Cir. 1993).

8. Juanita McNeil, a former hospital clerk, claims that she was the victim of discrimination at work where her supervising nurse and other nurses allegedly spoke Tagalog (a Filipino language not understood by McNeil) when giving instructions. As a result, McNeil claimed that her work performance was harmed. The hospital's position is that no discrimination took place.

   a. Explain McNeil's legal claim.

   b. Defend the hospital.

   c. Decide. Explain.

   d. May an employer lawfully impose an "English-only" rule in the workplace? For a journalistic account of these issues, see Junda Woo and Milo Geyelin, "Will Free Speech Mean Language Bias?" *The Wall Street Journal,* September 24, 1993, p. B12.

9. In *Personnel Administrator of Massachusetts* v. *Feeney,* 442 U.S. 256 (1979), a state policy of absolute hiring preference for veterans was upheld against a charge of gender-based discrimination in that few veterans are women. The disparate impact on women was clear, and Massachusetts' governing authorities can be assumed to have been aware of the "natural and probable consequence" of this preference. The Supreme Court found an absence of discriminatory purpose. Explain and justify that decision.

10. In many Title VII cases, a critical ingredient is that of identifying the relevant labor market. How would you counter Justice Stevens's argument in dissent in *Hazelwood School District* v. *United States,* 433 U.S. 299 (1976), that as a starting point the relevant labor pool should encompass the geographic area from which incumbent employees come?

11. When disparate impact analysis is applied to *objective* employment selection and promotion methods (such as standardized tests), intent need not be established to build a successful case. Now consider the situation where the employment selection or promo-

tion method in question is *subjective* in character (for example, letters of reference or interviews). Are those situations to be analyzed only under the disparate treatment standard, including its proof of intent requirement, or may the disparate impact analysis be employed, thus eliminating the intent issue? Explain. See *Clara Watson* v. *Fort Worth Bank and Trust,* 108 S.Ct. 2777 (1988).

Statutory Defenses

In a broad sense, business necessity, as explained above, is the principle defense to discrimination charges. However, as mentioned previously, Title VII affords four specific exemptions or defenses of particular note: (1) seniority, (2) employee testing, (3) bona fide occupational qualification, and (4) veterans' preferences. Attention is given to veterans' preferences in question 9 following the *Griggs* case. Bona fide occupational qualifications are addressed in the next section as a part of the sex discrimination materials. Seniority issues and employee testing standards are explored here.

Seniority.   Section 703(h) of the Civil Rights Act of 1964 provides that an employer may lawfully apply different standards of compensation or different conditions of employment pursuant to a bona fide (good faith) seniority system, provided such differences are not the product of an intent to discriminate. That is, the seniority system must not have been created for a discriminatory or other illegal purpose, and the seniority provisions must apply equally to all.

Seniority systems are either the product of the employer's initiative or of a collective bargaining agreement. Seniority is important because (1) those with less seniority are ordinarily the first to be laid off in the event of a workforce reduction and (2) benefits—including vacations and such working conditions as a choice of shifts—often depend on seniority.

Many complicated issues have arisen out of Congress's effort to abolish employment discrimination while preserving legitimate seniority plans. In sum, the dilemma is that a seniority system, otherwise entirely legitimate, sometimes has the effect of perpetuating past discriminatory practices. Employees once discriminated against in hiring or promotion suffer the further loss of reduced seniority. However, as established in the *Teamsters*[26] and *American Tobacco*[27] cases, the result of a bona fide seniority system may be to perpetuate discrimination, but such a result is illegal only if discriminatory intent is proved.

Layoffs.   In 1984, the U.S. Supreme Court addressed the difficult issue of whether, in times of employment reductions, employers may lay off workers according to seniority (thereby ordinarily reaching white males after women and minorities) or whether affirmative action requires retaining those low-seniority, protected-class employees while laying off white males of greater seniority. The *Firefighters* case answered the question when the Supreme Court, in effect, held that when layoffs are necessary the legal system may not protect newly hired workers by interfering with legitimate seniority systems.[28] In the *Firefighters* case, a federal district court had approved two affirmative action plans in Memphis, Tennessee, for increasing the number of blacks in the fire department. Soon thereafter, budgetary problems required Memphis to lay off 40 firefighters. The city faced the problem of whether to maintain its affirmative action program by laying off firefighters with greater seniority than the recently hired protected-class employees or to honor the provisions of the collectively bargained agreement on seniority, which, in effect, required laying off those most recently hired. The city decided to follow the collective bargaining agreement, and black firefighters filed suit. In the end, the Supreme Court upheld the seniority system despite its impact on affirmative action. The pursuit of affirmative action goals cannot upset legitimate seniority rights where layoffs are necessary. Thus, affirmative action plans may not "re-allocate jobs currently held."[29] However, as articulated in the *Cleveland Firefighters* case, *forward-looking* affirmative action (such as special training programs and special selection procedures for promotion, apprenticeships, and so on) is fully permissible.[30] In the Supreme Court's view, those forward-looking programs do not unnecessarily interfere with the rights of white employees.

Employee Testing.   Testing is, of course, central to professional personnel practice and to maximizing employee productivity, but testing has often been, both intentionally and unintentionally, a primary vehicle in perpetuating discrimination. Recall that only job-related tests supported by detailed, statistical evidence as to their scientific validity are lawful.

The Uniform Guidelines on Employee Selection Procedures, adopted by the EEOC and other federal agencies, provide standards specifying acceptable hiring practices for covered business and government employers. The guidelines reflect the EEOC's interpretation of the act and, as such, are not binding on the courts. However, the judiciary accords great deference to the guidelines. In essence, the guidelines embrace the standards that professional industrial psychologists have established for determining test validity.

The Four-Fifths Rule.   The guidelines are rather specific regarding the meaning of disparate or adverse impact. An employer will generally be presumed in noncompliance with the guidelines if the selection rate (such as the percentage passing a test, being hired, or being promoted) for any protected class is less than 80 percent of the selection rate for the group with the highest rate. The employer falling below that standard must prove the job relatedness of the employment practice in question and demonstrate that a good faith effort was made to find a selection procedure that lessened the disparate impact on protected classes.

Part Three—Sex Discrimination

EQUALITY FOR WOMEN

By most measures, even after years of struggle, women continue to occupy a distinctly secondary role in American life. More than 30 years after the passage of the 1963

Equal Pay Act, women earn from 70 to 74 cents (depending on the study) for every dollar earned by men.[31] The figures are even more dispiriting for minority women. In 1991, black women earned 62 cents and Hispanic women earned 54 cents for every dollar earned by white men.[32] The female/male pay gap was 59 cents on the dollar in 1977, so we have made progress, but the bulk of that progress is actually attributable to a decline in men's wages in recent years.[33]

Depends on the Job.   As displayed in the accompanying table, in certain specific occupations, particularly those paying by the hour, women's pay much more closely equals that of men; but in white-collar roles, women's pay sometimes sinks, on the average, to as low as half that of men.[34] Claims that the disparity is due to differences in credentials by sex were challenged in a recent scholarly study finding that in a sample of 800 corporate managers, "if women were men with the same credentials, they would earn about 18 percent more."[35]

Indeed, Americans generally agree that women are not treated fairly. A 1992 Gallup poll of 684 adults found only 36 percent of those responding believed that women and men are treated equally in seeking promotions.[36]

Pay More?   Adding to the humiliation is a new study suggesting that not only do women make less but they pay more. A 1993 book by a Ralph Nader associate Fran-

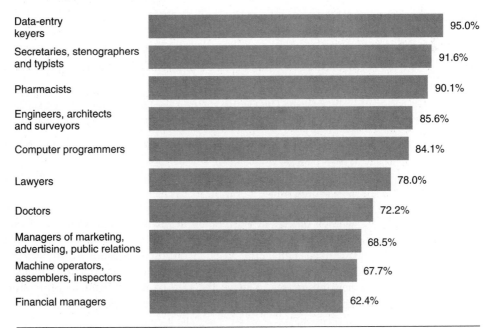

Across-the-board dollar disparity
Women's median wages for selected jobs in 1992 as a percentage of men's median wages for the same jobs.

Job	Percentage
Data-entry keyers	95.0%
Secretaries, stenographers and typists	91.6%
Pharmacists	90.1%
Engineers, architects and surveyors	85.6%
Computer programmers	84.1%
Lawyers	78.0%
Doctors	72.2%
Managers of marketing, advertising, public relations	68.5%
Machine operators, assemblers, inspectors	67.7%
Financial managers	62.4%

Source: Bureau of Labor Statistics. Reported in Joan Rigdon, "Three Decades after the Equal Pay Act, Women's Wages Remain Far from Parity," *The Wall Street Journal,* June 9, 1993, p. B1.

ces Whittelsey charges that women pay more than men for such things as cars, health care, dry cleaning, and clothing. For example, the book reports a Northwestern University law professor's study showing that white women paid an average of $150 more than white men for identical cars, while black women paid about $800 more.[37] According to the study, black men pay about $400 more per car than white men.

Abroad.   Women's frustration over the disparities noted here will not be allayed by a look around the balance of the world. In Japan, on the average, women earn only about half of what men earn, but in all other industrialized countries, the United States ranks on the low end of the scale. According to a University of Illinois study using data from the late 1980s:

INTERNATIONAL

[T]he ratio of female-to-male weekly wages ranged from 80 percent to 90 percent in Australia, Denmark, France, New Zealand, Norway and Sweden. Other countries in western Europe, and the U.S., had ratios of roughly 65 percent to 75 percent, with the U.S. on the low side.[38]

Questions

1. If we generally agree that women are not treated fairly in the workplace, why do we not correct the situation?
2. How do you explain why women, on the average, appear to pay more than men for many products and services?

Glass Ceilings (and Walls)

In 1992, *Fortune* asked: "When Will Women Get to the Top?"[39] Not for a long time, according to a poll of CEOs of 201 of the nation's largest companies:

[O]nly 16 percent believe it is "very likely" or "somewhat likely" that they could be succeeded by a female CEO within the next decade. And only 18 percent think it's "very likely" that even after 20 years a woman would be picked to run their companies.[40]

Not only do women confront a "glass ceiling" as they seek promotion, but recent studies suggest that many women are unable to move laterally out of traditional female roles (e.g., communications and staff support) and into power roles such as sales and production.[41]

Of course, women have made important strides in recent years. The percentage of women officers in Fortune 50 firms more than doubled—from 2.2 to 5.1 percent—between 1990 and 1992.[42] Furthermore, in the early 1990s, some 6.1 million women occupied managerial roles, as opposed to about 3.5 million in 1983.[43] Another very encouraging sign is that women now own some 5.4 million businesses and are starting new businesses at twice the rate of men.[44] And in professional life, generally, the changes have been striking. During the 1980s, the number of female doctors doubled, while women lawyers and dentists tripled. Indeed, in 1990, one in four lawyers was a woman.[45]

Mommy Track?

In recent years, Felice Schwartz, a long-time crusader for women's professional advancement, has called for a broader view of the glass ceiling and sex discrimination in the workplace. While women clearly have been the victims of bias, Schwartz argues, in essence, that women are simply different than men and that they should expect differing career paths. Independent of the need for power and the influence of traditional societal roles, men, she says, are more driven, more ambitious, and willing to work harder than women. Schwartz advocates what has been labeled a "mommy track" (for example, flexible hours or part-time work) for so-called career and family women. This approach would permit business to keep those women on the job rather than losing them entirely to family considerations.[46]

Question

1. To many women's rights advocates, Schwartz's proposal was an affront to their years of struggle for gender equality. Clearly, women continue to be disadvantaged in the workplace. Do you favor Schwartz's mommy track approach to dealing with that problem, or would that simply make the situation worse? Explain.

Women in Japan

To add some perspective to this topic and to achieve a sense of the cultural variables that influence sex discrimination, consider the following account of the role of women in Japan.

INTERNATIONAL

WHAT IT'S LIKE TO BE A WOMAN IN JAPAN

Carol Rose

It is just past lunchtime at the Oki agricultural collective. Women dressed in bright blue and yellow bonnets are loaded into pickup trucks for the drive to the cucumber fields, where they will toil beneath the blazing summer sun all afternoon.

But just before the trucks pull away, the man who

heads the collective motions for one of the women to come to the central office where I am to interview a group of men.

She is needed to serve tea.

It is a scene repeated time and again throughout my travels in Japan. Whether at a remote farmhouse or a modern office complex in downtown Tokyo, it is always women who serve the tea and then vanish without a word.

To most Americans, the relationship between the sexes in Japan is a constant source of indignation and bewilderment . . .

* * * * *

. . . Japanese women appear long-suffering, hiding shyly behind screens or simpering or giggling. They rarely participate in conversation with men, even when Western women are present. In most Japanese homes, the wife appears only long enough to serve tea and sweets, before shuffling back into the kitchen.

Despite lingering signs of discrimination, the status of Japanese women in the postwar era has improved dramatically. Today, virtually all women finish high school and attend the same courses given men. Around 23 percent of Japanese university students are women.

But equality in education has not yet translated into equality in jobs. Japanese law prohibits discrimination based on gender. But common practice is summed up in a recent Japanese popular magazine: "Because of marriage or childbirth, it is understandable that companies, for the sake of their long-term interests, entrust highly paid positions to men."

Want-ads in the newspaper are filled with job openings for women under 22 years of age. Older and more educated women have a difficult time getting a job, since employers fear they might demand retirement benefits. Women are discouraged from staying at a job beyond the age of 25, which is considered the proper time for marriage.

Once a woman quits her job, however, it is virtually impossible for her to ever again work full time . . .

Women who do stay on the job earn only 50 cents for every dollar earned by men in the same job . . .

But nowhere is the gender imbalance more striking than in rural Japan. Staying with a farm family near Esashi City, 400 miles north of Tokyo, it is easy to see why young Japanese women are leaving the farm in search of greater opportunity in the cities.

Kinichi Oikawa, a farm wife, gets up more than one hour before the rest of the family and is out in the barn shoveling manure while her husband and 26-year-old son sleep. She then prepares breakfast while they read the morning paper. At night, she is the last person to bathe, following the traditional Japanese custom that men in the family bathe first (women have traditionally been considered dirty in Japan and thus are believed to soil the waters of the communal family bath).

Asked if she resented the hardships of farm life, Oikawa giggles and hides her face.

* * * * *

On the surface, the outlook for Japanese women appears bleak. But there is a subculture in which women have enormous power.

Wives control the purse strings in nearly every family; husbands get an allowance. While the house belongs to the husband, the furnishings belong to the wife. Divorce in Japan is uncommon, about one-quarter the U.S. rate. When it does occur, women are entitled to half of the family possessions.

Child-rearing is also a source of power. Since most men work long hours, six days a week, they rarely participate in family activities. Education of the children is strictly controlled by the mothers, as are marriage arrangements.

The result is not always pleasant. Denied opportunities to better themselves, Japanese women often seek success through their sons. As a result, many are called "Kyoiku Mama" or "education mothers" because they constantly push their children to excel in school.

But few Japanese women expressed envy of my position as an American woman. One farm wife asked if I was forced into a career because I could not find a husband. "A woman's happiness is in home and marriage," she said. A young male government worker, who has traveled extensively in the United States, said he thought Japanese women were less lonely than those in America.

He may be right. At birth, Japanese women have a clear position in the family and in society, while American women are breaking out of traditional roles. Freedom presents American women with difficult choices. But they are choices rarely available in Japan.

Source: *Des Moines Register,* August 30, 1987, p. 3C. © *Des Moines Register.* Reprinted by permission.

ANALYSIS OF SEX DISCRIMINATION

Under Title VII of the 1964 Civil Rights Act, sex discrimination analysis proceeds in essentially the manner outlined earlier in the chapter—disparate treatment and disparate impact are the key tests. An important extension of disparate treatment analysis is sex plus discrimination. *Sex plus* is the term applied to those situations where an employer has attempted to distinguish between male and female workers by imposing a second employment criterion (in addition to sex) on one gender but not on the other. For example, in *Phillips* v. *Martin Marietta,*[47] the employer refused to hire women with preschool-age children but welcomed men with preschool-age children. For the assembly trainee position for which Phillips applied, 75 to 80 percent of those hired had been women. The Supreme Court struck down the sex-plus classification. What consequences might have been anticipated from a contrary ruling?

Bona Fide Occupational Qualification

As explained earlier, Title VII permits discrimination under limited circumstances. Among those exemptions or defenses is the bona fide occupational qualification (BFOQ). Discrimination is lawful where sex, religion, or national origin is a BFOQ reasonably necessary to the normal operation of that business. The exclusion of race and color from the list suggests Congress thought those categories always unacceptable as bona fide occupational qualifications. The judicially created defense of business necessity is applicable to racial classifications. The BFOQ was meant to be a very limited exception applicable to situations where specific inherent characteristics are necessary to the job (e.g., wet nurse) and where authenticity is required (e.g., actors).

The BFOQ defense is lawful only if the following conditions are met:

1. Proof of a *nexus* between the classification and job performance, and
2. "*necessity*" of the classification for successful performance, and
3. that the job performance affected by the classification is the "*essence*" of the employer's business operation.[48]

Nexus. Will the classification affect job performance? For example, will "maleness" depreciate performance in a job requiring manual dexterity, or will "femaleness" depreciate performance in a laboring job requiring night work and long hours? The courts have thoroughly rejected distinctions based on such stereotypes.

Necessity. Mere customer preference or, in general, higher costs will not justify an otherwise discriminatory employment practice. Thus, that restaurant customers prefer to be served by women or that hiring women will require the addition of another washroom or that hiring blacks, for example, will anger customers and cause a decline in income are not justifications for discrimination.

Essence. An employer can lawfully insist on a woman to fill a woman's modeling role because being female goes to the essence of the job. However, airlines, for example, cannot hire only women as flight attendants even if females are shown to perform the "nonmechanical" portions of the job better than most men. Those duties "are tangential to the essence of the business involved."[49]

Many employers have simply assumed that women could not perform certain tasks. Women were thought to be insufficiently aggressive for sales roles, and women were denied employment because they were assumed to have a higher turnover rate due to the desire to marry and have children. Those stereotypes are at the heart of sex discrimination litigation generally and sex as a BFOQ particularly.

Dothard v. *Rawlinson,* a 1977 Supreme Court case, offers a good example of the BFOQ analysis.[50] Dianne Rawlinson sought employment as a prison guard in Alabama. She was a 22-year-old college graduate with a degree in correctional psychology. She was denied employment because she failed to meet the 120-pound weight requirement for the job. The state also required such employees to be at least 5 feet 2 inches tall. Alabama operated four all-male, maximum security prisons. The district court characterized the Alabama prison system as one of "rampant violence" and a "jungle atmosphere." Rawlinson sued, claiming employment discrimination. Resolve this case under the BFOQ analysis, including the defenses that would be raised by the state.

PARENT AND MANAGER?

Many of the most trying and poignant sex discrimination issues are those arising out of the increasing conflicts (particularly for women but increasingly for men) between being a parent and pursuing a career. Historically, the employed woman who became pregnant faced a serious threat to her professional future. In 1978, Congress amended the Civil Rights Act of 1964 with the Pregnancy Discrimination Act, which treats pregnancy discrimination as a form of sex discrimination. The table that follows summarizes some of the circumstances of pregnant employees and outlines the protections of the Pregnancy Discrimination Act.

In 1983, the Supreme Court interpreted the act to apply to employees' pregnant spouses. By a 7-to-2 vote the Court ruled that pregnancy-related expense benefits for the spouses of male employees must be equal to the pregnancy-related expense benefits accorded to married female employees.[51] Then, in 1987, the Court upheld a California law giving pregnant women a four-month leave from work and guaranteeing them their job back after the leave.[52] The 1993 Family Leave bill (see Chapter 12) provides further relief.

Pregnant Women in the Workforce

- 71% of all women who become pregnant are working at the time.
- 38% are in the workforce by the time their children are three months old.
- 58% are working by the time their children reach one year of age.

Among women who are working when they become pregnant:

- 50% are back in the labor force by the time their children are three months old.
- About 75% of those women return to the same job that they had before.
- 72% have returned to the labor force by the time their children are a year old.

Of the women who work sometime during their pregnancy:

- 50% work into their third trimester.
- Of those who work into their third trimester, 59% are back at work within three months of their children's births.

Source: "Work around Childbirth," Rand Corp.

The Pregnancy Discrimination Act makes it illegal for an employer with more than 15 employees to:

- Fire an employee for becoming pregnant.
- Refuse to hire a worker because she is pregnant.
- Demote or penalize a worker because she is pregnant.
- Refuse to promote a worker because she is pregnant.
- Deny disability leave if such a leave is available to other disabled workers.
- Deny health insurance for pregnancy if there is insurance available for other medical conditions.
- Deny fringe benefits, such as the crediting of vacation days, seniority, or pay increases, while a woman is on leave for childbirth if other disabled employees continue to accrue such benefits.

Source: Reported in Kathleen Hughes, "Pregnant Professionals Face Pressures at Work as Attitudes toward Them Shift," *The Wall Street Journal*, February 6, 1991, p. B1. Reprinted by permission of *The Wall Street Journal*, © 1991 Dow Jones & Company, Inc. All Rights Reserved Worldwide.

Questions

1. If women take several years off from work to bear and begin raising children, are their careers likely to be permanently impaired? Explain.
2. Ethel Roskies, a University of Montreal psychologist, reporting the results of a survey of successful professional women: "The woman who gives up marriage and

children in order to further her career is making a bad bargain." "We found that single, childless women are significantly more depressed, report lower self-esteem and lower life satisfaction than married women with children."[53] Comment.

FETAL PROTECTION

In 1991, the Supreme Court decided perhaps the most significant civil rights case in two decades. The *Johnson Controls* decision addresses the dilemma of whether fertile women may lawfully be denied jobs involving exposure to substances that may cause harm to their fetuses.

UAW v. JOHNSON CONTROLS, INC.
499 U.S. 187 (1991)

Justice Blackmun

In this case we are concerned with an employer's gender-based fetal-protection policy. May an employer exclude a fertile female employee from certain jobs because of its concern for the health of the fetus the woman might conceive?

I

Respondent Johnson Controls, Inc., manufactures batteries. In the manufacturing process, the element lead is a primary ingredient. Occupational exposure to lead entails health risks, including the risk of harm to any fetus carried by a female employee.

Before the Civil Rights Act of 1964 . . . became law, Johnson Controls did not employ any woman in a battery-manufacturing job. In June 1977, however, it announced its first official policy concerning its employment of women in lead-exposure work:

[P]rotection of the health of the unborn child is the immediate and direct responsibility of the prospective parents. While the medical profession and the company can support them in the exercise of this responsibility, it cannot assume it for them without simultaneously infringing their rights as persons.

. . . Since not all women who can become mothers wish to become mothers (or will become mothers), it would appear to be illegal discrimination to treat all who are capable of pregnancy as though they will become pregnant.

Consistent with that view, Johnson Controls "stopped short of excluding women capable of bearing children from lead exposure," . . . but emphasized that a woman who expected to have a child should not choose a job in which she would have such exposure. The company also required a woman who wished to be considered for employment to sign a statement that she had been advised of the risk of having a child while she was exposed to lead . . .

Five years later, in 1982, Johnson Controls shifted from a policy of warning to a policy of exclusion. Between 1979 and 1983, eight employees became pregnant while maintaining blood lead levels in excess of 30 micrograms per deciliter . . . This appeared to be the critical level noted by the Occupational Health and Safety Administration (sic) (OSHA) for a worker who was planning to have a family . . . The company responded by announcing a broad exclusion of women from jobs that exposed them to lead:

> ". . . [I]t is [Johnson Controls'] policy that women who are pregnant or who are capable of bearing children will not be placed into jobs involving lead exposure or which could expose them to lead through the exercise of job bidding, bumping, transfer or promotion rights."

The policy defined "women . . . capable of bearing children" as "[a]ll women except those whose inability to bear children is medically documented." . . . It further stated that an unacceptable work station was one where, "over the past year," an employee had recorded a blood lead level of more than 30 micrograms per deciliter or the work site had yielded an air sample containing a lead level in excess of 30 micrograms per cubic meter . . .

II

In April 1984, petitioners filed . . . a class action challenging Johnson Controls' fetal-protection policy as sex discrimination . . . Among the individual plaintiffs were petitioners Mary Craig, who had chosen to be sterilized in order to avoid losing her job, Elsie Nason, a 50-year-old divorcee, who had suffered a loss in compensation when she was transferred out of a job where she was exposed to lead, and Donald Penney, who had been denied a request for a leave of absence for the purpose of lowering his lead level because he intended to become a father . . . The District Court certified a class [action.]

The District Court granted summary judgment for defendant-respondent Johnson Controls . . .

The Court of Appeals . . . affirmed the summary judgment by a 7-to-4 vote . . .

. . . Specifically, the court concluded that there was no genuine issue of material fact about the substantial health-risk factor because the parties agreed that there was a substantial risk to a fetus from lead exposure . . . The Court of Appeals also concluded that, unlike the evidence of risk to the fetus from the mother's exposure, the evidence of risk from the father's exposure, which petitioners presented, "is, at best, speculative and unconvincing." . . .

* * * * *

With its ruling, the Seventh Circuit became the first Court of Appeals to hold that a fetal-protection policy directed exclusively at women could qualify as a BFOQ . . .

III

The bias in Johnson Controls' policy is obvious. Fertile men, but not fertile women, are given a choice as to whether they wish to risk their reproductive health for a particular job . . .

* * * * *

. . . Respondent does not seek to protect the unconceived children of all its employees. Despite evidence in the record about the debilitating effect of lead exposure on the male reproductive system, Johnson Controls is concerned only with the harms that may befall the unborn offspring of its female employees . . .

* * * * *

We hold that Johnson Controls' fetal-protection policy is sex discrimination forbidden under Title VII unless respondent can establish that sex is a "bona fide occupational qualification."

IV

Under . . . Title VII, an employer may discriminate on the basis of "religion, sex, or national origin in those certain instances where religion, sex, or national origin is a bona fide occupational qualification reasonably necessary to the normal operation of that particular business or enterprise." . . . We therefore turn to the question whether Johnson Controls' fetal-protection policy is one of those "certain instances" that come within the BFOQ exception.

* * * * *

Johnson Controls argues that its fetal-protection policy falls within the so-called safety exception to the BFOQ. Our cases have stressed that discrimination on the basis of sex because of safety concerns is allowed only in narrow circumstances. In *Dothard* v. *Rawlinson,* this Court indicated that danger to a woman herself does not justify discrimination . . . We there allowed the employer to hire only male guards in contact areas of maximum-security male penitentiaries only because more was at stake than the "individual woman's decision to weigh and accept the risks of employment."

Similarly, some courts have approved airlines' layoffs of pregnant flight attendants at different points during the first five months of pregnancy on the ground that the employer's policy was necessary to ensure the safety of passengers . . .

We considered safety to third parties in *Western Airlines, Inc.* v. *Criswell,* . . . in the context of the ADEA. We focused upon "the nature of the flight engineer's tasks," and the "actual capabilities of persons over age 60" in relation to those tasks . . . We stressed that in order to qualify as a BFOQ, a job qualification must relate to the "essence," . . . or to the "central mission of the employer's business" . . .

The concurrence [not reprinted here] ignores the "essence of the business" test and so concludes that "the safety to fetuses in carrying out the duties of battery manufacturing is as much a legitimate concern as is safety to third parties in guarding prisons (*Dothard*) or flying airplanes (*Criswell*)." . . . By limiting its discussion to cost and safety concerns and rejecting the "essence of the business" test that our case law has established, the concurrence seeks to expand what is now the narrow BFOQ defense. Third-party safety considerations properly entered into the BFOQ analysis in *Dothard* and *Criswell* because they went to the core of the employee's job performance. Moreover, that performance involved the central purpose of the enterprise . . . The concurrence attempts to transform this case into one of customer safety. The unconceived fetuses of Johnson Controls' female employees, however, are neither customers nor third parties whose safety is essential to the business of battery manufacturing. No one can disregard the possibility of injury to future children; the BFOQ, however, is not so broad that it transforms this deep social concern into an essential aspect of batterymaking.

Our case law, therefore, makes clear that the safety exception is limited to instances in which sex or pregnancy actually interferes with the employee's ability to perform the job . . . Johnson Controls suggests, however, that we expand the exception to allow fetal-protection policies that mandate particular standards for pregnant or fertile women. We decline to do so. Such an expansion contradicts not only the language of the BFOQ and the narrowness of its exception but the plain language and history of the Pregnancy Discrimination Act.

The PDA's amendment to Title VII contains a BFOQ standard of its own: unless pregnant employees differ from others "in their ability or inability to work," they must be "treated the same" as other employees "for all employment-related purposes." . . . In other words, women as capable of doing their jobs as their male counterparts may not be forced to choose between having a child and having a job.

* * * * *

V

We have no difficulty concluding that Johnson Controls cannot establish a BFOQ. Fertile women, as far as appears in the record, participate in the manufacture of batteries as efficiently as anyone else. Johnson Controls' professed moral and ethical concerns about the welfare of the next generation do not suffice to establish a BFOQ of female sterility. Decisions about the welfare of future children must be left to the parents who conceive, bear, support, and raise them rather than to the employers who hire those parents . . . Title VII and the PDA simply do not allow a woman's dismissal because of her failure to submit to sterilization.

Nor can concerns about the welfare of the next generation be considered a part of the "essence" of Johnson Controls' business. Judge Easterbrook in this case pertinently observed: "It is word play to say that 'the job' at Johnson [Controls] is to make batteries without risk to fetuses in the same way 'the job' at Western Air Lines is to fly planes without crashing." . . .

* * * * *

VI

A word about tort liability and the increased cost of fertile women in the workplace is perhaps necessary . . .

More than 40 States currently recognize a right to recover for a prenatal injury based either on negligence or on wrongful death . . . According to Johnson Controls, however, the company complies with the lead standard developed by OSHA and warns its female employees about the damaging effects of lead. It is worth noting that OSHA gave the problem of lead lengthy consideration and concluded that "there is no basis whatsoever for the claim that women of childbearing age should be excluded from the workplace in order to protect the fetus or the course of pregnancy." . . . Instead, OSHA established a series of mandatory protections which, taken together, "should effectively minimize any risk to the fetus and newborn child." . . . Without negligence, it would be difficult for a court to find liability on the part of the employer. If, under general tort principles, Title VII bans sex-specific fetal-protection policies, the employer fully informs the woman of the risk, and the employer has not acted negligently, the basis for holding an employer liable seems remote at best.

* * * * *

The tort-liability argument reduces to two equally unpersuasive propositions. First, Johnson Controls attempts to solve the problem of reproductive health hazards by resorting to an exclusionary policy. Title VII plainly forbids illegal sex discrimination as a method of diverting attention from an employer's obligation to police the workplace. Second, the spectre of an award of damages reflects a fear that hiring fertile women will cost more. The extra cost of employing members of one sex, however, does not provide an affirmative Title VII defense for a discriminatory refusal to hire members of that gender . . . Indeed, in passing the PDA, Congress considered at length the considerable cost of providing equal treatment of pregnancy and related conditions, but made the "decision to forbid special treatment of pregnancy despite the social costs associated therewith." . . .

We, of course, are not presented with, nor do we decide, a case in which costs would be so prohibitive as to threaten the survival of the employer's business. We merely reiterate our prior holdings that the incremental cost of hiring women cannot justify discriminating against them.

VII

*   *   *   *   *

It is no more appropriate for the courts than it is for individual employers to decide whether a woman's reproductive role is more important to herself and her family than her economic role. Congress has left this choice to the woman as hers to make.

Reversed and remanded.

Questions

1. What reasoning supported the Supreme Court's judgment that sex was not a BFOQ in this case?
2. *a.* What reasoning supported the Supreme Court's judgment that employer liability for a prenatal injury "seems remote at best"?
   b. Do you agree with the Court's reasoning on the liability issue? Explain.
3. Make the argument that the *Johnson Controls* decision will result in job losses in American industry and a reduced ability for American business to compete in the international market.
4. What steps would you expect businesses to take in an effort to cope with the implications of the *Johnson Controls* decision?
5. Assume a worker is warned of fetal hazards on the job and voluntarily signs a release excusing the employer of liability for any injuries that may follow. Would that release be legally binding in a subsequent fetal injury case? Explain.
6. Can a hospital lawfully agree to patients' demands for physically intimate care only by those of the same sex? Explain. See *Carey* v. *New York State Human Rights App. Bd.,* 61 A.D. 2d 804, 402 N.Y.S. 2d 207 (1978).
7. How might an airline justify a policy forbidding the assignment of pregnant flight attendants to flight duty? Is such a policy lawful? Explain. See *Condit* v. *United Airlines, Inc.,* 558 F.2d 1176 (4th Cir. 1977), cert. denied, 435 U.S. 934 (1978). Compare *Burwell* v. *Eastern Air Lines, Inc.,* CA4, 1980, 23 FEP Cases 949.
8. The Southern Pacific railroad denied employment as an agent-telegrapher to Rosenfeld, a woman. The railroad cited hard work (some 80-hour weeks and some lifting of 50

pounds or more) and California labor laws restricting hours of work and weights to be lifted by women.
  a. Is sex a BFOQ under these facts? Explain.
  b. Does the California statute govern this situation? Explain.
  c. The *Rosenfeld* court articulated the following very narrow test of those circumstances under which sex is a legitimate BFOQ: "sexual characteristics, rather than characteristics that might, to one degree or another, correlate with a particular sex, must be the basis for the application of the BFOQ exception." Explain the court's test and offer an example of a job wherein sex would clearly constitute a BFOQ. See *Rosenfeld* v. *Southern Pacific Co.,* 444 F.2d 1219 (1971).

SEXUAL HARASSMENT

Broadly, sexual harassment consists of unwelcome sexual advances, requests for sexual favors, and other verbal or physical conduct of a sexual nature. That conduct in a work setting constitutes sex discrimination in violation of Title VII.

Well-settled case law and federal guidelines have established two categories of sexual harassment:

1. *Quid pro quo sexual harassment.* In these cases, continued employment or an employment benefit such as a promotion are conditioned by a manager or a supervisor on the employee's willingness to engage in sexual conduct—that is, a boss expects a sexual opportunity in trade for a job benefit.
2. *Hostile environment sexual harassment.* In these cases, no employment benefit need be lost or gained. Rather, the question is one of whether the work environment has become offensive and abusive because of the pervasive presence of, for example, sexual aggression, sexual jokes, pornographic pictures, sexually derogatory comments, and so on. That hostile environment may be the product of conduct by managers, supervisors, coworkers, or even those not actually employed by the firm in question.

Sexual harassment claims under Title VII may be supplemented by various civil and criminal actions. For example, assault, battery, breach of contract, and criminal assault are all possibilities, depending on the circumstances.

The evidence suggests that sexual harassment at work is widespread. Thirty-one percent of the women and 7 percent of the men surveyed in a 1994 nationwide Harris Poll indicated that they had been the victims of sexual harassment at work. However, 63 percent of those surveyed said there is no sexual harassment in their workplace.[54] A 1992 survey of *Working Woman* readers reported a 60 percent rate of harassment.[55]

Sexual harassment charges filed at the federal level fell under 5,000 in 1989. Then Anita Hill's dramatic sexual harassment allegations against now U.S. Supreme Court Justice Clarence Thomas in his Senate confirmation hearings apparently spurred a new surge in filings, as these totaled 10,608 in 1992.[56]

What Is It?   Not surprisingly, a continuing difficulty in dealing with sexual harassment lies in identifying it. At this writing in 1994, the Equal Employment Opportunity Commission (EEOC) has proposed new guidelines (expressing the federal government's opinion but not carrying the weight of law) defining harassment (not limited to sexual harassment) as "verbal or physical conduct that denigrates or shows hostility or aversion toward an individual because of his/her race, color, religion, gender, national origin, age, or disability" where, in brief, that behavior creates an intimidating, hostile, or offensive working environment. That harassment could take the form of written or graphic material or "epithets, slurs, negative stereotyping, or threatening, intimidating or hostile acts that relate to race, color, religion, gender, national origin, age or disability."[57]

At the workplace level, the confusion can be considerable. A 1992 Roper Poll summarized 22 situations and asked the respondents which of them constituted sexual harassment. Clear majorities found sexual harassment in only three of the situations. Those involved direct questions about sexual practices and being required to sleep with the boss in exchange for a raise. Strong majorities rejected a finding of sexual harassment in such situations as:

- A compliment about a coworker's appearance.
- Asking a coworker for a date.
- A woman looking "up and down" a man as he walks by.
- Referring to women as "girls."

A middle ground of great confusion included such situations as:

- A male boss calling a female "honey."
- A man looking "up and down" a woman as she walks by.
- Men in the office repeatedly discussing the appearance of female coworkers.[58]

In Grade School?   In an interesting and important development, we are now witnessing a surge of claims of sexual harassment in the schools among children as young as 8 or 9. Claims of unwelcome touching, lewd sexual comments, and unkind gender-based comments that were once lumped in the "boys will be boys" file are now the subject of litigation. Indeed, in 1993, a Minnesota high school female received $40,000 from the Chaska School District as a settlement of her claims that school officials had ignored her complaints of sexual harassment. She had discovered her name on a list of 25 female students about whom male students had written lewd sexual comments.[59]

Question

1. What would you do in the following situation: You are a university administrator and you receive a complaint from two female graduate students. These women share an office with a male graduate student who displays on his desk a 5 × 7-inch photo of his wife in a chain-mail bikini. Is the male student guilty of environmental sexual harassment? Explain.[60]

In the case that follows, the Supreme Court recently addressed the question of when mere sexist behavior in the workplace crosses over to become actionable sexual harassment.

HARRIS v. FORKLIFT SYSTEMS, INC.
114 S.Ct. 367 (1993)

Justice O'Connor

In this case we consider the definition of a discriminatorily "abusive work environment" (also known as a "hostile work environment") under Title VII of the Civil Rights Act of 1964.

I

Teresa Harris worked as a manager at Forklift Systems, Inc., an equipment rental company, from April 1985 until October 1987. Charles Hardy was Forklift's president.

The Magistrate found that, throughout Harris' time at Forklift, Hardy often insulted her because of her gender and often made her the target of unwanted sexual innuendos. Hardy told Harris on several occasions, in the presence of other employees, "You're a woman, what do you know" and "We need a man as the rental manager"; at least once, he told her she was "a dumb ass woman." Again in front of others, he suggested that the two of them "go to the Holiday Inn to negotiate [Harris'] raise." Hardy occasionally asked Harris and other female employees to get coins from his front pants pocket. He threw objects on the ground in front of Harris and other women, and asked them to pick the objects up. He made sexual innuendos about Harris' and other women's clothing.

In mid-August 1987, Harris complained to Hardy about his conduct. Hardy said he was surprised that Harris was offended, claimed he was only joking, and apologized. He also promised he would stop, and based on this assurance Harris stayed on the job. But in early September, Hardy began anew: While Harris was arranging a deal with one of Forklift's customers, he asked her, again in front of other employees, "What did you do, promise the guy . . . some [sex] Saturday night?" On October 1, Harris collected her paycheck and quit.

Harris then sued Forklift, claiming that Hardy's conduct had created an abusive work environment for her because of her gender. The United States District Court for the Middle District of Tennessee, adopting the report and recommendation of the Magistrate, found this to be "a close case," but held that Hardy's conduct did not create an abusive environment. The court found that some of Hardy's comments "offended [Harris], and would offend the reasonable woman," but that they were not

> so severe as to be expected to seriously affect [Harris'] psychological well-being. A reasonable woman manager under like circumstances would have been offended by Hardy, but his conduct would not have risen to the level of interfering with that person's work performance.

Neither do I believe that [Harris] was subjectively so offended that she suffered injury . . . Although Hardy may at times have genuinely offended [Harris], I do not believe that he created a working environment so poisoned as to be intimidating or abusive to [Harris].

In focusing on the employee's psychological well-being, the District Court was following Circuit precedent. See *Rabidue* v. *Osceola Refining Co.,* 805 F. 2d 611, 620 (CA6 1986), cert. denied, 481 U. S. 1041 (1987). The United States Court of Appeals for the Sixth Circuit affirmed in a brief unpublished decision.

We granted certiorari to resolve a conflict among the Circuits on whether conduct, to be actionable as "abusive work environment" harassment (no *quid pro quo* harassment issue is present here), must "seriously affect [an employee's] psychological well-being" or lead the plaintiff to "suffe[r] injury."

II

Title VII of the Civil Rights Act of 1964 makes it "an unlawful employment practice for an employer . . . to discriminate against any individual with respect to his compensation, terms, conditions, or privileges of employment, because of such individual's race, color, religion, sex, or national origin." As we made clear in *Meritor Savings Bank* v. *Vinson,* 477 U. S. 57 (1986), this language "is not limited to 'economic' or 'tangible' discrimination. The phrase 'terms, conditions, or privileges of employment' evinces a congressional intent 'to strike at the entire spectrum of disparate treatment of men and women' in employment," which includes requiring people to work in a discriminatorily hostile or abusive environment. When the workplace is permeated with "discriminatory intimidation, ridicule, and insult," 477 U. S., at 65, that is "sufficiently severe or pervasive to alter the conditions of the victim's employment and create an abusive working environment," Title VII is violated.

This standard, which we reaffirm today, takes a middle path between making actionable any conduct that is merely offensive and requiring the conduct to cause a tangible psychological injury. As we pointed out in *Meritor,* "mere utterance of an . . . epithet which engenders offensive feelings in a employee," does not sufficiently affect the conditions of employment to implicate Title VII. Conduct that is not severe or pervasive enough to create an objectively hostile or abusive work environment—an environment that a reasonable person would find hostile or abusive—is beyond Title VII's purview. Likewise, if the victim does not subjectively perceive the environment to be abusive, the conduct has not actually altered the conditions of the victim's employment, and there is no Title VII violation.

But Title VII comes into play before the harassing conduct leads to a nervous breakdown. A discriminatorily abusive work environment, even one that does not seriously affect employees' psychological well-being, can and often will detract from employees' job performance, discourage employees from remaining on the job, or keep them from advancing in their careers. Moreover, even without regard to these tangible effects, the very fact that the discriminatory conduct was so severe or pervasive that it created a work environment abusive to employees because of their race, gender, religion, or national origin offends Title VII's broad rule of workplace equality . . .

We therefore believe the District Court erred in relying on whether the conduct "seriously affect[ed] plaintiff's psychological well-being" or led her to "suffe[r] injury." Such an inquiry may needlessly focus the factfinder's attention on concrete psychological harm, an element

Title VII does not require. Certainly Title VII bars conduct that would seriously affect a reasonable person's psychological well-being, but the statute is not limited to such conduct. So long as the environment would reasonably be perceived, and is perceived, as hostile or abusive, there is no need for it also to be psychologically injurious.

This is not, and by its nature cannot be, a mathematically precise test. We need not answer today all the potential questions it raises . . . But we can say that whether an environment is "hostile" or "abusive" can be determined only by looking at all the circumstances. These may include the frequency of the discriminatory conduct; its severity; whether it is physically threatening or humiliating, or a mere offensive utterance; and whether it unreasonably interferes with an employee's work performance. The effect on the employee's psychological well-being is, of course, relevant to determining whether the plaintiff actually found the environment abusive. But while psychological harm, like any other relevant factor, may be taken into account, no single factor is required.

III

Forklift, while conceding that a requirement that the conduct seriously affect psychological well-being is unfounded, argues that the District Court nonetheless correctly applied the *Meritor* standard. We disagree. Though the District Court did conclude that the work environment was not "intimidating or abusive to [Harris]," it did so only after finding that the conduct was not "so severe as to be expected to seriously affect plaintiff's psychological well-being," and that Harris was not "subjectively so offended that she suffered injury." The District Court's application of these incorrect standards may well have influenced its ultimate conclusion, especially given that the court found this to be a "close case."

[Reversed and remanded.]

Justice Scalia, concurring

Meritor Savings Bank v. *Vinson,* 477 U. S. 57 (1986), held that Title VII prohibits sexual harassment that takes the form of a hostile work environment. The Court stated that sexual harassment is actionable if it is "sufficiently severe or pervasive 'to alter the conditions of [the victim's] employment and create an abusive work environment.' " Today's opinion elaborates that the challenged conduct must be severe or pervasive enough "to create an objectively hostile or abusive work environment—an environment that a reasonable person would find hostile or abusive."

"Abusive" (or "hostile," which in this context I take to mean the same thing) does not seem to me a very clear standard—and I do not think clarity is at all increased by adding the adverb "objectively" or by appealing to a "reasonable person's" notion of what the vague word means. Today's opinion does list a number of factors that contribute to abusiveness, but since it neither says how much of each is necessary (an impossible task) nor identifies any single factor as determinative, it thereby adds little certitude. As a practical matter, today's holding lets virtually unguided juries decide whether sex-related conduct engaged in (or permitted by) an employer is egregious enough to warrant an award of damages. One might say that what constitutes "negligence" (a traditional jury question) is not much more clear and certain than what constitutes "abusiveness." Perhaps so. But the class of plaintiffs seeking to recover for negligence is limited to those who have suffered harm, whereas under this statute "abusiveness" is to be the test of whether legal harm has been suffered, opening more expansive vistas of litigation.

Be that as it may, I know of no alternative to the course the Court today has taken. One of the factors mentioned in the Court's nonexhaustive list—whether the conduct unreasonably interferes with an employee's work performance—would, if it were made an absolute test, provide greater guidance to juries and employers. But I see no basis for such a limitation in the language of the statute. Accepting *Meritor's* interpretation of the term "conditions of employment" as the law, the test is not whether work has been impaired, but whether working conditions have been discriminatorily altered. I know of no test more faithful to the inherently vague statutory language than the one the Court today adopts. For these reasons, I join the opinion of the Court.

Justice Ginsburg, concurring

Today the Court reaffirms the holding of *Meritor Savings Bank* v. *Vinson:* "[A] plaintiff may establish a violation of Title VII by proving that discrimination based on sex has created a hostile or abusive work environment." The critical issue, Title VII's text indicates, is whether members of one sex are exposed to disadvantageous terms or conditions of employment to which members of the other sex are not exposed. As the Equal Employment Opportunity Commission emphasized, the adjudicator's inquiry should center, dominantly, on whether the discriminatory conduct has unreasonably interfered with the plaintiff's work performance. To show such interference, "the plaintiff need not prove that his or her tangible productivity has declined as a result of the harassment." *Davis* v. *Monsanto Chemical Co.,* 858 F. 2d 345, 349 (CA6 1988). It suffices to prove that a reasonable person subjected to the discriminatory conduct would find, as the plaintiff did, that the harassment so altered working conditions as to "ma[k]e it more difficult to do the job."

Questions

1. Based on the majority opinion, what kinds of "circumstances" would be helpful in determining whether a working environment is hostile or abusive?
2. Justice Scalia (see his concurring opinion) is clearly uncomfortable with what he takes to be the vague standard set down by the majority. Why, then, did he vote with the majority?
3. Summarize Justice Ginsburg's suggested test for establishing a hostile or abusive work environment.
4. *a.* What test did the majority settle on to define sexual harassment of the kind in the *Harris* case?
   b. What constitutional challenge might be raised to that test? Explain.
   c. Are you comfortable with the majority's test in *Harris?*
5. The lower federal courts have been struggling with the question of whether sexual harassment should be "measured" by the standard of the "reasonable *person*" or by the standard of the reasonable *man* or the reasonable *woman.*

a. Does the *Harris* decision settle that question? Explain.

b. Why does it matter?

6. Could an employer successfully defend against a female employee's claim of a hostile work environment (e.g., male supervisors regularly questioning female subordinates about their sexual activities and preferences) by offering testimony from other female employees that they are untroubled by the conduct? See *Morgan* v. *Hertz Corp.,* 27 FEP 990 (W.D. Tenn. 1981) as reported in Vern E. Hauck and Thomas G. Pearce, *"Vinson:* Sexual Harassment and Employer Response,*" Labor Law Journal* 38, no. 12 (December 1987), pp. 770, 772.

7. Soon after her employment in the federal Environmental Protection Agency Paulette Barnes was allegedly the subject of social and sexual advances from her supervisor (not the defendant and appellee in the case). Despite firm refusals, the supervisor is alleged to have repeatedly sought her company after working hours and suggested on numerous occasions that her employment status would be enhanced were she to engage in a sexual relationship with him. She had made clear her insistence on a purely professional relationship. Then, according to Barnes, her supervisor and other administrators began a program of harassment, including taking many duties from her. Ultimately her job was abolished in apparent retaliation for her resistance to the unwanted advances. She then filed a complaint with the EEOC.

   Decide. Explain. See *Barnes* v. *Costle,* 561 F.2d 983 (D.C. Cir. 1977). (Costle was an administrator of the Environmental Protection Agency and was a litigant in this case solely by reason of his official position.)

8. A nurse in a California hospital filed a claim under state law alleging that she was the victim of environmental sexual harassment because she witnessed a doctor's repeated harassment of other women employees. The plaintiff alleged that the doctor pulled nurses onto his lap, kissed them, and made other sexual advances. The plaintiff claimed that witnessing those acts, which were not directed toward her, had caused her to suffer headaches, stomach aches, and diarrhea.

   How would you rule on the nurse's claim? Explain. For a journalistic account of the lawsuit, see Philip Hager, "Court . . . Sex Harassment Suit Filed by Bystander," *Los Angeles Times,* January 19, 1990, p. A3.

Harassment Abroad?

A recent study suggests that sexual harassment pervades the workplaces of the world, with 21 percent of French women, 58 percent of Dutch women, and 74 percent of British women reporting that they had experienced sexual harassment at work.[61] Of course, the notion of sexual harassment differs widely from culture to culture, and of the 23 nations studied, only 6 in addition to the United States had statutes defining or mentioning sexual harassment. The report concludes that the United States has been in the forefront in addressing sexual harassment.[62]

The brief article that follows notes the Japanese decision to officially address sexual harassment.

JAPAN DEFINES SEXUAL HARASSMENT

Richard Holman

The Japanese government for the first time defined sexual harassment in the workplace and urged companies to try to prevent such incidents.

The Labor Ministry characterized harassment as unpleasant speech or conduct with sexual references or connotations that create a difficult working environment. It said managers and workers have found it difficult to identify and deal with the issue.

For years, Japanese women have endured sexual remarks by male bosses and colleagues, but few spoke up for fear of ridicule or reprisals in the male-oriented society. A quarter of women surveyed by the ministry had been harassed at work.

The ministry, which wants to make it easier for companies to take positive steps to guard against harassment, seeks a budget for the next fiscal year to start an educational campaign for companies.

Source: *The Wall Street Journal,* October 20, 1993, p. A11. Reprinted by permission of *The Wall Street Journal,* © 1993 Dow Jones & Company, Inc. All Rights Reserved Worldwide.

EQUAL PAY

Title VII affords broad protection from discrimination in pay because of sex. The Equal Pay Act of 1963 directly forbids discrimination on the basis of sex by paying wages to employees of one sex at a rate less than the rate paid to employees of the opposite sex for equal work on jobs requiring equal skill, effort, and responsibility and performed under similar working conditions (*equal* has been interpreted to mean "substantially equal"). The act provides for certain exceptions. Unequal wage payments are lawful if paid pursuant to (1) a seniority system, (2) a merit system, (3) a system that measures earnings by quantity or quality of production, or (4) a differential based on "any other factor other than sex." The employer seeking to avoid a violation of the Equal Pay Act can adjust its wage structure by raising the pay of the disfavored sex. Lowering the pay of the favored sex violates the act.

Paying women and men the same amount for the same work is simple enough in principle, but the legal issues have proved slippery, indeed. For example:

1. Is travel reimbursement a "wage"? Maternity payments?[63] [According to the federal government—No.]
2. Must the plaintiff establish a *pattern* of sex-based wage discrimination?[64] [According to the federal government—No.]
3. Are jobs unequal in effort and thus "unequal work" when a part of one job includes tasks that females are physically unable to perform?[65] [No, if those tasks do not constitute a substantial part of the job.]

In the leading case of *Corning Glass Works* v. *Brennan,* the Supreme Court was faced with the question of whether different shifts constituted differing "working conditions."[66] Women had been engaged in glass inspection on the day shift. Corning added a night shift of inspectors, which, due to state "protective" laws, was composed entirely of males. The night shift demanded and received higher wages than the female day inspectors. The Supreme Court held that the time of day in and of itself is not a *working condition.* That term, the Court said, refers to "surroundings" and "hazards." However, shift differentials could lawfully constitute a "factor other than sex" if established by the employer.

COMPARABLE WORTH

Equal pay for equal work is hardly a radical notion, but equal pay for work of comparable value would, if fully realized, dramatically alter the nature of the American labor market. *Comparable worth* calls for determining the compensation to be paid for a position based on the job's intrinsic value in comparison to wages being paid for other jobs requiring comparable skills, effort, and responsibility and having comparable worth to the organization.

The argument is that the dollar value assigned to jobs held predominantly by men is higher than the value assigned to jobs held predominantly by women. To proponents of comparable worth, such disparities cannot be explained by market forces. They argue that women are the continuing victims of sex discrimination in violation of Title VII of the Civil Rights Act of 1964.

A variety of studies have contrasted pay scales in traditionally female jobs with those in traditionally male jobs where the jobs are judged to be of comparable worth. For example, licensed practical nurses in Illinois in 1983 earned an average of $1,298 per month, while electricians earned an average of $2,826.[67] A 1987 Child Welfare League study fixed the median salary of garbage collectors at $14,872 annually, as compared with $12,800 for child care workers.[68] The same study found social workers with master's degrees earned about $21,800 per year, while auto salespeople averaged $22,048.[69]

A number of companies and state governments practice some form of comparable worth, but most continue to rely on the market as the best measure of worth.

The U.S. Supreme Court has yet to directly explore the substance of the comparable worth debate. In the *Gunther*[70] case, the Court held, in effect, that Title VII does not forbid the comparable worth theory. However, the federal appeals court decisions to date have rejected the comparable worth theory in the context of Title VII sex discrimination.[71]

SEXUAL STEREOTYPES

Ann B. Hopkins, a Price Waterhouse manager, was hoping in 1982 to be promoted to partner. She had earned at least $34 million in consulting contracts for the firm, a record exceeding that of the 87 other candidates for partner—all of whom were male. Despite her success, Hopkins was denied partnership. She left the firm and filed a sex discrimination claim. The firm says she was an "overbearing, arrogant, and abrasive manager." [72] She argued that her occasional cursing and her sometimes brusque manner would have been overlooked had she been a male. At trial, she introduced the partners' written evaluations, which included such words and phrases as "macho," "lady partner," and "charm school." One mentioned that "she may have overcompensated for being a woman." Hopkins testified that a chief partner suggested she wear makeup, have her hair styled, walk more femininely, and so on. Based on that evidence and expert testimony, Hopkins claimed she was a victim of sexual stereotyping. The firm offered evidence in support of its contention that Hopkins' personality and interpersonal skills were the issue in the case. One consultant said he left the firm in part because of what he perceived to be the difficulty in working with Hopkins, whom he accused of once "screaming obscenities over the phone at him for 'up to' 45 minutes." [73]

Hopkins won at the district court level, where the court found that Price Waterhouse was guilty of sex discrimination. [74] The District of Columbia Court of Appeals affirmed, finding "ample support for the district court's finding that the partnership selection process was impermissibly infected by stereotypical attitudes toward women." [75] The court went on to hold that Price Waterhouse had to show that bias as a consequence of sexual stereotyping was not the decisive factor in the decision to deny promotion. The case then went to the U.S. Supreme Court. How would you rule on this claim of sexual stereotyping as sex discrimination? See *Price Waterhouse* v. *Hopkins,* 109 S.Ct. 1775 (1989). If you find for Hopkins, would you order Price Waterhouse to offer her the partnership she sought? Explain.

Part Four—Religious Discrimination

In general terms, discrimination on the basis of religion is to be analyzed in the manner of the other protected classes specified by Title VII. "Religion" is not limited to orthodox faiths, but it does exclude mere shams designed to legitimize otherwise impermissible conduct. The Supreme Court has defined the necessary faith as a "sincere and meaningful belief occupying in the life of its possessor a place parallel to that filled by the God of those admittedly qualified." [76]

In the absence of an appropriate defense (for example, BFOQ), an employer, of course, cannot decline to hire or otherwise discriminate against an individual or group on the grounds of religion. The plaintiff's problem in such cases is to offer proof that religious bias was the motivation for the disputed employment practice. Discrimination on the grounds of religion is permissible if "an employer demonstrates that he is unable to reasonably accommodate an employee's or prospective employee's religious observance or practice without undue hardship on the conduct of the employer's business." Thus, the primary issue in the area of religious discrimination has come to be that of determining "reasonable accommodation" in varying factual settings.

The leading case is *Trans World Airlines, Inc.* v. *Hardison,* in which the sabbatarian plaintiff worked in a parts warehouse that operated around the clock, seven days a week. [77] Because of a transfer, Hardison was at the bottom of the departmental seniority list and was unable to take his Sabbath off. The company conferred with Hardison and permitted the union to seek a swap of shifts or a change in jobs, but the efforts were unsuccessful. A seniority modification could not be agreed on, and the company rejected Hardison's request for a four-day week because the solution would have required the use of another employee at premium pay. The Supreme Court's opinion in the case reduced the employer's duty to a very modest standard: "To require TWA to bear more than a de minimis cost in order to give Hardison Saturdays off is an undue hardship." Saturdays off for Hardison would have imposed extra costs on TWA and would have constituted religious discrimination against other employees who would have sought Saturday off for reasons not grounded in religion. The *Hardison* court also took the position that the collective bargaining agreement's seniority provisions need not give way to accommodate religious observance. The Court found sufficient accommodation in TWA's reducing weekend shift sizes and allowing voluntary trading of shifts.

By contrast, the Supreme Court declined to review a federal court of appeals decision holding that an employer failed to reasonably accommodate an employee who declined to work on Sundays when the employer made no effort to find substitutes, did not permit employees to post bulletin-board notices seeking substitutes, and did not itself use the bulletin board to seek volunteers to replace the employee.[78]

Part Five—*Affirmative Action*

The struggle for civil rights in the workplace sometimes cannot be achieved, in the short run, simply by avoiding discriminatory practices. Obviously, obeying the law is expected of all. However, as a matter of social policy, we have decided that mere compliance with the civil rights laws, guaranteeing equal opportunity in the workplace, is not always adequate to correct the wrongs of discrimination. Among other problems, a great deal of time ordinarily would need to pass before the lingering effects of past discrimination would no longer be felt if we were to do nothing more than not practice discrimination. Therefore, we have decided as a society to implement the policy that we label *affirmative action* as a means of remedying past wrongs and preventing the same in the future. In following an affirmative action plan, employers consciously take positive steps to seek out minorities and women for hiring and promotion opportunities, and they often employ goals and timetables to measure progress toward a workforce that is representative of the qualified labor pool.

Affirmative action efforts arise in two ways: (1) courts may order the implementation of affirmative action after a finding of wrongful discrimination, and (2) employers may voluntarily adopt affirmative action plans. Some may do so because they believe it is a wise management strategy or because they approve of affirmative action as a matter of social policy, or both. Others may adopt affirmative action because they wish to do business with the federal government. All government contractors must meet the affirmative action standards of the Office of Federal Contract Compliance Programs. As discussed above, those standards consist essentially of established goals and timetables for strengthening the representation of "underutilized" minorities and women.

Good Policy?

Affirmative action is one of the most hotly disputed social issues in contemporary life. Minorities and women have been the victims of discrimination. Should white males "pay" for those wrongs? Critics decry affirmative action as "reverse discrimination." They argue that affirmative action is paternalistic and encourages the view that minorities and women can progress only with the aid of white males.[79] Studies confirm that affirmative action plans stigmatize minorities and women in the minds of coworkers. Minorities and women are often assumed to have achieved their positions via "quotas" and not as the result of their efforts and abilities.[80]

Now, many white males feel that they are surrounded and under siege by the forces of affirmative action and multiculturalism. Even if so, *Newsweek* argues that being a white man is still a very comfortable role in contemporary America:

> But is the white male truly an endangered species, or is he just being a jerk? It's still a statistical piece of cake being a white man, at least in comparison with being anything else. White males make up just 39.2 percent of the population, yet they account for 82.5 percent of the Forbes 400 (folks worth at least $265 million), 77 percent of Congress, 92 percent of state governors, 70 percent of tenured college faculty, almost 90 percent of daily-newspaper editors, 77 percent of TV news directors. They dominate just about everything but NOW and the NAACP.[81]

THE LAW

Quotas?

The most interesting recent developments in affirmative action have involved higher education. In 1992, the U.S. Department of Education's Office of Civil Rights accused the very prestigious Boalt Hall School of Law at the University of California at Berkeley of affording unfair racial/ethnic preferences in admissions under its program that set goals of 23 to 27 percent minority enrollment. Applicants were divided into ethnic or racial groups and compared only with applicants from their own group. The University denied any wrongdoing but reached a settlement with the government that forbids future discriminatory approaches.[82] The irony of the Boalt Hall situation is that the government inquiry was prompted by complaints that many highly qualified *Asian* applicants were denied admission because the "goal" for Asians was 5 to 7 percent of the class.[83]

The government argued that the plan violated the famous U.S. Supreme Court decision in the *Bakke* case, where a white male claimed that he was the victim of "reverse discrimination" when he was denied admission to the University of California at Davis medical school even though he had better objective credentials than a number of minority students who were granted admission under the University's "quota" system.[84] That ruling appeared to forbid quotas while permitting consideration of race as a factor in affirmative actions plans. However, subsequent decisions (e.g., see *Paradise,* p. 601) permit quotas under very extreme circumstances.

Race-Based Aid

Many colleges and universities offer some race-specific financial aid. Surveys show that less than 1 percent of scholarships are tied to race, but the issue has become somewhat explosive on symbolic grounds.[85] In 1993, Education Secretary Richard Riley announced the government's policy that such aid is lawful from the federal government's point of view. Riley took the position that such aid helps to right the wrongs of the past. The constitutionality of race-targeted aid is being tested in the courts.

Question

1. The highly competitive University of Texas School of Law employs the Texas Index (TI), a combination of grade point average and Law School Admission Test score as the primary measure of suitability for admission. Michael Greve reported in *The Wall Street Journal:*

   For the entering class of 1989, the median TI score was 76 [out of a possible 88] for Anglo Texas residents, 64 for blacks, and 66 for Mexican-Americans. A university memorandum explains helpfully that "a resident Mexican-American with a Texas Index between 65 and 69 had almost a 90 percent chance of admission." A similarly situated Anglo had less than a 1 percent chance of admission.[86]

   Comment.

Conservative View

The Supreme Court of the late 1980s and early 1990s, reflecting more judicially conservative nominees and perhaps the tone of the times, took a close look at affirmative action plans. In the most notable of these cases, *Richmond* v. *Croson,*[87] the Court ruled that the Constitution limits the power of state and local governments to reserve a percentage of their business for minority contractors (so-called minority set-asides). Those set-asides are impermissible if they involve quotas or if they are not directed explicitly to the correction of well-documented cases of discrimination in the past. Nearly 40 states and 200 cities and counties were forced by the decision to review their set-aside programs.

On the other hand, the Court upheld the constitutionality of Federal Communications Commission policies giving minorities preference in competing for broadcasting licenses.[88] The decision is especially notable because it holds for the first time that Congress has the power, via affirmative action, not just to correct the effects of past discrimination, but also to promote diversity.

A minority of justices on the present court believe that affirmative action is permissible only if directed to specific, identified victims of past discrimination. In rejecting that view, the majority supports carefully tailored consideration of race and sex in hiring and promotion situations. However, as discussed earlier in this chapter, such relief is impermissible where it would result in laying off those with seniority (typically, white males).

AFFIRMATIVE ACTION IN PRACTICE

United Steelworkers of America v. *Weber* is perhaps the clearest Supreme Court statement to date about the permissible boundaries of affirmative action.[89] Weber, a white male, challenged the legality of an affirmative action plan that set aside for black employees 50 percent of the openings in a training program until the percentage of black craft workers in the plant equaled the percentage of blacks in the local labor market. The plan was the product of a collective bargaining agreement between the Steelworkers and Kaiser Aluminum and Chemical. In Kaiser's Grammercy, Louisiana, plant only 5 of 273 skilled craft workers were black, while the local workforce was approximately 39 percent black. In the first year of the affirmative action plan, seven blacks and six whites were admitted to the craft training program. The most junior black employee accepted for the program had less seniority than several white employees who were not accepted. Weber was among the white males denied entry to the training program.

Weber filed suit, claiming Title VII forbade an affirmative action plan that granted a racial preference to blacks where whites dramatically exceeded blacks in skilled craft positions but there was no proof of discrimination. The federal district court and the federal court of appeals held for Weber, but the U.S. Supreme Court reversed. Therefore, under *Weber,* race-conscious affirmative action remedies can be permissible. Several qualities of the Steelworkers' plan were instrumental in the Court's favorable ruling:

1. The affirmative action was part of a *plan.*
2. The plan was designed to "open employment opportunities for Negroes in occupations which have been traditionally closed to them."
3. The plan was temporary.
4. The plan did not unnecessarily harm the rights of white employees. That is—
   a. The plan did not require the discharge of white employees.
   b. The plan did not create an absolute bar to the advancement of white employees.

Therefore, affirmative action in situations like that in *Weber* does not constitute unlawful reverse discrimination.

The Supreme Court clarified the law's affirmative action commands a bit further in the *Burdine* case, in which the Court asserted that Title VII does not require the employer to hire a minority or female applicant whenever that person's objective qualifications were equal to those of a white male applicant. Therefore, "the employer has discretion to choose among equally qualified candidates, provided the decision is not based upon unlawful criteria."[90]

JOHNSON v. TRANSPORTATION AGENCY
107 S.Ct. 1442

Justice Brennan

Respondent, Transportation Agency of Santa Clara County, California, unilaterally promulgated an Affirmative Action Plan applicable . . . to promotions of employees. In selecting applicants for the promotional position of road dispatcher, the agency, pursuant to the plan, passed over petitioner Paul Johnson, a male employee, and promoted a female employee applicant, Diane Joyce. The question for decision is whether in making the promotion the Agency impermissibly took into account the sex of the applicants in violation of Title VII of the Civil Rights Act of 1964. The District Court for the Northern District of California . . . held that respondent had violated Title VII. The Court of Appeals for the Ninth Circuit reversed. We granted certiorari.

I

A

In December 1978, the Santa Clara County Transit District Board of Supervisors adopted an Affirmative Action Plan (Plan) for the County Transportation Agency . . .

* * * * *

The agency stated that its plan was intended to achieve "a statistically measurable yearly improvement in hiring, training and promotion of minorities and women throughout the Agency in all major job classifications where they are underrepresented." As a benchmark by which to evaluate progress, the agency stated that its long-term goal was to attain a work force whose composition reflected the proportion of minorities and women in the area labor force. . . .

* * * * *

The agency's plan . . . set aside no specific number of positions for minorities or women, but authorized the consideration of ethnicity or sex as a factor when evaluating qualified candidates for jobs in which members of such groups were poorly represented. One such job was the road dispatcher position that is the subject of the dispute in this case.

B

On December 12, 1979, the agency announced a vacancy for the promotional position of road dispatcher . . . Dispatchers assign road crews, equipment, and materials, and maintain records pertaining to road maintenance jobs. The position requires at minimum four years of dispatch or road maintenance work experience for Santa Clara County . . .

Twelve county employees applied for the promotion, including Joyce and Johnson. Joyce had worked for the county since 1970, serving as an account clerk until 1975. She had applied for a road dispatcher position in 1974, but was deemed ineligible because she had not served as a road maintenance worker. In 1975, Joyce transferred from a senior account clerk position to a road maintenance worker position, becoming the first woman to fill such a job. During her four years in that position, she occasionally worked out of class as a road dispatcher.

Petitioner Johnson began with the county in 1967 as a road yard clerk, after private employment that included working as a supervisor and dispatcher. He had also unsuccessfully applied for the road dispatcher opening in 1974. In 1977, his clerical position was downgraded, and he sought and received a transfer to the position of road maintenance worker. He also occasionally worked out of class as a dispatcher while performing that job.

Nine of the applicants, including Joyce and Johnson, were deemed qualified for the job, and were interviewed by a two-person board . . . The scores awarded ranged from 70 to 80. Johnson was tied for second with a score of 75, while Joyce ranked next with a score of 73. A second interview was conducted by three Agency supervisors, who ultimately recommended that Johnson be promoted. Prior to the second interview, Joyce had contacted the county's Affirmative Action Office because she feared that her application might not receive disinterested review. The office in turn contacted the agency's affirmative action coordinator, whom the agency's plan makes responsible for keeping the director informed of opportunities for the agency to accomplish its objectives under the plan. At the time, the agency employed no women in any skilled craft position, and had never employed a woman as a road dispatcher. The coordinator recommended to the director of the agency, James Graebner, that Joyce be promoted.

Graebner, authorized to choose any of the seven persons deemed eligible, thus had the benefit of suggestions by the second interview panel and by the agency coordinator in arriving at his decision. After deliberation, Graebner concluded that the promotion should be given to Joyce. As he testified: "I tried to look at the whole picture, the combination of her qualifications and Mr. Johnson's qualifications, their tests scores, their expertise, their background, affirmative action matters, things like that . . . I believe it was a combination of all those."

. . . Graebner testified that he did not regard as significant the fact that Johnson scored 75 and Joyce 73 when interviewed by the two-person board.

Petitioner Johnson filed a complaint with the EEOC alleging that he had been denied promotion on the basis of sex in violation of Title VII.

II

In reviewing the employment decision at issue in this case, we must first examine whether that decision was made pursuant to a plan prompted by concerns similar to those of the employer in *Weber.* Next, we must determine whether the effect of the plan on males and nonminorities is comparable to the effect of the plan in that case.

The first issue is therefore whether consideration of the sex of applicants for skilled craft jobs was justified by the existence of a "manifest imbalance" that reflected underrepresentation of women in "traditionally segregated job categories." In determining whether an imbalance exists that would justify taking sex or race into account, a comparison of the percentage of minorities or women in the employer's work force with the percentage in the area labor market or general population is appropriate in analyzing jobs that require no special expertise . . . Where a job requires special training, however, the comparison should be with those in the labor force who possess the relevant qualifications . . .

* * * * *

. . . [W]omen were concentrated in traditionally female jobs in the agency, and represented a lower percentage in other job classifications than would be expected if such traditional segregation had not occurred. Specifically, 9 of the 10 paraprofessionals and 110 of the 145 office and clerical workers were women. By contrast, women were only 2 of the 28 officials and administrators, 5 of the 58 professionals, 12 of the 124 technicians, none of the skilled craft workers, and 1—who was Joyce—of the 110 road maintenance workers.

* * * * *

As the agency plan recognized, women were most egregiously underrepresented in the skilled craft job category, since *none* of the 238 positions was occupied by a woman. In mid-1980, when Joyce was selected for the road dispatcher position, the agency was still in the process of refining its short-term goals for skilled craft workers in accordance with the directive of the plan. This process did not reach fruition until 1982, when the agency established a short-term goal for that year of three women for the 55 expected openings in that job category—a modest goal of about 6 percent for that category.

* * * * *

. . . Given the obvious imbalance in the skilled craft category, and given the agency's commitment to eliminating such imbalances, it was plainly not unreasonable for the agency to determine that it was appropriate to consider as one factor the sex of Ms. Joyce in making its decision. The promotion of Joyce thus satisfies the first requirement enunciated in *Weber,* since it was undertaken to further an affirmative action plan designed to eliminate agency work force imbalances in traditionally segregated job categories.

We next consider whether the agency plan unnecessarily trammeled the rights of male employees or created an absolute bar to their advancement. In contrast to the plan in *Weber,* which provided that 50 percent of the positions in the craft training program were exclusively for blacks, and to the consent decree upheld last term in *Firefighters* v. *Cleveland,* which required the promotion of specific numbers of minorities, the plan sets aside no positions for women. The plan expressly states that "[t]he 'goals' established for each division should not be construed as 'quotas' that must be met." Rather, the plan merely authorizes that consideration be given to affirmative action concerns when evaluating qualified applicants . . . No persons are automatically excluded from consideration; *all* are able to have their qualifications weighed against those of other applicants.

In addition, petitioner had no absolute entitlement to the road dispatcher position. Seven of the applicants were classified as qualified and eligible, and the agency director was authorized to promote any of the seven. Thus, denial of the promotion unsettled no legitimate, firmly rooted expectation on the part of the petitioner. Furthermore, while the petitioner in this case was denied a promotion, he retained his employment with the agency, at the same salary and with the same seniority, and remained eligible for other promotions.

Finally, the agency's plan was intended to *attain* a balanced work force, not to maintain one . . .

* * * * *

III

The agency earmarks no positions for anyone; sex is but one of several factors that may be taken into account in evaluating qualified applicants for a position. As both the plan's language and its manner of operation attest, the agency has no intention of establishing a work force whose permanent composition is dictated by rigid numerical standards.

We therefore hold that the agency appropriately took into account as one factor the sex of Diane Joyce in determining that she should be promoted to the road dispatcher position. The decision to do so was made pursuant to an affirmative action plan that represents a moderate, flexible, case-by-case approach to effecting a gradual improvement in the representation of minorities and women in the agency's work force. Such a plan is fully consistent with Title VII, for it embodies the contribution that voluntary employer action can make in eliminating the vestiges of discrimination in the workplace.

Affirmed.

* * * * *

Justice Scalia, with whom the Chief Justice joins, and with whom Justice White joins in Parts I and II, dissenting

---

* * * * *

Several salient features of the plan should be noted. Most importantly, the plan's purpose was assuredly not to remedy prior sex discrimination by the agency. It could not have been, because there was no prior sex discrimination to remedy. The majority, in cataloguing the agency's alleged misdeeds, neglects to mention the district court's finding that the agency "has not discriminated in the past, and does not discriminate in the present against women in regard to employment opportunities in general and promotions in particular." This finding was not disturbed by the Ninth Circuit.

* * * * *

The most significant proposition of law established by today's decision is that racial or sexual discrimination is permitted under Title VII when it is intended to overcome the effect, not of the employer's own discrimination, but of societal attitudes that have limited the entry of certain races, or of a particular sex, into certain jobs.

* * * * *

The agency here was not seeking to remedy discrimination—much less "unusual" or "egregious" discrimination . . .

In fact, however, today's decision goes well beyond merely allowing racial or sexual discrimination in order to eliminate the effects of prior societal *discrimination.* The majority opinion often uses the phrase "traditionally segregated job category" to describe the evil against which the plan is legitimately (according to the majority) directed. As originally used in *Steelworkers* v. *Weber* that phrase described skilled jobs from which employers and unions had systematically and intentionally excluded black workers . . . But that is assuredly not the sense in which the phrase is used here. It is absurd to think that the nationwide failure of road maintenance crews, for example, to achieve the agency's ambition of 36.4

percent female representation is attributable primarily, if even substantially, to systematic exclusion of women eager to shoulder pick and shovel. It is a "traditionally segregated job category" *not* in the *Weber* sense, but in the sense that, because of long-standing social attitudes, it has not been regarded *by women themselves* as desirable work . . . There are, of course, those who believe that the social attitudes which cause women themselves to avoid certain jobs and to favor others are as nefarious as conscious, exclusionary discrimination. Whether or not that is so (and there is assuredly no consensus on the point equivalent to our national consensus against intentional discrimination), the two phenomena are certainly distinct. And it is the alteration of social attitudes, rather than the elimination of discrimination, which today's decision approves as justification for state-enforced discrimination. This is an enormous expansion, undertaken without the slightest justification or analysis.

Questions

1. Explain the majority's reasoning in upholding the promotion of a female over a marginally better-qualified male.
2. Justice Scalia, in a portion of his dissent not reproduced above:

   A statute [Title VII of the Civil Rights Act of 1964] designed to establish a color-blind and gender-blind workplace has thus been converted into a powerful engine of racism and sexism, not merely *permitting* intentional race- and sex-based discrimination, but often making it, through operation of the legal system, compelled.

   Do you agree? Explain.
3. In 1972, a federal district court found that Alabama's public safety department had violated the equal protection clause of the Fourteenth Amendment by systematically excluding blacks from employment as state troopers. The court ordered the department to hire one black for every white hired until blacks held 25 percent of the trooper positions. In 1974, the court found that the department had employed strategies and policies that frustrated full relief. Then, in 1981, black troopers sought an order requiring a one-for-one policy in promotions pending departmental implementation of a valid promotion policy of its own. A federal district court then ordered the department to initiate that one-for-one promotion policy, assuming sufficient qualified black candidates, until the 25 percent standard was reached. In the mid-1980s, about 27 percent of the arresting officers were black, but none held a position higher than sergeant. The promotion decision was appealed to the U.S. Supreme Court. Decide. Explain. See *United States* v. *Phillip Paradise,* 107 S.Ct. 1053 (1987).
4. The Equal Employment Opportunity Commission engaged in a lawsuit to prevent a labor union and its apprenticeship program from engaging in discrimination against black and Hispanic individuals. The district court found evidence of discrimination and, among other things, set a 29 percent nonwhite membership goal based on the percentage of nonwhites in the labor pool in New York City. The union was twice found in contempt for failure to comply, and the membership goal was raised to 29.23 percent. The U.S. Supreme Court upheld the plan, finding that Title VII does not prohibit race-conscious relief as a remedy where such circumstances as persistent or particularly egregious discrimination obtain.

   Write a dissenting opinion. See *Sheet Metal Workers* v. *Equal Employment Opportunity Commission,* 106 S.Ct. 3019 (1986).

Part Six—Additional Discrimination Topics

THE AMERICANS WITH DISABILITIES ACT (ADA)

In 1990, Congress and President Bush approved the Americans with Disabilities Act, among the most far-reaching pieces of protective legislation in the nation's history. The ADA forbids discrimination in employment, public accommodations, public services, transportation, and telecommunications against the 43 million Americans who are disabled. The act seeks to remove barriers to a full, productive life for disabled Americans while eliminating humiliations, such as the following, that have often accompanied impairments:

> The Kentucky woman who was dismissed from a job because her AIDS-stricken son moved back home.
>
> The blind Harvard Law School graduate who wrote to 600 corporations three times over without receiving a single job offer.
>
> The college that refused to hire a severely arthritic woman because trustees thought "normal students shouldn't see her."
>
> The paralyzed Vietnam veteran who must use the service entrance to restaurants because the regular doorways are too narrow for his wheelchair.[91]

While the act guarantees access to public transportation, shopping malls, restaurants, doctors' offices (and all public accommodations and services), as well as access to the telephone for 24 million hearing-impaired and 3 million speech-impaired Americans, we will limit our exploration to the employment provisions of the new legislation.

Prior to the passage of the ADA, disabled individuals were protected by federal law (the Rehabilitation Act of 1973) against employment discrimination only in public-sector jobs and those jobs in the private sector where employers received federal grants or contracts. The ADA both forbids private-sector employment discrimination against disabled workers and applicants and amends and updates the Rehabilitation Act, affirming broad protection in public-sector and publicly funded employment. Small businesses with fewer than 15 employees are exempted from the employment elements of the act.

A disabled person is (1) one who has a physical or mental impairment that substantially limits one or more major life activities, (2) has a record of such an impairment, or (3) is regarded as having such an impairment. Major life activities include caring for oneself, seeing, hearing, learning, and working, for example. One who has a history of cancer, for example, might "have a record of such an impairment." And one might be viewed by others as impaired because of, for example, a physical deformity when, in fact, that condition does not impair job performance in any material way.

Disabilities

Blindness, hearing loss, mental retardation, cosmetic disfigurement, anatomical loss, and disfiguring scars are examples of covered disabilities. Alcoholism, drug abuse, and AIDS are covered. However, the act specifically excludes job applicants and employees who *currently* use illegal drugs when the employer acts on the basis of such use. Thus, the act covers those who are rehabilitated and no longer using illegal drugs, those in rehabilitation and no longer using illegal drugs, and those erroneously regarded as using illegal drugs. Employers may expect the same performance and behavior from alcoholics and drug abusers as from all other employees. In sum, the act treats alcoholism and drug addiction as medical problems and protects those who are overcoming their impairments.

Specifically excluded as disabilities are homosexuality, bisexuality, exhibitionism, gambling, kleptomania, and pyromania, among others. Questions regarding which conditions constitute disabilities will continue to require litigation. For example, in interpreting the federal Rehabilitation Act and state disability laws, some courts have treated obesity as a disability while others have not.

Accommodation.   An employer may not discriminate in hiring or employment against a *qualified person* with a disability. A qualified person is one who can perform the *essential functions* of the job. The act requires employers to make *reasonable accommodations* for disabled employees and applicants. Reasonable accommodations might include such things as structural changes in the workplace, job reassignment, job restructuring, or new equipment.

Hardship.   The employer's primary defense is that of *undue hardship.* The employer need not make an accommodation to a disabled person if that adjustment would be unduly expensive, substantial, or disruptive. The employer can call on the hardship defense only after an appropriate accommodation has been identified. All new facilities must be accessible to disabled parties unless structurally impractical, but Congress appears to have intended that changes to existing facilities should not be required if they would involve large expense.

The ADA does not require affirmative action plans or quotas. Unqualified applicants need not be hired, and one who cannot perform the essential functions of the job after reasonable accommodations may be discharged.

structurally impractical

THE ADA IN PRACTICE

In the first nine months after the ADA went into effect, over 8,500 complaints were filed with the EEOC.[92] The government expects about 12,000 cases annually, although the early figures suggest that estimate may be exceeded. Back impairments constituted 14 percent of the early claims, while mental illness, including stress, accounted for 8.3 percent.[93] Alcoholism, drug addiction, AIDS, and sex-related claims all prompted a great deal of controversy in the drafting of the ADA, but are accounting, collectively, for less than 10 percent of the complaints.[94]

Compliance Costs

The EEOC has estimated that the average cost per disabled employee of complying with the ADA will be $261.[95] A *Wall Street Journal* survey of 79 companies found 61 percent of the respondents feeling that compliance with the law would be easy while 28 percent think it will be difficult.[96] The Principal Financial Group explained its compliance experience in accommodating the needs of a hearing-impaired employee:

> The Principal made accommodations for a deaf pension-department employee for less than $300. This involved hiring an interpreter for the job evaluation (approximately $40 for two hours/once per year), restructuring the job (no cost), purchasing a Telecommunicative Device (TDD)to enable the employee to use the telephone ($239), and educating other employees in the department (no cost).[97]

First Case

The decision that follows led to the first jury verdict under the ADA. Note that we are dealing here with a federal district court decision addressing a summary judgment motion. The reasoning in this case may or may not hold up as ADA cases proceed up through the appeals system.

U.S. EQUAL EMPLOYMENT OPPORTUNITY COMMISSION v. AIC SECURITY INVESTIGATION, LTD.
820 F. Supp. 1060 (N.D. Ill 1993)

Judge Guzman

Background Facts

This action is brought pursuant to Title I of the Americans with Disabilities Act of 1990 and Title I of the Civil Rights Act of 1991. The EEOC and the Intervening Plaintiff, Charles Wessel ("Wessel"), allege that AIC [a commercial security firm] discriminated against Wessel on the basis of his disability, terminal cancer, by discharging him from his position as Executive Director at AIC. [AIC moved for a summary judgment.]

Wessel was hired . . . in February 1986 . . . In his position of Executive Director, Charles Wessel was the Chief Executive of the security guard division. The Executive Director position which Wessel held was at all times during his employment the highest management position in AIC, and accordingly, Wessel was responsible for the overall management and profitability of AIC. The position of Executive Director required, as an essential function, overall management and direction of the 300 plus employees of the company, from all management level personnel to watch commanders and ultimately hundreds of security guards employed by AIC . . .

Wessel is a widely recognized leader in the security guard industry, having worked in the industry for approximately thirty years . . .

When Wessel started with AIC, he had emphysema caused by smoking 2–4 packs of cigarettes a day for approximately 25 years and 8–10 cigars a day for 15 years, and he had a back injury rendering him 20 percent disabled under his V.A. disability. In June, 1987, Wessel was diagnosed with lung cancer. Following surgery and recuperation Wessel returned to work at AIC. In July, 1991, Wessel suffered pneumothorax during a biopsy and went into respiratory arrest. Thereafter, Wessel was again diagnosed with lung cancer, this time affecting his right lung. Surgery was performed, and following a period of treatment and recuperation, Wessel again returned to work as Executive Director of AIC. In April, 1992, Wessel was initially diagnosed with 2 tumors, and subsequently, in June, 1992, with 2 additional tumors, for a total of 4. Wessel's doctors considered his condition to be terminal and he was told sometime in April, 1992 that he had six to twelve months to live. Wessel has received radiation treatments since this diagnosis but these treatments have been palliative, that is, not for the purpose of a cure, but to prolong and assure some quality of Wessel's life.

Wessel continued to work at AIC throughout the course of the treatments, although on the days when the radiation treatments were scheduled in the afternoon, he had to leave work at approximately 2:30 P.M. The amount of time Wessel was absent from work is disputed. The EEOC and Wessel allege that Wessel had two treatments in July of 1992 and he did not miss a full day of work on either of those two days nor did he miss any other work in July of 1992. AIC claims that he missed 15 workdays in April and May of 1992, several days in June, 1992 and 2 days in July, 1992. Further, between July 29th and August 13th, 1991 Wessel missed 16 days of work when he experienced a pneumothorax during his routine one-day biopsy. He missed 2 half days and one full day in August of 1991, and he missed approximately 33 days between October 3rd and November 4th, 1991 for surgery to remove his right lung. Dr. Nomanbhoy, Wessel's primary treating physician, restricted Wessel's driving because of lesions in the occipital lobe of the brain and in December of 1992 Wessel experienced seizures . . . Larry Roberts, the Executive Vice President of AIC's Systems Division, offered Wessel a driver which Wessel refused.

On or about June 10, 1992, Mrs. Vrdolyak [AIC's sole shareholder] hired Beverly Kay to work for AIC. On July 28, 1992, Kay had a meeting with Wessel. During that meeting, Kay apprised Wessel that Mrs. Vrdolyak had decided that it was time for Wessel to retire. On July 30, 1992, Kay advised Wessel by telephone that his employment at AIC was terminated effective July 31, 1992. Wessel was paid through July 31, 1992. Prior to his termination from AIC, Wessel was never subject to any warnings relating to his performance, his attendance, or any disciplinary action.

Discussion

* * * * *

[The U.S. Supreme Court:] "at the summary judgment stage the judge's function is not himself to weigh the evidence and determine the truth of the matter but to determine whether there is a genuine issue for trial." *Anderson v. Liberty Lobby, Inc.,* 477 U.S. 242, 106 S.Ct. 2505.

* * * * *

Therefore, this court must determine whether the EEOC has offered any evidence to create a genuine issue of fact as to AIC's summary judgment claim against the EEOC and Wessel . . .

Disputed Issues of Fact Remain as to Whether Wessel Was Able to Perform the Essential Functions of His Job

AIC first contends that Wessel cannot meet his initial burden of proof that he was a qualified individual with a disability. In particular, AIC argues that regular, predictable, full-time attendance was an essential function of the position of Executive Director which Wessel could not perform regardless of any reasonable accommodations.

To support this contention AIC points to the deposition testimony of Wessel in which Wessel stated as follows:

Q

... When you went to work on a given day, did you typically know everything that, every issue that you were going to confront that day, or did things come up on a daily basis?

A

Absolutely, I did not know what was going to come up. We're in a business that is subject to surprises. Nothing is routine. There is no day-to-day "do this," "do that."

Q

Hectic pace, your workplace?

A

Sometimes.

Q

Need for quick decisions?

A

Often.

Likewise, Wessel testified that a "normal" workday had been 8:00 to 8:30 A.M. to 6:00 to 6:30 P.M. at night, but this changed significantly in 1991 and 1992. AIC also points to Wessel's testimony regarding the search for his replacement in which Wessel stated: "No, Ed was one who came in at five to ten after 9 and left at five to ten before 5. And then once I told him that I was terminal and he'd either better get in shape or they were going to look elsewhere, he did make an effort. This testimony, AIC argues, clearly indicates that AIC, and indeed, Wessel himself, would exclude individuals from any consideration for the Executive Director position unless they could put in the necessary long hours.

AIC claims that during the last 12 months of his employment at AIC, Wessel was absent approximately 25 percent of the time . . .

The EEOC's response to these arguments puts forth the counter-argument that while it is undisputed that Wessel was required to miss a certain amount of work for surgery and treatment of his cancer during his employment at AIC, there remains a genuine issue of material fact as to whether Wessel's absence resulted in his not being able to perform the essential functions of the position of Executive Director. The EEOC points to the deposition testimony of David Pack, Wessel's supervisor for all but one month of his employment, who stated the following:

Q

Did it affect the hours he put in at work?

A

No. He put in quite a few hours.

Thereafter, Pack stated that although Wessel missed time for surgery and treatment, it was no different than instances when other employees at AIC had to take time off for surgery. In addition Pack elaborated that typically Wessel worked long hours and Saturdays and did "a ton of work at home."

Similarly, Kenneth Bartels, an AIC customer who dealt with Charles Wessel for years testified that his ability to contact Wessel at AIC did not change at all in 1992, from what it had been in prior years . . .

The EEOC finally argues that perhaps the most telling indication that a genuine issue of fact remains as to whether Wessel's absences, necessitated by surgery and treatment, resulted in his inability to perform the essential functions of the position of Executive Director is the complete absence of any evidence in the record that Wessel was ever advised by anyone at AIC that his lack of attendance was interfering with the performance of his duties.

* * * * *

In light of these disputed facts a genuine issue remains as to whether as of July 29, 1992, Wessel was a "qualified individual with a disability" as that term is defined. To be sure, attendance is necessary to any job, but the degree of such, especially in an upper management position such as Wessel's, where a number of tasks are effectively delegated to other employees requires close scrutiny. Further, an executive such as Wessel more than likely handled a number of his business matters through customer contact, and this usually is done by phone or in person at the customer's site . . . Therefore, a genuine issue of fact remains as to whether Wessel was meeting that threshold of both attendance and regularity necessary to perform his job successfully at the time he was discharged . . .

AIC's next argument raises the allegation that Wessel was unable to perform his job because of alleged short term memory problems. This allegation is supported by Wessel's deposition testimony that in part stated "My short-term memory is somewhat limited, but by the—an hour from now I remember everything."

AIC also contends that the people who worked with Wessel on a daily basis during his course of employment with AIC during 1992 observed Wessel exhibiting severe short-term memory loss directly related to his performance of the functions of this job as Executive Director. AIC also emphasizes that in July of 1992, Wessel was involved in a serious problem with one of AIC's largest accounts. Apparently a contract renewal was mistitled when mailed to a renewal account and in a second instance an incorrect estimate was submitted to an AIC customer . . .

AIC claims that in order to insure the survival of the company, Wessel's job responsibilities were being transferred to other AIC personnel as his condition deteriorated . . . Finally, AIC points out that Wessel upon his termination immediately became qualified for total disability Social Security benefits.

Once again, I agree with the EEOC that Mr. Wessel's alleged short-term memory loss and its effect on Mr. Wessel's qualification to perform his job as Executive Director is a disputed issue of fact. It is important to note that Wessel's own testimony was "[m]y short-term memory is somewhat limited, but the—an hour from now I remember everything." The fact that Wessel admits to some limitation of his short-term memory is not evidence of the severity of such or that the limitation had any impact on Wessel's performance. In fact, deposition testimony reveals that the lobes of Mr. Wessel's brain where the tumors were located were not the lobes where the short-term memory function takes place . . . Further, AIC's contentions that "there is simply no accommodation for memory loss" is contradicted by AIC's own expert witness, Dr. Peter Lewitt, who stated in his deposition that if memory is a problem, for example, writing things down and keeping logical notes is one strategy to improve a deficient memory . . .

As to the two errors that AIC has alleged, Wessel acknowledges that he failed to catch both and explained that they were the result of clerical error . . .

Therefore a factual question exists, as to whether Wessel's errors can lead to a finding that Wessel could not perform the essential functions of this position of Executive Director . . .

As to AIC's assertion that over time, Wessel's job responsibilities were being transferred to other AIC employees because of Wessel's alleged inability to perform such, this assertion is refuted by the testimony of David Pack . . . Specifically, Pack stated in his affidavit that "Wessel maintained overall responsibility for all of these essential functions throughout his employment." Pack further testified that to the extent that Wessel began to delegate and transfer some of his functions to others, the reasons for the transfer were unrelated to Wessel's illness . . .

Finally, there is substantial evidence in the record to create a genuine issue on the question of whether Wessel could perform the essential functions of his job. AIC's audited financials show that the profits of AIC's division under Wessel's direction increased from July 31, 1991 to July 31, 1992, while the overall profits of AIC decreased. Likewise, there is disputed evidence to refute the allegation that Wessel was unable to perform the "essential functions" of labor negotiations, supervising investigations, tracking litigation and development of policy. Therefore, there exists disputed material issues of fact and summary judgment must be denied.

A Disputed Issue of Fact Remains as to Whether Wessel Could Not Perform His Job without Risk of Injury to Both Himself and the Employees with Whom He Worked, Regardless of Any Reasonable Accommodation

. . . This argument stems from Wessel's treating physician's recommendation that he not drive a car because of his potential to suffer a seizure. Wessel's refusal to discontinue driving, AIC argues, poses a direct threat to other AIC employees, the public at large, as well as exposes to AIC to potential liability.

* * * * *

In the instant case, AIC does not assert and cannot demonstrate that driving is an essential function of Wessel's job. Even if they had, an accommodation, i.e., alternative mode of transportation, could be provided . . .

Disputed Facts Remain as to the Medical Evidence regarding Mr. Wessel's Condition as It Relates to His Ability to Perform His Job

AIC in their reply . . . primarily argue that the record is clear that all four physicians who are to give expert medical testimony at trial have declared Wessel unable to perform his former position of Executive Director for AIC. Allegedly this conclusive medical testimony is not disputed anywhere.

. . . I disagree with AIC's statement that this medical testimony is not disputed anywhere. Dr. Nomanbhoy in his deposition clearly stated that he had never observed Mr. Wessel suffering from memory problems and that up until a few weeks ago when Mr. Wessel fell he had no qualms in answering that Mr. Wessel could still perform his job . . .

Conclusion

For the reasons listed above, AIC's motion for summary judgment is **denied.**

Afterword

When the *AIC* case went to trial in 1993, a federal jury found for Wessel and awarded $22,000 in back pay, $50,000 in compensatory damages, and $500,000 in punitive damages. Judge Guzman subsequently upheld the back pay and compensatory awards, but he reduced the punitive award to $150,000 in order to remain within the ADA-prescribed cap of $200,000.[98]

Questions

1. What decision was Judge Guzman required to make in order to resolve the summary judgment motion?
2. *a.* Based on your reading of the facts, would you have dismissed Wessel, had you been in charge? Explain.
   b. Based on your reading of the facts, would you have found for Wessel if you had been sitting on the federal jury? Explain.
3. Based on the outcome of this case, does the ADA impose an undue burden on the American business community? Explain.
4. In your opinion, should drug addiction be treated as a disability under the law? Explain.
5. Several million Americans suffer from diseases having a genetic cause or an important genetic ingredient (e.g., Alzheimer's disease, hemophilia, and sickle-cell anemia). We now have tests to identify those genetic predispositions before the diseases actually manifest themselves. Should employers be allowed to test job applicants for genetic "imperfections" and use that information to deny them jobs—since the presence of a gene associated with a disease signals the likelihood of large medical bills in the future? Explain. See David Stipp, "Genetic Testing May Mark Some People as Undesirable to Employers, Insurers," *The Wall Street Journal,* July 9, 1990, p. B1.
6. In 1988, Robert T. McGregor enrolled at the Louisiana State University Law Center, but he twice failed to achieve the program's minimum grade point requirements. McGregor

suffers from pain and fatigue that resulted from a series of accidents. He had asked LSU to allow him to enroll in law school on a part-time basis, but the school has a firm full-time policy and is committed to having all first-year students enrolled in the same courses at the same time. McGregor sued LSU, claiming a violation of Section 504 of the Rehabilitation Act of 1973. Decide. Explain. See *McGregor v. Louisiana State University,* 3 F. 3d 850 (5th Cir. 1993).

AGE DISCRIMINATION

The Age Discrimination in Employment Act (ADEA) forbids employers (including state and local governments), employment agencies, and labor organizations from discriminating because of age against employees 40 years of age or older, thus eliminating mandatory retirement for most occupations. The ADEA permits both private lawsuits and action by the EEOC.

Age discrimination is established under disparate treatment/disparate impact analysis similar to that for race and sex, although three Supreme Court justices recently (and pointedly) noted that no *high court* decision has incorporated disparate impact into ADEA law.[99]

BFOQ

The chief defense available to the employer-defendant is the bona fide occupational qualification. In essence, an employer must demonstrate that only employees of a certain age can safely and/or efficiently complete the work in question. Thus, in *Hodgson* v. *Greyhound Lines,*[100] the bus company defended its policy of hiring intercity drivers 34 years of age or younger. Greyhound demonstrated that its safest drivers were those 50 to 55 years of age with 16 to 20 years of driving experience with Greyhound—two qualifications that those 40 years of age or older (the protected class) could not attain. Given that evidence, the company was able to lawfully maintain its policy.

Cases

In recent years, we have seen an explosion of age discrimination complaints. Nearly 23,000 claims were filed with the federal and state governments in the first half of 1992, a total equaling that for all of 1985.[101] Most complaints do not reach court. Many result in dismissals, but those that are settled can be very expensive, ranging typically from $50,000 to $400,000 per worker.[102] Claims often arise simply from ill-advised remarks:

> Claims vary from allegations that managers spoke of getting "new blood" or told older people they were "slowing down" to charges that workers were coerced into retirement. A 41-year-old former claims representative for Allstate Insurance Co. who said a company

official told her that Allstate wanted a "younger and cuter" image, won a $2.8 million award.[103]

Allstate planned to appeal.

Layoffs

The huge layoffs of the early 1990s have hit hard at older workers. In 1993, McDonnell Douglas agreed to pay $20.1 million to settle EEOC charges of age discrimination in laying off or forcing retirement for 10,000 St. Louis employees.[104] Nine hundred were at least 55 years old, and the EEOC argued that 370 fewer workers should have been cut from that group.[105] McDonnell Douglas contends it did not discriminate.

While the case law has been split in instances where older, higher paid employees were laid off in order to reduce costs, a 1993 Supreme Court decision appears to have settled some of those cases where disparate treatment is at issue. In *Hazen Paper*[106] (see question 4, p. 612), the Court held that no disparate treatment exists when the motivating factor in the decision is something other than the employee's age (such as salary, pension status, years of service, or seniority), even though that factor may be correlated to age.

Europe

As the next article reveals, the United States has a much firmer age discrimination policy than do most European nations.

INTERNATIONAL

FORTYSOMETHINGS FACE GREATER JOB DISCRIMINATION IN EUROPE THAN HERE

Chris Conte

Age discrimination is illegal in the U.S., but European employers legally can—and often do—refuse to consider job applications from older people, reports the Wyatt Co. The consulting firm says many Europeans who lose jobs after age 45 can only find short-term contracts or temporary work. A lawsuit recently forced the British Civil Service to modify its practice of only recruiting people who are under 30, though.

Employers in most European countries also can force employees to retire when they reach the normal age of eligibility for pensions—between 55 and 67, depending on the country. But some countries require advance notice for such lay-offs, and others require extended jobless benefits for workers who don't have pensions or some other source of retirement income.

Questions

1. Metz alleges that he was fired in violation of the ADEA. He had been a plant manager for a company that was experiencing financial problems. His employer notified him that the plant would be closed and he would be laid off. The company then sent the assistant manager of another plant, Burzloff, to Metz's plant to inspect it and make repairs. Burzloff requested that he be allowed to manage Metz's plant; the employer approved this request and discharged Metz. At the time of his layoff, the 54-year-old Metz had a salary of $15.75 an hour; when the 43-year-old Burzloff replaced Metz, his salary was $8.05 per hour.[107]

    Metz had worked for Transit for 27 years. He had received raises each year, even though the company was not profitable during some of those years. The company decided its poor financial performance did not justify retaining Metz, whose salary was comparatively high. Metz was not asked to take a pay cut before he was dismissed. The court framed the issue in the case in this manner:

    > The sole issue on appeal is whether the salary savings that can be realized by replacing a single employee in the ADEA age-protected range with a younger, lower-salaried employee constitutes a permissible, nondiscriminatory justification for the replacement.[108]

    Resolve that issue. Explain. See *Metz* v. *Transit Mix, Inc.,* 828 F.2d 1202 (7th Cir. 1987).

2. Assume you own a clothing store designed to appeal primarily to the "young adult" market. In your opinion, should the law permit you to hire only "young adults" as salespersons? Explain.

3. Under its collective bargaining agreement, Trans World Airlines maintained a policy of automatically transferring flight captains to positions as flight engineers when they were disqualified from their pilot's role for reasons other than age (for example, medical disability or a labor force reduction). Under the agreement, the captains were entitled to "bump" any less-senior flight engineer. However, pilots who were retired on reaching age 60 were not automatically entitled to move into a flight engineer position. Rather, they were allowed to remain with TWA only if they had secured a flight engineer position prior to their 60th birthday. They could do so only by submitting a bid in the hope that a vacancy would arise prior to their 60th birthday. Three pilots, forced to retire by TWA, filed suit, claiming a violation of the Age Discrimination in Employment Act, which forbids differential treatment of older workers "with respect to a privilege of employment." Does the ADEA *require* TWA to grant transfer privileges to disqualified pilots? Explain. See *Trans World Airlines, Inc.* v. *Thurston,* 469 U.S. 111 (1985).

4. Walter Biggins, a then 62-year-old chemist, believed he deserved a raise from $44,000 to $100,000 annually from his small, family-owned Holyoke, Massachusetts, employer, Hazen Paper Co.[109] Initially courteous discussions descended to rancor, and Biggins was fired weeks before his pension was to vest. He was entitled to damages under ERISA (see Chapter 12), but Biggins also claimed age discrimination. A jury found a willful violation of the ADEA. The federal district court overruled the jury on the willfulness issue. The Court of Appeals reversed, giving considerable weight to evidence of pension interference, including testimony that

Hazen had offered to keep Biggins as a consultant, in which capacity he would not have received his pension.

As mentioned earlier, the Supreme Court ruled that an employer does not violate the ADEA by firing an older employee to prevent pension benefits from vesting. Why did the Court reach that decision? See *Hazen Paper Company* v. *Walter F. Biggins,* 113 S.Ct. 1701 (1993).

CHAPTER QUESTIONS

1. Can an employer lawfully request age-related information on employment applications? Explain.
2. Can a private organization lawfully dismiss an employee on the grounds of homosexuality when that sexual preference does not interfere with job performance? Explain.
3. At this writing in 1994, Congress is considering legislation that would designate both young (under age 21) and old (over 65) drivers as "high risks." In your view, would such legislation constitute impermissible age discrimination? Explain.
4. Title VII disparate impact cases do not require a showing of purposefulness or intent to establish unlawful discrimination. A finding of discrimination under the Fifth and Fourteenth Amendments does require such a showing. Would you favor amending Title VII to require direct, explicit proof of actual discriminatory purpose? Explain.
5. Pan American Airways, Inc., maintained a policy of excluding men from positions as flight attendants. The policy was challenged on sex discrimination grounds. Pan American defended its policy with a survey showing that 79 percent of all passengers preferred being served by females. Then Pan Am offered expert testimony to show that the passenger preference was attributable to "feminine" qualities possessed by few males. The district court ruled for Pan Am on the grounds that "all or substantially all" [the test articulated in *Weeks* v. *Southern Bell Telephone,* 408 F.2d 228 (5th Cir. 1969)] men were unable to successfully fulfill the duties of flight attendants. The decision was appealed. Decide. Explain. See *Diaz* v. *Pan American Airways, Inc.,* 311 F. Supp. 559 (S.D. Fla. 1970), 442 F.2d 385 (5th Cir.), cert. denied, 404 U.S. 950 (1971).
6. Can a Polynesian restaurant lawfully limit employment to "brown-skinned persons" in those jobs visible to the public? Explain.

7. Would a readily visible office wall display of nude and seminude female figures located in a common work area (for example, one poster, on display for eight years, depicted a "woman with a golf ball on her breasts and a man standing over her, golf club in hand, yelling 'fore.'") in combination with obscene comments about women on a routine basis (for example, "whores," "All that bitch needs is a good lay.") give rise to an intimidating, hostile, or offensive working environment within the meaning of the sexual harassment law? Explain. See *Rabidue* v. *Osceola Refining Co.,* 805 F.2d 611 (6th Cir. 1986). But see *Robinson* v. *Jacksonville Shipyards,* 760 F. Supp. 1486 (M.D. Fla. 1991).
8. Ali Boureslan, a naturalized United States citizen who was born in Lebanon and was working in Saudi Arabia, was discharged by his employer, Arabian American Oil Company, a Delaware corporation. Boureslan sued ARAMCO under Title VII of the Civil Rights Act of 1964, claiming that he was discriminated against because of his race, religion, and national origin. The lower court ruled that Title VII does not reach U.S. citizens employed abroad by American firms. Boureslan appealed to the U.S. Supreme Court. Decide. Explain. See *Equal Employment Opportunity Commission* v. *Arabian American Oil Company,* 111 S.Ct. 1227 (1991).
9. *a.* Assume your employer is hosting a conference at a local hotel to examine the latest insights in total quality management. Further assume that one of the participants is hearing-impaired, a fact that was unknown both to your employer and to the hotel. If an interpreter is not provided, can your employer and/or the hotel be sued under the ADA? Explain.
   b. A physician recommended that the New York board of bar examiners accord a visually impaired bar applicant four days rather than the

standard two in which to complete the bar examination. Must the board comply with that recommendation in order to provide "reasonable accommodation" as required under the ADA? See *D'Amico* v. *New York State Board of Law Examiners*, 813 F. Supp. 217 (1993).

10. Define *affirmative action*.

11. A flight attendant was discharged in 1968 in accordance with her employer's "no marriage" rule. The rule was later abolished. She was rehired in 1972 and sought to have her seniority based on her original date of hire rather than the time at which she was rehired. She argued that the seniority system operated to perpetuate past discrimination. She brought suit against the airline. Decide. Explain. See *United Airlines, Inc.* v. *Evans*, 431 U.S. 553 (1977).

12. Blacks employed at the Georgia Power Company were concentrated in the four lowest job classifications, which were maintained as separate seniority units under a collective bargaining agreement. Workers moving to higher classifications were required to forfeit all accumulated seniority. All other classifications were overwhelmingly composed of whites. Movement from those classifications did not require seniority forfeiture. A consent decree in 1979 settled a Title VII lawsuit. The company agreed to count blacks' total time for seniority. Then, with the Supreme Court's *Teamsters* decision, the union that was a party to the consent decree argued that the law had been altered and the old seniority system was bona fide. Thus, the union sought to have the consent decree rescinded. Decide. Explain. See *U.S.* v. *Georgia Power Co.*, 634 F.2d 929 (1981).

13. Thornton worked as a manager at a Connecticut retail store. In accordance with his religious beliefs, Thornton notified his manager that he could no longer work on Sundays as required by company (Caldor, Inc.) policy. A Connecticut statute provided that "No person who states that a particular day of the week is observed as his Sabbath may be required by his employer to work on such day. An employee's refusal to work on his Sabbath shall not constitute grounds for his dismissal." Management offered Thornton the options of transferring to a Massachusetts store where Sunday work was not required or transferring to a lower-paying supervisory job in the Connecticut store. Thornton refused both, and he was transferred to a lower-paying clerical job in the Connecticut store. Thornton claimed

a violation of the Connecticut statute. The store argued that the statute violated the Establishment Clause (see Chapter 5) of the First Amendment, which forbids establishing an official state religion and giving preference to one religion over another or over none at all. Ultimately the case reached the U.S. Supreme Court.

   a. Decide. Explain.

   b. Do the religious accommodation provisions of Title VII of the Civil Rights Act violate the Establishment Clause? See *Estate of Thornton* v. *Caldor, Inc.*, 472 U.S. 703 (1985).

14. A male employee of a private social service organization was dismissed after three years of employment. The employee filed suit, contending he was a victim of sex discrimination forbidden under Title VII. The employee contended his discharge was in retaliation for his resistance to his male supervisor's sexual advances. The employer argued that Title VII does not reach such claims. Decide. See *Wright* v. *Methodist Youth Services, Inc.*, 511 F.Supp. 307 (DC NIll. 1981).

15. A woman sought a freightyard job. Her application was denied because she failed to meet the company's requirement of two years' truck-driving experience or truck-driving training. The woman believed she was a victim of sex discrimination.

   a. Build a case on her behalf.

   b. Build a case for the trucking company.

   c. Decide the case. Explain. See *Chrisner* v. *Complete Auto Transit, Inc.*, 645 F.2d 1251 (1981).

16. Must your local country club admit qualified applicants regardless of race, religion, sex, and so on? Explain.

17. In 1972, a trucking firm hired one black worker and one white worker as temporary employees. The white worker had more experience, but when a full-time position became available the black employee was selected. The hiring manager acknowledged that the decision was made to meet the "attainment levels" of the employer's informal affirmative action plan. The affirmative action plan was not "organized," and the manager was allegedly only "vaguely aware" of the employer's minority hiring expectations. The white worker filed suit, claiming Title VII violations. In particular, he alleged that the company's racial preference amounted to an impermissible quota system. Decide. Explain. See *Lehman* v. *Yellow Freight System*, 651 F.2d 520 (1981).

18. A new Texas airline, flying out of Dallas' Love

Field, was in a precarious financial posture. A campaign was mounted to sell itself as "the airline personification of feminine youth and vitality." In commercials, its customers, who were primarily businessmen, were promised "in-flight love," including "love potions" (cocktails), "love bites" (toasted almonds), and a ticketing process (labeled a "quickie machine") that delivered "instant gratification." A male was denied a job with the airline because of his sex. He filed a Title VII action. The airline argued that attractive females were necessary to maintain its public image under the "love campaign," a marketing approach that the company claimed had been responsible for its improved financial condition. Decide. Explain. See *Wilson* v. *Southwest Airlines Co.,* 517 F.Supp. 292 (ND Tex. 1981).

19. An employer assigned customers to employees based on the race or national origin of the customer. For example, Hispanic customers were assigned to Hispanic employees. Otherwise, employees were treated equally as to pay and working conditions. Is the employer guilty of employment discrimination? Explain. See *Rogers* v. *EEOC,* 454 F.2d 234 (5th Cir. 1971).

20. Should obesity be treated as a *disability* as that term is defined in the Americans with Disabilities Act? Explain.

21. Is sexual harassment a problem that should properly be addressed via federal intervention (EEOC)? Explain.

22. On balance, have the feminist movement and accompanying legal victories improved the quality of life for American women? For American men? Explain.

23. In the late 1980s and early 1990s, one in four young black men was in prison, on parole, or on probation. Witnesses testifying before a Senate committee looking into the condition of black males in America called for government and business to cooperate in providing more jobs and better education for young black males. And they suggested that government should provide more assistance to black children in order to reduce problems later in their lives.
    a. Do you approve of those suggestions? Explain.
    b. What role would you assign to the business community in addressing the problems of young black males? Explain.

24. In general, women pay smaller life insurance premiums than men, but women's health insurance premiums substantially exceed those of men. Insurance companies point to differences in risks and subsequent claims patterns to explain the rate differentials. Should all states pass legislation requiring insurance companies to charge equal insurance fees for equal coverage regardless of sex? Explain.

25. Elizabeth Hishon, an attorney employed by the Atlanta law firm of King and Spaulding, alleged that the firm had engaged in sex discrimination in failing to elevate her to the rank of partner. King and Spaulding argued that Title VII should not apply to partnership decisions because those "promotions" change the individual's status from "employee" to "employer." They further contended that the freedom of association guarantees of the Constitution permit them to choose whomever they wish as partners. Is Hishon's claim governed by Title VII? Explain. See *Hishon* v. *King and Spaulding,* 467 U.S. 69 (1984).

26. An EEOC guideline defines sexual harassment as "unwelcome sexual advances, requests for sexual favors, and other verbal or physical conduct of a sexual nature" when submission to the conduct affects employment decisions and/or the conduct interferes with work performance or creates a hostile work environment. In your opinion, is the guideline fair and workable? Explain.

27. The author of a *Harvard Law Review* article argues for discrimination claims based on appearance:

    > The most physically unattractive members of our society face severe discrimination . . . The unattractive ("those individuals who depart so significantly from the most commonly held notions of beauty that they incur employment discrimination") are poorly treated in such diverse contexts as employment decisions, criminal sentencing, and apartment renting. Although appearance discrimination can have a devastating economic, psychological, and social impact on individuals, its victims have not yet found a legal recourse.

    Should we treat some aspects of appearance (for example, shortness, obesity, and unattractive facial characteristics) as disabilities, thus forbidding discrimination based on those characteristics? Explain. See Note, "Facial Discrimination: Extending Handicap Law to Employment Discrimination on the Basis of Physical Appearance," *Harvard Law Review* 100, no. 8 (June 1987), p. 2035.

28. The accompanying ad for foreign exchange dealers

appeared in the December 11, 1987, issue (p. 22) of *The Nation,* an English-language newspaper published in Bangkok, Thailand.

 a. Analyze the legality of the ad based on American law.

 b. Should American firms abroad adhere to American antidiscrimination policies even if those policies might put the American firms at a competitive disadvantage or offend the values and mores of the host country? Explain.

An American Bank
invites applications for
CORPORATE FOREIGN EXCHANGE DEALERS
for its Bangkok branch

Qualifications:

- Thai national
- Age 23–30 years, preferably male
- University graduate in Finance, Economics or related field
- 1–2 years dealing experience
- Good command of both spoken and written English

Salary is negotiable and attractive benefits will be provided for the successful candidates. The bank offers excellent opportunities for career advancement.

Send application stating details of qualifications and experience, present salary and a recent photo to

The Nation
Class 1191
GPO Box 594
Bangkok 10501

---

29. Philosopher Hugh Lehman applies equal pay and comparable worth principles to the practice of transnational corporations establishing manufacturing operations in Third World nations where labor costs are reduced:

> If the principle of equal pay for work of equal value is valid as a principle of justice, then it appears that the practice of paying workers in Third World countries at a lower rate than workers doing the same jobs in industrialized nations is unjust.[110]

Comment.

30. Blacks make up 12 percent of the U.S. population, and that share is growing slowly. Three percent of the population is Asian, while 9 percent is Hispanic, and both are growing rapidly. Asians and Hispanics combined outnumber blacks on college campuses. Asians have surpassed all other groups of Americans, including whites, in median income. Commentator Stephen Buckley:

> Today blacks are faced with a somber choice. We can go it alone, fighting against the swelling tide of Asian and Hispanic power, or we can forge coalitions with those groups—and with whites who are sympathetic to minority concerns. We can admit, at least tacitly, that blacks can't maintain or expand our power without their help.[111]

Comment.

31. As discussed in this chapter, American law forbids a variety of forms of discrimination. At the same time, we revere personal freedom. For example, we protect the First Amendment rights of neo-Nazi groups and the Ku Klux Klan, notwithstanding their racist goals. Do you favor recent legislation banning "hate speech"? Should we pass laws forbidding "group defamation"—malicious and degrading remarks directed to a racial or ethnic group? Explain.

NOTES

1. Benjamin Holden, "Parent of Denny's Restaurants, NAACP Agree on Plan to Boost Minorities' Role," *The Wall Street Journal,* July 1, 1993, p. A3.

2. Benjamin Holden, "Denny's Chain Settles Suits by Minorities," *The Wall Street Journal,* May 24, 1994, p. A3.

3. 347 U.S. 483 (1954).

4. 163 U.S. 537 (1896).

5. A portion of the material in this paragraph is drawn from William P. Murphy, Julius G. Getman, and James E. Jones, Jr., *Discrimination in Employment* 4th ed. (Washington: Bureau of National Affairs, 1979), pp. 1–4.

6. Ann Hagedorn and Thomas F. O'Boyle, "Marriott Settles," *The Wall Street Journal,* March 7, 1991, p. B8.

7. Larry Hugick, "Blacks See Their Lives Worsening," *The Gallup Poll Monthly,* no. 319, April 1992, p. 26.

8. June O'Neill, "The Changing Economic Status of Black Americans," *The American Enterprise* 3, no. 5 (September–October 1992), p. 71.

9. Dorothy Gaiter, "Diversity of Leaders Reflects the Changes in the Black Community," *The Wall Street Journal,* May 6, 1992, pp. A1, A8.

10. Jeff Howard, "The Third Movement: Developing Black Children for the 21st Century," in *The State of Black America 1993,* ed. Billy Tidwell (New York City: National Urban League, 1993), p. 26.

11. Facts on File, "June Jobless Rate Edges Up to 7%," *Facts on File World News Digest,* July 8, 1993, p. 502 B1.

12. Tidwell, *The State of Black America,* p. 245.

13. Hilary Stout, "Americans' Health Improves but Blacks Suffer Higher Death Rates than Whites," *The Wall Street Journal,* June 26, 1992, p. B6.

14. Ibid.

15. Scripps Howard News Service, "Black Americans Rank Low in U.N. Study," *Waterloo Courier,* May 18, 1993, p. B6.

16. Christopher Conte, "More Schooling Is the Key to Improving Wages of Black Workers," *The Wall Street Journal,* May 11, 1993, p. A1.

17. Ibid.

18. O'Neill, "The Changing Economic Status of Black Americans," p. 72.

19. Associated Press, "Census Report Shows Hispanics Still Struggling," *Waterloo Courier,* August 23, 1993, p. A10.

20. Associated Press, "Racial, Ethnic U.S. Balance Faces Change," *Waterloo Courier,* September 29, 1993, p. A1.

21. "Hate Rises," *Parade,* May 13, 1990, p. 15.

22. Bill Conlin, "How *Life* Magazine Stereotyped Joe DiMaggio," *Des Moines Register,* January 24, 1988, p. 11D.

23. William Kazer, "'Darkie' Manufacturers Fail to Brush Off Charges of Racism," *The Nation,* (Bangkok, Thailand), December 11, 1987, p. 30.

24. Joseph Boyce, "L.A. Riots and the 'Black Tax,'" *The Wall Street Journal,* May 12, 1992, p. A16.

25. See *St. Mary's Honor Center* v. *Hicks,* 113 S.Ct. 2742 (1993).

26. *International Brotherhood of Teamsters* v. *United States,* 97 S.Ct. 1843 (1977).

27. *American Tobacco* v. *Patterson,* 456 U.S. 63 (1982).

28. *Firefighters Local Union No. 1784* v. *Stotts,* 467 U.S. 561 (1984).

29. See Malcolm H. Liggett, "Recent Supreme Court Affirmative Action Decisions and a Reexamination of the *Weber* Case," *Labor Law Journal* 38, no. 7 (July 1987), p. 415.

30. *Local No. 93, International Association of Firefighters* v. *City of Cleveland,* 478 U.S. 501 (1986).

31. Joan Rigdon, "Three Decades after the Equal Pay Act, Women's Wages Remain Far from Parity," *The Wall Street Journal,* June 9, 1993, p. B1.

32. Ibid.

33. Ibid.

34. Ibid.

35. Ibid.

36. Gallup Poll for Accountants on Call, "Profiles of the American Worker." Reported in *HR Focus* 69, no. 8 (August 1992), p. 13.

37. Cox News Service, "Women Pay More for Less," *Des Moines Register,* May 18, 1993, p. 4A.

38. Lindley Clark, "The Pay Gap Narrows—Slowly," *The Wall Street Journal,* July 2, 1993, p. A6.

39. Anne Fisher, "When Will Women Get to the Top?" *Fortune* 126, no. 6 (September 21, 1992), p. 44.

40. Ibid.

41. Julie Lopez, "Study Says Women Face Glass Walls as Well as Ceilings," *The Wall Street Journal,* March 3, 1992, p. B1.

42. Fisher, "When Will Women Get to the Top?" p. 44.

43. Al Neuharth, "Risk-Taking Women Create Own Ceilings," *USA Today,* August 14, 1992, p. 15A.

44. Ibid.

45. Alan Otten, "Male Professions Are Much Less So," *The Wall Street Journal,* November 15, 1993, p. B1.

46. Elizabeth Ehrlich, "The Mommy Track," *Business Week,* March 20, 1989, p. 126.

47. 400 U.S. 542 (1979).

48. Mack A. Player, *Federal Law of Employment Discrimination in a Nutshell,* 2nd ed. (St. Paul, Minn.: West Publishing, 1981), p. 202.

49. See generally *Diaz* v. *Pan American World Airways, Inc.,* 442 F.2d 385 (5th Cir.), cert. denied, 404 U.S. 950 (1971).

50. 97 S.Ct. 2720.

51. *Newport News Shipbuilding & Dry Dock Co.* v. *EEOC,* 462 U.S. 669 (1983).

52. *California Federal Savings and Loan Association* v. *Mark Guerra, Director, Department of Fair Employment and Housing,* 479 U.S. 272 (1987).

53. Associated Press, "Study of Career Women Finds Children Add to Satisfied Lives," *Des Moines Sunday Register,* November 22, 1992, p. 5A.

54. Gannett News Service, "Poll Gauges Workplace Harassment," *Des Moines Register,* March 28, 1994, p. 3A.

55. Ronni Sandroff, "Sexual Harassment—The Inside Story," *Working Woman,* June 1992, p. 47.

56. Barbara Jorgensen, "Warning: Sexual Harassment Can Be Dangerous to Your Company's Health," *Electronic Business,* May 1993, p. 1.

57. BNA, *Fair Employment Practices,* 403:526 (October, 1993).

58. Alan Otten, "Uncertainty Persists on Sexual Harassment," *The Wall Street Journal,* July 29, 1992, p. B1.

59. *Minneapolis-St. Paul Star Tribune,* "School to Pay Ex-Student $40,000 in Harassment Case," *Waterloo Courier,* April 6, 1993, p. B8.

60. Note Book, "Chris Robinson, a Graduate Student . . ." *The Chronicle of Higher Education,* June 16, 1993, p. A33.

61. Associated Press, "Study: Sexual Harassment Pervasive Worldwide," *Waterloo Courier,* November 30, 1992, p. A3.

62. Ibid.

63. Refer to the Department of Labor's Interpretive Bulletin, as reported in Sullivan et al., *Federal Statutory Law,* p. 596.

64. Ibid., pp. 598–601.

65. Ibid., p. 608, reporting *Shultz* v. *American Can Co.—Dixie Prods.,* 424 F.2d 356 (8th Cir. 1970).

66. 417 U.S. 188 (1974).

67. Council on the Economic Status of Women, State of Minnesota, "Men's, Women's Comparable Jobs," *Des Moines Sunday Register,* January 8, 1984, p. 3C.

68. "Child Care Workers Near Pay Bottom," *Waterloo Courier,* January 3, 1988, p. A8.

69. Ibid.

70. *County of Washington* v. *Gunther,* 452 U.S. 161 (1981).

71. See, e.g., *Spaulding* v. *The University of Washington,* 740 F.2d 686 (1984).

72. Michael J. McCarthy, "Supreme Court to Rule on Sex-Bias Case," *The Wall Street Journal,* June 14, 1988, p. 33.

73. Ibid.

74. *Hopkins* v. *Price Waterhouse,* 618 F.Supp. 1109 (1985).

75. *Hopkins* v. *Price Waterhouse,* 825 F.2d 458, 468 (1987).

76. *United States* v. *Seeger,* 380 U.S. 163 (1965).

77. 432 U.S. 63 (1977).

78. *EEOC* v. *Ithaca Industries,* 849 F.2d 116 (4th Cir. 1988), cert. denied, 109 S.Ct. 306 (1988).

79. Clint Bolick, "The Great Racial Divide," *The Wall Street Journal,* November 30, 1992, p. A10.

80. Gannett News Service, "Affirmative Action Brands Workers, Qualified or Not," *Des Moines Register,* August 31, 1992, p. 6A.

81. David Gates, "White Male Paranoia," *Newsweek,* March 29, 1993, pp. 48, 49.

82. Scott Jaschik, "Education Department Says Affirmative-Action Policies of Berkeley's Law School Violated Federal Anti-Bias Laws," *The Chronicle of Higher Education,* October 7, 1992, p. A21.

83. Michael Greve, "The Newest Move in Law Schools' Quota Game," *The Wall Street Journal,* October 5, 1992, p. A12.

84. *University of California Regents* v. *Bakke,* 438 U.S. 265 (1978).

85. Tamara Henry, "Race-Based Scholarships Now 'Proper'" *USA Today,* March 19, 1993, p. A1.

86. Greve, "The Newest Move," p. A12.

87. *City of Richmond* v. *Croson,* 109 S.Ct. 706 (1989).

88. *Metro Broadcasting, Inc.* v. *FCC,* 497 U.S. 1050 (1990).

89. 99 S.Ct. 2721 (1979).

90. *Texas Department of Community Affairs* v. *Burdine,* 450 U.S. 248 (1981).

91. Associated Press, "Congress on Verge of Passing Landmark Disabilities Bill," *Waterloo Courier,* December 3, 1989, p. B1.

92. Karen Matthes, "ADA Update: The First Year in Review," *HR Focus* 70, no. 7 (July 1993), p. 3.

93. Editorial, "Lawyers Disable Disability," *The Wall Street Journal,* January 11, 1993, p. A14.

94. Ibid.

95. Gary Coulton and Roger Wolters, "Employee and Management Rights and Responsibilities under the Americans with Disabilities Act (ADA): An Overview," *Employee Responsibilities and Rights Journal* 6, no. 1 (March 1993), p. 55. Citing Equal Employ-ment Opportunity Commission, "Equal Employment Opportunity for Individuals with Disabilities." *Federal Register* 56 (40) (1991), pp. 8,577–8,603.

96. Albert Karr, "Compliance Costs Are Often Modest under the New Disability Law," *The Wall Street Journal,* August 4, 1992, p. A1.

97. Catherine Bennett and Max Johnson, "Complying with Disability Act Isn't Costly," *Des Moines Register,* July 29, 1992, p. 7A.

98. "$500,000 ADA Award Slashed," *Chicago Daily Law Bulletin,* June 7, 1993, p. 1.

99. *Hazen Paper Company* v. *Walter F. Biggins,* 113 S.Ct. 1701 (1993).

100. 499 F.2d 859 (7th Cir. 1974).

101. Junda Woo, "Ex-Workers Hit Back with Age-Bias Suits," *The Wall Street Journal,* December 8, 1992, p. B1.

102. Ibid.

103. Ibid.

104. Kevin Salwen, "EEOC Warns against Layoffs Based on Age," *The Wall Street Journal,* March 2, 1993, p. A4.

105. Ibid.

106. 113 S.Ct. 1701 (1993).

107. "Age Discrimination," 56 U.S.L.W. 2155 (1987), summarizing *Metz* v. *Transit Mix, Inc.*

108. *Metz* v. *Transit Mix, Inc.,* 828 F.2d 1202, 1205 (7th Cir. 1987).

109. See Paul M. Barrett, "How One Man's Fight for a Raise Became a Major Age-Bias Case," *The Wall Street Journal,* January 7, 1993, p. A1.

110. Hugh Lehman, "Equal Pay for Equal Work in the Third World," *Journal of Business Ethics* 4, no. 6 (December 1985), p. 487.

111. Stephen Buckley, "Minorities Compete for Status," *Waterloo Courier,* August 8, 1993, p. E-2.

14

EMPLOYMENT LAW III: LABOR–MANAGEMENT RELATIONS

Part One—Introduction

Union membership has declined dramatically in recent years. Only about 11 percent of private sector workers belong to unions.[1] The causes are many:

> Stagnant incomes, a declining manufacturing sector, foreign competition, high unemployment, deregulation, a changing work force, and a high-tech workplace have all meant trouble in the union hall.[2]

Strikes have declined to the lowest levels since World War II.[3] Unions can no longer promise wage increases in excess of those earned by nonunion employees. Broadly, unions simply do not have the power today that they enjoyed in the past. Nonetheless, labor law remains a very important vehicle for maintaining workplace productivity and fairness. The article that follows describes the kind of worker–management conflict that labor law is designed to prevent and resolve.

TO SOME SMALL FIRMS, IDEA OF COOPERATING WITH LABOR IS FOREIGN

Kevin G. Salwen

Nearly four years into his company's labor dispute, a bitter Art Nevill wonders if the business will be able to survive.

Sales at the company he runs and half-owns, Refuse Compactor Service Inc., have slipped so much from nearly $7 million in 1989 that "I'll be lucky to do $2 million this year," he says.

And no one can put a price tag on the emotional toll. A deteriorating labor situation at Refuse Compactor culminated in a strike. It left Jesus Vela, a former welder at the company, finding only day-to-day work and separated from his wife. At home, "little problems would become big problems," he laments in Spanish.

One day Mr. Nevill hit a picketing worker with a forklift. Later, he became so angered by strikers shouting obscene comments and making lewd gestures at his wife that he grabbed a United Auto Workers picket sign and burned it.

Certainly that wasn't the message President Clinton was promoting at a Chicago conference . . . to boost labor-management cooperation. Companies in this country must know "that you can grow and prosper by treating workers as indispensable partners," the president told a group of 400 corporate executives, labor leaders and academics . . .

But many small businesses think such concepts as worker-management teams are a big company's game. "For the smallest firms, you start talking about things like that and they die laughing," says William Dennis, senior research fellow at the National Federation of Independent Business, a small-business lobbying group.

Roots in a Power Struggle

Indeed, at small companies, the democracy Mr. Clinton is urging can run smack into autocracy. Owners often say "it's my plant. I own it. I created it and no one is going to tell me how to run it," says Melvin Welles, chief administrative law judge at the National Labor Relations Board.

*   *   *   *   *

Many small-business owners clearly work closely with their workers. But while small firms outnumber large firms overall, they are far less likely to be unionized than large ones, and most NLRB complaints are filed by unions. Two-thirds of unfair labor practice complaints are filed against employers with fewer than 100 workers, according to NLRB figures. Increasingly, unions target small firms for membership expansion; last year, they won certification at firms with fewer than 50 workers at a rate twice that

of companies with more than 500, the Bureau of National Affairs calculates.

The labor conflict at Refuse Compactor shows what can go wrong when a proud, independent owner faces workers making demands on that independence.

Mr. Nevill started Refuse Compactor in the San Fernando Valley in 1970 with $200. "Building the business was fun," he recalls. He and partner Gene Butterfield hired one employee, and together they started making large trash bins.

But Mr. Nevill wasn't an easy man to work for. "He used to scream at you every day," says Javier Soriano, who joined Refuse as a welder in 1976. Mr. Soriano tells of asking Mr. Nevill to give Mr. Vela, who spoke no English, a 25-cent raise to $6.50 an hour. "Art said he could do it if he took the money from me," Mr. Soriano says.

Charges of Safety Violations

Mr. Soriano, who would become cochairman of the union-bargaining committee, says Mr. Nevill also forced welders to work in the rain and safety inspectors cited Refuse for a string of problems in the early 1980s. Mr. Nevill counters that the inspectors came in only after a "drunk" worker cut off three fingers in a machine.

Mr. Nevill acknowledges morale problems at the plant, but says they stemmed mostly from workers' comparing paychecks. The 47-year-old entrepreneur says he likes to give raises to the employees who work hardest. For the others, he says: "I told them to hustle more. You make me more money, you'll make more money. I'm not about to give raises to people who say, 'Pay me more money or I won't work hard.' That's not American."

Despite the work environment—or perhaps because of it—Refuse Compactor grew into a successful small manufacturing business. By 1989, it had hired a full-time salesman, two foremen and a plant manager. Sixty-four workers reported to them. The company had a backlog of more than two months . . .

But trouble was brewing. The mix of Mr. Nevill's cantankerous personality, workers' discontent over pay and two strong external forces—the UAW and the slowing California economy—would soon prove too much.

* * * * *

Experts Can Cushion the Clash

It isn't just the owner's fault. Workers, who often don't see what it takes to run a business or meet a payroll, frequently view their employer's success as an opportunity to get a share. At larger companies, labor experts say, that divergence is usually smoothed by a phalanx of trained managers and personnel professionals schooled in the science of labor disputes. But at smaller companies, which don't have the training resources or know-how, the clash can be devastating.

In the spring of 1989, Tony Abuanza and another employee stepped into Refuse Compactor's white cinder-block office building and told plant manager George Miller and Mr. Nevill's wife, Linda, that the workers wanted more pay, an extra week of vacation and another holiday. Mr. Miller told them to put their request in writing.

But workers apparently took that as rejection. A week later, the company received a letter from the UAW, saying that workers had signed cards seeking a vote on representation from the union. Within weeks, the workers, hoping for higher pay and relief from workplace pressure, voted the union in, 29–17.

With a third party involved in ensuing contract negotiations, relations between Refuse Compactor and its workers deteriorated quickly. Mr. Soriano says that in a meeting with about a dozen workers, Mr. Nevill told them that "the [expletive] union will never tell me what to do in my shop," adding, "How would you like it if I told you what to do in your house?"

Once the work force joins a union, labor officials say, many business owners initially take a hard-line stance but soften it as they grow accustomed to the new balance of power. Mr. Nevill never did.

Missteps by Union

That resistance in turn led to a string of miscalculations by the union. Frustrated by a lack of progress on a contract, the UAW, hoping to improve the workers' leverage, got strike authorization from them. The move never was meant to result in a walkout, says representative Ernie Shelton.

But Mr. Nevill, seeing his 20-year-old creation slip into outsiders' hands, presented a "final" offer, and called workers in to argue that the union was a bad idea. He compared the union with living in "Russia," several workers say, though Mr. Nevill denies he used that term. And, workers say, he gave some employees raises to win their backing, something Mr. Nevill also denies.

As Mr. Nevill fought back, the union, worried that its support was dwindling, turned its threat into reality: On Nov. 17, 1989, the workers called a strike.

Neither side expected more than a two-week impasse. At $100 a week in strike pay from the UAW, it would be tough for the workers to live. At the same time, the UAW felt that it couldn't show weakness lest it demonstrate to other business owners that a hard line would soften it.

Forty-three workers stayed out that first week, many walking the picket lines on industrial Foothill Boulevard in front of the plant property. Leaders of the union local bolstered the forces. By the second week, more than a dozen workers returned to their jobs.

Morale, Business Suffer

As the strike dragged on for weeks and then months, morale decayed. Gradually, the number of pickets shrank to 17, with many workers walking away to find other employment or return to Mexico.

Mr. Nevill's business began to suffer, too. Customers coming to the gate had to wait until strikers moved from in front of the driveway. Eventually, they declined to come. Truck drivers were prodded to keep away. Many did.

"It was very depressing," recalls Tom Rehder, a former Refuse foreman who has since gone to work for Cubic Container Manufacturing, a direct competitor. "It was like going to the dentist every day and having root canal. Except on the way to root canal, you'd get verbally abused."

As Refuse's backlog dwindled, even employees who had returned started to lose work. New orders weren't coming in. The salesman, frustrated, left, taking customers with him.

For the strikers and Mr. Nevill, emotion began to take over. One morning in January 1990, a truck driver came to the gate to pick up six tool boxes the company had made. But he refused to cross the picket line. So, Mr. Nevill, who wanted the $2,000 sale, agreed to bring the large steel boxes out to the street.

Climbing aboard the forklift, the owner began driving toward the gate. Five strikers, including welder Regulo Catalan, walked slowly across the driveway with blue and white UAW picket signs. "Mr. Arturo," as the workers called Mr. Nevill, hit Mr. Catalan in the arm with the tool boxes as he drove past.

Mr. Nevill loaded the tool boxes from the forklift onto the truck. The strikers had resumed their walking. Mr. Nevill climbed aboard the forklift again, and told the workers to get out of the way. Then, driving in reverse, he hit Mr. Catalan's leg. Mr. Nevill drove back to the plant property smiling, workers later testified to the NLRB.

Mr. Nevill, for his part, says the worker faked the accident. "He'd be dead if I ran over him," he says.

Weeks later, Mr. Nevill, his frustration mounting, confronted Mr. Soriano, swinging the factory gate into him and bruising his ribs. Mr. Nevill contends that the gate couldn't have injured the worker, and says Mr. Soriano was trying to be hit.

"The point of all of this is for the union to push as far as possible so that I react, and then they can file unfair labor practices," Mr. Nevill argues. "Sometimes, I wake up and think, 'This is America? This is what it has come to?'"

The UAW's lawyer, William Heine, counters that Mr. Nevill had "a suicide wish. He'd rather put himself out of business than negotiate with the union."

In August 1990, the 17 remaining strikers, many broke and disillusioned, offered to return unconditionally. Only three have been hired back. The two sides continue to wage a legal battle, as Refuse's business remains depressed.

On the wall of the UAW's meeting hall in North Hollywood, a sign proclaims "Progress Together." But in Refuse's case, as with many labor disputes, there are no winners—unless one counts lawyers and competitors.

The company's work force has dropped to about 15 from more than 60. The UAW local has spent far more than it can ever hope to recoup in union dues. And this May, the NLRB upheld an administrative law judge's ruling that Mr. Nevill had committed a string of unfair labor practices against his former workers, including swiping Mr. Catalan with the forklift.

In recent days, NLRB investigators have been poring over his records, trying to determine how much Mr. Nevill owes in back pay to the strikers. The union claims that Refuse should pay over $300,000.

Mr. Nevill, whose company had a loss of $280,000 in the quarter ended Dec. 31 (the most recent for which he has records), doesn't think he has the money. He is considering filing for bankruptcy protection if the back-pay claim is high.

Both sides remain disillusioned. The striking workers have long since given up hopes of working for Refuse again. Meanwhile, Mr. Nevill considers his business to be "back to 1975" in size. Concludes the owner: "I hope I never see another employee or another NLRB person in my life."

Questions

1. After reading this story of labor conflict, do your sympathies lie with Nevill or his employees? Explain.
2. As described in this *Wall Street Journal* article, do you think that Nevill's behavior was unfair and that he should be punished in some way under the law? Explain.
3. Should the legal system refrain so far as possible from playing a role in the dispute between Nevill and his workers since the business does, indeed, belong to Nevill and his partner? Explain.

Part Two—History

To understand contemporary labor relations and labor law, one must first know something about the history of labor conflict in this country and the causes of that conflict. The Industrial Revolution brought about vast changes—not only in terms of means and methods of production in the United States and throughout the world, but also in terms of the effects those changes had on the social order and the distribution of wealth.[4]

During a relatively short period of time, the United States moved from an agrarian to an industrial society. Goods formerly produced in the home or in small shops by a craftsman and a few apprentices suddenly became the products of factories employing hundreds of people. Then, because of the large number of workers, intermediaries were necessary to supervise and manage the operation of the workplace. The personal relationship that had once existed between workers and their employer disappeared.[5]

Competition among these developing firms in the late 1800s was fierce. Increases in demand often caused firms throughout an industry to expand their operations to keep pace with the growing market. However, since the firms within a given industry all increased output at the same time, production often exceeded the demand for goods.[6] To stay in business, companies had to cut production costs. Faced with fixed costs for raw materials and overhead expenses, companies found that one production cost could be reduced: the cost of labor. By paying workers as little as possible and making them work 14- or 18-hour days, employers could lower their total production costs. Thus, employers had an economic incentive for ignoring the human needs of the workers. The presence of an economic incentive to abuse workers, combined with the absence of the personal relationship between employer and worker, led to a severe deterioration of working conditions.[7]

Farmers and Immigrants

At the same time, two other situations had a significant influence on the development of labor conflict. The first was that workers often left the farms and moved to cities to be near their jobs. Unfortunately, that movement destroyed an important safety net. That is, if wages did not provide the full measure of living expenses, farm families still had their gardens and chickens and cows to use for food. Once these families moved to the cities, all expenses had to be covered by whatever wages were paid, no matter how meager an amount that might be.[8]

A second major factor generating labor conflict was foreign immigrants' influx into northern and midwestern industrial centers. The availability of people anxious to work meant competition for jobs was fierce and employers could fill jobs easily, regardless of low wages and deplorable working conditions.[9] In addition, some highly educated immigrants were escaping political and religious persecution in their homelands. These people brought to the United States ideas, philosophies, and experiences in class struggle and labor conflict, which presumably exacerbated a struggle that was coming to a head in any case.[10]

A Grim Picture

To say that working conditions for many people at this time were unpleasant or even dismal would be a vast understatement. The term *desperate* better describes the problem. Children were impressed into service as soon as they were big enough to do a job and then made to work 12- and 14-hour days.[11] Textile companies would send men called "slavers" to New England and southern farm communities to gather young women to work in the mills.[12] Employers built factory and mining towns where workers would be forced to rent company-owned tenements and buy provisions from company stores at exorbitant rates.[13] Reports such as the following about labor and living conditions in the forepart of the 20th century reveal the grim picture:

> When I moved from the North to the South in my search for work, I entered a mill village to work in a cotton mill as a spinner. There I worked 11 hours a day, five and a half days a week, for $7 a week. In a northern mill I had done the same kind of work for $22 a week, and less hours. I worked terribly hard . . .
>
> The sanitary conditions were ghastly. When I desired a drink of water, I had to dip my cup into a pail of water that had been brought into the mill from a spring in the fields. It tasted horrible to me. Often I saw lint from the cotton in the room floating on top of the lukewarm water. All of the men chewed tobacco, and most of the women used snuff. Little imagination is needed to judge the condition of the water which I had to drink, for working in that close, hot spinning room made me thirsty. Toilet facilities were provided three stories down in the basement of the mill in a room without any ventilation. Nowhere was there any running water . . .
>
> The married women of the South work extremely hard . . . They arise about five to take the cow out to the pasture, to do some weeding in the garden, and to have hot cakes ready for their husbands' breakfasts when they arise. Then they prepare their children for school and finally start their work in the mills at 6:30, where they work for 11 hours. Upon their return to their homes, they have housework to do. They have no conveniences . . .
>
> Everything in the village is company owned. The houses look like barns on stilts, and appear to have been thrown together. When I would go inside one of them, I could see outside through the cracks in the walls. The workers do all of their trading at the company

store and bank, and use the company school and library for they have no means of leaving the village . . .

I worked in the South for nine months, and during that time I could not reconcile myself to the conditions of the mills and village. Therefore, I left the South and returned to the North—back to the clock punching, speed-up and efficiency system of the northern mills.

Five years have passed since then, and I have learned through experience that I may go North, South, East, or West in my search for work, and find miserable working conditions for miserable wages. I know that the workers in any industry are in a most deplorable condition, but the workers of the South are in virtual slavery.[14]

Compare these working-class conditions with those of John D. Rockefeller, the great tycoon of the same era. Although Rockefeller was notoriously frugal, his estate at Pocantico Hills contained:

more than 75 buildings . . . Within his estate were 75 miles of private roads on which he could take his afternoon drive; a private golf links on which he could play his morning game; and anywhere from 1,000 to 1,500 employees, depending on the season.

. . . Rockefeller also owned an estate at Lakewood, which he occupied in the spring; an estate at Ormond Beach in Florida for his winter use; a townhouse . . . in New York; an estate at Forest Hill, Cleveland, which he did not visit; and a house on Euclid Avenue in Cleveland, likewise unused by him.[15]

Contrasting these conditions with those of the workers enables us to better understand the sense of injustice felt by many workers and the belief of many that a redistribution of wealth might provide the only solution to the class conflict.

ORGANIZING LABOR

The Knights of Labor, initially a secret society, was the first major labor organization in the United States. The Knights of Labor, led first by Uriah Stephens and then by Terence V. Powderly, had a large following during the 1870s and 1880s.[16] The order admitted any workers to its ranks, regardless of occupation, race, sex, or nationality; in fact, the only people excluded from the group were gamblers, bankers, stockbrokers, and liquor dealers.[17] The Knights of Labor dedicated itself to principles of social reform. For example, the group sought the protection of wage and hour laws, improved health care systems, and mandatory education.[18] The goals of the Knights of Labor were perhaps too broad and far-reaching to bring workers any relief from their immediate problems. Great philosophical divisions within the Knights brought about its rapid decline.[19]

Skilled Workers

Samuel Gompers, who built and developed the American Federation of Labor (AFL), had more practical, attainable goals in mind for his organization. Gompers, a worker in the cigar industry, saw the need to organize workers along craft lines so that each craft group could seek higher wages and better working conditions for its own workers, all of whom had the same type of skills and, presumably, all of whom shared the same occupational goals.[20] This approach, a national association of local unions directed to workers' pragmatic needs rather than the more politically motivated activities of the Knights of Labor, proved to be a successful formula for union organization.

Laborers

The Congress of Industrial Organizations (CIO) was organized in response to the need of an entire segment of the working population to which the AFL was virtually unresponsive.[21] The AFL consisted of unions of craft labor. By the 1930s, however, millions of workers were employed in highly compartmentalized jobs requiring very little skill. Assembly-line production required repetitive tasks that could be performed by untrained workers.[22] The interests of these unskilled workers differed greatly from those of skilled workers, and ordinarily the unskilled workers did not qualify for membership in most craft unions. Therefore, funneling these workers into the craft unions was not a particularly practical solution to their need for organization. Further, the members of the AFL were not willing to accept the idea of unions set up along industry, rather than craft, lines. John L. Lewis, Sidney Hillman, David Dubinsky, and a number of others saw the need for industrywide unionization in mass production industries. When their suggestions were rejected out of hand at the 1935 international meeting of the AFL, these people started the CIO.[23]

A great deal of competition existed between the AFL and the CIO through the 1930s and 1940s. The AFL remained attached to traditional notions of labor–management struggle, trying to achieve gains through intrafirm improvements. The CIO was less conventional (in its day) in its approach. It strove for industrywide improvements coupled with political solutions, such as price controls, low-cost housing, and foreign trade policies that would minimize competition from low-cost foreign labor.[24] After years of bitter conflict, the organizations agreed to stop raiding one another for members, and in 1955, the two groups united forces. They function together today as the AFL–CIO.[25]

UNIONS AND THE DEVELOPING LAW

Through the late 19th and early 20th centuries, employers had been very successful in discouraging union organizing. Two devices used by employers to inhibit union formations were "yellow dog" contracts and blacklists. A *yellow dog contract* was an employment agreement under which the employee was bound by the contract's terms not to become a member of a union. *Blacklists* were simply lists of union organizers or sometimes even participants in labor activities circulated among all the companies in an industry or geographic locale telling employers not to hire the people named on the lists because they were union instigators.[26]

The most effective legal means to halt a union in its incipiency was the court injunction. If a group of workers began picketing a factory, for example, an employer could easily obtain from a state or federal court an order forbidding the workers to continue such activities.

By 1932, public pressure had mounted so that Congress, in passing the Norris-LaGuardia Act (designed primarily to prevent antitrust problems), withdrew from the federal courts the right to issue injunctions against labor activities and clarified its legislative intent that the terminology "restraint of trade" that was the heart of the 1890 Sherman Antitrust Act was not meant to include the organization or activities of labor. The Norris-LaGuardia Act also specifically outlawed the use of yellow dog contracts. Even the Norris-LaGuardia Act proved ineffectual, however, because employers were still able to go into state courts to obtain injunctive relief.[27]

Labor Protection

From 1932 to 1935, labor tensions continued to mount. The nation was still caught in the Great Depression. Believing that one element essential to economic recovery was stability in the workforce, Congress addressed the labor "question" with comprehensive legislation in the form of the Wagner Act of 1935. This legislation, patterned after the Railway Labor Act of 1926, gave workers for the first time the unequivocal right to organize and engage in concerted activities for their mutual aid and benefit. To protect this right, Congress identified a number of "unfair labor practices" and made them illegal. These unfair labor practices were all activities that Congress feared employers might use to thwart workers' attempts to unionize and to undermine the economic power that would come from workers' newfound rights.[28] Through the Wagner Act, Congress also established the National Labor Relations Board (NLRB), an administrative agency charged with the responsibility of overseeing and ensuring fair union representation elections and investigating, prosecuting, and trying employers accused of unfair labor practices.[29]

Management Protection

Unions grew rapidly, and by 1947, Congress decided labor no longer needed such a protective watchdog and, in fact, thought management might need a little help in coping with ever-growing labor organizations.[30] Thus, Congress decided to "neutralize" its position vis-à-vis labor organizations by imposing some responsibilities on these organizations. Congress did so by enacting the Taft-Hartley Act, a series of amendments to the Wagner Act that identified as unfair labor practices certain activities unions used to hamper, rather than help, the collective bargaining process. The Taft-Hartley Act also added a provision to the existing labor legislation that ensured employers' right to speak out in opposition to union organizing—in effect, protecting their First Amendment right to freedom of speech. Thus, the Taft-Hartley Act signaled a move by the government away from unconditional support for labor toward a balance of rights between labor and management.[31]

Corrupt Union Leaders

Congressional hearings in the 1950s uncovered a new source of concern in the area of labor relations. This time, the problems were not between labor and management, although certainly friction between the two continued to exist. Attention now was focused on union leaders who were abusing their power. Once in power, some union leaders had prevented others from challenging their power by not holding meetings of the union's rank and file, not scheduling elections, and using union funds to promote their own election campaigns. Stories came to light accusing some union officials of accepting collective bargaining agreements with terms that were against the interest of their constituencies, in exchange for bribes paid to them by corporate management. These agreements were aptly called "sweetheart" deals. Evidence indicated certain union officials had looted their unions' treasuries.[32]

In response to the growing evidence that union leaders were benefiting at the expense of the membership, Congress in 1959 enacted the Labor-Management Reporting and Disclosure Act (LMRDA), also known as the Landrum-Griffin Act. This act contains provisions requiring unions to keep records of their funds, including statements of their assets, liabilities, salaries paid, and all other expenditures. It also prohibits unions from loaning money except under specified circumstances and in conformity with certain procedural rules. These financial statements and transactions must all be reported annually to the government.

Members' Rights

The Landrum-Griffin Act also contains a set of provisions often referred to as the "Bill of Rights" for the individual laborer. These provisions are designed to protect union members by requiring that union meetings be held, that members be permitted to speak and vote at these meetings, that every employee covered by a collective bargaining agreement have the right to see a copy of that agreement, and that a union member be informed of the reasons and given a chance for a hearing if the union wishes to suspend or take disciplinary action against that member, unless he or she is being suspended for nonpayment of dues.[33] Although these provisions had the potential for eliminating the internal union problems, court decisions have done much to emasculate the protections provided in Landrum-Griffin.

This historical progression—from labor's helplessness to active union organizing following passage of the Wagner Act in 1935, to restoration of balance between labor and management in 1947, and, finally, to a recognition of the powerlessness of the individual within the union—sounds very smooth and logical. The entire process has been likened by many to the swinging of a pendulum. One should not forget, however, that labor conflicts in the United States have often been attended by severe violence; have driven apart towns, factories, even families; and have raised emotions to higher pitches than perhaps any other social or political issue. Labor law must be understood within this context.

Part Three—Labor Legislation Today

THE STATUTORY SCHEME AND ITS GOALS

Today, labor–management relations are governed by the National Labor Relations Act (NLRA).[34] This act includes the Wagner Act, the Taft-Hartley Act, and portions of the Landrum-Griffin Act. The remaining provisions of the Landrum-Griffin Act make up the aforementioned Labor–Management Reporting and Disclosure Act and the "Bill of Rights of Members of Labor Organizations." These provisions deal with the internal operations of labor organizations and the relationship between the individual union member and the union itself, rather than with the relationship between the union and the employer.

The National Labor Relations Act, Section 1, sets out the following policy statement:

> It is declared to be the policy of the United States to eliminate the causes of certain substantial obstructions to the free flow of commerce and to mitigate and eliminate these obstructions when they have occurred by encouraging the practice and procedure of collective bargaining and by protecting the exercise by workers of full freedom of association, self-organization, and designation of representatives of their own choosing, for the purpose of negotiating the terms and conditions of their employment or other mutual aid or protection.

Given its constitutional authority to regulate commerce (see Chapters 5 and 7) Congress couches its findings and declarations of policy in terms of eliminating the obstructions to freely flowing commerce caused by labor conflicts. Note, too, that Congress identifies labor conflict to be due, in large part, to lack of bargaining power on the part of individual employees and, thus, sets out to correct the problem by promoting concerted activity by employees and collective bargaining between labor organizations and management. Keep these ideas in mind as you examine the choices made by Congress in regulating labor–management relations and the decisions made by the NLRB and the courts in interpreting and applying these statutory mandates.

Right to Organize

First, the NLRA gives employees the right to engage in concerted activity. Section 7 of the NLRA states:

> Employees shall have the right to self-organization, to form, join or assist labor organizations, to bargain collectively through representatives of their own choosing, and to engage in other concerted activities for the purpose of collective bargaining or other mutual aid or protection, and shall also have the right to refrain from any or all of such activities except to the extent that such right may be affected by an agreement requiring membership in a labor organization as a condition of employment.

Management Unfair Labor Practices

Second, as previously mentioned, the act describes and outlaws certain activities by employers that would hamper or discourage employees from exercising the rights granted to them in Section 7. Thus, Section 8(a) of the act makes it an unfair labor practice for an employer to:

1. Interfere with employees in the exercise of the rights given to them by Section 7.
2. Dominate, interfere, or assist with the formation of any labor organization (including contributing financial support to it).
3. Encourage or discourage membership in any labor organization by discrimination in regard to hire, tenure of employment, promotion, salary, or any other term of employment.
4. Discharge or take any other action against an employee because he or she has filed charges or given testimony under the act.
5. Refuse to bargain collectively with a duly certified representative of the employees.

These five provisions are designed to allow employees to organize in an atmosphere free from intimidation by the employer, with minds clear of the fear that the employer might be able to affect their jobs adversely because of their choice to participate in a labor organization. The provisions also ensure that the employer, through his or her position of authority, will not be able to interfere with union activities by either seizing control of the union or rendering it impotent by refusing to bargain collectively.

Union Unfair Labor Practices

Section 8(b) lists activities constituting unfair labor practices by a labor organization. Some of these provisions mirror some of the activities prohibited to employers. That is, at least since the enactment of the Taft-Hartley Act, the law is not sympathetic to labor organizations that try to use coercive tactics, threats of the loss of livelihood, or any other strong-arm methods to recruit members. Thus, a labor organization is not permitted to:

1. Restrain or coerce any employee in the exercise of his or her rights as granted by Section 7.
2. Cause or attempt to cause an employer to discriminate against an employee who has chosen not to join a particular labor organization or has been denied membership in such an organization.
3. Refuse to bargain collectively with an employer on behalf of the bargaining unit it is certified to represent.
4. Induce or attempt to induce an employer to engage in secondary boycott activities.
5. Require employees to become union members and then charge them excessive or discriminatory dues.
6. Try to make an employer compensate workers for services not performed.

7. Picket or threaten to picket an employer where the object of the picketing is to force the employer to recognize or bargain with a labor organization that is not the duly certified representative of a bargaining unit.

The remaining subparts of Section 8 cover a variety of problems: Section 8(c) protects the First Amendment rights of people involved in labor disputes while spelling out limitations on those rights. Section 8(d) describes and defines the duties of employers and labor organizations to bargain collectively over certain mandatory subjects. This section also sets up a "cooling-off" process under which a party who wishes to renegotiate a collective bargaining agreement must serve notice of its desire to do so 60 days in advance of the agreement's expiration date. Sections 8(e) and (f) describe situations in which it is impermissible for both employers and labor organizations to pursue their disputes in ways that extend those disputes beyond the confines of their own internal conflict.

NATIONAL LABOR RELATIONS BOARD (NLRB)

The NLRB is an administrative agency instrumental in regulating labor–management relations. Its primary tasks are designating appropriate bargaining units of workers (deciding which workers have a sufficient "community of interest" to afford them unity when bargaining); conducting elections for union representation within the chosen bargaining unit; certifying the results of such elections; and investigating, prosecuting, and adjudicating charges of unfair labor practices.[35]

Although the congressional mandate by which the NLRB was formed gives the agency jurisdiction theoretically to the full extent of the interstate commerce powers vested in Congress, the agency has neither the funding nor the staff to administer its duties to all of American industry. Thus, some limitations have been placed on the board by both statute and the agency's own decisions.

These restrictions on jurisdiction take two basic forms. (1) Employers: The board itself requires the portion of an employer's business involved in interstate commerce to exceed certain dollar amounts, which differ depending on the nature of the industry. Labor disputes involving firms falling beneath the minimum are assumed not to significantly affect commerce. (2) Employees: Entire groups of employees are excluded from coverage. For example, government employees, railroad and airline workers covered by the Railway Labor Act, agricultural workers, domestic workers, independent contractors, and supervisors and other managerial employees are not protected by the board.[36]

The NLRB and Worker Participation

Spurred by Japanese success and methods, American companies have been experimenting with a variety of strategies to improve productivity. Among them is increased worker participation in management decision making as a part of the more general effort at total quality management (TQM). President Clinton and Labor Secretary

Robert Reich are strong advocates of "quality circles" and TQM. However, as we have seen, the National Labor Relations Act, Sections 2(5) and 8(a)(2), provides that employer domination or interference with the formation or administration of any labor organization is an unfair labor practice. Broadly, the law is designed to prevent sham unions that, in fact, are dominated by management. Hence, in 1992 and 1993, the NLRB was called on to decide two cases involving the legality of some company-created labor–management committees designed to strengthen production quality. The article that follows describes the NLRB decisions and examines some of the political and industrial policy implications of preserving legitimate union interests on the one hand while striving for quality improvement via employee involvement on the other.

DUPONT IS TOLD IT MUST DISBAND NONUNION PANELS

Kevin G. Salwen

In a major blow to corporate worker-management teams, the National Labor Relations Board ordered DuPont Co. to disband seven such panels and to deal instead with the company's chemical workers union.

At the same time, the board attempted to lay out how companies can set up the increasingly popular labor-management teams.

The decision has been eagerly awaited by U.S. companies because it is the first major case to address the issue of safety committees in corporations where a union is present. Late last year, the NLRB ruled that worker-management teams at Electromation Inc. of Elkhart, Ind., were illegal "sham unions" because they set up "action committees" at a time when the Teamsters union was trying to organize the plant.

Legislative Hurdles

The DuPont ruling is a blow to the philosophy of Labor Secretary Robert Reich, who is a strong advocate of worker-management teams as a way of solving workplace problems. Mr. Reich has said repeatedly that he would seek legislation protecting the sanctity of worker-management teams if the NLRB's rulings have the effect of stifling such groups.

Such legislation wouldn't be easy to enact. Labor unions would fight efforts to curtail their already dwindling muscle within corporations, and they still hold much sway within the Democratic Party.

The NLRB was unanimous in deciding that the DuPont safety and fitness committees were illegal "labor organizations" under the National Labor Relations Act of 1935. The panels made decisions concerning safety in DuPont's Deepwater, N.J., facility, but those determinations were subject to the approval of management members on the teams, the board said. The union has several thousand members, all at the Deepwater facility.

Company Control

DuPont management dominated the committees in other ways as well, the NLRB decided. For example, the Wilmington, Del.-based chemical company set the size of each panel, and determined which employees would staff the committee if more than the required number volunteered. It also reserved the right to set up or disband any of the committees. Cumulatively, the board said, that meant the committees' administration was dominated by DuPont, rather than being an equal labor-management team.

Moreover, "some committees dealt with issues which were identical to those dealt with" by the Chemical Workers Association—and with even greater success, the board said. For example, the Antiknocks Area Safety Committee got a new welding shop for a worker who had complained of poor ventilation, while the union's attempt to resolve the same problem had failed.

Similarly, the committees decided on incentives and awards for workers, areas the NLRB said were "mandatory subjects of bargaining."

Guidelines Are Suggested

Still, the board attempted to create an outline from which companies could set up teams. For instance, such committees would need to avoid "dealing" with management as a union might. Specifically, the board indicated that the committees should exist "for the sole purpose of imparting information . . . or planning educational programs."

In addition, the board suggested that management

not dominate the panels, but rather be a participant with a commensurate number of votes—notably a minority.

Meanwhile, the board singled out as being legal the quarterly safety conferences that DuPont began in 1989. At those conferences, the board said, it was announced that bargainable matters couldn't be dealt with and that "the conference wasn't a 'union issue.'"

* * * * *

The board's decision upheld an administrative ruling issued last May. DuPont dispanded the seven committees soon after that administrative ruling. Now the company and union agree in advance on issues such as committee makeup and procedure before establishing a safety committee, company officials said.

Source: *The Wall Street Journal,* June 7, 1993, p. A2. Reprinted by permission of *The Wall Street Journal,* © 1993 Dow Jones & Company, Inc. All Rights Reserved Worldwide.

Questions

1. Will these NLRB decisions significantly curb the total quality movement? Explain.
2. Does the DuPont decision forbid worker–management cooperative decision-making efforts? Explain.
3. In your view, do the *DuPont* and *Electromation* decisions harm American industrial competitiveness? Explain.
4. Assume a union seeks a bargaining unit that would include all full-time and regular part-time employees at a supermarket, including head cashiers, produce managers, stock managers, and baggers. The unit would exclude meat department employees, salespeople, security guards, store managers, and assistant managers.
   a. Do you think a "community of interest" exists among these workers such that the board should approve this unit? Explain.
   b. If not, how should the group be changed?
   c. Do you need any additional facts before making your decision? Explain. See *Daylight Grocery Co., Inc.* v. *NLRB,* 678 F.2d 905 (11th Cir. 1982).

CHOOSING A BARGAINING REPRESENTATIVE—ELECTIONS

Petition

A union, employee, or employer initiates the formal organizing process by filing an election *petition* with the NLRB. The petition is sent to the employer, thus providing notice of union activity. The NLRB then assumes its authority to closely oversee the conduct of employer and union. Of course at that point, the employer is free to simply recognize its employees' interest in joining a particular union and to engage in bargaining with that union, although voluntary recognition is uncommon. Failing voluntary recognition, the process proceeds through the NLRB. The board will accept only those petitions supported by a substantial "showing of interest," which has been interpreted to mean the signatures of at least 30 percent of the employees in a bargaining unit. (In practice today, most unions will not proceed toward an election without 50 to 65 percent of the employees' signatures.) Those signatures accompany the petition, or they may appear on *cards,* which unions may provide to workers to affirm their interest in an election and/or in union representation.

Hearing

The NLRB ordinarily will hold a hearing within 21 days after the petition is filed to settle procedural issues such as whether a union contract already covers the employees or whether the election should be delayed. However, the crucial issue to be addressed in the hearing is normally whether the proposed bargaining unit (the designated employee group, for example, all hourly workers, all welders, or all craftpersons) is "appropriate" for the election.

Bargaining Unit

As noted above, the key consideration in establishing the appropriate employee bargaining unit is the *community of interest* among the employees. Thus, clerical employees are presumptively considered to be a separate bargaining unit because of their shared concerns, but with the consent of the parties, they might also be included in a larger bargaining unit consisting of production and maintenance workers, for example. Certain classes of employees, such as supervisors, are excluded from the bargaining unit. The bargaining unit may range from a portion of a plant to multiple employers in multiple plants. Plants may have more than one appropriate bargaining unit, depending on the composition of the workforce. The NLRB makes the decision regarding the appropriate bargaining unit based on a series of guidelines such as the physical location of the plants, physical contact among employees, similarity of wages, benefits, working conditions, differences in skill requirements among job categories, and common supervision.

The Election

After a variety of procedural requirements are satisfied, the NLRB will either direct an election or dismiss the petition. If the election proceeds, the union representative is selected by a majority vote of the employees. The board oversees the election to ensure the process is carried on under "laboratory conditions."[37] In other words, the elections must be held under circumstances that, to the extent possible, are free from undue or unfair influence by either the employer or by unions vying for the right to represent the bargaining unit.

Unfair labor practices are frequently committed at this juncture by employers anxious to prevent their plants from becoming organized. This is not meant to suggest that overzealous unions never commit unfair labor practices or that employers always do. However, employers who are resistant to unions have a great many natural advantages in the struggle against them. For example, the employer could distribute written arguments and objections to unions along with paychecks and thereby ensure that every employee sees the document. (Such an action, by itself, is *not* an unfair labor practice.)[38] The employer effectively has a captive audience. The employer generally is in better financial shape to stage a battle than the union is. Finally, and perhaps most importantly, the employer is the one who, in the final analysis, doles out or withholds benefits to the employees and provides them with jobs in the first place.

Free Speech

Despite these considerable inherent advantages, management also has the right to speak out against unions in the form of ads, speeches, and the like. Section 8(c) of the Taft-Hartley Act is designed to ensure employers' and labor organizations' traditional First Amendment rights so long as they do not overstep certain bounds:

> The expressing of any views, argument or opinion, or the dissemination thereof, whether in written, printed, graphic, or visual form, shall not constitute or be evidence of an unfair labor practice . . . if such expression contains no threat of reprisal or force or promise of benefit.

Threats of Reprisal or Force

Even within the confines of Section 8(c)'s language, problems often arise in determining whether antiunion arguments put forth by an employer are legitimate or whether they contain veiled threats. Suppose, for instance, that a company owner warns her employees that if she has to pay higher wages, she will be forced to go out of business and the employees will all lose their jobs. Such statements of economic "forecast" by employers have been the subject of a great deal of litigation. The following case explains the issues involved.

NLRB v. GISSEL PACKAGING CO.
395 U.S. 575 (1969)

[The president of Sinclair Company, one of four companies whose actions were being examined in this case, tried to dissuade his employees from joining a union. To that end, he informed them that, if the union won the election, it was bound to call a strike because the Teamsters were a "strike-happy" outfit. He told the employees on more than one occasion that the company's financial position was precarious and that a strike would likely force the plant to close. He suggested that the out-of-work employees would have a difficult time finding new jobs because of their age and lack of education. The union lost the election by a vote of 7 to 6 and filed objections to the election with the NLRB.

Both the NLRB and later the Court of Appeals agreed that the election should be set aside, despite the company's claim that it had merely been exercising its First Amendment rights to express its views to employees. The Supreme Court affirmed the Court of Appeals decision.]

Chief Justice Warren

We note that an employer's free speech right to communicate his views to his employees is firmly established and cannot be infringed by a union or the board. Thus, § 8(c) [29 U.S.C. § 158(c)] merely implements the First Amendment by requiring that the expression of "any views, arguments, or opinion," shall not be "evidence of an unfair labor practice," so long as such expression contains "no threat of reprisal or force or promise of benefit" in violation of § 8(a)(1). Section 8(a)(1), in turn, prohibits interference, restraint, or coercion of employees in the exercise of their right to self-organization.

Any assessment of the precise scope of employer expression, of course, must be made in the context of its labor relations setting. Thus, an employer's rights cannot outweigh the equal rights of the employees to associate freely, as those rights are embodied in § 7 and protected by § 8(a)(1) and the proviso to § 8(c). And any balancing of those rights must take into account the economic dependence of the employees on their employers, and the necessary tendency of the former, because of that relationship, to pick up intended implications of the latter that might be more readily dismissed by a more disinterested ear. Stating these obvious principles is but another way of recognizing that what is basically at stake is the establishment of a nonpermanent, limited relationship between the employer, his economically dependent employee, and his union agent, not the election of legislators or the enactment of legislation whereby that relationship is ultimately defined and where the independent voter may be freer to listen more objectively and employers as a class freer to talk.

Within this framework, we must reject the company's challenge to the decision below and the findings of the board on which it was based. The standards used below for evaluating the impact of an employer's statements are not seriously questioned by petitioner and we see no need to tamper with them here. Thus, an employer is free to communicate to his employees any of his general views about unionism or any of his specific views about a particular union, so long as the communications do not contain a "threat of reprisal or force or promise of benefit." He may even make a prediction as to the precise effects he believes unionization will have on his company. In such a case, however, the prediction must be carefully phrased on the basis of objective fact to convey an employer's belief as to demonstrably probable consequences beyond his control or to convey a management decision already arrived at to close the plant in case of unionization. If there is any implication that an employer may or may not take action solely on his own initiative for reasons unrelated to economic necessities and known only to him, the statement is no longer a reasonable prediction based on available facts but a threat of retaliation based on misrepresentation and coercion, and as such without the protection of the First Amendment. We therefore agree with the court below that "[c]onveyance of the employer's belief, even though sincere, that unionization will or may result in the closing of the plant is not a statement of fact unless, which is most improbable, the eventuality of closing is capable of proof." As stated elsewhere, an employer is free only to tell "what he reasonably believes will be the likely economic consequences of unionization that are outside his control," and not "threats of economic reprisal to be taken solely on his own volition."

Equally valid was the finding by the court and the board that petitioner's statements and communications were not cast as a prediction of "demonstrable 'economic consequences,'" but rather as a threat of retaliatory action. The board found that petitioner's speeches, pamphlets, leaflets, and letters conveyed the following message: that the company was in a precarious financial condition; that the "strike-happy" union would in all likelihood have to obtain its potentially unreasonable demands by striking, the probable result of which would be a plant shutdown, as the past history of labor relations in the area indicated; and that the employees in such a case would have great difficulty finding employment elsewhere. In carrying out its duty to focus on the question "[W]hat did the speaker intend and the listener understand?" the board could reasonably conclude that the intended and understood import of that message was not to predict that unionization would inevitably cause the plant to close but to threaten to throw employees out of work regardless of the economic realities. In this connection, we need go no further than to point out (1) that petitioner had no support for its basic assumption that the union, which had not yet even presented any demands, would have to strike to be heard, and that it admitted at the hearing that it had no basis for attributing other plant closings in the area to unionism; and (2) that the board has often found that employees, who are particularly sensitive to rumors of plant closings, take such hints as coercive threats rather than honest forecasts.

Affirmed.

Question

1. *a.* Why does the Court suggest the NLRB has a duty to determine what the speaker intended and what the listener understood?
   b. How does that differ from merely looking at what the employer actually said?
   c. Why is that difference important?

Promise of Benefit

While threats of force or reprisal are clearly objectionable elements in union campaigns, the rationale behind the prohibition against promises of benefit is not as intuitively obvious. In the case of *NLRB* v. *Exchange Parts Co.,* 375 U.S. 409 (1964), Exchange Parts sent its employees a letter shortly before a representation election that spoke of "the *Empty Promises* of the Union" and "the *fact* that *it is the Company that puts things in your envelope.*" After mentioning a number of benefits, the letter said:

"The Union can't put any of those things in your envelope—*only the Company can do that.*" Further on, the letter stated: "[I]t didn't take a Union to get any of those things and . . . it won't take a Union to get additional improvements in the future." Accompanying the letter was a detailed statement of the benefits granted by the company since 1949 and an estimate of the monetary value of such benefits to the employees.

In addition, the letter outlined further benefits, such as additional vacation days and overtime pay, that the company had recently decided to institute. In the representation election held two weeks later, the union lost. The Court of Appeals did not think the employer's action constituted an unfair labor practice. The Supreme Court disagreed. Justice Harlan stated:

> We think the Court of Appeals was mistaken in concluding that the conferral of employee benefits while a representation election is pending, for the purpose of inducing employees to vote against the union, does not "interfere with" the protected right to organize.
>
> The broad purpose of § 8(a)(1) is to establish "the right of employees to organize for mutual aid without employer interference." We have no doubt that it prohibits not only intrusive threats and promises but also conduct immediately favorable to employees which is undertaken with the express purpose of impinging upon their freedom of choice for or against unionization and is reasonably calculated to have that effect. In *Medo Photo Supply Corp.* v. *N.L.R.B.*, this Court said: "The action of employees with respect to the choice of their bargaining agents may be induced by favors bestowed by the employer as well as by his threats or domination." . . . The danger inherent in well-timed increases in benefits is the suggestion of a *fist inside the velvet glove.* [Emphasis added.] Employees are not likely to miss the inference that the source of benefits now conferred is also the source from which future benefits must flow and which may dry up if it is not obliged . . .

* * * * *

Reversed.

Union Persuasion

Employers, of course, are not the only parties affected by Section 8(c). Unions are also restricted in the type of preelection persuasion they employ. In cases involving promises of benefits made by the union, the board has been more reluctant to set aside elections than it has when such promises have been made by management. The board's reasoning is that employees realize that union preelection promises are merely expressions of a union platform, so to speak. Employees recognize that these are benefits for which the union intends to fight. Employers, on the other hand, really do hold within their power the ability to confer or withdraw benefits. Nonetheless, occasionally a union does promise a benefit in a manner that violates Section 8(c).

Racism, Propaganda, Misrepresentations

For both employers and employees, the circulation of racist propaganda designed to engender racial antipathy is grounds for setting aside an election.

Historically, the NLRB took a similarly firm stance regarding all manner of propaganda and misrepresentation. Frequently, the board has been asked to set aside elections tainted by falsehoods, allegations, misstatements, and the like. The board's position in this area has changed from the early view of setting aside elections where "trickery" of that kind was involved to its current position that misrepresentation alone will not constitute grounds for overturning an election. The burden is on the parties to correct *substantive* misrepresentations and sort out the truth via the marketplace of ideas. The board would intervene only where the *deceptive manner* of the misrepresentation (e.g., a forged document) made it impossible for the parties themselves to discern the truth. Some courts have endorsed the NLRB view. Others have not. The NLRB may once again change its position. Hence, "most parties remain cautious regarding possible misrepresentations, particularly in the very late stages of a campaign, when the other side will not have time to reply."[39]

Questions

1. *a.* What is the Court in *Exchange Parts Co.* talking about when it refers to the "fist inside the velvet glove"?
   b. Do you think the Court is justified in thinking that workers would be fooled or cowed by a sudden move by management to grant benefits? Explain.
   c. Do you think the efforts to unionize or negotiate would be undermined? Explain.
2. Suppose a union seeking to organize employees says that any employee who voices support for the union before the election will not have to pay union dues for a full year if the union is voted in.
   a. Do you see any difference between this and the *Gissel* case? Explain.
   b. Who do you think workers feel more threatened by—their employers or their peers? Explain.
   c. Should the Court's reasoning in this case be the same as it was in *Gissel?* Why? See *NLRB* v. *Savair Manufacturing Co.,* 414 U.S. 274 (1973).
3. Suppose the employees of Steno Office Supply, Inc., a large manufacturing firm, have petitioned the NLRB for an election. Company management personnel begin inviting workers to lunch to discuss the upcoming election and the likely "consequences" of unionization. These lunches are held at the local country club. During these discussions, at which employee comments are encouraged, although not forced, managers make allusions to the union organizer's sexual orientation. The comments, made in the form of jokes, suggest that homosexual favors may be required in lieu of dues.
   a. If the union loses the election, should the NLRB set the election aside because of the tactics used? Explain.
   b. Which, if any, of these tactics seem problematic?
   c. Would any one of the tactics by itself be enough to set aside the election? Explain.
   d. What standard should the board use in making its determination?
   e. What additional information might you want to have before making a decision in this particular case? See *General Knit of California,* 239 NLRB 619 (1978),

99 LRRM 1687, for a discussion of the historical standard. But see *Midland National Life Insurance,* 263 NLRB No. 24 (1982) for the current view.

4. The International Brotherhood of Electrical Workers (IBEW) won a representation election involving a group of Chicago Tribune Company employees. The company appealed the election to the NLRB, and the NLRB overruled the company's objections. The case proceeded to the federal court of appeals, where the company claimed, among other things, that the IBEW should be blocked from representing the workers because of alleged racial discrimination by the union. The company claimed that racial discrimination charges had been filed against the union, that the union had been a defendant in at least one discrimination law suit, and related claims. The company did not produce evidence that the alleged discrimination against employees was directly related to the election in question. Should certification be denied to the IBEW? Explain. See *NLRB* v. *Chicago Tribune Co.,* 943 F.2d 791 (7th Cir. 1991); cert. den., 112 S.Ct. 2301 (1992).

5. The United Food and Commercial Workers Union attempted to organize the 200 workers at a Lechmere, Inc., retail store located in a shopping plaza in Newington, Connecticut. After having little success at reaching workers via a newspaper ad, the union began placing handbills on cars in the shopping plaza parking lot. The lot was jointly owned by Lechmere and the developer of the other shops in the plaza. A long-standing Lechmere policy forbade all solicitations and handbills on its property. Each time the union sought to distribute handbills in the parking lot, the company ordered them to leave and the handbills were confiscated. The union then began distributing handbills from a grassy strip of public land adjacent to the lot and phoned or wrote to about 20 percent of the employees. Only one signed union authorization card was secured. The union then filed unfair labor practice charges against Lechmere, claiming that barring the union from the parking lot was a violation of the National Labor Relations Act. Decide. Explain. See *Lechmere, Inc.* v. *NLRB,* 112 S.Ct. 841 (1992).

Collective Bargaining

Section 8(a)(5) of the NLRA requires an employer to engage in collective bargaining with a representative of the employees. Section 8(b)(3) imposes the same duty on labor organizations. If the organization is the representative of the employees, that organization has an obligation to bargain collectively with the employer. Failure to bargain by either an employer or representative of the employees constitutes an unfair labor practice.

What is collective bargaining? What must one do to discharge the duty imposed? According to Section 8(d) of the National Labor Relations Act:

> [T]o bargain collectively is the performance of the mutual obligation of the employer and the representatives of the employees to meet at reasonable times and confer in good faith with respect to wages, hours, and other terms and conditions of employment . . . but such obligation does not compel either party to agree to a proposal or require the making of a concession.

Three distinct questions are raised by Sections 8(a)(5), 8(b)(3), and 8(d):

1. What duties are imposed on employers and employees' representatives by the requirement that they confer "in good faith"?
2. About which subjects must the parties bargain?
3. What are the implications of the union's recognition as the *exclusive* bargaining agent for a bargaining unit?

Bargaining in Good Faith.   Good faith is a murky area with no definitive answers. The NLRB and the courts look at the totality of the objective evidence in the negotiations to secure a sense of whether the parties intend to engage in serious negotiations. Over the years, various factors (none of which is conclusive in and of itself) have been identified by the board and the courts as being suggestive of good faith bargaining. Some of these include the following:[40]

1. There must be a serious attempt to adjust differences and to reach an acceptable common ground.
2. Counterproposals must be offered when another party's proposal is rejected. This must involve the give and take of an auction system.[41]
3. A position with regard to contract terms may not be constantly changed.[42]
4. There must be a willingness to incorporate oral agreements into a written contract.[43]

Surface Bargaining.   The NLRA itself specifies that a mere inability to reach an agreement or the failure to make a concession does not mean the parties have abrogated their duties to bargain collectively. But the board and the courts have rejected so-called surface bargaining, in which a party is merely going through the motions without manifesting a sincere intent to reach an understanding. In identifying surface bargaining, which indicates an absence of good faith, the board and the courts consider the total bargaining picture, including factors such as the four noted above.

However, an employer who faithfully attends bargaining sessions, makes some concessions, submits counterproposals, and "fulfills its procedural obligations" will not be found guilty of surface bargaining regardless of its other conduct in negotiations.[44] The fact that a party engages in "hard bargaining" by failing to yield on a major issue while conceding other issues does not result in a finding of surface bargaining.[45]

Take-It-or-Leave-It-Bargaining.   In the 1960s, General Electric made a "fair, firm offer" to its union and refused to budge unless the union could prove to GE's satisfaction that a change was appropriate. At the same time, GE built a massive publicity campaign to persuade the public and its employees that the union should accept GE's offer. This approach has come to be labeled "boulwarism" after GE vice president Lemuel Boulware, who created it. During the subsequent strike, the case went to court, where GE's tactics were struck down. The court did not explicitly reject take-it-or-leave-it bargaining, but rather rejected the total package as showing a lack of good faith bargaining. The inflexible position in combination with the marketing campaign effectively left GE without room to bargain meaningfully.[46]

Per Se Breach.   The board and the courts have struggled with the question of whether there are any actions that, if taken by one of the bargaining parties, would constitute a per se breach of the duty to bargain in good faith. Are there actions so detrimental to the bargaining process that use of them is enough to justify a finding of bad faith?

Suppose a union was in the midst of bargaining with management over terms of a new collective bargaining agreement and began using economic weapons against the employer while negotiations were proceeding. In the case of *NLRB* v. *Insurance Agents' International Union,* Insurance Agents' International Union was negotiating a collective bargaining agreement with Prudential Insurance Company of America.[47] The union decided to use its economic power to harass the company during these negotiations. The union's tactics included:

> [R]efusal for a time to solicit new business, and refusal (after the writing of new business was resumed) to comply with the company's reporting procedures; refusal to participate in the company's "May Policyholders' Month Campaign"; reporting late at district offices the days the agents were scheduled to attend them, and refusing to perform customary duties at the offices, instead engaging there in "sit-in-mornings," "doing what comes naturally," and leaving at noon as a group; absenting themselves from special business conferences arranged by the company; picketing and distributing leaflets outside the various offices of the company on specified days and hours as directed by the union; distributing leaflets each day to policyholders and others and soliciting policyholders' signatures on petitions directed to the company; and presenting the signed policyholders' petitions to the company at its home office while simultaneously engaging in mass demonstrations there.[48]

The NLRB thought the union's use of economic weapons against the company during a time when negotiations were not at an impasse showed bad faith on the part of the union, even though no evidence had been presented indicating the union had refused to cooperate at the bargaining table. The board's reasoning was that:

> [T]he respondent's [union's] reliance upon harassing tactics during the course of negotiations for the avowed purpose of compelling the company to capitulate to its terms is the antithesis of reasoned discussion it was duty-bound to follow. Indeed, it clearly revealed an unwillingness to submit its demands to the consideration of the bargaining table where argument, persuasion, and the free interchange of views could take place. In such circumstances, the fact that the respondent continued to confer with the company and was desirous of concluding an agreement does not *alone* establish that it fulfilled its obligation to bargain in good faith.[49]

Justice Brennan, writing the opinion for the Supreme Court, disagreed with the board, saying that:

> It is apparent from the legislative history of the whole act that the policy of Congress is to impose a mutual duty upon the parties to confer in good faith with a desire to reach agreement, in the belief that such an approach from both sides of the table promotes the over-all design of achieving industrial peace. Discussion conducted under that standard of good faith may narrow the issues, making the real demands of the parties clearer to each other, and perhaps to themselves, and may encourage an attitude of settlement through give and take . . . But apart from this essential standard of conduct, Congress intended that the parties should have wide latitude in their negotiations . . .
>
> . . . It must be realized that collective bargaining, under a system where the government does not attempt to control the results of negotiations, cannot be equated with an academic collective search for truth—or even with what might be thought to be the ideal of one . . .

The system has not reached the ideal of the philosophic notion that perfect understanding among people would lead to perfect agreement among them on values. The presence of economic weapons in reserve, and their actual exercise on occasion by the parties, is part and parcel of the system that the Wagner and Taft-Hartley Acts have recognized. Abstract logical analysis might find inconsistency between the command of the statute to negotiate toward an agreement in good faith and the legitimacy of the use of economic weapons, frequently having the most serious effect upon individual workers and productive enterprises, to induce one party to come to the terms desired by the other. But the truth of the matter is that at the present statutory stage of our national labor relations policy, the two factors—necessity for good-faith bargaining between parties, and the availability of economic pressure devices to each to make the other party incline to agree on one's terms—exist side by side. One writer recognizes this by describing economic force as "a prime motive power for agreements in free collective bargaining." . . .

[W]e think the board's approach involves an intrusion into the substantive aspects of the bargaining process . . .

The use of economic pressure, as we have indicated, is of itself not at all inconsistent with the duty of bargaining in good faith.[50]

Bargaining in Good Faith—Continued.   If using economic weapons during the negotiating process is not an exercise of bad faith and if the NLRB must close the door of the bargaining room, so to speak, and not judge what goes on behind it, can you think of any activities short of a complete refusal to bargain that would constitute lack of good faith?

Two practices have provided the major source of "bad faith" findings by the Supreme Court. The first arises when a company, during negotiations, announces that it cannot accede to higher wage demands, for example, without sending the company into bankruptcy. The union is willing to accept that limitation because, after all, it will do the employees no good to have high wages if they then lose their jobs as a result. The union, however, asks to see the company's books to verify that the company is, indeed, in the financial straits that it claims. If the company refuses to disclose such information to the union, this is a refusal to bargain in good faith.[51]

The second set of circumstances involves a situation in which the company institutes a change unilaterally during the bargaining period that affects one of the subjects of collective bargaining or offers better terms directly to the employees than the company has ever proposed to the union. For example, at the bargaining table, the company has only been willing to offer one week's paid vacation to employees of two years or less. Company officials then announce (not at the bargaining table but directly to the employees themselves) that effective immediately, all employees who have worked for six months or more are entitled to two weeks' paid vacation. According to the Supreme Court, such an action taken by the company would be strong evidence of bad faith.[52]

Mandatory Bargaining Subjects.   While employers and labor representatives are free to discuss whatever lawful subjects they mutually choose to discuss, Section 8(d) of the NLRA clearly sets out some *mandatory subjects* over which the parties must bargain. These are wages, hours, and "other terms and conditions of employment." Although these topics for mandatory bargaining seem simple enough, questions still arise frequently. For example, suppose the union and employer bargain over wages and agree to institute merit increases for employees. Must the employer also bargain over which employees are entitled to receive these increases or who will make the decision at the time the increases are to be given? Does the question of bringing in subcontractors to perform certain jobs fall within the scope of "wages, hours, and terms and conditions of employment," since the use of subcontractors may reduce the amount of work available to regular employees? Or does that subject belong more directly to the management of the firm? What about a decision to close a plant?

Generally, the board and the courts will balance three factors. First, they look to the effect of a particular decision on the workers—how direct is it and to what extent is the effect felt? Second, they consider the degree to which bargaining would constitute an intrusion into entrepreneurial interests or, from the opposite side, the degree of intrusion into union affairs. Third, they examine the practice historically in the industry or the company itself.[53]

Permissive and Prohibited Bargaining Subjects.   In the *Borg-Warner* case,[54] the Supreme Court approved and clarified the distinction between *mandatory and permissive bargaining subjects.* Those matters not directly related to wages, hours, and terms and conditions of employment and not falling within the category of *prohibited* subjects are considered permissive. Either party may raise permissive subjects during the bargaining process, but neither may pursue them to the point of a bargaining impasse. Refusal to bargain over a permissive subject does not constitute an NLRA violation and permissive subjects must simply be dropped if the parties do not reach agreement. Permissive subjects ordinarily would include such items as alteration of a defined bargaining unit, internal union affairs, and strike settlement agreements. *Prohibited bargaining subjects* are those that are illegal under the NLRA or other laws.

The Union as Exclusive Bargaining Agent.   Once a union has been elected and certified as the representative of a bargaining unit, it becomes the exclusive agent for all of the employees within that bargaining unit, whether they voted for the union or not. The exclusivity of the union's authority has a number of implications, but one is particularly relevant in determining whether an employer has failed to demonstrate good faith at the bargaining table. Specifically, the employer must deal with the certified representative who acts on behalf of all employees in the bargaining unit. The employer commits an unfair labor practice if he or she attempts to deal directly with the employees or recognizes someone other than the workers' chosen representative. In both instances, the issue is fairly straightforward. The employer is undermining the position of the representative by ignoring him or her.

Unilateral Change.   Somewhat less obvious than this direct violation, but based on the same reasoning, is the problem of an employer who, during the course of negotiations, institutes a unilateral change in employee benefits. For example, in the 1962 Supreme Court case of *NLRB* v. *Katz,* an employer made three unilateral changes.[55] He granted merit increases, changed the sick leave policy, and instituted a new system of automatic wage increases. This strategy was considered a failure to bargain in good faith because it effectively denied the union the right to joint participation in the decision making and because the employer's actions tended to obstruct the process and make the negotiations more difficult. If negotiations had come to a complete impasse before the employer instituted these changes, the Court might have decided differently. However, the employer clearly demonstrated a lack of good faith when it unilaterally granted better benefits than any offered at the bargaining table.

Can you imagine any instance in which the unilateral granting of benefits might be permissible? If raises are always given in December and labor negotiations are in progress during December in a given year, should the employer be permitted to grant pay increases without negotiating them? Is your answer conditional in any way?

UNION SECURITY AGREEMENTS AND RIGHT-TO-WORK LAWS

In order to maintain their membership, unions typically seek a collective bargaining clause requiring all employees to become union members after they have been employed for some period of time—generally, 30 days (*union shop agreements*)—or, at the least, requiring them to pay union dues and fees (*agency shop agreements*). These arrangements are lawful under the NLRA.

Twenty-one states have enacted so-called *right-to-work* laws, which prohibit union security arrangements in collective bargaining agreements. In these states, nonmembers receive all the benefits of having union representation. Needless to say, unionized plants are far less common in right-to-work states than in states without those laws.

Finally, at one time, unions with a great deal of bargaining leverage would insist on clauses in collective bargaining agreements that restricted employers from hiring anyone not already a union member. These *closed-shop agreements* are now prohibited by the NLRA.

Canada

The following article criticizes Canadian agency shop and closed shop practices and suggests something of the international economic pressure currently discouraging union organizing.

WORKERS SHOULD NOT
BE FORCED TO JOIN UNIONS

Diane Francis

Union bully-boy tactics are being challenged across Canada. Reform certainly is needed if this country is to ever survive the highly competitive 1990s and 21st century.

* * * * *

Of course, I believe that people should have the right to form a bargaining unit or to join a union.

This means, conversely, that people should also have the right to decline joining a bargaining unit or union.

That right does not exist across Canada and should. Most provincial laws adhere to the so-called Rand Formula that forces people to pay dues but relieves them of the requirement to join a union. The Rand Formula is bad enough. I don't believe that people should pay dues if they are not members of a union. But even worse are British Columbia's laws that go beyond the Rand Formula and clearly transgress civil rights by forcing workers to join a union against their will.

. . . [T]his month, the National Citizens' Coalition . . . took on British Columbia's unjust closed-shop labor laws. In a court challenge that will cost a bundle, the coalition will help Norma Janzen, 52, a teacher of learning-disabled children who was fired in 1990 because she refused to join a union.

Janzen taught children with special needs for 24 years. In June 1990, her school board and union negotiated a closed-shop provision. She refused to join both the union and the British Columbia Teachers Federation and lost her means of making a living.

"I entered this profession because I wanted to help young people and joining the union would have interfered with that goal," she said. "I had to stand by that principle even if it meant losing my job . . ."

The coalition will pay her costs and was contacted by a group of teachers called B.C. Teachers for Association, acting on her behalf. In Janzen's district of Langley, teachers were given one year to join the union. Those opposed appealed their case to the Industrial Relations Council but were unsuccessful. Her lawyer will argue that closed shops violate an individual's freedom of association, guaranteed by Section 2 (d) of the Charter of Rights and Freedoms.

Meanwhile, federal civil servant Paul Vidlak and Tory MP Rene Soetens . . . hope to attack the Rand Formula itself through a . . . bill that would give workers the choice of union membership and payment of dues—a law that New Zealand passed recently.

Vidlak and thousands of federal civil servants crossed the picket line nearly two years ago when the Public Service Alliance of Canada struck the federal government for a few days. Vidlak asked Treasury Board to stop deducting dues from his paycheques, but Treasury Board refused.

Another civil servant, Ernie Forsen, also crossed the picket line and was booted out of the PSAC union by Daryl Bean and his bully boys. Still on the hook to pay dues even though he's been kicked out, Forsen unsuccessfully attempted to take the federal government to small claims court in Ottawa to get his dues back. He estimates thousands of civil servants were also suspended from union membership, but the union refuses to disclose the figures to him.

"In my local there are 1,700 members and about 175 of us have been suspended for five years because we went to work. We did nothing illegal, nothing immoral and had every right to do what we did, and for that we are punished by a union we are forced to financially support," he said. "I'd also like to know the strike vote results, which the union refuses to disclose."

Forsen filed a grievance under Sections 91 and 92 of the Public Service Staff Relations Act and was rebuffed again; he was told his beef is with the union not the employer. Now he aims to get a judge to rule on whether his suspension violates Section 6 of the act that says "every employee may be a member of an employee organization."

Forsen says this section guarantees him membership in the union if he chooses, so PSAC had no right to boot him out. Conversely, he says, employees have a right not to belong and not to pay dues.

Source: Copyright 1993 Financial Post Ltd. *The Financial Post* June 22, 1993, p. 11. Reprinted by permission.

Questions

1. Explain the arguments supporting British Columbia's closed shop law.
2. Are labor unions retarding America's competitiveness in the world market? Explain.

ADMINISTERING THE AGREEMENT

One of the great virtues of collective bargaining agreements is that they ordinarily provide for a system by which labor–management disputes may be resolved. To avoid turning to the courts, the agreement ordinarily will spell out a series of steps for settling problems. If a difficulty arises that cannot be settled informally, the dissatisfied employee typically files a written complaint (*grievance*) with the union, which then discusses the matter with the company.

Failing a settlement, the dispute proceeds up the chain of authority in the company and the union. If all of these efforts fail, the dispute moves to *binding arbitration,* which often may be provided for in the collective bargaining agreement. An arbitrator is a neutral third party (or parties) who is mutually agreed on by labor and management. The arbitrator holds a hearing to receive each party's version of the facts. The arbitrator issues an opinion called an *award.* The arbitrator's decision may be appealed to the courts, but that decision ordinarily will not be overturned.

STRIKES

For many, the initial image of labor conflict is one of employees on strike, picketing a store or factory. Striking is, however, an extremely drastic measure under which employees must bear an immediate loss of wages while, in many instances, risking job loss.

Strikes are at a post–World War II low in the United States, although they remain a significant feature of the industrial scene.[56] A Deutsche Bank Research study of strikes during the 1980s found:

Nation	Average Workdays Lost During 1980s per 1,000 Employees
Spain	631
Great Britain	309
United States	118
Germany	27
Japan	9

Source: Christopher Conte, "Lost Labor," *The Wall Street Journal,* July 21, 1992, p. A1.

Strikes are of two kinds:

1. Those instituted by workers in response to the employer's commission of an unfair labor practice such as interfering with legitimate union activities.
2. Those used purely as economic weapons to persuade an employer to provide more favorable employee benefits or better working conditions.

Unfair Labor Practice Strikes.   In general, these strikers cannot be fired for their legitimate strike-related conduct. They may be replaced by temporary workers, but they are entitled to have their jobs back at the conclusion of the strike even if the replacements must be fired to provide openings.

Economic Strikes.   All strikes not involving unfair labor practices fall into this category. In what has been labeled "the most significant change in collective bargaining to occur since the passage of the Wagner Act in 1934," employers are now increasingly willing to *permanently replace* economic strikers.[57] Employers had enjoyed that right where necessary "in an effort to carry on the business" since a 1938 Supreme Court decision, but for practical reasons they had rarely exercised it.[58] Later Supreme Court decisions had imposed some limitations on that right. However, President Reagan's 1981 dismissal of 11,300 striking air traffic controllers effectively crushed their union (PATCO) and caused private-sector employers to reassess their long-standing reluctance to use replacements during and after strikes.[59]

The *TWA* decision that follows greatly strengthened management's hand in employing permanent replacements for economic strikers. In response, the Democratic majority in Congress forwarded legislation that would prohibit hiring permanent replacements for striking workers. However, at this writing in July 1994, that legislation has been blocked by a Republican filibuster.

TWA, INC. v. FLIGHT ATTENDANTS
489 U.S. 426 (1989)

Justice O'Connor

We decide today whether, at the end of a strike, an employer is required by the Railway Labor Act (RLA or Act) . . . to displace employees who worked during the strike in order to reinstate striking employees with greater seniority.

I

In March 1984, Trans World Airlines, Inc. (TWA) and the Independent Federation of Flight Attendants (IFFA or Union) began negotiations . . . on a new collective bargaining agreement . . . The existing collective bargaining agreement created a complex system of bidding the general effect of which was to insure that those flight attendants with the greatest seniority would have the best opportunity to obtain their preferred job assignments, flight schedules, and bases of operation as vacancies appeared, and to insure that senior flight attendants would be least affected by the periodic furloughs endemic to the airline industry . . .

For two years TWA and the Union unsuccessfully bargained over wages and working conditions . . . [O]n March 7, 1986, the Union went out on strike.

TWA informed its flight attendants before and during the strike that it would continue operations by hiring permanent replacements for striking flight attendants, by continuing to employ any flight attendant who chose not to strike, and by rehiring any striker who abandoned the strike and made an unconditional offer to return to any available vacancies.

TWA also informed its flight attendants that any vacancies created as a result of the strike would be filled by application of the seniority bidding system to all working flight attendants and that such job and domicile assignments would remain effective after the strike ended . . . Thus, at the conclusion of the strike, senior full-term strikers would not be permitted to displace permanent replacements or junior nonstriking flight attendants and could be left without an opportunity to return to work. TWA's promise not to displace working flight attendants after the strike created two incentives specifically linked to the seniority bidding system: it gave senior flight attendants an incentive to remain at or return to work in order to retain their prior jobs and domicile assignments; it gave junior flight attendants an incentive to remain at or return to work in order to obtain job and domicile assignments that were previously occupied by more senior, striking flight attendants.

As promised, TWA continued its operations during the 72-day strike by utilizing approximately 1,280 flight attendants who either did not strike or returned to work before the end of the strike and by hiring and fully training approximately 2,350 new flight attendants, some 1,220 of whom were hired during the first few days of the strike. On May 17, 1986, the Union made an unconditional offer to TWA on behalf of the approximately 5,000 flight attendants who had remained on strike to return to work. TWA accepted the offer but refused the Union's May 27th demand that TWA displace those prestrike employees who were working as of May 17 ("crossover" employees). Accordingly, TWA initially recalled only the 197 most senior full-term strikers to fill available job and domicile vacancies. By the terms of a poststrike arbitral agreement, these strikers and all subsequently reinstated full-term strikers returned to work as vacancies arose and with precisely the seniority they would have had if no strike had occurred. In May 1988, more than 1,100 full-term strikers had been reinstated with full seniority.

In an effort to reinstate all the full-term strikers by displacing the newly hired flight attendants and less senior crossover employees, the union proceeded on two fronts. First, it brought an injunction action alleging that the full-term strikers were not "economic strikers" but "unfair labor practice strikers" entitled to reinstatement by application of principles this Court has developed in interpreting the National Labor Relations Act (NLRA) . . . The district court ultimately ruled against the union on this claim . . . At the same time, the union filed the instant action contending that, even assuming the strike was economic, the full-term strikers were entitled to reinstatement either under the terms of the prestrike collective bargaining agreement or under the RLA itself. On cross motions for partial summary judgment, the district court held that the full-term strikers were not entitled to displace either the junior crossovers or the 1,220 new hires employed by TWA immediately after the strike commenced. (The motions did not require the district court to rule on the status of the remaining new hires.) The district court also held that 463 new hires not fully trained by the end of the strike could be displaced by full-term strikers . . .

* * * * *

. . . The Court of Appeals . . . affirmed the district court's ruling that full-term strikers could not displace the 1,220 fully trained new hires but could displace the 463 untrained new hires . . . The Court of Appeals, however, reversed the district court's ruling that more senior full-term strikers could not displace junior crossovers . . .

. . . Today, we reverse the Court of Appeals . . . and hold than an employer is not required by the RLA to lay off junior crossovers in order to reinstate more senior full-term strikers at the conclusion of a strike.

II

We have observed in the past that carefully drawn analogies from the federal common labor law developed under the NLRA may be helpful in deciding cases under the RLA . . .

* * * * *

. . . Both the RLA and the NLRA protect an employee's right to choose not to strike . . . and, thereby, protect employees' rights to "the benefit of their individual decisions not to strike." . . .

* * * * *

. . . The positions occupied by newly hired replacements, employees who refused to strike, and employees who abandoned the strike, are simply not "available positions" to be filled. As noted above, those positions that were available at the conclusion of the strike were filled "according to some principle, such as seniority, that is neutral . . ." That the prospect of a reduction in available positions may divide employees and create incentives among them to remain at work or abandon a strike before its conclusion is a secondary effect fairly within the arsenal of economic weapons available to employers . . .

. . . While the employer and union in many circumstances may reach a back-to-work agreement that would displace crossovers and new hires or an employer may unilaterally decide to permit such displacement, nothing in the NLRA or the federal common law we have developed under that statute requires such a result . . .

* * * * *

[RLA discussion omitted.]

IV

Neither the RLA itself nor any analogies to the NLRA indicate that the crossover policy adopted by TWA . . . was unlawful. Rather, the decision to guarantee to crossovers the same protections lawfully applied to new hires was a simple decision to apply the preexisting seniority terms of the collective bargaining agreement uniformly to all working employees. That this decision had the effect of encouraging prestrike workers to remain on the job during the strike or to abandon the strike and return to work before all vacancies were filled was an effect of the exercise of TWA's peaceful economic power, a power that the company was legally free to deploy once the parties had exhausted the private dispute resolution mechanisms of the RLA . . .

Reversed.

Questions

1. How would you vote on the proposed federal legislation banning the practice of permanently replacing economic strikers? Explain.
2. A provision of the federal Food Stamp Act denied food stamps to families while a member of the family was on strike, except where the family had been receiving food stamps prior to the strike. The legislation was challenged by union members.

> *a.* What constitutional objections would you raise to that legislation?
> *b.* Decide the case. Explain. See *Lyng* v. *Auto Workers,* 485 U.S. 360 (1988).
> 3. Can you envision any problems that are likely to arise as a result of the distinction drawn between economic strikers and unfair labor practice strikers?
> 4. What are the policy justifications for distinguishing between these two types of strikers?
> 5. Assume Mary Wills, a bottle inspector for Pop Soda Inc. and a member of a certified bargaining unit, struck along with other bottle inspectors to protest an allegedly unfair labor practice committed by the employer. The bottle inspectors offered to return to work after a one-week strike, and, although their positions were not filled, Pop Soda offered them entirely different positions as bottle sorters, telling the employees that they would shortly thereafter be returned to their regular inspector jobs. Wills was the only one who accepted this offer; the other employees insisted that they were legally entitled to their former jobs. Wills made subsequent inquiries, attempting to get her inspecting job back, but the company at no time made a proper offer for that position. After three and a half months of working as a bottle sorter, Wills resigned because of physical problems with her hand. She then made a claim to the NLRB that Pop Soda had committed an unfair labor practice by not reinstating her to her inspecting position. She asked for reinstatement and back pay.
>
> Do you think she is entitled to either or both of these remedies? See *The Coca-Cola Bottling Company of Memphis and International Brotherhood of Teamsters, et. al.,* 269 NLRB No. 160 (1983–84 CCH NLRB ¶ 16,259), decided April 23, 1984.

Notification of the Intent to Strike

Congressional desire to maintain industrial peace is manifested, in part, through the conditions imposed by Section 8(d) of the NLRA. These provisions are designed to prevent ill-conceived strikes by requiring that any party desiring to terminate or renegotiate a collective bargaining agreement must serve written notice on the other party at least 60 days prior to the expiration of the agreement then in force. Within 30 days of notifying the other party of its desires, the moving party must also notify the Federal Mediation and Conciliation Service and any state or local conciliation boards set up for the purpose of resolving that type of dispute. Failure to give this notice is considered a refusal to bargain in good faith. Moreover, any worker who goes on strike during this "cooling off" period loses his or her status as an employee for purposes of being protected by the NLRA. Such an employee may be discharged by the employer without any repercussions from the act.

The 60-day notification period allows both parties some leeway during which they can discuss and hopefully resolve their contract disputes before the old contract terminates. The notification provision ensures that neither employers nor employees are left in the lurch, unprepared for or unaware of the other party's dissatisfaction with the present bargaining agreement. Perhaps more important, the public is protected to a great extent. A strike in any sector of industry tends to have a ripple effect, creating disturbances throughout the economy.

Lockouts

Work stoppages sometimes take the form of *lockouts,* in which management shuts the door on some or all employees. Lockouts have become more common since the *TWA* decision. Lockouts take two forms:

1. *Defensive.* The company says it must keep employees out to protect itself against violence or sabotage.
2. *Offensive.* The company uses the lockout as a strategy to persuade the workers to accept its position.

Lockouts can be very potent weapons, since workers are not paid and many states do not offer unemployment compensation for those locked out. Since the *TWA* decision, workers have become more reluctant to strike when a contract expires, but management may now force the issue by ordering a lockout to persuade the union to accept company terms. For example:

> Warehouse workers at Hasbro, Inc. headquarters in Pawtucket, R.I., were locked out for two months. Hasbro executives argued they needed to cut costs and workers' salaries to remain competitive. The lockout ended after Teamsters Local 251 signed a three-year contract.[60]

Picketing and Boycotts

Primary Picketing.   In addition to strikes, unions often engage in picketing and/or boycotts in an effort to apply pressure to an employer and to broadly publicize their concerns. Picketing is the familiar process of union members gathering and sometimes marching, placards in hand, at a place of business. Peaceful, informational picketing for a lawful purpose is protected by the Labor-Management Reporting and Disclosure Act. However, some kinds of picketing are forbidden, and all picketing can be regulated by the government to ensure the public safety. So-called primary picketing is expressed directly to the employer with whom the picketers have a dispute. Primary picketing enjoys broad constitutional and statutory protection.

Secondary Picketing/Boycotts.   Secondary picketing or boycotting is directed to a business other than the target firm with whom the union is actually in conflict, and ordinarily it is unlawful. That is, unions are engaging in an unfair labor practice if they threaten or coerce a third party with whom they are not engaged in a dispute in order to cause that third party to cease doing business with the firm that is the real target of the union's concern. Assume Union A has a dispute with Company B. Direct, primary picketing, a strike, and the like against Company B would normally be permissible. But if A were to impose pressure via picketing, for example, on Company C, a supplier of Company B, that pressure would ordinarily constitute unlawful behavior. Thus, secondary picketing, secondary boycotts, and other forms of coercion against parties not the principals in a labor dispute are, with some exceptions, unlawful labor practices.

Questions

1. George A. Hormel & Co. and the United Food and Commercial Workers Union settled a long labor dispute. Thereafter, an unhappy employee drove his car in a parade and attended a rally, both of which were designed to encourage a nation-wide boycott of Hormel Products. The employee did nothing to signal his feelings beyond his presence at the two events.

   Employees may lawfully be dismissed for disloyalty to their employer. Supporting a boycott of an employer's products ordinarily constitutes disloyalty except where (1) the boycott is related to an ongoing labor dispute and (2) the support does not amount to disparagement of the employer's product.

   Was this Hormel employee engaged in protected activity such that his dismissal was unlawful? Explain. See *George A. Hormel and Company* v. *National Labor Relations Board,* 962 F.2d 1061 (D. of Col. Cir., 1992).

2. Two stevedoring companies in Fort Pierce and Port Canaveral, Florida, loaded Florida citrus fruit on ships bound for Japan. The International Longshoremen's Association (ILA) had a dispute with the two stevedoring companies and asked for the support of Japanese dockworkers' unions. The Japanese unions agreed and notified their membership and several Japanese stevedoring companies of that support. Concerned that their fruit might not be unloaded upon arrival in Japan, several American shipping companies diverted their ships for citrus loading from Fort Pierce and Port Canaveral to Tampa, Florida. The ILA thanked the Japanese unions for their help and asked that they continue. The result was that the Fort Pierce and Port Canaveral stevedoring companies were injured financially.

   Does the ILA conduct in this case constitute a violation of the National Labor Relations Act? Explain. See *Coastal Stevedoring Co.,* 313 NLRB 53 (1993).

EMPLOYEES' RIGHTS WITHIN OR AGAINST THE UNION

The Union's Duty of Fair Representation

As you have seen in previous sections of this chapter, the union is given statutory authority to be the *exclusive* bargaining agent for the employees in the designated bargaining unit. This means that even if an individual employee in the bargaining unit does not agree with union policies or is not a member of the union, he or she cannot bargain individually with the employer. Such an employee will still be bound by the terms of the collective bargaining agreement.

The Supreme Court has ruled that unions have a duty to fairly represent all members of the bargaining unit. Sometimes that task is difficult because of divergent interests within the unit (one of the reasons for taking great care in choosing an appropriate bargaining unit). For example, if a company is in difficult financial circumstances, it may tell union negotiators that the company must do one of two things to stay viable—lay off workers or give all employees a cut in salary. The workers who have seniority and would not lose their jobs in a layoff are likely to push for the former; workers with less seniority, who would normally be let go during a layoff, will prefer in most instances to retain their jobs even if they are forced to take a cut in wages.

This type of situation, however, is a far cry from those in which a union has arbitrarily or with purposeful intent discriminated against some segment of its rank-and-file membership. In addition to the racial discrimination found in many unions, sex discrimination was also rampant. Unions were notorious for negotiating contracts in which women were excluded from certain jobs and paid lower wages for performing work identical to their male counterparts. In recognition of the discrimination being practiced by many unions, Congress built special provisions into the Equal Pay Act of 1963 and the Civil Rights Act of 1964, making it illegal for unions to discriminate on the basis of race, color, creed, national origin, or sex.

The "Bill of Rights" of Labor Organization Members

The "Bill of Rights" for members of labor organizations is contained in Title I, Section 101 of the Labor-Management Reporting and Disclosure Act (LMRDA or Landrum-Griffin Act). The Bill of Rights was designed to ensure equal voting rights, the right to sue the union, and the rights of free speech and assembly. These rights of union members are tempered by the union's right to enact and enforce "reasonable rules governing the responsibilities of its members."[61]

Many people are extremely skeptical about the union leaders' ability and/or desire to be responsive to the interests of the membership rather than to their own needs for power or money. This skepticism is due, at least in part, to the information brought to light in congressional hearings in the late 1950s.

> Prior to the enactment of the LMRDA in 1959, the Select Senate Committee discovered widespread corruption, dictatorship, and racketeering in a number of large international unions. The committee found that the president of the Bakery and Confectionary Workers' International Union of America had "railroaded through changes in the union constitution which destroyed any vestigial pretenses of union democracy . . ." The committee likewise found Teamster officials joining with others to take over illegal gambling operations with an "underworld combine," and the top officers of the United Textile Workers of America avariciously misappropriating union funds. "Democracy [was] virtually nonexistent" in the International Union of Operating Engineers because the union was ruthlessly dominated through "violence, intimidation, and other dictatorial practices."[62]

Even though union members are guaranteed the rights of free speech and assembly, federal court cases, at both the district and circuit court levels, have made clear that unions are not obligated to provide space in union newspapers for articles containing viewpoints opposed to those of union leadership, nor is the union obligated to hold meetings at the behest of their membership even when the union constitution provides a procedural means for calling such a meeting. Moreover, the union meeting agenda can be set by the union leadership in such a way as to preclude discussion of particular issues. The union is permitted to establish "reasonable" rules to govern such situations.

Other federal court decisions have come down equally firmly in interpreting other "rights" guaranteed by the workers' Bill of Rights. Thus, although union members are entitled to vote in union elections, they do not have the right to demand a vote on a decision of whether to strike. Likewise, the union is not required to submit a proposed collective bargaining agreement to the membership for ratification or approval, although the Bill of Rights gives members the right to see a copy of the agreement under which they are working.[63]

As a result of these court rulings, one could make a tenable argument that employees are now caught in a double bind. Not only is the employer a potential source of trouble for the employee, but so may be the very union that was supposed to be his or her vehicle for relief.

THE FUTURE OF UNIONS

We began this chapter with a look at the declining fortunes of the American union movement. Our central concern remains the future of unions. The following article suggests early signs of renewed zeal.

UNIONS DISPLAY A REVIVAL OF MILITANCY

Dana Milbank and Wendy Bounds

Workers used to solve their disputes with companies by marching off the job. But when flight attendants at Alaska Airlines got into a tiff with the company over scheduling and work rules, they selected a more effective weapon: a "Campaign for Chaos."

"We are going into work every day," says Gail Bigelow of the Association of Flight Attendants. "But at any given time we could call a work stoppage. It could last a day or a half-hour, but the company will have no idea when it's coming."

In response, the unit of Alaska Air Group has ordered at least three managers and supervisors from headquarters to ride on every flight in case of a work stoppage, producing a slowdown at the upper levels. "It's been a long couple of weeks," says an Alaska Airlines spokesman.

After more than a decade of retreat, union militancy appears to be surging. Unions are taking on employers with publicity campaigns, creative strikes and shows of solidarity in the workplace. Some see the new spirit as a backlash against the 1980s that will reinvigorate labor.

'More Anger and Militancy'

"There's been more militancy at the rank-and-file level," says Jeff Faux, president of the Economic Policy Institute in Washington. "There's more stress on the job, and that means more anger and militancy."

He attributes the rise in activism to a decline in real wages and benefits and an assault on job security that includes the use of anti-union consultants and permanent replacements for strikers. At the same time, workers have found their upward mobility blocked, creating an overeducated and restless work force.

The new activism may, of course, amount to no more than a last stand for labor. Although U.S.

union membership has shown small gains, it continues to shrink as a proportion of the work force . . . Work stoppages, meanwhile, fell to the lowest level in 45 years in 1992, according to the Bureau of Labor Statistics. A labor-backed bill banning permanent replacements for striking workers faces bleak prospects. And recent contract negotiations have brought unions little improvement in pay and benefits.

Sar Levitan, director of George Washington University's Center for Social Policy, believes unions are more concerned with defending health and pension benefits for an aging membership than with winning new benefits or expanding their membership. "I don't see much of an offensive," he says.

But at the same time, union victories in representation elections reached 50% last year, the highest rate since 1984, according to an analysis by the Bureau of National Affairs . . .

The new militancy has some important differences from the past; unions these days are more likely to use boycotts and town meetings than picket lines and baseball bats. In the old days, the activism would have meant more strikes. But in today's pro-management labor landscape fostered by the Reagan and Bush administrations, workers realize that walking off the job often means getting fired. And in a weak economy, union workers are in no mood to lose their jobs to replacement workers.

Unions have been flocking to a variety of creative tactics . . . At American Telephone & Telegraph Co. last year, the Communications Workers set up an "electronic picket line" in which 70,000 people pledged to boycott AT&T if the union didn't get its way. The CWA estimates the threatened boycott would have cost AT&T $3 million to $5 million a week in lost revenue. An AT&T spokesman said the threat "sounds like a weapon" but denies that it had an impact.

Boycott of State Farm

In an ongoing dispute at A. E. Staley Manufacturing Co., in Decatur, Ill., the Allied Industrial Workers have pressured Staley representatives to resign from two bank boards and has launched a boycott of State Farm insurance, an indirect owner of the company, a unit of Britain's Tate & Lyle PLC.

The union also marched on Staley and State Farm offices and the state capitol. Instead of a strike, the union has been able to slow down work by scrupulously following safety rules workers had ignored before. Apparently frustrated by the union's tactics, the company locked out the workers. "There was an accumulated frustration built up in the '80s, one defeat after another," says Philip Mattera, research director for Corporate Campaign Inc., a New York consulting firm advising the union. "They're tired of being pushed around."

* * * * *

But there are limits to the effectiveness of this new spirit. Workers striking three plants owned by PPG Industries Inc. recently organized a display of inter-union solidarity. The workers, represented by the Aluminum, Brick and Glass Workers, organized a rally in downtown Pittsburgh at which hundreds of union faithful from five different unions circled PPG's glass headquarters. The protesters, some in camouflage suits, yelled slogans, waved flags and brandished banners that said things like "I'd rather die on my feet than live on my knees."

"I'm starting to see a lot of progress in the movement," said Mike Davin, a Teamster at the rally. "It's coming back."

Not so fast. PPG has declared that it will close two of the three plants on strike—claiming the closures are unrelated to the dispute.

The Mine Workers, meanwhile, are hoping to boost their fortunes by discarding their violent image in their selective strikes against coal companies. "We're no radicals here," says Mike Thomas, a worker at Ashland Coal Inc.'s Hobet No. 21 mine picketing along Highway 119 just up from Madison, W.Va. "We know the companies would like nothing more than to see us agitated, but we'll sit tight."

Violence during the strikes has been limited to companies' charges of rock-throwing, shooting at power equipment and igniting fires "of suspicious origin." Strikers from Mr. Thomas's Local 2286 trapped company supervisors for three hours in a school parking lot but didn't hurt anyone.

The Mine Workers' relatively peaceful solidarity has had some impact. As the union's selective strikes enter a third month, idling 14,000 workers, four coal producers have abandoned the 12-member Bituminous Coal Operators' Association and reached their own deals with the union.

But even an all-out victory for the Mine Workers would do little more than keep them from slipping further; their core demand is security in the few jobs they still have rather than improvements in pay and perks. "You'll never hear us mention wages," says John Ghiz, a 48-year-old miner on strike. "We have to be concerned that we'll even have a job."

Source: *The Wall Street Journal,* July 8, 1993, p. A2. Reprinted by permission of *The Wall Street Journal,* © 1993 Dow Jones & Company, Inc. All Rights Reserved Worldwide.

Questions

1. Do you expect labor unions to regain some of their lost power? Explain.
2. On balance, have labor unions been a beneficial force in American life? Explain.
3. *a.* Is America facing a dangerous imbalance in wealth between the well-educated, powerful management class and the poorer, undereducated laboring class? Explain.
   b. If so, can unions contribute meaningfully to correcting that imbalance? Explain.
   c. If not, do unions serve any meaningful role in contemporary life? Explain.

CHAPTER QUESTIONS

1. In year 1 of a collective bargaining agreement, the National Labor Relations Board operates under the *irrebuttable presumption* that a properly certified union has majority support of the employees. After that first year, the presumption of majority support becomes *rebuttable.* Thus the employer could lawfully withdraw recognition of the union after year 1 if it could provide the NLRB with adequate objective evidence of a "good faith doubt" that the union retained majority support.

   Curtin Matheson Scientific, Inc., was bargaining with the Teamsters union for a new collective bargaining agreement. After its final offer was rejected, Curtin Matheson "locked out" 27 bargaining unit employees. The Teamsters union then called an economic strike. Five employees crossed the picket line, and the company hired 29 permanent replacements for the 22 strikers. Curtin Matheson then withdrew recognition from its Teamsters local, saying that it had a good faith doubt that the union held the majority support of the workers. The company took that position based, in part, on its *presumption* that the replacements opposed the union. The union filed an unfair labor practice charge with the NLRB.
   a. Explain the reasoning that supports the company's *presumption* (without substantial evidentiary support) that the permanent replacements did not support the union.
   b. Can the NLRB lawfully adopt that *presumption?* Explain. See *National Labor Relations Board* v. *Curtin Matheson Scientific Inc.,* 494 U.S. 775 (1990).
2. In your opinion, what are the average blue-collar worker's biggest sources of job dissatisfaction? Can they be eliminated through collective bargaining? Explain.
3. In your opinion, what are the average white-collar worker's biggest sources of job dissatisfaction? What means do such workers have for eliminating those sources of dissatisfaction? Explain.
4. Imagine what the world will be like 50 years from

now. In what ways do you picture the worklife of the average American to have changed? Explain.

5. Imagine the ideal work world. How close does that picture come to the one you conjured up in response to question 4? What types, if any, of labor or other legislation would bring society closer to that ideal? Explain.

6. What societal changes over the past 30 years have affected the workplace the most, in your estimation? Has labor law kept pace with workplace changes? If not, what new legislation is necessary? Explain.

7. A union representing a bargaining unit comprising both men and women and multiple racial and ethnic groups demands to see detailed information that the employer keeps on wages paid to women and minorities, as well as hiring statistics about these members of the workforce.

   a. Should the employer be required to let the union see this data? Explain.

   b. What circumstances might affect your decision? See *Westinghouse Electric Corp.,* 239 NLRB No. 18 (1978).

   c. Suppose that, instead of asking for wage information, the union asked to see the questions, answers, and individual scores achieved by employees on psychological aptitude tests that the employer requires employees to take. If the employer refuses to turn these scores over, has it committed an unfair labor practice? Explain.

   d. Does this situation differ significantly from the previous situation? See *Detroit Edison Co.* v. *NLRB,* 440 U.S. 301 (1979).

8. Aavco Hardware Company learns that union organizers (not Aavco employees) have been passing out literature to Aavco employees in the Aavco parking lot, which is surrounded by a chainlink fence but does not have a closed gate or guardhouse. Aavco officials want to throw these "union instigators" off the property.

   a. Will the officials be committing an unfair labor practice if they do? Explain.

   b. Would it matter if Aavco had a general "no solicitation" rule? Explain.

   c. What if Aavco adopted a no solicitation rule only after the first union organizers started handing out literature? Explain. See *Central Hardware Co.* v. *NLRB,* 407 U.S. 539 (1972).

9. United Plant Guard Workers of America (UPGWA) sought union certification at Arbitron Security Services, Inc. The union and the company stipulated certain election procedures to be followed, including, among other things, the hours, date, and location at which balloting would be held and the posting of notices of the election. Several days before the election, the company posted notices of the election in several conspicuous locations. Two days before the election, the union mailed notices to employees listed on sheets supplied to the union by the company. The election was held on a regular payday. Out of 314 employees eligible to vote, a total of only 64 valid votes (26 of them for the union) were cast. The UPGWA petitioned the NLRB following the union's defeat, claiming that the low voter turnout led to the inference that notice of the election to the employees had been inadequate and that the election results should be set aside. What do you think the NLRB's response is likely to be? Explain. See *Iowa Security Services, Inc. and National Union, United Plant Guard Workers of America,* 269 NLRB No. 53 (1983–84 CCH NLRB ¶ 16,145), March 21, 1984.

10. A bargaining unit, consisting of 56 employees at the time of a union representation election, voted in favor of unionization by a vote of 29 to 23. The employer sought to have the election results nullified, alleging that six days prior to the election, a union official meeting with 20 employees had referred to a company vice president as a "stingy Jew." The company had witnesses to substantiate this claim, and the union did not deny it.

    a. Do you think the election results should be set aside? Explain. See *NLRB* v. *Silverman's Men's Wear, Inc.,* 656 F.2d 53 (3d Cir. 1981).

    b. Suppose, instead, union officers came to campaign meetings for a Japanese-owned company wearing T-shirts that said, "Remember Pearl Harbor" and "Japs speak with forked tongue and slant eyes." Do you think the result would be any different? Explain. See *YKK (U.S.A.) Inc. and Sandra M. Collins et al.,* 296 NLRB No. 8 (1983–84 CCH NLRB ¶ 16,158), March 8, 1984.

11. The Clayton Act (see Chapters 10 and 11) exempts union wage negotiations from the antitrust laws. Workers in many different and competing companies may lawfully join together to form a single bargaining unit (for example, the Teamsters union). Of course, the antitrust laws forbid competing companies from joining together in the manner workers are allowed to do. Economist Gary Becker of the

University of Chicago argues that the time has come to treat union conspiracies in the same manner as those of management. Becker argues for replacing traditional trade unions with company unions (unions limited in membership to a single company), such as those used in Japan. He says union shop laws and other protections could be strengthened so management could not dominate the union. He notes the general decline of union membership in the United States: "In 1955 one of every three members of the U.S. labor force belonged to a union, compared with 17 percent in 1987." He believes these declines are largely due to the growth of such protections as unemployment compensation, social security, medicare, and new barriers against unfair dismissals. Should labor unions be fully subject to the antitrust laws? Explain. See Gary Becker, "It's Time to Scrap a Few Outmoded Labor Laws," *Business Week,* March 7, 1988, p. 18.

12. Consider the following account of a contrast in labor–management relations in the United States and Japan.

> By 1989 Nippon Steel planned to reduce jobs in steel by 19,000 (41 percent of the work force). However, Nippon did not intend to dismiss "surplus personnel" or to offer voluntary retirement. Those workers were to be reemployed elsewhere in the steel division, or they were to be retrained for new jobs in other divisions. On the other hand, USX (the American leader in steel) released some 87,000 workers from 1980 to 1987. Of course, those workers received many benefits, such as jobless pay, insurance, and early retirements. Nonetheless, USX officials explained that company health took priority over worker welfare. Executive Vice President Bruce Johnson remarked that "it would have been futile to devise a human relations strategy ahead of a business strategy" during the massive cutbacks in steel.

Do you support the Nippon approach or that at USX, or are the situations simply not comparable? Explain. See Associated Press, "Japanese Job Traditions under Attack," *Des Moines Register,* October 8, 1987, p. 9S.

13. Section 8(a)(3) of the National Labor Relations Act permits a labor–management agreement requiring all employees to pay a sum equivalent to union dues even though they may not choose to become members of the union (an *agency shop*). Some employees who had chosen not to join the union but who were paying the equivalent of dues claimed that their money had been misused because the union allegedly spent funds on such activities as organizing the employees of other companies, lobbying, and participating in social, charitable, and political events. May a union lawfully expend nonmember dues in support of activities unrelated to collective bargaining? See *Communications Workers of America* v. *Beck,* 487 U.S. 735 (1988).

14. A union–management dispute led to an economic strike, at which point the employer hired replacement workers. At the end of the strike, the workforce consisted of 25 former strikers and 69 replacement workers. The agreement settling the strike provided that strikers would be recalled as vacancies arose. However, the employer did not follow the agreement when it recalled four workers (three of whom were replacements) and failed to consider any of 28 strikers who remained out of work.

Well-settled labor law provides that "economic strikers who have been permanently replaced but who have unconditionally offered to return to work are entitled to reinstatement upon the departure of the replacements." The NLRB found a violation of the National Labor Relations Act, and framed the issue as follows: "How should the layoff of the permanent replacement worker—who has a contractual right to recall—affect the reinstatement rights of unreinstated strikers? The NLRB ruled that it would require a showing that the laid-off replacements had no "reasonable expectancy of recall." Then the burden of proof would shift to the employer to justify its failure to recall strikers when vacancies arose. The NLRB decision was appealed. Decide. Explain. See *Aqua-Chem Inc.* v. *NLRB,* 910 F.2d 1487 (7th Cir., 1990); cert. den., 111 S.Ct. 2871 (1991).

15. Some employees were transferred from a unionized plant to a new location.
   a. Are the employees who were transferred to the new location still members of their original bargaining unit? Explain.
   b. What test should the National Labor Relations Board employ in deciding whether the employer must recognize and bargain with the

union in the new location? See *Gitano Group, Inc.,* 308 NLRB No. 173 (1992).

16. A field organizer for the International Brotherhood of Electrical Workers (IBEW) sought work with a nonunion electrical firm. In applying for a job as an electrician, the organizer told the company that he would use his time during lunch and after work in an effort to organize employees. Indeed, while his application was being processed, he organized a picket line at the company to protest low wages. The foreman then told the organizer that he would

not be hired because "it's kind of hard to hire you when you're out there on the other side, picketing." Had he been hired, the organizer acknowledged that he would have maintained some relationship with the union, and he would likely have later returned to full-time employment with the union.

Was the organizer unlawfully denied employment? Explain. See *Willmar Electric Service, Inc.* v. *National Labor Relations Board,* 968 F.2d 1327 (D. of Col. Cir., 1992); cert. den., 113 S.Ct. 1252 (1993).

NOTES

1. Kevin Salwen, "Is the Glass 89% Empty or 11% Full?" *The Wall Street Journal,* September 21, 1993, p. B13.

2. Louis Rukeyser, ed., *Louis Rukeyser's Business Almanac* (New York: Simon & Schuster, 1988), p. 60.

3. Ibid.

4. The historical and political background information used in this chapter was drawn from a number of sources and amalgamated in such a way that precise footnoting was difficult. Many of the sociological trends described, for example, are discussed in three or four sources. The author (first edition) would, therefore, like to acknowledge the works of the following people, whose research and insights proved to be invaluable resources on which to draw: Richard S. Belous, Hyman Berman, Angela Y. Davis, Richard Edwards, John J. Flagler, Eli Ginzberg, J. David Greenstone, Isaac A. Hourwich, and Sar A. Levitan.

    Amy Gershenfeld Donnella, the author of this chapter (first edition), would like especially to acknowledge and thank Professor Archibald Cox, from whom she took a course in labor law in 1978, and whose textbook and class lectures provided the cornerstone of her understanding of the subject. The author hopes that her own good fortune at having had the opportunity to study labor law under Professor Cox will translate into a richer educational experience for students using this textbook.

5. Archibald Cox, with Derek Bok and Robert A. Gorman, *Cases and Materials on Labor Law,* 8th ed. (Mineola, N.Y.: Foundation Press, 1977), pp. 7–8.

6. Richard Edwards, *Contested Terrain: The Transformation of the Workplace in the Twentieth Century* (New York: Basic Books, 1979), pp. 40–41.

7. John J. Flagler, *The Labor Movement in the United States* (Minneapolis: Lerner Publications, 1972), pp. 26–33.

8. Cox, *Labor Law,* p. 8.

9. Isaac A. Hourwich, *Immigration and Labor* (New York: Arno Press, 1969), pp. 125–45.

10. Cox, *Labor Law,* p. 9.

11. Flagler, *Labor Movement,* pp. 26–28.

12. Ibid.

13. Hourwich, *Immigration and Labor,* pp. 232–49.

14. Eli Ginzberg and Hyman Berman, *The American Worker in the Twentieth Century: A History through Autobiographies* (New York: Free Press, 1963), pp. 193–95, in *I Am a Woman Worker,* ed. Andria Taylor Hourwich and Gladys L. Palmer, Affiliated Schools for Workers, 1936, pp. 17 ff.

15. Flagler, *Labor Movement,* pp. 33 and 36, quoting Frederick Lewis Allen, *The Big Change . . .* 1900–1950.

16. Ibid., p. 47.

17. J. David Greenstone, *Labor in American Politics* (New York: Alfred A. Knopf, 1969), p. 21.

18. Cox, *Labor Law,* p. 11.

19. Greenstone, *Labor in American Politics,* p. 22.

20. Ibid., p. 23.

21. Flagler, *Labor Movement,* pp. 81–83.

22. Greenstone, *Labor in American Politics,* pp. 41–42.

23. Cox, *Labor Law,* pp. 86–87.

24. Ibid., pp. 87–88.

25. Ibid., p. 88.

26. Flagler, *Labor Movement,* pp. 54–56.

27. Cox, *Labor Law,* pp. 60–66.

28. Greenstone, *Labor in American Politics,* p. 83.

29. Ibid., p. 47.

30. Cox, *Labor Law,* p. 91.

31. Ibid., p. 94.

32. Ibid., pp. 1,107–08.

33. Ibid., p. 1,108.

34. The National Labor Relations Act is found in Title 29 U.S.C. § 151 et seq.

35. Cox, *Labor Law,* pp. 113–22.

36. Ibid., pp. 99–101.

37. See, for example, *Dal-Tex Optical Co.,* 137 NLRB No. 27 (1962), in which repeated references are made to the departure in the election process from "laboratory conditions."

38. See Section 8(c) of the Taft-Hartley Act.

39. Littler, Mendelson, Fastiff & Tichy, *The 1990 Employer,* vol. 2, p. U-17.

40. Benjamin J. Taylor and Fred Witney, *Labor Relations Law,* 4th ed., (Englewood Cliffs, N.J.: Prentice Hall, 1983), p. 406.

41. *Majure Transport Company v. NLRB,* 198 F.2d 735 (1952).

42. *NLRB v. Norfolk Shipbuilding & Drydock Corporation,* 172 F.2d 813 (1949).

43. *Southern Saddlery Company,* 90 NLRB 1205 (1950).

44. Littler et al., *The 1990 Employer,* vol. 2, p. V-13. Citing *Reichhold Chemicals, Inc.,* 288 NLRB no. 8 (1988).

45. Ibid. Citing *NLRB v. Crockett-Bradley, Inc.,* 598 F.2d 971 (5th Cir. 1979).

46. *NLRB v. General Electric Company,* 418 F.2d 736 (1969).

47. *NLRB v. Insurance Agents' International Union,* 361 U.S. 477 (1960).

48. 361 U.S. at 480–481.

49. 361 U.S. at 482, citing 119 NLRB 769–771.

50. 361 U.S. at 488.

51. *NLRB v. Truitt Mfg. Co.,* 351 U.S. 149 (1956).

52. *NLRB v. Katz,* 369 U.S. 736 (1962).

53. See, for example, *First National Maintenance Corporation v. NLRB,* 101 S.Ct. 2573 (1981).

54. 356 U.S. 342 (1958).

55. 369 U.S. 736 (1962).

56. Daniel Seligman, "Unions and Strikers: A Huge Nonproblem," *Fortune,* May 31, 1993, p. 175.

57. Littler et al., *The 1990 Employer,* vol. 2, p. V-6.

58. *NLRB v. Mackay Radio & Tel. Co.,* 304 U.S. 333 (1938).

59. Littler et al., *The 1990 Employer,* vol. 2, p. V-6.

60. Cliff Edwards, "Companies Turn Up Pressure by Locking Out Protesting Workers," *Waterloo Courier,* July 4, 1993, p. C3.

61. *United Steelworkers of America v. Sadlowski,* 457 U.S. 102 (1982).

62. *Sadlowski v. United Steelworkers of America,* 645 F.2d 1114, 1124 (D.C. Cir. 1981).

63. Zech and Kuhn, "National Labor Policy: Is It Truly Designed to Protect the Worker?" Selected Papers of the American Business Law Association: *National Proceedings,* 1982, at 442–43.

PART

V

BUSINESS AND SELECTED SOCIAL PROBLEMS

15

CONSUMER PROTECTION

●

INTRODUCTION

Consumer protection organizations argue that wrongs against buyers are common-place. Clearly, fraud, misleading advertising, faulty products, and the like exact a heavy price in personal injuries and dollars. Furthermore, as the following Sears episode suggests, wrongdoing or even the mishandling of allegations of wrongdoing can be extremely expensive for American businesses.

SEARS IS ACCUSED OF BILLING FRAUD AT AUTO CENTERS

Tung Yin

The California Department of Consumer Affairs accused Sears, Roebuck & Co. of systematically over-charging auto-repair customers, and the agency proposed revoking the company's license to operate 72 automotive centers in the state.

Prompted by a growing number of consumer complaints, the department conducted a yearlong under-cover investigation of billing practices at 33 Sears centers from Los Angeles to Sacramento. It found that its agents were overcharged nearly 90% of the time, by an average of $223. The department said Sears pressured repairmen to overcharge by setting punitive sales quotas. The agency alleged violations of state law including making false and misleading

statements, fraud, willful departure from accepted trade practices and false advertising.

* * * * *

A Sears spokesman said that "we strongly disagree" with the state's allegations . . .

Auto-repair fraud is considered common by law-enforcement officials and consumer groups, but most cases involve individual garages. The Sears case may be the biggest fraud action yet against an auto-repair operator. Moreover, although the investigation was conducted only within California, the department believes Sears's alleged overcharging extends to automotive centers in other states. Sears operates 850 auto-repair centers nationwide.

* * * * *

The investigation occurred in two phases. In the first, undercover agents took 38 cars with worn brakes but no other mechanical defects to 27 Sears automotive centers throughout California from December 1990 to December 1991. In 34 instances, or 89%, agents were told that additional and more expensive repairs were needed. The worst example was in the San Francisco suburb of Concord, where an agent was overcharged $585 to have the front brake pads, front and rear springs, and control-arm bushings replaced . . .

In the second phase, the department informed Sears of the investigation in December 1991, and then conducted 10 more tests in January, of which seven resulted in unnecessary repairs. The auto repair centers stopped selling unnecessary springs and shocks but still overcharged the agents, although the average amount was down to $100, the state said.

The department believes that pressure from corporate headquarters led to the overcharges. The complaints began shortly after Sears established a quota of parts and services and repair sales for every eight-hour shift [according to Jim Conran, department director]. Employees also were instructed to sell a certain number of shock absorbers or struts for every hour of work. Those who failed to meet these quotas, Mr. Conran said, had their work hours reduced or were transferred out of the department.

Sears responded that the department's undercover investigation was seriously flawed. In particular, the test cars were generally older than typical cars used in California, and therefore had problems the department wasn't focused on, said Dirk Schenkkan, an attorney . . . who has been retained by Sears in the matter.

Mr. Schenkkan also disputes the department's allegations on sales quotas. "That is not the practice," he said. "Sears has established sales goals as guides. These goals are based on surveys of the public's needs."

Source: *The Wall Street Journal,* June 12, 1992, p. B1. Reprinted by permission of *The Wall Street Journal,* © 1992 Dow Jones & Company, Inc. All Rights Reserved Worldwide.

Afterword

Following the California charges, Sears placed full-page ads in a number of newspapers denying the allegations. Chairman Edward Brennan acknowledged that "mistakes may have occurred," but Sears's policy was to recommend "preventive maintenance measures to help insure your safety, [including] recommending replacement of worn parts, when appropriate, before they fail. This accepted industry practice is being challenged by the bureau."[1]

Soon after the California troubles came to light, Sears was accused of similar misdeeds in New Jersey. However, undercover investigations in New York and Illinois found relatively few problems. Then, in late June 1992, after two weeks of unfavorable publicity, Brennan announced that he was accepting personal responsibility for the troubles and that the company was discontinuing the "quota" system of employee compensation that apparently provoked the problems. Nonetheless, legal pressure and declining sales persisted. In the months following the initial scandal, Sears estimated that its auto repair sales were off 15 percent nationwide, for a loss of approximately $700,000 per day.

Settlement.   Sears decided to negotiate. In what is believed to be the largest settlement of its kind in history, in September 1992, about three months after the charges were raised, Sears agreed to provide $50 in coupons for each purchase of certain Sears auto parts (e.g., shock absorbers) between August 1, 1990, and January 31, 1992. Ultimately, Sears paid approximately $15 million in refunds and other costs. While continuing to deny intentional wrongdoing, Sears agreed to substitute a salary plan for its commission system. At this writing in 1994, some states have announced that they intend to investigate Sears' practices once again because they believe that Sears has continued to use a variation on its original commission plan. Sears says that their compensation system safeguards against abuse.[2]

Corporate Concern.   Whether conduct like that alleged above is routine in the business community is the subject of dispute. But we do know that many companies not only obey the law as a matter of course but voluntarily impose on themselves standards in excess of the legal minima. For example, the Calderon Company of Locust Valley, New York, recalled one of its products, a child's mobile, when a 15-month-old boy was strangled by the mobile's 26-inch nylon cord. The mobile, which featured large stuffed animals, came with a warning label indicating it should not be used for children under age three. The warning label had been removed.[3] Similarly, Artsana of America of New York recalled its "Spinning Windmill Rattle" out of fear that the toy might be a choking hazard for children. The company had received no reports of actual choking incidents involving the toy.[4] The companies initiated these recalls in cooperation with the federal Consumer Product Safety Commission.

CONSUMERISM: PAST AND FUTURE

To the surprise of most, concern for the consumer is an ancient policy:

> Until the Age of Reason in England, nothing resembling the doctrine of caveat emptor [buyer beware] existed in the custom and usage of the trade. Throughout the Middle Ages, church manuals laid down strict standards for market conduct, including requirements for warranties of quality. In the marketplace, merchants who dealt with their neighbors on a face-to-face basis took care to safeguard the quality of their products.[5]

However, the market changed from the craftsperson, face-to-face approach of that era to the complexities of mass production. At the same time, the influence of the church in commercial matters receded profoundly. In America, scandals in foods and drugs and a general feeling of abuse by corporate giants led to what might be labeled the first wave of consumer protection. In 1906, Congress passed the Pure Food and Drug Act. Previously, drugs had been largely unregulated and the public was regularly victimized by "patent" medicines, often either valueless, addictive, or both. Upton Sinclair's book, *The Jungle,* brought the filthy conditions in the meatpacking industry vividly to the public eye. Then, in 1914, Congress created the Federal Trade Commission to stem "unfair methods of competition."

Second Wave

Consumer concerns were muted during World War I and the prosperous 1920s, but the Depression of the 1930s provoked a second wave of protection. In the private sector, Consumers Union and its magazine, *Consumer Reports,* was founded. President Roosevelt appointed a Consumers Advisory Board, and during his administration Congress passed the Food, Drug and Cosmetic Act of 1938, which provided for the seizure of food, drugs, cosmetics, and therapeutic devices that were adulterated or misbranded. Likewise, in 1938, Congress passed the Wheeler-Lea Amendment to the Federal Trade Commission Act, which extended FTC jurisdiction to "unfair and deceptive acts or practices in commerce."

Third Wave

The third major wave of consumer protection activity was felt in the mid-1960s, largely through the efforts of the quintessential consumer activist Ralph Nader. Nader's bestselling book, *Unsafe at Any Speed,* led to the demise of General Motors' Corvair. Nader has been an enormously influential voice in the passage of many pieces of legislation. He has attacked virtually every segment of American commerce. In concert with his "Nader's Raiders" (student aides) and other allies, he has marshaled untiring research, the law, and public opinion to reshape consumer protection law. He became such an aggravation to General Motors that the company hired a law firm that then hired private detectives to investigate Nader in the hope of discrediting him. The head of the detective agency allegedly encouraged his subordinates to find out what they could about Nader's "women, boys, etc." Nader learned of the scheme and sued GM. The suit was settled out of court, and GM President James Roche publicly apologized to Nader.[6]

For a variety of reasons, the consumer movement cooled in the late 1970s and 1980s. However, the public's strong appreciation for consumer protection is well documented. As commentator Robert Samuelson reminds us, America has changed.

> Twenty years ago, the vague concepts of "social responsibility" and "consumerism" barely existed; now (diluted, to be sure) they are the conventional wisdom, even in business . . . And, . . . Nader's social regulation—of everything from auto safety to pollution—has triumphed.[7]

COMMON LAW CONSUMER PROTECTION

Later in this chapter we will explore government efforts to protect us from misleading advertising, unfair lending practices, and the like. Before turning to that legislation, we need to appreciate the common law (judge-made law) that preceded and, in some respects, provided the foundation for the striking federal, state, and local initiatives of recent years. In addition to the product liability protection (negligence, warranties, and strict liability) discussed in Chapter 16, the injured consumer can look to several common law "protections," including actions for fraud, misrepresentation, and unconscionability.

Fraud and Innocent Misrepresentation

If the market is to operate efficiently, the buyer must be able to rely on the truth of the seller's affirmations regarding a product. Regrettably, willful untruths appear common in American commerce. The victim of fraud is entitled to rescind the contract in question and to seek damages, including, in cases of malice, a punitive recovery. While fraud arises in countless situations and thus is difficult to define, the legal community has generally adopted the following elements, each of which must be proven:

1. A misrepresentation of a material fact with knowledge of the falsehood.
2. Intent to deceive.
3. Justifiable reliance on the falsehood by the injured party.
4. Damages resulting from reliance on the falsehood.

In identifying a fraudulent expression, the law distinguishes between statements of objective, verifiable facts and simple expressions of opinion. The latter ordinarily are not fraudulent even though they are erroneous. Thus, normal sales "puffing" ("This baby is the greatest little car you're ever gonna drive") is fully lawful, and the consumer is expected to exercise her own good judgment in responding to such claims. However, if a misleading expression of opinion comes from an expert, and the other party does not share that expertise (e.g., the sale of a diamond engagement ring), a court probably would offer a remedy.

Silence.   In limited circumstances, silence may constitute fraud. Typically, that problem may emerge where Party A misunderstands the facts of the situation and Party B both knows the true facts and knows that A does not know those facts and cannot reasonably be expected to discover them. An example would be a cracked engine block, where the cracks were filled with a sealer and covered with a compound such that the crack is unlikely to be discovered even by capable inspection.[8] In such situations, the knowledgeable party may be under a duty to speak. Nonetheless, the general rule is that silence is fully permissible.

Of course, fraud can involve false conduct as well as false expression. A familiar example is the car seller who rolls back an odometer with the result that the buyer is misled.

A variation on the general theme of fraud is *innocent misrepresentation,* which differs from fraud only in that the falsehood was unintentional. The wrongdoer believed the statement or conduct in question to be true, but he or she was mistaken. In such cases, the wronged party may secure rescission of the contract, but ordinarily damages are not awarded.

Before plunging into the fraud case that follows, take a moment to reflect on the extreme complexity in reaching a societal judgment about which conduct should constitute a wrong. Is the use of an unmarked patrol car a fraud against the public? Is a party to a marriage contract guilty of fraud in failing to disclose his or her propensity to snore? Should a seller be expected to disclose all that is known about his or her product? Is a university guilty of fraud where it purports in its catalogs, inscriptions, and so on to purvey wisdom, but a student does not believe wisdom has been delivered?[9]

PELSTER v. RAY
987 F.2d 514 (8th Cir. 1993)

Circuit Judge Wollman

Vernon and Michelle Pelster bought a used car on which the odometer had been rolled back. The Pelsters brought claims against Gary Ray and Cletus Dwight Grace for rolling back the odometer. They alleged separate counts under federal and state odometer statutes and Missouri's common law of fraud. The Pelsters brought similar claims against Earl Wayne Morton ("Wayne Morton") and Joyce Morton for passing the rolled-back car through their wholesale auto auction, the South Central Auto Auction ("South Central") . . . The jury found for the Pelsters, assessing both compensatory and punitive damages against all four defendants. Ray and Grace were not present at the trial and have not filed an appeal. The Mortons, however, appeal . . .

I

The Pelsters began their odyssey through the world of used cars in the fall of 1988. Like countless other American families, they determined that they had outgrown their present automobile and decided to look for a dependable low-mileage used car that could accommodate "the kids and stuff." In the course of their car shopping, the Pelsters discovered a four-door 1986 Oldsmobile Cutlass Ciera (the "Ciera") on the lot of Modern Auto Co. ("Modern Auto") in Washington, Missouri. The Ciera was clean and appeared to have a low number of miles (37,344) on it. After a test drive and the usual thrust and parry of negotiation, the Pelsters bought the Ciera for $7,400, plus additional charges for a service agreement and financing.

As the Pelsters later learned, their new purchase was hardly the meticulously cared-for cream puff that all used car buyers dream about. Instead, the Ciera had just completed its travels through the shadowy netherworld of used car wholesalers and dealers. It had entered that world as a high-mileage lease car; by the end of its journey, however, the Ciera had emerged with the rejuvenated outward appearance of a clean low-mileage dream car.

Kevco Limited, an Ohio leasing company, originally bought the Ciera in December 1984 from a dealership in Columbus, Ohio. As is customary in the auto leasing business, Kevco Limited leased the Ciera for approximately two and a half years, and then in August 1988 sold the Ciera to Chase Motors, Inc. ("Chase Motors"). At the time of the transfer, Kevco Limited certified to Chase Motors that the Ciera's odometer reading of 95,804 miles was correct. Chase Motors obtained a new Ohio title, on the front of which was written the 95,804 mileage figure representing the miles on the car at the time Chase Motors bought it . . .

A few weeks later, Chase Motors sold the car to U.S. Wholesales through the Ohio Auto Auction. According to the Ohio Auto Auction check-in sheet, the mileage on the Ciera at that point was 96,242. U.S. Wholesales, or at least a group of individuals involved with U.S. Wholesales, appears to have been in the business of rolling back the odometers on used cars. U.S. Wholesales was a registered car dealer licensed to operate in Paragould, Arkansas, although it apparently conducted its operations in Murray, Kentucky. Information concerning the ownership, organization, and membership of U.S. Wholesales is sketchy, at best; it appears, however, that at least twenty or more individuals were involved with the organization in some manner. Those individuals included Dave Manier (identified by some as the owner of U.S. Wholesales), Larry Shelton, Gary Ray, Aaron "Red" Morris, Cletus Dwight Grace, and Tommy Jones. (The organization and all of these individuals will be collectively referred to as "U.S. Wholesales.")

On September 7, 1988, Dixon Motors of Washington, Missouri, bought the Ciera from U.S. Wholesales at South Central's weekly auction. Dixon Motors received the Ohio title listing Chase Motors as the owner of record. The mileage figure on that title stating the number of miles on the odometer at the time Chase Motors had purchased the vehicle had been changed from 95,804 to 35,804. In the reassignment section on the title's back, the writing showed that Chase Motors had sold the Ciera to U.S. Wholesales with a mileage reading of 36,242.

It is unclear exactly how the paperwork for the transfer between U.S. Wholesales and Dixon Motors changed hands. The paperwork does show that U.S. Wholesales and Dixon Motors did not complete the space for a second reassignment on the back of the Ohio title; instead, Dixon Motors received a separate Arkansas Dealer's Reassignment of Title form (the "dealer's reassignment") from U.S. Wholesales. Dealers and wholesalers commonly use such reassignment forms when transferring vehicles among themselves rather than completing the reassignment section on the back of the title itself. The dealer's reassignment contained what purported to be the signature of Dave Manier on behalf of U.S. Wholesales as seller. According to the dealer's reassignment, Manier's signature had been notarized by Vorea Tackett on September 6, 1988. It remains unknown who actually signed the dealer's reassignment (whether it was Dave Manier or somebody else on his behalf) and who Vorea Tackett was.

In her deposition, which counsel for the Pelsters read into evidence at trial, Joyce Morton admitted that she had completed part of the dealer's reassignment. She testified that she had written "miles 36904" near the top of the dealer's reassignment. She also testified that she had filled in Dixon Motors's name and address as buyer.

After Dixon Motors had obtained a fresh Missouri title in its own name, it sold the Ciera to Modern Auto on September 19, 1988. Dixon Motors completed the first reassignment section on the back of its Missouri title and there certified that, to the best of its knowledge, the Ciera had travelled 36,968 miles as reflected on the odometer . . .

As noted above, the Pelsters ultimately purchased the Ciera from Modern Auto. In addition to giving the Pelsters a vehicle invoice describing the terms of the sale, Modern Auto reassigned the Ciera's title to the Pelsters by completing a second reassignment on the back of the title that Modern Auto had received from Dixon Motors (the Missouri title listed in Dixon Motors's name). Also, as required by federal and Missouri law, Modern Auto completed an odometer statement certifying that, to the best of its knowledge, the Ciera's actual mileage was 37,344 and the odometer had not been altered or repaired. Vernon Pelster signed this odometer statement to acknowledge that he had received it.

The Pelsters first learned of the Ciera's true history when they received a letter from Tom Ley, an investigator for the Missouri Department of Revenue. The Pelsters subsequently filed this suit.

Both Vernon and Michelle Pelster testified that they had relied on the odometer itself and the odometer statement provided by Modern Auto in making their decision to purchase the Ciera . . .

The Pelsters called Tom Ley to the stand. Ley described himself as a criminal investigator specializing in vehicle theft and odometer fraud for the Missouri Department of Revenue. In outlining his qualifications and work experience, Ley stated that he had conducted 50–60 odometer fraud investigations in the five years that he had worked for the Department of Revenue.

Ley described the general investigative techniques that he customarily uses in his work. He testified that he attempts to trace a vehicle's title history back through its various owners to the manufacturer. He stated that in the course of an investigation he speaks with dealers and obtains from them whatever documentation they can provide, usually titles, odometer statements, repair records, and bills of sale. He further stated that he also talks to auto auctions; he seeks similar documents from them, often including the auction's check-in sheets (also known as "block sheets"), which contain a description of the car and its current odometer reading. He testified that he contacts former owners of the vehicle, seeking oral and written information about the vehicle's mileage. Finally, he stated that he obtains copies of titles, odometer statements, and other documents from government agencies in the various states in which the vehicle had been titled. He testified that he had followed this procedure in investigating the roll-back of the Ciera.

Ley described generally how the roll-back game operates. He explained how people alter or roll back a car's odometer. Ley also explained how people physically alter the vehicle's documentation (titles and odometer statements) to match the new numbers on the odometer. Finally, over the Mortons' objection, Ley testified regarding the general reputation among dealers and auctioneers as to where rolled-back cars originate. He stated that, according to the reputation, rolled-back cars often come from Kentucky; Paragould, Arkansas; Oklahoma; Texas; and Lebanon, Missouri.

Counsel for the Pelsters then directed Ley's testimony to the history of the Ciera. Counsel walked Ley through the various documents that accompanied the Ciera through its transfers, including copies of titles, odometer statements, and auction check-in sheets. Having explained the contents of these various documents, Ley opined that the Ciera had been rolled back during the time that it was in the possession of U.S. Wholesales and before it passed through South Central.

Counsel then led Ley through a more general discussion of his investigation of U.S. Wholesales and South Central. This testimony included a discussion of four cars (the "PH & H cars") originally owned by Peterson, Howell & Heather, a large auto leasing firm. Over the Mortons' objection, the magistrate judge admitted documents showing that the four PH & H cars had passed through South Central and W.W. Motors (Wayne Morton's separate auto dealership located in West Plains, Missouri) in late 1988, and that the odometers had probably been rolled back during the time they were in the possession of South

Central or W.W. Motors. All of this testimony constituted "similar acts evidence," which the Pelsters offered to prove that the Mortons knew that U.S. Wholesales was selling rolled-back cars through their auction and that the Mortons intended for subsequent purchasers to rely on false mileage representations made on the vehicles' titles and odometer statements.

Finally, counsel asked Ley to provide the general results of his investigation of U.S. Wholesales and South Central. Over the Mortons' objection, Ley testified that he had investigated 350 vehicles that had passed through South Central. Of those 350 cars, Ley testified that 300 of them had been rolled back when they went through South Central. Ley also testified that he had investigated 210 cars that U.S. Wholesales had rolled back. Of those 210 cars, Ley stated that U.S. Wholesales had sold 204 of them through South Central.

Counsel for the Pelsters also read into evidence excerpts from Wayne Morton's deposition. Wayne Morton testified that he had been involved in the automobile business since 1960, spending much of that time working as an employee or owner of auto auctions. He stated that in March 1988 he had started up South Central with Joyce Morton (then known as Joyce Adams), Clarence Page, and Suzanne Jones, verbally agreeing that all four would share the auction's profits. He testified that between March 1988 and January 1989, South Central handled approximately 200 to 250 cars per week. He asserted that part of his duties at South Central had included "supervising the office," yet he denied that he had known what paperwork was passing through the office and how the office workers were handling that paperwork. He further denied having any knowledge that Joyce Morton had been signing or notarizing titles and odometer statements for vehicles that had been sold at South Central, although he identified her signature on several titles and odometer statements at his deposition.

He admitted that Mel Dixon, owner of Dixon Motors, told him at some point during South Central's brief existence that Dixon Motors was being forced to buy back some cars that it had bought from U.S. Wholesales at South Central. He further admitted that Mel Dixon had said that the repurchase was due to "odometer discrepancies" with the cars. He stated that he had instructed Mel Dixon to meet with U.S. Wholesales at the next auction and settle the problem. He admitted that he had continued to do business as usual with U.S. Wholesales after he had received this notice that U.S. Wholesales had sold rolled-back cars at his auction. In fact, U.S. Wholesales was the largest volume seller of cars at South Central during its existence.

Wayne Morton also admitted personally rolling back and selling three cars in December 1988. He did this under the name of W.W. Motors and did not sell the three cars through South Central. He admitted in his testimony that he had pled guilty to charges involving the roll-back of these three cars. The Pelsters subsequently offered into evidence Wayne Morton's record of conviction on three counts of mail fraud relating to the three rolled-back cars.

Finally, counsel for the Pelsters read into evidence excerpts from Joyce Morton's deposition, in which she stated that she had worked in the office at South Central. She testified that her duties had included writing checks, collecting accounts receivable, handling payroll, and taking care of the paperwork on sale days. Contrary to her husband's description of South Central's procedures, she stated that she and her co-workers in the office customarily had filled out titles, dealer reassignments, and odometer statements on behalf of both buyers and sellers at the auction. She stated that in completing such paperwork she and her co-workers had merely transferred the mileage numbers from the check-in sheets without verifying their accuracy. She admitted that she had signed Dave Manier's signature on behalf of U.S. Wholesales several times and that she had often notarized Manier's signature when in fact one of her co-workers had signed his name. As noted above, she specifically admitted writing "miles 36904" on the dealer's reassignment for the Ciera.

The Mortons did not offer any testimony in their defense. At the conclusion of the Pelsters' case, the Mortons each moved separately for a directed verdict, which the magistrate judge denied . . . The jury returned a verdict in favor of the Pelsters, awarding actual damages in the amount of $6,400 and assessing punitive damages in the amount of $50,000 each against Grace, Ray, and Wayne Morton, and $25,000 against Joyce Morton.

II

The Mortons initially challenge the magistrate judge's denial of their motions for a directed verdict. To survive the motions for a directed verdict, the Pelsters needed to produce sufficient evidence to allow a reasonable jury to find that they had proven the following elements of Missouri common law fraud with respect to Wayne and Joyce Morton:

> (1) A representation. (2) Its falsity. (3) Its materiality. (4) The speaker's knowledge of its falsity or ignorance of its truth. (5) His intent that it should be acted on by the person and in the manner reasonably contemplated. (6) The hearer's ignorance of its falsity. (7) His reliance on its truth. (8) His right to rely thereon . . .

* * * * *

Having scrutinized the record, we find that the Pelsters introduced sufficient evidence to support a fraudulent concealment claim against Wayne Morton based on his superior knowledge. They presented evidence that a substantial number of cars with rolled-back odometers passed through their auction. Wayne Morton admitted that his duties included "overseeing the office." Given the overwhelming pervasiveness of the improper office practices of filling out titles and odometer statements, practices seemingly designed to hide altered odometers, the jury would be entitled to find that Wayne Morton knew that U.S. Wholesales was selling rolled-back cars through South Central. The jury could also reasonably make the next logical inference that Wayne Morton knew that the Ciera had been rolled back.

Having concluded that the Mortons, as wholesale auctioneers, had a duty not to affirmatively misrepresent or knowingly conceal a vehicle's true mileage, the question still remains whether the Pelsters sufficiently showed that any alleged fraudulent conduct by the Mortons proximately caused their damages. It is true that allowing a purchaser two or three links down the chain of title to sue a wholesale auto auction means that there will be intervening owners of the vehicle who may have known of the fraud and may have had a better opportunity than the wholesale auctioneer to disclose the misrepresentation. In this case, the Mortons argue that either Dixon Motors or Modern Auto could have disclosed the roll-back and ended the Ciera's fraudulent journey through the channels of commerce. They conclude that the conduct of the intermediate dealers insulates their conduct from liability. They emphasize that Mel Dixon was the one who told Wayne Morton that two other U.S. Wholesales cars had been rolled back.

* * * * *

If the Mortons believed that either Dixon Motors or Modern Auto had taken some intervening action that cut off their liability, the Mortons bore the responsibility to present evidence to that effect, which they failed to do. Moreover, mere proof that Mel Dixon knew that U.S. Wholesales was rolling back cars would not excuse any misrepresentation or concealment on the Mortons' part; such evidence may expose Dixon Motors to liability, but it would not constitute a superseding cause of the Pelsters' damages . . .

We conclude that the Pelsters introduced sufficient evidence to create a jury question on all elements of their fraud claim, including the presence of a misrepresentation by the Mortons and its proximate causation of the Pelsters' damages. The magistrate judge, therefore, properly denied the Mortons' motions for a directed verdict.

III

We now turn to the admissibility of Tom Ley's testimony . . .

The Mortons challenge the admission of Ley's testimony on several grounds. They assert that his testimony violated the rule against hearsay because he based his testimony on out-of-court statements made in oral conversations and written documents; concerned matters on which Ley lacked personal knowledge; and, to the extent it was based on the contents of documents, violated the best evidence rule.

Ley admitted in his testimony that he had obtained his information (oral and written) from numerous out-of-court sources, including previous owners, dealers, auctions, state agencies, a "confidential informant," and various individuals connected with U.S. Wholesales. During most of his testimony, it was unclear upon which of those sources of information Ley was basing his testimony. Presumably, Ley's ultimate conclusions that 300 of 350 cars auctioned at South Central had been rolled back and that U.S. Wholesales had been responsible for 204 of those 300 rolled-back cars were based on all of the sources he identified.

We find that Ley's testimony constituted inadmissible hearsay . . .

* * * * *

. . . The Pelsters claim that Ley was an expert witness, who may base his opinions upon facts or data "of a type reasonably relied upon by experts in the particular field in forming inferences or opinions." . . .

* * * * *

. . . [W]e find that Ley's conclusions were inadmissible, even if he had been properly qualified as an expert. The Federal Rules of Evidence provide for the admission of expert testimony where it will "assist the trier of fact to understand the evidence or to determine a fact in issue." Conversely, "[w]here the subject matter is within the knowledge or experience of lay people, expert testimony is superfluous." The test for determining the appropriateness of expert testimony is "the common sense inquiry whether the untrained layman would be qualified to determine intelligently and to the best possible degree the particular issue without enlightenment from those having a specialized understanding of the subject involved in the dispute."

In this case, any lay person has the ability to compare the odometer readings on two titles, odometer statements, or check-in sheets and decide whether and when the vehicle's odometer had been rolled back . . .

* * * * *

Having determined that Ley's conclusions were based on hearsay and were not proper subjects of expert testimony, we find that Ley's testimony regarding the results of his investigation prejudiced the defendants . . .

* * * * *

We acknowledge that the Pelsters are now faced with a formidable and tedious task on retrial. In addition to presenting evidence to show the presence of a representation, their reliance, and causation, they must produce admissible documents or testimony on enough rolled-back vehicles to persuade the jury that the Mortons knew of the falsity of the Ciera's odometer reading. How many vehicles they will need to trace for the jury and how to present such evidence are questions of their trial strategy.

[Reversed and remanded.]

Questions

1. Summarize the evidence suggesting that the Mortons, through their South Central Auto Auction, had engaged in fraud.
2. Explain the Mortons' argument that they were not the *proximate cause* of the plaintiffs' injuries.
3. Explain why the appeals court reversed and remanded the lower court decision.
4. A beautiful Victorian house overlooking the Hudson River in New York was sold. The buyer subsequently concluded that the house was haunted and sued to rescind the contract. The seller conceded that she had, on several occasions, asserted that the house was haunted and had publicized it as such in the news media, but she admitted that she had not conveyed that opinion to the buyer (not a local resident). Does that failure to disclose amount to misrepresentation such that the contract should be rescinded? Explain. See *Stambovsky* v. *Ackley,* 572 N.Y.S. 2d 672 (1991).
5. The plaintiff, Herbert Williams, bought an auto on March 1968, in Milwaukee, Wisconsin. Williams had sought an air-conditioned car. A salesman for the defendant, Rank & Son Buick, Inc., said the car was air conditioned, and Williams noted a knob on the dash labeled "Air." Williams drove the car for one and a half hours prior to purchase, and he otherwise had ample opportunity for inspection. Several days after the purchase Williams discovered that "Air" referred only to ventilation. The car was not air conditioned. Williams sued. Decide the case. See *Williams* v. *Rank & Son Buick, Inc.,* 44 Wis.2d 239, 170 N.W.2d 807 (1969).

UNCONSCIONABLE CONTRACTS

The efficiency and success of the American economy depends, in no small part, on the reliability of contractual relationships. The buyer must know that the goods will be delivered, and the seller must know that the bill will be paid. It is, therefore, only with the greatest reluctance that the legal system intervenes in freely bargained arrangements. Jurists adopted the concept of unconscionability to nullify or reform contracts that are so unfair or oppressive as to demand societal intervention. Mere foolishness or a want of knowledge do not constitute grounds for unconscionability, nor is a contract unconscionable and hence unenforceable merely because one party is spectacularly clever and the other is not.

Unconscionability is a concept not easily pinned down, and so it should be. The Uniform Commercial Code (UCC 2–302) governs unconscionability. Some situations are so patently unfair that justice requires intervention, but we wish to do so only in rare instances when (1) the bargaining power of the parties was so unbalanced that the agreement was not truly freely entered or (2) the clause or contract in question is so unfair as to violate societal values.

For example, in the leading case, *Williams* v. *Walker-Thomas Furniture Company,*[10] the U.S. Court of Appeals for the District of Columbia explicitly held that the unconscionability provision of the UCC should be enforced under appropriate circumstances. In that case, the question was whether a furniture contract was unconscionable where the balance due on each item purchased by a particular buyer remained due until payments had been made on *all* items purchased by that buyer. Under the contract, the seller had the right to repossess all of the items previously purchased if the buyer failed to complete payments on even one item in a series of transactions. In your view, is that contract unconscionable? Explain.

The case that follows illustrates the application of unconscionability reasoning in an interesting situation far afield from conventional consumer protection.

DON KING PRODUCTIONS, INC. v. DOUGLAS
742 F. Supp. 778 (S.D.N.Y. 1990)

[James "Buster" Douglas, a professional boxer, and his manager John P. Johnson (assisted by Johnson's lawyer, Stephen Enz) entered into a boxing promotion agreement with Don King Productions on December 31, 1988. Douglas received $25,000 at the time. The contract gave DKP exclusive promotional rights for Douglas's boxing for three years. DKP expressed its intent to promote a world championship bout for Douglas. In the event Douglas became world champion, the contract was to be automatically extended for the full period of the championship and two years thereafter. The agreement promised at least 10 bouts over three years, with purses to be negotiated but with floors of $25,000 and $10,000 in expenses for each.

Douglas participated in three bouts, the last of which was a heavyweight championship fight with Mike Tyson in Tokyo, Japan, on February 10, 1990. Douglas's contract provided for a total of $1.3 million for that fight. Douglas knocked out Tyson in round 10, thus becoming the world champion. However, King, who was also Tyson's promoter, protested the outcome, using various means including public claims of a "long count" in round 8 when Tyson had knocked Douglas to the mat.

Johnson and King met in February 1990 to discuss a Douglas match that King planned for the Trump Plaza in Atlantic City, New Jersey. At about that time, the Mirage Hotel of Las Vegas contacted Johnson seeking to schedule a bout there. On February 21, 1990, Douglas and Johnson signed a contract with Mirage. The contract provided for a reported total of $60 million for two fights but required Douglas to secure a release from the contract with King or a court order voiding the contract.

DKP then sued Douglas and Johnson for breach of contract and the Mirage for interference with contract. Douglas and Johnson asserted counterclaims for slander and intentional infliction of emotional distress based on King's claims that Tyson should have been declared the winner and that Douglas was not a deserving champion. Those claims were rejected by the court. Douglas and Johnson also claimed their contract with DKP was *unconscionable.*]

Judge Sweet

* * * * *

The Unconscionable Contracts Defense

Douglas and Johnson plead as an affirmative defense that the contracts they entered into with DKP are unconscionable. Under New York law . . . a determination of unconscionability

> requires a showing that the contract was both procedurally and substantively unconscionable *when made*—i.e., "some showing of an 'absence of meaningful choice on the part of one of the parties together with contract terms which are unreasonably favorable to the other party.'" *Gillman v. Chase Manhattan Bank, N.A.,* 534 N.E.2d 824, 828 (1988).

The factual contentions set forth in the Douglas/Johnson interrogatories to support the unconscionability defense—that the Tokyo conduct of King was unconscionable, that King is a powerful promoter, and that exclusive, extendable terms of the contracts are unreasonably favorable to King—are as a matter of law insufficient.

The Douglas/Johnson contention that the contracts "became unconscionable" *after* their inception owing to King's conduct during the Tokyo fight is unavailing . . . The doctrine of unconscionability implicates the circumstances and terms of a contract at the time of formation—not the parties' subsequent performance under it . . . The Tokyo performance by King . . . has . . . absolutely no bearing on the defense of unconscionability, which relates to substantive and procedural fairness of a contract "when made."

Douglas/Johnson next contend that King so dominates promotion of heavyweight fights that the Douglas–King contracts are inherently procedurally unconscionable . . . Douglas/Johnson make no allegation here that deceptive or high-pressure tactics were employed in concluding the contracts, that contract terms were concealed in fine print, or that there was a gross asymmetry in the experience and education of the parties, each of whom was represented by counsel throughout the course of their arms-length negotiations.

. . . [T]he unconscionability defense does not here implicate its primary use as "a means with which to protect the commercially illiterate consumer beguiled into a grossly unfair bargain by a deceptive vendor or finance company." *Marvel Entertainment Group, Inc. v. Young Astronaut Council,* No. 88–5141, 1989 WL 129504 (S.D.N.Y. October 27, 1989). Without some definite allegation of a defect in the contract negotiation process apart from King's stature in the boxing field, which alone does not suggest "inequality so strong and manifest as to shock the conscience and confound the judgment," (quoting *Christian v. Christian,* 365 N.E.2d 849, 855 (1977), defendants have failed to create an issue of procedural unconscionability requiring resolution by jury.

The contention that the contracts require Douglas to fight exclusively for DKP for the extendable terms of such contracts, which could amount to the rest of the boxer's professional life, equally fails to satisfy the requirement of substantive unconscionability. Only in "exceptional cases" is "a provision of [a] contract . . . so outrageous as to warrant holding it unenforceable on the ground of substantive unconscionability alone." *Gillman,* 534 N.E.2d at 829 . . .

Douglas and Johnson . . . cite no case considering or holding an exclusive services contract unconscionable on grounds of duration . . . The court therefore declines to revisit its prior legal determinations that the contract durational terms were definite in nature and the contracts were supported by sufficiently-definite price consideration to induce Douglas' promise to fight exclusively for DKP. The unconscionability defense accordingly shall be stricken, there having been no proffer or allegation sufficient to establish either its procedural or substantive elements.

* * * * *

[So ordered.]

Afterword

King, Douglas, and the Mirage settled their dispute. King agreed to assign the promotion rights to the Douglas–Evander Holyfield fight to the owner of the Mirage, Steve Wynn. Douglas agreed to pay $4 million to King. Douglas lost to Holyfield but left boxing having earned some $30 million.

Questions

1. *a.* Why did the court reject Douglas's unconscionability argument?
   b. Do you agree with the court? Explain.
2. What does the court mean by its statement that a contract must be "both procedurally and substantively unconscionable?"
3. Plaintiff Willie had listed his business in the Wichita, Kansas, Yellow Pages for 13 years. Plaintiff was expanding his business, and he entered into an agreement with the defendant phone company to include additional telephone numbers in the directory. Defendant inadvertently failed to include one of the numbers in the directory. The contract signed by the parties included a conspicuous exculpatory clause limiting the phone company's liability for errors and omissions to an amount equal to the cost of the ad. On discovering the omission, plaintiff had begun advertising the number on television at a cost of approximately $5,000. Plaintiff contends the exculpatory clause is unconscionable and, therefore, unenforceable. Decide. Explain. See *Willie* v. *Southwestern Bell Telephone Company,* 549 P.2d 903 (Kan. 1976).
4. A door-to-door salesman representing Your Shop at Home Services, Inc., called on Clifton and Cora Jones, who were welfare recipients. The Jones couple decided to buy a freezer from the salesman for $900. Credit charges, insurance, and so on were added to that $900 base so that the total purchase price was $1,439.69. Mr. and Mrs. Jones signed a sales agreement that accurately stipulated the price and its ingredients. The Joneses sued to reform the contract on unconscionability grounds. They had paid $619.88 toward the total purchase price. At trial, the retail value of the new freezer at the time of purchase was set at approximately $300.
   a. What is the issue in this case?
   b. Decide. Explain. See *Jones* v. *Star Credit Corp.,* 298 N.Y.S. 2d 264 (1969).

THE CONSUMER AND GOVERNMENT REGULATION OF BUSINESS

Having established the common law foundation for consumer protection, we now turn to some of the many governmental measures that provide shelter in the often unforgiving marketplace. States and localities have adopted a wealth of protective measures, but those cannot be meaningfully summarized here. We will look primarily at a sample of federal activity. The reader is urged to continue confronting the question of the proper balance between the free market and government intervention.

The Federal Trade Commission (FTC)

Rule Making.   The Federal Trade Commission was created in 1914 to prevent "unfair methods of competition and unfair or deceptive acts or practices in and affecting commerce." In conducting its business, the FTC performs as a miniature government, with extensive and powerful quasi-legislative and quasi-judicial roles. The primary legislative direction is in issuing *trade regulation rules* to enforce the specific intent of broadly drawn congressional legislation. That is, the rules define with particularity those acts or practices that the commission deems unfair or deceptive. Violations of trade regulation rules are punished by civil penalties, injunctions, and other appropriate redress.

In the same vein, the FTC issues *industry guides,* which are the commission's interpretations of laws it enforces. The guides provide direction to the public, and although they do not have the force of law, a failure to observe the guides might result in adjudication.

The FTC's quasi-legislative role is well illustrated by its long and vigorously contested investigation of various funeral industry practices. After 10 years of inquiry, the FTC voted to require funeral directors to both itemize prices and quote them over the phone. Furthermore:

> [T]he rule requires funeral directors to "unbundle" funeral packages and allow customers to choose the services they want. It also prohibits embalming without a relative's permission, and forbids undertakers from misrepresenting the law to customers, such as saying embalming is required by a state when it is not.[11]

Critics of the rule argued that it was based more on anecdotes than on solid evidence. Supporters pointed to the great expense associated with funerals and the likelihood that consumers would not engage in careful shopping when dealing with the stress of a death.

Widespread public concern about environmental issues has led many marketers to emphasize the environmental protection advantages of their products. In 1992, the Federal Trade Commission issued industry guides to help prevent misleading "green" advertising and labeling. Broadly, the guidelines require a reasonable foundation in competent scientific evidence for any environmental claim. For example, ads or labels using the word *biodegradeable* must be supported by evidence demonstrating that the product will completely decompose within a reasonably short period of time after normal disposal.[12]

Questions

1. Why should the funeral industry be required to meet standards (for example, itemizing prices) not required in other industries?
2. How would you vote on the funeral industry rule? Explain.
3. Why were environmental claims given particular attention by the FDA?

Adjudication.   On its own initiative or as a result of a citizen complaint, the FTC may conduct investigations into suspect trade practices. At that point, the commission may drop the proceeding, settle the matter informally, or issue a formal complaint. An informal settlement normally takes the form of a consent agreement in which the party under investigation voluntarily discontinues the practice in question but is not required to admit guilt.

Car Rentals.   In 1992, Dollar Rent-A-Car and Value Rent-A-Car both agreed to settle FTC charges that they had failed to disclose mandatory "extra" charges when giving price quotations to potential customers. The FTC claimed that ads and telephone quotes failed to reveal extra charges such as required airport surcharges or fees for drivers beneath age 25. Neither company admitted any wrongdoing, and both said the alleged violations occurred under previous owners.[13]

Where an agreement cannot be reached, the commission may proceed with a formal complaint. In that case, the matter proceeds essentially as a trial conducted before an administrative law judge. Both the government and the "accused" party may be represented by counsel, and the proceeding is conducted in accordance with due process of law. If the government prevails, the judge may issue a cease and desist order forbidding further wrongful conduct. That order may be appealed to the full commission and to the federal Court of Appeals (assuming proper grounds for appeal).

The FTC is designed to prevent wrongdoing. Hence, it has no authority to impose criminal sanctions. Although it can impose fines, the commission often engages in more creative remedies—for example, ordering corrective advertising to counteract previous, misleading ads or requiring contracts to be altered. In the case of "high-pressure sales," the commission has allowed the consumer a cooling-off period in which to cancel a contract.

Deceptive Practices.   FTC regulatory efforts range across the spectrum of consumer activity. For example, the FTC issued a rule specifying that mail-order sellers are in violation of the Federal Trade Commission Act if they solicit orders through the mail without a reasonable expectation that the goods can be shipped in 30 days or less. The FTC has pursued broad-scale regulatory initiatives against a number of industries, including insurance, used autos, and credit cards; but perhaps the best examples of FTC rule-making and adjudicatory actions lie in the area of advertising.

Unfair and deceptive trade practices, including those in advertising, are forbidden under Section 5 of the Federal Trade Commission Act. The term *unfair* has been only loosely defined. We will focus our inquiry on deception, particularly deception in advertising. Historically, the commission has pursued a variety of deceptions in advertising. For example, bait-and-switch tactics are forbidden. In those cases, the seller ordinarily advertises a product at very low prices to attract customers. Then the customer's attention is deliberately switched to another more expensive product. Under the commission's *ad substantiation program,* advertisers are engaging in unfair and deceptive practices if they make product claims without some reasonable foundation for those claims. Advertisers must be able to produce sound evidence that their product performs as promoted.

Test. The courts have traditionally found unlawful deception in those acts or practices having "a tendency or capacity to deceive." The FTC follows a narrower interpretation, requiring a three-part inquiry into the impact of the ad on the *reasonable* consumer: "1. what claims are conveyed in the ad; 2. are those claims false or misleading; and 3. are those claims material to prospective consumers?"[14] Proof of actual deception is not necessary; rather a showing of some probability of deception is sufficient. The words in an ad must be examined in their total context, and the commission may consider evidence regarding consumers' actual interpretation of those words. Reasonable consumers are something like "ordinary people." However, ads directed to a specific subset of the population are measured by the reasonableness standards of that subset. *Materiality* refers to those situations where the ad is likely to affect what consumers actually do when buying products. Where an advertiser omits information that might be considered germane to the claim, the FTC will employ the materiality standard to determine whether the ad is deceptive as a consequence of the omission—that is, did the omission affect consumer choice?[15]

The Market. Of course, the power of the market itself remains the first line of consumer protection against deception. In 1993, Target Stores accused Wal-Mart of misleading customers with ads that overstated the price of some Target products. Target publicized its charges by running large ads in nine newspapers nationwide. For example, a Target spokesperson said Wal-Mart in Cedar Rapids, Iowa, advertised Famous Amos cookies at $1.67 and claimed that Target's price was $2.49 while Target said its price was actually $1.69.[16] The importance and the sensitivity of these truth-in-advertising issues is illustrated by the following discussion of Wal-Mart's recent decision to phase out its most prominent slogan.

WAL-MART BOWS TO PRICING REALITY BY CHANGING 4 LETTERS

Bob Ortega

In a move that shows how hard it is to be the discount leader in today's bargain-basement retailing environment, Wal-Mart Stores Inc. has begun phasing out its slogan "Always the low price. Always."

The new line, already cropping up in TV campaigns: "Always low prices. Always."

* * * * *

"The fact is, no one always has the lowest price. That's just the nature of this industry," says a spokeswoman for Dayton Hudson Corp.'s Target stores.

Indeed, Target recently complained to several Better Business Bureaus and ran a campaign accusing Wal-Mart of using misleading price comparisons in ads contrasting prices at the two chains.

Target's ads, which ran under headlines stating, "This Never Would Have Happened if Sam Walton Was Alive," provoked a furious public response from Wal-Mart. But they also helped advocates of changing the company's slogan win a continuing internal debate, according to one of those involved.

* * * * *

Of course, none of this is to say Wal-Mart is dropping its price-cutting strategy. As it has for years, the company consistently beats the competition in most categories, according to a series of independent studies. But the claim of the low price all the time has become riskier.

"Consumers take these things very, very literally," says retail consultant Russell Ferstandig, president of Competitive Advantage Consulting. "As soon as they find any evidence, no matter how minor, that the message isn't true, there's a strong negative reflex reaction." He adds: "This new statement is a much easier message for the consumer to believe; and it's much harder to blow a hole in."

Source: *The Wall Street Journal,* May 21, 1993, p. B1. Reprinted by permission of *The Wall Street Journal,* © 1993 Dow Jones & Company, Inc. All Rights Reserved Worldwide.

Afterword

At this writing in May 1994, Wal-Mart continues to phase out the use of the language "Always the low price." As stores are remodeled, ads run their course, and so on, that phrase, according to the Wal-Mart plan, will be replaced by language such as "Watch for falling prices" and "Roll back, America."

Questions

1. Should the Federal Trade Commission intervene if a company like Wal-Mart advertised "always the low price" when, in fact, its prices, on the average, might be the lowest, but its prices for individual items were not always the lowest? Explain.
2. Some Kraft, Inc., advertisements claimed its Kraft Singles cheese slices contained the same amount of calcium as 5 ounces of milk and more calcium than most brands of imitation cheese. Kraft argued that at least some of its ad claims were true because the slices were made from 5 ounces of milk and thus have a high calcium content. The government pointed out that about 30 percent of that calcium is lost in the process of converting milk to cheese, such that the ads resulted in an exaggeration of the actual calcium content. Are those ads deceptive? Explain. See *Kraft Inc.,* v. *F.T.C.,* 970 F. 2d 311 (1992).
3. For years, American Home Products had claimed via advertising that its product, Anacin (a painkiller), had a unique formula that was superior in effectiveness to all other nonprescription painkillers. In fact, the only active painkilling ingredient in Anacin was aspirin. The Federal Trade Commission found that American Home Products was engaging in deceptive advertising. The commission ordered AHP to stop its deceptive advertising and required AHP to support any future claims about the superiority of its product as a painkiller with two scientifically valid studies. AHP appealed the commission's decision. Decide. Explain. See *American Home Products* v. *F.T.C.,* 695 F.2d 681 (3d Cir. 1982).

4. Listerine mouthwash has been marketed since 1879 with no change in its formula. Beginning in 1921, Listerine was advertised as being effective in preventing, curing, and alleviating colds and sore throats. The Federal Trade Commission found those claims to be untrue and ordered Listerine's producer, Warner-Lambert, to desist from those claims and to include the following words in its Listerine ads for approximately one year: "Contrary to prior advertising, Listerine will not prevent colds or sore throats or lessen their severity." Warner-Lambert appealed. Decide. Explain. See *Warner-Lambert* v. *Federal Trade Commission,* 562 F.2d 749 (D.C. Cir. 1977), cert. den., 435 U.S. 950 (1978).

Sale Pricing.   When is a sale truly not a sale? Do some retailers offer phony markdowns based on fictitious, inflated "original" or "regular" prices? In 1964, the Federal Trade Commission issued guides requiring proof that a former price was genuine. However, since 1970, the FTC has largely ignored price advertising cases. The FTC has preferred to focus on deception in health, safety, and product performance because those are areas where consumers are believed to be less able to protect themselves. Consequently, many states and localities have recently asserted their own authority in this area. Consider the following account of an important recent state court case in this area.

MAY UNIT ILLEGALLY DECEIVED CUSTOMERS IN ITS ADVERTISING PRACTICES, COURT RULES

James P. Miller

A Colorado state court found that May Department Stores Co. illegally deceived customers, in a widely watched case involving the company's advertising practices.

The ruling affects only the Denver-based May D&F unit of the St. Louis department-store operator, but it's considered likely to have a wide impact in the retail industry, where promotional pricing practices are drawing increasing scrutiny from state officials around the nation.

May D&F said it is "disappointed" by the decision. "We believe our advertising practices are fair and appropriate," the company said, adding that it is considering an appeal.

. . . Colorado Attorney General Duane Woodard claimed that May D&F duped consumers by artificially inflating its so-called original or regular prices, and then promoting discounts from those prices

as bargains. The state sought an injunction against the practices, under the state's Consumer Protection Act.

May denied the charges . . .

. . . Judge Larry J. Naves wrote that May D&F's practices didn't comply with the Federal Trade Commission Guides Against Deceptive Pricing . . .

The case, which May opted to fight rather than to settle out of court as other retailers have done in similar cases, deals with the pricing of such mundane items as saucepans, rotisseries, coffee-makers, mattresses and glassware. But it has provided an intriguing view of how retail price promotions can make consumers think they're getting a better deal than they really are.

In general, May acknowledged that in certain sections of the store it offered items at what it called the "original" or "regular" price for 10 days at the start of a six-month selling season. But few items moved at these levels. The company then would drop the price, and advertise the items as below "original price." Further discounts from those realistic prices were touted as sales prices of limited duration, as "15-hour specials" and the like. At the end of the six-month season, the items were briefly marked up again to the generally noncompetitive levels for another 10-day period that would re-establish the next 170 days' prices as "bargains."

The court found that the state "has proven by a preponderance of the evidence that May D&F violated all three" of the deceptive practices alleged in the complaint.

"May D&F's 'original' price for practically all of its merchandise in the Home Store [section] was a fictitious high price established as a reference price for the purpose of subsequently advertising bargain reductions from that price," the judge wrote. "The clear expectation of May D&F was to sell all or practically all merchandise at its 'sale' price." . . .

The court enjoined May D&F from establishing a reference price for the sole purpose of future markdowns unless it "fully and completely" discloses to consumers its method of determining those original prices at the same time, in its ads. It also is prohi-bited from using price terms "which have meanings unique to May D&F," unless it also publishes a glossary of such terms. The order prohibits the unit from advertising sales of limited duration "in such manner as to communicate to consumers a false sense of urgency to purchase," when similar price levels are routinely scheduled throughout a selling season.

The court ordered May D&F to pay an $8,000 fine to the state—much less than the more than $1 million the state had sought—and directed the company to pay costs and attorney fees to the state; an official at the attorney general's office estimated that would total $250,000 to $400,000.

The attorney general's office called the ruling "not only a significant decision but a major victory. The court agreed with our position in all respects." An official said such practices hurt not only consumers, but also work to the "disadvantage of small-business competitors who can't compete with these kinds of advertising shenanigans."

Source: *The Wall Street Journal,* June 28, 1990, p. B4. Reprinted by permission of *The Wall Street Journal,* © 1990 Dow Jones & Company. All Rights Reserved Worldwide.

Afterword

At this writing in 1994, the May case is back at the trial level to resolve some remaining penalty issues. The case was reviewed by the Colorado Court of Appeals and the Colorado Supreme Court, both of which agreed that the May Company had violated the Colorado Consumer Protection Act. See *The May Department Stores Company* v. *The State of Colorado,* 17 BTR 1782 (Col. 1993).

Questions

1. Explain what the court held to be May D&F's wrongful practices.
2. How would the free market operate to protect the consumer in situations such as that described in the May D&F article?
3. On balance, would American society be better off if we abolished laws forbidding unfair and deceptive advertising and instead allowed the free market to work its will in this area? Explain.

The Consumer Product Safety Commission (CPSC)

The Consumer Product Safety Commission (CPSC), created in 1972, is responsible for reducing the risks in using some 15,000 consumer products, including toys, lawn mowers, washing machines, bicycles, portable heaters, and household chemicals. Each year, about 22,000 deaths and 30 million injuries are associated with those products.[17] In 1992, lawn mower injuries alone sent 50,000 people to hospital emergency rooms and an estimated 135,000 were injured by lawn care products generally.[18]

The CPSC has had some success in fulfilling its mission:

> The commission, established during the Nixon Administration, had a pretty good track record for a while. Thanks to CPSC action, kids now have flame-retardant sleepwear, chain saws are safer and aerosol cans are less hazardous. Slats on cribs are spaced to prevent babies' strangling to death. Injuries from the blades of rotary lawnmowers, which once stood at about 80,000 a year, are down dramatically after the CPSC ordered design changes.[19]

Nonetheless, the CPSC is a generally benign presence in Washington, D.C., after 12 years of cuts that reduced the agency's budget by half. The Reagan and Bush administrations favored greater reliance on voluntary industry standards and counted on market forces to protect the consumer. President Clinton appears more sympathetic to the role of the CPSC, and his 1994 appointee to chair the commission, Ann Brown, has moved to streamline the commission's work. She has ordered the commission staff to complete some eight years of work on safety standards for riding lawnmowers, and she wants the commission to address such issues as the safety of baby walkers (discussed later in this chapter) and the safety of string in the necks and waists of children's clothing. However, two of the three commission seats are occupied by Bush appointees, and money for aggressive initiatives is in short supply.

Firmer Rules? Unhappy with CPSC inactivity, Congress passed the Consumer Product Safety Improvement Act of 1990, which strengthened the original act and requires the agency to undertake safety initiatives for some specified hazards, including cigarette lighters, indoor pollutants, and automatic garage door openers. In 1993, the new garage door rule went into effect, requiring safety features to prevent humans and animals from being crushed accidentally by closing doors. The CPSC reported that 54 children were killed by garage doors between 1982 and 1992.[20] The new rule requires one of three safety mechanisms:

> a control button that has to be held constantly to make the door close, an electric-eye sensor or a door-edge sensor like those on elevators.[21]

All of the necessary technology is readily available and is expected to add $20 to $25 to the cost of an opener.

Question

1. Given the lives to be saved versus the additional cost for improved openers, do you support the new rule? Explain.

Duties.   The commission's authority extends over the full range of consumer products (glass, toys, ladders, saws, stoves, and so on). Its duties are many, but the heart of its activities may be summarized as follows.

1. Data Collection.   The commission conducts research and collects information as a foundation for regulating product safety. The commission's National Electronic Injury Surveillance System (NEISS) collects data from many hospital emergency rooms across the country. The hospitals report all injuries involving consumer products. Analysis of that database then suggests directions for more intensive investigations.

2. Rule Making.   The commission, via its rule-making authority, promulgates mandatory consumer product *safety standards.* The commission invites any person or group to submit a safety standard for the product in question. Industry trade associations have been more active in submitting "offers" to set standards, but consumers and consumer groups (such as the Consumers Union) have been encouraged to participate. Safety standards essentially are technical specifications requiring certain minimums in strength, design, flammability, corrosiveness, labeling, and so on. The commission issues *performance standards,* which specify the minimum level of service expected from a product. For example, a ladder may be required to hold a specified amount of weight. Similarly, the commission issues *labeling standards,* which may require the attachment of a warning label to certain products. For example, the CPSC has provided that children's sleepwear must meet certain flame-resistance standards, must be labeled to show that they meet those standards, must be labeled with care instructions to preserve flame retardants (where used), and production and distribution records must be maintained so that the product's history can be traced. Because safety is not free, proposed product standards must include a statement of the anticipated economic and environmental impact.

Standards are processed under traditional due process requirements, including publication in the *Federal Register,* notice to affected parties, and hearings. Affected parties may petition a federal Court of Appeals to reverse CPSC rules.

3. Compliance.   The CPSC is empowered to use a variety of strategies in securing compliance. Manufacturers must certify before distribution that products meet federal safety standards. Agents of the commission may inspect manufacturing sites. The commission can mandate specific product safety testing procedures, and businesses other than retailers are required to keep records sufficient for the commission to see that they are in compliance with safety standards.

4. Enforcement.   In cases of severe and imminent hazards, the commission may seek an immediate court order to remove a product from the market. In less urgent circumstances, the commission may proceed with its own administrative remedy. Because it prefers to secure voluntary compliance, the commission may urge the company to issue public and/or private notices of a defect, or it may seek the repair or replacement of defective parts. Where voluntary negotiations fail, the commission may proceed with an adjudicative hearing, conducted in the manner of a trial, before an administrative law judge or members of the commission. The decision may be appealed to the full commission and thereafter to the appropriate U.S. Court of Appeals. In its first six years, the CPSC issued approximately 1,200 product recalls. Failure to comply with safety provisions may result in civil and/or criminal penalties.

Only a few products have actually been banned from the market. For example, in 1988, Congress required the CPSC to ban most lawn darts. The play items had resulted in at least three deaths and several thousand injuries. Most lawn dart injuries have been suffered by children. In recent years, the CPSC has been hotly criticized for regulatory footdragging—particularly in the area of child safety.

Baby Walkers. The American Medical Association and others believe that baby walkers are unreasonably dangerous and, in 1992, petitioned the CPSC to ban them. According to the AMA, the walkers are associated with an average of one death annually. In 1991, 29,000 injuries, of which 9,500 were considered severe, were connected to walkers.[22] In 1994, the commission voted to begin a formal rule-making action, but it also will continue negotiations directed toward voluntary guidelines.

Critics say additional regulation is foolish and that the problem lies principally with poor supervision by parents:

> Four out of five walker-related accidents were preventable with baby gates and adult supervision: 77 percent of the infants fell down stairs and 4 percent fell off a porch or out a door.[23]

The critics contend that few injuries associated with walkers are actually the product of the walker itself, and they remind us that more than 99 percent of the babies using walkers are not injured.[24]

Question

1. What action would you take in the baby walker controversy? Explain.

CONSUMER FINANCE LAW

For a considerable portion of American history, frugality was a virtue of the first rank. Saving was esteemed. Borrowing for consumer goods was, to many, foolish and a sign of weakness or decay. Today, we live in quite another world. We are encouraged to experience the good life by spending lavishly. To do so we may well need to borrow. Purchases on credit are not only tolerated, they are encouraged. Our shift to a commercial world predicated on the extension of credit opened seductive new windows of pleasure for the consumer, but the spread of indebtedness as a way of life led to new problems and, in some instances, abuses for both the debtor–consumer and the creditor–business. Predictably, and perhaps necessarily, we turned to the law for relief.

CREDIT REGULATIONS

Congress and the states have extended a variety of protections to the consumer seeking and securing credit. We will take an abbreviated look at several particularly important pieces of creditor protection legislation.

Truth in Lending Act (TILA)[25]

As we increasingly turned to credit financing, consumers often did not understand the full cost of buying on credit. TILA is part of the Consumer Credit Protection Act of 1968. Having been designed for consumer protection, it does not cover all loans. The following standards determine TILA's applicability:

1. The debtor must be a "natural person" rather than an organization.
2. The creditor must be regularly engaged in extending credit or arranging for the extension of credit.
3. The purpose of the credit must be "primarily for personal, family, or household purposes" not in excess of $25,000. However, "consumer real property transactions" are covered by the act. Hence, home purchases fall within TILA provisions.
4. The credit must be subject to a finance charge or payable in more than four installments.

Following the enactment of the TILA, the Federal Reserve Board developed regulations (labeled Regulation Z) detailing the specific requirements of the act. TILA was designed both to protect consumers from credit abuse and to assist consumers in becoming more informed regarding credit terms and costs so they could engage in comparison shopping. Congress presumed the increased information would stimulate competition in the finance industry. The heart of the act is the required conspicuous disclosure of the finance charge (the actual dollar sum to be paid for credit) and the annual percentage rate (APR) (the total cost of the credit expressed at an annual rate). The finance charge includes not just interest but service charges, points, loan fees, carrying charges, and others. TILA disclosure requirements apply to both *open-end* (for example, VISA and MasterCard) and *closed-end* (loans of a fixed amount for a definite time) transactions.

Questions

1. A health spa sells some memberships for cash and some on an installment basis. The price is the same whether the buyer pays cash or buys on the installment plan. The spa has an arrangement with a financing agency to sell the installment contracts to the agency at a discount (a price lower than the face value of the contract).

   a. How would you argue that the installment contract sales are in violation of TILA and Regulation Z?

   b. How would you rule on such a case? See *Joseph* v. *Norman's Health Club, Inc.,* 532 F.2d 86 (8th Cir. 1976).

Credit and Charge Cards

TILA provides that credit cards cannot be issued to a consumer unless requested. Cardholder liability for unauthorized use (lost or stolen card) cannot exceed $50, and the cardholder bears no liability after notifying the issuer of the missing card.

The Fair Credit and Charge Card Disclosure Act of 1988 creates extensive disclosure requirements for card issuers. The act requires notification of various cost factors when card issuers solicit applications. Details vary, depending on whether the card application was solicited by mail, telephone, or "take ones" (e.g., a magazine insert). In general, issuers must disclose key cost features, including APR, annual membership fees, minimum finance charges, late payment charges, and so on. Similarly, when an account is opened and regularly thereafter, the customer must be informed of cost features such as the interest rate, the balance on which interest will be computed, and so on. Billing statements must include such information as the APR, monthly rates, and the balance due.

Equal Credit Opportunity Act (ECOA)

In a society historically beset with discrimination, it is hardly surprising that credit was often denied on the basis of prejudices and stereotypes. In 1974, Congress enacted the Equal Credit Opportunity Act to combat bias in lending. Credit must be extended to all creditworthy applicants regardless of sex, marital status, age, race, color, religion, national origin, good faith exercise of rights under the Consumer Credit Protection Act, and receipt of public assistance (e.g., food stamps or Aid to Dependent Children). ECOA was in large part a response to anger over differing treatment of women and men in the financial marketplace. Creditors often would not loan money to married women under the woman's own name. Single, divorced, and widowed women were at a great disadvantage, vis-à-vis their male counterparts, in securing credit; and frequently women who married had to reapply for credit under their husband's name.

In addition to forbidding explicit discrimination in granting credit, ECOA includes a variety of provisions limiting the information that a creditor can require in processing an application. In general, the creditor cannot seek information that could be used to engage in discrimination. Hence, among others, inquiries as to marital status, income from alimony, child support, maintenance payments, birth control practices, and child-bearing plans are either forbidden or limited.

MILLER v. AMERICAN EXP. CO.
688 F.2d 1235 (1982)

Circuit Judge Boochever

Facts

Maurice Miller, plaintiff's late husband, applied for and received an American Express credit card in 1966. His account was denominated a Basic Card Account. Later in 1966, plaintiff Virginia Miller applied for and was granted a supplementary card. Her application was signed by her husband as the basic cardholder and by her. Mrs. Miller agreed to be personally liable for all charges made on her supplementary card. Her card bore a different account number from her husband's card, was issued in her own name, required a separate annual fee, and bore a different expiration date from Mr. Miller's card. The Millers used their American Express cards until Mr. Miller passed away in May, 1979. Two months after her husband's death, Mrs. Miller attempted to use her card during a shopping trip and was informed by the store clerk that her account had been canceled. This was the first notice she received of the cancellation. Subsequently, Amex informed her that her account had been canceled pursuant to a policy of automatically terminating the account of a supplementary cardholder upon the death of a basic cardholder. Amex invited her to apply for a basic account. Her application for a new account consisted merely of filling out a short form, entitled "Request to Change Membership status from Supplementary to Basic Card Member," which did not require any financial or credit history data. Amex issued Mrs. Miller a new card, apparently on the basis of her 13-year credit history in the use of the card it had just canceled. Mrs. Miller brought suit against Amex for violation of the ECOA.

[T]he district court . . . awarded summary judgment to Amex without specifying its reasons.

Analysis

The issues on this appeal are whether Amex's policy of canceling a spouse's supplementary account upon the death of the basic cardholder violates the ECOA and whether a plaintiff must always show discriminatory intent or effect to establish an ECOA violation. The facts are undisputed, therefore, we must decide whether the substantive law was correctly applied . . .

The ECOA makes it unlawful for any creditor to discriminate with respect to any credit transaction on the basis of marital status . . .

In order to carry out the purposes of the ECOA, the board promulgated the regulations codified at 12.C.F.R. §§ 201.1 *et seq.* Section 202.7(c)(1) provides that a creditor shall not terminate the account of a person who is contractually liable on an existing open-end account on the basis of a change in marital status in the absence of evidence of inability or unwillingness to repay.

Mrs. Miller's Amex card was canceled after her marital status changed from married to widowed. Under § 202.7(c)(2), Amex could have asked her to reapply for credit, but instead it first terminated her card and then invited reapplication. There was no contention or evidence that her widowhood rendered Mrs. Miller unable or unwilling to pay, indeed, Amex's prompt issuance of a new card to her indicates that she was considered creditworthy.

* * * * *

Termination on the Basis of Marital Status: Proof of Credit Discrimination

The ECOA outlaws credit discrimination on the basis of marital status. Amex argues that it was entitled to summary judgment because Mrs. Miller did not attempt to show that Amex's policy of canceling all supplementary cardholders on the death of the basic cardholder either was adopted with discriminatory intent or had an adverse impact on widows as a class. In light of the purposes of the ECOA, we do not think such a restrictive interpretation of the regulation is warranted.

* * * * *

The conduct here was squarely within that prohibited by § 202.7(c). Mrs. Miller's account was terminated in response to her husband's death and without reference to or even inquiry regarding her creditworthiness. It is undisputed that the death of her husband was the sole reason for Amex's termination of Mrs. Miller's credit. Amex contends that its automatic cancellation policy was necessary to protect it from noncreditworthy supplementary cardholders. The regulations, however, prohibit termination based on a spouse's death in the absence of evidence of inability or unwillingness to repay. Amex has never contended in this action that the death of her husband rendered Mrs. Miller unable or unwilling to pay charges made on her card . . .

We hold that Amex violated the ECOA and regulations thereunder in its termination of Mrs. Miller's supplementary card. For this reason, we reverse . . .

Circuit Judge Poole, dissenting

The majority today holds in effect that a credit practice need not be discriminatory to violate the Equal Credit Opportunity Act (the Act). Because this holding is contrary to the clear language and purpose of the Act, I respectfully dissent.

* * * * *

Violation of § 202.7(c)

It is a fact that American Express canceled appellant's supplementary card after the death of her husband. Section 202.7(c), however, does not prohibit the termination of an account after a change in an applicant's marital status; it prohibits only the termination of an account "on the basis of" such a change. Since the change in appellant's marital status was not the basis for American Express's decision to cancel her supplementary card, there has been no violation of § 202.7(c).

* * * * *

American Express's practice is not discriminatory since cancellation of supplementary cards is an evenhanded and uniform consequence suffered by all supplementary cardholders and is not at all operative because of a change in a cardholder's marital status. The majority's holding thus does not contribute to the eradication of credit discrimination. Rather, it prevents American Express from treating all supplementary cardholders alike and instead forces it to give preferential treatment to those supplementary cardholders who happen to have been married to the basic cardholder. Such a result stands the act on its head.

* * * * *

Questions

1. Explain the majority's reasoning.
2. Do you agree with the majority opinion or that of the dissenting judge? Explain.
3. Does ECOA increase or decrease the cost of credit? Explain.
4. Mrs. John P. Harbaugh applied for a Master Charge credit card. Her application included information regarding her employment as a teacher, her salary, and so on. She forwarded the application to Continental National Bank and Trust Company. In response, Continental issued two credit cards in the name of John P. Harbaugh. Mrs. Harbaugh understood that she could use the cards, and that she could sign them Mrs. John P. Harbaugh or Mrs. Helen D. Harbaugh. However, she was unsatisfied with that arrangement and filed suit, claiming discriminatory denial of credit based on the sex or marital status of the applicant in violation of the ECOA. Although she could use the card issued in her husband's name, Mrs. Harbaugh indicated she wanted to have her own account and her own credit rating "in case something should happen to her husband." In fact, the bank did establish Mrs. Harbaugh's own account but under the name John P. Harbaugh because the bank's computer system deleted courtesy titles like Mrs. The bank argued that the deletion of courtesy titles was consistent with the legal requirements of a credit-granting policy "neutral as to sex." Testimony at trial indicated that Mrs. Harbaugh's account under the name John P. Harbaugh would not establish a separate credit history in her own name. But under federal law, creditors are required to send notice that married women can have credit information for joint accounts reported in both the husband's and the wife's names. Mrs. Harbaugh was so notified, and she understood she could use that mechanism to establish her own credit history. Given these conditions, Mrs. Harbaugh made two alternative claims: "(1) the bank was under an affirmative duty to use the courtesy title 'Mrs.' in opening her account or (2) if the courtesy title of 'Mrs.' was deleted, the bank was under a duty to ensure that she receive a separate credit history in her own name."

   How would you rule on Mrs. Harbaugh's claims? Explain. See *Harbaugh* v. *Continental Ill. Natl. Bank,* 615 F.2d 1169 (1980).

Fair Credit Reporting Act (FCRA)

For most of us, a favorable credit rating is necessary to the full enjoyment of American life. We seek credit so commonly that the three major credit bureaus (Equifax, TRW, and Trans Union) have 400 million records on 160 million people.[26] Given these conditions, it is essential that credit information be accurate, that the information be used only for proper purposes, and that credit inquiries not unnecessarily disturb the consumer's privacy. Congress passed the FCRA in 1970, in recognition of both the potential for abuse in gathering and reporting credit information and the necessity for accurate, fair credit reports.

Rather than conduct their own credit investigations, businesses commonly turn to firms such as TRW that specialize in gathering, storing, and reporting that information. Those credit bureaus (or, in the language of the act, "consumer reporting agencies" that regularly engage in the business of gathering and reporting consumer credit data to third parties) are covered by the terms of the act. The key requirements of the FCRA are as follows:

1. Consumer Rights. If requested, consumer reporting agencies must—with certain exceptions—provide each consumer with the information in his or her file. However, the consumer does not have the right to see the file itself. Inaccurate, obsolete, and unverifiable information must be removed. If the contents of the file remain in dispute, the consumer has the right to include in the file a brief statement of her or his version of the issues in question. If a consumer should be denied employment, credit, or insurance because of an agency report, the user of the report must so inform the consumer, and the consumer must be advised as to the origin of the credit report.

2. Reporting Agency Responsibilities. In brief, agencies are required to follow reasonable procedures to ensure that information is both accurate and up-to-date. Consumer credit reports can be furnished only for the following purposes without the consumer's permission or a court order: (*a*) credit, (*b*) insurance, (*c*) employment, (*d*) obtaining a government benefit, or (*e*) other legitimate business purpose involving a consumer. Inasmuch as protection of privacy is one of the stated purposes of the act, it is interesting that Congress imposed no limitation on the kinds of information that may be included in a file. Hence, sexual practices, political preferences, hair length, friendships, organizational memberships, and the like can lawfully be reported.

3. User Responsibilities. Those who purchase a consumer credit investigation must inform the consumer in advance of the pending inquiry.

When a consumer is denied credit, employment, or insurance, or where financial charges are increased because of an adverse credit report, the consumer must be apprised of the name and address of the consumer reporting agency that provided the information.

4. Penalties. Both civil and criminal penalties, including damages, fines, and imprisonment, are possible under the FCRA. The primary enforcement burden lies with the Federal Trade Commission.

Privacy. A 1990 Louis Harris poll found 71 percent of the Americans surveyed agreeing with the statement that "Consumers have lost all control over how personal information about them is circulated and used by companies."[27] Personal privacy in this information era may become our most pressing consumer protection issue. But the Harris poll also shows that consumers want all the advantages of our consumer society, such as ready access to credit cards and the ease of purchasing by mail.[28] The credit industry reminds us that our highly efficient, credit information sharing system is a cost-effective way of permitting sellers to open credit to many more consumers than would otherwise be the case. And they argue that shoddy, unfair work by credit bureaus is quickly punished by the market.

Government Intervention. In the 1990s, government regulators have taken an activist stance toward privacy issues. In 1991, TRW settled lawsuits with 19 states and the FTC resolving claims of unfairness in credit reporting. TRW agreed to set up toll-free numbers for consumer questions, make its reports more readable, and establish new rules for responding to consumer complaints.[29] The 1991 Telephone Consumer Protection Act attempts to curb annoying "junk" calls. Telemarketers now cannot lawfully call before 8 AM or after 9 PM; and, if called, you can ask to be placed on their federally mandated do-not-call list. Consumer groups had sought a national data bank of people not wanting to be called, but the Federal Communications Commission said that approach would cost $20 million to establish and $10 million annually to operate.[30]

In 1993, the FTC challenged TRW and Trans Union for selling confidential credit information to junk mailers. TRW agreed to desist. Trans Union indicated that it will fight the FTC in court, arguing that its practices are legal.[31]

The editorial that follows builds the argument for continuing legal intervention to protect consumer privacy.

TIGHTEN CREDIT LAW TO PROTECT PRIVACY

Much of your privacy—yes, even secrets you'd sooner no one knew about—is up for sale.

Credit bureaus, which gather information about you when you apply for credit or a loan, have got the goods on you. Three companies—TRW, Equifax and Trans Union—have information on about 90 percent of us.

They know how much money you make, how much money you spend—and on what. They know what your bank balance is and if you pay your bills on time. They know if you've been unemployed or have a bad driving record.

They know a lot about you, more than is needed for that loan. But they've found there is money in your personal profile, so the bureaus and the smaller bureaus they deal with repackage the data and sell it without your permission.

The buyers are banks and retailers, telemarketers and mail-order houses, which, in turn, bombard you with unsolicited sales calls and junk mail.

The Fair Credit Reporting Act of 1970 was intended to protect your privacy. But the computer age has made compiling data easier—and has exposed loopholes in the law.

Opponents . . . will tell you that this information saves marketing businesses money by allowing them to target their advertising to the age and income group best suited for their products or services.

They'll tell you they provide a service that allows consumers to get credit quickly.

And they're right.

But they'll also tell you the 1970 law is working.

Tell that to John J. Casson, 54, of Brooklyn, N.Y. He was harassed by a department store about the delinquent account of a person with a similar name. He thought the problem was corrected, until he had a loan rejected. Negative data about the other person had been put in his files.

Tell that to John Krizek, 57, of Van Nuys, Calif. While he was going through a divorce, much of his assets were tied up in an escrow account, resulting in some unpaid bills. Even after the divorce was settled and the bills paid, problems remained on his record. Four years later, he's still not sure they're fixed.

Tell that to J. Danforth Quayle, 43, of Washington, D.C. A *Business Week* editor paid a $500 fee and a credit bureau gave the editor access via his home computer to its data base. It included the credit records of the vice president. Quayle was not amused. No one would be.

Like a rumor, too often this information is passed behind your back. Like a rumor, too often this data is inaccurate—up to 40 percent by some estimates—and can tarnish your reputation. Like a rumor, too often it's almost impossible to correct unless you find everyone to whom it was passed.

That's why Congress must change the law.

- Credit information should be used only for transactions initiated by the consumer, or sold for other purposes only with the consumer's permission.
- You should be told of adverse information and get a free report each year to check for errors; mistakes should be corrected within 30 days.
- Banks should not be allowed to prescreen your records in order to offer you preapproved lines of credit.

Your privacy should not be for sale. What these companies are selling, you already own.

Source: *USA Today,* June 19, 1990, p. 10A. Copyright 1990, *USA Today.* Reprinted with permission.

Fair Credit Billing Act (FCBA)

The FCBA, passed in 1974, provides a mechanism to deal with the billing errors that accompany credit card and certain other credit transactions. The credit card holder who receives an erroneous bill must complain in writing to the creditor within 60 days of the receipt of the bill. If so, the creditor must acknowledge receipt of the complaint within 30 days. Then, within two billing cycles but not more than 90 days, the creditor must issue a response either acknowledging or denying the error. If the former, appropriate adjustments must be made. If the latter, the creditor must explain why the bill is correct. After filing its response, the creditor must wait 10 days before reporting the account as delinquent. If the consumer continues to dispute the accuracy of the bill, the creditor must file notice of the continuing dispute with any third party to whom notice of the delinquency is directed. Penalties for a creditor in violation of the act are quite modest. The creditor forfeits the right to collect the amount in question and any accompanying finance charges, but the forfeiture cannot exceed $50 for each charge in dispute.

Truth in Savings Act

Under this new federal law, which became effective in 1993 (1994 for credit unions), banks and savings institutions must (among other things) (1) fully disclose the fees and terms of their checkings and savings accounts, (2) express interest on deposits in the form of an *annual percentage yield (APY)* that includes compounding, and (3) pay interest on deposits in full on a daily basis. However, as the *Des Moines Register* reported, these protections come at a price:

> Truth is not cheap.
>   Nor, when it comes to banking, is it easy.
>   It takes 166 pages to explain the federal government's new Truth in Savings Act.
>   Iowa bankers estimate that compliance with the act could cost them more than $20 million a year in mailing charges alone. And there's the cost of new computer hardware and software that many banks will need to buy to comply with the proposed rules.[32]

DEBTOR PROTECTION

Generosity of spirit and deed is one of the more noble dimensions of the American character. Hence, for charitable reasons as well as for some "hard-nosed" economic considerations, the American legal system has enacted careful protections for those who find themselves indebted.

Debt Collection

The Fair Debt Collection Practices Act (FDCPA) of 1977 (amended in 1986) is designed to shield debtors from unfair debt collection tactics by debt collection agencies and attorneys who routinely operate as debt collectors. The act does not extend to creditors who are themselves trying to recover money owed to them. Several thousand debt collection agencies nationwide pursue those who are delinquent in their debts. The agencies are normally paid on a commission basis and are often exceedingly aggressive and imaginative in their efforts.

The FDCPA forbids, among others, the following practices:

1. Use of obscene language.
2. Contact with third parties other than for the purpose of locating the debtor. (That provision is an attempt to prevent harm to the debtor's reputation.)
3. Use of or threats to use physical force.
4. Contact with the debtor during "inconvenient" hours. For debtors who are employed during "normal" working hours, the period from 9 PM to 8 AM would probably be considered inconvenient.
5. Repeated phone calls with the intent to harass.
6. Contacting the debtor in an unfair, abusive, or deceptive manner.

The Federal Trade Commission is responsible for administering the FDCPA. A wronged debtor may also file a civil action to recover all actual damages (for example, payment for job loss occasioned by wrongful debt collection practices as well as damages for associated embarrassment and suffering). A civil penalty up to $1,000 as well as attorneys' fees and court costs may also be collected.

The next reading suggests some of the problems in debt collection practices.

DEBT COLLECTORS' AGGRESSIVE TACTICS BRING MOUNTING PROTESTS FROM IRATE CONSUMERS

Lucinda Harper

In tough economic times, opportunity stops knocking and bill collectors start calling. With debts harder to collect, there are increasing complaints that more collection agencies are turning to hardball tactics—some even breaking the law—to pursue past-due accounts.

For Linda and Daniel Warnick of Grantsville, Md., the nightmare began last year when their 17-year-old daughter, Stacey, and her boyfriend stole their Chevron credit card and began running up $1,300 in gasoline, oil and interest charges while joy riding. Then Mr. Warnick lost his job as a construction worker, and Stacey became pregnant, contracted toxemia and was hospitalized.

Enter Allied Bond & Collection Agency of Trevose, Pa., which was given the task of collecting the debt for Chevron. On top of all her other woes, Mrs. Warnick says she started receiving as many as six phone calls a day from an Allied Bond collector. According to Mrs. Warnick, the collector verbally abused her over the telephone and threatened her with imprisonment.

"He called me a liar and told me I should kick my daughter out of the house for stealing my credit card and to file charges against her," says Mrs. Warnick, a bakery worker. She says that when the collector demanded that she send him a packet of postdated checks to cover the debt, she complied. After Mr. Warnick's job ran out and the Warnicks warned Allied that their checking account was depleted, Allied continued to cash the checks, overdrawing the account. Allied refused to comment for this article.

Booming Business

For years, collection agencies have devised creative ways to track down debtors. But today, Americans are defaulting in ever-growing numbers on debts they piled up during the free-spending 1980s. Delinquencies have risen 30% this year, reports RAM Research, a Frederick, Md., bankcard research firm. That means booming business for collection agencies. But with the continuing weak economy, collecting debts takes more ingenuity.

"Collection agencies are taking a bold new approach to collecting their money. Collectors have been banging on people's doors and asking for merchandise or payment and bothering debtors even after they have filed for bankruptcy," says Cassandra Ayers, assistant vice president for Financial Service Systems, a Washington-based debt-counseling service. "But they have got to realize that with the economy the way it is, people just don't have the money. And if it comes down to eating or paying off their credit cards, they are going to eat."

The Fair Debt Collection Practices Act protects debtors . . .

But cases of agencies ignoring that law seem to be proliferating. Although they have no figures, Federal Trade Commission officials report a steady rise in consumer complaints about debt collectors over the past few years . . .

Tied-Up Telephone Lines

When Tina Marshall fell behind on her Chase Manhattan credit-card bill, for instance, debt collectors bombarded her employer, the Thomassen Lincoln Mercury car dealership in Rockville, Md., with phone calls. Maureen Duffy, the dealership's business manager, says that on one morning in June, telephone lines at the dealership were tied up for almost two hours with calls from the Great Lakes Collection Bureau in Buffalo, N.Y.

"We're a car dealership, and we really don't have time to deal with this," complains Ms. Duffy, who became so exasperated she called the Maryland Attorney General's Office and solicited its assistance; the office intervened, without making any formal charges, and the calls stopped. Great Lakes Collection Bureau, while it said it wouldn't address the circumstances of Ms. Marshall's account, said that "it is not our practice or policy" to harass debtors.

* * * * *

When Kia Puriefoy got into credit trouble in New York, a collection agency at one point "called my landlord, told her I was in credit trouble and asked if I paid my rent," she says. Ms. Puriefoy says that when she was just starting out in the film industry a few years ago, she used a credit card to charge food from the gourmet shop at Macy's and soon had a bill of more than $1,000. Now a free-lance assistant director, she says she recently made her final payment on her Macy's debt but has since gone into default on a fitness-center bill. "It's been just really tough," she says.

* * * * *

The bleak job market, slow income growth and the high indebtedness of U.S. consumers have all played their part in that debt-recovery trend. Collection agencies say they have also seen a big increase in white-collar deadbeats and among people with previously stellar credit histories.

The American Collectors Association, the trade group for collection agencies, concedes that times are hard for creditors and that they are in turn tougher with debtors. Agency executives say accounts are being turned over to them a lot sooner from anxious businesses. They add that creditors are more likely than ever to switch collection agencies if they don't see fast results. But despite such pressures, the association says most companies stay within the law.

Moreover, collection agencies complain that debtors themselves are growing more clever in evading debts, often making empty payment promises and screening their telephone calls . . .

Still, a few collectors acknowledge harassment does occur. They blame agency pressures, describing heated competition between collectors seeking recognition for the results they get.

Lee Reyes of Lorton, Va., for instance, has been in the debt-collection business about seven years. She has worked as a collector at several agencies and now finds companies that need debt-collection services for Mid-Atlantic Collections in Laurel, Md. "I have seen some of my co-workers [at other agencies] call and scream at people and misrepresent themselves," says Ms. Reyes.

Ms. Reyes, who is 26 years old, says she was often the top collector at the agencies where she worked, averaging $40,000 a month in collections in an industry where $30,000 is considered good. She describes a dog-eat-dog world where employees are often encouraged to do "whatever they have to" to get a debtor to pay up.

The best response to abusive tactics, experts say, is to go to the authorities. After complaining to the Maryland Collection Agency Licensing Board, Mrs. Warnick got a letter from Allied Bond's general manager saying that her account would no longer be handled by the collector about whom she had complained. The agency also returned the remaining postdated checks.

Source: *The Wall Street Journal,* December 3, 1991, p. B1. Reprinted by permission of *The Wall Street Journal,* © 1991 Dow Jones & Company, Inc. All Rights Reserved Worldwide.

Questions

1. Why shouldn't debt collectors be able to use aggressive tactics of the nature described in this article in order to compel payment of legitimate bills?
2. In your view, does the fundamental problem lie with the debt collectors or the debtors? Explain.

3. *a.* Do you approve of the six general FDCPA prohibitions discussed above? Explain.

   b. Would you add further protections? Explain.

Bankruptcy

Our culture encourages indebtedness. For various reasons, some debtors become encumbered beyond reasonable hope of recovery. Those individuals and organizations may, under appropriate circumstances, seek relief under the terms of our bankruptcy laws. Bankruptcy has become common in American life. We wish to afford a fresh beginning to the debtor and to avoid rendering the debtor an unproductive, helpless burden on society. We also want the involved creditors to recover as much of their losses as possible. So, although the reasons for our bankruptcy provisions are in large part quite pragmatic, it is nevertheless touching that we retain the humane recognition that some of us occasionally need a lift to overcome our ill fortune or foolishness.

Bankruptcy Boom.   Bankruptcies skyrocketed during the 1980s and 1990s. Bankruptcy filings in 1992 reached 971,517, up 178 percent over a 10-year period.[33] Both corporate and personal filings were up sharply, but over 900,000 of the total belonged to individuals. Corporate filings, while up from 10 years ago, are down a bit from the high in 1987.[34] Filings reach across all income classes. Creditors' lawyers argue that many consumers simply do not understand that bankruptcy is often not the easy way out that they seek. A personal bankruptcy filing may remain on an individual's credit record for as long as 10 years, thereby imperiling the capacity to secure loans for often vital purchases such as homes and autos.[35]

The Law.   Our attention will be limited to the principal federal statute, the Bankruptcy Reform Act of 1978.

Bankruptcy is an adjudication relieving a debtor of all or part of her liabilities. Any person, partnership, or corporation may seek debtor relief. Three forms of bankruptcy action are important to us:

1. *Liquidation* (Chapter 7 of the Bankruptcy Act), in which all assets except exemptions are distributed to creditors.
2. *Reorganization* (Chapter 11), in which creditors are kept from the debtor's assets while the debtor, under the supervision of the court, works out a plan to continue in business while paying creditors.
3. *Adjustment of debts of an individual with regular income* (Chapter 13), in which individuals with limited debts are protected from creditors while paying their debts in installments.

"Straight" Bankruptcy.   A Chapter 7 liquidation petition can be *voluntarily* filed in federal court by the debtor (individual, partnership, or corporation), or creditors can seek an *involuntary* bankruptcy judgment.

In a voluntary action, the debtor files a petition with the appropriate federal court. The court then has jurisdiction to proceed with the liquidation, and the petition becomes the *order for relief.* The debtor need not be insolvent to seek bankruptcy.

An involuntary bankruptcy can be compelled only if the creditors have an individual or aggregate claim of at least $5,000. The debtor may challenge the bankruptcy action. The court will enter an order for relief if it finds the debtor has not been paying his or her debts when due or if most of the debtor's property is under the control of a custodian for the purpose of enforcing a lien against that property.

After the order for relief is granted, voluntary and involuntary actions proceed in a similar manner. Creditors are restrained from reaching the debtor's assets. An interim bankruptcy trustee is appointed by the court. The creditors then hold a meeting, and a permanent trustee is elected. The trustee collects the debtor's property and converts it to money, protects the interests of the debtor and creditors, may manage the debtor's business, and ultimately distributes the estate proceeds to the creditors. Both federal and state laws permit the debtor to exempt certain property, which typically includes a car, a homestead, some household or personal items, life insurance, and other "necessities." Normally, a dollar maximum is attached to each. For example, the federal exemptions include a vehicle, not to exceed $1200 in value and household goods/personal belongings not to exceed $4000.

The debtor's nonexempt property is then divided among the creditors according to the priorities prescribed by statute. Secured creditors are paid first. If funds remain, "priority" creditors, such as those responsible for administering the debtor's estate, are paid. Then, funds permitting, general creditors are paid. Each class must be paid in full before a class of lower priority will be compensated. Any remaining funds will return to the debtor.

When distribution is complete, the bankruptcy judge may issue an order *discharging* the debtor of any remaining debts except for certain statutorily specified claims. Those include, for example, alimony, child support, taxes, and educational loans. The debtor might fail to receive a discharge if the debtor had received a discharge in the previous six years, if property was concealed from the court, or if good faith in the bankruptcy process was lacking in other respects.

Reorganization.   Chapter 11 is the bankruptcy proceeding most commonly employed by corporations, but its provisions also apply to other debtors, including partnerships and individuals. As explained in the following article, Chapter 11 allows financially troubled businesses to continue in operation while debt adjustments are arranged.

PULLING A COMPANY THROUGH CHAPTER 11 IS A RISKY BUSINESS AS HURDLES ABOUND

Laurie P. Cohen

Companies that file for protection from creditors under Chapter 11 of the federal Bankruptcy Code hope to work out a way to pay off their debts and continue in operation.

But the road through bankruptcy court is a perilous one, and only one out of eight companies reorganizes successfully. The rest cease operations, according to the Federal Office of Court Administration.

* * * * *

Here is a step-by-step look at what bankruptcy experts say a company faces once it embarks on a Chapter 11 reorganization:

• The case is assigned to a federal bankruptcy judge in the district where the filing is made. The judge's role during the case is to resolve conflicts that may arise . . .

• A U.S. trustee, who is employed by the Justice Department, will be appointed by the bankruptcy judge and will explain to the debtor company and its counsel the reporting and operating requirements for the district where the filing is made.

• Usually within a day of the filing, the company and its lawyers will submit to the court a list of the company's 20 largest creditors. The company must close its existing bank accounts and its books and begin new accounts and books as of the date the filing is made.

• Within days, the company's executives will meet with the company's bank lenders to work out a basis for continuing to operate. The company will attempt to negotiate a credit line with its banks that will provide funds to pay suppliers and employees. Banks are usually willing to cooperate, rather than risk losing all. Some suppliers may seek assurances that they will be paid in advance for merchandise sold while the company is in Chapter 11 proceedings. The banks will want to enable the company to make such guarantees.

• The U.S. trustee will attend to the administrative details of the bankruptcy and supervise day-to-day problems. He will then appoint one or more creditors committees, culled from the list of top creditors. These committees will appoint chairmen and will hire their own lawyers, investment bankers and accountants . . .

• If the creditors believe that the company's management isn't operating the business as a fiduciary ought to, the creditors can ask the judge to appoint an outside trustee to manage the company's affairs before it emerges from bankruptcy. This isn't a common occurrence, although it did happen in the Eastern Airlines case.

• With its funds for continuing operations in place, the company can begin the task of reorganizing its operations. Its investment bankers will consider whether the company can take existing creditors' debt and restructure it on improved or extended terms. The bankers will also determine whether it may be best for the company to bring in a "white knight" partner who can provide new financing, or whether assets ought to be sold.

• The company will negotiate with its various creditor groups, and the creditors will negotiate with each other. Virtually all of the creditor groups will want to be paid out before the others, which, of course, isn't feasible. A compromise will likely be reached at the end of an arduous negotiating process.

• Finally, if all goes well, a plan of reorganization will be produced by the company's investment bankers and lawyers. The plan will be voted on by creditors and confirmed by a federal bankruptcy judge. Once confirmed, the company will be ready to emerge from Chapter 11 proceedings. In a major corporate bankruptcy, the entire process generally takes at least six months and may take as much as two years.

Source: *The Wall Street Journal,* January 16, 1990, p. A10. Reprinted by permission of *The Wall Street Journal,* © 1990 Dow Jones & Company. All Rights Reserved Worldwide.

Adjustment of Debts.   Under Chapter 13 of the Bankruptcy Reform Act, individuals (not partnerships or corporations) can seek the protection of the court to arrange a debt adjustment plan. Chapter 13 permits only voluntary bankruptcies and is restricted to those with steady incomes and limited debts ($100,000 unsecured, $350,000 secured). After the necessary petition is filed, creditors are restrained from reaching the debtor's assets. A trustee is appointed, and the debtor files a plan for repayment.

Further Reforms?.   Distress over skyrocketing bankruptcy filings and the very slow, expensive bankruptcy process have caused Congress to struggle with additional reform legislation. At this writing in May 1994, new legislation is expected to be approved along the lines described in the following article.

LOSSES IN BANKRUPTCIES SPUR LENDERS TO STRIVE TO PROTECT THEMSELVES

Kenneth H. Bacon

Bankruptcy cost Dominic Antonelli his 103-foot yacht, his 12-acre suburban estate and his stake in Virginia's Natural Bridge, a much-visited rock formation once owned by Thomas Jefferson.

Still, he didn't come out all that badly. According to his attorneys, he was allowed to keep assets totaling $5 million, including cash and stocks, and his creditors agreed to pay him about $400,000 a year for his help in unwinding the tangle of real-estate partnerships he had set up. So bankruptcy was kind to the overextended parking-lot and real-estate magnate—especially considering that when he filed in 1991, he and his wife listed debts of $250 million and assets of $120 million.

Lots of people are using bankruptcy to hang onto a sizable slice of their wealth while sidestepping a pile of debt. They are the most visible distortion in a larger system in need of an overhaul. Bankruptcy proceedings can drag on for years, allowing debtors to stiff creditors and avoid settlement as long as possible.

"It's sickening," says James Coe, president of First Federal Savings & Loan in Delta, Ohio, who complains that the rules are stacked in favor of the debtors. For example, he notes that many homeowners can stay in their houses for as long as a year essentially cost-free after they default on mortgage payments.

Fighting Back

Tired of endless bankruptcy proceedings and outraged by dodgy debtors, lenders are fighting back. Visa U.S.A. has set up a nationwide network of lawyers to seek settlements from bankrupt cardholders. Many lenders are working harder to protect themselves. Robert Duncan, chairman of Magnolia Federal Bank, says the Hattiesburg, Miss., thrift has increased the down payments required to get home mortgages. "Bankruptcy has had an impact on credit availability," he says.

* * * * *

Corporate bankruptcies, especially, can turn into marathons, often enriching armies of lawyers and accountants at the expense of creditors. LTV Corp. is just emerging from bankruptcy proceedings after seven years. Often the delays help the companies in bankruptcy, but sometimes they have the opposite effect, ensnaring managers of troubled companies in court proceedings instead of giving them time to run the business. That can make it even harder for the companies to get a fresh start, as the law intended.

In Mr. Antonelli's case, the threat of protracted negotiations led creditors to agree to a generous settlement. Otherwise, they risked months of costly litigation that would have drained off the assets that they hoped to share. Fees for the nearly 100 lawyers, accountants and appraisers involved in the case were running as high as $1 million a month, all paid by the debtor . . .

Bankruptcies have exploded since a 1978 revision of the bankruptcy law made it easier to wipe out debts in court . . .

One factor behind the surge is the treacherous economic climate of the past decade, with lurches in interest rates, collapsing real-estate values and banking and thrift-institution crises.

Fading Stigma

But lenders also blame an attitudinal sea change that seems to have all but wiped away the stigma of bankruptcy. "Bankruptcy has become an acceptable strategy" for dealing with various economic problems, says Norman Owen, the vice president for credit management at Levi Strauss & Co.

For example, a business professor earning $50,000 a year at Western Maryland College filed for bankruptcy after borrowing $191,000 on 27 credit cards to "support his lifestyle," according to a Visa deposition. Asked in a deposition about the debt buildup, the professor explained, "Hey, it was the Eighties."

Although Visa and card-issuing banks are working harder to recover money from bankrupt cardholders, critics say they won't attack the culture of credit that often leads to bankruptcy. Michael Staten, director of Purdue University's Credit Research Center, contends that creditors' laxity in screening potential borrowers explains why bankruptcy doesn't carry its former stigma. His research shows that with card issuers aggressively pursuing new customers, more than 16% of deadbeats can obtain new lines of credit within one year of filing for bankruptcy.

"Conventional wisdom holds that former bankrupts can begin the task of reestablishing credit through small, secured installment loans obtained from local lenders who are in a position to know and monitor the borrower's financial status," Mr. Staten says. In fact, he says, bankrupts frequently can get new credit cards, car loans and retailers' charge cards shortly after declaring for bankruptcy.

Corporate bankruptcies have also come under attack for letting poor performers off the hook. "There is an element of reverse Darwinism," says Bruce Simon, a lawyer who represents labor unions in bankruptcy proceedings. This is particularly true in industries plagued with overcapacity, such as steelmaking and airlines. "You end up getting survival of the unfittest," he says. "For every LTV or Sharon Steel that is preserved, there is a Bethlehem Steel that suffers" because it competes with a reorganized company that reduced its debt and sometimes evaded other obligations.

Robin Phelan, president-elect of the American Bankruptcy Institute, an educational group, concedes that "the authors of the Bankruptcy Code probably didn't contemplate that businesses could remain in Chapter 11 for long periods of time without paying certain obligations and thus could gain a competitive advantage, particularly in price-sensitive industries."

And like the individuals that get new credit cards soon after declaring bankruptcy, companies often find it easier to borrow money after they file than before. The reason: Loans to companies in bankruptcy get preferred status, in a distribution of assets, over many other debts. Earlier this year, Leslie Fay Cos. filed for Chapter 11 protection following an accounting scandal that scared away the dressmaker's lenders. Right after the filing, Citibank agreed to lend the cash-strapped company $100 million.

A Flight into Oblivion

But sometimes, bankruptcy proceedings become so prolonged and complex that companies don't emerge intact. Eastern Airlines is often cited as the prime example of a company that, with bankruptcy-court approval, frittered away a net worth of more than $1 billion during a futile two-year effort to fly its way out of trouble and reorganize under Chapter 11.

Last year, Congress tried and failed to pass a bankruptcy-reform bill. The measure had strong support from consumer lenders, such as credit-card issuers with soaring bankruptcy losses, but a group of big banks, led by J. P. Morgan & Co., turned against it at the last minute. They feared losing out as a result of provisions requiring Chapter 11 companies to put payments to pension plans and employee health care above other creditors' claims.

This year, the bill stands a much better chance of passing. One aim of the legislation is to accelerate corporate reorganizations under Chapter 11 . . .

* * * * *

Speed-Up Maneuvers

The bankruptcy bill would limit total extensions to one year and expand bankruptcy courts' power to expedite cases. It also proposes creation of a new Chapter 10 pilot program for businesses with debts totaling less than $2.5 million in an effort to find ways to experiment with accelerated procedures for small companies.

But the law wouldn't stop still-solvent companies from filing and continuing to operate under Chapter 11. They have been able to use bankruptcy proceedings to escape obligations or limit liabilities for environmental or product-liability problems. Johns Manville Corp. (now Manville Corp.) sought protection to limit asbestos claims. A. H. Robins, now a unit of American Home Products Corp., did the same to handle claims concerning the Dalkon Shield contraceptive device. Continental Airlines entered Chapter 11 to break a union contract, and Trans World Airlines used it to escape pension obligations.

"Over the last decade or more, the bankruptcy courts have been given the task of developing an industrial policy," Mr. Simon says. "To deregulate industries [such as airlines] and leave the fallout from these decisions to the bankruptcy courts is absurd."

Generally, banks and finance companies support the legislation, although big banks and other major lenders to bankrupt companies are trying to knock out provisions that would require debtors to meet certain health and pension obligations. One provision would require companies in Chapter 11 to use proceeds from new loans to pay retirement benefits first rather than to finance continuing operations. The American Bankers Association has warned Congress that this would discourage banks from lending to Chapter 11 companies and "force many additional companies into Chapter 7 liquidation," in which assets are sold off to meet creditors' claims, and the company folds.

The bill's primary change for individuals would seek to encourage debtors to reorganize their finances and pay off their debts over three to five years under Chapter 13, rather than liquidating all their assets to pay a percentage of their debts under Chapter 7. The bill would raise to $1 million from $350,000 the ceiling on personal debts for a Chapter 13 filing. Many debtors would rather work out a payment plan under Chapter 13 because it leaves them with a much better credit rating after emerging from bankruptcy. Creditors also prefer Chapter 13 reorganization because they usually end up with more money.

Source: *The Wall Street Journal*, June 17, 1993, p. A1. Reprinted by permission of *The Wall Street Journal*, © 1993 Dow Jones & Company, Inc. All Rights Reserved Worldwide.

Questions

1. *a.* Should we try to restore the social stigma that once attached more firmly to filing for bankruptcy? Explain.
   b. In general, have we simply become too *forgiving?* Explain.
2. Can you cite reasons for the bankruptcy boom beyond those mentioned in the article?
3. Should those filing for bankruptcy under Chapter 7 not be allowed to exempt equity in their homes and autos? Explain.

TOO MUCH GOVERNMENT PROTECTION?

Broadly, the central question in this chapter, as for the entire book, is whether we in America need more or less government intervention in our commercial lives. The article that follows raises the same issue in the United Kingdom in the somewhat whimsical context of beer foam.

'CREAMY HEADS MEAN LESS BEER FOR OUR MONEY'

Associated Press

When an Englishman orders a pint of beer, he's serious about wanting a full 20-ounce pint and may well demand that the glass be topped off if there's too much foam.

But under pressure from the beer industry, the government is quietly wavering on a pre-election promise to make every pint a full one, effective next year.

Brewers estimate that filling each glass full would cost about 400 million pounds or $628 million a year—a burden to thousands of pub owners who would get fewer servings per barrel.

So the government says it will reconsider things as it throws out cumbersome and unnecessary regulations on business.

This does not sit well with British beer drinkers, who down 28 million pints a day.

* * * * *

Drinkers advocate the use of 22-ounce glasses with a line near the top marking off the 20-ounce pint, so bartenders could pour beer up to the line and the foamy head would not be counted.

*   *   *   *   *

"Obviously if a lot of the beer is froth, you're not getting a full pint of beer," said Stephen Cox, a spokesman with the Campaign for Real Ale, a group of beer activists who fight the takeover of small breweries by giant companies.

"We're getting these massively creamy heads and less beer for our money."

Granted, the government has not abandoned the full-pint rule. But officials have backed off their rhetoric from March 1992, a month before a hotly contested national election.

Edward Leigh, then the consumer affairs minister, publicized his full-pint campaign with a news release titled "Leigh raises a full liquid pint to consumers."

He said investigators had found drinkers were getting 5 percent less than a full pint on average—and as much as 17.5 percent short in some pubs.

The government decreed that by April 1994, a pint would be a pint.

But in February, regulators quietly included the full-pint rule in a wide-ranging review to abolish unnecessary red tape.

The Brewers Society, an industry trade group, contends that consumers should decide whether a pint measures up.

Drinkers can insist that glasses be topped off and boycott pubs that come up short, spokesman Tim Hampson said.

"We're having civil servants imposing on the drinkers what a beer should look like, and for most people, a beer is a personal thing," Hampson said.

Many southern English beer drinkers like their brew to come to the top of the glass with no foam, but northerners are partial to a creamy top.

The debate will go on. But Paul Bright, who was sipping bitter at the Sir Christopher Hatton pub near London's diamond district, said a little less beer in the glass makes no real difference.

"By the end of the night, you're spilling it anyway," Bright said.

Source: *Des Moines Register,* May 4, 1993, p. 85. Reprinted by permission of the copyright holder, the Associated Press.

Questions

1. Does a foam head on a glass of beer sold and advertised as a "pint" constitute a misleading or deceptive consumer practice? Explain.
2. Is this issue best left to consumers to deal with, as the Brewers Society argues? Explain.
3. *a.* Is the amount of foam in a glass of beer an issue in the United States?
   b. Should it be? Explain.
4. Is a consumer misled when sold 16 ounces of potato chips in a bag large enough to hold three times that weight and volume? Explain.

CHAPTER QUESTIONS

1. In sum, would the consumer's lot be improved if we sharply reduced or eliminated the many consumer protection efforts outlined in this chapter? Explain.
2. Once the government decided to intervene in the free market on behalf of consumers, two broad options presented themselves: (*a*) the government could have limited its effort to generating and distributing information to consumers or (*b*) the government could have set safety standards for all products. Assuming the government were forced to choose one or the other but not elements of both, which option should it choose? Explain.
3. The federal government has struck down professional and state regulations forbidding advertising

by doctors and advertisements for some products (for example, contact lenses). Why did the government open the door to advertising in those areas?

4. Consumers sometimes abuse sellers. One familiar technique is shoplifting. Of course, shoplifting is a crime. However, the criminal process is cumbersome and often does not result in monetary recoveries for sellers. As a result, at least 43 states now have laws permitting store owners to impose civil fines, the collection of which is usually turned over to a lawyer or collection agency with a threat to sue in civil court, file criminal charges, or both if payment is not forthcoming. Fines may range from $50 to $5,000 or more, depending on the value of the item stolen.
   a. Defense lawyers say this civil fine system is unfair. Why?
   b. On balance, is the civil fine approach to shoplifting a good idea? Explain.

5. In recent years, Congress has considered legislation banning tobacco advertising. Leaving health and legal issues aside, international marketing professor J. J. Boddewyn of the City University of New York argues that an advertising ban would be ill advised. Boddewyn explains that tobacco advertising is banned in five free market countries (Italy, Iceland, Singapore, Norway, and Finland). Per capita tobacco consumption did not decline in those countries following the advertising prohibitions; indeed, it increased by margins ranging from 3 percent in Finland to 68 percent in Italy. A study in five nations found only 1 percent of the 7- to 15-year-old children interviewed pointed to advertising as the most important reason for their decisions to begin smoking. The influence of parents, siblings, and friends was easily the dominant factor as they understood their decisions. And the results of the survey were the same across the five nations, even though one nation actually banned tobacco advertising (Norway), two significantly restricted it (Australia and the United Kingdom), and two employed modest restrictions (Spain and Hong Kong).[36]
   a. What arguments would you raise in favor of a ban on tobacco advertising?
   b. How would you vote on such a bill? Explain.

6. Cite some examples of consumers abusing businesspeople.

7. In 1989, 9,700 Americans visited emergency rooms to care for injuries from fireworks (down from a high of 12,600 injuries in 1986).[37] Since 1966, the federal government has limited the power and kinds of fireworks that can be purchased in the United States. And 13 states have banned fireworks of all kinds.[38]

For many children and their parents, firecrackers, Roman candles, skyrockets, and sparklers for the Fourth of July and other special occasions—a $200 million industry—have provided joy and memorable moments.

Chemistry professor John Conkling, executive director of the American Pyrotechnics Association, says that fireworks are on America's "list of endangered species":

> We could have a video game Fourth of July in the not-too-distant future, sitting in our living rooms and watching animated fireworks displays on our television screens.[39]

Various individuals and organizations, including the National Fire Protection Association, are lobbying for a complete ban on fireworks except for use by licensed professionals in public displays.
   a. Professor Conkling argues that backyard fireworks use is safe if practiced with common sense. How do we decide whether the fun and economic benefits of fireworks justifies the resulting injuries?
   b. Should we leave this issue to parents and the free market? Explain.
   c. Broadly, have government regulations on such things as gambling, three-wheeled all-terrain vehicles, fireworks, and dangerous toys taken an unnecessary toll in reduced fun in American life? Explain.

8. According to survey data, consumers in six industrialized nations overwhelmingly favor the creation of "National Departments of Consumer Protection." A consumer protection agency was approved by 65 percent or more of those surveyed: in Australia (80 percent), Canada (82 percent), England (74 percent), Israel (86 percent), Norway (65 percent), and the United States (74 percent).[40] Would you favor the creation of such a body? Explain.

9. The Consumer Product Safety Commission reported that in 1992, 39,000 people were injured while using chain saws.[41] Based on these figures, should chain saw sales be banned until a safer prod-

uct is produced? If enacted, would such a ban be effective? Explain.

10. Swedish law requires safety messages to be included in ads to children. ("Always wear a helmet when skateboarding.") In the Netherlands, ads for candy must include a picture of a toothbrush.[42] Should those policies be adopted in the United States? Explain.

11. Professor and advertising scholar J. J. Boddewyn argues that (*a*) "There are more lies in personal ads than by all business combined—from 'apartment with river view [from the bathroom,]' to 'attractive woman wants to meet man.'" (*b*) "Some government ads are downright misleading"; "armed forces recruitment posters . . . promise you will 'see the world' but do not include a warning [from the Surgeon General?] that you could be shot at and die."[43] Comment.

12. The plaintiff, a wholesaler, reached an agreement with Philco, a manufacturer, to distribute Philco appliances to retailers. The plaintiff agreed to carry an adequate inventory of Philco parts. The agreement provided that either party could terminate the contract with 90 days' written notice. In the event of termination, the wholesaler agreed on demand to resell and deliver its remaining Philco stock to Philco. The resale price was to be agreed. The agreement was terminated, but Philco declined to exercise its option to repurchase. The wholesaler was unable to sell most of the remaining Philco inventory and demanded that Philco repurchase, but Philco declined. The plaintiff brought suit, claiming the contract was unconscionable. Decide. Explain. See *W. L. May Co., Inc.* v. *Philco-Ford Corporation,* 543 P.2d 283 (Or. 1975).

13. Bankruptcy laws differ from nation to nation. In this era of global corporations, explain some of the problems that may arise out of the failure of the industrial nations to agree on an international bankruptcy treaty.

14. Roseman resigned from the John Hancock Insurance Company following allegations of misuse of his expense account. He reimbursed the account. Subsequently, he was denied employment by another insurance firm after that firm read a Retail Credit Company credit report on him. The credit report included accurate information regarding Roseman's resignation. Was Retail Credit in violation of the Fair Credit Reporting Act in circulating information regarding the resignation? Explain. See *Roseman* v. *Retail Credit Co., Inc.,* 428 F.Supp. 643 (Pa., 1977).

15. Dun & Bradstreet, Inc., a credit reporting agency, erroneously reported to five subscribers that Greenmoss Builders had filed for voluntary bankruptcy. A correction was subsequently issued. Greenmoss, remaining dissatisfied, filed suit for defamation. The Supreme Court has held—in *New York Times* v. *Sullivan,* 376 U.S. 254 (1964)— that a public official cannot recover damages for defamation in the absence of a showing that the statement was made with "actual malice"—knowledge that it was false or with reckless disregard for whether it was false. Here, the credit report in question was not a matter of public importance. Must the plaintiff, Greenmoss, show actual malice by Dun & Bradstreet? Explain. See *Dun & Bradstreet, Inc.* v. *Greenmoss Builders, Inc.,* 472 U.S. 749 (1985).

16. The Ogilvy & Mather ad agency found in a [1987] survey that only 59 percent of people . . . "like advertising a lot or a little," compared with 68 percent in a similar 1985 study. What's more, half of the consumers surveyed consider most ads to be in poor taste, while just 43 percent felt that way two years ago. Even the number of people who believe ads provide useful information has slipped: 71 percent versus 76 percent in 1985.[44]

a. Is advertising doomed to a continuing decline in respect and influence? Explain.

However, Ogilvy found that consumers around the world are generally less cynical than Americans about advertising:

People in Hong Kong, Colombia, Brazil, and Britain are much bigger fans of advertising, according to a multinational study conducted by Ogilvy. Consumers in Hong Kong and Colombia praise advertising as a way to obtain valuable information about products, while most Brazilians consider ads entertaining and enjoyable. In the six countries Ogilvy studied, only West Germans dislike ads more than Americans.[45]

b. How do you account for Americans' greater skepticism regarding advertising?

NOTES

1. "Sears Places Ads Denying California Charges on Cars," *The Wall Street Journal,* June 15, 1992, p. B5.

2. Gilbert Fuchsberg, "Sears Reinstates Sales Incentives in some Centers," *The Wall Street Journal,* March 7, 1994, p. B1.

3. "State Announces Recall of Toys," *Des Moines Register,* November 11, 1987, p. T1.

4. Ibid.

5. D. Rothschild, "The Magnuson-Moss Warranty Act: Does It Balance Warrantor and Consumer Interests?" *George Washington University Law Review* 44 (1976), pp. 335 and 337, as reported in Donald Rothschild and David Carroll, *Consumer Protection Reporting Service* (Owings Mills, Md.: National Law Publishing Corporation, 1983), vol. I, p. Intro–2.

6. See, for example, "The U.S.'s Toughest Customer," *Time,* December 12, 1969, pp. 89–98.

7. Robert J. Samuelson, "The Aging of Ralph Nader," *Newsweek,* December 12, 1985, p. 57.

8. *Lindberg Cadillac Co.* v. *Aron,* 371 S.W.2d 651 (1963).

9. See *Trustees of Columbia University* v. *Jacobsen,* 53 N.J. Super. 574, 148 A.2d 63 (1959).

10. 350 F.2d 445 (C.A.D.C. 1965).

11. Daniel Mintz, "FTC Votes Funeral Rate Disclosures," *Des Moines Register,* July 29, 1982, p. B5.

12. Roy Brown, "Federal Trade Commission Guides for the Use of Environmental Marketing Claims," in "Legal Developments in Marketing," *Journal of Marketing* 57, no. 2 (April 1993), p. 110.

13. Michael Katz, "FTC Forces Car Rental Firms to Reveal All," *The Wall Street Journal,* August 8, 1992, p. B4.

14. *Kraft* v. *F.T.C.,* 970 F.2d 311 (7th Cir. 1992) at 314.

15. Gary T. Ford and John E. Calfee, "Recent Developments in FTC Policy on Deception," *Journal of Marketing* 50 (July 1986), pp. 82, 98.

16. Larry Ballard, "Target Accuses Wal-Mart of False Advertising," *Waterloo Courier,* March 25, 1993, p. B5.

17. Michael Lemov and Malcolm Woolf, "Underreporting Defects Is Risky," *The National Law Journal,* December 14, 1992, p. S6.

18. *Boston Globe,* "Thousands Hurt in Mowing Accidents," *The Montreal Gazette,* June 21, 1993, p. B4.

19. Viveca Novak, "The Grinch that Stole the CPSC," *The National Law Journal,* December 19, 1992, p. 2,921.

20. *The Washington Post,* "Garage Doors Covered by New Rules," *Waterloo Courier,* January 3, 1993, p. E6.

21. Ibid.

22. Diana Lundin, "Will Consumer Groups Put the Brakes on Walkers for Babies?" *Des Moines Register,* December 26, 1992, p. T1.

23. Amy Eskind, "Bringing Up Baby," *The Wall Street Journal,* April 13, 1993, p. A14.

24. Ibid.

25. The materials in this section are drawn, in part, from Rothschild and Carroll, *Consumer Protection Reporting Service.*

26. Jeffrey Rothfeder, "Is Nothing Private?" *Business Week,* September 4, 1989, p. 74.

27. Associated Press, "Poll: Loss of Privacy Feared by Consumers," *Waterloo Courier,* June 12, 1990, p. B8.

28. Ibid.

29. Michael Miller, "TRW Agrees to Overhaul Its Credit-Reporting Business," *The Wall Street Journal,* December 11, 1991, p. B1.

30. *Newsday,* "New Federal Law Chills Pesky Telephone Solicitations," *Waterloo Courier,* December 20, 1992, p. A6.

31. Michael Miller, "FTC Takes Aim at Trans Union, TRW Mail Lists," *The Wall Street Journal,* January 13, 1993, p. B1.

32. David Elbert, "Dark Side to Reform Measure," *Des Moines Register,* June 14, 1992, p. G1.

33. Kenneth Bacon, "Losses in Bankruptcies Spur Lenders to Strive to Protect Themselves," *The Wall Street Journal,* June 17, 1993, p. A1.

34. Ibid.

35. Amy Marcus, "Declaring Insolvency Called a Bad Solution," *The Wall Street Journal,* February 21, 1990, p. B1.

36. J. J. Boddewyn, "Smoking Ads Don't Get People Hooked," *The Wall Street Journal,* November 21, 1986, p. 24.

37. Associated Press, "Fireworks Expert Sees Tradition Dying," *Des Moines Register,* July 4, 1990, p. 4A.

38. Ibid.

39. Ibid.

40. Hiram Barksdale et al., "A Cross-National Survey of Consumer Attitudes towards Marketing Practices, Consumerism, and Government Regulations," *Columbia Journal of World Business* 17, no. 2 (Summer 1982), pp. 71, 83.

41. Joanne Ball Artis, "Pattern of Injuries Cited in Wood-Chipper Case," *Boston Globe,* August 19, 1993, p. 34.

42. J. J. Boddewyn, "The Global Spread of Advertising Regulation," *MSU Business Topics,* Spring 1981, pp. 5, 9.

43. Ibid., p. 12.

44. Ronald Alsop, "Advertisers Find the Climate Less Hostile Outside the United States," *The Wall Street Journal,* December 10, 1987, p. 25.

45. Ibid.

16

PRODUCT LIABILITY

●

INTRODUCTION

Product liability law governs litigation for injuries resulting from defective products. As recently as the early 1960s, product liability was little more than an obscure corner of the law. Strict liability, today's primary weapon for the plaintiff in a defective product action, did not exist. Through a steady accumulation of judicial decisions and legislative enactments, product liability litigation is now so common and often so successful that it has changed the business community's manufacturing and distribution practices while, arguably, imposing a "liability or accident tax" on consumers. For example, approximately 30 percent of the cost of a stepladder, one-third of the price of a small airplane, and 95 percent of the price of childhood vaccines are attributable to the cost of dealing with personal injury lawsuits involving those products.[1]

A Conference Board survey revealed that as a result of product liability concerns:

47% of American manufacturers have withdrawn products from the market, 39% have declined to introduce new products, 25% have discontinued product research, 15% have laid off workers, and 8% have closed plants.[2]

Much of the American business community believes that our legal liability system is simply out of control. These concerns have led to repeated but as yet unsuccessful efforts by Congress to pass legislation reforming our tort (personal injuries not arising out of contracts) liability system.

On the other hand, a 1994 study by Jury Verdict Research of 90,000 cases indicates that juries seem to be increasingly unsympathetic to product liability claims. The study revealed that juries in 1992 found for plaintiffs in about 43 percent of the product liability cases while in 1987 plaintiffs had prevailed in 54 percent of those cases. Similarly, about 75 percent of the jurors interviewed by the consulting firm, FTI Jury Analyst Group, said that they believe jury awards are too large and about two-thirds of those jurors believe that we have too many lawsuits.[3]

We will explore both the technical dimensions of product liability actions and the policy dispute regarding the fairness and wisdom of contemporary product liability law. The three major causes of action are negligence, breach of warranty, and strict liability.

Part One—Negligence

In dangerously simplified terms, *negligence* is a breach of the duty of due care. To paraphrase *Black's Law Dictionary,* a negligent act is the failure to do what a reasonable person, guided by those considerations that ordinarily regulate human affairs, would do or doing what a reasonable person would not do. Thus, a producer or distributor has a duty to exercise reasonable care in the entire stream of events associated with the development and sale of a product. In designing, manufacturing, testing, repairing, and warning of potential dangers, those in the chain of production and distribution must meet the standard of the reasonably prudent person. Failure to do so constitutes negligence. Furthermore, rather recent decisions extend potential liability to those situations in which a product is being put to an unintended but reasonably foreseeable *misuse.*

Historically, product producers were ordinarily protected from negligence liability under the combined effects of the doctrines of privity and caveat emptor (let the buyer beware). *Privity* is the label applied to the legal relationship arising when parties enter a contract. As a consequence of the privity requirement, wronged consumers could reach only those in the chain of distribution with whom a contractual relationship (privity) had been established. Therefore, consumers ordinarily could not recover against a remote manufacturer. Under the caveat emptor principle, the vendor was liable for defects only to the extent that an agreement was reached to provide for that liability. In previous centuries, consumers might have expected to deal face to face with the product producer. Therefore, the privity and caveat emptor notions held at least the superficial legitimacy of a buyer and seller, presumed to be of equal bargaining power, protecting their own interests in an equitable contract. However, the development of elaborate, multilayered systems of production and distribution prompted a revision of legal standards. In a famous 1916 New York state decision (*MacPherson* v. *Buick Motor Co.*), brilliant jurist Benjamin Cardozo held that an action could be maintained against a remote manufacturer of an automobile with a defective wheel that broke and caused injury.[4] In so doing, Cardozo put aside the view that the plaintiff's right to recovery grew only out of a contractual relationship. Cardozo's view has since been uniformly adopted, thus permitting victims of negligence to bring actions against all wrongdoers in the chain of production and distribution.

To establish a successful negligence claim, the plaintiff must meet each of the following requirements:

1. *Duty.* The plaintiff must establish that the defendant owed a duty of due care to the plaintiff. In general, the standard applied is that of the fictitious reasonable man or woman. That "reasonable person" acts prudently, sensibly, and responsibly. The standard of reasonableness depends, of course, on the circumstances of the situation.

2. *Breach of duty.* The plaintiff must demonstrate that the defendant breached the duty of due care by engaging in conduct that did not conform to the reasonable person standard. Breach of the duty of due care may result from either the

commission of a careless act or the omission of a reasonable, prudent act. Would a reasonable man or woman discharge a firearm in a public park? Would a reasonable person foresee that failure to illuminate one's front entry steps might lead to a broken limb?

3. *Causation.*

    a. Cause in fact. Did the defendant's breach of the duty of due care actually cause the harm in question? Commonly, the "but for" test is applied to determine cause in fact. For example, but for the defendant's failure to stop at the red light, the plaintiff pedestrian would not have been struck down in the crosswalk.

    b. Proximate cause. The plaintiff must establish that the defendant's actions were the proximate cause of the injury. As a matter of policy, is the defendant's conduct sufficiently connected to the plaintiff's injury as to justify imposing liability? Many injuries arise from a series of events—some of them wildly improbable. Did the defendant's negligence lead directly to the plaintiff's harm, or did some intervening act break the causal link between the defendant's negligence and the harm? For example, the community's allegedly negligent maintenance resulted in a blocked road, forcing the plaintiff to detour. While on the detour route, the plaintiff's vehicle was struck by a plane attempting to land at a nearby airport. Was the defendant's negligence the proximate cause of the plaintiff's injury?[5]

4. *Injury.* The plaintiff must have sustained injury, and, due to problems of proof, that injury must be physical.

Proximate cause may be the most obscure ingredient in the test for negligence. Establishing proximate cause often requires addressing the slippery notion of foreseeability and its relation to duty, as illustrated by the *Watters* case.

WATTERS v. TSR, INC.
904 F.2d 378 (6th Cir. 1990)

Circuit Judge David A. Nelson

This is a wrongful death case in which the plaintiff [Sheila Watters] appeals from an order granting summary judgment to the manufacturer of a parlor game called "Dungeons & Dragons." The plaintiff alleges that her son was an avid player of the game, and it came to dominate his mind to such an extent that he was driven to suicide.

* * * * *

I

* * * * *

TSR's Dungeons & Dragons game is one in which the players assume the roles of characters in "adventures" suggested in illustrated booklets. These adventures, set in an imaginary ancient world, are narrated and orchestrated by a player known as the Dungeon Master.

The results of various encounters between characters are determined by using dice in conjunction with tables provided in the published materials.

The rules of the game do not call for the physical acting out of any role. The game is usually played at a table or in some other comfortable setting. We have seen no indication in the record that the game's materials glorify or encourage suicide, or even mention it. It does not appear that the materials allude in any way to guns. Many schools and libraries use Dungeons & Dragons as a learning tool and as a means of promoting creativity. More than a million copies have been sold, according to TSR's records . . .

Mrs. Watters describes her son, Johnny Burnett, as a "devoted" Dungeons & Dragons player who became absorbed by the game to the point of losing touch with reality. She claims that as a result of his exposure to the game, "he lost control of his own independent will and was driven to self-destruction." The record does not disclose Johnny's age at the time of the tragedy.

TSR moved for summary judgment on various grounds, including these: [(1) First Amendment claim—omitted]; (2) TSR owed no duty to refrain from distributing the game or to warn of the possible consequences of playing it; and (3) Johnny Burnett having died at his own hand, the suicide was an intervening or superseding cause of his death. Granting summary judgment to the defendant on First Amendment grounds, the district court did not reach any of the state law issues.

* * * * *

III

"Actionable negligence," under Kentucky law, "consists of a duty, a violation thereof, and consequent injury." . . . "Every person owes a duty to every other person to exercise *ordinary care* in his activities to prevent any *foreseeable injury* from occurring to such other person" . . .

* * * * *

The plaintiff's complaint alleges that the defendant violated its duty of ordinary care in two respects: it disseminated Dungeons & Dragons literature to "mentally fragile persons," and it failed to warn that the "possible consequences" of playing the game might include "loss of control of the mental processes." To submit this case to a jury on either theory, it seems to us, would be to stretch the concepts of foreseeability and ordinary care to lengths that would deprive them of all normal meaning.

The defendant cannot be faulted, obviously, for putting its game on the market without attempting to ascertain the mental condition of each and every prospective player. The only practicable way of insuring that the game could never reach a "mentally fragile" individual would be to refrain from selling it at all—and we are confident that the courts of Kentucky would never permit a jury to say that simply by marketing a parlor game, the defendant violated its duty to exercise ordinary care.

As to the supposed breach of a duty to warn, Kentucky law imposes a general duty on manufacturer and suppliers to warn of dangers known to them but not known to persons whose use of the product can reasonably be anticipated . . .

Johnny Burnett was certainly one of the class of people whose use of the game could reasonably have been anticipated, and there is no contention that he or his mother, Mrs. Watters, knew of any danger in using it. (An affidavit executed by Mrs. Watters indicates that she knew the game was often played at the public library; that Johnny and his friends played the game constantly after school and on weekends over a period of several years; and that never, either before or during the period when he and his friends were immersed in the game, did Johnny cause his mother any problems.) But if Johnny's suicide was not foreseeable to his own mother, there is no reason to suppose that it was foreseeable to defendant TSR.

In moving for summary judgment on the breach of duty question, defendant TSR put Mrs. Watters to her proof on foreseeability and knowledge—on whether TSR knew of some danger that made the suicide foreseeable. Mrs. Watters was not free simply to rest on her pleadings; she was required, by affidavits, depositions, answers to interrogatories, or the like, to "designate 'specific facts showing that there [was] a genuine issue for trial.'" . . . This she failed to do. Aside from one vague reference to hearsay about the game's "dangerous propensities"—Mrs. Watters' affidavit concluded with a sentence reading, in its entirety, "I have subsequently read in many publications including the Paducah Sun of the dangerous propensities of the game Dungeons & Dragons"—the record sets forth no "specific fact" showing that the defendant's game was in fact dangerous or that the defendant had knowledge of any danger when the materials that Johnny and his friends had been using for so many years were manufactured and sold.*

The actual content of the materials in question would hardly have given TSR reason to foresee that players of the game would become more susceptible to murder or suicide than non-players. The materials make it clear that Dungeons & Dragons is a "let's pretend" game, not an incitement to do anything more than exercise the imagination. And the imaginary world referred to in the booklets—a world of magical spells, hidden treasures, and fantastic monsters—does not appear to be a world in which people kill themselves or engage in acts of wanton cruelty toward other people. We are not dealing here with the kind of violence or depravity to which children can be exposed when they watch television, or go to the movies, or read the fairy tales of the Brothers Grimm, for example.

Television, movies, magazines, and books (including comic books) are far more pervasive than the defendant's games. Were the courts of Kentucky prepared to say that works of the imagination can be linked to a foreseeable danger of antisocial behavior, thereby giving rise to a duty to warn, one would expect to find Kentucky caselaw to that effect in lawsuits involving television networks, book publishers, or the like. There is no such caselaw. And what little authority exists outside Kentucky favors the defendant, not the plaintiff. See for example, *Zamora v. Columbia Broadcasting System,* 480 F.Supp. 199 (S.D.Fla. 1979) (no cause of action stated against three major television networks for allowing the plaintiffs' minor child to become so "intoxicated" by television violence that he was "stimulated, in-

---

*We have found two decisions, not cited in the briefs, mentioning claims that Dungeons & Dragons has dangerous propensities. In *State* v. *Molitor,* 729 S.W.2d 551 (Mo.Ct.App.1987), where a young woman was tied up and strangled after an all-night houseparty devoted to listening to music, consuming liquor, smoking marijuana and practicing martial arts, the defendant sought to introduce expert testimony suggesting that he had been "desensitized" at some point by playing Dungeons & Dragons. The appellate court sustained exclusion of the testimony on relevance grounds and because the defendant's offers of proof made no showing that he had, in fact, been "desensitized." In *People* v. *Ventiquattro,* 138 App.Div.2d 925, 527 N.Y.S.2d 137 (1988), a fifteen-year-old boy who killed a companion with a shotgun gave the police several conflicting accounts of how the shooting occurred. In one account he stated that he was playing the game Dungeons & Dragons and shot the victim while fantasizing that it was his job to exterminate evil. Whether this particular account was truthful, and whether TSR ever learned of it, we do not know.

cited and instigated" to shoot and kill an elderly neighbor.) [and] *Herceg* v. *Hustler Magazine, Inc.,* 565 F.Supp. 802, (S.D. Texas 1983) (absent an allegation of incitement, no claim stated against magazine for publishing a description of "autoerotic asphyxiation" that allegedly prompted plaintiffs' decedent to hang himself).

* * * * *

IV

By itself, moreover, a breach of duty is not enough to warrant recovery; there can be no liability for negligence if the negligence is not shown to have "caused" the injury complained of. And the courts of Kentucky have long recognized that the chain of causation may be broken by "facts [that] are legally sufficient to constitute an intervening cause." . . .

Facts sufficient to constitute an intervening cause "are facts of such 'extraordinary rather than normal,' or 'highly extraordinary,' nature, unforeseeable in character, as to relieve the original wrongdoer of liability to the ultimate victim." . . .

* * * * *

The fact of Johnny Burnett's suicide is undisputed. The third paragraph of Mrs. Watters' complaint affirmatively avers "[t]hat on the 29th day of September, 1987 the deceased departed this world as a direct and proximate result of a gun shot wound self inflicted by said deceased." Whether that extraordinary and tragic occurrence was or was not a "superseding cause" is thus a legal issue that must be resolved by the court.

Courts have long been rather reluctant to recognize suicide as a proximate consequence of a defendant's wrongful act . . . Generally speaking, it has been said, the act of suicide is viewed as "an independent intervening act which the original tortfeasor could not have reasonably [been] expected to foresee." . . .

There are several exceptions to the general rule. Where a person known to be suicidal is placed in the direct care of a jailer or other custodian, for example, and the custodian negligently fails to take appropriate measures to guard against the person's killing himself, the act of self destruction may be found to have been a direct and proximate consequence of the custodian's breach of duty. *Sudderth* v. *White,* 621 S.W.2d 33 (Ky. App. 1981) . . .

* * * * *

Johnny was not known to be suicidal, as far as the plaintiff has told us, and he was not placed in the care or custody of defendant TSR. Accordingly, the plaintiff can derive no benefit from cases such as *Sudderth* v. *White* . . . The fact is, unfortunately, that youth is not always proof against the strange waves of despair and hopelessness that sometimes sweep seemingly normal people to suicide, and we have no way of knowing that Johnny would not have committed suicide if he had not played Dungeons & Dragons. Finally, of course, it does not appear that Mrs. Watters can show that Johnny was delirious or psychotic, or that he acted under an irresistible impulse or while incapable of realizing what he was doing.

On the contrary, Mrs. Watters' affidavit shows affirmatively that Johnny Burnett, who lived in her household throughout his life, never caused Mrs. Watters any problems. He went to school regularly, and he took care of a paper route. The record contains no affidavit from a psychiatrist or similar expert suggesting that he suffered from any psychosis. As far as the record discloses, no one had any reason to know that Johnny Burnett was going to take his own life. We cannot tell why he did so or what his mental state was at the time. His death surely was not the fault of his mother, or his school, or his friends, or the manufacturer of the game he and his friends so loved to play. Tragedies such as this simply defy rational explanation, and courts should not pretend otherwise.

Affirmed.

Questions

1. What was the central issue in this case?
2. What test does the court employ in determining whether the defendant, TSR, owed a duty to the deceased?
3. Why did the court conclude that the plaintiff, Watters, had failed to show that TSR had *caused* Johnny Burnett's death?
4. Plaintiff was seven month's pregnant and the mother of 17-month-old James. She was standing on the sidewalk, and James was in the street. A truck being negligently driven bore down on the boy, running him over. The shock caused the mother to miscarry and suffer actual physical and emotional injury. She brought suit against the driver for harm to herself and the infant child.
   a. What is the issue in this case?
   b. Decide the case. Explain. See *Amaya* v. *Home Ice, Fuel & Supply Co.,* 379 P.2d 513 (CA. S. Ct., 1963). But also see *Dillon* v. *Legg,* 441 P.2d 912 (CA. S. Ct., 1968).
5. Is a fireworks manufacturer liable for harm to children who ignited an explosive that had failed to detonate in the town's public display the previous day? Explain.
6. The mother of a 12-year-old boy who died in a shooting accident when a gun he was playing with accidentally discharged sued *Boys Life,* a magazine published by the Boy Scouts of America. The mother claimed that the boy was influenced to experiment with a rifle after reading a 16-page firearms advertising section in the magazine.
   a. What product liability claims would the mother raise?
   b. What constitutional defense would the Boy Scouts raise?
   c. Decide. Explain. See *Jan Way* v. *Boy Scouts of America,* 856 S.W.2d 230 (Tex. 1993).

CLASSES OF NEGLIGENCE CLAIMS

Personal injuries resulting from negligence are commonplace, but certain classes of problems deserve particular mention.

Manufacturing

Improper manufacturing, handling, and/or inspection of products often give rise to negligence claims. However, the extremely complex process of producing, distributing, and using a product sometimes so obscures the root of the injury in question that proof of fault is nearly impossible to establish. (See the section on *res ipsa loquitur,* which follows shortly.)

Another commonplace problem in manufacturing negligence is the situation where rapid technological advances provide safer manufacturing methods than were available at the time of the injury in question. For example, a hemophiliac, living in Kentucky, was diagnosed with AIDS in 1983 and died in 1985, whereupon his wife sued the manufacturer of the blood product that the deceased had used to combat his hemophilia. A federal court of appeals decision rejected the wife's claim that the drug company should have been employing a heat treatment process that was subsequently shown to be effective in inactivating the virus and that apparently had been successfully employed in Germany, but not in the United States, as early as the 1970s. The court said that under Kentucky law, "compliance with industry custom is evidence of non-negligence" and that heat treatment to prevent the spread of AIDS was not adopted in the United States until after 1984.[6]

Designing

Defective design of a product may provoke a negligence action. Two principal lines of analysis have emerged: (1) The *risk/utility test* holds that a product is negligently designed if the benefits of a product's design are outweighed by the risks that accompany that design. (2) The *reasonable expectations* test imposes on the manufacturer a duty to design its products so that they are safe not only for their intended use but for any reasonably foreseeable use as well. For example, in the leading case of *Larsen* v. *General Motors Corporation,*[7] a U.S. court of appeals found GMC guilty of negligence in the design of the steering assembly of a 1963 Chevrolet Corvair, even though the steering assembly had no causal relationship with the accident that led to the lawsuit. In that case, the plaintiff received severe injuries from a head-on collision in which the steering mechanism of the Corvair was shoved back into his head as he was driving the car. The court explained that auto accidents, as a class, are foreseeable:

> While automobiles are not made for the purpose of colliding with each other, a frequent and inevitable contingency of normal use will result in collisions and injury-producing impacts. No rational basis exists for limiting recovery to situations where the defect in design or manufacture was the causative factor of the accident, as the accident and the resulting injury . . . all are foreseeable.[8]

Question

1. Professor Kip Viscusi argues that we should exempt companies from liability for *design defects* where they can show "either compliance with a specific government regulation or the use of a hazard warnings program that is sufficiently effective that it leads to informed market decisions." See W. Kip Viscusi, *Reforming Products Liability Law* (Cambridge: Harvard University Press, 1991), p. 128. This book was reviewed by Suzanne Lambert, *Michigan Law Review* 90, (May 1992), p. 1,634.
   a. Explain what Viscusi is proposing.
   b. Explain the weaknesses in relying on government regulation as a method of consumer protection.
   c. Would you favor Viscusi's approach to design defect liability? Explain.

Warning

A negligence claim may arise from a supplier's *failure to warn* of a danger associated with the product. According to the *Restatement (Second) of Torts,* liability attaches if the supplier "knows or has reason to know that the chattel is or is likely to be dangerous for the use for which it is supplied" and "has no reason to believe" that the user "will realize its dangerous condition." Judicial decisions in duty to warn cases are influenced by such factors as the feasibility of an effective warning and the probable seriousness of the injury.

Laaperi installed a smoke detector in his bedroom, properly connecting it to his home's electrical system. Six months later, Laaperi's house burned and three of his children were killed. A short circuit, which caused the fire, also deprived the A.C.-powered smoke detector of electricity. Thus, the detector did not sound a warning. Laaperi then claimed that Sears, Roebuck, where he purchased the detector, was guilty of negligence for failing to warn him that a fire might disable his smoke detector such that no warning would issue. How would you rule in this case? See *Laaperi* v. *Sears, Roebuck & Co.,* 787 F.2d 726 (1st Cir., 1986).

RES IPSA LOQUITUR

As alluded to previously, problems of proof are sometimes so daunting as to render negligence law an ineffectual tool in serving the injured consumer. In part because of that condition, the courts have adopted the doctrine of *res ipsa loquitur* (the thing speaks for itself). The doctrine permits the court to infer the defendant's negligence even though that negligence cannot be proven—that is, the facts suggest that the plaintiff's injury must have resulted from negligence on the part of the defendant but the circumstances are such that the plaintiff is unable to prove negligence. The case that follows sets out the test for applying *res ipsa loquitur.*

PAT STALTER v. COCA-COLA BOTTLING COMPANY OF ARKANSAS AND GEYER SPRINGS FOOD CITY, INC.
669 S.W.2d 460 (Ark. 1984)

Justice Hickman

Pat Stalter, the appellant, was injured when a bottle fell through the bottom of a soft drink carton and broke while she was shopping at Food City, a Little Rock, Arkansas, grocery store. She sued Food City and Coca-Cola Bottling Company for damages. After hearing all the evidence, the trial court granted both appellees' motions for directed verdicts. We review the trial court's direction of a verdict . . .

Appellant was in Food City on December 10, 1981, with her employer, shopping for groceries. She lifted a carton of one-liter Coca-Cola bottles into her basket, and as she did, one of the bottles fell through the bottom of the carton and broke. A piece of glass went through her slacks, boot, and hose, and cut her leg. As the bottle dropped, she said that she hit her right hand against some object and injured it. She was immediately referred by a store employee to a clinic where the cut was stitched. She received other medical care later. Her employer verified her account and said that the carton was "mushy" and looked as though it had been wet for some time.

The Coca-Colas were in a display that was maintained by Coca-Cola Bottling Company. Two or three times a week the company visited the store, cleaned the shelves, and replenished and rotated the stock. A Coca-Cola employee testified that they do not manufacture the cartons they use. He said that their process insures that only a minimal amount of moisture is on the bottle when placed in the carton. Furthermore, he testified that the tensile strength of the carton is actually increased by moisture. The cartons are designed to be used three times but the employee stated that approximately half are reused and those are only reused once. Only a perfunctory visual inspection is made before reuse.

The appellant argues on appeal that the evidence should have been allowed to go to the jury on [the theory of] res ipsa loquitur . . .

[Strict liability and warranty claims omitted.]

Res ipsa loquitur is a doctrine that, when applied, allows the jury to infer negligence from the plaintiff's testimony of the circumstances surrounding the accident. The procedural effect of the application of the doctrine is that the burden shifts to the defendant to go forward with evidence to offset the inference of negligence. To apply the doctrine, the plaintiff must show that the injury was caused by an instrumentality under the control of the defendant, that the accident ordinarily would not happen in the absence of the defendant's negligence, and that there is no evidence of other causes of the accident.

In this case the appellant offered evidence that she was injured because of a damaged soft drink carton, that the carton was under control of both of the appellees, and that she was not at fault.

Problems in applying res ipsa loquitur arise where, as in this case, there are plural defendants and, although the plaintiff has been injured through negligence, he cannot positively point to the defendant responsible. The doctrine may be applied to plural defendants. The difficulty in such cases is that no one of the defendants has exclusive control of the instrumentality that allegedly caused the injury. That is why the trial court refused to apply res ipsa loquitur in this case. The control requirement is not always equivalent to exclusive control however. More than one defendant may be liable where both have a duty to the plaintiff and share control. Several injury cases involving soft drinks are illustrative of the position courts have taken.

* * * * *

In *Nichols* v. *Nold* [258 P.2d 317 (1953)] a soft drink bottle exploded, injuring the plaintiff. The Supreme Court of Kansas held that res ipsa loquitur should be applied to both the grocery store and the bottler because:

> The real test is whether defendants were in control at the time of the negligent act or omission which either at the time or later produced the accident. The fact that plaintiff did not know which one of the defendants was the cause of the accident, or when or where it took place, was the reason for naming them as parties defendant.

A different result was reached in *James* v. *Childs,* 166 So. 2d 77 (La. App. 1964). There the bottom of a soft drink carton gave way and a breaking bottle injured the plaintiff. The plaintiff sued the grocery store and the bottler. The Louisiana court held that res ipsa loquitur could only be applied to the bottler because the store had no duty to inspect the bottoms of the cartons, and because it was highly improbable that a customer or employee of the store caused the damage to the carton.

Although the facts of James v. Childs are very similar to those in this case, we disagree with the court's reasoning. Once the appellant explained how the accident happened, it was incumbent upon Coca-Cola and Food City to present proof that the accident was not their fault. Indeed, they both did try to shift the blame. Here, Coca-Cola admitted that they had control over the display; that they arranged it, replenished it, and otherwise maintained it. A Food City employee testified that Food City employees occasionally replaced drinks when the display was empty or replaced a carton that was out of place in the store. Beyond that evidence of shared control, both appellees also had a duty to the appellant. Food City had a duty to exercise ordinary care to maintain its premises in reasonably safe condition. Food City and Coca-Cola both had a duty to use due care in discovering obvious defects. The evidence of shared control of the carton, together with the duty each appellee owed the appellant, is such that the theory of res ipsa loquitur should have been presented to the jury. Where there are several defendants who are in control and burdened with the supervision of an instrumentality, it is for them to explain when that instrumentality injures someone . . .

* * * * *

. . . It will be for the jury to determine the respective liabilities of the parties, if any. We reverse and remand for proceedings consistent with this opinion.

Questions

1. What is the test for establishing *res ipsa loquitur?*
2. What reasoning did the court employ in holding that both defendants might be liable under the *res ipsa loquitur* theory?
3. In your opinion, does *res ipsa loquitur* impose an excessive and unnecessary burden on defendants, or—in this complicated era of mass production, with its very distant relationship between buyers and producers—is *res ipsa* appropriate? Explain.
4. A bartender, Parrillo, was opening a bottle of grenadine when it exploded, causing injury. Parrillo sued Giroux Company, the producer of the liquor. Giroux packaged the liquor itself after buying bottles from a manufacturer. Giroux visually inspected the bottles and ordinarily found defects in 1 of every 400 to 500 bottles. The evidence showed that Parrillo did not mishandle the bottle. Decide the case. Explain. See *Parrillo* v. *Giroux Co.,* 426 A.2d 1313 (R.I. 1981).

DEFENSES AGAINST NEGLIGENCE

Even if the plaintiff has proven all of the necessary elements of a negligence claim, the defendant may still prevail by establishing a good defense. Two of those defenses (and a variation) are of special importance.

Comparative Negligence

Most states have adopted comparative negligence as a defense. It involves weighing the relative negligence of the parties. Though the formula varies from state to state, typically the plaintiff's recovery is reduced by a percentage equal to the percentage of the plaintiff's fault in the case. Assume a plaintiff sustained $10,000 in injuries in an accident. If the plaintiff's own negligence is found to be 20 percent responsible for the injuries, then the plaintiff's recovery will be reduced to $8,000. When the plaintiff's fault actually exceeds that of the defendant, the plaintiff may be barred from recovery.

Contributory Negligence

Rather than employing the comparative negligence doctrine, a few states continue to follow the historic rule that any contribution by the plaintiff to his or her own harm constitutes a *complete bar to recovery.* If the plaintiff is found to have contributed in any way to her injury, even if that contribution is miniscule, she is unable to recover.

Assumption of Risk

A plaintiff who willingly enters a dangerous situation and is injured will not be permitted to recover. For example, if a driver sees that the road ahead is flooded, he will not be compensated for the injuries sustained when he loses control as he attempts to drive through the water. His recovery is barred even though the road was flooded due to operator error in opening a floodgate. The requirements for use of the assumption of risk defense are (1) knowledge of the risk and (2) voluntary assumption of the risk.

The case that follows illustrates the application of the contributory/comparative negligence defense.

INSURANCE CO. OF NORTH AMERICA v. PASAKARNIS
451 So.2d 447 (Fla. 1984)

Chief Justice Alderman

The facts of this case are simple and straightforward. While driving a jeep, without having fastened the available and fully operational seat belt contained therein, Richard Pasakarnis was injured in an accident caused entirely by John Menninger who had run a stop sign and struck Pasakarnis's jeep broadside. Pasakarnis was thrown from the jeep and landed on his posterior. As a result, he sustained a compression-type injury to his lower back. His treating physician testified that his injury was caused by his flying through the air and impacting on the pavement.

In their answer to the complaint, defendants, petitioners here, alleged as an affirmative defense that at the time of the accident, Pasakarnis had available for his use a seat belt which, had it been utilized, would have substantially reduced or prevented any bodily injuries to him; that Pasakarnis was negligent in failing to use this safety device; and that his damages should be reduced in proportion to his negligence. Pasakarnis moved to strike this affirmative defense, contending that, because he had no duty to wear a seat belt, the fact that he was not wearing his seat belt when this accident occurred does not establish a legal basis to reduce the amount of his damage award. The trial court granted the motion to strike, holding that expert testimony pertaining to the nonuse of seat belts and the causal relationship between nonuse and Pasakarnis's injuries would not be admissible at trial . . .

The defendants proffered the deposition of an engineer-accident analyst who stated that had Pasakarnis properly utilized his seat belt, it would have restrained him in the seat of the jeep and he would not have been ejected . . . Further, in response to the question of whether Pasakarnis would have been likely to suffer any injury inside the jeep itself if he had been restrained by his seat belt and shoulder harness at the time of impact, the expert opined that within a high degree of probability, Pasakarnis would not have sustained any injury.

The jury found that Menninger was 100 percent responsible for the accident and that the total amount of Pasakarnis's damages was $100,000 . . .

Upon appeal, the District Court of Appeal, Fourth District, affirmed the judgment of the trial court holding the seat belt evidence inadmissible. The Fourth District . . . elected to follow a line of authority which disallows evidence of failure to use an available operational seat belt. It found that the effectiveness of seat belts in preventing or limiting injury is still questionable and concluded that their nonuse should not be deemed prima facie unreasonable. It asserted judicial restraint as a compelling reason to answer the certified question in the negative and . . . decided that it was not within the province of the courts to legislate on the use of seat belts.

* * * * *

We disagree and find this issue particularly appropriate for judicial decision. In the past, this Court has not abdicated its continuing responsibility to the citizens of this state to ensure that the law remains both fair and realistic as society and technology change. In fact, the law of torts in Florida has been modernized, for the most part, through the courts.

* * * * *

In *Hoffman* v. *Jones*, we decided that contributory negligence as a complete bar to a plaintiff's action was unjust . . . In adopting the doctrine of comparative negligence, we explained that under this theory a plaintiff is prevented from recovering *"only that proportion of his damages for which he is responsible."*

* * * * *

. . . [W]e hold that the "seat belt defense" is viable in Florida. The seat belt has been proven to afford the occupant of an automobile a means whereby he or she may minimize his or her personal damages prior to occurrence of the accident.

. . . [A]utomobile collisions are foreseeable as are the so-called "second collisions" with the interior of the automobile. The seat belt has been a safety device required by the federal government for nearly 20 years.

* * * * *

Those jurisdictions adopting the "seat belt defense" have considered three different approaches: (1) plaintiff's nonuse is negligent per se; (2) in failing to make use of an available seat belt, plaintiff has not complied with a standard of conduct which a reasonable prudent man would have pursued under similar circumstances, and therefore he may be found contributorily negligent; and (3) by not fastening his seat belt, plaintiff may, under the circumstances of a particular case, be found to have acted unreasonably and in disregard of his or her best interests and, therefore, should not be able to recover those damages which would not have occurred if his or her seat belt had been fastened.

Because Florida does not by statute require the use of available seat belts, we reject the rule that failure to wear a seat belt is negligence per se as have the majority of jurisdictions. We also reject the second approach because contributory negligence is applicable only if plaintiff's failure to exercise due care causes in whole or in part the accident rather than enhancing the severity of the injuries. Rather, we adopt the third approach . . . Nonuse of the seat belt may or may not amount to a failure to use reasonable care on the part of the plaintiff. Whether it does depends on the particular circumstances of the case. Defendant has the burden of pleading and proving that the plaintiff did not use an available and operational seat belt, that the plaintiff's failure to use the seat belt was unreasonable under the circumstances, and that there was a causal relationship between the injuries sustained by the plaintiff and plaintiff's failure to buckle up. If there is competent evidence to prove that the failure to use an available and operational seat belt produced or contributed substantially to producing at least a portion of plaintiff's damages, then the jury should be permitted to consider this factor, along with all other facts in evidence, in deciding whether the damages for which defendant may otherwise be liable should be reduced. Nonuse of an available seat belt, however, should not be considered by the triers of fact in resolving the issue of liability unless it has been alleged and proved that such nonuse was a proximate cause of the accident.

[District Court decision quashed. Case remanded.]

Questions

1. Why did the court treat the failure to wear a seat belt as a comparative negligence issue rather than negligence per se or contributory negligence?
2. Does this decision mean citizens of Florida who fail to wear a seat belt will be denied recovery for any injuries they might suffer in a motor vehicle accident? Explain.
3. Justice Shaw in dissent in *Pasakarnis:*

   Despite statistics determining that seat belts can be effective in reducing the number of serious injuries and deaths caused by automobile accidents, a vast majority of the motoring public declines to use them. If one accepts the proposition that there is no common law or statutory duty to wear seat belts, and that the wearing of such belts has been rejected by a majority of the public despite the urging of industry and the federal government, then the duty this decision places upon the Florida motorist is at the very least based upon a debatable public policy determination best left to the legislature.[9]

   a. Should the seat belt issue have been left to the legislature? Explain.
   b. In your judgment, have America's courts, as a whole, assumed an undesirably aggressive, activist role that amounts to an intrusion on the legislative function? Explain.

4. Should the federal government pass a law requiring the use of seat belts at all times in automobiles? Explain.

5. Alvin Dillinger suffered injuries while driving a large Caterpillar dumpster. While proceeding up a hill at a grade of 7 percent with a full load, the transmission failed, resulting in an engine stall. The truck started rolling down the hill and Dillinger applied the foot brake. In accordance with winter rules, he had earlier properly disengaged the truck's front brakes, so when he applied the foot brake, he was relying on the rear brakes only. He thought the brakes were working correctly because he felt normal pressure. The truck did not stop, but he thought that was due to road conditions. He contemplated jumping but thought that too dangerous, given the vehicle's 10-foot height. The truck rolled off an embankment and Dillinger was thrown out, suffering serious injuries. Dillinger claims the accident was the result of improperly designed hydraulic hoses, which lost fluid and thus lost braking power. Dillinger brought a product liability action. Dillinger was not wearing a seat belt, and he failed to engage the alternative braking systems (e.g., emergency brake) that were available to him.

   a. Can the court properly allow the jury to hear testimony regarding Dillinger's failure to use the seat belt? Explain.

   b. Assuming Dillinger was negligent in failing to use one of the alternative braking methods, can that testimony be heard by the jury to show that Caterpillar did not cause Dillinger's harm? Explain. See *Dillinger* v. *Caterpillar,* 959 F.2d 430 (3d Cir. 1992).

6. Distinguish contributory negligence and assumption of risk.

7. David Clapham lost an eye when he was hit by a foul ball at Yankee Stadium in New York City. He sued the Yankees and the city, which owns the stadium, contending they were negligent in failing to extend the protective screen to reach the box seat he was occupying behind the Yankee dugout.

   a. What defense would you raise on behalf of the Yankees?

   b. Decide the case. Explain.

   c. What if Clapham had left the game early and was struck by a foul ball while walking through the city-owned parking lot?

Part Two—Warranties

As explained previously, negligence claims are often difficult to prove. For that reason and others, the wronged consumer may wish to raise a breach of warranty claim in addition to or in place of a negligence action. A *warranty* is simply a guaranty arising out of a contract. If the product does not conform to the standards of the warranty, the contract is violated (breached), and the wronged party is entitled to recovery. Note that a negligence claim arises from breach of the duty of due care, while a warranty claim arises from a breach of contract. The following sections describe how express and implied warranties are created. (Discussion of the warranty of good title is omitted. See UCC 2–312.)

EXPRESS WARRANTIES

The seller of goods affirms a fact or makes a promise regarding the character or quality of the goods. Warranties are governed primarily by the terms of the Uniform Commercial Code. The UCC is designed to codify and standardize the law of commercial practice throughout the United States. Forty-nine states have adopted all or the bulk of the UCC. Louisiana has adopted only portions.

> **UCC 2–313. Express Warranties by Affirmation, Promise, Description, Sample**
>
> (1) Express warranties by the seller are created as follows:
> - (*a*) Any affirmation of fact or promise made by the seller to the buyer which relates to the goods and becomes part of the basis of the bargain creates an express warranty that the goods shall conform to the affirmation or promise.
> - (*b*) Any description of the goods which is made part of the basis of the bargain creates an express warranty that the goods shall conform to the description.
> - (*c*) Any sample or model which is made part of the basis of the bargain creates an express warranty that the whole of the goods shall conform to the sample or model.

The philosophy undergirding UCC 2–313 is straightforward. The seller who seeks to enhance the attractiveness of his or her product by offering representations as to the nature and/or quality of the product must fulfill those representations or fall in breach of contract and be subject to the payment of damages.

Puffing

Perhaps the area of greatest confusion in determining the existence and coverage of an express warranty is distinguishing a seller's promise from a mere expression of opinion. The latter, often referred to as sales talk or puffing, does not create an express warranty. The UCC requires an affirmation of fact or promise. Hence, a statement of opinion is not covered by the code. For example, the sales clerk who says, "This is the best TV around," would not be guaranteeing that the television in question is the best available. The salesperson is expressing a view. We, as consumers, seem to be quite patient with sellers' exaggerations. If, on the other hand, the clerk said, "This TV has a solid walnut cabinet," when in fact it was a pine veneer stained to a walnut tone, a breach of warranty action might ultimately be in order. The test to be applied in such situations is one of reasonable expectations. An expression of opinion coming from an expert may well rise to the level of an affirmation of fact or promise because the buyer should reasonably expect to be able to rely on the expert's affirmations. For example, if a handwriting expert seeking to sell a purportedly rare historical document says, "This handwriting is clearly that of Adolph Hitler," that statement might well be treated as an affirmation of a fact.

IMPLIED WARRANTIES

A seller enters into a contract for the sale of goods and, as a consequence, an implied warranty arises by operation of law. That is, an implied warranty automatically attaches to the sale of goods unless the warranty is disclaimed (disavowed) by the seller.

Two types of implied warranties are provided for:

UCC 2–314. Implied Warranty: Merchantability; Usage of Trade

(1) Unless excluded or modified (Section 2–316), a warranty that the goods shall be merchantable is implied in a contract for their sale if the seller is a merchant with respect to goods of that kind. Under this section the serving for value of food or drink to be consumed either on the premises or elsewhere is a sale.

UCC 2–315. Implied Warranty: Fitness for Particular Purpose

Where the seller at the time of contracting has reason to know any particular purpose for which the goods are required and that the buyer is relying on the seller's skill or judgment to select or furnish suitable goods, there is unless excluded or modified under the next section an implied warranty that the goods shall be fit for such purpose.

The implied warranty of merchantability is a powerful tool for the wronged consumer in that the warranty arises automatically by operation of law. If the seller is a merchant regularly selling goods of the kind in question, the warranty of merchantability simply accompanies the sale unless the warranty is excluded via a disclaimer (explained below). The warranty arises even if the seller made no certification as to the nature or quality of the goods. UCC 2–314 enshrines the consumer's reasonable expectation that only safe goods of at least ordinary quality will appear on the market.

The implied warranty of fitness for a particular purpose likewise arises by operation of law, but only when the seller (merchant or not) knows (or has reason to know) that the goods are to be used for a specific purpose, and the seller further knows that the buyer is relying on the seller's judgment. If those conditions obtain, the warranty exists automatically unless disclaimed. For example, Chris Snapp engages an audio products clerk in a discussion regarding the proper stereo system for Chris's classic Austin Healey sports car. Chris explains the joy he expects to receive in driving his car along the winding Kentucky roads with the convertible top down and the stereo booming. Unfortunately, the stereo selected on the clerk's advice proves insufficiently powerful to be heard clearly above the rushing wind. Should Chris recover for breach of the implied warranty of fitness for a particular purpose? Merchantability?

DISCLAIMERS

Express warranties may be disclaimed (excluded) or modified only with great difficulty. In any contract displaying both an express warranty and language disclaiming that warranty (for example, sold "as is" or "with all faults"), the warranty will remain effective unless the warranty and the disclaimer can reasonably be read as consistent.

Implied warranties may be excluded or modified by following either of the two patterns explained in UCC sections 2–316(2) and (3)(a).

> (2) Subject to subsection (3), to exclude or modify the implied warranty of merchantability or any part of it the language must mention merchantability and in case of a writing must be conspicuous, and to exclude or modify any implied warranty of fitness the exclusion must be by a writing and conspicuous . . .
>
> (3) Notwithstanding subsection (2)
>
> *(a)* unless the circumstances indicate otherwise, all implied warranties are excluded by expressions like "as is," "with all faults" or other language which in common understanding calls the buyer's attention to the exclusion of warranties and makes plain that there is no implied warranty . . .

Finally, when a buyer, before entering a contract, inspects the goods (or a sample thereof), or declines to inspect, no implied warranty exists with regard to defects that should have been apparent on inspection [UCC 2–316(3)(b)].

The following case illustrates the evolution of warranty law in an increasingly complex commercial society.

HENNINGSEN v. BLOOMFIELD MOTORS, INC.
161 A. 2d 69 (N.J. 1960)

Justice Francis

Plaintiff Claus H. Henningsen purchased a [new] Plymouth automobile, manufactured by defendant Chrysler Corporation, from defendant Bloomfield Motors, Inc. His wife, plaintiff Helen Henningsen, was injured while driving it and instituted suit against both defendants to recover damages on account of her injuries. Her husband joined in the action, seeking compensation for his consequential losses. The complaint was predicated upon breach of express and implied warranties and upon negligence. At the trial the negligence counts were dismissed by the court and the cause was submitted to the jury for determination solely on the issues of implied warranty of merchantability. Verdicts were returned against both defendants and in favor of the plaintiffs. Defendants appealed . . .

On May 7, 1955, Mr. and Mrs. Henningsen visited the place of business of Bloomfield Motors, Inc. . . . They were shown a Plymouth which appealed to them and the purchase followed. The record indicates that Mr. Henningsen intended the car as a Mother's Day gift to his wife. When the purchase order or contract was prepared and presented, the husband executed it alone. The purchase order was a printed form of one page . . .

The testimony of Claus Henningsen justifies the conclusion that he did not read the two fine print paragraphs referring to the back of the purchase contract. And it is uncontradicted that no one made any reference to them, or called them to his attention. With respect to the matter appearing on the back, it is likewise uncontradicted that he did not read it and that no one called it to his attention.

The reverse side of the contract contains 8½ inches of fine print . . .

In the seventh paragraph, about two thirds of the way down the page, the warranty, which is the focal point of the case, is set forth.

7. It is expressly agreed that there are no warranties, express or implied, *made* by either the dealer or the manufacturer on the motor vehicle, chassis, or parts furnished hereunder except as follows . . .

The new Plymouth was turned over to the Henningsens on May 9, 1955 . . . That day, Mrs. Henningsen drove to Asbury Park. On the way down and in returning the car performed in normal fashion until the accident occurred. She was proceeding north on Route 36 in Highlands, New Jersey, at 20 to 22 miles per hour. The highway was paved and smooth, and contained two lanes for northbound travel. She was riding in the righthand lane. Suddenly she heard a loud noise "from the bottom, by the hood." It "felt as if something cracked." The steering wheel spun in her hands; the car veered sharply to the right and crashed into a highway sign and a brick wall . . .

The insurance carrier's inspector and appraiser of damaged cars, with 11 years of experience, advanced the opinion, based on the history and his examination, that something definitely went "wrong from the steering wheel down to the front wheels" and that the untoward happening must have been due to mechanical defect or failure; "something down there had to drop off or break loose to cause the car" to act in the manner described . . .

The Claim of Implied Warranty against the Manufacturer

. . . [W]e come to a study of the express warranty on the reverse side of the purchase order signed by Claus Henningsen. At the outset we take notice that it was made only by the manufacturer and that by its terms it runs directly to Claus Henningsen . . .

The terms of the warranty are a sad commentary upon the automobile manufacturers' marketing practices. Warranties developed in the law in the interest of and to protect the ordinary consumer who cannot be expected to have the knowledge or capacity or even the opportunity to make adequate inspection of mechanical instrumentalities, like automobiles, and to decide for himself whether they are reasonably fit for the designed purpose. But the ingenuity of the Automobile Manufacturers Association, by means of its standardized form, has metamorphosed the warranty into a device to limit the maker's liability . . .

The manufacturer agrees to replace defective parts for 90 days after the sale or until the car has been driven 4,000 miles, whichever is first to occur, *if the part is sent to the factory, transportation charges prepaid, and if examination discloses to its satisfaction that the part is defective.* It is difficult to imagine a greater burden on the consumer, or less satisfactory remedy . . .

The matters referred to represent only a small part of the illusory character of the security presented by the warranty. Thus far the analysis has dealt only with the remedy provided in the case of a defective part. What relief is provided when the breach of the warranty results in personal injury to the buyer? . . . But in this instance, after reciting that defective parts will be replaced at the factory, the alleged agreement relied upon by Chrysler provides that the manufacturer's "obligation under this warranty" is limited to that undertaking: further, that such remedy is "in lieu of all other warranties, express or implied, and all other obligations or liabilities on its part." The contention has been raised that such language bars any claim for personal injuries which may emanate from a breach of the warranty . . .

Putting aside for the time being the problem of the efficacy of the disclaimer provisions contained in the express warranty, a question of first importance to be decided is whether an implied warranty of merchantability by Chrysler Corporation accompanied the sale of the automobile to Claus Henningsen.

* * * * *

Chrysler points out that an implied warranty of merchantability is an incident of a contract of sale. It concedes, of course, the making of the original sale to Bloomfield Motors, Inc., but maintains that this transaction marked the terminal point of its contractual connection with the car. Then Chrysler urges that since it was not a party to the sale by the dealer to Henningsen, there is no privity of contract between it and the plaintiffs, and the absence of this privity eliminates any such implied warranty.

* * * * *

Under modern conditions the ordinary layman, on responding to the importuning of colorful advertising, has neither the opportunity nor the capacity to inspect or to determine the fitness of an automobile for use; he must rely on the manufacturer who has control of its construction, and to some degree on the dealer who, to the limited extent called for by the manufacturer's instructions, inspects and services it before delivery. In such a marketing milieu his remedies and those of persons who properly claim through him should not depend "upon the intricacies of the law of sales. The obligation of the manufacturer should not be based alone on privity of contract. It should rest, as was once said, upon 'the demands of social justice.' "

Accordingly, we hold that under modern marketing conditions, when a manufacturer puts a new automobile in the stream of trade and promotes its purchase by the public, an implied warranty that it is reasonably suitable for use as such accompanies it into the hands of the ultimate purchaser. Absence of agency between the manufacturer and the dealer who makes the ultimate sale is immaterial.

The Effect of the Disclaimer and Limitation of Liability Clauses on the Implied Warranty of Merchantability

. . . [W]hat effect should be given to the express warranty in question which seeks to limit the manufacturer's liability to replacement of defective parts, and which disclaims all other warranties, express or implied? In assessing its significance we must keep in mind the general principle that, in the absence of fraud, one who does not choose to read a contract before signing it, cannot later relieve himself of its burdens.

But in the framework of modern commercial life and business practices, such rules cannot be applied on a strict, doctrinal basis. The conflicting interests of the buyer and seller must be evaluated realistically and justly, giving due weight to the social policy evinced by the Uniform Sales Act, the progressive decisions of the courts engaged in administering it, the mass production methods of manufacture and distribution to the public, and the bargaining position occupied by the ordinary consumer in such an economy. This history of the law shows that legal doctrines, as first expounded, often prove to be inadequate under the impact of later experience. In such case, the need for justice has stimulated the necessary qualifications or adjustments.

In these times, an automobile is almost as much a servant of convenience for the ordinary person as a household utensil. For a multitude of other persons it is a necessity . . .

The traditional contract is the result of free bargaining of parties who are brought together by the play of the market, and who meet each other on a footing of approximate economic equality. In such a society there is no danger that freedom of contract will be a threat to the social order as a whole. But in present-day commercial life the standardized mass contract has appeared. It is used primarily by enterprises with strong bargaining power and position. Such standardized contracts have been described as those in which one predominant party will dictate its law to an undetermined multiple rather than to an individual. They are said to resemble a law rather than a meeting of the minds . . .

The warranty before us is a standardized form designed for mass use. It is imposed upon the automobile consumer. He takes it or leaves it, and he must take it to buy an automobile. No bargaining is engaged in with respect to it. In fact, the dealer through whom it comes to the buyer is without authority to alter it; his function is ministerial—simply to deliver it . . .

The gross inequality of bargaining position occupied by the consumer in the automobile industry is thus apparent. There is no competition among the car makers in the area of the express warranty.

* * * * *

Assuming that a jury might find that the fine print referred to reasonably served the objective of directing a buyer's attention to the warranty on the reverse side, and, therefore, that he should be charged with awareness of its language, can it be said that an ordinary layman would realize what he was relinquishing in return for what he was being granted? . . . *In the context* of this warranty, only the abandonment of all sense of justice would permit us to hold that, as a matter of law, the phrase "its obligation under this warranty being limited to making good at its factory any part or parts thereof" signifies to an ordinary reasonable person that he is relinquishing any personal injury claim that might flow from the use of a defective automobile . . .

The Dealer's Implied Warranty

The principles that have been expounded as to the obligation of the manufacturer apply with equal force to the separate express warranty of the dealer.

* * * * *

. . . [W]e conclude that the disclaimer of an implied warranty of merchantability by the dealer, as well as the attempted elimination of all obligations other than replacement of defective parts, are violative of public policy and void . . .

The Defense of Lack of Privity against Mrs. Henningsen

Both defendants contend that since there was no privity of contract between them and Mrs. Henningsen, she cannot recover for breach of any warranty made by either of them. On the facts, as they were developed, we agree that she was not a party to the purchase agreement. Her right to maintain the action, therefore, depends upon whether she occupies such legal status thereunder as to permit her to take advantage of a breach of defendants' implied warranties . . . We are convinced that the cause of justice in this area of the law can be served only by recognizing that she is such a person who, in the reasonable contemplation of the parties to the warranty, might be expected to become a user of the automobile . . .

It is important to express the right of Mrs. Henningsen to maintain her action in terms of a general principle. To what extent may lack of privity be disregarded in suits on such warranties? . . . [I]t is our opinion that an implied warranty of merchantability chargeable to either an automobile manufacturer or a dealer extends to the purchaser of the car, members of his family, and to other persons occupying or using it with his consent. It would be wholly opposed to reality to say that use by such persons is not within the anticipation of parties to such a warranty of reasonable suitability of an automobile for ordinary highway operation. Those persons must be considered within the distributive chain . . .

Affirmed.

Questions

1. Define the doctrine of privity of contract.
2. List those considerations that permitted the *Henningsen* court to disavow the privity requirement under the facts of that case.
3. Why was the Chrysler disclaimer ruled invalid?
4. A father asks his 11-year-old son to go to the kitchen, open a bottle of beer, and return with it. In opening the beer, the son's hand is cut when the bottle breaks. The father sues the bottler on behalf of his son. The father raises both negligence and breach of warranty claims. At trial, it is established that the son was not negligent. The bottler defends by establishing that the beer was purchased by the father. Decide. Explain.

MAGNUSON–MOSS WARRANTY ACT

While the Uniform Commercial Code embodies our primary expression of warranty rules, Congress has extended and clarified those rules by passing the Magnuson–Moss Warranty Act. Congress approved the act following a study that found widespread abuse of consumers. Warranties were often vague, deceptive, or simply incomprehensible to the average purchaser. The act, administered by the FTC, applies only to consumer products and only to written warranties. The act does not require offering an express written warranty, but where such a warranty is offered and the cost of the goods is more than $10, the warranty must be labeled *full* or *limited*. A full warranty requires free repair of any defect. If repair is not achieved within a reasonable time, the buyer may elect either a refund or replacement without charge. If a limited warranty is offered, the limitation must be conspicuously displayed.

If a warranty is offered on goods costing more than $15, the warrantor must "fully and conspicuously disclose in simple and readily understandable language the terms and conditions of the warranty." The FTC has developed various rules to implement the intent of the disclosure requirement. For example, if the warrantor requires return of the completed warranty registration card in order to "activate" the warranty, that return requirement must be clearly disclosed in the warranty.

The effect of the Magnuson-Moss Act has not been entirely consistent with Congress's hopes. In practice, many sellers may have either offered limited warranties or eliminated them entirely.

Part Three—Strict Liability

Negligence and warranty actions are helpful to the harmed consumer. However, rapid changes in the nature of commercial practice, as well as an increasing societal concern for consumer protection, led the legal community to gradually embrace yet another cause of action. *Strict liability in tort* offers the prospect of holding all of those in the chain of distribution liable for damages from a defective product, rather than imposing the entire burden on the injured consumer. Manufacturers and sellers are best positioned to prevent the distribution of defective products, and they are best able to bear the cost of injury by spreading the loss via pricing policies and insurance coverage.

Strict liability as an independent tort emerged in 1963 in the famous California case of *Greenman* v. *Yuba Products, Inc.*[10] In the ensuing two decades, most states, via either their judiciaries or their legislatures, have adopted strict liability in concept. The essence of the strict liability notion is expressed in Section 402A of the *Restatement (Second) of Torts.* (Note that the *Restatement of Torts* does not constitute law. Rather it is a summary of the law of torts as interpreted by a group of legal scholars.) In brief, 402A imposes liability where a product is sold in a *defective condition, unreasonably dangerous*[11] to the user. The 402A test:

1. One who sells any product in a defective condition, unreasonably dangerous to the user or consumer or to his property, is subject to liability for physical harm thereby caused to the ultimate user or consumer, or to his property, if
   a. the seller is engaged in the business of selling such a product, and,
   b. it is expected to and does reach the user or consumer without substantial change in the condition in which it is sold.
2. The rule stated in Subsection (1) applies although
   a. the seller has exercised all possible care in the preparation and sale of his product, and
   b. the user or consumer has not bought the product from or entered into any contractual relation with the seller.

COVERAGE

All of those engaged in the preparation and distribution of a defective product may be liable for any harm caused by the defect, regardless of proof of actual fault. Furthermore, although not addressed in Section 402A, the courts have extended strict liability coverage to reach injured bystanders. Coverage generally extends to both personal injuries and property damage, but in some states the latter is excluded. Some states limit strict liability recovery to new goods, and some have limited liability to a designated period (for example, 15 years) after the manufacture or sale of the product.

DEFENSES

Assumption of risk and *misuse of the product* are both good defenses and, if factually supported, can act as a complete bar to strict liability recovery. In theory, strict liability is a no-fault concept. Hence, *contributory negligence* should not constitute a useful defense. The South Dakota Supreme Court summarized the law in this area in 1979:

> Many courts have considered the question of what defenses are available in strict liability cases. Classifying them is difficult because all of the courts do not mean the same thing when they use the terms *contributory negligence* and *assumption of risk.* A reading of the cases from other jurisdictions satisfies us that regardless of the nomenclature used, they can be divided into four classifications:
>
> 1. The classical negligence defenses are all available.
> 2. A restricted species of contributory negligence is a defense.
> 3. Most jurisdictions hold that contributory negligence—whether classical or restricted—is not a defense.
> 4. Finally, California and Alaska hold that contributory negligence is not a defense, but plaintiff's recovery may be reduced on a theory of "comparative fault" which balances the user's negligence against the defectiveness of the product.[12]

In recent years, we are witnessing an increasing willingness to accept the comparative fault position attributed to California and Alaska.

The *Leichtamer* case that follows offers a good overview of strict liability reasoning.

LEICHTAMER v. AMERICAN MOTORS CORP.
424 N.E.2d 568 (Oh. 1981)

Justice Brown

This litigation arises out of a motor vehicle accident which occurred on April 18, 1976. On that date, Paul Vance and his wife, Cynthia, invited Carl and Jeanne Leichtamer, brother and sister, to go for a ride in the Vance's Jeep Model CJ–7. The Vances and the Leichtamers drove together to the Hall of Fame Four-Wheel Club, of which the Vances were members. The Vances were seated in the front of the vehicle and the Leichtamers rode in the back. The club, located near Dundee, Ohio, was an "off-the-road" recreation facility. The course there consisted of hills and trails about an abandoned strip mine.

While the Vance vehicle was negotiating a double-terraced hill [proceeding *down* the hill], an accident occurred. The hill consisted of a 33-degree slope followed by a 70-foot-long terrace and then a 30-degree slope. Paul Vance drove over the brow of the first of these two slopes and over the first flat terrace without incident. As he drove over the brow of the second hill, the rear of the vehicle raised up relative to the front and passed through the air in an arc of approximately 180 degrees. The vehicle landed upside down with its front pointing back up the hill. This movement of the vehicle is described as a pitch-over.

The speed that the Vance vehicle was traveling at the time of the pitch-over was an issue of dispute. The Leichtamers, who are the only surviving eyewitnesses to the accident, described the vehicle as traveling at a slow speed. Carl Leichtamer described the accident as occurring in this fashion:

> Well, we turned there and went down this trail and got to the top of this first hill . . . And Paul looked back and made sure that everybody had their seat belt fastened. That it was fastened down; and he pulled the automatic lever down in low and he put it in low wheel, four wheel, too . . . And then he just let it coast like over the top of this hill and was using the brake on the way down, too. We came to the level-off part. He just coasted up to the top of the second hill, and then the next thing I remember is the back end of the Jeep going over . . . When we got to the top of the second hill, the front end went down like this (demonstrating) and the back end just started raising up like that (demonstrating).

John L. Habberstad, an expert witness for American Motors Corporation, testified that the vehicle had to be traveling between 15 and 20 miles per hour. This conclusion was based on evidence adduced by American Motors that the vehicle landed approximately 10 feet from the bottom of the second slope, having traversed about 47 feet in the air and having fallen approximately 23.5 feet.

The pitch-over of the Jeep CJ–7, on April 18, 1976, killed the driver, Paul Vance, and his wife, Cynthia. Carl Leichtamer sustained a depressed skull fracture. The tailgate of the vehicle presumably struck Jeanne Leichtamer. Jeanne was trapped in the vehicle after the accident and her position was described by her brother as follows: "She was like laying on her stomach although her head was sticking out of the jeep and the—she was laying on her stomach like and the tailgate of the jeep like, was laying lower, just a little bit lower or right almost on her shoulders and then the back seat of the jeep was laying on her lower part of her back . . . [H]er legs were twisted through the front seat." Jeanne Leichtamer is a paraplegic as a result of the injury.

Carl and Jeanne Leichtamer, appellees, subsequently sued American Motors Corporation, American Motors Sales Corporation and Jeep Corporation, appellants, for "enhanced" injuries they sustained in the accident of April 18, 1976. The amended complaint averred that the permanent trauma to the body of Jeanne Leichtamer and the other injuries to her brother, Carl, were causally related to the displacement of the "roll bar" on the vehicle. Appellees claimed that Paul Vance's negligence caused the accident, but alleged that their injuries were "substantially enhanced, intensified, aggravated, and prolonged" by the roll bar displacement.

Paul Vance purchased his Jeep CJ–7 four-wheel-drive motor vehicle from a duly licensed, factory-authorized dealer, Petty's Jeep & Marine, Inc., owned and operated by Norman Petty. Vance purchased the vehicle on March 9, 1976. The vehicle came with a factory-installed roll bar. The entire vehicle was designed and manufactured by Jeep Corporation, a wholly owned subsidiary of American Motors. American Motors Sales Corporation is the selling agent for the manufacturer. Appellees did not claim that there was any defect in the way the vehicle was manufactured in the sense of departure by the manufacturer from design specification. The vehicle was manufactured precisely in the manner in which it was designed to be manufactured. It reached Paul Vance in that condition and was not changed.

The focus of appellees' case was that the weakness of the sheet metal housing upon which the roll bar had been attached was causally related to the trauma to their bodies. Specifically, when the vehicle landed upside down, the flat sheet metal housing of the rear wheels upon which the roll bar tubing was attached by bolts gave way so that the single, side-to-side bar across the top of the vehicle was displaced to a position 12 inches forward of and $14\frac{1}{2}$ inches lower than its original configuration relative to the chassis. The movement of the position of the intact roll bar resulting from the collapse of the sheet metal housing upon which it was bolted was, therefore, downward and forward. The roll bar tubing did not punch through the sheet metal housing, rather the housing collapsed, taking the intact tubing with it. That this displacement or movement of the intact roll bar is permitted by the thin nature of the sheet metal wheel housing to which it is attached and the propensity of the bar to do so when the vehicle lands upside down is central to the appellees' case.

The appellants' position concerning the roll bar is that, from an engineering point of view, the roll bar was an optional device provided solely as protection for a side-roll.

* * * * *

The other principal element of appellees' case was that the advertised use of the vehicle involves great risk of forward pitch-overs. The accident occurred at the Hall of Fame Four-Wheel Club, which had been organized, among others, by Norman Petty, the vendor of the Vance vehicle. Petty allowed the club to meet at his Jeep dealership. He showed club members movies of the performance of the Jeep in hilly country. This activity was coupled with a national advertising program of American Motors Sales Corporation, which included a multimillion-dollar television campaign. The television advertising campaign was aimed at encouraging people to buy a Jeep, as follows: "Ever discover the rough, exciting world of mountains, forests, rugged terrain? The original Jeep can get you there, and Jeep guts will bring you back."

The campaign also stressed the ability of the Jeep to drive up and down steep hills. One Jeep CJ–7 television advertisement, for example, challenges a young man, accompanied by his girlfriend: "[Y]ou guys aren't yellow, are you? Is it a steep hill? Yeah, little lady, you could say it is a steep hill. Let's try it. The King of the Hill, is about to discover the new Jeep CJ–7." Moreover, the owner's manual for the Jeep CJ–5/CJ–7 provided instructions as to how "[a] four-wheel-drive vehicle can proceed in safety down a grade which could not be negotiated safely by a conventional two-wheel-drive vehicle." Both appellees testified that they had seen the commercials and that they thought the roll bar would protect them if the vehicle landed on its top.

Appellees offered the expert testimony of Dr. Gene H. Samuelson that all of the physical trauma to the body of Jeanne Leichtamer were causally related to the collapse of the roll bar support. These injuries—fractures of both arms, some ribs, fracture of the dorsal spine, and a relative dislocation of the cervical spine and injury to the spinal cord—were described by Samuelson as permanent. He also testified that the physical trauma to the body of Carl Leichtamer was causally related to the collapse of the roll bar.

Appellants' principal argument was that the roll bar was provided solely for a side-roll. Appellants' only testing of the roll bar was done on a 1969 Jeep CJ–5, a model with a wheel base 10 inches shorter than the Jeep CJ–7. Evidence of the test was offered in evidence and refused. With regard to tests for either side-rolls or pitch-overs on the Jeep CJ–7, appellants responded to interrogatories that no "proving ground," "vibration or shock," or "crash" tests were conducted.

The jury returned a verdict for both appellees. Damages were assessed for Carl Leichtamer at $100,000 compensatory and $100,000 punitive. Damages were assessed for Jeanne Leichtamer at $1 million compensatory and $1 million punitive . . .

I(A)

Appellants' first three propositions of law raise essentially the same issue: that only negligence principles should be applied in a design defect case involving a so-called "second collision." In this case, appellees seek to hold appellants liable for injuries "enhanced" by a design defect of the vehicle in which appellees were riding when an accident occurred. This cause of action is to be contrasted with that where the alleged defect causes the accident itself. Here, the "second collision" is that between appellees and the vehicle in which they were riding.

I(B)

* * * * *

. . . [T]he vast weight of authority is in support of allowing an action in strict liability in tort, as well as negligence, for design defects. We see no difficulty in also applying Section 402A [*Restatement (Second) of Torts*] to design defects. As pointed out by the California Supreme Court, "[a] defect may emerge from the mind of the designer as well as from the hand of the workman." A distinction between defects resulting from manufacturing processes and those resulting from design, and a resultant difference in the burden of proof on the injured party, would only provoke needless questions of defect classification, which would add little to the resolution of the underlying claims. A consumer injured by an unreasonably dangerous design should have the same benefit of freedom from proving fault provided by Section 402A as the consumer injured by a defectively manufactured product which proves unreasonably dangerous.

* * * * *

Strict liability in tort has been applied to design defect "second collision" cases. While a manufacturer is under no obligation to design a "crash-proof" vehicle, an instruction may be given on the issue of strict liability in tort if the plaintiff adduces sufficient evidence that an unreasonably dangerous product design proximately caused or enhanced plaintiff's injuries in the course of a foreseeable use. Here, appellants produced a vehicle which was capable of off-the-road use. It was advertised for such a use. The only protection provided the user in the case of roll-overs or pitch-overs proved wholly inadequate. A roll bar should be more than mere ornamentation.

I(C)

We turn to the question of what constitutes an unreasonably dangerous defective product.

Section 402A subjects to liability one who sells a product in a "defective condition, unreasonably dangerous" which causes physical harm to the ultimate user. Comment *g* defines defective condition as "a condition not contemplated by the ultimate consumer which will be unreasonably dangerous to him." Comment *i* states that for a product to be unreasonably dangerous, "[t]he article sold must be dangerous to an extent beyond that which would be contemplated by the ordinary consumer who purchases it, with the ordinary knowledge common to the community as to its characteristics."

With regard to design defects, the product is considered defective only because it causes or enhances an injury. "In such a case, the defect and the injury cannot be separated, yet clearly a product cannot be considered defective simply because it is capable of producing injury." Rather, in such a case the concept of "unreasonable danger" is essential to establish liability under strict liability in tort principles.

The concept of "unreasonable danger," as found in Section 402A, provides implicitly that a product may be found defective in design if it is more dangerous in use than the ordinary consumer would expect. Another way of phrasing this proposition is that "a product may be found defective in design if the plaintiff demonstrates that the product failed to perform as safely as an ordinary consumer would expect when used in an intended or reasonably foreseeable manner."

* * * * *

Thus, we hold a cause of action for damages for injuries "enhanced" by a design defect will lie in strict liability in tort. In order to recover, the plaintiff must prove by a preponderance of the evidence that the "enhancement" of the injuries was proximately caused by a defective product unreasonably dangerous to the plaintiff.

* * * * *

[Part II omitted.]

III

Appellants . . . contend that it was error for the trial court to have admitted in evidence television commercials which advertised the Jeep CJ–7 as a vehicle to "discover the rough, exciting world of mountains, forests, rugged terrain." Appellants further contend that "a jury may not base its verdict upon such television commercials in the absence of a specific representation contained in the commercials as to the quality or merit of the product in question and in the absence from the plaintiff that the use of the product was in reliance upon such representations."[sic]

We hold that a product is unreasonably dangerous if it is dangerous to an extent beyond the expectations of an ordinary consumer when used in an intended or reasonably foreseeable manner. The commercial advertising of a product will be the guiding force upon the expectations of consumers with regard to the safety of a product, and is highly relevant to a formulation of what those expectations might be. The particular manner in which a product is advertised as being used is also relevant to a determination of the intended and reasonably foreseeable uses of the product. Therefore, it was not error to admit the commercial advertising in evidence to establish consumer expectations of safety and intended use.

Affirmed.

Justice Holmes, dissenting

The majority reaches its decision by virtue of the application in a second collision case of the doctrine of strict liability as contained in Section 402A of the Restatement of Torts 2d.

I am unable to join in this analysis. In a products liability action based upon an alleged design defect of the product, which allegedly has enhanced the plaintiff's injuries, I feel that the manufacturer should be held liable only when the plaintiff is able to prove that the manufacturer was negligent in adopting his chosen design.

It is my view that the proper rule to be applied in crashworthiness cases is set forth in *Larsen* v. *General Motors Corp.* as follows:

> The manufacturers are not insurers but should be held to a standard of reasonable care in design to provide a reasonably safe vehicle in which to travel.
>
> This duty of reasonable care in design rests on common law negligence that a manufacturer of an article should use reasonable care in the design and manufacture of his product to eliminate any unreasonable risk of foreseeable injury.
>
> There should be no requirements in the law that manufacturers must design their automotive products to withstand extraordinary accidents of unusual circumstance or severity . . .

* * * * *

As stated, there was a significant absence of specific proof as to any reliance by these plaintiffs upon the capability of the roll bar in a pitch-over situation or otherwise. Additionally, there was an insufficiency of proof that this type of an accident, involving a pitch-over of a Jeep, was a common accident and one reasonably foreseeable. In fact, the evidence would tend to controvert such a finding in that there was testimony from both plaintiffs and defense witnesses that pitch-overs are rare events which occur infrequently and only if the specific conditions necessary to bring it about exist.

American Motors presented testimony that the roll bars were installed on these Jeeps to aid in the protection of occupants in roll-over situations, not pitch-over accidents as was occasioned here.

* * * * *

There also was a failure of proof here as to any alternate safer design practicable under the circumstances of a pitch-over rather than a roll-over, and absence of any proof of any lessened or differential injuries that might have been sustained had an alternate design been installed in this jeep.

As stated, in the application of the proper standards here, the manufacturer's duty is to exercise reasonable care in the design of its product to eliminate any reasonable risk of foreseeable injury, but it need not be designed to make the vehicle accident proof.

Questions

1. Many courts now employ what is known as the risk/utility test in deciding design defect cases like *Leichtamer* under a strict liability analysis. The risk/utility test holds that a product is defective if the usefulness of particular elements of the product's design are outweighed by the dangers accompanying those elements. In *Leichtamer,* the court relied on the consumer expectations test.
   a. Explain the consumer expectations test.
   b. Criticize it.
2. The dissent in *Leichtamer* argued for the application of a negligence standard in this case. Had the court adopted that view, rather than relying on strict liability reasoning, would the decision have been different? Explain.
3. *a.* Why did the *Leichtamer* court apply strict liability to this case?
   b. Are you persuaded by the court's reasoning? Explain.
4. Does this decision have the effect of requiring the Jeep to be "accident proof" (as argued by the dissent) to avoid liability? Explain.

5. Had Jeep designed the vehicle without a roll bar of any kind, who would have won this case? Explain.

6. The deceased had rented an auto from the Hertz Corporation. A tire blew out, and a fatal crash resulted. The tire was manufactured by Firestone. The estate of the deceased filed suit against Hertz and Firestone. Evidence presented at trial caused the jury to believe that the dangerous condition of the tire arose after its manufacture.

   a. Can the plaintiff successfully raise a strict liability claim against Hertz? Explain.

   b. Against Firestone? Explain. See *Stang* v. *Hertz Corp.,* 83 N.M. 730, 497 P.2d 732 (1972).

7. Nancy Denny was driving her Ford Bronco II. She swerved to avoid a deer and suffered serious injuries when the Bronco tipped over. She sued on strict liability, negligence, and breach of implied warranty grounds. The jury found for Denny on warranty grounds but rejected the strict liability and negligence claims, finding that the Bronco was not defective. Denny was awarded $3 million. Ford appealed, saying that the jury's findings were inconsistent.

   a. Explain Ford's argument.

   b. Decide. Explain.

   c. The jury found Denny 60 percent responsible for her own harm. Does that finding change the results? Explain. See *Nancy Denny and Robert Denny* v. *Ford Motor Company,* 88-CV-1180, U.S. District Court, Binghamton, New York (1993).

LIMITS OF STRICT LIABILITY—MARKET SHARE LIABILITY?

The great test now for the courts in the strict liability area is to determine just how far this powerful doctrine should be expanded in providing recoveries for those injured by the multitude of products that are so central to our consumer society.

The next case summarizes the current judicial debate over extending negligence and/or strict liability reasoning to what has become a long line of cases in which plaintiff/daughters, while yet fetuses, were exposed to an allegedly defective drug (DES). DES, which was marketed from the early 1940s until 1971, was administered to prevent miscarriages. The drug received FDA marketing approval, but a warning was required indicating that the drug was experimental. Then, in 1971, FDA marketing approval was withdrawn, as evidence emerged linking DES to cancer in the daughters of those who took it. The California Supreme Court, in the groundbreaking DES case *Sindell* v. *Abbott Laboratories* (discussed in the *Smith* case, which follows shortly), condemned the defendant drug manufacturer:

> During the period defendants marketed DES, they knew or should have known that it was a carcinogenic substance, that there was a grave danger after varying periods of latency it would cause cancerous and precancerous growths in the daughters of the mothers who took it, and that it was ineffective to prevent miscarriage. Nevertheless, defendants continued to advertise and market the drug as a miscarriage preventative. They failed to test DES for efficacy and safety; the tests performed by others, upon which they relied, indicated that it was not safe or effective. In violation of the authorization of the Food and Drug Administration, defendants marketed DES on an unlimited basis rather than as an experimental drug, and they failed to warn of its potential danger.[13]

However, because of the passage of time, the loss of records, the large number of manufacturers, and other factors, the plaintiff/daughters ordinarily cannot identify the *specific* manufacturer responsible for the defective drug ingested by their mothers. The *Smith* case explores that problem.

SMITH v. ELI LILLY & CO.
560 N.E.2d 324 (Ill. 1990)

Justice Ryan

The plaintiff in this appeal alleges that she was injured by the drug diethylstilbestrol (DES) [a miscarriage preventative], which her mother ingested during pregnancy. She seeks relief against defendant DES manufacturers. The issue is whether, in a negligence and strict liability cause of action, Illinois should substitute for the element of causation in fact a theory of market share liability when identification of the manufacturer of the drug that injured the plaintiff is not possible . . .

I. Facts

The plaintiff, Sandra Smith, was born on July 13, 1953, in Chicago, Illinois. In 1978, . . . [a] biopsy revealed that plaintiff had a form of cancer known as clear cell adenocarcinoma of the vagina . . . Plaintiff alleges that the DES prescribed for her mother while plaintiff was *in utero* caused the cancer.

The trial court [and] the appellate court . . . adopted a theory of market share liability . . . We granted leave to appeal.

II. History of DES

* * * * *

In 1971, two medical studies suggested that there was a statistically significant association between the outbreak in young women of clear cell adenocarcinoma, a form of cancer, with the maternal ingestion of DES during pregnancy. Later that year the FDA banned the marketing of DES for use by pregnant women . . .

Beginning in the 1970s, hundreds of lawsuits were filed against manufacturers of DES by the daughters of women who took the drug while pregnant. These plaintiffs are commonly referred to as the "DES daughters." The seriousness of the injuries they suffer cannot be questioned and the hysterectomy required for Sandra Smith was not unusual . . .

III. Substantive Tort Principles

* * * * *

The plaintiff before us alleges that after extensive discovery she has been unable to identify the manufacturer of the DES her mother ingested. A number of circumstances contribute to the barrier in establishing causation in fact in DES cases. The effects caused by prenatal exposure to DES usually do not manifest themselves until at least after the child reaches puberty, and more years may pass before the cancer is linked to DES. During this long lapse, whatever records the doctor, pharmacy, or manufacturer maintained have often been lost or destroyed and the memories of the persons involved have faded. Further exacerbating the problem is the fact that during the 25 years that DES was used to treat pregnancy-related problems, as many as 300 companies manufactured the drug. The manufacturers were only required by law to maintain records for five years and many manufacturers have either gone out of business or destroyed their records or have only partial records available.

Although proof of causation in fact is ordinarily an indispensable ingredient of a *prima facie* case, the plaintiff points out that competing tort interests have compelled courts to create exceptions to the causation requirement. These exceptions to the rule have allowed a plaintiff to shift to a defendant or a group of defendants the burden of proof on the causation issue. Included within the exceptions are "enterprise liability," "alternative liability" and "market share liability."

* * * * *

. . . Currently, four states have adopted some form of this theory when confronted with the issue of imposing liability on drug manufacturers for injuries caused to women whose mothers ingested DES while pregnant. However, none of these states agree on the remedy or its application.

IV. Judicially Promulgated Market Share Theories
A. California

In *Sindell* v. *Abbott Laboratories* (1980), . . . the California Supreme Court rejected the plaintiff's three bases for her cause of action and instead modified the alternative liability theory, thus fashioning its form of market share liability. In reaching this conclusion, the court reasoned that in a contemporary complex industrialized society, advances in science and technology create fungible goods which may harm consumers and which cannot be traced to any specific producer. It then went on to give three policy reasons for developing market share liability. First, as between an innocent plaintiff and a manufacturer of a defective product, the manufacturer should bear the cost of the injury. Second, it believed that the manufacturer was in a better position to bear the cost involved in an injury. Third, because the manufacturer is in the best position to recognize defects in products and to guard against them, holding the producer liable for these defects would provide an incentive to product safety.

Under the remedy as fashioned in *Sindell,* the plaintiff must first join as defendants the manufacturers of a "substantial share" of the DES which her mother may have taken, and must prove a *prima facie* case on every element except identification of the direct tortfeasor. After joining the manufacturers, the burden of proof shifts to defendants to demonstrate that they could not have manufactured the DES that caused plaintiff's injuries. If a defendant fails to meet this burden, the court fashions a market share theory to apportion damages according to the likelihood that any of defendants supplied the product by holding each defendant liable for the proportion of the judgment represented by its share of that market. The intended result of the rule is that each manufacturer's liability for an injury is approximately equivalent to the damages caused by the DES it manufactured.

* * * * *

Other than the overall concept of market share liability, which will be addressed later in this opinion, the rule as specifically developed in *Sindell* has been extensively criticized, and as of this date only one federal district court has adopted it in the same form . . .

* * * * *

[B. Washington and C. Wisconsin omitted.]

D. New York

The court of appeals of New York [developed] its own version of market share liability. [*Hymowitz* v. *Eli Lilly & Co.*]

New York's theory utilizes a national market [that] apportions "liability so as to correspond to the over-all culpability of each defendant, measured by the amount of risk of injury each defendant created to the public-at-large." . . . A defendant can exculpate itself only through proof that it did not participate in the marketing of DES for pregnancy use. The rule also provides that liability is several only, and is not to be inflated if all the manufacturers are not before the court.

V. Courts Which Have Rejected Market Share Liability

Other than these cases, the concept of market share liability has not received strong support . . .

The Iowa Supreme Court rejected the doctrine "on a broad policy basis." (*Mulcahy* v. *Eli Lilly & Co.* (Iowa 1986) . . . *Mulcahy* equated the theory with a court-constructed insurance plan which requires manufacturers to pay for injuries their product may not have caused . . . The court concluded "that awarding damages to an admitted innocent party by means of a court-constructed device that places liability on manufacturers who were not proved to have caused the injury involves social engineering more appropriately within the legislative domain." . . .

The Missouri Supreme Court agreed with the arguments of the drug manufacturers that market share liability was unfair, unworkable, and contrary to Missouri law and violated the state's public policy . . .

* * * * *

We conclude, therefore, that market share liability is not a sound theory, is too great a deviation from our existing tort principles, and should not be applied in cases brought by "DES daughters."

* * * * *

Acceptance of market share liability and the concomitant burden placed on the courts and the parties will imprudently bog down the judiciary in an almost futile endeavor. This would also create a tremendous cost, both monetarily and in terms of the workload, on the court system and litigants in an attempt to establish percentages based on unreliable or insufficient data . . .

If we were to allow courts and juries to apportion damages when reliable information is not available, the clear result would be that the determinations will be arbitrary and there will be wide variances between judgments, without sufficient explanation as to these differences . . .

Moreover, it is unrealistic to say that a true percentage of the market can be established by the defendants before the court. Throughout the history of the use of DES as a miscarriage preventative, hundreds of manufacturers produced the product and it is impossible to bring them before our courts. The defendants who do appear will have a difficult enough time to establish their market shares. Those who cannot meet this task but desire to reduce their potential liability will have the difficult burden of establishing the shares of manufacturers not before the court . . .

* * * * *

Plaintiff argues that the drug manufacturers are liable for their breach of duty to a foreseeable plaintiff. Under plaintiff's interpretation of duty, manufacturers of products for human consumption have a special responsibility and any manufacturer of DES can be held liable because it breached a duty owed to her. The appellate court accepted plaintiff's notion of duty, reasoning in part that drug manufacturers "owe a special duty of care to the public." . . .

The plaintiff and appellate court have too broadly interpreted the duty of a drug company and to whom it owes that duty. Both negligence and strict liability require proof that defendant breached a duty owed to a particular plaintiff . . . Each manufacturer owes a duty to plaintiffs who will use its drug or be injured by it. However, the duty is not so broad as to extend to anyone who uses the type of drug manufactured by a defendant.

* * * * *

. . . Justice Richardson, writing for the dissenters in *Sindell,* argued that market share liability makes the entire drug industry "an insurer of all injuries attributable to defective drugs of uncertain or unprovable origin, including those injuries manifesting themselves a generation later, and regardless of whether particular defendants had any part whatever in causing the claimed injury." . . . We agree with his conclusion that such a solution is an unreasonable over-reaction in attempting to achieve what is perceived as a socially satisfying result.

* * * * *

Reversed and remanded.

Justice Clark, concurring in part and dissenting in part

. . . I would adopt the theory of market share liability established by the court of appeals of New York in *Hymowitz* v. *Eli Lilly & Co.* . . . because I believe that the *Hymowitz* theory provides a fair and rational way to remedy the injustice presented by this case and avoids the shortcomings of previous theories of market share liability. I therefore dissent from the majority's outright rejection of market share liability.

Questions

1. Explain the general notion of market share liability.
2. Do you agree with the judgment of the Illinois Supreme Court in the *Smith* case? Explain.
3. How can a defendant avoid liability under the *Sindell* decision alluded to in the opinion?
4. A victim of asbestosis could not identify all of the manufacturers of the asbestos to which he was exposed. Should the court apply the market share theory of liability to this case? Explain. See *Celotex Corporation* v. *Copeland,* 471 So.2d 533 (Fla. 1985).
5. The City of Philadelphia and the Philadelphia Housing Authority sued various manufacturers of lead-based paints and their trade association seeking in excess of $100 million to help pay the cost of programs to reduce health problems associated with lead-based paint. The federal Department of Health and Human Services has concluded that lead poisoning is a serious threat to children's health in the United States. Some children ingest lead either by chewing on walls and other surfaces coated with lead-based paint or by breathing air containing dust from crumbling paint. Plaintiffs claimed that the defendants had known of these dangers for decades, and plaintiffs conceded that they had known of those dangers for a number of years. Plaintiffs sued on a variety of product liability grounds, among them the theory of market share liability. Only one trial court opinion in Pennsylvania has recognized the market share theory. Should the federal court of appeals apply market share reasoning to this case? Explain. See *City of Philadelphia* v. *Lead Industries Assn,* 994 F.2d 112 (3d Cir. 1993).

Afterword

In recent years, the potential burden to manufacturers from DES litigation has grown to include lawsuits involving the *granddaughters* of women who took the drug. However, the first decision in this emerging line of litigation favored the DES manufacturers,[14] as discussed in the following article.

THIRD-GENERATION DES LAWSUIT DISMISSED BY STATE APPEALS COURT

Amy Stevens and Christi Harlan

New York's highest state court ruled that Karen Enright, a nine-year-old girl with cerebral palsy whose grandmother took the pregnancy drug DES, has no legal standing to sue the former manufacturers of the drug.

Thousands of DES cases have been filed over the years by "DES daughters" who claimed they were damaged by exposure to the drug while they were in the womb. But this is the first ruling by any state's high court on whether liability for DES-related injuries should extend to a third generation.

* * * * *

The Enrights claim that the ingestion of DES by Karen's grandmother set in motion an unbroken chain of events that produced Karen's injuries. The appeals panel, in a 5–1 decision, ruled that the pharmaceutical companies are liable only for alleged injuries suffered by the women who took the drug and their children. The panel wrote that allowing third-generation suits to proceed might result in a decline in the development of new products.

Leonard Finz, the New York lawyer for the Enrights, said he is considering asking the U.S. Supreme Court to review the case or requesting that the state Legislature take up the issue. The decision, he said, has left thousands of "victims of a calamity of overwhelming proportions without a legal remedy."

Source: *The Wall Street Journal,* February 21, 1991, p. B7. Reprinted by permission of *The Wall Street Journal,* © 1991 Dow Jones & Company. All Rights Reserved Worldwide.

Part Four—Product Liability: A Summary Case

The 1992 California case that follows combines negligence, warranty, and strict liability claims in the commonplace situation where a consumer has been injured by the consumption of food.

MEXICALI ROSE v. THE SUPERIOR COURT OF ALAMEDA COUNTY AND JACK A. CLARK, REAL PARTY IN INTEREST
822 P.2d 1292 (Cal. 1992)

Chief Justice Lucas

---

* * * * *

[Plaintiff] Jack A. Clark was a customer at petitioners' [defendants'] restaurant. He ordered a chicken enchilada and sustained throat injuries when he swallowed a 1-inch chicken bone contained in the enchilada. He brought an action for damages based on theories of negligence, breach of implied warranty, and strict liability. He alleged defendant Mexicali Rose negligently left the bone in the enchilada and the food was unfit for human consumption. He also asserted he did not expect to find a bone, and it is not common knowledge there may be bones in chicken enchiladas . . .

* * * * *

. . . According to plaintiff, defendants could be held (i) liable in negligence for their failure to exercise reasonable care in the preparation of the food, (ii) liable for violating California's statutory implied warranty because a chicken bone in a chicken enchilada renders the latter unfit for human consumption under the implied warranty of merchantability and fitness of California Uniform Commercial Code sections 2314 and 2315, and (iii) strictly liable because the food item was "defective" under the theory of Restatement Second of Torts section 402A, comment i, imposing strict liability when food is "dangerous beyond that which would be contemplated by the ordinary consumer who purchases it, with the ordinary knowledge common to the community as to its characteristics."

The question we address, therefore, is whether a restaurant keeper may be held liable for serving food containing substances natural to the product that, when consumed by the patron, cause injury. As explained below, we agree with plaintiff that a "reasonable expectation" test is applicable in this context and, in part at least, is consistent with the development of tort law in our jurisdiction. Accordingly, we adopt that test as our own. As we further explain, although we conclude that under a reasonable expectation test plaintiff may not state a cause of action under the theories of strict liability or breach of the implied warranties of merchantability or fitness, we conclude that under the same test, he may state a cause of action in negligence based on defendants' asserted failure to exercise due care in the preparation of the chicken enchilada.

Mix and Its Progeny: The Foreign-Natural Test and the Reasonable Expectations of the Consumer

* * * * *

In *Mix,* the plaintiff swallowed a fragment of chicken bone contained in a chicken pot pie he consumed in the defendant's restaurant . . . We held there could be no liability under either an implied warranty or negligence theory . . . Although we conceded that it is frequently a question for the jury to determine whether an injury-producing substance present in food makes the food unfit for consumption, we maintained that a court in appropriate cases may find as a matter of law that an alleged harmful substance in food does not make the food defective or unfit for consumption. We explained our holding as follows:

> Bones which are natural to the type of meat served cannot legitimately be called a foreign substance, and a consumer who eats meat dishes ought to anticipate and be on his guard against the presence of such bones . . . Certainly no liability would attach to a restaurant keeper for the serving of a T-bone steak, or a beef stew, which contained a bone natural to the type of meat served, or if a fish dish should contain a fish bone, or if a cherry pie should contain a cherry stone—although it be admitted that an ideal cherry pie would be stoneless." We concluded as a matter of law that a chicken pot pie containing chicken bones is reasonably fit for consumption, and there could be no breach of the implied warranty . . .

* * * * *

More recently, however, courts addressing the foreign-natural distinction have deviated from strict application of *Mix* to conclude that the ultimate issue of liability should not be based on a determination whether the object causing injury was either foreign or natural, but instead should be based on whether the consumer reasonably should have anticipated the natural injury-producing substance in the food . . .

* * * * *

In sum, the trend developing in courts recently considering the issue whether a plaintiff may recover for injuries caused by a natural or foreign substance can be summarized as follows: If the injury-producing substance is natural to the preparation of the food served, it can be said that it was reasonably expected by its very nature and the food cannot be determined to be unfit for human consumption or defective.* Thus, a plaintiff in such a case

---

*Unfortunately, both dissents misrepresent the scope and application of our holding. The term "natural" refers to bones and other substances natural to the product served, and does not encompass substances such as mold, botulinus bacteria or other substances (like rat flesh or cow eyes) not natural to the preparation of the product served.

has no cause of action in implied warranty or strict liability. The expectations of the consumer do not, however, negate a defendant's duty to exercise reasonable care in the preparation and service of the food. Therefore, if the presence of the natural substance is due to a defendant's failure to exercise due care in the preparation of the food, an injured plaintiff may state a cause of action in negligence. By contrast, if the substance is foreign to the food served, then a trier of fact additionally must determine whether its presence (i) could reasonably be expected by the average consumer and (ii) rendered the food unfit for human consumption or defective under the theories of the implied warranty of merchantability or strict liability.

* * * * *

Defendants assert that "public policy and good common sense support the *Mix* rule." They contend that allowing a plaintiff to recover even in negligence for an injury caused by a natural substance is unreasonable because, they assert, this would place a burden on all restaurants to remove all bones. Defendants claim the better policy is "to encourage consumers to be careful."

As noted above, we agree with defendants to the extent they reason that a restaurant patron cannot expect a chicken pie to be free of all bones. Such an expectation would be unreasonable and unrealistic to the ordinary consumer and would not conform to either federal or state health and safety standards . . .

On the other hand, we disagree with defendants . . . that we should continue to preclude a plaintiff from attempting to state a cause of action in negligence when a substance natural to the preparation of the food product has caused injury . . .

. . . [W]e believe a patron can reasonably expect that a restaurateur will exercise reasonable care in preparing chicken enchiladas so that any natural substances contained in the food will not be either of such size, shape or quantity to cause injury when consumed. It is reasonably foreseeable that a sizable bone could cause the unsuspecting patron substantial injury if swallowed. Under these principles, we believe it is a question for the trier of fact to determine whether the presence of the injury-producing substance was caused by the failure of the defendants to exercise reasonable care in the preparation of the food, and whether the breach of the duty to exercise such care caused the consumer's injury. In so concluding, we emphasize that restaurateurs have available all the traditional defenses to a negligence cause of action, including comparative negligence.

The strict foreign-natural test of *Mix* should be rejected as the exclusive test for determining liability when a substance natural to food injures a restaurant patron. We conclude instead that in deciding the liability of a restaurateur for injuries caused by harmful substances in food, the proper tests to be used by the trier of fact are as follows:

If the injury-producing substance is natural to the preparation of the food served, it can be said that it was reasonably expected by its very nature and the food cannot be determined unfit or defective. A plaintiff in such a case has no cause of action in strict liability or implied warranty.

If, however, the presence of the natural substance is due to a restaurateur's failure to exercise due care in food preparation, the injured patron may sue under a negligence theory.

If the injury-causing substance is foreign to the food served, then the injured patron may also state a cause of action in implied warranty and strict liability, and the trier of fact will determine whether the substance (i) could be reasonably expected by the average consumer and (ii) rendered the food unfit or defective . . .

* * * * *

Based on the foregoing, we affirm the Court of Appeal judgment to the extent it directs the trial court to sustain defendants' demurrers to the implied warranty and strict liability causes of action, and we reverse the judgment directing the demurrer to plaintiff's negligence cause of action be sustained.

[Remanded.]

Justice Mosk, dissenting

The majority hold that processed food containing a sharp, concealed bone is fit for consumption, though no reasonable consumer would anticipate finding the bone. They declare in effect that the bone is natural to the dish, therefore the dish is fit for consumption. The majority never explain why this should be the rule, when it is universally held that in the analogous case of a sharp bit of wire in processed food, liability occurs under both the implied warranty of fitness and the theory of strict liability for defective consumer products.

* * * * *

A nutshell in a scoop of ice cream, a bit of crystalized corn in a serving of corn flakes or a chunk of bone in a hamburger is as harmful and unanticipated from the injured consumer's point of view as a bit of rock, glass or wire in the same food products. For social policy reasons we have long held the restaurateur strictly liable for injuries caused by unwholesome food, and there is no reason to abandon this social policy when the object in food that causes the injury is "natural."

It is a fallacy to assume that all objects which were a natural part of the ingredients of the food at an early stage of preparation are characteristic of the finished product or are anticipated by the consumer of the finished product. The more highly processed the food, the less it is to be anticipated that injurious natural objects such as shells or bones will be present.

* * * * *

I see no reason to breathe new life into an arbitrary and artificial distinction between natural and foreign defects in food products. This distinction is no longer followed in the majority of jurisdictions that have considered the matter in the last 30 years . . . I agree with the majority that when the consumer is injured by a foreign object, we should determine liability on warranty and strict liability theories on the basis of the reasonable expectation of the consumer. In the interest of public health, I would apply the same standard to so-called natural defects.

Questions

1. How did the court express the central issue in the *Mexicali* case?
2. *a.* In *Mexicali,* did the California Supreme Court adopt the foreign-natural test or the reasonable expectation test?
   b. Explain each.

3. Build a decision tree showing how to apply the *Mexicali* court's test to the question of whether a consumer who broke a tooth when biting a cherry pit in a cherry pie, for example, should be able to recover in negligence, warranty, and/or strict liability.
4. The plaintiff, born and raised in New England, was eating fish chowder at a restaurant when a fish bone lodged in her throat. The bone was removed and the plaintiff sued the restaurant, claiming a breach of implied warranty under the UCC. Evidence was offered at trial to show that fish chowder recipes commonly did not provide for removal of bones. Decide. Explain. See *Webster* v. *Blue Ship Tea Room, Inc.,* 198 N.E.2d (Mass. 1964).

Part Five—Product Liability and Public Policy

Tobacco

The tobacco industry is in a litigation war with consumers who claim that tobacco is a defective product and that tobacco advertising is false and misleading. Historically, plaintiffs had no success in claiming that tobacco smoking and chewing leads to cancer and other health problems. However, some recent decisions have produced tiny but threatening fissures in the tobacco industry's mighty armor, and litigation has expanded.

• In May 1994, 50 law firms, led by New Orleans personal injury lawyer Wendell Gauthier, announced that they had agreed to invest $100,000 each to pursue a class action lawsuit on behalf of all people addicted to cigarettes. Gauthier described his strategy as "You addicted me. You knew it was addicting, and now you say it's my fault."[15] [Congressional hearings in early 1994 examined the question of whether the tobacco industry has intentionally maintained addictive levels of nicotine in cigarettes—see Chapter 8.] Gauthier is also expected to argue that the tobacco companies have targeted teenagers who cannot make a free, knowledgeable choice about smoking.

Gauthier will team with such powerful plaintiffs' attorneys as Stanley Chesley of Cincinnati (sometimes called the "Master of Disaster" because of his victories in big personal injury cases) and the colorful Melvin Belli of San Francisco. That imposing coalition, if it holds together, promises to pose the biggest threat to date against the tobacco industry, which has yet to pay a penny in damages in civil injury suits. To this point, the tobacco companies have had to fight only one plaintiff at a time, and their superior resources have enabled them to crush those plaintiffs. Furthermore, Gauthier's addiction claim may be more convincing to jurors than earlier suits arguing that tobacco is a defective product and one requiring a warning before use. On the other hand, enormous hurdles lie before Gauthier's class action. First, the tobacco companies argue that the courts will not certify the smoking addiction claims as a class action. Their position is that each smoker's case is unique and thus should not be lumped together. Further, they feel that jurors continue to believe that smokers can quit if they wish to do so.[16]

• In May 1994, the state of Mississippi announced that it is suing the tobacco industry seeking tens of millions of dollars for the cost to the state of treating tobacco-related illnesses suffered by welfare recipients. The state is also asking the court to stop cigarette manufacturers from encouraging smoking by minors. The suit will take the form of a class action. Tobacco companies are expected to defend by saying that the state must bring a separate suit on behalf of each patient and that smokers make independent decisions to smoke. Other states may follow the Mississippi lead.[17]

• Apparently, for the first time in the United States, a court found that cigarette manufacturers could be held strictly liable for illness caused by smoking. The 1993 pretrial ruling came in a Mississippi state court. A family sued American Tobacco for the cancer death of Anderson Smith, who had smoked Pall Mall cigarettes for 45 years. However, the pre-trial ruling was rendered moot when the jury at trial found that the plaintiff died from a blood clot rather than from lung cancer or emphysema. State Supreme Court decisions in New Jersey and Louisiana permit juries to find tobacco companies liable for illness, but none have done so and now the legislatures in those states and several others have passed laws barring many strict liability claims.[18] Furthermore, in the first tobacco trial following the U.S. Supreme Court's leading decision in this area, the *Cipollone* case (discussed in the article that follows), an Illinois jury declined to find R. J. Reynolds Tobacco Co. liable for a dying man's cancer, saying, in effect, that the plaintiff had chosen to smoke and would need to bear the responsibility. The plaintiff, Charles Kueper, claimed that he had been encouraged to smoke through false and deceitful advertising.[19]

• Recently, Norma Broin, a flight attendant suffering from cancer, brought what is believed to be the first so-called passive smoking case against the tobacco industry.[20] She seeks to establish a class action on behalf of approximately 60,000 nonsmoking flight attendants who claim either to suffer from cancer and other diseases or to be at higher risk of illness due to long-term exposure to secondary smoke in flight cabins. Some airline employees have previously won workers' compensation claims from their employers under similar circumstances.[21]

• Tobacco companies have successfully fought a number of claims of responsibility for fires caused by untended cigarettes.[22] Those claims have been unsuccessful when brought by the smokers themselves because the tobacco companies have been able to argue that the smokers have a duty to properly care for the cigarettes. However, a new angle is being explored in a case currently under litigation. Philip Morris is being sued by the estate of a woman who died in a fire (along with her three children) started by her husband's untended cigarette.[23]

Cipollone.   Rose Cipollone died in 1984 after having smoked for 40 years. Prior to her death, she sued three cigarette companies. Her family carried on the litigation for nearly a decade, during which time they were awarded $400,000 (subsequently thrown out on appeal), and they won a partial victory in the U.S. Supreme Court in the leading tobacco liability case to date.[24] The following article explains the *Cipollone* decision.

TOBACCO INDUSTRY FACES
FRESH LEGAL DANGER
AFTER JUSTICES' RULING

Paul M. Barrett

The tobacco industry says it has never paid a dime on a suit from a smoker claiming health damage from cigarettes. That seems likely to change.

The Supreme Court yesterday exposed cigarette companies to new and uncertain legal risks that could have a major financial impact on the tobacco business. In a splintered and surprising decision, the court said smokers may file lawsuits alleging that cigarette makers hid or distorted the health dangers of tobacco.

Those are the types of claims—until now successfully blocked by the industry—that create the danger of huge jury awards and may force cigarette makers to begin offering sizable settlements of the sort they previously sniffed at.

"The smokers were at their eleventh hour," says Prof. Ronald Collins, a constitutional and commercial law expert at George Washington University. "Now they have a way to get to juries, and the fraud and conspiracy [charges] set you up for punitive damages."

"Substantial Impact"

There could be new dangers for other industries as well, including waste disposal and makers of cars, pharmaceuticals, medical devices, chemicals and pesticides. "If the court's opinion is to be taken at its word," says Kenneth Geller, a lawyer who represents firms in some of those businesses, "it could have a substantial impact in many other contexts."

* * * * *

That's because the justices, by a 7–2 vote, changed the law dramatically on the question of when federal statutes preclude state-level legal activity, including private lawsuits. By allowing suits against tobacco companies, the decision, written by Justice John Ste-

vens, reaffirmed that this heavily conservative court nonetheless isn't reflexively pro-business. The court said—apparently for the first time—that it would sharply limit companies' ability to argue that federal statutes bar more aggressive state regulation or lawsuits based on state law.

* * * * *

The tobacco companies, focusing on a narrow part of the ruling, hailed the decision as a victory. And indeed, for smokers, it still won't be easy to collect from the tobacco companies. Although some of Justice Stevens's colleagues said they would have gone further, his opinion bars suits charging tobacco companies with failing to provide adequate warnings. Nor can a plaintiff argue that using pictures of healthy people in cigarette ads is intended to "neutralize" the federally mandated warning language.

The "Achilles' Heel"

Instead, smokers will have to persuade juries that cigarette makers committed fraud or misrepresentation. That will still be a difficult task, especially considering that juries have been skeptical of awarding money to people who smoked for years and then complained about the health effects. But, as Mr. Geller acknowledges, "The name of the game is getting to the jury." If plaintiffs can create even a significant risk of big punitive-damage awards, he notes, "settlement value goes way up."

In addition, by allowing the fraud and conspiracy claims, the Supreme Court decision enables plaintiffs to move the question of responsibility from smokers to the industry itself. "The decision focuses attention on what truly is the potential Achilles' heel of the tobacco industry: whether their own research showed that smoking causes disease and whether they consciously sought to conceal that fact," says Matt Myers, counsel to the Coalition on Smoking or Health.

*   *   *   *   *

And, in fact, that's exactly why the tobacco companies claimed victory yesterday. They argued, essentially, that they're off the hook unless someone can prove they lied to the public, and they insist they didn't. At the very least, they say, plaintiffs will have to prove that the alleged misconduct was a reason they either started smoking or continued to light up—and without overwhelming evidence of industry misfeasance, juries aren't expected to be any more receptive to smokers' suits than they have been in the past, the tobacco companies say.

Ups and Downs

"There was so much information in the public realm about the dangers of smoking that it will be very difficult to find plaintiffs who are able to persuade a jury that they either began to smoke or continued to smoke because of misleading statements from the tobacco industry," says Victor Schwartz, a product liability expert in Washington, D.C., who has consulted for Philip Morris and R. J. Reynolds . . .

The justices' ruling . . . came on an appeal by Thomas Cipollone, whose mother, Rose, a smoker for 40 years, sued three tobacco companies in 1983, soon after her cancerous lung was removed. Mrs. Cipollone died in 1984, and her husband carried on the lawsuit until his death in January 1990. The suit was filed against Brooke Group Ltd.'s Liggett Group Inc., Philip Morris Cos.' Philip Morris Inc. unit, and Lorillard, a Loews Corp. unit.

In an unusual move, the tobacco companies agreed with Mr. Cipollone that the high court should hear the case. The companies said there are so many similar lawsuits pending that there was a need for the Supreme Court to rule.

The decision turned on a relatively technical issue involving the relationship between federal and state law. In 1965, Congress required tobacco companies

for the first time to put warning labels on cigarette packages, advising smokers beginning in 1966 that smoking "may be hazardous to your health." In 1969, Congress amended the law to require sterner warnings and to broaden language that pre-empted state legal activity in this area.

The central issue in the Cipollone case, and in tobacco liability litigation generally, is the degree to which the 1969 pre-emption provision blocks smokers' lawsuits.

The Cipollone suit, which has had a complicated history, made a number of allegations: that the cigarette companies failed to properly warn of health risks, that they made false statements and that they intentionally committed fraud and conspired to hide the truth about smoking.

Before the suit got to trial, a federal appeals court in Philadelphia ruled that the federal labeling law pre-empts claims based on a failure to warn or based on advertising of cigarettes. Despite that setback, the Cipollones eventually did get their case to a jury, in a trial that focused on disputes about pre-1966 advertising—before there was any question of federal preclusion of lawsuits.

The jury awarded $400,000 to the family for its claims against Liggett based on Mrs. Cipollone's smoking from 1942 through 1965. The award was for the cigarette companies' false statements about the lack of health risks in their pre-1966 advertising.

In 1990, the appeals court threw out the verdict and ordered a new trial, requiring the family to prove that Mrs. Cipollone relied on claims for the safety of cigarettes in the companies' advertising. The appeals court reiterated its earlier ruling that the federal labeling law bars lawsuits to hold tobacco companies liable for smoking after 1965. The Supreme Court reversed part of that decision and sent the case back for a new trial.

The critical passage of Justice Stevens's opinion holds that the high court should narrowly interpret congressional language that pre-empts state-level legal activity, and shouldn't infer that Congress meant to go further.

*   *   *   *   *

In this case, [Justice Stevens concluded] Congress meant to impose uniform federal standards for warnings in advertising—thus precluding claims that cigarette makers failed to warn their customers adequately. For similar reasons, he said that smokers may not file claims based on companies' alleged efforts to "neutralize" mandated warnings.

But lawsuits based on any affirmative false statements in the advertising aren't precluded, Justice Stevens said, because they are essentially promises, analogous to guarantees made in a commercial contract. Although no longer included in tobacco ads, assurances about cigarettes were common years ago, and suits may still be based on them.

In the '40s, R. J. Reynolds Tobacco Co. assured smokers that "More Doctors Smoke Camels." As late as the early '50s, Lorillard termed the micronite filter in its Kent cigarettes "so safe, so effective, it has been selected to help filter the air in hospital operating rooms."

"For folks who smoked in the '50s and '60s, you may get some express warranty claims," Mr. Myers says. "But by and large for today's population, the Supreme Court decision will focus attention on the tobacco industry's more recent activities"—such as allegedly suppressing evidence of tobacco's health effects. In addition, it's a safe bet that some plaintiffs' attorneys will explore whether advertisements for the low-tar, low-nicotine cigarettes currently on the market make implied health guarantees.

* * * * *

Any corporate records indicating industry concerns over the dangers of secondhand smoke could prove damning, says Laurence H. Tribe, the Harvard Law School professor, who argued on behalf of the plaintiff in the second round of the Cipollone case before the Supreme Court.

But lawyers for the industry maintain that all relevant corporate documents about smoking are already public because of the Cipollone litigation.

Source: *The Wall Street Journal,* June 25, 1992, p. A1. Reprinted by permission of *The Wall Street Journal,* © 1992 Dow Jones & Company, Inc. All Rights Reserved Worldwide.

Afterword

The *Cipollone* case was to return to a New Jersey federal court for retrial when lawyer Marc Edell and the Cipollone family agreed to drop their claim. The litigation had become too expensive to continue. Edell's firm had absorbed some $1 million in costs in the *Cipollone* case.[25] Further, he and other lawyers in the many years of tobacco litigation had been frustrated by the continuing refusal of the tobacco industry to turn over documents that, according to plaintiffs' lawyers, would show that the tobacco industry has long been aware of a link between smoking and disease.[26] At this writing in May 1994, *The New York Times* and *The Wall Street Journal* have reported that in 1963 Brown and Williamson Tobacco Company executives debated and decided against publicly releasing research showing a causal link between cigarette smoking and lung cancer (as well as some heart problems).[27]

Questions

1. Why have smokers generally been unable to recover, in cases like *Cipollone,* on strict liability and breach of the warranty of merchantability? See, for example,

Green v. *American Tobacco Co.,* 391 F.2d 97 (1968), cert. denied, 397 U.S. 911 (1970).

2. Would you favor legislation banning cigarette advertisements and promotions? Explain.

3. Plaintiffs seeking damages in smoking cases are attempting to avoid case-by-case apportionments of blame (e.g., the smoker was 90 percent liable for her injury and the tobacco company 10 percent liable) in favor of the risk/utility theory of liability. Under that theory, a jury might find a manufacturer free of negligence but still liable because the risks of using the product far exceed its benefits. Thus, the manufacturer would be held responsible for the *known and predictable* costs of the product to the public even if the manufacturer had warned of the product's dangers.

What do you think of the risk/utility approach to liability in tobacco cases? Explain.

Claims from Abroad—The Dalkon Shield

INTERNATIONAL

The Dalkon Shield, an intrauterine contraceptive device, was manufactured in the United States by A. H. Robins from 1970 to 1974, at which time the product was removed from the market because of multiplying cases of various serious medical problems associated with the shield. Thereafter, over 9,000 U.S. women filed liability claims against Robins, and by mid-1985 the company had paid some $378 million in damages. With further suits pending, Robins sought bankruptcy protection.

As the following article illustrates, one of the troublesome complications of contemporary product liability law is that corporate defendants such as Robins now must learn to manage claims from abroad, including the special problems of language, cultural differences, access to proof, differing economic standards, and so on, that accompany those claims.

PLAINTIFFS' LAWYERS MOVE TO PRESERVE EXCHANGE OF DATA

Milo Geyelin

Little noticed during the years of litigation over A. H. Robins Co.'s Dalkon Shield have been claims from 13,827 foreign women who were injured by the contraceptive. Now that Robins's bankruptcy-law reorganization is in its final stages, plaintiffs' lawyers for the foreign claimants and trustees who will administer claims settlements have begun discussing some of the complexities. The issues are particularly troubling to foreign claimants because Robins sold the Dalkon Shield abroad for more than a year after halting domestic sales in the early 1970s.

Language is a major problem facing foreign claimants. The trust has a Taiwanese nurse to help with claims resolution and both Portuguese and Spanish speaking employees. Yet snafus abound. When initial claim forms were mailed to Taiwanese women, groused Edward C. Y. Lau, a San Francisco plaintiffs' lawyer, they were written in English.

Some of the other issues: Should foreign claimants receive the full dollar value of their settlements or should the amounts be adjusted to reflect the value of the dollar where they live? What is the likelihood that a claim against Robins could succeed in a foreign country and should that be considered when deciding how much to pay abroad? Some countries, Sweden for example, don't have tort systems in which to bring negligence or product-liability lawsuits.

The most serious problem facing foreign claimants overall will be access to medical records. The trust will require some form of proof that the Dalkon Shield was used before paying a claim. The trouble is that medical records easily available in the U.S. may not be in foreign countries. And even if the records can be obtained, as in Sweden's socialized health-care system, for example, who will pay the cost of translation and certify its accuracy?

Source: *The Wall Street Journal,* July 25, 1989, p. B8. Reprinted by permission of *The Wall Street Journal,* © 1989 Dow Jones & Company. All Rights Reserved Worldwide.

CORPORATION PROTECTION?

We have seen that product liability law—particularly that of strict liability—has wrought a revolution in the degree of protection afforded to the consumer. Clearly, the courts and legislatures believed consumers had been relatively powerless in the face of defective products, and that powerlessness had become particularly pronounced as commercial practice left behind straightforward, face-to-face bargaining and entered an era of multiple and complex layers of parts suppliers, manufacturers, distributors, retailers, and so on. That imbalance of power was addressed in part by expanded product liability theories. In keeping with the generally egalitarian tone of the past two decades (for example, the civil rights and feminist movements), the law of consumer protection seemed to move toward the presumed ideal of righting every wrong. Now, predictably enough, the business community and others believe the balance of power has swung too profoundly in favor of the consumer. They see business laboring under an excessive burden, born of an unjust effort to shift losses to those with the deepest pockets.

Reform?

At this writing in 1994, Congress is considering legislation to reform our product liability laws. However, that legislation is given little chance of success. Similar proposals have been rebuffed each year for the past decade. At the same time, the business lobby has enjoyed considerable success in encouraging many state legislatures to impose limits on damage awards. Trial lawyers, consumer groups, labor unions, and others oppose reforms because they believe that the present laws are necessary to protect the public from dangerous products.

Reformers point to a variety of problems.

1. Product liability laws and judgments are ambiguous, and they vary from state to state and court to court. Thus, neither business nor the consumer can understand where liability lies.[28]
2. Product liability is beset with an "entitlement mentality" that increasingly awards damages to an injured plaintiff even where the producer bore no responsibility or where the plaintiff misused the product, thus contributing to her own harm.[29] Even the presence of "state-of-the-art" safety features may not protect the producer from liability.
3. The contingency fee system encourages plaintiffs and lawyers to file more suits since the financial risk of doing so is eliminated for the plaintiff and "spread" for the lawyer who hopes to occasionally strike it rich with a very large recovery.[30]
4. In cases involving more than one defendant, the doctrine of joint and several liability means that each culpable defendant is equally liable (and potentially fully liable) for paying the plaintiff's damages regardless of actual contribution to the injury. Thus, if a defendant cannot pay, the other defendants will be required to make up the difference. Obviously, joint and several liability has the effect of encouraging plaintiffs' lawyers to find ways to include at least one "deep pocket" among those being sued. In recent years, many states have abolished or modified their approaches to joint and several liability.
5. Broadly, damage claims have grown so numerous and damage awards so large (particularly punitive awards) that they have become a major burden for the economy. Production and innovation may be retarded. Many companies have simply discontinued certain products (e.g., trampolines and football helmets) because of liability fears. Other products never reach the market for the same reason. We as consumers pay more for our products in order to cover the cost of liability claims. And American companies have a reduced capacity to compete in the world market. The accompanying table illustrates the problem. Note that these awards involve tort claims generally, not merely those arising from defective products. And note that many large jury awards are either reduced or overturned on appeal.

The Five Largest Jury Awards in 1990*

$55.7 million	Insurance-fraud verdict against Woodmen of the World Life Insurance for misrepresenting policy terms to a Texas teacher's aide. On appeal.
$45.0 million	Finding against Brown Retail Group of Missouri for a car accident resulting in brain damage to a 42-year-old woman. Settled for $29.6 million.
$34.0 million	Judgment against Texaco in the leukemia death of a 31-year-old Kansas man exposed to benzene vapors in its products. On appeal.
$28.9 million	Negligence finding against Georgia Power Co. in the case of a man burned after touching a wire while gardening. Later settled for undisclosed amount.
$26.3 million	Verdict against Owens-Corning in the case of a 57-year-old man with asbestosis. Awaiting rulings on post-trial motions.

*Includes only judgments against companies.

Source: Lee Smith, "Trial Lawyers Face a New Charge," *Fortune*, August 26, 1991, p. 85.

Evidence

Not surprisingly, both the reformers and those defending our product liability system are probably correct in part. The following article summarizes a recent study by the well-regarded Rand Institute, which concludes that product liability, at least in the medical and pharmaceutical industries, is helpful in some respects and in need of reform in others.

RAND LIABILITY STUDY

Junda Woo and Milo Geyelin

A leading think tank is weighing in with another look at one of the legal profession's most heated controversies: Do product liability laws work to protect consumers or do they stifle innovation and hurt business?

The answer, from the Rand Institute for Civil Justice, in Santa Monica, Calif., is a mix of both. The Rand study, an economic analysis of the impact of personal-injury litigation on the pharmaceutical and medical industries, researched the effects of lawsuits on product availability, innovation, safety and pricing.

Liability has scuttled some good products, including some children's vaccines, but also has hastened the demise of "unacceptably risky" products, notably the Dalkon Shield intrauterine device, according to the study.

And while the risk and cost of liability have deterred innovation of some products that could benefit society, usually these products are in small markets with high capital requirements and low profits, according to the study. Products with "blockbuster" profit potential—such as the antidepressant Prozac and the sleeping pill Halcion—are routinely marketed despite litigation costs, the study said.

"Companies withdraw products because of liability only if the threat is perceived as sufficiently large in relation to profitability," according to the study.

Regarding safety, the study found that liability laws have led to improved medical devices, citing as examples mass litigation over the Dalkon Shield, the Bjork-Shiley heart valve and breast implants. But liability has had little impact on the safe design of pharmaceuticals, the study found, mostly because of the high threshold for marketing approval already required by the Food and Drug Administration.

The effect of liability on pricing also has been mixed. Products with high liability potential, such as the morning sickness drug Bendectin, were priced substantially higher as a result, the study found. But the price premiums for liability may often exceed the actual cost of lawsuits, depending on market conditions, according to the study. And for most products, the impact of liability has had negligible effects on pricing, the Rand report said.

"One of the important messages here is that liability is very complex, and it has good and bad effects," said Rand senior economist Steven Garber, who wrote the study.

The civil justice system could be made more predictable and efficient, he said, with several reforms. The study recommends exempting from liability companies that comply with FDA regulations, specifying more explicitly what kind of wrongful conduct merits punitive damages and improving procedures for weighing the credibility of expert testimony and scientific evidence.

Source: *The Wall Street Journal,* September 24, 1993, p. B6. Reprinted by permission of *The Wall Street Journal,* © 1993 Dow Jones & Company, Inc. All Rights Reserved Worldwide.

Questions

1. Much of the legal cost associated with product liability law is, of course, generated in attempting to prove or disprove fault. Strict liability, at least in theory, is a no-fault concept. Should we recast product liability law entirely in a no-fault mode? In so doing we would recognize the inevitability of defective products and careless consumers. Costs would be borne by all. Comment.

2. Tort claims sometimes arise out of accidents involving strangers, but often those episodes involve people who have some kind of relationship (e.g., buyer-seller or doctor-patient). In the latter set of circumstances, Professor Paul Rubin, among others, suggests that we should allow the parties to establish, in advance, a contract that would resolve the claims if an accident should happen. Thus, Rubin suggests, a physician and a patient might enter into an agreement in advance of treatment providing that the patient would sue only for limited damages (such as out-of-pocket medical expense and lost wages) in the event of malpractice.

   a. What benefits would consumers derive from such agreements?

   b. Why do the courts ordinarily refuse to enforce such agreements?

   c. Would you favor Rubin's approach to tort reform? Explain. See Paul Rubin, *Tort Reform by Contract* (Washington, D.C.: The AEI Press, 1993).

CHAPTER QUESTIONS

1. Plaintiff suffered a spider bite while trying on slacks in the dressing room of the defendant's Mode O'Day store. Plaintiff sued both the local retailer and the parent firm. She based her claim on negligence, breach of the implied warranty of fitness for a particular purpose, and strict liability.

   a. Defend Mode O'Day and the local retailer.

   b. Decide. Explain. See *Flippo* v. *Mode O'Day Frock Shops of Hollywood,* 248 Ark. 1, 449 S.W.2d 692 (1970).

2. A passenger ran after a train as it was leaving a station. Two railroad employees boosted the passenger aboard, but in doing so a package carried by the passenger fell beneath the wheels of the train and exploded. The package, unbeknownst to the employees, contained fireworks. The force of that explosion caused a scale many feet away to topple over, injuring the plaintiff, Mrs. Palsgraf. Mrs. Palsgraf sued the railroad on negligence grounds.

   a. Defend the railroad.

   b. Decide. Explain. See *Palsgraf* v. *Long Island R.R.,* 162 N.E. 99 (N.Y. 1928).

3. When police perform their duties negligently, courts now often allow plaintiffs to sue their employers (states and municipalities).

   a. Assume firefighters showed poor judgment in deciding to turn off the electrical system in a building during a fire, with the result that the building's sprinkler system was inoperative. Should the building's owners be allowed to recover on negligence grounds? Explain.

   b. Assume firefighters negligently diverted water from a building's sprinkler system to their hoses. Should the building's owners be able to sue the fire department for negligence? Explain. See *Harry Stoller and Company* v. *City of Lowell,* 587 N.E.2d (Mass. 1992). For a journalistic account, see Arthur Hayes, "Negligence Suits Pose a Threat to Firefighters," *The Wall Street Journal,* July 6, 1992, p. 11.

4. Two hemophilia patients who tested HIV positive after receiving a blood-clotting agent known as Factor VIII filed negligence and strict liability claims against four manufacturers of the agent. The plain-

tiffs could not specify which of the manufacturers actually produced the Factor VIII that led to their illnesses. Can the plaintiffs employ market share liability in this action? Explain. See *Doe* v. *Cutter Biological, Inc.,* 971 F.2d 375 (9th Cir 1992).

5. Alejandro Phillips, a young California man, was shot four times in the back at the opening of the movie "Boyz N the Hood," a depiction of growing up in a dangerous Los Angeles neighborhood dominated by gangs. Phillips was shot during a scuffle involving alleged gang members. According to his lawyers, Phillips himself was not a member of a gang. Dozens of similar violent episodes accompanied the opening of the movie. Phillips's lawyers accuse Columbia Pictures of negligence in marketing the film. They claim that the movie's advertising concentrated on the relatively minor episodes of violence in the movie and largely ignored the affirmative and pacifist ingredients at the core of the movie. They contend that Columbia should have anticipated violence as a consequence of that advertising approach. Phillips filed suit.
    a. Explain Phillips's legal claims.
    b. Defend Columbia.
    c. Decide. Explain. For a journalistic account, see Joanne Lipman, "Issue of Ads Leading to Violence Is Raised in Suit Tied to Movie," *The Wall Street Journal,* April 27, 1992, p. B10, and see "Film Patron Injury," *Entertainment Law Reporter,* Vol. 15, no. 1, p. 22.

6. Embs, the plaintiff, was shopping in a self-serve grocery store. A carton of 7UP was on the floor about one foot from where she was standing. She was unaware of the carton. Several of the bottles exploded, severely injuring Embs's leg. Embs brought a strict liability action against the bottler.
    a. Raise a defense against the strict liability claim.
    b. Decide. Explain. See *Embs* v. *Pepsi-Cola Bottling Co. of Lexington, Kentucky, Inc.,* 528 S.W.2d 703 (1975).

7. Plaintiff suffered injury from ingesting a defective prescription drug, MER/29. Plaintiff sued the druggist from whom the product was purchased in its original, unbroken package. The druggist issued the drugs under a doctor's instructions.
    a. Which causes of action might the plaintiff plausibly bring?

    b. Decide. Explain. See *McLeod* v. *W. S. Merrell Co., Div. of Richardson-Merrell,* 174 So.2d 736 (Fla. 1965).

8. Plaintiffs Dr. Arthur Weisz and David and Irene Schwartz bought two paintings at auctions conducted by the defendant, Parke-Bernet Galleries, Inc. The paintings were listed in the auction catalog as those of Raoul Dufy. It was later discovered that the paintings were forgeries. The plaintiffs took legal action to recover their losses. Parke-Bernet defended itself by, among other arguments, asserting that the "Conditions of Sale" included a disclaimer providing that all properties were sold "as is." The conditions of sale were 15 numbered paragraphs embracing several pages in the auction catalog. The bulk of the auction catalog was devoted to descriptions of the works of art to be sold, including artists' names, dates of birth and death, and, in some instances, black-and-white reproductions of the paintings. It was established at trial that plaintiff Weisz had not previously entered bids at Parke-Bernet, and he had no awareness of the conditions of sale. Plaintiffs David and Irene Schwartz, however, were generally aware of the conditions of sale. Is the Parke-Bernet disclaimer legally binding on the plaintiffs? Explain. See *Weisz* v. *Parke-Bernet,* 325 N.Y.S. 2d 576 (Civ. Ct. N.Y.C. 1971).

9. Lisa Mazur, a Philadelphia girl, received a measles vaccination at school in 1982 as part of a mass immunization program. The vaccination caused a fatal neurological disorder. Her parents sued the manufacturer, Merck & Co. Assume the vaccine was produced according to all applicable safety standards but that all such vaccines carry a small degree of risk of side effects or of mimicking the disease itself.
    a. Explain the Mazur family's legal claim.
    b. Decide.
    c. Assume Merck sold the drug through the federal Centers for Disease Control, which was required by contract with Merck to ensure that all patients received information about the potential risks of the vaccine. Would that arrangement change the outcome of the case? Explain. See *Mazur* v. *Merck,* 964 F.2d 1348 (1992).

10. A child contracted Reyes Syndrome after being given aspirin. The aspirin package contained an English language warning regarding a connection between Reyes Syndrome and aspirin, but the child's

Hispanic mother could not read the warning. Does the manufacturer have a duty to warn in a foreign language? Explain. See *Rameriz* v. *Plough,* 62 *Law Week* 2383 (1993).

11. Plaintiff-employee was operating a machine designed to flatten and then curve metal sheets. The metal was shaped by three long rollers. Plaintiff turned off the rollers to remove a piece of slag. He left the power on. In trying to remove the slag, he accidentally brushed a gear lever, which activated the rollers. His hand was drawn into the rollers, and injury resulted. At the time of the machine's manufacture, two safety mechanisms were available to prevent such accidents but the manufacturer of the machine (San Angelo) had not installed those mechanisms. What defense would you offer on behalf of the defendant machine manufacturer? Decide. Explain. See *Suter* v. *San Angelo Foundry and Machine Co.,* 406 A.2d 140 (N.J. 1979).

12. In June 1983, a San Diego, California, jury awarded $2.5 million to the family of a man killed while riding as a passenger in a Porsche Turbo 930. The plaintiff had argued, among other things, that the car was too powerful and too unstable for the average driver and that the manufacturer should have provided a warning regarding the power of the car. During the trial, the plaintiff's attorney received an internal anonymous memo from Porsche headquarters in West Germany that described the car's handling as "poisonous" and argued that the car had a tendency to oversteer. At the time of the accident, the car was traveling at 60 MPH in a 25-MPH zone. The jury voted 10 to 2 in finding the car unsafe for street driving.[31] Comment.

13. In the mid-1980s, the state of Colorado began enacting a series of tort reform measures in hopes of increasing insurance availability, reducing insurance rates, giving business a respite from litigation, and curbing what were believed to be unjustified jury awards. *The Wall Street Journal* summarized some of the measures and their results:

> State laws here protect ski resorts and dude ranches from lawsuits over accidental injuries. Bars are virtually immune from legal blame for the acts of drunk patrons. Jury awards for pain and suffering top out at $250,000. And defendants can't be forced to ante up more in damages just because they have the deepest pockets.[32]

After a few years of experience with the Colorado reforms, *The Wall Street Journal* observed that the results have been "quite mixed." Explain that judgment—how is tort reform likely to affect consumers, insurance firms, businesses, and lawyers?

14. Plaintiff James L. Maguire was seriously injured when the motor vehicle in which he was a passenger was struck by another motor vehicle. Plaintiff alleges that Vikki Paulson, the driver of the other vehicle, was intoxicated at the time of the accident. Following the accident, Paulson entered guilty pleas to (1) operating a motor vehicle while under the influence of alcohol, (2) involuntary manslaughter as a consequence of the death of another passenger riding with Maguire, and (3) failure to stop at a stop sign. During the time in question in the case, Pabst Brewing Company had engaged in an advertising campaign promoting the sale of its products. Plaintiff claims the defendant Pabst was liable for his injuries because (among other claims) its advertising promoting the consumption of alcohol by those who drove to taverns constituted a danger to highway safety and because the brewer had failed to warn consumers of the dangers of alcohol consumption. Decide. Explain. See *Maguire* v. *Pabst Brewing Company,* 387 N.W.2d 565 (Iowa 1986).

15. The plaintiff, a mother, claimed she went to the defendant physician to seek a therapeutic abortion. She further claimed the abortion was negligently performed, resulting in the "wrongful birth" of a healthy child. Plaintiff sought to recover, in a negligence action, for the costs of rearing the child. Decide. Explain. See *Nanke* v. *Napier,* 346 N.W.2d 520 (Iowa 1984). But see *Jones* v. *Malinowski,* 473 A.2d 429 (Md. 1984).

16. Suppose that you are the fourth purchaser of a 10-year-old home. After completion of the sale, you discover various defects in the home.
    a. Could you successfully sue the builder of the home? Explain.
    b. What claims of law would you raise?
    c. Would the outcome be influenced by whether the defects were latent (hidden) or patent (readily observable)? Explain. See, e.g., *Cosmopolitan Homes, Inc.* v. *Weller,* 663 P.2d 1041 (Colo. 1983). But see *Crowder* v. *Vandendeale,* 564 S.W.2d 879 (Mo. 1978), and *Redarowicz* v. *Ohlendorf,* 92 Ill.2d 171, 441 N.E.2d 324 (1982).

17. In 1985, two young adult males (18 and 20 years of age) shot themselves with a 12-gauge shotgun after drinking beer and listening to the "Stained Glass" album by the "heavy metal" band, Judas Priest. One man died immediately and the other three years later. The families of the two men sued the band and CBS Records on the grounds that subliminal messages in the music caused the men to shoot themselves. After listening to the evidence, the trial judge concluded that the subliminal message, "Do It," could be heard throughout the album, but he also concluded that the message was the result of a chance combination of sounds. The judge found for the defendants.

    Do you agree with the judge's decision? Explain. For a journalistic account of the case, see Amy Dockser Marcus and Arthur S. Hayes, "CBS Is Found Blameless in Music Suicides," *The Wall Street Journal,* August 27, 1990, p. B3.

18. In 1984, a woman was killed in an aerial tramway car at Palm Springs, California, when a piece of the tram machinery crashed through the Plexiglas roof of the car. The victim's blood splashed on two nearby passengers. Those passengers sued, seeking monetary damages for the emotional trauma of the episode. The passengers suffered nightmares, flashbacks, claustrophobia, and other complaints that they linked to the anguish of the tramway accident. So-called horror suits of this kind, where bystanders seek to recover for emotional injury from witnessing accidents, have become increasingly common in recent years.

    a. Raise the policy arguments against extending legal protection to those not themselves physically harmed in an accident such as that at Palm Springs.

    b. How would you rule on their claim? Explain. For a journalistic account of the case, see Philip Hager, "State High Court . . . Suit by 'Horror' Witnesses," *Los Angeles Times,* August 21, 1990, p. A3.

19. A man drowned on a family outing while using equipment rented from a canoe and inner-tube outfitter. His family sued, claiming the outfitter was negligent in failing to properly patrol the river and provide emergency assistance. The family won an $800,000 jury award. The parties later agreed to settle the case out of court. According to expert opinion, a 6-mile canoe trip costing $12 per person would cost more than $87 if lifeguards were to be required along rivers.

    a. In addition to the lack of safety equipment and personnel, what other claims are plaintiffs likely to raise in such situations?

    b. How might states act to protect recreational outfitters such as those who provide canoe, hiking, mountain climbing, and horseback riding?

    c. Some recreational outfitters, summer camps, motels, and others have responded to the threat of litigation by eliminating activities such as horseback riding and implements such as diving boards. The result, plaintiffs' lawyers argue, is increased safety. How do you feel about the reduction of summer recreation in exchange for increased safety? Explain. See Edward Felsenthal, "Modern Bathing Suits Spoil Summer Fun," *The Wall Street Journal,* June 24, 1993, p. B9.

NOTES

1. Peter Huber, *Liability: The Legal Revolution and Its Consequences* (New York: Basic Books, 1988), p. 3.

2. U.S. Senator Charles Grassley quoting from a Conference Board survey. Uniform Federal Product Liability Law (S. 640), Senate Hearing 102–1047, August 5, 1992, p. 31.

3. Edward Felsenthal, "Juries Display Less Sympathy in Injury Claims," *The Wall Street Journal,* March 21, 1994, p. B1.

4. 111 N.E. 1050 (N.Y. 1916).

5. *Doss* v. *Town of Big Stone Gap,* 134 S.E. 563 (1926).

6. *McKee* v. *Cutter Laboratories and Miles Laboratories,* 866 F. 2d 219 (6th Cir. 1989).

7. 391 F.2d 495 (8th Cir. 1968).

8. Ibid., p. 502.

9. *Insurance Co. of North America* v. *Pasakarnis,* 451 So.2d 447 (Fla. 1984) at 455–6.

10. 27 Cal. Rptr. 697, 377 P.2d 897 (1962).

11. Some states have eliminated the "unreasonably dangerous" standard from their strict liability tests.

12. *Smith v. Smith,* 278 N.W.2d 155 (S.D. 1979).

13. 163 Cal. Rptr. 132, 607 P.2d 924 (1980). Cert. den., 449 U.S. 912 (1980).

14. *Enright* v. *Eli Lilly & Co., 59 Law Week* 1134 (1991).

15. Eben Shapiro, "A Crafty Lawyer Turns Up the Heat on Tobacco," *The Wall Street Journal,* May 19, 1994, p. B1.

16. Ibid.

17. Junda Woo and Eben Shapiro, "Judge Gives Boost to Cigarette Suits," *The Wall Street Journal,* May 13, 1993, p. B5.

18. Ibid.

19. Associated Press, "Man Loses Suit against Tobacco Company," *Waterloo Courier,* January 31, 1993, p. A7.

20. Mark Hansen, "Second-Hand Smoke Suit," *ABA Journal* 78 (February 1992), p. 26.

21. Ibid.

22. John R. Wilke and Wade Lambert, "Cigarette Firms' Fire Liability Is Tested," *The Wall Street Journal,* May 12, 1992, p. B10.

23. Ibid.

24. *Cipollone* v. *Liggett Group,* 112 S.Ct. 2608 (1992).

25. Henry Reske, "Cigarette Suit Dropped," *ABA Journal* 79 (February 1993), p. 30.

26. Junda Woo, "Anti-Cigarette Suit Withdrawn in New Jersey," *The Wall Street Journal,* November 6, 1992, p. A3.

27. Eben Shapiro, "Tobacco Firms May Face New Pressure with Disclosure of Executive's Memo," *The Wall Street Journal,* May 9, 1994, p. 4A.

28. Robert H. Malott, "America's Liability Explosion," *Directors and Boards,* Spring 1986.

29. Ibid.

30. Ibid.

31. "Jury Finds Porsche Turbo Dangerous on Streets," *Des Moines Register,* June 30, 1983, p. 4A.

32. Milo Geyelin, "Overhaul of Civil Law in Colorado Produces Quite Mixed Results," *The Wall Street Journal,* March 3, 1992, p. A1.

CHAPTER 17

ENVIRONMENTAL PROTECTION

This natural inequality of the two powers of population, and of production in the earth, and that great law of our nature which most constantly keep their effects equal, form the great difficulty that to me appears insurmountable in the way to the perfectibility of society . . . No fancied equality, no agrarian regulations in their utmost extent, could remove the pressure of it even for a single century. And it appears, therefore, to be decisive against the possible existence of a society all the members of which should live in ease, happiness and comparative leisure.

Thomas Malthus, *An Essay on the Principle of Population*, 1798

Part One—Introduction[1]

We persist in assaulting the globe. In 1991, Saddam Hussein corrupted the Persian Gulf with the largest oil spill in history. Exxon has spent an estimated $3.5 billion in trying to clean up after the 1989 tragedy of the Exxon *Valdez* oil spill in Alaska. A considerable expanse of the former Soviet Union will remain uninhabitable for years as a result of the 1986 Chernobyl nuclear power plant accident.

Although the earth is a natural recycler of wastes—a very effective garbage dump—its ability to successfully neutralize the cumulative refuse of modern society is finite. Some concerns about pollution are centuries old, but the upsurge in population and increased industrialization and urbanization in the last 100 years have concentrated ever-increasing amounts of waste matter in small areas and put much greater pressure on the assimilative capabilities of the planet. Further, an improved understanding of the effects of various waste materials on the environment has generated widespread interest and public awareness of pollution problems.

PUBLIC OPINION

Environmental concerns may be the most prominent social cause of the 1990s. Public opinion polls consistently support the view that environmental degradation is an increasingly serious problem and that Americans must make sacrifices to correct that problem. For example, a 1992 national poll asked "Who should be responsible for cleaning up the environment?"[2] The results:

General public	41%
Industry	34
Government	22
All three equally	3

In that same poll, 92 percent of the respondents said that the government "should be doing more." Favored government initiatives included:

- More regulations on disposal of industrial waste—83 percent.
- Mandatory recycling—80 percent.
- More environmental information—76 percent.[3]

Perhaps more to the point, most Americans are willing to change their lives to aid the environmental cause. Also revealed by the poll: When asked what they are doing to "save the planet," 93 percent said they personally were helping—89 percent recycle garbage, 78 percent conserve electricity, 65 percent buy environmentally safe products, and 63 percent conserve water.[4]

Pay More?

Fortune magazine reported on a 1992 Roper poll:

[N]early two-thirds of those polled believe economic growth and environmental protection can go hand in hand, but if compromises between the two cannot be found, they clearly side with the environment. Americans say they are willing to divert money from other federal programs and make personal financial sacrifices to improve the environment.[5]

The table on page 767 summarizes the sacrifices that Americans say they are (and are not) willing to make in the environmental cause. Of course, what we would actually be willing to do when talk turns to action remains to be seen.

BUSINESS TO BLAME?

Business certainly is not the sole contributor to the environmental pollution we face. Individual citizens are primarily responsible for particulate matter discharged by wood-burning stoves, indoor pollution from cigarette smoking, and air pollution caused by our national one-worker-per-car commuting habits. Most forms of pollution, however, probably do have some business connection—whether direct or indirect. Thus, the subject matter of this chapter provides a superb opportunity to review the ethical considerations of business decision making and the overall social responsibility of business.

What Americans Will Do—And Won't

	Favor	Oppose		Favor	Oppose
Require people to separate garbage and solid waste for recycling	93%	6%	In metropolitan areas, require people who drive to work to take public transportation one day a week	57%	41%
Ban foam containers used by fast-food chains and other packaging that adds to the solid waste problem	84	14	Enforce stricter air quality regulations, increasing utility bills $10 per month	57	40
Require testing and repairs of your car each year for air pollution and emissions	80	19	Limit the number of large cars that could be produced	51	44
Ban disposable diapers, reducing the amount of solid waste in landfills	74	23	Add a 20-cent-per-gallon increase to the price of gasoline for cleaner fuels	48	50
Require pollution control equipment that would add $600 to the cost of a new car	68	28	Close pollution-producing factories, resulting in a loss of jobs	33	59

Source: Barbara Rosewicz, "Americans Are Willing to Sacrifice to Reduce Pollution, They Say," *The Wall Street Journal,* April 20, 1990, p. A12. Reprinted by permission of *The Wall Street Journal,* © 1990 Dow Jones & Company, Inc. All Rights Reserved Worldwide.

Question—Part One

1. Make a list of what you believe are the most serious environmental hazards we face today.
   a. To which of these hazards has business contributed?
   b. Without discussing whether it should, *can* business contribute solutions to any of these hazards? Explain.

Part Two—A Global Concern

Destruction of the Amazon Is "One of the Greatest Tragedies of History."

INTERNATIONAL

The skies over western Brazil will soon be dark both day and night. Dark from the smoke of thousands of fires, as farmers and cattle ranchers engage in their annual rite of destruction: clearing land for crops and livestock by burning the rain forests of the Amazon . . . Last year the smoke grew so thick that Porto Velho, the capital of the state of Rondonia, was forced to close its airport for days at a time. An estimated 12,350 sq. mi. of Brazilian rain forest—an area larger than Belgium—was reduced to ashes.

* * * * *

[The destruction of the forests] would be an incalculable catastrophe for the entire planet. Moist tropical forests are distinguished by their canopies of interlocking leaves and branches that shelter creatures below from sun and wind, and by their incredible variety of animal and plant life. If the forests vanish, so will more than 1 million species—a significant part of earth's biological diversity and genetic heritage. Moreover, the burning of the Amazon could have dramatic effects on global weather patterns—for example, heightening the warming trend that may result from the greenhouse effect . . .

To Brazilians, such pressure amounts to unjustified foreign meddling and a blatant effort by the industrial nations to preserve their economic supremacy at the expense of the developing world.[6]

Communist "Ecocide"

When the Soviet Union fell, we knew that problems remained for its people, but few of us imagined that the communist policy of production quotas and growth at any cost had threatened the core of life:

No other great industrial civilization so systematically and so long poisoned its land, air, water and people.[7]

A recent study details the shocking destruction:

- In 1990, the life expectancy of Moscow residents was 10 years below what it was in 1970.
- In some farming villages in the Caucasus region, pesticide use is so extreme that "cancer is the only cause of death."
- Nearly three-fourths of the surface water in the former Soviet Union is considered polluted.[8]

Most Polluted Place in the World

One particularly devastated section of the old Soviet Union has assumed the dubious title of dirtiest place on the planet:

In the Ust Kamenogorsk region of Soviet Central Asia, site of a nuclear-fuel explosion in September, there are so many chemical plants that sweeping the streets is banned so as not to stir up contaminants.

On the coast of the Baltic republic of Estonia, "gray snow" spewing from a cement factory hardens like mortar on village roofs.

About 30 miles from the 1986 nuclear disaster at Chernobyl, some farmers are told to leave their land and come back when it's safe—in 600 years.

The most-polluted place in the world—"no question in my mind"—is a lakeshore in Russia's heavily industrialized Ural Mountains, says Thomas B. Cochran, a physicist at the Natural Resources Defense Council in Washington. "No place else on Earth can you just stand, and get a lethal dose in an hour."

The deadly spot is on the shore of 100-acre Karachay Lake, which in the early 1950s became the repository for radioactive wastes from the nuclear-weapons production complex at Chelyabinsk, 900 miles east of Moscow.

The dose rate near the outlet pipe is "in the hundreds of roentgens per hour," Cochran says. An hour's dose is enough to kill a person within weeks. Surrounded by forest, the lake is cordoned off to everyone except heavily shielded workers stabilizing the contamination.[9]

Shifting Society's Pollution

Though Japan and Western Europe have tough environmental standards, anyone who travels the Third World quickly discovers it's a fantasy that the industrial countries are the polluted ones. Air quality in Mexico City, New Delhi, or Lagos makes Pasadena at noon seem like a mountain health spa. General pollution in Taiwan, South Korea, Poland, Brazil, Indonesia, and other developing nations far surpasses the West's.

Cold free-market analysis of this situation says Fine. The environment of the West is worth more, measured by property values, than in the developing world; so why not shift pollution there? Health in the West, measured by the courtroom standard of lifetime-earnings potential in dollars, is worth dramatically more than Third World health measured in bahts or rupees. So why not let somebody else get sick while enjoying cheap products made possible by distant pollution?

Shifting society's pollution to other lands is no more acceptable than exporting uncertified drugs. One of the Bush administration's first acts was a selfless order that U.S. firms not ship toxic wastes to undeveloped countries. Another step in the right direction might be a "pollution tariff"—a levy on products imported from countries not making good-faith steps toward ecological control. That would help American industry while pressuring foreign governments to protect their own citizens and workers.[10]

The Global Picture

The Wall Street Journal summarized the current state of the global environment:

A Layman's Guide to Key Environmental Issues

	Description	Pessimist's View	Optimist's View
Overpopulation	Now at 5.4 billion, the world's population is growing by about 95 million a year. If current trends continue, world population could nearly triple to 14 billion by the latter half of the next century.	Overpopulation worsens poverty, accelerates pollution, jeopardizes food supplies, spreads disease. Failure to curb population growth undermines economic progress and magnifies environmental decline.	Population growth is a natural partner of economic progress. The world's carrying capacity is vast, and natural resources are abundant. Technology and human ingenuity can solve any serious shortages, if they arise.
Biodiversity	Human activities continue to reduce biological diversity. Extinction rates are accelerating. Among the causes: poverty, pollution, excessive exploitation, habitat destruction and the introduction of alien species.	As economic development spreads, ecosystems are chopped into ever-smaller fragments, able to support fewer species. Genetic materials—for example, specimens of individual species—need to be protected and managed as sovereign resources.	Extinction of species from time to time is part of nature's way. Biotechnology and business need unfettered access to the world's natural resources to support scientific progress and economic growth.

	Description	Pessimist's View	Optimist's View
Deforestation	Forests are reeling from pressures of economic development. Clear-cutting destroys habitat and watersheds, increases erosion and reduces the world's ability to cope with greenhouse gases.	Deforestation threatens the entire planet. More than 90% of the world's land-dwelling plants and animals inhabit forests. Tropical deforestation is accelerating.	Trees are a renewable resource and the supply is abundant. Selective cutting of the forests brings needed jobs and income, spurring further economic development.
Ocean Pollution	The single greatest threat to the world's oceans is pollution from land-based sources, which account for about 70% of all the toxic chemicals, sediment, garbage and other pollutants at sea.	As toxic algae blooms spread, they deplete oxygen and block sunlight, killing fish and other life forms. Alarming threats are also posed by alien species introduced as cargo ships routinely discharge ballast water in foreign harbors.	The capacity of the oceans to "cleanse" themselves is enormous. Besides, most ocean pollution from land-based sources can be managed effectively by individual nations and through bilateral and regional arrangements.

Source: David Stipp and Frank Allen, "Forecast for Rio: Scientific Cloudiness," *The Wall Street Journal,* June 3, 1992, p. B1. Reprinted by permission of *The Wall Street Journal,* © 1992 Dow Jones & Company, Inc. All Rights Reserved Worldwide.

SOLUTIONS

How can solutions for these problems be found? Let's review the resolution mechanisms discussed throughout this text. We understand that most people want a cleaner environment, yet Adam Smith's "invisible hand," the free market (see Chapter 1), apparently is not of sufficient strength to guide the economy in that direction. The problem is not a failure in pricing system theory, but rather that the pricing system works to perfection, albeit in the wrong directions. This inconvenience can be traced to what economists call the *externality, free good,* or *commons* problem. Simply stated, producers have used the environment as a free garbage dump. In effect, producers can pollute a river and pass the costs (in the form of dirty water, dead fish, disease, and so forth) onto society as a whole. If a good can be obtained at no cost, an economist or a businessperson would be inclined to use as much of the *free good* as possible, and producers have done just that. There is no pricing incentive to minimize pollution if pollution has no direct cost to the company; in fact, the incentive is to maximize pollution. In this instance, the welfare of individuals acting in their own private interests does not coincide with the general good.

Collective Good

Another way in which an economist might examine the problem is as a *collective good.* If the citizens want a clean environment, the market would presumably reflect that desire by paying nonpolluting companies higher prices for their goods. Unfortunately, the benefits of clean air and water are not restricted to those paying for them through higher prices, because equal benefits are bestowed on those persons still trading (at lower prices) with polluting companies. Thus a clean environment benefits everyone equally, regardless of each individual's contribution toward it. A rational utility-maximizing strategy for each person, then, is to patronize cheaper, polluting firms to the exclusion of the more expensive nonpolluters, despite the desire of society for a clean environment. Therefore industries have no incentive not to pollute. Externalities and collective goods are instances of "market failure." (See Chapter 7.)

Ethics

Another solution mechanism for conflicts between business and society, which was discussed in Chapters 2 and 3, is letting the individual ethics of decision makers determine which course of action to take.

Of course, one of the many problems in relying on individual and/or corporate conscience to resolve environmental problems lies simply in identifying the "right" course of action. Even if disposed to do good, how does one choose, in the short term, between, for example, clean air and jobs?

Law

And what of the law? Obviously, international environmental problems cannot be cured merely by passing a new regulation in this country. Increasingly, the nations of the world are reaching understandings about cleansing the globe. In June 1992, environmental concerns drew together in Rio de Janeiro, Brazil, the largest gathering of heads of state in history. That remarkable assemblage for the Earth Summit testifies to the increasing global recognition of environmental problems and their critical role in international economic development and trade. Consider also the 1990 revision to the Montreal Protocol, a global environmental accord: "Driven by disturbing new evidence of a widening hole in the Earth's ozone layer, representatives of 53 nations agreed . . . to ban major ozone-destroying chemicals by the year 2000."[11] Similarly, in 1994, 64 nations added teeth to the 1990 Basel Convention (curbing transnational toxic waste shipment) by agreeing to immediately stop dumping toxic waste in developing countries. The United States, feeling, among other things, that certain materials such as scrap metal could properly be sent abroad for recycling if the receiving governments agree, has not ratified the Basel Convention.[12]

Global Warming

INTERNATIONAL

At this writing in 1994, President Clinton has proposed an initiative to help purify the global environment without leaning exclusively on federal dictates. We in the United States produce one-fifth of the world's greenhouse gases, and Clinton has pledged to reduce our emissions to 1990 levels by the year 2000. Clinton called for government, industry, and individuals to voluntarily comply with new standards for cutting back on "greenhouse" gas emissions such as carbon dioxide that appear to be raising global temperatures. Among other ingredients, the plan calls for tax incentives to encourage commuters to use public transportation, and it asks business to invest in antipollution programs in countries where they are doing business. Parts of the plan require congressional approval.[13]

Question—Part Two

1. How would you allocate responsibility for the impacts of our pollution (for example, acid rain in Canada, ocean dumping, oil spills in international waters, and American industry located in foreign countries and polluting locally) felt outside the United States? Explain.

Part Three—Environmental Protection in the United States

The United States has developed a wide variety of environmental protection laws and remedies, some of which are discussed in this part.

Throughout this discussion, keep in mind the central problem in environmental law—how much are we willing to pay? This is not an easy question to answer. For example, as a society, do we want clean air at any cost? How do we value human life so we can decide how much to spend to reduce the statistical incidence of a particular hazard, thereby saving some estimated number of lives annually? Must we sacrifice short-term economic development to achieve long-term environmental goals?

THE FEDERAL PRESENCE

Surprisingly, the federal government has long maintained a role in the protection of the environment. For example, an 1899 congressional enactment required a permit to discharge refuse into navigable waters. As it became apparent that private, state, and local environmental efforts were not adequate to the burgeoning problems, Congress began in the early 1970s to take a number of aggressive legislative initiatives.

National Environmental Policy Act (NEPA)

In 1970, President Nixon signed the National Environmental Policy Act (NEPA), which established a strong federal presence in the promotion of a clean and healthy environment. NEPA represents a general commitment by the federal government to "use all practicable means" to conduct federal affairs in a fashion that both promotes "the general welfare" and operates in "harmony" with the environment. A portion reads:

Public Law 91–190 (1969), 42 U.S.C. § 4331 *et seq.*

PURPOSE

Sec. 2. The purposes of this Act are: To declare a national policy which will encourage productive and enjoyable harmony between man and his environment; to promote efforts which will prevent or eliminate damage to the environment and biosphere and stimulate the health and welfare of man; to enrich the understanding of the ecological systems and natural resources important to the Nation; and to establish a Council on Environmental Quality.

The Council on Environmental Quality (CEQ) serves as an adviser to the president. Specifically, the CEQ must "assist and advise the president in the preparation of the [annual] Environmental Quality Report." The CEQ is a watchdog of sorts. It is required to conduct studies and collect information regarding the state of the environment. The council then develops policy and legislative proposals for the president and Congress.

But NEPA's primary influence results from its environmental impact statement (EIS) requirements. With few exceptions, "proposals for legislation and other major federal action significantly affecting the quality of the human environment" must be accompanied by an EIS explaining the impact on the environment and detailing reasonable alternatives. Major federal construction projects (highways, dams, and nuclear reactors) would normally require an EIS; but less-visible federal programs (ongoing timber management or authorizing the abandonment of a lengthy railway) may also require EIS treatment. A major private-sector action supported by federal funding or by one of several varieties of federal permission may also require an EIS. Hence, private companies receiving federal contracts, funding, licenses, and the like may be parties to the completion of an EIS.

Environmental Protection Agency (EPA)

In 1970, Congress created the Environmental Protection Agency (EPA) to oversee the public regulation of environmental issues. EPA duties include, among other things: (1) information gathering, particularly in surveying pollution problems, (2) research regarding pollution problems, (3) assisting state and local pollution control efforts, and (4) administering many of the federal laws directed to environmental concerns.

At this writing in 1994, Congress is considering, as it has for some years, the elevation of the Environmental Protection Agency to cabinet-level status. That legislation may not succeed. However, the CEQ has received increased funding from the Clinton administration. The president had originally intended to abolish the CEQ, but after political opposition, the administration changed direction and strengthened the council while also establishing the White House Office on the Environmental Policy. The Clinton CEQ will be responsible for NEPA compliance with general environmental policy being managed by the White House Office.

AIR POLLUTION

We depend on (indeed, we emotionally embrace) the automobile. In doing so, we have opened vistas of opportunity not previously imagined, but for the present at least we also have eliminated clean air. Motor vehicles discharge carbon monoxide, nitrogen oxide, and hydrocarbons as by-products of the combustion of fuel. Motor vehicles are the major source of air pollution, but industrial production and the combustion of fossil fuels in homes and industry are also significant contributors to the dilemma of dirty air. For most Americans, air pollution is simply an unpleasant fact of life. To the average Los Angeles resident, smog has been more central to daily activity than the area's beaches and mountains.

Progress?

Those discouraging words are facts of contemporary life, but it is also a fact that our hard work and vast expenditures may succeed in dissipating much of the gloom. As *Newsweek* recently reported, "Most barometers of air quality have been showing positive trends for years." [14] *Newsweek* attributes much of this salutary trend to the continuing replacement of old, "dirty" cars with newer, environmentally friendly models— 1993 models emit only about 1 percent as much pollution as cars of 20 years ago. [15] From 1982 to 1992, "overall U.S. smog incidence dropped by 8 percent," such that New York City, for example, fell from 71 "bad" carbon monoxide days in 1985 to 2 days in 1991 and 1 in 1992. [16]

Severe problems remain. Approximately 90 million people breathe unhealthy air, and recent improvements in smog conditions have resulted in part from the good fortune of cooler summers (smog is more likely in hotter weather). [17]

Clean Air Act of 1990 (CAA)

Early clean air legislation in 1963 and 1965 carried limited authority. The Clean Air Act Amendments of 1970 and 1977 gave the EPA the power to set air-quality standards and to ensure that those standards were achieved according to a timetable prescribed by the agency. Politics brought clean air to the fore in 1990, and a new Clean Air Act followed (see table on page 775). The Clean Air Act of 1990, which is being phased in over a period of years, generally requires tougher auto emission controls, cleaner burning gasoline, and new equipment to capture industrial and business pollution, all of which work toward the general goal of reducing airborne pollutants by about 50 percent. The act's virtues are summarized in the following remarks from the *Los Angeles Times:*

> Washington has revisited the federal Clean Air Act for the first time since the 1970s, and the winners are:
>
> —Southern California. The law itself will not create clean air. But it provides a framework for the region actually to meet federal health standards one day, something that has never quite been within our reach.

Clean Air Act at a Glance

Urban smog
- Aims to cut smog 15 percent in the first six years and 3 percent annually until federal air quality standards are met.
- Requires new emission controls on factories, businesses, and automobiles to meet smog reduction goals.

Motor vehicles
- Lowers limits on smog-causing hydrocarbon emissions by 40 percent (0.25 grams per mile) and nitrogen oxide emissions by 60 percent (0.41 gpm).
- Phases in alternative fuel cars for fleets and—under a California pilot program—for private cars.
- Requires on-board canisters to capture vapors during refueling and extends warranties on emission control equipment from 50,000 to 100,000 miles.

Airborne toxins
- Factories must install "maximum achievable control technology" to reduce release of 189 toxic chemicals by 90 percent by 2000.
- Additional controls required if needed to ensure an "ample margin of safety" from cancer-causing pollutants.

- Creates chemical safety board to investigate chemical release accidents.

Acid rain
- Coal-burning electric power plants must cut sulfur dioxide emissions by 10 million tons, or roughly in half, by 2000.
- Utilities may buy and sell "pollution credits" to reduce the cost of emisison controls at dirty plants and allow expansion.

Ozone depletion
- Phases out production of chemicals—such as chlorofluorocarbons (CFCs) and halons—that damage the stratospheric ozone layer by 2000.

Penalties
- Maximum $25,000 a day in civil penalty [generally limited to $200,000 maximum] for violators and possible criminal prosecution of corporate executives.
- Government may impose sanctions if states and cities fail to meet air quality standards.

Source: *Des Moines Register,* November 16, 1990, p. 2A. Reprinted by permission of the copyright holder, The Associated Press.

—Canada. Its lakes and forests will no longer be eaten alive by acid rain. By 1995, power plants in 21 states must reduce by 5 million tons the quantity of sulfuric acid that they now scatter into the atmosphere to mix with clouds and form acid rain. Another 5 million tons must be taken out of the air by 2000.

—A largely untested theory that market economics can play a role in controlling smog and acid rain. That's if government regulators make it worth something to polluting industries to reduce dirty emissions. A power plant that cuts emissions by, say, 10 percent more than the law requires can sell its "right" to pollute to another plant that needs to add that 10 percent to its own smokestacks to generate more power.[18]

Implementing the CAA

In 1993, a Senate report entitled "Three Years Later: Report Card on the 1990 Clean Air Act Amendments" accorded the government a B− "grade" in measuring progress toward implementing the very prescriptive provisions of the new, 800-page law.[19]

Cost-Benefit.   The central question is whether big benefits, like those noted above, are worth the cost—in the case of the Clean Air Act, about $25 billion annually. Currently, we are spending over $120 billion annually on total environmental cleanup, and that figure is expected to rise to nearly $180 billion by 2000, which would represent approximately 2.8 percent of the gross domestic product.[20]

Obviously, consumers will bear much of the cost of clean air. For example, new Ford cars are expected to rise in price by an average of $225 in the short term and by as much as $1,125 in the long term due to CAA requirements. Much of the $225 increase is attributable to replacing ozone-depleting chloroflourocarbons in air conditioners with hydroflourocarbons, which are believed to be harmless to the atmosphere.[21]

Business, Too, Will Pay. The heavy cost associated with clean air is well illustrated by a corner of the Clean Air Act that requires bigger businesses in severe air pollution regions of 11 states to reduce the number of people who drive to work or face penalties. Mass transit, where available, car pools, and company transportation are the likely options. Some estimates place the cost to employers at between $200 and $900 annually for each employee.[22]

The benefits have approached the miraculous in some instances, but the bill is very high. Now our task is to decide where we want to put our money and how much we want to pay for what many scientists believe to be rather trivial advances in air quality. *Fortune* explains:

> Take acid rain and ozone depletion. Most scientists agree that acid rain poses only a minor danger to rivers and lakes and no serious threat to human health. By contrast, the number of skin cancer deaths due to ozone depletion could rise from 500 a year currently to 100,000 by 2050. Yet Eileen Clausen, the EPA's director of atmospheric programs, figures the U.S. will spend about $1 billion annually for the next eight years to fight ozone depletion, and perhaps $4 billion a year "forever" to reduce acid rain.[23]

Passive Smoke

If the subject is clean air, smog immediately comes to mind, but in 1993 the EPA opened a new "indoor" front in its antipollution strategy by declaring that breathing secondhand tobacco smoke increases the risk of illness. As might be expected, this interesting initiative has been greeted with great publicity and a lawsuit from the tobacco industry, which seeks to have the EPA passive smoke report declared null and void on the grounds that the scientific evidence does not support the EPA conclusion.[24] The EPA report says that evidence conclusively establishes a link between inhaling secondhand tobacco smoke and illness. The report blamed passive smoke for approximately 3,000 lung cancer deaths annually in nonsmokers, and it attributes 150,000 to 300,000 annual cases of bronchitis and pneumonia in young children to that smoke.[25]

Implications? The report put immediate pressure on schools, work sites, restaurants, and other public places to make new arrangements for dealing with this so-called environmental tobacco smoke. Even sports stadiums have begun to ban smoking altogether or to restrict it to limited areas. The report may lead to tighter Occupational Safety and Health Administration regulations on smoke in the workplace. It may influence child custody decisions depending on whether one of the parents smokes, and it is likely that child abuse charges will be brought, in some instances, against parents who smoke around children who suffer from respiratory problems.

Questions

1. Automakers are particularly concerned about the economic impact of the Clean Air Act.

> By the end of the decade, worries Michael J. Schwarz, Ford Motor Co.'s manager of emission-control analysis and planning, "we'll be a nice, environmentally conscious company that's going broke because we can't interest customers in our cars." Schwarz's beef is that U.S. car manufacturers, already trailing the Japanese in key engineering areas, need to pour money into new-product design and development. And now, Detroit will have to divert some of those funds into cutting tailpipe emissions.[26]

   Comment.

2. Commentator James Flanigan made the argument that "the Clean Air Act properly understood is an economic force that will drive new technology . . . and increase U.S. competitiveness."[27] Explain his argument.

3. Estimates vary widely, but full implementation of the most stringent standards under the Clean Air Act amendments could increase the average price of a new car by $600.[28] Are you willing to pay an additional $600 (in current dollars) for each new car you purchase in your lifetime as *one part* of your financial contribution to clean air? Explain.

4. *a.* Given the new EPA position on passive smoke, could a full-time bartender successfully sue her employer if, 15 years from now, she develops lung cancer and the bar has allowed smoking during that entire time? Explain. Raise the competing issues.

   b. *Should* a bar be responsible for that illness? Explain.

WATER POLLUTION

As with the air, we have displayed a tendency to treat our water resources as free goods. Rather than paying the full cost of producing goods and services, we have simply piped a portion of that cost into the nearest body of water. The waste from production—indeed from the totality of our life experience—has commonly been disposed of in the water at a cost beneath that required to dispose of the waste in an ecologically sound fashion.

The corruption of our water system arose in a variety of ways. We have not always realized what we now know about the danger of wastes and the cleansing limits of our lakes and streams. The Gulf of Mexico provides a particularly alarming example. Industrial wastes, lawn chemicals, farm fertilizers, and household wastewater from all over the eastern two-thirds of the United States flow into the Gulf of Mexico, with the result that a patch of the gulf bottom waters up to 20 meters thick and about the size of New Jersey is effectively dead. Divers found no crab, shrimp, or fish in the dead zone. Nitrates from farm fertilizers encourage massive algae growth that sinks to the Gulf floor, decays, and consumes the available oxygen.[29] Approximately 10 percent of the freshwater runoff in the United States is used for industrial cooling. Often, the result is water that is inhospitable to aquatic life. Herbicides, pesticides, acid runoff from strip mining, and oil spills are more examples of our assault on the waterways. While scientists differ on the severity of the problem, we have learned that in recent years, airborne pollutants such as acid rain sometimes damage our water resources as well.

Federal Policy

The Clean Water Act (CWA), designed to "restore and maintain the chemical, physical and biological integrity of the nation's waters," establishes two national goals: (1) achieving water quality sufficient for the protection and propagation of fish, shellfish, and wildlife and for recreation in and on the water; and (2) eliminating the discharge of pollutants into navigable waters. The states have primary responsibility for enforcing the Clean Water Act, but the federal government, via the Environmental Protection Agency, is empowered to assume enforcement authority if necessary.

The goals of the Clean Water Act are to be implemented primarily by imposing limits on the amount of pollutants that may lawfully enter the water of the United States from any "point source" (typically a pipe). The National Pollutant Discharge Elimination System (NPDES) requires all pollutant dischargers to secure an EPA permit before pouring effluent into a navigable stream. The permit specifies maximum permissible levels of effluent. Typically, the permit also mandates the use of a particular pollution control process or device while requiring the permit holder to monitor its own performance and report on that performance to the state or the EPA, as appropriate.

Nonpoint Pollution.   Water runoff from the land commonly carries with it pollutants including silt, fertilizers, and pesticides. Virtually the entire U.S. coastline, as well as many bays, rivers, lakes, and other waterways, are affected by these nonpoint pollutants. The problems are multiple—for example, fertilizer runoff from agricultural land feeds algae, which spreads to the point that it consumes the oxygen in some inlets and coves, thus eliminating other plant and animal life. Existing legislation has been ineffectual, and nonpoint pollution remains largely unregulated.

Rewrite

At this writing in 1994, Congress is expected to rewrite federal clean water law. The primary initiatives are expected to be (1) an increase in pollution control spending (assuming deficit reduction targets are met) that would add $500 million annually to the existing $2 billion expenditure up to a total of $5 billion in the year 2000, and (2) increased attention to nonpoint pollution such as that from farmlands, streets, and construction sites.[30]

Clean Water Case

The case that follows illustrates the process by which the EPA and the states employ the Clean Water Act in determining whether water from a municipal waste treatment plant is clean enough to be dumped into a stream—a particularly difficult decision in this case, where pollution from one state flows by river into another state.

ARKANSAS v. OKLAHOMA
112 S.Ct. 1046 (1992)

Justice Stevens

Pursuant to the Clean Water Act . . . the Environmental Protection Agency (EPA) issued a discharge permit to a new point source in Arkansas, about 39 miles upstream from the Oklahoma state line. The question presented in this litigation is whether the EPA's finding that discharges from the new source would not cause a detectable violation of Oklahoma's water quality standards satisfied the EPA's duty to protect the interests of the downstream State. Disagreeing with the Court of Appeals, we hold that the Agency's action was authorized by the statute.

I

In 1985, the City of Fayetteville, Arkansas, applied to the EPA, seeking a permit for the City's new sewage treatment plant under the National Pollution Discharge Elimination System (NPDES). After the appropriate procedures, the EPA issued a permit authorizing the plant to discharge up to half of its effluent (to a limit of 6.1 million gallons per day) into an unnamed stream in northwestern Arkansas. That flow passes through a series of three creeks for about 17 miles, and then enters the Illinois River at a point 22 miles upstream from the Arkansas-Oklahoma border.

The permit imposed specific limitations on the quantity, content, and character of the discharge . . .

Respondents challenged this permit before the EPA, alleging that the discharge violated the Oklahoma water quality standards. Those standards provide that "no degradation [of water quality] shall be allowed" in the upper Illinois River, including the portion of the River immediately downstream from the state line.

Following a hearing, the Administrative Law Judge (ALJ) concluded that the Oklahoma standards would not be implicated unless the contested discharge had "something more than a mere de minimis impact" on the State's waters. He found that the discharge would not have an "undue impact" on Oklahoma's waters and, accordingly, affirmed the issuance of the permit.

On a petition for review, the EPA's Chief Judicial Officer . . . held that the Act and EPA regulations offered greater protection for the downstream State than the ALJ's "undue impact" standard suggested. He explained the proper standard as follows:

> [A] mere theoretical impairment of Oklahoma's water quality standards—i.e., an infinitesimal impairment predicted through modeling but not expected to be actually detectable or measurable—should not by itself block the issuance of the permit. In this case, the permit should be upheld if the record shows by a preponderance of the evidence that the authorized discharges would not cause an actual *detectable* violation of Oklahoma's water quality standards.

On remand, the ALJ . . . found that there would be no detectable violation of any of the components of Oklahoma's water quality standards. The Chief Judicial Officer sustained the issuance of the permit.

Both the petitioners and the respondents in this litigation sought judicial review. Arkansas argued that the Clean Water Act did not require an Arkansas point source to comply with Oklahoma's water quality standards. Oklahoma challenged the EPA's determination that the Fayetteville discharge would not produce a detectable violation of the Oklahoma standards.

The Court of Appeals did not accept either of these arguments. The court agreed with the EPA that the statute required compliance with Oklahoma's water quality standards, and did not disagree with the Agency's determination that the discharges from the Fayetteville plant would not produce a detectable violation of those standards. Nevertheless, relying on a theory that neither party had advanced, the Court of Appeals reversed the Agency's issuance of the Fayetteville permit. The court first ruled that the statute requires that "where a proposed source would discharge effluents that would contribute to conditions currently constituting a violation of applicable water quality standards, such [a] proposed source may not be permitted." Then the court found that the Illinois River in Oklahoma was "already degraded," that the Fayetteville effluent would reach the Illinois River in Oklahoma, and that that effluent could "be expected to contribute to the ongoing deterioration of the scenic [Illinois R]iver" in Oklahoma even though it would not detectably affect the River's water quality.

* * * * *

[Sections II and III omitted.]

IV

The parties have argued three analytically distinct questions concerning the interpretation of the Clean Water Act. First, does the Act require the EPA, in crafting and issuing a permit to a point source in one State, to apply the water quality standards of downstream States? Second, even if the Act does not *require* as much, does the Agency have the statutory authority to mandate such compliance? Third, does the Act provide, as the Court of Appeals held, that once a body of water fails to meet water quality standards no discharge that yields effluent that reach the degraded waters will be permitted?

In this case, it is neither necessary nor prudent for us to resolve the first of these questions. In issuing the Fayetteville permit, the EPA assumed it was obligated by both the Act and its own regulations to ensure that the Fayetteville discharge would not violate Oklahoma's standards. As we discuss below, this assumption was permissible and reasonable and therefore there is no need for us to address whether the Act requires as much . . .

Our decision not to determine at this time the scope of the Agency's statutory *obligations* does not affect our resolution of the second question, which concerns the Agency's statutory *authority*. Even if the Clean Water Act itself does not require the Fayetteville discharge to comply with Oklahoma's water quality standards, the statute clearly does not limit the EPA's authority to mandate such compliance.

Since 1973, EPA regulations have provided that an NPDES permit shall not be issued "[w]hen the imposition of conditions cannot ensure compliance with the applicable water quality requirements of all affected States." . . .

* * * * *

The regulations relied on by the EPA were a perfectly reasonable exercise of the Agency's statutory discretion. The application of state water quality standards in the interstate context is wholly consistent with the Act's broad purpose, "to restore and maintain the chemical, physical, and biological integrity of the Nation's waters." Moreover § 301(b)(1)(C) expressly identifies the achievement of state water quality standards as one of the Act's central objectives . . .

* * * * *

Arkansas argues that regulations requiring compliance with downstream standards are at odds with the legislative history of the Act and with the statutory scheme established by the Act. Although we agree with Arkansas that the Act's legislative history indicates that Congress intended to grant the Administrator discretion in his oversight of the issuance of NPDES permits, we find nothing in that history to indicate that Congress intended to preclude the EPA from establishing a general requirement that such permits be conditioned to ensure compliance with downstream water quality standards.

Similarly, we agree with Arkansas that in the Clean Water Act Congress struck a careful balance among competing policies and interests, but do not find the EPA regulations concerning the application of downstream water quality standards at all incompatible with that balance. Congress, in crafting the Act, protected certain sovereign interest of the States; for example, § 510 allows States to adopt more demanding pollution-control standards than those established under the Act . . .

For these reasons, we find the EPA's requirement that the Fayetteville discharge comply with Oklahoma's water quality standards to be a reasonable exercise of the Agency's substantial statutory discretion.

V

The Court of Appeals construed the Clean Water Act to prohibit any discharge of effluent that would reach waters already in violation of existing water quality standards. We find nothing in the Act to support this reading.

The interpretation of the statute adopted by the court had not been advanced by any party during the agency or court proceedings. Moreover, the Court of Appeals candidly acknowledged that its theory "has apparently never before been addressed by a federal court." . . .

Although the Act contains several provisions directing compliance with state water quality standards, the parties have pointed to nothing that mandates a complete ban on discharges into a waterway that is in violation of those standards. The statute does, however, contain provisions designed to remedy existing water quality violations and to allocate the burden of reducing undesirable discharges between existing sources and new sources. Thus, rather than establishing the categorical ban announced by the Court of Appeals—which might frustrate the construction of new plants that would improve existing conditions—the Clean Water Act vests in the EPA and the States broad authority to develop long-range, areawide programs to alleviate and eliminate existing pollution.

* * * * *

VI

The Court of Appeals also concluded that the EPA's issuance of the Fayetteville permit was arbitrary and capricious because the Agency misinterpreted Oklahoma's water quality standards. The primary difference between the court's and the Agency's interpretation of the standards derives from the court's construction of the Act. Contrary to the EPA's interpretation of the Oklahoma standards, the Court of Appeals read those standards as containing the same categorical ban on new discharges that the court had found in the Clean Water Act itself. Although we do not believe the text of the Oklahoma standards supports the court's reading . . . we reject it for a more fundamental reason—namely, that the Court of Appeals exceeded the legitimate scope of judicial review of an agency adjudication . . .

EPA regulations require an NPDES permit to comply "with the applicable water quality requirements of all affected States." This regulation effectively incorporates into federal law those state law standards the Agency reasonably determines to be "applicable." In such a situation, then, state water quality standards—promulgated by the States with substantial guidance from the EPA and approved by the Agency—are part of the federal law of water pollution control.

* * * * *

. . . In this case, the Chief Judicial Officer ruled that the Oklahoma standards—which require that there be "no degradation" of the upper Illinois River—would only be violated if the discharge effected an "actually detectable or measurable" change in water quality.

This interpretation of the Oklahoma standards is certainly reasonable and consistent with the purposes and principles of the Clean Water Act . . .

The EPA's application of those standards in this case was also sound. On remand, the ALJ scrutinized the record and made explicit factual findings regarding four primary measures of water quality under the Oklahoma standards: eutrophication, aesthetics, dissolved oxygen, and metals. In each case, the ALJ found that the Fayetteville discharge would not lead to a detectable change in water quality. He therefore concluded that the Fayetteville discharge would not violate the Oklahoma water quality standards. Because we agree with the Agency's Chief Judicial Officer that these findings are supported by substantial evidence, we conclude that the Court of Appeals should have affirmed both the EPA's construction of the regulations and the issuance of the Fayetteville permit.

* * * * *

In sum, the Court of Appeals made a policy choice that it was not authorized to make. Arguably, as that court suggested, it might be wise to prohibit any discharge into the Illinois River, even if that discharge would have no adverse impact on water quality. But it was surely not arbitrary for the EPA to conclude—given the benefits to the River from the increased flow of relatively clean water and the benefits achieved in Arkansas by allowing the new plant to operate as designed—that allowing the discharge would be even wiser. It is not our role, or that of the Court of Appeals, to decide which policy choice is the better one, for it is clear that Congress has entrusted such decisions to the Environmental Protection Agency.

[Reversed.]

Questions

1. Why did the EPA and ultimately the Supreme Court find that the Arkansas effluent would not violate the Clean Water Act even though that effluent would reach an Oklahoma stream whose water quality was already degraded?
2. Explain the court of appeals decision. Explain the Supreme Court's reversal of the court of appeals. In your opinion, which court reached the better conclusion? Explain.
3. The Environmental Protection Agency approved regulations to protect the public from contaminated drinking water. An estimated 90,000 illnesses (including diarrhea, nausea, vomiting, and stomach upsets) annually are attributed to germs in drinking water. The regulations apply stringent standards to water treatment systems in about 10,000 communities where drinking water is drawn from rivers and streams. The EPA estimates that the new regulations will require about $3 billion in initial capital expenditures and about $500 million annually in additional operating costs. As a result, rural home water bills were expected to increase by as much as $50 per month while urban bills were likely to rise by about $6 per month. In your view, are those additional costs justified by a dramatic reduction in the illnesses noted above? Explain. See "EPA: Cleaner Water Will Mean Higher Bills," *Des Moines Register,* June 23, 1989, p. 14T.

LAND POLLUTION

Pollution does not fit tidily into the three compartments (air, water, land) used for convenience in this text. Acid rain, as discussed above, debases air and water as well as the fruits of the water and land (fish and trees). Similarly, the problems of land pollution addressed in this section often do damage to the fullness of the natural world. For most of recorded history, we felt safe and comfortable in using the earth as a garbage dump. When we did begin to recognize emerging dangers, our initial concern was simply the problem of disposing of the enormous bulk of our solid wastes.

Garbage

Basically, the problem is that our lifestyles result in mountains of solid waste that grow higher every year. As of 1992, we were spending $30 billion annually for municipal trash collection, a figure that will rise to perhaps $75 billion by 2000.[31] Our total waste stream, which the EPA sought to curb by 25 percent, has, in fact, increased 13 percent since 1988.[32] Some initiatives by both business and government have sought to control the solid waste problem. For example, McDonald's has decided to stop using polystyrene packaging. And the public has become increasingly conscious of our waste-generating lifestyles:

> DIAPER WARS: Disposable diaper makers blamed consumer misunderstanding for survey results that show people support a ban on their product. About 16 billion disposables are sold each year. Because of environmental and health issues, bans or taxes are being considered in at least 20 states. A Gallup poll showed 43 percent of people support a ban. Officials say consumers don't realize cloth diapers take more energy to make and need water for cleaning.[33]

Recycling

Nine states have bottle bills that result, according to industry figures, in recycling about 80 percent of the beverage containers in those states. We dispose of 115 billion beer and pop cans annually. Those containers consume about 5 percent of our landfill space. According to the federal General Accounting Office, 70 percent of Americans favor a nationwide bottle bill, but Congress has never given its approval.[34]

In Germany, manufacturers are required by law to clean up the garbage they produce.[35] As a result, BMW, for example, uses junked BMWs to make plastics, with a goal of recycling 90 percent of each car. In total, the United States reuses about one-third as much of our waste as do Germany and Japan.[36] Of course, recycling is not a cure-all for our waste management problems. The article that follows examines some of the strengths and weaknesses of recycling.

RECYCLING IN SEATTLE
SETS NATIONAL STANDARD
BUT IS HITTING SNAGS

Bill Richards

It is Monday night—garbage night here—and as usual, Janice D'Acquisto is dancing in her trash can.

Knees bent, arms pumping, Ms. D'Acquisto jumps up and down in the 30-gallon can, mashing down a week's worth of leavings that she, her two daughters and her granddaughter have produced. Across the city others are performing similar can dances, known here as the "Seattle Stomp." To get residents to recycle, Seattle charges heavily for each extra barrel of garbage they put out. Hence the Stomp: "You climb in, jump around, and eventually it all fits in one can," Ms. D'Acquisto says proudly.

Human trash compacting wasn't quite what officials had in mind five years ago when Seattle announced a plan to recycle 60% of its garbage by

1998. Since then, Seattle's ambitious program has become a big-city benchmark, with a remarkable 42% of all the city's trash going into recycling bins and 90% of all single-family homes participating.

*   *   *   *   *

Sorting Things Out

But beneath this mound of hoopla a troubling fact has begun to emerge: Seattle's recycling program is quietly running out of steam. Most experts say the city won't come close to its 60% target without draconian steps like fining nonparticipants. Big waste generators like apartment complexes and small businesses have shown only tepid interest in recycling, or have rebelled. Some recycled materials, such as glass, are being stockpiled because they can't be sold and have even been dumped in landfills. Seattle has had to entangle itself in a risky, long-term commitment to shoulder the losses of recycling contractors.

*   *   *   *   *

As it happens, the chief motivation for Seattle's recycling effort, a purported garbage crisis owing to a lack of dumps, seems to have been a mirage. Regional landfills opened in Washington and Oregon since 1988 have the capacity to absorb Seattle's garbage for nearly another century, with or without recycling.

Savings in Doubt

Whether Seattle is saving money by recycling instead of dumping seems to be anyone's guess. A recent state study found that it costs $40 a ton less to recycle when Seattle's garbage is calculated by weight, as the city does. But when the study calculated the cost of the same garbage by volume, as haulers do, recycling and dumping came out costing about the same.

A significant shortfall in Seattle's high-profile program would have a magnified national impact. Dozens of cities and states have followed Seattle's example, banking on recycling large portions of their waste as a solution for their garbage problems. New Jersey, for example, last year targeted 60% of its solid

waste for recycling by 1996, and 22 other states aim to recycle at least 40%.

But as cities and states leap on the recycling bandwagon, a growing number of skeptics question whether ever-higher recycling targets are useful or necessary. "There has been a recycle-or-die movement that has made some false assumptions," contends Resource Recycling's Mr. Powell, who heads the industry's National Recycling Coalition. Recycling zealots, Mr. Powell says, believed they could avoid dumps and generate thousands of new jobs related to recycling materials. "That ain't gonna happen," he says.

Hedge Clippings

Critics like Harvey Alter, manager of the U.S. Chamber of Commerce's resources policy department, contend that recycling has built-in limits and no big city can hope to salvage much more than 30% of its garbage. Adding in yard waste such as leaves and hedge clippings may boost that another 10%, he says . . .

Seattle's recycling officials bristle at all this negativism. "I don't think 60% is pie in the sky, and we can back that up with a whole lot of analysis," says Raymond Hoffman, Seattle's senior recycling planner. He says Seattle can meet its target by composting food waste and adding more waste paper to its recyclables. The program also needs more business involvement, he says.

*   *   *   *   *

At the Elite Tavern in the city's Capital Hill district, manager Richard Lapray says he dropped out in May partly because recycling was costing his business nearly $150 a month to participate. "We were filling two bins a week with all kinds of broken colored glass, and I knew they couldn't recycle that stuff," Mr. Lapray says. "It was just ending up in a landfill somewhere, so why bother?"

Mr. Lapray isn't far off. Besides becoming a recycling model, Seattle also has become a model for recycling's built-in pitfall: The more active the program, the more it floods limited markets, depressing resale prices and raising program costs.

Green Glass Glut

Take green glass—please. The stuff fetched $30 a ton here two years ago. But Seattle collected 40,000 tons of the glass last year, overwhelming the state's lone commercial glass furnace, which can handle only 32,000 tons a year. Residents still dutifully toss their green glass bottles into recycling bins, but as the resale price has dropped to zero, haulers have been stockpiling it and hoping someone, somewhere, will take it off their hands.

City and state officials are searching hard for markets for used glass, plastic and paper. But pilot efforts by Procter & Gamble Co. to create outlets here for colored plastics and disposable diapers proved unprofitable and were dropped. Johnson Controls Inc., which makes plastic soda bottles, subsidized collection of the bottles here for the last four years, hoping a market would open up. It says it lost money and plans to drop the operation at the end of the year.

* * * * *

"Making this work is far more difficult than anyone envisioned when we started," says David Dougherty, director of the Clean Washington Center, a state-funded effort to find new markets for recycled material. Mr. Dougherty says finding markets for recyclables can be accomplished, "but it's going to be expensive." . . .

Others say Seattle is in over its head. "We told the bureaucrats, 'You're playing in a very sensitive marketplace,'" says Warren Razore, whose locally based company, Rabanco, has run recycling programs here since 1965.

Scant Cash for Trash

Mr. Razore says a mere 5% jump in the supply of some kinds of recyclables can depress their resale value by half. The price for newsprint bobbed from a high of $75 a ton at the start of the recycling program here in 1988 to $30 a ton three years after the city's program started. Newsprint now sells for around $45 a ton here, rising after California passed a law requiring newspapers to contain 23% recycled paper. But Mr. Razore says the newsprint price could plunge again when Los Angeles's fledgling recycling program hits its stride, dumping an expected 21,000 tons of newsprint a month on the market.

* * * * *

But all these problems may be beside the point, as far as Seattle is concerned. Even if the city's recycling program doesn't meet expectations, the *idea* of recycling seems more popular than ever.

Source: *The Wall Street Journal,* August 3, 1993, p. A1. Reprinted by permission of *The Wall Street Journal,* © 1993 Dow Jones & Company, Inc. All Rights Reserved Worldwide.

Questions

1. If landfills can continue to comfortably absorb waste, why is Seattle so zealously committed to recycling?
2. Should we support only those recycling programs that pay for themselves? Explain.

Solid Waste Disposal Act

To attack the massive garbage problem, Congress approved the Solid Waste Disposal Act of 1965. The act, in brief, leaves solid waste problems to states and localities, while the federal government offers research and financial support.

Toxic Substances Control Act (TSCA)

In 1976, Congress approved the Toxic Substances Control Act (TSCA) to identify toxic chemicals, assess their risks, and control dangerous chemicals. Under the terms of the TSCA, the Environmental Protection Agency requires the chemical industry to report any information it may have suggesting that a chemical poses a "substantial risk." The EPA is empowered to review and limit or stop the introduction of new chemicals.

Resource Conservation and Recovery Act (RCRA)

By 1976, the dangers of hazardous substances were becoming apparent to all, and Congress complemented the TSCA with the Resource Conservation and Recovery Act (RCRA). The act addresses both solid and hazardous wastes. Its solid waste provisions are more supportive than punitive in tone and approach. The federal government is authorized, among other strategies, to provide technical and financial assistance to states and localities; to prohibit future open dumping; and to establish cooperative federal, state, local, and private-enterprise programs to recover energy and valuable materials from solid waste.

Subtitle C of the RCRA is designed to ensure the safe movement and disposal of hazardous wastes. The generator of the waste must determine if that waste is hazardous under EPA guidelines and, if so, report the waste site and waste activities to the government. The waste generator must then create a manifest to be used in tracking the waste from its creation to its disposal. Along the "cradle-to-grave" path of the waste, all those with responsibility for it must sign the manifest and safely store and transport it. Once at a licensed disposal facility, the owner signs for the waste and returns a copy to the generator.

Disposal Sites.   Owners and operators of hazardous waste disposal sites must obtain government permits to begin operation. Those sites must be operated according to EPA standards, and remedial action must be taken should hazardous wastes escape from the sites.

Through the 1980s, the general thrust of RCRA was to replace land burial of hazardous waste with treatments that destroy those wastes and neutralize their toxicity. Then, in 1993, the EPA announced a crackdown on incinerators, which have been widely employed as an alternative to burial in dealing with toxic garbage. Under the new policy, announced in May 1993, the EPA imposed a moratorium of 18 months on all new hazardous waste incinerators, during which time the agency will be overhauling its rules governing hazardous waste burning and will develop strategies to force reduction of waste. The policy applies to incinerators, industrial boilers, industrial furnaces, and cement kilns that burn everything from general garbage to suspected cancer-causing agents such as dioxin. Each year, we burn 5 million tons of hazardous waste—enough to fill tank trucks stretching end to end from Washington, D.C., to Los Angeles.[37]

NIMBY.   The transportation and disposal of solid and hazardous waste have led citizens' groups as well as state and local governments to aggressive action under the general banner of "Not In My Backyard" (NIMBY). Citizens are contesting the siting of new landfills, shipments of nuclear waste, the creation of hazardous waste facilities, and the like. Some communities have passed ordinances forbidding the transportation of wastes through their boundaries. In 1992, the Supreme Court struck down Michigan and Alabama NIMBY statutes. The Michigan law prohibited private landfill operators from accepting solid waste from outside the county in question unless explicitly permitted to do so by the county. The Court held that the Michigan law discriminated against interstate commerce (see Chapter 7). The Court reached a similar conclusion in the Alabama case where the state imposed fees on all hazardous waste disposed of within the state but imposed a higher fee on garbage that came from out of state.[38]

Discrimination?

For some years, complaints have been raised that government decisions regarding hazardous waste disposal have had the effect of exposing black Americans to greater levels of toxic pollution than whites. For the first time, in 1993, the Clinton administration agreed to investigate those complaints. In ongoing lawsuits aimed at the situation, plaintiffs have argued that they need not prove that states or the federal government *intended* to discriminate in decisions such as choosing sites for hazardous waste disposal; rather, they need only show that the *effect* of the decisions is to disproportionately burden blacks. They believe that would be so even if the decisions were made on the basis of the cost of land, population density, and other conditions unrelated to race.

EPA chief Carol Browner has said, "I don't think that there is any doubt that low-income and minority communities have borne the brunt of our industrial life style."[39] And the data do show dramatic disparities in some cases. For instance, according to the *New York Times,* in Carville, Louisiana, where the population is 70 percent African-American, 353 pounds of toxic material per capita is released, while the statewide average per capita is 105 pounds.[40]

The discrimination theme has also played a prominent role in efforts to strengthen pesticide protection rules under the Federal Insecticide, Fungicide, and Rodenticide Act. After beginning the process in 1984, the EPA in 1992 issued new standards that apply to farm workers (farm owners and families are exempt from many of the rules) and employees in nurseries, greenhouses, and forests. In order to limit exposure to pesticides, which cause an estimated 1,000 fatalities annually, employers must train workers in pesticide safety, post safety information and warnings, use both English and Spanish in giving warnings, and bar workers from recently sprayed fields. Migrant labor advocates, while applauding the new rules, argued that they do not go far enough in training our 1.5 to 2.5 million hired farm workers about pesticide exposure.

NAFTA and Waste

> The following article illustrates the nature of hazardous waste problems and suggests that the recent passage of NAFTA may lead to significant cross-border waste management progress between Mexico and the United States. Here, California officials alleged that RSR, Corp., the world's largest auto battery recycler, hired a California company, Alco Pacifica, to ship battery lead from California to a processing plant in Mexico from which salvageable material was to be returned to California. However, prosecutors charged, the material was simply abandoned in Mexico, with little or no processing.[41]

NAFTA MAY GET LIFT
FROM PACT ON TOXIC SITE

Bob Davis

[Los Angeles] prosecutor David Eng and Mexican environmental officials [announced] a novel plan to clean up an abandoned lead-recycling plant outside Tijuana, Mexico . . .

Mr. Eng, an environmental prosecutor in the Los Angeles County District Attorney's office, has used a state law classifying lead slag as a hazardous waste to negotiate toxic-waste cleanups south of the border. In the deal, RSR Corp., a privately owned Dallas lead recycler, said it will pay $2.5 million and plead no contest to charges of improperly transporting lead waste from its Los Angeles smelter to Mexico.

$2 Million Cleanup

Of the $2.5 million fine, $2 million will be used to clean up the site, called Alco Pacifico de Mexico, said Los Angeles authorities and the companies involved. Los Angeles District Attorney Gil Garcetti also plans to donate $300,000 of the fine to a foundation that provides medical care for border-area residents. And the Mexican government will use the Alco Pacifico site's recoverable lead, valued at between $100,000 and $200,000, to help pay back wages of workers at the plant, which closed in 1991 after a strike.

The Los Angeles authorities could have prosecuted the case alone, but without the cooperation of the Mexican government the settlement wouldn't have helped clean up the site or provided benefits to people in the area.

* * * * *

Alco Pacifico has become a grim reminder of Mexico's difficulties in enforcing environmental standards. The 14-acre lead-recycling facility is in the arid hills outside Tijuana, next to dairies that feed the city. The plant has been shut for two years. The rusting furnaces are surrounded by hills of lead ash and slag, open to the wind.

Daniel Muno Garay, who owns one of the nearby dairies, said that over the past decade, 14 cows suddenly keeled over and died. Alco Pacifico managers paid for the losses. "When the animals first started dying, the dairy owner named his price for the animals," Mr. Muno said in an interview last year. "The second time, they would just go over (to Alco Pacifico) for the money."

Occasionally, Mexican regulators visited Alco Pacifico, Mr. Muno said. Plant managers would promise to install new equipment, he said, but the factory would start running at night to avoid the regulators' attention.

Source: *The Wall Street Journal,* June 15, 1993, p. A2. Reprinted by permission of *The Wall Street Journal,* © 1993 Dow Jones & Company, Inc. All Rights Reserved Worldwide.

Afterword

In December 1993, the chief executive of Alco Pacific, the California company that transported lead slag for RSR from Los Angeles to the Tijuana, Mexico, site, was sentenced to 16 months in jail on three felony counts of unlawful transportation of hazardous wastes to Mexico. That sentence was the sternest such prosecution ever in the United States.[42]

Questions

1. *a.* Do you think it is a moral wrong for black communities to be burdened with a disproportionate share of toxic waste?
   b. A legal wrong? Explain.
   c. In shipping wastes to underdeveloped countries, are U.S. firms guilty of racism? Explain.
2. Presumably, most of us bear some responsibility for the hazardous waste problem because our consumption preferences lead to the creation of waste. Because market decisions created the problem, should we let the market resolve it by permitting hazardous waste disposal in the most profitable fashion? Explain.
3. Hazardous waste sites are necessary, but few communities will accept them. Assume government intervention is necessary to manage the hazardous waste problem. Should the federal government pass legislation requiring all states and localities to accept all hazardous waste sites that comply with the federal government's disposal standards? Explain.

Superfund—Comprehensive Environmental Response, Compensation, and Liability Act of 1980 (CERCLA)

CERCLA, known as "Superfund," is designed to help clean up hazardous dumps and spills. In many instances, those responsible for hazardous dumps and spills cannot afford to pay for cleanup. Other hazardous sites have been abandoned. In both cases, the threat to the public is such that the government created the Superfund to attack those sites that are so dangerous that they have been included on the National Priorities List (NPL). The bulk of the fund is drawn from taxes on chemicals and petroleum. Private citizens suffering injury from hazardous wastes do not receive relief under the terms of CERCLA. Rather, they must pursue their claims through the judicial system.

Cost.   The NPL now includes some 1,245 sites and is expected to eventually grow to more than 3,000. Twelve to 15 years and $25 to $30 million have been required to clean the average site.[43] Total cleanup costs are estimated at $500 billion, and 50 years may be required for the job. Furthermore, some 35,000 additional sites need attention but are currently less threatening than those on the NPL.[44]

All parties responsible for any illegal hazardous waste discharge are strictly liable (with certain limitations) for all costs associated with the necessary cleanup. Unfortunately, many polluters have disappeared or are unable to pay. The result is that the government has been able to secure only about one-fifth of the cleanup costs that potentially could have been recovered from polluters.[45] Particularly frustrating is the sum of money devoted to the legal fees expended in protecting the interests of the many parties who are often involved in a Superfund case. For example:

> One critic recently cited the case of a Long Island, N.Y., site in which 136 law firms represent potentially responsible parties (PRPs) and another 72 law firms represent the PRPs' 442 insurers. Although the site was reportedly placed on Superfund's priority list more than eight years ago, no cleanup plan has yet been approved.[46]

In testimony before Congress, Du Pont's corporate counsel, Bernard Reilly, argued for greater use of privatization of Superfund cleanups. He pointed to a pair of sites in southern New Jersey:

> One landfill is being cleaned up by a chemical industry group at one-third the cost of the EPA-managed site.[47]

At this writing in 1994, President Clinton has proposed a plan for rewriting the Superfund law. The president seeks to relax cleanup standards in some instances with the expectation that costs may be reduced by as much as 25 percent. The plan also includes a new tax on commercial insurance companies that would be used to settle lawsuits by polluting businesses against their insurers and an arbitration system designed to remove Superfund cases from the courts. The administration thinks that the combined effect of these measures would be to halve Superfund litigation.[48]

Right to Know

Spurred by the Bhopal, India, chemical plant disaster, which resulted in the deaths of more than 3,000 people, Congress passed the Emergency Planning and Community Right-to-Know Act of 1986 as an amendment to the Superfund law. The act requires companies to notify the government if they release any extremely hazardous chemicals into the environment, and they must submit an inventory of their hazardous chemicals to the government. Each state must establish emergency response commissions, local emergency planning committees, and emergency plans to deal with chemical discharges. In general, information regarding dangerous chemicals must be released to the public on request. Beyond preparing for chemical release emergencies, the hope behind the law is that its disclosure requirements will enhance community awareness of chemical hazards, thus provoking sufficient community pressure to cause companies to voluntarily reduce their emissions.

ENFORCEMENT AND PENALTIES UNDER FEDERAL LAW

Because of the risks associated with pollution, environmental protection bodies have been given strong enforcement authority. Very often, violators initially are warned and a compliance schedule is set out. If corrective action is not forthcoming, sterner measures are followed including an administrative order to comply. Where problems persist or the difficulties are more serious, the government may initiate civil and/or criminal actions against both firms and managers. Penalties vary with the act in question, but the provisions of the Clean Air Act are typical in that civil fines of $25,000 per day up to a maximum of $200,000 (and higher under some conditions) are provided for. Individuals may be jailed for one or more years and fined. In some instances, an entire operation may be shut down.

Government action has increased over the years, and civil suits have remained the preferred mode of enforcement. "In 1982, according to EPA statistics, 112 civil and 29 criminal cases were referred to [the Justice Department.] In 1991, the numbers were 393 and 81."[49] The table on page 793 details the pattern of criminal enforcement of environmental laws.

A worrisome dimension of the criminal prosecution record is that small operators are much more likely to go to jail than are managers of big firms. According to a recent study, defendants from large companies who were found guilty had an 18 percent chance of going to jail, compared with a 43 percent chance for those from small businesses.[50]

Enforcement Mechanisms

Many environmental statutes require companies to monitor their own environmental performance and report that information (including violations) to the government. Government agencies generally have broad authority to conduct environmental inspections of both plants and records as necessary, although they will need to seek search warrants where criminal prosecutions are anticipated. Finally, many environmental statutes provide for the possibility of *citizen suits* wherein an individual is empowered to challenge government environmental decisions such as the granting of a permit, and generally to demand both governmental and private sector compliance with the law.

STATE AND LOCAL REGULATION

Under the "police powers" granted by the Constitution, as previously discussed in Chapter 7, state and local governments have the right to impose various controls on citizens to protect and maintain the public health and safety and its general welfare. State and local governments are increasingly acting in the area of environmental protection to do just that. Although rejected by voters by a two-to-one margin, a 1990 California environmental initiative (the so-called Big Green) is reflective of the activism at the state level.

Cracking Down on Environmental Crime

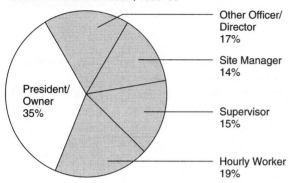

Who Is Charged
Posts of indicted individuals, 1983–90

- President/Owner 35%
- Other Officer/Director 17%
- Site Manager 14%
- Supervisor 15%
- Hourly Worker 19%

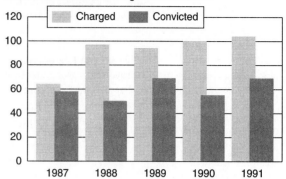

Charges and Convictions
Number of defendants charged and convicted*

Charged   Convicted

(years: 1987, 1988, 1989, 1990, 1991; scale 0–120)

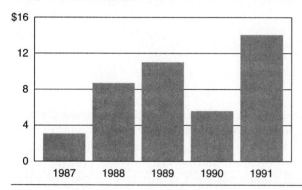

Fines Imposed
Fines, in millions of dollars*

(years: 1987, 1988, 1989, 1990, 1991; scale $0–$16)

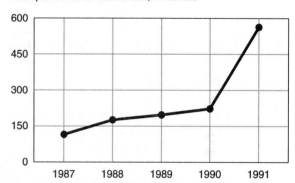

Prison Time
Total prison sentences served, in months*

(years: 1987, 1988, 1989, 1990, 1991; scale 0–600)

Source: Frank Allen, "Few Big Firms Get Jail Time for Polluting," *The Wall Street Journal,* December 9, 1991, p. B1. Reprinted by permission of *The Wall Street Journal,* © 1991 Dow Jones & Company, Inc. All Rights Reserved Worldwide. *Data are for fiscal years that ended September 30, 1991.

California's size and its role as an environmental pacesetter often copied by other states made Big Green a closely watched national barometer of how far the public would go for cleaner air, more trees and fewer pesticides. The initiative would have eventually banned a host of pesticides currently used on food crops. It would have set aside $300 million for buying ancient redwood trees, further strengthened California's already strict limits on air pollutants, permanently banned oil drilling off California's coast and set up a new elective office of Environmental Advocate empowered to enforce all state environmental laws.[51]

While California has led the way in environmental activism, most states have now joined the crusade. Ralph Rosenberg, former Iowa state legislator, explains:

The states have enacted right-to-know legislation to inform the public of hazardous materials. In addition, people are gaining a greater say in the location of hazardous waste facilities. Georgia recently required that the public be notified of applications for hazardous waste facilities.

* * * * *

States have passed laws aimed at fighting improper hazardous waste management. Indiana, for example, enacted a law that calls for buyers of property to be advised that they might be liable for environmental cleanup costs.

* * * * *

[T]he Iowa Legislature created a $200 million program to deal with leaking underground storage tanks and assist businesses in meeting federal standards.

These laws exemplify how society is beginning to hold itself environmentally accountable.[52]

Questions—Part Three

1. As one writer has asked, "What can be done to permit growth that balances the needs of business with the very real concerns of citizens about the quality of life in their communities?"[53]
2. Imagine what life would be like if all of the federal, state, and local laws previously discussed were repealed. Describe both short- and long-run impacts.

Part Four—Remedies Other than Legislation

THE COMMON LAW

Long before the federal government became actively involved in environmental issues, courts were grappling with the problem. As early as the 1500s, city officials were ordered by a court to keep the streets clean of dung deposited by swine allowed to run loose; the air was said to be "corrupted and infected" by this practice. Legal arguments have typically revolved around the right of a person to use and enjoy private or public property if such usage causes harm to a neighbor's property.

The doctrines of *nuisance* and *trespass* are paramount in common law environmental litigation. A private nuisance is a substantial and unreasonable invasion of the private use and enjoyment of one's land, while a public nuisance is an unreasonable interference with a right common to the public. Harmful conduct may be both a public and private nuisance simultaneously; the case law distinctions between the two are often blurred. A trespass occurs and liability is imposed with *any* intentional invasion of the right to one's exclusive use of one's own property.

The distinction between trespass and nuisance is fine, and the two may be coextensive. Nuisance and trespass causes of action have been entered for such offenses as fouling a neighbor's water, flooding another's land, or causing excessive noise, smell, or particulate matter on another's property. The remedies available to a successful plaintiff are monetary damages for the harm suffered and/or an injunction to prevent similar conduct by the defendant in the future.

Negligence and strict liability claims may also arise from pollution cases. For example, a company might well be guilty of negligence if it failed to correct a pollution problem where the technology and necessary resources were available to do so, and that failure caused harm to someone to whom the company owed a duty. In addition, certain activities, such as the use of toxic chemicals, might be so abnormally dangerous as to provoke a strict liability claim. (See Chapter 16 for a discussion of negligence and strict liability.)

Common law pollution remedies, while taking a backseat to federal and state laws, remain useful tools in addressing environmental harm. The *Boomer* case that follows is perhaps the most controversial common law treatment of an environmental nuisance.

BOOMER v. ATLANTIC CEMENT CO.
26 N.Y.2d 219 257 N.E.2d 870 (1970)

Judge Bergan

Defendant operates a large cement plant near Albany. These are actions for injunction and damages by neighboring land owners alleging injury to property from dirt, smoke and vibration emanating from the plant. A nuisance has been found after trial, temporary damages have been allowed but an injunction has been denied.

* * * * *

. . . The threshold question raised by the division of view on this appeal is whether the court should resolve the litigation between the parties now before it as equitably as seems possible; or whether, seeking promotion of the general public welfare, it should channel private litigation into broad public objectives.

A court performs its essential function when it decides the rights of parties before it. Its decision of private controversies may sometimes greatly affect public issues. Large questions of law are often resolved by the manner in which private litigation is decided. But this is normally an incident to the court's main function to settle controversy. It is a rare exercise of judicial power to use a decision in private litigation as a purposeful mechanism to achieve direct public objectives greatly beyond the rights and interests before the court.

* * * * *

It seems apparent that the amelioration of air pollution will depend on technical research in great depth; on a carefully balanced consideration of the economic impact of close regulation; and of the actual effect on public health. It is likely to require massive public expenditure and to demand more than any local community can accomplish and to depend on regional and interstate controls.

A court should not try to do this on its own as a by-product of private litigation and it seems manifest that the judicial establishment is neither equipped in the limited nature of any judgment it can pronounce nor prepared to lay down and implement an effective policy for the elimination of air pollution. This is an area beyond the circumference of one private lawsuit. It is a direct responsibility for government and should not thus be undertaken as an incident to solving a dispute between property owners and a single cement plant—one of many—in the Hudson River Valley.

The cement-making operations of defendant have been found by the court at Special Term to have damaged the nearby properties of plaintiffs in these two actions. That court, as it has been noted, accordingly found defendant maintained a nuisance and this has been affirmed at the Appellate Division. The total damage to plaintiff's properties is, however, relatively small in comparison with the value of defendant's operation and with the consequences of the injunction which plaintiffs seek.

The ground for the denial of injunction, notwithstanding the finding both that there is a nuisance and that plaintiffs have been damaged substantially, is the large disparity in economic consequences of the nuisance and of the injunction. This theory cannot, however, be sustained without overruling a doctrine which has been consistently reaffirmed in several leading cases in this court and which has never been disavowed here, namely that where a nuisance has been found and where there has been any substantial damage shown by the party complaining an injunction will be granted.

The rule in New York has been that such a nuisance will be enjoined although marked disparity be shown in economic consequence between the effect of the injunction and the effect of the nuisance.

* * * * *

. . . [T]o follow the rule literally in these cases would be to close down the plant at once. This court is fully agreed to avoid that immediately drastic remedy; the difference in view is how best to avoid it.

One alternative is to grant the injunction but postpone its effect to a specified future date to give opportunity for technical advances to permit defendant to eliminate the nuisance; another is to grant the injunction conditioned on the payment of permanent damages to plaintiffs which would compensate them for the total economic loss to their property present and future caused by defendant's operations. For reasons which will be developed the court chooses the latter alternative.

If the injunction were to be granted unless within a short period—e.g., 18 months—the nuisance be abated by improved methods, there would be no assurance that any significant technical improvement would occur.

* * * * *

Moreover, techniques to eliminate dust and other annoying by-products of cement making are unlikely to be developed by any research the defendant can undertake within any short period, but will depend on the total resources of the cement industry nationwide and throughout the world. The problem is universal wherever cement is made.

For obvious reasons the rate of the research is beyond control of defendant. If at the end of 18 months the whole industry has not found a technical solution a court would be hard put to close down this one cement plant if due regard be given to equitable principles.

On the other hand, to grant the injunction unless defendant pays plaintiffs such permanent damages as may be fixed by the court seems to do justice between the contending parties. All of the attributions of economic loss to the properties on which plaintiffs' complaints are based will have been redressed.

The nuisance complained of by these plaintiffs may have other public or private consequences, but these particular parties are the only ones who have sought remedies and the judgment proposed will fully redress them. The limitation of relief granted is a limitation only within the four corners of these actions and does not foreclose public health or other public agencies from seeking proper relief in a proper court.

It seems reasonable to think that the risk of being required to pay permanent damages to injured property owners by cement plant owners would itself be a reasonably effective spur to research for improved techniques to minimize nuisance.

[Reversed and remanded.]

* * * * *

Judge Jasen (dissenting)

It has long been the rule in this state, as the majority acknowledges, that a nuisance which results in substantial continuing damage to neighbors must be enjoined . . . To now change the rule to permit the cement company to continue polluting the air indefinitely upon the payment of permanent damages is, in my opinion, compounding the magnitude of a very serious problem in our state and nation today.

In recognition of this problem, the legislature of this state has enacted the Air Pollution Control Act . . . declaring that it is the state policy to require the use of all available and reasonable methods to prevent and control air pollution.

* * * * *

. . . It is interesting to note that cement production has recently been identified as a significant source of particulate contamination in the Hudson Valley. This type of pollution, wherein very small particles escape and stay in the atmosphere, has been denominated as the type of air pollution which produces the greatest hazard to human health. We have thus a nuisance which not only is damaging to the plaintiffs, but also is decidedly harmful to the general public.

I see grave dangers in overruling our long-established rule of granting an injunction where a nuisance results in substantial continuing damage. In permitting the injunction to become inoperative upon the payment of permanent damages, the majority is, in effect, licensing a continuing wrong. It is the same as saying to the cement company, you may continue to do harm to your neighbors so long as you pay a fee for it. Furthermore, once such permanent damages are assessed and paid, the incentive to alleviate the wrong would be eliminated, thereby continuing air pollution of an area without abatement.

* * * * *

I would enjoin the defendant cement company from continuing the discharge of dust particles upon its neighbors' properties unless, within 18 months, the cement company abated this nuisance.

* * * * *

I am aware that the trial court found that the most modern dust control devices available have been installed in defendant's plant, but, I submit, this does not mean that *better* and more effective dust control devices could not be developed within the time allowed to abate the pollution.

Moreover, I believe it is incumbent upon the defendant to develop such devices, since the cement company, at the time the plant commenced production (1962) was well aware of the plaintiffs' presence in the area, as well as the probable consequences of its contemplated operation. Yet, it still chose to build and operate the plant at this site.

Questions

1. What remedy was mandated by the *Boomer* court?
2. The defendant was required to pay a "tax" for the right to continue to pollute. In your opinion, was the court correct in imposing that "tax" rather than requiring further pollution abatement? Explain.
3. In a portion of the opinion not reprinted here, the dissenting Judge Jasen argues that the use of permanent money damages in place of an injunction has been limited to cases where "the use to which the property was intended to be put was primarily for the public benefit." Why might the denial of the injunction be acceptable in public benefit cases but not in cases of private benefit?
4. In a portion of the opinion not reprinted here, the dissenting Judge Jasen argues: "The promotion of the polluting cement company has, in my opinion, no public use or benefit." Do you agree? Explain.
5. Plaintiff Webb developed Sun City, a retirement village near Phoenix, Arizona. At the time, a distance of 2½ to 3 miles separated plaintiff's development from defendant Spur Industries' cattle-feeding operation. The feed lot was well managed and clean for a business of that character. Prior to the Sun City project the area around the feed lot had been largely undeveloped. Sun City and related growth brought large numbers of people in proximity to the cattle lot. As time passed, the two businesses expanded, until at the initiation of the suit, only 500 feet separated the two. Plaintiff filed suit to enjoin defendant's operation as a nuisance. Decide. Explain. See *Spur Industries, Inc.* v. *Del E. Webb Development Co.,* 494 P.2d 700 (1972).

THE FREE MARKET REVISITED

Our steady, even spectacular, strides forward in environmental protection have not dispelled the view, particularly among economists and businesspeople, that legislation is sometimes not the best remedy for environmental problems. To them, pollution control is not so much a matter of law as of economics. They believe that with proper incentives, the market will, in many instances, prove superior to legislation in preventing and correcting environmental problems. The general idea is well illustrated by New York City's efforts to deal with its daily production of 385 tons of sludge, which cannot legally be dumped into the ocean and which overwhelms local landfill capacity. Bio Gro Systems of Annapolis, Maryland, ships 100 tons of sludge daily by rail from New York City to Colorado and Arizona, where farmers are now on waiting lists to have the potent fertilizers spread on their land. The city pays Bio Gro but the sludge is free to farmers, whose reliance on chemical fertilizers has now been reduced.[54]

Cost-Benefit

From the free market point of view, environmental legislation very often imposes unacceptable costs. *Fortune* asked, "How much is America overpaying for environmental regulations?"[55] In 1990, our total bill for federal air and water legislation was estimated to be $320 billion, of which $79 billion came in direct costs while the balance was the result of reduced job growth, reduced capital formation, and lower savings.[56] According to economists Michael Hazilla and Raymond Kopp, those costs resulted in a 5.8 percent reduction in the gross national product.[57] Some of these costs appear to be excessive. For example, Brookings fellow Robert Crandall has calculated that solid and toxic waste cleanup regulations cost $5 to $9 billion annually. If that money saves half of the 1,100 additional annual cancers that the EPA attributes to the waste, the cost per cancer case prevented would be $10 to $18 million.[58]

The article that follows illustrates the particular environmental regulatory burden borne by small businesses.

SMALL FIRMS SPEND MUCH TIME, MONEY COMPLYING WITH ENVIRONMENTAL RULES

Eugene Carlson

Someday, William Anderson's costly struggle to rid his auto dealership of five small underground gas and oil tanks will be over for good. Someday, his Dreisbach Buick dealership on the outskirts of Pontiac, Mich., will be certified environmentally pristine by the state.

Someday—but not yet. Mr. Anderson has spent two years, and more than $100,000, on the task so far. Two holes the size of swimming pools have been dug and filled in the lot behind the dealership building. Consultants have been hired, soil and water tested, and reports filed in numbing detail. The five steel tanks have long since been cut up and sold for scrap. Yet, much remains to be done.

Mr. Anderson isn't some big-time polluter. While gas, oil and chemicals leaking from underground tanks have fouled water supplies around the U.S., there is no suggestion that his dealership's tanks were faulty. Over the years, occasional small oil and gas spills around the mouths of the tanks seeped into the ground, but tests indicate that the oily residue contaminated ground water no more than a few yards from the source. A consultant hired by Mr.

Anderson says the threat to drinking-water supplies is nil.

Nor is the 57-year-old car dealer a casualty of a bureaucracy run amok. By most accounts, Michigan is making a good-faith effort to implement a 1988 federal rule aimed at eliminating defective underground storage tanks. To escape liability risks, Mr. Anderson and thousands of other car dealers and service-station operators in the state are replacing their old tanks with new ones.

Rather, Mr. Anderson considers himself the victim of good intentions gone awry. "Ours is just one small business, and we're trying very hard to be a good citizen and comply with environmental regulations. If it wasn't tragic, it'd be comical," Mr. Anderson says.

Avalanche of Paper

Entrepreneurs say that environmental regulation is a particularly fast-growing part of their red-tape burden these days. Many business owners strongly support efforts to clean the nation's air and water and protect workers and consumers from hazardous materials. But they say the "green" movement also has created a growing regulatory labyrinth.

Large corporations typically have in-house experts to guide the company through the maze. But most small businesses lack the staff and resources required to track the avalanche of paper from environmental agencies.

Up to now, small-business managers have typically taken an ad hoc approach to environmental rules, scanning trade association newsletters for hints of rule changes and hiring consultants to explain the seeming gobbledygook. But regulation's lengthening reach is forcing some companies to change tactics. "We now have two employees with engineering degrees who do nothing but track [regulatory] paper," says Earlyn Church, vice president and co-owner of Superior Technical Ceramics Corp., St. Albans, Vt.

Sardonic Photograph

To demonstrate the magnitude of the problem, an employee at Bernhardt Furniture Co., Lenoir, N.C., put all the government forms dealing with disposal of dirty cleaning rags, the company's principal hazardous waste, in a pile and stood beside it for a sardonic photograph.

"He's 6 feet 2 inches, and the stack of forms is slightly taller than he is," says Alex Bernhardt, the company's president. Mr. Bernhardt says his company "could easily spend twice as much on [environmental] compliance in the next five years as on R&D and new machinery and equipment" combined.

*   *   *   *   *

Mr. Anderson's adventure in digging up his storage tanks reads like an environmental soap opera. Like many states, Michigan has tried to ease the pain of excavation by setting up a trust fund to pay for all but $10,000 of owners' removal costs. The fund, which totaled $41.6 million last April 30, is financed by a fee on wholesale sales of gas and oil.

To remain eligible for reimbursement, a tank owner has to follow a strict timetable, spending money at each step. But the reimbursement pipeline is clogged. Mr. Anderson, for instance, says he still hasn't seen a penny from the trust fund.

Among the expenses he says he has incurred since 1990: $500 for registering his tanks with the state; $375 to purchase a state-required surety bond; $1,100 to test the contents of the tanks before excavation; $25,000 to dig up the tanks; $73,000 to fill the holes; and roughly $12,000 in consulting fees.

State law stipulates reimbursement for approved expenses within 90 days. But Sarah Burton, the private consultant supervising Dreisbach Buick's tank-removal project, says payment typically takes "nine months to a year, easily." Meanwhile, she adds, "You have to keep forking out money to stay eligible."

Dreisbach Buick isn't on the ropes. Mr. Anderson says business has "dramatically improved" from last year. But he is angry over a program that requires him to spend large sums with no apparent payoff to his company or to the public. "It's terribly inefficient, and it's a criminal use of capital," he says. "I could take that money and buy 10 used cars and turn those cars in 60 days and make an average $1,000 each."

*   *   *   *   *

But now comes Phase II. Mr. Anderson's consultant says the state will undoubtedly order the car dealer to sink from four to 10 shallow wells around the perimeter of the old tank storage area to establish if oily water remains in the soil and, if so, to see how far it has seeped.

This means hiring a drill rig, monitoring the well and, perhaps, capturing the water and removing the pollutants. "A nice Phase II investigation with a report," Ms. Burton says. "We're talking $25,000."

Free Market Solutions

Recognizing that forced compliance with standards is only one, albeit necessary, ingredient in the struggle for a clean environment, the federal government has recently been aggressive in finding ways to employ the natural incentives and advantages of market-based reasoning and mechanisms in attacking pollution. The government, in trying to force power generators to cut sulfur dioxide emissions in half by the year 2000, is now employing a free market approach in which pollution rights can be bought and sold. The Clean Air Act provides for pollution allowances putting a ceiling on how much sulfur dioxide utilities can emit. Plants can keep their allowances in order to pollute, or they can install cleaner equipment and sell their allowances on the open market. One result of this approach is that environmental groups can now buy air pollution rights, allow them to expire, and prevent tons of pollution from reaching the air. However, the key result is suggested by the following article describing the emerging market in pollution rights, a market in which government pollution allowances are now a commodity being bought and sold on the Chicago Board of Trade and in private markets arranged by brokerage houses.

NEW RULES HARNESS POWER OF FREE MARKETS TO CURB AIR POLLUTION

Jeffrey Taylor

In this tidy community [Torrance, California] of bungalows and palm trees, where even lawn mowers and gas pumps are strictly regulated to fight pollution, Mobil Oil Corp. has just gained the right to spew an additional 900 pounds of noxious gas vapors each day.

So why aren't environmental activists storming the gates of the refinery?

Actually, Mobil is helping usher in a new era in environmental protection. For about $3 million, Mobil's refinery here recently acquired pollution "credits" from the nearby city of South Gate, Calif. South Gate had acquired the credits from General Motors Corp., which closed a plant there in 1985 and sold the city the property. The Torrance refinery will be emitting far less additional pollution than did General Motors.

Mobil bought the pollution rights under a rudimentary version of market-based environmental regulation. The program has been around since the 1970s, but its rules are so cumbersome that pollution "trades" like Mobil's are rare.

That will soon change. A growing number of regulators believe conventional "command and control" regulation—which allows each plant to pollute so much but no more—is failing to stop destruction of the environment. These authorities, encouraged by economists, want to harness the Earth's atmosphere to financial markets and let the markets rid the world of acid rain and global warming.

Using Markets or Else

"The 21st century is going to be about using markets to solve social and environmental problems," says Richard L. Sandor, an economist and a director of the Chicago Board of Trade. "Otherwise, the world is going to look like it does in the movie 'Blade Runner.' We're going to be stopping on the road for oxygen tanks."

Commodities exchanges such as the Board of Trade are competing to run legally sanctioned markets that would trade rights to emit sulfur dioxide, nitrogen oxide and reactive vapors like those emitted by Mobil's holding tanks. Utilities, refineries and manufacturers would buy and sell pollution rights, which are supposed to ease the transition to increasingly stringent emission limits. And investors will be able to use the instruments to speculate on the price of eliminating smog.

Not everyone is thrilled about market-based regulation of the environment. Some environmentalists think it is immoral to buy and sell the right to pollute. Others doubt regulators have the tools to enforce market-based programs, which require pinpoint accuracy in monitoring emissions. And some polluters are skeptical that regulators accustomed to commanding and controlling can give a market the freedom it needs to function.

Market Forces

Yet in Washington, California and elsewhere, proponents have won over opposition by arguing that traditional regulation gives polluters no incentive to reduce emissions lower than what is allowed. Markets, they say, will create strong competition among companies to find the cheapest and most technologically advanced ways to cut pollution.

A major catalyst for change was the 1990 U.S. Clean Air Act. Starting in 1995, the act will use a market-based program to force power plants across the country to cut emissions of sulfur dioxide, a pollutant that smells like rotten eggs and mixes with clouds to produce acid rain.

* * * * *

International Cooperation

Other, even more ambitious programs are in the works. Economists working for the United Nations and the Environmental Defense Fund are researching an international market to reduce emissions of carbon dioxide, the main cause of global warming. This would link countries with vastly different economies and environmental laws in a single pollution-control system . . .

The idea of turning pollutants into a marketable commodity isn't new. Early this century, a British professor named A. C. Pigou argued that a market price for cleaning air and water ought to be established and included among a polluter's expenses, like costs for labor and materials. It wasn't until 1975, however, that the U.S. Environmental Protection Agency created a limited pollution market by authorizing regional air-quality regulators to let companies buy and sell pollution credits.

The rules: To open a plant or add equipment, a company must offset new pollution by buying credits from a polluter reducing its output. The credits are denominated in pounds of pollution allowed per day and typically sell for $1,000 to $4,000 a pound.

* * * * *

Reducing the Total

By the year 2000, the law limits total sulfur-dioxide emissions by all utilities to 8.9 million tons a year, 10 million tons less than in 1985 . . .

In 1995, the first 110 plants will begin receiving pollution credits from the EPA, each of which allows one ton of sulfur-dioxide pollution a year. The EPA also will sell a few thousand extra credits in an annual auction. The hitch: Companies will only get enough credits for 30% to 50% of what they used to pollute.

For example, in 1985 Illinois Power Co.'s Baldwin No. 1 power plant in Baldwin, Ill., pumped out 89,300 tons of sulfur dioxide. In 1995, Baldwin will get 40,834 one-ton emission credits.

To manage this reduction, Illinois Power had several options under the Clean Air Act. It could burn coal with a lower sulfur content; install a smokestack "scrubber" to remove sulfur dioxide; or simply operate the plant less often. Or it could buy pollution credits, as available, from other utilities.

Illinois Power is investing in a scrubber that will cut the plant's emissions to 6,000 tons a year or less. The company plans to use the credits to offset pollution at some of its other power-generating stations, and may even have extra credits to save for the future or sell to other utilities.

The net effect? "Cleaner air," says Gerald M. Keenan, senior vice president of Palmer Bellevue Corp., a Chicago consulting firm that helps utilities manage Clean Air Act reductions. "This changes the whole calculus of what companies are going to do: how they fuel their plants, the capital improvements they'll make, how much they operate plants, everything."

* * * * *

One shortcoming of market-based regulation is that no one has yet devised a comprehensive way to apply it to the biggest polluter of all: automobiles. Another concern is that while it may result in cleaner air overall, it doesn't force a company to clean any particular plant. In fact, in some cases, it is possible for a plant to buy the right to pollute more than ever.

Orlando Minelli, a retiree who lives in the shadow of Mobil's Torrance refinery, is trying to sell his house and isn't happy that Mobil recently bought the right to increase the refinery's output of pollution. "It's hurting this area," he says.

Environmentalists say Mobil's pollution buy in Torrance underscores a broader theme of market-based regulation: As emissions trading becomes reality across the country, regulators need to be wary of sacrificing people like Mr. Minelli for some perceived greater good. "You have to have strong local health standards that supersede the emissions-trading program," says Mr. Goffman of the EDF.

Source: *The Wall Street Journal*, April 14, 1992, p. A1. Reprinted by permission of *The Wall Street Journal*, © 1992 Dow Jones & Company, Inc. All Rights Reserved Worldwide.

INTERNATIONAL

A Balance?　Of course, unbridled faith in the free market is not likely to be in our long-term best interests. Chile's experience under General Augusto Pinochet from 1973 to 1990 illustrates the risk. Pinochet put his faith in the free market. With privatization and deregulation, he brought Chile the most vibrant economy in South America. However, now that Pinochet is gone, the environmental price of unregulated growth is becoming apparent. Forests, streams, and valleys have been plundered. The result, as described in *Time* magazine, is most apparent in the smog-enshrouded capital, Santiago:

> A thick layer of contaminants settles almost daily over the city, trapped by cold air and mountains on all sides. The causes of the filth: haphazard development and an out-of-control bus system that Pinochet began deregulating in 1975. Two thirds of the smog's harmful elements come from the 11,000 privately owned buses that spew diesel fumes through the city. The government bought out 2,600 of the worst offenders. But pollution still reached lethal levels for two days in July, forcing the government to shut schools and factories and to warn parents to keep their children indoors.[59]

Questions

1. A pollution permit policy often results in shifting pollution from one site to another. Is that policy defensible? Explain.

2. According to a study completed for the government, the cost of controlling hydro-carbons ranged from $16,550 per ton in an auto-painting operation to $41 per ton for a gas terminal in the same area. Explain how the sale of emission allowances between those firms might protect the environment while reducing costs.

3. Suggested free market incentives for pollution control include government taxes or fees on pollution and government rules mandating refundable "deposits" on hazardous materials. Explain how those incentives would work.

4. A *Wall Street Journal* editorial commenting on the market for pollution rights:

> The best news about the introduction of a market for rights to avoid compliance is that the public will finally get a precise measure of the cost of environmental rules. Once that is known, voters can decide if the price is worth the result, or if the law should be changed to comply with what the public is willing to pay.[60]

Are we paying too much for environmental protection? Explain.

Part Five—The Business Response

The Exxon *Valdez* oil tanker struck a reef in Prince William Sound, Alaska, in 1989, and spilled 11 million gallons of oil, the worst such disaster in American history. An estimated 1,500 miles of shoreline were contaminated. More than 500,000 birds and mammals died. Facing 1,990 criminal charges, Exxon paid $100 million in restitution and $150 million in fines. Then, under a 1991 settlement, Exxon agreed to pay $900 million to settle state and federal civil claims for environmental damage. Exxon has also spent an estimated $2 billion in cleanup efforts in Prince William Sound. At this writing in May 1994, 14,000 Alaska natives, property owners, and fishermen are suing Exxon for $1.5 to $3 billion in compensatory damages and unspecified punitive damages on the grounds that the oil spill has severely damaged their livelihoods and culture.

Joseph Hazelwood, captain of the Exxon *Valdez,* who was not at the wheel at the time of the accident, was acquitted of charges that he was drunk and reckless but was found guilty of the lesser charge of "negligent discharge of oil" for which he was fined $50,000 and ordered to undertake 1,000 hours of cleanup work at Prince William Sound. That sentence is on appeal.[61]

New Climate

The *Valdez* spill established a climate in which the Congress and President Bush agreed on new legislation, the Oil Pollution Act of 1990, to dramatically increase shipowners' liability for spills, to require double hulls in new tankers and phase in double hulls in used tankers, and to establish new cleanup and prevention requirements.

However, the most far-reaching consequence of the spill is a heightened public consciousness of environmental issues, which has, in turn, forced the business community to embrace a new environmental sensitivity that *Business Week* has labeled

"The Greening of Corporate America—'Sometimes You Find that the Public Has Spoken, and You Get On with It.'"[62]

Similarly, *Fortune* reports:

> "The 1990s will be the decade of the environment." That's not the chief druid of Greenpeace talking, but rather the new president of the Petroleum Marketers Association of America in a November speech. Mere corporate ecobabble intended to placate the latest group of special-interest loonies? Any company that thinks that way will probably regret it. Exxon provides the obvious if inadvertent example of the bitter costs of seeming unconcerned about the environment. Not long after the March accident in Valdez, Alaska, 41 percent of Americans were angry enough to say they'd seriously consider boycotting the company.[63]

The Weight of the Law

Public opinion has been effective in motivating increased corporate environmental concern, but the weight of the law has clearly played an enormous role. A *National Law Journal* survey of 200 corporate general counsels reveals the feeling that corporations are caught in an ever-tighter legal squeeze of harsher penalties, tighter scrutiny, and more complex laws.[64] Most, however, believe that sound environmental practices improve long-term profitability, and they applaud closer attention to pollution. At the same time, two-thirds admitted that their businesses had operated at least some time in the past year in violation of environmental laws.[65] The press of the law on corporate operations is evident in these other findings from the survey:

- The environmental workload forced 67 percent of corporations to hire law firms specifically to handle green issues in the last year.
- Only 30 percent of the attorneys believed that full compliance with the matrix of U.S. and state environmental laws was possible.
- [O]nly 14 percent of the general counsel said over-regulation was forcing their companies to consider moving operations abroad.
- [A]bout 58 percent said their companies had performed voluntary cleanup of hazardous waste sites—costly actions designed to fend off future liabilities.

"Environmental law is no longer a black box you add on at the end" of management decision-making, said one general counsel. "It is moving away from mere compliance towards a time when a company that doesn't build environmental safety into its products will no longer be able to compete."[66]

Public Opinion

Legislation and a sense of social responsibility have helped shape the business community's approach to environmental issues. However, the most powerful engine behind the 1990s greening of the corporation is public opinion. Corporate America believes that the citizenry is now so serious about the environment that spending decisions will be influenced by environmental considerations. The articles that follow describe some of the strategies that businesses are embracing in response to heightened public concern.

INDUSTRIES ENLISTING IN "GREEN REVOLUTION"

Dick Rawe

Shoppers buying meat at Kroger grocery stores can choose between foamlike polystyrene trays or butcher paper.

At McDonald's, diners sip through thinner straws, saving a million pounds of plastic annually.

Retail giant Wal-Mart responded to consumer concerns with an ecological plan that seeks products from suppliers that are nonpolluting and biodegradable.

MacConnection, a computer sales firm, has switched from foam peanuts to shredded newsprint as packaging material to protect products during shipment.

The Ban the Box Coalition is fighting to eliminate longboxes used to ship CDs, saying they unnecessarily add to the waste stream.

These are but ripples in the rising tide of consumer-driven changes in packaging and recycling to reduce landfill waste at the source. In short, American business has joined the green revolution.

"There has been a striking change in response of industry to global issues," said Jan Beyea, senior scientist for the non-profit National Audubon Society. "Business is taking this issue seriously, realizing nobody can escape. Those businesses that have intimate contact with consumers are feeling tremendous pressure from consumers who want fewer environmentally damaging products.

"There are 600 proposed bans on plastics around the U.S. that have made the chemical industry sit up and take notice. It has forced companies that had been very cavalier about the environment to recognize that their business depends on changing the public image. It's an exciting time because you see public concerns translated into actions, a willingness to sit down and come up with solutions."

Americans produce about 160 million tons of waste annually, the U.S. Environmental Protection Agency estimates. We generate more per person than any other nation—about a pound a day more than the average person in West Germany, for example. Existing landfills are getting full, especially in the East and West Coast states, and resistance to opening new dumps is stiffening because nobody wants one for a neighbor.

"The feckless voyage of the garbage barge" has become a national symbol of America's solid waste dilemma, said the EPA's "Agenda for Action" report of 1988.

The public perception is that making plastic creates pollution, that plastics never deteriorate in landfills and that disposable diapers not only fill our landfills but also contribute to groundwater pollution.

In fact, the EPA said plastics constitute but 6.5 percent of landfill waste and disposable diapers less than 2 percent vs. 41 percent for paper and 18 percent for lawn waste. And plastics dug up out of landfills after 10 years were found to have deteriorated 50 percent, according to Riley Kinman, a University of Cincinnati professor who has probed and studied landfills for 20 years.

But the widespread perception otherwise has put pressure on companies to reduce plastic and paper in packaging.

"We tend to react with simple solutions," said Geoffrey Place, Procter & Gamble vice president [of] research and development. Sometimes, he added, what seems to be excessive packaging is necessary.

"We have packaging to prevent tampering, to protect food products and to prevent damage during shipments," he noted. "In some cases, we have regulatory requirements so packaging is not as useless as it is sometimes thought to be. At the same time there is a valid argument that we use more packaging than there needs to be. We need to retain what is vital and useful and eliminate the wasteful part of packaging."

Howard McIlvain, creative director for Libby Perszyk Kathman, a Cincinnati firm that designs packaging for a number of national firms, said environmental impact is a frequent topic during meetings to discuss a new product and packaging.

"Clients ask: Is it an efficient use of material? Is there waste in this packaging? Are we using recyclable material? Are we making sure that designation is clearly printed on the container or overwrap? Are we using thinner, or less material?"

He said one client, Valvoline, "clearly has at the top of its thinking" ways of promoting the proper disposal of oil and empty one-quart plastic bottles. Valvoline may eventually switch to gallon jugs to replace four 1-quart bottles, he said.

Here's what some other companies are doing:

- The Kroger Co.: The grocery firm has an 11-point source reduction and recycling program. "Buying meat over the counter just wrapped in butcher paper avoids the polystyrene tray," said Thomas Schlachter, assistant manager-store operations.
- H. J. Heinz Co.: By next year, half of the 400 million bottles of ketchup the company sells worldwide annually will be of recyclable PET (polyethylene terephthalate) plastic. The other half will be of recyclable glass.
- Procter & Gamble: The leader in the $3.8 billion laundry detergent market is expanding U.S. use of its Tide, Cheer, Oxydol and Gain brands in reformulated compact versions. P&G sells the compacts, which require less packaging, in 20 countries worldwide. P&G's disposable diapers are now only half as thick.
- Fuji Film: Fuji Photo Film U.S.A. Inc. said the company will replace plastic canisters in which film is sold in the U.S. with moisture-proof paper.
- McDonald's: The world's largest hamburger chain is switching to a tanker system for delivery of concentrates such as Coca Cola and orange juice to eliminate several million pounds of packaging annually.

Source: *Waterloo Courier,* October 21, 1990, p. C8. Reprinted with permission of the copyright holder, The Scripps Howard News Service.

Questions—Part Five

1. *a.* Should consumers boycott Exxon because of the *Valdez* oil spill? Explain.
   b. Would you do so? Explain.
2. *a.* Is the "greening of the corporation" a sincere corporate response to perceived environmental problems or a bottom-line, profit-maximizing response to consumer pressure—or both? Explain.
   b. Does it matter? Explain.
3. How might the government's ever-increasing environmental regulations along with the public's call for a new environmental consciousness favor big-business interests over those of small-business owners?

CHAPTER QUESTIONS

1. What advice would you give a developing country on an appropriate stance on environmental protection? Be realistic in terms of recognizing probable budget and technology constraints.

2. Economist B. Peter Pashigian: "It is widely thought that environmental controls are guided by the public-spirited ideal of correcting for 'negative externalities'—the pollution costs that spill over from private operations. This view is not wrong by any means. But it is suspiciously incomplete. After all, there are numerous studies of regulatory programs in other fields that show how private interests have

used public powers for their own enrichment."[67]
What forces in addition to correcting for negative externalities might be influencing the course of federal pollution control?

3. William Tucker argues that environmentalism is "essentially aristocratic in its roots and derives from the land- and nature-based ethic that has been championed by upper classes throughout history. Large landowners and titled aristocracies . . . have usually held a set of ideals that stresses 'stewardship' and the husbanding of existing resources over exploration and discovery. This view favors handicrafts over mass production and the inheritance ethic over the business ethic."[68]

Tucker goes on to argue that environmentalism favors the economic and social interests of the well off. He says people of the upper middle class see their future in universities and the government bureaucracy. They have little economic stake in industrial expansion. Indeed, such expansion might threaten their suburban property values.
Comment.

4. Culprits in indoor pollution include cigarette smoke, asbestos, carbon monoxide from heaters, and radon. The problem has been exacerbated in recent years by our success in "tightening" buildings as an energy conservation measure. The EPA is beginning to explore the question of indoor pollution. Assume the EPA finds a problem roughly as threatening to our welfare as that of external air pollution. Should the government intervene? Explain.

5. The Fifth Amendment to the Constitution provides that private property cannot be taken for public use without just compensation. Four oil companies had entered a lease agreement with the federal government for oil and gas rights in the Santa Barbara Channel, off the California coast. Two platforms supporting productive wells had been erected, and a third was requested. The request was granted, but before the platform was constructed one of the earlier wells experienced a "blowout," causing enormous ecological damage in the Santa Barbara Channel. The secretary of the interior then suspended all operations in the channel pending congressional cancellation of the leases. The oil companies brought suit. Does the indefinite suspension of oil-drilling rights constitute a "taking" in violation of the Fifth Amendment? See *Union Oil Co.* v. *Morton,* 512 F.2d 743 (1975).

6. Professor and business ethics scholar, Norman Bowie:

> Environmentalists frequently argue that business has special obligations to protect the environment. Although I agree with the environmentalists on this point, I do not agree with them as to where the obligations lie. Business does not have an obligation to protect the environment over and above what is required by law; however, business does have a moral obligation to avoid intervening in the political arena in order to defeat or weaken environmental legislation.[69]

   a. Explain Professor Bowie's reasoning.
   b. Do you agree with him? Explain.

7. Some argue that so-called frost belt states will be particularly insistent on maintaining strict air quality standards for new emission sources.
   a. Other than general concern for air quality, why would the frost belt states have a particular interest in maintaining those standards?
   b. Might the frost belt states be expected to modify that stand over time? Explain.

8. Economist Robert Crandall argues:

> [O]ur best chances for regulatory reform in certain environmental areas, particularly in air pollution policy, come from the states. Probably, responsibility for environmental regulation belongs with the states anyway, and most of it ought to be returned there.[70]

   a. What reasoning supports Crandall's notion that responsibility for environmental regulation belongs with the states?
   b. How might one reason to the contrary?
   c. If the power were yours, would environmental regulation rest primarily at the state or the federal level? Explain.

9. Why do plaintiffs typically experience great difficulty in prevailing in negligence actions alleging injury from toxic substances?

10. The doctrine of strict liability—originally applied to extrahazardous activities and more recently to defective products—could be extended to the area of toxic waste. Jeremy Main commented on that possibility in *Fortune* magazine:

> If strict liability were now extended to toxic wastes, then it would do a company no good to

plead that it had obeyed the laws and followed approved procedures when it disposed of its wastes. It would still be liable, even if the hazards are seen only in retrospect.[71]

Should the strict liability doctrine routinely be extended to toxic waste cases? Explain.

11. The Pennsylvania Coal Company owned coal land in the drainage basin of the Meadow Brook. The company's mining operation released water into the brook, thus polluting it. Sanderson owned land near the stream, and she had been securing water from it. However, the mining operation rendered the stream useless for Sanderson's purposes. Sanderson filed suit against the coal company. In 1886, a final verdict was rendered in the case. Should Sanderson prevail? See *Pennsylvania Coal Co. v. Sanderson and Wife,* 6 A 453 (1886).

12. In a realignment of resources, the U.S. Army decided to close the Lexington–Blue Grass Army Depot. The expected loss of over 2,600 jobs caused various parties to file suit in an effort to stop the closing. The plaintiffs contended that the Army and the Department of Defense violated the National Environmental Policy Act by failing to file an environmental impact statement. NEPA requires an EIS in all cases of "major federal actions significantly affecting the quality of the human environment." Decide. Explain. See *Breckinridge* v. *Rumsfeld* 537 F.2d 864 (1976), cert. denied, 429 U.S. 1061 (1977).

13. A number of groups and individuals filed suit to block Duke Power's planned construction of nuclear power plants in North and South Carolina. The plaintiffs challenged the federal Price-Anderson Act, which provided that damages resulting from nuclear incidents would be limited to $560 million. In the event of damages exceeding $560 million, the act provided that Congress would review the situation and take appropriate action. The district court had ruled that there was a "substantial likelihood" that Duke would not be able to complete the plant unless protected by the act. The district court ruled that the $560 million limit in the act violated the constitutional requirement that neither life nor property may be taken by the government without due process of law. The case was appealed to the U.S. Supreme Court. Decide. Explain. See *Duke Power Co.* v. *Carolina Environmental Study Group, Inc.,* 438 U.S. 59 (1978).

14. Some critics claim that the current fever for using material suitable for recycling has the effect of focusing an unsound degree of attention on landfill space while ignoring total environmental efficiency.

> Several cities—for example, Portland, Ore., and Newark, N.J.—have essentially banned polystyrene food packages, yet a Franklin Associates comparison of polystyrene packaging and its alternative, paperboard containers, showed that the polystyrene hamburger clamshell uses 30 percent less energy than paperboard. Its manufacturing results in 46 percent less air pollution, and 42 percent less water pollution.[72]

Would fast-food companies exhibit poor judgment if they replaced polystyrene with paperboard? Explain.

15. Lynn Scarlett, solid-waste management authority:

> [T]oo many local governments have failed to charge anything—or anything like the actual costs—for collecting and disposing of garbage. Cities such as Baltimore, Denver, and Los Angeles do not directly charge households for garbage collection. In fact, a study of more than 200 U.S. cities found that 39 percent charge no direct fees at all for garbage service, giving consumers little incentive to "conserve" on their waste production. Instituting pricing for collection and disposal will remedy that. Seattle's introduction of per-can charges a few years ago encouraged more than 70 percent of all residents to recycle and reduce waste.[73]

Comment.

16. More than half of EPA spending is directed to Superfund and to helping build sewage treatment plants. Make the argument that the EPA is directing its resources to highly visible but relatively low-risk problems while giving inadequate attention to visually obscure, serious issues.

17. For sometime now, the government has been buried in the seemingly insoluble conflict between loggers and environmentalists in the northwest United States. The object of their conflict is a threatened species, the northern spotted owl. At this writing in 1994, the government is struggling with new measures to ease the restrictions on logging in spotted owl territories by shrinking the 2,600-acre "owl circles" around spotted owl nests. The government proposal is unlikely to satisfy either side.

The Political Economy Research Center in Boze-man, Montana, proposes a market-based solution: Except for designated wilderness land, the government should put lumber rights up for auction. How would that approach work, and why might it be preferred to government rules about where logging is permitted?

18. The federal Endangered Species Act provides that all federal agency actions are to be designed such that they do not jeopardize endangered or threatened species. The act had been interpreted to reach to federal agency work or funding in foreign countries, but the federal government changed that interpretation in 1986 to limit the act's reach to the United States and the high seas. A group labeled De-

fenders of Wildlife filed suit, seeking to reinstate the original interpretation. The case reached the U.S. Supreme Court, where Justice Scalia wrote that Defenders of Wildlife would have to submit evidence showing that at least one of its members would be "directly" affected by the interpretation. In response, one member of Defenders of Wildlife wrote that she had visited Egypt and observed the endangered Nile crocodile and hoped to return but feared that U.S. aid with the Aswan High Dam would harm the crocodiles.

  a. Why did Scalia call for that evidence?
  b. Decide the case. Explain. See *Lujan* v. *Defenders of Wildlife,* 112 S.Ct. 2130 (1992).

NOTES

1. The author owes a debt to coauthor James Freeman for his significant contributions to this chapter.

2. Mark Clements, "How Much Do We Care?" *Parade,* June 14, 1992, p. 16.

3. Ibid.

4. Ibid.

5. Faye Rice, "Next Steps for the Environment," *Fortune* 126, no. 8 (October 19, 1992), p. 98.

6. Eugene Linden, "Playing with Fire," *Time,* September 18, 1989, p. 76. Copyright 1989 The Time Inc. Magazine Company. Reprinted by permission.

7. Associated Press, "Soviets Gone, but 'Ecocide' Lingers as a Grim Legacy," *Waterloo Courier,* April 13, 1992, p. A1.

8. Ibid.

9. Joy Aschenbach, "Damaged Soviet Ecology Finally Out in the Open," *Waterloo Courier,* October 30, 1990, p. C9.

10. Gregg Easterbrook, "Cleaning Up," *Newsweek,* July 24, 1989, pp. 26, 33. © Newsweek, Inc. All rights reserved. Reprinted by permission.

11. Larry Stammer, "53 Nations Pledge to Ban Ozone Destroyers by 2000," *Los Angeles Times,* June 30, 1990, p. A1.

12. Catherine Bolgar, "Toxic Waste Exports Banned," *The Wall Street Journal,* March 28, 1994, p. B17.

13. Catalina Camia, "Clinton Offers Plan on Global Warming," *Congressional Quarterly,* October 23, 1993, p. 2,879.

14. Gregg Easterbrook, "Winning the War on Smog," *Newsweek,* August 23, 1993, p. 29.

15. Ibid.

16. Ibid.

17. Ibid.

18. Editorial, "Something Special in the Wind," *Los Angeles Times,* October 31, 1990, p. B6.

19. *Courier* Wire Services, "Implementation of Clean Air Act Brings B-Minus for EPA," *Waterloo Courier,* November 15, 1993, p. A2.

20. Rice, "Next Steps," p. 98.

21. Timothy Noah, "Clear Benefits of Clean Air Act Come at a Cost," *The Wall Street Journal,* November 15, 1993, p. B1.

22. Wade Lambert, "Businesses Must Wean Workers from Their Cars," *The Wall Street Journal,* November 4, 1993, p. B1.

23. Rice, "Next Steps," p. 98.

24. Associated Press, "EPA Report on Smoking Is Challenged," *Des Moines Register,* June 23, 1993, p. 4A.

25. Ibid.

26. Vicky Cahan, "A Clean-Air Bill Is Easy. Clean Air Is Hard," *Business Week,* November 5, 1990, p. 50.

27. James Flanigan, "Clean Air Act Will Fuel New Technologies," *Los Angeles Times,* October 31, 1990, p. D1.

28. Rose Gutfeld, "Clean-Air Proposal Eventually May Add as Much as $600 to Car Sticker Prices," *The Wall Street Journal,* October 11, 1990, p. B1.

29. Associated Press, "Midwest Flooding Doubled Gulf's 'Dead Zone,'" *Waterloo Courier,* November 19, 1993, p. A3.

30. Janet Hook and the *Congressional Quarterly* staff, "Clinton Controls Fall Agenda, Although Not Its Results," *Congressional Quarterly,* September 4, 1993, pp. 2,295, 2,315.

31. Rice, "Next Steps," p. 100.

32. Ibid.

33. Kathleen Lavey, "Nationline," *USA Today,* June 14, 1990, p. 3A. Copyright 1990, *USA Today.* Reprinted with permission.

34. Editorial, "As Tidy as Iowa," *Des Moines Register,* March 31, 1992, p. 6A.

35. Rice, "Next Steps," p. 100.

36. Ibid.

37. Bureau of National Affairs, "Hazardous Waste, EPA Issues New Strategy, Freeze on Hazardous Waste Incineration," *Daily Report for Executives,* May 19, 1993, p. 95.

38. 61 *Law Week* 3105 (August 18, 1992).

39. John Cushman, "U.S. to Weigh Blacks' Complaints about Pollution," *New York Times,* November 19, 1993, p. A16.

40. Ibid.

41. Andrea Ford, "Firm Agrees to Clean Up Tijuana Site," *Los Angeles Times,* June 16, 1993, p. A3.

42. Dianne Solis, "Jail Term Given in Cross-Border Pollution Case," *The Wall Street Journal,* December 16, 1993, p. A13.

43. Peter Prestley, "The Future of Superfund," *ABA Journal,* August 1993, p. 62.

44. Ibid.

45. Associated Press, "EPA Finds Cleanup Lawsuits Are More than It Can Handle," *Des Moines Register,* June 21, 1993, p. 5A.

46. Prestley, "Future of Superfund," p. 65.

47. Rice, "Next Steps," p. 100.

48. Timothy Noah, "Details of Plan to Revise Superfund Law Are Spelled Out, Draw Mixed Reviews," *The Wall Street Journal,* February 4, 1994, p. A10.

49. Henry Reske, "Record EPA Prosecutions," *ABA Journal,* March 1992, p. 25.

50. Frank Edward Allen, "Few Big Firms Get Jail Time for Polluting," *The Wall Street Journal,* December 9, 1991, p. B1.

51. Charles McCoy, "Environmental Initiative Rejected in California," *The Wall Street Journal,* October 8, 1990, p. A12.

52. Ralph Rosenberg, "No Free Lunch in Nature's Cafe," *State Government News* 33, no. 1 (January 1990), p. 24.

53. Christopher B. Leinberger, "Curbing Growth Controls," *The Wall Street Journal,* January 22, 1987, Reprinted by permission of *The Wall Street Journal,* © 1987 Dow Jones & Company, Inc. All Rights Reserved Worldwide.

54. Frank Edward Allen, "Western Farmers Love New York Sludge," *The Wall Street Journal,* November 24, 1992, p. B1.

55. Louis Richman, "How Zealous Greens Hurt Growth . . . ," *Fortune* 125, no. 6 (March 23, 1992), p. 26.

56. Ibid.

57. Ibid.

58. Ibid.

59. Brook Larmer, "The Greening of Santiago," *Newsweek,* August 10, 1992, p. 41.

60. Editorial, "Efficient-Markets Pollution," *The Wall Street Journal,* March 2, 1992, p. A12.

61. *State of Alaska* v. *Joseph J. Hazelwood,* 866 P.2d 827 (1993).

62. Emily T. Smith and Vicky Cahan, "The Greening of Corporate America," *Business Week,* April 23, 1990, p. 96.

63. David Kirkpatrick, "Environmentalism: The New Crusade," *Fortune* 121, no. 4 (February 12, 1990), p. 44. © 1990 Time Inc. Magazine Company. All rights reserved.

64. Marianne Lavelle, "Environment Vise: Law, Compliance," *The National Law Journal,* August 30, 1993, p. S1.

65. Ibid.

66. Ibid., p. S2.

67. B. Peter Pashigian, "How Large and Small Plants Fare under Environmental Regulation," *Regulation* (March–April 1983), p. 19.

68. "Tucker contra Sierra," *Regulation* (March–April 1983), pp. 48–49.

69. Norman Bowie (with Kenneth Goodpaster), "Corporate Conscience, Money and Motorcars," in *Business Ethics Report, High-lights of Bentley College's Eighth National Conference on Business Ethics,* ed. Peter Kent, 1989, pp. 4, 6.

70. Robert Crandall, "The Environment," in "Regulation—The First Year," *Regulation* (January–February 1982), pp. 19, 29, 31.

71. Jeremy Main, "The Hazards of Helping Toxic Waste Victims," *Fortune* 108, no. 9 (October 31, 1983), pp. 158, 166.

72. Lynn Scarlett, "Make Your Environment Dirtier—Recycle," *The Wall Street Journal,* January 14, 1991, p. A12.

73. Ibid.

THE CONSTITUTION
OF THE UNITED STATES
OF AMERICA

●

Preamble

We the People of the United States, in Order to form a more perfect Union, establish Justice, insure domestic Tranquility, provide for the common defence, promote the general Welfare, and secure the Blessings of Liberty to ourselves and our Posterity, do ordain and establish this Constitution for the United States of America.

Article I

Section 1. All legislative Powers herein granted shall be vested in a Congress of the United States, which shall consist of a Senate and House of Representatives.

Section 2. (1) The House of Representatives shall be composed of Members chosen every second Year by the People of the several States, and the Electors in each State shall have the Qualifications requisite for Electors of the most numerous Branch of the State Legislature.

(2) No Person shall be a Representative who shall not have attained to the Age of twenty-five Years, and been seven Years a Citizen of the United States, and who shall not, when elected, be an Inhabitant of that State in which he shall be chosen.

(3) Representatives and direct Taxes shall be apportioned among the several States which may be included within this Union, according to their respective Numbers, which shall be determined by adding to the whole Number of free Persons, including those bound to Service for a Term of Years, and excluding Indians not taxed, three fifths of all other Persons.[1] The actual Enumeration shall be made within three Years after the first Meeting of the Congress of the United States, and within every subsequent Term of ten Years, in such Manner as they shall by Law direct. The Number of Representatives shall not exceed one for every thirty Thousand, but each State shall have at Least one Representative; and until such enumeration shall be made, the State of New Hampshire shall be entitled to chuse three, Massachusetts eight, Rhode Island and Providence Plantations one, Connecticut five, New York six, New Jersey four, Pennsylvania eight, Delaware one, Maryland six, Virginia ten, North Carolina five, South Carolina five, and Georgia three.

---

[1]Refer to the Fourteenth Amendment.

(4) When vacancies happen in the Representation from any State, the Executive Authority thereof shall issue Writs of Election to fill such Vacancies.

(5) The House of Representatives shall chuse their Speaker and other Officers; and shall have the sole Power of Impeachment.

Section 3. (1) The Senate of the United States shall be composed of two Senators from each State, chosen by the Legislature thereof,[2] for six Years; and each Senator shall have one Vote.

(2) Immediately after they shall be assembled in Consequence of the first Election, they shall be divided as equally as may be into three Classes. The Seats of the Senators of the first Class shall be vacated at the Expiration of the Second Year, of the second Class at the Expiration of the fourth Year, and of the third Class at the Expiration of the sixth Year, so that one third may be chosen every second Year; and if Vacancies happen by Resignation, or otherwise, during the Recess of the Legislature of any State, the Executive thereof may make temporary Appointments until the next Meeting of the Legislature, which shall then fill such Vacancies.[3]

(3) No Person shall be a Senator who shall not have attained to the Age of thirty Years, and been nine Years a Citizen of the United States, and who shall not, when elected, be an Inhabitant of that State for which he shall be chosen.

(4) The Vice President of the United States shall be President of the Senate, but shall have no Vote, unless they be equally divided.

(5) The Senate shall chuse their other Officers, and also a President pro tempore, in the Absence of the Vice President, or when he shall exercise the Office of President of the United States.

(6) The Senate shall have the sole Power to try all Impeachments. When sitting for that Purpose, they shall be on Oath or Affirmation. When the President of the United States is tried, the Chief Justice shall preside: And no Person shall be convicted without the Concurrence of two thirds of the Members present.

(7) Judgment in Cases of Impeachment shall not extend further than to removal from Office, and disqualification to hold and enjoy any Office of honor, Trust, or Profit under the United States: but the Party convicted shall nevertheless be liable and subject to Indictment, Trial, Judgment, and Punishment, according to Law.

Section 4. (1) The Times, Places and Manner of holding Elections for Senators and Representatives, shall be prescribed in each State by the Legislature thereof; but the Congress may at any time by Law make or alter such Regulations, except as to the Places of chusing Senators.

(2) The Congress shall assemble at least once in every year, and such Meeting shall be on the first Monday in December, unless they shall by Law appoint a different Day.[4]

Section 5. (1) Each House shall be the Judge of the Elections, Returns, and Qualifications of its own Members, and a Majority of each shall constitute a Quorum to do Business; but a smaller Number may adjourn from day to day, and may be authorized to compel the Attendance of absent Members, in such Manner, and under such Penalties as each House may provide.

(2) Each House may determine the Rules of its Proceedings, punish its Members for disorderly Behavior, and, with the Concurrence of two thirds, expel a Member.

(3) Each House shall keep a Journal of its Proceedings, and from time to time publish the same, excepting such Parts as may in their Judgment require Secrecy; and the Yeas and Nays of the Members of either House on any question shall, at the Desire of one fifth of those Present, be entered on the Journal.

---

[2]Refer to the Seventeenth Amendment.
[3]Ibid.
[4]Refer to the Twentieth Amendment.

(4) Neither House, during the Session of Congress, shall, without the Consent of the other, adjourn for more than three days, nor to any other Place than that in which the two Houses shall be sitting.

Section 6. (1) The Senators and Representatives shall receive a Compensation for their Services, to be ascertained by Law, and paid out of the Treasury of the United States. They shall in all Cases, except Treason, Felony and Breach of the Peace, be privileged from Arrest during their Attendance at the Session of their respective Houses, and in going to and returning from the same; and for any Speech or Debate in either House, they shall not be questioned in any other Place.

(2) No Senator or Representative shall, during the Time for which he was elected, be appointed to any civil Office under the Authority of the United States, which shall have been created, or the Emoluments whereof shall have been encreased during such time; and no Person holding any Office under the United States, shall be a Member of either House during his Continuance in Office.

Section 7. (1) All Bills for raising Revenue shall originate in the House of Representatives; but the Senate may propose or concur with Amendments as on other Bills.

(2) Every Bill which shall have passed the House of Representatives and the Senate, shall, before it becomes a Law, be presented to the President of the United States; If he approve he shall sign it, but if not he shall return it, with his Objections to the House in which it shall have originated, who shall enter the Objections at large on their Journal, and proceed to reconsider it. If after such Reconsideration two thirds of that House shall agree to pass the Bill, it shall be sent together with the Objections, to the other House, by which it shall likewise be reconsidered, and if approved by two thirds of that House, it shall become a Law. But in all such Cases the Votes of both Houses shall be determined by yeas and Nays, and the Names of the Persons voting for and against the Bill shall be entered on the Journal of each House respectively. If any Bill shall not be returned by the President within ten Days (Sundays excepted) after it shall have been presented to him, the Same shall be a Law, in like Manner as if he had signed it, unless the Congress by their Adjournment prevent its Return in which Case it shall not be a Law.

(3) Every Order, Resolution, or Vote, to Which the Concurrence of the Senate and House of Representatives may be necessary (except on a question of Adjournment) shall be presented to the President of the United States; and before the same shall take Effect, shall be approved by him, or being disapproved by him, shall be repassed by two thirds of the Senate and House of Representatives, according to the Rules and Limitations prescribed in the Case of a Bill.

Section 8. (1) The Congress shall have Power To lay and collect Taxes, Duties, Imposts and Excises, to pay the Debts and provide for the common Defence and general Welfare of the United States; but all Duties, Imposts and Excises shall be uniform throughout the United States;

(2) To borrow money on the credit of the United States;

(3) To regulate Commerce with foreign Nations, and among the several States, and with the Indian Tribes;

(4) To establish a uniform Rule of Naturalization, and uniform Laws on the subject of Bankruptcies throughout the United States;

(5) To coin Money, regulate the Value thereof, and of foreign Coin, and fix the Standard of Weights and Measures;

(6) To provide for the Punishment of counterfeiting the Securities and current Coin of the United States;

(7) To Establish Post Offices and Post Roads;

(8) To promote the Progress of Science and useful Arts, by securing for limited Times to Authors and Inventors the exclusive Right to their respective Writings and Discoveries;

(9) To constitute Tribunals inferior to the supreme Court;

(10) To define and punish Piracies and Felonies committed on the high Seas, and Offenses against the Law of Nations;

(11) To declare War, grant Letters of Marque and Reprisal, and make Rules concerning Captures on Land and Water;

(12) To raise and support Armies, but no Appropriation of Money to that Use shall be for a longer Term than two Years;

(13) To provide and maintain a Navy;

(14) To make Rules for the Government and Regulation of the land and naval Forces;

(15) To provide for calling forth the Militia to execute the Laws of the Union, suppress Insurrections and repel Invasions;

(16) To provide for organizing, arming, and disciplining, the Militia, and for governing such Part of them as may be employed in the Service of the United States, reserving to the States respectively, the Appointment of the Officers, and the Authority of training the Militia according to the discipline prescribed by Congress;

(17) To exercise exclusive Legislation in all Cases whatsoever, over such District (not exceeding ten Miles square) as may, by Cession of particular States, and the Acceptance of Congress, become the Seat of the Government of the United States, and to exercise like Authority over all Places purchased by the Consent of the Legislature of the State in which the Same shall be, for the Election of Forts, Magazines, Arsenals, dock-Yards, and other needful Buildings;—And

(18) To make all Laws which shall be necessary and proper for carrying into Execution the foregoing Powers, and all other Powers vested by this Constitution in the Government of the United States, or in any Department or Officer thereof.

Section 9. (1) The Migration or Importation of Such Persons as any of the States now existing shall think proper to admit, shall not be prohibited by the Congress prior to the Year one thousand eight hundred and eight, but a Tax or duty may be imposed on such Importation, not exceeding ten dollars for each Person.

(2) The privilege of the Writ of Habeas Corpus shall not be suspended, unless when in Cases of Rebellion or Invasion the public Safety may require it.

(3) No Bill of Attainder or ex post facto Law shall be passed.

(4) No Capitation, or other direct, Tax shall be laid, unless in proportion to the Census or Enumeration herein before directed to be taken.[5]

(5) No Tax or Duty shall be laid on Articles exported from any state.

(6) No Preference shall be given by any Regulation of Commerce or Revenue to the Ports of one State over those of another; nor shall Vessels bound to, or from, one State be obliged to enter, clear, or pay Duties in another.

(7) No money shall be drawn from the Treasury, but in Consequence of Appropriations made by Law; and a regular Statement and Account of the Receipts and Expenditures of all public Money shall be published from time to time.

(8) No Title of Nobility shall be granted by the United States: And no person holding any Office of Profit or Trust under them, shall, without the Consent of the Congress, accept of any present, Emolument, Office or Title, of any kind whatever, from any King, Prince, or foreign State.

Section 10. (1) No State shall enter into any Treaty, Alliance, or Confederation; grant Letters of Marque and Reprisal; coin Money; emit Bills of Credit; make any Thing but gold and silver Coin a Tender in Payment of Debts; pass any Bill of Attainder, ex post facto Law, or Law impairing the Obligation of Contracts, or grant any Title of Nobility.

---

[5]Refer to the Sixteenth Amendment.

(2) No State shall, without the Consent of the Congress, lay any Imposts or Duties on Imports or Exports, except what may be absolutely necessary for executing its inspection Laws: and the net Produce of all Duties and Imposts, laid by any State on Imports or Exports, shall be for the Use of the Treasury of the United States; and all such Laws shall be subject to the Revision and Controul of the Congress.

(3) No State shall, without the Consent of Congress, lay any Duty of Tonnage, keep Troops, or Ships of War in time of Peace, enter into any Agreement or Compact with another State, or with a foreign Power, or engage in War, unless actually invaded, or in such imminent Danger as will not admit of delay.

Article II

Section 1. (1) The executive Power shall be vested in a President of the United States of America. He shall hold his Office during the Term of four Years, and, together with the Vice President, chosen for the same Term, be elected as follows:

(2) Each State shall appoint, in such Manner as the Legislature thereof may direct, a Number of Electors, equal to the whole Number of Senators and Representatives to which the State may be entitled in the Congress; but no Senator or Representative, or Person holding an Office of Trust or Profit under the United States, shall be appointed an Elector.

(3) The Electors shall meet in their respective States, and vote by Ballot for two Persons, of whom one at least shall not be an Inhabitant of the same State with themselves. And they shall make a list of all the Persons voted for, and of the Number of Votes for each; which List they shall sign and certify, and transmit sealed to the Seat of the Government of the United States, directed to the President of the Senate. The President of the Senate shall, in the Presence of the Senate and House of Representatives, open all the Certificates, and the Votes shall then be counted. The Person having the greatest Number of Votes shall be the President, if such Number be a Majority of the whole Number of Electors appointed; and if there be more than one who have such Majority, and have an equal Number of Votes, then the House of Representatives shall immediately chuse by Ballot one of them for President; and if no Person have a Majority, then from the five highest on the List the said House shall in like Manner chuse the President. But in chusing the President, the Votes shall be taken by States, the Representation from each State have one Vote; A quorum for this Purpose shall consist of a Member or Members from two thirds of the States, and a Majority of all the States shall be necessary to a Choice. In every Case, after the Choice of the President, the Person having the greater Number of Votes of the Electors shall be the Vice President. But if there should remain two or more who have equal Votes, the Senate shall chuse from them by Ballot the Vice President.[6]

(4) The Congress may determine the Time of chusing the Electors, and the Day on which they shall give their Votes; which Day shall be the same throughout the United States.

(5) No person except a natural born Citizen, or a Citizen of the United States, at the time of the Adoption of this Constitution, shall be eligible to the Office of President; neither shall any Person be eligible to that Office who shall not have attained to the Age of thirty-five Years, and been fourteen Years a Resident within the United States.

(6) In case of the removal of the President from Office, or of his Death, Resignation or Inability to discharge the Powers and Duties of the said Office, the Same shall devolve on the Vice President, and the Congress may by Law provide for the Case of Removal, Death, Resignation or Inability, both of the President and Vice President, declaring what Officer shall then

---

[6]Refer to the Twelfth Amendment.

act as President, and such Officer shall act accordingly, until the Disability be removed, or a President shall be elected.[7]

(7) The President shall, at stated Times, receive for his Services, a Compensation, which shall neither be encreased nor diminished during the Period for which he shall have been elected, and he shall not receive within that Period any other Emolument from the United States, or any of them.

(8) Before he enter on the Execution of his Office, he shall take the following Oath or Affirmation: "I do solemnly swear (or affirm) that I will faithfully execute the Office of President of the United States, and will to the best of my Ability, preserve, protect, and defend the Constitution of the United States."

Section 2. (1) The President shall be Commander in Chief of the Army and Navy of the United States, and of the militia of the several States, when called into the actual Service of the United States; he may require the Opinion, in writing, of the principal Officer in each of the executive Departments, upon any Subject relating to the Duties of their respective Offices, and he shall have Power to grant Reprieves and Pardons for Offenses against the United States, except in Cases of Impeachment.

(2) He shall have Power, by and with the Advice and Consent of the Senate, to make Treaties, provided two thirds of the Senators present concur; and he shall nominate, and by and with the Advice and Consent of the Senate, shall appoint Ambassadors, other public Ministers and Consuls, Judges of the supreme Court, and all other Officers of the United States, whose Appointments are not herein otherwise provided for, and which shall be established by Law; but the Congress may by Law vest the Appointment of such inferior Officers, as they think proper, in the President alone, in the Courts of Law, or in the Heads of Departments.

(3) The President shall have Power to fill up all Vacancies that may happen during the Recess of the Senate, by granting Commissions which shall expire at the End of their next Session.

Section 3. He shall from time to time give to the Congress Information of the State of the Union, and recommend to their Consideration such Measures as he shall judge necessary and expedient; he may, on extraordinary Occasions, convene both Houses, or either of them, and in Case of Disagreement between them, with Respect to the Time of Adjournment, he may adjourn them to such Time as he shall think proper; he shall receive Ambassadors and other public Ministers; he shall take Care that the Laws be faithfully executed, and shall Commission all the Officers of the United States.

Section 4. The President, Vice President and all civil Officers of the United States, shall be removed from Office on Impeachment for, and Conviction of, Treason, Bribery, or other high Crimes and Misdemeanors.

Article III

Section 1. The judicial Power of the United States, shall be vested in one supreme Court, and in such inferior Courts as the Congress may from time to time ordain and establish. The Judges, both of the supreme and inferior Courts, shall hold their Offices during good Behaviour, and shall, at stated Times, receive for their Services a Compensation, which shall not be diminished during their Continuance in Office.

Section 2. (1) The judicial Power shall extend to all Cases, in Law and Equity, arising under this Constitution, the Laws of the United States, and Treaties made, or which shall be made, under their Authority;—to all Cases affecting Ambassadors, other public Ministers and Con-

---

[7]Refer to the Twenty-Fifth Amendment.

suls;—to all Cases of admiralty and maritime Jurisdiction;—to Controversies to which the United States shall be a Party;—to Controversies between two or more States;—between a State and Citizens of another State,[8]—between Citizens of different states;—between Citizens of the same State claiming Lands under the Grants of different States, and between a State, or the Citizens thereof, and foreign States, Citizens or Subjects.

(2) In all Cases affecting Ambassadors, other public Ministers and Consuls, and those in which a State shall be a Party, the supreme Court shall have original Jurisdiction. In all the other Cases before mentioned, the supreme Court shall have appellate Jurisdiction, both as to Law and Fact, with such Exceptions, and under such Regulations as the Congress shall make.

(3) The trial of all Crimes, except in Cases of Impeachment, shall be by Jury; and such Trial shall be held in the State where the said Crimes shall have been committed; but when not committed within any State, the Trial shall be at such Place or Places as the Congress may by Law have directed.

Section 3. (1) Treason against the United States, shall consist only in levying War against them, or, in adhering to their enemies, giving them Aid and Comfort. No Person shall be convicted of Treason unless on the Testimony of two Witnesses to the same overt Act, or on Confession in open Court.

(2) The Congress shall have Power to declare the Punishment of Treason, but no Attainder of Treason shall work Corruption of Blood, or Forfeiture except during the Life of the Person attainted.

Article IV

Section 1. Full Faith and Credit shall be given in each State to the public Acts, Records, and judicial Proceedings of every other State. And the Congress may by general Laws prescribe the Manner in which such Acts, Records and Proceedings shall be proved, and the Effect thereof.

Section 2. (1) The Citizens of each State shall be entitled to all Privileges and Immunities of Citizens in the several States.

(2) A Person charged in any State with Treason, Felony, or other Crime, who shall flee from Justice, and be found in another State, shall on demand of the executive Authority of the State from which he fled, be delivered up, to be removed to the State having Jurisdiction of the Crime.

(3) No Person held to Service or Labour in one State, under the Laws thereof, escaping into another, shall, in Consequence of any Law or Regulation therein, be discharged from such Service or Labour, but shall be delivered up on Claim of the Party to whom such Service or Labour may be due.[9]

Section 3. (1) New States may be admitted by the Congress into this Union; but no new State shall be formed or erected within the Jurisdiction of any other State; nor any State be formed by the Junction of two or more States, or Parts of States without the Consent of the Legislatures of the States concerned as well as of the Congress.

(2) The Congress shall have Power to dispose of and make all needful Rules and Regulations respecting the Territory or other Property belonging to the United States; and nothing in this Constitution shall be so construed as to Prejudice any Claims of the United States, or of any particular State.

Section 4. The United States shall guarantee to every State in this Union a Republican Form of Government, and shall protect each of them against Invasion; and on Application of

---

[8]Refer to the Eleventh Amendment.
[9]Refer to the Thirteenth Amendment.

the Legislature, or of the Executive (when the Legislature cannot be convened) against domestic Violence.

Article V

The Congress, whenever two thirds of both Houses shall deem it necessary, shall propose Amendments to this Constitution, or, on the Application of the Legislatures of two thirds of the several States, shall call a Convention for proposing Amendments, which, in either Case, shall be valid to all Intents and Purposes, as part of this Constitution, when ratified by the Legislatures of three fourths of the several States, or by Conventions in three fourths thereof, as the one or the other Mode of Ratification may be proposed by the Congress; Provided that no Amendment which may be made prior to the Year One thousand eight hundred and eight shall in any Manner affect the first and fourth Clauses in the Ninth Section of the first Article; and that no State, without its Consent, shall be deprived of its equal Suffrage in the Senate.

Article VI

(1) All Debts contracted and Engagements entered into, before the Adoption of this Constitution shall be as valid against the United States under this Constitution, as under the Confederation.

(2) This Constitution, and the Laws of the United States which shall be made in Pursuance thereof; and all Treaties made, or which shall be made, under the Authority of the United States, shall be the supreme Law of the Land; and the Judges in every State shall be bound thereby, any Thing in the Constitution or Laws of any State to the Contrary notwithstanding.

(3) The Senators and Representatives before mentioned, and the Members of the several State Legislatures, and all executive and judicial Officers, both of the United States and of the several States, shall be bound by Oath or Affirmation, to support this Constitution, but no religious Test shall ever be required as a Qualification to any Office or public Trust under the United States.

Article VII

The Ratification of the Conventions of nine States shall be sufficient for the Establishment of this Constitution between the States so ratifying the Same.

[Amendments 1–10, the Bill of Rights, were ratified in 1791.]

Amendment I

Congress shall make no law respecting an establishment of religion, or prohibiting the free exercise thereof; or abridging the freedom of speech, or of the press; or the right of the people peaceably to assemble, and to petition the Government for a redress of grievances.

Amendment II

A well regulated Militia, being necessary to the security of a free State, the right of the people to keep and bear Arms, shall not be infringed.

Amendment III

No Soldier shall, in time of peace be quartered in any house, without the consent of the Owner, nor in time of war, but in a manner to be prescribed by law.

Amendment IV

The right of the people to be secure in their persons, houses, papers, and effects, against unreasonable searches and seizures, shall not be violated, and no Warrants shall issue, but upon probable cause, supported by Oath or affirmation, and particularly describing the place to be searched, and the persons or things to be seized.

Amendment V

No person shall be held to answer for a capital, or otherwise infamous crime, unless on a presentment or indictment of a Grand Jury, except in cases arising in the land or naval forces, or in the Militia, when in actual service in time of War or public danger; nor shall any person be subject for the same offence to be twice put in jeopardy of life or limb; nor shall be compelled in any criminal case to be a witness against himself, nor be deprived of life, liberty, or property, without due process of law; nor shall private property be taken for public use, without just compensation.

Amendment VI

In all criminal prosecutions, the accused shall enjoy the right to a speedy and public trial, by an impartial jury of the State and district wherein the crime shall have been committed, which district shall have been previously ascertained by law, and to be informed of the nature and cause of the accusation; to be confronted with the witnesses against him; to have compulsory process for obtaining witnesses in his favor, and to have the Assistance of Counsel for his defence.

Amendment VII

In Suits at common law, where the value in controversy shall exceed twenty dollars, the right of trial by jury shall be preserved, and no fact tried by jury, shall be otherwise re-examined in any Court of the United States, than according to the rules of the common law.

Amendment VIII

Excessive bail shall not be required, nor excessive fines imposed, nor cruel and unusual punishments inflicted.

Amendment IX

The enumeration in the Constitution, of certain rights, shall not be construed to deny or disparage others retained by the people.

Amendment X

The powers not delegated to the United States by the Constitution, nor prohibited by it to the States, are reserved to the States respectively, or to the people.

Amendment XI [1798]

The Judicial power of the United States shall not be construed to extend to any suit in law or equity, commenced or prosecuted against one of the United States by Citizens of another State, or by Citizens or Subjects of any Foreign State.

Amendment XII [1804]

The Electors shall meet in their respective states and vote by ballot for President and Vice-President, one of whom, at least, shall not be an inhabitant of the same state with themselves; they shall name in their ballots the person voted for as President, and in distinct ballots the person voted for as Vice-President, and they shall make distinct lists of all persons voted for as President, and of all persons voted for as Vice-President, and of the number of votes for each, which lists they shall sign and certify, and transmit sealed to the seat of the government of the United States, directed to the President of the Senate;—The President of the Senate shall, in the presence of the Senate and House of Representatives, open all the certificates and the votes shall then be counted;—The person having the greatest number of votes for President, shall be the President, if such number be a majority of the whole number of Electors appointed; and if no person have such majority, then from the persons having the highest numbers not exceeding three on the list of those voted for as President, the House of Representatives shall choose immediately, by ballot, the President. But in choosing the President, the votes shall be taken by states, the representation from each state having one vote; a quorum for this purpose shall consist of a member or members from two-thirds of the states, and a majority of all the states shall be necessary to a choice. And if the House of Representatives shall not choose a President whenever the right of choice shall devolve upon them before the fourth day of March next following, then the Vice-President shall act as President, as in the case of the death or other constitutional disability of the President.[10]—The person having the greatest number of votes as Vice-President, shall be the Vice-President, if such number be a majority of the whole number of Electors appointed, and if no person have a majority, then from the two highest numbers on the list, the Senate shall choose the Vice-President; a quorum for the purpose shall consist of two-thirds of the whole number of Senators, and a majority of the whole number shall be necessary to a choice. But no person constitutionally ineligible to the office of President shall be eligible to that of Vice-President of the United States.

Amendment XIII [1865]

Section 1. Neither slavery nor involuntary servitude, except as a punishment for crime whereof the party shall have been duly convicted, shall exist within the United States, or any place subject to their jurisdiction.

Section 2. Congress shall have power to enforce this article by appropriate legislation.

Amendment XIV [1868]

Section 1. All persons born or naturalized in the United States, and subject to the jurisdiction thereof, are citizens of the United States and of the State wherein they reside. No State shall make or enforce any law which shall abridge the privileges or immunities of citizens of the United States; nor shall any State deprive any person of life, liberty, or property, without due process of law; nor deny to any person within its jurisdiction the equal protection of the laws.

Section 2. Representatives shall be apportioned among the several States according to their respective numbers, counting the whole number of persons in each State, excluding Indians not taxed. But when the right to vote at any election for the choice of electors for President and Vice President of the United States, Representatives in Congress, the Executive and Judicial officers of a State, or the members of the Legislature thereof, is denied to any of the male inhabitants of such State, being twenty-one years of age,[11] and citizens of the United States, or

---

[10]Refer to the Twentieth Amendment.
[11]Refer to the Twenty-Sixth Amendment.

in any way abridged, except for participation in rebellion, or other crime, the basis of representation therein shall be reduced in the proportion which the number of such male citizens shall bear to the whole number of male citizens twenty-one years of age in such State.

Section 3. No person shall be a Senator or Representative in Congress, or elector of President and Vice President, or hold any office, civil or military, under the United States, or under any State, who having previously taken an oath, as a member of Congress, or as an officer of the United States, or as a member of any State legislature, or as an executive or judicial officer of any State, to support the Constitution of the United States, shall have engaged in insurrection or rebellion against the same, or given aid or comfort to the enemies thereof. But Congress may by a vote of two thirds of each House, remove such disability.

Section 4. The validity of the public debt of the United States, authorized by law, including debts incurred for payment of pensions and bounties for services in suppressing insurrection or rebellion, shall not be questioned. But neither the United States nor any State shall assume or pay any debt or obligation incurred in aid of insurrection or rebellion against the United States, or any claim for the loss or emancipation of any slave; but all such debts, obligations and claims shall be held illegal and void.

Section 5. The Congress shall have power to enforce, by appropriate legislation, the provisions of this article.

Amendment XV [1870]

Section 1. The right of citizens of the United States to vote shall not be denied or abridged by the United States or by any State on account of race, color, or previous condition of servitude.

Section 2. The Congress shall have power to enforce this article by appropriate legislation.

Amendment XVI [1913]

The Congress shall have power to lay and collect taxes on incomes, from whatever source derived, without apportionment among the several States, and without regard to any census or enumeration.

Amendment XVII [1913]

(1) The Senate of the United States shall be composed of two Senators from each State, elected by the people thereof, for six years; and each Senator shall have one vote. The electors in each State shall have the qualifications requisite for electors of the most numerous branch of the State legislatures.

(2) When vacancies happen in the representation of any State in the Senate, the executive authority of such State shall issue writs of election to fill such vacancies: *Provided,* That the legislature of any State may empower the executive thereof to make temporary appointments until the people fill the vacancies by election as the legislature may direct.

(3) This amendment shall not be so construed as to affect the election or term of any Senator chosen before it becomes valid as part of the Constitution.

Amendment XVIII [1919]

Section 1. After one year from the ratification of this article the manufacture, sale, or transportation of intoxicating liquors within, the importation thereof into, or the exportation thereof from the United States and all territory subject to the jurisdiction thereof for beverage purposes is hereby prohibited.

Section 2. The Congress and the several States shall have concurrent power to enforce this article by appropriate legislation.

Section 3. This article shall be inoperative unless it shall have been ratified as an amendment to the Constitution by the legislatures of the several States, as provided in the Constitution, within seven years from the date of the submission hereof to the States by the Congress.[12]

Amendment XIX [1920]

(1) The right of citizens of the United States to vote shall not be denied or abridged by the United States or by any State on account of sex.

(2) Congress shall have power to enforce this article by appropriate legislation.

Amendment XX [1933]

Section 1. The terms of the President and Vice President shall end at noon on the 20th day of January, and the terms of Senators and Representatives at noon on the 3rd day of January, of the years in which such terms would have ended if this article had not been ratified; and the terms of their successors shall then begin.

Section 2. The Congress shall assemble at least once in every year, and such meeting shall begin at noon on the 3rd day of January, unless they shall by law appoint a different day.

Section 3. If, at the time fixed for the beginning of the term of the President, the President elect shall have died, the Vice President elect shall become President. If the President shall not have been chosen before the time fixed for the beginning of his term or if the President elect shall have failed to qualify, then the Vice President elect shall act as President until a President shall have qualified; and the Congress may by law provide for the case wherein neither a President elect nor a Vice President elect shall have qualified, declaring who shall then act as President, or the manner in which one is to act shall be selected, and such person shall act accordingly until a President or Vice President shall have qualified.

Section 4. The Congress may by law provide for the case of the death of any of the persons from whom the House of Representatives may choose a President whenever the right of choice shall have devolved upon them, and for the case of the death of any of the persons from whom the Senate may choose a Vice President whenever the right of choice shall have devolved upon them.

Section 5. Sections 1 and 2 shall take effect on the 15th day of October following the ratification of this article.

Section 6. This article shall be inoperative unless it shall have been ratified as an amendment to the Constitution by the legislatures of three-fourths of the several States within seven years from the date of its submission.

Amendment XXI [1933]

Section 1. The eighteenth article of amendment to the Constitution of the United States is hereby repealed.

Section 2. The transportation or importation into any State, Territory, or possession of the United States for delivery or use therein of intoxicating liquors, in violation of the laws thereof, is hereby prohibited.

Section 3. This article shall be inoperative unless it shall have been ratified as an amendment to the Constitution by conventions in the several States, as provided in the Constitution, within seven years from the date of the submission hereof to the States by the Congress.

---

[12]Refer to the Twenty-First Amendment.

Amendment XXII [1951]

Section 1. No person shall be elected to the office of the President more than twice, and no person who has held the office of President, or acted as President, for more than two years of a term to which some other person was elected President shall be elected to the office of President more than once. But this Article shall not apply to any person holding the office of President when this Article was proposed by the Congress, and shall not prevent any person who may be holding the office of President, or acting as President, during the term within which this Article becomes operative from holding the office of President or acting as president during the remainder of such term.

Section 2. This article shall be inoperative unless it shall have been ratified as an amendment to the Constitution by the legislatures of three-fourths of the several States within seven years from the date of its submission to the States by the Congress.

Amendment XXIII [1961]

Section 1. The District constituting the seat of Government of the United States shall appoint in such manner as the Congress may direct:

A number of electors of President and Vice President equal to the whole number of Senators and Representatives in Congress to which the District would be entitled if it were a State, but in no event more than the least populous state; they shall be in addition to those appointed by the states, but they shall be considered, for the purposes of the election of President and Vice President, to be electors appointed by a state; and they shall meet in the District and perform such duties as provided by the twelfth article of amendment.

Section 2. The Congress shall have power to enforce this article by appropriate legislation.

Amendment XXIV [1964]

Section 1. The right of citizens of the United States to vote in any primary or other election for President or Vice President, for electors for President or Vice President, or for Senator or Representative in Congress, shall not be denied or abridged by the United States or any State by reason of failure to pay any poll tax or other tax.

Section 2. The Congress shall have power to enforce this article by appropriate legislation.

Amendment XXV [1967]

Section 1. In case of the removal of the President from office or of his death or resignation, the Vice President shall become President.

Section 2. Whenever there is a vacancy in the office of the Vice President, the President shall nominate a Vice President who shall take office upon confirmation by a majority vote of both Houses of Congress.

Section 3. Whenever the President transmits to the President pro tempore of the Senate and the Speaker of the House of Representatives his written declaration that he is unable to discharge the powers and duties of his office, and until he transmits to them a written declaration to the contrary, such powers and duties shall be discharged by the Vice President as Acting President.

Section 4. Whenever the Vice President and a majority of either the principal officers of the executive departments or of such other body as Congress may by law provide, transmit to the President pro tempore of the Senate and the Speaker of the House of Representatives their written declaration that the President is unable to discharge the powers and duties of his office, the Vice President shall immediately assume the powers and duties of the office as Acting President.

Thereafter, when the President transmits to the President pro tempore of the Senate and the Speaker of the House of Representatives his written declaration that no inability exists, he shall resume the powers and duties of his office unless the Vice President and a majority of either the principal officers of the executive departments or of such other body as Congress may by law provide, transmit within four days to the President pro tempore of the Senate and the Speaker of the House of Representatives their written declaration that the President is unable to discharge the powers and duties of his office. Thereupon Congress shall decide the issue, assembling within forty-eight hours for that purpose if not in session. If the Congress, within twenty-one days after receipt of the latter written declaration, or, if Congress is not in session, within twenty-one days after Congress is required to assemble, determines by two-thirds vote of both Houses that the President is unable to discharge the powers and duties of his office, the Vice President shall continue to discharge the same as Acting President; otherwise, the President shall resume the powers and duties of his office.

Amendment XXVI [1971]

Section 1. The right of citizens of the United States, who are eighteen years of age or older, to vote shall not be denied or abridged by the United States or by any State on account of age.

Section 2. The Congress shall have power to enforce this article by appropriate legislation.

THE SECURITIES ACT
OF 1933 (Excerpts)

Definitions

Section 2. When used in this title, unless the context otherwise requires—(1) The term "security" means any note, stock, treasury stock, bond, debenture, evidence of indebtedness, certificate of interest or participation in any profit-sharing agreement, collateral-trust certificate, pre-organization certificate or subscription, transferable share, investment contract, voting-trust certificate, certificate of deposit for a security, fractional undivided interest in oil, gas, or other mineral rights, any put, call, straddle, option, or privilege on any security, certificate of deposit, or group or index of securities (including any interest therein or based on the value thereof), or any put, call, straddle, option, or privilege entered into on a national securities exchange relating to foreign currency, or, in general, any interest or instrument commonly known as a "security," or any certificate of interest or participation in, temporary or interim certificate for, receipt for, guarantee of, or warrant or right to subscribe to or purchase, any of the foregoing.

Exempted Securities

Section 3. (a) Except as hereinafter expressly provided the provisions of this title shall not apply to any of the following classes of securities:

* * * * *

(2) Any security issued or guaranteed by the United States or any territory thereof, or by the District of Columbia, or by any State of the United States, or by any political subdivision of a State or Territory, or by any public instrumentality of one or more States or Territories, or by any person controlled or supervised by and acting as an instrumentality of the Government of the United States pursuant to authority granted by the Congress of the United States; or any certificate of deposit for any of the foregoing; or any security issued or guaranteed by any bank; or any security issued by or representing an interest in or a direct obligation of a Federal Reserve bank. . . .

(3) Any note, draft, bill of exchange, or banker's acceptance which arises out of a current transaction or the proceeds of which have been or are to be used for current transactions, and which has a maturity at the time of issuance of not exceeding nine months, exclusive of days of grace, or any renewal thereof the maturity of which is likewise limited;

(4) Any security issued by a person organized and operated exclusively for religious, educational, benevolent, fraternal, charitable, or reformatory purposes and not for pecuniary profit, and no part of the net earnings of which inures to the benefit of any person, private stockholder, or individual;

* * * * *

(11) Any security which is a part of an issue offered and sold only to persons resident within a single State or Territory, where the issuer of such security is a person resident and doing business within, or, if a corporation, incorporated by and doing business within, such State or Territory.

(b) The Commission may from time to time by its rules and regulations and subject to such terms and conditions as may be described therein, add any class of securities to the securities exempted as provided in this section, if it finds that the enforcement of this title with respect to such securities is not necessary in the public interest and for the protection of investors by reason of the small amount involved or the limited character of the public offering; but no issue of securities shall be exempted under this subsection where the aggregate amount at which such issue is offered to the public exceeds $5,000,000.

Exempted Transactions

Section 4. The provisions of section 5 shall not apply to—
(1) transactions by any person other than an issuer, underwriter, or dealer.
(2) transactions by an issuer not involving any public offering.

* * * * *

(4) brokers' transactions executed upon customers' orders on any exchange or in the over-the-counter market but not the solicitation of such orders.

Prohibitions Relating to Interstate Commerce and the Mails

Section 5. (a) Unless a registration statement is in effect as to a security, it shall be unlawful for any person, directly or indirectly—
(1) to make use of any means or instruments of transportation or communications in interstate commerce or of the mails to sell such security through the use or medium of any prospectus or otherwise; or
(2) to carry or cause to be carried through the mails or in interstate commerce, by any means of instruments of transportation, any such security for the purpose of sale or for delivery after sale.
(b) It shall be unlawful for any person, directly or indirectly—
(1) to make use of any means or instruments of transportation or communications in interstate commerce or of the mails to carry or transmit any prospectus relating to any security with respect to which a registration statement has been filed under this title, unless such prospectus meets the requirements of section 10; or
(2) to carry or cause to be carried through the mails or in interstate commerce any such security for the purpose of sale or for delivery after sale, unless accompanied or preceded by a prospectus that meets the requirements of subsection (a) of section 10.
(c) It shall be unlawful for any person, directly or indirectly to make use of any means or instruments of transportation or communication in interstate commerce or the mails to offer

to sell or offer to buy through the use or medium of any prospectus or otherwise any security, unless a registration statement has been filed as to such security, or while the registration statement is the subject of the refusal order or stop order . . .

Registration of Securities and Signing of Registration Statement

Section 6. (a) Any security may be registered with the Commission under the terms and conditions hereinafter provided, by filing a registration statement in triplicate, at least one of which shall be signed by each issuer, its principal executive officer or officers, its principal financial officer, its comptroller or principal accounting officer, and the majority of its board of directors or persons performing similar functions.

APPENDIX

THE SECURITIES EXCHANGE ACT OF 1934 (Excerpts)

Definitions

Section 3. (a) When used in this title, unless the context requires—

* * * * *

(4) The term "broker" means any person engaged in the business of effecting transactions in securities for the account of others, but does not include a bank.

(5) The term "dealer" means any person engaged in the business of buying and selling securities for his own account, through a broker or otherwise, but does not include a bank, or any person insofar as he buys or sells securities for his own account, either individually or in some fiduciary capacity, but not as part of a regular business.

* * * * *

(7) The term "director" means any director of a corporation or any person performing similar functions with respect to any organization, whether incorporated or unincorporated.

(8) The term "issuer" means any person who issues or proposes to issue any security; except that with respect to certificates of deposit for securities, voting-trust certificates, or collateral-trust certificates, or with respect to certificates of interest or shares in an unincorporated investment trust not having a board of directors of the fixed, restricted management, or unit type, the term "issuer" means the person or persons performing the acts and assuming the duties of depositor or manager pursuant to the provisions of the trust or other agreement or instrument under which such securities are issued; and except that with respect to equipment-trust certificates or like securities, the term "issuer" means the person by whom the equipment or property is, or is to be, used.

(9) The term "person" means a natural person, company, government, or political subdivision, agency, or instrumentality of a government.

Securities and Exchange Commission

Section 4. (a) There is hereby established a Securities and Exchange Commission (hereinafter referred to as the "Commission") to be composed of five commissioners to be appointed by the President by and with the advice and consent of the Senate. Not more than three of such commissioners shall be members of the same political party, and in making appointments members of different political parties shall be appointed alternately as nearly as may be practicable.

Transactions on Unregistered Exchanges

Section 5. It shall be unlawful for any broker, dealer, or exchange, directly or indirectly, to make use of the mails or any means or instrumentality of interstate commerce for the purpose of using any facility of any exchange within or subject to the jurisdiction of the United States to effect any transaction in a security, or to report any such transaction, unless such exchange (1) is registered as a national securities exchange under . . . this title, or (2) is exempted from such registration upon application by the exchange because, in the opinion of the Commission, by reason of the limited volume of transactions effected on such exchange, it is not practicable and not necessary or appropriate in the public interest or for the protection of investors to require such registration.

Regulation of the Use of Manipulative and Deceptive Devices

Section 10. It shall be unlawful for any person, directly or indirectly, by the use of any means or instrumentality of interstate commerce or of the mails, or of any facility of any national securities exchange—

(a) To effect a short sale, or to use or employ any stop-loss order in connection with the purchase or sale, of any security registered on a national securities exchange, in contravention of such rules and regulations as the Commission may prescribe as necessary or appropriate in the public interest or for the protection of investors.

(b) To use or employ, in connection with the purchase or sale of any security registered on a national securities exchange or any security not so registered, any manipulative or deceptive device or contrivance in contravention of such rules and regulations as the Commission may prescribe as necessary or appropriate in the public interest or for the protection of investors.

Registration Requirements for Securities

Section 12. (a) It shall be unlawful for any member, broker, or dealer to effect any transaction in any security (other than an exempted security) on a national securities exchange unless a registration is effective as to such security for such exchange in accordance with the provisions of this title and the rules and regulations thereunder.

THE NATIONAL LABOR
RELATIONS ACT (Excerpts)

Rights of Employees

Section 7. Employees shall have the right to self-organization, to form, join, or assist labor organizations, to bargain collectively through representatives of their own choosing, and to engage in other concerted activities for the purpose of collective bargaining or other mutual aid or protection, and shall also have the right to refrain from any or all of such activities except to the extent that such right may be affected by an agreement requiring membership in a labor organization as a condition of employment as authorized in section 8(a)(3).

Unfair Labor Practices

Section 8. (a) It shall be an unfair labor practice for an employer—

(1) to interfere with, restrain, or coerce employees in the exercise of the rights guaranteed in section 7;

(2) to dominate or interfere with the formation or administration of any labor organization or contribute financial or other support to it: *Provided,* That subject to rules and regulations made and published by the Board pursuant to section 6, an employer shall not be prohibited from permitting employees to confer with him during working hours without loss of time or pay;

(3) by discrimination in regard to hire or tenure of employment or any term or condition of employment to encourage or discourage membership in any labor organization: *Provided,* That nothing in this Act, or in any other statute of the United States, shall preclude an employer from making an agreement with a labor organization (not established, maintained, or assisted by any action defined in section 8(a) of this Act as an unfair labor practice) to require as a condition of employment membership therein on or after the thirtieth day following the beginning of such employment or the effective date of such agreement, whichever is the later, (i) if such labor organization is the representative of the employees as provided in section 9(a), in the appropriate collective-bargaining unit covered by such agreement when made, and (ii) unless following an election held as provided in section 9(e) within one year preceding the effective date of such agreement, the Board shall have certified that at least a majority of the employees eligible to vote in such election have voted to rescind the authority of such labor organization to make such an agreement: *Provided further,* That no employer shall justify any discrimination against an employee for nonmembership in a labor organization (A) if he has reasonable

grounds for believing that such membership was not available to the employee on the same terms and conditions generally applicable to other members, or (B) if he had reasonable grounds for believing that membership was denied or terminated for reasons other than the failure of the employee to tender the periodic dues and the initiation fees uniformly required as a condition of acquiring or retaining membership;

(4) to discharge or otherwise discriminate against an employee because he has filed charges or given testimony under this Act;

(5) to refuse to bargain collectively with the representatives of his employees, subject to the provisions of section 9(a).

(b) It shall be an unfair labor practice for a labor organization or its agents—

(1) to restrain or coerce (A) employees in the exercise of the rights guaranteed in section 7: *Provided,* That this paragraph shall not impair the right of a labor organization to prescribe its own rules with respect to the acquisition or retention of membership therein; or (B) an employer in the selection of his representatives for the purposes of collective bargaining or the adjustment of grievances;

(2) to cause or attempt to cause an employer to discriminate against an employee in violation of subsection (a)(3) or to discriminate against an employee with respect to whom membership in such organization has been denied or terminated on some ground other than his failure to tender the periodic dues and the initiation fees uniformly required as a condition of acquiring or retaining membership;

(3) to refuse to bargain collectively with an employer, provided it is the representative of his employees subject to the provisions of section 9(a);

(4) (i) to engage in, or to induce or encourage any individual employed by any person engaged in commerce or in an industry affecting commerce to engage in, a strike or a refusal in the course of his employment to use, manufacture, process, transport, or otherwise handle or work on any goods, articles, materials, or commodities or to perform any services; or (ii) to threaten, coerce, or restrain any person engaged in commerce or in an industry affecting commerce, where in either case an object thereof is—

(A) forcing or requiring any employer or self-employed person to join any labor or employer organization or to enter into any agreement which is prohibited by section 8(e);
(B) forcing or requiring any person to cease using, selling, handling, transporting, or otherwise dealing in the products of any other producer, processor, or manufacturer, or to cease doing business with any other person, or forcing or requiring any other employer to recognize or bargain with a labor organization as the representative of his employees unless such labor organization has been certified as the representative of such employees under the provisions of section 9: *Provided,* That nothing contained in this clause (B) shall be construed to make unlawful, where not otherwise unlawful, any primary strike or primary picketing;
(C) forcing or requiring any employer to recognize or bargain with a particular labor organization as the representative of his employees if another labor organization has been certified as the representative of such employees under the provisions of section 9;
(D) forcing or requiring any employer to assign particular work to employees in a particular labor organization or in a particular trade, craft, or class rather than to employees in another labor organization or in another trade, craft, or class, unless such employer is failing to conform to an order or certification of the Board determining the bargaining representative for employees performing such work:

Provided, That nothing contained in this subsection (b) shall be construed to make unlawful a refusal by any person to enter upon the premises of any employer (other than his own employer), if the employees of such employer are engaged in a strike ratified or approved by a representative of such employees whom such employer is required to recognize under this Act: *Provided further,* That for the purposes of this paragraph (4) only, nothing contained in such paragraph shall be construed to prohibit publicity, other than picketing, for the purpose of truthfully advising the public, including consumers and members of a labor organization, that a product or products are produced by an employer with whom the labor organization has a primary dispute and are distributed by another employer, as long as such publicity does not have an effect of inducing any individual employed by any person other than the primary employer in the course of his employment to refuse to pick up, deliver, or transport any goods, or not to perform any services, at the establishment of the employer engaged in such distribution:

(5) to require of employees covered by an agreement authorized under subsection (a)(3) the payment, as a condition precedent to becoming a member of such organization, of a fee in an amount which the Board finds excessive or discriminatory under all the circumstances. In making such a finding, the Board shall consider, among other relevant factors, the practices and customs of labor organizations in the particular industry, and the wages currently paid to the employees affected;

(6) to cause or attempt to cause an employer to pay or deliver or agree to pay or deliver any money or other thing of value, in the nature of an exaction, for services which are not performed or not to be performed; and

(7) To picket or cause to be picketed, or threatened to picket or cause to be picketed, any employer where an object thereof is forcing or requiring an employer to recognize or bargain with a labor organization as the representative of his employees, or forcing or requiring the employees of an employer to accept or select such labor organization as their collective bargaining representative, unless such labor organization is currently certified as the representative of such employees:

(A) where the employer has lawfully recognized in accordance with this Act any other labor organization and a question concerning representation may not appropriately be raised under section 9(c) of this Act.

(B) where within the preceding twelve months a valid election under section 9(c) of this Act has been conducted, or

(C) where such picketing has been conducted without a petition under section 9(c) being filed within a reasonable period of time not to exceed thirty days from the commencement of such picketing; *Provided,* That when such a petition has been filed the Board shall forthwith, without regard to the provisions of section 9(c)(1) or the absence of a showing of a substantial interest on the part of the labor organization, direct an election in such unit as the Board finds to be appropriate and shall certify the results thereof: *Provided further,* That nothing in this subparagraph (C) shall be construed to prohibit any picketing or other publicity for the purpose of truthfully advising the public (including consumers) that an employer does not employ members of, or have a contract with, a labor organization, unless an effect of such picketing is to induce any individual employed by any other person in the course of his employment, not to pick up, deliver or transport any goods or not to perform any services.

Nothing in this paragraph (7) shall be construed to permit any act which would otherwise be an unfair labor practice under this section 8(b).

(c) The expressing of any views, argument, or opinion, or the dissemination thereof, whether in written, printed, graphic, or visual form, shall not constitute or be evidence of an unfair labor practice under any of the provisions of this Act, if such expression contains no threat of reprisal or force or promise of benefit.

(d) For the purposes of this section, to bargain collectively is the performance of the mutual obligation of the employer and the representative of the employees to meet at reasonable times and confer in good faith with respect to wages, hours, and other terms and conditions of employment, or the negotiation of an agreement, or any question arising thereunder, and the execution of a written contract incorporating any agreement reached if requested by either party, but such obligation does not compel either party to agree to a proposal or require the making of a concession . . .

* * * * *

Representatives and Elections

Section 9. (a) Representatives designated or selected for the purposes of collective bargaining by the majority of the employees in a unit appropriate for such purposes, shall be the exclusive representatives of all the employees in such unit for the purposes of collective bargaining in respect to rates of pay, wages, hours of employment, or other conditions of employment: *Provided,* That any individual employee or a group of employees shall have the right at any time to present grievances to their employer and to have such grievances adjusted, without the intervention of the bargaining representative, as long as the adjustment is not inconsistent with the terms of a collective-bargaining contract or agreement then in effect: *Provided further,* That the bargaining representative has been given opportunity to be present at such adjustment.

(b) The Board shall decide in each case whether, in order to assure to employees the fullest freedom in exercising the rights guaranteed by this Act, the unit appropriate for the purposes of collective bargaining shall be the employer unit, craft unit, plant unit, or subdivision thereof: *Provided,* That the Board shall not (1) decide that any unit is appropriate for such purposes if such unit included both professional employees and employees who are not professional employees unless a majority of such professional employees vote for inclusion in such unit; or (2) decide that any craft unit is inappropriate for such purposes on the ground that a different unit has been established by a prior Board determination, unless a majority of the employees in the proposed craft unit vote against separate representation or (3) decide that any unit is appropriate for such purposes if it includes, together with other employees, any individual employed as a guard to enforce against employees and other persons rules to protect property of the employer or to protect the safety of persons on the employer's premises; but no later organization shall be certified as the representative of employees in a bargaining unit of guards if such organization admits to membership, or is affiliated directly or indirectly with an organization which admits to membership, employees other than guards.

(c) (1) Whenever a petition shall have been filed, in accordance with such regulations as may be prescribed by the Board—

(A) by an employee or group of employees or an individual or labor organization acting in their behalf alleging that a substantial number of employees (i) wish to be represented for collective bargaining and that their employer declines to recognize their representative as the representative defined in section 9(a), or (ii) assert that the individual or labor organization, which has been certified or is being currently recognized by their employer as the bargaining representative, is no longer a representative as defined in section 9(a); or

(B) by an employer, alleging that one or more individuals or labor organizations have presented to him a claim to be recognized as the representative defined in section 9(a); the Board shall investigate such petition and if it has reasonable cause to believe that a question of representation affecting commerce exists shall provide for an appropriate hearing upon due notice. Such hearing may be conducted by an officer or employee of the regional office, who shall not make any recommendations with respect thereto. If the Board finds upon the record of such hearing that such a question of representation exists, it shall direct an election by secret ballot and shall certify the results thereof.

* * * * *

(3) No election shall be directed in any bargaining unit or any subdivision within which, in the preceding twelve-month period, a valid election shall have been held. Employees engaged in an economic strike who are not entitled to reinstatement shall be eligible to vote under such regulations as the Board shall find are consistent with the purposes and provisions of this Act in any election conducted within twelve months after the commencement of the strike. In any election where none of the choices on the ballot receives a majority, a run-off shall be conducted, the ballot providing for a selection between the two choices receiving the largest and second largest number of valid votes cast in the election.

THE CIVIL RIGHTS ACT OF 1964, TITLE VII (Excerpts)

Definitions

Section 701

* * * * *

(j) The term "religion" includes all aspects of religious observance and practice, as well as belief, unless an employer demonstrates that he is unable to reasonably accommodate to an employee's or prospective employee's religious observance or practice without undue hardship on the conduct of the employer's business.

(k) The terms "because of sex" or "on the basis of sex" include, but are not limited to, because of or on the basis of pregnancy, childbirth or related medical conditions; and women affected by pregnancy, childbirth, or related medical conditions shall be treated the same for all employment-related purposes, including receipt of benefits under fringe benefit programs, as other persons not so affected but similar in their ability or inability to work, and nothing in Section 703(h) of this title shall be interpreted to permit otherwise. This subsection shall not require an employer to pay for health insurance benefits for abortion, except where the life of the mother would be endangered if the fetus were carried to term, or except where medical complications have arisen from an abortion: *Provided,* That nothing herein shall preclude an employer from providing abortion benefits or otherwise effect bargaining agreements in regard to abortion.

Unlawful Employment Practices

Section 703. (a) It shall be an unlawful employment practice for an employer—

(1) to fail or refuse to hire or to discharge any individual, or otherwise to discriminate against any individual with respect to his compensation, terms, conditions, or privileges of employment, because of such individual's race, color, religion, sex, or national origin; or

(2) limit, segregate, or classify his employees or applicants for employment in any way which would deprive or tend to deprive any individual of employment opportunities or otherwise adversely affect his status as an employee, because of such individual's race, color, religion, sex, or national origin.

(b) It shall be an unlawful employment practice for an employment agency to fail or refuse to refer for employment, or otherwise to discriminate against, an individual because of his race, color, religion, sex, or national origin, or to classify or to refer for employment any individual on the basis of his race, color, religion, sex, or national origin.

(c) It shall be an unlawful employment practice for a labor organization—

(1) to exclude or to expel from its membership, or otherwise to discriminate against, any individual because of his race, color, religion, sex, or national origin;

(2) to limit, segregate, or classify its membership or applicants for membership or to classify or fail or refuse to refer for employment any individual, in any way which would deprive or tend to deprive any individual of employment opportunities, or would limit such employment opportunities or otherwise adversely affect his status as an employee or as an applicant for employment, because of such individual's race, color, religion, sex, or national origin; or

(3) to cause or attempt to cause an employer to discriminate against an individual in violation of this section.

(d) It shall be an unlawful employment practice for any employer, labor organization, or joint labor management committee controlling apprenticeship or other training or retraining, including on-the-job training programs to discriminate against any individual because of his race, color, religion, sex, or national origin in admission to, or employment in, any program established to provide apprenticeship or other training.

(e) Notwithstanding any other provision of this title, (1) it shall not be an unlawful employment practice for an employer to hire and employ employees, for an employment agency to classify, or refer for employment any individual, or for any employer, labor organization, or joint labor management committee controlling apprenticeship or other training or retraining programs to admit or employ any individual in any such program, on the basis of his religion, sex, or national origin in those certain instances where religion, sex, or national origin is a bona fide occupational qualification reasonably necessary to the normal operation of that particular business or enterprise, and (2) it shall not be an unlawful employment practice for a school, college, university, or other educational institution or institution of learning to hire and employ employees of a particular religion if such school, college, university, or other educational institution or institution of learning is, in whole or in substantial part,owned, supported, controlled, or managed by a particular religion or by a particular religious corporation, association, or society, or if the curriculum of such school, college, university, or other educational institution or institution of learning is directed toward the propagation of a particular religion.

* * * * *

(h) Notwithstanding any other provision of this title, it shall not be an unlawful employment practice for an employer to apply different standards of compensation, or different terms, conditions, or privileges of employment pursuant to a bona fide seniority or merit system, or a system which measures earnings by quantity or quality of production or to employees who work in different locations, provided that such differences are not the result of an intention to discriminate because of race, color, religion, sex, or national origin; nor shall it be an unlawful employment practice for an employer to give and to act upon the results of any professionally developed ability test provided that such test, its administration or action upon the results is not designed, intended, or used to discriminate because of race, color, religion, sex, or national origin. It shall not be an unlawful employment practice under this title for any employer to differentiate upon the basis of sex in determining the amount of wages or compensation paid or to be paid to employees of such employer if such differentiation is authorized by the provision of Section 6(d) of the Fair Labor Standards Act of 1938 as amended (29 U.S.C. 206(d))

* * * * *

(j) Nothing contained in this title shall be interpreted to require any employer, employment agency, labor organization, or joint labor-management committee subject to this title to grant preferential treatment to any individual or to any group because of the race, color, religion, sex, or national origin of such individual or group on account of an imbalance which may exist with respect to the total number of percentage of persons of any race, color, religion, sex, or national origin employed by any employer, referred or classified for employment by any employment agency or labor organization, admitted to membership or classified by any labor organization, or admitted to, or employed in, any apprenticeship or other training program, in comparison with the total number or percentage of persons of such race, color, religion, sex, or national origin in any community, State, section, or other area, or in the available work force in any community, State, section, or other area.

Other Unlawful Employment Practices

Section 704. (a) It shall be an unlawful employment practice for an employer to discriminate against any of his employees or applicants for employment, for an employment agency, or joint labor-management committee controlling apprenticeship or other training or retraining, including on-the-job training programs, to discriminate against any individual, or for a labor organization to discriminate against any member thereof or applicant for membership, because he has opposed any practice, made an unlawful employment practice by this title, or because he has made a charge, testified, assisted, or participated in any manner in an investigation, proceeding, or hearing under this title.

(b) It shall be an unlawful employment practice for an employer, labor organization, employment agency, or joint labor-management committee controlling apprenticeship or other training or retraining, including on-the-job training programs, to print or cause to be printed or published any notice or advertisement relating to employment by such an employer or membership in or any classification or referral for employment by such a labor organization, or relating to any classification or referral for employment by such an employment agency, or relating to admission to, or employment in, any program established to provide apprenticeship or other training by such a joint labor-management committee indicating any preference, limitation, specification, or discrimination, based on race, color, religion, sex or national origin, except that such a notice or advertisement may indicate a preference, limitation, specification, or discrimination based on religion, sex, or national origin when religion, sex, or national origin is a bona fide occupational qualification for employment.

THE AMERICANS WITH DISABILITIES ACT, TITLE I

Section 101 Definitions

As used in this title:

(1) Commission—The term "Commission" means the Equal Employment Opportunity Commission established by section 705 of the Civil Rights Act of 1964 (42 U.S.C. 2000e–4).

(2) Covered entity—The term "covered entity" means an employer, employment agency, labor organization, or joint labor-management committee.

(3) Direct threat—The term "direct threat" means a significant risk to the health or safety of others that cannot be eliminated by reasonable accommodation.

(4) Employee—The term "employee" means an individual employed by an employer.

(5) Employer—

    (A) In general—The term "employer" means a person engaged in an industry affecting commerce who has 15 or more employees for each working day in each of 20 or more calendar weeks in that current or preceding calendar year, and any agent of such person, except that, for two years following the effective date of this title, an employer means a person engaged in an industry affecting commerce who has 25 or more employees for each working day in each of 20 or more calendar weeks in the current or preceding year, and any agent of such person.

    (B) Exceptions—The term "employer" does not include—

        (i) the United States, a corporation wholly owned by the government of the United States, or an Indian tribe; or

        (ii) a bona fide private membership club (other than a labor organization) that is exempt from taxation under section 501(c) of the Internal Revenue Code of 1986.

(6) Illegal use of drugs—

    (A) In general—The term "illegal use of drugs" means the use of drugs, the possession or distribution of which is unlawful under the Controlled Substances Act (21 U.S.C. 812). Such term does not include the use of a drug taken under supervision by a licensed health care professional, or other uses authorized by the Controlled Substances Act or other provisions of Federal law.

    (B) Drugs—The term "drug" means a controlled substance, as defined in schedules I through V of section 202 of the Controlled Substances Act.

(7) Person, etc.—The terms "person," "labor organization," "employment agency," "commerce," and "industry affecting commerce," shall have the same meaning given such terms in section 701 of the Civil Rights Act of 1964 (42 U.S.C. 2000e).

(8) Qualified individual with a disability—The term "qualified individual with a disability" means an individual with a disability who with or without reasonable accommodation, can perform the essential functions of the employment position that such individual holds or desires. For the purposes of this title, consideration shall be given to the employer's judgment as to what functions of a job are essential, and if an employer has prepared a written description before advertising or interviewing applicants for the job, this description shall be considered evidence of the essential functions of the job.

(9) Reasonable accommodation—The term "reasonable accommodation" may include—

    (A) making existing facilities used by employees readily accessible to and usable by individuals with disabilities; and

    (B) job restructuring, part-time or modified work schedules, reassignment to a vacant position, acquisition or modification of equipment or devices, appropriate adjustment or modifications of examinations, training materials or policies, the provision of qualified readers or interpreters, and other similar accommodations for individuals with disabilities.

(10) Undue hardship—

    (A) In general—The term "undue hardship" means an action requiring significant difficulty or expense, when considered in light of the factors set forth in subparagraph (B).

    (B) Factors to be considered—In determining whether an accommodation would impose an undue hardship on a covered entity, factors to be considered include—

        (i) the nature and costs of the accommodation needed under this Act;

        (ii) the overall financial resources of the facility or facilities involved in the provision of the reasonable accommodation; the number of persons employed at such facility; the effect on expenses and resources, or the impact otherwise of such accommodation upon the operation of the facility;

        (iii) the overall financial resources of the covered entity; the overall size of the business of a covered entity with respect to the number of its employees; the number, type, and location of its facilities; and

        (iv) the type of operation or operations of the covered entity, including the composition, structure, and functions of the workforce of such entity; the geographic separateness, administrative, or fiscal relationship of the facility or facilities in question to the covered entity.

Section 102 Discrimination

(a) General Rule—No covered entity shall discriminate against a qualified individual with a disability because of the disability of such individual in regard to job application procedures, the hiring, advancement, or discharge of employees, employee compensation, job training, and other terms, conditions, and privileges of employment.

(b) Construction—As used in subsection (A), the term "discriminate" includes—

    (1) limiting, segregating, or classifying a job applicant or employee in a way that adversely affects the opportunities or status of such applicant or employee because of the disability of such applicant or employee;

    (2) participating in a contractual or other arrangement or relationship that has the effect of subjecting a covered entity's qualified applicant or employee with a disability to the discrimination prohibited by this title (such relationship includes a relationship with an employment or referral agency, labor union, an organization providing fringe benefits to an employee of the covered entity, or an organization providing training and apprenticeship programs);

    (3) utilizing standards, criteria, or methods of administration—

(A) that have the effect of discrimination on the basis of disability; or

(B) that perpetuate the discrimination of others who are subject to common administrative control;

(4) excluding or otherwise denying equal jobs or benefits to a qualified individual because of the known disability of an individual with whom the qualified individual is known to have a relationship or association;

(5) (A) not making reasonable accommodations to the known physical or mental limitations of an otherwise qualified individual with a disability who is an applicant or employee, unless such covered entity can demonstrate that the accommodation would impose an undue hardship on the operation of the business of such covered entity; or

(B) denying employment opportunities to a job applicant or employee who is an otherwise qualified individual with a disability, if such denial is based on the need of such covered entity to make reasonable accommodation to the physical or mental impairments of the employee or applicant;

(6) using qualification standards, employment tests or other selection criteria that screen out or tend to screen out an individual with a disability or a class of individuals with disabilities unless the standard, test or other selection criteria, as used by the covered entity, is shown to be job-related for the position in question and is consistent with business necessity; and

(7) failing to select and administer tests concerning employment in the most effective manner to ensure that, when such test is administered to a job applicant or employee who has a disability that impairs sensory, manual, or speaking skills, such test results accurately reflect the skills, aptitude, or whatever other factor of such applicant or employee that such test purports to measure, rather than reflecting the impaired sensory, manual, or speaking skills of such employee or applicant (except where such skills are the factors that the test purports to measure).

(c) Medical Examinations and Inquiries—

(1) In general—The prohibition against discrimination as referred to in subsection (A) shall include medical examinations and inquiries.

(2) Preemployment—

(A) Prohibited examination or inquiry—Except as provided in paragraph (3), a covered entity shall not conduct a medical examination or make inquiries of a job applicant as to whether such applicant is an individual with a disability or as to the nature of severity of such disability.

(B) Acceptable Inquiry—A covered entity may make preemployment inquiries into the ability of an applicant to perform job-related functions.

(3) Employment entrance examination—A covered entity may require a medical examination after an offer of employment has been made to a job applicant and prior to the commencement of the employment duties of such applicant, and may condition an offer of employment on the results of such examination, if—

(A) all entering employees are subjected to such an examination regardless of disability;

(B) information obtained regarding the medical condition or history of the applicant is collected and maintained on separate forms and in separate medical files and is treated as a confidential medical record, except that—

(i) supervisors and managers may be informed regarding necessary restrictions on the work or duties of the employee and necessary accommodations:

(ii) first aid and safety personnel may be informed, when appropriate, if the disability might require emergency treatment; and

(iii) government officials investigating compliance with this Act shall be provided relevant information on request; and

(C) the results of such examination are used only in accordance with this title

(4) Examination and Inquiry—

(A) Prohibited examinations and inquiries—A covered entity shall not require a medical examination and shall not make inquiries of an employee as to whether such employee is an individual with a disability or as to the nature or severity of the disability, unless such examination or inquiry is shown to be job-related and consistent with business necessity.

(B) Acceptable examinations and inquiries—A covered entity may conduct voluntary medical examinations, including voluntary medical histories, which are part of an employee health program available to employees at that work site. A covered entity may make inquiries into the ability of an employee to perform job-related functions.

(C) Requirement—Information obtained under subparagraph (B) regarding the medical condition or history of any employee are subject to the requirements of subparagraphs (B) and (C) of paragraph (3).

Section 103 Defenses

(a) In general—It may be a defense to a charge of discrimination under this Act that an alleged application of qualification standards, tests, or selection criteria that screen out or tend to screen out or otherwise deny a job or benefit to an individual with a disability has been shown to be job-related and consistent with business necessity, and such performance cannot be accomplished by reasonable accommodation, as required under this title.

(b) Qualification Standards—The term "qualification standards" may include a requirement that an individual shall not pose a direct threat to the health or safety of other individuals in the workplace.

(c) Religious Entities—

(1) In general—This title shall not prohibit a religious corporation, association, educational institution, or society from giving preference in employment to individuals of a particular religion to perform work connected with the carrying on by such corporation, association, educational institution, or society of its activities.

(2) Religious tenets requirement—Under this title, a religious organization may require that all applicants and employees conform to the religious tenets of such organization.

(d) List of Infectious and Communicable Diseases—

(1) In general—The Secretary of Health and Human Services, not later than 6 months after the date of enactment of this Act, shall—

(A) review all infectious and communicable diseases which may be transmitted through handling the food supply;

(B) publish a list of infectious and communicable diseases which are transmitted through handling the food supply;

(C) publish the methods by which such diseases are transmitted; and

(D) widely disseminate such information regarding the list of diseases and their modes of transmissibility to the general public. Such list shall be updated annually.

(2) Applications—In any case in which an individual has an infectious or communicable disease that is transmitted to others through the handling of food, that is included

on the list developed by the Secretary of Health and Human Services under paragraph (1), and which cannot be eliminated by reasonable accommodation, a covered entity may refuse to assign or continue to assign such individual to a job involving food handling.

(3) Construction—Nothing in this Act shall be construed to preempt, modify, or amend any State, county, or local law, ordinance, or regulation applicable to food handling which is designed to protect the public health from individuals who pose a significant risk to the health or safety of others, which cannot be eliminated by reasonable accommodation, pursuant to the list of infectious or communicable diseases and the modes of transmissibility published by the Secretary of Health and Human Services.

Section 104 Illegal Use of Drugs and Alcohol

(a) Qualified Individual with a Disability—For purposes of this title, the term "qualified individual with a disability" shall not include any employee or applicant who is currently engaging in the illegal use of drugs, when the covered entity acts on the basis of such use.

(b) Rules of Construction—Nothing in subsection (A) shall be construed to exclude as a qualified individual with a disability an individual who—

(1) has successfully completed a supervised drug rehabilitation program and is no longer engaging in the illegal use of drugs, or has otherwise been rehabilitated successfully and is no longer engaging in such use;

(2) is participating in a supervised rehabilitation program and is no longer engaging in such use; or

(3) is erroneously regarded as engaging in such use, but is not engaging in such use; except that it shall not be a violation of this Act for a covered entity to adopt or administer reasonable policies or procedures, including but not limited to drug testing, designed to ensure that an individual described in paragraph (1) or (2) is no longer engaging in the illegal use of drugs.

(c) Authority of Covered Entity—A covered entity—

(1) may prohibit the illegal use of drugs and the use of alcohol at the workplace by all employees;

(2) may require that employees shall not be under the influence of alcohol or be engaging in the illegal use of drugs at the workplace;

(3) may require that employees behave in conformance with the requirements established under the Drug-Free Workplace Act of 1988 (41 U.S.C. 701 et seq.);

(4) may hold an employee who engages in the illegal use of drugs or who is an alcoholic to the same qualification standards for employment or job performance and behavior that such entity holds other employees, even if any unsatisfactory performance or behavior is related to the drug use or alcoholism of such employee; and

(5) may, with respect to Federal regulations regarding alcohol and the illegal use of drugs, require that—

(A) employees comply with the standards established in such regulations of the Department of the Defense, if the employees of the covered entity are employed in an industry subject to such regulations, including complying with regulations (if any) that apply to employment in sensitive positions, in such an industry, in the case of employees of the covered entity who are employed in such positions (as defined in the regulations of the Department of Defense);

(B) employees comply with the standards established in such regulations of the Nuclear Regulatory Commission, if the employees of the covered entity are employed in an industry subject to such regulations, including complying with regulations (if any) that apply to employment in sensitive positions in such an industry, in the case of employees of the covered entity who are employed in such positions (as defined in the regulations of the Nuclear Regulatory Commission); and

(C) employees comply with the standards established in such regulations of the Department of Transportation, if the employees of the covered entity are employed in a transportation industry subject to such regulations, including complying with such regulations (if any) that apply to employment in sensitive positions in such an industry, in the case of employees of the covered entity who are employed in such positions (as defined in the regulations of the Department of Transportation).

(d) Drug Testing—
   (1) In general—For purposes of this title, a test to determine the illegal use of drugs shall not be considered a medical examination.
   (2) Construction—Nothing in this title shall be construed to encourage, prohibit, or authorize the conducting of drug testing for the illegal use of drugs by job applicants or employees or making employment decisions based on such test results.

(e) Transportation Employees—Nothing in this title shall be construed to encourage, prohibit, restrict, or authorize the otherwise lawful exercise by entities subject to the jurisdiction of the Department of Transportation of authority to—
   (1) test employees of such entities in, and applicants for, positions involving safety-sensitive duties for the illegal use of drugs and for on-duty impairment by alcohol; and
   (2) remove such persons who test positive for illegal use of drugs and on-duty impairments by alcohol pursuant to paragraph (1) from safety-sensitive duties in implementing subsection (c).

Section 105 Posting Notices

Every employer, employment agency, labor organization, or joint labor-management committee covered under this title shall post notices in an accessible format to applicants, employees, and members describing the applicable provisions of this Act, in the manner prescribed by section 711 of the Civil Rights Act of 1964 (42 U.S.C. 2000e–10).

Section 106 Regulations

Not later than 1 year after the date of enactment of this Act, the Commission shall issue regulations in an accessible format to carry out this title in accordance with subchapter II of chapter 5 of title 5, United States Code.

Section 107 Enforcement

(a) Powers, Remedies, and Procedures—The powers, remedies, and procedures set forth in sections 705, 706, 707, 709, and 710 of the Civil Rights act of 1964 (42 U.S.C. 2000e–4, 2000e–5, 2000e–6, 2000e–8, and 2000e–9) shall be the powers, remedies, and procedures this title provides to the Commission, to the Attorney General, or to any person alleging discrimination on the basis of disability in violation of any provision of this Act, or regulations promulgated under section 106, concerning employment.

(b) Coordination—The agencies with enforcement authority for actions which allege employment discrimination under this title and under the Rehabilitation Act of 1973 shall develop procedures to ensure that administrative complaints filed under this title and under the Rehabilitation Act of 1973 are dealt with in a manner that avoids duplication of effort and prevents imposition of inconsistent or conflicting standards for the same requirements under this title and the Rehabilitation Act of 1973. The Commission, the Attorney General, and the Office of Federal Contract Compliance Programs shall establish such coordinating mechanisms (similar to provisions contained in the joint regulations promulgated by the Commission and the Attorney General as part 42 of title 28 and part 1691 of title 29, Code of Federal Regulations, and the Memorandum of Understanding between the Commission and the Office of Federal Contract Compliance Programs dated January 16, 1981 (46 Fed. Reg. 7435, January 23, 1981)) in regulations implementing this title and Rehabilitation Act of 1973 not later than 18 months after the date of enactment of this Act.

Section 108 Effective Date

This title shall become effective 24 months after the date of enactment.

GLOSSARY OF LEGAL TERMS

A

act of state doctrine   The view that a judge in the United States or another country does not have the authority to challenge the legality of acts by a foreign government within that foreign government's own borders.

adjudication   The formal pronouncement of a judgment in a legal proceeding.

administrative law   That branch of public law addressing the operation of the government's various agencies and commissions. Also the rules and regulations established by those agencies and commissions.

Administrative Procedure Act   A federal statute specifying the procedural rules under which the government's agencies and commissions conduct their business.

ad valorem   (Latin) According to value. Hence, an **ad valorem** tax would be based upon the value of the item in question rather than, for example, a fixed rate for all such items.

affidavit   A written statement sworn to by a person officially empowered to administer an oath.

affirmative action   A government/private sector program, springing from the civil rights movement, designed to *actively promote* the employment and educational opportunities of protected classes rather than merely forbidding discrimination.

affirmative defense   A portion of defendant's answer to a complaint in which the defendant presents contentions which, if proved true, will relieve the defendant of liability even if the assertions in the complaint are correct.

agent   A person entrusted by a principal to act on behalf of that principal; one who is authorized to carry out the business of another.

alternate dispute resolution   The growing practice of employing strategies other than conventional litigation to solve conflicts. Those strategies include negotiation, arbitration, and mediation with variations like "minitrials" and "rent-a-judge" arrangements.

amicus curiae   A "friend of the court" who, though not a party to the case, files a brief because of a strong interest in the litigation.

annual percentage rate   The rate of interest charged for borrowing money as expressed in a standardized, yearly manner that allows for comparison among lenders' fees.

answer   The defendant's first pleading in a lawsuit, in which the defendant responds to the allegations raised in the plaintiff's complaint.

appeal   The judicial process by which a party petitions a higher court to review the decision of a lower court or agency in order to correct errors.

appellant   The party filing an appeal.

appellee   The party against whom an appeal is filed.

arbitration   An extrajudicial process in which a dispute is submitted to a mutually agreeable third party for a decision.

arraignment   A criminal law proceeding in which a defendant is brought before a judge to be informed of the charges and to file a plea.

assault   A show of force that would cause the reasonable person to believe that they are about to receive an intentional, unwanted, harmful physical touching.

assumption of risk   An affirmative defense in a negligence case in which the defendant seeks to bar recovery by the plaintiff by showing that the plaintiff knowingly exposed himself or herself to the danger that resulted in injury.

at-will employee   An individual not under contract for a specified term and therefore, under the general rule, subject to discharge by the employer at any time and for any reason.

B

bait-and-switch advertising   An unlawful sales tactic in which the seller attracts buyer interest by insincerely advertising a product at a dramatically reduced price while holding no genuine intent to sell the product at that price. The seller then disparages the "bait" and diverts the buyer's attention to a higher-priced product (the switch), which was the sales goal from the first.

battery   An intentional, unwanted, harmful physical touching.

beyond a reasonable doubt   The level of proof required for conviction in a criminal case.

blue sky laws   Statutes regulating the sale of stocks and other securities to prevent consumer fraud.

bona fide   In good faith; honestly.

bona fide occupational qualification (bfoq)   A defense in a discrimination claim where employer argues that a particular religion, sex, or national origin is a necessary qualification for a particular job.

boycott   A confederation or conspiracy involving a refusal to do business with another or an attempt by the confederation to stop others from doing business with the target person or organization.

brief   A written document setting out for the court the facts, the law, and the argument of a party to the lawsuit.

burden of proof   The party with the burden of proof (normally the plaintiff in a civil suit and the state in a criminal case) is required to prove the truth of a claim or lose on that issue.

C

capacity   A required element in an enforceable contract. Capacity refers to the mental ability to understand the nature and consequences of a contract.

capitalism   Private ownership of the means of production with a largely unrestricted marketplace in goods and services.

cause in fact   The actual cause of an event. One of the required elements in a negligence claim.

cause of action   Facts sufficient to support a valid civil lawsuit.

caveat emptor   Let the buyer beware.

cease and desist order   An instruction from an agency instructing a party to refrain from a specified act.

certiorari   A legal procedure affording an appellate court the opportunity to review a lower court decision. Also a writ asking the lower court for the record of the case.

civil law   The branch of law dealing with private rights. Contrast with criminal law.

class action   A legal action brought by one on behalf of himself or herself and all others similarly situated.

comity   Courtesy. Nations often recognize the laws of other nations not because they must do so but because of the tradition of comity; that is, goodwill and mutual respect.

commerce clause   That portion of the United States Constitution that provides for federal regulation of foreign and interstate trade.

commercial speech   Speech directed toward a business purpose. Advertising is an example of commercial speech. Such speech is protected by the First Amendment, but not to the degree that we protect other varieties of speech.

common law   Judge-made law. To be distinguished from statutory law as created by legislative bodies.

comparable worth   The legal theory that all employees should be paid the same wages for work requiring comparable skills, effort, and responsibility and having comparable worth to the employer.

comparative negligence   A rule of law in which the plaintiff's recovery in a negligence suit is reduced by a percentage equal to the percentage of the plaintiff's contribution to his or her own harm. Contrast with contributory negligence.

complaint   The first pleading filed by the plaintiff in a civil lawsuit.

conglomerate merger   A merger between firms operating in separate markets and having neither a buyer–seller nor competitive relationships with each other.

consent decree   A settlement of a lawsuit arrived at by agreement of the parties. Effectively, an admission by the parties that the decree is a just determination of their rights.

consideration   A required element in an enforceable contract. The thing of value passing between the parties which results in a benefit to the one making the promise or a detriment to the one receiving the promise.

conspiracy   An agreement between two or more persons to commit an unlawful act.

contingent fee   An arrangement wherein an attorney is compensated for his or her services by receiving a percentage of the award in a lawsuit rather than receiving an hourly wage or specified fee.

contract   An agreement that is legally enforceable by the courts.

contributory negligence   A defense in a negligence action wherein the defendant attempts to demonstrate that the plaintiff contributed to the harm on which the litigation was based.

Contributory negligence acts as a complete bar to the plaintiff's recovery. Contrast with comparative negligence.

copyright   The creator's (artist, author, etc.) right to control the copying and distribution of his or her work for a period of time specified by statute.

counterclaim   A cause of action filed by the defendant in a lawsuit against the plaintiff in the same suit.

criminal law   Wrongs against society that the state has seen fit to label crimes and that may result in penalties against the perpetrator(s). Contrast with civil law.

D

d.b.a.   Doing business as.

deceptive advertising   Advertising practices likely to mislead the reasonable consumer where the practice in question is material in that it affected consumer choice.

declaratory judgment   A judicial action expressing the opinion of the court or articulating the rights of the parties without actually ordering that anything be done.

de facto   In fact. Actually. As **de facto** school segregation which is caused by social and economic conditions rather than by government act.

defamation   A false and intentional verbal or written expression that damages the reputation of another.

defendant   The party in a civil suit against whom the cause of action was brought and, in a criminal case, the party against whom charges have been filed.

de jure   Legitimate. Lawful. Of right. As **de jure** school segregation which is caused by government order and thus is legally correct even if morally wrong.

deposition   A discovery procedure wherein a witness's sworn testimony is taken out of court, prior to trial, for subsequent use at trial.

derivative action   A lawsuit by a stockholder on behalf of the corporation to protect the organization's rights against the conduct of an officer or director.

dicta   Statements in a judicial opinion that are merely views of the judge(s) and are not necessary for the resolution of the case.

directed verdict   Party to a lawsuit makes a motion asking the judge to instruct the jury to reach a particular decision because reasonable minds could not differ about the correct outcome of the case.

discovery   Legal procedures by which one party to a litigation may obtain information from the other party. Depositions and interrogatories are examples of discovery procedures.

disparate impact   Employment discrimination theory in which a facially neutral employment practice (such as requiring a high school diploma for new hires) results in an unfair and adverse impact on a protected class.

disparate treatment   Theory of employment discrimination wherein an individual or group is intentionally disfavored via actual discriminatory policies and practices.

diversity of citizenship   One standard by which federal courts may gain jurisdiction over a lawsuit. Plaintiffs and defendants must be from different states and more than $50,000 must be at issue.

divestiture   In antitrust law, a remedy wherein the court orders a defendant to dispose of specified assets.

dividend   A shareholder's earnings from his or her stock in a corporation.

double jeopardy   The United States Constitution provides that the same individual may not be tried twice in the same tribunal for the same criminal offense.

due process   A constitutional principle requiring fairness in judicial proceedings and that government laws and conduct be free of arbitrariness and capriciousness.

dumping   The commercial practice of selling goods in a foreign market at a price substantially beneath that charged in the domestic market.

E

embargo   Government order prohibiting importation of some or all products from a particular country.

embezzlement   The fraudulent and unauthorized taking of the money of another while charged with the care of that money.

eminent domain   The state's power to take private property for public use.

en banc   All of the judges hearing a case as a group rather than individually or in panels.

enjoin   To require. A court issues an injunction requiring a certain act or ordering a party to refrain from a certain act.

environmental impact statement   Documents that must be filed under the terms of the National Environmental Policy Act whenever a federal agency undertakes action (such as the building of a highway) that may have significant environmental consequences. The documents must detail the environmental impact of the proposed action.

equal protection   The Fourteenth Amendment to the United States Constitution provides that all similarly situated individuals are entitled to the same advantages and must bear the same burdens under the law.

equity   A body of law based on fairness wherein monetary damages will not afford complete relief.

establishment clause   The First Amendment to the United States Constitution forbids the United States government from creating a government-supported church or religion.

estoppel   A legal doctrine providing that one may not assert facts that are in conflict with one's own previous acts or deeds.

exclusive dealing contract   An agreement under which a buyer agrees to purchase all of its needs from a single seller or under which a seller agrees to dispose of all of its production to a single purchaser.

exculpatory clause   Portion of a contract that seeks to relieve one of the parties to the contract from any liability for breach of a duty under that contract.

exemplary damages   Same as punitive damages

existentialism   A philosophy emphasizing the individual's responsibility to make herself what she is to become. Existence precedes essence.

expropriation   Seizure by a national government of property and/or rights of a foreign firm within the national government's own borders.

F

featherbedding   A labor law term describing the practice where workers were paid even though they did not perform any work. Featherbedding is a violation of federal labor law.

federalism   The division of authority between the federal government and the states to maintain workable cooperation while diffusing political power.

federal question   Litigation involving the federal constitution, statutes, and treaties. The federal courts have jurisdiction over cases involving federal questions.

felony   A crime of a serious nature ordinarily involving punishment by death or imprisonment in a penitentiary.

fiduciary   One who holds a relationship of trust with another and has an obligation to act in the best interests of the other. As one who manages property on behalf of another.

franchise   A marketing arrangement in which the franchisor permits the franchisee to produce, distribute, or sell the franchisor's product using the franchisor's name or trademark.

fraud   An intentional misrepresentation of a material fact with intent to deceive where the misrepresentation is justifiably relied on by another and damages result.

free exercise clause   First Amendment provision guaranteeing all Americans the right to pursue their religious beliefs free of government intervention (with limited exceptions).

full faith and credit clause   Provision of the United States Constitution requiring each state to recognize the laws and judicial decisions of all other states.

G

G7   An association embracing seven of the world's leading industrial powers (Canada, France, Italy, Germany, Japan, the United Kingdom, and the United States) designed to improve worldwide economic and political conditions.

garnishment   Action by a creditor to secure the property of a debtor where that property is held by a third party.

General Agreement on Tariffs and Trade (GATT)   An international treaty setting rules to achieve cooperation in worldwide trade practices including the specific goal of lowering tariffs, subsidies, and other barriers to free trade. Over 100 nations are members of the GATT.

good faith   Honesty; an absence of intent to take advantage of another.

grand jury   A body of people convened by the state to determine whether the evidence is sufficient to bring a criminal indictment (formal accusation) against a party.

gray market   Transactions conducted outside the usual supplier-approved channels of distribution. These transactions (unlike **black market** sales) are lawful but are often discouraged by suppliers. The gray market operates parallel to the "officially" authorized chain of distribution.

grease   Payments to low ranking authorities for the purpose of facilitating business in another nation. Not forbidden by the Foreign Corrupt Practices Act if legal in the host nation.

greenmail   In order to avoid an unfriendly takeover, a corporation may be forced to buy back its own stock from a raider at an inflated price.

H

herfindahl-hirschman index   Calculation used by the Justice Department to determine the degree of economic concentration in a particular market and to determine the degree to which a proposed horizontal merger would further concentrate that market. Computed by squaring the market share of each firm in a market and summing those totals.

horizontal merger   Acquisition by one company of another company competing in the same product and geographic markets.

I

indemnify   Reimburse one who has suffered a loss.

in personam jurisdiction   The power of the court over a person.

indictment   A grand jury's formal accusation of a crime.

information   A prosecutor's formal accusation of a crime.

injunction   A court order commanding a person or organization to do or not do a specified action.

insider   A term used in securities law broadly designating one who is in possession of nonpublic information and, more narrowly, referring to those who are officers, directors, or 10 percent (or more) owners of an enterprise.

inside trading   Unfairly employing inside information to trade on the market with individuals not having the benefit of that inside information.

interrogatories   An ingredient in the discovery process wherein one party in a lawsuit directs written questions to another party in the lawsuit.

invasion of privacy   Violating one's right to be left alone by publicizing personal information, using a likeness without permission, eavesdropping, and the like.

J

judgment notwithstanding the verdict (judgment n.o.v.)   A judge's decision overruling the finding of the jury.

judicial review   A court's authority to review statutes and, if appropriate, declare them unconstitutional. Also refers to appeals from administrative agencies.

jurisdiction   The power of a judicial body to adjudicate a dispute. Also the geographical area within which that judicial body has authority to operate.

jurisprudence   The philosophy and science of law.

jury instructions   A judge's directions to the jury explaining the law that must be applied in the case at hand.

K

keiretsu   Japanese cartels of vertically related firms working together in a collaborative fashion.

L

letter of credit A statement from a financial institution such as a bank guaranteeing that it will pay the financial obligations of a particular party.

libel A tort where a falsehood is communicated in writing to at least one third party.

lien A claim against a piece of property in satisfaction of a debt.

limited liability Shareholders of a corporation ordinarily cannot be sued for actions of the corporation and thus normally can lose only the amount invested in the firm.

long-arm statute A state enactment that accords the courts of that state the authority to claim jurisdiction over people and property beyond the borders of the state so long as certain "minimum contacts" exist between the state and the people or property.

M

malpractice Improper or negligent conduct in the performance of duties by a professional such as a doctor or lawyer.

mediation An extrajudicial proceeding in which a third party (the mediator) attempts to assist disputing parties to reach an agreeable, voluntary resolution of their differences.

merger The union of two or more business organizations wherein all of the assets, rights, and liabilities of one are blended into the other with only one firm remaining.

misdemeanor A criminal offense less serious than a felony normally requiring a fine or less than a year in a jail other than a penitentiary.

monopoly Market power permitting the holder to fix prices and/or exclude competition.

moot An issue no longer requiring attention or resolution because it has ceased to be in dispute.

most favored nation An element of the General Agreement on Tariffs and Trade (GATT) which provides that the parties (e.g., the United States and the People's Republic of China) to an international trade agreement promise to extend to each other any favorable trading terms (e.g., exemptions from tariffs) that are offered to other trading partners.

motion A request to a court seeking an order or action in favor of the party entering the motion.

motion for a directed verdict A request by a party to a lawsuit arguing that the other party has failed to prove facts sufficient to establish a claim and that the judge must, therefore, enter a verdict in favor of the moving party.

N

nationalization A country taking over a private business often without adequate compensation to the ex-owners.

negligence The omission to do something that a reasonable person, guided by those ordinary considerations that ordinarily regulate human affairs, would do, or an action that a reasonable and prudent person would not take.

nolo contendere　A no-contest plea in a criminal case in which the defendant does not admit guilt but does submit to such punishment as the court may accord.

nuisance　A class of wrongs that arises from the unreasonable, unwarrantable, or unlawful use by a person of his or her property that produces material annoyance, inconvenience, discomfort, or hurt.

O

oligopoly　An economic condition in which the market for a particular good or service is controlled by a small number of producers or distributors.

ordinance　A law, rule, or regulation enacted by a local unit of government (e.g., a town or city).

over-the-counter securities　Those stocks, bonds, and like instruments sold directly from broker to customer rather than passing through a stock exchange.

P

partnership　An association of two or more persons where they agree to work together in a business designed to earn a profit.

patent　A right conferred by the federal government allowing the holder to restrict the manufacture, distribution, and sale of the holder's invention or discovery.

per curiam　"By the court." Refers to legal opinions offered by the court as a whole rather than those instances where an individual judge authors the opinion.

per se　By itself; inherently.

peremptory challenge　At trial, an attorney's authority to dismiss prospective members of the jury without offering any justification for that dismissal.

plaintiff　One who initiates a lawsuit.

pleadings　The formal entry of written statements by which the parties to a lawsuit set out their contentions and thereby formulate the issues on which the litigation will be based.

police power　The government's inherent authority to enact rules to provide for the health, safety, and general welfare of the citizenry.

precedent　A decision in a previously decided lawsuit that may be looked to as an authoritative statement for resolving current lawsuits involving similar questions of law.

predatory pricing　Selling below cost with the intention of driving a competitor out of business.

preemption doctrine　Constitutional doctrine providing that the federal government "preempts the field" where it passes laws in an area thus denying the states the right to pass conflicting laws or, in some cases, denying the states the right to pass any laws in that area.

prima facie case　A litigating party may be presumed to have built a prima facie case when the evidence is such that it is legally sufficient unless contradicted or overcome by other evidence.

privatization　The many strategies for shifting public-sector activities back to private enterprise. Those strategies include contracting out government work to private parties, raising the user fees charged for public services, selling state-owned property and enterprises, and returning government services such as garbage collection to the private sector.

privity of contract   The legal connection that arises when two or more parties enter a contract.

procedural due process   Constitutional principle requiring that the government assure fundamental fairness to all in the execution of our system of laws.

promissory estoppel   Court enforcement of an otherwise nonbinding promise where the recipient of the promise (the promisee) has relied on the promise (made by the promisor), has suffered injury, and justice cannot be secured without enforcing the promise.

proximate cause   Occurrences that in a natural sequence, unbroken by potent intervening forces, produce an injury that would not have resulted in the absence of those occurrences.

proxy   Written permission from a shareholder to others to vote his or her share at a stockholders' meeting.

punitive damages   Damages beyond compensatory damages accorded for the purpose of imposing punishment for the egregious nature of the defendant's conduct.

Q

quantum meruit   (Latin) As much as he deserves. Describes a plea for recovery under a contract implied by law. Fair payment for work performed.

quid pro quo   Exchanging one thing of value for another. In sexual harassment law, quid pro quo cases are those where employment benefits are conditioned on the subordinate's submission to sexual advances.

R

redlining   Most commonly, the practice of refusing to make loans in economically unstable areas with the result that minorities are sometimes discriminated against in securing credit.

release   Agreement to relinquish a right or a claim. Sometimes labelled a "waiver" or a "hold harmless" clause.

remand   To send back. For example, a higher court sends a case back to the lower court from which it came.

res   A thing, object, or status.

resale price maintenance   Manufacturer's effort to restrict the price at which its product is resold.

res ipsa loquitur   "The thing speaks for itself." Negligence doctrine under which the defendant's guilt is not directly proved but rather is inferred from the circumstances that establish the reasonable belief that the injury in question could not have happened in the absence of the defendant's negligence.

res judicata   "A thing decided." A doctrine of legal procedure preventing the retrial of issues already conclusively adjudicated.

respondeat superior   "Let the master respond." Doctrine holding the employer liable for negligent acts committed by an employee while in the course of employment.

restraints of trade   Contracts, combinations, or conspiracies resulting in obstructions of the marketplace, including monopoly, artificially inflated prices, artificially reduced supplies, or other impediments to the natural flow of commerce.

reverse   Overturn the decision of a court.

right-to-know laws   Federal and state laws and regulations requiring employers to assume the affirmative responsibility of acquainting employees with hazardous substances and conditions in the workplace.

right-to-work laws   State legislation forbidding or restricting labor contracts that permit employment only for those who belong to unions.

S

secondary boycott   Typically, a union strategy that places pressure not on the employer with whom the union has a dispute but rather with a supplier or customer of that employer in the hope that the object of the boycott will persuade the employer to meet the union's expectations.

security   A stock, bond, note, or other investment interest in an enterprise designed for profit and operated by one other than the investor.

separation of powers   The strategy of dividing government into separate and independent executive, legislative, and judicial branches, each of which acts as a check on the power of the others.

sexual harassment   Unwelcome sexual advances, requests for sexual favors, and other unwanted physical or verbal conduct of a sexual nature.

shareholder   One holding stock in a corporation.

shark repellant   Various kinds of corporate behaviors designed to make a company unattractive to potential acquirers.

slander   A defamatory statement orally communicated to at least one third party.

small claims courts   Courts of limited powers designed to hear cases involving modest sums of money (often limited to about $1000) in hearings free of many of the formalities and burdens associated with the more conventional judicial process.

sovereign immunity   The government's right to exclude itself from being sued for damages in all but those situations where it consents to be sued. In international law, sovereign immunity permits a nation to decline to be sued in the courts of other nations.

standing   A stake in a dispute sufficient to afford a party the legal right to bring or join a litigation exploring the subject of the dispute.

stare decisis   "Let the decision stand." A doctrine of judicial procedure expecting a court to follow precedent in all cases involving substantially similar issues unless extremely compelling circumstances dictate a change in judicial direction.

statute   A legislative enactment.

strict liability   The imposition of legal liability in a civil case as a matter of policy even though the defendant has exercised due care and has not been proved negligent.

subpoena   An order from a court or administrative agency commanding that an individual appear to give testimony or produce specified documents.

substantive due process   Due process clause of the Constitution requires that a statute be fair and reasonably related to a legitimate government purpose so that persons are not improperly deprived of their property rights.

summary judgment   A judicial determination prior to holding that no factual dispute exists between the parties and that, as a matter of law, one of the parties is entitled to a favorable judgment.

summons   A document originating in a court and delivered to a party or organization indicating that a lawsuit has been commenced against him, her, or it. The summons constitutes notice that the defendant is expected to appear in court to answer the plaintiff's allegations.

sunset legislation   A statute providing that a particular government agency will automatically cease to exist as of a specified date unless the legislative body affirmatively acts to extend the life of the agency.

supremacy clause   An element of the U.S. Constitution providing that all constitutionally valid federal laws are the paramount law of the land and, as such, are superior to any conflicting state and local laws.

T

takeover bid   A tender offer designed to assume control of a corporation.

tender offer   Public offer to buy shares in a company from the current shareholders under specified terms and at a specified price often for the purpose of taking over the company in question.

tort   A civil wrong not arising from a contract.

totalitarianism   A rigid, undemocratic government according power to a particular political group and excluding all others from access to political influence. The Soviet Union, Nazi Germany, and Fascist Italy were totalitarian states.

trademark   A word, name, or other distinctive symbol registered with the government and used exclusively by the owner to identify its product.

trademark infringement   Unauthorized use of the trademark of another.

treble damages   An award of damages totaling three times the amount of actual damages, authorized by some statutes in an effort to discourage further wrongful conduct.

tying contract   A sales or leasing arrangement in which one product or service may be bought or leased only if accompanied by the purchase or lease of another product or service as specified by the seller–lessor.

U

ultra vires   Corporate conduct beyond the scope of activities provided for under the terms of incorporation.

unconscionability   A contract so one-sided and oppressive as to be unfair.

union shop   In labor law, the situation where all employees of a company must join a union in order to retain employment. Forbidden in right-to-work states.

usury   Charging an interest rate exceeding the legally permissible maximum.

V

venue   The specific geographic location in which a court holding jurisdiction should properly hear a case, given the convenience of the parties and other relevant considerations.

verdict   The jury's decision as to who wins the litigation.

vertical merger   A union between two firms holding a buyer–seller relationship with each other.

voir dire   The portion of a trial in which prospective jurors are questioned to determine their qualifications, including absence of bias, to sit in judgment in the case.

W

waiver   Relinquishing a legal right—as the situation where one agrees not to sue if injured while participating in a particular activity, such as attending a baseball game.

warranty   Any promise, express or implied, that the facts are true as specified. For example, in consumer law, the warranty of merchantability is a guaranty that the product is reasonably fit for the general purpose for which it was sold.

workers' compensation laws   State statutes providing fixed recoveries for injuries and illnesses sustained in the course of employment. Under those statutes, workers need not establish fault on the part of the employer.

Y

yellow-dog contract   An illegal agreement under which an employee promises not to join a union.

Table of Cases

Subject Index